A HISTORY OF EASTERN EUROPE

Praise for the first edition:

'This book is an ambitious undertaking. The book excels in urging readers to "think again" about the succession of regimes and ideologies that have shaped, destroyed and resurrected Eastern European nations.'

Contemporary Review

Eastern Europe has a most complicated and troubled history, one not simply defined by Communist rule and Soviet domination. In *A History of Eastern Europe* Robert Bideleux and Ian Jeffries provide comprehensive coverage of this complex past, from antiquity to the present day.

This new edition provides a thematic historical survey of the formative processes of political, social and economic change which have played paramount roles in shaping the evolution and development of the region. Subjects covered include:

- Eastern Europe in ancient, medieval and early modern times
- the legacies of Byzantium, the Ottoman Empire and the Habsburg Empire
- the impact of the region's powerful Russian and Germanic neighbours
- rival concepts of 'Central' and 'Eastern' Europe
- the experience and consequences of the two World Wars
- varieties of fascism in Eastern Europe
- the impact of Communism from the 1940s to the 1980s
- post-Communist democratization and marketization
- the eastward enlargement of the EU.

Including two new chronologies – one for the Balkans and one for East Central Europe – *A History of Eastern Europe* is the ideal companion for all students of Eastern Europe.

Robert Bideleux is a Reader in the School of Humanities at the University of Wales, Swansea. **Ian Jeffries** is a Reader in the School of Business, Economics and Law also at the University of Wales, Swansea. They have both published extensively on the Balkans, East Central Europe and Russia.

IN SYSTEM

A HISTORY OF
EASTERN EUROPE
CRISIS AND CHANGE

Second edition

ROBERT BIDELEUX AND IAN JEFFRIES

Routledge
Taylor & Francis Group

LONDON AND NEW YORK

First published 1998
by Routledge
2 Park Square, Milton Park, Abingdon, Oxon OX14 4RN

Simultaneously published in the USA and Canada
by Routledge
270 Madison Ave, New York, NY 10016

Second edition published 2007

Routledge is an imprint of the Taylor & Francis Group, an informa business

© 2007 Robert Bideleux and Ian Jeffries

Typeset in Great Britain by Saxon Graphics Ltd, Derby
Printed and bound in Great Britain by Antony Rowe Ltd, Chippenham, Wiltshire

British Library Cataloguing in Publication Data
A catalogue record for this book is available from the British Library

Library of Congress Cataloging in Publication Data
Bideleux, Robert.
A history of Eastern Europe : crisis and change / Robert Bideleux and Ian Jeffries. --2nd ed.
p. cm.
Includes bibliographical references and index.
1. Europe, Eastern--History. I. Jeffries, Ian. II. Title.
DJK38.B53 2007
947--dc22

2006100591

ISBN 13: 978–0–415–36626–7 (hbk)
ISBN 13: 978–0–415–36627–4 (pbk)
ISBN 13: 978–0–203–01889–7 (ebk)

ISBN 10: 0–415–36626–7 (hbk)
ISBN 10: 0–415–36627–5 (pbk)
ISBN 10: 0–203–01889–3 (ebk)

For our parents

Contents

List of maps

List of tables

Preface to the second edition

The central purpose of this book is to provide a thematic historical survey and analysis of the formative processes of political, social and economic change which (in our judgement) have played the
paramount roles in shaping the development of East Central Europe and the Balkans – regions
which in recent times have had the great misfortune of being sandwiched between the former Tsarist
and Soviet empires, on the one side, and Germany and Italy, on the other.

For this second edition, we have removed much of our earlier coverage of medieval and early
modern Poland, Hungary and the Kingdom of Bohemia (the Czech Lands) in order to make room
for (i) a great deal of new material on the Byzantine and Ottoman Balkans; (ii) some new perspectives on medieval and early modern East Central Europe; (iii) much fuller coverage of the two
World Wars and the Holocaust; and (iv) major updates on the transformations which have been
taking place in East Central Europe and the Balkans since 1989, including a new conceptual framework for analysing these changes and the eastward enlargement of the EU. The admission of eight
East Central European and Baltic states into the European Union in May 2004 was a momentous
event, comparable in long-term importance to the Revolutions of 1989, and it has therefore received
a fairly thorough evaluation in this new edition. Readers who have a particular interest in late medieval and early modern East Central Europe will, we hope, still be able to obtain access to copies of
the first edition, which provided more detailed analyses of this region during those periods.

The new text, revisions and statistical tables for this new edition of *A History of Eastern Europe*
were prepared by Robert Bideleux, who also took the opportunity to tighten up the previous text
wherever possible. Nevertheless, the book remains the result of nearly two decades of fruitful collaboration between two authors who have shared a longstanding interest in East Central Europe, the
Balkans and Russia, and strong commitments to liberal and civic values and interdisciplinarity.

When we first started collaborating on this project, we originally envisaged that Robert Bideleux's
largely thematic historical surveys and analyses of the Balkans and East Central Europe would be
complemented by separate chapters on the evolution of the individual states in these regions during
the twentieth century, all to be contained within a single volume. A natural division of labour recommended itself at the outset: Robert Bideleux would mainly provide the overarching thematic, historical and political analyses, narratives and perspectives, while Ian Jeffries would mainly provide more
detailed accounts and analyses of economic and political change in individual countries since 1989.
However, as we became increasingly aware of the bearing of the more remote past on the increasingly
complex problems of the post-Communist present, our joint project expanded into three large volumes.
The present book, first published in 1998 and the first volume of this trilogy, was very largely written
by Robert Bideleux, albeit with indispensable inputs from Ian Jeffries at every stage. The second
volume, published in early 2007 and entitled *The Balkans: A Post-Communist History*, was more of a
joint effort. It provides more detailed treatments of individual Balkan countries during the twentieth
and early twenty-first centuries, paying particular attention to the period since 1989. The almost

completed third volume deals with the East Central European states, mainly since the end of Communist rule. Taken together, these three volumes seek to provide the most comprehensive survey and analysis of political and economic change in the modern Balkans and East Central Europe available in English. Nevertheless, this first volume can also be read as a free-standing thematic analysis and interpretation of political, economic and (to lesser degrees) social and cultural change in the Balkans and East Central Europe from the Roman period to 2006.

Even a book as large as this one has to be selective. We took an early decision to limit the space devoted to diplomatic activity, partly because this has already received abundant attention from diplomatic historians, but mainly because we believe that, on the whole, it has been of less consequence than the interaction of broader and more persistent political, economic, social and cultural forces. To be sure, we have endeavoured to outline and discuss major diplomatic actions and events which have had enduring effects on the Balkans and East Central Europe, notably the Congress of Vienna (1815), the Berlin Congress of 1878, the peace settlements of 1919–20, and the notorious 'percentages agreement' between Churchill and Stalin in October 1944. On the whole, however, we find ourselves in agreement with the following statement by Professor Norman Davies, the most prominent British historian of Poland: 'Very few, if any, of the diplomatic memoranda concerning Poland's future ever exerted a decisive influence on the course of events. Many of them . . . remained a dead letter . . . Others were simply ignored. The most important of them did nothing but express the pious aspirations of their authors or confirm the details of political settlements already accomplished . . . At . . . critical moments, matters were decided not at the conference table, but by the situation on the ground and by the men who held the reins of practical power. At moments of less importance, diplomatic action counted for even less . . . The Polish nation grew from infancy to maturity regardless of the diplomats, and it owes them no debt of gratitude' (Davies 1981b: 15). Much the same could be said in relation to other East Central European countries and the Balkans.

Similarly, we have endeavoured to minimize the attention devoted to significant external actors, such as Bismarck and Napoleon. Although such figures loom very large in the writings of some diplomatic historians, we would humbly submit that the Iron Chancellor and the Corsican upstart had rather less impact on the history of the Balkans and East Central Europe than did several other 'off-stage' actors, among whom Marx, Lenin, Stalin, Khrushchev, Brezhnev, Gorbachev, Christ, Luther, Calvin, Mussolini and Hitler most readily spring to mind, and we have to draw a line somewhere.

Much more regrettable is the fact that we have had to limit our coverage of many important cultural and intellectual developments. Proper coverage of these themes would have doubled or trebled the size of this book. Nevertheless, we have been able to give some attention to the impact of Christianization, the Renaissance, the Reformation, the Counter-Reformation, the Enlightenment, nationalism and Marxism, albeit often in highly summarized forms. Half a loaf is better than none.

It is also necessary to say a few preliminary words about the extent and nomenclature of the regions covered by this book. The naming and demarcation of European regions is always controversial and loaded with implicit and/or contentious claims and connotations. Fortunately, there is fairly widespread agreement that Poland, Hungary, the Czech Republic, Slovakia and Slovenia constitute an identifiable region, to which we apply the name East Central Europe; and that to the south of this lies another identifiable region comprising Greece, Albania, Bulgaria, Romania, Serbia, Croatia, Bosnia and Herzegovina, Kosova and the Republic of Macedonia, which is commonly referred to as 'the Balkans' or 'the Balkan Peninsula'. Nevertheless, there have been long disputes as to where exactly the Balkans end and East Central Europe begins. Although most Westerners (especially historians) include Croatia and Romania in the Balkans, for centuries Transylvania (now northern Romania) and Croatia were key components of the Kingdom of Hungary, which in turn became part of the Habsburg domains. Should they therefore be included in East Central Europe? Many (perhaps most) Romanians and Croatians appear to believe that their countries have more in common with East Central Europe than with the Balkans. However, we have argued elsewhere that their deeply entrenched 'vertical' power relations and power structures and the resultant relative weakness of the rule of law, limited government and civil society have more in common with the predicaments of their Balkan neighbours than those of East Central Europe (see Bideleux and Jeffries 2007: 5–16, 127–8, 141–3, 179–82, 199–201, 210, 214–15, 218, 230–1, 581–7, 591–2). Conversely, partly because Slovenia was a key component of interwar Yugoslavia and later of the Socialist Federal Republic of Yugoslavia, many historians have treated it as part of the Balkans, rather than as part of East Central Europe. However, we have become convinced that during most of its history the territory and inhabitants of what was to become Slovenia have had considerably more in common with the Austro-German lands than with Slovenia's southern neighbours, and that since the early 1990s Slovenia has displayed far greater 'structural similarities' (political, economic and social) to East Central Europe than to the Balkans. Implicitly, this was a major reason why Slovenia was included in the admission of eight East Central European and Baltic states into the European Union in May 2004, whereas Romania and Bulgaria were not allowed to enter until January 2007, and Croatia seems unlikely to be allowed to join until 2009 or 2010. Clearly, the issues involved are not merely matters of academic interest, but have directly affected international perceptions of the standing of particular countries in the European 'pecking order'.

Nevertheless, despite the very negative images generated by the conflicts between Yugoslav successor states between 1991 and 1995 and the high incidence of poverty, organized crime and corruption in the post-Communist Balkan states, we also believe that the widely assumed 'superiority' of East Central Europe over the Balkans has been greatly exaggerated by those who conveniently forget that East Central Europe was a major incubator of fascism, the Kafkaesque state, and racial and religious hatreds and atrocities during the twentieth century. It is neither fair nor acceptable to contrast alleged Balkan 'vices' with sanitized and idealized visions of East Central European 'virtues'. The post-Communist states in the Balkans have indeed experienced far greater inter-communal tensions, abuse of power, organized crime, corruption and poverty than those in East Central Europe, but this need not mean that they are innately, culturally or morally inferior to their East Central European counterparts. During much of its past the Balkan Peninsula was one of the most economically, technologically and politically sophisticated and law-governed areas in what has come to be known as 'Europe', and we see no intrinsic (cultural or 'civilizational') reasons why it could not become so again in the future. In our view, the peninsula's problems in modern times have been caused mainly by circumstances and power structures which can be changed, especially by the prospect and impact of membership of the EU, rather than by so-called 'Balkan' attitudes, mentalities and mindsets. These are in large measure products of lazy and exaggerated caricatures and stereotypes of the Balkans propagated by the Western media and, to lesser degrees, by Western academia.

The English language lacks an appropriate and widely acceptable collective name for the Balkans and East Central Europe. In German they have aptly been called *Zwischeneuropa* ('in between Europe'). This has the advantage of encapsulating their principal modern predicament, that of 'living between East and West . . . between Germany and Russia, or, in early modern times, between Turks and Habsburgs' (Burke 1985: 2). However, there is no similarly apt English name. The nearest equivalent is 'the lands between', but this has never passed into common usage.

We are fully aware that since the mid-1980s it has been fashionable to refer to these regions either as 'Central Europe' or as 'Central and Eastern Europe'. For reasons set out more fully in the Introduction, we have resisted the temptation to follow suit. In the perceptions of most West Europeans, the term 'Central Europe' has long referred primarily to Germany and Austria (the former 'Central Powers'), and it still has strong connotations of *Mitteleuropa* and Austrian and German imperialism. Furthermore, the incorporation of these 'lands between' into an expanded conception of Central Europe implicitly (and perhaps deliberately) overstates the degrees to which they have been part of the European 'mainstream' in modern times. That is to say, it underestimates the degrees to which these regions have been relegated to Europe's 'peripheries' or 'semi-peripheries' since the seventeenth century. It also implicitly understates the magnitude of the political, economic and social changes which both of these regions have had to make during their so-called 'return to Europe'. Furthermore, the widespread practice of referring to these regions as 'Central and Eastern Europe' or the 'Central and East European countries' (CEECs) is a vague and lazy expedient which merely muddies the waters even more.

Therefore, *faute de mieux*, the title of this book continues to refer to these 'lands between' as 'Eastern Europe' – the name by which they generally came to be known during the east–west partition of Europe from 1945 to 1989. This is in no way intended to impugn or belittle their 'Europeanness' and/or their 'European credentials', which remain second to none. Rather, it merely amounts to a pragmatic endeavour to distinguish them both from a 'Central Europe' centred on Germany and Austria and from the Commonwealth of Independent States (the CIS, comprising the former Soviet republics other than the three Baltic States – Estonia, Latvia and Lithuania). Having devoted more than thirty years to studying and writing about the peoples and states of *Zwischeneuropa*, whose 'European credentials' are amply endorsed in this book, we have no desire to slight or to denigrate them in any way.

Some books on 'Eastern Europe' have dealt with the Baltic States alongside Poland, Hungary and former Czechoslovakia, that is, as part of East Central Europe, on the grounds that they formally achieved independent statehood within the eastern zone of Europe from 1918 to 1940 and that their forebears were to varying degrees united with Poland in the great Polish-Lithuanian Commonwealth from the sixteenth to the eighteenth century (for example, the Baltic States were included in Rothschild (1974) and Crampton (1994)). However, the Baltic States and their forebears constitute an intermediate category of their own, because from the eighteenth century to 1991 (with relatively brief interruptions) they were integral parts of the Russian Empire and later the Soviet Union. Since the late eighteenth century, consequently, the political, social, cultural and economic affairs of the territories which evolved into the Baltic States have been much more strongly intertwined with those of Russia and the Soviet Union than with those of Poland, Hungary, the Czech Lands, Slovakia and Slovenia. In this book, therefore, we have made only occasional reference to the Baltic States – mainly during the post-1989 period, in which their affairs have again become more closely linked to those of East Central Europe.

Professor George Blazyca (who tragically died of cancer in his prime in 2005), Professor Raymond Pearson, Dr Gareth Pritchard, Professor Jack Morrison and, above all, Dr Eleanor Breuning provided copious and constructive comments on the manuscript of the first edition, which prompted many changes and clarifications. Eleanor, in particular, made many stylistic improvements and picked up significant mistakes. However, Robert Bideleux takes full responsibility for any remaining errors and controversial or questionable judgements, as he has formulated almost all the themes, arguments and positions put forward in this book (although those in chapter 35 had important inputs from Ian Jeffries) and has never shied away from controversy.

We also wish to reaffirm our appreciation of the invaluable support and assistance we received from Heather McCallum on the first edition in 1997–8, and to thank Eve Setch, Sue Dixon and Vicky Peters at Routledge for their patience and help during the preparation of this second edition. Ian Critchley, our desk editor for the first edition, was a big help during the final stages of its production. For this second edition, Carol Fellingham Webb has been a very responsive copy-editor, and Helen Brocklehurst has read and provided many constructive comments on chapter 29.

Finally, Robert would like to express heartfelt thanks to Catherine Lee for providing indispensable stimulus and unstinting support during the preparation of this second edition, to Ian Jeffries for maintaining his faith in and support for the project, and to Alison, Chantal and Kieran Bideleux for their forbearance during the writing of the first edition (1990–7). Alison Bideleux also provided much appreciated books and comments on the Byzantine Empire and on certain aspects of the Renaissance, without which the first edition would have been much the poorer.

Chronologies

BE = Byzantine Empire

CDB = central Danubian basin

ECE = East Central Europe

HE = Habsburg Empire

OE = Ottoman Empire

Chronology of Balkan history

BCE (before common era, BC)

*c.*3000–*c.*1450	A non-Indo-European **Minoan civilization** emerged in Crete, centred on the palace of Knossos. This civilization (and the hieroglyphic script which it initially used) appears to have had ties with and to have been markedly influenced by Egypt, and perhaps to lesser degrees by Anatolia (Asia Minor), the Levant (Syria and Lebanon), Mesopotamia and Sicily. Its palaces and towns appear to have been unfortified.
*c.*2000–1600	**Inflows of 'proto-Greeks'**, probably from the Caucasus region and speaking an Indo-European language, into mainland Greece and the Aegean islands, gave rise to a proto-Greek **'Helladic civilization'**.
*c.*1750–	Minoans developed the so-called **'linear A' script**.
*c.*1600–1450	Emergence of a **'Mycenaean' Greek culture** centred on Mycenae (in Peloponnese) and the Aegean islands. Fortified palaces were built, and the inhabitants of mainland Greece and Minoan Crete developed the so-called **'linear B' script** (an early form of Greek). By 1450 Mycenaean trading networks extended from Sicily to the Levant (present-day Lebanon and Syria).
*c.*1450	**Minoan palaces on Crete plundered and destroyed** by Mycenaean Greeks, who seized control.
*c.*1200	**Mycenaean siege and capture of port-city of Troy**, which had hitherto controlled the Dardanelles access to the Marmara and Black seas, severely strained Mycenaean resources.
*c.*1150	**Disintegration of Mycenaean power, networks and towns**.
*c.*1150–900	**Greece's so-called 'Dark Ages'**: mainland Greece was invaded by fierce and less sophisticated **'Dorian Greeks'** from further north. Decay or destruction of Mycenaean towns, palaces and forts.
*c.*800–321	**Rise of Greek islands and 'city-states'**.
770s–	Greek colonies were established in Italy and along the Adriatic coast.
776	First pan-Hellenic Olympic Games, held at Olympia.
*c.*760	**Homer's *Iliad* written down.**
750s–	**Emergence of the Greek alphabet**, adapted from the alphabet developed by the Phoenicians, whose power extended from the Levant to the western Mediterranean, where they founded the port-city of Carthage in 814.
753	**'Founding' of Rome**.
730s–	Greek colonies were founded on **Corfu** (Corcyra) and **Sicily**.

650s–640s	Emergence of **'tyrants'** (dictators) in many Greek city-states.
	Beginnings of Greek settlement on the Black Sea coasts.
545–546	**Persian conquests** of Greek settlements in western Anatolia.
508–505	**Inauguration of 'democracy' in Athens**.
499	Greek revolt against Persian rule in western Anatolia, supported by Athens and other Greek city-states.
490	Persian attempt to conquer Greece defeated at Marathon.
480	Persian forces sacked Athens, but were defeated at Salamis, Platea and Mycale. Athens recovered quickly, exploiting its fleet of slave-powered galleys.
*c.*480–*c.*430	**Heyday of 'classical Greek civilization'**, whose leading lights included Pericles (495–429), Aeschylus (*c.*524–456), Sophocles (*c.*495–406), Herodotus (*c.*484–*c.*420), Socrates (*c.*470–399), Thucydides (*c.*460–*c.*400), Plato (*c.*428–*c.*347), and Aristotle (384–322).
478	Anti-Persian 'League of Delos' was founded by Athens.
461–451	War between Athens and Sparta (first Peloponnesian War).
443–429	Athens flourished under Pericles.
*c.*429–*c.*146	**Decline of the Greek city-states.**
431–403	Mutually debilitating war between 'democratic' Athens and militaristic Sparta and its allies (second Peloponnesian War).
362	Sparta eclipsed, while other Peloponnesian city-states regained autonomy.
338	**Philip II of Macedon** (reg. 359–336) subjugated Greek city-states. He was assassinated in 336 and succeeded by his son.
336–323	**Alexander the Great (of Macedon)** and his generals rapidly overran Egypt, Anatolia, the Levant, Mesopotamia, Persia and northern India, but this hastily assembled empire rapidly unravelled after Alexander died of a fever in 323.
321	Macedon occupied Athens and terminated its 'democracy'.
321–301	Alexander's leading generals established their own personal kingdoms: Cassander seized Macedon and Greece, Lysimachus took Thrace, Seleucus acquired Babylon and much of Persia, Ptolemy retained Egypt, but Antigonus lost out.
307	Macedon crushed Athenian bid to regain independence.
298–290	**The Roman Republic conquered most of Italy**.
280–272	Rome subjugated Greek colonies in mainland Italy.
272	Celtic marauders sacked Greek temples at Delphi.
264, 262	Rome conquered Greek Messana and Agrigentum in Sicily.
264–241	Rome captured Carthaginian cities in Sicily and gained ascendancy in the Mediterranean.
229–228	**Rome campaigned against piracy in Adriatic Sea and imposed military protectorate on southern Illyria** (Albania).
214–205	Rome fought Macedon (which had entered an alliance with Carthage in 215) and captured Greek Syracuse and Tarentum in Sicily.
200–197	After subjugating Carthage in 202, Rome mauled Macedon and detached its major Greek and Anatolian possessions.
196	Roman occupiers of Corinth proclaimed Greece to be 'free'.
171–168	Rome again fought and defeated Macedon (along with its ally Epirus), annexed Corfu and installed client rulers in southern Illyria, but Illyria's inhabitants intermittently rebelled against Roman overlordship until AD 9.

155	**Roman forces invaded Dalmatia** (northern Illyria, now Croatia and Bosnia) and destroyed its main town, Delminium.
149–146	**Rome finally crushed Macedon, Carthage and Corinth, conquered the remaining Greek city-states, and incorporated Macedon and mainland Greece into a new Roman province of Macedonia**, within which Athens and Sparta held privileged status.

Roman ascendancy in the Balkans, 146 BC–AD 395

140	Rome conquered **Epirus** (added to the province of Macedonia).
118–117	Rome crushed major rebellions in Dalmatia.
88–86	Athens and other Greek cities entered an anti-Roman alliance with King Mithridates VI of Pontus (Anatolia). The Roman consul Sulla retaliated by sacking Athens and Piraeus and reconquering much of Greece.
67, 58	Rome conquered Crete and Cyprus, respectively.
48	Julius Caesar finally triumphed over Pompey in Thessaly.
44	Corinth was refounded as a Roman city, subsequently becaming the capital of the Roman-Greek province of Achaea (hived off from Macedonia).

Common Era (CE, AD)

6–10	**Rome crushed major rebellions against Roman overlordship in Illyria and turned it into the Roman province of Dalmatia**.
46	Thrace became a Roman province.
85, 89	Dacia's King Decebalus made major incursions into the Romans' Balkan province of Moesia.
101–6	**Dacia (now Wallachia and Transylvania) was incorporated into the Roman Empire** by Emperor Trajan.
250, 267	Germanic Goths raided and plundered Thrace, Macedonia and Greece.
257–9	Persecution of Christians in Roman Empire, including the Balkans.
260–302	**Period of Roman religious toleration allowed Christianity to spread in the Balkans, as elsewhere**.
271	Mounting 'barbarian' incursions led to **Roman withdrawal from Dacia**.
285	**Emperor Diocletian** (reg. 284–305), a soldier and self-made Roman Emperor from Dalmatia, partitioned the increasingly unwieldy Roman Empire between himself and three of his Balkan colleagues. In 305 he retired to his great palace in Split.
302–10	**Renewed persecution of Christians** in Roman Empire.
311, 313	New **edicts of toleration** in Roman Empire..
312	**Emperor Constantine I (reg. 306–37)** defeated the co-rulers of the subdivided Roman Empire and reunited it under his own rule. Attributing his major victory in 312 to God's favour, he finally ended persecution of Christians in the Roman Empire and fostered an imperial cult combining elements of emperor-worship, Graeco-Roman paganism and Christianity.
324	**Constantine I founded Constantinople** (now Istanbul) on the site of the Greek trading colony of Byzantium (established *c.*600 BCE), making it the capital of the Roman Empire in 331. This laid the foundations of the **Eastern Roman Empire** known to modern historians as the **Byzantine Empire (BE)** or **Byzantium**.

325	Constantine I convoked the **Church Council of Nicea** in a vain attempt to unite Christian churches around agreed doctrinal definitions, beliefs and practices.
378–95	Germanic Visigoths invaded and pillaged mainland Greece.
391	**Emperor Theodosius (reg. 379–95) made Christianity the official religion of the Roman Empire**, including the western and southern Balkans. The Olympic Games and pagan temples and oracles were closed down.
395	**Goths invaded the Balkans**, as far south as Greece. **The Roman Empire was divided into an Eastern and a Western Empire.** This consolidated the ascendancy of Greek-speakers, the Greek language and Eastern Orthodox Christianity in the burgeoning Byzantine Empire and the preponderance of Latin and Roman Catholicism in the waning Western Roman Empire.

Byzantine (East Roman) dominion over the Balkans, 395–1204

Late fourth century	**Byzantium deflected most of the Germanic marauders westwards** by paying them 'subsidies' (tribute, bribes).
400	Massacre of Goths invited to Constantinople.
406–9	**Vandals overran Gaul (France) and Iberia (Spain).**
410	**Visigoths captured and sacked Rome.**
447	**Huns** (nomadic warriors and pastoralists led by Attila) invaded Thrace and extracted large 'subsidies' from Byzantium.
453	**Ostrogoths** raided Byzantine domains.
455	**Vandals captured and sacked Rome.**
476	The 'barbarian' Odoacer deposed the last Western Roman Emperor.
527–65	**Reign of Byzantine Emperor Justinian.**
533–40	Byzantium (re)conquered northern-west Africa, Corsica, Sardinia and the Balearic Islands.
535–40, 547–55	Byzantium (re)conquered almost all of Italy.
540	**Turkic Bulgars ravaged Macedonia and Thrace**, whereupon Justinian launched a costly fortification of BE's Danubian frontier against 'barbarian' maurauders.
540–629	**Mutually debilitating power struggle between Persia and BE**, mainly for control of Anatolia and the Black Sea.
541–4, 558, 573, 587	**BE was decimated by bubonic plague epidemics**.
552–5	Byzantium reconquered most of Spain, completing a short-lived reunion of the core domains of the Roman Empire.
553	Itinerant monks brought **silk worms** to Constantinople, launching a successful Byzantine silk industry.
567, 585	Visigoths expelled Byzantine forces from western and central Spain. Last Byzantine garrisons departed in 624.
582	**Turkic Avars** captured Byzantine Sirmium (now Sremski Mitrovica in Serbia) and obtained Byzantine 'subsidies'.
580–590s	Major **Slav incursions into Byzantine Balkans**, initially in co-operation with Avar overlords.
599–600, 608, 618	**BE was again decimated by bubonic plague epidemics**.
617	Slav incursions reached the walls of Constantinople.

625, 640, 697, 700	**BE was again decimated by bubonic plague epidemics**.
626	Persia and Avars unsuccessfully besieged Constantinople.
629	**BE decisively defeated Persia**.
636–42	**Arab Muslim Empire overran debilitated Persia and Byzantine Syria, Lebanon, Palestine and Egypt**. This facilitated subsequent Arab conquest of north-west Africa (Byzantine Carthage fell in 699).
649, 654	The Arabs captured Cyprus and Rhodes.
674–8	**Unsuccessful Arab siege of Constantinople**, defeated mainly by Byzantine use of 'Greek fire' against the Arab fleet.
675–81	**Emergence of a Bulgar–Slavic polity,** formally recognized by BE in 681.
717–18	**Constantinople was unsuccessfully besieged by 80,000 Arabs**.
726	Against strong opposition, BE's victorious 'iconoclastic' **Emperor Leo III prohibited 'worship of images'**. Byzantine territories in north-central Italy rebelled against this ban, and in 727 BE lost control of all except Ravenna.
733	Leo III transferred the Balkans, Sicily and Calabria from Roman Catholic to Byzantine ecclesiastical jurisdiction.
746	BE recaptured Cyprus from the Arabs.
746–7	**BE was again decimated by a plague epidemic**.
751	Byzantium lost Ravenna, its last possession in north-central Italy.
827	Crete and Sicily were captured by Saracens.
*c.*855	**Constantine**, a Byzantine scholar in Thessaloniki, devised the **'Glagolitic' script** for the Slavic languages.
862	The ruler of Greater Moravia asked BE to send him teachers who could propagate Christianity in a language intelligible to Slavs.
863	Constantine and his brother **Methodius** went to Greater Moravia to further develop a Slavic written language, liturgy and scriptures. From 867 to 869 Constantine and Methodius were hosted by the Pope in Rome, where Constantine became a monk and adopted the name **Cyril** before dying in 869. The **Cyrillic script** which he devised was named after him.
865	Bulgaria's **Khan Boris** (reg. 852–89 and 893) was baptized and made Eastern Orthodox Christianity his country's official religion.
870–85	Methodius resumed his mission in Moravia. By the time of his death in 885, he and his assistants had translated the Bible into **Church Slavonic**. Germanic and Catholic opponents then hounded Methodius and Cyril's disciples out of Greater Moravia and suppressed their Slavonic liturgy.
885	Khan Boris invited the disciples of (Saints) Cyril and Methodius to Bulgaria. There they further developed the **'Cyrillic' alphabet** and the **Church Slavonic language**, the twin foundations of the major South Slav and Eastern Slav languages.
890–3	Khan Vladimir (reg. 889–93) tried to de-Christianize Bulgaria.
893	Ex-Khan Boris deposed his son Vladimir and reinstated Christianity as Bulgaria's official religion.
900s–920s	**First Bulgarian Empire**: **Tsar Simeon** (reg. 893–927) conquered most of Macedonia, Serbia, Albania, Wallachia and Thrace and tried to capture Constantinople.
926	Tsar Simeon established an **autocephalous Bulgarian Orthodox Church**, with its own patriarchate seated at **Preslav**.
925	Byzantium recaptured Cyprus from the Arabs.
968–9	Preslav was captured by Kiev Rus.

970–1	**Most of the Balkan Slavs were brought back under Byzantine rule**. Their clergy were subsequently Hellenized and subordinated to the patriarchate of Constantinople.
1014–19	The last redoubts of Bulgarian independence were brutally crushed by BE's Emperor **Basil 'the Bulgar-slayer'**.
1050	Pope prohibited use of Eastern Orthodox rites in Italy.
1054	**Final 'schism' (rupture) between ('Latin') Roman Catholic and Eastern Orthodox Christendom**, as the Pope 'excommunicated' the Eastern Orthodox Church.
1055	**Seljuk Turks** from Central Asia took control of Baghdad and embarked on conquests in Armenia and Anatolia.
1061	Norman invasion of Sicily threatened power of BE in eastern Mediterranean and Adriatic.
1071	**BE lost Bari and Brindisi**, its last Italian strongholds, to the Normans. **It was also decisively defeated by the Seljuk Turks at Manzikert**. This opened Anatolia to Turkish conquest.
1081–2	**BE granted Venice free access to Byzantine ports and control of their main habours and customs offices**, in return for (empty) Venetian promises of naval assistance against the Normans and the Turks.
1095	**Pope Urban II launched a military Crusade ('Holy War') to liberate the Holy Lands from 'the Infidel'**. Crusaders captured Nicea (capital of the Seljuk Turks), Antioch and Jerusalem (1097–9), but proved unable to retain them.
1147–8	Largely ineffectual **Second Crusade**, during which Norman Sicily captured Byzantine Corfu and pillaged Athens, Corinth and Thebes.
1166	Rebellion in Serbia led by **Stefan Nemanja**, founder of Serbia's future **Nemanja dynasty**.
1171	Byzantine Emperor Manuel I ordered the **arrest of all Venetians on BE territory and the confiscation of their property**, in a bid to overcome Venice's economic stranglehold on BE, but he felt obliged to restore all Venetian privileges and confiscated property in 1175.
1185–6	**Bulgarian rebellion** led by tax-averse Bulgarian boyars (landlords) at **Trnovo**.
1187	BE formally recognized a resurrected Bulgarian principality under Ivan I Asen (reg. 1187–96) and his brothers Petur Asen (reg. 1196–7) and Kaloyan Asen (reg. 1197–1207).
1188–92	Inconclusive **Third Crusade**; Crusaders captured Cyprus, Acre and Jaffa.
1202	**Fourth Crusade (1202–4)**, financed and transported mainly by Venice, captured port of Zadar.
1204	Instead of liberating the Holy Lands, **Catholic Crusaders sacked Constantinople and temporarily ended the Eastern Orthodox BE**. Venice made strategic acquisitions in the Adriatic and Greece, while several short-lived 'Crusader states' were established in the Balkans. Bulgaria's ruler **Kaloyan** seized this opportunity to expand his Balkan domains.

Western (Catholic) rule in Constantinople, 1204–61

1204	The **'Latin Emperor' Baldwin**, installed in Constantinople by the Fourth Crusade, attempted to subjugate the burgeoning Second Bulgarian Empire.

1205	**Kaloyan** captured Emperor Baldwin and further extended his own domains.
1217	Greek Orthodox ruler of Epirus subjugated most of Macedonia.
1222–4	Greek Orthodox Epirus conquered Thessaloniki and Thessaly.
1227	Under pressure from Hungary, the papacy proclaimed a **Crusade against alleged heretics in Bosnia**.
1230	**Second Bulgarian Empire: Tsar Ivan II Asen (reg. 1218–41)** conquered Epirus, Macedonia, Albania, Serbia, southern Wallachia and northern Greece, becoming the dominant Balkan power. He also restored an autocephalous Bulgarian Orthodox Church and unsuccessfully besieged Constantinople in 1235–6.
1237–42	**Mongol invaders shattered Bulgaria's economy and power**.
1243	**Mongol invaders shattered the Seljuk Turks' economy and power.**
1246–9, 1256–8	The Greek Orthodox rulers of Nicaea (Iznik) and northern Anatolia subjugated most of the southern Balkans, profiting from the misfortunes of Epirus, Bulgaria and the Seljuk Turks.

The restoration and final decline of Byzantium, 1261–1453

1261	**Michael Palaeologus, the Greek Orthodox ruler of Nicaea (Iznik), captured Constantinople**. The last 'Latin Emperor' and his Venetian backers fled by sea.
1299–1300	A Turkic frontier warrior known as **Osman** founded an Osmanli (alias Ottoman) statelet in northern Anatolia.
1326	**Osman captured the strategic city of Bursa (Brusa).**
1329, 1337	Osman's son **Orkan** (reg. 1326–62) captured Nicaea (Iznik) and Nicomedia (now Izmit), BE's last Anatolian strongholds.
1330–55	An Eastern Orthodox and largely Slavic **Serbian Empire**, comprising Serbia, Montenegro, Macedonia, Bulgaria, Albania and northern Greece, was established by **Stefan Uros III** (1321–31) and **Stefan Dusan** (1331–55).
1345	**Ottomans annexed the emirate of Karasi on the Dardanelles**, while assisting Byzantine functionary John Cantacuzene's bid for BE's throne.
1346	Stefan Dusan established an autocephalous **Serbian Orthodox Church and Patriarchate** and was crowned as 'Tsar and Autocrat of the Serbs and Romans'.
1347	**John Cantacuzene** seized the Byzantine throne with Ottoman help.
1349	John Cantacuzene married Sultan Orkhan's daughter Theodora and invited 20,000 Ottoman mercenaries to the Balkans to help defeat Stefan Dusan's Serbian bid for Balkan supremacy.
1352, 1354	**The Ottomans captured Cimpe (Tzympe) and Gallipoli**, strategic bridgeheads on the Balkan Peninsula.
1355	Stefan Dusan died while launching a siege of Constantinople, whereupon his hastily assembled empire rapidly disintegrated.
1361	The **Ottomans captured Adrianople** (now Edirne), making it their capital and using it to establish full control of eastern **Thrace** and **Philippopolis** (now Plovdiv).
1364	The Ottomans defeated large Catholic and Orthodox Christian forces near **Adrianople.**

1371	The Ottomans defeated major Orthodox/Balkan Slav armies in the **Maritsa valley**, gateway to the central Balkans.
1380–6	**Bitolj** (Monastir), **Sofia** and **Nis** fell to the Ottomans.
1386–7	The Ottomans captured **Thessaloniki** and most of Macedonia.
1389	The **Battle of Kosovo** between the Ottomans (with numerous Orthodox Christian allies) and a coalition of Serb, Bosnian, Bulgarian, Albanian and Wallachian Orthodox Christian forces was technically a draw, with heavy losses and royal deaths on both sides. Yet it barely halted Ottoman advances.
1391–2	**The Ottomans largely completed their conquest of lands inhabited by Orthodox South Slavs.**
1392–5	**Timur the Lame** (Tamerlane), who had launched a Central Asian Empire in Samarkand in 1369, conquered and plundered Persia, Mesopotamia, New Sarai (capital of the Tatar Golden Horde) and Astrakhan.
1395–1402	**The Ottomans unsuccessfully besieged Constantinople.**
1396	Ottomans routed a Catholic anti-Turkish Crusade at **Nicopolis**.
1402	**Ottoman power was temporarily shattered by Timur** at the Battle of Ankara.
1402–13	Struggles between rival claimants to the Ottoman throne gave Balkan Christian polities a (largely wasted) breathing space.
1413–21	Ottomans regrouped and recovered under **Sultan Mehmet I**.
1422	**Second unsuccessful Ottoman siege of Constantinople**.
1442–68	Ottomans met with tenacious **Albanian resistance**, led by **Gjergj Kastrioti (Skenderbeg)**.
1444	Ottomans decimated Hungarian-led Catholic forces at **Varna**.
1448	Ottomans routed a grand coalition of Christian forces at the second (and more decisive) **Battle of Kosova**.
1453	**Fall of Constantinople** to massive Ottoman bombards and 150,000 Ottoman troops, ending more than a thousand years of Byzantine ascendancy in the Balkans.

Ottoman ascendancy in the Balkans, 1453–1913

1453	A *berat* (**charter**), given to Patriarch Gennadius by Sultan Mehmet II, promised considerable **religious/cultural toleration and autonomy for non-Muslim 'peoples of the Book'** (Christians and Jews).
1456–9	**Ottoman reconquest of Serbia and mainland Greece.**
1463	Ottoman conquest of Bosnia.
1467–79	Ottoman conquest of Albania.
1482–3	Ottoman conquest of Herzegovina.
1499	Ottomans subjugated Montenegro.
1476, 1521	Ottoman reduction of Wallachia and Moldavia to vassal status.
1475–1783	Ottoman exclusion of foreign shipping from the Black Sea.
1490s–1520s	Approximately 100,000 Jewish refugees from Spain and Portugal were welcomed into the Ottoman Empire (OE).
1516–17	Ottoman conquest of the Levant, Palestine, Egypt and the Hijaz transformed OE into the chief guardian of the Muslim Holy Places and Sunni orthodoxy.
1521	Ottomans captured Belgrade.
1526	**Battle of Mohacs: Ottomans decisively defeated Hungary**.

1529	**Unsuccessful Ottoman siege of Vienna**.
1604–1829	OE restricted grain exports from imperial domains, to help ensure the security and cheapness of grain supplies to Istanbul.
1683	**Second unsuccessful Ottoman siege of Vienna**.
1687–99	**Habsburg 'liberation' or '(re)conquest' of Hungary, Transylvania and Croatia**.
1699	**Peace Treaty of Karlowitz**, with OE as the defeated party.
1711–1821	**The 'Phanariot regime'**: OE exercised suzerainty over Wallachia and Moldavia indirectly, through mainly Greek clergy, servitors and merchant princes. They siphoned off taxes, fines and bribes for their own enrichment, but paid the Ottomans for the privilege of doing so.
1716–17	Habsburg Empire (HE) conquered most of Serbia and parts of Bosnia and Wallachia.
1736–9	OE regained some lost Balkan territory.
1768–74, 1782–3, 1787–92	**Russo-Turkish Wars**: Russia obtained a great deal of territory and a 'protectorate' over Balkan Orthodox Christians.
1797–1813	**Bonapartist France occupied Croatia and Slovenia** and fostered the **'Illyrian Provinces'**.
1804–13	**Serbian insurrection** led by **Karadjordje**; crushed in 1815.
1806–12	**Russia conquered eastern Moldavia ('Bessarabia'**, now Moldova), where it extended and intensified serfdom.
1809	Britain occupied the Ionian Islands (until 1864).
1815–17	**Northern Serbia** won full autonomy under **Milos Obrenovic**.
1821	**Greek revolt** against Ottoman overlordship in **Moldavia** (leader Alexandros Ypsilantis); and Romanian revolt against Phanariots in **Wallachia** (leader Tudor Vladimirescu). Both revolts were crushed, but the Phanariot regime was terminated.
1821–8	**Greek War of Independence**; victorious in 1827–8, owing to Russian, British and French backing.
1829–33	**Russia occupied Moldavia and Wallachia** and imposed 'Organic Statutes' (ostensibly liberalizing reforms).
1837	**Anglo-Ottoman trade treaty** helped to open up OE markets.
1839–76	**Tanzimat (restructuring) reforms of the OE**.
1853–6	**Crimean War**: OE, with Anglo-French backing, rejected Russian demands for Russian control of Christian 'Holy Places' on Ottoman territory. In 1853 Russia occupied Moldavia and Wallachia and sank the Ottoman Black Sea fleet. In 1854 HE occupied Moldavia and Wallachia (until 1857), while Britain and France declared war on Russia, which was defeated in 1855–6.
1859	**Personal union of Wallachia and Moldavia** under Alexandru Ioan Cuza (reg. 1859–66).
1861–2	Administrative union of Wallachia and Moldavia.
1864	Britain ceded **Ionian Islands** to Greece.
1864–5	**Cuza emancipated Romania's serfs**, but the terms of their emancipation were made increasingly onerous for them after Cuza was overthrown by powerful boyars in 1866.
1866–1914	Wallachia and Moldavia were consolidated into a Romanian state by Prince Carol of Hohenzollern-Sigmarinen.
1875–6	**Rebellions in Bosnia and Bulgaria** were bloodily suppressed in 1876, whereupon **Serbia and Montenegro declared war against OE**.

1876	Political crisis in the OE resulted in the promulgation of a liberal constitution establishing a parliamentary system.
1877–8	**Russo-Turkish War**: OE was severely defeated.
1878	**Treaty of San Stefano**, negotiated between OE and Russia, awarded Bulgarians a large independent state. However, the subsequent **Berlin Congress** (of Europe's Powers) decided to halve Bulgaria's size, restore Ottoman suzerainty over Bulgaria, recognize **Serbian, Romanian and Montenegrin independence**, and allow a **Habsburg occupation of Bosnia-Herzegovina**. Sultan Abdulhamit II (reg. 1876–1909) suppressed the OE's parliament and the constitution of 1876.
1879	Albanian insurgents launched an armed **League of Prizren**, in a bid to save Albania and Kosova from being carved up by Serbia, Montenegro, Greece and Bulgaria.
1885	Bulgaria annexed largely Bulgarian-inhabited **eastern Rumelia**.
1897	Union (*enosis*) between Crete and Greece was defeated by OE.
1903	Macedonian Slavs staged a bloodily suppressed **uprising in Krusevo**; Serbia's king and queen were gruesomely murdered during a military coup.
1908	**HE formally annexed Bosnia-Herzegovina**, enraging many South Slav nationalists. **Bulgaria gained full independence**. The **'Young Turk' Revolution** ended Sultan Abdulhamit's autocracy in OE, raising hopes of further liberalization, but by 1909 obdurate Turkish nationalists were in control.
1909–12	Several **Albanian uprisings against Ottoman rule**, abetted by Serbia and Montenegro.
1912–13	**Balkan Wars**: Serbia, Montenegro, Bulgaria and Greece largely expelled OE from Balkans (only Istanbul and southern Thrace remained Turkish). Major **Serb atrocities** in annexed Kosova. **Greece**, having gained southern Macedonia, southern Epirus, Crete and most Aegean Islands, nearly doubled in size. Aggrieved by its relatively meagre gains, Bulgaria fought and lost a war against Serbia, Montenegro, Greece and OE. This further reduced Bulgaria's gains, while Romania annexed South Dobrudja.

The post-Ottoman Balkans, 1913–45

1913	Europe's Powers fostered a weak **Albanian state**, comprising barely half the territory inhabited by Albanians.
1914 (28 June)	**Bosnian Serb assassination of the Habsburg Crown Prince Franz Ferdinand and his wife** in Sarajevo during a state visit on the anniversary of the 1389 Battle of Kosovo.
1914 (July)	**Habsburg ultimatum to Serbia** demanded Serb submission to Habsburg overlordship. Serbia accepted all bar one of the demands, yet **HE declared war on Serbia** – thereby engulfing Europe in conflict.
1914–15	**Serbia twice repelled large Habsburg invasion forces**, but it could not withstand the **entry of OE and Bulgaria into the war on the side of the Central Powers** (HE and Germany). Serbia's government, royal family and armed forces escaped across Albania's mountains to Corfu in late 1915, but many Serbs perished en route or in Corfu.
1916	**Romania** entered the war on the side of the Entente (France, Britain and Russia) in August, but was swiftly defeated and plundered by the Central Powers.

1917	**Greece** entered the war on the side of the Entente in July and facilitated an Entente invasion of central and eastern Balkans via Thessaloniki, in return for later Anglo-French backing for Greek expansion into Anatolia.
1918	**Bulgaria collapsed and surrendered in September, OE did so in October, and the Central Powers in November. HE disintegrated in October.**
1918 (Dec)	**Romania expanded greatly**, Greece expanded significantly, and **a Serb-dominated South Slav (Yugoslav) kingdom was established**, but Bulgaria incurred territorial losses (confirmed by Treaty of Neuilly in 1919) and Albania's prospects seemed grim.
1919	**Greece invaded Anatolia**, with Anglo-French backing.
1919–23	Increasingly authoritarian peasantist regime in Bulgaria under **Aleksandur Stamboliski**.
1920–2	**Greek forces were routed by the Turks**, who brought most Turkish-inhabited areas of the Balkans and Anatolia into the new Turkish Republic. Subsequently, Greece and Turkey 'exchanged' (expelled) ethnic minorities, reciprocally.
1920–3	**Albania**, having been occupied by neighbouring states during First World War, gradually (re)gained independence.
1923	**Treaty of Lausanne** stabilized Turkey's new borders; **Mustafa Kemal** 'Ataturk' became its president.
1923–6	**Aleksandur Tsankov's 'White terror'** against the Bulgarian left.
1924	Mustafa Kemal abolished the Caliphate.
1920s	**The Balkans struggled to achieve political and economic stability and viability**. The principle of **national self-determination** fostered irredentism, minority problems and instability (more than harmony and stability). It rendered most borders open to challenge – and minorities vulnerable to 'ethnic cleansing'.
1924–39	**Ahmed Zogu** (later King Zog) subjected Albania to authoritarian rule.
1928–31	Romania's **National Peasant Party** initiated promising reforms, but was undermined by the 1930s Depression.
1929–41	Royal authoritarian rule in **Yugoslavia**.
1930s	**The Balkans were hugely damaged by the collapse of world commodity prices and European 'beggar my neighbour' protectionism.**
1933–40	The rich Western democracies' reluctance to keep their markets open to other countries' exports and to offer economic and technological assistance drove most of the Balkan ruling elites into the seemingly warmer embrace of fascist states, which appeared to offer preferential access to much-needed markets, capital and technology.
1935	Croatian *Ustasa* assassinated Yugoslavia's King Alexander.
1935–40	Military dictatorship in **Greece**.
1935–44	Royal dictatorship in **Bulgaria**.
1938–40	Royal authoritarian rule in **Romania**.
1939 (Apr)	Italian annexation of **Albania**.
Oct 1940–1941	An unsuccessful Italian invasion of **Greece** was rescued by Germany in 1941.
1941–5	**Yugoslavia, Albania and Greece** suffered rapacious military occupations by fascist states, giving rise to Europe's strongest Communist-led anti-fascist resistance movements. Pro-Axis **Romania** experienced traumatic

territorial amputations in 1940, the Holocaust in 1941–3 and Soviet occupation in 1944–5, but pro-Axis **Bulgaria** escaped relatively unscathed.

The Balkans under Communist dominance, 1945–89

1945–52	While **Greece** suffered a **civil war (1946–9)** and an initially repressive **monarchist regime** backed by Britain and the USA, **Romania, Bulgaria, Yugoslavia and Albania** suffered the rigours and privations of full-blown **Stalinist Communism**.
1945–85	Dictatorship of **Enver Hoxha** in Albania.
1948	Tito's **Yugoslavia** was 'excommunicated' by the USSR.
1953–89	The Balkan states, including Greece, underwent **rapid expansion of industry, cities, education and health care**. **Greece** was gradually (albeit erratically) opened up and liberalized under pressure and with assistance from the West. During the 1960s and 1970s **Yugoslavia**, with its mass tourism and more than a million Yugoslav *gastarbeiter* working in the West, became the most open, liberal, marketized and Westernized of the Communist states and appeared to be heading in directions not dissimilar to Greece, although resurgent inter-ethnic tensions gave grounds for misgivings from 1968 and especially 1981 onwards. By contrast, **Romania**, **Bulgaria** and especially **Albania** remained ensnared by **'national Stalinism'**. The brutal purges, prison camps and terror of the late 1940s and early 1950s were scaled back, but right up to 1989 there was very little liberalization or openness.
1954–89	Dictatorship of **Todor Zhivkov** in Bulgaria.
1961	Albania severed links with the USSR and turned to China instead.
1965–89	Dictatorship of Nicolae Ceausescu in Romania.
1968–74	**Greece under the 'Colonels regime'** (military rule) became a pariah state, until an attempt to 'unite' Cyprus with Greece by force of arms precipitated a Turkish military occupation of northern Cyprus and the overthrow of the 'Colonels regime'.
1974–2007	Return to civilian rule, the Westernizing economic and cultural impact of mass tourism, and Greek entry into the European Community in 1981 strongly reinforced the Greek path towards increased liberalization and openness.
1978	**Albania broke with China**, becoming a 'hermit state'.
1980	**Tito**, the dictator who had held Yugoslavia together, died.
1981	Greece joined the EC.
1985–91	Half-hearted liberalization under **Ramiz Alia** in Albania.
1989 (Nov)	Breakdown of Communist rule in **Bulgaria**.
1989 (Dec)	Violent emergence of **National Salvation Front in Romania**.
1990	Collapse of Communist rule in **Yugoslavia**.
1991–2	Increasingly violent **disintegration of Yugoslavia** (the SFRY) and the breakdown of Communist rule in **Albania**.

The Balkan post-Communist states, 1990s–2007

1990s–2007	The Balkan post-Communist states have been engaged in ongoing battles for democratic scrutiny and accountability, political and economic

liberalization, fundamental rights, limited government and the rule of law. The biggest impediments arose in Bosnia, Serbia and Croatia, where the break-up of the SFRY enabled ruling elites to exploit ethnic collectivism to pernicious ends. The inherited power structures also proved remarkably resistant to fundamental restructuring in Romania and Bulgaria. However, from the late 1990s onward, internal pressures for restructuring and reform were strongly reinforced by the incentives and requirements of membership of the EU and (to lesser degrees) NATO.

1990–9	**Franjo Tudjman**'s corrupt authoritarian nationalist rule in Croatia.
1990–2000	**Slobodan Milosevic**'s corrupt, authoritarian and intermittently nationalist rule in Serbia.
1991–5	**'Homeland war'** between Croatia and Serbia.
1992–5	**Bosnian War**: Bosnia-Herzegovina was torn apart.
1992	**Romania and Bulgaria signed 'Europe Agreements'** (enhanced Treaties of Association with the EC)
1994–5	**NATO** belatedly intervened in Bosnia-Herzegovina.
1995 (Nov)	The Bosnian War was ended by the US-brokered **Dayton Accords**, which established a decentralized, consociational and confederal Bosnia and Herzegovina under UN tutelage.
1997	Several so-called **'pyramid schemes' collapsed in Albania** (January), which was engulfed by **insurgency** (February–June).
1998–early 1999	Serb forces engaged in ethnic cleansing of Kosovars in **Kosova**.
1999	**Kosova War**: NATO bombed Serbia into submission and placed Kosova under a UN protectorate. EU leaders decided that it was too risky to leave the Balkan post-Communist states 'out in the cold' any longer and allowed Romania and Bulgaria to become official candidates for EU membership (October– December). **Tudjman**'s **death** (December) revived Croatia's prospects.
2000 (Sept–Oct)	**Overthrow of Milosevic** revived Serbia's prospects.
2001	**Macedonia was engulfed in civil war** between the Slav Macedonian majority and the large ethnic Albanian minority (February-July), yet **signed an SAA with the EU** (April).
2001 (Oct)	**Croatia signed an SAA with the EU**.
2002 (Dec)	A European Council in Copenhagen decided that Romania and Bulgaria could be allowed to enter the EU in 2007 or 2008, provided further reforms were implemented.
2003 (June)	At the Thessalonki European Council, the western Balkan post-Communist states were formally assured by EU leaders that they too would be allowed to join the EU in due course – the question was no longer 'whether' but merely 'when'.
2004 (Mar)	**Romania and Bulgaria entered NATO**.
2004 (17–18 Mar)	Inter-ethnic conflict was briefly reignited in Kosova**.**
2005 (Oct)	**The EU decided to start membership negotiations with Croatia and Turkey**. As of April 2007, Croatian entry by 2009 was still deemed possible.
2005 (Dec)	**Macedonia became an official candidate for EU membership**, but actual negotiations were held in abeyance during 2006.
2006 (May)	**EU suspended SAA negotiations with Serbia**, because of its persistent failure to arrest and hand over those indicted by the ICTY for war crimes

and crimes against humanity. **Montenegro** voted in favour of independence from Serbia, and became independent the following month.

2006 (June)	**Albania signed an SAA with the EU.**
2006 (Sept)	The EU commission recommended that **Romania and Bulgaria** be allowed to enter the EU in January 2007, albeit subject to continued monitoring and safeguard provisions.
2006 (Nov)	NATO leaders invited Montenegro and Serbia to join Partnership for Peace. They also announced that in 2008 Croatia, Albania and Macedonia would be formally invited to become NATO members.
2006 (Dec)	A European Council reaffirmed that the Western Balkan states would be admitted into the EU in due course, albeit still without specifying any time-frame.
2007 (Jan)	**Romania and Bulgaria entered the EU.** The ultra-nationalist Serbian Radical Party won the largest share of the vote in Serbian parliamentary elections, but insufficient to form a government.
2007 (Mar)	**UN envoy Martti Ahtisaari recommended that Kosova should become an independent state**, with its own constitution, flag and armed forces, but **under EU supervision**, during 2007. **Montenegro signed an SAA with the EU.** Serbia was told that it could become an official candidate for EU membership as early as 2008, provided it co-operated fully with the ICTY.
2007 (April)	A major crisis erupted in Romania when premier Calin Popescu Tariceanu (leader of the Liberal Party) sacked his main coalition partners (the Democratic Party) and the non-party ministers whose reforms had secured the admission of Romania into the EU, while parliament voted to suspend and impeach President Traian Basescu (leader of the Democratic Party), accusing him of having repeatedly violated the Constitution. These shenanigans aroused fears that Romania was back-tracking on its reforms and would incur punitive sanctions.
2007 (May)	The attempted impeachment of Basescu was overturned by a popular referendum, temporarily defusing the Romanian crisis. Russia repeatedly threatened to use its UN veto to block Kosova's formal secession from Serbia.
2007 (June)	The EU resumed SAA negotiations with Serbia, after a new Serbian coalition government increased Serbian cooperation with the ICTY.

Chronology of East Central European history

BCE

c.1300–*c*.400	So-called **Lusatians** inhabited parts of the present territory of Poland and the Czech Republic.
c.500–*c*.350	**Scythian incursions** into ECE.
c.370– *c*.400	Beginnings of **Celtic settlement** in ECE.
c.100–	Celts began to be assimilated and/or displaced westwards by incursions of **Germanic peoples** into ECE.
c.50	Beginnings of **Dacian incursions** into the central Danubian basin (CDB).
10–9	**Romans** subjugated the mainly Celtic inhabitants of what are now western Hungary and Slovakia, which were incorporated into the Roman province of **Pannonia**, and also began to trade with the lands between the River Vistula and the Baltic Sea.

CE (AD):

c.106–*c*.271	**Transylvania** was part of the Roman province of Dacia.
c.180s–*c*.230s	Gradual **Roman withdrawal** from ECE in the face of recurrent **Gemanic ('barbarian') incursions**.
c.250–*c*.400	Germanic Vandals settled in what is now Poland.
360s–410s	**Huns**, horse-borne nomadic steppe pastoralists and warriors from Central Asia and/or Mongolia, began major incursions into the Volga basin, ECE and the Balkans, living off the lands they ravaged. Their stirrups, equestrian skills, small but fast and rugged horses, hit-and-run tactics, and light but effective bows and arrows and swords enabled them to run rings around European opponents. Their depredations intensified the southward and westward migrations of the Germanic warrior peoples ('barbarians') who assailed the Roman Empire.
420s–455	Unified and led by **Rugila** (d. 434) and his nephews **Attila** (reg. 434–53) and **Bleda** (reg. 434–45) from a base on the River Tisza in the CDB (present-day Hungary), the Huns repeatedly ravaged central Europe, the Balkans and northern Italy, extorting large payments of 'tribute'.
454–5	Various Germanic rulers joined forces to defeat the Huns, who were finally driven back into the Eurasian steppes. The resultant power vacuum in ECE was mainly filled by Germanic warrior peoples.
c.510–*c*.600	First archaeological evidence of **Slavs** in Slovakia and Moravia.

*c.*568–780s	Turkic **Avars**, originally horse-borne nomadic pastoralists and warriors from the Eurasian steppes, established their ascendancy over the CDB and northern Balkans.
*c.*623–*c.*658	**Samo** (a Frankish merchant-adventurer) united the Slavs in Moravia, Slovakia, northern Austria and eastern Bohemia, overthrew Avar overlordship, and repeatedly raided Frankish territories.
660s–770s	**Reassertion of Avar overlordship** in CDB.
700s–800s	First archaeological evidence of Slavs in the present territory of Poland, which was then sparsely inhabited.
780s–814	**Emergence of (Germanic) Frankish Empire under Charlemagne**.
791, 795–6	**Franks inflicted major defeats on Avars**. Some Avars were baptized into Roman Catholic Christianity and accepted Frankish overlordship, but others elected a new kagan and maintained armed resistance to Frankish domination. A Catholic Church synod entrusted the **Christianization** of the CDB to the archbishopric of Salzburg, but Christianization of lands further north (present-day Bohemia, Moravia and Slovakia) was assigned to the bishopric of Passau.
791 or 803	Charlemagne established **the Ostmark** (later Austria) as a fortified eastern outpost of his nascent empire and Catholic Christendom. He was crowned as Holy Roman Emperor by the Pope in 800.
800s–810s	Emerging Slav potentates liquidated the remnants of Avar power and occupied Avar forts and palaces. Slav principalities arose around **Nitra** and in **Moravia**.
828	First Christian Church in ECE was consecrated at **Nitra** (in present Slovakia) by the Catholic Archbishop of Salzburg.
831	Moravia's ruling elite embraced Catholic Christianity.
*c.*833	**Mojmir I**, ruler of Moravia (820s–846), conquered the Slav principality of Nitra.
862	**Prince Rastislav** (reg. 846–70) asked BE to send teachers who could propagate Christianity in a language intelligible to Slavs. The Byzantine scholars **Methodius** and **Constantine**, who had developed a 'Glagolitic' Slavonic script in Thessaloniki, arrived in Greater Moravia in 863 to develop further a Slavic written language and liturgy.
867–9	Constantine and Methodius were hosted by the Pope in Rome, where Constantine became a monk and adopted the name **Cyril** before dying in 869. The **Cyrillic script** which he devised was named after him.
870–85	Methodius returned to Moravia with the rank of papal legate and archbishop and, despite Frankish opposition and interference, continued his mission. He and his assistants completed a translation of the Bible into **Church Slavonic** before his death in 885.
870	Rastislav was overthrown by his nephew **Svatopluk** (reg. 870–94), with backing from Germanic Catholic opponents of Eastern Orthodox Christianity. After Methodius died in 885, Svatopluk and his Frankish Catholic allies hounded Methodius and Cyril's disciples out of Greater Moravia and suppressed their Slavonic liturgy there, but their work was resumed in Bulgaria and became the basis of the major South Slav and Eastern Slav languages.
898–900	Successive **Magyar invasions** of the CDB.
900–7	**Magyar occupation of Transdanubia, Slovakia, parts of Transylvania**

	and the Ostmark (now Austria). 'Western Slavs' became lastingly separated from 'South Slavs'. **Full disintegration of Greater Moravia** facilitated the **emergence of a Slav polity in Bohemia**, ruled by the **Premyslid dynasty** until 1306.
904	**Arpad**, deputy leader of the Magyar confederacy, seized power and founded Hungary's **Arpad dynasty** (reg. 904–1301).
933, 955	**Germanic forces decisively defeated Magyar forces**, restoring the Ostmark to Germanic control and initiating the sedentarization of the Magyars.
c.958–1128	Much of Poland was ruled by the **Piast dynasty**, supposedly descended from a legendary ninth-century founder named Piast.
965–6	Polish ruler **Mieszko I** (reg. c.958–92) embraced Catholic Christianity.
970–97	Hungary's ruler **Geza** subordinated and sedentarized the Magyar warrior clans and in 973 adopted Catholic Christianity.
c.1000	**Roman Catholic Churches** were established in Poland and Hungary; Geza's son **Istvan** (reg. 997–1038) received a royal crown from the Pope.
1046, 1061	Rebellions by Magyar pagans were ruthlessly suppressed.
1097	**Hungary occupied inland Croatia and Dalmatia**; its ruler Koloman (reg. 1095–1116) was crowned King of Croatia and Dalmatia in 1102. Various Dalmatian ports, fearing Venetian power, subsequently opted for Hungarian overlordship.
1126–1288	Gradual subjugation and Christianization of pagan Prussians (Balts) by the Roman Catholic **Order of Teutonic Knights**.
1138–1320	Political fragmentation of the Piast realm.
1146	**Vienna** became the capital of the Ostmark.
1222	Hungary's ruler **Andras II** promulgated a **Golden Bull** limiting the prerogatives of the monarchy and the Church and recognizing rights to resist perfidious rulers (cf. England's Magna Carta, 1215).
1241–2	Poland and Hungary were severely devastated by Mongol armies.
1264	The ruler of Krakow promulgated a **Charter of Jewish Liberties** (the **Statute of Kalisz**); many of Europe's Jews later settled in Poland.
1273	Rudolf of Habsburg was elected (Germanic) Holy Roman Emperor.
1282(–1918)	**Emperor Rudolf established the Habsburgs as the hereditary rulers of the Austrian Crown Lands**.
1301–8	Baronial anarchy in Hungary, after extinction of Arpad dynasty.
1308–82	Hungary was ruled by the **Anjou dynasty**, which benefited from surges in gold and silver mining and new trade links with Germany, the Baltic and the Balkans.
1308–1454	Teutonic Knights controlled the strategic port of **Gdansk** (Danzig).
1310–1437	Bohemia was ruled by the cosmopolitan **Luxembourg dynasty**.
1320–70	(Re)unification of Piast Poland.
1346–78	Bohemia's ruler **Charles of Luxembourg** served as Holy Roman Emperor, made Prague the empire's chief city (1350–1400), and founded Prague's **Charles University** (1348).
1361	A university was established in **Pecs**.
1362	**Grand Duchy of Lithuania** defeated the Mongol (Tatar) Golden Horde and seized most of Ukraine.
1365	A university was established in **Vienna**.

1363–74	**Konrad Walhauser** and **Jan Milic** sowed the seeds of a proto-Protestant Reformation in Prague. The Bible was translated into Czech in the 1370s.
1374	In Poland, the **Statute of Kosice** extended the prerogatives and privileges of the nobility, clergy and (to lesser degrees) burghers.
1378–1419	Turbulent reign of **Vaclav IV** in Bohemia.
1386(–1572)	Poland's aristocracy forced **Queen Jadwiga** (aged eleven) to marry **Jogaila**, Grand Duke of pagan Lithuania. This **dynastic union** founded Europe's largest polity – an elective monarchy, ruled by the (Lithuanian) **Jagiellonian dynasty** until 1572.
1387–1437	Hungary was ruled by **Zsigmund of Luxembourg** (married to Maria of Anjou), who became Holy Roman Emperor in 1410 and also inherited the Bohemian throne from his brother Vaclav IV in 1420.
1380s–1410s	Fierce debates in Prague between mainly **Czech church reformers**, led by **Matej of Janov** (*c.*1350–93) and later **Jan Hus** (*c.*1371–1415), and mainly German conservatives (Catholics).
1400	Krakow's **Jagiellonian University** received a large bequest from Queen Jadwiga and became Poland's premier university.
1403	The mainly German 'masters' of Prague University published and condemned a Wyclifite list of **'Forty-Five Articles'** or heresies, which they accused the Czech reformers of propagating.
1410	Poland-Lithuania defeated the Teutonic Knights at **Battle of Grunwald**.
1414–17	A **Catholic Church Council was convened at Constance**, in an attempt to restore church unity and authority. It burned Jan Hus and Jeronym Prazhsky to death as heretics in 1415 and 1416, respectively.
1415	Leading Czech noble supporters of Jan Hus formed a **Hussite League** to defend and promote his teachings and reforms. A (mainly Germanic) **Catholic League** was formed to oppose them.
1416	Czech reformers gained control of most of Bohemia's churches.
1419	Under pressure from the Pope and Emperor Zsigmund, from February to July King Vaclav IV forcibly restricted the Hussite reform movement. Radical Hussites gathered on a hilltop in southern Bohemia known as **Mount Tabor** to defy the restrictions and launched the so-called **Taborite movement**, which seized control of Prague in July–August and again in October. Emperor Zsigmund persuaded moderate/propertied Hussites to back down in December, while Catholics launched a counter-offensive.
1420	Radical Hussites established demotic armies, commanded by the brilliant military tactician **Jan Zizka** (1360–1424) and ultimately expelled the mostly Germanic Catholic forces from most Czech towns and cities, including Prague.
1420–95	Papal prohibition on Catholic merchants from entering Bohemia.
1421	The noble-dominated Bohemian Diet dethroned Zsigmund in Bohemia.
1421–34	**Hussite Wars**: radical Hussite/Taborite forces, led by Jan Zizka until 1424 and by Prokop the Shaven thereafter, fought off eight further invasions of Bohemia by Catholic forces. Hussite armies also made brief incursions into Slovakia, Silesia, Thuringia, Bavaria and Poland, in bids to propagate the **Hussite Reformation** and extirpate their enemies.
1425	In Poland, nobles were granted security from arbitrary arrest and seizure of property (this 'habeas corpus' was extended to Lithuania in 1434).

1434	Conservative Hussite nobles and Prague patricians supported a brutal Catholic suppression of radical Hussites, thereby ending the Hussite Wars.
1437–9	Hungary and the Czech Lands were briefly ruled by a Habsburg, Albrecht (Zsigmund's son-in-law), but he died of plague in 1439.
1438–1740	Only Habsburgs became Holy Roman Emperors.
1442–3	**Janos Hunyadi**, a soldier of fortune from Transylvania, inflicted major defeats on Ottoman forces in the Balkans.
1439–44	Hungary was ruled by a Jagiellonian, Wladyslaw (Ulaszlo), who was defeated and killed by Ottoman forces at Varna.
1448–71	Bohemia was ruled by **Jiri of Podebrad**, the conservative 'Oliver Cromwell' of the Hussite Reformation.
1454	The major Baltic ports of **Gdansk, Elblag (Elbing) and Torrun (Thorn)** switched allegiance from the Teutonic Knights to Poland-Lithuania, where the **Statute of Nieszawa** (1454) stipulated that troops and new taxes were henceforth to be raised only by noble consent.
1454–66	**The Teutonic Order** lost a **Thirteen Year War** against Poland-Lithuania. Its remaining domains submitted to Polish overlordship.
1450s	**Printing presses** were established in Bohemia.
1456	Janos Hunyadi broke a Turkish siege of Nandorfehevar (Belgrade) and routed Ottoman forces, but then died of plague.
1458–90	Renaissance Hungary reached its apogee under Janos Hunyadi's son, **King Matyas Hunyadi**.
1465	A Hungarian university was established in Pozsony (Bratislava).
1471–1526	Bohemia was ruled by weak (later absentee) **Jagiellonian monarchs**.
1472–3	**Printing presses** were established in Poland and Hungary.
1478–90	Hungary occupied Moravia.
1485–90	Hungary occupied eastern Austria, including Vienna.
1485	Catholics and Hussites negotiated a pact of mutual religious toleration in Bohemia (repeatedly renewed until 1620s).
1490–1526	Hungary (as well as Bohemia) was ruled by weak **Jagiellonian monarchs**.
1490s–1510s	**Enserfment**: major legal restrictions were imposed on peasant mobility and other peasant freedoms in Bohemia, Poland-Lithuania, Hungary, Brandenburg, Mecklenburg, Prussia and Russia. **Inflows of Jewish refugees** from Spain and Portugal, especially to Poland and OE.
1505	In Poland-Lithuania, henceforth, no major innovation was to be introduced without the consent of the Sejm.
1506	Habsburg Emperor Maximilian I (reg. 1493–1519) married his grandson to the daughter of Lajos I, King of Hungary and Bohemia.
1513	First books in the vernacular were published in Poland.
1514	A Hungarian **'people's Crusade'** against the Turks became a popular revolt against the nobility and rich monasteries, who brutally crushed it.
1518	In Poland-Lithuania agricultural tenants lost the right to appeal to crown law courts (against their landlords), and in 1520 the Sejm increased their statutory labour obligations (*corveé*) from twelve to fifty-two days per annum.
1519–56	Holy Roman Emperor **Charles V** sought to unify Roman Catholic Christendom under Habsburg dominance.
1521	Hungary lost Nandorfehevar (Belgrade) to the Ottomans.

1525	**Dissolution of the Teutonic Order**. East Prussia and the major port-city of Gdansk entered the Kingdom of Poland as semi-autonomous entities.
1526	At **Mohacs,** Ottoman forces routed Hungarian forces and occupied much of Hungary. Lajos II, the King of Hungary and Bohemia, died while fleeing. The Habsburgs claimed the vacant Hungarian and Bohemian thrones.
1520s	**Lutheranism** spread rapidly among German-speaking townspeople in much of ECE.
1529	**Ottomans reinvaded Hungary and unsuccessfully besieged Vienna.** A Polish university was established at Wilno (Vilnius) in Lithuania.
1530s–1580s	Rapid spread of **Protestantism** (especially Calvinism) among the nobilities and commoners of ECE.
1541	**The OE captured Buda and imposed a lasting tripartite partition of Hungary**: central Hungary came under direct Ottoman rule; Transylvania became an autonomous principality under Ottoman overlordship; Slovakia and Transdanubia stayed under Habsburg rule.
1541	Books were printed in Hungarian in Hungary for first time.
1561	**Dissolution of the Order of Livonian Knights**. Livonia and the major port-city of Riga entered the Kingdom of Poland as semi-autonomous entities.
1565	Polish-Lithuanian burghers were barred from foreign trade and travel.
1569	The **Union of Lublin** established a **Polish-Lithuanian Commonwealth** (*Rzeczpospolita*).
1573	A **Confederation of Warsaw** (dominated by aristocrats) elected Henri de Valois as King of Poland-Lithuania, adopted a **Statute of Toleration**, and gave nobles exclusive rights to exploit the timber and minerals on their landholdings.
1575	Adoption of the so-called **Czech Confession**.
1576–86	The able warrior **Stefan Bathory** served as King of Poland-Lithuania, but lost the right to ennoble commoners (other than for military prowess).
1580s–1590s	Under **Emperor Rudolf II** (reg. 1577–1611), Prague became the capital of the Holy Roman Empire and a major centre of the arts and sciences.
1587–1668	Poland-Lithuania was ruled by staunchly Catholic-absolutist members of the Swedish **Vasa dynasty**, thereby embroiling the Commonwealth in the Roman Catholic Counter-Reformation and in Swedish conflicts and ambitions.
1596	A **Uniate Church**, which employed Eastern Orthodox rites but accepted papal authority, was established in Poland-Lithuania. Its members were mainly Ukrainian, Belarussian and (in later centuries) Romanian.
1599(–1918)	Pro-Habsburg Catholic royalists monopolized all key posts in Bohemia.
1605	A Polish-backed pretender was installed as Tsar of Muscovite Russia, only to be deposed in 1606.
1610	**Wladyslaw Vasa**, the son of Poland-Lithuania's King Zygmunt III Vasa, became Tsar of Muscovite Russia, but he was overthrown in favour of the Romanovs in 1613.
1611	In Poland-Lithuania, commoners were barred from buying landed estates.
1618	Bohemian Protestants, Utraquists and liberal-minded Catholics began to rebel against Habsburg Catholic absolutism.
1618–48	The devastating **Thirty Years War** between largely Catholic and largely Protestant forces for control of ECE (especially Bohemia).

1619	Bohemia's Diet voted to depose the Habsburgs from the Bohemian throne, which it offered to the Protestant ruler of the Palatinate.
1620 (Nov)	Austrian Habsburg forces crushed Bohemia's rebel forces at the **Battle of the White Mountain**, near Prague.
1621	The Dutch United Provinces joined the anti-Habsburg 'Protestant cause'.
1626	Denmark joined the anti-Habsburg 'Protestant cause'.
1630	Sweden joined the anti-Habsburg 'Protestant cause'.
1648	The **Treaty of Westphalia** terminated the Thirty Years War and the 'wars of religion' which had afflicted Europe since the 1520s.
1648–54	A huge anti-Polish **Cossack-cum-peasant rebellion in Ukraine** resulted in major territorial and population losses, signalling the start of Poland-Lithuania's protracted decline (1648–1795).
1640s–1740s	ECE experienced a so-called **'feudal reaction'** (steadily rising rents and dues, further erosion of peasant rights, liberties and landholdings, intensification of serfdom, extension of manorial cultivation, and erosion of the position of towns and burghers), increasing anti-Semitism and a full-blown Roman Catholic Counter-Reformation.
1655–60	**Much of Poland was devastated by Swedish invaders**, intent on annexing Pomerania and Livonia and dominating northern Europe.
1673–96	The able warrior **Jan Sobieski** served as King of Poland-Lithuania.
1683	Forces led by Jan Sobieski defeated a major **Ottoman siege of Vienna** and launched a successful counter-offensive against the OE. By saving and strengthening the fickle Austrian Habsburgs, Sobieski unwittingly contributed to Poland-Lithuania's future demise.
1686–99	**'Reconquest' of Hungary, Transylvania and Croatia** by the HE from the OE.
1697–1764	Poland-Lithuania was led by feckless and inept Kings of Saxony.
1700–21	The **'Great Northern War'**: a rash Saxon–Polish-Lithuanian invasion of Swedish Livonia and Riga precipitated devastating Swedish counter-invasions of Poland-Lithuania, which in turn precipitated devastating Russian interventions.
1701	The Hohenzollern Elector of Brandenburg and Duke of Prussia unified his domains at Poland-Lithuania's expense.
1709	Sweden was decisively defeated by Russia in 1709, but this in turn precipitated Russian expansion at Poland-Lithuania's expense.
1703–11	**Anti-Habsburg insurgency in Hungary and Transylvania**.
1711	The **Treaty of Szatmar** bought off Hungary's landed aristocracy by granting Hungary a decentralized **'county system'** of aristocratic self-administration and liberties and a separate legal system.
1717	Proclamation of **free trade** in the Adriatic Sea and the subsequent development of **Trieste** and **Fiume (Rijeka)** as the HE's major 'free ports'.
1740–8	The **'War of the Austrian Succession'**: the succession of Habsburg Emperor Karl VI's daughter Maria Theresa was contested by King Albert of Bavaria, who was elected Holy Roman Emperor in 1740.
1745	**Maria Theresa** (reg. 1740–80), having ceded Lower Silesia to Prussia, had her husband Francis of Lorraine elected as Holy Roman Emperor, retrieving the imperial line.
1756–63	The **'Seven Years War'** pitted the HE, France and Russia against Britain, Hanover and Prussia.

1764(–95)	**Stanislaw Poniatowski**, ex-lover of Russia's Empress Catherine II (reg. 1762–96), became the dynamic (last) King of Poland-Lithuania.
1764–6	Major 'self-strengthening' reforms in Poland-Lithuania.
1767	The Sejm, surrounded by Russian troops, had to repeal the reforms.
1765–90	The **enlightened despotism** of Maria Theresa's son, **Emperor Josef II**.
1767	The obligations of the peasantry were limited by law in German Austria.
1768–72	Polish-Lithuanian uprising against Russian overlordship in Podolia, amid Ukrainian and Cossack pogroms against Jews and Poles.
1772	**First Partition of Poland-Lithuania** between Russia, Prussia and HE.
1773	The Pope dissolved the **Jesuit Order**. In Poland-Lithuania and in HE, the state took over its schools, academies and other assets, to facilitate a rapid expansion of state schooling and state universities.
1775	A **customs union** was established between German Austria and the Czech Lands. The obligations of the peasantry were limited by law in the Czech Lands.
1778	Liberal and self-strengthening reforms and new code of laws promulgated in Poland-Lithuania.
1781	Josef II issued a **Patent of Toleration** (towards Lutherans, Calvinists and Orthodox Christians, but not for sects and Jews) and **largely abolished serfdom** in German Austria and the Czech Lands.
1782	Josef II dissolved approximately 700 monasteries and convents and outlawed mendicancy.
1785–90	Josef II imposed a centralized Germanic administration on Hungary, so as to extend his radical reforms to the 'Hungarian half' of the HE.
1789	Josef II introduced a more uniform and progressive tax system in German Austria and the Czech Lands.
1790s	Start of a **reactionary backlash** in HE against Josef II's reforms and against the French Revolution, especially under **Emperor Franz II** (reg. 1792–1835).
1791	Radical new constitution promulgated in Poland-Lithuania.
1792	Russia invaded Poland-Lithuania and backed opponents of reform.
1793	**Second Partition of Poland-Lithuania**, this time between Russia and Prussia alone (without Habsburg participation).
1792–7	The HE fought unsuccessfully against revolutionary France.
1794	Partitioning Powers brutally suppressed a radical nine-month Polish-Lithuanian rebellion headed by Tadeusz Kosciuszko.
1795	**Third (and complete) Partition of Poland-Lithuania** between Russia, Prussia and HE.
1797–1801	More than 25,000 Poles fought for France in 'Polish Legions'.
1799–1800	HE fought against revolutionary France.
1805	Napoleon defeated HE and Russia at Austerlitz and occupied Vienna.
1806	**Dissolution of the Holy Roman Empire**, at Napoleon's behest.
1807–13	Napoleon sponsored a French-controlled **Grand Duchy of Warsaw** with 2.5 million inhabitants.
1809	Napoleon defeated HE at Wagram. Southern Poland incorporated into the Grand Duchy of Warsaw, whose population rose to 4.2 million.
1809–48	**Clemens Metternich** served as Habsburg chief minister.
1811	HE declared bankruptcy.

1812	Nearly 100,000 Poles participated in Napoleon's 600,000-man **invasion of Russia**, launched from the Grand Duchy of Warsaw.
1813–15	Russian forces routed Napoleon and occupied the Grand Duchy of Warsaw.
1813–14	Britain, Prussia, Russia and HE comprehensively defeated Napoleon.
1814–15	**Congress of Vienna**, dominated by Metternich. HE ceded southern Netherlands (future Belgium) to the Dutch, but secured its dominance of northern and central Italy and a 300-state German Confederation. **Poland-Lithuania was re-partitioned** between HE, Prussia and Russia, which controlled a Warsaw-centred **'Congress Kingdom'**.
1830–2	**Cholera epidemics** in Poland and north-east Hungary.
1830	Polish cadets' uprising in Warsaw (November). Count **Istvan Szechenyi**, Hungary's leading liberal-paternalist reformer, published *Hitel* (*Credit*).
1831–2	Warsaw's Sejm voted to dethrone the Romanovs in the Congress Kingdom, during a major bloodily suppressed **Polish rebellion** against Russian rule.
1832	Count **Istvan Szechenyi** published *Verlag* (*Enlightenment*).
1833–8	Hungarian nationalist **Lajos Kossuth** wrote radical *Parliamentary Reports* and *Municipal Reports*.
1837–40	Detention and trial of Lajos Kossuth.
1830–46	Substantial industrialization and urbanization in German Austria and the Czech Lands.
1840	Hungary's Diet declared Hungarian to be Hungary's official language (in place of Latin), alienating ethnic minorities (63 per cent of the population).
1845–7	Widespread **grain crop failures and potato blight** in ECE.
1846	Polish nobles and ethnic Ukrainian peasants mounted bloodily suppressed **uprisings in western and central Galicia** (Habsburg Poland).
1847	**Italian 'patriots'** protested against Habsburg rule in Lombardy and Veneto. Election of Lajos Kossuth to Hungary's Diet.
1848	**Revolutions of 1848** ended Bourbon absolutism in Sicily and Naples (January), asserted Hungarian self-rule (March), and deposed the Orleanist monarchy in France (February), Metternich in Austria (March), the Habsburgs in Veneto (March), and Pope Pius IX in Rome (November). **Frantisek Palacky** rejected invitation to represent the Czechs in the German liberal-nationalist *Vorparlament* of 1848–9 and formulated the **'Austro-Slav'** stance in favour of a federalized Habsburg Empire (April). Bohemia received charter granting autonomy and parity between Czech and German (April). **Slavonic Congress** convened in Prague on 2 June, but was suppressed after street fighting between Prague students and Habsburg troops precipitated **Habsburg artillery bombardment of central Prague** (17 June). A **constituent assembly** for the 'Austrian half' of the Habsburg Empire opened in Vienna on 22 July and passed **Act of Peasant Emancipation** on 7 September. Radicals seized control of Vienna, 6–31 October, but were defeated by military encirclement, hunger and thirst. On 2 December, Habsburg Emperor Ferdinand (reg. 1835–48) abdicated in favour of nephew **Franz Josef** (reg. 1848–1916).
1849	Austrian constituent assembly dissolved (7 March). **HE subsequently crushed revolutions** in Hungary (with Russian help), Lombardy and Veneto.
1849–59	**'Neo-absolutism'** in HE.

1851	**Abolition of the customs 'wall'** between the 'Austrian' and 'Hungarian' halves of HE.
1851–4	Major state programme of **railway construction** in HE.
1852–9	So-called **'Bach regime'** of centralized rule by Habsburg officials.
1853–6	**Crimean War**: OE, with Anglo-French backing, rejected Russian demands for Russian control of Christian 'Holy Places' in OE. In 1853 Russia occupied Moldavia and Wallachia and sank OE's Black Sea fleet. In 1854 HE occupied Moldavia and Wallachia (until 1857), while Britain and France declared war on Russia, which was defeated in 1855–6.
1859	**HE lost Lombardy to Piedmont** (helped by France), **'Bach regime' was discredited, and Bach resigned**.
1860	In the 'Austrian half' of the HE, noble-dominated provincial diets gained increased powers, as did an imperial Reichsrat (council), in which the diets gained increased representation. Hungary's pre-1848 'county system' of local administration and the pre-1848 powers of its diet were restored, but its leaders boycotted the Reichsrat.
1861	Tsar Alexander II announced **imminent emancipation of serfs in the Russian Empire** (February). HE's Reichsrat was elevated to a bicameral quasi-parliament, with upper house nominated by the emperor and lower house selected by regional diets (February), but diets of Hungary and Croatia (from 1861), Bohemia (from 1863) and Galicia (from 1864) boycotted the Reichsrat.
1863	A major **Polish nationalist uprising** in 'Russian Poland' was crushed.
1864	**Serfs emancipated in Russian Poland**, on relatively favourable terms.
1866	**HE defeated by Prussia** in brief war for dominance of Germany. HE also lost Veneto.
1867	The defeats of 1866 resulted in an **Austro-Hungarian 'Compromise'** (*Ausgleich*), establishing a **Dual Monarchy**.
1868	**Croatia and Galicia ('Austrian Poland') gained limited autonomy**. In Galicia, Polish was subsequently granted equal status with German in schools, law courts, public administration and at Jagiellonian University. Passage of major **Nationality and Education Acts in Hungary**.
1867–73	**HE underwent an economic boom** (the *Gründerzeit*).
1873	The *Gründerzeit* ended in a major **economic crash**. Board established to promote comprehensive elementary schooling in Galicia.
1875–90	Hungary was governed by the repressive nationalist **Kalman Tisza**, who strongly promoted **'Magyarization'**.
1878(–1918)	HE 'temporarily' occupied **Bosnia-Herzegovina**.
1879(–1918)	HE and Germany concluded a **Dual Alliance**.
1879–93	Ascendancy of **Count Taafe's conservative 'iron ring'** in Austrian half of HE; increased economic **protectionism and cartelization**.
1905–6	**Major unrest in Hungary and 'Russian Poland'**, and a major **crisis in relations between Hungary and Austria**.
1907	First **manhood suffrage** elections to Austrian Reichsrat.
1908	**HE formally annexed Bosnia-Herzegovina**.
1914 (Mar)	Austrian **Reichsrat prorogued** (until 1916).
1914 (28 June)	**Assassination of Habsburg Crown Prince Franz Ferdinand and his wife** by a Bosnian Serb in Sarajevo.
1914 (July)	HE demanded Serb submission to Habsburg overlordship. Serbia accepted

	all but one of the demands, but **HE declared war on Serbia** – engulfing Europe in conflict.
1914 (Sept)	HE suffered defeats in Serbia and Galicia
1914–17	**Josef Pilsudski's Polish Legions** supported Central Powers against Russia.
1915	HE helped by Germany and Bulgaria in Balkans (from October).
1916 (Aug–Oct)	HE suffered defeats on Russian front, but Germany proclaimed a German-controlled Kingdom of Poland.
1916 (Oct)	Austrian premier **Karl Stürgh assassinated** by Friedrich Adler.
1916 (Dec)	Emperor **Franz Josef died**; succeeded by **Karl VI**.
1917	USA sided with the Entente, but HE defeated Italian forces at Caporetto (October) and the Bolshevik Revolution relieved pressure on Central Powers (November–December).
1918	Proclamation of **Woodrow Wilson's '14 Points'** (January). Russia promised Poland independence (30 March). Surrenders of Bulgaria (September) and OE (October) accelerated **collapse and disintegration of HE (October) and surrender of Central Powers (November). Pilsudski took control in Poland (November).**
1919	**Bela Kun's 'National Bolshevik' regime in Hungary** (March–July). **Treaty of St Germain** ratified reduction of Austria to a small rump state, prohibited from uniting with Germany.
1919–20	**Russo-Polish War** caused further devastation in Poland.
1919–44	**Admiral Horthy's authoritarian regime in Hungary**.
1920	**Treaty of Trianon** confirmed loss of two-thirds of Hungary's territory.
1920s	ECE struggled to achieve political and economic stability and viability. Principle of **national self-determination** fostered irredentism and rendered minorities vulnerable to 'ethnic cleansing'.
1926–35	**Marshal Pilsudski's authoritarian rule in Poland**.
1930s	**ECE was hugely damaged by the collapse of world commodity prices and increased 'beggar my neighbour' protectionism.**
1931	**ECE's major banks collapsed**, exacerbating the economic depression. Persecution of Poland's large Ukrainian minority.
1933–8	Right-wing authoritarian rule in Austria.
1934–40	Conservative dictatorships in Estonia and Latvia.
1938 (Mar)	Germany annexed Austria (*Anschluss*).
1938 (Sept)	At Munich, Britain, France and Italy endorsed **dismemberment of Czechoslovakia** by Germany.
1939 (Mar)	**Germany completed the destruction of Czechoslovakia.**
1939 (Aug)	**Nazi–Soviet Non-Aggression Pact**
1939 (Sept)	**Germany and USSR invaded Poland; start of Second World War.**
1941 (June)	**Axis Powers invaded USSR.**
1943 (Apr)	**Jewish uprising in Warsaw ghetto**, ferociously crushed.
1944 (Aug)	**Polish uprising in Warsaw**, ferociously crushed.
1944 (Oct)	Churchill's **'percentages agreement'** with Stalin in Moscow.
1945 (Jan)	At **Yalta**, the 'Big Three' agreed on east–west partition of Europe.
1945 (May)	**Defeat of Germany**; end of Second World War in Europe.
1945–7	Semi-parliamentary regimes in ECE.
1947	USA launched **ERP**. USSR initially welcomed it, but later forced Poland, Hungary and Czechoslovakia to forgo 'Marshall Aid'.
1948–9	Berlin blockade. **Consolidation of Communist dictatorships in ECE.**

1949	Formation of **Comecon (the CMEA)**
1953	Death of Stalin, followed by **anti-Communist uprisings** in East Germany, Poland and Czechoslovakia.
1954–64	**Nikita Khrushchev** led the CPSU and the Soviet bloc into a **partial 'thaw'**.
1955	Soviet forces withdrew from Austria and Finland. **Formation of the Warsaw Pact** as Soviet bloc counterpart to NATO.
1956 (Feb)	Khrushchev made a speech denouncing Stalin.
1956 (June–Nov)	**Major unrest in Poland**.
1956 (Oct–Nov)	**Hungarian Revolution**, crushed by Soviet forces.
1961	**Berlin Wall** built. **Albania broke with USSR** and turned to China. **Janos Kadar**, Hungary's Communist dictator, proclaimed: 'Those who are not against us are with us.'
1963–8	**Czechoslovak reform movement**, culminating in '**Prague Spring**'.
1964–83	**Leonid Brezhnev** led the CPSU and 'froze' the Soviet bloc.
1968	Inauguration of Hungary's '**New Economic Mechanism**'.
1969	Willy Brandt's '**Ostpolitik**' inaugurated **East–West détente**.
1975	The **Helsinki Accords**, culmination of East–West détente, promoted European security and human rights.
1977	**Charter 77**, a high-profile Czech human rights movement, was born.
1980	Emergence of 10 million member **Solidarity union** in Poland.
1981 (Dec)	**Martial law in Poland**; repression of Solidarity.
1982–3	**Yuri Andropov** led the CPSU into half-hearted reforms.
1983	Martial law was lifted in Poland.
1983–5	Konstantin Chernenko led CPSU into a new 'freeze'.
1985–91	**Mikhail Gorbachev** led the CPSU and the Soviet bloc into far-reaching *perestroika* (restructuring) and *glasnost* (openness).
1989 (July)	**PHARE aid programme**, co-ordinated by the EC, was launched.
1989	Poland's '**Roundtable' talks** (February–April) led to contested elections in June.
1989 (Sept)	Hungarians became free to escape to the West.
1989 (Nov)	**'Fall' of the Berlin Wall; end of Communist rule in ECE**.
1990	Freely contested **multi-party elections** were held in Hungary and Czechoslovakia. Poland underwent '**shock therapy**' and 'big bang' restructuring under a Solidarity-led government, but this tore Solidarity apart.
1991	Poland, Hungary and Czechoslovakia signed '**Europe Agreements**' (enhanced Treaties of Association with the EC).
1993	EU leaders agreed on '**Copenhagen Criteria**' for EU membership (June). Reformed ex-Communists won parliamentary elections in Poland (September).
1993 (Jan)	The Czech Republic and Slovakia underwent a '**velvet divorce**'.
1994–5	The EU Commission prepared '**pre-accession strategies**' for ECE.
1995 (Dec)	EU leaders adopted '**Madrid Criteria' for EU membership** (in relation to 'administrative and judicial capacity').
1997 (July)	The EU Commission published *Agenda 2000*, a road-map for EU enlargement.
1997 (Dec)	EU leaders decided to **start EU membership negotiations with Poland, Hungary, the Czech Republic, Slovenia and Estonia**.

1999 (Apr)	Poland, Hungary and the Czech Republic entered **NATO**.
1999 (Oct–Dec)	EU leaders decided to include Slovakia, Lithuania, Latvia, Romania and Bulgaria in EU membership negotiations.
2002 (Nov)	NATO invited Slovenia, Slovakia and the Baltic states to enter NATO in 2004.
2002 (Dec)	A **European Council in Copenhagen** finalized the (ungenerous) terms on which ECE and the Baltic States could enter the EU.
2003	EU Treaties of Accession were approved by **referenda** in ECE and the Baltic States.
2004 (Mar)	**Slovenia, Slovakia and the Baltic States entered NATO.**
2004 (May)	**ECE and the Baltic States entered the EU**, in time to participate in elections to the European Parliament in June.
2004–7	In ECE and the Baltic States, **economic growth, FDI inflows, and asset inflation mainly accelerated in the wake of EU membership**. However, these booms and the latent inflationary pressures appeared to be unsustainable in the longer term. Fears were also expressed that, having done everything necessary to gain entry into the EU in 2004, these countries had relaxed their self-discipline and were **falling back into some 'bad old habits' and/or illiberal attitudes in 2006–7**.
2007 (Jan)	**Slovenia** became the first formerly Communist-ruled state to adopt the euro as its currency. During 2006 the booming **Estonia and Lithuania** came very close to meeting the 'convergence criteria' for entry into the 'euro-zone', but were refused entry because their inflation rates slightly exceeded the permitted levels. **Slovakia** was aiming to qualify for entry into the euro-zone in 2009, and in 2007 Estonia chose 2011 as its new target date for entry. However, 'eurosceptical' governments in **Poland** and the **Czech Republic** were clearly in no hurry to adopt the euro, while Latvia (which had 6 per cent inflation rate in 2006) and deficit-stricken Hungary would find it very difficult to meet the euro-zone 'convergence criteria' before 2012 at the earliest.

Abbreviations

ARFY	Alliance of Reform Forces of Yugoslavia (Savez reformskih snaga Jugoslavije)
BANU	Bulgarian Agrarian National/Popular Union
BCE	Business Central Europe
BK	Balli Kombetar (National Front, in 1940s Albania and Kosova)
BP	before present
CEFTA	Central European Free Trade Area
CIS	Commonwealth of Independent States (the former Soviet republics, other than the Baltic States)
CMEA	Council of Mutual Economic Assistance, established by the Soviet bloc states in 1949
COCOM	Co-ordinating Committee for Multilateral Trade Controls
CPSU	Communist Party of the Soviet Union
CSCE	Conference on Security and Co-operation in Europe (1975–94, forerunner of OSCE)
EBRD	European Bank for Reconstruction and Development (inaugurated in 1991, it publishes useful *Transition Reports*)
EC	European Community (established in 1965 through the merger of the ECSC, the EEC and Euratom)
ECSC	European Coal and Steel Community (established in Paris in 1952)
EEC	European Economic Community (established in Rome in 1958)
EEN	*Eastern Europe Newsletter*, latterly known as *Eastern Europe*
EFTA	European Free Trade Association (established in Stockholm in 1960)
EPU	European Payments Union
ERP	European Recovery Programme, 1947–51 (assisted by the Marshall Plan)
EU	European Union (inaugurated under the terms of the Maastricht Treaty in 1993)
FBiH	Federation of Bosnia and Herzegovina (the predominantly Bosniak and Croat sector or 'entity' in Bosnia)
FRY	Federal Republic of Yugoslavia (Serbia and Montenegro only, 1992–2003)
FT	*Financial Times* (an invaluable source of current information and analysis)
FYROM	Former Yugoslav Republic of Macedonia (officially, the Republic of Macedonia or ROM)
G7	Group of Seven major advanced capitalist states
G8	Group of Eight (comprising the seven major advanced capitalist states plus Russia)
G24	Group of twenty-four liberal-capitalist democracies ('the West' plus Japan)
GATT	General Agreement on Tariffs and Trade (forerunner of the WTO)
GDP	Gross Domestic Product
GDR	German Democratic Republic, alias 'East Germany' (1949–89)

GMP   Gross Material Product (the measure of national income deployed by Communist regimes)
ICG   International Crisis Group (a Brussels-based NGO which publishes very useful on-line reports)
ICTY   International Criminal Tribunal for former Yugoslavia
IDPs   internally displaced persons
IHT   *International Herald Tribune* (an invaluable compendium of American commentary and analysis)
IMF   International Monetary Fund
JNA   Yugoslav People's Army
KGB   Soviet state security police
KOR   Committee for Workers' Defence (Poland, 1970s–1980s)
LCY   League of Communists of Yugoslavia
MAP   Membership Action Plan (for NATO membership)
NATO   North Atlantic Treaty Organization (established in 1949)
NDH   Independent State of Croatia (1941–5, dependent on Nazi Germany for its existence)
OECD   Organization for Economic Co-operation and Development (successor to the OEEC)
OEEC   Organization for European Economic Co-operation (precursor of the OECD)
OSCE   Organization for Security and Cooperation in Europe (known as the CSCE from 1975 to 1994)
PHARE   Pologne, Hongrie: activité pour la restructuration économique (launched in 1989 as the main EU-co-ordinated Western aid programme for East Central European, Baltic and Balkan post-Communist states)
PPS   Polish Socialist Party
reg.   reign
ROM   Republic of Macedonia
RS   Republica Srpska (the predominantly Bosnian Serb 'entity' within Bosnia and Herzegovina)
SAA   Stabilization and Association Agreement (a tailored Treaty of Association with the EU)
SFRY   Socialist Federal Republic of Yugoslavia (the former Communist-ruled Yugoslavia)
SKJ   League of Communists of Yugoslavia (1950s successor to the Communist Party of Yugoslavia)
SPS   Socialist Party of Serbia (founded in 1990 by Slobodan Milosevic)
SRS   Serbian Radical Party (founded and led by the wayward Serbian ultra-nationalist Vojislav Seselj)
TACIS   Technical Assistance to the Commonwealth of Independent States
TEMPUS   Trans-European Mobility Scheme for University Studies
TOL   Transitions Online (www.tol.cz) (a very useful information service on Europe's post-Communist states)
UN   United Nations
UNCTAD   UN Conference on Trade and Development
VJ   Yugoslav army (the Serbian-controlled army of the Serbian-controlled rump FRY, 1992–2003)
WEU   Western European Union (launched on UK initiative in 1954–5, comprising the European members of NATO)
WTO   World Trade Organization (successor to GATT)

Introduction: Crisis and change in the Balkan Peninsula and East Central Europe

THE PLIGHT OF 'THE LANDS BETWEEN'

This book offers a thematic history and analysis of the lands which lie between Germany, Italy and the former Tsarist and Soviet empires. German writers used to refer to these lands as *Zwischeneuropa*. Unfortunately, this apt term has no neat equivalent in English. The closest approximation is 'the lands between', as used in the titles of several major books and articles on the region (for example, Palmer 1970 and Croan 1989). This has the virtue of encapsulating the essential misfortune of these regions in modern times, that of being sandwiched between overwhelmingly powerful empires: Germanic on the one side and Ottoman, Tsarist or Soviet on the other. In the words of the Czechoslovak dissident Milan Simecka: 'We live in the awareness that our unhappy situation on the borders of two civilizations absolves us from the outset from any responsibility for the nation's fate. Try as we might, there is nothing we can do to help ourselves' (Simecka 1985: 159). Indeed, as relatively small and vulnerable 'latecomers' to a Europe of sovereign nation-states, the peoples of the Balkans and East Central Europe acquired their modern national independent statehood and territories at least partly by the grace and favour of Europe's Great Powers. Acute awareness of this uncomfortable predicament has helped to perpetuate widespread 'national insecurity' among these peoples. This has fostered fatalistic assumptions that these peoples and regions would usually be *acted upon*, rather than act in accordance with their own interests and needs, and that powers based outside these regions would make territorial dispositions to suit themselves – as indeed they did, most notably in the peace treaties of 1648, 1713, 1815, 1878 and 1918–19, the successive partitions of Poland in 1772, 1793 and 1795, the brutal dismemberment of Czechoslovakia in 1938–9, the even more brutal dismemberment of Yugoslavia in 1941, the infamous 'percentages agreement' between Stalin and Churchill in October 1944, and the Yalta and Potsdam agreements of 1945.

The medieval and early modern history of these 'marchlands' was blighted by persistent warfare against marauders and interlopers from both East and West: Avars, Huns, Magyars, Bulgars, Mongols and Turks from Asia; and German colonists, Venetian traders and Catholic Crusaders from the West. Over the span of many centuries, the battle lines between Roman Catholic and Eastern Orthodox Christianity and (to lesser degrees) between Christianity and Islam shuttled back and forth across the Balkans and parts of East Central Europe. Viewed in an even longer perspective, the peoples of *Zwischeneuropa* acted as 'a buffer between the West and Asia, allowing the Western nations to develop in comparative security their own civilization, while the fury of the Asiatic whirlwinds spent itself on their backs. And throughout these centuries their powerful neighbours in the West exploited their weakness to encroach on their territory and ruin their economic life' (Seton-Watson 1945: 21–2). Successive layers of conquerors, interlopers and colonists settled in these lands, occasionally establishing states of their own, giving rise to 'many disputed frontier regions and several inextricably mixed populations' (pp. 11, 74).

Map 1   The Balkans and East Central Europe: geographic zones

The inhabitants of the Balkans and East Central Europe have frequently faced threats or hazards on two fronts, as well as cultural and colonial penetration from both East and West. The eminent Polish writer Witold Gombrowicz once mused: 'What is Poland? A country between East and West, where Europe somehow all but comes to an end, a transitional country where East and West mutually weaken each other. But . . . our country is a little bit of a parody of the East and of the West . . . Our "superficiality", our "carefreeness" are essentially aspects of an irresponsible infantile relationship to culture and life, our lack of faith in reality. The origin of this may be that we are neither properly Europe or Asia' (quoted by Kiss 1987: 130, 135–6).

This book endeavours to analyse and explain the historic divergence of the Balkans and East Central Europe from western Europe and (to lesser degrees) from each other. The most important differences have concerned their divergent forms and conceptions of Christianity, 'feudalism', absolutism and nationhood, their contrasting responses to the late medieval and early modern 'crises of feudalism', the relatively late emergence and retention of serfdom in much of East Central Europe (as in Russia) and in parts of the Balkans (chiefly Romania, Croatia and Bosnia), the long survival of imperial polities in both regions, the resultant late establishment of independent nation-states throughout the region, and the emergence of asymmetrical 'periphery–core' relationships between the eastern and western halves of Europe during the modern era.

We have consistently used (lower-case) 'western Europe' and 'eastern Europe' as broad geographical expressions, referring respectively to the western and eastern 'halves' of Europe. We recognize that, like (upper-case) 'Eastern Europe', 'Western Europe' only became a formal political and economic entity in the wake of the Yalta and Potsdam agreements of 1945. Indeed, 'Western Europe' did not achieve institutional expression until the establishment of the Council of Europe, the Organization of European Economic Co-operation (OEEC), the European Coal and Steel Community (ECSC), the Western European Union (WEU) and the European Economic Community (EEC) during the late 1940s and 1950s. Thus, while it is sometimes convenient or even necessary to draw broad-brushed distinctions between 'eastern Europe' and 'western Europe', we are fully aware that neither of these areas ever became a unified or monolithic entity.

THE STRUCTURE OF THE BOOK

Part I The Balkan Peninsula from the Graeco-Roman period to the First World War

Part I endeavours to explain how the Balkan Peninsula, which was in many respects the cradle of European civilization and long included some of Europe's most highly developed economies and societies, became 'Balkanized' – making this term a byword for acutely debilitating and allegedly endemic fragmentation, inter-ethnic conflict, underdevelopment, and loss of political and economic autonomy. In particular, we challenge the widely accepted view that the main responsibility for the decline and fractious disunity of the peninsula in modern times can be laid at the door of the 'alien' and sometimes stultifying and oppressive Ottoman Empire – a view long propagated in the post-Ottoman Balkan media, educational institutions, and 'official' and/or nationalist histories of the region and its peoples. The proponents of these perspectives have tended to be less concerned with historical veracity than with special pleading, national myth-making, the 'justification' of territorial claims and the nursing of longstanding grievances. This is not to deny that similar patterns are to be found in many other parts of the world, but simply to alert readers to the pernicious and often anachronistic uses and abuses of history by modern nationalist as well as Communist historians. For example, modern 'national' histories of Serbia and Bulgaria have tended to portray the medieval Serbian and Bulgarian kingdoms as embryonic nation-states whose potentially glorious development was brutally cut short by alien conquerors and subsequently stifled by several centuries of Ottoman imperial rule, and to regard the maximum territorial extensions of these (far from 'national') medieval kingdoms as the 'natural' or 'historic' boundaries of their nations. During the twentieth century historical 'memories' of these aggressive medieval polities were metamorphosed into modern nationalist programmes of territorial aggrandizement, backed up by terrible 'ethnic cleansing'.

Instead of treating such evils as part of the Ottoman 'impact' and/or 'legacy' in the Balkans, our account emphasizes that there were already strong portents of political, cultural and economic decline and fragmentation in the Balkans *long before the Ottomans appeared on the scene*; that these problems contributed to the ease with which the Ottomans subjugated the peninsula; and that such problems were (to varying degrees) alleviated during the fifteenth- and sixteenth-century apogee of Ottoman rule. Admittedly, the so-called Pax Ottomanica broke down during the seventeenth century, and the later sclerosis of the Ottoman system eventually impeded many efforts to modernize the Balkan economies and education systems, impairing the capacity of the inhabitants of the Balkans to meet and adapt to the challenges of a changing world. Yet, while the Ottomans can be 'accused' of having *prolonged and/or failed to resolve* many of the problems which they inherited in their Balkan domains, few of those problems were of the Ottomans' own making.

Nevertheless, by seriously delaying the development of independent nation-states, liberalism and the rule of law on the Balkan Peninsula, the dogged persistence of the Ottoman imperial polity did unwittingly contribute to the emergence of exclusive and illiberal 'ethnic' conceptions and definitions of 'the nation', rather than more inclusive and liberal ones. 'Ethnic' nationalism has tended to elevate the rights of collectivities above those of individuals, even those of the individual members of ethnic majorities (Kohn 1944: 330; Sugar 1971a: 11; and Ramet 1997: ch. 1). The terrible 'ethnic purification' or 'ethnic cleansing' undertaken in parts of the Balkans between 1912 and 1921, between 1941 and 1945, and during the 1990s can thus be seen as the logical culmination of the exclusive and illiberal conceptions and definitions of nationhood which developed mainly as a result of the late survival of supranational imperial polities in this region and the weak development of the rule of law. To be sure, the 'activist' forms of nationalism and radicalism fostered by the French Revolution had a similarly intolerant and even murderous potential, especially in the hands of a Robespierre or a St Just. In western Europe, however, this was counteracted and held in check by a relatively strong development of the rule of law, the separation of powers, liberalism and liberal concepts of limited government. In western Europe, most political communities have been governed and held together by common bodies of law with clear distinctions between the public and private domains and strong constitutional restraints on the acquisition and use of power within specific historically determined jurisdictions and territories. Unfortunately, there have been fewer and weaker checks and safeguards against illiberal 'activist' doctrines, movements and states in the eastern than in the western half of Europe. During the twentieth century 'activist' forms of politics repeatedly replaced *law* with *ideology* and a shared sense of *mission* or *purpose* as the basis of political community, had scant regard for constitutional restraints on the acquisition and use of power, subordinated individuals to an all-embracing and highly intrusive political order, and refused to regard existing frontiers and jurisdictions as inviolable (O'Sullivan 1983: 35–7). It could conceivably be argued that this, rather than the prevalence of illiberal 'ethnic' nationalism per se, has been the most crucial respect in which the eastern half of Europe has differed from the western half in modern times. However, if *limited government and the rule of law* represented *adequate* safeguards against ethnic excesses, it would be difficult to explain the triumph of Nazism in Weimar Germany, a country which prided itself on having a *Rechtsstaat* (in sharp contrast to the Balkans and Russia's domains). Germany's vaunted rule of law proved incapable of preventing the Nazi revolution, while the fact that the German nation and national state were conceived and defined in *ethnic* rather than *territorial* terms encouraged successive generations of pan-German nationalists (culminating in Nazism) to strive to unite all Germans in a single German superstate, with ultimately devastating consequences for Europe and even for Germany itself. The triumph of Nazism in Germany in 1933 suggests that the prevalence of 'ethnic' nationalism was at least as important as the inadequacy of legal and constitutional safeguards in explaining the large-scale occurrence of lethal 'ethnic purification' and/or 'ethnic cleansing'.

Ethnic cleansing and genocide have not been monopolized by any one religious or ethnic group. At one time or another during the twentieth century, such crimes against humanity have also been carried out on a large scale by predominantly Catholic Croats, Hungarians, Poles and Lithuanians, by predominantly Orthodox Romanians, Serbs and Ukrainians, by predominantly Protestant Latvians and north Germans, and by predominantly Muslim Bosniaks, Albanians and Turks. Rather than point fingers of blame at the particular religious and ethnic groups who have committed such atrocities at various times and places, we consider that the root cause of this terrible malady has been the 'ethnic' conception and definition of nationhood, which prevailed at least partly as a result of the predominance of supranational imperial polities in central and eastern Europe up to the end of the First World War. Since it was very difficult in central and eastern European conditions to emulate the western European practice of defining 'civic nations' on the basis of pre-existing proto-national polities, the intelligentsias who inhabited the central and eastern European empires conceived, fostered, imagined and constructed 'ethnic nations' instead. In this respect, the peoples of the Balkans and East Central Europe were to a large extent victims of circumstance and/or potentially lethal 'received ideas'. These peoples were not inherently more vicious or more incapable of living at peace with their neighbours than were western Europeans, various of whom had over a longer time-span committed enormous barbarities against Jews, Moors, Gypsies, Catalans, Basques, Native Americans, Asians, Africans and the Irish, among others.

In our view, the surgical creation of several 'ethnically purified' or 'ethnically cleansed' nation-states in the Balkans has been the painful and tragic outcome of the prevalence of exclusive 'ethnic' conceptions of the nation and of the principle of national self-determination, both of which put high premia on 'ethnic homogeneity' or 'ethnic purity', exacerbated by the attendant weakness of liberal values and legal constraints on 'ethnic' excesses. Indeed, in a region where nations have been defined in narrowly ethnic terms, the promotion of the principle of national self-determination has been an open invitation to inter-ethnic conflict and 'ethnic cleansing'. There is therefore a danger that there will continue to be a potential for inter-ethnic conflict and human tragedy in the Balkans until its various peoples either abandon 'ethnic' nationalism or, *faute de mieux*, are finally 'resettled' into ethnically 'cleansed' or 'purified' nation-states, surgically carved out of the former ethnic patchworks. A similarly barbaric logic was responsible for the 'ethnic purification' of Germany, Austria, the Czech Lands, Slovakia, Poland and Hungary during the 1940s. Even this would not be a real solution, however, because inter-ethnic hatreds could still persist between ethnically 'homogenized' states. Furthermore, the fact that anti-Semitism has persisted in countries whose formerly substantial Jewish minorities have been almost completely eradicated provides a warning that ethnic 'purification' or 'cleansing' does not of itself remove the roots of inter-ethnic hatred, quite apart from the fact that 'ethnic purification' can leave a country morally, culturally and technologically stunted and impoverished. Lasting and self-renewing cultural, material and spiritual vigour are to be found in ethnic and cultural *diversity*, most dramatically in countries such as Canada and the USA, rather than in ethno-cultural homogeneity. Ultimately, the only sure way to escape the problems generated by 'ethnic nationalism' is to replace it with more liberal and inclusive 'civic' forms of identity, allegiance and community. In Part V and in Bideleux and Jeffries (2007), we argue that this can be achieved in full only by allowing the more cosmopolitan and commodious supranational civil order of the European Union to supersede the congenitally 'ethnocratic' framework of the nation-state.

Part II East Central Europe from the Roman period to the First World War

The main aim of Part II is to analyse the evolution of East Central Europe from the emergence of its medieval polities until the First World War. Part II begins by emphasizing the acute paucity of reliable information on the peoples and polities of East Central Europe prior to the tenth century AD. It then examines the various reasons for the rise and decline of the medieval and early modern Kingdoms of Poland, Hungary and Bohemia, each of which had at least half a millennium of independent existence before eventually succumbing to alien imperial control. While briefly summarizing their major problems and achievements and the traditions, values and orientations which they bequeathed to posterity, we also give attention to the power, privileges and internal divisions of the East Central European nobilities and the impact of Christianization, the Renaissance and the Reformation(s).

This is followed by an account of the rise and fall of the Habsburg Monarchy, with three closely interrelated aims: (i) to explain why most of East Central Europe fell far behind the emerging national or proto-national states of western Europe with regard to urbanization, industrialization, agricultural development, and science and technology during the seventeenth and eighteenth centuries; (ii) to examine the reasons why East Central Europe came under supranational imperial control from 1526 (Kingdom of Bohemia), 1711 (Hungary) or 1772/95 (Poland-Lithuania) until 1918, while the West was steadily evolving towards a system of national states; and (iii) to assess the long-term impact and legacies of the Habsburg Empire in East Central Europe and the northern Balkans. This paves the way for an assessment of the Revolutions of 1848, an analysis of the impressive economic and cultural revivals in Hungary, German Austria and the Czech Lands during the nineteenth century, and a discussion of the precocious development of so-called 'finance capitalism' and 'monopoly capitalism' during the final decades of the Habsburg Empire (Lenin and Bukharin added remarkably little to Hilferding's path-breaking ideas on these matters).

Our account of the legacies of the Habsburg Empire discusses the causes and catastrophic consequences of the almost 'racial' chasm that opened up between the Austro-Germans and the Austro-Slavs from 1848 onward. The resultant political blind-spots, mutual misunderstandings and mutual mistrust encouraged the erstwhile Austro-German 'liberals' to sell out to Habsburg neo-absolutism and impaired the potential for healthy social and political co-operation, thereby 'poisoning the wells' of liberalism and democracy for a considerable time to come. It also helped to sow the seeds of the racial crimes committed against millions of Jews, Gypsies and Slavs by the Third Reich and millions of 'willing collaborators' between 1938 and 1945. We emphasize the dire consequences of the development of (pan-)German 'ethnic' nationalism as a major political force in East Central Europe from 1848 to 1945, not out of Germanophobia, but simply to stress the ultimately devastating (and not always premeditated) effects of 'ethnic nationalism' in a multi-ethnic region. The results should be seen as an illustration of the general dangers posed by insidious 'ethnic nationalism', rather than as a peculiar product of 'the German national character' (as so many Germanophobes have seen it). On a smaller scale (because they have involved much smaller nations), Magyar, Romanian, Croatian and Serbian 'ethnic nationalisms' have displayed similarly lethal tendencies, while their Bulgarian, Albanian, Greek, Turkish, Polish, and Slovak counterparts have not been completely free of them. While the Jews were undeniably the biggest victims of the growth of 'ethnic nationalism', ethnic exclusivism and ethnic 'purification' or 'cleansing' in 1940s Europe, this ought not to be allowed to obscure the devastating effects which it has sometimes also had on Gypsies, Slavs and Kosovars.

Each East Central European, Baltic and Balkan nation has tended to portray its own treatment of ethnic minorities as exemplary, while criticizing or condemning that of others. Such attitudes, which were (and have continued to be) routinely reflected in the media, history books and political pronouncements, generally co-existed with widespread policies of forcible assimilation of ethnic minorities. This contributed to a general lowering of standards of conduct and culture, both through a form of 'moral brutalization' of the perpetrators and by turning the school system into 'a kind of chauvinistic nursery' that stunted the mental development of its pupils (Jaszi 1929: 330, 340–1).

Lastly, in dealing with the external relations of the Habsburg Empire, we emphasize that the termination of the empire's longstanding policy of co-operation with Russia in the Balkans (from the 1770s to the 1840s), followed by the Habsburg alliance with Germany from 1879 onward, divided Europe into two mutually hostile power blocs. The ensuing rivalry, arms race and collision course eventually engulfed Europe in the First World War, which in turn precipitated the disintegration of Europe's eastern empires. We highlight the roles of the problems and miscalculations of the Habsburg Monarchy and its tangled relations with Serbia in bringing about this momentous and highly destructive chain of events.

Part III From national self-determination to fascism and the Holocaust: the Balkans and East Central Europe, 1918–45

Part III offers explanations for the failure of various (often half-hearted) attempts to establish independent and democratic nation-states and viable national market economies in the Balkans and East Central Europe between the two World Wars and for the ways in which these failures contributed to the spread of fascism in these regions, along with its lethal culmination in the Holocaust. While giving due weight to external factors beyond the control of the rulers of East Central Europe and the Balkans, our main emphasis is on the inherent defects of the 1919–20 peace settlements in these regions and of the underlying 'ethnic' concepts and definitions of nationhood and national self-determination. We broadly concur with Sir Lewis Namier's contention that healthy constitutional development is most likely to occur within civic polities which take existing states and territories as their starting points, instead of trying to make states and territories correspond exclusively to particular ethnic groups. 'Self-determination . . . contests frontiers, negates the existing state and its inner development, and by [fostering] civil and international strife is apt to stultify constitutional growth' (Namier 1946: 26–7). Ethnic ultra-nationalism and fascism took national self-determination to its logical conclusion, with often horrific consequences.

We then discuss the origins and the severe impact of the 1930s Depression. This exacerbated inter-ethnic tensions and tendencies towards economic nationalism, authoritarianism and fascism, and effectively undermined any remaining hopes for the development of liberal capitalism, liberal democracy and progressive social reform in the interwar Balkan, Baltic and East Central European states.

Part III also provides radical reappraisals of the nature of the agrarian problems and poverty of the interwar Balkans and East Central Europe, the impact of the 1920s land reforms, and the significance and potential of the strong and interesting peasantist movements in these regions, before going on to examine rival interpretations of the nature, spread and significance of fascism in the Balkans and East Central Europe. We emphasize that 'ethnic' and 'integral' nationalism favoured 'ethnic collectivism' (collective as against individual rights and obligations), economic nationalism, étatisme and authoritarianism, and often predisposed its adherents towards fascist or quasi-fascist solutions to political, economic and ethnic problems.

Finally, Part III gives considerable attention to official Communist interpretations of fascism and of the pivotal struggle between Communism and fascism. Widespread tendencies to dismiss these interpretations as crude oversimplifications have contributed to serious underestimation of their seminal roles in Communist thinking at that time on how to extend Communist power and influence in Europe through the military defeat and/or armed overthrow of fascism.

Part IV In the shadow of Yalta: the Communist-dominated Balkans and East Central Europe, 1945–89

Part IV provides an interpretation of the rise and fall of Communist rule in the Balkans and East Central Europe. It is widely accepted that the success or failure of the Communist regimes came to depend on the maintenance of sustained economic growth and rising consumption levels. These were objectives that none of them could easily attain on their own, in an autarkic fashion. Therefore, they would ultimately depend on how successfully they could escape or surmount the initially self-imposed austerities and constraints of 'boxed-in' self-reliance and central planning by promoting transnational and/or supranational economic co-operation, division of labour and integration within the Council of Mutual Economic Assistance (CMEA), known in the West as Comecon, which also offered increased (preferential) access to the vast markets and mineral resources of the Soviet Union. Thus the failure of Comecon to promote a high degree of integration between its members ultimately contributed to the downfall of the Balkan and East Central European Communist regimes. We analyse in addition some of the social and political factors that contributed to the collapse of Communist rule and the significance of the Revolutions of 1989.

Part V Post-Communist transformations

The book concludes with an appraisal of the major problems and dilemmas that have had to be confronted during the transitions to democracy and market economies and the repossession of untrammelled national sovereignty by the post-Communist states, the ultimately successful entry of the East Central European states into the European Union in May 2004, and the deep-seated structural impediments which have substantially delayed the entry of the post-Communist Balkan states into the EU. We argue that both the prospect and the attainment of EU membership have profoundly changed the frameworks and the incentive structures within which East Central European states, politicians, businesses and citizens have tackled the problems of democratization, political and economic liberalization, and (above all) establishing the rule of law, limited government and rule-governed civil associations. These changes have helped to consummate a profound shift from the preponderance of 'vertical' power relations and structures (which have ensnared and afflicted them for so long) to a growing preponderance of 'horizontal' power relations and structures. These changes are not only creating the crucial legal and institutional infrastructure on which to build vigorous liberal democracy, liberal capitalism, limited government and the rule of law, but are also greatly assisting diverse interests, ethnicities, value systems and belief systems to co-exist with greatly reduced mutual friction and impairment. Both here and in greater detail in Bideleux and Jeffries (2007), we argue that the prospect and the gradual attainment of EU membership have also started to bring about similar changes in the post-Communist Balkan states – much more belatedly, but with growing momentum. The prospects for liberal democracy, liberal capitalism, limited government and the rule of law in the post-Communist Balkans crucially depend on the European Union keeping faith with the promises which it repeatedly made between 1999 and 2005 that the whole of the Balkans – and not just Romania, Bulgaria and possibly Croatia – will gain membership of the EU in due course. The fate of these countries rests partly in their own hands, but also in those of the existing members of the European Union.

MORE THAN A NAME: THE CONTROVERSIES OVER 'CENTRAL' AND 'EASTERN' EUROPE

Many natives of 'the lands between' violently object to the Western habit of referring to their region(s) as 'Eastern Europe'. In the opinion of Jacques Rupnik, 'From Prague to Budapest, from Cracow to Zagreb, the rediscovery of Central Europe will remain one of the major intellectual and political developments of the 1980s and will no doubt be a vital ingredient in the reshaping of the political map of Europe in the post-Yalta era' (Rupnik 1990: 250).

In an influential essay first published in French in 1983 and then published in English as 'The Tragedy of Central Europe' in 1984, the Czech writer Milan Kundera proclaimed that Hungary,

Czechoslovakia and Poland were (in spirit at least) part of the West. 'What does Europe mean to a Hungarian, a Czech, a Pole?' he asked. 'For a thousand years their nations have belonged to the part of Europe rooted in Roman Christianity. They have participated in every period of its history. For them, the word "Europe" does not represent a phenomenon of geography, but a spiritual notion synonymous with the word "West". The moment Hungary is no longer European – that is, no longer Western – it is driven from its own destiny, beyond its own history: it loses the essence of its identity.' In Kundera's view, geographic Europe (extending from the Atlantic to the Ural Mountains) had long been 'divided into two halves which evolved separately: one tied to ancient Rome and the Catholic Church, the other anchored in Byzantium and the Orthodox Church'. After the Second World War, however, 'the border between the two Europes shifted several hundred kilometres to the west', and as a result several nations which had always considered themselves to be Western woke up to discover that they were now in the East (Kundera 1984: 33).

From Kundera's standpoint, Roman Catholic Poland, Hungary and Czechoslovakia constituted 'the eastern border of the West' rather than the western border of the East. (Perhaps deliberately, he omitted to mention Catholic Slovenia and Croatia.) In his view the East meant, above all, Russia; and 'nothing could be more foreign to Central Europe and its passion for variety than Russia: uniform, standardizing, centralizing' (p. 33). Indeed, 'on the eastern border of the West – more than anywhere else – Russia is seen not just as one more European power but as a singular civilization, an *other* civilization . . . Russia knows another (greater) dimension of disaster, another image of space (a space so immense entire nations are swallowed up in it), another sense of time (slow and patient), another way of laughing, living, and dying. That is why the countries in Central Europe feel that the change in their destiny that occurred after 1945 is not merely a political catastrophe: it is also an attack on their civilization' (p. 34).

Kundera was especially alert to the dangers of pan-Slavism: 'The Czechs . . . loved to brandish naively their "Slavic ideology" as a defence against German aggressiveness. The Russians, on the other hand, enjoyed making use of it to justify their own imperial ambitions. "The Russians like to label everything Russian as Slavic, so that later they can label everything Slavic as Russian", the great Czech writer Karel Havlicek declared in 1844, trying to warn his compatriots against their silly and ignorant enthusiasm for Russia.' Kundera emphasized that for a thousand years the Czechs 'never had any direct contact with Russia. In spite of their linguistic kinship, the Czechs and the Russians have never shared a common *world*: neither a common history nor a common culture.' Moreover, the relationship between the Poles and the Russians 'has never been less than a struggle of life and death. Joseph Conrad . . . wrote that "nothing could be more alien to what is called in the literary world the 'Slavic spirit' than the Polish temperament with its chivalric devotion to moral constraints and its exaggerated respect for individual rights"' (p. 34).

Following the publication of this famous essay, there was growing insistence on calling the region comprising the Czech Lands, Slovakia, Poland and Hungary 'Central' rather than 'Eastern' Europe. This was much more than a semantic quibble. It went to the heart of the region's self-image and aspirations. The debates about 'Central' and 'Eastern' Europe were a form of soul-searching about what the peoples and states of the region were or should be. Moreover, the campaign to (re-)establish a lapsed conception of 'Central' Europe became an integral part of 'the long revolution against Yalta' – against the Allies' decision to partition Europe into Soviet and Western spheres of influence in 1945 (Feher 1988). This campaign therefore merits serious consideration, even if it raised more problems than it solved. Its central contention was that the Yalta Conference in 1945 'created a geopolitical entity, "Eastern Europe", which as a polity or a community of destiny had never before existed' (Feher 1988: 20).

Writing on the eve of the Revolutions of 1989, the Czechoslovak dissident Miroslav Kusy declared that 'Eastern Europe' was merely 'a political power-bloc of the Comecon and Warsaw Pact states' and that any sense of 'East Europeanness' that its inhabitants might have had was 'tantamount to the feelings shared by an eagle and a lion living alongside each other in a zoo' (Kusy 1989: 93). 'The project of Central Europe has been gradually filling the historical and political vacuum created by the deconstruction of Eastern Europe' (Feher 1989: 415).

This 'rediscovery of Central Europe' had a major impact on the way in which the history of the region was perceived. According to the eminent Polish-American historian Piotr Wandycz, 'Bohemia (later Czechoslovakia), Hungary and Poland did belong to the Western civilization. Christianity and all that it stood for had come to them from Rome or, to put it differently, the Western impact was the dominant and lasting one.' Thus the peoples of East Central Europe 'became part of the West' and 'were shaped by and experienced all the great historical currents: Renaissance, Reformation, Enlightenment, the French and Industrial Revolutions. They differed drastically from the East.' Bordering on Russia and the Ottoman domains, these marchlands 'regarded themselves, and were regarded by others, as the bulwark of Christendom . . . Their eastern frontiers marked the frontiers of Europe' (Wandycz 1992: 3).

Similarly, the prominent Hungarian academic Peter Hanak argued that 'Central Europe' was 'the Eastern zone of the West', rather than 'the Western "rim" of the East'. In his view, the Austro-Hungarian Empire was 'the eastern frontier of liberal constitutional rule up to the First World War. This political system (in spite of its limitations and transgressions) carried forward and upheld the heritage of European humanism, enlightenment and liberalism . . . The Monarchy (including Hungary) . . . stood in the middle between the fully-fledged parliamentary democracy in the West and autocracy in the East. This is precisely the meaning of the term: Central Europe'. Therefore, 'the fact that the peoples of this region . . . have often been at loggerheads, riven by conflicts and hatreds, is no argument against the historical existence of the entity. On the contrary, this is proof of its existence: it is neighbours who are mostly cursed by anger, hatred and strife' (Hanak 1989: 57, 68–9).

It has often been claimed that as a result of their location on the exposed eastern frontiers of Western Christendom, defending Western civilization against Asiatic and/or Russian 'barbarism', it was the Poles, the Czechs and the Hungarians who developed the clearest perceptions of what Europe was – and thus became more fervently 'European' and 'Western' than the West. 'European-ness' and feelings of 'being European' have usually been most highly prized, not by those who take them for granted, but by those who live in greatest fear of losing them. 'Central Europe longed to be a condensed version of Europe itself in all its cultural variety, a small arch-European Europe' (Kundera 1984: 33). Hugh Seton-Watson claimed that 'nowhere in the world is there so widespread a belief in the reality, and the importance, of a European cultural community as in the countries lying between the EEC and the Soviet Union' (Seton-Watson 1985: 14).

East Central Europe and Croatia played pivotal roles in defining and popularizing the very idea of 'Europe' during the Renaissance. Until the fifteenth century, the concept of Europe had been 'a neutral geographical expression'. It fell to Polish, Hungarian, Bohemian, Austrian and Croatian publicists, who feared that Europe was under mortal threat from the steadily advancing Ottoman 'menace', to proclaim that they and their Catholic rulers were defending 'not merely European territory but specifically European values against Muslim aggression' (Coles 1968: 148; Goldstein 1999: 32–4). The 'Polish Pope' John Paul II declared in June 1991: 'We do not have to enter Europe, because we helped to create it and we did so with greater effort than those who claim a monopoly of Europeanism' (Kumar 1992: 460). This belief was very important to the East Central European and Balkan intelligentsias during the 1980s and 1990s, and it helped their countries to persevere with exceedingly arduous processes of economic and institutional reform after 1989. It also informed their drive for reintegration into the European 'mainstream', latterly epitomized by the EU and (to lesser degrees) NATO.

In 1993, in response to the question 'Why should the post-Communist countries of Europe seek membership of NATO?', the then Czech president Vaclav Havel stated that there were three main reasons why his own country should do so. 'First, the Czech Republic lies in the very centre of Europe, which has traditionally been a crossroads for different spiritual trends and geopolitical interests.' The Czechs had learned from bitter experience that 'we must take an active interest in what goes on in the rest of Europe. Such matters always affect us more than they do many other countries. This is why we have a heightened sense of obligation to Europe.' However, the Czechs did not want 'to take without giving. We want an active role in the defence of European peace and democracy. Too often, we have had direct experience of where indifference to the fate of others can lead, and we are determined not to succumb to that kind of indifference.' Secondly, Czechs 'share the values on which NATO was founded and which it exists to defend. We are not just endorsing such values from the outside; over the centuries we have made our own contribution to their creation and cultivation. Why then should we not take part in defending them?' Thirdly, the Czechs have 'vivid memories of the Munich crisis in 1938 when, without consulting us, part of our country was bargained away to Hitler. Munich meant not only the failure of the Western democracies to confront the Nazi evil – a failure for which the West had to pay dearly – but the collapse of the European collective security of the time. This experience tells us how important it is for a country so exposed to be firmly involved – in its own interests and the general interest – in a working system of collective security.' More generally, the Czech Republic, Hungary, Poland, Slovakia and Slovenia 'clearly belong to the Western sphere of European civilization. They . . . are simply declaring an affinity with an institution they belong to intrinsically, where they see their own security interests best served and where they can actively participate' (Vaclav Havel, writing in *IHT*, 20 October 1993, p. 4).

Nevertheless, in glossing over the many cultural, economic and historical divergences between western Europe and East Central Europe (at least since the seventeenth century, if not before then) and in claiming that their homelands have long been Western in spirit, the new champions of 'Central Europe' encouraged their compatriots seriously to underestimate the scale of the economic, political and cultural adjustments which would have to be made if they were really to (re)join and become fully accepted as part of the West. While no one can deny either the 'European credentials' of East Central Europe or the fact that this region is very different from Russia, that does not of itself make the region 'Western'.

One of the primary aims of this book is to offer fair but hard-headed analyses of some of the historic differences between the western half of Europe, on the one hand, and East Central Europe and the Balkans, on the other. These differences emerged long before the advent of Communist rule and the Cold War partition of Europe, and the legacies could not be expunged or overcome overnight. One of the dangers in attempting to lull the governments and citizens of these countries into thinking that their region was already *innately* Western was that this would make them less likely to accept either the magnitude or the necessity of undergoing the painful adjustments required by entry into the European Union and NATO. Their so-called 'return to Europe' could not succeed on the basis of wishful thinking and self-delusion. This was not a trivial issue. It was a matter of immense practical as well as academic importance.

Another complication was that the name 'Central Europe' had widely differing meanings and connotations for Poles, Czechs, Slovaks, Hungarians, Croats, Slovenes, Austrians, Germans, Ukrainians, Belarussians, Lithuanians, Gypsies and Jews, let alone for the British, the French, the Russians and the Italians. For example: does (or did) Kundera's 'Central Europe' include the many millions of former Ukrainian, Belarussian and Lithuanian inhabitants of interwar Poland, Hungary and Czechoslovakia? After all, they and their ancestors had participated in many of the same formative historical processes and cultural experiences as did the Poles, the Czechs and the Magyars. For centuries they were all part of the same 'middle European' world. On the other hand, would it be fair and consistent to treat Ukrainians and Belarussians differently from their Russian 'cousins', who are fellow 'East Slavs'? Similarly, was or is it either fair or rational to regard East Central

Europe as more 'Western' than the Balkan Peninsula? The areas that became Poland and the Czech Lands were never part of the Roman Empire, whereas most of the Balkan Peninsula (most of which Kundera implicitly excluded from his concept of the 'Roman' or 'Latin' West) had been part of the Roman Empire for centuries.

An even greater complication is that most Western conceptions of 'Central Europe' have above all included Germany and Austria. From its inception, the concept of 'Central Europe' (alias *Mitteleuropa*) was redolent of pan-Germanism, of German and Austrian imperialism, and of Germanic economic and cultural hegemony over East Central Europe and the Balkans. The geographer Joseph Partsch, in his book *Mitteleuropa* (published in 1904), proclaimed that 'All of Central Europe belongs, knowingly or unknowingly, to the sphere of German civilization' (quoted by Schwarz 1989: 145). Friedrich Naumann's best-selling book entitled *Mitteleuropa* (published in Berlin in 1915) interspersed German imperialist rhetoric with hymns of praise to nature, mountaineering, travel, the Danube and Central European art, and with imperial condescension towards non-German cultures: 'Central Europe will be German in its core, will use German . . . as a matter of course, but must show indulgence and flexibility towards the other languages involved, for only then can harmony prevail' (p. 101). Nevertheless, in Naumann's view, 'Central Europe came about through Prussian victories' (pp. 57–8) (quoted by Schwarz 1989: 147). Similarly, in an essay published in Vienna in 1930, Albrecht Haushofer declared that 'Central Europe . . . owes its creation to the Germans. It would not exist without them' (quoted by Schwarz 1989: 146). It was in this context that Tomas Garrigue Masaryk, the founder and first president of Czechoslovakia, coined the name 'East Central Europe' during the First World War, as a counterblast to German use of the term *Mitteleuropa* 'as a justification for imperial Germany's expansionist plans' (Garton Ash 1986: 210). Masaryk defined East Central Europe as 'the lands between East and West, more particularly between the Germans and the Russians' (Kumar 1992: 446). This is also our own preferred usage.

It is also not easy to reconcile Kundera's idealization of 'Central Europe' as a bearer and custodian of supposedly higher or more civilized Western values with the role of Central and East Central Europe as a crucible of extremely illiberal ideas, projects and doctrines, culminating in pan-German imperialism, Nazism, mass genocide and Auschwitz. In the words of the Croatian writer Miroslav Krleza, 'Central Europe doesn't represent for me, on the aesthetic level, a separate universe . . . Naumann's beloved theory of the unity of *Mitteleuropa* has been variously used either as a political pretext (pan-German or Austro-imperialism . . .) or as a nostalgic longing for the past' (quoted by Matvejevic 1989: 183–4). However, at least some of those who have championed the revival of the concept of 'Central Europe' since the 1980s may have been consciously or unconsciously wanting to substitute German for Russian influence in East Central Europe and (to lesser degrees) the Balkans, in the hope that Germany would rapidly regenerate these regions and reintegrate them into the European 'mainstream'. The promotion of overarching identities has often involved opportunistic and potentially hazardous games.

Latter-day champions of 'Central Europe' have been overly inclined to blame the region's misfortunes on Russia. Admittedly, by comparison with the greater pluralism (if not always tolerance) of the West and East Central Europe, Russia's political and cultural traditions undoubtedly appear monolithic, exclusive, and intolerant of nonconformity and dissent. In the opinion of the Hungarian philosopher Mihaly Vajda, 'in Russia one cannot find the main features of the civilization we call European . . . The leading value of Europe is *freedom* . . . the freedom of the individual limited only by that of others' (Vajda 1986: 168). Nevertheless, Russia and/or the Soviet Union cannot be held wholly or even largely responsible for the suppression of East Central European traditions of pluralism and observance of the rule of law. Of course, it would be very nice to believe that 'Central Europe' was a bed of roses until the Red Army arrived in 1945. However, as remarked by the Czechoslovak dissident Milan Simecka, it was not Soviet Russia but Nazi Germany that 'tore up by the roots that certain decency of political and cultural standards which the Central European nations managed to preserve more or less intact up to 1937 . . . At the moment the tragedy of Central Europe began to unfold, Eastern influences were negligible . . . The cancer which finally put paid to what had gone before was nurtured on Western European history and fed on the decaying legacy of Western European intellectual movements' (Simecka 1985: 158–9). In 1987, with impeccable intellectual honesty, Simecka noted that after the Second World War 'the Central European nations were neither as politically mature, nor quite as innocent as Kundera would have us think . . . with everyone trying to grab as much as they could for themselves . . . The "leading value" in those days was the "national interest", so-called, not internal freedom' (Simecka 1987: 179). Indeed, 'one of the reasons why the influence of the "other civilization" [Russia] was so effective was because, to a certain extent, we provided it with fertile soil' (p. 180).

In some ways, the Kafkaesque world invented in East Central Europe prefigured the Communist states. Timothy Garton Ash similarly pointed out that 'specifically *Central* European traditions . . . at least facilitated the establishment of Communist regimes in Hungary and Czechoslovakia . . . A superbureaucratic statism and formalistic legalism taken to absurd (and sometimes already inhuman) extremes were, after all, particularly characteristic of Central Europe before 1914.' He asked, rhetorically, 'what was really more characteristic of historic Central Europe: cosmopolitan tolerance, or nationalism and racism?' (Garton Ash 1986: 195). In the words of Vaclav Havel: 'We are struggling not only against the heritage of Communism, but also against the many problems that have cursed our history in the more distant past' (Havel 1994b: 163).

Out of an understandable desire to differentiate their own 'homelands' as sharply as possible from the Eastern Orthodox world, writers such as Kundera (1984), Szucs (1988), Hanak (1989) and Wandycz (2001) have considerably exaggerated the 'otherness', oppression, uniformity, centralization, peasant poverty, economic stagnation and absence of private initiative and enterprise in what they term 'the East', especially imperial Russia. In point of fact, late Tsarist Russia experienced a sizeable economic boom. It was buoyed up by significant advances in peasant agriculture, rising popular literacy, expectations and consumption levels, growing regional and occupational specialization, Western-style class differentiation, foreign direct investment and the emergence of millions of small and some 'big time' capitalist entrepreneurs. The Tsarist Empire was never as static, monolithic or centrally controlled as the over-used notion of a Russian 'Oriental despotism' would seem to suggest (see Blanchard 1989; Bideleux 1987: 11–18; 1990; 1994.)

Those who have professed to believe in the actual or potential unity and cohesion of 'Central Europe' probably underrated the force of the predominantly centrifugal tendencies of its constituent peoples. The notion that a specific set of shared values binds these countries together would be more convincing if these values were not largely confined to small groups of intellectuals. In the vision of 'Central Europe' propounded above all by Vaclav Havel, the Hungarian writer Gyorgy Konrad and the Polish historian and dissident Adam Michnik during the 1980s, citizens would, relying on their own initiative and moral resources, create their own democratic institutions and autonomous associations ('civil society') in order to compensate for the failure of the state to encourage and to nourish them, under regimes that were committed to the suppression of all independent political and cultural activity (Glenny 1990: 186). Thus Gyorgy Konrad argued that in contrast to the West, where civil society controlled the state, Central Europe was characterized by the independence or separation of civil society from the state. Central Europe was a region in which civil society had had to reject and distance itself from the state, increasingly replacing official state values, ideologies and structures with its own autonomous ones. 'On no account were we West Europeans, but we are not East Europeans either' (Konrad 1984: 91–114). During the 1970s and 1980s East Central European dissidents developed a common set of values emphasizing social self-organization and self-defence, non-violence, the priority of the individual over the state and society, and the primacy of individual human rights (Garton Ash 1986: 197–204). 'Truth and certain elementary values such as respect for human rights, civil society, the indivisibility of freedom and the rule of law – these were the notions that bound us together and made it worth our while to enter again and again into the unequal struggle with the powers that be' (Havel 1994b: 215). The starting point of such struggles was 'neither the will to power nor an ideological vision of the world, but rather a moral stance', intended to promote 'a climate of solidarity, creativity, co-operation, toler- ance and deepening responsibility' (pp. 216–17).

The revival of notions of 'Central Europe' during the 1980s proved decidedly short-lived. Fol- lowing the collapse of Communist rule and Soviet hegemony in 1989, the memory of East Central European dissident collaboration against a common oppressor quickly faded and, with the notable exception of Vaclav Havel, the former dissident intellectuals who had gained high office in the new post-Communist regimes soon fell from grace, while 'Central European' ideals foundered amid growing inter-state rivalries and competition for Western investment, economic assistance and political favour. The dissolution of Czechoslovakia into the Czech Republic and Slovakia on 1 January 1993 was a further setback for the concept of East Central Europe as a cohesive entity based upon shared values, beliefs, experiences and aspirations.

Even Kundera acknowledged that 'Central Europe is not a state; it is a culture or a fate. Its borders are imaginary and must be drawn and redrawn with each new historical situation' (Kundera 1984: 35). In 1986 Gyorgy Konrad similarly acknowledged that 'Central Europe' was not a reality but a project or an aspiration: 'What is revolutionary about the idea of Central Europe is precisely the fact that today it is only a dream. By contrast with the political reality of Eastern Europe and Western Europe, Central Europe exists only as a cultural counterhypothesis . . . If there is no Central Europe, there is no Europe . . . If we don't cling to the utopia of Central Europe we must give up the game . . . Being Central European does not mean having a nationality, but rather an outlook on the world' (Konrad 1986: 113–16). Pedrag Matvejevic, a professor at the University of Zagreb, declared that 'Central Europe, or what actually remains of it, is engaged in the laborious process of recover- ing from the losses it has suffered . . . Central Europe is abandoning itself to sweet memories, strug- gling with difficulty against its own provincialism, and often proving itself ill-equipped to rejuvenate its old traditions' (Matvejevic 1989: 190). Even Kundera admitted that 'the nations of Central Europe have used up their strength in the struggle to survive' (Kundera 1984: 34).

As argued by Timothy Garton Ash (1986: 212), 'If the term "Central Europe" is to acquire some positive substance, then the discussion will have to move forward from the declamatory, the senti- mental and the incantational to a dispassionate and rigorous examination both of the real legacy of historic Central Europe – which is as much one of divisions as of unities – and of the true conditions of present day East Central Europe.' This present book can be seen as a contribution towards the first of these two tasks.

We do not doubt the existence of East Central Europe as a fairly distinct cultural and historical region which essentially comprises the easterly territories of the former Habsburg Empire and is clearly distinguishable from Germany, Italy and Switzerland as well as from the southern and eastern Balkans and Russia. Nevertheless, we also see greater justification for treating East Central Europe as *the most Westernized part of Europe's East* than for regarding it as *the most easterly extension of Europe's West*. We adopt this stance out of respect and affection (rather than low regard) for this region, which we have been studying for most of our working lives. This stance may offend those East Central Europeans who insist that they and their ancestors have long felt them- selves to be part of 'the West', but it is based neither on ignorance nor on ill will. More importantly, as mentioned above, it recognizes the magnitude of the social and cultural as well as economic adjustments which East Central Europeans have had to make in order to realize their desire to (re-)enter into the European 'mainstream'.

GRADATIONS OF DIFFERENCE: THE GRADUAL EMERGENCE OF EAST–WEST DIVISIONS WITHIN EUROPE

From the eleventh to the seventeenth century, despite the enduring schism between the Roman Catholic and the Eastern Orthodox churches in 1054, few people emphasized or focused upon East–West differences within 'Christendom', which was the preferred appellation for 'Europe' in those times (Wandycz 1992: 2). It was only after the Mongol invasions of 1237–41 that western Europeans 'began to conceptualize the existence of an East European area' (Curta 2005: 3). Indeed, Larry Wolff has persuasively argued that it was only during the Enlightenment that Europe's East–West divide came to be seen as more significant than its longstanding North–South divide: 'The invention of Eastern Europe was a subtly self-promoting and sometimes overtly self-congratulatory event in intellectual history, whereby Western Europe also identified itself and affirmed its own precedence' (Wolff 1994: 360). Until the eighteenth century, Europe's *North–South* differences – between a warmer, more 'civilized' and more city-orientated, Graeco-Roman, '*Mediterranean south*' and a cooler, more dour and more rural Germanic or Slavic '*barbarian north*' – were much more deeply embedded in public perceptions than were Europe's East–West differences, such as those between Western 'Latin Christendom' and Eastern 'Orthodox Christendom'. Wolff argued that a new mental-mapping construct which came to be called 'Eastern Europe' was invented by Western Europe's writers, thinkers, travellers and chattering classes during the eighteenth-century 'Enlightenment', as a result of which Poland-Lithuania and Russia found themselves rudely reassigned – and in effect demoted – from 'northern' to 'eastern' Europe. The earlier religious-cum-cultural cleavage between Eastern Orthodox Christendom and Western/Latin Christendom had been much less far-reaching than the new East–West divide constructed by Enlightenment *philosophes* and authors of travelogues. The Enlightenment fostered and propagated new and deeply condescending and demeaning Western perceptions of – and attitudes towards – the eastern half of Europe. These new perceptions and attitudes helped to crystallize new cultural and geopolitical power relations and divisions between the western and eastern halves of Europe, and these salient East–West power relations and divisions within Europe became even more entrenched during the nineteenth and twentieth centuries (Wolff 1994).

Nevertheless, the beginnings of an East–West divide in Europe can be traced back to the East–West partitions of the Roman Empire in 285 and 395 AD and to the mounting divergence and eventual schism between Eastern Orthodox and Western (Roman) Catholic Christianity. In the 'barbarian peripheries' of western and north-western Europe, the fifth-century disintegration of the Western Roman Empire prepared the ground for the gradual emergence of fissiparious, decentralized and almost constantly warring feudal polities which, more by luck than by design, eventually nurtured a precocious development of both agrarian and urban capitalism in the interstices of western feudal society. Thus the fragmentation, disunity and heterogeneity which have often been perceived as inherent systemic handicaps of western European polities and societies during the medieval period proved to be unexpectedly advantageous in the early modern era, when relatively decentralized, heterogeneous and fragmented power structures permitted or even fostered the emergence of competitive and dynamic economies and societies based on relatively free market forces, the cash nexus, increasingly impersonal rule of law and contract, and increasingly secular and law-governed civil societies. This subsequently set the scene for the emergence of proto-national monarchies, proto-industrial economies and embryonic 'civic' nation-states.

The extreme fragmentation of western European polities from the sixth to the eighth century AD facilitated the emergence of unusually decentralized societies within which power was dispersed downwards to relatively autonomous landed nobilities, ecclesiastical lords and burghers. In an influential essay on the origins of Europe's deep-seated East–West divisions, the Hungarian philosopher Jeno Szucs has emphasized the seminal importance of the ways in which this made possible an enduring separation of 'state' and 'society' in western Europe (Szucs 1988: 298–9). It also allowed the Roman Catholic Church to escape from 'caesaropapism' and the tutelage of the state and to assert the autonomy of its spiritual authority and domain (pp. 299–300). This was in marked contrast to the position of the Eastern Orthodox Church, which remained relatively subservient to the state in the Balkans and Russia. Moreover, the separation of the temporal and spiritual spheres in western Europe eventually made it possible to extricate politics from religious ethics and theology and facilitated the development of secular political thought and secular conceptions of authority. 'The West's separation of the sacred and the secular, the ideological and political spheres, was uniquely fruitful, and without it the future "freedoms", the theoretical emancipation of "society", the future nation-states, the Renaissance and the Reformation alike could never have ensued' (Szucs 1988: 300). Indeed, 'The really important feature of West European development from the Middle Ages onwards was the gradual separation of state and society. Out of West European political and social disintegration and fragmentation there arose new urban communities within which the attitudes and behaviour of individuals were shaped less and less by tradition . . . And – most importantly – relations among various social groups were settled increasingly by contract' (Vajda 1988: 341). Such processes were experienced only to very limited degrees in the medieval Balkans, were nipped in the bud from the twelfth century onwards in medieval Russia, and developed only in truncated forms in medieval East Central Europe.

While it is commonly accepted that the Protestant parts of Europe attached much greater importance to mass education and allowed a greater latitude for debate, enquiry and dissent than did the states that remained Roman Catholic, it is less widely appreciated that, for all its authoritarianism, bigotry and fear of popular education, the Roman Catholic Church continued to attach much more importance to scholarship and to the education of its own clergy and the ruling classes than did the Eastern Orthodox Church, which tolerated quite abysmal levels of ignorance and blind prejudice among its clergy and laity alike. Similarly, the enduring rearguard resistance of the Roman Catholic Church against extensions of temporal authority over spiritual matters (even in Communist Poland and Hungary in more recent times) has often been contrasted with the greater subservience of the Eastern Orthodox Church to temporal rulers, be they Byzantine, Bulgar, Serb, Ottoman, Tsarist or Communist, although Steven Runciman rightly warned against the temptation to exaggerate this contrast (Runciman 1968: 7). The greater independence of the Roman Catholic Church from temporal rulers was not necessarily something inherent in Roman Catholicism. Rather, the political disintegration and chaos into which western Europe was plunged by the so-called 'barbarian' invasions and the collapse of the Western Roman Empire allowed the Roman Catholic Church to assert and consolidate its independence from western Europe's temporal rulers, whereas the Eastern Orthodox Church remained in a kind of 'Babylonian captivity' in the Byzantine, Ottoman, Tsarist and Soviet empires. During the ninth century Charlemagne temporarily re-established an imperial polity in western Europe, 'utilizing the last reserves of the Frankish institutions' as well as the last vestiges of Roman imperial tradition. However, 'these reserves had already been exhausted, and the temporary edifice was destroyed once and for all by a new element that arose from below – vassalage' (Szucs 1988: 300). Subsequent attempts to relaunch an all-embracing Holy Roman Empire merely succeeded in delaying the emergence of a unified German state until the late nineteenth century.

Fortunately for medieval western Europe, the forms of vassalage that fortuitously emerged there were able to preserve or regain the considerable autonomy that had been won by the nobility, the Church and the towns during the so-called 'Dark Ages' and established reciprocal and quasi-contractual relations between rulers and their vassals (Szucs 1988: 300–1). Between about 1050 and 1300 the western European 'feudal' economies enjoyed a period of dynamic expansion, attended by the rise of towns, cities and city-states, major technical and organizational advances in agriculture, industry, finance and commerce, substantial increases in living standards and in the size and social status of nobilities and urban patriciates, and significant extensions in the rights and liberties of the more prosperous strata. In contrast to the experience of Eastern Orthodox Christendom and the great Asiatic despotisms, moreover, western European vassals were rarely required to engage in total self-abasement to their overlords. They were normally allowed to hold their heads erect and clasp the hand of their liege lord, instead of having to grovel at his feet. Indeed, a cardinal feature of western European feudalism was that it began to enshrine a basic concept of 'human dignity as a constitutive element in its political relations' (Szucs 1988: 302). Furthermore, political fragmentation, decentralization and the consequent multiplicity of small jurisdictions (each with its own feudal courts and customary laws) offered a fertile soil for the development of the rule of law and of a relatively autonomous Christian lay culture, morality and scale of values which rulers, for the most part, felt bound to respect (Szucs 1988: 302–3). Thus administrative, military, fiscal and judicial functions came to be separated from the personal authority of the ruler and were distributed among various layers of feudal society. Hence the growing autonomy of the nobility, the Church, the towns and the law courts fostered the development of 'civil society', 'civil liberties' and contractual market relations in western Europe. This extended freedoms downward, accelerating the conversion of servile obligations into cash nexuses and the gradual dissolution of serfdom (Szucs 1988: 305–6).

The concept of 'civil society' (*societas civilis*) came into use in the mid-thirteenth century to refer to this growth of autonomous institutions and activities. The West gradually accepted the notion that rulers (even supposedly 'absolute' rulers) had to respect and operate within the laws of the realm and were thus responsible or even subservient to 'society' seen as an abstract legal entity (Szucs 1988: 308). In the West, significantly, it was increasingly assumed that 'civil society' should control the ruler and/or the state, whereas the much weaker forms of 'civil society' that have emerged (if at all) in the eastern half of Europe (including East Central Europe) have usually been seen as acting in opposition to the ruler/state. In other words, while the West assumed an increasingly co-operative and consensual relationship between 'civil society' and the ruler/state, the East assumed a rather more combative and antagonistic relationship between its relatively stunted 'civil society' and its generally stronger rulers and states.

Between the fifteenth and eighteenth centuries, these East–West contrasts were magnified by the emergence of an economically and technologically dynamic and geopolitically hegemonic 'capitalist world-system' centred on Europe's Atlantic seaboard, in relation to which East Central Europe, the Balkans and Russia were relegated to the roles of less developed and increasingly subordinate 'semi-peripheries' which produced and exported raw or semi-processed primary commodities in exchange for western European manufactured goods and commercial-cum-financial services. However, we argue that this East–West division of labour within Europe came about later, more gradually and for more endogenous reasons than proposed by Immanuel Wallerstein (1974a, 1974b). (See pp. 91–109, 140–1, 155–90 below, and McGowan 1981: 2–9.)

Not only human-made political, cultural and institutional factors have impeded the development of East Central Europe and the Balkans. Much of East Central Europe is quite landlocked by comparison with western Europe, which is much better served by navigable rivers and its coastal waters, while much of the Balkan Peninsula has a relatively impenetrable mountainous terrain (indeed, the word means 'mountains'), as German occupation forces discovered to their great cost in Yugoslavia, Greece and Albania from 1941 to 1945. Much of western Europe also has moister and more temperate climates, longer growing seasons and a less mountainous terrain than does most of the eastern half of Europe, and it has been much less prone to soil erosion than the Balkans. Natural advantages of this sort made it easier for western European centres of trade and craft industry to link up with one another commercially. Such a trade network was established as early as the 1180s, according to the eminent French medievalist Georges Duby, who calls this one of the 'main turning points in European economic history' (Duby 1974: 257–70). At the opposite pole, 'No such network of commercial centers connected Balkan and Byzantine territory by that date or afterwards . . . The Balkan lack of coastal access or navigable rivers combined with the Ottoman wheat monopoly, designed to provision Constantinople at artificially low prices, to keep other urban grain markets from becoming integrated into a "national market". It typically cost more than the purchase price to transport 100 kilograms of wheat just 100 kilometres. Bulk trade could hardly flourish under these conditions' (Lampe 1989: 180, 184).

These factors help to explain the relatively low population densities and the comparative scarcity of large towns and cities in the Balkans and East Central Europe. This, together with the restrictive effects of the so-called 'second serfdom' in East Central Europe, further limited commercial opportunities and the size of markets. The Balkans and East Central Europe had a combined population of only about 22 million in 1700, about the same population as that of France at that time, while the only really significant urban markets within these regions during the early eighteenth century were Constantinople (400,000), Vienna (120,000), Prague (50,000) and Warsaw (30,000) (Okey 1982: 21, 32). With these significant exceptions, early modern East Central Europe and the Balkan Peninsula remained overwhelmingly rural worlds. Disadvantages of these sorts, combined with the growth of western European colonial commerce and the displacement of the world's major trade routes away from the Mediterranean and the Baltic towards Europe's Atlantic seaboard, caused both East Central Europe and the Balkans to fall far behind maritime western Europe, which developed increasingly secular and urban 'civic' societies with much greater freedom of thought, occupation and commerce.

At least until the early seventeenth century, however, western Europe (whichever way it is defined) was not strikingly 'more developed' or 'more advanced' economically and technologically than the Balkans and East Central Europe. This was partly because average levels of economic development, education and per capita income were almost everywhere very much *lower* than they have been since the Industrial Revolution, with the consequence that the *scope* for East–West economic, social and cultural disparities was also much *less* in the distant past than it has become in the modern industrial and post-industrial eras, the riches of which have made possible greatly increased inter- and intra-regional inequalities. Furthermore, parts of the Balkan Peninsula were widely regarded (and certainly thought of themselves!) as having higher levels of learning, morality, culture, and economic capability than the relatively remote, sparsely populated and less developed 'barbarian peripheries' of northern and western Europe, at least until the sack of Constantinople by north-west European Crusaders in 1204 (Haldon 1997: 16) and probably up to the passing of the sixteenth-century apogee of the Ottoman Empire (Braudel 1995: 89–92). Similarly, parts of East Central Europe (e.g. Bohemia) were probably as 'developed' or 'advanced' as much of western and north-western Europe until the 1610s (see pp. 140–1, 155–9, 176–9, below).

The relatively centralized, absolutist, rigid and stifling power structures which remained dominant in the eastern half of Europe until the First World War were outwardly imposing and splendid, but their long-term effects were stultifying. The Byzantine (Eastern Roman) Empire was succeeded by the Ottoman Empire from 1453 until the nineteenth or early twentieth century (varying from one area to another). Even those areas of East Central Europe which had seemed to begin to develop along lines similar to those of western Europe from the tenth to the sixteenth century gradually fell under an eventually debilitating Catholic-absolutist Habsburg control. At first this took relatively mild and tolerant forms, following the crushing defeat of Hungarian and Bohemian forces at the hands of the Ottomans at the Battle of Mohacs in 1526. However, East Central European absolutism became much more ascendant, far-reaching, oppressive and restrictive in the wake of the Habsburg victories over Central and East Central Europe's Protestant forces during the devastating Thirty Years War (1618–48), and even more so following the Habsburg 'liberation' or reconquest of Hungary between 1686 and 1699. These major setbacks were accompanied by widespread de-urbanization, emigration of merchants and craftsmen, and increased seigneurial power over downtrodden and increasingly enserfed peasantries. This was the case not only in the Habsburg domains as such but also in the adjacent Polish-Lithuanian Commonwealth prior to its gradual dismemberment by its absolutist Habsburg, Romanov and Hohenzollern neighbours in 1772, 1793 and 1795.

However, it was the north-western European Industrial Revolution, combined with the growing specialization of both East Central Europe and the Balkans in less sophisticated and generally less remunerative primary products, which dramatically widened Europe's East–West disparity in per capita national income from around two to one to about three to one within the space of some fifty years during the nineteenth century (Berend 1986: 339). This fundamental economic disparity widened still further during the twentieth century and it will persist well into the twenty-first century, even on the most optimistic assumptions. If the Balkan and East Central European states continue to be dogged by the kinds of crisis that they have repeatedly experienced in modern times, it will be an even longer haul.

THE BALEFUL CONSEQUENCES OF 'ETHNIC NATIONALISM' AND 'ETHNIC COLLECTIVISM'

While in western Europe the outcome of the late medieval and early modern 'crisis of feudalism' generally hastened the formation and consolidation of proto-national states (usually national monarchical states), the outcome of the corresponding eastern European crises facilitated the emergence and consolidation of 'absolutist' multinational imperial polities which managed to retain control of the greater part of the eastern half of Europe until 1918 (Anderson 1979, *passim*). A major consequence was that in western Europe modern nationalist doctrines developed *after* (or, in some cases, even as a result of) the establishment of proto-national states, whereas in the eastern half of Europe modern nationalism was incubated within multinational imperial polities, *before* the creation of nation-states. This in turn meant that, whereas western European nations were mostly conceived and defined in inclusive 'civic' terms (as the people of particular states and territories) and nationalism was mainly used to foster unificatory national identities and allegiances to existing states (which often encompassed culturally heterogeneous populations), in the eastern half of Europe nations were destined to be conceived and defined in more exclusive cultural or 'ethnic' terms, since these nations neither derived from nor corresponded to the existing multinational imperial states within which they resided. This seemingly innocuous east–west divergence was in many ways the most fateful difference between western and eastern European polities and societies during the late nineteenth and twentieth centuries. 'Between the wars, nationalism was the curse of eastern Europe – a political curse, in that national grievances, real or unreal, provided pretexts for oppressive rule and strong points for Nazi domination – and an economic curse, in that the national tariff walls were an obstacle to development' (Warriner 1950: 64).

Even if exclusive and frequently illiberal 'ethnic' nationalism was not the 'original sin' or the 'root of all evil' in twentieth-century East Central European and Balkan politics, it came pretty close to being that. It 'poisoned the wells' of liberalism and democracy in these regions, both before and after the emergence of independent nation-states. It also severely distorted and impeded the rule of law, equality of opportunity and the neutral operation of market economies. Inter-ethnic tensions, jealousies and conflicts threw up major road-blocks on the tortuous paths to pluralistic liberal democracy and market systems, even where they did not result in outright war. Conversely, the failure of liberalism and the rule of law to put down deeply entrenched roots in Balkan and East Central European societies made it all the more difficult to curb or constrain 'ethnic' excesses. 'The dominant nationality in each country indiscriminately looks upon the state as its very own, however undemocratic it may be' (Vajda 1988: 344). In nineteenth- and early twentieth-century East Central Europe and the Balkans, most experiments in democracy degenerated into intolerant majoritarianism, trampling underfoot the rights of minorities – and ultimately those of the majorities as well.

Under the sway of ethnic nationalism and ethnic collectivism, democratization empowered and buttressed the claims of potentially oppressive collectivities much more than it empowered and buttressed the rights of individuals. So long as each dominant ethnic group believed that it had exclusive title to particular states and territories, there would always remain considerable potential for violent inter-ethnic conflict in these benighted and war-scarred regions.

The belated initiation and the even later completion of the nation-building and state-building processes and the prominence of 'ethnic' or 'integral' nationalism in twentieth-century eastern Europe is thus mainly to be explained by many centuries of political, social and economic conditions and structures significantly different from those in western Europe. As will be made plain in Parts I to III, we do not accept the frequently alleged existence of *innate* differences in the 'ethnic make-up' and 'temper' of the two halves of Europe. We believe that this kind of cultural stereotyping and caricature often borders on racial prejudice and racism. In our view, *the distinctive political and cultural complexions of the eastern European nations and the nation-states which they sooner or later created were not innate but structurally determined.* Regrettably, the structures and contexts within which nationalism emerged in the eastern half of Europe did not reinforce but came into conflict with the development of tolerance and mutual respect. In western Europe, civil society (in the sense of a vigorous, autonomous and pluralist associations operating increasingly within the rule of law) has mainly 'defended pluralism and its autonomy against the encroachments of the state', but its potential counterpart in the eastern half of Europe frequently became 'the mainstay of a national identity that was often endangered by the foreign ruler or foreign state' and 'the principal defender of nationhood'. This engendered 'a certain uniformism and intolerance in the name of a common stand against the non-national or anti-national forces', that is the 'mentality of the besieged fortress' (Wandycz 1992: 8). Before the kingdoms of Bohemia, Hungary and Poland-Lithuania fell under the control of alien absolutist empires during the seventeenth and eighteenth centuries, multi-ethnic 'political nations' had indeed begun to emerge in East Central Europe. 'It was the interruption of statehood . . . that vitiated the process of nation forming along the Western lines. The result was an evolution toward a different concept of nationhood, coloured by the romantic outlook, conceived in terms of ethnicity and cultural-linguistic criteria' (Wandycz 1992: 7).

After several centuries under the 'imperial heel', mainly in the so-called 'prison-house of nations', the long submerged or subjugated peoples of East Central Europe were finally 'liberated' in the wake of the First World War. Even after the disintegration of Europe's eastern empires, however, the eastern and western halves of Europe continued to diverge in important respects. Some of these were portrayed in François Delaisy's influential *Les Deux Europes* (1924), Henry Tiltman's still fascinating *Peasant Europe* (1934), and David Mitrany's *Marx against the Peasant* (1951).

Miklos Duray, an outspoken member of the Hungarian minority in Slovakia during the 1980s, argued that, quite apart from their distinctive social and economic structures, the political systems and cultures of the states that emerged from the disintegration of the Habsburg, Tsarist, Hohenzollern and Ottoman empires were fatally scarred by 'the absolutization of the national idea', that is, by an intolerant majoritarianism or 'totalitarian nationalism' that erected new barriers and aroused new conflicts between nations (Duray 1989: 98–9). 'Within the political designs of the new states which emerged victorious on the historical stage, there was room only for their own power interests, for the interests of the ruling nation. There was no room for the national and cultural interests of the defeated nations . . . nor was there any provision for protecting the interests and identity of the national minorities . . . It was in this respect that Eastern Central Europe most clearly divorced itself from the West' (pp. 101–2), even *before* the advent of either Soviet hegemony or Communist dictatorship. Similarly, following the demise of the Nazi 'New Order' in 1945, 'The situation positively invited unrestrained behaviour because the concept of ethnic totality, no less alien to modern European traditions than Hitlerite or Stalinist ideas, had become the rule' (p. 104). Duray lamented that the seven decades since 1918 had seen 'no great improvement in conditions for a settlement between neighbouring countries in Eastern Central Europe, despite the fact that the countries of the area share such a similar past' (p. 110). The potential consequences were serious: 'Political pluralism emerged in Western Europe particularly as a means of resolving social, political and ideological conflicts . . . Such a concept of pluralism is absent from the traditional political culture of the Eastern Central European countries. It can even be said to run counter to our traditions' (pp. 112–13). Such a situation was conducive to the primacy of the politics of values which are inherently non-negotiable and absolute, rather than 'the politics of interests, characterized by pragmatic calculation, bargaining and compromise' (Batt 1994b: 37).

The rule of law, the pluralism and the liberal democracies and market economies of western Europe were only achieved after a century or more of struggle and hard-won incremental gains. In the wake of the demise of Europe's Communist regimes in 1989–91, there was still no guarantee that the struggles to establish liberal democracy and liberal capitalism (which had been tortuous, erratic and protracted in the West) could be telescoped into just one or two decades in East Central Europe and the Balkans, not least because these regions did not appear to offer very auspicious soil for political, social and cultural toleration and the rule of law. It has rarely (if ever) been possible to acquire a truly democratic system and a functioning market economy 'off the peg', as it were, in the way that one does when one purchases a ready-made suit. It was bound to be much easier for Europe's post-Communist states to emulate the outward trappings of Western liberal democracy and liberal market economies than their inner substance. After all, as Havel candidly acknowledged, Communist rule was 'far from being simply the dictatorship of one group of people over another. It was a genuinely totalitarian system, that is, it permeated every aspect of life and deformed everything it touched, including all the natural ways people had evolved of living together.' The Communist regimes fostered 'a specific structure of values and models of behaviour . . . When Communist power and its ideology collapsed, this structure collapsed along with it. But people couldn't simply absorb and internalize a new structure immediately, one that would correspond to the elementary principles of civic society and democracy.' The early 1990s were thus fraught with danger: 'In a situation where one system has collapsed and a new one does not yet exist, many people feel empty and frustrated. This condition is fertile ground for radicalism of all kinds, for the hunt for scapegoats, and for the need to hide behind the anonymity of the group, be it socially or ethnically based. It encourages hatred of the world, self-affirmation at all costs, the feeling that everything is now permitted and the unparalleled flourishing of selfishness . . . It gives rise . . . to political extremism, to the most primitive cult of consumerism, to a carpet-bagging morality . . . the eruption of so many different kinds of old-fashioned patriotism, revivalist messianism, conservatism and expressions of hatred' (Havel 1994b: 221–2). It has proved much harder for Europe's post-Communist states to overcome the deep-rooted 'home-grown' legacies of exclusive and illiberal 'ethnic' nationalism and ethnic collection than to throw off the largely alien and externally imposed ideological heritage of Marxism-Leninism.

Nevertheless, it has inevitably taken a considerable time for post-Communist states to shake off all the legacies of Communist rule. The Communist regimes lasted much longer than the fascist regimes of the 1930s and 1940s and, as a consequence, there was almost *universal complicity* in Communist wrongdoings. Corruption, illegality and reliance on the black market were matters of daily survival, and many people refrained from speaking up on behalf of those falsely accused of wrongdoings (or sometimes even informed on their neighbours) in order to protect a son, a daughter, a parent or a close friend. It has been neither possible nor desirable to try to round up all the chief villains and to subject them to Nuremburg-style trials. Wholesale 'purges' and witch-hunts invariably get out of hand, generate crude score-settling and new miscarriages of justice, claim too many innocent victims, and jeopardize healthy political activism (see Krastev 2004). In his New Year's Day address on 1 January 1990, President Havel prudently warned his fellow Czechs to refrain from seeking scapegoats for the effects of Communist rule: 'We have to accept this legacy as a sin we committed against ourselves. If we accept it as such, we will understand that it is up to us all, and up to us alone, to do something about it. We cannot blame the previous rulers for every-thing, not only because it would be untrue, but also because it would blunt the duty that each of us faces today: namely, the obligation to act independently, freely, reasonably and quickly' (Havel 1994b: 15).

For all these reasons, it was bound to take two to three decades for the inhabitants of these states to burn this legacy out of their souls. Seventeen years on, there were still frequent strongly voiced demands for retribution against former Communist officials in East Central Europe (especially Poland) and in the Baltic States. However, it would be wisest to emulate the successful example of post-Francoist Spain by drawing a line under the past, burying the hatchet and concentrating on building a better future. As a strategy for coming to terms with and overcoming past misdeeds, the South African Truth and Reconciliation Commissions offer a more appropriate and effective model than judicial inquisitions and judicial retribution, which run the risk of producing new miscarriages of justice and perpetuating social enmity, insecurity and cycles of revenge. It is safer to bury hatch-ets than to keep swinging them around. The major witch-hunt against former 'informers' and Com-munist 'agents' launched by President Lech Kaczynski and premier Jaroslaw Kaczynski (his twin brother) in Poland in 2006 threatened the survival of both liberalism and democracy far more than did the continuing presence of a few thousand unexposed and unpunished former 'informers' and Communist 'agents' in significant jobs in Polish state, ecclesiastical and educational institutions and the media. Like McCarthyism in the USA during the 1950s, the 'cure' propounded by the Kac-zynskis was much more dangerous than the alleged 'disease'. Fortunately, most of the Balkan and East Central European post-Communist states have prudently resisted the strong temptation to engage in similar large-scale witch-hunts, recognizing that the maintenance of liberal and demo-cratic values (rather than vengance) should be their paramount concern.

CRISIS AND CHANGE

The development of East Central Europe and the Balkans never has been and never will be just a 'staggered' and 'inferior' repetition of the development of western Europe. Each region has always had, and will continue to have, an agenda and a dynamic of its own. In East Central Europe and the Balkans, to a much greater extent than in western Europe, fundamental changes in political, social and economic structures or systems have tended to occur as a result of convulsive or cataclysmic crises, such as those that occurred during the Revolutions of 1848–9, in the wake of the Austro-Prussian War of 1866 and the stock-market crash of 1873, after the Balkan Wars of 1876–8 and 1912–13, amid the political upheavals of 1905–8, after the two World Wars, during the 1930s Depression, during the de-Stalinization upheavals of 1953–6, and in the wake of the collapse of the Communist systems in 1989–91. The striking frequency and magnitude of these crises, along with the consequent preponderance of erratic, eruptive or convulsive patterns of change, account for the sub-title of this book. Crises have repeatedly destabilized the precarious foundations and structures of East Central European and Balkan regimes and societies, thereby creating opportunities for radical and/or reactionary change. Gradual, evolutionary or incremental change on the Western pattern has not been wholly absent, but it has been much less prominent than in western Europe. During the nineteenth and twentieth centuries, moreover, the somewhat belated appearance of rail-ways, big cities, large-scale industrialization, cyclical booms and slumps, population explosions, the rapid uprooting of millions of people from the countryside to the towns, mass emigration, mass education, mass nationalism, political parties and trade unions greatly increased the region's social and political instability and turbulence and accelerated the pace of change. Societies in flux tend to experience acute political, social and cultural disorientation and despair, producing much pain and suffering as well as explosions of literary, intellectual, musical and artistic creativity and innovation.

In regions characterized by sporadic and eruptive patterns of change, political stabilization probably depends on wholesale social 'engineering' more than on piecemeal 'constitutional tinkering' (Longworth 1994: 114). The region has repeatedly experienced periods of feverish social and/or political reform, such as the reforms of Emperor Josef II during the 1780s, the Revolutions of 1848–9, the immediate aftermaths of the two World Wars and the period since 1989, interspersed with long periods of political immobilism or even retreat. During the twentieth century, however, crises have tended to 'break down the already precarious structure of mass society' and thus to increase the chances of success 'for anti-democratic mass movements' (Kornhauser 1960: 113).

In these respects, the modern social and political dynamics in East Central Europe and the Balkans have been quite amenable to the forms of 'revolution from above' favoured by Communist, fascist and authoritarian nationalist regimes. Nevertheless, this does not mean that we should automatically accept Alexander Gerschenkron's influential thesis that, as a result of the 'relative backwardness' of pre-1914 eastern Europe, the state had to play a much larger developmental role there than it did in the industrialization of western Europe (Gerschenkron 1962: 5–30, 353–64). He argued that the initial poverty of these predominantly agrarian economies, the increasing economies of scale and capital intensity of many industrial technologies, and the increasingly important 'linkages' and 'complementarities' between various industrial sectors and infrastructural investment (especially in railways) were constantly expanding the capital requirements of industrialization and the critical minimum effort needed to launch it as a self-reinforcing and sustainable process. In his view, these expanding financial requirements could only be met by the state and/or specialized investment banks, in most cases partly by attracting and harnessing inflows of Western loan capital and foreign direct investment. In such 'backward' economies, increased state enterprise, contracts, investment subsidies and other developmental expenditures had to be financed mainly by increased taxation of the preponderant agricultural sector. This 'fiscal squeeze' was bound to reduce effective demand for industrial and agricultural consumer goods, thereby increasing the importance of state contracts, investment subsidies and other forms of protectionism in sustaining demand for industrial products (especially producer goods), while forcing the primary sector to expand its exports, which would in turn help to service the foreign debt and finance much-needed imports of Western machinery and equipment.

Gerschenkron's critics have shown that he implicitly underestimated the roles played by the state and sometimes even by banks in the early stages of western European industrialization. The forms of state intervention and bank finance employed during western European industrialization may have been different, but they were often none the less crucial. For example, the state made decisive contributions to the economic successes of eighteenth-century England, not least through its increasingly liberal trade policies, the Enclosure Acts, the Acts of Union with Scotland and Ireland, and the promotion of British maritime supremacy and colonial power, while banks played a leading role in the Industrial Revolution in Scotland (Cameron 1966: 60–99). Moreover, the economic roles of the state, investment banks and foreign direct investment and the capital intensity of certain industries increased almost everywhere in the late nineteenth and early twentieth century. These trends were not peculiar to Europe's so-called 'backward economies' or 'late industrializers'. They had as much or more to do with escalating arms races and the growth of defence expenditures and military-industrial complexes than with the needs of civilian economic development (let alone public welfare provisions, which remained rather modest until the 1940s). Indeed, while parts of pre-1914 eastern Europe did develop some large-scale and capital-intensive industries (e.g. oil, steel and chemicals) for military reasons or where specific natural resource endowments warranted it, in most areas industrialization continued to be based mainly on gradually expanding production of low-technology and labour-intensive consumer goods such as textiles, processed foods and drinks (Bideleux 1987:

15, 17, 55–6, 259–61). It was not until the First World War and the subsequent emergence of autarkic and étatiste regimes (whether fascist or Communist) that the eastern European economies began to conform more closely to the Gerschenkronian model, albeit primarily for military and ideological reasons. It is anachronistic to try to project these patterns backward on to the pre-1914 period, as Gerschenkron did. Moreover, it was certainly not necessary or inevitable for economic development to be directly funded and controlled by the state in a dirigiste or 'neo-mercantilist' manner in Europe's less developed economies. The 1980s and 1990s witnessed a massive world-wide retreat from corporatism and collectivism and, on the doctrinal level, a 'neo-liberal' counter-revolution against the 'neo-mercantilism' of the preceding decades, not least in the so-called 'developing countries'. The retreat from centrally planned 'command economies' dovetailed with that trend.

The traumatic experience of Communist dictatorship and Soviet domination was but a brief episode in the history of East Central Europe and the Balkans, which has been more profoundly affected by other political, cultural and economic influences which lasted far longer than the Communist experiment, even if that remains the most vivid memory. In large measure it is those older, deeper and temporarily suppressed influences that have been reasserting themselves most strongly since 1989. This makes it all the more important to try to understand the underlying trends in the history of Europe's post-Communist states and the turbulent or conflicting emotions which these arouse among their inhabitants.

At the same time, we have to bear in mind that the ever-changing present is constantly shifting our perspectives on the past. Our current vantage-point is not something fixed. 'Every present has a past of its own, and any imaginative reconstruction of the past aims at reconstructing the past of this present' (Collingwood 1946: 247). Hence the process of writing history is never completed, and 'every generation must rewrite history in its own way; every new historian, not content with giving new answers to old questions, must revise the questions themselves'. Indeed, the historian is 'part of the process he is studying . . . and can see it only from the point of view which at this present moment he occupies within it' (p. 248). These observations are particularly pertinent to successive reappraisals of Balkan and East Central European history. The Revolutions of 1989 and their aftermath have not only presented many old questions in a new light. They have also raised many questions about the past of the new present. This book attempts not only to cast fresh light on many old questions, but also to pose and tentatively answer many new questions.

Part I

The Balkan Peninsula from the Graeco-Roman period to the First World War

1 The gradual 'Balkanization' of the Balkan Peninsula

The Balkan Peninsula, along with the nearby Aegean and Ionian seas and islands, the Black Sea, and the northern and western parts of Asia Minor (Anatolia), is widely perceived to have been the 'birthplace' or 'fountainhead' of European civilization. Indeed, during 'Late Antiquity' (the late Roman period) and at least until the twelfth century AD, the Balkan Peninsula remained either *the* most or *one* of the most 'advanced', 'civilized' or 'developed' regions of Europe, economically and technologically as well as culturally (Haldon 1997: 16). By the late nineteenth century, however, the formerly 'primitive' and 'barbarian' peoples of north-western Europe were ruling the roost and calling the shots, whereas the Balkan Peninsula had degenerated into one of the most conflict-prone and least developed regions in Europe. Somewhat nonsensically, considering that the concept of 'Europe' was first invented by the ancient Greeks and that the proponents of 'European' (and indeed 'Western') civilization are fond of tracing its roots back to the ancient Greek civilization which flourished in and around the Balkan Peninsula and its adjacent seas and islands, by the late twentieth century many xenophobic Western and Central Europeans had come to regard many (perhaps most) of the inhabitants of the Balkans as less 'European' and less 'civilized' than themselves and had even started questioning whether Balkan states should be eligible to join the European Union.

The overarching purpose of Part I of this book is to shed light on the protracted decline in the Balkan Peninsula's standing relative to other parts of Europe and on the deep historical roots of some of the problems which have latterly afflicted this far from happy region. This does not mean that we see the major problems that have afflicted the Balkans in recent times as products of 'ancient' ethnic and/or religious hatreds, still less that we view them as manifestations of an age-old 'clash of civilizations'. On the contrary, we regard many of the problems afflicting the Balkans as products of 'modernity' – this is especially the case for the nationalist ideologies and doctrines which emanated from Germanic Central Europe and the West. Others have been products of 'postmodern' tendencies towards fragmentation. Only a few have been peculiar and/or endemic to this peninsula.

In the Balkans during the twentieth century, to be sure, 'history' became a battleground upon which and/or in whose name terrible atrocities were repeatedly committed by nationalist, religious and Communist fanatics and ideologues. Particular care therefore needs to be taken to guard against the ethnic biases, cultural determinism and cultural or even racist stereotyping exhibited in many accounts of modern and even medieval Balkan history.

The biggest source of distortion in modern historical writing on the Balkans has been the strong tendency for Greek, Albanian, Romanian, Bulgarian, South Slavic, Balkan émigré and Western historians to succumb to varying degrees of anti-Ottoman, anti-Turkish or Islamophobic bias. During the nineteenth and twentieth centuries, historians in or from the Balkans (including some of 'Balkan descent' in the West) often presented very partisan views and implicitly or explicitly championed the territorial and/or cultural claims of particular ethnic and/or religious groups. Events that took place centuries ago were frequently treated as if they were recent occurrences. Indeed, these were still 'live issues' that sometimes aroused strong hatreds, resentments, jealousies or national pride. Appropriately enough, the Balkans are in many ways just a reflection and a microcosm of the 'Europe' which they so seminally helped to create. They are 'Europe' writ small. Modern conflicts, and even the more 'postmodern' Yugoslav conflicts of the 1990s, were to varying degrees intensified by over-heated memories of classical and medieval heroes, battles, atrocities, acts of valour and imperial projects. Until the 1990s, sometimes ludicrous or tragic obsessions with the distant past continued to inflame relations between, for example, the peoples of the former Yugoslavia, between the Greeks and their neighbours, between Romanians and Hungarians (especially over and between the respective communities in and territorial claims to Transylvania), and between Albanians and their neighbours (especially over Kosova, Epirus and western Macedonia). History and the misuse of history in pursuit of pernicious nationalist goals bedevilled Balkan politics and state-building from the early nineteenth century to the 1990s. On 10 December 1992, for example, more than one million Greeks (about one-third of the population of Athens) took part in mass protests against the decision of their Macedonian Slav neighbours to call their newly independent state the 'Republic of Macedonia'. Similarly, on 31 March 1994 more than a million Greeks demonstrated in Thessaloniki (Salonika) in support of their country's economic sanctions against the Republic of Macedonia. The Greek state even prosecuted and imprisoned some of its own citizens for daring to publicize the Macedonian Slav case and the existence of a significant Slav minority in northern Greece. In the eyes of many Greek nationalists there was and is no such thing as a 'Macedonian Slav' nation or nationality, and those Greeks who say otherwise have sometimes been treated and even prosecuted as 'traitors' to their country.

Such attitudes and the recent conflicts in the Balkans have partly derived from obsessive preoccupations with 'history' as perceived and narrated by modern nationalists. Even 'medieval studies in Southeastern Europe have always been a key area of confrontation for competing nationalistic discourses' (Curta 2005: 35). Reflecting on his experiences as an international negotiator during the conflicts between the Yugoslav successor states (1991–5), David Owen wrote: 'Nothing is simple in the Balkans. History pervades everything . . . It is not sufficient to explain away the frequently broken promises, the unobserved ceasefires, merely as the actions of lying individuals. They were also the product of South Slavic history' (Owen 1996: 1–2). Noel Malcolm, an eminent specialist on Bosnia and Kosova, noted that during the early 1990s the major perpetrators of violence in the Yugoslav successor states tried not only to ruin their enemies' future, but also to expunge the evidence and destroy the cultural and architectural heritage of their enemies' past (Malcolm 1994: xxiii). Such obsessions with history are by no means peculiar to the Balkans – for example, Hitler's occupations of France and Yugoslavia in 1940 and 1941, respectively, and the ways in which he subsequently treated both countries were in large measure motivated by his desire to settle 'historic' German and Austrian grievances. Nevertheless, such obsessions undeniably played significant roles in the conflicts which have bedevilled the modern and postmodern Balkans.

The Balkan Peninsula was known to the Ottoman Turks as 'Rumelia', to eighteenth-century Europeans as 'Turkey-in-Europe', to medieval Christendom as 'Romanie', and to the classical world as Illyricum, Macedonia and Thrace (Stoianovich 1967: 4). During the nineteenth century the term 'Balkans' (derived from a Turkish term for mountains) was aptly applied to the region. The term 'Balkanization' came into use in the early twentieth century, with reference to the problems which afflicted the post-Ottoman Balkans:

> With the decline of Ottoman power and the rise of national states the Balkan Peninsula lost whatever unity it had – the unity of subjection to an outside power. The facts of geography and the nature of the Ottoman system had kept the region a mosaic of different nationalities; together with the particularism which the new nationalism introduced, they left its peoples exposed to their own internecine conflicts and to the influence or domination of the great powers of Europe.

Thus there emerged . . . the classic model of what the world has come to know as Balkanization – a group of small, unstable and weak states, each based on the idea of nationality, in an area in which nation and state did not and could not coincide; all with conflicting territorial claims and with ethnic minorities that had to be assimilated or repressed, driven into unstable and changing alignments among themselves, seeking support from outside powers . . . and in turn being used by those powers for the latter's strategic advantage. (Campbell 1963: 397)

The resultant 'international anarchy . . . found its logical outcome in two great periods of war, from 1912 to 1922 and from 1939 to 1945'; and, during the second of these, 'nationalism, which in a generally liberal and democratic form had inspired the Balkan peoples in the long struggle for freedom and independence, finally helped to open the gates to Hitler' and engulfed the nations involved 'in the fires of hatred and massacre' (Campbell 1963: 397–8).

How did the Balkan Peninsula reach such a sorry state? According to many Western as well as Balkan historians of the peninsula, the explanations are mainly to be found in the baleful impact of four to five centuries of Ottoman overlordship. Depending on the area in question, this lasted from the fourteenth or fifteenth century to the nineteenth or early twentieth century. Peter Sugar, a major Western historian of the Balkans, proclaimed that 'South-eastern Europe became "Balkanized" under Ottoman rule' (Sugar 1977: 287). In his view, 'Ottoman conquest destroyed the larger units represented by the [former] states of South-eastern Europe' and in their place created 'a multitude of theoretically self-contained units which were small enough to be powerless but large enough to be functionally useful' (p. 279). However, 'The result was a very strict, over-organized socio-economic structure that soon ossified and was, at the same time, amazingly lenient. This licence prevented the enserfment of the South-eastern European peasantry and allowed the population, both urban and rural, to organize on a small communal basis under the leadership of its own elected officials . . . and facilitated their rebirth in the form of modern nations' (pp. 279–80). Sugar also argued that 'the most important change that Ottoman rule brought to South-eastern Europe was the large-scale demographic transformation of the area', including the northward displacement of the Serbs, Romanian migrations into the Banat and the Crisana, and Albanian migrations into Kosova, Epirus and Macedonia. These migrations produced 'a mosaic of hopelessly interwoven population patterns' (p. 283). Consequently, 'Ottoman social organization and the migratory patterns created by the forces that the Ottomans had set in motion were responsible for the appearance of South-eastern Europe's major modern international problem: large areas inhabited by ethnically mixed populations' (p. 284).

Despite ascribing 'Balkanization' primarily to the impact of Ottoman rule on the peninsula, Sugar's writings nevertheless remained unusually free of anti-Ottoman cultural bias. In a more blatantly anti-Ottoman vein, Wayne Vucinich claimed that:

Ottoman rule had a devastating effect on the cultural life of most of the conquered nations. In the Balkans, for example, learning virtually dried up, and art deteriorated from the exquisite medieval masterpieces to simple primitive creations. Once on a cultural level with the rest of Europe, the Balkan peoples had fallen far behind by the nineteenth century. There were several reasons for this. The Ottoman regime obliterated many of the spiritual and material resources of the subject peoples. Medieval states were eradicated, scions of conquered nobility killed off, churches and monasteries demolished, lands devastated, settlements destroyed, and large segments of the population dispersed. The Christian communities, deprived of their own resources for development, were given no comparable substitute. Moreover, they were isolated from cities and the mainstream of civilization, and restricted to a rural and pastoral life. As a result of long Turkish rule, the Balkan peoples became 'the most backward' in Europe. Like the Turks themselves, they were bypassed by the Renaissance. (Vucinich 1965: 68–9)

In place of such monocausal and ethnocentric explanations of the so-called 'Balkanization' of the Balkan Peninsula, and in order to present the undeniably important impact of the Ottoman Empire on the Balkans in a more balanced and nuanced historical perspective, we emphasize the interplay of diverse cultural, demographic, economic, locational and natural-environmental factors and the wider international or geographical context, including the interference and impact of other imperial powers. In our view, the deteriorating fortunes of the Balkan Peninsula from the seventeenth century to the Second World War cannot be blamed monocausally or ethnocentrically on 'the Ottoman impact'. Most of the underlying causes were largely beyond the control of the Ottoman Empire (see pp. 87–9, 95–107). It has become increasingly clear to us that much that has been attributed to the 'Ottoman impact' was either already in existence or incipient or merely inherited and perpetuated (rather than initiated) by Ottoman overlordship, and that many other evils were inflicted on the region by the major European powers which increasingly manipulated and 'meddled' in Balkan affairs for their own ends. The Ottoman impact on the Balkans has presented both the Balkan peoples and many Western historians of the Balkans with a convenient and superficially persuasive *scapegoat*, which has helped to divert attention from the ways in which their own cultures, institutions, rulers and histories must share the 'blame' for their deteriorating predicament. During the twentieth century it has also provided for pretexts for Bulgarian, Serbian/Yugoslav and Greek oppression of Turkish, Albanian and other Muslim minorities in the Balkans.

Rather than blame 'Balkanization' on any one of the successive conquering and colonizing peoples who have intruded into the peninsula, it is much fairer to emphasize the roles of location, accessibility and terrain in enticing and facilitating wave upon wave of inward migration and conquest. The terrain of much of the Balkan Peninsula is 'a jumble of mountainous valleys and cul-de-sacs that unquestionably produce local isolation' for its ethnically diverse inhabitants, who have therefore tended to cluster into numerous small pockets. Nevertheless, a network of major river valleys (such as the Morava–Vardar corridor and the Sava and Maritsa valleys) connects the eastern Mediterranean with the Danube basin, the Dardanelles, the Bosphorus and Asia Minor. This has provided easy access for foreign invaders and colonists from both East and West to this strategic crossroads between 'Europe' and 'Asia' (Kostanick 1963: 2).

In his still unsurpassed synoptic history of the Balkans, Leften Stavrianos emphasized that the location and the accessibility of the peninsula encouraged frequent and prolonged invasions. 'The struggle against these invasions . . . hindered the process of racial assimilation which has been the characteristic development in Western Europe. The complex terrain is also an important factor. If the peninsula had been a plateau instead of a highly mountainous and diversified region, it is probable that the various races would have amalgamated to a considerable degree. A common Balkan ethnic strain might have evolved' (Stavrianos 1958: 12). Unusually complex ethno-cultural tapestries or mosaics were formed and perpetuated in the Balkan Peninsula, in contrast to the somewhat larger and seemingly more homogeneous ethno-cultural units which were forged by the proto-national monarchical states of late medieval and modern western Europe. Contrary to Sugar's claim that 'South-eastern Europe became "Balkanized" under Ottoman rule' (Sugar 1977: 287), Stavrianos pointed out that 'By the fifteenth century the Slavs were in firm possession of a broad belt from the Adriatic to the Black Sea. The dispossessed Illyrians were concentrated in present-day Albania and the scattered Thraco-Dacians were reappearing as the nomadic Vlachs of the central highlands and as the Romanians of the newly-emerging trans-Danubian states, Moldavia and Wallachia. This ethnic distribution that took place in the Byzantine period has persisted with slight changes to the present' (Stavrianos 1958: 32).

The migrations and processes of acculturation and assimilation which occurred under Ottoman rule did result in some significant alterations to the ethnic complexions of Bosnia, Kosova and Croatia. These continued up to the 1990s and fuelled rival territorial claims to all or parts of these areas. Nevertheless, Stavrianos is much more accurate than Sugar: a complex Balkan ethnic mosaic was largely established *before* rather than *during* Ottoman rule, and mosaics of this sort are to be found even in areas which were only briefly or slightly affected by that rule. However, these later migrations did not greatly augment the overall complexity of the ethnic patchwork in the Balkans. Crucially, *the Ottoman system was essentially a response to (rather than the cause of) the ethno-cultural complexity of the region.* Therefore, even if the Ottoman Empire had never been established, the later spread of the ideas of nationalism, national self-determination and the nation-state would still have had highly disruptive and potentially explosive consequences within the Balkan ethnic mosaic. These consequences cannot and should not be blamed on 'the Ottoman impact'.

For millennia, the Balkan Peninsula has served as a major 'crossroads' and 'bridge' between civilizations and continents. The metaphor of the Balkans as a 'bridge' has long informed local conceptualizations of its role in history, most famously in Ivo Andric's Nobel Prize-winning novel *The Bridge over the Drina* (1945). Such an area was bound to be unsettled in times of conflict.

When the Balkans are compared and contrasted with western Europe, it is often insufficiently recognized that most western European nations are also *amalgams* of many different ethnic and linguistic 'strains'. France comprises Frankish, Norman, Gallic, Iberian and Ligurian 'strains' (among others), while Italy has long been an ethnic 'melting pot'. Britain, Belgium, the Netherlands, Switzerland and Spain also very visibly incorporate diverse ethnic and linguistic groups. In this regard, the crucial difference between the Balkans and western Europe lies not in the presence or absence of a multiplicity of component linguistic and ethnic 'strains', but rather in the *particular circumstances* which favoured or made possible the extensive fusion or unification of diverse 'strains' into relatively discrete and homogeneous units in western Europe and the equally extensive perpetuation of separate ethnic identities and allegiances in the Balkans. Indeed, *'the unique feature of Balkan ethnic evolution is that virtually all the races that have actually settled there, as distinguished from those that have simply marched through, have been able to preserve their identity to the present'* (Stavrianos 1958: 13). Conversely, few of the peoples who have settled in the Balkans during the past two or three millennia have evolved and amalgamated into clearly delineated nation-states, partly because of the distinctive physical geography of the Balkans and partly because of the relatively late survival of multi-ethnic imperial polities in the eastern half of Europe. These two factors have been the main contributors to the preservation of the peninsula's unusually complex ethno-linguistic diversity and mosaics.

SOME PROBLEMS POSED BY MARIA TODOROVA'S *IMAGINING THE BALKANS* (1997)

Among the many academic books on the Balkan Peninsula published since 1989, *Imagining the Balkans* (1997) by the Bulgarian émigré historian Maria Todorova has been the most influential and talked about. The book provides many valuable insights into Balkan identities and culture(s) and the ways in which they are perceived, both within and outwith the Balkans. Professor Todorova has become the best-known writer on so-called 'Balkanism'. Nevertheless, this influential book is flawed in ways that illuminatingly illustrate the potential pitfalls facing those who venture into this difficult terrain.

Professor Todorova reaffirms the current standard view that 'By the beginning of the twentieth century . . . "Balkanization" had not only come to denote the parcelization of large and viable political units but also had become a synonym for a reversion to the tribal, the backward, the primitive, the barbarian . . . What has been emphasized about the Balkans is that its inhabitants do not care to conform to the standards of behaviour devised as normative by and for the civilized world' (Todorova 1997: 3). Thus, what had begun simply as 'a geographical appellation' was 'transformed into one of the most powerful pejorative designations in history, international relations, political science, and nowadays, general intellectual discourse' (Todorova 1997: 7).

The occasional objections from aggrieved inhabitants of the peninsula that the new 'Balkan' identity was a spurious, unwarranted and pernicious concoction imposed or projected upon them by overbearing and manipulative foreign imperial powers *do* carry *some* weight. Todorova plausibly contends that, somewhat like the concept of 'the Orient', the construct of 'the Balkans' has 'served as a repository of negative characteristics against which a positive and self-congratulatory image of the "European" and the "West" has been constructed' (Todorova 1997: 188). She claims that 'the rhetoric of Balkanism, created [in] and imported from the West, has been completely internalized' by the Balkan intelligentsia (p. 57), but this is an oversimplified overstatement. Indeed, by affirming several times that the idea of 'the Balkans' *does* relate to a substantive phenomenon, she implicitly casts doubt on claims that this conceptualization was in effect created in and imported from the West. She acknowledges that, while 'some accept, although reluctantly, their Balkanness, while others renounce any connection with it, what is common for all Balkan nations is the clear consensus that the Balkans exist, that there is something that can be defined as Balkan, although it may be an undesired predicament and region' (p. 57). 'There is no doubt in anybody's mind that the Balkans exist' (p. 161). 'The Balkans have a concrete historical existence', and therefore 'the question of whether or not they actually exist cannot even be posed for the Balkans' (p. 12). Inasmuch as this is 'actually' the case, then we are not dealing merely with pernicious figments of the imagination, whether Western or otherwise, but with a more tangible reality.

A more fundamental problem with Todorova's analysis is her insistence that, in so far as 'the Balkans' and a Balkan identity are 'really existing' phenomena and thus rather *more* than mere figments of the imagination, they are largely attributable to what she calls (for short) 'the Ottoman legacy'. She does acknowledge the widely held view that the nature and identity of this peninsula have primarily been 'shaped' by two 'historical legacies' of 'crucial' importance: (i) 'the millennium of Byzantium with its profound political, institutional, legal, religious and cultural impact'; and (ii) 'the half millennium of Ottoman rule that gave the peninsula its [modern] name and established the longest period of political unity it had experienced' (Todorova 1997: 12). Nevertheless, she assigns primacy to the Ottoman legacy: 'Not only did part of southeastern Europe acquire a new name – Balkans – during the Ottoman period, it has been chiefly the Ottoman elements or the ones perceived as such that have mostly invoked the current stereotypes'; and therefore 'it seems that the conclusion that the Balkans are the Ottoman legacy is not an overstatement' (Todorova 1997: 12). Even though she explicitly acknowledges the importance of 'the Byzantine legacy' in shaping the culture, ideas, discourses, attitudes and orientations of the majority of inhabitants of this peninsula (chiefly on pp. 162–7 and 179–83), she nevertheless repeats her claim that 'it is the Ottoman elements . . . or the ones perceived as such that are mostly invoked in the current stereotype of the Balkans' (p. 162).

Having thus largely equated the 'Balkan' attributes of the peninsula and its inhabitants with 'the Ottoman legacy', she then asserts that, since their secession from the Ottoman Empire, 'The countries defined as Balkan (i.e. the ones that participated in the historical Ottoman sphere) have been moving steadily away from their Ottoman legacy, and with this also from their balkanness' (Todorova 1997: 183). Consequently, 'De-Ottomanization has been regarded as a process that was to achieve the coveted ideal of the polar opposite of being Ottoman (or Oriental), namely, steady Europeanization, Westernization, or modernization of society' (p. 180). She also makes the controversial claim that, in 'practically all spheres, except the demographic and the sphere of popular culture', the 'break' with 'the Ottoman legacy as continuity . . . was enacted almost immediately after the onset of political independence and, as a whole, was completed by the end of World War I; thereafter it was relegated to the realm of perception' (p. 181).

These claims are highly questionable in several respects, the most obvious one being that it would be almost unprecedented for peoples who have lived under the dominion of an alien imperial power for several centuries to shake off the greater part of that power's legacy so soon after attaining political independence. Just consider how long it is taking for former British, French, Spanish and Portuguese colonies to surmount and exorcize the legacies of colonial rule (which was considerably shorter than Ottoman dominion over the Balkans!), or how long it is taking the former satellites of the Soviet Union to shake off the legacies of a mere four decades of relatively indirect Soviet overlordship.

Furthermore, Todorova's claim that the (re)conceptualization and (re)construction of this peninsula as '*the Balkans*' was largely a product of the Ottoman impact upon that peninsula implicitly deflects or offloads too much of the 'blame' for the allegedly negative aspects of the peninsula's condition, predicament and characteristics on to the Ottomans and their 'legacy'. Such a claim implicitly absolves the peninsula's inhabitants and/or their much older Byzantine-Christian traditions and heritage from responsibility for most of the various unsavoury attributes that have been (often unjustly) projected on to them since the late nineteenth century. She is unfairly implying that these allegedly negative attributes are largely the fault of the Ottoman impact, while at the same time failing to question very deeply and explicitly whether this impact was really as negative as has often been (rather glibly) assumed. Many of the most exciting and/or positive attributes of the Balkan Peninsula, not least in West European perceptions, also derive from the impact of several centuries of Ottoman rule on its inhabitants, architecture, art, dress, textiles, furnishings, cuisine and music. In these respects, it is difficult to see much *practical* difference between Todorova's treatment of the Ottoman legacy and the way in which Vucinich and most Balkan nationalist historians portray the impact of Ottoman rule as the root of most of the evils that have afflicted this peninsula since the fall of Byzantium in 1453.

To be sure, Todorova deploys far more nuanced and sophisticated language and concepts than do the many extremely crude and one-sided Balkan nationalist histories of the Ottoman Balkans. Yet the end result appears to be virtually the same: to scapegoat the Ottoman impact and implicitly to absolve the peninsula's preponderantly non-Turkic peoples and cultures from any major share of responsibility for the terrible afflictions which have been visited upon them, often by fellow inhabitants of the same peninsula. By conveniently and self-righteously offloading or deflecting much of the responsibility for most of the peninsula's modern-day evils on to a now defunct imperial power, this approach to presenting and conceptualizing the peninsula's modern history is not only profoundly distorting and misleading, but also discourages the formerly subjugated peoples from confronting and coming to terms with their own respective roles in and partial responsibility for the many things that have subsequently 'gone wrong' *for* and especially *between* them. This self-exculpatory Ottoman-bashing approach has been one of the banes of Balkan history, and Professor Todorova's reformulations continue in much the same rut, albeit with much greater flair and sophistication. However, as we stress in chapters 5–7, the Ottoman Empire largely took over, harnessed and perpetuated (rather than suppressed or destroyed) the ongoing cultures, identities and power structures of the peninsula's overwhelmingly Christian populations. *The modern Balkans have therefore been shaped far more profoundly by their predominantly Christian heritage than by 'the Ottoman legacy'*, which by comparison was almost 'epiphenomenal'.

It is much more plausible that a Balkan identity emerged and/or was perceived and constructed mainly on the basis of the growing national assertiveness of the peninsula's Christian populations and identities, in response to the gradual decline and retreat of Ottoman rule during the eighteenth and nineteenth centuries, rather than as a product of the (predominantly Islamic) Ottoman impact and legacy. In her stimulating *Inventing Ruritania: The Imperialism of the Imagination* (1998), Vesna Goldsworthy has cogently argued that 'perceptions of the peninsula emerge fully shaped only after a specific Balkan identity came into being, distinct from the Ottoman Empire. The struggle against Ottoman rule, which drew European attention to the peninsula in the first half of the nineteenth century, posits the region as an imaginary European sphere. For as long as they were ruled by Islamic rulers, the largely Christian Balkan nations were seen as enslaved Europeans. The moment when the newly independent Balkan states are supposed to be joining Europe is, however, also the moment when they are symbolically differentiated from it and a new – "Balkan" – Other is created' (Goldsworthy 1998: 11). This more nuanced and sophisticated interpretation of the emergence of the new '*Balkan*' identity is considerably more consistent with the nature and content of what emerged, as well as with the timing of its emergence. The newly emerging 'invented' or constructed overarching 'Balkan' identity and its constituent national or ethnic identities comprised not only a few overtly exotic and '*Oriental*' features implanted or infused into the peninsula's society and culture by the Ottoman Turks and Islam, but also many of the perceived ethno-cultural traditions and characteristics of the specifically Christian inhabitants of the peninsula. These were seen (and have continued to be seen) as much more central to '*Balkan*' identity and identities than were (and are) the specifically Ottoman Turkish and Islamic elements highlighted by Todorova. If 'the Ottoman legacy' had supplied the major ingredients in the new 'Balkan' identity, as Todorova claims, then one would expect this new identity to have been 'imagined', 'invented' or constructed during the Ottoman Empire's sixteenth- and early seventeenth-century heyday, when 'the Ottoman impact' on the peninsula was at its strongest and most widespread, rather than during the empire's protracted early eighteenth- to early twentieth-century retreat and decline, when its impact was considerably weakened. In practice the new name seems to have come into use, and both an overarching '*Balkan*' identity and new '*Balkan*' national identities seem to have been 'imagined' and/or constructed, *during and after* the emergence of initially autonomous and later independent Balkan 'nations' and states during the nineteenth and early twentieth century. At that time, as Vesna Goldsworthy aptly puts it, they 'fulfilled a need for a short-hand reference for the new states crystallising in the territory previously known as Turkey in Europe' (Goldsworthy 1998: 3).

It is also noteworthy that, unlike the construction of many other 'Oriental' identities, the discovery, 'imagining', 'invention' or construction of an overarching Balkan identity and its constituent national or ethnic identities was not primarily a discourse among politicians, officials, writers and thinkers in the service of foreign imperial powers (including the Ottoman Empire), nor was it simply imposed on the Balkan Peninsula by outsiders. Rather, it was a multidirectional *dialogue* between outsiders and the native inhabitants of the peninsula, partly in response to the emergence of new independent-minded entities (peoples, nations and states) at that time. Many members of the peninsula's growing and increasingly assertive and self-conscious nationalist intelligentsias, who were supported by smaller numbers of prospering Orthodox Christian entrepreneurs who helped to finance the nationalist revolutions, school-building and church-building which culminated in the establishment of first autonomous and later independent Balkan states, participated actively in the 'discovery' and/or 'construction' of new Balkan identities.

At the same time, however, the processes by which this peninsula came to be known as 'the Balkans' and perceived as qualitatively 'Balkan' were unable to escape the impact of parallel processes by which internal as well as Western perceptions of the peninsula came to be partially '*Ottomanized*' and/or '*Orientalized*'. Partly as a result of the often visible, alluring or fascinating effects of Ottoman rule on Balkan forms of dress, architecture, art, music and cuisine, the peninsula came to be perceived by many of its educated inhabitants, as well as by many Western and Central Europeans, as part of an exotic, despotic and erotic 'Near East' which was *partially 'Oriental' and therefore not fully 'European'* or, more commonly, *only ambiguously 'European'*. This occurred in spite of the fact that by the time of the 'Greek War of Independence' (1820–8) educated Western and Central Europeans had fully 'rediscovered' the notion that the idea of Europe had been invented on this self-same peninsula by the ancient Greeks in the fifth century BC (see Herodotus *c.*420 BC [1996]: 91, 228, 394) and even though the southern Balkans were by then widely regarded as the 'fountainhead' or 'birthplace' of European conceptions of democracy, nurturing hopes that a newly independent Greece could be quickly drawn back into Europe's so-called 'mainstream'. Consequently, Todorova is on firmer ground in arguing that 'In the realm of ideas, balkanism evolved partly as a reaction to the disappointment of the West Europeans' "classical" expectations in the Balkans, but it was a disappointment within a paradigm which had already been set as separate from the oriental' (Todorova 1997: 20). 'Unlike orientalism, which is a discourse about an imputed opposition' between the Orient and the Occident, 'balkanism is a discourse about an imputed ambiguity' (p. 17). Todorova therefore treats Balkanism, not as a form of Orientalism, but as 'a seemingly identical, but actually only similar, phenomenon' (p. 11).

The partial 'Orientalization' of the peninsula and of Western and Central European perceptions of it, which (unlike Balkanism) can indeed be attributed in large measure to the impact of five centuries of Ottoman rule, was probably a major reason why the neo-Ottoman expression *'the Balkans'* caught on so firmly during the late nineteenth and early twentieth century and why it is still explicitly or implicitly considered to be apt by many Western and local writers and commentators on the peninsula's history, politics and culture. The term 'Balkan Peninsula' was coined by the German geographer August Zeune in his book *Goea. Versuch einer wissenschaftlichen Erdbeschreibung* (Berlin: 1809), while the earliest published use of the term *'the Balkans'* in the English language was apparently by Robert Walsh in his *Narrative of a Journey from Constantinople to England* (London: 1828). 'Only by the middle of the nineteenth century was it applied by more authors to the whole peninsula', which hitherto had been variously known as Rumeli or Rumelia (Ottoman names for their province of Rum, 'the land of the Romans', named after the eastern Roman Empire which latter-day historians call 'Byzantium'), 'Turkey-in-Europe', 'European Turkey', the Greek or Hellenic Peninsula, the Illyrian Peninsula, the Slavo-Greek Peninsula, or the South Slavic Peninsula (Todorova 1997: 25–7, 249–50).

Nevertheless, 'the Balkans' and 'Balkan identity' were neither conceived nor constructed solely or even mainly on the basis of 'the Ottoman legacy'. The latter was always just one of several ingredients. Other major ingredients included the rich philosophical, literary, architectural, sculptural and other artistic legacies of the ancient Greek polities; the rich religious, artistic, architectural, musical and intellectual legacies of the Byzantine Empire (the most important and influential polity on the peninsula from the 320s AD to 1204); the architectural and infrastructural legacies of Roman Illyricum and Dalmatia; and the real and the imagined legacies of the pre-Roman Illyrians and Thracians. John Allcock has rightly emphasized that 'the Balkans' were only partly conceived as Oriental and/or Ottomanized. 'Alongside, and closely related to, the construction of the Balkans in terms of their location on the decaying fringes of the Orient stands another and competing set of images. They are equally complex, evocative and deeply rooted in history. This is the notion that its peoples are heirs to the Classical World, and their lands the homes of great civilizations' (Allcock 2000: 229–31). Importantly, these elements exalt rather than belittle or denigrate the Balkans and Balkan identity.

Furthermore, the construction of both an overarching 'Balkan identity' and more localized 'Balkan identities' during the nineteenth century was massively influenced by the great 'rediscovery' and celebration of 'folk culture(s)' by folklorists, philologists and ethnographers, as well as by collectors, recorders, exhibitors and performers of folk music, folk tales, folk art, popular customs, popular costumes and even peasant housing (culminating in the establishment of peasant museums, like the excellent ones in central Bucharest and in Suceava in Romania). These movements contributed potently to the further development of the Balkan written languages and Balkan literatures, art, architecture and music. During the twentieth century new ways of seeing, hearing, reproducing and using Balkan folk art and music provided rich and exciting sources of inspiration for artistic, sculptural, architectural and musical innovation, producing important international figures such as the Romanian sculptor Constantin Brancusi (1876–1962), the Croatian sculptor Ivan Mestrovic (1883–1962), the Romanian composer/violinist Georghe Enescu (1881–1955) and the Serbian composer Ljubica Maric (1909–2003). Although Central and Western Europeans such as the artist Henri Matisse have been attracted and inspired by these 'discoveries' partly because of their perceived 'exotic' and 'primitive' qualities, these identity-building discoveries usually had little to do with Orientalism and/or 'the Ottoman legacy'. Therefore, any attempt to reduce 'Balkanism' and the construction of Balkan identities to 'the Ottoman legacy' is highly misleading and sells both the Balkan Peninsula (and also Western and Central European responses to it) very short. There was vastly more to 'Balkanism' and Balkan identities than Todorova suggests, and they were by no means perceived only in a negative light. They also aroused great admiration, fascination, curiosity and even creative inspiration among many well-educated West and Central Europeans, as well as among the peninsula's inhabitants. It was partly for such reasons that in the early twentieth century Bucharest came to be known as 'little Paris', while cities such as Belgrade and Zagreb also became renowned for the vibrancy of their intellectual and artistic life and 'café cultures'.

Equating 'Balkanism' or 'Balkan identity' with 'the Ottoman legacy' raises additional problems in relation to those parts of the Balkan Peninsula which were relatively little affected by direct Ottoman rule (primarily Croatia and the 'Danubian Principalities' of Wallachia and Moldavia). Ottoman legacies have been much more diluted in Croatia and Romania, yet this has not stopped these countries from being considered parts of the Balkan Peninsula. Nor has it prevented these countries from sharing many traits, attitudes, formative experiences and important dimensions of cultural heritage with their more southerly neighbours on this same peninsula, even though it has long been apparent that many (perhaps most) of their inhabitants (especially intelligentsia) prefer to be considered part of 'Central' Europe rather than 'the Balkans'. Slovenia has at times been considered 'Balkan' because of having been part of both interwar and Communist Yugoslavia, yet Ottoman influences barely exist at all in Slovenia, which never experienced Ottoman rule.

Unfortunately, it became all too easy for outside observers to consider 'Balkanization' to be a congenital condition of the peoples of the Balkan Peninsula and, by attributing it to innate or genetically determined 'Balkan' characteristics and mentalities, to succumb to facile and fatalistic assumptions that the inhabitants of this peninsula are somehow not capable of thinking and behaving in more peaceful and 'civilized' ways. Assumptions of this sort have underlain Western and Central European perceptions of politics and conflict in the Balkans almost continuously since the late nineteenth century. Such perceptions were strongly aroused by the so-called 'Bulgarian atrocities' of April 1876, when irregular *bashibazouks* (mainly Muslim Slav forces in the service of the Ottoman Empire) were accused of having killed around five thousand Bulgarian Christians (mainly women and children), many of whom were burned alive in a church in which they had taken refuge (Crampton 1997: 81–2). These perceptions were reinforced by the particularly grisly murder of the King and Queen of Serbia during a military *coup d'état* in 1903, and were strengthened still further by the gruesome atrocities which many thousands of armed combatants in the Balkan Peninsula inflicted on hundreds of thousands of civilians (often fellow citizens of the same state) during the Balkan Wars of 1912–13, during the First and Second World Wars, during the aftermaths of those wars, during the Yugoslav conflicts of 1991–5, and in Kosova in 1999. There is no denying that such actions were extremely barbaric and shocking. Nevertheless, it needs to be pointed out that the often prurient Western accounts of such terrible occurrences all too easily portray them as peculiarly 'Balkan', 'alien', 'other', 'un-European' and even exotic and 'Oriental', apparently forgetting that equally terrible occurrences have occurred in twentieth-century Germany, Austria, Poland, Hungary, Czechoslovakia, Spain, Ireland, France, the Netherlands, Belgium and Italy, and that (appalling though they were) all such occurrences in the Balkan Peninsula were dwarfed by the scale of the barbarism and atrocities committed by hundreds of thousands of ethnic Germans and their mostly Austrian, French, Italian, Dutch, Belgian, Baltic, Hungarian, Croat, Romanian, Ukrainian and Belarussian collaborators against millions of civilians (mostly Jewish and Gypsy compatriots) during the Second World War. This is *not* said to exonerate in any way the many barbarities committed by inhabitants of the Balkan Peninsula, but simply to *keep things in perspective* and to emphasize that the Balkans have no monopoly on European barbarism. Judging by the record of their colonial and/or wartime attributes, Western and Central Europeans have no grounds whatsoever to feel either morally superior to, or more 'civilized' than, the inhabitants of the Balkans. Therefore, despite using the expressions 'the Balkans', 'Balkan' and 'Balkanization', this book in no way suggests that the peoples, states and societies of the Balkan Peninsula are morally or culturally 'inferior' to the peoples, states and societies of Western and Central Europe, even though they are at present economically much poorer, less privileged and (partly as a consequence of this) less secure and in some cases more brutalized or desperate. It is far too easy for Westerners living in comparatively comfortable circumstances to adopt smugly self-righteous and 'superior' attitudes towards standards of conduct in the Balkans, and they would do well to reflect on how Westerners would behave in similar circumstances (the actions of some American and British soldiers in Iraq in 2003–4 and of some Americans following the devastating hurricanes in New Orleans in September 2005 gave some idea).

Some writers on the Balkan Peninsula claim that 'the "politically correct" term Southeastern Europe has more or less replaced the Balkans, because it has become impossible to define a country as "Balkan" without having to explain oneself' (Goldsworthy 2002: 34). Other specialists on the region argue that the overarching transformation in the region since the end of Ottoman rule has been the (re)conversion of 'the Balkans' into 'South-eastern Europe' (Todorova 1997; Lampe 2006). The major problem with such views is that the expression 'South-eastern Europe' refers to a much larger area which nearly always also includes Turkey, Cyprus and Moldova and perhaps ought also to include Georgia, Armenia, Ukraine and Azerbaijan, which also have strong (albeit variously contested) claims to be considered part of Europe. If (as we believe) these countries can be included in a 'Greater Europe' defined in functional and empirical terms, rather than on the basis of outmoded cultural, religious or racial prejudices and preconceptions, then they are manifestly located in the south-eastern part of it! We therefore continue to refer to the Balkan Peninsula as 'the Balkans' because that remains the name which most immediately and precisely indicates to most people the region under discussion. If a less controversial and politically and culturally loaded and sufficiently widely recognized name for this peninsula were available, we could use that instead, but this has not occurred. Furthermore, while it is difficult to deny that the types of problem conveyed by and encapsulated in the more obviously pejorative concept of 'Balkanization' do reflect *some* significant aspects or components of the predicaments in which the peoples and polities on this peninsula have had the misfortune to find themselves since the late nineteenth century, we are also fully aware that this is far from being the whole story and that the notion of 'Balkanization' is fraught with dangers of highly misleading *caricature* and *stereotyping*, which we have striven to avoid.

2 The Balkan Peninsula in the Graeco-Roman period

The first major civilization on the landmass which has come to be called 'Europe' was that of ancient Greece. Heavily influenced by the Minoan civilization in Crete (*c*.3400–*c*.1450 BC), an advanced 'Bronze Age' Hellenic civilization (that of the Achaeans) developed around Mycenae, Tiryns, Pylos, Athens and Thebes from *c*.1600 BC. In the wake of the destructive Dorian invasions, however, mainland Greece entered a period of decline from *c*.1100 BC. The Dorians, who spoke the Doric dialect of the Greek language, were better armed but less 'civilized' than their Achaean cousins, many of whom migrated to Greek colonies in coastal Asia Minor.

Starting around 480 BC, 'classical' Greek civilization flourished in and around the emerging mercantile city-states of Athens, Sparta, Thebes, Argos and Corinth, located in Attica and the Peloponnesus. Guided by philosophers and historians in place of priests and prophets, 'classical' Greece developed a new ethics, literature, drama, art and architecture, based upon secularism and humanism. This was the age of Aeschylus, Sophocles, Euripides, Aristophanes, Herodotus, Thucydides, Plato and Aristotle.

During the same period addional Greek colonies were founded along the Black Sea, Adriatic, Ionian and Aegean coasts and up the River Danube, increasing Hellenic influence on other inhabitants of the Balkan Peninsula, including those who are commonly referred to as Thracians (inhabiting the eastern Balkans or present-day Bulgaria and Romania), Illyrians (inhabiting the western Balkans, comprising present-day Albania, Croatia and Bosnia) and Macedonians (inhabiting the central Balkans), although the frequent claims that 'Illyrians' and 'Macedonians' were distinct and clearly identified peoples who were direct ancestors of the modern inhabitants of these same territories are far from proven and probably spurious (see Wilkes 1992: 3, 11–12, 38, 167, 218, 265, 268–71; and Bideleux and Jeffries 2007: 24, 184, 331–2, 407–8). However, the Greek city-states dissipated their energies and resources in chronic internecine warfare and were eventually conquered by Philip II of Macedon (reg. 359–336 BC) and his famous warrior-son Alexander the Great (reg. 336–323 BC), whose far-flung and short-lived empire extended from Egpyt through Asia Minor, Syria and Mesopotamia (Iraq) to Persia and the Punjab.

Starting around 229 BC, there were Roman incursions into the western Balkans, ostensibly to protect Roman shipping in the Adriatic Sea, but also to promote Roman dominance over the region. Following protracted power struggles and warfare, the nascent Roman Empire subjugated southern Illyria (parts of present-day Albania, Bosnia, southern Croatia and northern Greece) in 168–6 BC, mainly as a result of the crushing defeats it inflicted on the kingdoms of Macedon and Epirus in 168 BC. The Romans went on to conquer Macedonia in 148 BC, present-day mainland Greece between 150 and 146 BC, the western Balkans between 6 and 9 AD, and Dacia (present-day Romania) between AD 100 and 106. The inhabitants of Illyria, whoever they were, kept up intermittent resistance to Roman overlordship until AD 9, when Rome decided to crush them once and for all.

Although the Romans came as conquerors, they retained a high regard for the older and more venerable Greek culture and civilization, which they sought to preserve and assimilate. Greek was granted equal status with Latin as one of the two official languages of imperial administration, the law courts, commerce and learning. It was no accident that the New Testament was written and disseminated in Greek rather than in Latin. The hybrid Graeco-Roman civilization which developed in the Balkans in Roman times was predominantly Hellenic, especially in the south and east. However, the Latin/Roman impact was strong in the prosperous province of Illyricum (Illyria), where irrigated agriculture, viticulture, textile manufacture and the mining of gold, silver, iron and lead flourished under Roman rule. Several Illyrian soldiers of humble origin even rose to the rank of emperor (Claudius II, Aurelian, Probus, Diocletian and Maximian). The language became Latinized (and Italian is still widely understood along the Adriatic coast, where it was later reinforced by Venetian influences). Even though Roman rule in Dacia only lasted from AD 106 to 275, modern Romanians are taught to think of themselves as descendants of the Romanized Dacians (Thracians) and Roman colonists who inhabited this imperial outpost, and the modern Romanian language has retained (or retrieved) its predominantly Latin roots.

Graeco-Roman civilization, which was initially concentrated in a few coastal areas, was gradually disseminated more widely. Indeed, the construction of remarkable Roman military and commercial highways across the peninsula effectively linked the major new towns in the interior, including Singidunum (Belgrade), Serdica (Sofia), Philippopolis (Plovdiv), Naissus (Nis) and Hadrianopolis (Adrianople/Edirne), with major ports such as Dyrrachium (Durres), Salonika (Thessaloniki), Byzantium (Constantinople/Istanbul), Tomis (Constanta), Odessos (Varna), Mesembria (Nesebur), Epetion (Split) and Trogurium (Trogir). During their heyday, these flourishing Roman towns in the Balkans boasted impressive temples, villas, palaces, sewage systems, baths and aqueducts, of which the 'remains' have became important tourist attractions in modern times. These towns established considerable fiscal and judicial control over their rural hinterlands.

GROWING DIVERGENCE BETWEEN THE WESTERN AND EASTERN SECTORS OF THE ROMAN EMPIRE

Between the second and fourth centuries AD the centre of gravity of the Roman Empire gradually shifted from the western to the eastern Mediterranean. Commerce and banking were more highly developed in the eastern Mediterranean, which was traversed by the great trade routes carrying Asian products to European markets. The eastern provinces were also deliberately fortified by the Roman Empire, both militarily and economically, in order to fend off growing threats from 'barbarian' marauders from north-central Europe, the Eurasian steppes and a burgeoning Persian Empire. As a consequence, metal-working, arms production, irrigated agriculture, viticulture, fishing, textiles, leatherwork, food-processing, communications and mining were actively promoted in the Balkans and Asia Minor (Haussig 1971: 31–4).

Escalating frontier warfare fostered the emergence of able 'self-made' frontier commanders, often from humble Balkan origins, as the new imperial 'strongmen'. Political power slowly slipped from the civilian Roman Senate and senatorial aristocracy in Italy to the ascendant frontier commanders, who increasingly became the new Roman emperors and provincial governors. These professional soldiers and military 'usurpers' doubled the size of the Roman army to about 600,000 men and broke up the unwieldy legions into smaller and more mobile detachments backed up by heavy cavalry, especially under the emperor Diocletian (AD 284–305), while the Balkan and Danubian provinces became 'seedbeds of talent' (Brown 1971: 24–5, 41).

Eastern Mediterranean agriculture was characterized by a marked prevalence of small, independent and self-motivated peasant farmers and a relative absence of deeply entrenched and oppressive landed aristocracies. Stimulated by the military exigencies and high social mobility and fluidity of the 'frontier' regions, it became more responsive and productive than its western counterparts. In

Italy, by contrast, agricultural productivity and incentives were impaired by a growing concentration of landholdings in the hands of a class of increasingly inattentive, parasitic, wealthy, corrupt and oppressive absentee landlords (latifundists), especially the close-knit senatorial aristocracy, who also increasingly resisted imperial demands for taxes and military service. Roman military and administrative efficiency atrophied in Italy, where falling productivity and growing dependence on relatively expensive imported foods and raw materials increased Italian prices and the cost of living, depressing both the position of the labouring classes and the competitiveness of industries. Italy lost its lead in ceramics to Germany, in wine production to Gaul and North Africa, and in metal goods, armaments, textiles, leatherwork and glassware to the Balkans and Anatolia, which managed to lure away many of Italy's skilled workers and craftsmen (Haussig 1971: 26–8).

The Balkan Peninsula was not without senatorial landlords, but they 'can scarcely have owned a twentieth of the East' and were dwarfed by those of Italy (Treadgold 1997: 114). Indeed, 'the power of the eastern senatorial elite was to a large extent moderated . . . by a greater density of cities and by the continued existence throughout the eastern regions of a middling group of landowners. There was, moreover, a greater number of more or less autonomous peasant communities, subject fiscally directly to the state; while the landowning elite in the East never came to dominate either the central imperial establishment or the civil bureaucracy in the way that the western senatorial establishment did' (Haldon 1995: 17).

Perceiving that Rome was increasingly unable to retain control of its overextended and increasingly unwieldy empire, Emperor Diocletian (himself of humble Balkan origin) decided to divide the empire between himself and three of his Balkan colleagues in AD 295. He also instigated more systematic taxation based on official land registers and communal village responsibility for payment of imperial taxes, which jointly bound the peasantry more tightly to their domiciles.

EMPEROR CONSTANTINE I (REG. AD 306–37), CONSTANTINOPLE AND THE EMERGENCE OF THE EASTERN ROMAN (BYZANTINE) EMPIRE

In 312, not long after Diocletian's 'retirement' in 305 AD to his remarkable palace in Split (Salonae) on the Dalmatian coast, the empire was forcibly reunited by Emperor Constantine I (AD 306–37), who defeated his co-rulers in battle in AD 312 and AD 323–4 respectively. Constantine subsequently attributed his decisive victory in AD 312 to intervention by the Christian God, and he ostensibly converted to Christianity (Grant 1978: 300–8). This gave a major boost to the Christianization of the emerging Eastern Roman Empire. As recently as AD 257–9 and 302–10 the Roman Empire's Christian inhabitants had been subjected to systematic official persecution. From AD 260 to 302, however, Christianity had profited from a prolonged period of toleration, renewed by official edicts of religious toleration in 311 and 313, although as yet no more than 10 per cent of the imperial population was Christian (Woodhouse 1977: 22). Indeed, Christians only slightly outnumbered Jews, who at that time constituted 8 per cent of the imperial population (Haussig 1971: 45). In deciding to give official backing to Christianity, it appears that Constantine was influenced by the ideas of 'Christian Apologists' such as Lactantius and Eusebius, who argued that Christianity had found a *modus vivendi* with Roman civilization and that it could be the salvation (in more senses than one) of the beleaguered Roman Empire (Brown 1971: 84, 86). Constantine certainly sought to use Christianity to bolster his imperial authority and to re-establish the empire on new foundations, although Christianity did not actually become the official religion until AD 391, under Emperor Theodosius I (reg. 379–95). Constantine sought to blend Graeco-Roman paganism, philosophy and emperor-worship with Christianity, rather than root out the non-Christian elements in imperial culture.

In AD 324 Constantine laid the foundations of a new imperial capital, a 'new Rome', on the site of the small Greek trading colony of Byzantium, which had been established in 660 BC in a strategic position on the Bosphorus. Here he grouped around himself a new civilian ruling class who reversed the previous trend towards military rule and led the eastern half of the Roman Empire towards 'a new identity, as the empire of Constantinople' (Brown 1971: 88, 138). Constantinople became the crucible of a new civilization, an amalgam of Christian, Eastern, Hellenistic and Roman elements. Modern historians of this empire have given it the name 'Byzantium', alias 'the Byzantine Empire', although this was not what it was called at the time.

In AD 395, following the death of Theodosius I, the Roman Empire underwent a lasting East–West division, consolidating 'Greek' predominance in the revamped Eastern Roman empire and 'Latin' predominance in the disintegrating Western Roman Empire. Faced with concurrent threats of 'barbarian' invasion from north-central Europe and the Eurasian steppes, the Eastern Roman Empire offered the so-called 'barbarian' invaders bribes ('subsidies') and other inducements to refrain from further raids and attacks. It also enlisted some 'barbarians' into imperial service and in AD 400 treacherously massacred a force of 'barbarian' Goths who had been invited to reside in Constantinople.

These stratagems successfully deflected the main 'barbarian' invasions away from the Balkans and Anatolia into Italy, Spain and Gaul. While the Vandals were preparing to invade Gaul and Spain in AD 406–9, the Visigoths invaded Italy in 402 and they devastated Rome in 410, after the rich and vain Roman senators had refused to buy them off (much as they had increasingly refused to render the taxes and recruits needed to maintain effective West Roman armies). The official rulers of the Western Roman Empire retreated to Ravenna, but it never recovered from these blows and the last Western Roman emperor was deposed by Germanic 'barbarians' in AD 476.

Consequently, whereas parts of the Balkans were to remain under imperial rule for another 1,400 years (until 1913), the Western Roman empire fragmented into a multiplicity of 'barbarian' states. It is widely believed that the disintegration of the Western Roman Empire ushered in several centuries of economic, cultural and technological stagnation or even regression in the region. The scale, timing, causes and geographical extent of the ensuing stagnation and/or retrogression are still matters of vigorous debate. Nevertheless, it seems fairly clear that this process of fragmentation was also what made possible the eventual emergence of more or less discrete nation-states in early modern western Europe, long before anyone even dreamed of establishing such states in the Balkans (or in East Central Europe, for that matter). The destruction of the Western Roman imperial polity by Germanic 'barbarians' during the fifth century further strengthened the position of the already emerging latifundia and landed aristocracies in what we now call western Europe. This in turn made possible the subsequent emergence of decentralized 'feudal' polities, economies and societies, from which increasingly secure private property in land, laws regulating and upholding private contracts and property rights, private property as the basis of independent and pluralistic sources of power and wealth, so-called 'improving landlordism', increases in agricultural productivity and surpluses, and increasing scope for large-scale commercial, agricultural and industrial capitalism fitfully *emerged* over the next twelve to fifteen centuries. Thus the 'barbarian' destruction of the Western Roman Empire inadvertently set the stage for the future emergence of Western feudalism, capitalism and nation-states. In the Balkans, by contrast, the long survival of a tenacious and more vertically structured imperial polity helped to perpetuate many of the legal, administrative, military, cultural and economic achievements of the Eastern Roman Empire, yet in the long term this retarded the emergence of decentralized feudal (and subsequently capitalist) economies and societies and nation-states. Thus the long-term significance of these divergent political, cultural and socio-economic trajectories, reinforced by the east–west division of the Roman Empire in 395, the 'barbarian' devastation of Rome in 410 and the formal deposition of the last Western Roman emperor in AD 476, was quite momentous. The illustrious civilization preserved by the Eastern Roman Empire ('Byzantium') eventually lost out to a more fluid and decentralized West, which fostered a precocious development of feudalism, capitalism and nation-states, and ultimately proved more economically, culturally and technologically dynamic than the more vertically structured and imperial polities, economies and societies which predominated until the First World War in the Balkans and (albeit from much later and very different starting points) in East Central Europe and Russia.

3　The Byzantine ascendancy and its impact, AD 395–1204

The cosmopolitan, neo-Roman and Greek-dominated Byzantine Empire lasted from AD 395 to 1204, with a feeble reprise from 1261 to 1453. The resilience and longevity of this empire rested in large measure on its Graeco-Roman heritage, and on the nodal and almost impregnable position of Constantinople, controlling the Bosphorus channel. With its 'eminently defensible' site, a superb natural harbour, and a commanding position on the only sea lanes between the Mediterranean and the Black Sea and on the best land route between Europe and south-west Asia, Constantinople became the major meeting point between East and West, between Roman law, administration and military technology, Greek philosophy, paganism and the three main monotheistic religions (Judaism, Christianity and Islam). Constantinople is tentatively estimated to have had about 200,000 inhabitants in AD 450, 200,000–250,000 in 610, around 100,000 in 780 (after recurrent epidemics of plague), about 200,000 in 1025 and 300,000 in 1200, after which it plunged to about 50,000 between 1400 and 1450 (Treadgold 1997: 139, 279, 405, 700, 840). These cautious estimates should be set against extravagant claims that the population expanded to around 500,000 at its peaks (e.g. Woodhouse 1977: 21, 34).

Although Constantinople was repeatedly endangered by external military threats, it fell into enemy hands on only two occasions: in 1204 and in 1453. So long as Constantinople itself survived intact, the Byzantine Empire remained capable of remarkable recoveries, such as those that were to occur after the formidable Arab, Avar, Slav, Bulgar and Seljuk Turkish invasions of Byzantine dominions between the seventh and the eleventh centuries. Constantinople was the economic heart of the Byzantine Empire, the industries, commerce, movable wealth and thousands of merchants and craftsmen of which were to remain heavily concentrated within its great walls (Andreades 1948: 70). Even when much of its hinterland fell into enemy hands, as was the case from time to time, Constantinople could still derive considerable revenue, wealth, naval-mercantile power and recuperative potential from its control of the Bosphorus. In this respect, the Byzantine Empire went into terminal decline only when (in desperation) it surrendered control of its trade, customs revenues and shipping to the ambitious and aggressive Italian maritime and mercantile city-states from 1082 onwards, because this gradually closed off the empire's powers of recuperation. However, even after its revenues, trade and shipping fell under alien control, Constantinople nevertheless remained one of the great emporia of the eastern Mediterranean world (Haussig 1971: 313).

One thousand years of Byzantine ascendancy and influence had a much deeper and more enduring impact on the Balkans than did the subsequent four to five centuries of Ottoman overlordship. Despite the widespread survival of Turkish cuisine, coffee houses, bazaars, mosques and minarets, it is certain that the art, architecture, customs, values, beliefs and physical appearance of most Balkan towns and villages owe much more to the Byzantine heritage than they do to the Ottomans and Islam. Byzantine missionaries, merchants and officials propagated Byzantine legal ideas, literature, literacy, and Orthodox Christianity, art and architecture among the many non-Hellenic inhabitants of the Balkans. Although Europe's spiritual and temporal rulers continued to pay lip-service to Christian unity, the associated East–West divisions within Christendom steadily deepened up to and beyond the formal 'schism' between the Roman Catholic and Byzantine Orthodox churches in 1054, which gave a sharper doctrinal edge to Europe's most enduring East–West divide. As seen in chapter 1, the claims of Balkan historians such as Maria Todorova that specifically 'Balkan' culture(s) and identities were primarily products of 'the Ottoman impact' or 'the Ottoman legacy' have been profoundly misleading. On the contrary,

> The modern culture of the Balkans . . . had evolved by the fifteenth century through a process of Byzantinization. For the South Slavs, and the Albanians and Rumanians for that matter, Byzantium was . . . the great educator, the great initiator, the source of both religion and civilization. Her missionaries spread the gospel among the barbarians, and with it they brought Byzantine legal ideas, literature, art, trade, and everything else that constitutes a distinctive civilization. (Stavrianos 1958: 32)

The modern Balkan states were to inherit a 'culture which was basically Byzantine but modified by centuries of Muslim domination' (Jelavich and Jelavich 1963: xv). Byzantium's subjects were 'enthusiastic "Romans". They called themselves *Rhomaioi* for the next thousand years and in the medieval Near East the Byzantine Empire was known as *Rum*, "Rome", and Christians as "Romans", *Rumi*', although they exhibited little veneration for Rome as such; they expressed their imperial loyalties 'not through the brittle protocol of senatorial or civic institutions, but directly – by falling on their knees before statues and icons of the emperor' (Brown 1971: 42).

Significantly, the Greeks still refer to themselves as 'Romioi' (Romans), and Byzantine Orthodox Christianity internalized even more pagan and 'Oriental' influences than did Western Catholic Christianity. Indeed, even though Christianity is widely regarded as part of the defining 'essence' of the West and Western culture and identity, Christianity – like Judaism and Islam – was one of the multitude of cults which emanated from what in the twentieth century came to be called 'the Middle East' (this now commonplace expression originated in an American naval manual as late as 1902). It was from the ancient Syro-Iranian and Egyptian civilizations that Byzantium and Christianity assimilated monasticism, the cult of icons (veneration of images) and the veneration of Mary as the Mother of God (the Theokotos), partly as concessions to the Syro-Iranian and Egyptian cults of the Great Mother goddess (Artemis, Cybele, Isis) with which early Christianity found itself in competition. Nike, the pagan goddess of Victory, furnished the prototype for Christian depictions of angels. The widespread cult of the sun god and of the emperor as such a god engendered Christian depictions of Christ and the apostles as sun gods emitting an aura or nimbus (rays of light) and of Christ as an emperor or sun king. This was also the origin of the decision to celebrate Christmas on 25 December, the 'birthday' (feast day) of the sun god (Haussig 1971: 36–8, 43). Many similarly pagan and/or 'Eastern' elements found their way into Western Christianity as well, but they were even stronger in Byzantine Christendom. Thus the Roman cult of the emperor as a god, 'linking the cult of the sun god with the imperial cult', was 'reconciled' with the adoption of Christianity by fostering a new cult of the Christian Byzantine emperor as the head of the Byzantine Church and as the focus of imperial loyalty and obedience. 'He who denied the doctrine pronounced by the Emperor was a traitor to the Empire and had sinned against the person of the Emperor' (Haussig 1971: 40). Similarly, the basilica and the simple domed edifice, both of which had previously been associated with pagan emperor-worship and used as mausoleums for members of the imperial family, were promoted as the standard forms of church architecture. Likewise, the higher clergy were dressed up in imperial robes to emphasize that they were the emperor's servants and representatives, while churches were decorated with imperial portraits in order continually to remind worshippers of their omnipotent, omnipresent and divinely 'anointed' ruler.

The formal adoption of Christianity as the official state religion and as a basis of imperial cohesion and authority in AD 391 encouraged or even obliged the East Roman state to try to uphold, impose or strive for Christian unity and 'orthodoxy' ('right belief'). The official East Roman or Byzantine Church rapidly came to see itself as 'the Orthodox Church', whereas other Christian tendencies and denominations were regarded as 'heterodox' and potentially subversive 'deviations'. However, recurrent imperial endeavours to find or devise doctrinal compromises and to impose these on Coptic (Egyptian), Syrian, Nestorian and Armenian Christians in vain attempts to achieve Christian-cum-imperial unity in the East Roman domains produced results quite the opposite of what the imperial authorities intended: they hardened positions and intensified mistrust and antagonisms. Nestorian Christians found it necessary to take refuge in the Persian Empire, while the Roman papacy and the older patriarchates of Antioch, Alexandria and Jerusalem were alienated by imperial assertion of the primacy of the new ('upstart') patriarchate of Constantinople, which was under direct imperial patronage and control and therefore lacked their supposed spiritual independence and integrity. Over the centuries more than one in three Constantinople patriarchs were dismissed by the emperor (Soisson 1977: 112). This encouraged both the (Western) Roman Catholic Church and the (Eastern) 'monophysite' Armenian, Coptic, Syrian and Nestorian churches repeatedly to challenge and repudiate the religious authority of Constantinople. The more Constantinople tried to conciliate and accommodate the 'monophysite' Eastern churches (which, prefiguring Islam, insisted on the 'oneness' of God), the more it succeeded in alienating the Western church and the Popes in Rome. Thus the Byzantine Church became separated from other 'Eastern' Christian churches (chiefly those of Armenia, the Levant, Persia and Egypt) as well as from the Western (Roman Catholic) Church (Haussig 1971: 44–5).

BYZANTINE SOCIETY

Recent estimates suggest that the Byzantine Empire had a population of 16 million in AD 457. Constantinople, with about 200,000 inhabitants, and Thessaloniki, with about 70,000, were the only large cities in the Balkans. The empire had about 930 settlements with the legal status of cities, but 'their average size cannot have been much more than one thousand [inhabitants]. Many had only a few hundred people . . . As in villages, these cities' populations included many peasants who went out daily to cultivate the surrounding fields.' Overall, 'perhaps a million lived in cities of more than 10,000, perhaps another million lived in lesser cities, and roughly 14 million in villages that no one pretended were cities' (Treadgold 1997: 137–42). Indeed, until Asia Minor was lost to the Seljuk Turks in the eleventh century, most of the Byzantine Empire's cities were not in the Balkans but in Anatolia (Browning 1975: 93–4). During the sixth century, moreover, 179 of the 265 towns in the Balkan provinces and their offshore islands were located in the south – in Thessaly, Achaea, Macedonia, Epirus and Crete. There were far fewer towns in the northern Balkans, which were much more thinly populated and rural.

The classic Balkan *polis*, with baths, theatres, temples, numerous merchants and craftsmen, and a relatively autonomous patriciate, had been largely confined to the Greek-speaking south and east. In the more Latinized northern and western Balkans the towns were mainly more recently established forts (*kastra*) or garrison towns, dominated by garrison commanders and imperial officials (Browning 1975: 89–93). From the end of the sixth century, however, the distinction between a *polis* and a *kastron* became blurred: 'The term *kastron* had three meanings – a simple castle, the citadel of a town or the whole of a fortified town. Some *kastra*, which were intended mainly as places of refuge for the rural population in case of attack, had room for only a very restricted permanent population . . . *Kastra* which were no more than fortified villages were very common and the [Byzantine] administration treated them as essentially rural communities . . . Nevertheless, the emphasis on the rural character of Byzantine towns should not be overdone . . . Byzantium was not distinct from the rest of Europe in having farmers living in urban settlements. It was a general phenomenon throughout Europe up to the eighteenth century' (Harvey 1989: 200–1). This characterization of Byzantine *kastra* is remarkably consistent with the various types of *kastra* which still abound in rural Greece today, which are virtually indistinguishable from small villages.

IMPERIAL RESURGENCE AND OVEREXTENSION UNDER JUSTINIAN I (REG. AD 527–65)

After the devastating fifth-century 'barbarian' invasions, a fairly unified Roman Empire was briefly re-established by the dynamic Byzantine Emperor Justinian I, who greatly increased the efficiency (and oppressiveness) of the central administration and tax collection. He spent his much augmented revenues on massive construction projects, including the refortification of the empire's exposed northern (Danubian) frontiers, and on blandishments or 'subsidies' (bribes) to its potential enemies (Woodhouse 1977: 33). He also instigated an ambitious codification of Roman law. Justinian's legal codes eroded slavery, strengthened serfdom, reduced sexual inequalities in the laws of succession and inheritance, permitted divorce, outlawed rape and castration, introduced some safeguards against arbitrary detention, imprisonment and crucifixion, brought Christianity into the law and made Church property inalienable, thereby accelerating the (already excessive) enrichment of the monasteries (Soisson 1977: 41–5). Viewed in a longer perspective, however, Justinian contributed to a 'hardening' of East–West differences.

Citizens and senators of Constantinople rose against their dynamic, big-spending and autocratic emperor during the 'Nika' ('Vanquish') riots of AD 532, during which half the city went up in flames. Urged on by his wife Theodora, a former circus prostitute, Justinian initiated a very ambitious and showy reconstruction of central Constantinople. Its cathedral of Hagia (St) Sophia became the largest and tallest church building in Europe. Justinian and his outstanding general Belisarius also accomplished an unexpectedly rapid Byzantine reconquest of north–west Africa, Corsica, Sardinia and the Balearic Islands between 533 and 540, which in turn helped to make possible (and finance) a Byzantine reconquest of more than nine-tenths of Italy from the (Germanic) Ostrogoths between 535 and 540. In 540, however, while most Byzantine forces were committed to these western conquests, Byzantine Syria was occupied by Persia, and Macedonia and Thrace were invaded by Tukic Bulgars. Byzantine forces were recalled from Italy and the western Mediterranean to repel these threats. However, between 541 and 544 the population and armed forces of the Byzantine Empire were decimated by a massive epidemic of plague, while the north African province mutinied. The Ostrogoths seized their chance to regain most of Italy between 542 and 548. In response, the Byzantine Empire invaded Persia in 541 and concluded peace with it in 545. This allowed Byzantium not only to restore its control of north Africa and (re)conquer Italy, but also to (re)conquer most of Spain between 547 and 555, thereby (re)uniting most of the core territories of the earlier Roman Empire under Byzantine rule. However, Justinian had greatly overextended his empire, leaving its Balkan and Anatolian heartlands dangerourly exposed, over-taxed, over-centralized, under-provided, crisis-prone and vulnerable.

THE MYSTERIOUS EMERGENCE OF THE SLAVS, SIXTH TO EIGHTH CENTURY AD

Between the sixth and the eighth century AD, numerous Avar, Bulgar and Slavic warriors invaded the territories which have become Serbia, Slovenia, Croatia, Bosnia-Herzegovina, Macedonia, peninsular Greece, Bulgaria and southern Romania (Browning 1975: 33–4; Evans 1960: 28). These incursions, which mainly comprised Slavs with smaller admixtures of Turkic and Iranian warrior peoples, displaced large numbers of Greeks, Thracians, Illyrians and 'Romanized' Dacians and Vlachs either southward or into the mountains, dramatically altering the ethnic geography of the Balkans.

Map 2 The Balkans and East Central Europe: seventh to eighth centuries

It has long been widely assumed that (i) the Slavs originated somewhere between the Vistula, the Dniepr and the Carpathians; (ii) they had long practised stock-breeding, fishing, hunting and cool temperate agriculture and lived in humble wooden or mud houses which were frequently partly sunk into the ground to provide greater warmth in winter, in small settlements which were often located on river banks; (iii) unlike the nomadic steppe warriors, who were fast-moving horsemen, they moved on foot or in dugout boats; (iv) they wore no body armour, but carried shields, spears or bows, avoided head-on military encounters on open terrain, and made skilful use of ambushes; (v) they had no political organization higher than tribal forms, and their hitherto clan-based kinship and settlement patterns were giving way to nuclear families settled in territorial (rather than consanguinary) villages; and (vi) they overran the Balkans mainly by sheer weight of numbers, rather than through any intrinsic military superiority (Browning 1975: 30–2; Evans 1960: 26).

However, Florin Curta and Paul Barford have cogently argued that these assumptions are mere conjectures and that no one really knows how, when or even where the early Slavs originated and what they were like (Curta 2001, 2006; Barford 2001). Both highlight the spuriousness of the attempt of the sixth-century Byzantine writer Jordanes to identify the so-called 'Sclavenes' who suddenly appeared out of the blue on Byzantium's metaphorical radar screens during the sixth century as descendants of 'ancient Venethi' from the River Vistula and/or Pripet marsh regions (in what are now the Polish-Belarussian borderlands); and they also point out that there were no contemporary reports of any large-scale migrations of Slavs from such regions of origin into the Balkans and cast doubt on whether such migrations ever took place (Curta 2001: 39–43, 75, 113, 336–7; Barford 2001: 45–6, 286–7). In addition, Curta puts forward an ingenious conjecture of his own concerning the origins of the so-called 'Sclavenes' perceived by sixth-century Byzantine authors. In place of 'a great flood of Slavs coming out of the Pripet marshes', Curta postulates that 'the name "Sclavene" was a purely Byzantine construct, designed to make sense of a complex configuration of *ethnies* on the other side of the northern frontier of the Empire' (Curta 2001: 3, 118–19). 'Slavs did not become Slavs because they spoke Slavic, but because they were called so by others' (p. 346). 'The making of the Slavs was less a matter of ethnogenesis and more one of invention, imagining and labeling by Byzantine authors. Some form of group identity, however, which we may call ethnicity, was growing out of the historical circumstances following the fortification of the Danube *limes*. This was therefore an identity formed in the shadow of Justinian's forts, not in the Pripet marshes . . . That no "Slavs" called themselves by this name [until the twelfth century] not only indicates that no group took on the label imposed by outsiders, but also suggests that this label was more a pedantic construction than the result of systematic interaction [let alone investigation] across ethnic boundaries' (p. 350). Thus, in place of the hitherto prevalent notion of a great Slav migration from origins somewhere in Poland or Belarus during the sixth and seventh centuries, Curta suggests that there were relatively short-range inflows of unknown peoples from just north of the Danube (present-day Romania), and that these were most probably not a single ethnic group or even speakers of a common 'Slavic' language. They were called 'Sclavenes' by Byzantine authors for lack of any hard information about who they were – and the label eventually stuck and began to be imbued with more specific ethnographic content. This conjecture is reiterated in Curta (2005: 59–61). Nevertheless, Curta's thesis remains nothing more than yet another conjecture and, while it does appear to offer a more-or-less plausible explanation of the emergence of the Balkan Slavs, it has nothing to say about the subsequent emergence of either the 'Western' Slavs' (the forebears of the Poles, Czechs and Slovaks) or the 'Eastern Slavs' (the forebears of the Russians, Ukrainians and Belarussians). Consequently, Curta has only established that no one really knows for sure how, when or where the Slavs originated. The equally mysterious emergence of the other ('Western') Slavs who eventually populated most of East Central Europe is discussed in similar terms on pp. 137–9, below.

Whoever the Slavs were and wherever they originated, their influx into previously Byzantine

Balkan domains was greatly facilitated by the prior abandonment of many northern Balkan towns and forts by their previous inhabitants, who had gradually been driven southward by two centuries of intermittent raids and invasions by 'barbarian' marauders (Browning 1975: 34–42; Haldon 1997: 93, 114). It appears very likely that the Byzantine Empire was severely weakened by epidemics of bubonic plague which decimated the indigenous Balkan populations in AD 542, 558, 573, 587, 599–600, 608, 618, 625, 640, 697, 700 and 746–7 and created a demographic vacuum which virtually sucked in Slav settlers from the north (Biraben and Le Goff 1975: 62–71). This helps to explain why Slav incursions appear to have met with relatively weak resistance and managed to penetrate as far south as the Peloponnesus (Morea). Indeed, if bubonic plague was as virulent from 542 to 747 as it was in the more famous epidemics of the 1340s to 1380s, a loss of nearly one-third of the population seems plausible. Warren Treadgold has conjectured that the empire's population, having risen from about 16 million in AD 457 to about 19 million in 540, may have fallen to just 13 million by 610 (within the boundaries of 457), with the decrease being largely attributable to the impact of plague (Treadgold 1997: 216, 278).

The Byzantine Empire was further weakened by a protracted power struggle from AD 540 to 629 with a new Persian Empire, which overran Syria while Armenians rebelled against Byzantine overlordship in eastern Anatolia. These challenges eroded Byzantine control over most of the Italian, Spanish and North African territories (re)conquered by Justinian. Persia was finally defeated by Byzantium in AD 629. However, the struggle left Byzantium and Persia too drained and debilitated to resist the meteoric rise of Arab Muslim power between 636 and 642. The Persian Empire was easily conquered by the Arab Muslim Empire in AD 637–41 and most of its subjects subsequently accepted Islam. Similarly, Byzantium lost Syria, Palestine and Egypt to the Arab Muslim Empire in AD 636–42. This opened the way for an Arab Muslim conquest of North Africa, although Byzantine Carthage held out until AD 699. The Byzantines also managed to repel two massive Arab assaults on Constantinople in AD 674–8 and AD 717–18 respectively, before finally stemming the tide of the Arabs' north-westward expansion in 738.

The threats posed by the Persians and the Arabs to Byzantium's survival helped the 'Slav' and Turkic Bulgar raiders, who later became settlers, to consolidate their incursions into the Balkans. The Slavic and Bulgar tribal confederations which were established in the Balkans in the mid-seventh century were 'not yet states in the true sense . . . They were temporary . . . and lacked a standing military force, an administration or a strictly defined state territory.' However, the onset of class differentiation soon called into existence 'organs of government and coercion to protect the interests of the now wealthy tribal aristocracy and to ward off possible attacks' (Hristov 1985: 26). In AD 681, while it was still under severe threat from the Arabs, Byzantium was obliged to concede diplomatic recognition to an embryonic Bulgar-Slav state.

In 1830, when Greece was establishing its national independence from the Ottoman Empire, the historian Jakob Philipp Fallmerayer provoked a furore by arguing that the Greeks had been wholly displaced from peninsular Greece by large hordes of Slav settlers during the sixth and seventh centuries, and that this negated the modern Greeks' claims to lineal descent from the extraordinarily creative ancient Greeks:

> The [ancient] Hellenic race in Europe is exterminated . . . The immortal works of the spirit of Hellas and some ancient ruins . . . are now the only evidence of the fact that long ago there was such a people as the Hellenes . . . For not a single drop of real pure Hellenic blood flows in the veins of the Christian population of modern Greece. (Fallmerayer 1830: iii, quoted in Vasiliev 1952: 177)

However, Fallmerayer greatly overstated his case. Much of northern and western Greece and the Peloponnese was extensively settled by Slavs and did escape Byzantine control, but eastern and parts of central Greece, the Aegean coast and the major Greek islands and coastal cities were never overrun by Slavs and many of these places received numerous Greek refugees. Starting in the late seventh century, moreover, the Slav-settled areas of Greece were gradually re-Hellenized by the Byzantine Empire, the (Greek) Orthodox Church and Greek-speaking merchants and colonists, aided by the establishment of effective new Byzantine military administrations known as *themata* (Browning 1975: 39–42). Thus, 'even though the Peloponnese itself was under Slav control for more than two hundred years, there was no question of any permanent Slavonization of Greek territory. Little by little the Byzantine authorities in Greece and the other coastal regions managed to regain lost ground.' Nevertheless, 'The greater part of the Balkan peninsula, the whole interior, became completely a Slav country and from now onwards is referred to in Byzantine sources as the region of "Sclavinia"' (Ostrogorsky 1968: 94).

However, there is little doubt that demographic decline, repeated Persian, Arab, Avar and Bulgar attacks, and substantial inflows of people(s) whom the Byzantines decided to call 'Slavs' brought about serious urban contraction ('ruralization') in the Balkans from the sixth to the eighth century. Reduced population diminished demand for and production of agricultural products, which in turn curtailed demand for urban goods and services. In addition, Balkan towns lost their former fiscal and judicial control over their rural hinterlands, and both the towns themselves and the imperial state became much less able to afford the costs of maintaining buildings and fortifications. The great exception to these trends was Constantinople, which enjoyed an earlier and more pronounced recovery as a result of its overriding commercial, political and strategic importance, but there was no comparable mitigation of the sorry plight of the provincial towns, many of which were depopulated or abandoned (Harvey 1989: 21–8).

There is also a major ongoing debate concerning the long-term impact of the Slav influx on the social structure and rural landscape of the Balkan Peninsula. Various Russian Byzantinists have argued that large-scale Slavic colonization introduced full-blown communal land tenure with periodic redistribution of landholdings, paralleling their view of Russia's emergence and development. The case for this perspective was made most forcefully by E.E. Lipshich (1945, 1947). Drawing on the ideas of the nineteenth-century Russian Byzantinists Vasily Grigorevich Vasilievsky, Fyodor I. Uspensky and Konstantin Nikolaevich Uspensky, she interpreted the famous seventh- or eighth-century Byzantine 'Farmer's Law' as evidence of the existence of village communities with collective fiscal responsibilities and wide-ranging communal practices. If there really was massive-scale 'Slav' settlement in the Balkan Peninsula, whose pre-existing populations were undoubtedly decimated by epidemic diseases, endemic warfare and frequent crop failure, it is intuitively very plausible to suppose that the new Slav settlers could have disseminated their (allegedly) communal traditions of village organization and landholding, even though the surviving documentary evidence for this supposition is very thin. The major problems are that we cannot be certain of the extent to which 'the Slavs' (whoever they were and wherever they originated) *really had* developed communal traditions of village organization and landholding *prior to* their influx into the Balkans, and that there is *no reliable information* on the scale of the 'Slavic' influx. Nineteenth-century Russian Slavophiles believed as an article of faith that 'the Slavs' had possessed strong communal traditions 'from time immemorial' (Aksakov 1889: 65). It also became an article of Soviet historiographical dogma in the 1930s to 1950s that supposedly 'Slavic' peasantries had been in existence for centuries past and had developed strong communal traditions by the sixth or seventh century AD, following or even accompanying an alleged decline of Slavic tribalism (Grekov 1959: 99–100; Liashchenko 1949: 69–71). However, there have been many non-Russian and even some Russian historians of the Slavic peoples who are equally insistent that communal customs and institutions did not develop to any very marked degree among the Slavs who settled in the Balkans during the Byzantine era (Lemerle 1979: 41–6; Kaplan 1992: 185–218; Vasiliev 1952: 245–7; Ostrogorsky 1942: 198–9; 1968: 135–6), or that they emerged among South Slavs only in later centuries in the form known as the *zadruga*. There are also prominent Russian and Russian émigré historians of Russia and/or the Balkans who have contended that Slavic village commune systems only developed in early modern times and essentially for pragmatic 'reasons of state' – primarily for fiscal motives and/or to control peasant mobility and/or to prevent the 'proletarianization' of the peasantry. This so-called 'statist' perspective, first formulated by the eminent nineteenth-century Russian liberal jurist Boris Chicherin, was upheld by Pyotr Struve (1942: 426) and Georgii Ostrogorsky (1968: 134–6), among others. Indeed, Ostrogorsky argued that the transformations which occurred between the sixth and eighth centuries stopped short of establishing a Russian-style village commune system in the Balkans:

> It is scarcely conceivable that the old landed estates could have survived to any significant extent the assaults of the Avars and Slavs . . . and the Persians and then the Arabs . . . As far as can be seen, they did in fact largely disappear, and were replaced by smallholders . . . and the *stratioti* who formed the new army of the themes. Thus . . . a great change took place in the countryside which placed the social structure of the Empire upon a new foundation and directed its development along new paths . . . The new pattern of the Byzantine village is most clearly reflected in the famous *Farmer's Law* . . . The peasants whose legal relationships are regulated by the *Law* are free landowners. They have no obligations to any landlord but only to the state, as taxpayers. There are no restrictions on their freedom of movement. This does not imply that there are no serfs at all in this period, but it does imply that the free peasantry formed a large class . . . The *Farmer's Law* pays particular attention to the individual's title to his personal property. Nevertheless, the inhabitants of a village formed a community . . . This village community had nothing to do with the type of community organization distinguished by common cultivation and periodical redistribution of land which was once thought to have existed in Byzantium and whose origin was attributed to the influence of the 'primitive' Slav community life introduced by Slav migration. This theory . . . is based on false hypotheses; its supporters had constructed their supposed primitive Slav communes after the model of the Russian *mir* system which is now recognized as a product of a later period . . . Byzantium never had a [village] community organized on the basis of common cultivation and, if we rely on the sources, we can find no such community among the Slavs either. Byzantium certainly had [fiscal village] communities of the kind described above and these were found long before the Slav settlement . . . There is no doubt that the Slavs played an extremely important part in the revival of the Byzantine Empire in the seventh century. This was not because they imported a specifically Slav type of community organization . . . but because they brought new energy and strength into the enfeebled state. (Ostrogorsky 1968: 134–6)

Paul Lemerle agreed that the state's concerns in the Farmer's Law were 'purely fiscal', reflecting the collective fiscal responsibility of the village community towards the state, and that the law 'reveals no derogation from, no restriction on, the principle of individual property' (Lemerle 1979: 43). He conceded that the law contained hints of the existence of common lands periodically redistributed by the commune and of occasional reapportionment of land and fiscal obligations within the commune in order to equalize tax burdens in the wake of the departure or extinction of particular households, but he saw these merely as pragmatic adjustment mechanisms to facilitate the meeting of fiscal obligations and also to maintain individual private property as the norm (pp. 43–7). For Lemerle, as for Ostrogorsky, the main significance of the Slavic invasions was demographic. Lands depopulated by the impact of prolonged warfare, disease and economic crises were 'stocked afresh with hands', thereby helping the Byzantine Empire to recover from its demographic catastrophes (pp. 48–50). However, Lemerle rejected Ostrogorsky's claims concerning the decline of big landed property. In Lemerle's view, this survived largely intact (albeit not completely unscathed), while the lack of reference to great landed property in the Farmer's Law did not necessarily imply that it had ceased to be important (pp. 51–7). He also questioned the significance of the properties held by soldiers in return for military service, to which Ostrogorsky had attached so much importance in the period from the seventh to the ninth century (p. 59).

Lemerle's claims regarding the resilience of big landed property are broadly supported by the Marxist Byzantinist John Haldon, but with the qualification that there was a change in the composition of the landowning elite: a shrinkage of the old senatorial aristocracy and its landholdings was offset by the rise of a (new) more meritocratic 'provincial landed elite', which increased its wealth and landholdings on the basis of military and administrative prowess and state service (Haldon 1997: 128–30, 155–72). Nevertheless, Haldon warns that the Byzantine landed elite, 'powerful as it was, never dominated urban and rural life and economic relations to the extent that seems to have occurred in the West', because in the Byzantine Empire power 'remained more diffuse, the state always managed to retain an effective fiscal control, and the rural population, while oppressed and exploited, remained more . . . heterogeneous in social and economic terms than in the West' (Haldon 1997: 31).

Soviet medievalists also claimed that allegedly large inflows of Slav settlers in villages characterized by extensive communal practices brought about a historic transition in the Byzantine Balkans from slavery or the 'ancient'/'slave' mode of production (which was rather questionably portrayed as the main basis of agriculture in the Graeco-Roman world) to 'higher' and more autonomous communal forms of peasant society and agriculture. This in turn was portrayed as having paved or cleared the way for a more vigorous development of serfdom, which Soviet historians regarded as the basis of a 'higher' (i.e. more productive) 'feudal' mode of production and as a 'regeneration' of the Byzantine Empire's economic and social foundations (Grekov 1959: 32–7; see also Haldon 1995: 7–8).

However, these Soviet claims are unconvincing. While slavery undoubtedly existed, 'slaves do not appear to have played a role of any significance in overall production in the late Roman and Byzantine world' and they had already been superseded by other modes of production long before the Slav invasions (Haldon 1995: 16). Nevertheless, the repopulation of the Balkans by significant inflows of 'Slavs' between the sixth and the ninth century may have further reduced the importance of slavery in the Balkan Peninsula, while correspondingly increasing the importance of independent peasant proprietorship, nucleated rural settlement patterns and relatively autonomous village communities with collective fiscal responsibility, even if slavery did not disappear completely (Lemerle 1979: 51, 65; Haldon 1997: 132–41, 152–3). However, in spite of the strength of conviction and argumentation on all sides in these debates, there is no way of knowing which of these positions is empirically soundest. There is not enough reliable and unambiguous information on which to be able to base such judgements, despite the abundance of ingenious conjectures and counter-conjectures.

THE ALLEGED HARDENING OF BELIEFS, ATTITUDES AND BOUNDARIES, FIFTH TO NINTH CENTURY AD

Peter Brown has argued that, as a result of protracted struggles with Persia (AD 540–629) and the explosive expansion of the Arab Muslim Empire along the southern shores of the Mediterranean (637–47), the Byzantine Empire came to see itself as the Christian fortress of the Near East: 'Byzantines regarded themselves no longer as citizens of a world empire, but as a Chosen People ringed by hostile, pagan nations . . . In such a closed society, treason was equated with unbelief. The hardening of boundaries reflects an inner rigidity' (Brown 1971: 172, 174). The adoption of Christianity as the official imperial religion in AD 380 had already resulted in greater exclusiveness and intolerance towards non-Christians. 'The Christian Church differed from other oriental cults, which it resembled in so many ways, through its intolerance' (Brown 1971: 65). The ensuing restrictions on the building of synagogues and on the rights of Jews to hold public office, to marry non-Jews and to appear in court culminated in the abolition of the Jewish patriarchate in AD 425, as well as in Christian boycotts of Jewish traders and doctors and Christian pogroms (assaults) on Jews, Jewish properties and synagogues. Byzantium gradually came to see itself 'no longer as a society in which Christianity was merely the dominant religion, but as a totally Christian society', with the result that paganism was suppressed and the non-Christian became a social outcast (Brown 1971: 174). However, there are weighty objections to this perspective (see pp. 77–81, 86 and 90, below).

The rise of Christian monasticism

Since the 380s AD there had also been a steady growth of Christian monasticism. Monastic orders became the 'shock troops' of Christianity, asserting Christianity as the imperial religion and assaulting pagans, Jews and heretics, egged on by emperors who shared their prejudices (Brown 1971: 104). From the fifth century onwards, much of the wealth which would previously have been channelled into public and private construction and investment was diverted into the coffers of the Church and monasteries 'for the remission of sins' or to cover the costs of acquittal at the Last Judgment (p. 108). By AD 527 there were at least a hundred monasteries in and around Constantinople alone (Woodhouse 1977: 26). Before long, as Byzantine monks and missionaries propagated Orthodox Christianity among the other inhabitants of the southern and eastern Balkans and Roman Catholic rivals did the same in the north-western Balkans, the region as a whole became littered with monasteries. Bulgaria, for example, came to have 150 (Hristov 1985: 70). Many of them were massive and some have remained standing or even in full operation to this day. In this way a significant part of the Balkans' wealth and manpower was siphoned off by a partly parasitic social group, who 'sterilized' much of that wealth in the form of beautiful but 'non-productive' monastic and ecclesiastical buildings and magnificent religious ornamentation.

The impact of Christian monasticism in the Balkans was not wholly negative, however. 'The monasteries harnessed the chronic underemployment of the towns and villages' by mobilizing many thousands of zealous monastic retainers and staffing hospitals, soup-kitchens, alms houses and nursing, ambulance, burial and carrying services (Brown 1971: 110). In addition, Byzantine monks and missionaries played seminal roles in the creation of South Slav written languages and literary cultures, which in turn provided the 'cultural toolkits' through which Christian teachings and literacy were disseminated among most of the South Slavs (Curta 2006: 5).

The roles of (Saints) Cyril and Methodius in the genesis of 'Church Slavonic' and Slavonic literature

Constantine (later Cyril) and Methodius, two Byzantine monks who may conceivably have been of South Slavic extraction, devised the first Slavonic alphabet (the so-called 'Glagolitic' script) around AD 855, in order to make it possible to start (i) translating Byzantine religious writings into Slavonic languages, (ii) converting the Balkan Slavs to (Orthodox) Christianity and (iii) creating Slavonic literary cultures. In AD 863, at the invitation of Prince Rastislav, the two brothers were sent by the Byzantine Orthodox Church to Moravia on a mission to counteract the growth of Germanic/Roman Catholic influence in that region. However, their arrival in Moravia aroused strong Germanic/Roman Catholic opposition to their mission. The brothers then spent several years in Rome defending their development and use of a Slavonic written language and script for evangelical and liturgical purposes, even though this departed from the principle that the three languages which had supposedly been 'Divinely ordained' for use in the Christian liturgy and for propagation of the Christian scriptures were Hebrew, Latin and Greek. While they were in Rome, Moravia's Prince

Rastislav was deposed, imprisoned and blinded by his nephew Svatopluk, acting in league with Germanic Roman Catholics. In AD 885, after both Cyril and Methodius had died, their Orthodox disciples were hounded out of Moravia by the ascendant Germanic Catholics and Prince Svatopluk enforced a papal ban on use of the Slavic liturgy which Cyril, Methodius and their followers had devised. However, the fugitives were given sanctuary by Khan Boris of Bulgaria, who had already decided (for reasons of state) to adopt Byzantine Orthodox Christianity as his country's official religion and to foster a Slavonic written language, as a means both of absorbing and competing with the magnificent and imposing cultural attainments of Byzantium and of enhancing Bulgaria's wider international standing. In Bulgaria the disciples of Cyril and Methodius resumed the work of translating Byzantine religious literature, this time into so-called 'Old Bulgarian' (alias 'Church Slavonic'). For this purpose they adapted the Glagolitic and Greek alphabets to create the so-called 'Cyrillic' script (named after Cyril). With relatively minor modifications, this was to become the template upon which the written national languages of other Eastern Orthodox Slavs, such as the Serbs, the Ukrainians and the Russians, were gradually to be hammered out under the (far from disinterested) guidance of Eastern Orthodox clergy. Over many centuries, this has fostered enduring linguistic and 'spiritual' bonds (as well as rivalries) between Bulgarians, Macedonians, Serbs, Montenegrins, Russians, Belarussians and Ukrainians, all of whom still use archaic 'Church Slavonic' ('Old Bulgarian') for some ecclesiastical or liturgical purposes. More immediately, as was (even) acknowledged in a semi-official Marxist history of Bulgaria published under Communist rule, 'Christianity also brought the Bulgarians closer to the culturally most advanced European nations and enabled them to attain a higher level of development' (Hristov 1985: 33–40). Orthodox clergy and Christianity were to fulfil similar functions for Serbia and Montenegro (and for Kiev Rus, the first Russo-Ukrainian state).

Rendering unto Caesar

There was, however, a 'downside' to all this. During the tenth century, as observed in the case of Bulgaria by Hristov (1985: 44), 'more and more peasants began losing their land and became bound to the estates of the secular and church feudals'. The official Church preached that the world had been ordered this way by God and that growing concentration of wealth 'should not arouse envy, discontent or resistance, because nothing in the world ever happened against God's Will' (p. 44). It is indeed hard to deny the emphasis in official Christianity (here, as elsewhere) on divinely ordained roles and hierarchies, on uncritical and uncomplaining obedience to social 'superiors', and on 'rendering unto Caesar that which is Caesar's'. Since considerably less than one-third of the Balkan population ever became Muslims, fatalistic and hierarchical 'official' Christianity should be seen as a more plausible source of the alleged 'Balkan fatalism' which historians like Vucinich (1963: 90–1; 1965: 69) prefer to attribute to the influence of alleged Islamic 'fatalism' under Ottoman rule.

The alleged 'narrowing' of Byzantine cultural horizons

Some Western historians have argued that the Byzantine and neo-Byzantine Balkans experienced the triumph of an intolerant 'middlebrow' Christian culture, shared by both rulers and ruled (Brown 1971: 181). Shorn of the bulk of its western and Asiatic territories, the Byzantine world became less cosmopolitan, more inward-looking, and more narrowly and homogeneously Greek and Orthodox in its culture and attitudes (Baynes and Moss 1948: 13). Its characteristic manifestations were Christian hagiographies ('Lives of the saints'), icons, Orthodox Church music (unaccompanied devotional chants and liturgies) and cults around 'holy relics' (Brown 1971: 181–3). During the same centuries the more centralized autocracy bequeathed by Emperor Justinian I (AD 527–65) also 'fatally weakened' the independence of the imperial bureaucracy, the provincial cities and the scholar-gentry, the traditional social pillars of secular classical education and culture (p. 180). The great challenges posed by the seventh-century Arab Muslim Empire allegedly 'completed the Christianization of the public life' of Byzantine cities, submerging 'the last vestige of a secular culture' (pp. 186–7). In the new religious culture 'a man was defined by his religion . . . He did not owe allegiance to a state; he belonged to a religious community . . . The arrival of the Arabs merely cut the last threads that had bound the provincials of the Near East to the Roman Empire . . . This was the final victory of the idea of the religious community over the classical idea of the state' (pp. 186–7). Thus a narrowing of mental/cultural horizons and a retreat from secular humanism and learning is alleged to have begun in the medieval Balkans, long before the arrival of the Turks.

However, these kinds of 'Orientalizing' Western perceptions of the late and neo-Byzantine Balkans were rejected by Sir Steven Runciman, a much more renowned and sympathetic authority on the Byzantine and neo-Byzantine Balkans. He contended that the 'decline' of the Byzantine Empire was purely territorial, economic and military, and that:

> paradoxically, the culture of Byzantium was never so brilliant as in the two centuries before its fall [to the Turks in 1453]. The art of the period was perhaps the most beautiful and certainly the most human that Byzantium ever produced; and it was produced so long as there was money to pay for it. The intellectual brilliance lasted on to the end, led by scholars whose vigour and origi- nality were as fine as any of their forefathers' and whose renown spread to foreign lands. Many of these scholars hoped that regeneration might still be achieved, even though it might involve integration with the West and an abandonment of ancient traditions. (Runciman 1968: 16)

Runciman elaborated convincingly on these more favourable perspectives in his classic books on *The Last Byzantine Renaissance* (1970) and on *The Fall of Constantinople 1453* (1969: 5–6, 14–15, 189). Furthermore, Florin Curta has emphasized the cultural sophistication attained by the first Bul- garian empire during the tenth century (Curta 2006: 147–8, 213–29).

Indeed, far from experiencing cultural and intellectual 'retrogression' and 'falling behind the West', the successive intellectual and cultural 'renaissances' which took place in the Byzantine Empire and some neo-Byzantine polities during the last centuries of the empire's existence made major contribu- tions to – and helped to lay the foundations of – the twelfth-century and the fourteenth- to sixteenth- century Renaissances centred on western Europe (especially France and Italy, respectively). Much the same was true of *the Byzantine diaspora*, which included the large numbers of Byzantine Orthodox artists, intellectuals and clergy who decamped to Italy in pursuit of richer and/or more secure livings during the fifteenth century. Until the fall of Constantinople in 1453, the Byzantine and neo-Byzantine domains did far more than western Europe to maintain and propagate the heritage of ancient Greek and Roman philosophy, law, rhetoric and medicine, and they were therefore in less need of a Renais- sance to 'rediscover' that heritage. Furthermore, the world-renowned development of painting in Italy from the mid-thirteenth to the mid-fifteenth century was in large measure derivative from models, pigments and techniques developed in Byzantium. These Byzantine influences are most vividly visible in eleventh- and twelfth-century Sicilian art and in later paintings by Cimabue (1240–1302), Duccio (1260–1318), Simone Martini (1284–1344), Pietro Lorenzetti (*c.*1280–1348), Ambrogio Lorenzetti (d. 1348) and other members of the magnificent Siena School, as well as in those of Giotto (1266– 1337), Paolo Veneziano (*c.*1290–1362) and Fra Angelico (d. 1455). Their Byzantine-inspired paint- ings were much freer, more abstract, less representational, more fluid and more ethereal than later Italian art (especially the Baroque), which became much heavier and lost much of the earlier warmth, vigour, verve and translucence of colour by becoming more rigidly representational and dominated by the grandiose tastes and demands of the Roman Catholic Church and/or ostentatiously wealthy Italian patrons, who increasingly used art merely to flaunt their own opulence and self-importance and to make political statements.

THE STRATEGIC INTERFACE BETWEEN ISLAM AND WESTERN CHRISTENDOM

The Arab conquest of Syria, Palestine, North Africa, Spain, the Balearic Islands, Corsica, Sardinia, Sicily, Crete, Cyprus and Armenia during the seventh and eighth centuries ended exclusive European control of the Mediterranean. These conquests also disrupted Europe's established lines of trade and communication with Asia, which may have caused a temporary contraction of European and Mediterranean commerce.

From the late seventh to the tenth century, Byzantium responded by using its still considerable naval power in the eastern Mediterranean to prevent goods from the East (spices, medicinal herbs, dyes, myrrh, precious stones, silks, cottons, fine fabrics, sugar) from being shipped directly from Syrian and Egyptian ports to western Europe. Instead, it redirected them through Byzantine ports (especially Constantinople), where they were subjected to very high customs duties, shipping charges and profit mark-ups, before being re-exported to western and central Europe, mainly through Italian (especially Venetian) distribution agents. This sowed the seeds of Venetian maritime-commercial power, which would eventually rival and undermine that of Byzantium. Byzantium also continued to dominate trade with the East via the Black Sea, including grain, furs, metals and amber from the Black Sea littoral. Control of European trade with Asia helped Byzantium to protect and foster its own industries and crafts. The Byzantine state 'virtually stopped its eastern import trade from bringing Syrian or Egyptian goods into the empire. Only raw materials were allowed to be imported. In this way its own industries and sales were safeguarded' (Haussig 1971: 172–3). Byzantine luxury and craft industries reached their peak between the ninth and eleventh centuries, producing fine fabrics, silks, carpets, paper, ceramics, leather goods, carvings, icons and metal-work (especially goblets, ewers, enamels and bronzes). Two monks had smuggled some silkworm eggs into Byzantium from Asia as early as AD 553 and 'from these precious eggs were derived all the varieties of silk-worm that stocked the western world for over a thousand years. The silks of the Byzantine Empire became famous throughout medieval Europe' (Darby 1967: 49). Byzantium had also discovered from Persia the secret of how to make luxury paper from rags, while from the Arabs it had learned how to make and use decorative ceramic tiles and faience (majolica) (Haussig 1971: 169).

During the ninth and tenth centuries, however, the Arabs broke through the Byzantine blockade and then turned the tables on Byzantium by capturing strategic Mediterranean islands and control of the Straits of Messina and then imposing a naval blockade on the Adriatic and the Aegean seas. Concurrently, high-cost Byzantine exports and re-exports were gradually being priced out of western and central European markets, partly as a result of excessive Byzantine customs tolls, shipping fees and mark-ups, and over-restrictive guild regulations. All this encouraged the rising Italian maritime-commercial powers (above all Venice) to trade directly with the Arab world, thus bypassing Byzantium and contributing to its incipient commercial and industrial decline (Haussig 1971: 306–7). By the twelfth century Byzantine trade was no longer predominantly in luxury and craft goods, as it had been from the sixth to the tenth century. Constantinople was gradually reduced to an entrepôt for unprocessed primary products.

In spite of the commercial and military 'stand-off', however, there was still a degree of mutual respect, commerce and cultural cross-fertilization between Byzantium and the Muslim states. 'Mosques were built in Constantinople, just as Christian churches remained open in Muslim territory. Rarely were either attacked or desecrated' (Woodhouse 1977: 44). It is now commonly accepted that Arab mathematics, science, astronomy, navigation techniques, philosophy, medicine, aesthetics, design, art and architecture and the concept of the university were transmitted to Europe partly via Byzantium, partly via Moorish Spain (al-Andalus) and Sicily, and later partly via Venice and Genoa, and that they made large seminal contributions to what most Europeans still fondly imagine to have been essentially European 'Renaissances' during the twelfth century and more famously between the fourteenth and sixteenth centuries (see Jardine 1996; Jardine and Brotton 2000; Brotton 2002; MacLean 2005: ix–x, xiv–xix, 1–21, among others).

THE TERRITORIAL, ECONOMIC AND MILITARY DECLINE OF BYZANTIUM

The massive territorial losses caused by Arab, Avar, Bulgar, Turkic and Slav territorial encroachments appear to have reduced the empire's population from approximately 17 million in AD 610 to just 7 million in 780, although it subsequently recovered to about 12 million in 1025 (as its territory doubled between 780 and 1025), before plunging to about 5 million in 1097 and partially recovering to 8 million in 1143 and 9 million in 1200 (Treadgold 1997: 403, 570, 700). The net contraction of the imperial territory and population made it increasingly difficult for Byzantium to raise sufficient revenues to pay the salaries of its officials. This encouraged the sale of offices, increased reliance on tax farmers, and the growth of official corruption, nepotism and extortion, which thus became endemic in the Balkans long before the establishment of the Ottoman Empire (Haussig 1971: 178). 'Officials regarded their office as a means of amassing as much wealth as possible. Responsibility towards the state and integrity were non-existent' (p. 177). However, Balkan historians such as Vucinich (1963: 89–90; 1965: 120) and Sugar (1977: 288) have seen fit to 'blame' the Ottoman regime for patterns of official corruption and extortion which it merely inherited and perpetuated.

Until the tenth century the imperial administration had regulated prices, wages, rents, interest rates and the activities of industrial and commercial guilds. It had also imposed compulsory loans and periodically debased the coinage, reducing confidence in the currency and in financial rewards. From the tenth century, however, Byzantine state regulation of prices, wages, rents, guilds and grain marketing broke down. This reduced the role of the state in the economy and thus freed the economy from restrictive and distorting state tutelage. Yet it also reduced the capacity of the state to protect Byzantine industries through tariffs and import restrictions. 'No longer was any attempt made to protect the home market by tariffs, or by limiting exports and imports.' Instead, 'the Empire resorted to bartering its sovereign rights in return for military aid from other powers'. Byzantium thus surrendered its economic independence to foreign commercial powers and 'ceased to be a great economic power' (Haussig 1971: 310). The silk industry was lost to Italy when the Normans captured Corinth and Thebes in 1147 and transported silkworms and workers to Sicily, which was then under Norman rule (p. 309). Furthermore, shipping firms gradually relocated from Byzantium to Italian cities to escape the excessive taxation (p. 313). The Byzantines thus switched from proactively 'carrying their wares to foreign ports' to passively 'waiting for the foreign purchaser to come to them' (Andreades 1948: 67). By the twelfth century 'Byzantine trade was no longer predominantly concerned with luxury goods, as it had been . . . between the sixth and tenth centuries' (Haussig 1971: 313). Instead, Constantinople had become an entrepôt for foodstuffs (grain, olive oil and sunflower oil) and raw materials (wool and flax) required by expanding west European cities and textile industries.

In 1071 Byzantium was dealt two lethal blows. It lost Bari, its last Italian stronghold, to the Normans. And at the Battle of Manzikert it was decisively defeated by the rising power of the Seljuk Turks, who proceeded to take control of Asia Minor, depriving Byzantium of a major source of revenue and recruits. Henceforth, Byzantium would desperately cast around for new expedients and allies, in a vain endeavour to arrest its ineluctable decline.

In 1082, in return for an empty promise of Venetian naval assistance against the Normans and the Turks, Byzantium granted Venetian shippers free access to the main Byzantine ports, along with control of the main harbour facilities (including warehouses) and of key public offices. However, Venice proved a fickle ally and did little to halt the encroachments of either the Normans or the

Turks. The treaty of 1082 became a slowly tightening 'noose around the neck of the Byzantine Empire . . . condemning her to slow death by strangulation' (Haussig 1971: 318). In an attempt to escape this predicament, Byzantium made similar concessions to Pisa and Genoa (Venice's arch-rivals). In 1171 it even arrested all Venetians on Byzantine soil, and confiscated their warehouses. However, it had to back down when, in retaliation, Venice flexed its muscles and seized the island of Chios, valued for its production of mastic (p. 318). In these ways the infamous Ottoman 'capitulations', which conferred trading privileges on certain Western powers in the subsequent Ottoman Empire, were clearly prefigured in Byzantium and were not a peculiarly Ottoman invention – nor initially a sign of weakness, as they were first granted during the heyday of Ottoman power.

LANDLORDS AND PEASANTS IN THE BYZANTINE BALKANS

The contraction of the imperial tax base and increased reliance on corrupt and extortionate tax farmers placed crushing burdens on the peasantry and led to the growth of debt servitude, foreclosures and the usurpation of peasant land by rich tax farmers, provincial administrators and a rising class of 'feudal' frontier barons who gained the upper hand in imperial affairs after the tenth century (Haussig 1971: 184–5, 304–8). The lives of Balkan peasants became increasingly dominated by oppression by and dread towards tax collectors, imperial administrators, big landowners, money-lenders and various foreign predators (Baynes and Moss 1948: xxix).

Georgii Ostrogorsky, probably the most influential historian of Byzantium, similarly argued that Byzantine economic strength was also being sapped by excessive taxation of the peasantry and townspeople and a steadily increasing concentration of land, power and wealth in the hands of parasitic monasteries and big private estate-owners, who were gradually enserfing much of the labour force. After the reign of Basil II (996–1025), the Byzantine state abandoned its former policy of protecting peasant and military smallholders. Taxation, which was increasingly indulgent towards monasteries and secular landlords, became increasingly oppressive for the mass of the population. The peasantry, hitherto the backbone of the Byzantine economy, was rendered incapable of working on an economic basis (Ostrogorsky 1968: 322–3, 329–31, 392–4; 1942: 210–11).

However, just as Ostrogorsky exaggerated the sixth- to ninth-century decline of large-scale pro-prietorship, so he may have exaggerated the extent of its recovery or re-establishment from the tenth to the early thirteenth century. Paul Lemerle has argued that the 'powerful' (*les puissants*) who emerged during the eleventh and twelfth centuries, and who were increasingly exploitative of and parasitic upon the peasant population or 'the weak' and 'the poor', were 'not, as is usually said, great landlords (although of course they may become so), but dignitaries, and above all officials . . . who use their authority or influence to exert pressure on those persons of inferior social – but not necessarily economic – standing who are the rural proprietors, the "poor" as the texts say' (Lemerle 1979: 95). In contrast to the 'feudal' societies of western Europe, where baronial control of large landed estates, villages and numerous peasants was the major *source* of baronial power and wealth, in the Byzantine domains the acquisition of large landholdings (large, that is, by Balkan though not necessarily by western European standards) was not so much a source as an *expression* of the power and wealth of powerful personages. 'The powerful' rarely, if ever, became *feudal barons* in the western European sense. Instead, their power and wealth derived from *their positions as agents of the state*, able to exploit their positions to *extort, embezzle, exploit, cheat and corrupt*, but much less interested in either *productive economic activity* or the *consolidation of truly independent private property*. Thus the Byzantine population ended up with the worst of both worlds: mounting inequality and exploitation and oppression by 'the powerful', without compensating incentives for vigorous development of independent private property and private enterprise (including so-called 'improving landlordism').

Alan Harvey has painted a much rosier picture of the Byzantine Balkans from the tenth to the thirteenth century, which he regards as a period of demographic recovery and economic advance. He argues that, even in the absence of hard evidence of 'any advances in agricultural technology', we should nevertheless consider 'how effectively resources were exploited within the limits of the technology available' (Harvey 1989: 120). In his view, this period saw a growing concentration of agricultural landholdings in the hands of larger landowners (p. 71). Their revenues must therefore have been increasing and in consequence they must have had 'greater resources to make improvements to their properties', which in turn must have led to increased investment in 'the acquisition of tools and ploughing animals, the construction of buildings . . . bridges, roads, drainage and irrigation schemes, water-mills and the planting on a large scale of vines, olives and other fruit trees. At the same time, demographic increase ensured that a sufficient supply of manpower was available' (p. 121). Towns, which had generally contracted sharply during the sixth and seventh centuries, 'began to recover from the ninth and tenth centuries and expanded significantly in the eleventh and twelfth centuries' (p. 56), thereby stimulating demand for agricultural commodities, whose increasing production in turn made possible the growth of towns. 'As the population increased from the tenth century onwards, the land had to be cultivated more intensively and there was a greater need for effective irrigation.' This in turn was facilitated by 'concentration of land in the hands of wealthy landowners', who were 'able to mobilise resources to implement large irrigation projects, ensuring the more effective exploitation of agricultural potential' (p. 135). He also claims that this potential was being increased by environmental factors. The accelerating erosion of soil from increasingly deforested and over-grazed Balkan hillsides and mountainsides was resulting in ever larger quantities of upland soil being carried downstream by rivers, thereby silting up estuaries and depositing soil on the floors of lower-lying river valleys (p. 136). Some peasants (especially those in the vicinity of towns and/or near streams) allegedly compensated for their growing disadvantages in arable farming by specializing in viticulture, arboriculture (olives and fruit), market gardening, and rearing sheep and goats (pp. 141–4, 149–51, 155), to which we could add apiculture (honey and wax). Furthermore, fisheries became 'a major source of food and revenue' in coastal areas and near rivers and lakes (p. 158).

The main implications of Harvey's hypotheses are that mainly poor upland peasants lost out to wealthier and increasingly productive lowland landlords, including the rich monasteries such as those of Mount Athos, and that this increased inequality raised overall agricultural investment and productivity. 'The economic consequences of the increasing predominance of large estates has . . . been misjudged. Large landowners had the resources to make significant improvements to their properties. They also had access to a sufficiently large supply of manpower to ensure that the land was properly cultivated . . . The alluvial plains, which could yield very high returns, needed an adequate supply of manpower to be cultivated effectively . . . These activities enabled a greater range of crops to be grown' (p. 161). 'The most dynamic element in the rural economy was the efforts made by powerful landowners to improve their properties' (p. 159). 'The most important alluvial plains, on whose grain production Constantinople was dependent, were those of Thrace, Macedonia and Thessaly . . . The Venetians regularly exported wheat from Thrace and Macedonia and the Bulgarian plains', while the Genoese developed exports 'mainly from the coastal areas of the Black Sea and the Thracian plain' (Harvey 1989: 139). Harvey concludes that the pattern of Byzantine agrarian development in this period thus 'corresponds in general terms to that of the medieval West much more closely than has usually been allowed' (p. 244). In both areas, in his view, increased agricultural production mainly resulted from expansion of the cultivated area and 'more effective exploitation of agricultural potential within the limits of the technology available' under the impact of demographic recovery, rather than technological innovation, whose significance in western Europe in this period he considers to have been exaggerated. Although medieval Byzantine agriculture has often been compared unfavourably with that of north-western Europe because of its non-adoption of the heavy iron plough with a mouldboard and of the overshot vertical-wheel type of water-mill, as well as the more limited adoption of three-fold crop rotation, Harvey points out that such innovations would have been largely or entirely unsuited to the much drier climates and the thinner and drier soils characteristic of the Balkans and Asia Minor (pp. 122–5, 129–33, 257ff.). He claims that 'there is no indication of any serious shortage of iron implements in Byzantium' (p. 257) and that economies were becoming increasingly monetized and commercialized both in Byzantium and in western Europe (p. 259). In his view, the main socio-economic differences between Byzantium and western Europe lay in (i) the greater importance of the state in the Byzantine economy, largely because the heritage of the Roman Empire had survived more intact in Byzantium than in western Europe (pp. 2, 268); and (ii) the fact that Byzantine towns were 'so dominated by the landowning elite that the mercantile and industrial groups were never able to gain firm control' of them, with the consequence that 'the long-running struggles for power between townsmen and their feudal overlord, so familiar in the west, did not occur in Byzantium' (p. 261).

However, Harvey's theses are based almost entirely on conjecture – on his view of what *might* or *must* have been taking place. He does not furnish much evidence to back up his bold claims, many of which could be sheer wishful thinking. Georgii Ostrogorsky took a much more pessimistic view of late Byzantine agrarian trends: 'The difficulty in making proper use of the larger estates', in his view, 'was partly due to the primitive conditions of economic technique; for in this respect the Byzantine Empire, so far ahead in culture, was in many ways far behind the West' (Ostrogorsky 1942: 220). Unfortunately, as yet no one has even come close to establishing in what century the levels of economic development and technological capability in parts of western Europe substantially overtook those attained in the Byzantine Empire. We are thus far from possessing answers to these pivotal questions.

THE FINAL SCHISM BETWEEN THE EASTERN ORTHODOX AND ROMAN CATHOLIC CHURCHES, 1054

The doctrinal and conceptual divisions within the Christian world deepened during the centuries preceding the final rift or 'schism' between the Roman Catholic and the Byzantine Orthodox churches in 1054. These East–West cleavages were even more fundamental and significant than the later ones within Western Christianity (primarily, though not exclusively, between the Roman Catholic and Protestant churches). They solidified and gave a sharper doctrinal edge to an enduring East–West divide within the nascent 'European' civilization, although Christianity and 'Christendom' were *never* coterminous with *any* of the extant conceptions of 'Europe'. Beyond the never-resolved battle for primacy between Rome and Constantinople, between the Pope of Rome and the Patriarch of Constantinople, and between Western and Eastern Christendom, there were ever-widening linguistic, semantic, doctrinal, liturgical and organizational differences between the two churches, for example over relatively new Roman Catholic practices such as the celibacy of priests, the use of unleavened bread and refusal to administer 'Communion in both kinds' (both bread and wine) to lay Christians, as well as the Roman Cathlolic doctrine of the 'double procession of the Holy Spirit'. In these and other respects, the Eastern Orthodox Church remained much 'truer' to the teaching and practices of the early Church(es) than did the Roman Catholic Church, and its claims to 'orthodoxy' were thus justifiable. There were also divergent attitudes to icons, relics, Mary the Mother of Jesus, and the relationship between the believer and God (reflected in the divergent internal layouts of Orthodox and Catholic churches), as well as differences in the fingers and movements to be used in making the sign of the cross. In 1050 a Papal Synod banned the use of Orthodox rites in Italy. The Orthodox Patriarch retaliated by banning the use of Catholic rites in Constantinople and by closing the Catholic churches there when they refused to comply. Finally, the papal legate sent to negotiate with Constantinople in 1054 'excommunicated' the Orthodox Church (Woodhouse 1977: 65; Haussig 1971: 315).

4 The Crusades, the emergence of South Slav polities and the decline of Byzantium, 1095–1453

The victories of the Seljuk Turks, especially at Manzikert (1071), raised the spectre of a Muslim-Turkish threat to 'Christendom'. This prompted Pope Gregory VII (1073–85) to promote the idea of a Christian Crusade or Holy War to 'liberate' the 'Holy Lands' (Palestine and Syria), eliminate the Turkish 'menace' and ensure the security of both Byzantine Orthodox and Roman Catholic Europe. However, Byzantium was to be irretrievably damaged by the Crusades, even though they were originally intended to 'save' it from the 'Infidel' threat.

It fell to Pope Urban II (1088–99) to launch the First Crusade in 1095. The Pope appealed for a few thousand Christian volunteers, but both he and the Byzantine Emperor Alexius I (1081–1118) were somewhat alarmed by the nature and magnitude of the response. Huge, disorderly and predatory armies of Frankish and Norman warriors, ruffians and adventurers were motivated as much by an appetite for plunder, profiteering and territorial gain as by pious concern for either the 'liberty' of the Holy Lands or the security of Byzantium and Christendom.

The First Crusade (1095–9) captured Nicaea (the Seljuk capital) in 1097, Antioch in 1098 and Jerusalem in 1099. But, having accomplished their declared mission, the Crusaders turned to further plunder, territorial aggrandizement and fighting among themselves, allowing the Turks to counter-attack successfully from 1112 onwards. The inconclusive Second Crusade (1147–8) and the Third Crusade (1188–92) were followed by a catastrophic Fourth Crusade (1201–4), during which the increasingly powerful Venetian Republic diverted the lawless and unscrupulous Crusaders away from the Holy Lands and against Byzantium. Indeed, Emperor Alexius III (1195–1203), who had been driven to conclude a humiliating peace and accommodation with the Turks in 1197 (in order to protect his rear), was a renegade and a traitor to the Christian cause in the eyes of many Catholic Crusaders. Having forced him to abandon the Byzantine throne to his pliant younger brother in 1203, they captured, looted and vandalized Constantinople itself in 1204, massacring many of its Orthodox Christian, Muslim and Jewish inhabitants and desecrating many of its Orthodox churches and cathedrals. They divided most of the imperial possessions among themselves and, amid the battered remnants of Byzantium, they proclaimed a Catholic 'Latin Empire' under Count Baldwin of Flanders and a Venetian Catholic patriarch, subservient to both Venice and the Pope. Some of the (mainly Norman) Crusaders were in a sense forebears of the rowdy north-west European 'lager louts' who descend on the Balkan beaches each summer! After this long-remembered bout of Roman Catholic treachery, plunder, desecration and massacres, many Orthodox Christians concluded that they would prefer Muslim rule to Latin (Catholic) rule. This was to be a major reason why so many Orthodox Christians later rejected the humiliating and hegemonic terms on which a few Western Catholic rulers offered Byzantium token assistance against the Ottoman Turks at various times between 1439 and 1453 and 'accepted the Turkish conquest . . . as a merciful release from Latin domination' (Woodhouse 1977: 98). On the whole, indeed, the Ottomans treated Orthodox Christians and the Orthodox Church with rather more respect than the Catholic Crusaders did.

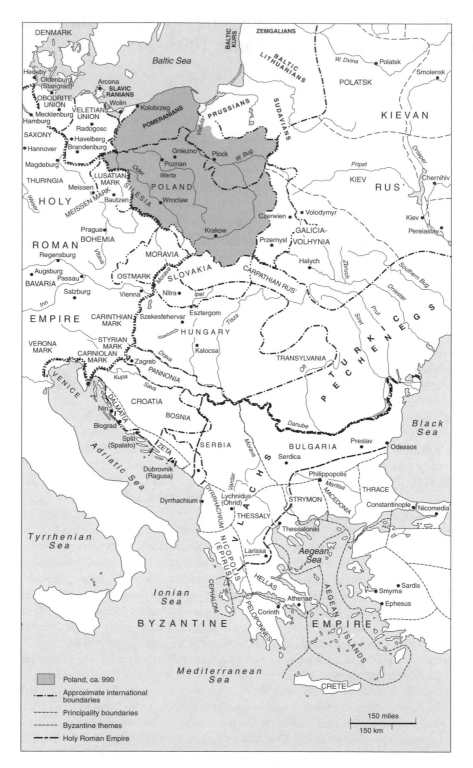

Map 3   The Balkans and East Central Europe: early medieval kingdoms in the second half of the eleventh century

For centuries to come, this contrast continued to influence the attitudes of Slavic Orthodox Christians towards their Catholic neighbours (in Italy, Croatia, Slovenia, Austria and Hungary).

The Byzantine Empire did not die in 1204, however. Within a year 'Emperor' Baldwin had been defeated and captured by the Bulgars, who resented the Crusaders' attempts to foist a Roman Catholic 'Latin Empire' on the Balkans Peninsula. Some Byzantine exiles, refugees and clergy rallied to a small neo-Orthodox Christian state in Anatolia, with its capital in Nicaea. This rather grandiosely named 'Empire of Nicaea' was slowly but steadily built up into the foremost neo-Byzantine successor state by the erstwhile Byzantine functionary Theodore I Laskaris (reg. 1205–22), his able son-in-law John Vatazes (reg. 1222–54), Vatazes's son Theodore II Laskaris (1254–58) and the regent Michael Palaeologus (reg. 1259–82). However, some other Byzantine exiles, refugees and clergy gave their support to a rival Greek Orthodox Christian state which has come to be known as the 'Despotate of Epirus'. Its core territory comprised what is now north-western Greece and southern Albania. During the 1220s the able and ruthless ruler of Epirus, Theodore Angelos Doukas (reg. 1215–30), won a string of military victories over his rivals and seemed destined to (re)capture Constantinople and relaunch the Byzantine Empire under his own leadership. However, this prospect threatened the ambitions of Bulgaria's Tsar Ivan Asen II (reg. 1218–41), who in 1230 defeated, captured and blinded Theodore Angelos Doukas and incorporated his territories into an expanding second Bulgarian Empire in the Balkans. In alliance with Nicaea, Ivan II Asen (unsuccessfully) laid siege to Constantinople in 1235–6 and then invaded Nicaean territory. Nevertheless, this Bulgarian bid for supremacy over the Balkans was halted by an epidemic in Bulgaria in 1237 (which killed Ivan II Asen's wife and one of their sons, and was seen by the Tsar as Divine retribution), by the death of Ivan II Asen in 1241, and finally by a devastating Mongol invasion of the eastern Balkans in 1241–2 (Ostrogorsky 1968: 434–8). This cleared the way for the rulers of Nicaea to bring much of the southern Balkans under Nicaean and Greek Orthodox control in 1246–9 and 1256–8. In 1261 this Greek Orthodox counter-offensive against the Catholic western European and Venetian interlopers in the Balkans culminated in an alliance with the powerful city-state of Genoa (which was engaged in a power struggle with its arch-rival Venice) and the (re)capture of Constantinople by Michael Palaeologus, who established the final and longest-lasting Byzantine dynasty (1261–1453). The Venetians and the last 'Latin emperor' were forced to flee by sea. Epirus was subjugated by Byzantium in 1263–4. However, the restored Byzantine state 'was but the pitiful remains of an empire' (Diehl 1948: 37). In return for naval assistance crucial to the (re)capture of Constantinople, Genoa was granted possession of strategic east Mediterranean islands, the Golden Horn (the prime position in Constantinople) and the right to collect 85 per cent of the customs revenues on sea traffic through the Bosphorus.

The Balkan economy and the stagnating civilizations of the eastern Mediterranean suffered further disruptions and destabilization in the wake of renewed Crusades in 1212, 1217–21, 1229, 1239, 1249, 1290 and 1343. These Roman Catholic 'Holy Wars' deepened and hardened religious divisions and antagonisms, both between Roman Catholic and Eastern Orthodox Christendom and between the Christian and Muslim worlds, without achieving any lasting 'liberation' of the 'Holy Lands'. The Crusades temporarily reduced the fruitful interaction and cross-fertilization between the Balkans and the Middle East, which had been at the heart of the eastern Mediterranean's extraordinary cultural creativity and ferment over so many centuries, but they did not end it. On the contrary, there has never been 'any lack of contact between Islam and the West. Despite periods of warfare, European merchants for centuries carried on a lively commerce' (Bulliet 2004: 6).

Angeliki Laiou has argued that 'the few surviving documents' from the late fourteenth and early fifteenth century yield 'a very gloomy picture of the Byzantine countryside', which had been 'devastated and depopulated' by the ravages of warfare and plague, with the result that 'men were scarce and land plentiful but uncultivated. Productivity was very low' (Laiou 1977: 7). On the basis of a study of agrarian conditions and trends in Byzantine-ruled southern Macedonia from the late thirteenth to the early fifteenth century, using the *praktika* (inventories of possessions) and fiscal documents kept by monasteries at that time and preserved in the monastic archives of Mount Athos (pp. 10–12), she has argued that 'during the last two centuries of its existence Byzantine society became heavily feudalized', because 'revenues from land were distributed by the Palaeologian Emperors among their followers and among civil and military officials in the form of *pronoia*', which were in origin prebendal grants conditional on state service (p. 4). Furthermore, 'many *pronoiai* soon became hereditary', as *pronoia*-holders increasingly ignored their service obligations. Thus 'what had been primarily a grant of revenues often became a grant of territorial rights as well. The countryside was parcelled out among landlords great and small; their revenues consisted of the taxes which the peasants had originally paid to the state, plus a part of the surplus, paid as rent . . . The peasant became a *paroikos*, a dependent peasant, as groups of families or entire villages were granted to the landlords', who (Laiou claims) were little interested in land unless it came with a captive supply of cheap labour to work it (p. 5). 'If a free, independent, landowning peasant did exist in this period, he is virtually invisible, and he is certainly invisible in the *praktika*' (p. 11). In Laiou's view, 'the Macedonian village of the fourteenth century had lost or was rapidly losing its independence. Its inhabitants were becoming dependent peasants of lay or monastic proprietors. The village had lost many of its collective rights and responsibilities with regard to the fisc, and yet in some respects it had retained a certain cohesion and some vestiges of its function as a community. In the eyes of the fisc, it preserved its existence as a unit composed of land and its inhabitants; it even had a few collective obligations – not however, to the state, but to the landlord. Finally, the village probably acted as a unit in its economic relations with the landlord, and preserved its judicial and administrative functions' (p. 64). She concluded that 'The life of the Macedonian peasant in the fourteenth century was very difficult. He was oppressed; he had little property and little freedom, and was at the mercy of natural and human hazards. Death was a constant companion. Disease had played an important role in the shortness of life of the peasant population; but economic exploitation and political upheavals exacerbated the already difficult conditions of existence' (p. 298).

However, it is hazardous to base generalizations about conditions and trends in the Byzantine countryside on a study of one region (southern Macedonia), relying largely on one type of source material (monastic *praktika*). On Laiou's own admission, very few non-monastic *praktika* have survived; one would inherently expect the peasants living on monastic land to be *paroikoi*; and 'the documentation which survives in the monastic archives deals almost exclusively with dependent peasants, *paroikoi*' (pp. 10–11), because monasteries had little interest in preserving a propertied peasantry on their domains (p. 213) and peasants were primarily of interest to the monasteries as sources of revenue and labour services (p. 221).

Jacques Lefort has challenged the doom-laden perspectives on the late Byzantine countryside propounded by historians in the Ostrogorsky (1968) and Laiou (1977) moulds. Along similar lines to Alan Harvey (1989) (see pp. 58–60), Lefort conjectured that significant population growth took place in the Balkans between the tenth century and the ravages of plague from 1347 onwards, and that this population increase resulted in a major intensification, diversification and more rational spatial organization of Balkan agriculture, with increased use of irrigation, water diversion for mills, crop rotation, catch cropping, increased construction of dividing walls and ditches, increased regulation of grazing, fishing and wood-cutting, and the introduction of industrial crops such as flax and mulberry cultivation/sericulture (Lefort 1993: 104–7). He argued that a relatively mobile population and a monetized economy encouraged increased commercialization and specialization and the growth of fairs and village crafts (pp. 110–11). He downplayed the significance of 'the generalized use of the word "paroikos" to refer to peasants' from the eleventh century onwards and challenged its use as evidence of 'a massive change in the status of the peasantry' (p. 112). Instead, starting in the tenth century, the state increasingly repaid services or granted rewards by assigning fiscal revenues from certain villages to particular officials or beneficiaries. 'Because the taxpayers of these villages no longer paid their taxes to the state but to a beneficiary, it became the habit . . . to call these taxpayers "paroikoi", even though they were still owners' (p. 112). Furthermore, 'the distinction between owner and tenant peasants was becoming blurred', because 'certainly from the thirteenth century onward . . . most of them were both owners and tenants' (p. 112). Lefort rejected claims that the average size of peasant landholdings was diminishing, because the estimates involved differed from one another by as much as 400 per cent and were therefore 'worthless' (p. 108). All that can safely be concluded is that we are dealing with hypotheses and counter-hypotheses, rather than hard information. No one knows for sure what the dominant trends and conditions were in late Byzantine rural society or its economy.

THE RISE OF THE FIRST SOUTH SLAV STATES

Relatively sedentary or sedentarized 'Slavs' either 'emerged' or 'arrived' in the eastern Balkans during the fifth and sixth centuries (see pp. 46–9). Meanwhile, semi-nomadic Turkic warriors and traders known as Bulgars established tribal confederations in this same area and gained an ascendancy over its Slavic peasant inhabitants during the seventh and eighth centuries (Crampton 1997: 8). 'The Bulgars seem to have lived in round yurt-like houses inherited from their steppe past . . . while the Slavs lived in square, half-underground houses with a stove in one corner . . . Different types of pottery are associated with the two peoples. But we soon find evidence of mixed settlements; as none of these settlements can be dated with any certainty, too much importance should perhaps not be attached to this archeological evidence' (R. Browning 1975: 47).

The Bulgar tribal confederations were not yet fully fledged states, since they still lacked standing armies, permanent administrations and clearly defined territories, but the Bulgars 'soon coalesced into a ruling elite which gradually established its political mastery over the much more numerous but militarily and organizationally weaker Slavic peasantry'; and the subsequent intermarriage and assimilation of the Bulgars into the much larger Slavic population was 'aided by the conversion of most Slavs and Bulgars to Byzantine Orthodox Christianity during the ninth century', thereby giving rise to a more unified realm which came to be known as Bulgaria (Crampton 1997: 12–16).

Most of Bulgaria lies to the north of the 'olive line' – the northern limit of olive cultivation, warm temperate (Mediterranean) agriculture and Hellenic life-styles (Browning 1975: 22, 53). Medieval Bulgarian agriculture was characterized by extensive stock-breeding (sheep, cattle and pigs, but few horses, despite the steppe origins of the Bulgars), apiculture (for both honey and wax, the latter being widely used as lamp fuel), and the cultivation of wheat, millet, barley, oats, vines and flax, using light wooden scratch-ploughs rather than heavy, wheeled, ironclad ploughs (pp. 80–2).

The main agricultural labour force was provided by the Slavs. Originally organized in communes based on kinship, with a fairly egalitarian system, they were early forced to pay a part of their surplus to the Bulgar state, which also transported and settled them in tribal units in new areas. Over and above the tribute which they paid to the state, many of them were quasi-feudal dependents of members of the nobility. The stages by which they reached this state of dependence are not recorded, but can be imagined: the tribal leaders become owners of the tribal land, and then become fused with the Proto-Bulgar aristocracy. Ninth- and tenth-century sources show peasants falling into groups: free peasants, *epoikoi*, Slavonic *epigi*, owing dues [only] to the state; peasants dependent on a lord, *paroikoi*, Slavonic *paritsi*; a third class, in some ways less free than the *paritsi* were the *otrotsi*, whose status resembled that of a slave. At the lowest level of the nobility we find the *Kmet*, probably in origin the head of a free commune . . . The *Zhupan*, originally a Slavonic tribal leader, had become absorbed into the Bulgar ruling class. (Browning 1975: 86–7).

It appears likely that, relative to the core Byzantine domains, the process of forming larger landed estates was less advanced, there were more independent peasant smallholders, there were much lower levels of urbanization, and 'the largest and most flourishing urban communities were those gathered around a royal court – military-administrative cities', because 'the heritage of classical urban life had been more definitively broken in Bulgaria than in Thrace and peninsular Greece . . . The massive military fortifications still surviving not only at Plishka and Preslav, but at Vidin, Ohrid and elsewhere, underline the military character of the early Bulgarian cities' (Browning 1975: 87, 94–101).

The first Bulgarian Empire, AD 890s–970

The multifaceted decline and tribulations of Byzantium left the Balkans with a power vacuum which was filled first of all by short-lived Bulgarian and Serbian empires and only later by the Ottoman Turks. The establishment of the first Bulgarian Empire was initiated by Khan (Prince) Boris (reg. AD 852–89 and 893). In order to accelerate the cultural assimilation and unification of his Slavic and Bulgar Turkic subjects and facilitate their communion with Europe's predominantly Christian states, Khan Boris forcefully fostered Byzantine Orthodox Christianity as Bulgaria's official religion from AD 864 onwards and, as mentioned in chapter 3, he subsequently invited followers of the Byzantine missionary monks Cyril and Methodius to devise a Slavonic written language for his realm. For this purpose, the so-called Cyrillic script was adapted from the so-called Glagolitic alphabet, which Cyril and Methodius had already devised for use in developing a written Slavonic language and liturgy in Moravia during the 860s, as well as from the Greek alphabet. Tsar Simeon (reg. AD 893–927), the illustrious Byzantine-educated and Greek-speaking son of Khan Boris, conquered most of Macedonia, Serbia, Albania, Wallachia (Vlachia) and Thrace, and pronounced himself 'Tsar of the Bulgars and Autocrat of the Romans' (i.e. Byzantine Orthodox Christians). (The title 'Tsar' was cognate with 'Caesar'.) He vigorously promoted the new Slavic literary culture and an 'autocephalous' (self-governing) Bulgarian Orthodox Church, and in AD 926 he established a Bulgarian Orthodox patriarchate at Preslav, his showy new capital. He could probably have united all the South Slavs under his rule, if he had not squandered his hard-won resources on several unsuccessful attempts to capture Constantinople, the last of which was cut short by his untimely death in AD 927 (Stavrianos 1958: 26). Simeon's son Peter (reg. AD 927–69) made peace with Byzantium, married a Byzantine princess and gained recognition both of the Bulgarian Orthodox patriarchate and of himself as Tsar of the Bulgarians, but his dominions were repeatedly ravaged by Magyar and Pecheneg marauders and in AD 968–9 Preslav was captured by Kiev Rus. The Byzantine forces sent to 'liberate' Bulgaria from Russian rule brought most of it back under Byzantine control in AD 970–1, although a Bulgarian 'rump' state survived in Macedonia until 1019. The last bastions of Bulgarian resistance were savagely subjugated by the Byzantine emperor 'Basil the Bulgar slayer' between 1014 and 1019. In 1014 around 14,000 Bulgarian warriors were taken prisoner and then blinded, in order to shock their kith and kin into submission to Byzantium. The reimposition of Byzantine rule led to the abolition of the Bulgarian Orthodox patriarchate and the Hellenization of the Orthodox clergy, although the Bulgarian Slavonic liturgy and literature somehow survived ('miraculously', according to nationalist mythology), while Bulgaria's big landowners ('boyars') mostly collaborated and enriched themselves at their peasants' expense.

The short-lived second Bulgarian Empire, 1230–41

A rebellion initiated by a group of tax-averse Bulgarian boyars at Trnovo in 1185 evoked reluctant Byzantine recognition (in 1187) of a new Bulgarian principality centred on Trnovo and ruled by the Asen family. Taking advantage of the conflicts and chaos precipitated by the Third Crusade

(1187–92) and of the capture of Constantinople by the Fourth Crusade in 1204, Bulgaria's new rulers rapidly expanded their domains. In 1205 they defeated and captured Count Baldwin of Flanders, the first 'Latin' emperor, who had rashly attempted to subjugate Bulgaria in 1204. In 1230 Tsar Ivan II Asen (reg. 1218–41) defeated Epirus and gained control of Macedonia, Albania, Serbia, southern Wallachia and northern Greece, establishing a second Bulgarian Empire embracing most of the Balkan Peninsula. He emulated Tsar Simeon by proclaiming himself 'Tsar and Autocrat of the Bulgarians and Romans' and by restoring an autocephalous Bulgarian Orthodox Church and Patriarchate in 1235. Nationalist and Communist histories of Bulgaria have often argued, with good reason, that the emergence of this second Bulgarian state was crucial to the long-term survival of a Bulgarian Slav culture and identity, in that it largely arrested the Hellenization which had occurred under restored Byzantine rule.

According to a Marxist history of Bulgaria published under the Communist regime, 'The Second Bulgarian State was typically feudal . . . It was then that the feudal mode of production became predominant, with its typical division of society into two main classes: boyars and dependent peasants. The boyars owned as inalienable property vast acreages of land, part of which, called "master's land", was tilled by serfs and farmhands. The remaining land was lent to the peasants to sustain themselves. There was also a comparatively large number of free peasants' (Hristov 1985: 53–4). However, this *Marxist* usage of the term 'feudal' refers to *a mode of production and a pattern of social relations of production based upon the appropriation of various forms of land rent and labour services from an increasingly dependent peasantry.* For clarity, it needs to be distinguished from *non-Marxist* usages of the term 'feudal', which refer to *highly decentralised political, cultural and juridical superstructures based upon the vassalage and fealty of castle-dwelling 'feudal barons' controlling local or regional jurisdictions of their own.* The former phenomenon could well have been emerging in medieval Bulgaria, but there are few indications that it served as a basis for the emergence of the latter phenomenon. Contrary to the claims of many non-Marxists, this need not mean that the official Marxist perspectives on medieval Bulgaria are incorrect or unsound. However, it does mean that the Bulgarian 'feudalism' to which they refer was by no means the same phenomenon as the 'feudalism' which most non-Marxist historians have regarded as characteristic of parts of western Europe during the same period. The word 'feudal' is often applied to widely differing phenomena, which could more usefully be given different names. The Marxist historian John Haldon has very sensibly argued that, in order to avoid unnecessary confusion, the mode of production which Marxists have called 'feudal' could more aptly be termed the '*tributary mode of production*', because it essentially involved the levying of various forms of 'tribute' in cash or in kind from dependent peasants (Haldon 1993: 40–51; 1995: iv, 10–12, 26–7). This clarification deserves to be more widely adopted, to reduce the widespread tendency for historians to argue at cross-purposes by using the same words (in this case 'feudal' and 'feudalism') to refer to quite different phenomena!

Starting in 1237 and 1242, the second Bulgarian Empire was hit by a devastating succession of Mongol/Tatar invasions, and thereafter rapidly disintegrated. The quarrelsome self-serving boyars were unwilling either to accept a strong central administration and standing army or to unite against external foes. They preferred to enhance their own local power and autonomy at the expense of both the state and the peasantry. In 1277 downtrodden and repeatedly plundered Bulgarian peasants rallied around Ivailo, a humble swineherd, who drove out the Tatars, married a widowed Bulgarian Tsarina and had himself crowned as Tsar. However, he sought boyar and ecclesiastical support against the Tatars and Byzantium, and the peasantry thereupon deserted their 'peasant Tsar'. In 1280, while negotiating with the Tatars, Ivailo was murdered by his hosts. With him died any immediate hope of a 'liberated' Bulgaria.

The short-lived Serbian Empire, 1320s–1350s

In 1330 Bulgaria was subjugated by a nascent Serbian Balkan Empire established by the Serbian rulers Stefan Uros III (1321–31) and Stefan Dusan (1331–55). The latter's empire embraced Serbia, Montenegro, Macedonia, Bulgaria, Albania and northern Greece. Like Bulgaria's Tsar Simeon before him, however, Stefan Dusan threw away his chance of welding the South Slavs into a coherent and durable Balkan Slav state. Had either of them concentrated on such a feasible goal, the Balkans could have developed into a much less fractious and vulnerable region. Even the inhabitants of Albania and northern Greece could have been gradually Slavicized through migration, intermarriage and cultural assimilation, for there was at that time a common religion (Eastern Orthodox Christianity), whereas ethnic identities and allegiances were still more fluid than 'fixed'. However, neither Simeon nor Stefan Dusan could resist the lure of Constantinople, known to southern Slavs as 'Tsarigrad' (the Tsar's city), and the overweening pretensions of a neo-Byzantine autocracy. In 1346, with lavish Byzantine pomp and ceremony, Stefan Dusan established an autocephalous Serbian Orthodox Church and Patriarchate and had himself crowned as 'Tsar of the Serbs and Romans', a title which he soon expanded to 'Tsar and Autocrat of the Serbs, Romans, Bulgarians and Albanians' (Darby 1968: 98). In 1355, however, just as he was launching his long-planned conquest of Constantinople in alliance with the powerful maritime republics of Ragusa (Dubrovnik) and Venice, he died of a fever. Thereafter, his far from unified state disintegrated almost as rapidly as it had been assembled. It proved to be 'a phantom empire . . . The adoption of a Byzantine style masked, without eliminating, the centrifugal social tendencies represented by unruly . . . and self-interested magnates' (Coles 1968: 22), many of whom defected to the Ottomans during the 1380s and 1390s.

In retrospect, Bulgarian and Serbian nationalists and 'national' historians have naturally tended to see the medieval Bulgarian and Serbian kingdoms as nascent or embryonic nation-states, the 'glorious' national development of which was rudely cut short by foreign conquerors and subsequently stifled by several centuries of Ottoman Turkish rule. They have also been inclined to treat the maximum extensions of their medieval kingdoms as 'the natural historical boundaries for their nations' (Jelavich 1983a: 27). Historical memories of these aggressive medieval kingdoms have translated into modern nationalist political programmes of territorial aggrandizement, causing immense bloodshed in the twentieth century. In practice these unstable and very loose-knit medieval kingdoms were very prone to internal disintegration (even before they succumbed to foreign conquerors) and their boundaries bore little correspondence to ethnic boundaries. These polities should be seen not so much as close forebears of the modern Bulgarian and Serbian nation-states, but rather as attempts by Bulgarian and Serbian 'upstarts' to create Orthodox Balkan empires modelled on Byzantium, aimed at usurping its imperial power, status and mission. They aspired, not to destroy Byzantium, but 'to occupy the imperial city and to claim for themselves the prestige and position of the Byzantine emperor' (Jelavich 1983a: 12). They imitated Byzantine court ceremonial, architectural styles, and patterns of government and culture (p. 13). National identities were still inchoate and fluid at that time, and were much weaker than the widely shared identification with Orthodox Christianity and a Byzantine (or neo-Byzantine) civilization. The predominantly Orthodox Christian Southern Slavs were developing conceptions of themselves as God's new 'chosen people' and of their shared (Church) Slavonic language as a 'holy language' akin to Greek, Roman and Hebrew – the languages in which the scriptures had originally been written. During the medieval era, their self-images and their consciousness of belonging to a wider community almost certainly owed much to more shared religion (and religous ties) and to a shared language than to perceptions of shared ethnicity or national consciousness. Ethnic, linguistic and literary differentiation and perceptions of ethnic, linguistic and literary differences appear to have been of more recent origin, mainly *after* rather than *before* the Balkans and the greater part of the Orthodox Slav community fell under Ottoman control and became more segmented.

From 1205 until 1355 it had seemed a racing certainty that one or another of the nascent South Slav polities would in due course conquer Byzantium and 'enter upon the Byzantine inheritance', and that such a state could have constituted an effective 'bulwark' against Ottoman expansion into Europe (Coles 1968: 21). However, history rarely conforms to a pre-ordained script. The rapid disintegration of Stefan Dusan's empire after 1355, followed by the momentous defeats suffered by Balkan Christian forces at the hands of the Ottomans in 1371 and 1389, allowed the Turks suddenly to erupt into the power vacuum created in the Balkans by the decline and contraction of both Byzantium and the South Slav polities.

5   The rise of the Ottoman (Osmanli) state, 1326–1453

Christian Europe ('Christendom') was caught almost completely off guard by the remarkably rapid rise of the Ottoman 'menace' (as contemporaries perceived it). Its capacity to resist the Ottoman advance was further reduced by such factors as the deep divisions between and within Roman Catholic and Eastern Orthodox Christendom, the deadly rivalries between Venice, Genoa, Ragusa and Constantinople, and the devastating effects of the Black Death (bubonic plague). This spread westwards from Constantinople in 1347, decimating and terrorizing whole populations for several decades. (Bubonic plague persisted in the Balkans and Anatolia until the nineteenth century.) By the early fifteenth century the massively depleted population of the Balkan Peninsula had begun to recover, as bubonic plague had 'lost some of its virulence', but by then the Byzantine Empire was too shrunken to be able to profit from this. Largely deprived of its former hinterlands, Constantinople became 'merely a safe and convenient harbour' for ships plying between the Mediterranean and the Black Sea (Treadgold 1997: 840).

Successive waves of Turkic nomadic pastoralists, warriors and marauders had been fanning out from Central Asia into Anatolia, the Black Sea region and the Middle East since the eighth or ninth century AD, partly in search of fresh pastures and hunting grounds and partly in response to pressure from the Mongols on their eastern and northern flanks. The Seljuk Turks in particular had blazed a trail for large-scale Turkic colonization and Islamicization of Anatolia since the eleventh century. Turkic colonization gradually displaced northwards the formerly dominant Armenians and Byzantine Greeks, and Anatolia became a favourite stomping ground for large numbers of Muslim Turkic freebooters and frontiersmen known as *ghazis* (derived from the Arabic word for 'raid').

THE HOUSE OF OSMAN (1300–1922) AND ITS INITIAL CONQUESTS

The Ottomans were named after Osman, who was born around 1258 and founded a small independent state in northern Anatolia in 1299 or 1300. Osman's father, Ertugrul, was a Turkic Muslim frontier warrior who had been awarded a small fief near Sogut during the thirteenth-century decline and fragmentation of the Seljuk Empire. Osman's gradual extension of his father's domains at the expense of both Byzantium and rival Turkic potentates culminated in his conquest of the city of Brusa (Bursa) on the southern shores of the Sea of Marmara in 1326. This strategically located city became the capital of the nascent Osmanli or 'Ottoman' state. The neighbouring Balkan and Anatolian states were preoccupied with more immediate threats, such as the Mongol and Tartar marauders who periodically 'erupted' from Eurasian steppes, so they took little notice of the emergence of the Ottomans. Osman's son Orkhan (reg. 1326–62) captured the last important Byzantine cities in northern Anatolia: Nicaea (Iznik) in 1329 and Nicomedia (Izmit) in 1337.

Military success attracted growing numbers of Turkic and Muslim *ghazis*, adventurers and freebooters into the service of the House of Osman, whose followers were not members of a particular tribe or clan, but rather a mixture of many kinds of Turkic and Turkicized peoples who chose to follow Osman and/or subsequent rulers (Sultans) of the Osmanli state (Sugar 1977: 12–13). Nor were the Ottoman Sultans 'purely' of 'Turkish ethnicity' (if you believe such a concept really matters!). Orkhan, Murat I (1362–89), Bayezit I (1389–1402), Murat II (1421–44 and 1146–51) and Mehmet II (1444–46 and 1451–81) married 'European' Christian princesses in order to seal dynastic alliances with various Balkan Christian rulers, while Sultan Bayezit I was actually the son, grandson and husband of Christian Balkan European princesses (Sugar 1977: 15–16, 21). In our estimation, with the (partial) exception of formal religious affiliation, there were more commonalities than differences between Ottoman Muslim and Balkan Christian ruling elites. Furthermore, although this is far too big a controversy to treat adequately in this book, we also broadly accept claims that the commonalities between Christianity, Islam and Judaism – the three great monotheist religions with common origins in the Old Testament – have been much more fundamental than the mostly epiphenomenal and widely exaggerated differences between them, that these three religions are best viewed as different branches of a single river rather than as three completely separate and dissimilar rivers, and that over the past 1,300 years there has actually been far less antagonism between Christians and Muslims than among Christians towards Jews (cf. Bulliet 2004; Dalrymple 2005).

The major challenge confronting the early Ottoman Sultans was how to harness and provide fulfilling outlets for the energies, appetites and religious fervour of their most numerous followers, especially the *ghazis*. 'The ever-increasing numbers of Islamic warriors who were attracted to the expanding Osmanli frontier state had to be kept occupied in some manner. The obvious solution lay across the Straits, where infidel Balkan kingdoms . . . promised rich spoils for the ghazis and new glory for the faith' (Stavrianos 1958: 36).

After ending more than a thousand years of Byzantine power in Asia Minor in 1337, Ottoman Turks first entered the Balkans in 1345 as mercenaries (about six thousand in all) in the service of an able Byzantine official and usurper named John Cantacuzene. They assisted him in his successful seizure of the Byzantine imperial throne, completed in 1347. Having strengthened this 'unholy alliance' by marrying off his daughter Theodora to Sultan Orkhan, Emperor Cantacuzene invited another 20,000 Ottoman mercenaries to the Balkans in 1349 to help him fight off Serbian encroachments on Byzantine territory. These first forays into the Balkans whetted Ottoman Turkish appetites for new conquests and booty, with the result that the Ottomans returned (uninvited this time!) in 1352 and 1354 to capture Tzympe (Cimpe) and Gallipoli respectively. From their new strategic bridgeheads on the northern (European) shores of the Dardanelles and the Sea of Marmara, the Ottoman Turks found it remarkably easy to expand into the power vacuum created by the accelerating decline and contraction of the Serbian and Byzantine empires. By 1365 the Ottomans had consolidated their hold on eastern Thrace (including Plovdiv) and had transferred their capital from Bursa (Brusa) to Adrianople (Edirne) in the south-eastern Balkans. This area, roughly corresponding to the present-day Turkish toehold in Europe, along with the city of Constantinople after it fell to the Turks in 1453, remained the only part of the Balkans ever to be intensively colonized by the Turks.

The first major Catholic and Orthodox Christian forces dispatched to arrest the Ottoman advance into the Balkans were cut to shreds near Adrianople (Edirne) in 1364. A similar fate befell the Orthodox South Slav armies sent down the Maritsa valley to head off the Turks in 1371. These traumatic Christian defeats effectively left the way open for the Turks to advance into the very heart of the Balkans. They were able to capture Bitolj (Monastir) in 1380, Sofia in 1385, Nis in 1386, Salonika (Thessaloniki) in 1387, and Kolarovgrad (Shumen), Provadija (Pravadi) and Novi Pazar in 1388.

On 15 June 1389 (28 June by the Eastern Orthodox calendar), according to Balkan Orthodox Christian and nationalist (especially Serbian) historiography, the Ottomans decisively defeated a grand coalition of Serb, Bulgarian, Albanian, Bosnian and Wallachian Orthodox Christian forces on Kosova Plain, shattering the last remnants of the defunct Serbian Empire. However, the revisionist historians John Fine jnr. and Noel Malcolm have told a somewhat different story. 'Though Serbian myth and poetry have presented this battle as a cataclysmic defeat in which the flower of Balkan chivalry perished . . . the truth is a little less dramatic. Losses were heavy on both sides' (Malcolm 1994: 20). At the close of battle, the remnants of the Orthodox Christian forces withdrew, but the Ottoman forces withdrew as well, both because they now lacked the numbers and strength to continue their offensive against the Balkan Christians and because a Serb who had ostensibly deserted to the Ottoman side managed to assassinate Sultan Murat. Murat's eldest son Bayezit, who commanded the Ottoman forces, felt obliged to pull back his remaining troops in order to make sure of his own succession to the Sultanate. 'Thus, since the Turks also withdrew, one can conclude the battle was a draw' (Fine 1987: 410). Indeed, since the Serb and Bosnian forces had seemingly held off an Ottoman assault, they initially claimed that they had 'won', and they were hailed as saviours of Christendom. However, whereas the Serbs had lost a large part of their forces in holding the Turks to a temporary draw, the Ottomans still had many thousands of fresh troops in reserve and were able to complete their conquest of the Orthodox Serb lands (other than Bosnian-ruled Hum and parts of Zeta/Montenegro) by 1392. Thus, although the Serbs may not have formally lost the Battle of Kosova in 1389, 'they lost the war because they were no longer able to resist the Turks effectively' (pp. 411–18).

A significant factor in these Ottoman victories was the regularity with which some Balkan Orthodox Christians either fought on the Ottoman side or else went over to the Ottomans in the crucial hour of battle. This partly reflected the fact that the declining and shrinking Orthodox Christian states commanded very little residual loyalty, support or credibility. In time-honoured fashion, 'rats' were deserting the 'sinking ships'. It was also the result of Ottoman success in inducing many of the weak and vulnerable Christian princes and boyars lying in their path to acknowledge Ottoman overlordship (suzerainty) and contribute men, money and supplies ('tribute') to the Ottoman war machine, in return for lenient treatment, partial assimilation into the Ottoman aristocracy and retention of their landholdings and privileged social positions. Many Orthodox Christian princes, boyars and soldiers of fortune were to make successful careers out of 'loyal' service to the Ottoman state. Some of these opportunists even converted to Islam in order to safeguard and/or enhance their prospects under Ottoman domination.

Furthermore, many Balkan Christian traders, artisans and peasants had good reason to prefer the 'order', stability, firmness and certainty offered by the Ottomans in their prime (during the so-called 'Pax Ottomanica') to the anarchy, instability, uncertainty, depredations and excessive taxation characteristic of the twilight years of the Balkan Christian states, on the eve of the Ottoman conquest. The increasingly downtrodden Balkan peasantry had suffered grievously from the insecure, unstable and anarchic conditions, the excessive fiscal and seigneurial exactions of the warring Balkan Christian rulers, officials and landowners, and the introduction and/or intensification of some forms of serfdom in some areas. The new Ottoman overlords were no worse than their Christian predecessors and in some quarters they were regarded as liberators. During the fifteenth and sixteenth centuries,

> the Ottomans restored to state proprietorship, or control, the bulk of the lands found in the hands of local lords . . . In many cases, it is true, they reassigned part of these lands to their previous owners, but these lords were now made Ottoman *timar*-holders under strict state control . . . Under the new regime, many corvées and other feudal obligations were simply abolished. Taxation and exemptions, the status of groups and individuals, and land titles were all regulated by laws issued by central government . . . Their administration and execution were entrusted to the district kadis [judges] and begs [commanders] . . . The Ottoman system imposed more simplified and initially lighter taxes . . . than the former Byzantine-Balkan system. (Inalcik 1997: 15–16)

The Ottoman conquests were also facilitated by the weakness of their Balkan opponents, who fielded armies numbering 'usually only hundreds rather than thousands' of troops and who not only refused to co-operate with one another but also fought among themselves (Fine 1987: 604).

In addition, the preponderant Orthodox Christian inhabitants of the Balkans had less reason to fear the relatively tolerant Ottomans than the Hungarians, who had repeatedly attempted to impose Roman Catholicism upon them (Fine 1987: 608). The gradualness of the process of establishing Ottoman control, beginning with vassalage or suzerainty and the co-optation of Christian talent, reduced resistance (p. 607) and 'contributed greatly to the long-range success of the Ottomans' (p. 610). Nevertheless, 'many Ottomans and Balkan Christians would have explained Ottoman success more simply, seeing it as resulting from the will of God, be it divine favour towards the Ottomans or divine anger at the Christians for their sins. This belief surely contributed to Ottoman success' (pp. 610–11).

During the 1390s, following the legendary Battle of Kosova Plain (1389), almost all the Orthodox Christian areas of the Balkans fell under Ottoman domination. The Orthodox rulers or princes of Serbia, Bulgaria, Macedonia, Bosnia, Albania and mainland Greece mostly became vassals of the Sultan, while the Byzantine Empire 'was reduced to the great city and its immediate surroundings' (Sugar 1977: 21–3). Only Constantinople, Ragusa (Dubrovnik), Montenegro, the mainly Italian-controlled Greek archipelagos and the Roman Catholic north-west corner, which was best-placed to receive assistance from the rest of Catholic Christendom, were able to resist further Ottoman encroachments, which were constrained by lengthening supply lines. However, when several Roman Catholic powers mobilized a new Crusade against the Turks in 1396, their Catholic armies were decimated by the Turks – with support from Orthodox Serbs – at Nicopolis.

Meanwhile, having almost encircled the imperial city, Sultan Bayezit I had initiated an eight-year siege of Constantinople in 1395. However, the Ottomans still lacked both the fire-power and the naval strength to break its great walls and its maritime lifeline to the outside world (as also proved to be the case during the second Ottoman siege of Constantinople in 1422).

Then in 1402, like a bolt from the blue, the Samarkand-based Tatar/Turkic empire of Timur the Lame ('Tamarlane') burst out of Central Asia into Anatolia. At the decisive Battle of Ankara in July 1402, Timur defeated and captured Sultan Bayezit I, whose Turkic forces deserted to Timur's Tatar/Turkic side, whereas the Balkan Christian vassals remained loyal to the Sultan. Timur thus temporarily weakened the Ottomans' Anatolian power base, before withdrawing to Central Asia in 1403 almost as suddenly and unexpectedly as he had arrived. During the ensuing reduction in Ottoman power, which was prolonged by an eleven-year power struggle between Bayezit's four sons (1402–13), several Balkan Christian principalities regained their political independence and Byzantium regained some lost territories. It was thus still uncertain who would become the undisputed overlord of the Balkans (Sugar 1977: 28).

However, the core territories of the House of Osman were reunited in 1413 under Sultan Mehmet I (1413–21). Not only Turkish colonists and *ghazis*, but also many Balkan Christian peasants and various Muslim and Christian commercial interests favoured the restoration of a 'Pax Ottomanica'. Ottoman possessions and the power of the *ghazis* had survived more or less intact in the south-eastern Balkans, as Timur had not ventured that far. Consequently the relaunched Ottoman Empire sprang from a south-eastern Balkans power base, whence the Ottomans conquered the rest of the southern, central and eastern Balkans, numerous Mediterranean islands, Hungary, Anatolia, Transcaucasia and most of the Arab Muslim world over the next two centuries. 'The Balkans became the backbone of the Ottoman Empire not only politically in the wake of Timur's blow in 1402, but also as the main source of supply for foodstuffs and raw materials to the Ottoman capitals of Edirne and [after 1453] Istanbul' (Inalcik 1997: 256).

During the 1420s, however, Venice still held a string of strategic islands and ports all around the Balkan peninsula. Many Aegean and Adriatic islands either remained under Venetian control until the 1790s or became autonomous havens for Greek and South Slav pirates. Most of the islanders soon found Roman Catholic Venetian rule to be ruthlessly exploitative and mercenary – indeed, 'more oppressive than that of the Turks', with the result that many eventually 'preferred . . . the Turks to the Venetians as masters' (Woodhouse 1977: 108, 113). The Venetians taxed the islanders much more heavily than the Ottomans were wont to do, denied them any local self-government (in marked contrast to Ottoman preservation of Christian local religious-cum-cultural autonomy), strictly controlled their trade (preventing either diversification or competition with Venetian traders), and encouraged Catholic priests to proselytize among Orthodox Christians, while deterring Orthodox priests from proselytizing among Catholics. Corfu, for example, was largely transformed into a single-crop colonial plantation economy. Olives and olive oil were produced for export, with results that are still visible today – the island became in effect one huge olive grove peppered with crumbling Venetian towns and forts.

In 1422 the second Ottoman siege of Constantinople failed like the first. Anxious Balkan Christian princes began to look to Hungary for alliances and protection. The Hungarian warlord Janos Hunyadi, aptly described by Stavrianos as a 'Christian ghazi', led these forces to a series of victories over the Ottomans up to 1443 (Stavrianos 1958: 50–2). Nevertheless, the tide finally turned in the Ottomans' favour when Sultan Murat II (reg. 1421–44 and 1446–51) roundly defeated 'Christian coalitions' of Hungarians, Venetians and Balkan princes at Varna in 1444 and at the (less famous but more decisive) second Battle of Kosovo in 1448.

THE OTTOMAN CAPTURE OF CONSTANTINOPLE, 1453

Sultan Mehmet II (reg. 1444–46 and 1451–81) followed up his father's great victories with the third and final siege of Constantinople in 1453. This time the Ottomans were in a position to close the Bosphorus to Byzantine shipping and to deploy cannons and bombards big enough to blast holes through the city walls which had withstood twenty previous sieges. The city's population had dwindled to fewer than 75,000, of whom only 5,000 were equipped to fight. These were vastly outnumbered by the 150,000-strong Ottoman siege army (Stavrianos 1958: 55–6). For the Ottomans the conquest of Constantinople had become a strategic imperative. 'The existence of a Christian citadel . . . in the middle of the Sultan's lands in a very strategic position was a threat . . . So long as there was a Christian emperor and a patriarch independent of Ottoman power, the Sultan's Christian subjects . . . had to be considered as potentially revolutionary elements' (Sugar 1977: 65–6).

The Ottoman conquest of Constantinople eliminated the major strategic bridgehead which could have been used in any future Christian counter-offensive against Ottoman power in the Balkans. For the Ottomans, however, the capture of Constantinople involved much more than military and prudential considerations. Constantinople was still a great entrepôt situated at the centre of several major trade and communications networks which, despite the gradual decline and contraction of the Byzantine Empire, stood ready to be reactivated by any burgeoning imperial power that was strong enough to capture the imperial city, restore the prestige and authority of its imperial mantle, and reinvigorate its networks. This was the main reason why so many rising and aspiring imperial powers (including the Arab, Bulgarian, Serbian and Seljuk empires) had attempted to capture Constantinople and why the Russian Empire would later try repeatedly to take Constantinople from the Ottomans. Its strategic position and nodal situation at the interface between southern Europe and south-western Asia made it the ideal location for the capital of an empire extending or aspiring to extend into both continents.

The capture of Constantinople completed the transformation of the Ottomans from 'an oriental "horde" operating within a fairly fluid zone of operation . . . into one of the great historic imperialisms' (Coles 1968: 26). By conferring control of the narrow sea passage between the Mediterranean and the Black Sea, it also furnished the Ottomans with vast new 'reservoirs' of food, raw materials and manpower, because the (mainly Greek and Genoese) Black Sea traders 'plied a rich trade with Europe' in cereals, horses, metals, fish, timber and slaves, much of which could henceforth be diverted to Ottoman use (p. 27). This also weakened Italian maritime-commercial dominance of the eastern Mediterranean, which had partly depended on privileged access to Byzantium and the Black Sea region.

After the capture of Constantinople, the rest of the Christian Orthodox Balkans quickly fell into the Ottomans' laps. Besides Bulgaria, which had already been subjugated as part of the encirclement of Constantinople, the Ottomans conquered Serbia (minus Belgrade) and mainland Greece in 1456–9, Bosnia in 1463, Albania in 1467–79, Herzegovina in 1482–3, Montenegro in 1499 and Belgrade in 1521. Wallachia and Moldavia submitted to Ottoman overlordship in 1476 and 1512, respectively. Only Montenegro, Wallachia and Moldavia retained large measures of autonomy, albeit as vassals of the Sultan. Then, having briefly occupied central Hungary in 1526 and 1528, the Ottomans more lastingly conquered most of Hungary proper as well as hitherto Hungarian-ruled Croatia and Transylvania from the 1540s until the 1690s. On the Balkan mainland only Austrian-controlled Slovenia, the resilient maritime-commercial Republic of Ragusa, several Venetian-ruled Dalmatian and Albanian ports, plus various Aegean and Adriatic islands, remained effectively outside Ottoman control. At times, even Venice and Ragusa nominally accepted Ottoman suzerainty in return for privileged commercial access to Ottoman ports. By 1485 the Ottoman Empire was obtaining more than 80 per cent of its revenues from its Balkan domains, and the proportion was still nearly 40 per cent in 1527–8, after its conquest of extensive Arab domains (Inalcik 1997: 55, 83). Control of the Balkans became the mainstay of Ottoman imperial power.

6   The Balkans during the heyday of Ottoman power, 1453–1686

Many nationalist, Communist and Christian historians of the Balkan 'nations' and 'proto-nations' have painted lurid pictures of the impact of the Ottoman conquest on South-eastern Europe, none more so than some of the semi-official pseudo-Marxist 'national' histories published under Communist rule. Even though Marxists were supposed to eschew nationalism and ethnocentrism, they often outdid non-Marxist nationalist historians, partly in an endeavour to prove the 'patriotic credentials' of the authors and of their Communist masters. A typical Marxist-Leninist history of Bulgaria stated:

> Bulgaria's fall under Turkish rule ushered in the grimmest period in the history of the Bulgarian people, a period of almost 500 years of foreign domination. During it, the very existence of the Bulgarians as a nationality was threatened as a result of . . . the brutal oppression and exploitation to which they were subjected by the Turkish conquerors. Foreign domination held back the development of the country's productive forces, severed the Bulgarians' contacts with all other nations and put an end to their free cultural development. Bulgaria's conquest by the Turks was accompanied by the destruction of whole towns and villages and by an extermination, enslavement and eviction of the population. Hitherto prospering towns and villages were reduced to ruins and the land was turned into a desert. The population of whole regions was forced to seek refuge in the mountains and in remote areas . . . Heavy taxes, duties and fees were also imposed . . . The Turkish conquest led to a decline of crafts and trade . . . Many craftsmen and merchants perished . . . others were sold into slavery . . . The Turkish authorities . . . resorted to violence, bribery and lies to force the Bulgarian population to give up Christianity . . . Many churches and monasteries . . . were destroyed . . . and for a long time it was forbidden to restore the demolished churches . . . The Bulgarian feudal class . . . was annihilated. (Hristov 1985: 63–5)

However, this would actually be a more fitting description of the initial impact of *Communist* rule in Bulgaria (p. 65). Another such history of Bulgaria claimed that a 'considerable part of the Bulgarian population was killed under the Turkish rule . . . It has been established that under Turkish rule, the Balkan population inhabiting the Balkan peninsula was reduced to half' (Gyuzelev 1981: 30). Another contributor claimed:

> The Bulgarians also suffered a demographic catastrophe as a result of the Ottoman invasion. It is difficult to estimate the exact number of people killed in the invasion, but the available data indicate a mass annihilation. Enslavement also decreased the number of Bulgarians. Tens of thousands were sold in slave markets . . . The invader's policy of strengthening the Turkic element in the Balkans with a view to the gradual assimilation of the Christian elements also resulted in onerous demographic changes. Great masses of Christians, who were replaced by Moslems, were compelled to move to Asia Minor. (Markova 1981: 35)

However, such allegations cannot be taken at face value. In many parts of the world during the four centuries between AD 1440 and 1840, some villages and towns were depopulated, fell into ruin or disappeared, while others expanded or even arose from nothing. These were normal responses to economic and social change. Many large villages disappeared or largely disappeared in Britain during the same period, without any violent destruction and pillage by foreign conquerors having taken place. Significant numbers of Balkan Christians were undoubtedly killed or dispossessed by the Turks for their roles in resisting the Ottoman conquest. However, for centuries before the Ottoman conquest of the Balkans, Catholic and Orthodox Christians had been busily killing and forcibly converting each other (as well as some non-Christians) in and around the Balkans, while forcibly 'relocating' substantial numbers of people from the Balkan Peninsula to Anatolia (and sometimes vice versa). There is little or no evidence that the levels of carnage, forced conversion and forced 'resettlement' significantly increased either during or after the establishment of Ottoman rule in the Balkans. On the contrary, it is often argued that the initial 'Pax Ottomanica' represented a marked improvement on the preceding disorders, depredations and internecine conflicts between rival Christian camps (Stavrianos 1958: 99–100, 112–14; Woodhouse 1977: 101, 104, 108; Inalcik 1997: 15–16).

The Balkan Christian princes and nobility were steadily reduced in number, admittedly. However, this seems to have occurred, not through 'forced' Turkification and Islamicization, but rather by natural wastage and by gradual assimilation of native Balkan nobles landlords, officials and tax-collectors into the landed classes and officialdom of the Ottoman Empire. This often involved voluntary conversion to Islam, along with the adoption of Turkish names, dress, manners and life-styles. There was some initial Turkification of Thrace and the eastern Balkans: 'Along with the Ottoman policy of transferring disorderly nomadic groups into the Balkans in order to Turkify and secure new conquests, a large-scale voluntary immigration took place during the fourteenth century' (Inalcik 1997: 34–5). By the early sixteenth century about 50,000 Muslim nomadic households and about 700,000 non-Muslim households were registered as living in the Balkan dominions of the Ottomans (Inalcik 1997: 26, 37). However, little of this was brought about by mass killings, deportations or forced conversions.

OTTOMAN RELIGIOUS TOLERATION AND PERPETUATION (RATHER THAN DESTRUCTION) OF THE BYZANTINE LEGACY

In the Balkans, on the whole, the early Ottoman rulers adopted 'a chivalrous and tolerant attitude towards the mainly Christian inhabitants of the lands they conquered. Some of these Christians converted to Islam, but even those who did not frequently welcomed the firm justice of Ottoman rule in contrast to the anarchic misgovernment of the decadent Byzantine Empire' (Mansfield 1992: 23).

In 1453, when the Muslim Sultan Mehmet II captured Constantinople, the citadel of Eastern Orthodox Christendom, he did not proceed to destroy it, as he could so easily have done (or as Christian Crusaders would almost certainly have done if they had captured the citadel of Islam). The looting and pillage by victorious troops was brought under control within a few days and was far less destructive and traumatic than the sack of Constantinople by Crusaders in 1204. Moreover, according to the Greek historian George Arnakis (1963: 127), 'Ottoman policy, for the most part, was not hostile to the Orthodox Church. The reason is obvious. It was essential to keep the Orthodox subjects of the Sultan from uniting with the Catholic Church, which was associated with the struggle to drive Islam out of Europe.'

Sultan Mehmet II was determined that the Ottoman Empire would be more than an Islamic and Turkish Sultanate. It would also be the heir and successor of Byzantium, the East Roman Empire. The Ottoman Sultans purposefully preserved Constantinople, added to its architectural splendours, repopulated it and made it into the capital of their expanding imperium. The city's population recovered from between 50,000 and 70,000 in 1453 (Treadgold 1997: 840; Stavrianos 1958: 56) to between 500,000 and 800,000 in 1600, making it by far the largest city in Europe (Coles 1968: 47).

Then as now, Muslim doctrine specifically required political and religious toleration of Christians and Jews as 'peoples of the Book' (the Bible) and as fellow believers in the One God, so long as they did not engage in violent resistance or treachery against Islam (although, if they did do this, they could legitimately be 'punished'). Moreover, because of their preoccupation with military, territorial and Islamic matters, the Ottoman rulers were from the outset content to leave much of their empire's important commercial, administrative, political, diplomatic and ecclesiastical business in largely unsupervised Christian hands. The Ottoman Empire was neither 'exclusively Islamic' nor 'exclusively Turkish'; rather, 'it was a dynastic Empire in which the only loyalty demanded of all its multifarious inhabitants was allegiance to the sultan. The loyalty demanded of those who did not hold office consisted in no more than not rebelling and paying taxes in cash, kind or services. Even these were often negotiable. It was in the end the person of the sultan and not religious, ethnic or other identity that held the Empire together' (Imber 2002: 3).

Sultan Mehmet II, whose wives included two Christian princesses, personally selected a new Christian Patriarch of Constantinople in 1453 (the previous incumbent having fled to Rome in 1451). He was 'not the barbaric despot often evoked in the western historical imagination . . . While directing the siege of Constantinople, Mehmed employed several Italian humanists who "read to the Sultan daily from ancient historians such as Laertius, Herodotus, Livy and Quintus Curtius and from chronicles of the popes and Lombard kings". Mehmed and his predecessors had spent decades conquering much of the territory of the classical Graeco-Roman world to which fifteenth-century Italian humanism looked for much of its inspiration . . . Mehmed appeared surprised at Italy's anxiety regarding his conquest of Greece. Claiming that the Turks and Italians shared a common Trojan heritage, he presumed that Italians would be pleased at his victory over a mutual old enemy' (Brotton 2002: 50).

The new patriarch, known as Gennadius, was a popular anti-Catholic monk and theologian who had orchestrated Byzantine opposition to the unpopular (and unratified) terms for a reunion of the churches, negotiated at the Council of Florence in 1439. Gennadius and his followers preferred to submit to the Sultan rather than to accept the vague and elusive support which the Pope and some Catholic states had been prepared to offer in return for abject Byzantine submission to the papacy and Roman Catholicism. That would have been more than most Orthodox Christians could stomach (it also encouraged the Russians to establish their own Orthodox patriarchate in due course). The Ottomans soon silenced (or drove into exile) the few remaining advocates of the ill-fated reunion of the churches. It suited the Ottomans to keep the major Christian churches divided and at each others' throats (though they scarcely needed any encouragement in this!). Few Orthodox Christians could ever have accepted the arrogantly supremacist Roman Catholic terms for a reunion of the churches. 'The essence of Orthodox belief was that with the confluence at Constantinople of Roman and Christian theories of terrestrial and celestial empire, the world had achieved its final order . . . Not only . . . was all future improvement or innovation impossible, but also error was unthinkable' (Woodhouse 1977: 30). For Orthodox Christians, Orthodoxy represented a kind of perfection. Any deviation from it was heterodox. Therefore, the Orthodox Church could neither submit nor make any concessions to Roman Catholicism and the papacy, whose doctrines were (from the Orthodox standpoint) not just false, but pernicious. The Orthodox Church was a profoundly conservative force, fiercely resistant not only to Roman Catholicism, but also to the Renaissance, the Reformation and the Scientific Revolution. The fact that these had so little impact or resonance in the Ottoman dominions in the Balkans is usually attributed to various alleged effects of Ottoman rule, but the influence of the Orthodox Church and the Byzantine heritage were much more to 'blame', precisely because their influence was so much more pervasive in the Balkans. Indeed, because late medieval Balkan Orthodox Christendom was convinced that it had preserved and combined all that was best in classical Graeco-Roman civilization with the highest and truest form of Christianity, it complacently felt no need of a Renaissance or a Reformation or a Scientific Revolution. Through all their afflictions, Balkan Orthodox Christians consoled or deluded themselves that they had already attained unsurpassable religious and cultural perfection.

With Ottoman support, the Constantinople patriarchate was largely able to halt the Venetian-backed Roman Catholic 'proselytizing offensive' down the Balkan Adriatic coast, which had penetrated as far south as Albania. It was also able to reassert its primacy among Orthodox patriarchates and to reduce the autonomy of the South Slav, Romanian and Albanian Orthodox churches. Ottoman conquests in the Balkans and the Near East helped to reassert the (hitherto waning) authority of the Constantinople patriarchate over the various Orthodox churches within Ottoman jurisdiction. These considerable setbacks to the development of separate South Slav, Albanian and Romanian national identities persisted until the re-emergence of autocephalous 'national' Orthodox churches in the newly independent Balkan states during the nineteenth century. However, 'in the eyes of the Turks, there was no essential difference between Greek and non-Greek Orthodox Christians' (Arnakis 1963: 127). The Ottomans, therefore, saw no legitimate 'ethnic' or 'proto-national' objection to the extension of the Constantinople patriarchate's jurisdiction over all Balkan Orthodox Christians, or to the (implicit) dominance of Greeks over Albanians, Romanians and South Slavs.

Nevertheless, the new Russian Orthodox patriarchate in Moscow remained outside the jurisdiction of the Ottomans and Constantinople. So, when Moscow declared itself to be 'the Third Rome', in succession to Byzantium, it gradually emerged as a rival source of support, religious authority and spiritual leadership for many Balkan Orthodox Christians after the fifteenth century. This has remained the case ever since.

For the Ottomans, however, the Constantinople patriarchate was the one that mattered. Mehmet II in person installed the new patriarch, Gennadius, 'with full Byzantine ritual and enhanced powers' (Woodhouse 1977: 95). In so doing he signalled his determination to inherit the Byzantine imperial mantle, to respect the customs and sensibilities of his Orthodox Christian subjects, and to rule his Balkan domains indirectly, through the Constantinople patriarchate. As part of this investiture Mehmet II gave Gennadius an imperial charter or *berat* granting the Orthodox Church and the Constantinople patriarchate considerably wider powers, prerogatives and privileges than they had previously been permitted under the Byzantine emperors. The *berat* recognized the Ecumenical Patriarch as the head of the Orthodox *millet* (religious community) and as a high-ranking *pasha* and *vezir* (official) of the Ottoman Empire, 'responsible for all the behaviour and loyalty of all the Sultan's Orthodox subjects' (Sugar 1977: 46). The *berat* gave him and his Synod 'the authority to settle all matters of doctrine, to control and discipline all members of the church, to manage all church property and to levy dues on laity and clergy alike' (Stavrianos 1958: 104). There was to be much less doctrinal meddling and political interference in church affairs under the Muslim Sultans than there had been under the meddlesome Byzantine emperors. The Orthodox Church and its clergy were exempted from Ottoman taxation and were granted ecclesiastical autonomy (p. 60). In addition, they were given conspicuous roles in 'the assessing and collecting of taxes due to the state' (Sugar 1977: 46). This sometimes made them unpopular. The *berat* also promised freedom of conscience and worship. 'Orthodox Christians were free to keep sacred books and icons in their homes and to attend church services unmolested' (Stavrianos 1958: 104). Finally, the *berat* granted the Orthodox Church extensive jurisdiction over civil and family matters, including marriage, divorce and inheritance, since Ottoman family and civil laws were perceived *not* to be readily applicable to non-Muslim populations.

In due course Orthodox ecclesiastical courts and magistrates came to handle not only family matters, but almost all civil litigation between Christians, while 'Orthodox bishops functioned in their dioceses virtually as prefects over the Christian population' (Stavrianos 1958: 104). In parallel to the Ottoman bureaucracy, the Orthodox Church acquired numerous administrative and legal functions (in addition to traditional ecclesiastical ones) and came to see itself as 'a state within a state . . . as the *de facto* ruler and protector of the Christians' (Sugar 1977: 46–7). The Orthodox Church naturally saw itself as the mediator between Orthodox Christians and the Ottoman state and as the sole arbiter and interpreter of Christian interests and aspirations (although many Balkan Christians and nationalists *later* came to see the Church merely as a privileged, servile, venal and corrupt 'collaborator' with an alien 'enemy power' and 'oppressor'). Some of the Church's powers and functions were shared with local (elected) communal authorities in most Balkan villages, as the Ottomans permitted considerable local autonomy. 'Provided the taxes were paid, the Turks did not care what their subjects did with themselves. Local administration, trade and education were entirely their own affair' (Woodhouse 1977: 103–4).

The Ottomans never attempted any 'forced' and/or large-scale Islamicization of the Balkans, not least because *the vast majority of Balkan Orthodox Christians were much more valuable to the Ottomans as Christians than they would have been as either forced or voluntary converts to Islam.* Admittedly, the Ottomans did find it useful to win over small numbers of Balkan Christians to Islam as allies and collaborators. However, Islam prescribed that Muslims were to be liable to fewer and lower taxes than non-Muslims. The Ottomans, therefore, relied disproportionately on their Christian subjects for revenue. In addition, the Ottomans often forcibly recruited soldiers from the Christian populations of the Balkans to fight their Muslim rivals in Anatolia and in the Arab world. Islamic doctrine condemns 'aggressive' (i.e. unprovoked) warfare between Muslim states. According to the Quran, Muslims may only fight in self-defence or in retaliation. Thus the Ottoman conquests in the Muslim world were, initially at least, heavily reliant on the use of Christian recruits from the Balkans. Christians have often been 'scandalized' by the fact that most of these recruits were (involuntarily) dragooned into Ottoman service. Ottoman military recruitment and conduct were indeed frequently ruthless and brutal, but this was also the case in most of Europe both then and later. Even the English and later British navy used press-ganging, and escape from brutal English/British naval discipline was hard. Moreover, most of the young Christian boys who were enslaved, Islamicized and reared into the elite Ottoman forces were destined to become the most privileged and powerful soldier-administrators of the Ottoman Empire, even though they remained the obedient 'slaves' of the Sultan. This was by no means 'slavery' in the same sense that white European slave-owners employed black slaves as menial forced labourers on colonial plantations and in mines. Indeed, according to Stavrianos (1958: 501), only five of the forty-nine grand *vezirs* (prime ministers) who served the Ottomans between 1453 and 1623 were of Turkish extraction, whereas a majority were of Christian European origin – including at least eleven Slavs, eleven Albanians, six Greeks, one Armenian, one Georgian and one Italian. It is also significant that the Ottomans began their momentous conquest of the Arab world only in 1516–17, *after* they had conquered most of the Balkans. The Ottoman Empire was to be based not only on the commonly perceived Muslim-Turkic conquest of most of the Balkans, but also on a less widely recognized *Balkan* as well as Anatolian conquest of the major Arab peoples. In large measure, the Balkan subjects of the Ottoman Sultan (especially those who spoke Greek or Armenian) became important partners in the economic and administrative functioning of the multi-ethnic Ottoman Empire. 'Many of the Greek traders and Armenian bankers held honorary foreigner status under the *berat* system and were thus practically untouchable for the Ottoman government' (Zürcher 2001: 50).

During the eighteenth and nineteenth centuries, when Ottoman discipline and control gradually broke down, the religious toleration and safeguards established by the *berat* given to Gennadius in 1453 were sometimes violated. Then Christians (especially Armenians) sometimes became victims of 'outbursts of Muslim fanaticism or arbitrary actions by provincial officials' (Stavrianos 1958: 105), including illegal seizures of church property and harassment of (sometimes dissident) clergy

(p. 105), as well as the acts of genocide perpetrated by Turks against Armenian Christians during the 1890s and again during the First World War. (Quataert 2005: 186–8 and Zürcher 2004: 114–17 offer judicious analyses of this highly controversial matter.) Nevertheless, the plight of religious nonconformists remained 'much more favourable in the Ottoman Empire than in Christian Europe' (Stavrianos 1958: 90). Under Ottoman rule Balkan Christians never experienced the deliberate systematic persecution that Muslims and Jews suffered in Spain (p. 107), or European Jews incurred from European Christians during the nineteenth and twentieth centuries, or Balkan Christians and Muslims suffered at the hands of Balkan Christians in 1941–5 and 1992–5. The most eloquent testimony to Ottoman religious toleration came when around a hundred thousand Sephardic Jews (including many merchants, skilled craftsmen and professional men) who had been driven out of Christian Spain were welcomed into the Ottoman Empire between the 1490s and the 1520s. Spain's economic and cultural loss was the Ottomans' gain, as these Jews went on to play important roles in Ottoman commerce, crafts and city life (p. 90). Ottoman toleration was 'far ahead' of contemporaneous Christian practice (p. 60).

Under Ottoman rule, admittedly, Orthodox Christians were denied full civil and religious equality with Muslims. 'Non-Muslims were forbidden to ride horses or to bear arms. They were required to wear a particular costume to distinguish them from the true believers. Their dwellings could not be loftier than those of the Muslims. They could not repair their churches or ring their bells except by special permission . . . They were required to pay a special capitation tax . . . in place of military service. And until the seventeenth century the Orthodox Christians paid the tribute in children, from which Jews and Armenians were exempted' (Stavrianos 1958: 105). Furthermore, Christians could not file law suits against Muslims or give testimony against Muslims in Muslim courts, and it became increasingly necessary to be a Muslim in order to become an Ottoman official (Malcolm 1994: 65–6). Nevertheless, for doctrinal and pragmatic reasons, coercive Islamicization remained a rarity (see pp. 77–80).

The gradual spread of Islam in the Balkans was based not only on various forms of legal discrimination against Christians, but also on the growth of new largely Muslim towns such as Sarajevo and Mostar: 'Slaves who converted to Islam could apply for freedom . . . Converted and freed slaves were especially likely to end up in the expanding towns' (Malcolm 1994: 66–7). Nevertheless, contrary to the claims of the Bulgarian historians quoted earlier (on p. 76), it seems fairly clear that Islam was *not* imposed on the Balkans by force or through large-scale Turkish colonization of the Balkan Peninsula.

THE ISLAMICIZATION OF BOSNIA AND HERZEGOVINA (ALIAS HUM)

Many of the themes presented in the previous section are best illustrated in relation to Bosnia and Herzegovina, which (like Albania and Kosova) became extensively Islamicized under Ottoman rule. Europeans who regard Europe as essentially Christian, and/or Islam as essentially non-European, have often expressed puzzlement or surprise that Bosnia and Herzegovina came to be so extensively Islamicized. This therefore calls for an explanation.

There has long been an influential 'theory' that many or even most of the inhabitants of Bosnia and Herzegovina were adherents of a radical, heretical and violently persecuted Christian sect known as the Bogomils, founded in tenth-century Bulgarian Macedonia by a priest called Father Bogomil. Upholding a Manichaean dualist conception of the world as divided between the forces of Good (the spirit, light, God) and Evil (matter, darkness, the Devil), the Bogomils denounced the oppressiveness, extravagance, decadence and high living of the wealthy monasteries, the Church hierarchy and the (pseudo-)Christian ruling classes. In Bogomil eyes, wealth, luxury and material possessions were intrinsically evil. The Bogomils were to go further than any other section of Balkan society in welcoming the Ottoman Turks as 'liberators' who could finally free them from centuries of religious and political repression at the hands of the Christian 'Establishment' (both Orthodox and Catholic). According to this 'theory', in order to secure Ottoman protection after centuries of persecution by the Catholic and Orthodox churches, the (allegedly) mainly Bogomil inhabitants of Bosnia, Herzegovina and parts of Macedonia converted en masse to Islam. This was supposedly the origin of the so-called 'Bosnian Muslims' (now called 'Bosniaks'), who (according to this 'theory') are mostly descended from Serbs and other South Slavs who converted to Islam in order to escape 'official' Christian persecution of the 'Bogomil heresy' and became the dominant ethno-cultural group in Ottoman Bosnia-Herzegovina, remaining staunch supporters of Ottoman rule until Bosnia-Herzegovina was occupied by Austria-Hungary in 1878, to the great consternation of their Orthodox and Catholic Slav neighbours.

This 'Bogomil theory' has certain attractions. It seemingly offers a colourful and dramatic explanation of the conversion of a substantial section of Bosnia's population to Islam during the period of Ottoman rule. It presents this, not as a mundane and protracted process, but as a sudden 'mass conversion of Bogomils who, having held out for centuries against the competition and/or persecution of the Catholic and Orthodox Churches, finally preferred to transfer their allegiance to Islam'. The theory has therefore found particular favour among modern Bosnian Muslims. 'Instead of being seen as mere renegades from Catholicism or Orthodoxy (to which, at various times, Croats and Serbs have suggested that they should "return"), they could now be regarded as descendants of the membership of an authentically and peculiarly Bosnian Church; and their turning to Islam could be described not as an act of weakness, but as a final gesture of defiance against their Christian persecutors' (Malcolm 1994: 29).

Latterly, however, the still influential 'Bogomil theory' has been largely discredited by Fine (1976, 1987) and Malcolm (1994). They point out that medieval Bosnia was formally under the ecclesiastical jurisdiction of the Western (Catholic) Church and that its rulers were at least outwardly Catholic. Twelfth- and thirteenth-century allegations of the emergence of widespread heresy in Bosnia (upon which the 'Bogomil theory' of Bosnia's conversion to Christianity is based) emanated largely from outside Bosnia, chiefly from Hungary, Zeta (Montenegro), Spalato (Split) and Ragusa (Dubrovnik), each of which was advancing claims on Bosnian territory and/or seeking excuses to interfere in Bosnia's internal affairs (Malcolm 1994: 15, 31–2). By the fifteenth century the papacy and the Franciscan monastic order (which were engaged in a campaign to 're-Catholicize' Bosnia) had joined in the allegations of heresy in this remote and mountainous country (pp. 23, 41). Nevertheless, there is no reliable independent and/or internal evidence that the Bosnian Church had ever been Bogomil. The only allegations that this was a Bogomil church came from polities (Hungary, Spalato) and bodies (initially the Dominican Order and later the Franciscan Order) which had designs on Bosnia and therefore had a strong vested interest in making such allegations, which automatically makes them unreliable or even suspect. Moreover, 'the only apparent instance of a medieval source referring to "Bogomils" in Bosnia was almost certainly a forgery' (p. 31).

Fine has forcefully argued on the basis of largely indirect and/or circumstantial evidence that the Bosnian Church was 'essentially Catholic' (Fine 1987: 147), while Malcolm has contended equally forcefully on the basis of similarly indirect and/or circumstantial evidence that the Bosnian Church was influenced not by Bogomilism but by the monastic precepts and practices of the Byzantine Orthodox Church and that these (rather than a heretical theology) were what its leaders were required to renounce at a synod held in Bolino Polje in April 1203 (Malcolm 1994: 33–9). Disagreements of this sort and the indirect/circumstantial nature of the meagre available evidence indicate that we cannot be absolutely sure what the doctrines and practices of the Bosnian Church really were. For similar reasons, we also cannot take at face value the claims that they were really Bogomil, as *true* Bogomils were puritanically opposed to the wealth, power and high living of the established churches and their temporal patrons, whereas the Bosnian Church seems to have accepted wealth, power and royal patronage without qualms. Moreover, the separate Bosnian Church (distinct from both the Western/Catholic and the Eastern/Orthodox churches) was 'largely defunct even *before* the Turkish conquest' of Bosnia in 1463 and therefore could not have played a major role in the area's subsequent Islamicization (Malcolm 1994: 41–2, 56).

This still leaves unanswered the key question of how Muslims became the majority religious group in late Ottoman Bosnia. Part of the answer has been very firmly established: the process did not involve sudden mass conversions to Islam, but on the contrary was very gradual. Ottoman tax registers indicate that Muslims made up less than 10 per cent of the population in central and eastern Bosnia in 1468–9. In 1485 the sandzak of Bosnia still contained about 155,000 Christians and only 22,000 Muslims. By the 1520s, however, the Christian population had fallen to around 98,000, while the Muslim population had risen to 84,000. By the late sixteenth or early seventeenth century, Muslims were in a majority (Malcolm 1994: 52–3). Furthermore, as already mentioned, there is no evidence of 'massive forcible conversion' to Islam or of 'mass resettlement . . . of Muslims from outside Bosnia' during the first century of Ottoman overlordship (p. 54). It was not necessary for Bosnian landowners to adopt Islam in order to be allowed to retain their landholdings, nor did Bosnians have to become Muslims in order to prosper – the Ottoman domains were peppered with rich non-Muslim merchants (pp. 64–5). Admittedly, there was a steady exodus of Catholics escaping actual or anticipated persecution (pp. 52–6), but the much more favoured Orthodox Church actually gained new adherents, monasteries and churches in Bosnia and Herzegovina during the first two centuries of Ottoman rule, partly through the influx of large numbers of Orthodox Christians from Turkish-occupied Serbia (Donia and Fine 1994: 32, 37–40, 47), even though its ecclesiastical infrastructure remained too weak or rudimentary to resist the gradual Islamicization of this area (Donia and Fine 1994: 36–37, 43–44; Malcolm 1994: 52–7, 70–1). Moreover, in Bosnia's mainly remote and 'largely priestless' rural areas, 'Christianity (in whatever form) had probably become little more than a set of folk practices and ceremonies . . . The shift from folk Christianity to folk Islam was not very great; many of the same practices could continue, albeit with slightly different words or names . . . Many of the same festivals and holy days were celebrated by both religions' (Malcolm 1994: 58). Bosnian Muslims continued to venerate the Virgin Mary, Christian saints and icons, and often retained Christian names and patronymics (pp. 59–60).

THE ISLAMICIZATION OF KOSOVA, ALBANIA AND WESTERN MACEDONIA

For broadly similar reasons, the Islamicization of most ethnic Albanians in Kosova, Albania and western Macedonia was also very gradual, non-coerced and not dependent on Turkish colonization (Malcolm 1998: 93–115, 129–38, 164–5, 190–201, 228–35). As in Bosnia, these processes created 'European Muslims' (this is no more of a contradiction in terms than 'European Christians' or 'European Jews'). The descendants of 'indigenous Balkan' converts to Islam, rather than people of Turkish descent, made up the vast majority of the Balkan Muslims. It is therefore all the more ironic that during the nineteenth and twentieth centuries most of these Balkan Muslims, most of whom had not a drop of 'Turkish blood' in their veins, were popularly referred to as 'Turks'; and that between the 1880s and the 1980s post-Ottoman Serbia, Bulgaria and Yugoslavia expelled or forcibly 'repatriated' hundreds of thousands of them from Kosova, western Macedonia, Bulgaria and Bosnia to Turkey as if they were 'Turks'. It is even more ironic that both the Ottoman Empire and the Kemalist-nationalist Turkish Republic welcomed their 'return' to Turkey 'as Turks', when these people were mostly nothing of the sort!

THE ORIGINS OF THE SO-CALLED '*MILLET* SYSTEM'

The *berat* given to Gennadius in 1453 played a catalytic role in the process by which the Ottoman Empire gradually came to be organized on the basis of *religious rather than ethnic* communities and identities, with separate religious and civil jurisdictions and legal systems for each of the empire's major religious communities (sometimes called *millets*). This so-called '*millet* system', which is often portrayed as a rigid system of social and religious segregation or *apartheid*, has been a matter of intense historical controversy, comparable to the heated debates over the effects of the caste system in India and of (racial) *apartheid* in South Africa. It is all too easy to caricature and/or scapegoat the '*millet* system' as the root cause of many Balkan problems, implicitly or explicitly deflecting 'blame' away from other structures, institutions, attitudes and policies.

The expression '*millet* system' – implying something carefully worked out, consistent and co-ordinated – is a misnomer. It never was a 'system' in that sense. It evolved fortuitously, out of a series of ad hoc responses to complex situations and problems, and (like South African *apartheid*) it engendered anomalies and misfits. While it is important not to exaggerate the specifically Ottoman impact on the Balkans and the Near East, Ottoman adherence to Islam did help to foster and extend the powers, autonomy and responsibilities of Christian and Jewish communities in ways that might not otherwise have occurred.

In Anatolia the main foundation stone of Ottoman authority, legitimacy and administration was the Islamic legal code (the 'sharia'). This was administered, interpreted and subjected to continuous 'creative adaptation' to changing circumstances by learned Muslim religious scholars-cum-legal-experts (the *ulema*, including *muftis*/jurists and *kadis*/judges). However, the 'sharia' was increasingly supplemented by local customary laws (for which the Ottomans showed considerable respect) and by royal decrees ('kanuns' and hence 'kanun law'), especially on the many matters not covered or inadequately covered by Islamic doctrine (which had originated in very different circumstances several centuries earlier). Nevertheless, the Ottoman Empire, like many other Muslim states before and since, appears to have been relatively slow to develop secular, universalistic conceptions of law, authority and citizenship and of the rights and duties of citizens, which could more readily have accommodated its non-Muslim subjects in a more integrated and unified polity, although claims that this did not occur at all are false caricatures. The Muslim system of legal administration and authority was considered only to be appropriate for and applicable to predominantly Muslim populations. This did not give rise to too many difficulties during the infancy of the Ottoman state and in areas where non-Muslims constituted only scattered minorities of the Sultan's subjects, but it did pose some problems once the Ottomans conquered substantial Christian populations in the Balkans and Armenia. In response, Ottoman rulers permitted the development of separate (particu-larist) jurisdictions and systems of law for *each* of the major religious communities under their rule. Just as Muslims were already subject to Muslim juridical administration and laws, so Orthodox Christians remained subject to the juridical administration of the Orthodox Church and its Constan-tinople patriarchate, Armenian Christians to the juridical administration of the Gregorian (Arme-nian) Church and its *Catholicos*, and the Jewish religious community (the '*Yahuda millet*') to its own separate religious/juridical administration and its own elected head (the '*Haham basi*'). Similar arrangements were later adopted for the much smaller Roman Catholic and Protestant communities, primarily comprising (and catering for) the 'expatriate' foreign merchants resident in Istanbul/Con-stantinople and Izmir/Smyrna. In this way, the Christian clergy became a mirror image of the Muslim *ulema*, exercising an authority over Christians comparable to that which the legal and theo-logical experts of Islam wielded over Muslims. Conversely, the Sultan imitated Christian practice by organizing a regular hierarchy among the *ulema* (Coles 1968: 30–1).

According to Coles, 'The Ottoman Empire . . . was an impressive administrative artifact; but, held apart by religion, its components could never blend into a coherent whole. Such a system of arbitrarily contrived cohabitation was never likely to grow into an organic society. Any faltering or decline in the efficiency of the military establishment by means of which the Turks policed and defended their European empire was bound to reveal its essential disharmony and impermanence' (Coles 1968: 73). Similarly, Vucinich has claimed that the Ottoman Empire 'was enfeebled by its own deliberate policy of isolating from each other the several distinct component cultures. It failed to instill in its diverse subjects a sense of belonging. After the sixteenth century the inherent weaknesses of the Ottoman state stood forth fully revealed, and the empire entered a period of ineluctable decline' (Vucinich 1965: 3).

However, there are also more positive views of the role of the Ottoman '*millet* system' in the Balkans. Geography and historical circumstances had fragmented the Balkans, Anatolia and the Arab lands into an unusually large number of separate (but intermingled) religious, ethnic, social and economic groups with 'little in common aside from a mutual need for some unifying force to provide security and regulate the economic factors on which the livelihood of all depended' (Shaw 1962: 617). These paramount needs forced the diverse groups 'to accept the rule of vast political empires – often the creation of one of them'. However, successive empires were forced to accommodate these ineradicable diversities by maintaining 'communal and local groupings, while throwing . . . only a veneer of unity over the surviving internal disunity'. The Ottomans, by organizing these diverse groups into *millets* and guilds and 'by writing down and making into law what had previously been . . . customary', gave their Balkan and Middle Eastern subjects a 'means by which they could preserve their traditional institutions and practices under the veneer of a common loyalty to the Sultan' (p. 617). Thus, in their heyday, the Ottomans upheld a political and economic order in which Turks, Arabs, Balkan Christians, Armenians and Jews could peacefully and profitably co-exist to their mutual benefit. Instead of attempting to impose an Islamic and Turkic uniformity on their various Balkan, Middle Eastern and North African subjects, the Ottomans tolerated and protected religious and cultural diversity and a corresponding diversity of dress, mores and social conduct. The differing 'regulations of residence, clothing and social conduct' applied to members of the various *millets* were not 'products of malice or prejudice', but methods of regulating contact between 'persons of different religions, classes and ranks' so as to minimize the potential for friction or conflict: 'Each individual had a place in life determined by his class, rank, position and religion. Within the bounds (*hadd*) of this place, he was absolute . . . The whole purpose of the regulations called "discrimination" in the West was to reduce the possibility of friction and to supply visual signs of each person's *hadd*, so that others would know it, treat him in accordance with it and avoid infringing it, at least inadvertently' (Shaw 1962: 619). The rationale was that the only way that such diverse and intermingled peoples could live, work and trade together in peace, harmony and prosperity was by respecting, protecting and institutionalizing religious, racial and cultural differences. (The development trajectory of the Habsburg Empire in East Central Europe became similarly respectful towards such differences, for similar reasons.)

The Ottomans 'unwittingly strengthened the group solidarity of their subjects' by granting them 'a large measure of communal autonomy' and by enforcing 'regulations separating Muslims from non-Muslims', thereby allowing them 'to practice their faiths and to conduct their communal affairs with a minimum of intervention and taxation' and 'with a degree of peace and security that previously had been conspicuously absent' (Stavrianos 1958: 114). The organization of the Ottoman Balkans on the basis of *religious* (rather than ethnic) affiliations made it possible to unite most of the Ottomans' Balkan subjects into a single Orthodox *millet* and to unite almost all the rest (Turks and most Albanians and Bosnians) into a single Muslim *millet* (Stavrianos 1963: 195). Whatever the minor economic drawbacks, organizing society on the basis of religious affiliation appears to have been *far less* conducive to inter-communal strife (whether religious or ethnic) than the later organization of the Balkans on the basis of a multiplicity of intermingled and ill-defined 'national' groupings, in the wake of the decline of Ottoman control from the late eighteenth century onwards. In the Balkans, paradoxically, religion did not acquire more explosive and destructive power until the 'age of nationalism', during which in some (though by no means all) areas of the Balkans religions became suffused and transformed by poisonous 'ethnic' nationalism.

In response to such perceptions, Wayne Vucinich claimed that *millets* placed 'severe constraints' on the 'freedom' of their members:

The *millet* embraced neither a unified territory, nor a homogeneous ethnic group . . . It consisted of widely separated communities, isolated from each other, which enjoyed different social, political and economic privileges and were weakly linked through ecclesiastical administration . . . The *millet* system meant isolation . . . and isolation meant stagnation . . . While the *millet* system . . . enabled the Balkan peoples to preserve their traditions and ethnic individuality, it simultaneously retarded their social development. The rebuilding of their states was an enormous problem for the Balkan peoples. (Vucinich 1963: 87–8)

There are several objections to these criticisms. 'Stereotypes present distorted and inaccurate pictures of Ottoman subjects living in sharply divided, mutually impenetrable religious communities called *millets* that date back to the fifteenth century. In this incorrect view, each community lived apart, in isolation from one another, adjacent but separate. And supposedly implacable hatreds prevailed: Muslims hated Christians who hated Jews who hated Christians who hated Muslims. Recent scholarship shows this view to be fundamentally wrong on almost every score' (Quataert 2005: 175). For the most part, the diverse religious communities of the Ottoman Empire did not lead rigidly separated lives, but on the contrary intermingled peacefully and to mutual advantage. Furthermore, the so-called '*millet* system' was never *intended* to prepare the Balkan peoples for independent nation-statehood, but rather to foster peaceful and profitable co-existence of diverse peoples under Ottoman overlordship. By contrast, the various attempts to carve discrete nation-states out of the ethnic patchwork of the Balkans from 1804 to the early 1990s resulted in recurrent intercommunal tensions and conflict and massive bloodshed. In the context of the Balkan ethnic mosaic, the Western 'Wilsonian' concept of a political order based on 'national' states has proved to be a sure-fire recipe for human catastrophe, including the vicious circles of massive economic impoverishment and chronic high unemployment, which in turn have prolonged and exacerbated intercommunal tensions. If it had been feasible to retain a political order based on religious rather than 'national' (ethnic) communities and affiliations, this might conceivably have avoided the major human tragedies which occurred in the Balkans in 1912–18, 1941–5, 1992–5 and 1999. Some (conceivably irksome) personal restraints and reductions in economic efficiency (narrowly defined) would have been a small price to pay for greater peace and harmony, which (if achieved) could have fostered virtuous circles of greater prosperity and fuller employment.

THE 'RURALIZATION' AND/OR 'PASTORALIZATION' OF CHRISTIAN POPULATIONS

The biggest long-term social change which can be unambiguously attributed to the impact of Ottoman rule in the Balkans was the widespread 'ruralization' or 'pastoralization' of large parts of the Christian population, just as the biggest long-term social change wrought by later Communist rule was to be the reverse migration of most Balkan Christians from the countryside into the towns. In large measure this occurred because many urban opponents of Ottoman rule fled to the highlands or were taken captive (often as slaves) or took refuge in the Kingdom of Hungary (which included Croatia, the Banat and Transylvania or in Italian states), while many of those who 'collaborated' with the Ottomans were gradually assimilated into the ascendant Muslim military, merchant, tax-collecting, administrative and landholding classes, who tended to congregate for mutual protection in the major Turkish garrison towns. In general, 'Turks settled in the plains and river basins of the eastern and central Balkans and in the towns of the entire peninsula. Many Slavs abandoned the lowlands to settle in the uplands, where they Slavicized the Vlachs but adopted their pastoral habits' (Stoianovich 1967: 116).

The Ottomans repopulated, renovated and expanded many of the older Balkan towns, such as Adrianople, Monastir (Bitolj), Sofia, Belgrade, Salonika, Skopje (Uskub), Janina, Mostar, Banja

Luka, Hercegnovi, Athens and Philippopolis (Plovdiv). They also established major new towns, including Sarajevo, Travnik, Elbasan, Tirana and Novi Pazar, especially during the sixteenth-century commercial revival (Stoianovich 1960: 242–3; Vucinich 1962: 614). Thereafter, as urban populations became predominantly Muslim while rural populations became predominantly Christian, towns came to be seen as the abode of Muslim rulers, landlords, tax collectors, middlemen and agents of coercion, whereas villages came to symbolize 'the home of the oppressed and exploited Christian peasant, tax payer and food-producer', at least in the eyes of the Balkan Christians. 'The two societal components came to represent a struggle between two ways of life, which deepened and expanded as time went on . . . After the Ottoman Empire expired, the village–city conflict continued, even though the city lost its Turkish character. This unbridged chasm is one of the major present-day problems' (Vucinich 1962: 603). The accuracy of these observations was tragically reconfirmed during the early 1990s, when many of the violent conflicts in former Yugoslavia were (at least initially) not just between Orthodox Serbs, Catholic Croats and Bosnian Muslims, but also between villagers and townspeople, often cutting across religious and ethnic divides. The extreme cases were the sieges of several multi-ethnic Bosnian cities and towns by predominantly rural Bosnian Serbs.

Other consequences of this town–country antagonism were that throughout the Ottoman period 'peasants were the backbone of the insurrectionary movements against Turkish rule' and that it was mainly the peasantry (rather than townspeople) who kept alive oral traditions, Christianity, Christian art and music, epic poetry, folk memories of 'medieval independence and glory, Balkan machismo and "true patriotism"', with the result that the nineteenth-century national revolutions sprang from 'the village and not from the city' (Vucinich 1962: 603). It was only in the eighteenth century that South Slavs began to migrate to the towns in any numbers, and only in the next century that they developed their own national bourgeoisies. 'Until then . . . peasants were looked upon as "the real representatives" of the nation' (p. 614).

THE 'BALKAN CULTURAL RETARDATION' CONTROVERSY

Ottoman rule has also been accused of retarding the economic and cultural development of its Balkan Christian subjects by neglecting and restricting their educational development:

> The Ottoman Turks were unable to develop a dynamic civilization through an integration of the cultures of the conquered peoples . . . the Ottoman Empire was regulated by 'an anti-literate elite' . . . The state did not provide for the enlightenment of the people of non-Muslim millets, but discouraged every form of learning . . . To be sure, Greeks, Armenians, Tsintsars and Jews who lived in the major cities were exposed to learning, could study abroad and could buy favours . . . But the rest of the population was driven into the hills and mountains, relegated to the status of peasantry, and cut off from cultural centres. (Vucinich 1962: 610, 635)

Setting aside the habitual exaggeration of the extent to which Balkan Christians were 'driven' into the hills and mountains, such accusations are based on anachronistic views of the powers and responsibilities of the state. Most states refused to accept direct responsibility for providing either education or other forms of social investment until the nineteenth century, and some did not do so until the twentieth century. Many states viewed mass education with deep misgivings, fearing that it would equip and encourage people to question and challenge religious and monarchical authority and the political and social status quo. Ottoman neglect of direct state provision of education was not untypical of the early modern period the world over. The only major exceptions occurred in the Germanic and Scandinavian states and (less markedly) in the Dutch Netherlands and Scotland, influenced by Martin Luther's Protestant doctrine that every (male) Christian should be equipped both to read the Bible for himself and to pursue his true 'vocation' in 'this life' to the best of his ability. This was the main reason why Lutheran and Calvinist countries pioneered state provision of mass education, long before the onset of large-scale capitalist industrialization. The extensive literature on the so-called 'Protestant ethic' and the rise of capitalism has tended to miss and/or obscure this much more important and distinct advantage of predominantly Lutheran and/or Calvinist societies. In the Ottoman Empire, not surprisingly, the Muslim *millet* was at least as uneducated and illiterate as the Christian *millets*. As in most states, moreover, underprivileged religious groups did not automatically experience educational disadvantage. On the contrary, discrimination against such groups has often spurred quests for education in endeavours to overcome their social disadvantages. Thus Jews came to be among the best-educated religious groups in anti-Semitic Christian Europe, Parsees became the best-educated Indians, some Chinese religious minorities became the best-educated religious groups in south East Asia, Protestant minorities were more educated than their Catholic counterparts within Catholic Christendom, and Nonconformists became more educated than Anglicans in England. If Balkan Orthodox Christians were as educationally and culturally 'retarded' as most critics of Ottoman rule contend, then this was caused more by the continuing intellectual impoverishment and obscurantism of Eastern Orthodox Christianity and the Orthodox Church (which began long before the Ottoman era) than it was by undeniable Ottoman neglect and occasional restriction of educational provisions (for Muslims and Jews as well as for Christians).

Vucinich tried to parry widespread criticism of the (Balkan) Orthodox Church by arguing that it 'kept touch with the outside world (the Papacy, Venice, Austria and Russia) and facilitated the passage of a small amount of European influence through the Ottoman Curtain' and by blaming the Ottomans for the Church's undeniable decline: 'The long period of restrictive existence and close association with the Ottoman government had . . . a negative effect on the development of the Orthodox Church. Once a source of spiritual strength and intellectual power, the Church began to ossify', and it was 'forced to concern itself primarily with the physical preservation of its members. Theology and learning acquired a secondary importance and in these fields the Church stagnated' (Vucinich 1962: 609–10).

However, these superficially plausible arguments do not hold much water. Most Orthodox Christians were at least as uneducated, illiterate and culturally impoverished under the politically independent Orthodox Christian regime in Tsarist Russia as they were under the 'Ottoman yoke' in the Balkans. Furthermore, the Ottomans imposed no restrictions on the printing of books in non-Ottoman languages. Therefore, 'whatever harmful effects the absence of Ottoman printing may have had, it applied only to the Ottoman reading public, and cannot be used as an excuse for the non-Muslims' failure to take full advantage of the opportunities left to them', and the 'question that remains is why Christian millets did not develop within the conditions of autonomy left to them. Whatever iron curtain the Ottomans may have erected between themselves and the European Enlightenment . . . much of the Balkan cultural backwardness in Ottoman times came as a result of the extraordinary influence of their own ecclesiastics' (Shaw 1962: 622).

Indeed, the early modern Eastern Orthodox Church became 'profoundly hostile to the West', and Patriarch Gennadius and his successors 'opposed the West as the home of Catholicism and Protestantism and as the birthplace of the Renaissance. They rejected everything the Renaissance stood for', and they did so 'not only because it was heretical, but also because it was becoming modern. The inevitable result . . . was the intellectual isolation and stagnation of the Balkan peoples . . . Their intellectual horizon did not extend beyond the concepts of faith and local community affairs. Living in a static and self-contained Orthodox theocracy, they remained oblivious to the new learning, scientific advances and burgeoning of the arts that were transforming and revivifying the Western world' (Stavrianos 1958: 111). 'The iron curtain that cut off the Balkan Christians cannot be exclusively attributed to the Ottoman conquest. The profound anti-Westernism of the Orthodox Church was also responsible' (Stavrianos 1963: 186).

Despite the many accusations levelled against Ottoman rule in the Balkans, Stavrianos strongly played down the magnitude of the Ottoman impact: 'The Turks had little influence on Balkan culture. One reason was that they were separated from their subjects by religious and social barriers. Another was that the Turks resided mostly in the towns . . . The superficiality of Turkish influence allowed the Balkan peoples to develop their cultures freely' (Stavrianos 1958: 107–8), partly because 'the Turkish people were a minority in their empire and, furthermore, a minority whose energies were concentrated . . . upon war and conquest' (p. 91). Indeed, as late as June 1914 there were only about two million Turks resident in the Balkans: one million in and around Constantinople and another million scattered over other parts (p. 97). Most of the time, furthermore, the Ottomans had 'less trouble ruling their Christian subjects . . . than their Muslim subjects' (p. 112). Ottoman institutions later 'deteriorated and became corrupt and oppressive. But in doing so Ottoman rule became less dangerous for the Balkan peoples. It did not threaten their national identities and cohesiveness. Its inefficiency and flabbiness eliminated the possibility of denationalization' (p. 113). In these respects, Ottoman overlordship was much less of a threat to pre-existing cultural identities in the Balkans than were late Tsarist and German imperialism to those in East Central Europe.

THE SIXTEENTH TO MID-SEVENTEENTH-CENTURY APOGEE OF OTTOMAN POWER

In its prime, the vigour and dynamism of the Ottoman Empire and the numerical superiority and valour of its armed forces continually expanded its frontiers and the opportunities for plunder, promotion and personal enrichment. Careers 'wide open to talent projected a succession of outstandingly able men to the summit of power' (Coles 1968: 54–5). During the sixteenth century the Ottoman Empire not only conquered most of the Arab Muslim world, Azerbaijan, Georgia, most of Hungary (including Croatia and Transylvania), and numerous Mediterranean islands, but also inflicted major naval defeats on Venice, Genoa and Spain. In 1521 the capture of Belgrade, the major fortress at the confluence of the middle Danube and several important tributaries, opened the way for the conquest of Hungary (1526–44) and an unsuccessful siege of Vienna (1529) by Sultan Suleyman 'the Magnificent' (reg. 1520–66). However, the Austrian Habsburgs tenaciously refused to renounce their rival claim to the Hungarian throne (vacant since the decisive Ottoman victory over the Hungarians at the Battle of Mohacs in 1526), and in Hungary, with overextended supply lines, the Ottomans were 'campaigning at the limit of their operational capacity' (Coles 1968: 82–7, 103). From the 1530s onward, the Austrian Habsburgs encouraged and assisted Orthodox Serb refugees from Ottoman-ruled Serbia to settle in a semi-autonomous 'Military Frontier' zone (the *Vojna Krajina*) along the shifting border between the Habsburg and Ottoman dominions (and, not unrelatedly, between Western Catholic and Eastern Orthodox Europe). Over several centuries this contributed to the growth of belligerent Serb populations in Croatia and Vojvodina (then part of southern Hungary). This was how the so-called *Krajina* ('Frontier') areas of Croatia came to be populated largely by Serbs (who initiated the armed conflict in the former Yugoslavia in 1991). It was also the origin of the gradual Serbianization of Vojvodina (whose Hungarian minority now feels that it is an underprivileged Catholic minority discriminated against in 'its own' province).

The Ottomans were still strong enough to mount a second (albeit unsuccessful) siege of Vienna in 1683. Their European territory reached its maximum extent as late as 1676 (Coles 1968: 160), while their Arab Muslim dominions in Asia and North Africa went on expanding (albeit fitfully) during the eighteenth century. So long as the Ottomans seemed invincible, most Balkan Christians gave them little trouble. Indeed, as part of a successfully expanding empire, the Balkan population enjoyed a period of relative peace and harmony and comparatively low fiscal and 'feudal' exactions.

At least until the seventeenth century, moreover, the Ottoman Empire remained *highly receptive to new foreign ideas, products and technologies*, including those emanating from Asia as well as those from Europe. It was quick to assimilate the latest advances in the design, production and deployment of artillery, smaller firearms and ships. Indeed, the early Ottomans' secret of success had lain in 'their remarkable powers of assimilation' (Coles 1968: 71). Even though Westerners tend to think of the Ottomans as 'non-European', numerous Sultans married and/or were sons or grandsons of Christian princesses and were in close contact with other parts of Europe (see pp. 71, 78). The fifteenth-century Ottoman elite, including several Sultans, 'was largely composed of individuals of Balkan or other European origin' (Finkel 2005b: 159) and was strongly affected by the enquiring humanistic spirit of the Renaissance (Stavrianos 1958: 131–2). 'Ottoman Sultans saw themselves as partaking in a common civilization encompassing their realm and the West . . . Mehmed II was fascinated by the Spartans, the Athenians, the Romans and the Carthaginians, but he identified above all with Alexander of Macedon and Julius Caesar . . . Ottoman monarchs of the Renaissance period could match their European counterparts in splendour . . . and could probably surpass most of them in the quality of the poetry they wrote' (Finkel 2005b: 157, 162). Despite their recurrent military conflicts, the Ottoman and other European domains were symbiotic fellow components of a single *Oecumene* (known inhabited world) (Goffman 2002: 8–9). Paintings by Gentile Bellini and Constanzo da Ferrara documented for posterity the 'oneness' of Mediterranean Europe and the Ottoman domains in the late fifteenth century, in the eyes of contemporaries, every bit as much as Fernand Braudel's *The Mediterranean World in the Age of Philip II* (1975) did by other means for the sixteenth century. Demographically as well as culturally and economically, the subjects of the Sultans were indeed more 'European' than 'Asiatic', at least until 1516–17.

7   The Balkans during the waning of Ottoman power, 1687–1921

Limitation's of space preclude a full account of the military, economic and cultural decline and territorial contraction of the Ottoman Empire. It is also difficult to do justice to the rich literature and debates on the causes and consequences of these momentous processes. This chapter merely highlights the major landmarks, determinants, repercussions and explanations.

Following the failure of the second Ottoman siege of Vienna in 1683 the Austrian Habsburgs launched a major counter-offensive. They and their allies advanced deep into Ottoman territory in Hungary and Greece and on the Black Sea coast. The Ottomans were decisively defeated at the second Battle of Mohacs in 1687 and at Zenta in 1697. Thereupon Hungary, Croatia and Transylvania were to come under Austrian Habsburg control. The peace treaty of Karlowitz (1699) was the first that the Ottoman Empire had ever had to sign as the defeated party. It ceded extensive territories, long under Ottoman rule and regarded as part of the House of Islam, to the 'infidel'. 'The Treaty of Karlowitz marked a final, decisive turning point in the military balance between Europe and the Islamic world . . . After Karlowitz, the Turkish empire found itself on the defensive, seldom able to equal the strength of any European power' (Coles 1968: 195). The Habsburg Empire had become the dominant power in East Central Europe and was now poised to start encroaching on the Ottomans' Balkan dominions. It completed its conquest of Hungary and captured most of Serbia (including Belgrade) and parts of Bosnia and Wallachia in 1716–17. These gains were ratified by the Treaty of Passarowitz (Pozarevec) in 1718. Europe would never again feel seriously threatened by 'the Turkish menace'. On the contrary, Europe henceforth faced the so-called Eastern Question, created by the contraction of Ottoman power. This gradually produced a power vacuum in the Near East, 'and one of the basic problems of European diplomacy until the end of World War I was how to fill this vacuum' (Stavrianos 1958: 177). Ironically this new European concern signalled an implicit acceptance of the Ottoman Empire as a *European* power, albeit as 'the sick man of Europe'.

The Ottomans would have incurred even greater territorial losses in 1687–99 and 1716–18 but for the ongoing quarrels and divisions between the European powers. These enabled the Ottomans to recover some ground in the Balkans in 1736–9 and subsequently to be 'left in peace' for three decades. From 1768 onwards, however, this peace was repeatedly broken by the emergence of an even greater threat to the Ottoman Empire, namely the rapid extension of imperial Russia's power and influence into the Balkans, the Black Sea region and Transcaucasia. This was combined with growing Russian support for fellow Orthodox Slav Christians in Montenegro, Serbia and Bulgaria and, more erratically, for Greek, Romanian and Georgian Orthodox and Armenian 'Gregorian' Christians (that is, so long as they remained under Ottoman rule; thereafter Russian 'concern' waned). The Turks were repeatedly defeated by the Russians on all three fronts from 1768 to 1919. Thus Russia gained control of most of the Black Sea steppes in 1768–74; the Crimea, the Kuban and the Black Sea itself in 1782–3; the rest of the Black Sea steppes in 1787–92; (independent) northern Azerbaijan in 1806–8; eastern Moldavia ('Bessarabia') in 1806–12; and most of Caucasian Armenia in 1827–8. In addition, Russia gained a kind of commercial 'most favoured nation' status and a virtual 'protectorate' over Orthodox Christians throughout the Ottoman Empire in 1774. This encouraged Russian imperialists to dream of 'recapturing' Constantinople for Orthodox Christendom, especially during the 1780s and 1870s and again in 1915. More positively, Russo-British military intervention secured Greek independence from Turkey in the late 1820s, while Russia's major victories over the Turks in 1877–8 gained full independence for Serbia, Montenegro and Romania and virtual independence for Bulgaria from 1878 onwards. How did this contraction of Ottoman power come about?

'CULTURALIST' EXPLANATIONS OF OTTOMAN DECLINE

Some Western historians of the Near/Middle East, for example Bernard Lewis (1961, 2002, 2005: 398–400, 453), J.P. Coles (1968) and Peter Mansfield (1992), have long argued that from the sixteenth century onwards the Ottoman polity and its rulers became less receptive and less open-minded than before, partly as a result of the Ottoman conquest of the Arab Muslim heartlands in 1516–17. These conquests increased the weight and influence of the conservative Muslim *ulema* and other specifically Muslim interests in what became an increasingly Islamic empire. Significantly, the Ottomans' conquests in North Africa and what since 1902 has come to be known as 'the Middle East' were primarily precipitated by a determination to suppress a heterodox Shia rebellion in Anatolia in 1514. This prompted a punitive Ottoman offensive against the new Shia empire established in Persia and Mesopotamia (Iraq) by Ismail Safavi, the leader of a Shia sect and founder of Persia's Safavid dynasty (1500–1736). This in turn initiated more than two hundred years of intermittent warfare between the Ottomans and Persia. As a result, the Ottomans conquered then Mamluk-controlled Syria, Palestine, Egypt and western Arabia in 1516–17 in order to pre-empt a potential alliance between Egypt's Mamluk Sultan and Safavid Persia. Likewise, the subsequent Ottoman conquest of North Africa (excluding Morocco) forestalled the growth of the Shia state established by the Sadi Sharifs in Morocco in 1511 (incidentally bringing the Ottomans into protracted naval conflict with Christian Spain, which had finally been freed from the last vestiges of Muslim rule in 1492).

In so far as the Ottomans won support from their new Arab Muslim subjects, it was mainly as conservative upholders of Sunni Muslim orthodoxy and conformity against Shia Muslim heterodoxy and subversion. Coles has argued that, following the violent suppression of open manifestations of Shia heterodoxy in 1514–28, 'most Shia sympathizers on Ottoman territory reverted to their traditional ruse of outward conformity to Sunni practices' (Coles 1968: 67), while the Ottomans abandoned their previous cultural eclecticism in favour of a 'particularly rigid and exclusive Sunni orthodoxy', with the result that a hitherto 'restless and fluid society' was subjected to 'the discipline of a conservative system of Muslim instruction and belief' (pp. 72–4). Flushed with military success and 'sublime smugness vis-à-vis both heretics and unbelievers', the Ottomans 'increasingly neglected those elements in the intellectual heritage of Islam which might have enabled them to keep pace with . . . Europe' (p. 75). Furthermore, as a result of the Turkish conquest of the Arab Muslim heartlands in 1516–17, the Ottoman Sultan naturally became the 'Protector of the Holy Places' of Islam (Mecca, Medina, Jerusalem and Hebron) and the 'Caliph of Islam', although only the last few Sultans made full use of the latter title in (ultimately unsuccessful) attempts to reverse or arrest the disintegration of their (by then) enfeebled empire.

Lewis, Coles and Mansfield have repeatedly argued that the Ottomans' new custodial role in the Islamic world further restricted their room for manoeuvre in such matters as institutional reform, education, censorship, assimilation of Western ideas and knowledge, external relations and treatment of non-Muslims. Thus, while the Ottomans were able to accept Western-style weapons and ships, because these could be employed in the service of Islam against the Infidel, 'printing and clocks could not be accepted, for they served no such purpose, and might flaw the social fabric of Islam' (Lewis 1961: 41). The increased 'Islamicization' of the Ottoman Empire also inevitably reinforced the 'wide and unbridgeable gulf between the Ottomans and their Christian subjects' (Coles 1968: 73). Despite their laudable tolerance towards Orthodox Christians, the Ottomans could never accept them as equal partners, and there was no mutual bond based upon shared beliefs and objectives.

The Ottomans strengthened the hierarchical organization of the *ulema*, upheld a strict Sunni Muslim orthodoxy and mobilized Sunni Muslim support for further warfare against Shia Persia and Roman Catholic Europe. Unfortunately, such responses 'froze the intellectual life of the Ottoman Empire' (Coles 1968: 68). Superficially, a facade of Muslim unity and conformity in the Ottoman Empire contrasted favourably with the religious ferment, disunity and sectarian strife of Reformation Europe, but in the long run the contrast worked in Europe's favour: the heated debates and 'mutual vituperation' between (and within) the Christian churches and sects stimulated intellectual discourse and enquiry, while Ottoman rejection of any deviation from 'strictly traditional' Sunni Muslim ideas, idioms and precepts allowed Europe to 'outstrip' the Turks and the Arabs in field after field (p. 68). Thus the Ottoman-ruled areas of the Muslim world became trapped in 'a revived and intolerant orthodoxy whose champions were increasingly impervious to external stimuli' (p. 62).

For most Muslims, allegedly Europe thus became 'an outer darkness of barbarism and unbelief, from which the sunlit world of Islam had nothing to learn and little to fear' (Lewis 1961: 34). Dazzled by the initially impressive military might of the Ottoman Empire, they clung for too long to 'the dangerous but comfortable illusion of the immeasurable and immutable superiority of their own civilization' (p. 35). In addition, the Muslim doctrine of 'successive revelation' (the belief that God was only revealed *fully* and *finally* to the Prophet Mohammed, superseding previous revelations to the Jewish and Christian prophets) encouraged Muslims to discount and/or dismiss Western thought and civilization as products of earlier (and therefore imperfect and incomplete) Christian revelations (p. 40). Ottoman subjects were 'imprisoned within a social and political system which lacked the capacity for sustained development; whose values were fundamentally uncritical and uncreative; and whose elites found it impossible to advance beyond . . . violent and voluptuous parasitism' (Coles 1968: 117). Even Leften Stavrianos, who was usually more circumspect, could not resist having a poke: 'Ottoman culture was far from being scanty or inferior', yet 'it cannot be placed in the first rank of civilizations. It lacked the originality of a truly great civilization' (Stavrianos 1958: 90).

Following Lewis, Mansfield has argued that these changes contributed to Ottoman neglect of the developmental potential of trade and industry, which were increasingly left to non-Muslims. Allegedly, 'Ottoman militarism was combined with a contempt for industry and commerce. The consequence was that when the empire was still in its heyday it was already being overtaken in material strength by the more innovative . . . economies of the Christian European states' (Mansfield 1992: 32). Within the Ottoman Empire industry and trade 'were left to the non-Muslim conquered subjects . . . Thus the stigma of the infidel became attached to the professions which the infidels followed, and remained so after many of the craftsmen had become Muslim . . . Christians, bankers, merchants and craftsmen were all involved in the general contempt which made the Ottoman Muslim impervious to ideas or inventions of Christian origin and unwilling to bend his own thoughts to the problems of artisans and vile mechanics' (Lewis 1961: 35). Consequently, increasing Western penetration of the Ottoman Empire had 'little effect on the minds and beliefs of Muslims . . . Secure in the knowledge of the superiority of Islam, they showed no interest in the ways of non-Muslim peoples.' *This was in marked contrast to previous Muslim polities*, 'which had not hesitated to benefit from the wisdom and knowledge of other civilizations'. After the early sixteenth century, the only serious Ottoman attempts to copy Western and Central European advances were in the military and naval fields, including mathematics, navigation and cartography, but the effect was 'entirely superficial' (Mansfield 1992: 39).

OTTOMAN 'IMPERIAL OVEREXTENSION': THE NATURAL/LOGISTICAL LIMITS OF THE OTTOMAN 'PLUNDER MACHINE'

Many Western historians of the Balkans and the Ottoman Empire have also argued that the factors which had initially sustained or contributed to Ottoman power and territorial expansion ceased to operate once the empire stopped expanding or reached the alleged 'natural limits' of its expansion, and finally operated in reverse when the empire began to contract. 'The Ottoman systems of military organization, civil administration, taxation and land tenure were all geared to the needs of a society expanding by conquest and colonization into the lands of the infidel. They ceased to correspond to the different stresses of a frontier that was stationary or in retreat' (Lewis 1961: 27). 'The Turkish system was wholly unsuited to a settled way of life. Its merits were those of a machine for waging permanent war and maintaining permanent expansion. Only such a condition could provide the supply of slaves needed to man the administration and the forces and the booty and tax revenue necessary to support them . . . Both at the centre and at the periphery the system began to break down as the momentum of conquest became exhausted' (Woodhouse 1977: 114). Since lengthening lines of supply, chains of command and channels of communication meant that the empire could not continue to expand indefinitely, 'it contained within it the seeds of its own decay' (p. 100). A vicious circle was set in motion: 'Inefficiency bred oppression, and oppression inefficiency' (p. 115).

According to Eric Jones, 'The Ottoman state was a plunder machine which needed booty or land to fuel itself, to pay its way, to reward its officer class . . . With military expansion brought to a halt, the state came under severe stress. Revenues sank and the army and navy could not be properly maintained, which in turn reduced military options. The system turned to prey on itself' (Jones 1981: 185) By the seventeenth century the empire had become 'too large to be administered by so centralized a government as the Sultanate necessarily was' (Woodhouse 1977: 114). Furthermore, as the zone of depredation shifted from the empire's borderland to its core territories, the strain imposed upon Ottoman institutions by the cessation of territorial expansion and the decline in booty income engendered mounting political instability and disorder (Coles 1968: 170). Central control broke down, leading to widespread anarchy and local usurpation of political power, yet any move formally to devolve power to the empire's constituent territories could only have accelerated the incipient imperial disintegration.

Paul Kennedy has argued that by the late sixteenth century the Ottoman Empire was 'showing signs of strategical overextension, with a large army stationed in central Europe, an expensive navy operation in the Mediterranean, troops engaged in North Africa, the Aegean, Cyprus and the Red Sea, and the reinforcements needed to hold the Crimea against a rising Russian power' (Kennedy 1989: 13). Responsibility for overextending the Ottoman Empire has been pinned primarily on Sultan Suleyman 'the Magnificent' (reg. 1520–66), the last 'great' Sultan.

'Imperial overextension' also became a burdensome economic drain. 'Ottoman imperialism, unlike that of the Spanish, Dutch and English, did not bring much in the way of economic benefit' (Kennedy 1989: 13). There were initial 'spoils of war' from the conquest of Hungary, but Ottoman pillage devastated and depopulated the Hungarian economy, reducing its capacity to provide longer-term revenues (Sugar 1977: 284; Coles 1968: 87). 'The systematic rape of frontier areas enabled sixteenth-century Ottoman forces to live adequately off the land. This was no longer a possibility for seventeenth-century armies, which were often three or four times as large and operating in . . . depopulated countryside' (Coles 1968: 188, 191).

Economic development was undermined by the voracious demands and ambitions of the Ottoman 'war machine'. The share of military expenses in central government expenditure, which in previous centuries had only been around 10 per cent, rose by 1600 to around 50 per cent (Lampe and Jackson 1982: 26). 'The agricultural surplus over subsistence needs that is the first prerequisite of modern growth was mortgaged to maintaining the large military establishment needed to expand the empire' (p. 22). Powerful vested interests opposed a switch to more regular taxes and/or pocketed the proceeds for their own personal enrichment. The Ottoman system was more concerned with 'warfare' than 'welfare' (Vucinich 1962: 635).

CHANGES IN MODES OF WARFARE AND STATE ORGANIZATION

The seventeenth-century reversal of Ottoman military fortunes was undoubtedly attributable to exogenous (external) as well as to endogenous (internally generated) factors. In particular, the Thirty Years War (1618–48) familiarized East Central Europe with new forms of military organization and technology, including the use of light, mobile, powerful and accurate Swedish and Dutch artillery in support of highly trained, well-equipped, mobile, versatile and strongly disciplined professional infantry. This combination, analogous in some ways to the development of the 'Blitzkrieg' during the Second World War, could defeat even the most massive cavalry charge. This rendered the long formidable Ottoman *sipahi* (cavalry) largely redundant or obsolete. Likewise, the Ottomans' massive and unwieldy cannons and bombards, which had been ideal for laying siege to heavily fortified towns, were insufficiently mobile, accurate or versatile for effective use in support of infantry attacks. The janissaries ('yeni-cheris' or 'new troops'), the main body of Ottoman infantry, degenerated into increasingly corrupt and conservative part-time soldiers with extensive 'business interests', although this was as much an effect as a cause of declining Ottoman military proficiency and performance. The increasingly cash-strapped Ottoman rulers had allowed and even encouraged the janissaries to engage in privileged business 'side-lines' in order to supplement their rapidly depreciating state stipends, but these 'business interests' (including many monopolies and extortion or protection rackets) conflicted with their military duties (Lewis 1961: 30; Coles 1968: 186–91; Stavrianos 1958: 121–3). Interestingly, an analogous situation arose in Turkey during the 1980s, when the growth of the private business interests of Turkish generals greatly exacerbated corruption and conflicts of interests among the senior Turkish military.

Furthermore, the new techniques of warfare were fearfully expensive, causing the costs of waging war to rise at least six-fold in real terms between 1500 and 1650 (Coles 1968: 188–91). This escalation of military costs favoured the emergence of major European 'land powers' with strong tax-collecting bureaucracies (first France, later the Habsburg Empire, then Russia and finally Prussia/Germany), as they alone were fully able to meet these escalating costs. Weaker states, such as Poland, Hungary, Bohemia and the Italian city-states, were slowly swallowed up by these emerging 'superstates'.

The new warfare also depended on the emergence of sophisticated and expensive new munitions industries and supply systems, which the Ottoman Empire was slow to develop. The artisans of Constantinople were 'skilled and numerous, but hidebound and suspicious of innovation'. Their restrictive craft guilds were affiliated to the janissaries, 'whose jealous determination to preserve their traditional military techniques led them to reject all suggestions in military technology', whereas the Austrian Habsburgs could call on the metallurgical skills of Central Europe and were 'well placed to procure the elaborate and constantly changing equipment required for effective warfare' (Coles 1968: 191).

French, Dutch, British, Habsburg and Prussian rulers and states forged close alliances with rich merchants and bankers to help meet fast-growing financial needs which gave new impetus to the development of capitalism, but Ottoman rulers 'failed' to follow suit (Coles 1968: 190). The Ottoman Empire had some rich merchants and bankers, but 'they were never able to play anything like the financial, economic and political role of their European counterparts', mainly because most of them 'were Christians or Jews – tolerated but second-class subjects of the Muslim state' (Lewis 1961: 31). Despite their wealth, they were 'socially segregated; they could obtain political power only by stealth, and exercise it only by intrigue', and were therefore unable to establish conditions favourable to commerce and build a solid and stable foundation of banking and credit to bail the Ottoman state out of 'its perennial financial straits' (p. 32).

However, the 'What went wrong?' approach to the Ottoman Empire (and the Muslim world more generally) employed by Bernard Lewis and Paul Coles 'stands history on its head. The notion that something went wrong presumes a comparative perspective in which there is a clear notion of how things should have gone, against which the actuality of failure can be measured . . . The Muslim world never possessed a road map with a clearly marked path leading to a promised land of equality with Europe . . . The reason I can say this with confidence is that no one in Europe and North America knew where the ship they were saling on was heading' (Bulliet 2004: 47–9). This 'what went wrong' approach yields little more than Western complacency, arrogance, presumption and myopia, rather than a rigorous and realistic consideration of the options and possibilities confronting the Ottoman Empire's thinkers and leaders at the time, (Bulliet 2004: 47–93).

CHANGES IN THE OTTOMAN EMPIRE'S LANDHOLDING SYSTEMS

Many histories of the Ottoman Empire have long made great play of an alleged transformation of the landholding systems and rural social structure of the Balkan provinces between *c*.1600 and *c*.1800 as a major explanation of the decline of the empire and in particular its Balkan domains, relative to Western and Central Europe, from the late seventeenth to the late nineteenth century. This line of explanation can be comprehended only if it is placed in a wider and longer historical perspective and context.

Ottoman law, like Roman and Byzantine law before it, distinguished between three aspects of landownership: (i) *rabaka* or *dominium eminens* (ultimate jurisdiction); (ii) *tasarruf* or *usus* (possession); and (iii) *istiglal* or *fructus* (usufruct). Halil Inalcik, the doyen of Turkish Ottoman historians, has strongly emphasized the continuities rather than the contrasts between Byzantine and Ottoman patterns of landholding and land regulation (Inalcik 1997: 105–6, 143–53). During the first two centuries of the Ottoman Empire, 90 per cent all land came under the ultimate jurisdiction of the Ottoman Sultans (p. 105), who parcelled it out on temporary conditional tenure to their vassals and *sipahi* (cavalry officers) in the form of *timars* (conditional grants of land) held in return for loyal service to the Sultan, whilst leaving the rights of usufruct to the peasantry. As late as the 1528 census, 87 per cent of Ottoman territory was the property of the Sultan (Lampe and Jackson 1982: 24). Much of the rest belonged to religious bodies. Consequently, there was hardly any hereditary private ownership of land. Furthermore, the *sipahi* could demand about three days' labour *per year* from peasants resident in their *timars* (as against the two or three days *per week* demanded by Balkan lords in the late medieval Christian states). They were also allowed to collect 10–20 per cent of the harvest (towards the upkeep of their cavalry horses in the service of the Sultan) and to collect certain taxes (primarily the poll tax on adult non-Muslim males, levied in lieu of military service). Indeed, 'the force and extent of command from above was too powerful during the sixteenth century to permit local notables to carve out feudal and other customary rights for themselves' (Lampe and Jackson 1982: 23). As a result, the peasants living under Ottoman rule from the fourteenth to the sixteenth century were subject to considerably fewer and lighter state and seigneurial dues and other impositions than were the peasantries in many parts of western Europe at that time, and were relatively free and able to prosper under the Pax Ottomanica. This was the socio-economic basis of the initial successes of the Ottoman 'war machine'.

The conventional wisdom is that this initially very successful system underwent very damaging changes after the 1590s, when the *sipahi* cavalry became militarily obsolete and redundant and

Ottoman territorial expansion began to slow down, and even more so from the 1690s onward, when the Ottoman Empire began to contract. As mentioned above, overextended supply lines, along with dwindling and increasingly hard-won territorial conquests, reduced the scope for military plunder and for the acquisition of new landholdings. As a result, warfare was transformed from a highly profitable activity for its practitioners into a major drain on the Ottoman treasury, and this in turn reduced the state's capacity to pay its officials, who increasingly sought to offset this by resorting to extortion, bribe taking, embezzlement and other forms of corruption (p. 434). Furthermore, these changes allegedly reduced the motivation for the militarily obsolete *sipahi* and other Ottoman servitors to acquire new *timars* for themselves and their families through conquest, while also encouraging them to convert their existing *timars* and other landholdings into hereditary privately owned estates known as *çiftliks*. 'It was the de facto conversion of these types of lands by competing ayans [notables], armed irregulars, or members of the old prebendal class [the *timar*-holder], that signified a fundamental transformation in land tenure in the Ottoman Empire' (Kasaba 1988: 25). These groups allegedly diverted their resources and energies from preying upon the Sultan's *external foes* to preying upon his *internal subjects* instead. Simultaneously, the attractions of private landowner-ship were also much enhanced by rising urban and European demand for food, raw cotton and tobacco, which resulted in rapidly rising grain and land prices. Indeed, the 'most intense period of çiftlik formation' was the eighteenth century, during which 'çiftlik owners did not hesitate to use forceful means to tie the peasants to their estates . . . The Ottoman government was no longer in a position to intervene in this process. Local officials, especially the kadis [judicial officials], were often in collusion with the notables and other usurpers, and consequently the local courts were either unable or unwilling to adjudicate in ciftlik-related cases' (Kasaba 1988: 25).

As a result, during the seventeenth and eighteenth centuries the Ottoman servitor classes alleg-edly retreated from their former military traditions and vocations in favour of increasingly ruthless and mercenary exploitation of the land and its cultivators. This transformation was facilitated by diminishing central control over provincial 'notables' (*ayans*), which not only reduced the state's capacity to restrain embezzlement, private usurpation of state and/or peasant land, and the habitual rapacity of landlords, tax farmers, judges and other officials, but also encouraged state officials, tax farmers and other state agents to 'get in on the act' and pocket most of the proceeds, to the detriment of both the Ottoman treasury and the increasingly impoverished Balkan peasantry. Gradually *çiftlik*-holders enriched themselves, became powerful, and increasingly usurped provincial authority, becoming virtual kings in their own domains and a law unto themselves, thereby both profiting from and contributing to the growing anarchy, lawlessness, banditry, insecurity and protection-racketeering which bedevilled the Ottoman dominions during the eighteenth and early nineteenth centuries. 'By the beginning of the nineteenth century, *çiftlik* agriculture had become the prevalent form of production in much of Thessaly, Epirus, Macedonia, Thrace, the Marica Valley, Danubian Bulgaria, Kosova, the Metobija Basin, the coastal plains of Albania, parts of Bosnia, and western Anatolia. Almost all the export crops of the Ottoman Empire were drawn from these areas and, within them, *çiftliks* were especially concentrated around the main arteries of commerce and com-munication' (Kasaba 1988: 27).

The production and exportation of primary commodities (grain, cotton, raisins, olives, nuts, beans, figs, other fruit and vegetables, tobacco, pig meat) conspicuously increased, as did tax farming, extortion, embezzlement, bribe taking, usurpation of state and peasant land, and various other forms of corruption and abuse of power. By the 1780s, roughly 80 per cent of the taxes col-lected were being siphoned off by tax farmers and officials, while only around 20 per cent reached the Ottoman treasury, with the result that by then the revenues of the Ottoman state were only about 10 per cent of those of the French state (McGowan 1997: 714). Consequently, the previously for-midable military-cum-economic power of the Ottoman Empire fell even further behind that of the rising European powers.

ALLEGED INSTITUTIONAL TORPOR OF THE OTTOMAN REGIME

It has often been argued that the root problem of the Ottoman Empire was that the institutions it created, while highly effective during its first two or three centuries, 'could not be developed and transformed to meet changing needs and circumstances' (Mansfield 1992: 27). Until the early nineteenth century, key institutions such as the janissaries, the *ulema*, the Sultanate, the royal household, the 'Ruling Institution' and the '*millet* system' proved remarkably resistant to reform. Furthermore, 'Attempts to reform and revive the empire actually contributed to its break-up and decline' (p. 27). The Ottomans were allegedly prisoners of their past. They eventually perceived the need for military, institutional and economic reforms, but the vested interests threatened by such reforms (on whom the Ottomans were to some extent dependent for social, political or religious support) insisted that what was needed was stricter observance of past precedents and practices. It is conventionally argued that, in contrast to the Tsarist Empire under Peter the Great (1689–1725) and the more intelligent of his successors (Elizabeth, Catherine II, Alexander II), the Ottoman regime 'failed' to remodel itself on supposedly Western lines, because it was more constrained by the growing conservatism of its hitherto 'successful' official religion, because it could look back on a greater imperial past from which it was harder to escape, and because 'no Peter the Great came to the Ottoman throne who was willing . . . to use the autocratic powers of his office for revolutionary purposes' (Coles 1968: 185, 172).

Until the early nineteenth century, therefore, the Ottomans allegedly clung to the crumbling pillars of an outmoded social order which was 'well past its sell-by date'. Furthermore, when the Ottoman state finally did attempt to reform itself during the nineteenth century, it was allegedly more concerned with promoting stronger, more efficient and (increasingly) autocratic government than with promoting liberty, independent local initiative and private enterprise (Lewis 2002: 59). In 'failing' to foster an 'enterprise culture', and in attempting to maintain a paternalistic autocratic state, the Ottoman regime allegedly displayed a deep-seated inability to emulate the successes of its major European rivals.

However, the major proponents of this type of explanation of the relative decline of the Ottoman Empire seem to overlook the degrees to which its most immediate and threatening rivals, namely the Tsarist and Habsburg empires, were also increasingly controlling, bureaucratic and militaristic autocracies which were similarly uninterested in promoting liberty, independent local initiative and private enterprise. There were more parallels than differences between them.

THE HAREM AND THE ALLEGED DEBILITY OF OTTOMAN SULTANS

In western and central Europe the growth of bureaucracy and representative government was diminishing the importance and influence of monarchs. However, the Ottoman state, which is still widely perceived to have remained essentially an autocratic 'war machine', remained unusually dependent on the calibre of its Sultans. 'For two and a half centuries a remarkable succession of ten outstanding rulers led the empire from victory to victory' (Stavrianos 1958: 118), but their successors included an astonishing number of 'incompetents, degenerates and misfits' (Lewis 1961: 23). This striking contrast has often been attributed to major changes in Ottoman practices. It was long the custom for each incoming Sultan to have all his brothers and half-brothers murdered (Ottoman polygamy ensured that these were usually numerous). This ruthlessness, going beyond the Byzantine tradition of having actual or potential rivals blinded, reduced the risks of contested successions, political instability, civil war and biological inbreeding. From the early seventeenth century onwards, however, this custom was replaced by the confinement of all royal princes, with the exception of the sons of the reigning Sultan, to the royal harem under the watchful eye of royal eunuchs. Stavrianos claimed that 'Inevitably, they became mental and moral cripples' (Stavrianos

1958: 118). The damage thus inflicted on the dynasty was compounded by a change in the succession law in 1617. Henceforth the throne was to pass to the eldest male member of the royal family. 'This meant that future Sultans were to be drawn . . . from the brothers, uncles and cousins, who had passed their lives in . . . degenerating seclusion . . . It was only natural that they should continue to depend on the peculiar companions of their boyhood. These . . . now became imperial favourites, using the puppet sultans as tools . . . Ottoman history henceforth was the history of endless strife between various individuals and cliques' (pp. 118–19). Confinement of royal princes to the royal harem remained Ottoman practice until the early nineteenth century, by which time it was allegedly too late to repair the damage.

However, these lines of argument have been greatly overplayed and may not hold water. The nature and supposedly debilitating significance of the Ottoman 'harem' was greatly exaggerated by Western male officials and other male visitors to Istanbul/Constantinople. Such men were naturally denied access to the 'harem' – the Sultan's private household – and, partly as a consequence of having no first-hand knowledge of it, some gave free rein to their male fantasies concerning its supposed Oriental exoticism, eroticism, sensuality and irrationality. However, considering the chronic inbreeding and often cumulative mental and physical deformity or 'degeneracy' which afflicted many European royal families (and has been poignantly portrayed in various Velazquez portraits of the Spanish Habsburgs), it is by no means certain that the later rulers of the Ottoman Empire can be compared unfavourably with their western and Central European contemporaries in terms of upbringing and physical, mental and moral calibre. Ottoman polygamy continually brought 'new blood' into the ruling family and thereby avoided the hazardous inbreeding prevalent among other European royal families.

REVISIONIST PERSPECTIVES ON THE DECLINE IN OTTOMAN POWER, PERFORMANCE AND ECONOMIC FORTUNES

In order to gain a fuller and more balanced understanding of the reasons for the military, economic and cultural 'decline' and 'retardation' of the Ottoman Empire and the Ottoman domains in the Balkans compared with the West and Central Europe, we need to look beyond narrowly institutional and cultural factors. Under Ottoman rule the predominantly Muslim and the predominantly Orthodox Christian areas of the Balkans undoubtedly lagged behind the economic, educational and cultural development of Western and Central Europe, but it does not follow that Ottoman rule was solely or even primarily responsible for this. The predominantly Roman Catholic areas of the Balkans, which were mostly under Austro-Hungarian rule, also lagged behind Western and Central Europe in most respects, although they did develop more vigorously than the Muslim and Orthodox Christian areas. Orthodox Christian Russia also lagged far behind Western and Central Europe, albeit under the strong and independent Orthodox Christian Tsarist regime. In truth, the 'decline' and 'retardation' of the Balkans and the Ottoman Empire also involved natural and environmental-cum-locational factors which were largely beyond the control of rulers. Partisan historians of the Balkans have neglected or underplayed the role of the 'politically neutral' factors which partly exonerate the major human actors, among whom they prefer to apportion 'blame'.

DEMOGRAPHIC CONTRACTION

The population of the Ottoman Balkans, having increased during the 'Pax Ottomanica' of the fifteenth and sixteenth centuries, allegedly fell catastrophically from at least 8 million in 1600 to fewer than 3 million by 1750, according to some influential estimates (Lampe and Jackson 1982: 37–8, 48–9; McGowan 1997: 652). Unfortunately, it is not clear to what extent these population estimates were directly or indirectly influenced by apocalyptic Balkan nationalist and/or Communist portrayals of the impact of Ottoman rule on the peninsula. Were they based on sober and detached calculations by disinterested parties? There has been insufficient discussion or evaluation of the sources and methods used in reaching these pivotal population estimates.

Population estimates for the Ottoman Balkans (as for the empire generally) prior to the nineteenth century are extremely unreliable. No census was taken in any part of the empire before 1831 (McGowan 1997: 652). Ottoman tax registers offer the only potential systematic basis for population estimates between the fifteenth and the late seventeenth century, but these only covered the non-Muslim population (because Muslims were exempt from the main taxes) and only counted households (irrespective of size) rather than individuals. The most eminent Turkish historian has warned that it is 'not possible on the basis of these figures even to approximate the total non-Muslim population' (Inalcik 1997: 25). Estimates have been made, nonetheless. Ottoman poll tax registers recorded that there were 674,000 non-Muslim households liable to the poll tax in the Ottoman Balkans in 1491, and Inalcik has suggested that if 6 per cent of the population was tax exempt and if there were five persons per household, this would indicate a non-Muslim population of approximately 4 million in the Ottoman Balkans in 1491 (p. 26). However, even allowing for the Pax Ottomanica and a significant influx of Muslim inhabitants in the interim, this calls into question the above-quoted estimate of a population of 8 million in the Ottoman Balkans in 1600, a mere 109 years later. The average size of household and the Muslim and non-Muslim shares of the population are both likely to have changed considerably over time, especially as large-scale migration, warfare, epidemics and economic crises inevitably had differing effects on different sections of the population, making it virtually impossible to make reliable inter-temporal comparisons. After 1695 the tax registers shifted from a household to a per capita basis of assessment for the poll tax (McGowan 1997: 713), which makes comparisons of eighteenth-century tax-based population estimates with the pre-1695 household-based ones even more hazardous. All we can reliably assume is that the population of the Ottoman Balkans was generally rising during the fifteenth and sixteenth centuries and generally falling during the seventeenth and early eighteenth centuries. More extreme claims tell us more about the unreliability of the data on which they are based than about what was actually happening on the ground.

A leading Turkish scholar has attributed the nonetheless considerable population contraction of the Ottoman Empire to such factors as the spread and/or rising incidence of anarchy, lawlessness, insecurity, impoverishment and epidemics, and the consequent mass migrations of peasants from fertile but exposed lowlands to the relative safety of remote but infertile highlands and to the adjacent Austro-Hungarian and Russian empires (Faroqhi 1997: 442). Crisis-induced migration or 'flight' must have had crippling effects on the economic and fiscal base of the Ottoman state, severely reducing its capacity to hold its own against the increasingly powerful Habsburg and Tsarist empires.

However, this seventeenth- and early eighteenth-century population contraction was by no means peculiar to the Ottoman Balkans. It roughly coincided with similar demographic downswings across Spain, the southern half of Italy, eastern France, Germany, Poland and Hungary (Hobsbawm 1965: 7). In particular, Italy and the Iberian Peninsula experienced broadly comparable economic decline, impoverishment, vulnerability to plague epidemics, climatic cooling (the so-called 'Little Ice Age' of the seventeenth and early eighteenth century), and widespread banditry and insecurity (Hobsbawm 1965: 7, 18; Cipolla 1970: 121–6, 177–9, 196–214; Cipolla 1976: 233–43; Faroqhi 1997: 467). What seems to be most distinctive in the Balkan case is the large scale of the population migrations or flights which took place. These were undoubtedly exacerbated by the incipient military contest between the Ottoman, Habsburg and Tsarist empires for control of the Balkan Peninsula. The resultant warfare repeatedly displaced substantial numbers of inhabitants and cumulatively weakened the Ottoman Empire to the benefit of its European rivals between 1686 and 1920. It has also been argued that the Muslim inhabitants of the Balkans bore the brunt of the impact of plague and other infectious diseases, partly because they lived mainly in towns and partly because they reacted with unusual fatalism or passivity to such diseases, and that this further weakened their capacity to retain control of the Balkans during the eighteenth and nineteenth centuries (McNeill 1979: 176–7).

Even though Balkan commerce and population began to grow again in the eighteenth century, this revival was based almost entirely upon the export of primary commodities, which reinforced the increasingly dependent and peripheral position of the Balkan Peninsula and the Ottoman empire as a whole in the international economic system.

THE RISE OF THE ATLANTIC ECONOMIES AND THE PERIPHERALIZATION OF THE BALKAN PENINSULA AND THE OTTOMAN EMPIRE

The eastern Mediterranean was probably the part of the world most adversely affected by the great shift or relocation of international trade routes away from the Black, Red and Mediterranean seas, following the rise of the Atlantic economies, the development of western European transoceanic sailing ships, and the western European voyages of discovery to the 'New World' and around Africa to India and the Far East. The Portuguese rounded the Cape of Good Hope in 1497, reached Calicut in India in 1498, seized Goa in 1510 and captured Malacca (the key to control of the main 'spice islands') in 1511. The Portuguese thus succeeded in 'outflanking' the traditional trade routes through the eastern Mediterranean and across Syria, Egypt, Asia Minor and Persia to the East. They also became a scourge upon Muslim traders in the Red Sea, the Gulf and the Indian Ocean, while their forts and garrisons established Portuguese dominion over southern Arabia and the Gulf region. Nevertheless, despite the arrival of these Portuguese predators and 'interlopers', the lucrative over-land Near Eastern spice trade between Europe, India and the south-east Asian 'spice islands' enjoyed a strong revival following the Ottoman conquests in Syria, Palestine, Arabia and Egypt in 1516–17. Spices travelled much better on the overland caravan routes than on the long, dank, storm-tossed ocean voyage around the Cape of Good Hope.

After the sixteenth century, however, the spice trade and associated tolls and revenues steadily declined in the wake of the north-west European 'fodder revolution'. Over much of northern Europe new root crops and farming practices gradually made fresh meat available throughout the year, with the result that 'spices were no longer so essential to mask the taint of over-ripe meat' (Jones 1981: 179). In addition, from the seventeenth century onward, 'the establishment of Dutch and British power in Asia and the transference of the routes of world trade to the open oceans deprived Turkey of the greater part of her foreign commerce and left her, together with the countries over which she ruled, in a stagnant backwater through which the life-giving stream of world trade no longer flowed' (Lewis 1961: 28).

The consequences were enormous. The eastern Mediterranean and the Black Sea regions, which had long been the hub of inter-continental commerce, suffered much more than a quantitative contraction of commerce, shipping and entrepôt activities. They also largely missed out on the qualitative development of the Atlantic economy and the 'New World', together with the crucial stimuli and additional resources which the latter conferred (almost exclusively) on Western Europe. As Eric Jones has emphasized, the storehouse of natural resources in the 'New World' was 'broken into once and for all' by West Europeans, who appropriated these additional resources and markets in ways and on a scale which other parts of the 'Old World' could never repeat. This was a *one-off windfall*, and western Europeans got there first. Furthermore, the development options and possibilities of Western Europe were transformed by the additional fisheries, metal ores and forest products, natural fibres and food crops, and the expanding opportunities for commerce and capital accumulation which were made available by West European penetration and conquest of the 'New World' and, to a lesser degree, Asia (Jones 1981: 81–4). The Atlantic seaboard location and the adventurous, predatory and systematically exploratory and innovative maritime orientation of the

West European states gave them 'relatively cheap access to the rich, graspable resources of the Americas and the oceans and to large external markets' (pp. 227, 79–80).

This helped most of the north-western European states to sustain greatly expanded non-agricultural populations who were engaged in developing the manufacturing, mining, construction and service sectors of their economies. Thus the Mediterranean basin (including the Balkans) ceded its former position as the most urbanized macro-region in Europe to the rising Atlantic powers. In addition, transoceanic navigation provided powerful stimuli to the development of mathematics, astronomy, optics, clocks, cartography, time-keeping and physics, which in turn made possible many of the advances of the seventeenth-century (mainly, though not exclusively, north-western) European 'Scientific Revolution' and the emergence of more secular and scientific cultures in north-western Europe and a few adjacent areas (Cipolla 1970b). These changes assisted north-western Europe to steal a march both on the Mediterranean world and on largely landlocked East Central Europe in the scientific, commercial and later industrial revolutions. The types of shipping (including slave-powered galleys) and the navigation technologies which were still prevalent on the Mediterranean and Black seas were unsuitable for transoceanic trade.

RELEGATION TO DEPENDENT PRIMARY EXPORT ECONOMIES

The increasingly passive dependence of the Balkans on an exchange of primary exports for industrial imports culminated in the Anglo-Ottoman Trade Treaty of 1838, which gave Britain and other European powers the right to trade throughout the Ottoman domains, subject only to minor anchorage fees and a 3 per cent *ad valorem* tariff on imports. This opened the door to foreign economic domination of the Ottoman Empire, largely eliminated two of the main sources of Ottoman state income (revenue from import duties and revenue from state monopolies) and effectively debarred the state from protecting Ottoman industries against foreign competition. 'As European manufactures flooded in, the traditional handicrafts and textile industries suffered' and, although merchants and bankers profited from the countervailing growth of foreign demand for raw materials and of urban demand for food, 'much of the newly created wealth accrued to foreigners' (Mansfield 1992: 57, 65–6, 69).

These setbacks contributed to the gradual transformation of the Ottoman Empire and the Balkan 'successor states' into financial and commercial 'dependencies' or 'appendages' of Europe's advanced capitalist states. They became increasingly passive providers of food and raw materials for western and central European towns and industries and of outlets for western and central European manufactured goods and capital. During the second half of the nineteenth century, moreover, the Ottoman Empire became what would now be called a 'Third World debtor state', constantly in danger of having to default on its increasingly onerous foreign debt and debt-service payments (as it actually did in 1875). This had the usual damaging and demoralizing effects on investors' and business confidence, encouraging both Balkan and 'foreign' capitalists to concentrate on short-term and/or speculative commodity and property dealings rather than longer-term productive and infrastructural ventures.

NATURAL, ENVIRONMENTAL AND LOCATIONAL FACTORS IN BALKAN DECLINE

In as much as Balkan economic 'decline' and 'retardation' were partly attributable to centuries of environmental or ecological damage caused by over-grazing, deforestation and soil erosion on Balkan hillsides, millions of Balkan peasants and landowners must have played a part (albeit unwittingly and perhaps somewhat ineluctably) in an ecological vicious circle.

The mainly hilly or mountainous Balkan terrain was mostly considered unsuitable for cultivation.

Balkan landowners and hill farmers therefore kept relatively large numbers of sheep and goats (and, to a lesser extent, pigs, donkeys and mules). These animals, however, tend to close-crop grass and nibble at any foliage, young shoots and little saplings, often denuding hillsides of their natural vegetation cover, while their hooves loosen soil and small stones. This in turn makes it easier for soil to be washed away by the (sometimes torrential) Mediterranean rainfall and for the shortened grass to be scorched dry by the fierce summer sun, while the reduction in soil and vegetation cover also increases the loss of groundwater through evaporation and 'run off'. The ensuing desiccation of soils and vegetation in summer increases the risk of forest and bush fires and deforestation, while the latter further reduces soil retention, moisture retention and humidity and may lead to a drier climate. As a result, formerly lush and/or forested hillsides and mountainsides are indeed rendered suitable only for sheep, goats, donkeys and mules. The ecological damage steadily intensifies until the increasingly barren and desiccated terrain can no longer support even these hardy animals. They are then moved on in search of fresh pastures, on which the vicious circle can start all over again.

These appear to have been the basic mechanisms by which the Balkans (like most of Mediterranean Europe and the North African Littoral) have suffered from many centuries of cumulative ecological damage, transforming vast tracts of formerly lush, humid and fertile terrain into barren scrubland on which not even sheep, goats, donkeys and mules can thrive. The consequences have also been aggravated by more than two thousand years of uncontrolled felling of trees for fuel and timber-built dwellings, boats and ships. In the Balkans, as elsewhere in the Mediterranean basin, only quite draconian conservationist regimes could have averted the ecological devastation caused (largely inadvertently) by many millions of landowners and hill farmers over the centuries. However, it is unlikely that either the Ottomans or Byzantium or any of the other polities which have ruled the region could have enforced the necessary restraint, even if they had fully understood the need for it. It is conceivable that only some form of 'eco-fascism' could have done so.

In any case the long-term result was the gradual impoverishment of the Balkan highlands, which in turn reduced the potential rural tax base of the Balkan states and rural demand for the products of Balkan towns and craft industry and, on the supply side, restricted the potential resource base of Balkan processing industries reliant upon agricultural raw materials. This set the stage for the widespread depopulation of the degraded Balkan uplands through mass emigration in recent times and further reduced potential rural investment in education, infrastructure and market integration. Moreover, the negative consequences were not confined to the Balkan uplands, although until recently that was where much of the population lived.

The often marshy Balkan lowlands, on the other hand, were particularly prone to plague, malaria, scarlet fever, diphtheria and other epidemic diseases. The impressive drainage, aqueducts and other 'water works' of Roman times show what could have been done to develop the Balkan lowlands, but under medieval Byzantine, Bulgarian and Serbian rule, as well as under Ottoman rule, they were allowed to fall into disrepair and decay. This, combined with long periods of endemic disorder and warfare, was what had encouraged much of the Balkan population to migrate to less fertile but usually safer and healthier high ground. The fact that Ottoman taxation, like Byzantine taxation before it, fell much more heavily on arable land than on pasture also encouraged many peasant farmers to take to the hills and mountains, where taxes were harder to impose and collect. However, such responses merely increased the population pressure, over-grazing and ecological damage on the Balkan uplands.

Furthermore, the Mediterranean climate, thin soils and rugged terrain of most parts of the Balkans were inherently less suited to the new root crops (turnips, swedes, beets and potatoes), grasses, clovers, crop rotations, heavier ploughs, bigger horses, larger carts and elaborate mixed-farming systems which lay at the heart of the north-west European agricultural revolution than were the more temperate climate, deeper soils and gently undulating hills and plains of most parts of north-western Europe. Some significant new crops (e.g. maize, cotton and tobacco) were widely adopted by Balkan farmers in the seventeenth and eighteenth centuries. Yet, unlike the new crops adopted in north-western Europe, they lacked the potential to 'revolutionize' Balkan agriculture. The real Balkan agricultural revolution had to wait until the widespread development of modern irrigation, flood control, drainage, mechanization, tractors, paved roads, fast transport, horticulture, hydroponics, plastic sheeting and rural mass education between the 1950s and 1980s, both in the Communist-ruled Balkans and in Greece.

OTTOMAN LANDHOLDING SYSTEMS REVISITED

Since the 1970s revisionist agrarian research on the Ottoman Empire has increasingly indicated that the growth and significance of the so-called '*çiftlik* system' has been greatly exaggerated and misunderstood. The term *çiftlik* was used to cover anything from quite a small farm to a large estate to a property which was not directly farmed by its owner but served merely as a source of rents and dues from various types of tenant and share-cropper. It is therefore doubtful whether it deserves to be characterized as a 'system'. More importantly, its emergence seems to have been limited to areas offering favourable opportunities for commercial agriculture, initially orientated not so much towards European export markets as towards the major and more accessible urban market of Constantinople/Istanbul (Faroqhi 1997: 447–8). Indeed, *çiftlik* agriculture was largely absent from Serbia, Montenegro and Romania, while in Bulgaria it 'covered just 20 per cent of the cultivated land in the regions where it was most widespread and as little as 5 per cent elsewhere'. No more than 10 per cent of Bulgarian peasants were subject to the so-called '*çiftlik* system', and the typical *çiftlik* in southern Bulgaria, north-eastern Greece and Macedonia, where the terrain was most suitable for arable farming, was rarely more than 6 to 12 hectares (Lampe and Jackson 1982: 34–7; cf. McGowan 1981: 69–79). To put this in comparative perspective, the typical *çiftlik* was smaller than the average Russian peasant landholding (11 hectares in 1905) and not much more than the average-sized French farm (8.7 hectares in 1882) (see comparative data on farm sizes in Bideleux 1987: 238–40). As late as the eighteenth century, 'the vast majority of agricultural units were very small . . . Even in limited zones where monocultures such as cotton were characteristic, a larger unit might only be an agglomeration of smaller ones, without implying any change in land use or in technique. There was virtually no "high farming" on the Ottoman scene' (McGowan 1997: 681).

Furthermore, the growing power, income and wealth of provincial *ayans* ('notables' or 'potentates') and prominent Ottoman officials emanated not so much from changes in landholding as from fiscal extortion, protection rackets, bribery and embezzlement, all exacerbated by much reduced central control over provincial officials, landholders and tax collectors and by greatly increased reliance on tax farmers (Lampe and Jackson 1982: 37). These circumstances were reviving deeply entrenched neo-Byzantine traditions of corruption and extortion which have continued to afflict public life in the Balkans and Turkey to this day. In terms of depriving both the state and the peasantry of desperately needed income, the effects were at least as detrimental as those caused by the alleged changes in landholding and rural social structure would have been, but the root causes of the economic and fiscal damage were not the ones traditionally alleged. Far from *facilitating* the establishment and consolidation of private property in land, the growing conditions of anarchy, insecurity and lawlessness actually *impeded* the development of private property and private enterprise. This contributed to the increasing economic 'backwardness' of the Balkans vis-à-vis Western and Central Europe.

The tax farmers, money-lenders, merchants, judges, officials, janissaries and other (often former) soldiers who were emerging as local potentates and entrepreneurs simply took the line of least resistance – and least risk. They generally found it much easier to exploit *in situ* (through rents, share-cropping and extortion rackets) the peasants living on the landholdings they were acquiring, rather than to evict the peasants and turn the newly acquired 'farms' or 'estates' into more fully fledged and directly managed capitalist enterprises, owing to (i) the lack of clarity and the poor enforceability of Ottoman property laws, (ii) the difficulties in the way of evicting sitting peasants from usurped lands, (iii) poor transport conditions (and hence high transport costs), and (iv) the still restricted scope for export-orientated agriculture.

> It was often sufficient to abolish peasant security of tenure . . . Thereafter, everything the peasants produced beyond minimum subsistence requirements could be 'creamed off' by the *çiftlik*-holder. But the refusal of the Ottoman central administration to promote or legalize peasant dispossession, combined with limited commercial opportunities, made it unattractive for local power-holders to acquire landholdings in their own name, that is, carry peasant dispossession to its logical extreme. As a result, legal, semi-legal and illegal forms of rent payable by peasant smallholders remained the typical manner in which agricultural products were appropriated by the politically dominant group. Thus, local power-holders only rarely made the transition to agricultural entrepreneurship. (Faroqhi 1997: 448–51)

Increasingly protracted and disruptive warfare, endemic banditry and rising societal turbulence and insecurity, along with mass flight and other forms of migration, rendered unenforceable the sixteenth-century Ottoman regulations binding peasants to their villages and to the land (Faroqhi 1997: 436).

These factors, along with the absence of a hereditary landed nobility with a strong *esprit de corps* and a durable established power base, rendered a full-blown 'second serfdom' of the sort that emerged in East Central Europe and in Russia largely unworkable in the Ottoman Balkan context (Faroqhi 1997: 550). Admittedly, Fernand Braudel claimed that the Ottoman *çiftlik* system 'produced cereals, first and foremost' and that 'cereal-growing, in Turkey as in the Danube provinces or in Poland, when linked to a huge export trade, created from the first conditions leading to the "new serfdom" . . . These large estates everywhere debased the peasantry' (Braudel 1975: vol II, p. 725). His son-in-law Traian Stoianovich similarly claimed that in the Balkans 'from the second half of the sixteenth to the early part of the nineteenth century, the intermediate categories between the "freemen" and the slaves again grew in number, giving rise to what is sometimes described as the "second serfdom"' (Stoianovich 1967: 160–1).

However, Braudel's argument was based on a false analogy. 'There is no evidence at all to suggest that the [Ottoman agrarian] system was inspired by contemporary examples in Eastern Europe beyond the Danube, despite the fact that the [re-]shaping of the Ottoman land regime is simultaneous with the vast enserfments of Eastern Europe' (McGowan 1981: 46). The Balkan *çiftlik* properties were much smaller than the landed estates of East Central Europe and Russia and never gave rise to the lordly manor house cultures and hereditary castes of landed noble families that emerged in the latter regions (see pp. 104).

The initial impetus for the shift from *timar* to *çiftlik* forms of landholding was *internal* to the Ottoman Empire, responding to the growing obsolescence and redundancy of the *timar*-holding *sipahi* cavalry, and it *slightly pre-dated* the rise of the second serfdom in East Central Europe and Russia, which it therefore could not have *emulated*. The new Ottoman landholding system was thus 'home grown', not 'borrowed' or 'copied' from Europe. The Ottoman state 'did *not* erect a second serfdom, as Braudel supposed. It had no interest in doing so, since the government was not simply the instrument of a landholding class and had nothing to gain . . . from the degradation of the peasantry' (McGowan 1981: 73). Furthermore, the development and territorial extension of the *çiftlik* system was severely hampered by Ottoman restrictions on the exportation of grain from 1604 to 1829 (p. 36), by poor transport facilities, by Ottoman exclusion of foreign shipping from the Black Sea from 1475 to 1783 (p. xi), by the severe seventeenth-century population decline in the Ottoman domains (resulting from disease, warfare, banditry and mass migrations to safer havens), and by the resultant labour shortages. Thus, like Wallerstein in relation to East Central Europe (see pp. 17, 162–3), Braudel almost certainly *exaggerated* the geographical extent of the so-called 'second serfdom' and imagined that grain exports became the basis of this 'second serfdom' *about two or three centuries earlier than they actually did.* In the case of the Ottoman Empire, as in Russia, Hungary and Romania, grain exports became quantitatively important only during the nineteenth century, two centuries *after* the emergence of the *çiftlik* system.

The only parts of the Balkans where substantial 'second serfdoms' emerged were in Croatia (which, as part of the Habsburg Empire, was strongly influenced by Hungary), in Bosnia and in the semi-autonomous principalities of Wallachia and Moldavia (the core territories of modern Romania). Even in Wallachia and Moldavia, however, the economically dependent Romanian peasantry who worked on landed estates in the fifteenth and sixteenth centuries 'cannot really be called serfs because they retained some right to property and could even change their place of domicile' (Sugar 1977: 117). As the Romanian boyars (estate-owners) became more powerful and increased their demands for dues in cash, kind and labour during the seventeenth century, 'the peasantry was pushed down almost to the level of serfdom' (p. 126). However, the continuing high level of peasant mobility (including ease of flight to adjacent territories) made it difficult to enforce the serf laws which had been enacted in 1600 (McGowan 1997: 683). Between 1741 and 1746, for example, Wallachia lost half its peasant families through emigration (Sugar 1977: 137), and the full juridical enserfment of the Romanian peasantry on the 'second serfdom' model did not take place until the second half of the eighteenth century (pp. 137–8), when Wallachia and Moldavia became more integrated into the international economy and the opportunities for agricultural exports produced by forced labour expanded significantly.

What stands out most clearly from all of this is that the potentates who emerged and held sway over Balkan rural society under Ottoman overlordship, as in the previous Byzantine Empire, owed their power, positions and wealth not primarily to ownership or control of the land, but rather to their roles and prerogatives as agents of the state – whether as officials, military officers, judges or tax farmers. They enriched themselves at the expense of the peasantry, craftsmen, small merchants and the state mainly by embezzlement, by taking bribes, by running extortion rackets, and by levying far more in taxes and/or fines than they actually paid over to the treasury – that is mainly by blatantly corrupt practices based upon naked abuse of unlimited or unregulated power. In so far as they owned land, this was much more a *manifestation* than a *source* of their power and wealth. Furthermore, partly because the Ottoman rulers, like their Byzantine predecessors, insisted on (and for long periods succeeded in) maintaining 'eminent domain' over all land, it was relatively difficult for 'the powerful' under Byzantine and Ottoman rule to convert their state-provided positions of power and influence into *independent and secure landed wealth.* The same holds for rich merchants. Under the Ottomans 'even the largest merchants could not rival a middle-level member of the political class such as a junior governor (*sancabeyi*) in terms of wealth, to say nothing of officials higher up in the administrative hierarchy . . . Throughout the sixteenth and seventeenth centuries, even wealthy merchants remained under the control of the political class' (Faroqhi 1997: 546). Therefore, *the rich and powerful remained subservient to the state, on whose favour they continued to depend* to maintain and exploit their power and positions for financial gain, and consequently *private property in land and venture capital never became as securely and independently established as it did in western Europe.*

The primary orientations of 'the powerful' (*les puissants*) were towards *office, influence, corruption and extortion*, rather than towards productive investment and entrepreneurship – hence the conspicuous absence of 'improving landlordism' and 'high farming' in the Balkans. West European landed nobilities may have been just as rapaciously *exploitative* as Byzantine and Ottoman officials, military servitors, tax farmers and other intermediaries – we have no way of knowing. What has distinguished the majority of potentates in the Balkans, as in many other parts of the world which remained ensnared in severely dysfunctional and debilitating vertical power relations and power structures, is that they have remained largely *parasitic, non-developmental, rent-seeking, clientelistic* and tenaciously supportive of the status quo and of enervating forces of inertia.

The tenacious and deeply entrenched 'verticality' of Balkan power relations and power structures has been the chief cause of Balkan 'retardation' or 'relative backwardness' compared with western Europe. The origins of such power relations and power structures can be traced back to the late Roman period, when the Eastern Roman state intervened in the economy in order to promote economic development and ward off 'barbarian threats'. They unrelentingly persisted or reasserted themselves during the protracted declines of the Byzantine and Ottoman empires and under the nationalist, fascist and Communist regimes which succeeded these empires. Once entrenched, they become very difficult to extirpate, as has been witnessed most recently in Serbia under Slobodan Milosevic, in Croatia under Franjo Tudjman, and in Romania under Ion Iliescu, to name only the most conspicuous examples. It is in the nature of such power systems that *high proportions of the population become ensnared and complicit in their maintenance, and come to regard bribery, corruption and extortion as 'normal' means of survival and enrichment*, partly because anyone sufficiently ruthless and skilful at 'playing the game' can participate. Such systems and practices are compatible with considerable upward social mobility, but their long-term effects are regressive, debilitating and inimical to development. Society becomes a captive to these corrupt and corrupting intermediaries and power-brokers, who have a strong interest in suppressing or at least emasculating any rival (and especially independent) sources of power and wealth. Thus the agrarian and fiscal systems which emerged during the later centuries of Ottoman rule in the Balkans can be seen to have gradually revived and entrenched *a neo-Byzantine 'verticality' of power relations and power structures*, generating the endemic and systemic bribery, clientelism, corruption and extortion that have continued to debilitate public life and economic development in most of the Balkans down to the present. However, far from regarding this situation as peculiar to the Balkans, we see it as the condition in which the great majority of humanity finds itself. Only a few parts of the world have had the good fortune to escape this plight by entrenching the 'horizontal' power relations and power structures which both make possible and draw sustenance from the rule of law, equality before the law, limited government, representative government, a civil society and a civil economy.

All in all, it is clear that the relative decline in Balkan and Ottoman economic fortunes from the seventeenth to the nineteenth century was in large measure a result of forces outside Ottoman control. It cannot be attributed largely to cultural and institutional factors, let alone to the actual or alleged deficiencies of Ottoman rule.

OTTOMAN 'SELF-STRENGTHENING' DURING THE 'LONG' NINETEENTH CENTURY

It is unsound to view the final century and a half of the Ottoman Empire (1774–1922) as 'all doom and gloom'. There were major positive developments, which need to be offset against the more widely publicized disasters and setbacks which contributed to the empire's steady disintegration between 1877 and 1919 and its final demise on 1 November 1922. The widespread assumption that 'the sick man of Europe' was terminally ill is questionable. If it had not been surrounded by imperialist vultures, awaiting recurrent opportunities to tear away and 'gobble up' large parts of its territory, it is conceivable that the empire could have retracted into its most defendable core territories in a less debilitating and more dignified manner.

Since the 1960s, many Turkish and some Western specialists on Ottoman history have depicted the late Ottoman Empire in an increasingly favourable light, emphasizing the various ways in which it was actively 'Europeanizing' its methods of government and public administration, its legal systems, its schools and universities, and its armed forces. This emphasis on late Ottoman 'Europeanization' has become increasingly linked to a wish to see present-day Turkey become – and become widely accepted as – a modern secular European state, sufficiently 'European' to be eligi-ble for membership of the European Union (in addition to NATO, the Council of Europe and the OSCE, in each of which it has been a longstanding and significant member).

The most assertively revisionist accounts of the final hundred years of Ottoman rule are those by Justin McCarthy (1997, chs 5, 6 and 9, and, more strongly, 2001, chs 1–2). Far from seeing the late nineteenth-century Ottoman Empire as terminally 'sick', he emphasizes that 'the Empire's economy and its population were growing', reversing a century or two of contraction. 'Its administrative system was being thoroughly overhauled and renewed. The numbers of teachers and doctors were growing. Railroad lines, roads, telegraphs and shipping were all increasing at a rapid pace. The Ottomans were making their first tentative steps towards representative government, well ahead of most of the world' (McCarthy 2001: 3). The number of pupils enrolled in 'new model' state schools rose from 16,000 in 1867 to 300,000 by 1913, by which date as many again were attending non-state *millet* and foreign schools, including 23,000 at American Christian missionary schools. This in turn furnished an expanding readership for the press and the burgeoning book trade (p. 18). During the absolutist reign of Sultan Abdulhamit II (1876–1909), whom many Western accounts dismiss as a dyed-in-the-wool reactionary, the railway network trebled in size, the all-weather road network grew sixfold, average life expectancy rose significantly, and European-style public build-ings proliferated to accommodate a modern government apparatus (pp. 28, 33). However, McCar-thy's writings show little sympathy for (or understanding of) Balkan and Armenian Christians and their 'struggles' against Ottoman overlordship. By writing about these peoples simply as enemies of the Ottoman state (and implicitly as fair game for the Ottoman forces of repression), he shows rather more sympathy for the casualties and sufferings incurred by the Ottomans' Turkish and/or Muslim subjects than for those inflicted upon Christian underdogs (pp. 42–74, 87–94, 106–12). Indeed, he bluntly declares that 'The Ottoman Empire was not sick; it was wounded by its enemies, and finally murdered' (p. 3). In McCarthy's account, the 'enemies' in question quite clearly include not only the predatory imperial powers, but also Ottoman subjects seeking equal rights, self-government or independence. However, he has rightly pointed out that the (often armed) struggles of Balkan peoples and the Armenians for greater rights and autonomy and/or secession resulted in millions of Ottoman Muslims (not just Turks) becoming refugees or even dying, and that these suf-ferings have tended to be overlooked or downplayed in most Balkan and Western accounts of the 'decolonization' of the Ottomans' Balkan domains (McCarthy 1995).

More balanced and judicious revisionism on the Ottoman Empire is to be found in work by Donald Quataert (1993, 2005), Bruce McGowan (1981, 1997), Caroline Finkel (2005a, 2005b), Erik Zürcher (2004), Daniel Goffman (2002) Colim Imber (2002), Michael Palairet (1997) and, most illuminatingly of all, the writings of various eminent Turkish historians, including Halil Inalcik (1969, 1991, 1997), Suraiya Faroqhi (1997, 2004, 2005), Sevket Pamuk (1987, 2000), Kemal Karpat (1972, 1984), Rifa'at Ali Abou-El-Haj (1991), Cemal Kafadar (1995), Resat Kasaba (1988) and Caglar Keyder (1991). In contrast to McCarthy, Kasaba explicitly acknowledges that 'the abusive nature' of the power of Ottoman *çiftlik* owners and financial intermediaries 'provoked antagonism from the peasantry, who in the Balkans were mostly Christians – as opposed to the usurpers, who were mostly Muslims' (Kasaba 1988: 27).

Even though the eighteenth-century Ottoman Empire was 'the sick man of Europe', it was not yet a 'helpless victim of circumstances beyond its control . . . Ottoman merchants succeeded in organiz-ing craft industries and setting up efficient networks for distribution, and European traders attempting to break into Ottoman markets often found them tough competitors . . . To put it differently, the Ottoman economy possessed potential of its own, and was not inert and defenceless . . . Ottoman mastery of the caravan routes permitted Ottoman merchants to build and control their own trading networks. Away from the coastal areas, European imports before the second half of the eighteenth century were unable to compete with locally produced wares' (Faroqhi 1997: 470, 480, 526).

During the nineteenth century 'the Ottoman economy, far from being in ruins, exhibited some very impressive signs of vitality' (Kasaba 1988: 1). From the 1840s to the 1870s, its exports rose faster than its imports (p. 87). Ottoman exports of hand-made fine textiles, yarns and leather goods remained 'highly sought after' in Europe until the late eighteenth century and, after a sharp decline of Ottoman exports of hand-made goods between the 1790s and the 1840s, there was a strong growth of Ottoman exports of machine-made silk and carpets from the 1850s to 1914 (Quataert 2005: 135). There was also a dramatic growth and professionalization of the Ottoman state apparatus: the number of Ottoman 'civil officials' rose from 2,000 in the late eighteenth century to between 35,000 and 50,000 in 1908, while the number of 'army personnel' rose from 24,000 in 1837 to 120,000 in the 1880s (Quataert 2005: 62–3).

In addition, Georges Contogeorgis has emphasized the resilience and durability of what he calls the '*cosmosystème hellénique*' (rooted in the Greek city-based maritime mercantile tradition) from the Byzantine era through Ottoman times down to the present: 'Dans l'espace vital hellénique, la cité servit un nouvel apogée des sociétés grecques, à partir de XVIIe siècle, de manière à encourager l'élaboration . . . d'un projet de remplacement . . . du pouvoir despotique ottoman par un cosmopolitéia grecque . . . Le monde grec de la cité contrôle l'économie de l'Empire ottoman, constituant une des plus puissantes classes bourgeoises de l'époque, la seule de nature oecuménique et non pas "nationale", dont l'action se déploie aussi en Russie, dans l'espace austro-hongrois et tous le long des côtes méditerranéennes' (Contogeorgis 2003: 116). Indeed, 'the position of Constantinopolitan, insular [island-based] and maritime Greeks became stronger after 1650 than ever before' (Stoianovich 1960: 269), as Greek merchants and shipowners came to dominate Balkan, Aegean, eastern Mediterranean and Black Sea commerce and shipping.

These perspectives parallel the revisionist claims which are increasingly being put forward vis-à-vis seventeenth-, eighteenth- and nineteenth-century India, China and Japan (usefully synthesized in E.L. Jones (1988) and Pomeranz (2000)). During the seventeenth and eighteenth centuries the major 'Oriental empires' (Ottoman, Habsburg, Russian, Chinese, Mughal and Japanese) were not nearly as torpid, despotic, static, monolithic and non-capitalist as Western 'Orientalism' would have us believe. Western military and economic superiority was still incipient rather than decisive, and was not yet sufficient to allow the West to exercise a pervasive tutelage over these eastern empires or to penetrate their markets very deeply, not least because transport difficulties and costs still gave the eastern empires considerable natural protection against foreign commercial penetration. During the eighteenth century these 'eastern empires' experienced significant population growth, major expansions of their cultivated areas and livestock herds, increasing commercialization, interregional specialization, and widespread proto-industrialization. They were by no means 'realms of darkness', and they contributed to and shared in many of the economic and technological advances of the incipient scientific and industrial revolutions, which were by no means confined to the West (these themes are developed in Pomeranz 2002, Goody 1996 and Frank 1998, for Asia; in Good 1984 for the Habsburg Empire; and in Blanchard 1989 for the Russian Empire). In the Ottoman Empire, as in Russia, the Enlightenment and rapidly advancing commercialization of the economy gradually overcame the former introversion, complacency, anti-modernism and anti-Westernism of Eastern Orthodox Christian culture(s) and helped to lock these empires into seemingly inexorable modernizing trajectories – for better or worse.

8 The emergence of Balkan national states, 1817–1913

THE RISE OF AUTONOMOUS MUSLIM REBELS AND RULERS

The innumerable military humiliations suffered by the Ottomans from 1687 onwards also contributed to the weakening of central imperial authority over the provinces. However, it was not among the Balkan Christians, but among the Sultans' Muslim subjects in North Africa, Anatolia, Albania, Syria, Lebanon, Kurdistan and the Arabian Peninsula that provincial independence was first asserted and went furthest. In Egypt, Syria, Albania, Anatolia, Baghdad and Basra ambitious provincial governors, military commanders or adventurous pashas, mainly members of the ruling Ottoman or Mamluk (Arabic for 'slave') military classes, took advantage of 'the remoteness and weakness of the Sultan's authority to intercept larger shares of the revenues of their provinces and to transform them into virtually independent principalities' (Lewis 1961: 37).

These Muslim rebels and usurpers were not, for the most part, popular or proto-nationalist leaders. Nevertheless, in remote desert or mountainous areas such as Albania, Arabia, Libya, Lebanon, Kurdistan and the Anatolian interior, Muslim potentates with strong local roots and some popular support did emerge. Either way, however, the Ottomans' loss of authority and prestige and their increasingly apparent incapacity to defeat 'infidel' foes made strong impressions on many Muslim rebels and opportunists. For the Sultans' non-Muslim subjects in the Balkans and Armenia, conversely, the long line of military humiliations was a cumulative demonstration of Ottoman vulnerability, eroding the initial mystique of Ottoman invincibility and emboldening Christian 'upstarts' to begin openly challenging Ottoman authority.

THE IMPACT OF NATIONALIST DOCTRINES IMPORTED FROM WESTERN AND CENTRAL EUROPE

To twentieth-century minds, conditioned to thinking in 'national' terms, the surprise is not that Balkan Orthodox Christians eventually rebelled against Ottoman rule, but that most of them accepted it for so long. Nationalism did not become a potent factor in Ottoman imperial disintegration until the nineteenth century. Before then few Bulgarians, Serbs, Albanians, Greeks, Armenians, Kurds, Arabs or even Turks had developed a sense of cultural or ethnic identity that was *national* (in the modern sense of belonging to a clearly defined and accepted 'nation'), rather than religious or parochial. Thus most of the Sultans' Christian subjects accepted Ottoman overlordship until the nineteenth century. Until then the many localized rebellions were inspired by personal ambition, opportunism or specific economic, social or political grievances, rather than by more broadly based national or proto-national sentiments capable of transcending parochialism.

Between 1805 and 1809 most of Croatia and Slovenia were conquered by Napoleonic forces and, from 1809 to 1814, were united under French jurisdiction as *les provinces illyriennes* – a name

Map 4   The Balkans and East Central Europe, 1815

harking back to Roman Illyricum and the ancient 'Illyrians'. French rule introduced civil equality before the law, abolished servile obligations, and initiated schooling in the 'Illyrian' language (as Croatian then became known) and the first newspaper in the 'Illyrian' (Croatian) language. French rule thus reawakened Croation and broader South Slavic ethno-cultural consciousness, which had diminished during the seventeenth and eighteenth centuries (Djilas 1991: 20–1).

Nationalism, which was propagated mainly in the wake of the French Revolution and the Napoleonic Wars under a combination of Western, German, East Central European and Russian influences, had an even more explosive impact in the Balkans than in Western Europe. Like the Habsburg Empire, the Ottoman Empire was not a cohesive embryonic nation-state commanding the *active* allegiance of most of its subjects, but rather an agglomeration of disparate semi-autonomous groups. This reduced their willingness and capacity to resist foreign territorial encroachments, commercial penetration and military aggression. 'Since nationalism did not serve as a cement to hold the empire together, it functioned instead as a centrifugal force which eventually tore the empire apart. The absence of Ottoman nationalism left an ideological vacuum which was filled by the several Balkan, Arab and even Turkish nationalisms' (Stavrianos 1958: 130–1). Stanford Shaw emphasizes that 'National sentiment simply did not fit in with the order of society conceived of by even the most enlightened Ottomans of the time. They did not understand that nationalism had made impossible the maintenance of a millet system which had worked for centuries, no matter how much autonomy was to be given to each millet.' Increased autonomy for the separate *millets* could only accelerate imperial disintegration. From the 1870s to 1913, however, centralizing reformers took the opposite tack. They tried to reconcile the Balkan provinces to reductions in local autonomy 'by advocating an "Ottomanization" of the population, an end to the millet system and its replacement by a common citizenship for all subjects of the Sultan regardless of religion, race and class', but this was 'entirely rejected by Balkan nationalists' (Shaw 1963: 74). Thus the Ottoman Empire and Balkan nationalism were mutually irreconcilable forces. There was no way of satisfying the aspirations of both.

THE 'COMMERCIAL REVOLUTION' AND THE RISE OF CHRISTIAN AND JEWISH TRADERS AND 'MERCHANT CAPITALISM'

Under the impact of growing commerce with the rest of Europe and increasing anarchy and insecurity in the Ottoman provinces during the eighteenth century, each community or collectivity 'strove desperately to improve its own position, generally at the expense of other collectivities' (Stoianovich 1963: 625). The inability of the Ottoman state to resolve these conflicts eventually resulted in the revolutionary transition from an imperial social order based upon a rigid hierarchy of legally defined and strictly segregated social estates and religious communities, to new societies based upon more fluid social classes and national states (p. 625).

Stoianovich argues that a key factor in the 'spiritual and political awakening and cultural redirection of the Balkan peoples' was the growth of native merchant classes. Even though they comprised considerably less than 10 per cent of the population, 'they were the human catalysts that joined the Balkan peoples to Europe' both commercially and ideologically (Stoianovich 1960: 235). They financed 'the founding of schools and the dissemination of books in their respective national languages among their compatriots. They were also receptive to the ideas of the Enlightenment.' Some sought national independence 'even at the cost of social revolution' (p. 306). The eighteenth-century expansion of Western and Central European towns, populations and industry had expanded demand for Balkan primary exports of grain, hides, meat, wine, tobacco, vegetable oils, wax, raw silk, raw cotton, wool and timber, raising commodity prices and encouraging production of cash crops for export (p. 255). Maize and cotton cultivation expanded particularly rapidly. Growing European demand for Ottoman (and particularly Balkan) primary products, combined with the declining capacity of the enfeebled Ottoman state to provide effective stimuli, support and protection for

Ottoman (and especially Balkan) industries, transformed the Ottoman Empire (including most of the Balkans) into an exporter of food and raw materials and into an importer of 'European manufactured, processed, "colonial" and luxury goods, principally sugar, coffee, textiles, expensive Russian furs and Central European hardware and glassware' (p. 259). Even though these patterns of foreign trade contributed to a form of de-industrialization of the Balkans via the stagnation of many traditional craft industries, they nevertheless expanded the commercial opportunities for Balkan merchants, both as exporters and as importers. Indeed, 'Balkan merchants benefited from the change even more than European merchants' (p. 259). This was because foreign traders' ignorance of Balkan market conditions 'gave Balkan merchants . . . the opportunity to obtain control of most of the overland carrying trade, part of the maritime carrying trade and virtually the entire commerce of the Balkan interior. The commercial sector of the Balkan economy expanded, while the overall Balkan economy declined' (p. 263).

At first this expanding Balkan commerce was dominated by Greeks, Jews and Armenians. By the late eighteenth century, however, these groups had been joined by thrusting Serbian, Bulgarian, Macedonian, Bosnian and Albanian livestock dealers and muleteers and by Croatian and Albanian maritime traders, shipowners and seamen operating from the rugged Adriatic coast and islands, often as pirates (Stoianovich 1960: 269, 281, 283). Starting in the late eighteenth century, however, Ottoman/ Muslim landlords and officials attempted to choke off this expansion of Balkan Christian mercantile power, which was (correctly) perceived as posing a serious threat to Ottoman/Muslim social and political ascendancy (pp. 306–7). Perceiving their own interests to be threatened or poorly served by this Ottoman/Muslim ascendancy and reaction, 'Greek and Serbian merchants closed ranks temporarily with the peasantry and furnished the leadership of the Serbian (1804–15) and Greek (1821–29) wars of national liberation. By and large, however, both Greek and Serbian merchants favoured only limited social revolution. They desired to transfer property from the Turks and Muslims to themselves and, after that, to establish existing property on a secure basis' (p. 312).

THE GROWTH OF BALKAN BANDITRY, PIRACY AND REVOLUTIONARY CURRENTS

The mounting insecurity of life and property under Ottoman rule (particularly among non-Muslims) also revived (or reversed the former decline of) the extended family and the importance of kinship and clan associations such as the South Slav 'zadruga', especially in remote, rugged, highland and frontier areas (Stoianovich 1962: 631–2). This situation also strongly contributed to the growth of banditry and piracy in the Balkans and in the Adriatic, Ionian and Aegean islands. Visitors to these islands and adjacent mainland areas are constantly reminded of the extent to which they were used for piracy and of the fact that quite a few Adriatic and Aegean ports practically owed their existence to piracy. Thus in the early nineteenth-century Ottoman Balkans 'perhaps 10 per cent of the Christian population, at least in . . . the frontier areas, was organized militarily for the purpose of transforming or abolishing rather than defending the empire' (p. 632). These became the seed-beds of the Serbian and Greek national rebellions, which developed into Serbian and Greek wars of 'national liberation'. Moreover, when confronted with the tasks of bringing various Balkan clan, kinship, bandit, pirate, pastoral and trading associations under more unified and purposeful leadership and control, merchant, clan and bandit leaders engaged 'intellectuals' and publicists to propagate unifying nationalist ideologies and build up nationalist movements and organizations. These 'intellectuals' were among the early products of the new schools sponsored by Balkan merchants and/or had been educated abroad. There they had come into contact with the ideas of the European Enlightenment, the French Revolution and Napoleon's empire. Although they were far from numerous, they exerted an influence out of all proportion to their numbers. They managed to give the Balkan revolts 'a new ideological goal: the reorganization of society upon a class and national rather than a corporate and imperial basis . . . In this manner, the Balkan revolutions were fatefully linked to the French, or Western, Revolution' (p. 632). Above all they absorbed and propagated the idea of the national state as a body of individuals with equal rights and obligations before the law and divided into social classes on the basis of economic status and wealth, rather than rigidly segregated into social estates and religious communities prescribed and regulated by a supranational and theocratic imperial order.

THE IMPACT OF SECULARISM

Simultaneously, the gradual secularization of West European culture and ideas under the impact of the Renaissance, the Scientific Revolution and the Enlightenment paved the way for a sea change in the receptivity of Eastern Orthodox Christians to Western influences. 'So long as Western civilization was essentially Catholic or Protestant, it was unacceptable to Orthodox peoples. When it became primarily scientific and secular, it became acceptable, and even desirable, to a constantly growing proportion of the population' (Stavrianos 1963: 188). The eighteenth-century Enlightenment and the attendant growth of trade and contact with the West aroused demands for a reorientation towards Europe and 'pointed to a world beyond the horizons of the Orthodox East as a possible model for the future'. At the same time, however, this growing consciousness of 'alternatives beyond the world of Orthodox culture' planted anxieties and posed dilemmas which were to trouble modern Balkan consciences and fuel new (internal) ideological divisions and conflicts among the Balkan Orthodox peoples during the nineteenth and twentieth centuries (Kitromiledes 1995: 5).

TERRITORIAL FRAGMENTATION OF THE BALKAN PENINSULA

The Balkan national revolutions did not (and probably could not) take place in a clean sweep which might have permitted a quick and tidy reconstruction of Balkan societies on a uniform or consistent basis. Instead the revolutions proceeded erratically and sporadically during the whole period from 1804 to 1918 (and beyond), gradually embracing one locality after another and repeatedly exacerbating the political and religious/ethnic fragmentation ('Balkanization') of South-eastern Europe. These protracted, piecemeal and exceedingly disruptive processes were partly caused by external factors. These included Great Power rivalries and interventions, Austrian territorial expansion into the northern and western Balkans, the residual (albeit waning) power and influence of the Ottoman Empire and the attempts of several European Powers (including Britain) to prop up the 'sick man of Europe' (with the aim of blocking Russian imperial ambitions in the Balkans and of preserving an overall 'balance of power' in Europe). But they also reflected the very variegated ethnic geography, ethnic consciousness and social and economic conditions in the Balkans. Only once, during the Balkan War of 1912, did the major Balkan nations manage to unite against a common external foe, namely the Ottoman Empire. But that momentary unity was quickly followed by a 'fratricidal' Second Balkan War between the victorious Balkan states during 1913 and by an even more cataclysmic 'Third Balkan War' between 1914 and 1918, which engulfed Europe and precipitated the final dissolution of the Ottoman, Tsarist and Habsburg empires.

Not only were the Balkan provinces of the Ottoman Empire very diverse and disunited, but they also became 'ripe' for 'national revolutions' at widely separated junctures. Because of its close proximity to and economic dependence on Constantinople (Istanbul), Bulgaria was not ready for revolution until the 1870s. Moreover, the more divided, hesitant or even pro-Ottoman Muslim areas of Albania, Kosova, Bosnia and western Macedonia were not really 'ripe' for 'national' self-rule until well into the twentieth century. Albania had 'national' statehood thrust upon it in 1913, more as a result of Great Power rivalries than in response to native demands for national self-determination. In some respects, therefore, 'Balkanization' (including the wide scope for external interference

in Balkan affairs) was an inescapable consequence of the (inevitably) erratic, protracted and fragmentary unfolding of the Balkan 'national revolutions'. Discrete, relatively compact and homogeneous nation-states were (and still are) almost impossible to achieve in this exceptionally variegated,
strife-torn peninsula.

Nevertheless, against seemingly impossible odds, the Serbian and Greek revolutions 'effected
the almost complete transfer of property and property rights . . . to the new political classes and to
the peasantry . . . [and] . . . generated a current in favour of a new social order guaranteeing security
of property and founded upon the principles of freedom of contact, equality before the law, and
social mobility on the basis of free political and economic competition' (Stoianovich 1963: 312).
Although this new social order had to be 'fought for over and over again . . . many institutions
resembling those that had been introduced in Western Europe . . . were rapidly brought into being'
(Stoianovich 1967: 152–3). By engaging in struggles 'against domestic as well as foreign tyranny',
the nascent Balkan nations gradually succeeded in obtaining 'recognition of the principle of equality before the law' and the abolition of the former social hierarchy based upon hereditary legally
defined social status (p. 162).

'UNFINISHED REVOLUTIONS'

All the same, the Balkan national revolutions remained 'unfinished revolutions' in the sense that they
never fully established social structures that would have allowed them to consolidate and consummate
the formal/legal changes by fostering 'middle elements' that were 'sufficiently large, homogeneous
and independent . . . to be able to manage the abnormal social strains created by the two world wars,
a world economic crisis, Communist revolution, fascist counter-revolution, economic change, technological backwardness, a "population explosion" and conflict between a multiplicity of cultural and
political traditions' (Stoianovich 1967: 153). Indeed, many of the problems that arose after the 1860s
stemmed from 'the fact that equality before the law does not abolish economic inequality . . . [and yet]
. . . the latter inequalities were exacerbated by a "population explosion" which left the peasantries with
less and less land as they became more and more equal' (p. 162).

POPULATION EXPLOSIONS, SOCIAL DISCONTENT AND MASS EMIGRATION

The Balkan 'population explosion' exacerbated existing social, economic and ecological strains. In
the case of Serbia population density increased sixfold between 1800 and 1910 (Stoianovich 1967:
164), while that of Romania (Wallachia and Moldavia) rose fivefold between 1815 and 1912 (Stavrianos 1963: 200). By the 1900s the population was growing by about 1.5 per cent per annum in
each of the Balkan states; this was double the rate for the Austro-Hungarian Empire and 50 per cent
faster than the population growth of either Britain or Germany (Lampe and Jackson 1982: 164).
Consequently, in the case of Serbia, the forested area shrank by two-thirds between 1815 and 1900
and the per capita availability of meat, milk and beasts of burden fell by two-thirds over the period
1859–1905, forcing Serbs to switch to a more cereal-based diet (Stoianovich 1967: 89, 165). Such
changes, which also occurred in the other Balkan states, were closely interlinked with the resettlement of the long depopulated Balkan lowlands. But ecological damage continued apace, especially
in upland areas.

Nevertheless, because the Balkans had comparatively low population densities to begin with, the
Balkan states never became overpopulated in the Malthusian sense of being unable to feed their
burgeoning populations. On the contrary, except in the case of Greece, per capita production of
grain and potatoes remained comparatively high (Bideleux 1987: 250, table 11). Thus the Balkan
states became 'overpopulated' only in the sense that they could not provide livelihoods for all their
inhabitants, especially in rural areas where there was a growing pool of surplus labour. 'More

people were engaged in agriculture than were needed for the prevailing type of cultivation' (Stavrianos 1963: 200). This problem was exacerbated by a growing 'fragmentation' of peasant landholdings as they were passed on from generation to generation. Moreover, the smallness of Balkan industrial sectors (which employed less than 10 per cent of the workforce and contributed less than 10 per cent of national income in each of the Balkan states) meant that it was not possible to absorb surplus rural labour into industrial employment to any major extent before the First World War or even in the interwar period. In addition, although agriculture was far from becoming mechanized, there were numerous small improvements in modest agricultural equipment and implements (such as spades, hoes, scythes, sickles, carts, wheelbarrows, horseshoes and iron buckets). These improvements, together with the fact that farming was becoming more commercialized, cost conscious and productive, also helped to render growing proportions of the farm population underemployed or even superfluous.

In each of the Balkan states, therefore, there was increasing social discontent, both among the peasantry and among those who drifted to the towns in (frequently fruitless) quests for employment. 'The common dissatisfaction of Bulgarian, Serbian and Greek peasants appears to have been a shortage of money rather than food or other necessities; money not to pay taxes but to buy more manufactures and especially to buy more land, as a rational response to population pressure' (Lampe and Jackson 1982: 193). In Romania rural discontent erupted into a widespread peasant revolt in 1907, in which more than 10,000 people perished. In Bulgaria peasant discontent was channelled into growing support for the radical Bulgarian Agrarian National Union from 1900 until the early 1920s, when its leader, Stamboliski, established a violent but short-lived 'peasant dictatorship'.

Another consequence of the Balkan 'population explosion' was the growing stream of emigration from the Balkans to Western and Central Europe and, above all, to the 'New World'. Between 1876 and 1915 more than 319,000 Greeks, 92,000 Romanians, 80,000 Bulgarians and 1,380 Serbs emigrated to other continents. Thus about 10 per cent of the population of Greece had emigrated by 1912 (Lampe and Jackson 1982: 195–6), while as many as one-third of Montenegrin males did so (Stavrianos 1963: 206). Emigration was the Balkan safety-valve. It also generated reverse flows of return migrants and remittances, which in turn helped to fund trade deficits (particularly in Greece), new businesses and capital formation. On the other hand, emigration left behind unfavourable demographic structures. Those who emigrated were the bolder spirits, the potential entrepreneurs and able-bodied young males who had been nurtured and educated at Balkan expense.

THE 'RELATIVE RETARDATION' DEBATES

Most Balkan histories of the Balkans have rather simplistically blamed the economic, educational and technological 'backwardness' or 'retardation' of their region on the effects of Ottoman rule (Palairet 1997: 158). However, Peter Sugar has pointed out that it was not when the Ottomans were still in full control, but rather *during the nineteenth century* (when most of the region was being gradually 'liberated' from Ottoman rule) that the really striking disparities in terms of levels of development opened up between the Balkans, on the one hand, and north-western and Germanic Central Europe, on the other. There is much to be said for such a view. Interregional disparities in per capita levels of income and output widened *dramatically* as a result of the industrial revolutions which occurred in north-western and Germanic Central Europe during the late eighteenth and nineteenth century. In spite of the numerous allegations of Ottoman neglect, restrictions, repression and retardation of Balkan economic, educational, cultural and political development, until the nineteenth century most European countries were 'only slightly better off than those ruled from Istanbul' (Sugar 1977: 283). However, 'Intellectually, economically, and even politically, the "Balkans" lagged further behind "civilized" Europe and appeared much more "backward" in 1880 than they did in 1780' (p. 282).

Nevertheless, it is still conceivable that some of the effects of Ottoman rule, combined with the damaging consequences of the Balkan Wars and unsuccessful Ottoman attempts to hang on the Balkans, contributed to the alleged Balkan 'failure' to master and assimilate the economic and technical advances which occurred in north-western and Central Europe during the late eighteenth and nineteenth century. The latter clearly built upon prior developments or 'preconditions' which were conspicuously absent in the Balkans, and the Ottomans could therefore be 'accused' of having 'failed' to prepare the ground for nineteenth-century technological advance, industrialization, education and democratization. According to Sugar, 'the Ottoman period must be held responsible for bequeathing a totally inadequate, medieval manufacturing sector to the economies of the empire's successor states' (Sugar 1977: 285).

The Balkans, in common with Portugal, Spain and the Italian states (which during the sixteenth and seventeenth centuries lost their earlier leads in transoceanic navigation and commerce to England, Holland and France), were also handicapped by relatively low levels of educational provision compared with north-western and Central Europe, by the dead weight of their oversized, parasitic and obscurantist ecclesiastical hierarchies and numerous clergy and monastic complexes, by their relatively ineffective authoritarian systems of government, and by their relatively rugged, mountainous terrains, which constrained agricultural productivity and made inland transport and communications comparatively slow and expensive. These countries were short of navigable inland waterways, while the cost of constructing roads and railways over difficult terrain remained relatively high, thereby retarding market integration and the commercialization of the interior. For the most part, they also lacked the fortuitous combinations of coal and metal ore deposits which had given rise to numerous centres of heavy industry in north-western and Germanic Central Europe.

However, Charles Issawi has emphasized that, while the Balkans undoubtedly fell further *behind* north-western and Central Europe economically, educationally and technologically, by the same criteria they nevertheless pulled further *ahead* of other former Ottoman domains. 'Around 1800 the Balkans were in most respects no better off than most of the Middle East. Grain yields may have been slightly higher. Transport was probably no better: more carts were used and more rivers were navigable, but the terrain was muddier and rougher and camel transport was not available. In some areas, notably Bulgaria, handicrafts were more widespread, but the region lacked the high crafts of Istanbul, Cairo, Aleppo, and Isfahan. Literacy was probably slightly, though surely not much higher, but urbanization was far lower' (Issawi 1989: 16–18). By 1914, however, the Balkans had moved decisively ahead of the Middle East by most developmental criteria, perhaps partly because 'the Balkans obtained independence much earlier and, although Balkan governments were far from being models of stability and enlightenment, they were more responsive to national needs. They helped the economy by building infrastructure and extending credit and by bringing about some industrialization before World War I' (p. 17). Furthermore, 'an enormous majority of peasants came to own their land and, since for a long time population density was light, their plots were adequate'. Ownership of the land they cultivated gave peasant farmers powerful incentives to become more productive and in most of the Balkan states this tended to defuse the violent potential of class conflict. 'Only Romania had a large – and parasitic – landlord class and a very deprived peasantry, in spite of the agrarian reform law of 1864' (p. 17). The rapacious exploitation and oppression of vulnerable peasants by exceptionally corrupt and ruthless landlords and intermediaries ('arendas') is widely judged to have been the main underlying cause of the great Romanian peasant revolt of 1907, but in this regard Romania can be seen as the exception that proved the rule. In addition, the Balkan populations became 'distinctly more educated' than their Middle Eastern counterparts. By 1910 between 35 and 40 per cent of children aged five to fourteen were attending Balkan primary schools, and Balkan literacy rates surged ahead of those of Egypt, Anatolia and the rest of the Middle East. The Balkans have also had an 'important natural advantage over the Middle East:

higher and more regular rainfall, resulting in more forests, more water power and more navigable rivers' (Issawi 1989: 16–18).

Issawi's emphasis on the positive results of the fact that independent 'national' states emerged earlier in the Balkans than in the Middle East is compatible with our contentions that (i) the Ottoman conquest was not the chief cause of the relative retardation of the Balkans in comparison with the West, as this had begun before the Ottomans even appeared on the scene (see pp. 57–8, 63, 70), and (ii) in the main, Ottoman overlordship of the Balkans had merely perpetuated the Byzantine heritage (see pp. 77–9).

However, claims that economic development and educational advance were accelerated by the attainment of independent statehood have been strongly contested by Michael Palairet. He has demonstrated fairly cogently that Serbia, Bulgaria and Macedonia experienced moderate economic development during their respective final decades of Ottoman rule and that by the mid-nineteenth century Ottoman institutions were not inimical to private enterprise and economic development, whereas by contrast the economies of Serbia and Bulgaria regressed dramatically after they attained full self-government, as did the economy of independent Montenegro throughout the nineteenth century (Palairet 1997: 28–33, 41–57, 66–128, 142–52, 171–202, 298–370).

Where does this leave us? We conclude that, although the Balkans fell further behind northwestern and Germanic Europe economically and technologically from the eighteenth to the mid-twentieth century, they nevertheless pulled steadily ahead of their Middle Eastern neighbours; and the economically, technologically and educationally retarding impact of Ottoman rule, even for the nineteenth century, has often been greatly exaggerated, especially by Balkan historians of the Balkans.

THE PLIGHT OF THE PEASANTRY

According to Stoianovich, 'The only elements of the bourgeois rational society which seeped down to the peasant . . . were the power of the state to recruit, punish and tax' (Stoianovich 1963: 320–2). However, Stavrianos takes a more positive view of the consequences: 'The diffusion of the money economy . . . increased village contacts with the outside world and thereby affected the traditional pattern of village life. The peasant sensed that literacy was essential under the new order . . . Hence he readily accepted elementary schooling for his children whenever it was made available . . . The younger generation was soon questioning the assumptions and attitudes upon which peasant life had been based . . . A new spirit of individualism and a desire for self-advancement undermined the solidarity of village life and even of the family . . . Tea, coffee, sugar and other commodities lost their character as luxury goods and passed into more common use. Town-made lamps replaced home-made candles, and the more prosperous peasants also bought furniture and household utensils. Iron ploughs became more common, though the poorer peasants continued to use the home-made iron-shod variety. A few householders began to buy ready-made clothing . . . In some peasant homes even a few books began to appear' (Stavrianos 1963: 204).

These seemingly modest changes represented a radical break with the self-sufficiency of earlier decades and the end of the closed, introverted village worlds of medieval and early modern times. The *downside* of all this was that the spread of the money economy subjected Balkan peasants to the sometimes violent fluctuations of national and international markets. This increased rural economic inequalities, class differentiation and social (including ethnic) conflicts and antagonisms. Sadly, different ethnic groups which had often co-existed in relative peace and harmony for centuries were increasingly pitted against one another by market forces and by the scramble to create 'national' states and extend 'national' territories. Peasant 'land hunger' had *national* significance, as it still does in the Balkans today.

URBANIZATION, RAILWAYS AND INFANT INDUSTRIES

The newly independent Balkan states rapidly developed sizeable capital cities, standing armies, bureaucracies, railways and other trappings of modern statehood. Between 1878 and 1910, for example, the population of Bucharest expanded from 177,000 to 193,000, while that of Sofia rose from 20,000 to 103,000 and that of Belgrade from 30,000 to 90,000 (Lampe 1975: 72). Between 1885 and 1913 the value of foreign trade and budget receipts more than doubled in real terms in each of the Balkan states (except Greece), while per capita taxation roughly doubled (Spulber 1963: 348–9). Between 1870 and 1911 the railway network expanded as follows: Romania, from 248 to 3,479 km; Bulgaria, from 224 to 1,934 km; Serbia, from zero to 949 km; Greece, from 12 to 1,573 km (Mitchell 1978: 317–18). However, even in the 1920s the railway density per 1,000 square km remained much less than in Western and Central Europe: Albania, zero km; Greece, 22 km; Bosnia-Herzegovina, 25 km; Bulgaria, 28 km; Serbia, 29 km; Wallachia and Moldavia, 32 km; Croatia, 53 km; Transylvania, 55 km; Slovenia, 69 km; Italy, 67 km; France, 97; Germany, 123 km; Belgium, 370 km (Stoianovich 1967: 96). The underdevelopment of Balkan railways is sometimes attributed partly to the mountainous terrain, but we have not noticed any corresponding shortage of railways in even more mountainous Austria and Switzerland!

Stoianovich argues that nineteenth-century Balkan industrialization was stunted by the liberal Anglo-Ottoman trade treaty of 1837 and by the terms on which the new Balkan states gained Great Power recognition in 1878. In his view 'the highly industrialized countries' set out to impede Balkan industrialization 'by trying to preserve intact the provisions of the Congress of Berlin (1878), which denied Serbia, Bulgaria and Romania the right to establish protective tariffs' (Stoianovich 1967: 97). Elsewhere he claims that 'The Balkan states could not protect themselves against the competition of European manufacturers, either because existing treaties forbade them to erect protective tariffs . . . or because the bulk of their exports was earmarked for one or two European countries which could deprive them of a market if they tried to assert their economic independence. The . . . pursuit of a more coherent economic programme was therefore delayed until the end of the century' (Stoianovich 1963: 319).

However, the consequences were not quite as clear-cut as Stoianovich suggests. Some Balkan industrial development did take place in low-technology activities (such as food-processing, textiles, tobacco-processing, brewing and building materials), while Romania had developed the world's fifth largest oil industry by 1914. These were activities in which the Balkans enjoyed comparative cost advantages, thanks to the plentiful local availability of suitable raw materials and cheap labour. Free trade meant that the requisite industrial plant and equipment could be imported relatively cheaply from well-established low-cost foreign suppliers. Until well into the twentieth century the Balkan states lacked the capital, educational and technical resource base on which to build up sophisticated engineering and metallurgical industries. In such circumstances industrial protectionism would have been more likely to protect inefficient producers and the excess profits of local monopolists than to evoke dynamic entrepreneurship and successful innovation.

LUMPEN-BOURGEOISIES AND STUNTED CAPITALISM

Nevertheless, partly as a result of the stunted or retarded development of private enterprise, private capital and the middle classes, the forms of industrial capital which belatedly emerged in the newly 'independent' Balkan states were heavily dependent on state 'favours' and patronage, in the guise of selective protectionism, subsidies, lucrative contracts, tax exemptions, monopolies and privileged franchises. This provided very fertile ground for the luxuriant growth of corruption. This context was reinforced by extensive state ownership of public utilities, mines, forests, foundries, munitions plants and manufacturing enterprises. 'Far from being an autonomous force, [Balkan] capitalism was dependent upon the largesse of government bureaus and ministries . . . The capitalist class was dependent on the state; the state was dependent upon foreign capital' (Stoianovich 1963: 336). Balkan capitalists were thus no more 'independent' than were Balkan states.

In the Balkans, as in many developing countries in the Third World, the capitalist state was much more than a referee between competing interests and the provider of a minimum of law and order and public services. It became the ultimate patron, directing and controlling (as well as responding to) social and economic forces and pressures. That role, rather than democratic processes and 'mandates', was to provide the main sources of its power and legitimacy. It would also in part serve the interests of foreign capital or foreign 'imperialism'. Moreover, each of the Balkan states became heavily (and vulnerably) dependent on a very narrow range of primary exports (usually just two or three) to the main Western and Central European powers. The hazards of such dependence were to be brought home most painfully and fatefully in the 1930s.

WEAK STATES AND PERVASIVE CORRUPTION

Most of the Orthodox Christian populations of the Balkans gained and consolidated independent statehood and so-called 'self-government' between 1878 and 1914. The rest, along with most of the Roman Catholic and Muslim populations of the Balkans, had to wait until the final collapse of the Habsburg, Tsarist and Ottoman empires at the end of the First World War. The emerging 'national' states and cultures were quite aggressively demotic and strikingly free of aristocratic influence. Their preponderantly peasant cultures faced little competition from 'higher' aristocratic cultures (unlike Poland and Hungary). The native nobilities and Christian aristocratic cultures which had begun to flourish in the Balkans in medieval times had largely disappeared in the course of four to five centuries of Muslim-Turkish domination. Only the churches and the oral traditions of the Balkan peasantry had preserved the tattered remnants of the medieval Balkan Christian cultures.

The leaders of the newly 'independent' Balkan peoples generally made some attempt to mould nation-states on Western patterns, even though the new countries actually comprised quite variegated populations. However, the new polities were soon bedevilled by warring factions, with the result that weak and unstable regimes, lacking either democratic or truly 'national' legitimacy, resorted to repression, patronage, nepotism and cronyism to hold on to power. Governments 'made' elections rather than the other way around. As economies faltered and the rule of law lapsed, humble citizens rapidly lost faith in the new states and in the probity, efficacy and even-handedness of governments and continued to put more trust in local clienteles and kinship associations to protect their interests.

The Balkan regimes proclaimed the need for 'progress', 'order' and 'Europeanization', encouraged European investment in Balkan railways, banks and industry, defended the interests of the propertied classes, and sought to educate and 'Westernize' their compatriots, believing that industrialization and agricultural advance would automatically result from closer association with Europe's advanced capitalist powers. The new, largely 'self-made' Balkan elites, including state officials, entrepreneurs, politicians, military officers and members of the liberal professions, were relatively 'open' to both money and talent. Perhaps because the new Balkan 'national' states contained no long-entrenched upper classes who could claim to have been the doughty custodians of national 'honour' and identity, they inherited no aristocratic models of deportment and deference, no established 'rules of the game' to regulate the unseemly scrambles for office (and for the spoils of office), and few effective checks or restraints on the misuse of public office or the misappropriation of public funds to line the pockets of public office-holders and their proverbial 'friends and relations'. Everything was 'up for grabs' in this 'survival of the fattest' environment. The 'mercenary' approach to public office-holding was a legacy of centuries of indirect rule of the Balkans through Byzantine, Ottoman and other intermediaries, who were fully expected to use the spoils of office to recoup the expenses and repay the political debts incurred during their ascent to public office.

It is the custom to blame this state of affairs squarely on the legacy of Ottoman rule. Thus Sugar argues that, as a result of the considerable local autonomy granted to both Muslim and non-Muslim *millets* in areas directly under Ottoman rule, relatively large numbers of individuals acquired some political and administrative experience and that it was these former communal office-holders who 'took over political leadership with relative ease prior to or just after the establishment of the various independent Southeast European states'. Political and administrative problems were to arise, not from a lack of experience, but from the fact that self-serving and nepotistic Balkan office-holders and oligarchs had learned the tricks and techniques of political chicanery and corruption only too well. 'It was the Ottoman legacy and training that was reflected in their actions. This aspect of the Ottoman past was the most damaging of all the legacies bequeathed to the peoples of South-eastern Europe by their former masters.' Therefore 'the Ottoman political legacy must be considered the greatest problem faced by peoples who, once again, had become masters of their own destiny' (Sugar 1977: 286–8). According to Vucinich, 'The Ottoman social system fostered many undesirable habits (e.g. the bribe, or *bakhshish*, distrust of government and so forth) . . . The notion persists that it is perfectly permissible to cheat and steal from the government, a problem with which none of the successor states has been able to cope altogether successfully' (Vucinich 1965: 120).

Such maladies have undoubtedly afflicted political life in the new Balkan 'national' states ever since, but it is as misleading as it is unjust to 'blame' this legacy squarely on the Ottomans. Rather, the gradual decline and retreat of Ottoman control permitted the re-emergence of age-old patterns of corruption, nepotism, lawlessness, extortion, protection-racketeering and self-serving administration in the Balkans. These were experienced not just in those areas that had been under Ottoman rule, but throughout the Balkans, suggesting deeper and more pervasive causes. They had been conspicuous in the medieval Danubian and South Slav states and during the protracted decline of Byzantium.

GREAT POWER INTERVENTION AND RIVALRIES

The Balkan states were semi-dependent states whose fates were determined directly or indirectly by the 'Great Powers'. Since the decline of Byzantium, the Balkans have been repeatedly subject to Great Power interventions. The emergence of independent Balkan states between 1827 (Greece) and 1920 (Albania) owed as much to Great Power rivalries and interventions in the region as it did to internal developments. Russia played an especially important role in championing the emergence of independent Balkan states. 'Hajduks, klephts, armatoles and brigands were heroes in the Balkan nationalist pantheon', but the 'prosaic reality was that conventional military and naval forces were more important [than irregular forces] in determining political outcomes. The 160,000 troops launched by Russia across the Danube in 1877 did more than any hajduks or klephts to win freedom for Balkan Christians' (Mazower 2001: 99–100).

The so-called Eastern Question, which ran like a silver thread through European diplomacy from 1718 to 1918, was essentially the question of how the European powers should carve up the Balkan territories of the declining Ottoman Empire (Stavrianos 1963: 199). Greek independence was secured by Anglo-Russian military intervention in the Greek War of Independence during the 1820s. Serbia, Montenegro, Romania and Bulgaria gained their independence through Russia's victory in the Russo-Turkish War of 1877–8, although the precise outcomes were modified and ratified by the other European powers at the 1878 Berlin Congress (to the detriment of Bulgaria, which was forced to cede territory and settle for mere autonomy for the time being). Finally, Albania would probably have been carved up between Italy, Greece, Montenegro and Serbia but for the Great Powers' insistence on the creation of a separate Albanian state in 1912–13 and (again) in

1920. Charles and Barbara Jelavich (1963: xiv–xv) argue that 'Tsarist Russia, more than any other country, was responsible for the physical liberation of the Balkan peoples.' Indeed, Russia invaded parts of the Balkans in 1769–74, 1787–92, 1798–1812, 1829–34, 1848–51 and 1877–9. It was widely assumed that these Russian military interventions, together with pan-Slavic cultural and Orthodox religious ties, would eventually bring the Balkans under Russian domination. However, once they had been liberated from Ottoman rule, the new Balkan states soon discovered that Russia had little more to offer (apart from cultural goods, particularly music and literature, and some sub-sequent protection against potential Turkish, Austrian or Italian attacks). Thus it was primarily to Western Europe and Germanic Central Europe that the new states turned for models, assistance, trade, investment and inspiration.

The overarching thesis of chapters 3–8 is that the major afflictions of the modern Balkans have primarily resulted from dysfunctional and repeatedly reasserted 'vertical' power-relations and power-structures, rather than from cultural factors. While it is seldom possible to wholly discount the influence of particular 'mentalities', 'mindsets' and attitudes, it is crucially important to guard against the pitfalls of simplistic cultural stereotyping and to be aware of the degrees to which such attributes are *dependent* rather than *independent* variables. They are most often *consequences of* (or *responses to*), rather than prime *causes* of, dysfunctional power-relations, opportunity-structures and incentive-structures. We therefore reject the various forms of cultural essentialism, stereotyp-ing and caricatures which attribute the salient problems of the modern Balkan Peninsula to the sup-posedly innate and unchanging qualities, mentalities and attitudes of its inhabitants, as if they were various types of inferior or intrinsically delinquent species (see pp. 27–37, 58, 87–90, 96, 98–109, 121, 546–7). Quite the contrary, we proceed from the premise that the study of Balkan (and indeed Asian and Islamic) polities and societies must start in much the same way that Western polities and societies are usually studied and conceptualized: by examining their dominant power-relations, class-structures and institutions and the kaleidoscopic ways in which these have interacted with societal and cultural heterogeneity and fluidity, rather than by caricaturing dominant religions, value-systems, 'mentalities' and 'mindsets' as the alleged wellsprings of incorrigibly dysfunctional behaviour. The broader (radical) implications of our less simplistic and less prejudicial approach to the study of polities, societies and the relationships between power-relations, power-structures, culture and so-called 'social capital' have been spelled out more fully elsewhere (Bideleux 2005 and 2007).

9   The cataclysmic impact of war on the Balkans, 1912–18

For the Balkans, the First World War was a direct sequel to the Balkan Wars of October 1912 to May 1913 and June–July 1913, and for that reason it is sometimes dubbed 'the Third Balkan War'. In all, there were six consecutive years of armed conflict in the Balkans, from 1912 to 1918.

THE BALKAN WARS OF 1912–13

The major crises afflicting the Ottoman Empire in 1911–12 (including the loss of Libya to Italy) finally forced the Ottoman authorities to cede most of the demands of an autonomist insurrection which took place in Albania during the spring and summer of 1912. At that point, the Albanian nationalist movement seemed to be on the verge of attaining its immediate goal of full national autonomy under protective Ottoman suzerainty. However, this caused the governments and nationalist movements of Montenegro, Serbia, Greece and Bulgaria to fear that the Albanian autonomist movement was becoming a force strong enough to frustrate the attainment of their own self-aggrandizing territorial aspirations and thus encouraged them to military action to realize these aspirations at Ottoman and Albanian expense before it was too late to do so. On 17 October 1912, therefore, Serbia, Bulgaria, Greece and Montenegro formed a Balkan alliance which declared war on the Ottoman Empire, with the aim of expelling the Ottomans from Europe. The lightning victories of about 350,000 Montenegrin, Serb, Bulgarian and Greek troops over much smaller Ottoman forces during the Balkan War of October 1912 to May 1913 abruptly ended Ottoman power in the Balkans. Pec and Djakovica were annexed by Montenegro. Serbia seized control of Kosova, the Sandzak of Novi Pazar and much of north-western Macedonia, more than doubling the size of its territory. Greece captured southern Macedonia, southern Epirus, Crete and Samos, nearly doubling the size of its population and territory. But Bulgaria, which bore the brunt of the fighting against Ottoman forces, felt 'cheated' because it made only relatively modest territorial gains – in north-eastern Macedonia and in Thrace. During June and July 1913, Bulgaria rashly waged war against its (collectively much stronger) Serbian, Montenegrin and Greek allies in a bid to bring about what many Bulgarians saw as a 'fairer' distribution of the territorial spoils. However, Bulgaria's already weary and depleted armed forces were trounced by its former allies, who further increased their own territorial gains at Bulgarian expense. Simultaneously, the Ottoman Empire seized the opportunity to regain some of the territory it had lost to Bulgaria in Thrace, while Romania, which hosted the peace conference which negotiated the ensuing Treaty of Bucharest in August 1913, seized its chance to annexe southern Dobrudja from Bulgaria.

Many Bulgarians came out of the Balkan Wars of 1912–13 feeling that their country had been collectively raped by its neighbours, even though Bulgaria had helped to bring about both wars. This, rather than any deep-seated affinities with or attachments to the Germanic peoples, became the main reason why Bulgaria subsequently positioned itself in the opposite military 'camp' to most of its Balkan neighbours during the two World Wars, driven by a desire to avenge the ways in which it had been 'treacherously robbed' of the fruits of its victories over the Ottomans in 1913.

Richard Hall has provided estimates of casualties in the Balkan Wars of 1912–13 as shown in Table 9.1.

Table 9.1   Estimated casualties in the Balkan Wars, 1912–13

	Killed in combat	**Wounded or sick**	**Died of disease**
Bulgaria	14,000 + 18,000	50,000 + 60,000	19,000 + 15,000
Greece	5,169 + 2,563	23,502 + 19,307	n/a
Montenegro	2,836 + 240	6,602 + 961	n/a
Serbia	36,550	55,000 + another 19,000 killed, wounded or sick.	

Source: Hall (2000: 136–7)

For states as small as Bulgaria, Greece, Serbia and Montenegro, these were very heavy casualty rates. Hall also estimates that the Ottoman Empire lost around 100,000 killed or wounded in combat and perhaps as many again killed by disease (p. 137), but another source claims that nearly 1.5 million Muslims died and over 400,000 Balkan Muslims became refugees as a result of the Balkan Wars of 1912–13 (Hupchick 2002: 321). According to Justin McCarthy, 27 per cent of 'the Turks and other Muslims of the Ottoman Balkans had died, 35 per cent had become refugees' (McCarthy 1997: 354).

THE AFTERMATH OF THE BALKAN WARS OF 1912–13

After the Balkan Wars of 1912–13, Serbia was assumed to be in no condition to fight another war. Perhaps partly for that reason, key sections of the Austro-Hungarian establishment 'believed the time was ripe to crush Serbia once and for all', even though it was 'virtually certain the Russians would back the Serbs' and this raised the risk of dragging Europe's major powers into a much larger war. 'After the assassination in Sarajevo, the Serbian government made almost all the concessions the Austrians demanded. It was not enough. The third Balkan War in three years was started by Austria; within a week, thanks to the system of obligations imposed by the rival alliances of Europe, all the Great Powers had become embroiled' (Mazower 2001: 99). The case for giving the Habsburg Empire (rather than Germany, Russia or Serbia) primary responsibility for causing the First World War is presented more fully in chapter 20.

THE BALKANS DURING THE FIRST WORLD WAR

In the Balkans during the First World War, the conflict between Serbia and Austria-Hungary triggered further conflicts between Romania and Austria-Hungary and between the predominantly Christian peoples and the Turks. The Bulgarian state seized this opportunity to recreate a 'Greater Bulgaria', while the Greek state sought to achieve a 'Greater Greece' in 1918–20 as spin-off from serving as a base of operations for the Entente Powers against the Central Powers.

Serbia

The First World War began with ineffectual Austro-Hungarian artillery bombardment of Belgrade, which was located vulnerably close to Serbia's northern border. This was followed by Austro-Hungarian invasions of Serbia from Bosnia-Herzegovina. It was widely assumed that little Serbia, with just 4.5 million inhabitants, stood no chance against an empire with 50 million inhabitants. However, the battle-hardened Serb army, boosted by its victories in the Balkan Wars of 1912–13, not only repelled the enemy forces but also invaded Habsburg territory. By early December 1914 the over-confident Serb forces were overextended and Belgrade fell into enemy hands, but they regrouped and astonished the world by retaking Belgrade in mid-December. From January to September 1915 the military pressure on Serbia abated, not only because Austria-Hungary faced serious threats from Russia in Galicia (Austrian Poland), but also because in April 1915 the Entente signed a treaty promising Italy major territorial gains extending all the way from Vlore (in Albania) and coastal Dalmatia and Trieste up through Istria, Gorizia and Gradisca to Trentino and South Tyrol, in return for entering the war against Austria-Hungary in May 1915. However, tiny landlocked Serbia was unable to obtain fresh supplies from the Entente Powers and suffered heavy casualties, acute food and munitions shortages, and a major typhus epidemic. In September 1915, moreover, the Central Powers managed to entice Bulgaria into the war on their side by signing a treaty backing its claims to most of Macedonia and Kosovo. In October and November 1915, a three-way attack by Germany, Austria-Hungary and Bulgaria induced the Serbian army, government and royal family to retreat through Kosova, Montenegro and the freezing-cold Albanian highlands towards the Adriatic ports of Shkoder, Durres and Vlore. During that retreat many died of cold and/or disease, while others were killed by ethnic Albanians in retaliation for the terrible atrocities perpetrated by Serbs against ethnic Albanians during the Balkan Wars of 1912–13. The size of the Serb armed forces had already fallen from 450,000 (10 per cent of the population) in mid-1914 to 300,000 by mid-1915, but nearly half of these perished and fewer than 100,000 made it to the Adriatic coast, whence they were taken by the French navy to Corfu, where many more died of disease. The Serbs were lionized in the French and British press for their tenacity and bravery, although it is questionable how far the qualities involved differed from those for which they were vilified in 1913 and during the 1990s. The battered remnants of the Serb army subsequently participated in the Entente offensives launched against the Central Powers from Greek Thessaloniki during 1917–18, which finally succeeded in defeating Bulgaria during September 1918. Overall, of an initial population of about 4.5 million, around 750,000 Serbs perished between 1912 and 1918 (Okey 1982: 154).

Bulgaria

Bulgarians were deeply divided over whether to take part in the war, not least because the Balkan Wars of 1912–13 had cost a great number of lives and limbs, for no real gain. However, Bulgaria was finally lured into the First World War on the side of the Central Powers in September 1915, in the expectation that Germany and Austria-Hungary would help it to take back from Serbia and Greece the extensive sections of Macedonia and Kosova which it had hoped to win during the Balkan Wars of 1912–13. A staggering 800,000 of its 5 million inhabitants were eventually mobilized (Mazower 2001: 100) and, through its alliance with the Central Powers, its forces did succeed in re-establishing a 'Greater Bulgaria' from late 1915 to mid-1918. However, Bulgaria was bled dry by its Germanic allies and it consequently suffered mounting shortages of munitions, medicine and food. This not only stoked up Bulgarian peasant unrest, but also antagonized the Macedonian Slavs who had been 'liberated' from Ottoman and subsequent Serbian or Greek rule, only to find that they were treated just as badly by their new Bulgarian overlords. Bulgaria and its recently conquered territories were finally overrun by British, French, Serb and Greek forces during September 1918, whereupon Bulgaria had absolutely nothing to show for six years of costly and debilitating warfare. Overall, nearly 40 per cent of Bulgaria's young adult males had been conscripted into its armed forces between 1912 and 1918, and of these more than 150,000 perished and more than 400,000 were wounded (Bell 1977: 122). Peasant anger at the fruitless sacrifices, exactions, corruptness and ineptitudes of the ruling nationalist-royalist coalition erupted into the Radomir Rebellion of September 1918 and was only partly assuaged by Tsar Ferdinand's abdication in favour of his son Boris on 3 October 1918. The radical, peasantist and increasingly violent Bulgarian Agrarian National

Union, which had mobilized peasant opposition to Bulgaria's involvement in these fruitless wars, was swept into government from October 1918 until June 1923.

Romania

Romania was initially neutral during the First World War, despite having recently renewed a treaty of alliance which it had negotiated with the Central Powers in 1887 and despite being ruled by Ferdinand of Hohenzollern (reg. 1914–27), who was a member of the same royal family as Germany's Kaiser Wilhelm II (reg. 1890–1918). However, Russia launched a major offensive against the Central Powers in June 1916 and promised to back Romanian claims to predominantly Romanian-inhabited Transylvania, Banat and southern Bukovina. In August 1916, calculating that the tide was turning against the Central Powers and urged on by Romanian nationalists, King Ferdinand and the National Liberal Party leader Ionel Bratianu decided to take Romania into the war on the side of the Entente, in the expectation that this would indeed enable Romania to acquire Transylvania, Banat and parts of Bukovina from Austria-Hungary and that Romania would fare badly if it did not enter the war on what appeared to be the winning side. However, the Romanian forces which invaded Transylvania, Banat and Bukovina soon proved to be no match for those of the Central Powers, and in the meantime Russia's offensive had run out of steam. In December 1916, having lost more than 300,000 lives and any hope of relief from Russia, the Romanian government retreated to Iasi while German and Austro-Hungarian forces occupied Wallachia, including Bucharest and the vital Ploesti oilfields. During 1917 and most of 1918 the Central Powers extracted large forced deliveries of oil, grain and other strategic commodities. By then oil had become the lifeblood of the German and Austro-Hungarian war machines and Romania was still the world's fifth largest producer of oil – indeed, next to Russia, it was the largest oil producer in Europe. After the new Soviet regime in Russia signed the Treaty of Brest-Litovsk with Germany in March 1918, the Romanian government also signed a separate peace treaty with Germany in May, whereby Romania gained Bessarabia (present-day Moldova) in the east at Russian expense in return for territorial concessions to Austria-Hungary in the north and to Bulgaria in Dobrudja and for economic tribute.

After the forced withdrawal of the German and Austro-Hungarian occupation forces during the autumn of 1918, however, Romania hastily re-entered the First World War on the winning side on 10 November 1918 (the day before the war ended!). This led to Romania's inclusion among the 'victorious powers' and helped it to 'liberate' (occupy) Transylvania, Banat, Bukovina, Bessarabia and south Dobrudja in late 1918, at the expense of defeated Austria-Hungary, Bulgaria and Russia. After Romanian control of Transylvania, Banat and Bukovina was challenged by the aggressively expansionist and revanchist 'National Bolshevik' regime headed by Bela Kun in Hungary from March to July 1919, Romania's triumphant armed forces also occupied southern Hungary and the city of Budapest from early August to November 1919. In addition, Romanian control of Transylvania, Banat and Bukovina was consolidated by the flight of tens of thousands of Hungarians from these territories to a severely truncated Hungary. Romania roughly doubled the size of its territory and population in late 1918. However, around 335,000 inhabitants of Romania (about 5 per cent of the pre-war population) perished during the First World War, not counting the thousands of Romanians who had died while serving in the Austro-Hungarian and Russian armed forces.

Greece

During the First World War Greece (like Romania) initially remained neutral, because Greek sympathies were deeply divided between the Entente and the Central Powers. A major crisis had been brewing in Greece since 1908. In that year, the Young Turks came to power in the Ottoman Empire, Austria-Hungary formally annexed Bosnia-Herzegovina, Bulgaria became a fully independent

kingdom and stepped up its territorial claims in Macedonia, while Crete (which had been autonomous since 1878) declared *enosis* (union) with Greece. The Greek government's alleged timidity in
the face of Ottoman and Western obstruction of Greek nationalist demands for the incorporation of
Macedonia, Cyprus and Crete into a 'Greater Greece' resulted in a group of army officers seizing
power in Athens in August 1909, in the hope of establishing a more assertive and nationalistic
regime. In October 1910 this military cabal conferred the premiership on a prominent Cretan politician, Eleutherios Venizelos, who thereupon became the dominant figure in Greek politics until
1933. By playing a lead role in the Balkan Wars of 1912 and 1913, Venizelos succeeded in annexing southern Macedonia, southern Epirus, Crete and Samos, which altogether nearly doubled
Greece's population and territory.

Almost from the start of the First World War, Venizelos and his followers favoured entering the
war on the side of the Entente, with a view to winning Entente backing for Greek acquisition of
northern Epirus, much of Thrace, Cyprus, the Dodecanese Islands and western Anatolia (the Izmir
region), which altogether would have given Greece control of the Aegean Sea. The chief obstacle
was that King Constantine I, who had inherited the Greek throne in 1913, was a Germanophile, an
honorary field marshal in the German army and a brother-in-law of Kaiser Wilhelm II. His sympathies were quite clearly with the Central Powers, but, in view of the strength of pro-Entente sentiment in Greece, Constantine formally advocated neutrality.

In October 1915, at the invitation of Venizelos, British and French expeditionary forces were
landed in the major port of Thessaloniki, ostensibly to launch an offensive to liberate the Serbs.
However, even though these forces initially proved quite ineffectual, their arrival deepened the
antagonism between the king and the prime minister, prompting Venizelos to resign. In 1916,
however, Venizelos established a self-proclaimed Greek government in Thessaloniki, in opposition
to the legitimate royal government in Athens. In December 1916, Britain and France conferred official recognition on the Venizelos government and imposed a naval blockade on those parts of
Greece which opposed it. Using gunboat diplomacy, Britain and France forced Constantine to abdicate in favour of his son and go into exile in June 1917, whereupon Venizelos returned to Athens
and formally brought Greece into the war in July 1917. In September 1918 the 300,000 Greek,
Serbian, Italian, British and French troops operating out of Thessaloniki finally got their acts
together and advanced deep into Bulgaria, Macedonia and Kosova, causing Bulgaria to collapse
and capitulate. This in turn broke the main lines of trade and communication between the Ottoman
Empire and its Germanic allies and contributed to the Ottoman capitulation on October 1918. All
told, the Bulgarian collapse at the end of September 1918 'led the German military leaders to conclude that the war was lost' (Mazower 2001: 101).

THE OTTOMAN EMPIRE

Having suffered massive casualties and territorial losses at the hands of European enemies and
rivals in 1876–8 and 1911–13 and having experienced increasingly humiliating European tutelage
since the mid-nineteenth century, the Ottoman Empire sought to turn the outbreak of war in
Europe in 1914 to its own advantage. However, even though German military 'advisers'/instructors
had been strategically involved in training and modernizing Ottoman land forces since the 1830s
(while the British did the same for the Ottoman navy), and even though German firms had been
actively involved in developing Ottoman steel and armaments production and providing rails and
equipment for the so-called Berlin–Baghdad railway project, the entry of the Ottoman Empire into
the war on the side of the Central Powers was by no means inevitable. The Ottoman Empire's main
external economic and cultural links were still with Britain and France, whose war efforts could
have profited enormously from keeping the empire either neutral or even pro-Entente, and it would
almost certainly have been most prudent for the empire's rulers to have remained neutral while

obtaining promises and concessions by playing each side off against the other, instead of entering the war.

The major worry for Ottoman ruling elites (including the nationalist Young Turks) was that Britain and France were allied to the Russian Empire, which had been championing South Slav and Armenian interests as a way of bringing the Balkans, the Caucasus and the Caspian and Black seas more fully under Russia's sway and encroaching on the Ottoman Empire. Russia even entertained hopes of 'liberating' Constantinople, the Bosphorus Straits (Bogazici) and the Dardanelles from Muslim/Turkish control. In addition, Britain and France were the main holders of the Ottoman foreign debt and the chief upholders and beneficiaries of the so-called 'capitulations', which conferred 'extra-territorial' rights (privileges) on their own citizens on Ottoman territory, and of Western tutelage over 'the sick man of Europe'. Some British groups had a burgeoning interest in the suspected oil potential of Mesopotamia, the Gulf and the Arabian Peninsula and further strengthening British supply lines through Egypt, the Red Sea, Aden and the Gulf region to British India, while some French groups had designs on Syria and Lebanon. Therefore, victory for the Entente was almost bound to result in further major losses and humiliations for the Ottoman Empire – possibly fatal ones. Furthermore, on 28 July 1914 Britain's then navy minister Winston Churchill outraged Turkish public opinion by ordering the seizure of two warships which were being built in British shipyards for the Ottoman navy and had already been paid for by public subscription.

These worries and provocations helped the nationalistic Ottoman war minister Enver Pasha to persuade the Ottoman government to sign a secret alliance with Germany on 2 August 1914, the day before Germany declared war on France, and simultaneously to announce that the Ottoman Empire would no longer pay the burdensome interest charges on its huge foreign debt. On 10 August 1914, moreover, the Ottoman government allowed two German warships to escape the British navy by taking refuge in the Ottoman-controlled Dardanelles. The Ottoman government then pretended that these ships had been bought from Germany as replacements for the two warships impounded by Churchill the previous month. On 29 October 1914, sporting new Turkish names but still manned by Germans, these warships shelled the major Russian Black Sea ports of Odessa, Sevastopol and Nikolaev, sinking many Russian ships (Finkel 2005a: 527–9). 'This action sealed the Ottoman Empire's fate – Russia declared war [on Turkey] on 2 November, and Britain and France [followed suit] on 5 November. On 11 November 1914 Sultan Mehmed V Resad declared war on Britain, France and Russia. Two days later . . . "holy war" was proclaimed . . . addressed to all Muslims . . . The Ottoman Empire was an agricultural state which had thrown itself into an industrialized war. It could raise an army but lacked the capacity to support it adequately' (p. 529).

As has already been emphasized, the Balkan Peninsula had long been the mainstay of Ottoman power, accounting for the bulk of the empire's population, tax revenues, military recruits, educated administrators and international merchants, and control of the Balkans had been what made the Ottoman Empire into a European Great Power (pp. 73–5). By expelling the Ottoman Turks from almost all of their remaining Balkan domains (other than southern Thrace and Istanbul/Constantinople), the Russo-Turkish War of 1877–8 and the Balkan Wars of 1912–13 effectively ended the Ottoman Empire's Great Power status. By 1914, having lost Egypt, Libya and almost all of its former Balkan possessions, the still largely agrarian Ottoman Empire had only 26 million subjects (Quataert 2005: 112). It was now dwarfed by the Russian Empire's 167 million subjects, the German Empire's 69 million and the Habsburg Empire's 50 million. Moreover, the Ottomans' still far-flung territories remained hard to defend – overland travel from Istanbul took over a month to the border with Russia and two months to Mesopotamia (Finkel 2005a: 529). In military and geopolitical terms, the Ottoman Empire had become a relatively minor power, despite the still impressive (problematic) geographical extent of its domains.

Such huge disparities were the main reasons for the Ottoman Empire's heavy casualties during the First World War, in which about 325,000 Ottoman soldiers were killed in action, between

400,000 and 700,000 were wounded in action, of whom about 60,000 subsequently died, and about 400,000 soldiers died of disease, 'bringing the total number of Ottoman combatants who died to almost 800,000', while 'the only lasting military success achieved by the empire's army was the defence of the Dardanelles in 1915–16 – the Gallipoli campaign' (Finkel 2005a: 530). In addition, more than a million civilian subjects of the Sultan perished during the First World War, including 'at least 600,000 Armenian civilians' (Quataert 2005: 69) and between 300,000 and 500,000 Syrians (Mansfield 1992: 165). Besides Armenians, more than a million Turks became refugees, many of whom died (McCarthy 1997: 363, 365, 380).

The First World War delivered the *coup de grâce* to the Ottoman Empire, which was unable to survive the Arab Revolt of 1916–18, the amputation of Mesopotamia and Palestine by British forces during the war, and the extensive occupation of additional Ottoman territories by Greek, British, French and Arab forces in 1918–21. Mehmet VI, the last Ottoman Sultan, was evacuated from Constantinople on a British battleship in 1922 (he died in San Remo in 1926). A Turkish Republic was established in 1923, and the Caliphate was abolished by the new republic in 1924.

THE LONGER-TERM IMPACT OF THE FIRST WORLD WAR ON THE BALKANS

The First World War fostered (or at least accelerated) major changes in the position and social consciousness of the peasantry in the Balkans, as also in East Central Europe and Russia. During the war millions of peasant conscripts were mobilized into national and imperial armies which marched through or were billeted in thousands of villages, in most cases abruptly ending centuries of isolation from the 'outside' world. After participating in grim warfare and socio-economic upheavals and having had their horizons rapidly and often shockingly expanded, these soldiers routinely decided not to return to their old villages after the war ended. Those who did return to their villages (if only to participate in post-war land redistributions) frequently became restive and did not settle. Some, including a significant minority who had been prisoners of war in Russia, joined nascent Communist parties, while others backed radical nationalist, socialist or peasantist parties. In his classic study of the effects of the First World War on the Romanian peasantry, David Mitrany observed that, from the moment they entered the war, 'many new truths and doubts began to work on the peasants' minds', because they perceived that 'many of their sufferings were due to the failures of their betters as leaders and administrators' and everywhere they were 'extolled as heroes in speeches and articles which left a bitter taste when tested by the realities of their existence' (Mitrany 1930: 98).

Even before the war ended, Europe was 'changing hands'. In Western Europe, and initially in the East as well, property transfers took the form of widespread selling and letting of land by big landowners in response to war-induced shortages of labour, horses, capital and fuel, rising land values and property taxes (especially death duties), rationalization of estates and fear or anticipation of imminent peasant revolts. However, where peasants or peasant soldiers began to mutiny, desert and rebel, as they increasingly did in the Balkans, East Central Europe and Russia, land sales and land leasing were soon superseded by spontaneous land seizures as well as by more equitable and controlled land reforms. By whichever means, the upshot in much of Ireland, Italy and the Baltic region as well as in Russia, the Balkans and East Central Europe was the final abolition or abdication of seigneurial control of the countryside. This was the *coup de grâce* against 'feudalism' and a major watershed in European agrarian history. It also challenged the structure of authority and social deference to 'superiors' who had heedlessly squandered millions of (mainly peasant) lives. As Mitrany put it in relation to Romania, the First World War left the Romanian peasantry 'almost alone in the field, as undisputed masters . . . They have conquered the countryside decisively for their own class . . . The line of social contest has shifted from the village and now runs near the boundary between land and town, between agriculture and industry' (Mitrany 1930: 101). Much the same was true in much of the rest of the eastern half of Europe. The lines had been (re)drawn for forthcoming battles between peasantries and townspeople, in which the peasants were politically mobilized and/or represented by large and highly influential peasantist movements or (much less widely at first) by radical nationalist, fascist, socialist or Communist parties.

Part II

East Central Europe from the Roman period to the First World War

10   The disputed 'roots' of East Central Europe before the tenth century AD

The origins of the peoples and polities of medieval East Central Europe are shrouded in mist. There is little written documentation about the inhabitants of this area and their polities prior to the tenth century AD, and even for that century the information remains quite patchy and fragmentary. Until the tenth century AD East Central Europe was largely pagan and illiterate, with the result that it lacked a literate Christian clergy desirous and capable of keeping written records and/or writing political-cum-historical chronicles. Hence, for most of the first millennium AD, the claims which historians of East Central Europe have made about this area and its inhabitants are in large measure ingenious hypotheses or conjectures, based mainly on very ambiguous, patchy, inconclusive and mostly circumstantial linguistic and archaeological evidence, odd fragments of 'popular' or 'national' folk tales, the often unreliable accounts provided by highly tendentious Byzantine and/or Germanic (Frankish) chroniclers and other outsiders, and the heroic but highly subjective and frequently tendentious guesswork of philologists, archaeologists and historians. The hitherto influential interpretations of the history of early medieval East Central Europe, especially the emergence of the Slav people(s) between the sixth and tenth centuries AD, have been shown to be little more than fanciful and highly implausible conjectures, resting on very scanty, ambiguous and flimsy evidence (Barford 2001, 2005; Curta 2001, 2005). This is one of the main reasons why we have kept our coverage of early medieval East Central Europe quite brief. Curta and Barford have highlighted just how little reliable information and/or scholarly consensus there is on this subject. For the time being, very little can be said on this period of East Central European history and prehistory with any confidence or authority. Little is known with even modest certainty and clarity about *what* happened in East Central Europe up to and including the first millennium AD, let alone sequencing and patterns of causation and interrelation. A great deal of rethinking remains to be done, and we don't believe that anything is to be gained by fobbing readers off with another round of flimsy conjectures and nationalist and pseudo-ethnographic fairy tales. Already in her 1971 book on the emergence of the Slavs, which in its day was regarded as the 'most valuable overall survey in English' on the 'early medieval archaeology of eastern and central Europe' (Barford 2001: 2), Marija Gimbutas emphasized the paucity and unreliability of the archaeological evidence for the era under discussion:

> The drab archeological remains of migrating farmers and stock-breeders who did not build houses or temples of stone or clay and did not create any outstanding or individualistic artistic style have not attracted the interest of archeologists . . . The reconstruction of the prehistoric Slavic culture still awaits a meticulous modern archeologist. The general picture of the North Carpathian culture during the Bronze and Early Iron Ages . . . is a patchwork based on meager archeological data . . . Without the archeological materials, the ancient Slavic material culture, its developmental phases, chronology and cultural relations cannot be reconstructed. (Gimbutas 1971: 26)

Similarly, the Hungarian historian Laszlo Makkai said of his Magyar forebears, who migrated from the Volga steppes to the Central Danubian basin (Pannonia) during the ninth century: 'Conflicting information from the available sources has inspired a variety of theories about the Hungarian migration . . . All that is certain is that the majority of the Hungarians did not leave the Volga before the second half of the ninth century' (Makkai 1975d: 21).

Nevertheless, taking advantage of the patchy, fragmentary and ambiguous qualities of the available archaeological and philological evidence, the early history of East Central Europe has long been a battleground between contending 'national' schools of history, archaeology, philology and ethnography. Many of these have explicitly or implicitly advanced, supported or been associated with rival territorial claims, often by asserting that this or that 'people' or 'ethnic group' (usually their own alleged forebears) were the 'original', 'native' or 'indigenous' inhabitants of this or that area, and that other claimants to such territories were merely 'aliens', 'foreigners', 'transients' or 'interlopers' with no rights of possession or permanent settlement, even though many such 'people' or 'ethnic groups' had probably lived in these same areas for centuries.

THE EARLY HISTORY AND PREHISTORY OF EAST CENTRAL EUROPE

The territory of present-day Poland and the Czech Republic never became part of the Roman Empire, and their documented history does not begin until the tenth century AD – and, even then, only quite patchily so.

Within the current territory of Poland, archaeologists have found evidence of human habitation in the Iron Age (after 600 BC), in the Bronze Age (1800–400 BC) and even as far back as *c*.180,000 BP (in the Ojcow Caves near Krakow). Primitive agriculture can be traced back to about 2500 BC, and it appears that so-called Lusatians (named after the eastern German district in which they were first identified) inhabited this area between roughly 1300 and 400 BC. They built wooden forts, including a famous island fortress at Biskupin in eastern Pomerania sometime around 550 BC and traded with Scandinavia and the Danube basin. The area was invaded by Scythian nomads from around 500 BC, but there is also archaeological evidence of Celtic settlement from around 400 BC and of Germanic incursions from the first century AD. The northern and eastern sections of modern Poland were also extensively settled by Baltic tribes – forebears of the modern Latvians and Lithuanians (Davies 1981a: vol. I, 41, 44, xxxix).

The fact that Roman coins and artefacts have been widely discovered (sometimes in large quantities) in the lands between the Baltic and the Vistula suggests that Roman expeditionary forces and traders may have made forays into these territories (Geremek 1982: 14). Nevertheless, writers such as Tacitus clearly regarded the area as *terra incognita*. His remarks on the so-called 'Venedii' could just as credibly refer to Germanic as to Slavic inhabitants of the area (Davies 1981a: 45). Therefore, it is probably 'unwise to put the Slavonic tag on any archaeological finds prior to AD 500' within the post-1945 territory of Poland (p. 44).

Slavs of one sort or another probably first settled between the Odra and Vistula rivers during the seventh and eighth centuries AD (Davies 1981a: 27). However, in view of the innumerable human migrations through and into this region and the resultant richness of its ethnic mix, 'it is quite impossible to isolate anything . . . to distinguish Slavonic from non-Slavonic racial elements' (p. 46). Admittedly, the so-called 'Autochthonous School' of Polish archaeology, philology and ethnography postulated a direct line of ethnic descent from the (Bronze Age) Lusatians through the obscure Venedii of Roman times to the unambiguously Polish/Slavic tribes of the tenth century. However, this conjecture was contested by the older 'Prussian School', which treated the very same area as the 'ancestral homeland' of the *Früostgermanen* (the early East Germans) (pp. 39, 282). Furthermore, many archaeologists, historians and philologists have questioned the alleged Lusatian and Venedian 'roots' of the proto-Slavs. Some argue that the Slavs originated in the northern

Carpathian region, where they intermingled with Baltic, German, Illyrian, Thracian and Iranian peoples, and that a Slav diaspora began between the fifth and the eighth century AD, under the impact of invading Huns, Avars and other nomadic warriors from Asia (pp. 40–3).

There are no references to *Polanie* (Polanians or 'people of the open plain') before the tenth century AD, and even these references are only to a single Slavic tribe who inhabited one section of the Warta–Vistula basin. The earliest surviving *written* records concerning Slavic inhabitants in what is now Poland date from AD 965–6, when the Polish ruler Mieszko I (who died in AD 992) reportedly married a Czech princess, renounced paganism and adopted the Christian faith (Davies 1981a: 3–4). Their polity gave birth to the concept of *Polska* (Poland), which was probably derived from the Polish word *pole*, meaning a field or open flat terrain. However, even after the formal establishment of a Polish Church in AD 1000, the eleventh and twelfth centuries remain 'largely obscured by the deficiencies of the sources', because, other than the clergy, Polish society remained 'overwhelmingly illiterate' (p. 78). While it is quite conceivable that somewhere in the Odra (Oder) basin or in the Vistula basin there once lived people(s) who spoke 'a language or group of related languages from which modern Polish has since developed', it is impossible to trace the emergence of such people(s) and their language owing to 'the absence of any linguistic records prior to the thirteenth century' (p. 47). Even though many Poles have fervently believed that their forebears have long inhabited an ancient and continuous Polish *macierz* (motherland), 'it is impossible to identify any fixed territorial base which has been permanently, exclusively and inalienably Polish. Its territory, like the settlement patterns, cultural alignment and ethnic mix of its population, has been subject to continual transformations' (Davies 1981a: 24).

Within the current Czech Lands and Slovakia, human habitation has been traced back to about 70,000 BP, while the smelting of local metal ores (beginning with copper) dates from about 2000 BC (Kavka 1960: 9–11). Between the fourth century BC and the first century AD, the Czech Lands and Slovakia appear to have been inhabited by Celtic tribes. Some Roman writers later referred to one of these tribes as the *Boii* – whence the name 'Bohemia'. Around 50 BC Dacians (from present-day Romania and Bulgaria) made inroads into the central Danubian basin. The Czech Lands were also settled by so-called Lusatians, whose traces stretch as far back as the Bronze Age, and there have been claims that these people were Slavs and that they are the area's oldest identifiable inhabitants. Starting around 100 BC, the Celtic inhabitants of these areas began to be assimilated and/or displaced westwards by belligerent Germanic peoples from the north European plain. The latter engaged in sporadic frontier wars with the Romans until late in the second century AD. These Germanic peoples appear subsequently to have been displaced westwards by marauding warriors from Asia – by Huns during the fourth and fifth centuries, and by Avars during the sixth and seventh centuries.

It appears that the Slavic forebears of the Czechs and Slovaks 'emerged' (or possibly 'arrived') in the Czech Lands and Slovakia during the sixth or early seventh century. The Czech nation derives its name from the *Cechi*, one of these Slavic tribes. It appears fairly certain that around AD 623 or 624 a merchant-adventurer known as Samo successfully led a Slavic rising against the Avars and that, until his death in about 658, he was the ruler of a Slavic tribal confederation straddling Moravia and parts of Slovakia and Bohemia. However, the Slavs of Bohemia, Moravia and Slovakia then 'disappear' from the documented historical record for about 170 years – that is, until the emergence of autonomous Slavic principalities in Nitra (in what is now Slovakia) by the 820s and in Moravia in around 830. The oldest recorded Christian church in East Central Europe was consecrated at Nitra in 828 by the Germanic Archbishop of Salzburg, and the Slavic ruling family of Moravia was baptized by the Germanic Bishop of Passau in 831. In around 833 the ruler of Moravia, Mojmir I, conquered the principality of Nitra, achieving one of the few brief unions between Slavic inhabitants in the Czech Lands and Slovakia prior to the twentieth century. Following Mojmir's death in 846, Moravia was invaded by Frankish Germans, who installed a client named Rastislav on the

Moravian throne. Whether in order to escape Frankish tutelage or to fend off Germanic/Catholic encroachments on his new domains, in AD 863 Rastislav invited two Byzantine monks known as Constantine (later Cyril) and Methodius to start baptizing the leading families of Moravia (and later Bohemia) into Byzantine Orthodox Christianity. Moravia had already cultivated commercial and cultural connections with Byzantium and with the nascent Bulgar kingdom, and since around 855 these two linguistically gifted monks had been engaged in the momentous tasks of devising a Slavonic alphabet (the Glagolitic script) and translating parts of the Orthodox liturgy into this first *written* Slavonic language. However, the rapid religious and cultural inroads achieved by these remarkable brothers from Salonika provoked a violent Germanic/Catholic counter-offensive. In 870 the unfortunate Rastislav was overthrown, imprisoned and blinded by his noxious nephew Svatopluk, with Germanic Catholic assistance. In 885, after both Cyril and Methodius had died, their converts and disciples were hounded out of the Czech Lands and Prince Svatopluk enforced a papal ban on the old Slavonic liturgy. Following Svatopluk's death in 894, however, the Czechs of Bohemia broke away from the so-called Moravian Empire, which finally collapsed under successive Magyar invasions of the central Danubian basin between AD 898 and 906. However, a new Czech dynasty known as the Premyslid dynasty emerged in Bohemia and presided over the emergence of an autonomous Catholic Church in Bohemia. According to Czech national myth, this new dynasty (which endured until 1306) originated with a sturdy Bohemian ploughman named Premysil who married Princess Libuse, the valiant daughter of a ninth-century ruler of Bohemia, and 'lived happily ever after'.

Western Hungary and south-western Slovakia entered documented history in 10–9 BC, when their then predominantly Celtic inhabitants were subjugated by the Romans. At that time the low-lying central Danubian (alias Pannonian or Hungarian) plain was very marshy and sparsely populated. However, the hilly western sections (Transdanubia, including Lake Balaton and what are now Pecs and Budapest), as well as what are now Bratislava, Devin and Stupava in south-western Slovakia, were incorporated into the Roman Empire as the province of Pannonia. The principal Roman town was Aquincum, whose substantial remains (including two amphitheatres and several public baths) have latterly been excavated and are to be found in District III of modern Budapest. Other major Roman remains have been unearthed in Pecs, Sopron and Szombathely and, in Slovakia, near Stupava and Bratislava (Mannova 2000: 12). Archeologists have established that Roman Pannonia had an economy based upon grain cultivation, stock-breeding (especially horses), viticulture, fruit growing, and crafts such as stone cutting, carriage building and pottery. The Roman Empire's north-eastern border (*limes*) extended as far as the Danube, along which the Romans established watchtowers and encampments to ward off marauding 'barbarians'. Similarly, mountainous Transylvania became part of the Roman province of Dacia.

When the Romans retreated in the face of recurrent 'barbarian' assaults, the central Danubian plain was overrun by successive waves of horse-borne nomadic warrior peoples from the European steppes: the Huns during the fourth and fifth centuries; the Avars from the late sixth to the eighth century; and the Magyars during the late ninth and early tenth century. These devastating invasions appear to have induced the Celtic inhabitants of this very exposed plain to seek safer havens further west. During the interlude(s) between the dominion of the Huns and that of the Avars, there appear to have been substantial inward migrations of Germanic and Vlach (Romanian) settlers, who were subsequently subjugated by and compelled to pay tribute to the Avars and Magyars. The Avars in turn were subdued by the Franks in the late eighth century.

Between the 840s and the 890s the titular forebears of the Magyar (Hungarian) nation appear to have been driven out of a temporary base in the Volga basin by Pecheneg steppe-warriors. After brief sojourns on the Don, the Dnieper and the Dnestr, they overran the central Danubian basin (which they had previously raided) between AD 896 and 900. Up to 400,000 Magyars, named after their leading tribe, easily overwhelmed the area's existing mainly Slavic but also Germanic, Avar and Vlach inhabitants, whom they may have outnumbered by about two to one. The Magyars subsequently subjugated not only the central Danubian basin, but also Transdanubia, Slovakia, parts of Transylvania and, in 907, the Ostmark (Austria). In addition, they undertook numerous plundering raids into Italy until 926, into Germany until 955 and into the Balkans until the 960s. Some of their raids even extended across France into northern Spain. In 904 Arpad, who was the *gyula* or deputy chief of the Magyar tribal confederacy, seized power and initiated the Arpad dynasty, which ruled Hungary until 1301. Although German, Italian and Balkan rulers were terrorized into paying regular tribute to the Magyars, they gradually united against these marauders and Germanic armies inflicted severe defeats on the Magyars in 933 and 955 (restoring the Ostmark to Germanic control), while the Byzantine Empire succeeded in fortifying its Danubian frontier more effectively by the 970s. In addition, the Magyars were further induced to adapt to more sedentary European life-styles by the emergence of Kievan Rus, which limited the scope for Magyar marauding on the Black Sea steppes and curtailed the Magyars' contacts with the Turkic inhabitants of the Don and Volga basins. All of this left the Magyars as a major 'wedge' separating the Western Slavs from the Southern Slavs.

THE MUCH DISPUTED ORIGINS OF THE SLAVIC 'PEOPLES' OF MEDIEVAL EAST CENTRAL EUROPE (THE SO-CALLED 'WESTERN SLAVS')

In truth, all that can be stated with any certainty is that by the tenth century AD a 'people' or 'peoples' widely identified as a 'Slavic' linguistic-cultural group and/or a biological-racial group made up a majority of the inhabitants of East Central Europe; that East Central Europe's 'Slavic' inhabitants were gradually evolving into the 'Western Slavic' forebears of the Czechs, the Slovaks, the Poles, the Sorbs and the Lusatians; and that contacts and hence ties between these 'Western Slavs' and their 'Southern Slav' cousins in the Balkan Peninsula were sharply curtailed by the large inflows of Magyars into the central Danubian basin between 896 and 907 AD.

Paul Barford (2001, 2005) and Florin Curta (2001, 2005, 2006) have demonstrated that there is very little (if any) reliable information concerning the Slavic people(s) and their place(s) of origin prior to the seventh century AD. Data generated by dendrochronology (the use of tree rings for dating past events) indicate that in East Central Europe 'the so-called Slavic culture . . . cannot be dated earlier than ca. 700 AD' (Curta 2005: 9). Paul Barford, a leading British specialist on Polish archaeology, maintains that 'there is little evidence of a Slavic presence in Polabia [modern-day East Germany] or central and northwestern Poland before the end of the seventh or the early eighth century. Indeed, over most of the area, there is only sparse settlement . . . before the late 600s' (Barford 2005: 62). There are longstanding and still far from resolved disagreements as to when and how the Slavic ancestors of the Poles, the Czechs and the Slovaks 'emerged': whether they first appeared in their current 'homelands' at some point during the sixth or seventh century AD; how they originated; and, if they 'migrated' or 'arrived' from somewhere else, whence they came. Nor is there any consensus concerning the nature and timing of the processes by which the Slavic people(s) separated or coalesced into Western, Eastern and Southern Slav linguistic and ethnic groupings.

It now seems *highly unlikely* that there were large ethnically or linguistically identifiable Slavic populations in East Central Europe prior to the sixth century AD. Before that time, significantly, the Byzantine (East Roman) Empire was 'totally oblivious to the existence of a barbarian people called the Slavs on their northern border. The terms [designating Slavic peoples] seem to have been coined or adopted by East Roman writers as descriptions of a certain group of barbarians only in the 550s' (Barford 2001: 36). Furthermore, it no longer seems plausible that the forebears of the Western Slavs 'migrated' to East Central Europe from elsewhere. There is insufficient evidence to back up older hypotheses suggesting a large-scale displacement of identifiably Slavic populations from what is now Ukraine and/or Belarus into East Central Europe (Barford 2001: 16, 45–6; Curta 2001:

336–7; 2006: 56). The inhabitants of 'the vast spaces of the Russian Plain' during the third to seventh centuries AD, whose existence and characteristics were not recorded in written documents, 'had no common name, whether it was "Slavs" or anything else' (Dolukhanov 1996: ix–x), and they 'cannot be ascribed to any ethnic group' (Curta 2001: 13). Furthermore, it is implausible to suppose that large-scale Slavic population pools and movements of this sort could have gone completely unnoticed by contemporary neighbouring peoples and states. Yet the expansion of the Slavic peoples to become the most numerous ethno-cultural group(s) in East Central Europe, the Balkans and Russia by the ninth century AD was also too rapid to be explicable as a natural demographic explosion (Barford 2001: 16; Urbanczyk 2005: 142). 'The rate of reproduction involved to fill the new territories with descendants of a small original population, no matter how the figures are calculated, is biologically impossible' (Barford 2001: 46). Curta and Barford have cogently argued that it is simply *not known* how any of the Slav peoples (not just the Western Slavs) came into existence, although this has not stopped them and others from continuing the long tradition of putting forward ingenious and interesting conjectures and hypotheses on this endlessly fascinating mystery (see Curta 2001: 3, 13, 118–19, 335, 346–50; 2006: 59; Barford 2001: 46; Urbanczyk 2005: 143–7).

Whatever the case, if populations were in an endemic state of movement and flux in most parts of Europe through much of the first millennium AD, it is highly unlikely that God had already led the ancestors of the Poles, the Czechs and the Slovaks to proto-national 'homelands' over which they could justly maintain permanent and exclusive jurisdiction for ever more, against all comers and/or prior occupants. Instead of striving to project specious modern ethnic, national and territorial concepts and claims on to pre-modern multi-cultural societies within which modern ethnic and national identities had not yet crystallized (often in misguided attempts to ascribe the origins of modern ethnic and national conflicts to a pre-modern past), it is much safer and sounder to emphasize that the peoples of East Central Europe are all *mongrels*. Modern attempts to 'discover' or invent ethnically and/or biologically pure medieval pedigrees in pursuit of modern national, racial and territorial claims are largely preposterous. There is much to be said for the mischievous definition of a nation as 'a group of persons united by a common error about their ancestry and a common dislike of their neighbours' (Deutsch 1969: 3). Our attitude to these matters is similar to that of the Hungarian writer Paul Ignotus: 'The Hungarian nation . . . is supposed to be distinguished by its Asiatic race and language. All that has been said about its race is rubbish; language alone is the distinctive reality. Europe consists of racially impure nations, but Hungary tops the list for racial impurities. If the various Slav national groups to her north and south, the Austro-Germans to her west, and the Romanians to her east are all mixtures, Hungary is simply a mixture of these mixtures' (Ignotus 1972: 21). Thankfully, most Magyars (Hungarians) do not even attempt to claim that present-day Hungary has been their national 'homeland' since time immemorial, because it has been fairly unambiguously established that their 'Asiatic' Magyar forebears arrived in the territory which has come to be known as Hungary no earlier than the ninth and tenth centuries AD.

The uncertain mongrel origins of the peoples of East Central Europe do not make these peoples fundamentally different from those of southern, western or northern Europe. All of Europe's peoples have diverse and often very obscure racial and ethnic origins. The only significant differences are that: (i) there is even less reliable and unambiguous evidence about the ethnic composition, cultures, ways of life and social organization of the populations of East Central Europe during the first millennium AD than about those of southern Europe (including the Balkans) and parts of western and Germanic Europe; (ii) this has made it relatively easy for nationalistic (Western) Slavic historians, philologists and archaeologists to advance specious ethnic, racial and territorial narratives and claims with regard to the first millennium AD; and (iii) this in turn has contributed to the emergence of relatively narrow and exclusive ethnic and racial conceptions of the nation in modern East Central Europe.

Finally, it needs to be emphasized that the emergence of the medieval Polish, Czech and Magyar kingdoms substantially pre-dated modern conceptions of exclusive territorial jurisdiction and state-hood. The seats of power around which royal authority could be directly enforced were usually sep-arated by vast expanses of ill-defined border country controlled by 'marcher lords' who were, to varying degrees, laws unto themselves. 'Political power radiated from a few centres of authority, whose spheres of influence constantly waxed and waned and very frequently overlapped' (Davies 1981a: 33). In East Central Europe, much of the terrain of which was either densely wooded or marshy and (partly for these reasons) more difficult to traverse than most parts of western Europe, such conditions persisted until the middle of the seventeenth century in the Kingdom of Bohemia and until the end of the eighteenth century in Poland and Hungary. This makes it even less sound to try to link particular 'peoples' or ethnic groups to particular territories or (supposedly) continuously occupied 'national homelands', and to try to buttress modern territorial claims with bogus historical narratives of that sort.

11 The apparent convergence between East Central Europe and Western Christendom, from the tenth to the sixteenth century AD

From the tenth to the sixteenth century the cultural and economic 'distance' between East Central and Western Europe was considerably reduced. It appears that East Central Europe was being assimilated into Western (Roman Catholic) Christendom, economically as well as culturally and socially. This perspective has been strongly supported by Jerzy Topolski (1981: 375–9), Piotr Wandycz (2001: 36, 18–61), Jeno Szucs (1988: 331), Ivan Berend (1986: 331–2), Mihaly Vajda (1988: 343) and Andrew Janos (1982: 30–1), among others. Adhesion to the Western branch of Christianity, combined with a massive influx of German colonists, traders, priests, lawyers and administrators, brought East Central Europe into ever-closer communion with western European cultures. This is often perceived as at least partly offsetting the fact that most of East Central Europe (unlike the Balkans) did not have an indigenous 'Graeco-Roman heritage', as only small fractions of East Central Europe had ever been part of the Roman Empire.

Conversion to Christianity, combined with the inflows of German traders, clergy and settlers and increased contact with western Europe, hastened the development of written languages, theological and scientific learning and scholarship, jurisprudence, commerce, agricultural and mining techniques, more formal and regular methods of administration, and towns as seats of temporal and ecclesiastical administration, commerce, learning and civic culture. From the fourteenth to the sixteenth century, monarchical prerogatives were increasingly circumscribed and eroded in the kingdoms of Poland-Lithuania, Hungary and Bohemia, each of which also experienced significant development of commerce, crafts, mining and towns. Bohemia was Europe's major producer of silver by 1300, and the minting of a plentiful silver currency greatly assisted the monetization and commercialization of its economy (Kavka 1960: 34–5). By the fourteenth century heavy ploughs and the three-field system were being introduced into East Central European agriculture (Topolski 1981: 376; Wandycz 1992: 30). Later, East Central European ore mining was further stimulated by discovery of the *seiger* process for separating silver from copper ore, with the result that the minting of metallic money quintupled between 1460 and 1530 (Anderson 1979: 22).

East Central Europe's educated elites participated vigorously in the Renaissance, the Reformation and the early stages of the Scientific Revolution. Vernacular writing proliferated in East Central Europe from the thirteenth century onward. Major cosmopolitan universities were established in Prague in 1348, in Vienna in 1365, in Krakow in 1400 and in Vilnius in 1579. Universities were also established in Pecs in 1361 and at Pozsony/Bratislava in 1465, but these did not survive. The first printing presses were established during the 1450s in Bohemia and in 1473 in Poland and Hungary (compared with the 1460s in Italy and the 1470s in both England and France). Translations of the Bible into the vernacular appeared first of all in Germany and Italy, then in Bohemia and Hungary, and only after that in England and France (Wandycz 1992: 36–7). The first vernacular printed books were published in 1513 in the case of Poland and in 1541 in Hungary. During the sixteenth century about eight thousand titles were published in Poland, compared with some ten thousand in England (pp. 50–1).

At this time the Danubian lands 'belonged . . . more nearly to Western Europe than at any time before or since' (Evans 1979: xxii). By 1500 around 25 per cent of the population lived in towns in Moravia, about 20 per cent did so in Bohemia and in Poland proper (excluding the vast Grand Duchy of Lithuania), while about 15 per cent of the population was urban in Hungary, although such proportions were still far below the 50 per cent levels estimated for the Low Countries and northern Italy in the same period (p. 60). By 1600 there were even around 150 small 'towns' in Slovakia (Kirschbaum 1995: 64–5; Spiesz *et al.* 2006: 68). Furthermore, sixteenth- and early seventeenth-century Poland, Bohemia, Moravia, Transylvania and (less formally) Slovakia gained renown as havens of religious toleration, whereas in western Europe this was an epoch of religious bigotry and strife.

For fuller surveys of East Central Europe between the tenth and sixteenth centuries, readers are referred to Piotr Wandycz (2001: 18–61) and to the first edition of the present book (Bideleux and Jeffries 1998: 111–261). Here we highlight key features of the Renaissance and the Reformation(s) in the kingdoms of Bohemia, Poland-Lithuania and Hungary.

THE REFORMATION(S) AND THE RENAISSANCE IN THE KINGDOM OF BOHEMIA

Western Europeans mistakenly tend not only to think of the sixteenth-century Reformation(s) as occurring primarily in western Europe and as helping to differentiate western from eastern Europe, but also to overlook the fact that Europe's *first* full-blown Christian Reformation occurred in Jan Hus's Kingdom of Bohemia rather than in Martin Luther's Germany. The Hussite Reformation was medieval Bohemia's largest and most seminal contribution to Europe's cultural development and the most important harbinger of the sixteenth-century European Protestant Reformations.

The Czech Lands became renowned for their cultural and economic prowess under the increasingly cosmopolitan Luxembourg dynasty (1310–1437), whose King Charles (reg. 1346–78) also became Holy Roman Emperor in 1346. In 1348, Charles founded Prague University, the first in the Holy Roman Empire and East Central Europe. It was intended to be a genuinely universal and cosmopolitan institution, in which Czech and Polish would stand alongside Latin, Italian and German as languages of instruction; and it soon had around 7,000 students in a city of about 40,000 inhabitants (Bradley 1971: 38). In 1350 Charles decided to make Prague the capital of the 'Holy Roman Empire' – a status which it retained until 1400. He initiated the construction of a Prague 'New Town', whose population eventually exceeded that of the 'Old Town'. He also rebuilt the royal castle of Hradcany and numerous fortresses, churches and monasteries, erected a new stone bridge across the River Vltava (the famously elegant Charles Bridge, which still links the two halves of the capital) and launched the construction of the cathedral of St Vitus. He brought foreign architects and artists to embellish Prague with masterpieces of the late Gothic style, while his court and chancery became centres of art and learning (Kaminsky 1967: 7). Prague thus developed into a magnificent and truly European city which attracted merchants, nobles, clergy, architects and students from the Germanic world, France, Italy, Poland and Hungary. During the 1350s Charles tamed the unruly Czech magnates and outlawed baronial banditry, whereupon law and order descended on the countryside and the king's highways became relatively safe for traders. In the agricultural sector he actively promoted viticulture, fruit farming and commercial carp ponds and established special tribunals to adjudicate disputes between landlords and peasants. Commerce and the craft industry were also stimulated by Charles's public works programmes, a currency reform and an incipient codification of customary law (Bradley 1971: 35–6).

The Hussite Reformation in fifteenth-century Bohemia

However, the growing wealth of the Czech Lands and the Catholic Church also fostered moral laxity and corruption, against which the early fifteenth-century 'Hussite Reformation' emerged by way of reaction. In Bohemia, as in many other parts of Catholic Christendom, the Catholic Church was conspicuously in need of reform, partly because the accumulation of ecclesiastical riches had palpably become an end in itself. By the fourteenth century the Church owned more than one-third of the land in the Kingdom of Bohemia (Kavka 1960: 45). Senior clergy and the medicant orders were allegedly enriching themselves through all sorts of scams and abuses, including simony, pluralism and the charging of extortionate burial fees (Kaminsky 1967: 11, 20; Betts 1947: 375, 379). Furthermore, the expansion of Bohemia's economy and revenues, combined with the proliferation of its holy relics and shrines, a burgeoning traffic in indulgences and the increasing habit of making the confirmation of ecclesiastical appointments subject to financial payments to the papacy, was turning the Kingdom of Bohemia into a prime target for papal exploitation and scams.

Charles persuaded the preacher Konrad Waldhauser to settle in Prague in 1363. From then until his death in 1369, Waldhauser regularly chastized Prague's mostly German burghers for their avarice, pride, opulence and religious pusillanimity and lashed out against the vices and inadequacies of the mendicant orders and even the regular clergy 'who sought their own profit instead of attending to the care of the souls entrusted to them' (Kaminsky 1967: 1967). His teachings influenced the up-and-coming generations of Czech religious reformers, especially Jan Milic of Kromeriz and Matej of Janov.

In 1363 Jan Milic decided to renounce his life of comfort and official status as a senior royal servitor and to become an impecunious preacher. From 1364 until his death in 1374, Milic proclaimed that there were many signs that the long-awaited Day of Judgement was approaching and that Christendom was woefully unprepared for the anticipated Second Coming of Christ. He therefore urged Christians to take Holy Communion frequently and *sub utraque specie* ('in both kinds', i.e. both the bread and the wine), in order to be ready at all times for the Second Coming and the Last Judgement, in accordance with Christ's bidding at the Last Supper. Before long the main body of adherents of the Czech reform movement became known either as 'Utraquists', on account of their insistence that lay Christians as well as clergy should regularly take Holy Communion *sub utraque specie*, or as 'Calixtines', because the Communion chalice (*calix*) became their symbol and clarion call. In Roman Catholic custom (since the twelfth century) the taking of Communion wine was reserved for the clergy. Milic emphasized that this was contrary to Christ's explicit teaching and that, in God's eyes, lay Christians and their clergy ought to be (and indeed were) on a more equal footing.

In 1367 Milic was allowed to travel to Rome to present his views on the crisis of Christendom to the Pope and, when Milic was imprisoned by the Roman Inquisition on account of his criticisms of the Catholic clergy, Emperor Charles even intervened to secure his release. After his return to Prague, moreover, Milic was allowed to continue to preach unmolested from 1369 until his death. 'He attracted a band of preachers who joined him in his poor life, dependent on alms, constantly working among the people. Increasing numbers of the laity also adhered to his movement.' When Milic launched a mission to rescue and reform the city's prostitutes, King Charles gave him one of Prague's leading brothels. Having raised enough money to acquire some of the adjacent properties and having received others as gifts, Milic set up a community which he named 'Jerusalem', devoted primarily 'to the housing and upkeep of the harlots he had converted' (Kaminsky 1967: 12).

What really hit home were his condemnations of the lapses and failings of the Church. Milic denounced not only simony, but 'the prelates' luxury and concubinage, their wealth and pluralism, their practice of usury . . . He also followed Waldhauser in denouncing the privileges of the mendicant orders, who . . . sold indulgences and used their special status to accumulate riches.' Nevertheless, he repeatedly affirmed his allegiance to the papacy and his fervent desire that the Pope would act 'to restore the purity of the Church, preferably by calling a general council in Rome'. Thus his stance implied 'not subversion but restoration of ecclesiastical authority' (p. 11).

Jan Milic of Kromeriz was thus the true 'father' of the incipient Czech Reformation (Kavka 1994: 131). However, his 'Jerusalem' community did not long survive his death in 1374, and the practice of frequent lay Communion *sub utraque specie* was condemned by the 'masters' of Prague University in 1388, whereupon a Church Synod decreed that the laity could take Communion only once a month (Kaminsky 1967: 14, 18). In 1391, however, the movement which Milic had launched found a new focus in the Bethlehem Chapel. This emphasized zealous preaching of the Gospel to one and all, using the first Czech translation of the scriptures which became available in the 1370s (Kavka 1994: 132).

Milic did not develop an elaborate and coherent system of doctrine and belief. His ideas and activities had emerged as spontaneous ad hoc responses to particular problems. The task of mould-ing his precepts into a coherent corpus of religious doctrines was mainly taken up by Matej of Janov (*c.*1350–93), a Czech noble who had fallen under the influence of Milic in 1372 but studied at the University of Paris from 1373 to 1381. In Paris Janov also came across criticisms of ecclesiastical abuses, opulence and laxity written by William of St Amour during the previous century, and he incorporated these into his own *Regulae veteris et novi testamenti* ('Rules of the Old and New Tes-taments'). Janov strove to square the circle: 'to combine the ideal of pietism with that of the hierar-chical Church. His fervour, his erudition, the broad range of his thought, which dealt with the local problem in European terms and defined the current situation in terms of the whole of Christian history – these traits would later make his *Regulae* an inexhaustible source of inspiration', espe-cially for the more radical Czech religious reformers (Kaminsky 1967: 14–15, 22–3). Janov called for 'a restoration of the Church by a return to its apostolic origins and a consistent observance of the "Rules of the Old and New Testaments" . . . discarding all that could not be supported by the evi-dence of Scripture', although he tempered this strict biblicism with a 'belief in ongoing revelation by the Holy Spirit' (Kavka 1994: 132). His central message was that the lives of the clergy should be reformed and the true faith be preached to the laity, who should be united with Christ through frequent Communion *sub utraque specie*, under the leadership of 'the holy people, the community of the saints within the ecclesiastical establishment' (Kaminsky 1967: 21).

During the 1380s and 1390s the debates and contests between Bohemia's Christian reformers and conservatives became increasingly caught up in a struggle between Czech and German 'masters' for control of Prague University, whereupon the university's originally universalist and cosmopoli-tan ideals got submerged by waves of acrimony, intolerance and xenophobia. King Vaclav IV (reg. 1378–1419), who succeeded Emperor Charles, endeavoured to exploit these currents for his own political advantage, but was ultimately unable to control them. In 1403 the still dominant Prague Germans accused their Czech antagonists of being adherents and peddlers of the radical ideas of the dissident Oxford philosopher and theologian John Wyclif (c. 1330–84). Wyclif's major religious tracts, written between 1374 and 1384, argued that lay Christians should be able to read and inter-pret the Bible for themselves and in their own language. They also downplayed the differences between lay Christians and the clergy, denounced ecclesiastical wealth and luxury, denied papal supremacy, and rejected the doctrine of transubstantiation (the belief that the bread and the wine, respectively, become the body and the blood of Christ during Holy Communion). Wyclif's reli-gious teachings had already been condemned as 'heretical' by English Catholic bishops in 1382 and 1392, but in 1403 the mainly German congregation of the University of Prague 'raised the stakes' by condemning as 'heretical' a specially prepared list of forty-five Wyclifite tenets which came to be known as 'the Forty-Five Articles'. Wyclif's ideas were indeed being studied by like-minded Czechs at that time. Contacts between England and Bohemia had increased considerably after 1382, when England's King Richard II (reg. 1377–99) married the sister of Bohemia's King Vaclav IV.

The Czech reception of Wyclifism became a major focus of the above-mentioned conflict between Czech and German 'masters' (professors) at Prague University during the 1390s (Kaminsky 1967: 23–4). Wyclif's thought strongly influenced the Czech preacher and professor Jan Hus (c.1371–1415), and the Milic movement metamorphosed into a movement led by Hus (pp. 34–5). However, Hus did not simply appropriate Wyclif's ideas. The impact of the latter on the Hussite movement should be viewed, not as cause and effect, but in terms of parallel perceptions of (and responses to) the problems of fourteenth-century Catholic Christendom (pp. 24–5). 'Hus did copy whole pages and passages of Wyclif into his own works', but this occurred because 'the heritage of the Bohemian religious movement' *predisposed* him to do so (p. 36). Plagiarism and originality were viewed differently then. The cult of originality had not yet developed and plagiarism was commonplace, even at Oxford. Hus copied 'not slavishly but freely and creatively, disposing over the whole Wyclifite corpus with consummate skill . . . and converting the very difficult, often chaotic works of Wyclif into powerful, effective books' (Kaminsky 1967: 36). Thus Wyclif's ideas, as assimilated by the Hussite movement, strongly contributed to the emergence of a country-wide religious reformation which also had substantial repercussions in adjacent Hungary and Poland (Betts 1947: 382–3), whereas in their original forms and setting they merely caused a few ripples on the English mill-ponds.

Hus embraced Wyclif's premise that the 'law of Christ' (*lex Christi*) offered an 'absolutely self-sufficient' foundation for the administration of the Church and for all Christian thought and conduct. 'This law is embodied in Scripture, which is superior to all other sources of faith, especially to the traditions relied on by the Roman Church; by means of Scripture and using our own reason, we can learn God's truth' (Kavka 1994: 132). Hus accepted Wyclif's view that, since the reign of Emperor Constantine (AD 312–37), the Church had succumbed to 'the lure of wealth and power and betrayed its mission' (p. 133). In *De ecclesia* (1413), Hus declared that 'no one is truly the vicar of Christ . . . unless he follow him in every way of life' (Kaminsky 1967: 53). Hus expected the clergy as a whole to renounce wealth and dominion, to lead and influence by example, and to live on alms. He thought that ecclesiastical wealth had diverted the clergy from their religious mission to a preoccupation with gaining benefices (Kavka 1960: 46). Like Wyclif, Hus also expected the powerful (including senior churchmen) to forfeit respect and authority if they fell into a state of mortal sin. He also believed that 'everyone had the right, even the duty, to defy orders that were contrary to binding principles of justice, which were to be judged by a person's own reason' (Kavka 1994: 132–3).

Nevertheless, Hus also diverged from Wyclif in certain fundamentals. He did not support Wyclif's rejection of the doctrine of transubstantiation, nor did he fully share Wyclif's willingness to trust secular rulers to effect a thorough reformation of the Church 'from above'. Like Milic and Janov, Hus believed that a reformation of the Church had to be effected mainly 'from within' and 'from below', on the initiative of the community of truly committed Christian clergy and laity. To this end he favoured a return to the election of priests and prelates by the Christian community (on the model of the early Church), in place of appointments 'from above' (Kavka 1994: 133).

The conflict between Czech and German Catholics in Prague became fatally entangled with the politics of both the Holy Roman Empire and the so-called 'papal schism' of 1378–1417 (between rival Popes in Rome and Avignon). To cut a long story short, this resulted in Jan Hus being summoned to defend himself against charges of heresy at a gathering of Catholic Church leaders known as the Council of Constance (1414–17). This was convened at the behest of Vaclav's brother Sigismund, who in 1410 became Holy Roman Emperor in addition to being King of Hungary. The Council's main task was to re-establish the unity and authority of the Church.

Having received prior guarantees concerning his personal safety from Emperor Sigismund, who had a vested interest in resolving religious tensions in his brother's Kingdom of Bohemia (which Sigismund hoped to inherit), Hus welcomed this opportunity to expound and defend his views in front of the leaders of the Catholic Church, in the naive belief that they would give him a fair and honest hearing. After all, Hus was aiming to reform and rejuvenate the Roman Catholic Church – not to subvert it or to break with it (Kaminsky 1967: 222). At the very least, he sought recognition of a reformed Bohemian Church *within* the Roman Catholic communion. Hus staked everything on a public hearing at the Council of Constance, hoping that he could thereby secure the future of Europe's first Reformation – either as the start of a general European Reformation or as a more localized 'Reformation in one country'.

In breach of Emperor Sigismund's guarantees, Hus was imprisoned soon after his arrival in Constance on 4 November 1414. He was put on trial, condemned as a heretic, and was burned to death on 6 July 1415, not only for daring to criticize corrupt ecclesiastical practices, but also for voicing doctrinal disagreements with high and mighty prelates who had not come to Constance to engage in difficult disputes with an upstart professor from Prague. Instead of defending his actual views, Hus found that he was forced to defend himself against views attributed to the Czech religious reformers en bloc by their enemies, partly because they sought to tar all reformers with the same brush, and partly because they were reluctant actually to read the allegedly 'heretical' and/or 'subversive' writings which they were attacking. Confronted with the list of Forty-Five Articles, Hus responded to most of them that he did not and had not held such views ('nec tenui nec non teneo'), 'and in most cases he was precisely or substantially correct' (Kaminsky 1967: 53).

Hus's powerful denunciations of the vices of the clergy had undoubtedly helped to arouse hatred and to bring people on to the streets against the unrepentant Catholic clergy from 1408 onwards. Moreover, Wyclif's ecclesiology had implicitly denied the Roman Church 'its title to institutional holiness, and hence . . . its final authority . . . Hus here followed Wyclif without significant variation' (p. 38). Hus had at least *appeared* to argue that the Pope was 'Antichrist' (p. 40), that the papal *Curia* was 'the synagogue of Satan' (p. 53), and that prelates engorged in 'sin and vice' were 'enemies of Jesus Christ' (p. 38).

Nevertheless, many of the doctrines which Hus actually or allegedly propounded 'were not heretical at all'. 'He did, to be sure, take up the ideas of John Wyclif, but always with the necessary additions or subtractions to make them conformable to orthodoxy' (Kaminsky 1967: 35). 'He never ceased . . . to maintain that his programme was orthodox' (p. 5). His aim, like that of so many Christian reformers, was to restore the Church to its original purity, rather than to reject, subvert or split it. When accused of holding the view that 'To enrich the clergy is against the rule of Christ', he replied that 'clerics may legitimately have riches so long as they do not abuse them' (p. 54).

Unlike the more intransigent reformers, Hus's chief concern was to bring the Catholic Church as a whole into line with the teachings of the Gospels and St Paul (Kaminsky 1967: 79). This was not only why he went to Constance, but also the main reason why he refrained from endorsing the call for frequent lay Communion *sub utraque specie* until 21 June 1415, just two weeks before his death (p. 134). The more radical reformers had long insisted that this practice was not merely prudent and desirable (in order to keep the practitioner perpetually prepared for the Second Coming) and consistent with the practice of the early Church, but also indispensable to individual salvation. They cited John 6:53 ('Except ye eat the flesh of the Son of man and drink his blood, ye have no life in you') and Matthew 26:27–8 ('And he took the cup and gave thanks, and gave it to them saying, Drink ye all of it; for this is my blood of the new testament, which is shed for many for the remission of sins'). By contrast, Hus never argued that the taking of Communion wine (the chalice) was a prerequisite for salvation (Kaminsky 1967: 127). Hus seems to have accepted the Catholic doctrine that lay Christians needed to receive only the bread, because (i) the 'real presence' of Christ was integral to both the bread and the wine, (ii) John 6:53 was open to a more spiritual interpretation, and (iii) Christ's twelve Apostles were prototypes of the clergy, not the laity (p. 11). Until almost the end, therefore, Hus considered that the Czech reformers' growing insistence on the chalice for lay Christians was merely erecting an unnecessary additional barrier to a strongly desired accommodation with the Catholic Church. In different circumstances a compromise might have emerged, bearing in mind that lay Communion *sub utraque specie* had been common practice in the Catholic Church until the twelfth century and has always been so in the Eastern Orthodox Church. However, the Council of Constance had been convened expressly to re-establish the unity and authority of the Catholic Church, *not to accommodate diversity*. On 15 June 1415, therefore, lay Communion *sub utraque specie* was emphatically condemned (Kaminsky 1867: 6). The church leaders were 'not interested in an accommodation' (p. 222).

When Hus realized that the Council of Constance had thus precluded any possibility of an accommodation with the Czech reformers, he finally endorsed lay Comminion *sub utraque specie*, not out of a conversion to the idea that it was a prerequisite for salvation, but for the sake of greater doctrinal unity within the reform movement and increased consistency with his own calls for a return to the practices of the early Church. He understood that, if the reform movement was to survive, the reformers would have to close ranks in support of Utraquism. On 21 June 1415 Hus wrote as follows to the only other prominent Czech religious reformer still unconvinced of the need for lay Christians to partake of the Communion wine: 'Do not oppose the sacrament of the cup of the Lord which the Lord instituted through Himself and His apostle. For no scripture is opposed to it, but only a custom which I suppose has grown up by negligence. We ought not to follow custom, but Christ's example . . . I beseech you for God's sake to attack [the radical Utraquist] Master Jakoubek no longer, lest a schism occurs among the faithful that would delight the devil' (Hus 1972: 181–2).

The Council of Constance was not prepared to listen to unpalatable truths about Church malpractices from the likes of Jan Hus or his compatriot Jeronym Prazsky, who was similarly burned as a heretic at the Council's command on 30 May 1416. The burning of Jan Hus and Jeronym Prazsky as 'heretics' helped to confine Europe's first Reformation to the Czech Lands and to delay the onset of a wider European Reformation until Martin Luther's defiant stand in 1517.

The imprisonment, trial and burning of Jan Hus and intransigent condemnation of Utraquism by the Council of Constance precipitated popular protests and disorders in Bohemia and incensed the increasingly Utraquist Czech nobility. There were innumerable written complaints and petitions against the way that Hus had been treated, not only from the Czech Lands but also from the Polish nobility (Betts 1947: 381–2). During September 1415, 452 Czech nobles attached their seals to eight copies of a letter proclaiming that Jan Hus had lived 'piously and gently in Christ' and that his teachings had been Catholic and free from heresy. At Constance, their letter stated, 'Hus confessed to no crime, nor was he legitimately and properly convicted of any, nor were any errors or heresies . . . demonstrated against him'. Those who claimed that Bohemia and Moravia were teeming with doctrinal errors were denounced as foul liars and traitors. Finally, the letter warned that the signatories would appeal to a future Pope and that, in the meantime, they would 'defend and protect, to the point of shedding our blood, the Law of our Lord Jesus Christ and its devout, humble and constant preachers, disregarding all human statutes to the contrary' (quoted by Kaminsky 1967: 143). That same month many Hussite nobles formed a Hussite League, whose founding pact stated: 'We shall command that on all our domains and properties the Word of God be freely preached and heard . . . We have also agreed to enjoin all our clergy whom we have under us not to accept any excommunications from anyone except those bishops under whom we live in Bohemia and Moravia . . . But if any of the bishops under whom we live should seek to oppress us or our clergy by improper excommunications or by force . . . we shall not obey them . . . And if anyone should seek to oppress us with any other, foreign excommunications, and should invoke the secular arm in connection with the issuing of them, we ought and wish to be of assistance to each other . . . so that we may not be oppressed' (quoted on pp. 144–5). This was in effect a call for the Bohemian (Czech) Church to free itself from the jurisdiction of Europe's Roman Catholic Church and to become a self-governing body under the protection of the Hussite nobility, who promised to defend it against potential royal and/or episcopal oppression as well as foreign interference. At the same time Prague University reaffirmed its support for Hus (p. 159).

The immediate response of Bohemia's Catholic prelates, nobles and some royal officials (especially Bohemian Germans) was to harass and to threaten to excommunicate unsanctioned itinerant preachers and the many lay Christians who, in defiance of the Council's ban, continued to take Communion *sub utraque specie*. In October 1415 a Catholic League was launched in opposition to the Hussite League (Kaminsky 1967: 147, 157). In November 1415, under pressure from the Council of Constance, Prague's Archbishop Konrad of Vechty (a German) ordered Bohemia's Catholic clergy to punish defiant Czechs by refusing to administer any of the sacraments to them (other than baptism). However, this so-called 'interdict' backfired: 'With . . . the churches silent and empty, the priests and preachers of the Hussite party could move in and take over' (pp. 158–60). Moreover, since the Catholic clergy were reneging on their religious duties, Hussite nobles, preachers, professors and burghers stepped up the ongoing 'secularization' of ecclesiastical estates, which had accounted for 'perhaps a third of the cultivable land' (p. 149), and deprived many Catholic priests of their benefices (p. 156). During the winter of 1415–16 'a sizeable portion of the Bohemian church organization thus passed into Hussite hands' (p. 161). In February 1416 the Council of Constance retaliated by summoning the 452 Czech nobles whose seals had been appended to the defiant letter of protest against the burning of Jan Hus in September 1415 'to appear before it for judgement' (p. 149). Their failure to show up contributed to the Council's decision to have Jeronym Prazsky burned as a heretic on 30 May 1416. The Council also ordered the closure of Prague University (which had originally been a papal foundation), but the university defiantly ignored this command (Bradley 1971: 47). The heavy-handed actions of the Catholic Church merely helped to unite Czech religious dissidents behind Utraquism, with the result that 'by the end of 1416 the lay chalice was accepted by all who stood for the cause of Hus', although (like Hus) most of the 'masters' at Prague University 'still shrank from the radical position that Utraquist Communion was necessary to salvation' (Kaminsky 1967: 161).

From 1416 to 1418 royal as well as ecclesiastical authority collapsed, as both Hussite and Catholic nobles, peasants and townspeople increasingly took matters (and property) into their own hands. In 1418, however, the new Pope elected by the Council of Constance in November 1417 ordered King Vaclav IV to reassert royal and Roman Catholic control of Bohemia and even to force Hussites publicly to approve the condemnation and burning of Jan Hus (Kaminsky 1967: 266). In February 1419, after additional pressure and threats from Emperor Sigismund, who by then was fully expecting to inherit the Bohemian throne, Vaclav IV finally launched a concerted campaign to restrict Utraquism severely and to restore former ecclesiastical properties and benefices to their previous Catholic incumbents. From February to June 1419, the Hussites of Prague seemed meekly to submit 'to a barely tolerated existence in a few churches' (p. 269). They retained merely 'a portion of the Catholic church-structure', and were denied an independent Hussite Church (p. 268). Catholic church services were finally resumed (p. 268) and it appeared that the Catholics were regaining full control of Prague's religious life (p. 272).

Partly in response to these new restrictions and setbacks, in early 1419 Utraquists and many more radical Christians began regularly to congregate in remote places, mainly on hilltops, where they received lay Communion 'under both kinds' and listened to fiery (and often millenarian) preaching in an atmosphere of supercharged enthusiasm. This was the beginning of the radical 'Taborite' movement, named after one of the most influential of these religious encampments, located on a hill in southern Bohemia which was given the biblical name of Mount Tabor. These hilltop congregations were not merely a means of evading the royal restrictions on lay Communion 'under both kinds' in Prague and other major towns. Early Christian tradition identified Mount Tabor as the refuge in Galilee to which Christ and his disciples withdrew to get away from their persecutors and to pray and contemplate in peace and safety, and from which the disciples launched the early Christian Church soon after Christ's crucifixion (Kaminsky 1967: 282). Aptly, it was from the new Mount Tabor that Bohemia's radical Christians relaunched the Hussite movement and turned the tables on Vaclav IV and the Catholic Church in July 1419 (pp. 277–8).

After further hesitation, Vaclav IV went on to the offensive on 6 July 1419. He installed anti-Hussite magistrates (town councillors) in Prague New Town. These prohibited mass processions, forcibly removed parish schools from Hussite control and restored them to the Catholic Church, and imprisoned some lay Christians for the offence of taking Communion 'under both kinds'. On 22 July, however, tens of thousands of Czechs attended a 'nationwide congregation' at Mount Tabor, probably in preparation for action to bring Prague back under Hussite control and possibly to make contingency plans for the election of a new (Hussite) archbishop and/or king (Kaminsky 1967: 289–91). On 30 July a mass procession of radical Utraquists surrounded the Town Hall of Prague's New Town and evicted the anti-Hussite magistrates and other Catholics who were attending a meeting there, throwing about thirteen of them out of a high window to their deaths and killing several others as well. This initiated an enduring Czech tradition of throwing political opponents out of high windows, known euphemistically as 'defenestration'. Shortly afterwards new magistrates, Hussite 'men of substance' rather than impoverished radicals, were elected. They were duly confirmed in office by Vaclav IV, who grudgingly accepted what was in effect a Hussite coup reversing the Catholic gains of the previous months, but the Hussite victory was almost immediately placed in jeopardy by King Vaclav's death from an apoplectic stroke on 16 August 1419 (pp. 294–6).

In order to increase their unity, the Hussites and the religious radicals hurriedly promulgated a joint programme, the so-called Four Articles of Prague: (i) unimpeded preaching of the Gospel to everyone; (ii) Communion 'under both kinds' for all Christians; (iii) the clergy to be divested of all worldly power and wealth; and (iv) public punishment of mortal sins, irrespective of a culprit's class or status (Kavka 1994: 152). 'Among the sins to be punished . . . were, in addition to theft, drunkenness and gambling, the exaction of feudal rents and an increase in interest and taxes. This was a plain attack on certain forms of feudal oppression' (Macek 1958: 46–7).

Following Vaclav IV's death, Prague radicals 'attacked various churches and monasteries, destroyed the brothels and kept the city in turmoil . . . In the provinces, too, radical Hussites attacked, smashed and burned monasteries' (Kaminsky 1967: 298). The storm centres of radical sectarianism shifted for a time from Mount Tabor in southern Bohemia to Plzen in western Bohemia (p. 299). Since he was at that time preoccupied with Hungary's conflicts with the Turks and the Venetians, Emperor Sigismund instructed the Bohemian nobility to uphold the peace and the old religious status quo until the convocation of a Bohemian Synod and Diet, 'whose decisions would be referred to the Pope' (p. 303).

The more moderate or conservative Hussites (including most of the Hussite nobles, officials, patricians and masters of Prague University), who had hitherto advocated co-operation with temporal rulers as a means of reforming the Church and divesting it of undue power and wealth, concluded that they had little option but to submit to Sigismund's instructions and hope for the best. On 16 October 1419, therefore, there emerged 'a union of Catholics and conservative Hussites'. This evidently involved agreements to disagree about the meaning and practice of Holy Communion and to 'coexist in peace until Sigismund could come, take over the realm and procure a papal reconsideration of Utraquism' (Kaminsky 1967: 301–2). Even the magistrates of Prague's Old Town formally submitted to royal authority. During October many Taborite radicals rumbustuously withdrew from Prague, 'smashing images in churches and monasteries' as they went, while the royalist union hired 'German and other non-Czech mercenaries to maintain order' (p. 306).

In retaliation, Prague radicals led by the professional soldier Jan Zizka attacked and captured the royal fortress of Vysehrad on 25 October 1419, while in early November there were renewed inflows of provincial Taborites into the capital to reinforce the radicals. Contingents from western Bohemia (including Plzen) managed to reach Prague without a fight, but those from the south (from Usti) were ambushed by royalist nobles near Zivhost and suffered heavy casualities. On hearing of this battle, which marked the start of the Hussite Wars, Prague radicals expelled the royalists from

Prague's Old Town and Prague Castle (Kaminsky 1967: 307). On 13 November 1419, however, Prague's frightened magistrates concluded another truce with the royalists, surrendered the Vysehrad fortress and endeavoured to prevent any further destruction of images, churches and monasteries, in return for royalist pledges to tolerate Utraquism (p. 308).

Nevertheless, Catholics and royalists took advantage of this ostensible truce to hunt down Hussites and Taborites in the provinces. Many Taborites then congregated in 'five cities of refuge' (Plzen, Zatec, Louny, Slany and Klatovy), in keeping with adventist prophecies that at the Second Coming of Christ 'the evil would perish and be exterminated, while the good would be preserved in five cities' (Kaminsky 1867: 310–12). Meanwhile, Sigismund did not leave Hungary until early December 1419 and, instead of making straight for Prague, he ordered the Bohemian Estates to attend a Christmas Diet at Brno in Moravia. There he exacted oaths of obedience, promises that Hussite barricades and fortifications would be dismantled, and guarantees for the safety of Catholics who returned to Prague (pp. 313, 362).

However, the abject submission of the Prague patricians, the masters of Prague University and the Hussite nobility to the Emperor-King in December 1419 'inaugurated a period of reactionary resurgence' as Catholic priests, officials and burghers ('mostly Germans') returned to Prague boasting of 'a rosy future' under Sigismund, who 'replaced Hussite castellans and burgraves throughout Bohemia with Catholics' (pp. 314–15). Before long, royalist barons were 'rounding up' and sending Hussites and Taborites 'to the Germans who operated the Kutna Hora extermination centre' (p. 326). Prague's moderate Hussites helplessly looked on, realizing that 'they were silent partners in the extermination of their brethren' (p. 363).

Under increasingly savage persecution, Taborite radicals rapidly turned from New Testament piety, pacifism and withdrawal to Old Testament wrath, belligerence and appeals for divine retribution against Catholics, Germans and royalists (Kaminsky 1967: 320–2). 'Great masses of people were concentrated in the Taborite towns . . . lacking any regular means of support, and imbued with the conviction that everything outside their communities was foredoomed to total destruction. Such a situation could hardly fail to generate violence' (p. 323). The Hussite 'masters' of Prague University recognized a Christian right of self-defence (pp. 326–7), but there was also 'religious violence, orgiastic and ritualistic . . . to purge the world in preparation for . . . Christ's second coming' (p. 347). In March 1420 the hard-pressed Taborite radicals of Pisek, Usti and Plzen congregated in the disused fortress of Hradiste, which rapidly became the new 'city of Tabor, to which Hussites from all over the realm now came', while communal funds were initiated 'as the foundation of a new economic order, that of communism' (p. 335). The inhabitants were organized into four self-supporting demotic armies (one of which was commanded by Jan Zizka), each carrying out fortification work day and night (p. 336). These armies set about imposing Taborite hegemony over as much of south Bohemia as possible. In the process 'towns, fortresses, monasteries and villages of the enemy were conquered; victims were slaughtered . . . It was the total warfare called for by chiliast military doctrine' (p. 367). Many nearby villages ceased to exist as their inhabitants were drawn into Tabor (p. 336). Taborites took to heart Matthew 19:29: 'And every one that hath foresaken houses, or brethren, or sisters, or father, or mother, or wife, or children, or lands, for my name's sake, shall receive an hundredfold, and inherit everlasting life' (p. 316).

During these crucial early stages, Tabor's chances of survival were greatly enhanced by the fact that Sigismund was still preoccupied by his own preparations for a great military campaign against the Turks. Instead of moving directly from Brno to Prague, he proceeded to the Silesian city of Wroclaw, where he convoked an imperial Diet to drum up 'international' support for his projected crusade against the Ottomans. In January 1420, moreover, he implicitly abandoned his shrewd initial policy of keeping the moderate/conservative Hussites 'on side' by pursuing a gradualist strategy of suppressing the Hussite and Taborite rebels by slow strangulation. Instead, he made it known that, unless all Bohemia's religious dissenters immediately submitted to his authority, he would punish the Hussite community as a whole by force of arms, presumably so that he could then devote undivided attention and resources to fighting the Ottomans. In February 1420 he sent letters to barons, officials, prelates and magistrates all over Bohemia, warning them that anyone who refused either to renounce 'Wyclifism' or to ostracize and hunt down the Taborite congregations would be put to death (Kaminsky 1967: 332). In March 1420 Sigismund not only persuaded the Pope to sanction a Catholic crusade (holy war) against Wyclifites, Hussites and other heretics, but also authorized the execution of the Prague merchant Jan Krasa for refusing to accept a series of articles condemning Hus, Jeronym and Utraquism. This increased the motivation for Hussites 'to fight off the invading hordes of largely German crusaders'; thus Sigismund's 'stupidity' succeeded in rallying Hussites to the defence of the Four Articles of Prague (pp. 362–9).

Radical Hussites and Taborites carried out a 'radical coup' in Prague on 27 May 1420. The city magistrates who had submitted to Sigismund were deposed and more radical replacements were elected (Kaminsky 1967: 372). The coup was followed by a house-to-house visitation of non-Utraquists, who were given the choice of either accepting Communion *sub utraque specie* or going into exile (p. 374).

Sigismund finally arrived in Prague with an army of around a hundred thousand Catholic mercenaries and Crusaders in June 1420. He occupied Prague Castle, had himself crowned by Archbishop Konrad in Prague's cathedral (across the river from the city) and laid siege to the Old and New Towns. On 14 July, however, Sigismund's army was routed by Taborite forces under Jan Zizka at Vitkov Hill. Sigismund returned to Prague with another large army in November 1420, yet this too was routed by Zizka's remarkable Taborites. Hussite and Taborite forces fought off further invasions of Bohemia by Sigismund and his German/imperial allies in 1421, 1422, 1423–4, 1426, 1427 and 1431. All eight invasions helped divert Bohemia's religious dissenters from their own internal differences of opinion, quarrels and power struggles, which might otherwise have torn the kingdom apart. Their victories were attributable not only to strength of religious conviction, but also to the military wizardry and innovations of Jan Zizka, who pioneered the use of light artillery in open battle. Hitherto, Europeans had used artillery merely as siege weapons. Zizka deftly deployed field guns (howitzers) mounted on fortified wagons which (when the need arose) were rapidly chained together to form almost impregnable circular wagon-forts (laager), from within which his gunners and infantry-riflemen could freely fire at the relatively vulnerable enemy cavalry and attacking infantry. He also made skilful use of terrain, mobility and surprise tactics.

After Zizka's death (from plague) in 1424, Taborite armies were led with similar élan by the charismatic soldier-priest Prokop the Shaven, a highly educated man from a Prague patrician family. Their famed invincibility 'struck such terror in the hearts of the crusaders that . . . at Tachov (1427) and Domazlice (1431) the latter no sooner heard the rumble of the approaching wagons and the singing of the Hussite battle hymn "Ye Warriors of God" than they took to flight' (Kavka 1960: 50). Not content with the defence of Bohemia and Moravia, however, these Czech warriors 'believed that they had a divine mission to take the Word of God to other lands, and their terrible wagon armies rolled destructively through Silesia, Thuringia, Saxony, Bavaria, even in 1433 right through Poland to the mouth of the Vistula' (Hay and Betts 1970: 228).

Notwithstanding their military prowess, the Czech religious dissenters were far from united. In August 1420 the Taborites sought the suppression of any remaining ecclesiastical wealth, simony, images and relics, the subjection of the writings of the masters of Prague University to close scrutiny and censorship by Christian zealots, and the purging and public punishment of sins such as fornication, adultery, prostitution, usury, fraud, commercial trickery, trafficking in stolen goods, swearing, the sale and consumption of alcoholic drinks, clerical misdemeanours and the wearing of fancy clothes (Kaminsky 1967: 376–7). A crucial division between Taborites and moderate Hussites opened up in September 1420, when the Taborites decisively broke with the Roman Catholic Church by electing their own bishop (i.e. one not consecrated by the Pope or his appointees, in accordance with the so-called apostolic succession) and by giving their elected clergy much the same rights and status as lay Christians. 'Taborite Hussitism anticipated the Reformation of the sixteenth century in the reinstitution of the direct relationship between Christ and the lay person' (Kavka 1994: 134–5).

For the moderate adherents of Hus's own teaching, the 'great dream of a church regenerated first in Bohemia, then in the world' remained the paramount aim (Kaminsky 1967: 435). They still believed in the apostolic succession – the anointing of priests by bishops who had been consecrated either by the Pope or by prelates consecrated by him (p. 383). They also feared the egalitarian (and potentially destabilizing) implications of the election of bishops and other clergy. Thus, for political and social as well as religious reasons, they had no desire to burn their bridges with Rome. They even tried to legitimize the Hussite Church and re-establish episcopal authority through Archbishop Konrad, who joined the Hussites on 21 April 1421 (p. 437). In 1421 the still noble-dominated Bohemian Diet nevertheless declared Sigismund deposed and offered the Bohemian crown to Jogaila (Jagiello), the ruler of Poland-Lithuania, on condition that he agreed to accept and uphold the Four Articles of Prague. He politely declined this 'poisoned chalice', but offered his ineffectual nephew Zygmunt Korybutowicz as regent. However, he proved unacceptable to the radical Czech dissenters, who demanded a native Czech ruler and drove him back to Poland-Lithuania in 1427. For lack of a generally acceptable king, therefore, the noble-dominated Bohemian Diet became the 'sovereign' power in the land from 1420 to 1436 and again from 1439 to 1453. It even 'appointed and controlled the consistory of priests and masters of the university which governed the Hussite Church right down to 1620' (Hay and Betts 1970: 228). By 1422 moderate Hussites had regained the upper hand in Prague (Kavka 1960: 50). Until the final showdown in 1434, Prague and Tabor were rival power centres, each propagating its own religious, political and social programme and seeking to extend its dominion (Kaminsky 1967: 461). The Hussite Wars of 1419–34 were finally brought to a conclusion by an unstable compromise permitting a fragile Catholic–Hussite modus vivendi in 1433 and by the bloody suppression of the more radical Hussites by an alliance of conservative Hussites with Bohemian Catholics in 1434.

The Hussite Reformation had radical repercussions. It 'broadened the medieval concept of freedom as a personal privilege to be acquired by rank or service or money, into a universal moral principle' (Brock 1957: 22). In contrast to the rest of East Central Europe, Czech burghers obtained substantial representation in the Bohemian Diet, while the Catholic Church forfeited most of its formerly vast property and power. Ethnic Czechs made gains at ethnic German expense. Many Germans left Bohemia altogether, both as a result of their loss of control of Prague University to the Czechs in 1409 and as a result of the expropriation of ecclesiastical property and the urban upheavals of 1419–21. The Czechs thus regained majority status in Prague and several other towns (until the 1620s), while Czech became more established as the language of administration, education, scholarship and worship (Krofta 1936: 85–6; Kavka 1960: 53).

These gains had a downside, however. Patriotism easily degenerated into aggression and xenophobia. Religious and social unrest and recurrent warfare proved disruptive, draining and debilitating, while the substantial increases in the landholdings and power of the nobility, combined with incipient labour shortages, encouraged landowners to exact more onerous seigneurial dues from the peasantry. Many peasants tried to oppose this, but their resistance eventually evoked increased legal restraints on peasant freedoms in 1487, 1497 and 1500.

As a result of the German exodus, chronic instability, frequent warfare, increased use of the vernacular, and diminished use of Latin and German, the University of Prague ceased to be a major cosmopolitan institution of learning. Prague became a more 'parochial' city, while the Czech Lands became somewhat isolated and culturally/intellectually impoverished, at least until the early sixteenth century. 'By retarding, and for some time entirely preventing, the influx of new currents of thought from the civilized West, Hussitism checked the development of the Czech nation in more than one branch of culture' (Krofta 1936: 87). Large parts of Bohemia's artistic and architectural heritage fell victim to the iconoclasm of Hussite and Taborite bigots, who destroyed countless churches, monasteries, paintings and statues. Violent conflict, Hussite and Taborite philistinism, and the loss of royal and ecclesiastical patronage kept artists, architects and craftsmen from the production of new works of art and architecture, obliged many to change occupation and/or emigrate, and temporarily denuded Bohemia of indigenous artistic and architectural talent (p. 86). On the cultural front, Hussite Bohemia made significant advances only in vernacular education, literature and music (especially hymns and chorales). Desiring to make the vernacular Bible and liturgy increasingly accessible to the laity, the Hussites promoted popular literacy and vernacular education for girls as well as for boys (Kavka 1960: 52–3).

The Hussite and Taborite movements and the matching fanaticism and bigotry of their Catholic opponents engendered stultifying intolerance, a preoccupation with religion and a narrowing of cultural horizons. These legacies 'erected barriers against the cultural and artistic transformations emanating from the Italian Renaissance' (Macek 1992: 215). They concentrated attention on 'the ethical and religious conception of the world and man, impeded the spread of the classical legacy', and delayed the emergence of secular art (pp. 210–11). Whereas the University of Krakow fostered the spread of Renaissance humanism in late fifteenth-century Poland, the University of Prague 'carried on teaching the obsolete curriculum of the Middle Ages' (p. 199). Only about 8 per cent of the publications printed in Bohemia between 1480 and 1526 'could be classified as Renaissance literature' (p. 206), while the eventual revival of artistic activities there was not a home-grown phenomenon but rather an alien 'transplantation' from Italy (p. 212). This was not entirely the Czechs' fault, however, since successive Catholic crusades against Bohemia (1420–31) and papal prohibition of foreign merchants from entering Bohemia (1420–95) largely 'sealed off the Czech Lands from the sources of the Italian Renaissance' (pp. 198–9).

The extinction of the Luxembourg dynasty in 1437 precipitated a decade of renewed instability and tension. This was overcome by the strong rule of Jiri of Podebrad (reg. 1448–71), a powerful conservative Hussite who became the 'Oliver Cromwell' of the Hussite Reformation. From 1465 until his death in 1471, however, he was locked in conflict with a rebel Catholic League backed by Hungary's King Matyas Hunyadi (reg. 1458–90). This conflict induced Preobrady and the Bohemian Diet to try to win the support of the Jagiellon rulers of Poland-Lithuania by offering the Bohemian throne to the Jagiellon crown prince.

Under the weak Roman Catholic Jagiellon kings who ruled Bohemia from 1471 to 1526 (and who also gained the Hungarian throne in 1490), the Czech Lands fell under the control of an increasingly privileged, oppressive and self-serving baronial oligarchy which gradually emasculated the country's (royal) central government and its hitherto flourishing towns, burghers and yeoman farmers. When the Jagiellon King of Bohemia (and Hungary) was defeated by the Ottoman Turks at the Battle of Mohacs in 1526 and died while fleeing, the Bohemian Diet conferred the vacant Bohemian throne on the Habsburg dynasty, which thereupon gradually brought the Czech Lands under Austrian rule. At first the Habsburgs allowed the Kingdom of Bohemia considerable freedom and autonomy. Partly as a result, the sixteenth-century Protestant Reformation spread like wildfire in the Czech Lands – initially among the large German minority (in the 1520s to 1540s), but later among most of the Czech inhabitants as well (1530s to 1580s).

BOHEMIA'S SECOND (PROTESTANT) 'REFORMATION'

During the early 1520s the Kingdom of Bohemia began to be influenced by the doctrines of the German Protestant reformer Martin Luther, who occasionally wrote to prominent Utraquists and the 'citizens of Prague'. Although Luther's Catholic opponents warned him against treading the same path as 'the heretic Hus', he publicly acknowledged the importance of Hus's teaching. The

Hussite Reformation had established precedents which Europe's Protestant reformers took into account, and lay Communion *sub utraque specie* was in due course adopted by 'practically all the reformed churches' (Kavka 1994: 140). During the 1520s, significantly, there were two new editions of *De ecclesia* (1413), Hus's major work written in Latin for a cosmopolitan European readership (rather than in Czech for a local one). Both the Hussite and the Lutheran reformation featured radical Waldensian, millenarian and eschatological currents, belief in the 'priesthood of all believers' and in the ultimate authority of the Holy Scriptures, advocacy of the vernacular and popular education, and various proponents of predestination (conceptions of 'the elect'). Both clearly perceived that administrative reforms on their own could not remedy spiritual barrenness, and that 'good works' had to be supplemented by the gift of 'grace'.

However, the sixteenth-century Protestant Reformation differed from the earlier Hussite Reformation in several major respects. For the Czech Utraquists 'grace' had to be attained primarily by means of the frequent collective, miraculous, sacramental renewal of both clergy and laity through active participation in Communions 'in both kinds', whereas for the later Protestant reformers it was to be attained primarily by means of spiritual rebirth through faith and commitment to the Lord. For Utraquists, in other words, neither faith nor 'good works' would suffice; grace and salvation could only be ensured by frequent sacramental consumption of both the bread and the wine, whose significance was miraculous and mystical as well as spiritual. In contrast to Protestantism, Utraquist grace and salvation was a matter not primarily of getting one's theology right, but rather of proper and frequent administration of the Eucharist as a full and inclusive reenactment of the Last Supper, in strict accordance with Christ's command. It was in this respect that Czech Utraquism differed most fundamentally from Protestantism as well as Catholicism (Betts 1931: 347–50).

The main emphasis of the religious reformers in fourteenth- and fifteenth-century Bohemia had been on the perceived need to reform and simplify the institutions and practices of the Church in endeavours to bring them closer to the perceived spirit, teachings and morality of the Gospels, the Sermon on the Mount, the Last Supper and the early Church. The Hussites campaigned against icons, relics and indulgences, but they developed no doctrine of justification (salvation) by faith. They simply urged Christians *collectively* to try to live like Christ and in strict accordance with His received teachings. The later Protestant Reformation, by contrast, placed much greater emphasis on matters of theology, on the Letters of St Paul, on rejection of the Catholic concept of purgatory (and all that went with it) and, above all, on *individual* justification (salvation) by *faith*.

An important contextual difference between the Hussite and the Lutheran Reformation was that the former preceded, whereas the latter followed, the advent of mass printing and more widespread literacy   the key means of propagating radical ideas to a mass audience. Yet another was that Luther's language was spoken by many millions of Germans who were dispersed across much of Europe, whereas Hus's language was spoken by less than a million Czechs who were largely confined to one small country. If the Czechs had been as numerous and as widely dispersed as Germans, and if Hus had enjoyed access to mass printing technology, the Czech Hussite Reformation could well have become a wider European Reformation.

Rather than simply reinforcing the legacies of the Hussite Reformation, Lutheran (and later Calvinist) influences introduced further elements of diversity, complexity, fragmentation and friction into the religious, political and cultural mosaic of the Czech Lands. Ironically, in view of their earlier hostility to Hussitism, the groups who were most immediately receptive to Lutheran ideas were the German communities of Silesia and the Lusatias, the predominantly German towns of Moravia, and the largely German-inhabited northern borderlands of Bohemia and Moravia (Kavka 1994: 141). These Germans were responsive to Lutheran ideas partly because they had been largely bypassed by the (overtly Czech) Hussite Reformation, but also because Luther was a German who addressed fellow Germans in their own tongue. As in Poland-Lithuania and in Hungary, Lutheranism strengthened specifically German identities, becoming a badge of 'Germandom'.

Many of the Czechs of Moravia and Silesia had remained Roman Catholic, and their lands had not undergone nearly as much secularization of church property and suppression of ecclesiastical corruption and abuses as Bohemia had. They had tended to regard Hussitism, Utraquism and Taborite sectarianism as quintessentially Bohemian rather than as pan-Czech phenomena. Under Lutheran influence, however, some of them accepted that their Catholic ecclesiastical institutions and clergy needed reform.

Conversely, the Utraquist Czechs of Bohemia were not widely attracted by Lutheranism at first. They had already participated in a momentous Reformation of their own, towards which many felt great pride and/or attachment. Church lands had already been secularized and the most glaring ecclesiastical corruption and abuses had already been quashed. 'The dissatisfaction of the poorer classes in the population, especially the peasants, which was at the root of the German Peasants' War and the radical currents of the Reformation in general, had already found a vent in sects of the Taborite-Waldensian kind' (Kavka 1994: 141). Previous German hostility towards the Hussite Reformation inclined many Czechs initially to look askance at a Reformation masterminded and propagated by Germans. When (under Lutheran influence) the Utraquist general assembly approved a series of 'doctrinal and administrative innovations' in 1524, conservative Utraquists in Prague reacted 'against this foreign corruption' of their established faith and practices. 'Rioting and lynching forced the Utraquist leaders to abandon their reforms', and many Utraquists 'joined the Catholics in demanding the suppression of the German faith' (Bradley 1971: 64).

Before long, however, the Czech Utraquists began to split into 'old' and 'new' branches. 'The new Utraquists were openly Protestant and evangelical' (Bradley 1971: 70). By referring to their Hussite precursors as 'evangelicals', the new Utraquists and the Unity of Brethren postulated 'a continuity of tradition, a clear progression from Hus and Jerome of Prague, through the Bohemian Brethren to Lutheranism' (Tazbir 1994: 171). The Unity of Brethren was a proto-Protestant Utraquist movement which emerged in the second half of the fifteenth century. Its members subsequently attained fame for translating the Bible into Czech during the second half of the sixteenth century (the Bible of Kralice), and its best-known adherent was the seventeenth-century scholar and educator Jan Amos Komensky (Comenius). The pull of the 'reborn' Unity of Brethren towards Lutheranism and later Calvinism was heralded by the teachings of Lukas of Prague between 1495 and his death in 1528. 'The reform of the Church on the principle of "the law of Christ", as determined by Wyclif, Hus and most determinedly by the Taborites, appeared to Lukas merely as a means, not an end . . . According to Lukas, faith, as the only way to redemption, is required by God more than works. He thus anticipated Luther's teachings . . . Unlike Luther, however, Lukas did not reject works, holding them as the inseparable supplement to faith and its telltale signs' (Kavka 1994: 138–9). In 1546–7 some 'old' as well as 'new' Utraquists supported the German Protestant Union's defiance of Emperor Charles V and 'dared to send a small military contingent to the Duke of Saxony, the leader of the Protestant nobles in Germany' (Bradley 1971: 70).

Bohemia's delayed Renaissance, 1575–1617

The Kingdom of Bohemia was not severely oppressed during the reigns of Maximilian II (1564–77), Rudolf II (1577–1611) and Matthias (1611–17). Although Maximilian II initially refused formally to lift his father's prohibitions against Lutheranism and the Unity of Brethren in Bohemia, he refrained from implementing the Counter-Reformation (or Catholic Reformation) programme formulated by the Church Council of Trent (1545–7, 1551–2, 1562–3). He was rumoured to be a closet Lutheran, and he felt able to permit the 'free exercise of the Lutheran faith for nobles and their subjects' in Austria in 1568 (Evans 1979: 6). In Bohemia, 'he preferred to leave the Czechs alone so long as they paid their taxes and provided troops for the Turkish wars' (Bradley 1971: 73).

This encouraged the Bohemian Lutherans, Utraquists and Brethren to reach an agreement on a unified corpus of beliefs and practices, the so-called Czech Confession of 1575. The Bohemian Diet entrusted the final drafting to a commission comprising six magnates, six lesser nobles and six burghers. Nearly half the text was based upon the so-called Augsburg Confession agreed between German Protestant rulers in 1530. Another one-third was borrowed from the Confession adopted by the Unity of Brethren in 1567. The most important parts consisted of the Four Articles of Prague (1419), Hussite synodal resolutions dating from 1421, and potent passages from Czech hymns and from the writings of Hus. It was couched in such a way as to present the sixteenth-century Reformation as a continuation and a 'completion' of its Hussite predecessor, as was the accompanying ecclesiastical ordinance. At a stormy session of the Bohemian Diet in 1575, Maximilian II 'authorized the Czech Confession and Ordinance only orally and as valid only for the aristocracy . . . Even so, with this regulation of ecclesiastical affairs the Czech Kingdom ranked among those countries with the most extensive religious freedom' (Kavka 1994: 146).

Even though this outcome rested on Catholic and royal observance of a non-binding gentleman's agreement rather than a legally binding constitutional document, it was regarded as a victory for toleration and for the non-Catholic majority. Late sixteenth-century Bohemia prospered, relations between Czechs and Germans became quite cordial and, until 1599, Bohemian Protestants and Catholics even began to pride themselves on their mutual tolerance. Tolerance became 'the main precept of Bohemian politics, which informed the country's government throughout the sixteenth century: negotiation, based on respect for the demands of each party, as the best guarantee for ensuring concord . . . This principle, expressing itself in religious issues as the tolerance of other confessions, penetrated deeply into the personal relationships within the families of the nobility. In many cases members of the same house, even the same family, belonged to different churches, and this religious diversity was no hindrance in either private life or public activity' (Polisensky 1974: 85).

Under Rudolf II Prague became once again the political, commercial and cultural capital of the Holy Roman Empire and the hub of East Central Europe. Bohemia's nodal position, the buoyancy of its mining, agriculture and textiles, and the temporary abatement of the Ottoman–Habsburg struggle for control of Hungary from 1568 to 1592 allowed Rudolf II to indulge in extravagant patronage of art, architecture and music. He brought in numerous Dutch, German and Swiss artists and architects, as well as a few Italians, in order to give Prague a Late Mannerist 'facelift'. There was also a fine flowering of vernacular styles of art and architecture, not least among the numerous castles and palaces built by rich magnates. At the same time, Prague became one of the musical capitals of Europe, thanks to Rudolf's patronage of orchestras, choirs and polyphonic music. Rudolf II built up a major art collection, including works by Leonardo da Vinci, Raphael, Tintoretto, Titian, Brueghel, Dürer, Holbein and Cranach. Rudolf's Prague was also home to the Czech founder of meridian astronomy, Tadeas Hajek of Hajek, the German mathematician and astronomer Johannes Kepler and the Danish astronomer Tycho de Brahe, while in medicine Jan Jessenius pioneered dissection at Prague University.

THE RENAISSANCE IN POLAND-LITHUANIA

Education developed considerably during the fourteenth and fifteenth centuries, albeit from very low base levels. By 1500 more than 80 per cent of the 6,000 parishes in Wielkopolska and Malopolska had schools (Zamoyski 1987: 119) and most nobles had attained some degree of literacy (Wyrobisz 1982: 157). Under Kazimiercz IV (reg. 1446–92), approximately 15,000 students received an education at the revamped Jagiellonian University in Krakow. Among those admitted in 1491 was a certain Mikolaj Kopernik, alias Copernicus (1473–1543), whose *De revolutionibus orbium coelestium* (1543) transformed not only mankind's view of the universe and of man's position within it, but even mankind's conception of itself. Poland had less ideological baggage than Italy, France or Spain to obstruct the path of radical new ideas. In contrast to Renaissance Italy, in Poland there was 'little or no resistance to the progress of new ideas, and the Church encouraged their dissemination' (Zamoyski 1987: 68). During the reigns of Zygmunt I (1506–48) and Zygmunt II (1548–72) there were substantial inflows of Italian artists and architects who transformed the appearance of Polish palaces, castles and country mansions. Poland also produced significant church music and native painters, such as Marcin Czarny and Mikolaj Haberschrak. The printing of significant numbers of books in Polish from the 1520s onwards fostered increased uniformity of spelling and grammar, transforming this language into a lucid, harmonious and efficient vehicle of expression.

THE PROTESTANT REFORMATION IN POLAND-LITHUANIA

In Poland-Lithuania Lutheranism was perceived as a specifically German religious movement, and Lutheranism gained numerous adherents from the 1520s onwards among Poland's predominantly German-speaking burghers, especially in the Baltic ports and the towns of Silesia and Wielkopolska, reinforcing their sense of 'ethnic separateness' (Tazbir 1994: 168). By the 1540s, however, non-German Calvinism was attracting increasingly powerful and influential converts and patronage among the magnates and the middle ranks of the Polish-Lithuanian nobility, some of whom financed the establishment of several dynamic Calvinist academies and publishing houses as well as a Calvinist ecclesiastical infrastructure. Calvinism thus became rather fashionable among the cosmopolitan and sophisticated sections of the nobility, who sometimes 'persuaded' or put pressure on the inhabitants of their landed estates and adjacent settlements to accept this creed. By the 1560s Protestants had acquired a majority in the lower house of Poland's Sejm and among the lay members of the Senate (the upper house), but this was not representative of the *religious* inclinations of the nobility as a whole (Zamoyski 1987: 81). Prominent Catholic nobles often backed Protestant deputies in the Sejm in the expectation that these would most staunchly defend the political prerogatives and privileges of the nobility against the absolutist pretensions of Catholic kings, that is, for political rather than religious reasons. By 1569 Protestants comprised roughly 20 per cent of the nobility (Tazbir 1994: 170) and about 15 per cent of the population as a whole, although nearly one-third of the latter were German Lutheran townspeople (Davies 1981a: 183, 162). Emphasis on the political rather than strictly religious motives for supporting the Reformation in Poland is consistent with Janusz Tazbir's claims that, unlike their western European counterparts, Polish Calvinists continued to venerate certain 'national' saints and the Virgin Mary, to regard Mary as the 'patron of the entire "nation" of the nobility', and to celebrate Christmas and Easter in much the same manner as Catholics (Tazbir 1994: 212–13).

Protestant ideas were probably much less alarming to Catholics in Poland-Lithuania than they were in overwhelmingly Catholic countries, as in Poland-Lithuania Christianity was already multi-denominational long before the Reformation. The Roman Catholic Church had never wielded the almost unchallenged power and authority that it held in medieval southern and western Europe, and Polish and Lithuanian Catholics had been obliged to establish a modus vivendi with a large Eastern Orthodox population which (like Protestants) rejected the celibacy of parish priests, used the vernacular in the liturgy, and accepted Communion 'in both forms' – the bread and the wine (Tazbir 1994: 168). By the late fifteenth century Eastern Orthodox Christians already comprised approximately 40 per cent of the population, and Armenian (Gregorian) Christians another 1 or 2 per cent. Catholics comprised only 45 to 47 per cent of the population in 1569 (Davies 1981a: 162, 166, 172). Royal edicts against 'heresy' were increasingly thwarted by the independent-minded nobility and Sejm. 'In a state which possessed no strong central executive authority, and where the ecclesiastical courts could not enforce their rulings, religious uniformity could not be imposed' (p. 199). In 1555 apostasy from the Catholic faith was in effect legalized by a royal decree suspending the jurisdiction of ecclesiastical courts over lay courts. The jurisdiction of ecclesiastical courts was virtually annulled altogether in 1562–3 (Tazbir 1994: 169; Zamoyski 1987: 84).

THE RENAISSANCE IN THE KINGDOM OF HUNGARY (INCLUDING SLOVAKIA)

Late medieval Hungary was assimilated into Western/Catholic Christendom, in which Latin was the lingua franca of the educated elite and within which the humanist outlook, ethos and values and Roman concepts of law, property and contract gradually came to prevail during the Renaissance. In these respects at least Hungary became rather more Westernized than the Eastern Orthodox lands of the Balkans and Russia.

King Matyas Hunyadi (1458–90) was one of Europe's most educated monarchs, a true 'Renaissance Prince'. He corresponded with eminent humanists and built up one of Europe's finest libraries, the Biblioteca Corvina. This employed legions of scribes, humanists, book-binders and illuminators and became 'one of the major seats of learning in Central Europe, with its enormous quantities of ancient literary works and humanist writings' (Klaniczay 1992: 167). The library, which was named after the raven (*corvus*) in the Hunyadi family crest, was unfortunately destroyed during the sixteenth-century Ottoman invasions. Other fine libraries were established by some higher clergy and magnates. Hungary's first printing press went into operation in 1472–3, although the first book written in Hungarian (as against Latin) was not printed until 1533 (in Krakow). Matyas was one of the first monarchs to use print and even posters as instruments of political propaganda. He and the most prominent Hungarian humanists fostered the idea of Hungary as a prime custodian of European Christian and humanist values against the 'Turkish menace'. During his reign large numbers of foreign (mainly Italian) artists, architects and humanists were attracted to live and work in Hungary, including Galeotto Marzio, Antonio Bonfini, Bartolomeo Fonzeo, Aurelio Brandolino Lippo and Francesco Bandini (Klaniczay 1992: 166–7). Under Matyas 'Hungary became the first European country to adopt the Renaissance to any great extent' (Bialostocki 1985: 155). For a short time it was 'the most important centre of humanism and Renaissance art' north of the Alps (Makkai 1975b: 112). Hungary also produced distinguished humanists of its own, most notably the chancellor Janos Vitez and his nephew Janus Pannonius ('the first great Hungarian poet'), who became Bishop of Pecs. During the fifteenth century more than five thousand people from Hungary attended foreign universities, principally in Italy, Paris and (increasingly) Krakow and Vienna. In 1465 a university known as the Academia Istropolitana was established in Pozsony/Bratislava in Slovakia (Ister being the Greek name for the Danube). It had faculties of arts, theology, medicine and law, but all except the law faculty were transferred to Buda after 1490 (Mikus 1977: 18; Kirschbaum 1995: 57).

THE PROTESTANT REFORMATION IN HUNGARY (INCLUDING SLOVAKIA)

The turbulent sixteenth century was a period of cultural and religious fervent. Humanist writing and scholarship, along with Renaissance architecture and art, moved out of the narrow confines of the royal court and the higher clergy into the wider circles of the landed nobility and educated townspeople. Hungary's first Protestant reformers emanated 'from the ranks of the followers of Erasmus' (Makkai 1975a: 140).

Even before the Ottoman victory over Hungarian forces at the Battle of Mohacs in 1526, Martin Luther's ideas were making waves in royal circles, but Protestantism subsequently attracted much wider attention. The laws against Lutheranism promulgated between 1523 and 1525 became a dead letter after the death of King Lajos II at the Battle of Mohacs in 1526 (Peter 1994: 158). After 1530

Hungary's local authorities started allowing evangelical congregations to take over existing church buildings (p. 159) and many hitherto conformist clergy openly displayed evangelical convictions and disaffection towards the Catholic Church, found shelter with Protestant lay patrons and 'became the most fervent propagators of the new faith' (p. 160). Two practical attractions must have been that Protestant clergy had greater freedom to preach, write and conduct services in the vernacular rather than Latin, and were permitted to marry.

Calvinist ideas rapidly gained ground at the expense of both Lutheranism and Catholicism between the 1540s and the 1570s, under the potent leadership of Marton Kalmancsehi Santa, Istvan Szegedi Kis and Peter Melius Juhasz. These men founded and built up Hungary's predominantly Calvinist 'Reformed Church', which by the 1560s had become Hungary's largest religious denomination. By the 1570s 'between 80 and 85 per cent of the Christian population were Protestant' (Peter 1994: 161), and by 1600 nine-tenths of this hitherto overwhelmingly Catholic country had become Protestant (Klaniczay 1992: 172).

Between 1522 and 1564 about two hundred Slovaks studied at the Lutheran University of Wittenberg, and most Slovaks became Lutherans under the influence of Lutheran preachers and pastors from Wittenberg, the mainly German-inhabited mining towns (Banska Bystrica, Banska Stiavnica, Kremnica ans Zvolen), and a substantial influx of Hussites during the fifteenth century (who popularized the Czech Bible prepared by the Czech Brethren during the 1450s). A minority of Slovaks became Calvinist, partly under the influence of the mainly Calvinist Magyar nobility. Between 1520 and 1600, about eighty-three schools were established in Slovakia, fewer than ten of which were Catholic. Moreover, there was greatly increased use of the Czech written language ('the biblical language'), especially among Slovak Lutherans, many of whom began to consider themselves and their church to be Czech rather than Slovak (see Spiesz *et al.* 2006: 65–7; Mannova 2000: 115–21; Kirschbaum 1995: 67–8).

The anarchical conditions resulting from the tripartite division of Hungary during the 1540s made it increasingly difficult for either the rulers or the Catholic Church to stem (let alone turn) the tide of the Protestant Reformation, while the absence of systematic persecution of Protestants turned Hungary into a relatively safe haven for Protestant refugees from Bohemia and the southern German states. Predominantly Protestant Transylvania became renowned throughout Europe for its religious toleration. During the 1560s, moreover, a Unitarian Church was established in eastern Hungary (Peter 1994: 161). In Transylvania Unitarianism briefly became an officially recognized religious denomination, on an equal footing with Calvinism, Lutheranism and Catholicism, although the Eastern Orthodoxy of the region's Romanian peasants was merely tolerated.

Alongside politically moderate forms of Protestantism, radical Anabaptism also gained a popular following in Hungary, starting in the troubled 1520s. However, it evoked serious repression from the landed nobility during the 1530s (Peter 1994: 160). A partly Protestant-inspired peasant uprising against the Turks and landlordism in the Tisza region in 1570 met with a similar response (Makkai 1975a: 141). Anabaptists subsequently 'retreated into defensive communities of zealots who lived a simple peasant life of self-help and discipline' (Evans 1979: 10).

The influence of Lutheran ideas was strongest among Hungary's German-speaking townspeople and in Slovakia, while Unitarianism was largely confined to Transylvania. By contrast, Calvinist and (in smaller measure) Anabaptist ideas attracted numerous Magyar adherents in all three sectors of partitioned Hungary.

Most of Hungary's landed nobility embraced Calvinism during the mid- to late sixteenth century, partly as a way of restricting monarchical and ecclesiastical power and laying hands on crown and church property. The significant patronage enjoyed by Hungarian Protestantism came not from monarchs and urban patriciates but from Calvinist landowners who rather anticipated the famous principle of *cuius regio, eius religio* by expecting the inhabitants of their domains to adopt the religion of their 'lords and masters'. Calvinist concepts of 'predestination' and 'the elect' evidently appealed to the *amour-propre* of sections of the nobility in Hungary, as well as in Poland, Lithuania, Bohemia and France.

While the Renaissance heightened Hungarian receptiveness towards the Reformation, the Reformation gave the Hungarian Renaissance a second wind. Protestants established numerous schools and printing presses. They preached, held services and printed books in the vernacular. The first Magyar grammar was published by the Protestant Matyas Devai Biro in 1538. The first complete printed Hungarian translation of the New Testament was published by Protestants in 1541. The Calvinist colleges established in Debrecen, Sarospatak and Marosvasarhely, together with the Unitarian college in Koloszvar, became Hungary's most renowned centres of learning. Under Protestant influence, 'a golden age of vernacular culture came into being' from 1570 to 1600, during which time books were printed in all the vernaculars spoken in Hungary (Peter 1994: 163).

The first complete translation of the Bible into Magyar, published at Vizsoly in 1590, had a major impact on the further development of the Magyar language. Magyars were 'provided with a rich abundance of reading matter, largely supplied by Protestant authors'; nearly half the printed works published in Hungary between 1570 and 1600 were produced in 'popular editions'; and 75 per cent of these were published in Magyar rather than in Latin (Peter 1994: 165–6). Nevertheless, Hungary was a partial exception to the frequent claim that Protestant insistence on the laity reading the Bible for themselves and being educated to do so was the driving force behind the development of vernacular languages and literary cultures during the Reformation. The fact that the first complete Magyar translation of the Bible was not published until 1590 indicates that in Hungary the Reformation 'did not put the Bible directly into the hands of the common people . . . Indeed, one eminent Calvinist bishop complained that the Reformation had done little to change the "total absence of culture" among the lower classes' (Peter 1994: 165). Thus, despite its formal numerical triumph, the Reformation put down shallower roots in Hungary than in countries with stronger urban sectors and larger and more educated Bible-reading publics. This in turn helps to explain the ease with which Hungary was partially re-Catholicized during the seventeenth and eighteenth centuries.

In sharp contrast to northern Germany and England, Hungary's conversion to Protestantism was not abetted by Protestant rulers. Western Hungary, on the contrary, became Protestant in the face of consistent (albeit ineffectual) royal support for the Catholic Church. Even after 90 per cent of the faithful had defected to the Protestant camp and only between 300 and 350 Catholic parishes remained, 'the entire hierarchy of the Roman Church was preserved', and Catholic bishops continued to be appointed to sees which were now under Ottoman rule (Peter 1994: 161–2). This meant that, when Hungary's Catholics finally bestirred themselves to mount a more vigorous Counter-Reformation during the seventeenth and eighteenth centuries, the mighty infrastructure of the Catholic Church was still at their disposal. They were slow to join the fight, but they had not thrown away their weapons.

12   The 'parting of the ways': the underlying divergence of East Central Europe from western Europe between the late fifteenth and late eighteenth century

Some of the major proponents of the view that East Central Europe underwent considerable 'Westernization' between the tenth and sixteenth centuries nevertheless admit that this 'Westernization' remained somewhat 'shallow' and 'superficial' (Wandycz 1992: 6). The eminent Hungarian economic historian Ivan Berend emphasized that during these centuries East Central Europe (like Russia) did not witness the establishment of 'feudalism in the Western sense': some of the outward forms of feudalism may have been introduced, but 'the substance of feudalism was never integrated into the social fabric of East European life' (Berend 1986: 331). According to Perry Anderson, 'The frontier character of Eastern social formations rendered it extremely difficult for dynastic rulers to enforce liege obedience from military settlers and landowners, in an unbounded milieu where armed adventurers and anarchic velleities were often at a premium . . . There were few organic ties binding the various aristocracies together' (Anderson 1979: 243).

East Central Europe's towns were mostly 'alien' German and Jewish enclaves. They were not strong enough to challenge or counter balance the power of either the landed nobility or the ruler. Nor were they sufficiently integrated with their Slavic or Hungarian hinterlands to be able to reshape society in the way that the rise of towns, cities and city-states did in western Europe. 'Commodity production, and with it the money economy, had not penetrated to the extent that it had in the West' (Gunst 1989: 66). Many western European towns soon developed beyond their initial roles as military, ecclesiastical or administrative strongholds into centres of commerce and production. By contrast, sixteenth-century eastern European 'towns' usually remained little more than administrative centres, way stations, collection points, garrisons or chartered villages (pp. 57–9). They were seats of consumption rather than production. It was only their size (and sometimes legal status) that gave them an urban appearance. With the possible exceptions of Bohemia and Moravia, eastern European townspeople failed to match either the degrees of independence and political representation or the range of civil liberties won by their western European counterparts. The significance of such contrasts was laid bare by the differing responses of the eastern and western halves of Europe to their respective late medieval 'crises of feudalism'.

Between about 1300 and 1450, while the economies of East Central Europe and Russia underwent dynamic expansion, many parts of western Europe were convulsed by Malthusian crises which were reflected in widespread famines, epidemics, drastic declines in population, and widespread social and political unrest. From the late sixteenth to the late eighteenth century, however, the western European economic crises and Malthusian constraints on both economic and population growth were gradually overcome through the expansion of interregional and overseas commerce, advances in agricultural, industrial and maritime organization and technology, territorial consolidation of states, and alliances between proto-national monarchies and nascent bourgeoisies.

All of these developments facilitated bourgeois and/or monarchical assaults on feudal privilege and particularism, and promoted increased economic specialization and the introduction or development of new products. 'European feudalism – far from constituting an exclusively agrarian economy – was the *first* mode of production in history to accord an autonomous structural base to urban production and exchange' (Anderson 1979: 21). Western Europe also experienced major inflows of precious and semi-precious metals, initially from Germany and East Central Europe and later from the New World, which increased the money supply and price levels, facilitated trade with Asia, encouraged the commercialization of agriculture and accelerated the dissolution of serfdom, mainly between 1450 and 1620.

However, while western Europe was gradually *overcoming or recovering from* its late medieval 'Malthusian' economic crises between the late sixteenth and mid-eighteenth centuries, during that same period East Central Europe was becoming increasingly engulfed in deep-seated socio-economic crises, which were manifested in famines, epidemics, dramatic demographic declines, and widespread urban and rural unrest. The demographic ('Malthusian') aspects of the East Central European crisis were compounded by the devastating effects of warfare, including the recurrent Ottoman military depredations in Hungary and Austria (especially from the 1520s to the 1680s), the catastrophic impact of the Thirty Years War (from 1618 to 1648), and the deeply debilitating wars which the Polish-Lithuanian Commonwealth fought against Sweden between 1655 and 1709 and against Russia during the seventeenth and eighteenth centuries.

In contrast to what took place in western Europe, moreover, the crises in early modern East Central Europe and also in Russia helped to bring about reactionary alliances between actual or aspiring absolute monarchs and big landowners. These resulted in large-scale extension and/or strengthening of serfdom and substantial de-urbanization, to the great detriment of most peasants and townspeople.

The major exception to the strengthening of absolutism in early modern East Central Europe was the Polish-Lithuanian Commonwealth. This vast polity experienced de-urbanization and major extensions of serfdom, but its extremely numerous and already powerful landed nobility contrived to strengthen itself even further vis-à-vis the monarchy and central government (as well as at the expense of the peasantry and townspeople) by achieving near-monopolies of political and economic power. In the longer term, however, Poland-Lithuania's partial divergence from the prevailing political trend towards absolutism in East Central Europe merely paved the way for the late eighteenth-century 'Partitions' of the Commonwealth between absolutist Russia, Prusssia and Austria, with the overall result that its inhabitants ultimately did not escape the overriding trends towards dramatic extension and entrenchment of absolutism in early modern East Central Europe.

The earlier western European crises had in the long run enhanced the economic importance and political leverage of the commercial classes and the towns, especially in the nascent capitalist 'core' economies of north-western Europe, led by the Netherlands and England, and this helped to accelerate and complete the dissolution of serfdom. Throughout most of East Central Europe and Russia, by contrast, the crises of the sixteenth and seventeenth centuries downgraded the political and economic position of towns and townspeople and resulted in major extensions and intensifications of serfdom, which helped to prolong its existence until the mid-nineteenth century. Indeed, the legislative strengthening of eastern European serfdom had already begun during the 1490s in Hungary, Poland, Brandenburg, Mecklenburg, Prussia, Bohemia and Russia, during the preceding economic upswing. Mounting labour shortages (relative to rapidly expanding cultivated areas and mining operations) and rising prices and living costs, combined with the fact that most landowners lacked sufficient finance to take full advantage of the expanding urban and export markets for eastern European grain, cattle, timber and metal ores, evoked concerted action to restrict the rights and mobility of the peasantry, who could then be subjected to increased compulsory dues in kind and labour obligations. A fundamental East–West socio-economic divergence began within Europe in this period:

> While western Europe was evolving capitalist conditions, the region east of the Elbe sharply deviated from that experience . . . Serfs were again bound to the soil . . . and feudal dues paid in crops and labour . . . gradually replaced the customary money rent. This change began at about the end of the fifteenth century . . . The two halves of Europe clearly split . . . The division of labour that took place in the modern world economy then forming reduced the countries of Eastern Europe to the role of suppliers of cereals and livestock. (Berend 1986: 334–5)

The 'Western model' of early modern society was based upon the elimination of serfdom, whereas 'the Eastern was based on prolonging it' (Szucs 1988: 312). Ironically, by expanding demand for eastern European primary commodity exports, the western European economic recovery further entrenched the position of this so-called 'second serfdom' in eastern Europe, 'causing the great estates cultivated by forced labour to become the typical Eastern partner in the East–West division of labour that developed' (p. 313).

According to the influential Marxist agrarian historian Robert Brenner, 'the peasantry of the East was much less well-positioned to resist the seigneurial reaction than was its Western counterpart, basically because the lords had led and dominated the process of colonization by which North-eastern Europe had been settled' and the region was therefore subjected to 'an extraordinarily tight form of feudal property relations' under the so-called 'second serfdom' (Brenner 1989: 44). The significance of this system went far beyond the narrowly economic sphere. It established a profound difference between eastern and western European society. 'This difference had important cultural and moral dimensions, affecting not only the serfs, whom it degraded, but their owners, many of whom were corrupted by the almost absolute power they wielded over them'; and the heritage of serfdom has influenced 'popular and elite attitudes down to the present day' (Longworth 1994: 298). Indeed, this so-called 'second serfdom' became much more widely prevalent in East Central Europe than in the Balkans, where it was largely confined to Romania, Croatia and Bosnia-Herzegovina (see pp. 51–2, 58, 67, 72,104–7).

Immanuel Wallerstein has argued that from the sixteenth century onwards East Central Europe was incorporated into a peripheral and dependent role in an emerging 'capitalist world economy' whose core was situated in north-western Europe, especially the Netherlands and England. Viewed in this perspective, the intensification and extension of serfdom in early modern East Central Europe was not a 'pre-capitalist' or 'feudal' phenomenon but a specific product and manifestation of emergent capitalism. It was analogous to the coercive 'cash crop labour systems' implanted in the Americas, where servile forced labour similarly became a commodity to be bought and sold in economies that were likewise reorientated towards the production of primary commodities for profit and for export to the north-western European core states. These latter allegedly appropriated most of the 'surplus value' generated by the 'world economy' as a whole and held the underdeveloped peripheries in subordinate 'dependent' roles (Wallerstein 1974a, 1974b).

The sixteenth century certainly saw the beginnings of qualitatively significant exports of grain, timber and livestock from the Baltic hinterland to north-western Europe, and these exports mainly emanated from large landed estates employing serf labour. However, Piotr Wandycz rightly points out that the so-called 'second serfdom' which arose in early modern eastern Europe 'took a long time in crystallizing and was less the product of the agrarian boom than of the tightening market that followed' during the seventeenth century (Wandycz 1992: 59). One must also beware of the temptation to exaggerate the role of external market forces in the extension and intensification of eastern European serfdom. Only tiny proportions of the grain produced in the eastern half of Europe were exported to western Europe during the sixteenth century. Such exports were largely confined to areas with easy riverine access to the major Baltic ports, for example, along the Vistula to Gdansk (Danzig). Grain exports from relatively landlocked Austria, Bohemia, Moravia and Hungary were at that time either negligible or non-existent. Even in the case of Poland exports amounted to only about 12 per cent of total grain output, according to Wandycz (1992: 58), and they may not have exceeded 2.5 per cent of total grain output (Topolski 1981: 391). Grain exports from the Baltic region to western Europe were still 'marginal in relation to total demand and supply' (p. 392). Furthermore, Hungarian, Russian and Romanian grain exports did not really 'take off' until the construction of railway networks in the second half of the nineteenth century, even if southern Poland, Hungary, Wallachia and Moldavia were already participating actively in the trans-European cattle trade (p. 397). For logistical reasons, sixteeenth-century East Central European agricultural trade was largely geared to local urban markets (p. 396).

Wallerstein's influential thesis that the sixteenth-century Baltic grain and timber exports to the nascent urban-industrial 'core' economies of north-western Europe restructured the East Central European economies and reduced them to a dependent peripheral status in the emerging 'capitalist world economy' therefore jumped the gun by two or three centuries. In reality, the affinities between the East Central European economies and their retardation relative to those of the West were more attributable to internal factors, especially to similarities of social structure, than to external ones (Kochanowicz 1989: 119). Furthermore, as Daniel Chirot has argued, the gradual emergence of East Central European economic dependence on the West from the seventeenth to the early twentieth century produced neither the uniformly negative and stultifying effects postulated by Marxist 'dependency' theorists nor the uniformly positive stimuli and 'demonstration effects' postulated by 'modernization' or 'Westernization' theorists (Chirot 1989a: 8–10).

Nevertheless, the promising economic and cultural trends in East Central Europe during the late medieval and Renaissance eras were indeed nipped in the bud by the combined effects of the Ottoman onslaughts, the widespread religious warfare of the seventeenth century, the expansion of intolerant absolutist empires, the attendant reinforcement of seigneurial privilege and agrarian serfdom, the resultant decline of towns, and persecution and/or emigration of religious dissenters, free-thinkers and (within the Habsburg Empire) Jews. The emigrants included substantial numbers of merchants, nobles and craftsmen. These mainly took refuge in Protestant Germany, Scandinavia, Britain and the Netherlands, whose economic and intellectual gains were to be East Central Europe's loss.

Admittedly, various manifestations of 'absolutism' also emerged in early modern western Europe. There, however, 'the very term "absolutism" was a misnomer', because no Western monarchy ever exercised 'absolute power over its subjects, in the sense of an untrammelled despotism' (Anderson 1979: 49). Thus Jean Bodin, the leading sixteenth-century theoretical exponent of French 'absolutism', took for granted the existence of strict limitations on the powers of the 'absolute' monarch: 'It is not within the competence of any prince in the world to levy taxes at will on his people, or to seize the goods of another arbitrarily'; the reason being that, 'since the sovereign prince has no power to transgress the laws of nature, which God – whose image he is on earth – has ordained, he cannot take the property of another without a just and reasonable cause' (quoted by Anderson 1979:50). Similar assumptions were to be found in the writings of other leading Western theoreticians of absolutism, such Hobbes and Grotius, as noted by Szucs (1988: 320).

Perry Anderson has provided an incisive and persuasive formulation of the most important differences between the Western and Eastern manifestations of 'absolutism'. The absolutist state in the western half of Europe was 'the redeployed political apparatus of a feudal class which had accepted the commutation of [seigneurial] dues. It was a *compensation for the disappearance of serfdom*, in the context of an increasingly urban economy which it did not completely control and to which it had to adapt.' The absolutist state in the eastern half of Europe, by contrast, was '*a device for the consolidation of serfdom*, in a landscape scoured of autonomous urban life or resistance. The manorial reaction in the East meant that a new world had to be implanted from above, by main force. The dose of violence pumped into social relations was correspondingly far greater' (Anderson 1979: 195; italics in the original). The maturation of absolutist states in the eastern half of Europe during the seventeenth century 'dealt a death-blow to the possibility of a revival of urban independence in the East. The new monarchies – Hohenzollern, Habsburg and Romanov – unshakeably assured the political supremacy of the nobility over the towns . . . In the Czech Lands, the Thirty Years' War finished off the pride and growth of the Bohemian and Moravian cities' (p. 205). Ironically, the Polish nobility successfully warded off the 'absolutist' ambitions of their own monarchs, only to be defeated by Russian, Prussian and Austrian absolutism (alias 'the Partitioning Powers') in 1772, 1793 and 1795.

The structure and outward forms of 'absolutism' were even more strongly shaped by the requirements of *warfare* in seventeenth- and eighteenth-century East Central Europe and Russia than they had been in sixteenth- and seventeenth-century western Europe. The East Central European and Russian nobilities were in large measure service nobilities, who routinely wore uniforms during their everyday lives because they represented the strong arm of the state. In Russia and in the Austrian domains of the Habsburg Monarchy as well as in Prussia, 'The entire State thus acquired a military trim. The whole social system was placed at the service of militarism' (Anderson 1979: 213). The harshness and the militarism of the 'absolutist' states in East Central Europe and Russia were also responses to widespread seigneurial fear of the ever-present dangers of peasant revolts against the rigours and degradations of serfdom (p. 212). Anderson concludes that 'in Eastern Europe, the social power of the nobility was unqualified by any ascendant bourgeoisie such as marked Western Europe: seigneurial domination was unfettered. Eastern Absolutism thus more patently and unequivocally displayed its class composition than [did] its Western counterpart. Built upon serfdom, the feudal cast of its State structure was more blunt and manifest' (p. 430).

The resultant political and social rigidities severely cramped East Central European development during the seventeenth and eighteenth centuries. Towns and the embryonic urban merchant classes went into temporary decline, partly as a result of the above-mentioned religious persecution, emigration and devastating warfare, and partly because the major noble producers of exportable grain, timber and livestock surpluses established direct relations with western European merchants and financiers, bypassing the often ethnically 'alien' Baltic towns and middlemen. In the case of Poland, moreover, laws passed as early as 1496 by the ascendant nobility prohibited burghers and merchants from owning land, travelling abroad or engaging in foreign trade. 'Polish merchants therefore remained primarily local middlemen. They did not specialize to any great extent and, more importantly, banking did not become an important part of their operations, as was happening among the larger Western European merchants . . . Polish towns and burghers were unable to become autonomous social or political forces. They were unable to forge national bonds among themselves, or to act as a uniting force. Nor were they available for use by the kings against the encroachment of noble power' (Kochanowicz 1989: 112, 114). In the case of the more landlocked Habsburg Empire, the landed nobility increasingly acquired and exploited restrictive local monopolies of activities such as grain milling and the selling of wines and spirits (Gunst 1989: 71). The proportion of its population living in towns had fallen to 8 per cent by 1735 and was still only 8.6 per cent in 1840 (Hanak 1989: 63). Levels of urbanization were even lower in the southern and eastern Balkans.

13 The emergence of Austrian Habsburg hegemony over East Central Europe, 1526–1789

The historical roots, ethos and 'mission' of the Habsburg Empire can be traced back to the *Ostmark* (Eastern March; hence the name *Österreich* or Eastern Realm, Latinized into Austria). This was founded in AD 803 by Emperor Charlemagne as a fortified eastern outpost of Roman Catholic (Western) Christendom and of the new (Franco-German) Holy Roman Empire, of which he had been crowned Emperor by the Pope in AD 800. From 803 to 1918 the enduring purpose and over-riding 'mission' of the Ostmark was to stand guard over the Danubian gateway into Catholic Chris-tendom and ward off potential Slav, 'infidel' and 'barbarian' incursions from the East. Throughout its long history the Austrian realm had the somewhat rigid, hard-edged, embattled spirit and mental-ity of a beleaguered 'frontier state'. It continued to see itself as the bastion of specifically 'Ger-manic' Catholic values in a sea of hostile Slavs, long after its Czech, Slovak, Slovene, Croat and Polish neighbours were converted to Catholicism. This nurtured a strong sense of internal as well as external 'threat', and the Austrian military eventually became 'far more . . . an instrument for maintaining inner cohesion than of a defence against foreign aggressors' (Jaszi 1929: 137).

Austria, like Prussia, emerged on the basis of successive eastward migrations of belligerent German colonists into East Central Europe and the northern Balkans. The Germans who migrated north-east-wards (including the infamous Teutonic Knights) created the nucleus of the future Prussian state, while German settlers in Bohemia, Moravia, Hungary, Transylvania, Croatia and Slovenia became the allies and 'shock troops' of the nascent Austrian state and diffused Germanic-Catholic urban civilization, education, architecture and farming practices among the Slavs, Magyars and Romanians of East Central Europe and the northern Balkans.

Between 976 and 1246 the Ostmark was consolidated and extended into Styria and Carniola by the Babenburg dynasty. However, the House of Babenburg came to an abrupt end in 1246, when the reign-ing duke died in battle with neighbouring Hungary. In 1251, however, the vacant Babenburg fiefs were seized, not by the King of Hungary, but by King Premysl Otakar II of Bohemia, a rival contender for the imperial crown of the Holy Roman Empire. But in 1273 the princes of this largely Germanic impe-rial confederation decided to elect Rudolf of Habsburg, a magnate with extensive possessions in south-western Germany, to the imperial throne. In 1276 and 1278 he inflicted decisive defeats on Bohemia and in 1282 he established his descendants as the hereditary rulers of the Austrian Crownlands (a posi-tion which the Habsburgs retained until 1918). From 1306 to 1307 a Habsburg occupied the Bohemian throne, and from 1437 to 1439 the Habsburg Emperor Albrecht V occupied both the Hungarian and the Bohemian thrones in the first of several attempts to bring Hungary and/or Bohemia under Austrian German rule. The Habsburgs also acquired Carinthia in 1335, Tyrol in 1363, Istria in 1374, Vorarlberg in 1375, Trieste in 1382, Gorizia in 1500 and Friuli in 1511. Vienna, which became the capital of the Ostmark in 1146, was raised to the status of a bishopric in 1469. From 1438 to 1740, only Habsburgs were to be elected to the imperial throne of the Holy Roman Empire, which became in effect a Habsburg family heirloom.

Following the Ottoman capture of Constantinople in 1453, the strategically exposed and vulnerable Kingdom of Hungary endeavoured to expand and strengthen itself at Austria's expense. The Hungarian King Matyas Hunyadi even captured Vienna in 1485. After his death in 1490, however, the increasingly disunited and beleaguered Hungarian realm turned to Austria for a defensive dynastic alliance against the Turks, cemented by the intermarriage of the respective royal families. Thus the Habsburg Holy Roman Emperor Maximilian I (reg. 1493–1519), who was greatly enriched by his own 'dynastic' marriage to the heiress of Burgundy (including the Low Countries) in 1477, not only married his *son* to the daughter of the co-rulers of Castile and Aragon (Spain) in 1496, but also married his *grandson* to the daughter of the King of Hungary and Bohemia in 1506. These 'dynastic marriages' paved the way for a phenomenal expansion of the Habsburg dominions and an even greater expansion of Habsburg revenues from silver mining in Central Europe and Spanish America as well as from Belgian and Spanish maritime commerce in Europe, the Americas and Asia.

The Habsburg Holy Emperor Charles V (reg. 1519–56) came into this extraordinary territorial inheritance just as the Protestant Reformation was getting under way in central and northern Europe and as the Ottoman Turkish threat to Western (Roman Catholic) Christendom was reaching its peak. As ruler of Burgundy, the Low Countries, Spain, Spanish America, parts of Italy and the Holy Roman Empire, he saw himself as the supreme arbiter and divinely anointed custodian of Roman Catholic Christendom, mirroring the position of Sultan Suleyman I 'the Magnificent' (reg. 1520–66) in the Muslim world at that time. Charles V saw Protestant 'heresy' as a fundamental challenge to his imperial authority and legitimacy, as well as to the religious unity of his vast dominions. However, in the course of his indefatigable warfare against both external (Ottoman) and internal (Protestant) enemies, he frittered away the vast revenues from the silver mines of Spanish America, bankrupted the major Central European finance houses (the Fuggers and the Welsers, who had derived their fortunes from mining and metallurgy), ruined Europe's richest entrepôt (the port-city of Antwerp), and drove many thousands of economically valuable Protestant merchants, artisans and financiers into exile from his increasingly bigoted Roman Catholic dominions.

In 1526 the then King of Hungary and Bohemia was routed by the Ottoman Sultan Suleyman the Magnificent at the Battle of Mohacs, and he died while fleeing. The Austrian Habsburg King Ferdinand I (reg. 1517–64) thereupon laid claim to the vacant Hungarian and Bohemian thrones. Ferdinand I's succession to the Bohemian throne was quickly approved by the noble-dominated Bohemian Diet, which now looked to the Austrian Habsburgs to give Bohemia the unity, military protection and 'strong government' which it urgently required in the face of the growing 'Turkish menace', and by late 1527 he had forced most of the Magyar aristocracy to accept his claim to the Hungarian throne and to pay increased dues (ostensibly 'tithes') to strengthen Hungary's defences against the Turks. However, Sultan Suleyman I had no intention of allowing defeated Hungary to fall under Habsburg control. He reinvaded Hungary in 1529 and, in an attempt to deter or pre-empt future Austrian Habsburg counter-offensives, laid siege to Vienna. However, this stretched Ottoman military resources, techniques and supply lines beyond their limits and capabilities. Supported by Martin Luther and Lutheran as well as Catholic German princes, the Austrian Habsburgs stood their ground and eventually forced the Sultan to retreat and abandon the siege of Vienna. These were the opening shots in an enormously taxing and protracted struggle between the Ottomans and the Austrian Habsburgs for control of Hungary, culminating in a second unsuccessful Ottoman siege of Vienna in 1683 and the subsequent Habsburg expulsion of the Ottomans from most of Hungary between 1686 and 1699. This power struggle with the Ottomans was to become one of the two main crucibles within which Austrian absolutism, militarism and obscurantism were to be forged. The other was the Thirty Years War (1618–48), fought in East Central Europe. Indeed, whether they were conscious of it or not, the Habsburgs appeared to be engaged in a bid for the mastery of Europe.

After the eventual abdication of Charles V, who had dissipated so much of the Habsburgs' strength and riches to so little avail, the Austrian Habsburg Ferdinand I became Holy Roman Emperor (reg.

1556–64). Emperor Ferdinand and his successors consolidated the East Central European territories of the Austrian Habsburgs. They agreed to relinquish the Low Countries, Italy and Spanish America to the Spanish Habsburgs, who continued to squander the rest of their 'American silver' revenues on ill-fated and/or misconceived military exploits, such as the Spanish Armada which was largely destroyed by Sir Francis Drake in 1588 and their attempted subjugation of the northern Netherlands (1566–1648).

Notwithstanding the Habsburgs' staunch adherence to Roman Catholicism, which was crucial to their legitimacy, authority and self-regard, Protestantism attracted a considerable following in East Central European from the 1520s onward. By the 1580s Protestants of various hues were in a majority in Bohemia and Hungary. Even in Lower Austria (including Vienna), the Roman Catholic Church experienced a slump in church attendance, fee income, donations and recruitment to the priesthood. Protestant leaders extracted pledges of religious toleration from their Habsburg rulers in 1568 in Lower Austria, in 1575 and 1609 in Bohemia, and in 1608 in Moravia and north-western Hungary, at moments when the Habsburgs urgently needed Protestant as well as Catholic support in their struggles against the Muslim Turks in Hungary and in the north-western Balkans, where the Austrian Habsburgs began to foster a fortified 'Military Frontier' (*Vojna Krajina*) in an eventually successful endeavour to ward off Ottoman encroachments.

Starting in 1599, the Habsburgs increasingly allowed militant Catholic royalists to monopolize Bohemia's key administrative and juridical positions and to discriminate actively in favour of Catholics and Catholicism. Czech and German Protestant nobles and burghers, along with many Utraquists and liberal Czech and German Catholics, felt that their existing liberties and Bohemian autonomy and tolerance were being increasingly threatened or compromised by a dangerous Catholic absolutist cabal.

THE THIRTY YEARS WAR (1618–48) AND ITS LEGACIES

The ensuing armed conflict between Bohemia and the Habsburgs emboldened the Bohemian Diet formally to terminate Habsburg rule in Bohemia in August 1619 and then to confer the Bohemian throne on Frederick, Elector of the Palatinate, who was then Germany's leading Protestant prince. This 'internationalized' the conflict. With help from Maximilian of Bavaria, the Spanish Habsburgs and the (Protestant) Elector of Saxony, however, the Austrian Habsburgs crushed the Bohemian insurgents at the fateful Battle of the White Mountain (near Prague) in November 1620. In the violent aftermath of this decisive battle, which heralded further decades of conflict and nearly three centuries of subjugation, Bohemia's population declined by at least one-quarter, while more than half of its landed property passed into the hands of Catholic loyalist magnates and soldiers of fortune. They took over Bohemia's administration, suppressed traditional Bohemian rights and liberties, intensified serfdom and greatly increased levels of taxation.

Whether motivated by bad consciences at having abandoned their Bohemian brethren to a terrible fate or by fear of the Habsburgs' increasingly dominant position in Europe, emerging Protestant powers such as Holland (1621), Denmark (1626) and Sweden (1630) belatedly took up arms in the name of the anti-Habsburg 'Protestant cause'. This further escalated and prolonged this devastating European war, whose legacy of destruction was to be felt for at least a century after its formal termination by the Peace of Westphalia in 1648. East Central Europe, especially Bohemia, bore the brunt of the resultant devastation and carnage.

The Thirty Years War also forced East Central Europe to develop and/or assimilate new methods of warfare based upon the use of well-trained, flexible and mobile professional infantry, supported by light, accurate, mobile and powerful Dutch and Swedish artillery. These were enormously expensive but extremely effective. In the eastern half of Europe, only centralized states with powerful, innovative bureaucracies and systems of public finance could afford them. Europe's belligerents were no longer able to base their war efforts on old-fashioned plunder and 'spoils of war', because their battlegrounds soon became too devastated and drained of movable resources to sustain that kind of warfare. This circumstance favoured the rising Habsburg Empire to the detriment of its smaller, weaker or less centralized neighbours, much as it subsequently favoured the rise of the Russian and Prussian empires. With the mining, metallurgical and technical resources of East Central Europe at their command, the Austrian Habsburgs were relatively well placed to meet the rapidly rising industrial and technical demands of the new forms of warfare. These factors not only helped the Habsburgs to strengthen their grip on East Central Europe, but also gradually tipped the military balance against the Ottomans in the protracted struggle for control of Hungary and the Balkans (Coles 1968: 186–91). The Austrian Habsburgs would have emerged even stronger if they had not simultaneously persecuted and driven into exile so many Protestant, Jewish and free-thinking merchants, artisans and financiers. Indeed, 'the Habsburgs were distinguished by neither heroism nor intelligence; but their tenacity was unequalled, their ambition unbounded and their luck phenomenal' (p. 118).

The other results of the Thirty Years War included the fragmentation of Europe's German-speaking peoples into more than three hundred states, most of which came under the dominance of Habsburg Austria for 150 years, and the triumph of absolutism and bigotry over free-thinking and tolerance in the greater part of East Central Europe. The ascent of the Austrian Habsburg ruler Ferdinand II to the role of crusading emperor (reg. 1619–37) made him 'master in his own house'. His more flexible and sophisticated heir, Ferdinand III (reg. 1637–57), consolidated this achievement once peace was established. Indeed, by the 1640s Ferdinand III enjoyed the immeasurable advantage that his regime 'now represented the only possible embodiment of order in Central Europe' and therefore had to be accepted by 'all who sought peace and recovery' (Evans 1979: 76).

After the Peace of Westphalia (1648), therefore, the Catholic Counter-Reformation was able to proceed 'with greater intensity' and 'on a firmer base' in East Central Europe (Evans 1979: 117). 'Ecclesiastical and civil authorities combined to create a new kind of unity' (p. 140). Nevertheless, the Peace of Westphalia also marked the end of the 'wars of religion' which had racked Europe since the early sixteenth century. Henceforth, wars would be fought mainly for selfish dynastic, commercial and geopolitical reasons rather than ideological ones, until the return to much more disruptive and destructive ideological warfare following the French Revolution. Although wars continued to be fought against Islam, these gradually became secular non-ideological power struggles for control of Hungary and the Balkans, and ceased to be religious or ideological 'holy wars'.

In post-1648 Europe, with the partial exception of the Balkans, religious affiliation became a purely internal matter for each state rather than a pretext for warfare and for interference in each other's internal affairs. The Peace of Westphalia formalized a new European states system which was in principle based upon the exclusive jurisdiction of each state within its own territory, although in reality the major powers continued to violate the sovereignty of their weaker neighbours when they saw fit to do so – the most notorious example of this being the successive Partitions of Poland-Lithuania between Russia, Prussia and Austria from 1772 to 1795.

THE SEVENTEENTH- AND EARLY EIGHTEENTH-CENTURY CULTURAL AND ECONOMIC RETARDATION OF THE AUSTRIAN HABSBURG DOMAINS

The triumphalism of Austrian absolutism and Counter-Reformation Catholicism, which was further reinforced by a string of Habsburg victories over the Turks in Hungary between 1686 and 1699, engendered a deepening intellectual and cultural 'freeze' in East Central Europe in the later seventeenth and early eighteenth century. Many thousands of 'heretics – Protestants, Jews and free-thinkers – were harassed, persecuted and driven into exile, many of them taking refuge in Protestant England, Scotland, Holland, Scandinavia and northern Germany. This accelerated the shift of European intellectual, scientific, technological and financial leadership from Catholic Europe to predominantly Protestant north-western Europe, where it intersected with the north-west European 'commercial revolution' and dramatic developments in the Atlantic economy. The latter gave rise to additional stimuli from 'new' non-European products such as cotton, silk, indigo, potatoes, tobacco, sugar, cocoa, coffee and tea. These in turn gave rise to new commercial, industrial, agricultural and scientific possibilities, including the vile profits of slavery and the Atlantic slave trade and major developments in shipping, shipbuilding, navigation and hence mathematics, optics, horology and physics (the principal thrusts of the Scientific Revolution). Such possibilities were largely closed off to the relatively landlocked and hidebound Habsburg Empire from the 1620s until the belated but vigorous development of the Enlightenment, 'enlightened despotism' and inland commerce in Central and East Central Europe and Russia during the mid- to late eighteenth century.

By strengthening Catholic absolutism and the ascendancy of big landowners and serfowners in East Central Europe, while inadvertently contributing to the commercial and scientific revolutions in north-western Europe, the Catholic Counter-Reformation and the effects of the Thirty Years War (1618–48) and the Habsburg 'reconquest' of Hungary (1686–99) powerfully contributed to a widening gap and a temporary 'parting of the ways' between north-western and East Central Europe. While north-western Europe actively fostered capitalism and an increasingly secular, scientific and rationalist civilization, East Central Europe was experiencing increased bigotry, obscurantism and 'refeudalization', including an intensification of serfdom and a concentration of landholdings in fewer and less 'progressive' hands.

In most of East Central Europe, as emphasized by the eminent Czech historian Josef Polisensky, the consequences were 'incalculably deleterious, setting back the development of communities by nearly a century and burdening them with a shortsighted, incompetent upstart nobility which could only prosper at the expense of the peasantry' (Polisensky 1974: 263). The biggest reversal of fortunes occurred in Bohemia, where 'refeudalization . . . delayed any further development and fettered all economic initiative', and caused antagonisms between Czechs and Germans to 'grow in intensity', as Germans came to dominate Bohemia and as the Empire's administration fell into 'the hands of the new "Austrian" nobility which had made its fortune through confiscations' (p. 264). Furthermore, in so far as Catholic magnates enriched themselves by dispossessing Protestants, Utraquists and anti-Habsburg Catholics, they also compromised their own integrity and independence. Until well into the nineteenth century, consequently, the 'decapitated' Kingdom of Bohemia lacked effective and independent champions of its particular interests. Meanwhile, an emerging East–West division of labour within Europe was encouraging East Central Europeans to specialize in the production and export of primary products by large estates employing serf labour, in exchange for north-west European manufactured goods produced by wage labour. This placed East Central Europe in an increasingly subordinate, inferior, semi-colonial role vis-à-vis north-western Europe (Polisensky 1974: 260). Overall, these appear to have been the most important causes of the economic, technological and cultural retardation of East Central Europe relative to north-western Europe during the seventeenth and early eighteenth century.

From the 1640s to the 1740s, at the height of the 'feudal reaction', East Central Europe experienced steadily rising rents and dues, the erosion of peasant rights and landholdings, the extension of manorial cultivation and the intensification of serfdom. Big landowners (including the Catholic Church and the royal family) became more actively involved in the administration of their estates and in the production and marketing of timber, linen and woollen textiles, hard liquor and minerals (such as iron, copper, coal and salt) as well as grain. They increasingly bypassed urban middlemen and fostered rural industries which could undercut urban crafts and guilds. They often employed Jews as their commercial agents. In response, non-Jewish burghers became more restrictive, defensive and anti-Semitic. This exacerbated the relative decline of towns. Big landowners also increasingly employed Jews as stewards or bailiffs ('front men') in their dealings with the peasantry, thereby contributing to the growth of peasant anti-Semitism. The lesser nobility, on the other hand, became increasingly dependent on employment in the army, the bureaucracy and the Roman Catholic Church. Nevertheless, they faced mounting competition from able and well-heeled commoners. This fuelled demands for special educational provisions for the sons of the lesser nobility.

'RECONQUEST', COUNTER-REFORM AND WARFARE, 1683–1711

The spectacular failure of the second (and final) Turkish siege of Vienna in 1683 opened the way for a successful Austrian counter-offensive against the Ottomans. This resulted in a Habsburg 'reconquest' of the Hungarian plain, Croatia-Slavonia and Transylvania between 1686 and 1699. Unfortunately, this 'reconquest' was accompanied by pillage, by widespread persecution of Hungarian Protestants (who had been relatively safe under Turkish suzerainty) and by a massive redistribution of land into the hands of an 'implanted' Catholic loyalist aristocracy and Catholic soldiers of fortune who had taken part in the 'glorious crusade' against the Turks. This rapacity and persecution gave rise to widespread anti-Habsburg insurgency in Hungary, Croatia, Slavonia and Transylvania from 1703 to 1711. The rebels took full advantage of the fact that most of the Austrian Habsburg armed forces were tied up in the War of the Spanish Succession (1701–14) in western Europe at that time. The Austrian Habsburgs failed in their very costly bid to obtain the vacant Spanish throne. In concert with England and Holland, however, they won control of the southern Netherlands and valuable Italian territories (Tuscany, Lombardy, Parma and Sardinia), while defeating King Louis XIV's bid for Bourbon hegemony over western Europe.

In 1711, as the warfare in both western Europe and Hungary took ever-mounting tolls, the Magyar propertied classes agreed to a compromise peace with the hard-pressed Austrian Habsburgs. The resultant Treaty of Szatmar (1711) gave Hungary a highly decentralized system of aristocratic self-administration, aristocratic 'liberties' (including freedom of conscience and exemption of landowners from direct taxation) and a separate legal system. This served as the basis for aristocratic 'loyalist' collaboration with the Austrian Habsburgs from 1711 to 1847 and for Hungary's special status within the Austrian Habsburg Empire.

POST-WAR RECOVERY AND MERCANTILISM, 1711–40

Emperors Josef I (1705–11) and Karl VI (1711–40) were somewhat less bigoted, more pragmatic and more conciliatory than their immediate predecessors. The relatively peaceful, mercantilist reign of Karl VI was also notable for the promotion of manorial and cottage industries (especially linen and woollen textiles), large-scale state-subsidized 'manufactories' (non-mechanized factories), mining, metallurgy and luxury craft industries (including porcelain, glassware, silk, lace, leather goods and clothes). These mainly developed in and around Vienna and in Bohemia-Moravia, with ancillary centres of mining and heavy industry in Styria and Silesia. Trade with the eastern Mediterranean and the Ottoman domains was encouraged by the proclamation of free trade in the Adriatic in 1717, by the 1718 peace treaty with Turkey (which also permanently ceded the 'Banat of Temesvar' to Austrian Habsburg control), by the development of Trieste and Fiume (Rijeka) as 'free ports', by the construction of highways from these ports to Vienna, and by the 'busting' of Venetian monopolies and trade privileges in the Adriatic and in the eastern Mediterranean/Ottoman domains. An exotic new world was opening up to the East Central Europeans.

THE BEGINNINGS OF 'ENLIGHTENED DESPOTISM' UNDER MARIA THERESA, 1740–80

From 1740 to 1780 the Habsburg Monarchy benefited from the 'enlightened despotism' of its de facto ruler Maria Theresa, a shrewd 'Erastian' or 'Reform' Catholic who strongly encouraged the use of church wealth for state and philanthropic purposes, including the beginnings of mass education in German Austria and in Bohemia-Moravia (in direct competition with the German/Lutheran states) and the more extensive provision of hospices and poor relief. However, despite Karl VI's extraordinary efforts to secure Bohemian (1720), Croatian (1721), Hungarian (1722), Transylvanian (1723), Belgian (1724), Lombard (1725) and the German princes' recognition of his daughter's claims to the whole Habsburg inheritance (through a legal device known to historians as 'the Pragmatic Sanction'), the succession of Maria Theresa was contested by King Albert of Bavaria, who was 'elected' to the imperial throne when Karl VI died in 1740.

During the resultant 'War of the Austrian Succession' (1740–8), Maria Theresa eventually succeeded in getting her husband Francis of Lorraine elected as Holy Roman Emperor in 1745. While real power remained in her own hands, she was obliged to cede mineral-rich Lower Silesia to King Friedrich II ('the Great') of Prussia – a territorial concession which unwittingly helped to set in motion the process of Prussian aggrandizement which eventually culminated in German unification and the overshadowing of the Habsburg Empire by Germany during the nineteenth century.

From 1749 to 1756, in the aftermath of the War of the Austrian Succession, there was a major burst of reform and centralization in Austria proper and in Bohemia-Moravia, although not in the Austrian Habsburgs' Hungarian, Croatian and Transylvanian dominions. These changes were designed to expand the revenue base of the Habsburg state sufficiently to support a standing army of 108,000 men. They were mainly implemented by parvenu bureaucrats under the guidance of Chancellor Friedrich Haugwitz, in the teeth of strong opposition from the older nobility and noble-dominated provincial diets or estates. In emulation of Prussia, moreover, a land register was established to serve as the basis for more systematic taxation of the hitherto under-taxed wealth of the landed nobility and for legal checks on any further erosion of peasant landholdings by big landowners. The latter marked the start of a paternalistic policy of 'peasant protection' which helped to arrest and eventually reverse the relative decline of independent peasant agriculture in East Central Europe, with important political, social and economic consequences for the later rise or resurgence of a number of submerged and downtrodden 'peasant nations' during the nineteenth and twentieth centuries.

The Seven Years War (1756–63), which pitted the Habsburg Empire, France and Russia against Britain, Hanover and Prussia, was followed by a more prolonged period of retrenchment, reform and relative peace (1763–92). The overriding aims of state policy during this period were to expand the Habsburg revenue base sufficiently to support a standing army of 300,000 men, whilst endeavouring to avoid costly and disruptive military engagements so as to provide a breathing space for steady economic growth.

THE 'ENLIGHTENED DESPOTISM' OF EMPEROR JOSEF II, 1765–90

In 1765 Josef II, Maria Theresa's austere but enlightened son, inherited the imperial crown (on the death of his father). He became a very active promoter of reform, although ultimate power and authority still remained with his mother. His reign saw the emergence of a reforming alliance of the Habsburgs with the lesser nobility, the burgher class, the peasantry and 'Erastian' or 'Reform' Catholics, against the overprivileged Church and aristocracy, but only in the 'Austrian' half of the empire.

In 1767 statutory limitations on the labour-service obligations of the peasantry were enacted in German Austria. A Czech peasant revolt prompted similar changes in the Czech Lands in 1775. Regular taxation of the massive riches of the Catholic Church was instituted in 1769. And in 1773, with papal consent, the Habsburgs dissolved the wealthy and overweening Jesuit order and its large network of schools and academies for the offspring of the upper classes, paving the way for a rapid expansion of more utilitarian state education, based upon an extensive network of elementary and secondary schools (*Normalschulen* and *Realschulen*). These soon placed German Austria and the Czech Lands in the forefront of European educational development, almost on a par with Protestant north Germany, Switzerland, Holland and Scandinavia and far ahead of France, Britain, southern Europe and Russia. This educational system laid the foundations for a brilliant intellectual and cultural renaissance in the Habsburg Empire from the late eighteenth to the early twentieth century. It eventually produced such major figures as the psychologist Sigmund Freud, the writers Franz Kafka, Karel Capek, Jaroslav Hasek, Arthur Schnitzler and Hugo von Hofmannsthal, the philosophers Ernst Mach and Tomas Masaryk, the Marxists Otto Bauer, Rudolph Hilferding and Georg Lukacs, the economists Karl Menger, Eugen von Böhm-Bawerk, Ludwig von Mises, Friedrich von Hayek and Joseph Schumpeter, the painters Gustav Klimt and Oskar Kokoschka and, last but not least, the composers Bela Bartok, Zoltan Kodaly, Bedrich Smetana, Antonin Dvorak, Leos Janacek, Franz Schubert, Hugo Wolf, Anton Bruckner, Gustav Mahler, Alexander von Zemlinsky, Arnold Schönberg, Alban Berg and Erich Korngold, among others.

Indeed, contrary to popular belief, the Habsburg Empire did not go into long-term 'decline' during the nineteenth century, other than in a purely military and territorial sense. As a Great Power it was eventually eclipsed by the emerging German Empire. It also lost territory to the processes of German and Italian unification. Economically, culturally and intellectually, however, the Habsburg Empire continued to develop vigorously right up to the First World War. By 1913 the *per capita* national income of German Austria was only about 10 per cent below that of Germany and roughly on a par with that of France (Good 1984: 241).

THE 1780S: JOSEF II'S HYPERACTIVE DECADE OF REFORMS

The death of Maria Theresa in 1780 ushered in a frenzied decade of reform under Josef II, who was now freed from the constraints imposed by his more cautious mother. In 1781 he not only abolished personal serfdom and many compulsory peasant dues ('banalities') in German Austria and the Czech Lands, but he also issued a Patent of Toleration for Lutherans, Calvinists and Orthodox Christians, albeit not for smaller Christian sects and for Jews. (He felt that the time was not yet ripe either for 'Jewish emancipation' or for the 'unleashing' of evangelical Christians.) He also relaxed censorship in order to mobilize public opinion and evoke a ferment in favour of reform. However, he was too authoritarian, impatient, impulsive and convinced of his own 'rightness' to act on a basis of formal accountability. Any notion that he should have to account for his actions or introduce elements of democracy was anathema to this benign yet idiosyncratic autocrat, unfairly portrayed as an oaf in Milos Forman's celebrated film *Amadeus*.

In 1782 Josef II ordered the dissolution of around 700 'contemplative' monasteries and convents and outlawed mendicancy (begging) by monks, while permitting the continued existence of about 1,400 monasteries and convents which ostensibly supported or provided 'really useful' trades, charity and health care. In 1784 he instituted a total ban on the importation of most manufactures, so as to protect Austro-Czech industries and foster greater imperial *Autarkie* (self-sufficiency). This also encouraged Swiss, German, British and French firms to establish subsidiaries within Austria. In 1785 he suspended Hungary's aristocratic 'liberties' (i.e. privileges) and local self-administration and imposed an Austrian-controlled central administration, with a view to extending his radical reforms to Hungary while sweeping aside Magyar aristocratic and ecclesiastical opposition to his programme. His major aims in Hungary were to establish more effective and equitable taxation, to abolish personal serfdom and to unify the Hungarian market.

The reign of Josef II was also characterized by active promotion of the German language and German culture. The German Society popularized the works of German writers. In 1772 the company of French actors was replaced by Germans at the Court Theatre, which Josef II reorganized into the Deutsches Nationaltheater in 1776. In 1782, at the emperor's command, it commissioned and staged the first major German-language opera, Mozart's *Die Entführung aus dem Serail*. (Even more significantly, one of Vienna's suburban theatres commissioned and staged Mozart's *Die Zauberflöte* in 1791.) More controversially, Josef II ordered the imposition of German (in place of Latin) as the official language of administration in Hungary in 1784, but this was reversed after his death in 1790. German nevertheless strengthened its hold as the lingua franca of officialdom and 'high culture' in East Central Europe.

In the revolutionary year of 1789, finally, Josef II introduced a uniform 12 per cent tax on the gross yield of both noble and peasant land (as recorded in official registers), combined with a statutory limitation of the seigneurial and ecclesiastical dues payable by the peasantry to just 18 per cent of the gross yield of their land, in both German Austria and the Czech Lands. After tax, therefore, peasants in these areas were henceforth to retain a statutory 70 per cent of the gross yield of their land (as an incentive to produce and sell more), while state revenues would increase at the expense of the nobility and the Catholic Church.

Overall, Josef II's reforms, which intervened in almost all matters, amounted to an astonishing one-man revolution. However, this apparent strength was also his major weakness. His revolutionary policies lacked 'the support of a revolutionary class' (Taylor 1976: 19). Paradoxically, his aims could only have been achieved in full by a real revolution, yet that would have destroyed the Habsburg Monarchy. On a more critical note, Robert Kann has characterized the achievements of Josef II as 'the system of the enlightened police state: everything for the people; nothing by the people . . . It was rigid and uncompromising.' At its core was 'the notion that only one man can rule and govern and that all those entrusted with the manifold tasks of government should receive their authority from him' (Kann 1974: 184). Josef II has often been affectionately or ironically described as 'the people's emperor' and as a role model for the fascist and Communist rulers in East Central Europe during the twentieth century.

AUSTRIA'S 'HOME-GROWN' ECONOMIC RESURGENCE, 1760s–1780s

Finding itself unable to compete very successfully in the emerging Western capitalist 'world economy' centred on the Atlantic seaboard, the Habsburg Empire settled for an East–West division of labour within its own relatively autarkic domains. This led to a customs union of Austria proper with Bohemia, Moravia and Habsburg Silesia in 1775 and to a substantial expansion of interregional trade and specialization. That in turn stimulated river improvements, canal construction, a network of hard-surfaced highways (more than 700 km by 1800), market integration, further expansion of cottage and manorial industries, the proliferation of water-powered mills and factories (there were at least 280 'manufactories' in Austria by 1790) and the revival of towns as centres of trade and industry. These changes, combined with the resultant acceleration in population growth, helped to bring about extensions of the cultivated area, the diffusion of new crops (such as maize and potatoes), the introduction of new cropping systems and livestock breeds (such as Merino sheep), the loosening and erosion of serfdom, rising real incomes, the emergence of new forms of textile and clothing production (especially cotton), and advances in flour milling, baking, brewing, wine making and distilling. The increased emission and use of paper money, which was induced by growing state expenditure on the army, arms production, education and infrastructure and by the ensuing budget deficits, also increased financial liquidity and the commercialization and expansion of the economy. By 1789, as a consequence, 'conditions over much of the Habsburg Empire were ripe for the introduction of factory industry: capital, skills and enterprise were available, and the institutional framework was reasonably favourable' (Gross 1973: 247). By then German Austria, Slovenia and the Czech Lands had become net exporters of manufactures. In 1782–3 finished goods made up 66 per cent of their exports and only 16 per cent of their imports (Good 1984: 25).

The most dramatic economic and social transformations occurred in Bohemia, Moravia and

Habsburg Silesia. The emasculation of political ambition and activity in the Czech Lands since the Thirty Years War (1618–48) had gradually encouraged both nobles and burghers to seek comfort and alternative outlets for their energies, education and talents in the development of urban and rural textile, food-processing, brewing, distilling, woodworking, glassware and metallurgical industries, thereby capitalizing on their relatively diverse and plentiful agricultural, mineral, timber and water resources, and nodal situation. The increasing commercialization of agriculture as well as industry and the accelerating development of cottage, manorial and urban craft/manufacturing industries hastened the dissolution of serfdom, and laid the economic and social foundations for the nineteenth-century Czech 'national renaissance' and the transformation of the Czech Lands into the industrial hub of the Habsburg Empire.

All these economic and social changes broke down social barriers, increased social 'mixing' (including intermarriage between persons of different classes, religions and nationalities) and enhanced social, geographical and occupational mobility. This allowed more and more people to find and pursue their 'true vocations' (the activities in which they could excel or perform their best), instead of remaining trapped within the confines of the social, religious, ethnic and occupational groups into which they had been born. This increased social fluidity, by promoting a fuller and more productive utilization of human resources, was a crucial stimulus to modern economic growth and to the movement away from relatively rigid and restrictive social, ethnic and religious hierarchies and mental horizons. Potentially the biggest beneficiaries of these changes were those groups which had hitherto been most restricted, namely, serfs and Jews. Their gradual emancipation made possible new flowerings of hitherto suppressed human talents.

14 Poland-Lithuania, 1466–1795

A dynastic union between Poland and Lithuania in 1386 under the Jagiellonians, followed by momentous Polish-Lithuanian victories over the Teutonic Order in 1410, 1454 and 1466, turned this realm into a major European power and Europe's largest state. From 1471 to 1526, following the establishment of Jagiellon kings on the thrones of Hungary (1440–4, 1490–1526) and Bohemia (1471–1526), the Jagiellons governed about one-third of mainland Europe (Zamoyski 1987: 50) and appeared to have gained the upper hand over the Habsburgs in the contest for supremacy over East Central Europe. Furthermore, even though Polish magnates had increased their power and wealth at the expense of the monarchy during the thirteenth and fourteenth centuries, the Jagiellon Grand Duke Kazimiercz IV managed to get himself elected and crowned as King of Poland in 1446–7 without conceding much to the magnates (Fedorowicz 1982: 92). In order to win over the nobility at the start of the Thirteen Years War against the Teutonic Order (1454–66), Kazimiercz IV issued the Statute of Nieszawa (1454), which stipulated that no new taxes could be levied nor armies raised without the consent of the noble-dominated provincial assemblies (*sejmiki*), whose meetings were regularized during the fifteenth century. He thereby mobilized the provincial nobility (the 'gentry') as a counterweight to the magnates, much as some western European monarchs mobilized, enfranchised and increasingly relied upon the towns to reduce their dependence upon the landed aristocracy (pp. 93–3).

The frequently alleged decline in the power of the Polish-Lithuanian monarchy during the fifteenth and sixteenth centuries has been greatly exaggerated. At least until 1573, the power of the monarch tended to increase rather than to diminish, precisely because several kings successfully mobilized the middle ranks of the nobility (the 'gentry') against the power of the magnates. The major concessions granted to the nobility as a whole in 1374, 1425, 1454, 1505 and 1562–9 should be seen as 'attempts at strengthening that authority by gaining the support of the gentry' against the magnates, rather than as 'a weakening of royal authority' (Wyczanski 1982: 97). This resulted in increased centralization and more effective administration, while eroding magnate influence (p. 148). Wyczanski's thesis is a useful antidote to the frequent and easy temptation to project back on to the fifteenth- and sixteenth-century Polish-Lithuanian monarchy some of the problems of political impotence and paralysis which certainly did afflict it between the mid-seventeenth and the late eighteenth century, and thus to perceive the gradual decline and eventual extinction of the Polish-Lithuanian realm as an ineluctable and predetermined process.

In 1526, however, the childless Jagiellon King of Hungary and Bohemia was defeated and killed by the Ottoman Turks at the Battle of Mohacs. The Hungarian and Bohemian crowns thereupon passed to Ferdinand of Habsburg, who had married the sister of Hungary and Bohemia's deceased King Lajos (Ludwik), who was himself married to a Habsburg. However, the resultant shift of power from the Jagiellons to the Austrian Habsburgs came about only gradually, since even under Habsburg overlordship Bohemia retained considerable autonomy until 1620, while most of Hungary fell under the control of the Ottomans and/or their Transylvanian vassals from the 1530s to the 1680s.

THE SIXTEENTH- AND EARLY SEVENTEENTH-CENTURY HEYDAY OF POLAND-LITHUANIA

Far from being in decline, Poland-Lithuania entered its heyday – economically, culturally, spiritually and even politically – during the sixteenth century. Both economically and in other respects there was a significant narrowing of the gap between Poland and the southern and western regions of Europe from the fourteenth to the sixteenth century. Still relatively remote and sparsely populated, Poland largely escaped the ravages of the Black Death and the associated crises which had convulsed western Europe during the fourteenth century. Instead, Poland entered an economic and demographic upswing which persisted into the sixteenth century (Zamoyski 1987: 59). Freer navigation was established on Poland's major rivers: the Vistula, the Bug, the Odra and the San. Roads were improved, pack horses gave way to wheeled transport, and a more unified market began to emerge. This, coupled with a 300 per cent rise in Poland's primary commodity prices during the sixteenth century, stimulated mining, agricultural production and the grain trade (Davies 1981a: 128–9). The sixteenth-century European inflation and 'price revolution', which increased grain prices much more than those of manufactures, greatly improved Poland's terms of trade. This made it easier for the landed classes to increase their expenditures on education and foreign study-travel – especially to Italy, where Polish students generally made up a quarter of the student body at the University of Padua between 1501 and 1605 (Zamoyski 1987: 108).

By 1500 15 per cent of Poland's population lived in 'towns' with 500 or more inhabitants (excluding the Grand Duchy of Lithuania). Gdansk was Poland's largest city, with about 30,000 inhabitants, followed by Krakow (18,000), Lwow (8,000), Torun/Thorn (8,000), Elblag/Elbing (8,000), Poznan (6,000–7,000), Lublin (6,000–7,000) and Warsaw (6,000–7,000) (Bogucka 1982: 138). By 1600 25 per cent of Poland's population resided in 'towns' with 500 or more inhabitants. Gdansk had about 70,000 inhabitants, followed by Krakow (28,000), Warsaw (20,000–30,000), Poznan (20,000) and Lwow (20,000) (p. 139). This growth of towns went hand-in-hand with the growth of the Jewish population, which numbered 450,000 or 4.5 per cent of the total population of the Polish-Lithuanian Commonwealth by 1648. Substantial numbers of Jewish refugees came to Poland from Spain after 1492 and from Portugal after 1496. They were no longer confined to commercial and financial occupations or even to the towns. They founded their own craft guilds, 'left their traditional urban refuges' and 'played an important pioneering role in the development of the south-eastern lands, especially in the Ukraine' (Davies 1981a: 440). Like the Christian burgher communities, the Jews developed their own institutions of self-government, culminating in the creation of their own judicial and legislative council of the Four Lands in 1580.

The Lutheran Reformation delivered the *coup de grâce* to the Teutonic Order. In 1525 the disconsolate Teutonic Knights converted to Lutheranism en masse, and the Grand Master Albrecht von Hohenzollern asked Poland's King Zygmunt I (reg. 1506–48) to turn East Prussia into a secular fiefdom of the Polish crown with himself as its hereditary duke (Davies 1981a: 143, 295). The erstwhile Teutonic state of Livonia, comprising much of what is now Latvia and Estonia, was similarly converted into a secular Polish fiefdom under a hereditary duke in 1561, while the major port-city of Riga was incorporated into the Kingdom of Poland with much the same privileges and autonomy as Gdansk (pp. 146–7).

The birth of the Polish-Lithuanian Commonwealth (Republic), 1569–76

The realm of the Jagiellons was, like that of the Austrian Habsburgs, an agglomeration of territories with widely differing populations, customs and forms of governance. 'The force holding this structure together was neither a feudal bond, nor a bureaucratic system, nor a military hegemony, but a broad consensus whose physical embodiment was the Jagiellon dynasty itself' (Zamoyski 1987: 92).

During the 1560s, Poland's ageing King Zygmunt II was childless and the imminent extinction of the Jagiellon dynasty posed the fraught question of whether the Polish-Lithuanian union could 'continue to exist in its present form' (Zamoyski 1987: 92). Fearful of the predatory expansionism of Russia's Tsar Ivan the Terrible (reg. 1533–84), Poland's Sejm and Senate met in joint session with their Lithuanian counterparts at Lublin in 1569, in order to sanction a new Act of Union. This 'Union of Lublin' established that the two Sejms and the two Senates would henceforth meet as one in the new union's new capital, the small but centrally located city of Warsaw. This *Rzeczpospolita Obojga Narodow* (Commonwealth or Republic of the Two Nations) was to constitute a single polity, with a unified market and a single currency. In principle, Lithuanian nobles were gradually to acquire much the same rights and status as their Polish counterparts, but some Lithuanian magnates justifiably feared that their previous dominance and privileges would be diluted and that the once mighty Grand Duchy of Lithuania would become the junior partner in this marriage of convenience. Their attempts at stonewalling were punished when Zygmunt II formally transferred Lithuania's Ukrainian provinces (Podlasie, Volhynia and Kiev) to the Kingdom of Poland (Davies 1981a: 152–3).

Following Zygmunt II's death in 1572, more than 40,000 Polish and Lithuanian nobles attended a vast Convocation Sejm on a large field outside Warsaw to elect a new king in 1573. They chose Prince Henri de Valois, who (together with his brother King Charles IX of France) had recently taken part in the notorious St Bartholomew's Eve massacre of some 20,000 French Protestants (*Huguenots*) on 24 August 1572. However, this choice was rendered more comprehensible by the main rival contenders: Tsar Ivan the Terrible; Prince Ernest of Habsburg; King Johan III of Sweden; and the Transylvanian soldier of fortune Stefan (Istvan) Bathory. The Habsburgs, like the Russian and Swedish candidates, were hoping to accomplish a dynastic annexation of Poland-Lithuania, which was still the largest state in Europe. France, by contrast, was trying to construct an anti-Habsburg coalition. The Polish-Lithuanian nobility appear to have opted for the candidate who they thought would best safeguard the union, their own privileges and the Commonwealth's independence. Before confirming the election of Henri de Valois, they made him swear to uphold and abide by a new quasi-constitutional document, which became known as the *Acta Henriciana* and which every subsequent monarch-elect was similarly required to accept before being confirmed as king. It enjoined the king (i) to maintain and respect the elective nature of the Polish-Lithuanian monarchy; (ii) to convoke the Sejm at least once every two years, in accordance with the terms laid down in the Union of Lublin; (iii) to respect the principle of religious toleration enshrined in the celebrated Statute of Toleration, which was passed by the Confederation of Warsaw in 1573; (iv) to obtain the Sejm's approval for any imposition of new taxes, declaration of war or summons of the nobility to military service (*levée en masse*); and (v) to recognize the nobility's right to resist, disobey or even withdraw their allegiance from the king if he broke any of these solemnly biding promises (Fedorowicz 1982: 110; Davies 1981a: 334).

In the event Henri de Valois was quickly dismayed by the apparent poverty and monotony of the Polish countryside and bored by the seemingly interminable courtly deliberations in Latin and/or Polish (which he did not understand). When his brother Charles IX died childless in May 1574, Henri returned home to become the new King of France.

In 1575, with their restive and leaderless Commonwealth under attack by Ivan the Terrible in Livonia and by Crimean Tatars in Ukraine, the Polish-Lithuanian nobility wisely elected as king the able Transylvanian Stefan (Istvan) Bathory, whose military prowess had already resulted in his election as Prince of Transylvania in 1571 (Davies 1981a: 416–23). Besides having to accept the *Acta Henriciana* before his coronation in 1576, Bathory was also required to swear a *Pacta Conventa* (Covenant) with regard to his conduct of foreign policy and his management of crown finances, thereby setting another precedent for future royal elections (pp. 334–5). Nevertheless, 'the king retained important powers and considerable room for manoeuvre', which the astute and energetic Bathory (reg. 1576–86) deployed to great effect. As king, he controlled the crown estates (one-sixth of the land and population) and wielded considerable powers of patronage, including the control of appointments to executive, judicial and ecclesiastical offices and to tenancies of lucrative royal properties and monopolies. He acted as the nominal commander-in-chief of the union's armed forces, had the major say in foreign policy, and wielded the power to issue edicts in all spheres not reserved to the Sejm, to convene and dismiss the Sejm, to set its agenda and sign its resolutions into statutory law (p. 336).

Religious toleration and ecumenicism in sixteenth-century Poland-Lithuania

The sixteenth-century Polish-Lithuanian nobility actively resisted the forms of religious persecution which plagued southern and western Europe at that time. When the Bishop of Poznan tried to have four 'heretics' burnt at the stake in 1554 and 1555, the accused were rescued by armed posses of nobles, many of whom were practising Catholics. One of them pointed out: 'It is not a question of religion, it is a question of liberty' (Zamoyski 1987: 84).

The Confederation of Warsaw which elected Henri de Valois as King of Poland-Lithuania in 1573 also passed a Statute of Toleration which stated: 'Whereas in our Commonwealth there is no small disagreement in the matter of the Christian faith, and in order to prevent that any harmful contention should arise from this, as we see clearly taking place in other kingdoms, we swear to each other, in our name and in that of our descendants for ever more, on our honour, our faith, our love and our conscience, that albeit we are *dissidentes in religione*, we will all keep the peace between ourselves, and that we will not, for the sake of our various faiths and differences of church, either shed blood or confiscate property, deny favour, imprison, or banish and . . . we will not aid or abet any power or office which strives to this' (quoted by Zamoyski 1987: 90–1).

This Statute of Toleration did not propose sanctions against those who attacked Protestant churches, homes, shops, funerals or cemeteries. Nor did it prevent the closure of Protestant churches and the expulsion of Protestants from Krakow in 1591, from Poznan in 1611 or from Lublin in 1627 (Tazbir 1994: 174). Roman Catholicism remained the official (state) religion. Nevertheless, the Statute encompassed almost all Christian denominations, including Orthodox Christians and the Polish Brethren. It was an astonishing 'agreement to disagree', way ahead of its time. It was a potent inspiration and the Commonwealth's greatest contribution to the Renaissance humanist spirit of toleration which ought to have pervaded late sixteenth-century Europe, in place of the mounting religious bigotry and fractiousness unleashed by the German, western and southern European Reformations and Counter-Reformations. The Statute was largely observed and upheld by the subsequent rulers of Poland-Lithuania, although there were some *illegal* lynchings and executions during periods of acute crisis (such as the 1650s and the 1700s). According to a Calvinist account of the Polish-Lithuanian Counter-Reformation, there were only twelve executions or sectarian killings of Protestants in Poland-Lithuania between 1550 and 1650, compared with more than 500 in England and nearly 900 in the Netherlands over the same period (Zamoyski 1987: 91). Indeed, for all their alleged religious ardour, Poles have committed *far fewer* atrocities against 'their own people' than most other European peoples have done. They have usually pulled back from the brink of violent internal conflict, even if they have not always refrained from persecution of Jewish and Ukrainian minorities and violent conflict with their neighbours. The motivation has undoubtedly included a strong self-interested desire for ethnic 'self-preservation', but there has also been a larger comprehension that freedom is indivisible – hence modern Poland's national slogan, 'For our freedom – and yours'.

During the middle years of the sixteenth century, there were 'repeated attempts to devise a form of Confession acceptable to all' (Davies 1981a: 183), with the aim of keeping the peace in this multi-cultural society. In 1555 a majority of deputies in the lower house of the Sejm even went so far as to demand the establishment of an ecumenical (inter-denominational) church which would perform its rites in the vernacular, allow priests to marry, offer Communion in both forms (the bread and the wine) and vest ultimate control of the Church in a Polish-Lithuanian Synod free of papal interference. King Zygmunt II (reg. 1548–72), who took an active interest in Protestantism and ecclesiastical reform while remaining a Catholic, referred the matter to Rome, having famously stated: 'I am not the king of your conscience,' (i.e., he regarded religion as a private and personal matter and he upheld freedom of conscience). However, this enlightened outlook must have been incomprehensible to a Western Pope, who merely reprimanded the king for 'allowing his subjects to formulate such heretical demands' (Zamoyski 1987: 86).

In 1595–6 the Commonwealth's ecumenicism also contributed to the creation of the Uniate Church, which unfortunately was blighted from birth. This hybrid church was Eastern Orthodox in its rites and customs (it retained the Slavonic Orthodox liturgy and the marriage of priests), but it gave allegiance to the Pope and the Vatican *Curia* rather than to the Orthodox Patriarch in Constantinople. Its establishment was partly a result of Polish Catholic attempts to render the Commonwealth's Eastern Orthodox inhabitants (who comprised about 40 per cent of the population) less susceptible to Muscovite Russian influence and to bind them more closely to the politically dominant Catholics (who made up 45–47 per cent of the population). It also arose out of various attempts by many Orthodox Christian clergy and nobles in Ukraine and (to lesser degrees) Belarus to draw closer to the Roman Catholic Church and the Polish nobility in the wake of the fall of Constantinople to the Ottomans in 1453 and the subsequent northward offensives of the Turks and the Crimean Tatars. Furthermore, the fall of Constantinople had encouraged Muscovite Russia to aspire to the leadership of all Eastern Orthodox peoples. This was the origin of Muscovite claims that Moscow was 'the Third Rome' (after Rome itself and Constantinople) and the chrysalis of a 'rising' world power and world civilization. In Polish-Lithuanian eyes, however, Muscovite ambitions were menacingly imperialist, while many of the lands to which the Tsars laid claim 'belonged to the Republic and had never belonged to Muscovy' (Davies 1981a: 387).

In 1588, during a pastoral visit to the Commonwealth, the Eastern Orthodox Patriarch of Constantinople seems to have authorized the Orthodox Bishop of Luck to open negotiations with the Catholic Bishop of Luck with a view to attaining greater mutual recognition and local co-operation between their respective dioceses (Zamoyski 1987: 160). The following year, however, a fully fledged Orthodox patriarchate was established in Moscow, further inflating the latter's territorial and pastoral ambitions and pretensions in Ukraine and Belarus. In response and with Jesuit encouragement, some of the Commonwealth's Orthodox bishops sent a letter to the Pope in 1595, asking him to admit the Orthodox Christians of Ukraine and Belarus into the Roman Catholic Church without requiring them to renounce their Eastern Orthodox/Slavic customs and liturgy. The Jesuits exerted pressure on the Pope to assent to this arrangement, probably to open the way to increased Polonization of the Orthodox Christians of Ukraine and Belarus and facilitate their future conversion to Roman Catholicism. The Pope was thus persuaded to issue a Bull purportedly ending the schism between the Orthodox and the Catholic churches in the Commonwealth. However, the manoeuvre backfired, because many of the Orthodox clergy and laity felt indignant that they had not been consulted and that they had been 'sold out' to the Roman Catholic Church by some high-handed and/or corrupt bishops and nobles, under pressure from the Jesuits. Therefore, the joint Synod which assembled in Brzesc (Brest) on 8 October 1596 to consummate the establishment of the so-called Uniate Church was wracked by acrimony and dissent. Many Orthodox Christians (including several bishops) refused to accept the Union of Brest and the day ended with the rival churches excommunicating one another.

Within the Commonwealth those Orthodox Christians who accepted the Union of Brest and the Uniate Church came to be known as the *unici* (uniates), while those who refused to do so were denounced as *dysunici* ('disuniates') and *dissidentes* (dissidents). For the next thirty-seven years, the latter were harassed and deprived of any official recognition and status. However, treating the

Orthodox Christians of Ukraine and Belarus as dissidents and schismatics merely encouraged them to look east, to the burgeoning Russian Orthodox Church. The realization that this was happening eventually persuaded the Commonwealth's Catholic authorities to relent and rehabilitate the Orthodox hierarchy in 1633 (Davies 1981a: 175).

All in all, this clumsy attempt to unite the Commonwealth's principal churches increased rather than reduced its religious divisions and antagonisms. It also contributed to the emergence of enduring antagonisms between Orthodox Eastern Slavs (Russians, Ukrainians and Belarussians) and Poles. Many Polish Catholics have tended to regard compatriots who are attracted to Eastern Orthodoxy, to Eastern Slavic culture or (more recently) to Marxism-Leninism as 'dissidents' and as actual or potential 'traitors' to Poland and its national religion. The situation also encouraged the formerly Orthodox nobles in Ukraine and Belarus to embrace full-blown Catholicism rather than the hybrid Uniate Church. In breach of the founding agreements, the Commonwealth never granted the Uniates the same status and representation as Catholics, and Uniate numbers were steadily eroded by desertions to either Eastern Orthodoxy or Roman Catholicism.

A further consequence was that both the Uniate Church and Eastern Orthodoxy became increasingly identified as banners and rallying points for peasant antagonism towards the increasingly Catholicized and Polonized nobility in the borderlands of Ukraine and Belarus. This was most evident during the tumultuous years between 1648 and 1668, but there were also significant 'after shocks' during the warfare and unrest which occurred during the 1700s, 1733–5 and 1792–4, during the Polish uprisings of 1830–1, 1846 and 1863, during the two World Wars and their aftermaths, and during the 1930s Depression. These antagonisms also contributed to significant revivals of Eastern Orthodoxy in Ukraine and Belarus during the seventeenth and eighteenth centuries. However, most of the areas inhabited by Eastern Orthodox Christians were lost to Russia during the second half of the seventeenth century, with the result that Uniates still constituted about 33 per cent of the Commonwealth's population in 1772, as against 43 per cent for Catholics, 10 per cent for Eastern Orthodox Christians, 8 per cent for Jews, and by then only 4 per cent for Protestants (Davies 1981a: 162). The Uniates who came under Russian rule were even more badly treated by successive Russian regimes than Eastern Orthodox Christians had been by the Polish-Lithuanian Commonwealth. Many Russian Orthodox bigots and Russian nationalists regarded them as traitors and apostates. Sadly, the Union of Brest has brought nothing but strife, bitterness and grief.

The Indian summer of the *Rzeczpospolita*, 1576–1648

King Stefan Bathory (reg. 1576–86) rapidly reformed the Polish-Lithuanian army and judiciary, almost doubled royal revenues, and brought to heel overmighty magnates, the fractious Dnieper Cossacks and the the city of Gdansk, which had supported the Austrian Habsburgs, and secured substantial 'voluntary' donations by the Church, Gdansk and others to the royal coffers (Davies 1981a: 425–8). He thus gained the wherewithal to roll back the Russian advance into Livonia and 'carry the fight into enemy territory' by subduing Polotsk and besieging Pskov, thereby inducing Ivan the Terrible to renounce his claims to Livonia, Polotsk, Velizh and Ushviata and to sue for peace in 1581–2 (pp. 429–31).

Bathory's brief but robust reign clearly demonstrated that an able and energetic ruler of the Polish-Lithuanian Commonwealth could still mobilize and deploy considerable strength and that, if the nobility had continued to select monarchs on the basis of proven ability, this elective monarchy could have been at least as effective as a hereditary one – perhaps more so, since it would have been less susceptible to the hazards of dynastic inbreeding. For the most part, however, the Commonwealth's nobles were less concerned with the common weal than with short-term tactical considerations and safeguarding their own sectional interests, prerogatives and privileges. They therefore mainly opted for weak monarchs.

The royal election of 1587 was primarily a contest between Sigismund Vasa, the Polish-speaking son and heir apparent of Sweden's King Johan III Vasa, who had married a staunchly Catholic Jagiellon princess from Poland, and Archduke Maximillian of Habsburg, the brother of the Habsburg Emperor Rudolf II. In 1587, as Habsburg Spain was preparing to launch a great naval armada against England, the Habsburg 'mafia' seemed poised to establish its supremacy over Europe. This encouraged Polish-Lithuanian magnates and nobles, fearful of the Catholic-absolutist Austrian Habsburgs, pre-emptively to engineer the election of the 21-year-old Vasa prince as King Zygmunt III of Poland-Lithuania. They also defeated a Habsburg attempt to gain the Polish-Lithuanian throne by force. Ironically, the Catholic-absolutist aspirations of Zygmunt III Vasa soon proved to be every bit as strong as those of the defeated candidate, but by then it was too late to undo the mistake. The Commonwealth was saddled with a monarch who was congenitally at odds with its constitution.

Thus began eighty-one years of Vasa rule (1587–1668) and a consequent embroilment in Swedish affairs, for which the Commonwealth would pay an unforeseeably high price. Furthermore, Zygmunt III soon alienated his original Polish-Lithuanian supporters by marrying a Habsburg archduchess, by proving highly susceptible to Jesuit and Habsburg influence, and by (mis)using his Polish-Lithuanian throne as a power base for several abortive attempts to roll back the Protestant Reformation and ensconce Catholic-absolutist ('divine right') rule in both the Commonwealth and Sweden. No matter how often he was forced to apologize and back down in public, he remained unrepentant at heart. This meant that the Polish-Lithuanian nobility could never trust him to respect and uphold their cherished liberties, institutions and procedures. The upshot was 'a succession of fruitless and damaging collisions with the institutions of the Commonwealth' (Zamoyski 1987: 136).

Zygmunt III's reign (1587–1632) coincided with the Commonwealth's 'golden age' and was the longest in Polish-Lithuanian history. Yet even on his deathbed he remained less interested in the Commonwealth per se than in using its still considerable power in the Baltic region to contain the Reformation and bring his native Sweden back into the Catholic fold. Thus he not only squandered his kingdom's resources, but also sowed the seeds of the catastrophes which befell the Commonwealth during the reign of his second son, Jan Kazimiercz Vasa (1648–68).

When his father Johan III died in 1593, Zygmunt III went to Sweden to claim his inheritance, but he met with sullen hostility from the Swedish aristocracy. Fearing that he might be deposed from his Commonwealth throne *in absentia*, he returned to Poland-Lithuania in 1594, leaving behind Duke Karl of Söddermannland (his Protestant uncle) as regent in Sweden. Zygmunt III made another attempt to establish himself as king in Sweden in 1598, but that equally bruising encounter encouraged the hostile Diet to depose him from the Swedish throne in 1599. This action signalled the start of the open hostilities between an increasingly Protestant Sweden and an increasingly Catholic Commonwealth, which were to drag on intermittently until 1709. The stakes were raised in 1604, when Zygmunt III's uncle (the former regent) was elected King Karl IX of Sweden. The Protestant Vasas succeeded in transforming Sweden into one of Europe's Great Powers and in turning the tables on their Catholic cousins in Poland-Lithuania, both by championing the Protestant cause in East Central Europe and by repeatedly annexing the Baltic's south-eastern shores.

The opening shots in this protracted battle for supremacy in the Baltic region were fired in the 1600s and again in the 1620s, when first Livonia and later Pomerania repeatedly changed hands. These conflicts were inflamed by the religious factor, as the predominantly Protestant merchants and patriciates of several south-eastern Baltic ports gradually switched their allegiance from the Commonwealth to Protestant Sweden. A treaty signed at Stumdorf (Stumska Wies) in 1635 temporarily suspended the Catholic Vasas' claim to the Swedish throne (it was not finally renounced until 1660) and restored the Prussian and Pomeranian ports to the Commonwealth, while confirming Sweden's hold on Livonia, but this was merely the calm before the Swedish storm that was to devastate the Polish-Lithuanian Commonwealth during the late 1650s.

Meanwhile, very different storms were brewing in Muscovy. The extinction of the long-reigning Riurik dynasty in 1598 rapidly plunged Russia into a period of political disintegration, crop failure, pestilence and social unrest known as the Time of Troubles. These tribulations, allied to dark suspicions concerning the means by which Tsar Boris Godunov (reg. 1598–1605) had gained his crown, threw up a number of pretenders to the Muscovite throne. Two of these so-called 'false Dmitris', both of whom claimed to be the reputedly murdered yet 'miraculously saved' younger son of Ivan the Terrible, managed to enlist Polish-Lithuanian and Jesuit support for their claims to the Russian throne. The first of these pretenders entered Moscow and gained the Tsarist crown virtually unopposed in 1605, but the following year he was overthrown and killed during an uprising orchestrated by the prominent Russian magnate Vasily Shuisky, who thereupon had himself elected Tsar (1606–10).

In 1607 another 'false Dmitri' garnered support from sections of the Polish-Lithuanian nobility with designs upon large tracts of Muscovite territory. In 1609 Tsar Shuisky and King Karl IX of Sweden entered a military pact against Poland-Lithuania, whereupon Zygmunt III obtained papal and Jesuit support for a Catholic crusade against Orthodox Russia and Protestant Sweden. When the main Muscovite army was crushed by Polish-Lithuanian forces at Klushino in 1610, the Muscovite nobility deposed Shuisky and transferred their allegiance to Zygmunt's son Wladyslaw, whom they elected Tsar (1610–13). However, Zygmunt III's over-zealous insistence that Muscovy had to become Catholic provoked a rash of Russian anti-Catholic rebellions and the election of a new Russian Orthodox Tsar, Mikhail Romanov (reg. 1613–45), who quickly launched a successful Russian counter-offensive.

Poland-Lithuania thus bungled its best opportunity to dismember its most dangerous foe. Norman Davies has warned that 'The idea that the Republic of Poland-Lithuania, with its modest military resources and creaking finances, could ever have contemplated "occupying" or "subjugating" the vastnesses of Russia is preposterous . . . The Poles were only able to intervene at all because powerful factions among the Muscovite boyars [aristocrats] were pressing them to do so' (Davies 1981a: 455). This may be true, but there is a big difference between 'occupying' or 'subjugating' Russia and fostering its potential for fragmentation. Poland-Lithuania failed to wrest maximum long-term advantage from Muscovy's tribulations, and the Russians managed to tip the scales in their own favour between 1654 and 1668.

In the eyes of contemporaries, however, the years between 1630 and 1648 appeared to herald a new era of peace and prosperity for the Commonwealth. The aggressive proclivities of the Austrian Habsburgs and the Protestant Vasas were otherwise engaged, Muscovy was preoccupied with internal reconstruction, Poland-Lithuania appeared to be under no immediate threat, and Zygmunt III was smoothly succeeded by his son Wladyslaw IV (reg. 1632–48), who was able to mediate between states caught up in the Thirty Years War.

Nevertheless, a colossal crisis was brewing. In 1640 and 1644 Podolia and Volynia were ravaged by marauding Crimean Tatars, who made off with thousands of captives. These raids prompted King Wladyslaw IV to plan a major military campaign against the Crimean Tatars and their Ottoman overlords in alliance with Muscovy and the Dnieper Cossacks, who were promised substantial shares of the spoils. However, the Sejm did not trust Wladyslaw IV and managed to obstruct his preparations in 1647–8, whereupon the already armed and mobilized Dnieper Cossacks made common cause with the Crimean Tatars *against* the Polish-Lithuanian Commonwealth. This Cossack revolt, combined with several disastrously bungled attempts to bring the Cossacks to heel, ignited a massive explosion of peasant unrest in Ukraine. At that time Ukraine was home to large numbers of runaway serfs, religious dissenters and peasants hostile to the southward spread of Polish-Lithuanian landlordism, serfdom and rack-renting Jewish 'middlemen'. The huge Cossack-cum-peasant rebellion of 1648–54 abruptly terminated the Commonwealth's 'golden age' and marked the start of its long and calamitous decline (1648–1795).

CATALYSTS OF DECLINE, 1648–1764

In May 1648 Wladyslaw IV, the only person who could easily have placated the mutinous Cossacks, suddenly died. His younger brother, Jan Kazimiercz, was immediately sworn in as the new king during a hastily arranged ceasefire, but the truce was soon broken by Ukraine's most powerful magnate, Prince Jarema Wisniowiecki, whose attempts to repress the rebel Cossacks misfired. This merely added fuel to the flames of rebellion, with the result that the conflict rumbled on until the Cossack leader Bogdan Khmelnitsky placed his unruly Cossacks under Tsarist 'protection' in 1654.

In addition, Polish Jews became prime targets of murderous pogroms between 1648 and 1656, during which time the Jewish population fell by nearly 100,000, especially in the south and east where Jewish middlemen had increasingly become revenue collectors and debt collectors on behalf of the Polish aristocracy, the crown and even the Catholic Church (Davies 1981a: 467). In response, the Jewish community subsequently retreated into itself. 'The masses of Polish Jewry lived in desperate poverty, in an increasingly hostile environment', which helped the Rabbinate gradually to reassert ' a medieval grip' over the orthodox Jewish community, yet simultaneously encouraged the growth of Hasidism, a mystical and ecstatic Jewish cult which attracted the growing numbers of impoverished Jewish slum-dwellers and social outcasts.

In 1655, taking advantage of the wounds inflicted upon Poland-Lithuania by the Russian-backed rebels in Ukraine, King Karl X of Sweden (reg. 1654–60) suddenly occupied Pomerania and proceeded to lay waste Warsaw, Krakow and many other Polish towns and cities. This orgy of killing and destruction brought relatively minor gains to Sweden, yet it had an intensity approaching that of the Nazi and Soviet devastation of Poland during the Second World War. Karl X 'was only interested in keeping Pomerania and Livonia, and treated the rest of Poland as occupied territory. He and his generals immediately began exporting everything they could lay hands on . . . Protestant Swedes also took to burning down churches, having first emptied them of everything portable' (Zamoyski 1987: 169–70). The malnourished, ravaged and disease-stricken population of Poland-Lithuania was reduced by a quarter between 1648 and 1660, and some towns took more than a century to regain their 1640s' population levels (Bogucka 1982: 140–1).

Incensed by the invaders' indiscriminate slaughter and pillage and by the bigoted burning and desecration of Catholic churches and shrines, the Poles succeeded in rallying their scattered and decimated forces in order to fight off the Swedish vultures. The Catholic defenders of the fortified monastery of Jasna Gora near Czestochowa were allegedly assisted by the miraculous intervention of the Black Madonna, whose portrait graces the abbey church to this day. News of this first defeat of the Swedes at Jasna Gora boosted the morale of the Commonwealth's troops, turned the tide and encouraged King Jan Kazmiercz to return from exile. Ever since then the Black Madonna of Jasna Gora has remained the most prominent focus of Polish patriotism, successive Catholic revivals and the nationwide cult of the Virgin Mary.

Besides Jasna Gora, centres such as Gdansk and Lwow also managed to ward off the Swedish juggernaut, while countries such as the Netherlands and Denmark came to the Commonwealth's assistance (reasoning that their enemy's enemy was their friend). After Khmelnitsky's death in 1657, moreover, the Cossacks vacillated between allegiance to Russia and allegiance to the Commonwealth and increasingly fought among themselves. When childless Jan Kazimiercz abdicated in 1668, grieving the death of his wife, the Commonwealth's Vasa dynasty finally spluttered to an ignominious end.

While the Commonwealth's relative decline had undoubtedly begun by the 1650s, its capacity for regeneration proved to be remarkable. Its resources, if fully mobilized and well directed, were still considerable. Moreover, its territorial vastness and diversity meant that its decline took place sporadically and unevenly over a long time-span, while its 'decentralized traditions of defence, finance and executive power were perpetuated' (Davies 1981a: 58). The military prowess of its cavalry from the early fifteenth to the late seventeenth century was based on the spectacularly high mobility, surprise tactics and weight-effective weaponry made possible by the inter-breeding of Tatar and European horses, the use of light Tatar saddles, and a reliance on the hybrid curved sabre modified from Tatar models by the Magyars and the Poles to give a 'uniquely high ratio of cutting-power to effort expanded' (Zamoyski 1987: 154–6). These weapons, equestrian skills and surprise tactics allowed the Commonwealth to develop an economy of strength which was eventually to prove fatal to its own defences (Majewski 1982: 182–3, 186, 189). 'Victory was repeatedly achieved at low cost and with little apparent effort, and this had a pernicious effect' (Zamoyski 1987: 156). While most of the monarchies in late sixteenth-century Europe were typically spending 60–70 per cent of their revenues on military items, the figure for Poland was nearer 20 per cent (p. 103). The Commonwealth briefly built up a navy between the 1560s and the 1640s, which even inflicted a defeat on the Swedish navy in 1627. However, the *szlachta* (middling and lesser nobility) and the Sejm liked paying for a navy even less than for a large standing army, with the result that after the crisis of the 1650s the navy was allowed to run down and the Commonwealth became dependent on Dutch and English maritime power (p. 156). Yet the Sejm repeatedly voted down proposals for a larger standing army (i) for reasons of cost and (ii) from fear that it could have been used to suppress the 'liberties' of the *szlachta* and establish an absolute monarchy (p. 103). The Commonwealth even failed to develop a regular diplomatic corps and a central chancellery capable of devising and pursuing a coherent foreign policy (p. 175).

One seemingly minor consequence of the Commonwealth's tribulations was eventually to prove the most lethal. In 1656 and 1657 the Hohenzollern ruler of Brandenburg and Prussia deftly played off the Swedes and the Poles against one another so as to obtain full sovereignty over his fiefdoms, which subsequently became the nucleus of a Kingdom of Brandenburg-Prussia and a new incubator of Germanic imperialism.

In 1669, in defiance of Habsburg and Bourbon candidatures for the Polish-Lithuanian throne, the nobility elected the rich but feckless Ukrainian magnate Michal Korybut Wisniowiecki as their new king. He died in 1673 after eating too many gherkins, while parts of his seemingly moribund kingdom were being invaded by the Ottomans. The Commonwealth was spared further ravages and humiliation by the military prowess of the magnate Jan Sobieski, who unexpectedly annihilated the invading Turkish forces and was thereupon elected king by the grateful nobility.

Unfortunately, instead of drastically augmenting the Commonwealth's permanent and professional establishment, its tax base and its arms production, the illustrious warrior-king Jan Sobieski (reg. 1673–96) preferred to rely on the courage, dedication, *esprit de corps*, equestrian skills, mobility, light Oriental sabres and tactical prowess of amateur noble volunteers and cavalrymen like himself. This sufficed in the short term, but in the long run it proved no match for the large professional armies, bureaucracies, tax revenues and armaments industries which were being built up by the Commonwealth's neighbours, who were increasingly outspending and outgunning it. Sobieski 'led by his own private example, dispensing his personal fortune in the service of the state', and he inspired 'the Republic to unparalleled efforts, in short bursts. But he left the outdated machine virtually exhausted . . . At the end of the reign, unpaid soldiery constituted a generalized plague in many provinces' (Davies 1981a: 478).

When the Ottomans besieged Vienna in 1683, the Austrian Habsburgs readily entrusted the defence of their own domain and of Catholic Christendom to Jan Sobieski, who had successfully harried the Turks during the 1670s. However, even though the Polish king covered himself with glory during the relief of Vienna in autumn 1683 and in the subsequent counter-offensive against the Turks, his celebrated victories benefited his own Commonwealth much less than the emergent Austrian Habsburg Empire. Furthermore, the resultant diversion of Polish-Lithuanian military resources towards the Danubian basin left the Commonwealth incapable of forestalling the final abandonment of all Ukraine to Russia in 1686.

The war-weary, bankrupt and increasingly anarchic Commonwealth was largely at the mercy of its more powerful neighbours during the royal election of 1697, in which Sobieski's son Jacub (favoured by the Habsburgs) lost out to Friedrich-August of Saxony (alias August II, 1697–1733), who was backed by Tsar Peter the Great. In principle, the Catholic Saxon king had good reason to share the Commonwealth's fear of the waxing power of the Swedish Vasas and the Hohenzollerns, and this personal union between Saxony and the noble *Rzeczpospolita* therefore made sense as a new defensive alliance against the new Protestant powers. Yet in reality this vainglorious and over-sexed Saxon monarch (who fathered some three hundred children) merely precipitated a protracted and hugely destructive military contest between Sweden and Russia, much of which was fought on Polish-Lithuanian territory.

August II rashly started the Great Northern War (1700–21) by attacking Swedish Livonia (including Riga) in the vain hope of bolstering his lack-lustre status in the eyes of his new Polish-Lithuanian subjects and of the other European powers. This act of folly provoked a devastating Swedish occupation of various parts of Poland-Lithuania from 1702 to 1709 and of Saxony from 1706 to 1709. Indeed, the Swedes were invited into Lithuania by a dissident Lithuanian magnate in 1702. This prompted other sections of the Lithuanian nobility to appeal for Russian military intervention *against* the Swedes. August II only regained his Saxon and Polish-Lithuanian thrones courtesy of the defeat of Karl XII of Sweden by Peter the Great in 1709 at the momentous Battle of Poltava, which finally extinguished Swedish power on the south-eastern shores of the Baltic Sea. Meanwhile, the Commonwealth's territories had changed hands several times, as a result of which its population contracted by a quarter (Leslie 1971: 6), and in 1701 the Hohenzollern Elector of Brandenbug and Duke of Prussia seized the opportunity to unite his separate domains and proclaim himself 'King Friederich I of Prussia'.

After his historic victory at Poltava in 1709, Peter the Great could easily have annexed large swathes of Polish-Lithuanian territory to Russia. However, he opted for indirect control of the Commonwealth through King August II, who owed his own restoration wholly to Russian military intervention. Peter presumably regarded the Commonwealth as too severely ravaged by seven years of fighting to be worth annexing.

In 1715, still smarting at the armed reimposition of unpopular and discredited Saxon rule, a so-called 'confederation' of Polish-Lithuanian nobles and magnates vowed 'to expel the Saxons lock, stock and barrel', but their plans were thwarted by renewed Russian military intervention and arbitration between 1715 and 1717 (Davies 1981a: 499–500). In 1716 Russian officials persuaded August II permanently to withdraw his Saxon troops from the Commonwealth in return for the Polish-Lithuanian nobility's 'silent consent' to statutory limitations on the size of the Commonwealth's armed forces (roughly 20,000 combatants) and tax revenues (pp. 500–2). This humiliating agreement was underwritten by Russia, which also undertook to guarantee the much-devalued 'liberties' of the Polish-Lithuanian nobility and of Orthodox Christians. However, 'The "Golden Freedom" which most of the noble citizens were taught to regard as the glory of their Republic had lost its meaning in a land where nine-tenths of the population lived in poverty and servitude' (p. 513). These new arrangements were rubber-stamped by a special one-day 'silent' session of the Sejm, which met surrounded by Russian troops on 30 January 1717. Thus began the centuries of Russian domination of Poland, from 1709 to 1989, with brief interruptions from 1806 to 1814 and from 1915 to 1945, employing an array of techniques anticipating those employed by the Soviet Union from 1945 to the 1980s. Indeed, the Commonwealth had lost something even more fundamental than territory: its self-respect. 'The Polish political classes, appalled by the realization of their subjugation, flitted easily from abject indifference to desperate rebellion, defending their remaining privileges with a truculence that always seemed to invite the impending disaster' (Davies 1981a: 500–1).

The emasculation of the central authorities and the Sejm left the Commonwealth to an even greater extent than before under the devolved control of the magnates, while the official armed forces were severely underfunded and were increasingly left to fend for themselves as best they could by means of billeting, pilfering and extortion rackets. These conditions encouraged an uncontrolled proliferation of private (baronial) armies which increasingly took the law into their own hands (Davies 1981a: 502–4). Indeed, by 1763 the Commonwealth's official armed forces were outnumbered 11:1 by those of Prussia, 17:1 by those of Austria and 28:1 by those of Russia (p. 504). It suited these states increasingly to use the Commonwealth 'as a battleground on which to settle their differences inexpensively', and 'whenever the Poles took steps to put their house in order both Russia and Prussia took counter-steps to see that nothing changed' (p. 513).

When August II died in 1733, the Polish-Lithuanian nobility elected the native nobleman Stanislaw Lesczynski as their new king, with French backing and against Russia's wishes. However, Russia insisted on a second (rigged) election which installed its preferred Saxon candidate, August III (son of August II), who had promised to cede Livonia to Russia once elected. The city of Gdansk, which raised an army in support of Lesczynski, was occupied by Russian forces in 1734. August III spent only two years in Poland-Lithuania during his thirty-year 'reign' (1734–64), and only one Sejm passed any legislation. 'The country seemed to run itself solely on the momentum of its own inertia' (Zamoyski 1987: 212).

Nevertheless, the Commonwealth's decline was not solely precipitated by political and military miscalculations and misfortunes. The excessive size and privileges of the nobility, the excessive concentration of power and wealth in the hands of the magnates, the renewed spread and intensification of serfdom, and the decline of the Vistula grain trade, the urban sector and Polish Protestantism also played important roles, albeit with effects that were not so very dissimilar from those experienced in Hungary, Bohemia and Austria. Furthermore, since magnates with private armies increasingly controlled the lesser nobility and the provincial law courts and were not held in check by the enfeebled central authorities, the plight of the peasantry deteriorated still further (Zamoyski 1987: pp. 212–14).

The excessive size, privileges and stratification of the nobility

The nobility comprised 6.6 per cent of the Commonwealth's population in 1569, rising to about 9 per cent by 1700 (Davies 1981a: 215). By 1569 the nobility owned approximately 60 per cent of the Commonwealth's territory, as against 25 per cent in church ownership and 15 per cent still owned by the crown. In practice, however, many crown and ecclesiastical properties were controlled by secular magnates (p. 218). However, while some magnates owned mini-kingdoms, most nobles were materially not much better off than the peasantry. 'In the Republic as a whole, well over half the nobility did not possess land' (pp. 228–9). Nevertheless, to be a member of the *szlachta* was rather 'like being a Roman Citizen'. The *szlachta* constituted the political nation, whereas the rest of the population (the *plebs*) 'did not count politically' (Zamoyski 1987: 92). While the magnates endeavoured to establish a narrow oligarchy, the rest of the nobility (the *szlachta*) fought for their own predominance within the political nation (p. 93). Royal ennoblements did not exceed two thousand between 1569 and 1696, virtually turning the nobility into a closed caste. By 1600 only rich Gdansk patricians could hope to gain admission to the nobility (Davies 1981a: 237; Maczak 1982: 127). The major landmarks are indicated in the chronology (pp. xxxiii–xxxv).

Much significance has been attached to the infamous *liberum veto*, the right of just one dissenting deputy to prevent a legislative, financial or procedural decision of the Sejm from taking effect. It reflected the very high premium on achieving unanimity or consensus in a society where the political executive could govern only with the overwhelming assent of the political nation. 'Laws and decisions which were passed in the face of opposition could not have been properly enforced' (Davies 1981a: 339). The first occasion on which the time-honoured principle of unanimity was mischievously invoked as a technicality in order to paralyse the conduct of the Sejm's legitimate business was on 9 March 1652, during the crisis in Ukraine (Zamoyski 1987: 183). However, the damaging effects of the *liberum veto* have been somewhat exaggerated. Its misuse was more a symptom than a cause of the Commonwealth's political problems. After 1652, it was not misused again until 1666 and 1668. It was only under August II (reg. 1697–1733) and August III (reg. 1734–63) that it was systematically abused in order to paralyse the passage of legislation and the conduct of state business, mainly by Sejm deputies acting in the pay and on the instructions of mischievous magnates and/or predatory powers, especially Russia. 'By posing as champions of the "Golden Freedom" . . . they could ensure that the Republic remained incapable of organizing itself or offering resistance' (Davies 1981a: 347). The final attempt to (mis)use the *liberum veto* 'was registered in 1763 by a deputy in Russian pay, who was laughed out of the Sejm. The power of veto had existed for well over a hundred years before it was used, and it continued to exist for thirty [years] after it was last invoked' (Zamoyski 1987: 207).

More persistently damaging was *the right of 'confederation'*, involving an association of nobles sworn to pursue a particular cause or grievance until 'justice' was achieved, and expressing the nobility's right to resist unjust laws and/or to withdraw allegiance from a king who violated his coronation oath to respect and uphold the laws of the realm. In principle, confederation was not an act of rebellion but a constitutional process undertaken for the common good and in the name of the law. During the seventeenth and eighteenth centuries, however, it was increasingly invoked for nefarious purposes, often at the instigation of a foreign power (especially Russia). Armed confederations were formed as early as 1302, 1382–4 and 1439, but major ones also emerged in the 1560s, 1573, 1606–8, 1656, 1672, 1704, 1715, 1733, 1767, 1768–72 and 1793 (Davies 1981a: 339). Although they usually claimed to be defending the 'Golden Freedom', their cumulative effects were even more debilitating than France's relatively short-lived *frondes*, to which they bore more than a passing resemblance.

During the first half of the seventeenth century the fiscal revenues accruing to the Polish-Lithuanian state were only about one-tenth of those accruing to the French state, mainly because the nobility, the clergy and Gdansk were largely exempt from taxation, at least until the introduction of a 'relatively insignificant' poll tax in 1662 (Zamoyski 1987: 130). The nobility maintained a political, social and economic hegemony which 'overwhelmed and eliminated all alternative loci of power and shaped the . . . state in its own image to suit its own needs' (Fedorowicz 1982: 5–8). The last noble *leveé en masse* occurred in 1667, yet the less the nobility served in the Republic's armed forces, 'the more they believed in the myth of their chivalric role. The less they participated in government, the more indispensable they believed themselves to be' (Zamoyski 1987: 182, 221). This all-pervasive hegemony inhibited the development of a bourgeois ethos and bourgeois values even in the towns. The ease with which the nobility contrived to promote and protect its perceived sectional interests had an enervating effect. 'At no point in this divinely ordained process of gathering in the good things due to them did the *szlachta* need to make an investment or calculate with market forces: notions of thrift, risk, investment and the value of money were ignored' (Zamoyski 1987: 57). This left the Commonwealth's propertied classes poorly prepared for the psychological shift to a European world increasingly based upon markets, entrepreneurship, innovation and industry (in more senses than one). Paradoxically, the same social groups which brought the Commonwealth to the brink of ruin later initiated energetic programmes of renewal and reform. History rarely adheres to a predictable, pre-ordained script.

The 'second serfdom' and the rise and decline of Vistula–Baltic grain trade

The expansion of the corporate privileges of the nobility coincided with the rise of the Vistula/ Baltic grain trade and the renewed spread and intensification of serfdom, although the directions and relative magnitudes of the causal connections have long been subject to heated debate. There is, however, little doubt that serfdom as such pre-dated the meteoric rise of the Vistula/Baltic grain trade during the fifteenth and sixteenth centuries. It therefore seems likely that the latter merely accelerated (rather than caused) the spread and intensification of serfdom in early modern Poland-Lithuania. Indeed, substantial increases in the external demand for and prices of grain exerted increased pressure 'on the one element in the rural economy, labour, which was capable of more intensive exploitation. In order to meet the demand, noble landowners exacted more work and harsher conditions from their peasants' (Davies 1981a: 280). However, since the renewed spread and intensification of serfdom was not confined to regions which actively participated in the booming Baltic grain trade, this cannot have been the only major influence. Many commercial backwaters also succumbed to the so-called 'second serfdom'. Changes in seigneurial and governmental mentalities and ideologies also contributed. Nor can these retrograde social and economic trends be simply attributed to the growing power of the nobility and the increasing weakness of the central state in Poland-Lithuania, for serfdom was also being intensified and extended in early modern Russia, where the central state became even stronger than the nobility, other than during acute crises such as the 'Time of Troubles' (1598–1613) and the 'Khovanschina' (1682–9). Many Marxists have argued that this is 'a distinction without a difference', in the sense that central and eastern European despotisms were just as expressive of and subservient to the class interests of the landed nobility as was the Polish-Lithuanian 'nobles' republic'. In our view, however, the interests, ambitions and responsibilities of the state represented a different mix of social, economic and political considerations which often overrode and/or conflicted with those of the landed nobility, even when the latter remained the most influential class; and it is therefore misguided and misleading to treat them as synonymous. Thus while the relatively decentralized and market-driven spread and intensification of serfdom in Poland-Lithuania appears to have gone hand-in-hand with the growth of local seigneurial power and autonomy and the gradual emasculation of the state, the strengthening and extension of serfdom in neighbouring Russia was undertaken at least partly in order to bind every social group (not just the serfs) to the service and overall control of an all-powerful Tsarist state. There were additional variations in the political and economic causes and consequences of the 'second serfdom' in Hungary, Austria, Bohemia, Brandenburg-Prussia, Croatia and Romania, further emphasizing that there was no regular systematic correlation between state weakness, seigneurial power and the spread and/or intensification of serfdom during the early modern era.

The faltering of Polish-Lithuanian grain exports from the 1620s onwards, combined with the dire consequences of the Swedish invasions (1655–60 and 1702–9) and anti-Turkish wars (1672–6 and 1683–91), introduced further complications. 'Faced with ruin, landowners looked not for long-range solutions but for drastic measures to deal with their pressing obligations . . . Losing his surplus production, the peasant also lost his chance for economic independence . . . He now limited himself to subsistence farming and fell ever more into dependence on the manor' (Kaminski 1975: 262). The 'second serfdom' was therefore fostered 'both by the rise of the Vistula trade and also, paradoxically, by its decline . . . Having toiled . . . to build the prosperity of the Republic's Golden Age, the serfs were now to be driven even harder to mitigate the effects of its misfortunes' (Davies 1981a: 285, 290). This prompts Davies to remark: 'How much more fortunate was England, whose sheep nibbled their way through Feudalism at an early date'! (p. 296).

However, in spite of increased restrictions on peasant mobility, the transfer of legal jurisdiction over the peasantry from the central state to the local landed nobility and the resultant inability of the peasantry to obtain legal protection and redress against oppressive landlords through the law courts, research thus far indicates that the Commonwealth's peasants 'never lost their legal entity. A peasant could appear in court as plaintiff and defendant, he had full rights of ownership of moveable property, and in some cases he could buy, sell and bequeath land' (Kaminski 1975: 267). In these respects, if not others, their status remained somewhat higher than that of Russia's serfs. However, the smaller landlords' attempts to save themselves at the peasants' expense 'could not work for long', with the result that their estates diminished in size and number, while landholdings became increasingly concentrated in the hands of the magnates (p. 263).

The Vistula/Baltic grain trade never fully recovered from the devastation inflicted on the Commonwealth between 1648 and 1666 by Cossack rebels in the south and by foreign invasions from the north and east. In 1655 alone, for example, Gdansk lost about one-fifth of its inhabitants through the effects of plague and siege (Davies 1981a: 288). The Commonwealth's foreign trade was further disrupted by the anti-Turkish wars of 1672–6 and 1683–91 and, altogether more seriously, by the renewed Swedish onslaughts of 1702–9. 'The decline of the Vistula trade after 1648 coincided with the decline of the power and prosperity of the Republic as a whole' (p. 287). Furthermore, external trade remained 'predominantly in foreign hands, which meant that a large part of the profit was made outside the country', and the great reduction in grain exports was not offset by any significant increase in manufactured exports, which were limited to 'a few low-quality finished products such as beer, rope and cloth' (Zamoyski 1987: 175).

The Vistula grain trade had already started to decline before 1648. It seems to have peaked in 1618–19. After that the economic life of the whole of East Central and northern Europe was disturbed by the Thirty Years War (1618–48), even though the Commonwealth contrived to keep out of it. By the 1640s Dutch merchants operating from Gdansk were experiencing difficulties in filling their ships with adequate supplies of Polish grain. Furthermore, once the established trading relationships had been ruptured by the catastrophes of the 1650s and the 1700s, they proved difficult to restore. The confidence of foreign merchants and Polish producers was badly shaken and, after western European customers had been forced to seek out suppliers elsewhere, it was hard to win them back again after hostilities abated (Davies 1981a: 288–9). In addition, it is often argued that the productivity of Poland's landed estates had hit a ceiling by 1600, after which the landlords' main recourse was to work their peasants ever harder, in vain attempts to offset falling productivity with ever-increasing inputs of forced labour (p. 285). The Polish-Lithuanian Commonwealth lacked the fiscal resources and concerted political resolve needed to overcome these limitations through state initiatives to reclaim heathlands, upgrade agricultural techniques, improve the available waterways and modernize the Baltic ports, in the manner adopted by neighbouring Prussia (p. 290).

At this same time advances in agricultural and drainage techniques were raising agricultural productivity in north-western Europe, while new sources of low-cost grain were being opened up in southern Europe, Russia and Brandenburg-Prussia, causing a further long-term erosion of the Commonwealth's comparative advantage in grain production and a deterioration in its terms of trade. In particular, the Polish-Lithuanian Baltic ports and hinterland faced mounting competition from Riga, Königsberg, Stettin, Lübek, Rostok and, in the eighteenth century, St Petersburg. By then the limitations of the Vistula as a natural waterway were also becoming apparent. Since dykes were never built along its flood-prone middle reaches, it was unsuited to the more modern forms of river traffic that were beginning to develop elsewhere in Europe (Davies 1981a: 291). The *coup de grâce* was to be the loss of Gdansk to the Kingdom of Prussia in 1772.

Urban decline

As a result of the catastrophes of 1655–60 and 1702–9, the Commonwealth's urban population fell by 60–70 per cent, to little more than 10 per cent of the total, and it was still below 20 per cent of the total in *c*.1750 (Bogucka 1982: 140). The privileges which successive Polish-Lithuanian kings had granted to the nobility had never been fully extended either to the Jewish or to the non-Jewish townspeople (burghers). The mainly German or Jewish leaders of the urban communities had rarely sought direct representation in the Sejm, preferring instead to deal with the king or to ask the local *woewoda* (palatine) to act on their behalf (Zamoyski 1987: 102). The potential emergence of Polish-Lithuanian towns was also impeded by their failure to foster either common institutions or regular

communication and alliances among themselves (Fedorowicz 1982: 115). This reduced their efficacy as counter weights to noble power. In 1565, moreover, the noble-dominated Sejm passed a law
prohibiting native burghers from travelling abroad to engage in trade, with the result that the latter
fell increasingly under the control of foreign merchants and financiers and the agents of the landed
nobility, to the great detriment of the towns and of the economy as a whole (Malowist 1959: 186–
7). The landed nobility also contributed to the decline of the towns by 'intensifying the export of
foodstuffs and primary products and favouring the import of manufactures . . . which was harmful
to the industrial production of the country' (p. 188). Thus the decline of the Commonwealth's urban
sector cannot be blamed entirely on the barbarities of Swedish invaders. It was partly
self-inflicted.

The Catholic Counter-Reformation

Starting in the later sixteenth century, the Catholic Counter-Reformation contributed to the Commonwealth's decline by reducing its cultural pluralism and vigour, its tolerance of diversity, its
receptiveness to foreign (especially Western) influences and ideas, and the importance given to elementary schooling and humanist learning and enquiry. Whatever its religious merits, it resulted in
cultural and intellectual impoverishment and a narrowing of mental horizons.

During the sixteenth century the Catholic Church retained control of its great wealth and extensive ecclesiastical infrastructure, despite the widespread 'defections' of the nobility and townspeople to Protestantism. It therefore retained the wherewithal to mount a potent counter-offensive
against the Reformers. The Jesuits, the shock troops of the Catholic Counter-Reformation, were
introduced into the Commonwealth in 1564–5 on the initiative of Cardinal Stanislaw Hosius. Piotr
Skarga (1536–1612), who rose to become the confessor and personal adviser of the militantly Catholic King Zygmunt III Vasa (reg. 1587–1632), argued that Poland-Lithuania would have to be
'reconquered for Rome, not by force . . . but by virtuous example, teaching, discussion . . . and per-
suasion' (Zamoyski 1987: 89–90). Skarga and other Jesuits 'ranged themselves behind the Crown,
particularly after the accession of their ally Zygmunt III' (p. 147).

By 1642 forty-seven Jesuit colleges had been established in the Commonwealth (Davies 1981a:
168). The Jesuit College in Vilnius was raised to university status in 1589. Jesuit schools and colleges churned out thousands of young nobles imbued with 'a ready-made set of religious, social and
political principles' opposed to the humanism of the fifteenth and early sixteenth century, which
had 'created such fertile ground for Protestantism' (Zamoyski 1987: 147). They fostered the notions
that 'to be Polish was to be Catholic' and that the various forms of Protestantism, Orthodoxy,
Armenian Christianity and Judaism were essentially 'foreign', even though Catholicism too had
originated as a 'foreign' import. 'Poles who were Protestant began to be viewed as eccentric, even
suspicious' (p. 149). Jesuit education largely 'confined itself to inculcating into its pupils a religious, social and political catechism and teaching them enough Latin and Rhetoric to enable them
to drone on for hours at political meetings' (Zamoyski 1987: 181). The ensuing retreat from genuine
outward-looking, universalist Latin humanism compounded the Commonwealth's growing cultural
and intellectual isolation. 'Xenophobia, bigotry and sheer ignorance combined to create an attitude
which extolled anarchy and substituted drink for thought' (p. 221). Poland-Lithuania came to be
seen as a bulwark of Catholic Christendom against the Turkish, Tatar and Russian hordes. The
Commonwealth's energies and resources were increasingly used up in struggles against these foes,
to the ultimate benefit of its regional rivals.

Nevertheless, the influence of the Jesuit Order should not be overstated. Up to the time of its dissolution in 1773, the Jesuits never controlled more than 70 of the Republic's 1,200 religious houses.
Their influence should be seen as running in parallel with the expansion of other (less Machiavellian)
contemplative, teaching and mendicant orders (Davies 1981a: 168). The number of (largely para-

sitic) monasteries rocketed from 220 in 1572 to 565 in 1648, while the foundation of Benedictine and Carmelite monasteries marked the beginning of a mystical tradition in Polish religious life (Zamoyski 1987: 145). Whether this was more 'cause' than 'effect' is open to question, but the gentle cult of the Virgin Mary became especially strong in Poland-Lithuania, where more than a thousand Marian shrines were flourishing by the seventeenth century, each with its own 'miraculous' icon of the Mother of God (Davies 1981a: 171).

As a result of Protestant male chauvinist neglect of the spiritual needs and aspirations of women, the wives of the Protestant nobility often remained open or covert adherents of the Catholic faith and continued to raise their offspring as Catholics (Zamoyski 1987: 90). This contributed to a decline of about two-thirds in the number of Protestant chapels between 1569 and 1600 and, as Calvinism became less fashionable, the Protestants lost their majority in the Senate. The waning of Polish Protestantism was also closely related to the pervasive 'change in the intellectual climate' across most of Catholic Europe, as the rationalism and pragmatic humanism of the early sixteenth century gave way to an 'agonizing search for absolutes' (p. 145).

The Reformation was further weakened by humanist intellectuals turning away from Protestantism, 'disillusioned by the intolerance of its leaders, its confessional fragmentation, and its increasingly arid intellectual debates reminiscent of the controversies of Scholasticism' (Tazbir 1994: 178). The Commonwealth's Protestants also failed to make many converts among the peasants. The Reformation had an inbuilt 'urban bias', partly because towns offered 'concentrations of population, nodes of communication and significant locations for intellectuals and important churchmen'. It made relatively little headway among agrarian populations, not just in Poland, but also in France, Italy, Portugal and Spain (Scribner 1994: 221–2). Religious reform nevertheless managed to overcome such barriers both in rural Bohemia, where it became 'closely associated with national identity, regardless of urban or rural context', and in rural Hungary, where its leading advocates immersed themselves in village and small-town life and were thus able 'to address the needs of Hungarian popular culture' (p. 223). In Poland-Lithuania, however, Lutheranism remained too closely identified with the sectional interests of German burghers, while Calvinism was too tied up with the concerns and aspirations of particular sections of the nobility. In north-western Europe the dynamics of the Renaissance and the Reformation were in some respects related to the rise of urban civilization and the drive to establish urban hegemony over the countryside (pp. 219–21), often in alliance with Renaissance and/or Protestant rulers (p. 2). Thus the lesser number and size of East Central European towns and their actual contraction during the late sixteenth and much of the seventeenth century, combined with the frequent alliance of East Central European rulers with members of the nobility (even though many of these were then Protestant) rather than with the towns, contributed to the eventual defeat of the East Central European Renaissance(s) and Reformation(s).

The contraction of Protestantism among the Commonwealth's nobles was accelerated by the great favour which the long-reigning Zygmunt III consistently showed towards Catholics in the exercise of his still considerable royal patronage (Zamoyski 1987: 145). The number of non-Catholics in the Senate plummeted from forty-one in 1587 to five by 1632 (Tazbir 1982: 204). The Protestant communities also contracted sharply as a result of the devastating Swedish Protestant invasions of the Commonwealth during the 1650s and the 1700s. The Swedes urged the Commonwealth's Protestants to transfer their allegiance to Sweden and quite a few did so. This elicited savage retribution from the Catholic side, obliging many Polish and Lithuanian Protestants to return to Catholicism 'as proof of their patriotism' (Davies 1981a: 198).

In 1638, after two Protestant students had desecrated a Catholic roadside shrine, the Sejm ordered the closure of the prestigious Unitarian Academy at Rakow, along with its printing press (Tazbir 1994: 175). The other illustrious Unitarian Academy at Leszno, whose rector from 1628 to 1656 was the famous Czech philosopher and pedagogue Jan Amos Komensky (alias Comenius), was sacked and burnt by Polish troops at the start of the Swedish invasion of 1655–60 because it refused to hand over its Swedish garrison (Davies 1981a: 189). In 1658 the Unitarians were even banished from the Commonwealth for refusing to take up arms to defend their country in a time of great peril (Zamoyski 1987: 144). The pacifist Quakers were similarly forced to emigrate from the Gdansk region in 1660. In 1668, moreover, the Sejm ordained that no Catholic could apostatize to another faith (on pain of exile), while in 1673 non-Catholics were debarred from entry into the ranks of the nobility, and in 1733 the Sejm barred non-Catholics from holding public office or serving in the Sejm (pp. 145, 221). Thus during the late seventeenth and early eighteenth century the Counter-Reformation did heavily curtail the hitherto fruitful participation of Protestants (especially nobles) in the political and cultural life of the Commonwealth, but 'it paid dearly for this success', since the resultant diminution of the Commonweath's political pluralism and cultural diversity 'brought about intellectual stagnation in the camp of the victors' (Tazbir 1982: 216–17).

Nevertheless, non-Catholics were rarely sentenced to death for their religious beliefs in Poland-Lithuania. They were more commonly sent into exile or given token fines. Moreover, the reductions of the political rights of non-Catholic nobles in the late seventeenth and early eighteenth century were reversed in 1768 and 1773, long before equivalent concessions were granted to Catholics in Protestant Britain (1829) or Sweden (1849) (Tazbir 1994: 179). Polish Catholicism continued to be characterized not so much by 'external militancy' as by 'extreme inward piety' (Davies 1981a: 170). Significantly, the anti-Islamic Crusades had never attracted many Polish participants, because the Islamic threat was 'too close and too well known to hold much glamour', whereas medieval Poland had repeatedly been threatened by Teutonic Crusaders who spent more time fighting fellow Catholics than 'converting the heathen' (p. 165). Polish Catholicism developed a martyr complex, seeing Poland as 'the Christ among nations', rather than an aggressive crusading spirit. Furthermore, in the absence of a powerful monarchy or central state on whose support it could call, in Poland-Lithuania the Catholic Church was unable to employ the more draconian methods of conversion and reconversion which proved effective in Spain, Italy and Bohemia (p. 170).

CRUEL TWISTS OF FATE: HOW THE COMMONWEALTH'S BELATED RECOVERY MERELY HASTENED ITS DEATH

In 1771, on the eve of the first Partition (1772), the Commonwealth was still one of the largest states in Europe. With 730,000 square kilometres of territory, it was larger than either France or Spain (albeit smaller than the Tsarist and Habsburg empires) and it had a population of about 11 million, exceeded only by that of France, Russia and the Habsburg empire (Wandycz 1974: 3). Moreover, for fifty-five years (1735–90) the Commonwealth managed to keep out of protracted European wars. Its magnates even began to promote some rudimentary industrial development, despite (or, more probably, because of) the stagnation of its staple grain and timber exports and, after the first Partition in 1772, the loss of unrestricted access to the Baltic via the lower Vistula and Gdansk. The new industries mainly consisted of labour-intensive 'low-tech' manorial enterprises located on landed estates which used servile labour to produce items such as cloth, clothing, footwear, furnishings, vodka, glassware, pottery, porcelain, ironware, utensils, swords, carriages and even rifles for 'captive' or sheltered internal markets. There were also significant peasant handicraft industries located in 'industrial villages', while the central authorities built some larger-scale textile and armaments manufactories in and around Warsaw, whose population rocketed from 30,000 in 1760 to 150,000 by 1792. In addition, the wealthy bishopric of Krakow established what was eventually to become Poland's heavy industrial heartland (Zamoyski 1987: 238–9). Ironically, the Commonwealth's non-participation in major European wars and the irksome limitations on the size of its armed forces fortuitously freed up resources for other purposes and contributed to a significant economic and demographic recovery. Between 1750 and 1790 the Commonwealth's population expanded on average by about 1.2 per cent per annum, faster than that of either France or even

England (Grochulska 1982: 247). Yet, in spite of these promising economic and demographic up-turns, the social structure of the eighteenth-century Commonwealth was not altered fundamentally. In 1770, on the eve of the first Partition, the nobility comprised 8–10 per cent of the population, Jews (mostly urban) about 10 per cent and non-Jewish burghers about 7 per cent. Most people were still peasants, of whom about 64 per cent lived on land controlled by the nobility, around 19 per cent on crown estates and approximately 17 per cent on church land. The nobility controlled about 78 per cent of all land, the crown 13 per cent and the Catholic Church 9 per cent (Wandycz 1974: 5–6).

Following the death of August III in 1764, the Commonwealth's Russian overlords rigged the royal election in favour of Stanislaw Poniatowski, a former lover of Russia's Empress Catherine the Great (1762–96). Once crowned as King Stanislaw-August (reg. 1764–95), however, the new Polish ruler refused to play a meek and compliant role. He had an intelligent and educated mind of his own, which was no doubt partly what had attracted the German Grand Duchess Catherine to him in the first place, before she became Russia's Tsarina in 1761 (initially as the wife of Tsar Peter III, who was murdered, allegedly with her connivance, in 1762). Even the 'confederated' Sejm which elected Stanislaw-August enacted several 'progressive' reforms, including provisions for majority voting in the provincial *sejmiki*, customs duties and the establishment of new fiscal and military commissions to enhance the Commonwealth's tax-collecting and defence capabilities. In 1765 he established a new academy, while in 1766 Chancellor Andrzej Zamoyski proposed constitutional reforms involving abolition of the *liberum veto*. Alarmed by the Commonwealth's attempts to reform itself, Russia and Prussia jointly threatened to invade it if the reforms were not repealed and the 'confederated' Sejm not dissolved forthwith. They also decided to stir up trouble for the Commonwealth by jointly demanding that Eastern Orthodox and Lutheran Christians should have the same rights to hold office as Catholics, even though neither Russia nor Prussia accorded similar rights to its own religious minorities! Russian troops then moved in to support two rebel 'confederations': a Lutheran one at Torun (Thorn) and an Eastern Orthodox one at Luck. In October 1767 the offending Sejm was hastily reconvened and, surrounded by Tsarist troops, forced to accede to Russia's demands. These included reaffirmations of the *liberum veto*, the right of 'confederation', elective monarchy, the noble monopoly of landownership and public office, and 'the landowner's power of life and death over his peasants' (Zamoyski 1987: 225–6).

During the late 1760s, in any case, the Polish-Lithuanian political classes were becoming polarized into mutually antagonistic armed camps and the new ('upstart') king seemed powerless to prevent this. The 'scandalous' means by which he had attained the throne, along with his generally conciliatory and accommodating stance (including his acquiescence in the Sejm's weak-kneed capitulation to Russian pressure), provoked hot-headed demands for his dethronement and exile. In February 1768, at the town of Bar in Podolia, a confederation of Polish and Lithuanian magnates and their noble 'hangers on' began a 'war of independence' which Russia's famous general Alexander Suvorov took nearly four years to defeat, even after the 'confederates' were attacked in the rear in 1768 by insurgent Orthodox Christian peasants and Cossacks, who between them murdered some 200,000 Polish Catholics and Jews before they themselves were 'suppressed with matching severity' (Davies 1981a: 519). Indeed, by the early 1770s the Commonwealth as a whole was a boiling cauldron of social, political and religious unrest. However, the Russo-Turkish War of 1768–74 tied up many of the Tsarist troops who might otherwise have been used to 'pacify' this unruly Republic. Empress Catherine therefore became increasingly receptive to Prussian proposals for a Partition of Poland-Lithuania between Russia, Prussia and Austria.

However, it was the Habsburgs who set the dastardly ball rolling by unilaterally annexing Spisz in 1769 and Nowy Torg in 1770. The first trilateral Partition of Poland-Lithuania was then agreed in 1771 and implemented in 1772 (amid protests from more liberal-minded countries such as Britain, the Netherlands and Denmark). The Commonwealth was deprived of 35 per cent of its population and 29 per cent of its former territory. Russia not only consolidated its grip on Livonia and Courland, but also annexed the (ethnically Belarussian) provinces of Polotsk, Witebsk, Mscislaw and Homel, amounting to 12.68 per cent of the Commonwealth's former territory and 1.3 million of its erstwhile inhabitants. Austria annexed several southern provinces, totalling some 11.17 per cent of the Commonwealth's former territory and 2.1 million of its erstwhile inhabitants. Prussia 'modestly' helped itself to a small but invaluable section of Baltic coast, amounting to 'only' 4.94 per cent of the Commonwealth's former territory and 'a mere 580,000' of its erstwhile inhabitants (Davies 1981a: 521–2). However, this not only joined up the hitherto discontiguous territories of the Kingdom of Brandenburg-Prussia, but also gave it a stranglehold on the Commonwealth's main artery: its riverine access to Gdansk and the Baltic Sea. Indeed, Prussia was quick to impose 'draconian duties' and tolls on Polish grain shipped down the Vistula for export to other parts of Europe (Zamoyski 1987: 229).

Norman Davies has emphasized that the 'special sense of outrage which attended the fate of the Polish Republic was partly due to the fact that European princes had eaten a fellow European. But it was also due to the particular moment. Poland was partitioned on the eve of the birth of Nationalism and Liberalism, and thus became a symbol of all those people for whom self-determination and the consent of the governed provide the guiding principles of political life' (Davies 1981a: 525). It is therefore scarcely surprising that the Commonwealth's fate eventually became a *cause célèbre* among liberal-minded Europeans. Nevertheless, one must guard against falling into the traps of special pleading, double standards and the temptation to idealize and romanticize the so-called 'political nation' of the Polish-Lithuanian Commonwealth. The moral issues were not quite as clear cut as some of its champions would have us believe. After all, the vast majority of its inhabitants, especially the non-Polish and non-Lithuanian peasantries, had been denied any form of self-determination and had been governed without consent, even before the Partitions. They had lived under the oppressive dominance of Polish and Lithuanian nobles ('the political nation'), many of whom were dyed-in-the-wool serfowners, and it is very doubtful whether the Commonwealth could have survived the introduction of genuine 'self-determination' and 'government by consent'. Furthermore, most of the Polish and Lithuanian landed nobility continued to enjoy extensive local powers and prerogatives under their new overlords (especially in so-called 'Galicia', the area which came under Habsburg rule), to considerably greater degrees than was the case for many other subordinated ethnic groups in nineteenth-century Europe. Therefore, the widespread view that the fate of the privileged 'political nation' of the Polish-Lithuanian Commonwealth was *especially* deserving of sympathy and solicitude because it was a 'great' and 'historic' nation (i.e. which had long been ranked among the oppressors rather than the oppressed) is one that we find hard to swallow! We doubt that the Commonwealth's downtrodden peasants shed many tears over the slight diminution in the power and status of their privileged, haughty and often cruel, callous or repressive 'masters', who received a kind of come-uppance and a relatively small taste of their own medicine at the hands of the Partitioning Powers. Neither Polish nor non-Polish peasants showed much inclination to support the subsequent attempts of the Polish and Lithuanian nobilities to recover their former political independence, most notably during the abortive 'nationalistic' noble uprisings of 1830–1 and 1863–4 within the territories that fell under Tsarist rule. Significantly, many Polish and some Western writers on Polish history habitually refer to 'the Partition of Poland' and to the terrible fate of 'the Poles' in such a way as to imply that the fate and the feelings of Lithuania and the Lithuanians were of less account or of a lower order than those of Poland and the Poles, and they often overlook the substantial participation of Lithuanian nobles in the so-called 'Polish uprisings' of 1830–1 and 1863–4. Historically conscious Lithuanians feel slighted by this Polish *hauteur*, which contributed to the subsequent coolness of relations between the Polish and Lithuanian political classes.

Some historians of Poland like to compare the status of the 'political nation' within the Polish-

Lithuanian Commonwealth to that of Roman citizens within the Roman Empire (for example, Zamoyski 1987: 92–3). However, while one can find instructive positive parallels, there were also some darker ones. In both cases many of the human beings living under the same rule were either serfs or slaves with no rights of representation, redress or self-determination, and yet the privileged strata unquestioningly accepted such gross inequalities as part of the 'natural' and/or 'divinely ordained' social order. Moreover, one does not have to be Irish, black or Indonesian to perceive elements of myopia, self-deception or hypocrisy in British and Dutch 'liberal' outrage at the fate of the Polish-Lithuanian Commonwealth at the hands of the Partitioning Powers.

In our view, anyone who is fully committed to self-determination on an equal and liberal footing for all nations and/or is genuinely outraged by the oppression of one nation by another cannot legitimately regard some nations as 'greater' or 'nobler' or more 'elevated' than others. In particular, we see no acceptable grounds for placing either the Poles or the 'political nation' of the former Polish-Lithuanian Commonwealth on a higher 'moral pedestal' than other formerly subjugated peoples of East Central Europe and the Balkans, least of all those who continued to be downtrodden by the Polish nobility. Karl Marx was probably right to argue that the (social) emancipation of Europe was impossible without the (political) liberation of Poland, but he should also have spared some thought for those Europeans whose overriding wish was to be freed from oppression by the Poles!

The political situation in the truncated Commonwealth stabilized surprisingly quickly after the 1772 Partition, at least until the death of Friedrich the Great in 1786. The political classes became increasingly polarized between the so-called 'Russian party' (those who accepted the status quo as a basis for more or less willing collaboration with Russia) and the 'patriotic party' (those who sought to strengthen the Commonwealth in the hope of eventually overturning an ignominious and vexatious status quo). Russia's Tsarina Catherine the Great could count on the active support of (i) some of the leading magnates, whose privileges and prerogatives she had promised to maintain; (ii) many (perhaps most) of the Commonwealth's Orthodox and Lutheran Christians, whose positions she had promised to protect; and (iii) a substantial number of Sejm deputies and Catholic bishops, some of whom were in Russian pay. Large numbers of Poles 'willingly served the interests of the Partitioning Powers. After fifty years of fractional politics and "Russian protection", there was no shortage of citizens who made their careers by working . . . on behalf of foreign paymasters . . . Men who dared to risk their lives and careers by protesting . . . were few and far between . . . In the Sejm of 1773, at the first Partition, only two honest men could be found' (Davies 1981a: 525–7).

However, while it is possible to cite the names of numerous magnatial 'collaborators' and various Sejm deputies, military commanders, high officials and Catholic bishops who owed their wealth and/or positions to such 'collaboration', the Commonwealth was far from being a passive victim. It may have been powerless to fight off its assailants, but this should not be mistaken for either complicity or consent. The 'Russian party' did not include all the leading magnates and Catholic clergy. Nor did the Sejm always meekly comply with Russian demands, except on the (not infrequent) occasions when it had to conduct its business at the point of a Russian bayonet (and even then it sometimes dragged its feet). Many patriotic Poles and Lithuanians were of course stunned or caught off guard by the first Partition, which was a *fait accompli* by the time that they had fully grasped the enormity, the cynicism and the surgical precision of the amputations which had been inflicted on the Commonwealth. Nevertheless, the initial numbness, paralysis and sense of shock gradually gave way to anger and bitter contempt. As in Poland of the 1970s and 1980s, 'patriots' began to satirize their predicament and then discovered or invented social and intellectual 'spaces' within which they sought to exercise and assert an inner spiritual freedom, in defiance of the seemingly all-powerful Russian overlords.

The 'patriotic party', which enjoyed the advantage of occupying the moral high ground, came to rely on the support of (i) a steadily increasing leaven of outspoken 'patriots' in the middle and lower ranks of the nobility; (ii) a nascent, increasingly articulate and politically conscious 'national intelligentsia' recruited mainly but not exclusively from the nobility; and (iii) a cautious, vain and hedonistic yet unusually astute and dedicated king, who fostered a ferment of 'enlightened' political debate and cultural regeneration. A significant number of 'enlightened' magnates, including Ignacy and Stanislaw Potocki, Andrzej Zamoyski, Stanislaw Malochowski, Adam Kazimiercz Czartoryski, Stansilaw Lubomirski, Michal Kazimiercz Oginski and Karol Radiwill, 'devoted their fortunes and their influence to the same cause, while less exalted figures, including many of the clergy, worked assiduously to put plans into action' (Zamoyski 1987: 237, 245–6).

The Commonwealth's incipient political and cultural rebirth was assisted by external factors. The contemporaneous European Enlightenment provided many useful models of political and social criticism and satire and fuelled the ferment of ideas, while the American Revolution supplied further sources of constitutional and military experience and inspiration. Indeed, the Commonwealth's future military hero, Tadeusz Kosciuszko (1746–1817), received royal approbation for his participation in the American War of Independence (in which he achieved the rank of brigadier-general), before he embarked on a radical reorganization of the Polish-Lithuanian armed forces in 1789 – Year One of the French Revolution, which was yet another potent example and inspiration. Just as importantly, Catherine the Great and the Tsarist establishment were deeply distracted by the powerful peasant, Cossack and Volga Tatar rebellion of 1773–5 (about which some standard histories of Poland-Lithuania are curiously silent). This rebellion mobilized an area larger than France under the Cossack leader Yemelyan Pugachëv, who claimed to be Catherine's murdered husband Peter III and proclaimed the abolition of serfdom and Tsarist military service in the areas he controlled. The gargantuan task of suppressing this uprising obliged the Tsarist state to lower its guard and reduce its troop levels in the Commonwealth. This opened an unexpected window of opportunity for Polish-Lithuanian political revival and reform.

In 1773 the same king and Sejm that had 'approved' the first Partition established a Commission for National Education entrusted with reorganizing all schools, universities and colleges (including those run by the churches) into a single country-wide education system. The Commission was headed by a team of enlightened aristocrats, including Ignacy Potocki, Adam Kazimiercz Czartoryski, Andrzej Zamoyski, Joachim Chreptowicz and Bishop Ignacy Massalski. It was endowed with part of the wealth of the Jesuit Order (which was dissolved at the Pope's behest in 1773) and it 'laid down curricula, chose and published textbooks, and supervised standards and teachers', as part of 'a war on obscurantism . . . whose aim was the social and political regeneration of the state, based upon the re-education of society'. In 1778, furthermore, Chancellor Andrzej Zamoyski published a new *Code of Laws* which reasserted royal prerogatives, made state officials accountable to the Sejm, subjected the clergy and church finances to state supervision, and increased the rights of the cities and the peasantry, but in 1789 its ratification by the Sejm was blocked by a 'combination of clerical bigotry and Prussian intrigue' (Zamoyski 1987: 230).

Stanislaw-August had already established a weekly periodical called *The Monitor* (modelled on Addison's *The Spectator*) and a new National Theatre in 1765. However, during the late 1770s and the 1780s there was a veritable explosion of new satirical periodicals and plays. By 1792 one in forty-five inhabitants was a subscriber (and one in twenty a reader) of at least one of the new periodicals. The hundreds of newly written plays were largely imitative of genres established by playwrights such as Molière, Voltaire and Sheridan (Zamoyski 1987: 231). The reformers dressed ostentatiously in French styles, quoted the *philosophes* and preached temperance, in the course of their campaigns against the atavistic dress, narrow 'know-nothing' outlook and alcoholic haze of the Sarmatian nobility.

The king also lavishly patronized painting, music and architecture by commissioning portraits and compositions, establishing five choirs and orchestras, attracting Pasiello and Cimarosa to Warsaw as court composers, and building (among other things) one of Europe's most elegant and refined palaces at Lazienki. Although all this ran up large debts, he 'believed passionately in the educational value of the arts' and argued that he was attempting to bequeath to posterity a significant cultural statement which would serve to inspire future generations and keep alive his vision of an intellectually and spiritually regenerated Commonwealth. In this mission he was undoubtedly successful (Zamoyski 1987: 240–4).

Stanislaw-August, who had come to the throne without either personal wealth or an illustrious lineage, was widely despised as a *parvenu* and as Catherine's ex-lover. He consequently had to rely on his intelligence, patience, tact and charm. As a former deputy in the Sejm, he was familiar with its workings and mentalities. He was also very aware of 'the considerable influence and powers still at the disposal of the Crown' and he exploited them to the full in pursuit of his aims, which were 'not so much a policy as a vision'. Even more importantly, from his reading and travels across Europe he had gained 'an appreciation of the state as an institution, a concept hitherto absent from Polish political thought' (Zamoyski 1987: 236–7). His efforts to mobilize society through and in support of the state had a revolutionary impact on the nobility, who since the 1650s had come to accept (and even idealize) anarchy as a 'normal' condition. The Commonwealth had appeared to be held together by little more than the force of inertia.

The nascent intelligentsia was recruited mainly (but not exclusively) from the various rungs of the nobility. Yet it partly transcended class divisions and came to be united by a common educational background, outlook, mission to enlighten, and ethos of service to society, which it aimed to transform. This was a new Enlightenment version of older conceptions of the nobility as the political nation. It sought to transform the basis of the nobility's claims to lead the country from noble birth and descent to the more meritocratic criteria of educational ethos, training and mission. The ranks of the intelligentsia were rapidly expanded by the reformed schools, colleges and universities of the 1770s and 1780s, which churned out thousands of missionaries of Enlightenment and enemies of obscurantism (Zamoyski 1987: 237). However, the Polish-Lithuanian Enlightenment was primarily the work of some 700–800 people who published works that contributed to the intellectual and cultural ferment of the late eighteenth century (Grochulska 1982: 249).

Friedrich the Great of Prussia, the chief instigator of the first Partition of Poland-Lithuania, died in 1786 and his successor, Friedrich Wilhelm II (reg. 1786–97), was widely thought to be concerned at Russia's excessive aggrandizement and therefore more favourably disposed towards the Commonwealth's attempts to reform and rehabilitate itself. In a parallel bid to gain the goodwill of Catherine the Great, Stanislaw-August inveigled the empress to his royal palace at Karniow in 1787 and offered her his country's military support in the forthcoming Russo-Turkish War (through which she hoped to acquire one or more Black Sea ports for Russia), in return for (i) permission to expand the Commonwealth's armed forces; (ii) Polish-Lithuanian participation in the anticipated commercial and territorial gains in the Black Sea region; and (iii) an implicit rehabilitation of the full sovereignty and international standing of the truncated Commonwealth, by allowing it to participate in a formally equal partnership with Russia. In the event, Catherine rejected these proposals. Confident that the Commonwealth's more avaricious magnates would support Russia's Black Sea exploits *unconditionally* (in the well-founded expectation of private participation and gains), she saw no reason either to accept the king's offer or to condone the Commonwealth's reforms. It suited her to keep Poland-Lithuania in a hobbled and prostrate position and, in a private letter, she even remarked that 'truth to tell, there is no need or benefit for Russia in Poland becoming more active' (quoted by Davies 1981a: 529).

Thereupon, in a vain attempt to curb Tsarist expansionism, Prussia concluded an alliance with Britain and the Netherlands and signalled that the Commonwealth could count on Prussia's approval if it were to deepen its reforms and reassert its sovereignty. With this apparent Prussian 'go-ahead', the Sejm which had been convoked in 1788 dared to embark on a more sweeping reform and rehabilitation programme. It immediately voted for increased defence expenditure and vested control of the army and foreign policy in Commissions of the Sejm. In 1789, encouraged by the unexpected turn of events in France and by Russia's continuing embroilment in its war with the Turks (1787–91), the Sejm even instituted a (then radical) 10 per cent tax on income from noble land and a 20 per cent tax on income from church land. It also appointed a Commission to prepare a new written constitution and decided to prolong its own session for as long as necessary to see this constitutional reform project through to completion (Zamoyski 1987: 246).

The draft constitution was finally unveiled on 3 May 1791. It retained the monarchy (which was expected to become hereditary, even though the king was a bachelor) and the privileged positions of the Catholic Church and the nobility. But it made the king's ministers (redesignated 'guardians of the laws') accountable to the Sejm, it restored freedom of worship and it abolished the *liberum veto* and the right of confederation. Moreover, burghers were to be accorded 'the same rights and privileges' as the nobility, while peasants were promised 'the protection of the law and government of the country', and the standing army was to be expanded to 100,000 men (Davies 1981a: 534). This new constitution was approved by the Sejm immediately and by the *sejmiki* in February 1792.

Russia signed a peace treaty with the Ottomans in January 1792, however, and by May of that year Catherine was moving 96,000 Russian troops into the Commonwealth, ostensibly in response to appeals for 'help' from a confederation convoked by members of the 'Russian party' at Torgowica in order to restore the Commonwealth's former 'Golden Freedom' (especially the *liberum veto*). Prussia, which had been invaded by revolutionary France in April 1792, was not in a position to respond to the Commonwealth's appeals for assistance (even if its ruler had been inclined to do so). By April 1792, moreover, the increasingly alarming course of the French Revolution had succeeded in uniting Europe's reactionary monarchies against the possibility of yet another revolutionary state – in their own 'backyard'. Commanded by Tadeusz Kosciuszko and Josef Poniatowski (the king's nephew), the Commonwealth's armies put up a brave fight, but the odds were overwhelmingly stacked against them. In August 1792, with the aim of averting a greater catastrophe, Stanislaw-August announced his government's capitulation to the Russian-backed Confederation of Torgowica and ordered the Commonwealth's troops to hold their fire. 'It was a shocking betrayal, executed for the most humane of motives. Faced by the Russians' threefold numerical superiority . . . he wanted to save his country unnecessary suffering. The Army dispersed. The commanding officers left hurriedly for exile. Warsaw was occupied without opposition' (Davies 1981a: 536).

In August 1792, on the eve of a Prussian invasion of north-western Poland, Russia and Prussia agreed on a second Partition of the Commonwealth, which was implemented in early 1793. Russia absorbed the remnants of the Grand Duchy of Lithuania (250,000 square kilometres), while Prussia annexed not only Gdansk and Torun but also Wielkopolska and most of Malopolska, Poland's historic 'ethnic heartlands' (580,000 square kilometres). Austria, which kept its hands clean on this occasion, got nothing. After three months of foot-dragging, this second Partition was eventually ratified in October 1793 by a Sejm whose members had been cowed and intimidated by Russian arrests, beatings, imprisonments and threats to sequestrate their property.

From March to November 1794, however, there was a nine-month Polish-Lithuanian insurrection against the Russian and Prussian occupation forces, whose presence (along with the virtual cessation of government) had contributed to an economic collapse and the radicalization of the population. Having returned from exile, Kosciuszko proclaimed an Act of Insurrection in Krakow on 24 March 1794 and assumed dictatorial powers. On 4 April 4,000 Commonwealth troops and 2,000 peasants armed with scythes famously defeated a Russian army at Raclawice, encouraging the citizens of Warsaw and Vilnius (Wilno) to join the insurrection. In May the Supreme Council proclaimed the emancipation of the serfs, confiscated church wealth, introduced an (unprecedented) graduated income tax and commandeered all factories. Desperately short of rifles, the insurrection employed novel combinations of artillery bombardment, cavalry charges and mass attacks by peasant scythemen. By 16 November, however, the insurrection had been brutally crushed by

Russia, Prussia and (belatedly) Austria, who in 1795 carved up the last remnants of the Common-wealth between them. Russia again took the lion's share (120,000 square kilometres), but the 48,000 square kilometres allocated to Prussia included Warsaw, while Austria grabbed 47,000 square kilo-metres around Krakow (Davies 1981a: 522). Overall, as a result of the three Partitions, Russia obtained 61 per cent of the former Commonwealth's territory and 45 per cent of its population (augmenting the Tsarist Empire's territory and population by a mere 3 per cent and 16 per cent, respectively). Prussia obtained 20 per cent of the former Commonwealth's territory and 23 per cent of its population (expanding its own territory and population by a massive 50 per cent and 40 per cent, respectively). The Habsburg Empire acquired 19 per cent of the former Commonwealth's ter-ritory and 32 per cent of its population (expanding the Habsburg domains by 25 per cent and 17 per cent, respectively) (Skowronek 1982: 262–3).

In the final analysis, the insurrection of 1794 could have succeeded only if it had received major help from revolutionary France, but the latter left the Commonwealth to the tender mercies of its absolutist neighbours. 'Europe regarded the fall of the insurrection with indifference and accepted the liquidation of the Polish[-Lithuanian!] state without any greater protest. Ironically, Poland[-Lithuania] was extinguished in the end not because of anarchy but because it had become a force capable of revolutionizing central and eastern Europe' (Gierowski 1982: 237).

15   Revolution and 'reaction': the Habsburg Empire, 1789–1848

The outbreak of the French Revolution in 1789 and the death of Josef II in 1790 led to a substantial retreat from reform under his brother, Leopold II (1790–2), the erstwhile 'enlightened' ruler of Tuscany. As sops to the empire's alarmed and agitated aristocracies, Leopold II immediately rescinded his brother's controversial land taxes and restored Hungary's aristocratic 'liberties' and self-administration (as 'guaranteed' by the Treaty of Szatmar in 1711). In 1791, in a vain attempt to counter balance these concessions to 'Reaction', he introduced a police reform which established a right of habeas corpus and citizens' rights of information, while giving the police public health responsibilities (for example, concerning quarantine regulations). He also increased the representation of peasants and burghers in the provincial Diets or Estates.

The retreat from reform turned into headlong flight during the long and reactionary reign of Emperor Franz II (1792–1835). Amid mounting unrest, his reign began with a purge of reformers from the central imperial administration, a reaffirmation of traditional seigneurial and ecclesiastical privileges, and a substantial reversal of the enlightened reforms of Maria Theresa and Josef II. The whole climate changed.

Revolutionary France declared war on an increasingly reactionary Habsburg Empire in April 1792. The Habsburgs unsuccessfully fought back against revolutionary France and the subsequent Bonapartist regime from April 1792 to October 1797, from March 1799 to July 1800, from September to December 1805 and from April to July 1809. The Habsburg war efforts were severely constrained by the restored fiscal privileges and preferences of the landed nobility, the Catholic Church and the Kingdom of Hungary and by far from 'meritocratic' military and social hierarchies. As a result of successive military defeats, the Habsburgs lost the southern Netherlands (which had already rebelled against Habsburg rule in 1789) and, temporarily, their Italian and South Slav possessions and some of their German and Alpine territories. (Napoleon even occupied Vienna itself in 1805.) In 1804, when Napoleon crowned himself Emperor of the French (with the Pope's blessing), the Habsburgs relaunched or reconstituted their remaining Austrian German, Bohemian, Hungarian and Polish (Galician) dominions as 'the Habsburg Empire' (not wishing to be upstaged by the 'Corsican upstart'). But in 1806, to forestall an Austrian attempt to unite the Germanic world against France, Napoleon obliged the newly established 'Confederation of the Rhine' to force Franz II to abdicate as Holy Roman Emperor and formally end the defunct (Germanic) Holy Roman Empire.

The succession of costly and unsuccessful wars, the ensuing losses of territory and revenues and the consequent soaring budget deficits (financed to a large extent by printing paper money) induced the Habsburgs to declare their state financially bankrupt in 1811. This 'state bankruptcy' shook the confidence of both domestic and foreign investors and reduced the empire's international credit rating in subsequent decades. More generally the recurrent warfare, the disruption of established trade networks and the 'Continental System' (Napoleon's attempted economic blockade of Britain) isolated the Habsburg Empire from the new products and technologies of the British Industrial Revolution and caused serious setbacks to the significant industrial development achieved in German Austria and the Czech Lands in the eighteenth century. A few industries (for instance, cotton textiles and sugar refining) may have benefited temporarily by being sheltered from British competition, but they either collapsed (sugar) or went into severe recession (cotton textiles) when the restoration of peace and freer trade exposed them to a 'cold blast' of foreign competition after 1815.

THE METTERNICH ERA, 1809–48

From 1809 to 1848 the conduct of Habsburg foreign policy fell into the capable but ultra-conservative hands of Count (from 1813 Prince) Clemens Metternich. In 1821 he also became court and state chancellor, with wider responsibility for imperial affairs. Metternich knew (or quickly learned) how to play a very weak hand to maximum advantage. He contrived to keep the brittle Habsburg Empire out of wars it could not win, to let others bear the brunt of its European battles and (when it was clear which way the wind was blowing) to become the chief peace-broker among the victors. He thus made Vienna the hub of European affairs from 1814 to 1848, and he understood that what remained of the Habsburg Empire could preserve the illusion of being a 'Great Power' only if its power was used very sparingly. Metternich regained by diplomacy much of the territory and influence that his immediate predecessors had lost through ham-fisted warfare. Under his guidance, the Habsburg Empire found itself a new European 'mission' and hence a new lease of life as a major bulwark against revolution (whether radical, liberal or national).

In Metternich's eyes the interests of Europe coincided with the interests of the Habsburg Empire. The Monarchy was a 'European necessity'. Therefore, what was good for the Habsburgs had to be good for Europe. From his ultra-conservative standpoint, there could be no difference or conflict between the two. His most remarkable achievement (or good fortune) was that Europe's other Powers became persuaded of this too, at least until the disruptive rise of a unified Germany and a unified Italy upset these stabilizing assumptions from the 1860s onward. The upshot was that Metternich not only guided the foreign policy of the Habsburg Empire, but through it influenced the destiny of Europe. Without Metternich, some have argued, nineteenth-century Europe would have developed along much more liberal lines.

In March 1813, hard on the heels of Napoleon's disastrous invasion of Russia in 1812, Prussia declared war on France. At first 'Austria stood on the sidelines and offered only "armed mediation" between the warring parties' (Kann 1974: 226). However, after a badly shaken Napoleon yielded to Austria's sizeable territorial demands virtually without a fight, Austria joined a 'grand alliance' of Russia, Sweden and Britain and went to war against France in August 1813, despite soaring budget deficits and inflation. Napoleon was decisively defeated at the Battle of Leipzig in October 1813. When he nevertheless rejected Metternich's conciliatory offer of recognition within the 'natural frontiers' of France, the grand coalition went on to depose Napoleon, occupy Paris and restore the French Bourbons in the spring of 1814. Partly as a result of the moderating influence and geographical calculations of Metternich, the peace terms imposed on France by the subsequent Congress of Vienna (September 1814–June 1815) were a model of restraint.

Metternich skilfully headed off Russian and Prussian demands for the imposition of more punitive peace terms on France, because these could have opened the way for the establishment of a Russian-backed Prussian ascendancy in Germany in return for Prussian acceptance of complete Russian control of Poland (to the detriment of Austria on both counts). He entered a secret alliance with the British and the French delegations to resist the Russian and Prussian designs on Poland and Germany, while also accepting the Russian Tsar's proposal of a conservative 'Holy Alliance' of Russia, Prussia and Austria to uphold the political and territorial status quo. This was more in keeping with Metternich's preferred emphasis on 'legitimacy', on full restoration of the 'status quo ante' wherever possible, on territorial 'compensation' where necessary and on maintenance of a European 'balance of power', as the appropriate foundations for a (conservative) 'new European order' .

Through the territorial settlements agreed at the Congress of Vienna in 1815 Metternich seemed to secure a more compact and easily defended Habsburg Empire. In compensation for the permanent loss of the economically valuable but strategically vulnerable southern Netherlands (Belgium), the Habsburgs secured most of northern and central Italy (Lombardy, the Veneto, Trentino, Tuscany, Modena, Piacenza and Parma) and a conservative/Catholic alliance with the papacy and the Papal States. In place of a sham/defunct 'Holy Roman Empire', which had been fragmented into more than three hundred states under the terms of the Treaty of Westphalia (1648), Metternich secured a seemingly more coherent and effective 'German Confederation' of thirty-nine states (including British-ruled Hanover, Danish-ruled Holstein, Dutch-ruled Luxembourg, Bohemia and four city-states), under the authority of a bicameral Bundestag (or confederal Diet) in Frankfurt am Main and a permanent Austrian 'presidency'. Originally established as an instrument of mutual defence against French revanchism and/or Russian imperialism, it soon became an instrument for maintaining the internal status quo, for blocking internal change, for Great Power interference in the internal affairs of the smaller German states and for closer co-operation between political police and censors in a reactionary struggle against the (real or imaginary) internal security threats posed by nascent German nationalism, liberalism and student radicalism, from 1817 to 1848.

In September 1819, under pressure from Metternich following the March assassination of the notable playwright August von Kotzebue by the German nationalist student Karl Sand, the Bundestag of the German Confederation in Frankfurt unanimously approved a draconian set of decrees adopted by a congress of German states in Karlsbad in August 1819. Up to 1848 these notorious 'Karlsbad Decrees' (renewed for an indefinite period in 1824) subjected the 'Germanic world' (including Bohemia) to wide-ranging police powers, elaborate and irksome censorship, a purge and police surveillance of universities, a prohibition of all student societies, networks of police 'spies' and 'informers', and blacklists of suspect individuals, that is, the paraphernalia of a modern *Polizeistaat* (police state). In 1820, moreover, Article 13 of the German Confederation was modified to concentrate all sovereign power in the hands of rulers and to curb both the granting of 'constitutions' and the 'consultative' roles of representative bodies such as provincial diets. In 1832 and 1834, following the revolutions in various parts of Europe in 1830–1, these provisions and the supporting networks of police, censors, spies and informers were strengthened still further, leading to the suppression of several diets and universities.

The Habsburg Empire thus re-emerged as the dominant reactionary Power in East Central Europe as well as in the Italian peninsula. This also strengthened its position in Dalmatia, Croatia, the Adriatic and the eastern Mediterranean. However, appearances were deceptive. In the longer term the imposition of an alien, repressive and ultra-conservative Austrian hegemony in Italy aroused an Italian nationalist backlash which would culminate in successive wars of Italian unification (1848–9, 1859–60 and 1866, with a 'postscript' in 1915–18). The greatly reduced political fragmentation of the 'Germanic world' after 1815 made Austrian dominance far less complete and less secure than it had been in the seventeenth and eighteenth centuries. Medium-sized German states (for example, Bavaria, Saxony and Hanover) could hope to gain greater freedom of manoeuvre for themselves by playing off Prussia against Austria. For its part Prussia used its acquisition of the Rhineland in 1815, its espousal of free trade from 1818 onwards, and the development of the Deutsche Zollverein (German Customs Union) and a more integrated German economy from 1834 onwards to bind the more industrialized German states more closely to itself and to marginalize Austria. Indeed, Prussia could afford to pursue its German interests and ambitions more single-mindedly than Austria and, for geographical reasons, almost any integrated German market and transport system had to involve Prussia and the Rhineland, but could (and increasingly did) bypass Austria. In implicit acknowledgement of Prussia's growing role and status as 'the other Power' in Germany, Austria increasingly relied on Prussia to 'police' and 'protect' the German Confederation. 'In theory, Austria and Prussia were combined in the defence of Germany; in practice, Austria left the main task to Prussia and discovered, too late, the penalty of her adroitness' (Taylor 1976: 34).

Furthermore, expansion into the Balkans had set the Habsburg Empire on a potential 'collision course' with the Russian Empire, which was busily expanding its 'fraternal' influence on Orthodox Serbia, Montenegro, Bulgaria and, less durably, on non-Slavic Romania and Greece. Indeed, Russia's acquisition of Bessarabia (present-day Moldova) in 1812 had brought it within reach of the River Danube. Almost any further expansion by Russia into the Balkans would have led to Russian control of the mouth and lower reaches of the Danube, the main artery of the Habsburg Empire. Finally, by advancing into the Balkans, the Habsburgs were storing up potentially explosive 'South Slav problems' for the future, just to add to their easily inflammable Magyar, Italian, German and Bohemian problems.

The quickening pace of economic and social change

Nevertheless, these slowly germinating problems remained under wraps until 1848. Despite (or perhaps because of) the repressive conservatism and stability of the Metternich era, the Habsburg Empire achieved a steady economic recovery during the 1820s and significant economic growth in the 1830s and early 1840s. For the period 1830–45, in the 'Austrian half' of the empire, it has been estimated that average annual growth rates were in the region of 2.5–3.3 per cent for aggregate industrial output, 7 per cent for mining output, 4–5 per cent for metallurgy, 4 per cent for engineering, 4 per cent for textiles (7 per cent for cotton) and 2 per cent for food-processing (5 per cent in the case of sugar refining). Crop production grew at an average annual rate of 1.2–1.4 per cent. In contrast, population growth was only 0.7 per cent per annum (Good 1984: 45–8, 69). On the same territory, the non-agricultural workforce had grown to about 28 per cent of the total by 1850, but in Bohemia the proportion was 36 per cent (pp. 46–7). The very existence of an adequate statistical basis for such estimates is itself indicative of significant economic and administrative attainments in mid-nineteenth-century Austria, especially Bohemia.

The establishment of the Danube Steamship Navigation Company in 1831 was a major milestone in the development of the Danube as the 'main artery' of the Habsburg Empire, since steam-powered vessels could easily navigate *upstream* as well as down. During the 1830s and early 1840s Hungary became a significant exporter of grain, wool, timber and flour up the Danube to Austria and Germany. This immediately stimulated the construction of Hungary's first large-scale flour mills and steam-powered saw mills, which in turn helped to stimulate the commercialization of Hungarian agriculture, major extensions of grain cultivation and livestock-rearing, significant drainage, irrigation and river-improvement schemes, and increased employment of wage labour in place of serfs. In German Austria and the Czech Lands, by contrast, the major developments in the same years were in food-processing, brewing, distilling, textiles, metallurgy, mining and machine-building, drawing upon greater supplies of capital and a more educated and technologically receptive workforce. During the 1830s and 1840s there was a revival of the refining of beet-sugar, in which the Habsburg Empire (and especially the Czech Lands) was destined to become a world leader in both output and technology. Large-scale brewing of beer began to develop in Vienna, Prague and Plzen (the home of the famous Pilsener lager process). The growth of urban demand for food, drinks, clothing, timber, agricultural raw materials and transport improvements, and the increase in interregional trade and specialization encouraged the growth of more productive and more market-oriented agriculture, land improvements, capital accumulation and the diffusion of new and more remunerative root and forage crops, crop rotations and livestock breeds in both halves of the Habsburg Empire. In 1836 the ocean-going Austrian Lloyd Steamship Company was established, operating services from Fiume and Trieste. Between 1835 and 1839 Austria's first steam-powered railways were built north and south of Vienna, using Austrian-made rails. More than 140 km of railway had been opened by 1839, 378 km by 1842 and 1,025 km by 1848, although only 46 km had been opened in Hungary by 1846.

From 1815 to 1848, in East Central Europe as well as in western Europe, there occurred a steady drift of population away from the land and 'industrial' villages into large towns and cities. By 1850 Vienna had about 444,000 inhabitants (compared with 247,000 in 1800), Budapest had 178,000 (54,000 in 1800), Prague had 118,000 (75,000 in 1800) and Krakow had 50,000 (24,000 in 1800). The Revolutionary and Napoleonic Wars of 1792–1814 had unsettled thousands of rural communities and had mobilized and/or uprooted millions of people. Many of the millions of men who had fought in those wars (often in foreign lands) later found it difficult to settle back into their former homes, villages and occupations. Many had acquired 'wanderlust', while others were just plain restless, often perhaps without quite knowing why.

In addition, war, revolution, agrarian change and the continuing rise of capitalism were helping to burst the constricting bonds of serfdom and so-called 'feudalism', which still tied tens of millions of peasants to virtually hereditary domiciles, social positions and occupations. Compared with semi-industrial Britain, however, much lower proportions of the uprooted or displaced persons who drifted into the larger towns and cities on the Continent were being absorbed into regular paid employment. In Continental Europe industrialization had not yet assumed such massive proportions as it had done in Britain. Instead of being thoroughly incorporated into a relatively stable and settled urban proletariat or upper/lower middle class, as in Britain, the Continental 'flotsam and jetsam' remained relatively unincorporated 'lumpenproletarians' (if they were uneducated) or members of an unincorporated and insecure 'lumpen' intelligentsia or 'lumpen' bourgeoisie (if they were educated). Thus the increasingly overcrowded large towns and cities on the Continent were being swollen by tens of thousands of homeless and unemployed persons (vagrants, waifs and beggars), prostitutes, petty criminals, casual labourers, opportunists and fortune-hunters.

The Continent was suffering not so much from the development of industry as from insufficient expansion of industrial and commercial employment, despite impressive rises in industrial output. Indeed, the beginnings of mechanization (especially in textile production), falling transport costs, the advent of railways and the growing scale, concentration and productivity of Continental European industry were undercutting and making redundant millions of urban as well as rural handicraftsmen (especially handloom weavers), who found it increasingly difficult to compete with the products of factory industry, whether these were domestic or imported. Some rural centres of handicraft industry achieved successful transitions to large-scale mechanized production and became 'little Manchesters' (including parts of Bohemia, German Austria and the Rhineland). But their successes merely exacerbated the plight of the majority of handicraft centres, many of which ultimately failed to adapt and survive, particularly during the 'hungry' 1840s (this was particularly the case in areas such as Silesia, Flanders, south-western Ireland and rural Hungary, which experienced significant rural 'de-industrialization' from the 1830s to the 1850s).

Yet because industrialization and the construction of railways not only destroyed old crafts, but sometimes gave rise to new craft employments or gave some existing handicraft industries larger markets, the *overall* numbers of Continental Europeans dependent on the land and/or handicraft industries did not decline dramatically in absolute terms, even though their share of the total population was falling significantly. The crucial point is that these 'traditional' occupations were unable to absorb Europe's burgeoning population growth. In the main it was this 'surplus' labour (surplus to the requirements of traditional activities) which increasingly drifted to the larger towns and cities, desperately seeking new ways of making a living, even if this meant engaging in petty crime,

prostitution, begging or scavenging. Such phenomena are nowadays assumed to be more characteristic of Third World industrialization (which has also generally failed to generate sufficient paid
employment). But it is pertinent to remember that Continental Europe passed through a similar
phase in the middle decades of the nineteenth century and that this constituted the basic socio-economic context of the 1848 Revolutions. Socially, the latter were arguably more the result of the
insufficient development (rather than the development) of capitalism. Those who had either lost or
not yet found secure footholds in Europe's emerging urban-industrial civilization furnished many
of the 'foot soldiers', 'rent-a-mobs' and malcontents who participated in the Revolutions of
1848–9.

THE POLITICAL AND CULTURAL RESURGENCE OF HUNGARY, 1790–1848

During the 1790s and 1800s, stimulated by the supply needs of the warring European armies and
the disruption of agricultural production in Europe's major war zones, grain and wool prices had
more than quadrupled. In response to these exceptional wartime conditions, Hungary's production
and exports of grain and wool had dramatically risen (both in volume and, especially, in value).
Magyar landowners had increased both the area and the methods of grain cultivation. The Magyar
nobility had been able greatly to expand its consumption of Western-style foods, drinks, clothing,
furnishings, glassware, silverware and even books and newspapers (including many imported products), and several wealthy aristocrats had begun to sponsor a new generation of 'improving landlords' and 'enlightened' gentlemen farmers, in emulation of British role-models. Acting in
conjunction with the ideas, attitudes and policies of the late eighteenth-century 'Enlightenment' and
'enlightened despotism', these new circumstances and stimuli had initiated a 'cultural revolution'
involving fundamental changes in the mentality, outlook, life-styles and aspirations of Hungary's
increasingly educated and assertive nobility, who made up the top 5 per cent of the population
(Deak 1979: 4).

The Magyar nobility was disproportionately large because it included anyone who could claim
descent from the numerous family retainers, vassals and other feudal servitors of the medieval
Arpad dynasty and, in addition, the descendants of the large numbers of warriors who had been
ennobled in order to augment the recruitment of fighting men into the armies of the rival rulers of
Hungary during the Turkish Wars of the sixteenth and seventeenth centuries. By the 1780s, 108
aristocratic families (the 'magnates') controlled about 40 per cent of all fiefs in twenty-seven counties of Hungary (including Croatia-Slavonia, but excluding Transylvania). Another 40 per cent of
all fiefs belonged to a much more numerous section of the nobility known as the 'bene possession-
ati'. In the early nineteenth century the latter started to refer to themselves as the 'gentry', using
either the actual English word or its Magyarized form (*dzsentri*). They began to ape the manners,
ideas and life-styles of their English 'cousins'. But four-fifths of the nobility, who numbered around
389,000 people (including dependents) in 1787 and about 617,000 in 1839, were in no sense *sei-
gneurs* or 'feudal lords'. They were mostly either smallholders or minor state officials or the minions
of rich magnates, and were distinguished from commoners only by their formal fiscal exemptions
and legal immunities and their rights of participation in local 'noble assemblies' and in elections to
the lower house of the Hungarian Diet (Janos 1982: 17–19). The poorest nobles were commonly
known as the 'sandaled' nobility because they could not afford fine boots. Until the early nineteenth
century membership of the Magyar 'nobility' was virtually synonymous with membership of the
Magyar political 'nation' (*natio*). In effect 'Magyar was a class term: it meant an owner of land
exempt from the land-tax, or one who attended the county assemblies and took part in the elections
to the Diet' (Taylor 1976: 26–7). Burghers also enjoyed local self-administration and token representation in the Hungarian Diet, but the burgher 'estate' largely consisted of Germans (and, from
the 1840s, Jewish immigrants from Poland, Austria and Russia) rather than Magyars.

From 1792 to 1809, in repeated attempts to elicit increased Magyar 'contributions' of money and men to successive war efforts against France, the Austrian Emperor (Franz) had wooed and flattered the Magyar nobility/'nation'. During the sessions of the Hungarian Diet in 1809, he had even had to pose as a 'Hungarian patriot' in order to counter Napoleon's appeal for a Hungarian revolt against the Habsburgs (Taylor 1976: 44). But in 1811, when the Austrian state declared itself bankrupt, the Hungarian Diet had refused to accede to Habsburg attempts to devalue the Hungarian currency (to reduce it to parity with the greatly depreciated Austrian currency). The Diet was in the end prorogued by the infuriated emperor, who refused to call another Hungarian Diet until 1825, violating his constitutional duty to convoke a Diet at least once every three years (Kann 1974: 237).

Furthermore, the termination of the Napoleonic Wars in 1814 was followed by steep declines in the effective demand for and the prices of grain and wool. This brought financial ruin to large sections of the Magyar nobility who had borrowed heavily during the boom years of the 1790s and 1800s or who were living beyond their means. Many more experienced acute difficulties in adjusting to the straitened economic circumstances of the post-1814 decade and to an increasingly competitive commercial environment thereafter, having grown accustomed to greatly increased expenditures on 'status consumption'. (These difficulties of adjustment were reflected in the Magyar saying: 'A gentleman is never in a hurry, never shows surprise and never pays his debts'!) Many items which had until recently been 'luxuries' reserved for the very rich had come to be seen as 'daily necessities', including tea, coffee, sugar, white bread, newspapers, books, perfumes, cosmetics and, above all, regular changes of clothing. The magnates were cushioned by the sheer size of their estates, but the smaller landholdings of the 'gentry' could less easily sustain their rising 'cashflow' requirements, while the landless or near-landless 'lesser nobility' stood little chance at all. Consequently the sons of the 'gentry', as well as the still rapidly proliferating 'lesser nobility', were hurled into an unseemly scramble for further education and state or professional employment. By 1846 Hungary had 33,000 'college graduates' and 'twice as many licensed attorneys *per capita* as the more developed western provinces of the . . . Empire', but only a fraction found employment commensurate with their qualifications and 'most of the students lived in abject poverty, supporting themselves by manual labour and the collection of alms' (Janos 1982: 42–3). Thus the Magyar nobility became a seething cauldron of frustrated professional and social ambitions as well as endemic economic anxiety and political discontents. There was a growing realization that these problems could only be resolved by the creation of a Magyar state to provide jobs for the unemployed sons of the Magyar nobility.

In the same period, not unrelatedly, the Magyar nobility became increasingly conscious of the extent to which Hungary had fallen behind the economic and cultural/technological development of north-western Europe. The gap had widened significantly since the fifteenth and sixteenth centuries. As a major producer and exporter of gold, silver, copper, cattle and grain, occupying a strategic position on the overland trade routes between the Baltic and the eastern Mediterranean, Renaissance Hungary had attracted large numbers of German merchants and artisans who had built up substantial craft industries and towns. Hungary's urban economy and culture had declined during the seventeenth and eighteenth centuries, however, as its gold and silver mines neared exhaustion and European trade gravitated towards the Atlantic.

Eighteenth-century Hungary was a landlocked commercial backwater, whose craft industries also suffered from Habsburg commercial discrimination in favour of the industrial interests of German Austria and Bohemia. By 1787 the population of the 'free royal cities' was only 6 per cent of the total (with up to 60 per cent of so-called 'townspeople' at least partly dependent on agriculture); and urban representation had been reduced to a single seat in the lower house of the Hungarian Diet (as against fifty-five for the 'noble' counties) (Janos 1982: 30–3). There was a serious growth of vagrancy and banditry, while agriculture was dominated by oppressive and inefficient systems of serfdom and some districts regressed to a primitive barter economy. Nevertheless, 'the fertility of the land and the favourable ratio of land to population provided adequate nutrition for most' (p. 33), while tales of the country's religious tolerance, natural wealth and availability of 'vacant' land attracted about a million (mainly German-speaking) immigrants between 1711 and 1780 and a significant Jewish immigration thereafter.

Starting in the 1790s, however, statistical enquiries and the writings of foreign visitors began to quantify and to publicize the degree to which Hungary had lagged behind Austria, the German states and north-western Europe. Many formerly 'hallowed' objects of Magyar pride and mythology, even the vaunted 'liberties' (that is, privileges) of the Magyar aristocracy, began to be questioned or to be seen either as hindrances to effective remedial action or as sources of ignorance, superstition, oppression, filth and shame. For instance, the Frenchman Marcel de Serres, in his *Voyage en Autriche* (published in Paris in 1814) wrote that 'The Hungarians are naturally indolent . . . Although Hungary is a naturally fertile country, the inhabitants have no idea how to extract the riches of the soil . . . Ignorant and superstitious, the Hungarians are bad agriculturalists and equally little attracted to trade' (cited by Janos 1982: 47–9).

While many Magyars took offence at such portrayals, others began to call for fundamental reforms. During the 1830s the leading reformer was a wealthy magnate, Count Istvan Szechenyi (1791–1860), widely revered as the 'father' of modern Hungary (even by his critics). An admirer of English trade and industry and especially 'improving landlordism' and the Whigs, Szechenyi advocated a liberalization of Hungary's restrictive land laws, the abolition of serfdom and the expansion of education and credit so as to facilitate the buying, selling and mortgaging of land in order to encourage both foreign and domestic investment in a commercial-agricultural revolution led by magnates like himself. In his view, the ensuing increases in agricultural productivity and incomes would adequately compensate the landlord class for the loss of serf labour and 'feudal' dues (persuading them to forgo their time-honoured tax exemptions), and raise popular purchasing power, expand the domestic market for both agricultural and industrial products, and generate the farm surpluses needed both to service the foreign debt and to feed and finance an expanding industrial sector. This 'virtuous circle' would, he hoped, transform the Magyars into 'one big happy family', headed by the magnates of course. This aristocratic, neo-physiocratic 'agriculture-first' strategy was primarily expounded in his two major works, *Hitel* (*Credit*, published in 1830) and *Verlag* (*Enlightenment*, published in 1832), which later became 'bibles' of Hungarian liberal-conservative paternalism. According to this programme, mass education, civil equality before the law and hence the abolition of serfdom were needed to transform all adults into fully fledged, legally responsible economic actors and contractual partners in economic transactions. Furthermore, he advocated the substitution of Magyar for Latin as Hungary's official language on purely pragmatic grounds, in order to enable more people to participate fully in civic and economic life, and not out of a chauvinistic desire to submerge the vernacular languages of Hungary's large non-Magyar minorities. Indeed, he counselled against his compatriots' persistent attempts to *impose* the Magyar language on the Croat, Slovak, Romanian and Ruthene minorities. Ever a gradualist and 'loyalist' aristocrat, Szechenyi aimed to achieve his programme 'organically', in collaboration (not confrontation) with the Habsburgs and the non-Magyar minorities. He eschewed confrontation, radicalism and strident nationalism, in the belief that his projects (and, equally, his class) needed the support and stability that the multinational empire could provide.

Szechenyi led by example. He donated a year's income from his estates to found a Hungarian Academy (to rehabilitate Magyar culture). He established the 'National Casino' (as a debating society) and instigated river improvements, urban renewal and the building of a permanent bridge between Buda and Pest, while in the Diet he battled against the entail laws, designed to keep landed estates intact down the generations. He seemingly preferred voluntary to state action. But most of his peers were in no hurry to renounce their fiscal and feudal/seigneurial privileges. The Hungarian Diet would approve only a very watered-down manumission law (1826), permitting the liberation of serfs on an individual basis, at the serfowners' discretion. Not until after the Revolutions of 1848–9 did a chastened Magyar aristocracy accept the bulk of Szechenyi's programme, albeit partly as a post-revolutionary *fait accompli*.

In 1831 there was a significant peasant revolt in north-eastern Hungary, precipitated partly by the Polish uprising of 1830–1 in Russian Poland and partly by the terrifying cholera epidemics which swept across Poland, Russia and Austria as well as Hungary in 1831. Many peasants regarded the pills that they were told to swallow, the chemicals that were poured into public wells and the treatments that were administered in makeshift cholera clinics as desperate attempts by the frightened ruling classes to poison the 'menacing' lower classes. They started attacking officials, landowners, clergy and Jews. The Hungarian peasant revolt was ruthlessly suppressed, with more than one hundred rebels being executed. After this, fear of peasant revolt polarized the Magyar 'political nation' into advocates of repression and advocates of reform (Deak 1979: 22). Indeed, until 1848, it robbed both the government and the nobility of the courage and political will needed to introduce social and agrarian reforms to relieve the plight of the peasants, most of whom were serfs.

During the 1840s, however, the political initiative had passed to more radical, impatient and stridently nationalistic Magyar 'gentry', headed by the demagogic Lutheran lawyer and journalist Lajos Kossuth (1802–94). One must beware of Austrian, Czech and Slovak claims that Kossuth was a Slovak 'convert' to Magyarism. His mother was German, but his father's Magyar descent can be traced back to 1263 (Deak 1979: 9–10). (But no doubt some wag will ask: 'What about before that?'!) Kossuth flattered and won the hearts of the Magyar nobility by referring to them all as 'gentry' and by reassuring them that, despite their provincial prejudices and xenophobia, they were the true embodiments and custodians of the Magyar nation and its 'national virtues'. As the indefatigable writer and producer of Hungary's first (hand-written) *Parliamentary Reports* from 1833 to 1836, the popular *Municipal Reports* from 1837 to 1838 and the widely read *Pesti Hirlap* (*Pest News*) newspaper from 1841 to 1844, Kossuth played upon the hopes, prejudices and anxieties of the Magyar nobility. In his view, the 'gentry' would no longer acquiesce in the leadership of the 'loyalist' aristocracy in the Hungarian Diet. On the contrary, the ascendant radical nationalists increasingly dictated terms or laid down the law to the magnates, the Habsburgs and the Viennese bureaucracy, who were increasingly thrown on to the defensive. Kossuth was not even silenced by a three-year detention from 1837 to 1840. On the contrary, he became a national *cause célèbre*, not least for the political skill with which he conducted his own defence during his trial (Deak 1979: 32–3).

In the economic sphere Kossuth rejected the decentralized, laissez-faire, 'agriculture first' (neo-physiocratic) development strategy favoured by Szechenyi. Instead, Kossuth advocated industrial subsidies and a more centralized and interventionist strategy of state-induced industrialization, drawing upon Friedrich List's *National System of Political Economy*, first published in 1841 and still famous for its 'infant industry' argument for tariff protection. In 1843 Kossuth co-authored a memorandum attributing Hungary's relative backwardness to its 'colonial dependence' on Austria, to a scarcity of technical personnel and to 'the existence of social and political institutions diametrically opposed to industrial interests', and advocating the development of 'national industry' by all available means, including industrial subsidies and tax concessions. When this was rejected by the 'loyalist' aristocracy and the imperial authorities, Kossuth supported the first-ever Magyar boycott of imported industrial goods in 1844. In 1846, echoing Listian economic nationalism, Kossuth wrote that 'those who do not possess the independent levers of civilization are only a people or race, but cannot be treated as a nation. Among these levers the most significant are trade and manufacturing industries. Without them one can exist as a country, but not as a nation' (quoted in Janos 1982: 66–8).

Between the early 1820s and the mid-1840s Hungary underwent a 'phenomenal' political, social and cultural transformation (Deak 1979: 61). During the early 1820s, with its Diet unconvoked, 'its agriculture medieval, its trade in crisis, its society old-fashioned and rigid', and the Magyar language 'unused except in colloquial speech', Hungary was 'one of the more backward and less influential provinces' of the Habsburg Empire; by the mid-1840s, however, 'the Diet was frequently in session . . . political parties had been constituted . . . newspapers poured out social criticism and political programmes; the country's internal administrative machinery had become almost entirely Magyar; Hungarian literature was thriving . . . the social structure had become less rigid', and serfdom was about to be abolished (pp. 61–2). Nevertheless, Hungary's resurgence was 'built on shaky foundations. Created not by a rising industrial bourgeoisie but by the landed nobility, Hungarian progress lacked solid economic backing' (p. 62). Indeed, despite some 'modest successes' in agriculture, trade, transportation and industry, 'Hungary's economy was falling behind the western parts of the Monarchy' (p. 62). The latter had ten times as many capitalist enterprises, employed fifteen times as many steam engines and produced six times as much pig and cast iron as did Hungary (p. 50). For a short time the Magyar leaders could conceal their economic weaknesses behind a 'facade of modernistic slogans and an excellent political organization', but this bluff could succeed 'only as long as neither the Court nor the Austro-German (and Czech) ruling circles were able to adopt similar slogans and political organization' (p. 62).

In 1844 the Diet declared Magyar to be the official language of the Kingdom of Hungary, even though Magyars comprised only 37 per cent of the population (45 per cent if Croatia-Slavonia is excluded) (Janos 1982: 11). By disadvantaging non-Magyars, including German-speaking imperial officials, the 1844 language law gave the Magyar nobility a near-monopoly of state employment in Hungary. Moreover, it imposed Magyar as the language of secondary education for non-Magyars (even in Croatia-Slavonia), as if Hungary was a unitary and culturally homogeneous kingdom (Kann 1974: 288). Indeed, Kossuth was openly demanding 'the unity of the lands of the Crown of King Istvan' (a euphemism for centralization, aggressive 'Magyarization' and suppression of the residual autonomy and/or separate cultural identities of the Croats, Slovaks, Transylvanian Romanians and Carpathian Ruthenes). Of course, many non-Magyars voluntarily assimilated into the 'dominant' ethnic group through intermarriage and/or in the hope of more rapid social and occupational advancement. This applied *a fortiori* to the so-called 'Saxon Germans' of Transylvania (who managed to maintain their centuries-old privileged position by 'collaborating' with the Magyars) and to the Jews, who were granted a Bill of Rights and membership of the burgher estate by the Hungarian Diet in 1840 (despite an initial royal veto in response to anti-Semitic lobbying from German townspeople). In 1847 Kossuth was finally elected to the Hungarian Diet, where he stepped up the Magyar nationalists' campaign to make Hungary 'their own'.

THE CZECH CULTURAL 'RESURGENCE', 1809–49

The remarkable Czech linguistic and cultural 'revival' was a largely accidental by-product of the social, administrative and educational reforms of Emperor Josef II (1765–90) and of the vigorous Czech economic development. In order to assist and encourage some of his (mainly German) imperial officials to learn Czech more effectively, Josef II had sanctioned the establishment of university chairs in Czech language and philology. Contrary to official intentions, however, these chairs became 'research centres of nationalism' and helped to elevate Czech 'from the humble position of a means of communication for peasants to that of an academic discipline and literary instrument' (Bradley 1971: 113–14).

In 1809 the first comprehensive Czech grammar was published by Father Josef Dobrovsky, director of the Hradiste seminary. He persuaded many of his fellow clergy and former pupils to produce sermons and poetry in 'formal Czech', using his grammar. At that time the Czech language had 'no fixed grammar and consisted only of spoken dialects' (Bradley 1971: 114). Josef Jungmann, prefect of the Academic Gymnasium in Prague, went on to publish an authoritative guide to Czech literary style. He also translated various foreign works into Czech, both to show that Czech was a competent vehicle of cultural expression (p. 122) and to persuade the authorities to permit the teaching of Czech in secondary schools (Kann 1974: 385).

Before long the Czech language was developing rapidly as the major outward manifestation of Czech national identity and as the preferred means of mass literary communication of the new generations of Czech teachers, clergy, lawyers, writers, journalists, professors, doctors, engineers, scientists, architects, musicians, merchants and industrialists, who proved to be the main beneficiaries of Josef II's social and educational reforms and the chief 'missionaries' of the Czech national resurgence. This Czech cultural 'resurgence' both benefited from and contributed to the development of the Bohemian Society of Sciences (established in 1784), the Czech Association for the Encouragement of Industry (1833) and, above all, the journal and the Czech Publishing Committee (*Matica ceska*) of the Bohemian Museum, which were established by the Czech historian and nationalist Frantisek Palacky in 1827 and 1830, respectively. During the 1820s and 1830s the Czech patriot V.M. Kramerius became a regular publisher of Czech 'revival' books and journals, including one prophetically entitled *Cechoslovak* (1820–5). Two 'revival' journals (*Ceska vcela* and *Kvety ceske*) survived from the 1830s to 1849, when they were shut down by the imperial authorities. An enduring Czech newspaper (*Prazske noviny*) emerged in the 1830s. 'The institutionalization of Czech cultural efforts had immediate and far-reaching effects . . . Czech literature really began to flourish and to create a large reading public' (Bradley 1971: 122–3). Aided by large-scale rural–urban migration the Czech intelligentsia began to reverse the seventeenth-century Germanization of Bohemia's towns and cities. Nevertheless, it is significant that, even in the later nineteenth century, some leading Czech writers, composers and intellectuals still found it easier or more advantageous to write in German (for example, Franz Kafka and Bedrich Smetana).

The dominant role of the non-noble intelligentsia in the nineteenth-century Czech 'revival' has been contrasted with the similarly hegemonic role of the nobility in the concurrent Magyar revival, in an attempt to explain the strongly cultural and apolitical orientation of the Czech renaissance: 'The Czechs, in contrast to the Hungarians, would not be *political* nationalists, for the Czech nobility refused to assume political leadership . . . Czech nationalism had to be cultural, for only Czech intellectuals were prepared to take up its cause. Thus, between 1780 and 1880, with a short interruption in 1848, Czech nationalism was expressed in poetry and prose, in books of research and in plays, in operas and music, in journals, newspapers, museums and national theatres, but hardly at all in social and political terms' (Bradley 1971: 115). However, this Czech–Magyar contrast is not as clear cut as it might appear. Landless, impecunious but educated Magyar nobles were so thick on the ground that they in effect became the Magyar intelligentsia which led the national 'revival'. Figures such as Lajos Kossuth, Jozsef Eötvös and Ferenc Deak were just as much members of the intelligentsia as of the nobility. The Magyar magnates were closer counterparts to the Bohemian nobility, not just in terms of wealth and privilege, but also in their vacillating and ambivalent attitudes towards nationalism and revolution (both groups tried to run with the hare and hunt with the hounds). Moreover, the notions that an intelligentsia cannot exercise political leadership and that intelligentsia nationalism had to be more cultural than political are refuted by the Russian as well as the Magyar example. Bradley was on stronger ground with regard to the significance he attaches to the role of historians in the Czech revival (Bradley 1971: 114–16).

Well before the Bohemian Diet designated Frantisek Palacky (1798–1876) the 'official historian' of Bohemia in 1829, the historians G. Dobner, B. Piter, A. Voigt and M. Pelcl played pivotal roles in the Czech 'revival'. Significantly, Dobner, Piter and Voigt were Germans, who, through their historian's enthusiasm for setting the historical record straight and for championing history's underdogs, became fervent 'converts' to the Czech national cause. In a sense this was just one of several illustrious examples of the pioneering role of eighteenth- and nineteenth-century German intellectuals in promoting 'rediscoveries' and 'revivals' of Slavic cultures, languages and history.

But the Czech case was special. Living cheek by jowl with Germans (and before the forging of a modernized and standardized written Czech language) many Czech commoners had become as Germanized as the last remnants of the Czech nobility. 'History alone could convince them that they were a separate nation capable of pursuing a unique national existence' (Bradley 1971: 114).

This explains both the Czech nationalists' obsession with Czech history and the striking ascendancy of historians (especially Palacky) in the Czech national movement in the early to mid-nineteenth century. That in turn helps to account for the Czech national leadership's seemingly Quixotic and anachronistic preoccupation, from the 1840s to the 1870s, with reclaiming the 'historic rights' of the (long defunct) Kingdom of Bohemia. They dreamed of restoring the former legislative and fiscal autonomy of the Bohemian Diet and of re-establishing the fine ideal of Bohemia as a tolerant multi-cultural home of both Czechs and Germans (and of Catholics and non-Catholics), peacefully co-existing, sharing power and prospering as they had done in the sixteenth century. This also partly explains Palacky's conciliatory attitude towards the Bohemian Germans and the German-dominated Bohemian Diet (and vice versa, at least until March 1848). This attitude is often glibly dismissed as 'conservative' and 'backward-looking', but that is misleading. It was really derived from a high-minded humanist desire to resurrect the 'Bohemian model' of tolerance, co-operation and power sharing which had been so wantonly destroyed by the Habsburgs in the seventeenth century.

THE METTERNICH REGIME

The Metternich regime had built dams to hold back the rising tides of nationalism, liberalism, radicalism and discontent. In 1848 these dams burst, partly because the political heartlands of Continental Europe were all convulsed by powerful social and ideological currents (and the Habsburg Empire could not be hermetically insulated from them) and partly because they went hand-in-hand with the mushrooming growth of new social classes. These new social classes, the bourgeoisie and the proletariat, could not easily be accommodated within the existing social hierarchies, rooted as these were in specifically pre-industrial economies and societies. Only countries which were in a real sense on the political peripheries of Continental Europe (Britain, Ireland, Scandinavia, Russia, Serbia, Greece, Albania, Spain and Portugal) failed to experience the revolutions in 1848.

Although the Habsburg Empire under Metternich was a *Polizeistaat* in the sense that the state employed censorship, police spies and informers, interception of mail, arbitrary powers of arrest, travel restrictions and mandatory registration of residence, servants, hotel visitors and Jews, there was another (somewhat contradictory) side to the coin. Metternich professed to believe in a *Rechtsstaat*, a 'law-governed society'. The 'supranational' imperial government in Vienna (unlike its post-1867 Magyar counterpart in Budapest) did make some attempt to be impartial in its treatment of the various 'nationalities', despite the troublesome growth of pan-German nationalism and the preponderance of Austrian Germans in the imperial administration. Metternich believed in 'pure' rather than 'constitutional' monarchy. He did not support arbitrary monarchy, which he equated with 'Oriental despotism'. He expected the monarch to take advice, to pursue 'orderly practices of government' and to uphold the laws, the justice, the social order and the Roman Catholic precepts upon which monarchical authority and legitimacy ultimately rested (and which the Monarchy would violate at its peril). Essentially, Metternich saw the Habsburg Empire as 'a system in which a variety of nationalities co-existed within a monarchical framework based on social hierarchy and the rule of law' (Sked 1989: 25, 16).

The nineteenth-century Habsburg bureaucracy was relatively competent, conscientious, impartial, professional, law abiding and free from corruption, in comparison that is with the states located further south and east in Europe. This legacy of a relatively 'law-governed' administrative tradition and society (even more than the higher levels of education, technology and economic development) became the crucial advantage of the Czech Republic, Slovenia and (in smaller measure) Hungary and Slovakia over most of Europe's other post-Communist states after the Revolutions of 1989. This legacy was what placed them (along with Poland and the Baltic States) at the front of the queue for membership of the European Union and made them the preferred locations for Western companies and investment in Europe's post-Communist states. The rule of law is a prerequisite for the proper functioning of both democracy and market economies, especially in relation to international dealings and transactions. Market economies can, of course, operate without democracy. However, if they are to be fully consummated, both require the rule of law and a fairly impartial state capable of consistently upholding and enforcing the rules and contracts on which they rest, as a basis for autonomous and pluralistic political, social, cultural and economic activity.

Fortunately for German Austria, the Czech Lands, Austrian Poland, Hungary, northern Italy and Slovenia, Metternich's Habsburg Empire largely rested on dynastic 'rights' and 'legitimacy', international treaties and international law. Consequently, the 'rule of law' was essential to its survival, even if it was never fully upheld and enforced. By nineteenth-century standards, the state kept relatively few political prisoners and made little (if any) use of torture. Foreign (even 'prohibited') literature circulated widely, while the police were in fact too few in number to exercise effective control during a major crisis. Thus in Vienna in 1848 Metternich could only rely on a garrison of 14,000, a police force of 1,000 and a municipal guard of 14,000 (most of whom were bandsmen), while the Habsburg Empire as a whole was arguably *under-policed* (Sked 1989: 44–52, 82–3).

16　The 'Revolutions of 1848': the Habsburg Empire in crisis

THE INCIPIENT DESTABILIZATION OF EAST CENTRAL EUROPE

The political stability which East Central Europe lost in 1848, with the fall of the Metternich regime, was not regained until 1948, with the full imposition of Stalinist control, after an intervening century of endemic instability and crisis. After 1848 Habsburg absolutism was perpetually on the defensive. 'The dynastic idea was challenged and, once challenged, could never recover the unconscious security of the past. The "Austrian idea" became an idea like any other, competing for intellectual backing; and the dynasty survived not on its own strength, but by manoeuvring the forces of rival nations and classes' (Taylor 1976: 56–7). In the final analysis, 'the Habsburg Monarchy and nationalism were incompatible; no real peace was possible between them. Metternich saw this more clearly than many of his successors' (p. 40). This was at the heart of the subsequent endemic instability and crisis up to 1918 and even beyond, when the problem became one of what would take the Habsburg Empire's place. The Revolutions of 1848–9 also made some Europeans fully aware for the first time of the difficulties of accommodating a unified German polity in a Europe mainly made up of much smaller nations and states (or would-be states). Indeed, the Czech leaders of 1848 were the first people to be directly confronted by 'the German problem', which loomed so large in European affairs thereafter. For these and other reasons 1848 was a 'defining moment' in the emergence of modern Europe, especially in East Central Europe.

It is difficult to provide an adequate overview of the polycentric and kaleidoscopically interacting events of 1848–9. The Revolutions within the Habsburg Empire 'took place in several theatres and on several levels. All were interrelated. This factor can never be fully shown in a historical presentation, which cannot tell all at the same time' (Kann 1974: 299). Moreover, there were major interactions and overlaps between internal and external events; for example, between the Revolutions and the Austro-Prussian competition for predominance in the German-speaking world, or between the Austrian wars against Piedmont-Sardinia and the Revolutions in Lombardy and Venetia. Besides, the Revolutions in the Habsburg Empire 'flared up in some places, then quietened down to move to other scenes, to break out again in the old places. There is no centre or continuity in the revolutionary events' (p. 300). Nevertheless, Sir Lewis Namier emphasized that the Revolutions of 1848–9 were 'born at least as much of hopes as of discontents' and their 'common denominator was ideological'; for this reason he called them 'the revolution of the intellectuals – *la révolution des clercs*' (Namier 1946: 4).

The Revolutions of 1848–9 were preceded by some local grain harvest failures and severe potato blight in 1845–7 and by industrial recession in 1847. In February 1846, moreover, an unsuccessful revolt of the Polish nationalist nobility in semi-autonomous Krakow sparked off a major rebellion of the impoverished and downtrodden serfs of western and central Galicia against their Polish 'masters' (see pp. 180, 295–6). This contributed to the climate of heightened social tension and economic distress and added to the already menacing problems of vagrancy, banditry and urban unemployment. Between 1847 and 1850, moreover, many parts of Europe were convulsed by a massive cholera epidemic. The terrible gastric symptoms of that relatively unfamiliar disease and woeful ignorance about its nature and transmission, combined with the heavy concentration of the millions of victims among the lower orders (including vagrants, waifs, beggars and lumpenproletarians), fuelled false rumours that the disease was spread by physical contact with human 'vermin' and that the terrified upper classes were attempting to 'poison off' large segments of the dirty, 'dangerous', fast-growing and semi-criminalized lower orders. Such rumours further exacerbated the tensions and mutual distrust between social classes and between the rulers and the ruled. In the end, however, the Revolutions of 1848–9 were defeated because, except in Hungary, 'ultimate control of the state-machine, and still more of the armies of the Great Powers on the European Continent, remained with the Conservatives' (Namier 1946: 31).

OPENING SHOTS: ITALY, 1847–8

The opening shots in the Revolutions of 1848–9 were fired in Italy. In 1847, in Habsburg-ruled Lombardy and Venetia, democrats and 'patriots' put strong pressure on the leading 'moderates' to petition Emperor Ferdinand for self-government and civil liberties. Tensions rose as the police attacked a peaceful demonstration in Milan in September 1847, encouraging northern Italian democrats and 'patriots' to back a ('no smoking') boycott of the (Habsburg) state tobacco monopoly. In retaliation, on 3 January 1848 the Austrian authorities provoked violent clashes between unarmed civilians and their armed forces, which were commanded by the octogenarian Field Marshal Radetzky, as 'justification' for the imposition of martial law.

The embattled northern Italian 'patriots' and democrats were spurred on by the news of successful popular uprisings against Neapolitan Bourbon absolutism in Sicily (12–27 January 1848), the promulgation of liberal constitutions in the Kingdom of Naples and Sicily (29 January) and in Tuscany (11 February), the forced abdication of King Louis Philippe in France (24 February) and the forced resignation of Metternich in Vienna (13 March). On 18 March, workers and craftsmen led by young Italian 'patriots' and democrats launched an anti-Habsburg uprising in Milan. However, before the radicals could consolidate their initial ascendancy, Lombardy's propertied classes (who were terrified of both 'republican anarchy' and far-reaching 'social revolution') seized the initiative and appealed to the adjacent Kingdom of Piedmont and Sardinia for military assistance against the Austrian army and (implicitly) against the radical 'patriots', democrats and populace. Radicals and republicans were fobbed off with empty assurances that the invading Piedmontese army commanded by King Carlo Alberto would not simply annex Lombardy but would accept the result of a plebiscite and that, once the Habsburgs were decisively defeated, Italy's constitution and destiny would be discussed and settled by the country as a whole. In Venice, by contrast, aided by the fact that Habsburg troops were already being withdrawn in response to the crisis in Lombardy, radical democrats led by Daniele Manin seized power on 22 March 1848 and quickly proclaimed a new Venetian Republic. With the Habsburgs seemingly 'finished' in Italy, the 'client' rulers of Parma and Modena also capitulated within days.

Nevertheless, King Carlo Alberto and the Italian 'patriots' failed to press home their initial advantages. Their fatal delays, disorganization and tactical errors allowed Field Marshal Radetzky to regroup the Habsburg forces, defeat Piedmont-Sardinia (twice over, in July 1848 and March 1849), reconquer Austria's Italian possessions (summer 1849) and restore the status quo ante.

THE END OF THE METTERNICH REGIME, MARCH 1848

News of the dramatic events in Italy in January 1848 and of the fall of the French monarchy on 24 February 1848 soon travelled by train, post and telegraph to many parts of the Habsburg

Empire and the Germanic world. However, these 'ripples' from France and Italy merely acted as catalysts. Habsburg absolutism was already under increasing challenge in German Austria, Bohemia and Hungary *before* 1848, as was Prussian absolutism in northern Germany and the Rhineland.

By the end of February 1848 radical and nationalist students had taken to the streets in Buda and Pest. On 3 March 1848 Lajos Kossuth, as leader of the radical-nationalist Magyar nobility in the Hungarian Diet, called for the liberation of Hungary from Austrian tutelage and came to Vienna to incite rebellion at the very nerve centre of the Habsburg Empire. On 11 March 1848 radical Czechs and Germans met in Prague to demand a restoration of the unity, civil liberties and self-government of the long defunct Kingdom of Bohemia (in other words, a return to the pre-1620s Bohemian constitution and quasi-statehood). In early March, amid growing street demonstrations in Vienna and a run on the banks, the Habsburgs panicked and prepared to ditch Metternich, in the hope that this would calm the rapidly spreading unrest.

On 13 March 1848, egged on by those who resented or envied Metternich's position and power and by the search for a scapegoat, the Diet of Lower Austria (the Vienna region) openly demanded his resignation. This demand was immediately taken up by protesters on Vienna's streets. When no one rallied to his defence, Metternich complied. However, instead of defusing the crisis, his resignation merely created a power vacuum and encouraged the malcontents to step up their agitation and demands. The Habsburgs temporarily lost control of events, as power passed to the provinces and city streets, and the Habsburg Empire came closer to disintegration in 1848–9 than at any other time before the First World War. The unrest in Vienna and the fall of Metternich caused imperial paralysis and a loss of direction and authority in what had become a very centrally directed polity, leaving the confused provincial authorities to flounder about without clear or practicable instructions. The Revolutions of 1848–9 laid bare the latent tensions and contradictions between and within the various peoples that made up the Habsburg Empire.

THE HUNGARIAN REVOLUTION OF 1848–9

In March 1848, following the resignation of Metternich, the Hungarian Diet renounced all Viennese authority and jurisdiction over Hungary and retained only a 'personal union' of the Kingdom with the Habsburg Monarchy (including the presence of a Habsburg viceroy in Budapest). The Diet legislated for the establishment of a sovereign Magyar national state, to comprise all 'the lands of the Crown of St Istvan' (that is, including Transylvania, Slovakia and Croatia). This was to have its own army, foreign policy, budget, currency and government responsible to a fully fledged parliament elected on a uniform franchise limited to the 'top' 6.5 per cent of the population (about the same as in Great Britain at that time). Most remarkably, this instinctively conservative Diet also abolished serfdom, tithes, the tax exemptions of the nobility and the entailment of feudal estates. By arguing that, unless the 'gentry' took the lead in promoting radical reform, 'real' radicals would mobilize the restive and largely non-Magyar peasantry (mostly serfs) against the (largely Magyar) propertied classes, 'Kossuth, alone in Europe, persuaded his followers to outbid the radicals instead of seeking dynastic protection against them' (Taylor 1976: 59). This was a major feat but more was to follow. Archduke Stefan, the Habsburg viceroy in Hungary, timidly surrendered his power to a Magyar government under Count Lajos Batthyany, with Kossuth as minister of finance, Count Istvan Szechenyi as minister of public works, Ferenc Deak as justice minister and Jozsef Eötvös as education minister (that is, a coalition of magnates and 'lesser' nobility).

On 11 April 1848, the so-called March Laws and associated changes were ratified by Emperor Ferdinand, formally legalizing the Hungarian Revolution and the creation of a separate Hungarian state (p. 63). Indeed, Istvan Deak called his major study of Hungary under Kossuth *The Lawful Revolution* (1979), on the grounds that these changes gained the requisite 'royal assent' and that the

Magyars merely seized upon the fall of the (somewhat unconstitutional) Metternich regime as an opportunity to reassert the Hungarian right of self-government which was supposed to have been enshrined in the Treaty of Szatmar (1711) and reaffirmed by the terms on which the Hungarian and Transylvanian diets approved the Pragmatic Sanction in 1722–3. In this sense the Hungarian Diet of March–April 1848 was more truly 'reactionary' than 'revolutionary' (Sked 1989: 58–9). Indeed, the Magyar leaders were 'respectable' and socially conservative men of property, who did not see themselves as revolutionaries and who would have been terrified at the prospect of a 'real' (social) revolution directed against the propertied classes.

The Transylvanian Diet, dominated by fearful Magyar and 'Saxon' German landowners, voted for the full incorporation of Transylvania into a unitary Hungary. However, alarm about the possible consequences of this change helped to trigger rebellions among the largely Romanian peasants of Transylvania and among the Serbs of the Military Frontier regions. Most peasants were also disappointed that the agrarian reforms had not gone far enough and would leave many of them just as poor, dependent and vulnerable as before. Indeed, many a landowner was in no hurry to apply the reforms to his own estate(s) and became a law unto himself.

Croatian resentment of the huge concessions to the Magyars led Emperor Ferdinand to appoint the Croat officer, landowner and 'patriot' Josip Jelacic as *ban* (viceroy) of Croatia in March 1848. But in June, under Magyar pressure, Jelacic was seemingly dismissed, although he in fact continued to act on the Habsburgs' behalf. His formal reinstatement in September 1848 signalled the start of a Croatian military offensive against the Magyars. This soon escalated into all-out war between Hungary and Austria and the deeply divided Batthyany government had to resign. The Hungarian parliament (elected in June 1848) handed power to a Committee of National Defence headed by Kossuth. He quickly organized and provisioned a remarkably successful 170,000-strong Magyar national army (known as the *honved* battalions), repressed the rebellions and dissent among the non-Magyar minorities, fought off the initial Croat and Austrian German invasions of Hungary and consolidated his position as a virtual dictator. In April 1849, at the peak of his apparent power and success, he proclaimed a republic and formally 'deposed' the Habsburgs in Hungary.

Kossuth's Hungarian Republic was probably doomed from the start, however. The odds were stacked against it. Lacking significant military-industrial capacity, Hungary was hopelessly outgunned. It had been seriously weakened by the rebellions and lack of support among its mostly peasant and/or non-Magyar inhabitants. Its mere existence threatened monarchical legitimacy, the European 'balance of power' and Russia's hold on Poland. (This virtually guaranteed that Russia would intervene militarily, as actually occurred in June–August 1849.) Even the 'liberal' governments of Britain and France tacitly welcomed its demise, because of the importance of the Habsburg Empire to the stability of East Central Europe, the containment of Russia and the European balance of power. Thus Kossuth's regime remained bereft of allies (other than Polish 'patriots', who were ultimately more of a liability than an asset). In the end the Magyars chose to surrender to Russian rather than Austrian *force majeure* in August 1849, but 'Austrians' incurred about 50,000 war deaths to the Russians' 543 (not counting 11,028 cholera victims). The Magyars also incurred about 50,000 war deaths (Sked 1989: 102). The blood-letting did not stop there. About 150 Magyars (including thirteen generals) were executed for their prominent roles in the Hungarian Revolution and 1,765 were imprisoned, although Kossuth himself escaped into permanent exile. Hungary was then punitively subjected to a decade of centralized absolutist 'direct rule' from Vienna, that is, by Austrian German officials. However, many of the reforms enacted by the Hungarian Revolution of 1848–9 (especially the abolition of serfdom and of the tax exemptions of the nobility) were maintained, if only as further punishments for the mutinous Magyar gentry. Ironically Austrian direct rule was even imposed on Croatia, Transylvania and the Military Frontier regions, which thus received as a 'reward' what the Magyars suffered as a punishment.

While recognizing that it would have been very hard for the Magyar leadership to resist the seductive opportunities for national assertion which presented themselves in 1848, Istvan Deak has soberly concluded that 'Szechenyi was right and Kossuth was wrong: Hungary ought not to have embarked on its great political venture without having first developed economic strength and a bourgeois society' (Deak 1979: 62). In our view, the Hungarian Revolution of 1848–9 was premature, foolhardy and afflicted by a fatal schizophrenia, but nationalists are often blind to harsh realities. On one level, this was a liberal universalist revolution, bestowing rights and obligations without religious or ethnic discrimination or favour. Yet it was also a Magyar nationalist revolution in which non-Magyars could fully participate only if they accepted the primacy of the Magyar language and aspirations and the transformation of the formerly multi-cultural and cosmopolitan Hungarian state into an expressly Magyar state. Similar tensions between liberalism and nationalism have bedevilled every step towards constitutional government, the rule of law and liberal democracy in the eastern half of Europe ever since, but the first open manifestations of this perennial eastern European problem and dilemma occurred in Hungary in 1848–9.

THE SMALLER 'NATIONAL AWAKENINGS' IN CROATIA, SLOVAKIA, TRANSYLVANIA AND RUTHENIA

During the 1840s aggressive 'Magyarization' policies had begun to antagonize and politically to 'awaken' some members of the Croat, Slovak, Ruthene and Transylvanian Romanian peoples or 'proto-nations'. This was to be the Magyar nationalists' biggest blunder, strongly contributing to the defeat of the Hungarian Revolution of 1848–9 – and later to the complete dismemberment of the 'thousand-year-old Kingdom of Hungary' in 1918–19.

The initial Slovak, Ruthene and Transylvanian Romanian responses to the threats posed by Magyar nationalism and 'Magyarization' policies were severely muted by their lack of 'political and territorial organization' (Kann 1974: 287), as well as by their relatively low levels of socio-economic development and national-historical consciousness at that time. By contrast, the nobility of autonomous Croatia reacted strongly from the onset. Ironically, Croatian nobles had hitherto been staunch allies of the Magyar nobility, united in a joint defence of their local autonomy and class privileges against threats both 'from above' (the Habsburg emperors and the imperial bureaucracy) and 'from below' (the downtrodden peasantry). Since 1591 the Croatian Sabor (Diet) had regularly sent delegates to take part in the deliberations of the Hungarian Diet. Having tasted direct rule from Vienna (1767–78), the Sabor resolved to return to indirect rule by Hungary in 1779. After the centralizing rule of Josef II (1780–90), the Sabor voluntarily transferred the voting of taxes ('contributions') and control of the 'common affairs' of Croatia and Hungary to the Hungarian Diet (1790). The Sabor even resolved that Magyar should be taught in Croatian schools (1827) and that a knowledge of Magyar should be required of Croatian officials (1830). 'There had been no hostility between Hungarian and Croat nobles. Indeed Croat privileges owed their survival to the association with Hungary; in isolation the Croat nobles would have shared the fate of the Czechs' (Taylor 1976: 27). However, the Croatian nobility quickly came to resent Magyar attempts to *impose* more far-reaching 'Magyarization' on Croatia during the 1840s. Besides their longstanding alliance with the Magyar nobility, the Croatian nobility also had strong traditions of military service in the imperial armed forces and of loyalty to the Habsburg emperor, and 'Magyar nationalism pushed the Croat nobles into the arms of the Habsburgs' (p. 28). In 1847 the Sabor itself succumbed to linguistic nationalism and declared Serbo-Croat to be the official language of Croatia-Slavonia (in place of both Magyar and Latin). This put it in direct conflict with the Hungarian Diet. In 1848–9 Croatian troops commanded by Baron Josip Jelacic played prominent roles in the suppression of the Hungarian and Viennese Revolutions. However, the subsequent Habsburg failure to reward the Croatian loyalism of 1848–9 either by fully restoring Croatian autonomy in the 1850s or by protecting Croatia against the renewal of aggressive 'Magyarism' from 1875 onwards eventually drove many

Croats into a cultural and political rapprochement with their Orthodox South Slav 'cousins', the Serbs, from whom they had hitherto been separated by a religious chasm.

FRANTISEK PALACKY, 'AUSTRO-SLAVISM' AND THE CONCEPTION OF THE HABSBURG EMPIRE AS 'A EUROPEAN NECESSITY'

For Bohemia and Moravia 1848 was a moment of truth. It brought home to many Czechs the realization that, despite their irksome lack of political autonomy, they could at least defend and develop their own national language, culture, identity and economy within the polyglot Habsburg Empire, and that the preservation of this multinational state offered the best (and perhaps the only) safeguard against absorption and eventual submergence in a Greater Germany, as envisaged by the German liberals and nationalists of the Frankfurt Vorparlament (Pre-Parliament) of 1848–9 (and as achieved by Hitler in 1938–9). In the eyes of the Frankfurt and Bohemian Germans, the defunct Kingdom of Bohemia was just as much part of the Germanic world as was German Austria. Consequently, the German liberal-nationalist Vorparlament invited Frantisek Palacky, as the acknowledged Czech spokesman and leader, to take part in their deliberations. The invitation was sent in a fraternal rather than predatory or imperialistic spirit. Nevertheless, it elicited Palacky's famous frosty reply of 11 April 1848:

> I am unable, gentlemen, to accept your invitation . . . The object of your assembly is to establish a federation of the German nation in place of the existing [con]federation of princes, to guide the German nation to real unity . . . and in this manner expand the power and strength of the German Reich. Although I respect such effort and the sentiments upon which it is based, I cannot, precisely for the reason that I respect it, participate in it . . . I am not a German . . . I am a Bohemian of Slavonic blood. (Palacky 1948: 303–4)

Palacky maintained that the Czech nation had 'never regarded itself as pertaining to the German nation . . . The whole union of the Czech lands, first with the Holy Roman (German) Empire and then with the German confederation, was always a mere dynastic tie' (Palacky 1948: 304). The second reason for Palacky's unwillingness to participate in the German Vorparlament was that its implicit purpose was 'to undermine Austria as an independent empire and indeed to make her impossible for all time', whereas from his standpoint the Habsburg Monarchy was 'an empire whose preservation, integrity and consolidation is, and must be, a great and important matter not only for my own nation but also for the whole of Europe, indeed, for humanity and civilization itself' (p. 305).

Palacky warned that 'along the frontiers of the Russian Empire there live many nations widely differing in origin, in language, in history and morals – Slavs, Wallachians [Romanians], Magyars and Germans . . . Turks and Albanians – none of whom is sufficiently powerful to bid successful defiance to the superior neighbour on the East [Russia] for all time. They could do so only if a close and firm tie bound them all together as one. The vital artery of this necessary union of nations is the Danube. The focus of power of such a union must never be diverted far from this river, if the union is to be effective and remain so. Assuredly, if the Austrian state had not existed for ages, it would have been a behest for us in the interests of Europe and indeed of humanity to endeavour to create it' (Palacky 1948: 306). Playing upon European (and especially German) Russophobia, Palacky pointed out that the vast and almost impregnable Russian state was expanding 'decade by decade' and that its seemingly unstoppable expansion was threatening to establish 'a universal monarchy, that is to say, an infinite and inexpressible evil . . . such as I, though heart and soul a Slav, would nonetheless profoundly regret from the standpoint of humanity' (p. 305). Palacky denied that he was anti-Russian: 'On the contrary, I observe with pleasure and sympathy every step forward which that great nation makes within its natural borders along the path of civilization.' Nevertheless, 'the bare possibility of a universal Russian monarchy has no more determined opponent or foe than myself – not because that monarchy would be Russian but because it would be universal' (p. 305). However, the Habsburg Empire could remain a fully effective bulwark against external threats to East Central Europe and the Balkans only if it assumed a federalized form. In its own long-term interests, the Monarchy would have to accept 'the fundamental rule . . . that all the nationalities and all the religions under her sceptre should enjoy complete equality of rights and respect . . . Nature knows neither dominant nor underyoked nations. If the bond which unites a number of diverse nations in a single political entity is to be firm and enduring, no nation can have cause to fear that the union will cost it any of the things which it holds most dear. On the contrary, each must have the certain hope that in the central authority it will find defence and protection against possible violation by neighbours of the principles of equality' (p. 306).

Palacky's influential compatriot Karel Havlicek expressed a similar view in 1848: 'Complete independence for the Czechs at this time, when only tremendous empires are being formed in Europe, would be very unfortunate. We could not be anything but a very weak state, dependent upon other states, and our national existence would be constantly imperilled. On the other hand, in a close union with the other Slavs in Austria, we would enjoy a large measure of independence . . . and, at the same time, considerable advantages from the association with a powerful state. All we can do is to co-operate frankly and sincerely in building and maintaining the Habsburg Empire' (quoted by Kann 1950a: 166). Palacky provided further clarification of his so-called 'Austro-Slav' stance in 1864:

We Bohemians certainly wish sincerely for the preservation and unity of Austria. Considering that by our own efforts we could scarcely create an independent sovereign state, we can preserve our historico-political entity, our particular nationality and culture and, finally, our economic life nowhere and in no better way than we can in Austria. That means in a free Austria, organized on the basis of autonomy and equality. We have no hopes and no political perspectives beyond Austria. (quoted by Kann 1950b: 138)

Palacky saw the Habsburg Empire as an indispensable 'bulwark' against otherwise unchecked Russian or German or Magyar dominion over large swathes of East Central Europe and the Balkans and as a 'guardian of Europe against Asiatic elements of every possible type' (Palacky 1948: 306). Thus historical and geopolitical considerations obliged Palacky 'to turn, not to Frankfurt, but to Vienna, to seek there the centre which is fitted and predestined to ensure and defend the peace, the liberty and the rights of my nation. But *your* endeavours, gentlemen, seem now to me to be directed . . . not only towards ruinously undermining, but even utterly destroying, that centre to whose authority and strength I look for salvation . . . If Europe is to be saved, Vienna must not sink to the role of a provincial town. If there exist in Vienna people who ask to have Frankfurt as their capital, we can only cry: Lord, forgive them, for they know not what they ask!' (p. 307).

The notion of the Habsburg Empire as a 'European necessity' was also backed by Lord Palmerston, the longserving nineteenth-century British foreign secretary and prime minister. In 1848 he told the British House of Commons:

Austria is a most important element in the balance of European power. Austria stands in the centre of Europe, a barrier against encroachment on the one side and against invasion on the other. The political independence and the liberties of Europe are bound up, in my opinion, with the maintenance and integrity of Austria as a great European Power; and therefore anything which tends . . . to weaken Austria, but still more to reduce her from the position of a first-rate Power . . . must be a great calamity to Europe and one which every Englishman ought to deprecate and try to prevent'. (Bourne 1970: 296)

Similarly, on 27 June 1848 the Russian foreign minister Count Charles von Nesselrode stated that the void which the disappearance of the Habsburg Empire 'would create would be so enormous and the difficulty of filling it so great, that it ought to continue for a long time yet, given the lack of any-thing to put in its place' (quoted by Sked 1989: 18). In 1860 even Karl Marx acknowledged that 'the circumstance which legitimates the existence of Austria since the middle of the eighteenth century is its resistance to the advances of Russia in Eastern Europe' (quoted by Jaszi 1929: 9).

Palacky's open letter to the Frankfurt Parliament in 1848 served notice that, in Czech eyes, Bohemia and Moravia belonged to the Slavic rather than the Germanic world and that the western-most Slavs were no longer passively prepared to allow their fate to be decide by others. This in turn awakened both Bohemian and Austrian Germans to the fact that they could not blithely assume that their interests would happily and 'fraternally' coincide with those of the Czechs and that the Czechs would follow their lead. This heralded the underlying antagonism between the Czechs and both Bohemian German and Austrian German liberals which would increasingly bedevil both Bohemian and Austrian/imperial politics from the 1860s until the very end of the Habsburg Empire. That antagonism prevented the creation of a harmonious liberal alliance capable of transcending narrow nationalist interests and dashed any real hope of liberalizing, democratizing or federalizing the Monarchy and of reconciling the Czechs and Germans in Bohemia. It portended great dangers, not just for the peoples immediately affected, but eventually (in 1938–9) for Europe as a whole.

Nevertheless, Palacky's 'historicism' and idealism could conceivably have provided a practical basis for a mutually acceptable *modus vivendi* in Bohemia from 1848 onwards *if* the Czechs and the Bohemian Germans had been willing and able to work out their own local constitutional, cultural and economic arrangements in isolation from the wider imperial and Germanic worlds. Many Bohemian Germans, including members of the rich aristocracy, had had their fill of austere, arro-gant, restrictive and interfering Habsburg absolutism and were ready to make common cause with the conciliatory Czech leadership in the 1840s. When news of Metternich's fall reached Prague in mid-March 1848, it initially evoked profound feelings of hope, liberation and mutual goodwill.

In mid-March 1848 the Bohemian Diet, dominated by Germans and great landowners, took the lead in demanding the restoration of the so-called *Staatrecht* (right of autonomy) of the erstwhile Kingdom of Bohemia, as it had done already in 1846 (Bradley 1971: 124; Taylor 1976: 50). This demand was less radical than it sounds, as it would have further enhanced the dominant position of the Bohemian German privileged class. The Diet elected a so-called 'National Committee' which was quickly joined by Czech nationalist leaders. Together they sent a delegation to Vienna on 20 March 1848 to present their demands for a resurrection of Bohemian liberties and autonomy. However, these and a set of more radical demands presented at the end of March were nonchalantly shrugged off by the new imperial prime minister, Count Anton Kolovrat, himself a very rich Bohe-mian magnate. He merely offered formal linguistic parity for Czech and German in Bohemian schools and administration, which had already been achieved in practice.

THE SLAVONIC CONGRESS OF JUNE 1848 AND THE HABSBURG BOMBARDMENT OF PRAGUE

While they were in Vienna seeking a restoration of Bohemian autonomy in March 1848, members of the Czech delegation bumped into Slav petitioners from other parts of the empire. Together they came up with the idea of convoking an ('Austrian') Slavonic Congress. Contrary to common belief, this was originally intended to be more of an academic than a political gathering. Organized by lin-guists, writers and historians (including Palacky), it was summoned to discuss Slavonic philology, literature and (academic) theories of Slavonic unity. Profiting from the new freedom of speech and assembly, they invited about 150 Slavs of varying distinction to congregate in Prague in early June 1848 (Bradley 1971: 126). In the event, more than three hundred delegates from all the Slav nations except Bulgaria took part, turning it into a pan-Slavic rather than a narrowly Austro-Slavic congress (Macurek 1948: 329–30). Moreover, many participants turned up in national costume.

On 8 April 1848, meanwhile, Bohemia had received a charter granting administrative autonomy as well as full equality of Czech with German. On 29 May the imperial governor of Bohemia, Count Leo Thun, reacted to the accelerating decline of Viennese authority by establishing a de facto 'provisional government', composed of moderate Czechs and Bohemian Germans. This initially gained Habsburg approval and, but for an unexpected turn of events in Prague, it could conceivably have consummated the incipient restoration of Bohemian autonomy (Taylor 1976: 68).

The opening session of the Slavonic Congress in Prague on 2 June 1848 passed off largely without incident. Meeting in the 'eye' of the 1848 Revolutions, however, the congress could not avoid getting drawn into politics. It produced two major political documents. One, a loyal Address to the Emperor, detailed the autonomist demands of his Slav subjects and vehemently denounced pan-German and German liberal calls for a Greater Germany (including large chunks of the Habsburg Empire). The other, a more radical Manifesto of the First Slavonic Congress to the Nations of Europe, contrasted the conquering martial traditions of 'the Latin and Germanic nations' with the allegedly pacific and libertarian traditions of the Slavs (conveniently overlooking Tsarist militarism and expansionism and the military exploits of the medieval Polish, Serb and Bulgarian kingdoms). 'We Slavs reject and hold in abhorrence all dominion based on main force [*force majeure*] and evasion of the law; we reject all privileges and prerogatives . . . We demand unconditional equality before the law, an equal measure of rights and duties for all.' The Manifesto also announced that the Slavonic Congress had 'proposed to the Austrian Emperor, under whose constitutional rule the majority of us live, that the imperial state be converted into a federation of nations all enjoying equal rights'. At the very least, the Slavs ought to gain 'the same rights . . . as the German and Magyar nations already enjoy'. In addition, the Manifesto called for an end to the tripartite partition of Poland and the 'inhuman and violent' treatment of the various Slav inhabitants of the Kingdom of Hungary. It asked the Austrian Germans, Prussia and Saxony to accord their Slav subjects greater dignity and respect. It demanded that the Slavic subjects of the Ottoman Empire 'be enabled to give free play to their national aspirations in state form'. Finally, it proposed 'that a general European Congress of Nations be summoned for the discussion of all international questions'. (A full English translation of the Manifesto was published in Beardmore (1948), from which these quotations are taken.)

However, while this Slavonic Congress called for the 'liberty, fraternity and equality of all nations' and the liberty and equal rights of all individuals, irrespective of nationality, most of the prominent German and Magyar nationalists and liberals of 1848 continued to think in terms of *supremacy* and *overlordship* over the other peoples of East Central Europe and the northern Balkans, upheld most of the existing *privileges* of the propertied classes, subscribed to a *hierarchy* of nations, and scorned or sneered at the loftier aspirations of the Slavonic Congress.

Further sessions of the Slavonic Congress were planned to discuss closer co-operation between the 'Austrian' Slavs. Since late May, however, Prague had been subject to heavy-handed policing by rather 'jumpy' imperial forces commanded by Prince Alfred Windischgrätz, who made provocative public pronouncements and placed heavy artillery on the heights overlooking the city centre. Moreover, despite its largely apolitical orientation, the Czech 'revival' had engendered a highly charged cultural ferment which intensified the excited and expectant atmosphere in Bohemia in 1848. On 12 June, following a peaceful rally and mass in the central (now St Wenceslas) square, scuffles broke out between students and the troops who were patrolling the streets. The military over-reacted, barricades sprang up and Prague was engulfed in six days of bloody street fighting, which was only brought to an end by several hours of heavy artillery bombardment of the city centre on 17 June. Windischgrätz became the first 'hero' of the Counter-Revolution (before Radetzky in August), and even the Frankfurt Vorparlament considered sending troops to assist in putting down the revolt (Taylor 1976: 70).

The Slavonic Congress was disbanded and Prague was placed under martial law, tying down troops who were more needed elsewhere. Convinced that the initial clashes (which his own heavy-handedness had provoked) were the work of Czech agitators and revolutionaries, Windischgrätz instigated a witch-hunt for the (non-existent) 'ringleaders' and detained ninety-four 'suspects'. The Slavonic Congress held in Prague in June 1848 led many Austrian and Bohemian Germans to see the Slavs as traitors, ingrates and potential threats to the survival of the Habsburg Empire and of their own variously privileged positions within it (Rath 1957: 255, 258). 'Germans in Bohemia denounced the Congress as high treason. After this display of Slavic unity they were . . . convinced that only a close union with Germany could save them from Slav domination' (p. 260). Behind Slav solidarity, Austrian and Bohemian Germans saw the spectre of Russian imperialism (p. 254). Furthermore, when South Slavs started referring to Austrian Germans as 'oppressors' and criticized the primacy of German in Slovene and Croatian secondary schools, such 'impertinence' from an 'inferior race' drew Austrian German ripostes that only Germans and instruction in German could initiate Slavs into 'the great cultural community of central Europe' (p. 257).

Elections to an Austrian constituent assembly were held in July 1848, while Prague was still under martial law. Oafish Windischgrätz claimed that martial law made the elections much freer, even though one duly elected Czech deputy was subsequently arrested as an alleged 'insurrectionist'. To cap it all, the German 'liberal' majority in the Austrian constituent assembly refused even to discuss Czech proposals for limited Bohemian autonomy. Czech leaders viewed these rebuffs 'as national discrimination, or even persecution' (Bradley 1971: 127). In May 1849, finally, there was a further witch-hunt against Czech students and radicals (alleged 'conspirators'), many of whom were sentenced to long prison terms or driven into exile in western Europe. Other Czechs emigrated to the USA, forming the nucleus of a later significant community of Czech-Americans.

THE REVOLUTIONS OF 1848–9 IN VIENNA

At the nerve centre of the Habsburg Empire, meanwhile, the fall of Metternich on 13 March 1848 had resulted in a succession of supposedly 'liberal' constitutionalist governments headed by Count Franz Anton Kolowrat (17 March–4 April), Count Karl Ficquelmont (4 April–3 May), Baron Franz von Pillersdorf (3 May–8 July) and Baron Johann von Wessenberg (19 July–20 November). None of them was able to assert much authority, either inside or outside Vienna. All four proved too slow, hidebound and hesitant to deliver timely and satisfactory constitutional concessions and practical reforms. Thus they repeatedly lost the political initiative to impatient and exasperated radicals, who temporarily succeeded in pushing many Austrian German townspeople leftward and towards direct action. Consequently there were several successive waves of revolution in Vienna in 1848, each more radical than its precursor.

In mid-March 1848 there was a liberal-constitutionalist revolution, which was to a considerable extent engineered and stage-managed by fractious anti-Metternich elements within the ruling classes (including several Habsburg archdukes and Archduchess Sophie, the scheming mother of Franz Josef). They manipulated public hostility towards Metternich for their own ends, as a means of extracting very limited constitutional concessions and changes of personnel (little more than a 'changing of the guard'). Remarkably, almost nothing was done to avert the 13 March demonstrations and riots that toppled Metternich (Rath 1957: 55). This averted a potential bloodbath. What is more, the Habsburgs proved only too willing to make a scapegoat of their most unpopular minister, who was not as powerful as many people believed, while his old rivals and protégés were ready and waiting to step into his shoes. However, some of the supposed 'liberals' were in fact conservatives who merely envied or resented Metternich's power and influence and wished to take his place.

The declared aims and concerns of the Austrian German 'liberals' on the eve of their March 1848 Revolution were remarkably limited. Since the 1830s a crescendo of 'liberal' criticism of the Metternich regime had found various means of expression via foreign publications, especially in books and newspapers which were published in the German states and illegally imported and circulated among the well-educated propertied classes, in circumvention of the Austrian censors and police surveillance (Rath 1957: 10–11, 19–31). Oppositional literature was discussed and circulated by 'liberal' clubs, which developed very close links with the Lower Austrian Diet, the liberal nobility, some state functionaries and the Lower Austrian Manufacturers' Association (pp. 28–32). Before 1848, however, 'none of the . . . "liberal" writers . . . expressed a desire for a constitution, a bill of rights, popular sovereignty or a genuine "liberal" parliament' (p. 27). No one was demanding freedom from search, freedom of assembly, abolition of the monarchy or ministerial accountability to a directly elected parliament (p. 44). 'Except for Archduke Louis, no member of the imperial family was attacked . . . In all the oppositional literature, not once was a demand made for revolution' (Rath 1957: 27). Austria's 'liberal' opposition was only calling for religious toleration, a relaxation of censorship and police powers, freedom of trade(s), abolition of monopolies, decentralization of government, consultative assemblies and more competent ministers (Sked 1989: 53–5).

In 1848, like their counterparts elsewhere in Europe, Austrian 'liberals' wanted neither popular sovereignty nor universal rights of political participation. On the contrary, they desired a constitution which would enhance the rights and privileges of the 'respectable' propertied classes by guaranteeing them the prerogative of co-operating with the monarch in making laws and approving taxes and by prohibiting royal violations of their rights as property-owning, tax-paying and law-abiding subjects. Thus 'the moderate liberals of the March revolution . . . merely wanted a parliament of property-holders to check the Emperor's absolute powers and advise him on legislation' (Rath 1957: 3–4, 194). Austria's burgeoning middle class, believing that they had 'the brains, the know-how and the money' required by the state, deeply resented their continued exclusion from privilege and high society. 'They yearned to replace the absolutist state with a liberal monarchy over which they could exercise considerable control' (p. 16). Yet neither the haute bourgeoisie, which looked to the state for ennoblements and protection, nor the professional and functionary classes, which looked to the state for employment, pensions and subsidized education, were particularly revolutionary. But a major problem for these middle classes was that the expansion of higher education had far outstripped the state's capacity to provide white-collar employment for graduates. This gave rise to large numbers of unemployed graduates and disaffected students, creating an impoverished, alienated and radicalized intelligentsia (Sked 1989: 78–80). Such people would do their best to push the 1848 Revolutions further to the left, in Austria as in other parts of central and eastern Europe.

On 15 March 1848, having finally agreed to convoke a representative assembly which would negotiate a constitution, Emperor Ferdinand was cheered and 'serenaded' by immense crowds gathered in Joseph Square. That night there were great torchlit processions through the city, which was ablaze with lights. 'Thousands of people – Germans, Hungarians, Italians, Bohemians, Poles and Jews – jostled each other in brotherly harmony to celebrate the dawn of a new freedom. Total strangers embraced one another on the streets and joined in singing' (Rath 1957: 86–7). The carnival atmosphere continued the next day, when Kossuth successfully negotiated self-government for Hungary and was carried shoulder-high through the streets of Vienna. (The general euphoria prefigured the scenes of jubilation in Berlin and Prague in November and December 1989, when the Communist dictatorships collapsed.) 'All classes of malcontents had worked together to bring on the revolution' (p. 88). Yet as soon as the propertied 'liberals' had gained what they wanted, they immediately initiated mass arrests of the lower-class radicals, rioters and demonstrators who had helped them to secure the resignation of Metternich and the promise of an assembly to draw up a constitution. By the night of 15 March the jails were already full to overflowing (p. 88). As far as the 'liberal' propertied classes were concerned, the March Revolution had served its purpose and they began to fear that the 'moderate' political revolution which they had initiated might slip out of their control and lead to a more violent social revolution. So they threw their weight behind efforts to restore law and order. 'They now wanted peace and stability so that they could reconstruct society in accordance with their interpretation of the revolutionary idea and . . . take full advantage of the privileges they believed the revolution had assured them' (Rath 1957: 4, 88, 224). After the Revolution lurched to the left on 15 and 29 May, moreover, large numbers of 'liberals' defected to the 'ultra-conservative camp' (p. 274).

However, the radical intelligentsia, university students and Vienna's 'under-privileged' classes felt increasingly cheated, slighted and alienated. They even felt 'betrayed' by the new government's acts of repression, by the lack of further reform, by the filling of government posts with stalwarts of the previous regime and by Emperor Ferdinand's decisions to 'grant' (unilaterally) a very limited and elitist constitution (on 25 April) and a very restrictive electoral law (on 11 May), in contravention of his promises to convoke a representative body which would freely determine the constitution. Ferdinand also upset a widespread assumption and expectation that this body would be elected on a broad franchise, even though he had never promised that.

On 15 May 1848, amid mounting popular unrest and major political confrontations between the supposedly 'liberal' government and both the (student) Academic Legion and the (burgher) National Guard, 'the radical democrats, who believed in popular sovereignty, were victorious over the moderate liberals of the March Revolution. The radicals had won recognition of the principles of universal suffrage and popular sovereignty, in that the Emperor and the government had been forced to agree to submit "the Emperor's constitution" to a democratically elected parliament for alteration as it saw fit' (Rath 1957: 194).

On 17 May, ostensibly fearing for Ferdinand's safety, the royal family evacuated him and his wife to Innsbruck. For many conservatives and property-owners the news that the Habsburg Emperor had been 'forced to flee' from his capital was a cause for alarm, but other people (including the government) felt let down, betrayed or even affronted. It certainly helped to polarize public opinion, while his subsequent reluctance to return to Vienna further reduced the popular esteem and affection which 'Ferdi the Benevolent' had hitherto enjoyed (despite many harsh or unkind judgements on the emperor's debilitating epilepsy).

A bungled government attempt to suppress the (student) Academic Legion on 25 May rallied National Guardsmen, workers and parts of the lower middle class to the students' defence. This led to the establishment of a more effective organ of 'people's power', a revolutionary Committee of Citizens, National Guards and Students, popularly known as the Security Committee (or Committee of Public Safety). From 26 May to 23 August the students and their proletarian and petit bourgeois allies were 'the recognized leaders of Vienna. Their Security Committee watched over every move of the authorities and superintended the police and the military' (Rath 1957: 218). The government was implicitly reduced to the status of an interim 'caretaker administration', with rapidly dwindling authority over other parts of the Habsburg Empire. By mid-summer there were in effect separate governments for German Austria, Bohemia, Moravia, Galicia, Hungary, Croatia, Lombardy and Venetia, while Austrian German allegiances were divided between the government, Vienna's Security Committee, the Court Camarilla at Innsbruck, the duly elected Austrian constituent assembly and the German National Assembly in Frankfurt.

The crucial task which Vienna's Security Committee had to set itself, in view of its radical (partly 'utopian socialist') ideology and its need of lower-class support, was to alleviate the mounting unemployment, dwindling food supplies, soaring living costs and deepening destitution of Vienna's lower classes. It therefore established a Labour Committee to expand the public works projects on the Prater and along the Danube and the Wien which the 'liberals' had initiated in March 1848 to relieve politically dangerous poverty and unemployment. But the projects soon brought themselves and the Revolution into disrepute. 'Much of the work, the cost of which was borne by the city, was useless. More and more workers were occupied with the pointless earthworks in the Prater. They were poorly supervised and . . . workers were quick to learn that they could earn a day's wage by doing little more than report for work' (Rath 1957: 220). By early June these projects were employing more than 20,000 people (over a fifth of Vienna's workforce) and drawing workers away from cash-strapped private workshops and factories. Attempts to bring the escalating costs and abuses under control provoked mass protests on 15–17 June and 21–23 August. These were suppressed by National and Civic Guards, fatally fracturing the fragile unity of the radical coalition. The public works programme ultimately failed its intended beneficiaries and alienated its former well-wishers. Within Vienna this fairly comprehensive failure probably sealed the fate of the 1848 Revolution. Yet the experiment was probably doomed from the outset, given the disruptive effects of the Revolution on markets, business confidence, revenues and labour discipline, the intermittent destruction of factories, machinery and property, and Vienna's increasing inability either to assure or pay for essential supplies of food and raw materials, underlining the impossibility of ('utopian') 'socialism in one city'.

Austria's long-awaited constituent assembly (elected on a broad but indirect franchise in June) finally opened on 22 July 1848. It fully exposed the inner contradictions of the Habsburg Empire. Its legitimacy and competence as an imperial institution were inevitably compromised by the fact that Hungary, Lombardy and Venetia were not (and did not want to be!) represented in it, while the Austrian and Bohemian Germans had already elected deputies to the German National Assembly in Frankfurt, which had opened on 18 May and was supposed to be negotiating either a federal or a confederal constitution for a 'united Germany' (including German Austria and, despite Czech objections, Bohemia). Moreover, almost half the Austrian Reichstag deputies were Slavs, who initially objected to the official assumption that parliamentary debate would be conducted exclusively in German. A substantial number of Slav deputies knew little or no German. Furthermore, 25 per cent of the deputies were peasants, rather than more educated and bilingual townspeople. However, since German was the only feasible lingua franca, the Slavs eventually relented on condition that all proceedings be translated into the mother-tongues of the non-German deputies, severely slowing up the assembly's business! Another problem was the over-representation of the bourgeoisie (60 per cent of all deputies) and the corresponding under-representation of other social classes. This multi-ethnic assembly also wasted much of its time bickering over the order of business and the composition of committees (Rath 1957: 274–9).

The upshot of all this was the (perhaps inevitable) failure of the constituent assembly to seize the political initiative, live up to expectations or gain much public confidence and support. Moreover, the lesson that the multi-ethnic Habsburg Empire was perhaps not really governable on the West European 'liberal' (constitutional monarchy) model lowered Austrian German resistance to the restoration of Habsburg absolutism. This formally took place on 7 March 1849, when the Reichstag was forcibly dissolved by the new 'strong man' Prince Felix Schwarzenberg (who had been prime minister of Austria since 21 November 1848). Schwarzenberg's *coup d'état* evoked barely a whimper of protest, partly because the constituent assembly had already marginalized itself by withdrawing from Vienna to Kromeriz (Kremsier) in Moravia to escape the hazards of the violent Viennese uprising which began on 6 October 1848.

THE FINAL DISSOLUTION OF SERFDOM, 1848–50

The most important legislation enacted by the short-lived Austrian Reichstag was the Act of Peasant Emancipation, passed on 7 September 1848. This has long been regarded as 'the greatest achievement of the Revolutions of 1848–49' (Taylor 1976: 72). Indeed, these revolutions occurred in predominantly peasant societies, whose only irresistible force was the peasants' desire be free of the *Robot* (compulsory labour services to landlords) and other 'feudal dues'. This elemental force ran along different channels from urban radicalism. Moreover, 'the peasant revolt against the *Robot* made their lords revolutionary as well, or at least unreliable supporters of imperial authority'. Even the loyalty of the magnates was shaken once the implicit bargain between them and the Habsburgs was broken. The Monarchy had not kept the peasants down, so the landed classes looked around for new allies (p. 57). Indeed, since 1846 the Austrian and Hungarian ruling classes had been dreading possible recurrences of the kind of peasant jacquerie that had ravaged Austrian Poland in February and March of that year.

Nevertheless, the Peasant Emancipation Act was little more than a formal endorsement and elaboration of an imperial manifesto of 11 April 1848, which promised 'to liberate the peasants from all services and dues incumbent on the land by 1 January 1849' (Rath 1957: 127). On 24 September 1848 about twenty-thousand people (including many peasants from surrounding areas) paraded through Vienna in celebration of the 'abolition of serfdom'. Many radical democrats blithely assumed that, since they had been instrumental in 'giving' the former serfs their freedom, the peasantry would in turn gratefully back them in their own (characteristically urban) radical demands (p. 316). But the urban radicals were to be bitterly disappointed and this sense of disappointment (allied to mutual incomprehension and differing agendas) would later bedevil relations between peasant and urban radical movements, culminating in the fateful mutual suspicion, mistrust and recrimination between peasant and Marxist parties in Eastern Europe from the 1900s to the 1940s. In the event many peasants felt disappointed with (or even cheated by) the limited scope and hard-nosed terms of the 1848 Emancipation Act and the persistence of some forms of 'feudal' dependence on big landowners. They especially resented the indignity and hardships of having to pay for some of their new 'freedoms' and the land allotted to them (particularly since their former 'masters' received partial compensation for loss of services, income and land), while the big landed estates remained largely intact and continued to account for nearly half of all farmland, instead of being broken up and distributed among the peasants and farm labourers who had worked them for centuries. Moreover, the failure to allot any land at all to cottars and farm 'servants'/labourers gave these groups more reason to feel anger rather than gratitude towards the constituent assembly radicals and 'liberals'. On the other hand, those peasants who *were* satisfied by the scope and terms of the emancipation act felt less gratitude to the constituent assembly than to the Habsburg emperor, for it was his manifesto of 11 April 1848 that first proclaimed the imminent abolition of serfdom and it was 'his' officials who implemented it. The contented sections of the peasantry 'lost all interest in continuing the revolution' and favoured the restoration of law and order (p. 127). By late September most peasants were 'probably indifferent to the outcome of the revolution' (p. 316), since it had moved in directions and on to an agenda in which they could have little direct interest or role. Some, especially the 'loyalist' Austrian German Catholic peasantry, were decidedly 'hostile to the radicals' (pp. 120, 316).

Either way, by delivering the *coup de grâce* against serfdom and temporarily defusing the agrarian question and the class struggle between the peasantry and the landed nobility, the Emancipation Act diminished the peasants' interest in continuing the Revolution. Thenceforth, the centre of gravity of imperial politics shifted from class struggle to inter-ethnic or 'national' struggles or, in other words, to a political terrain that was to be much more congenial to the right than to the left, to 'reaction' rather than 'revolution' or 'reform'. For several decades this gave East Central European politics a powerful push to the right.

Nevertheless, in Austria as in Hungary, the Peasant Emancipation Act 'swept away the underpinnings upon which the economy of most noble landowners had rested'. The latter forfeited the goods, services and cash dues hitherto provided by 'their' peasants, as well as their former tax exemptions and parts of their landed estates. 'Their indemnification fell short of compensating them for their material losses, and was further reduced by declines in the value of indemnification bonds' (Blum 1978: 425). Their difficulties were compounded by noble nonchalance, extravagance and lack of entrepreurial expertise and business acumen. 'The high grain prices of the 1850s and 1860s enabled most of them to survive despite their inefficiency.' However, when international grain prices fell in the face of growing competition from cheap American and Russian grain in the 1870s and 1880s, the Austro-Hungarian estate-owners' financial losses multiplied. Many had to sell all or parts of their estates or lost them to creditors (p. 426). Moreover, the loss of their seigneurial role 'stripped the concept of nobility of its essential meaning' (p. 419). For centuries the official pretext for the privileges and prerogatives of the landed nobility had rested on their supposed care and responsibility for the peasants in their charge, but the emancipation acts largely transferred these powers and functions to the state. Furthermore, the emancipation acts made everyone (at least nom-inally) equal before the law. There was to be one law for all subjects, holding out the prospect of 'equal civil, personal and property rights' for all, although many inequities persisted in practice (p. 440). For example, the mobility and civil rights of farm 'servants'/labourers were severely restricted in Hungary well into the twentieth century (p. 430). However, 'these lingering relics of times past were destined to disappear', as the individual gained increased freedom to choose an occupation and a marriage partner, to move about at will, to sign contracts, to buy and sell goods and services and to do as he or (sometimes) she wished with his or (very rarely) her property (pp. 440–1). At the same time, the emancipation acts gave a powerful new impetus to the undermining and dissolution of the time-honoured bases of power, authority, hierarchy, deference and obedience in East Central Europe, which culminated in the collapse of the Habsburg Empire in 1918.

THE POLITICAL POLARIZATION OF VIENNA, 1848–9

Meanwhile, the fragile unity of the radical democratic coalition in Vienna had been ruptured when Civic and National Guards, who had hitherto formed part of that coalition, savagely suppressed workers' protests against wage cuts (on the public works projects) on 23 August 1848. This 'bloody act of treachery', as workers and radicals saw it, also temporarily reasserted the tenuous authority of the 'liberal' government which had ordered the wage cuts and the Guards' repression of the ensuing protests.

Faced with the gathering strength of the (regrouped) counter-revolutionary forces after 23 August (and not just in Vienna but also in Bohemia and northern Italy), there emerged a desperate (almost Quixotic) 'last ditch' attempt by an increasingly beleaguered radical minority (drawn from the intelligentsia, the lower middle class, the students, the civil militias, the Vienna garrison and the working class) to save the increasingly imperilled 'revolutionary gains' by seizing control of Vienna from 6 to 31 October 1848.

There was no longer any middle ground by October. Hence either the radicals had to triumph or the reactionaries would do so. This was 'make or break' time. The catalysts of Vienna's 'October Revolution' were the menacing 'pincer' movements of the Croatian royalist forces commanded by Jelacic, Bohemian royalist forces commanded by Windischgrätz, and the Habsburgs' northern Italian forces commanded by Radetzky, plus the 'liberal' government's attempt to make the politi-cally divided grenadiers of the Vienna garrison join in the counter-revolutionary offensive against Kossuth's Hungary in early October 1848. A potent underlying factor in this October insurrection was, however, Vienna's accelerating economic collapse. By late September major segments of Vienna's lower middle and working classes were experiencing acute hardship, bordering on starva-tion (Rath 1957: 320). The insurrection began with a mutiny of Vienna's Richter battalion on the morning of 6 October, after it had been ordered to march against the Magyars. The mutineers were supported by radicals, students and disaffected workers and Guardsmen, who went on a rampage which culminated in the gruesome murder and mutilation of War Minister Latour later that day.

On 7 October 1848 Emperor Ferdinand, who had eventually returned to Vienna on 12 August, fled to Moravia, where he was soon followed (at a respectful distance) by most of the 'liberal' government, much of the constituent assembly and many senior bureaucrats, virtually abandoning Vienna to the rebels. Nevertheless, despite the unrest and near starvation in Vienna, 'there was little robbery or plundering'. This was testimony to 'the great respect of even the most extreme radicals for property rights'. However, no one knew what to do. 'Everyone was issuing orders simultaneously, but nobody wanted to obey anyone else . . . Courage was no substitute for leadership' (Rath 1957: 339). A last-minute Magyar attempt to relieve the rebels and break the Habsburg siege of Vienna on 30 October was easily defeated (pp. 356–7). The Viennese rebels were finally forced to surrender on 31 October by a combination of military encirclement, hunger and thirst. Many townspeople greeted the triumphant Habsburg forces as 'liberators', not only from the hunger and thirst, but also from the reign of terror unleashed by some despairing rebels during the last days of the siege (pp. 351–3). Windischgrätz then imposed censorship and martial law, prohibited political clubs and public meetings, placed more than two thousand people in political detention and executed nine of the rebel leaders (pp. 363–4). His brother-in-law, Prince Felix Schwarzenberg, launched a new government of conservative 'loyalists' and renegade 'liberals' on 21 November, persuaded Emperor Ferdinand to abdicate in favour of his eighteen-year-old nephew Franz Josef on 2 December and dissolved the constituent assembly on 7 March, with a soon-broken promise that a new constitution drawn up by the new government would come into effect when the emergency ended (pp. 364–5). The counter-revolutionaries could now turn their full attention to Hungary, where the Magyar nationalist revolution was decisively defeated in August 1849, snuffing out the (forlorn) 'last hope' of the 1848 radicals.

THE FATEFUL FISSURE: GERMANS VERSUS SLAVS

The central reason why the 1848 Revolutions within German Austria and Bohemia neither developed to the same degree as their counterparts in Hungary and northern Italy nor achieved anything as tangible as the overthrow of the monarchy in France lay in the inability of the major protagonists in German Austria and Bohemia to unite around a common overarching goal, or to share a single clearly identifiable focus. Magyar and Italian radicals were in broad agreement on the paramount aim of self-government, whether within or without the Habsburg Monarchy, while in France there was almost unanimous applause at the abdication of King Louis Philippe. But the emergence of a pan-German National Assembly at Frankfurt in the spring of 1848 confronted most Austrian and Bohemian Germans with very difficult choices between Greater Germany and Greater Austria, between pan-Germanism and a supranational Habsburg Empire. Their unwillingness and/or inability to make a clear-cut choice between these two alternatives gave their political behaviour a fatal hesitancy and indecisiveness in 1848–9. This in turn allowed the Habsburg civil and military authorities to make the choice for them, in favour of a Greater Austria and a forceful reassertion of Habsburg absolutism.

The Austrian Revolutions of 1848–9 also failed because they helped to polarize rather than harmonize national sentiments and aspirations within the Austro-Hungarian Empire. The various political factions in Vienna in 1848 were united in their hostility to the Czechs, even though the Czechs merely aspired to 'the same liberties the Viennese had gained during the March revolution' (Rath 1957: 145). The subsequent granting of autonomy and equality of Czech with German in Bohemia 'deeply angered' the Austrian Germans who were aspiring to 'a German empire that was to embrace all the lands of the historic Holy Roman Empire. They could not comprehend how any sensible people could voluntarily decline to share the future in store for the German race' (p. 146).

During the spring and early summer of 1848, with Hungary and Bohemia reasserting their autonomy, northern Italy in the throes of secession and a few Poles plotting against the 'Partitioning Powers', many Austrian and Bohemian Germans concluded that they had little to lose and much to gain from a 'united Germany'. They cared little about the effects that such an *Anschluss* (union) with other German states would have on the non-German nationalities of the Habsburg Empire. Moreover, the 'vast majority of the Viennese' considered the revolutionary concessions gained in Germany to be 'their own' and the creation of the German National Assembly in Frankfurt to be the prelude to the establishment of their own constituent assembly and Reichstag. For many Austrian Germans 'the liberal reforms . . . in Austria were of secondary importance to those . . . in Germany. In this sense the Viennese Revolution of 1848 was as much a German as an Austrian revolution.' This was particularly true of the Viennese students and radicals, many of whom were 'ardent proponents of union with Germany'. They wanted Austria to merge with other German lands in order to create 'a single democratic state comprising all the German-speaking peoples in central Europe' (Rath 1957: 133, 251). Thus they could make common cause with Italian and Magyar radicals and nationalists against the Habsburgs because they fully expected and accepted the secession of northern Italy and Hungary. Yet Austrian and Bohemian German radicals were also among the most militant, obdurate and inconsiderate German nationalists and chauvinists vis-à-vis the Czechs and the South Slavs, who did not relish the prospect of even a democratic Greater Germany (pp. 145–53, 255–66).

On the whole, 'Austro-Germans were incapable of understanding that, to non-Germans, "freedom" meant freedom from age-old German domination as well as from absolutism. Their feelings of superiority prevented them from admitting that the aspirations of subject nationalities for freedom were as natural and as honest as the longings of the Germans for political liberation' (Rath 1957: 267). Such attitudes and blind spots help to explain the subsequent deterioration in inter-ethnic relations within the 'Austrian half' of the Habsburg Empire. They also sowed the seeds of the crimes committed against the Slavs of East Central Europe and the Balkans by Hitler, the Nazis and disproportionately large numbers of Austrian and Bohemian Germans between 1938 and 1945. In relation to the Poles, the Czechs and the South Slavs, the eminent Anglo-Hungarian historian Sir Lewis Namier maintained that the German 'liberals' and nationalists of 1848 were 'in reality forerunners of Hitler' (Namier 1946: 33).

The 1848 Revolutions and the 'coming of age' of German nationalism thus confronted Austrian Germans with a fateful dilemma which contributed significantly not only to the defeat of these revolutions, but also to the collapse of the Habsburg Empire in 1918, to the demise of the 'first' Austrian Republic in 1938, and to the dismemberment of Czechoslovakia in 1938–9. As Germans, did they want to become full participants in a united German Reich? Or did they prefer to preserve and pursue their distinctively 'Austrian' identity, interests and statehood? This dilemma was not finally resolved until 1945–6, when 'Austrians' found it expedient to bury and forget their longstanding demands for *Anschluss* with Germany, in a remarkable fit (or feat) of 'collective amnesia' and an attempt to disassociate themselves from the crimes of Nazi Germany, to which Hitler and countless other Austrians had so strongly contributed. The Revolutions of 1848–9 and the attendant 'flowering' of German nationalism posed an analogous dilemma for the Bohemian (alias 'Sudeten') Germans. Their dilemma was only resolved in the end by the expulsion of more than three million Bohemian/Sudeten Germans from the Czech Lands in 1945–6. The purpose of highlighting these long-term consequences of the emergence of pan-German 'ethnic' nationalism as a major political force from 1848 to 1945 is not to encourage (let alone to endorse) 'Germanophobia', but to emphasize the frequently horrific and often unintended effects of 'ethnic' nationalism in the multi-ethnic mosaic of East Central Europe and the Balkans. The ultimately devastating effects of the rise of pan-German 'ethnic' nationalism were (to be precise) the most momentous manifestations of a more general problem, rather than a specific expression of 'German national character' (if there is such a thing). On smaller scales (because they involve much smaller nations), Magyar, Croat and more recently Serbian 'ethnic' nationalisms have produced similar consequences, while Bulgarian, Romanian, Albanian, Greek, Turkish, Slovak and Polish 'ethnic' nationalisms have sometimes manifested the potential to do so.

In 1848 even the Habsburgs were torn between their Germanic 'mission' and their Danubian 'destiny'. On 29 June 1848 the German National Assembly in Frankfurt resolved (by 436 votes to 85) to nominate the popular Habsburg Archduke Johann as 'imperial regent' of the (stillborn) 'united Germany'. Yet, on 22 July 1848, the same Habsburg Archduke opened the Austrian constituent assembly in Vienna. He thus became the formal president of two rival constituent assemblies, relating to two very different polities. Always with an eye to the main chance, the Habsburgs were in a sense hedging their bets. Indeed, court circles and Viennese radicals and 'liberals' shared a belief that the remodelling of the Habsburg Empire should be carried out 'in accordance with the wishes of the "master nations"'. Indeed, Austrian German 'liberals' and radicals assumed that the Habsburg Empire was 'a German state which would also play the chief part in a new liberal Germany, and they pressed as strongly for elections to the German national assembly in Frankfurt as for a constituent assembly in Austria' (Taylor 1976: 63).

However, Austria's privileged property-owning 'liberals' and conservatives were already questioning whether Austria would really be better placed as a border province of a united Greater Germany than as the metropolitan core of its own multinational Danubian empire. The Austrian 'liberal' government voiced its reservations in the *Wiener Zeitung* as early as 21 April 1848: 'Filled with the desire to have a close union with Germany, Austria will gladly seize any opportunity to prove its loyalty to the common German cause. However, it can never completely renounce the special interests of the different parts of its territory . . . It cannot approve any unqualified submission to the assembly of the German confederation or give up its independence in internal administration . . . In so far as this is irreconcilable with the nature of a confederation, Austria is not in a position to join one' (quoted by Rath 1957: 139–40). Metropolitan Vienna and Austria's propertied classes certainly had more to lose than to gain from a unified 'Greater Germany', but it took them a while to accept that they could not both *have* their *Kuchen* (cake) and eat it.

17 The empire strikes back: counter-revolution, neo-absolutism and reform in the Habsburg Monarchy, 1849–1918

THE ETHNIC AND TERRITORIAL CONFIGURATION OF AUSTRIA-HUNGARY, 1850s–1914

In 1910 this sprawling, mountainous, ramshackle empire extended over 257,478 square miles, making it Europe's second largest state (only Tsarist Russia was larger). Its 50 million inhabitants comprised thirteen significant 'nationalities' or national groupings. No ethnic group was dominant in numerical terms, as the following division shows: Germans, 22 per cent; Magyars (Hungarians), 18 per cent; Czechs, 12 per cent; Poles, 10 per cent; Ruthenes/Ukrainians, 8 per cent; Romanians, 6 per cent; Jews, 5–6 per cent; Croats, 5 per cent; Serbs, 4 per cent; Slovaks, 4 per cent; Slovenes, 3 per cent; Italians, 2 per cent; and Bosnian Muslims, 1 per cent (Kann 1974: 606–7). These official statistics have been rounded and adjusted slightly to allow for the Jews, who were not an officially recognized 'nationality' and were mostly lumped in with the Germans and Magyars. The numbers of Jews can be roughly surmised from the census returns on religious affiliations, in which Roman Catholic dominance clearly stands out: Roman Catholics (including 'Uniates', alias Ukrainian Catholics of the Orthodox rite), 77 per cent; Protestants, 9 per cent; Jews, 4 per cent; and Muslims, 1 per cent (Kann 1974: 607–8). Significant numbers of Jews had converted to Christianity or, especially if they were Marxists, had become atheists. Therefore Jews must have made up rather more than 4 per cent of the population. In the Habsburg Empire Jews were exceptionally prominent in the business community and in the liberal professions, especially law, medicine and the press, and they contributed powerfully to the development of capitalism, liberalism, Marxism, intellectual life in general and publishing. However, their glittering successes in these fields tragically made them favourite targets of Austrian reactionaries, racists and malcontents, sowing the seeds of the 1939–45 Holocaust. The two largest ethnic groups, the Germans in the west and the Magyars (Hungarians) in the east, were substantially outnumbered by their Slav subjects (Czechs, Slovaks, Poles, Ruthenes, Croats, Serbs, Slovenes and Bosnian Muslims), who altogether made up 46 per cent of the empire's population.

The 'Austrian' half of the empire comprised an untidy agglomeration of disparate territories which had been fully subjugated and brought under direct Viennese rule by the Austrian Habsburgs over a span of several centuries. At the heart of these Austrian 'Crownlands' (*Kronländer*) lay German Austria (*Deutsch Österreich*: the 'German Eastern Realm'). This included semi-industrial Lower Austria (capital Vienna), agrarian Upper Austria (capital Linz), semi-industrial Styria (capital Graz) and the Alpine, extensively forested and predominantly pastoral Western Lands (the Tyrol, Salzburg, Vorarlberg and Carinthia). The nobility, the officials and the burghers of German Austria dominated the western-cum-northern half of the empire in partnership with the Roman Catholic Church, the military, the mostly German-speaking estate-owners and burghers of the Kingdom of Bohemia (comprising the Czech Lands, or Bohemia, Moravia and parts of Silesia), and the Polish aristocracy and clergy of Galicia and Bukovina. These last two provinces made up 'Austrian Poland', annexed by the Habsburgs during the successive 'Partitions' of the former Polish-Lithuanian Commonwealth between Russia, Prussia and Austria (1772–95).

The regions subject to the most direct forms of Austro-German rule were the following: the predominantly Slovene provinces of Carniola, Gorz (Gorizia) and Istria (including the important predominantly Italian-speaking port of Trieste), which were annexed in the fourteenth century; the largely Croatian province of Dalmatia, annexed in 1797; and the partly Serbian, partly Croatian, but predominantly Bosnian/Muslim provinces of Bosnia-Herzegovina, militarily occupied in 1878 and formally annexed in 1908.

The Habsburgs ruled the eastern half of the empire in explicit or implicit partnership with the wealthy Magyar aristocracy of the constitutionally separate and more unified Kingdom of Hungary. The latter constituted a natural physical unit: the fertile, saucer-shaped Hungarian plain, through which flowed the River Danube and its major tributary, the Tisza, was almost encircled by the rim of mainly forested and/or pastoral highlands which comprised the greater part of Slovakia, Ruthenia, Transylvania, Banat and Croatia-Slavonia. From 1711 to 1848 the Habsburg-controlled Kingdom of Hungary had a distinct, highly decentralized and aristocratic *comitat* ('county') system of administration, which made for weak central government but nevertheless allowed considerable local autonomy. This helped Hungary to preserve a separate legal, administrative and cultural tradition and identity and fend off the sporadic Habsburg drives for greater political and administrative centralization and uniformity, which were largely confined to the western ('Austrian') half of the empire. From 1848 to 1860, in retribution for the Magyar nobility's enthusiastic participation in an abortive Hungarian 'national revolution' of 1848–49, Hungary was subjected to a punitive spell of Austrian 'direct rule'. However, in the wake of a humiliating and debilitating succession of Habsburg/Austrian military defeats in both Italy (1859 and 1866) and Germany (1864 and 1866), the empire was transformed into a so-called 'Dual Monarchy' from 1867 to 1918. Under this regime, the Magyar aristocracy and lesser nobility were allowed to establish a dynamic central government within the Kingdom of Hungary, in place of the earlier decentralized *comitat* system of local aristocratic administrative autonomy, but they used this to pursue aggressive and increasingly repressive 'Magyarization' (cultural assimilation) of their Slovak, Ruthene, Croatian and Romanian subjects. From the 1870s to the 1890s, partly as a consequence of the natural coherence of the Kingdom of Hungary as a physical and economic unit and the very secure political and cultural hegemony of the Magyar 'Establishment' over its non-Magyar subjects, whose national 'awakenings' had still barely begun, 'Magyarization' appeared to progress very effectively. Assimilation in this era was still largely voluntary, motivated by hunger for social and economic advancement, especially for Jews and (to lesser degrees) Slovaks and Romanians. In practice, however, the Magyar 'Establishment' was alienating and antagonizing hitherto 'loyal' or submissive subjects and fanning the embers of embittered and vengeful Slovak, Romanian and Ruthenian/Ukrainian nationalisms, which found expression in the rapid development of Slovak, Romanian, Croatian and Ruthene/Ukrainian autonomist and separatist movements between 1900 and 1918.

Until the coming of the railways the Habsburg Empire remained essentially a loose assemblage of localized, autarkic manorial and village economies, remotely presided over by a weakly developed state which was buttressed by the Roman Catholic Church, the landed nobility and administrative/garrison towns. Only gradually did the coming of railways, the expansion of trade in grain and timber, the growth of industrial villages and towns and the development of capitalism erode local isolation and autarky and increase the influence and power of the state and the national market.

It has been argued that even the core territories of the empire lacked economic and geographical coherence: 'Bohemia was connected through her rivers with the economy of Germany; Galicia and the Bukovina were cut off from the rest of the Monarchy by mountains; Vorarlberg was connected to the textile-producing regions of Switzerland and Swabia; the Monarchy lacked any river route to her main Adriatic ports; the Danube was extremely difficult to navigate; and two-thirds of the Monarchy was covered by hills and mountains' (Sked 1989: 198). This difficult terrain made the costs of railway and canal construction much higher than in Western Europe, impeding imperial integration.

However, others have argued that the Habsburg Empire did have underlying bonds which drew its diverse peoples together. The eminent Hungarian sociologist Oscar Jaszi wrote that 'Though this Empire as a whole did not have a unified national and geographical basis, still important popular forces were at work to form a vague feeling of solidarity in the nucleus of the Empire among Austria, Bohemia, Hungary and Croatia' (Jaszi 1929: 38). The prominent Habsburg historian Robert Kann referred to 'the community of interests of the peoples of the Danubian area from the time when Bohemia, Hungary, Croatia and the hereditary [Austrian] German lands were united together in 1526–27 down to . . . 1918' (Kann 1967: 30).

The East Central European core territories of the Habsburg Empire shared an overlapping visual and cultural heritage, especially in music, in literature or in the distinctive atmosphere, architecture and cuisine of East Central European towns. For many East Central European thinkers (as noted in the Introduction), as well as for many external observers of the region, these commonalties have been what has most vividly defined East Central Europe as a distinct region, entity or civilization, and there are many substantial grounds for accepting this.

The unifying 'main artery' of the empire was the Danube, as has been most evocatively portrayed by Claudio Magris (1989). Both before the river became fully navigable and even after the advent of railways, the Danube river basin was the natural line of communication linking Bavaria, Linz, Vienna, Bratislava (capital of Slovakia), Budapest (capital of Hungary), Szeged (on the Tisza, a major tributary into the Hungarian plain), Slavonia, Zagreb (the Croatian capital, on the Sava, another tributary) and, beyond the empire, Belgrade (capital of Serbia), Wallachia (Romania) and the Black Sea. From 1784 onwards the Ottoman Empire began to allow international river traffic to have access to Belgrade, Wallachia and the Black Sea, whereupon the Magyars began to straighten their sections of the Danube. From the later nineteenth century, river improvements on the Hungarian plain and in Romania began to be combined with flood control, drainage and irrigation schemes, as grain cultivation and exports expanded. The Danube Steamboat Navigation Company was established in 1831 and by the 1870s it was operating 140 steamers up and down the river.

The 1878 Berlin Congress assigned Austria-Hungary the prime responsibility for making improvements to the treacherous Iron Gates gorge, running between the Carpathians and the Balkans. Channels were cut through the cataracts on this section of the river in 1895–9. Between 1901 and 1913 river traffic through the Iron Gates doubled. (It mainly comprised Romanian oil and agricultural products, which were exported upstream to East Central Europe and Germany, and some coal and industrial products, shipped downstream to the Black Sea states from Central Europe.) By 1913 Danube river freight amounted to some 13 million tonnes per annum, although this was still far below the 60 million tonnes per annum carried on the Rhine in Western Europe. It was singularly unfortunate that the Danube flowed *away from* Europe's main centres of trade, industry and population, rather than *towards* them.

FROM LIBERAL 'COUNTER-REVOLUTION' TO NEO-ABSOLUTISM, 1849–60

In the wake of the political defeat of the 1848 Revolutions, the chastened Austrian German 'liberals' looked to the Habsburg state to carry out the economic 'anti-feudal' and unifying elements of the 'liberal' programme by autocratic means, much as Prussian German 'liberals' had looked to the Hohenzollern state to do the same within the German Zollverein (Customs Union) established in the 1830s. The 'liberal' propertied classes had suffered a real scare in 1848. Having slightly lifted the lid of the 'Pandora's Box' of democracy, they had seemingly lost control to 'radicals' who

wanted to advance beyond limited, orderly and elitist 'democracy for the rich' towards a more egalitarian 'democracy for the masses', threatening the privileged positions and prerogatives of the rich.
On further reflection, therefore, 'repentant liberals' concluded that it would be far safer to rely on
monarchical power and authority to implement vital parts of the 'liberal' programme in a more
strictly controlled manner ('from above'). Thus many 'liberals' sold out to the dynasty in the belief
that they could 'use' it to attain important 'liberal' objectives. These included an imperial customs
union; the construction of railways; the promotion of industry, banks and joint stock companies; the
rule of law (the setting up of a *Rechtsstaat*); 'responsible' quasi-constitutional government; the
further suppression of seigneurial privilege; the abolition of the hereditary rights of landlords in
local jurisdiction/administration; the erosion of the powers of landlord-dominated provincial diets;
the creation of a more uniform and more unitary state; and the opening of official careers to (mainly
bourgeois) 'talent'.

However, while considerable 'progress' was made on all these fronts from the 1850s to the
1870s, it was achieved at a high political price. Paradoxically, 'liberal progress' gave a new lease
of life to a fundamentally illiberal Habsburg absolutism. The dynasty used an army of tamed and
compliant 'liberals' to attain conservative dynastic aims, to create a larger, stronger and more
modern dynastic power base, to centralize the state, to reduce the roles of local/feudal 'particularism' and the landed nobility, to greatly extend the power and competence of the imperial bureaucracy and to establish a Kafkaesque 'Big Brother' state in East Central Europe, long before the
arrival of Communist dictatorship.

Emboldened by the apparent completeness of their political and military victories over the
radical, 'liberal' and nationalist movements of 1848, the Schwarzenberg government and Emperor
Franz Josef were not content merely to restore the status quo ante. They had no wish to return to the
immobilism, muddle and inertia of the Metternich era. They also tried to efface all memory of the
humiliations and compromises of 1848. Instead of fully reinstating the aristocratic imperial councils, provincial diets, local 'feudal' jurisdictions and the Hungarian *comitat* system, all of which had
provided platforms for the 'liberals' of 1848, the victors decided to press home their victory by
bringing to fruition Josef II's dream of a Germanic *Gesamtstaat*. This envisaged a centralized and
unitary empire ruled directly from Vienna by a highly professional German-speaking imperial
bureaucracy, the military, and provincial and local plenipotentiaries. Overbearing German-speaking
imperial officials and military commanders elbowed aside not only the 1848 'liberals', but federal-
ist aristocratic conservatives as well.

The Bach System, 1852–9

The chief architect of this so-called 'neo-absolutism' was Schwarzenberg's first justice minister
and subsequent interior minister, Alexander Bach, a renegade 'liberal' lawyer who had played a
prominent role in the March 1848 'liberal' Revolution in Vienna before gravitating towards the
'law and order' camp in the summer. Even before the sudden death of Schwarzenberg in April
1852, Bach emerged as the *éminence grise* of the neo-absolutist regime (although Emperor Franz
Josef allowed the office of prime minister formally to lapse, becoming in effect his own chief minister). Under the so-called 'Bach System', professional middle-class German bureaucrats overrode
traditional local autonomies and noble prerogatives and brushed aside historic claims and privileges
with an almost Jacobin fanaticism. Hungary, they argued, had forfeited its former constitutional
rights in 1848 by rebelling against Austria and by formally deposing the Habsburgs. Treated as a
newly conquered country, Hungary was to be administered by officers and officials imported from
Austria. Known as the 'Bach hussars', they were dressed up in ostentatious pseudo-Hungarian uniforms (braided tunics, swords and hats with feather cockades). Likewise, Croatia, Transylvania,
Slovakia, Bohemia and Galicia were allowed even less autonomy than before. 'The Habsburg

Empire became, for the first and last time, a fully unitary state. There was a single system of administration, carried out by German officials on orders from Vienna; a single code of laws; a single system of taxation' (Taylor 1976: 85).

Economic liberalization, market integration and the first railway boom, 1850s

The neo-absolutist regime stimulated trade and economic growth by dissolving many former monopolies, state ventures and guild restrictions, by liberalizing the mining laws, by reducing external tariffs and by abolishing the 'tariff wall' between Austria and Hungary. The Habsburg state also embarked on a railway-building programme between 1851 and 1854 in order to boost and further integrate the post-revolutionary imperial economy. By 1854, 70 per cent of the 1,433 km rail network was state owned. But the state incurred budget deficits, exacerbated by the high costs of the 1848 Revolutions and the ensuing wars with Hungary and Piedmont, the expenses of railway construction, the indemnification of ex-serfowners and the commercially disruptive effects of the 1854–6 Crimean War between Russia, on the one side, and Britain, France, Piedmont and the Ottoman Empire, on the other. In 1854–5, therefore, the state decided to privatize its railways and to leave further railway construction to private interests, albeit with state-guaranteed dividends and duty-free importation of rails and rolling stock. This largely involuntary volte-face was presented as a major sop or concession to the 'repentant liberals'. It also stimulated a large influx of foreign (especially French) investment in Austrian banks and railways.

This economic liberalization and market integration allowed Hungarian landowners to export grain, timber and livestock products more freely to Austria, undercutting many Austrian German and Czech farmers and driving some of them off the land into the developing urban sector. It also turned Hungary into a freely accessible 'captive market' for Austrian German and Bohemian textile and producer goods industries, to the detriment of Hungary's underdeveloped textile and craft industries and to the consternation of Magyar nationalists. The burgeoning Hungarian flour-milling, sugar-refining, brewing, distilling, wine-making and leather-goods industries (in which Hungary either had or soon achieved comparative cost advantages) benefited from unimpeded access to the expanding Austro-Bohemian market, and Hungarian exports of flour and sugar increased dramatically as a result. In the longer term Hungarian economic development was also accelerated by growing inflows of foreign (especially Austrian German and Jewish) capital and producer goods, which re-equipped Hungary's industries, expanded and modernized its infrastructure, and eventually created some significant engineering enterprises (notably the Ganz works). There emerged a symbiotic relationship between the Austrian and Hungarian economies (Komlos 1981: 10–12).

These developments enhanced the importance of Vienna as a commercial, financial and industrial centre, assisted the political stabilization of Habsburg neo-absolutism and temporarily revived Austrian claims to economic, cultural and political ascendancy in the Germanic world, winning the allegiance of many pan-German 'liberals' as well as nationalists. In December 1850 Prussia renounced its bid for a north German union and agreed to a restoration of the German Confederation under Austria's presidency. However, unlike 1860s Prussia, Austria could not afford to consummate its renewed ascendancy over Germany by brazenly and unreservedly mobilizing and appealing to German nationalism. Austria therefore repeatedly lost out to Bismarck's Prussia in the German wars of unification in 1864, 1866 and 1870.

Emperor Franz Josef (reg. 1848–1914)

Emperor Franz Josef played a pivotal role in the return to absolutism. Sworn in as emperor in December 1848, after the court camarilla finally decided that Emperor Ferdinand should abdicate, the new eighteen-year-old monarch did not consider himself to be bound by the promises and concessions which had been extracted from his 'Uncle Ferdi' under duress and in violation of 'divinely ordained' dynastic rights. Born plain 'Franz', he adopted the additional name 'Josef' in an attempt to invoke the spirit and claim the mantle of 'people's emperor' Josef II. Eventually, his adopted name came to signify a combination of obduracy and 'firmness' (like his great-uncle Franz) and 'reform from above' (like Josef II). In his dull and dreary devotion to duty, the dynasty and the defence of the Habsburg patrimony, Franz Josef became the archetypal Austrian bureaucrat, the epitome of imperial inertia and routine. 'It was a perpetual puzzle to him that he could not make his Empire work merely by sitting at his desk and signing documents for eight hours a day' (Taylor 1976: 78). His limited vision, his lack of fixed ideas, and his ruthless opportunism were what enabled him to survive so long amid the eddying currents of the later nineteenth and early twentieth century. He saw himself as the servant of *all* his subjects. Yet he was not willing to share with them any control over the major instruments of state power and coercion, namely the armed forces, the imperial bureaucracy, the police and the decisions of war and peace. Franz Josef and his chief ministers lacked a coherent, clear-sighted programme for the future. 'At the heart of the counter-revolution lay not strength and direction but dissension and confusion' (Sked 1989: 134).

The Catholic Church and the Concordat of 1855

The drift and disorientation were camouflaged (and the vacuum was filled) by a reassertion of absolutism and the powers of the Catholic Church. Imposing forms marked a lack of modern substance capable of meeting the needs of a rapidly industrializing and increasingly educated and sophisticated empire. The Monarchy became more and more anachronistic as a political organization, precisely because its economic, military and cultural strength continued to develop. The Concordat of 1855 gave the Roman Catholic Church an unprecedented degree of independence and control of education, censorship and family law. Non-Catholics were banned from teaching in Catholic/state schools and new restrictions were imposed on the Jews, while a 'spirit of intolerance paralyzed intellectual life'. The Habsburg Empire was in effect subjected to another Catholic counter-revolution, one enforced by police informers and spies (Kann 1974: 321–2). However, like the renewal of absolutism, this artificial revival of the church was an attempt 'to defeat the modern spirit with weapons taken from a seventeenth-century museum' (Taylor 1976: 89).

THE ERRATIC RETREAT FROM NEO-ABSOLUTISM, 1859–66

The 'Bach System' survived only until 1859. A stock exchange crisis in 1857 shook investors' confidence in the regime, which also committed fatal blunders in the foreign policy field. During the Crimean War the perfidious Habsburgs refused to reciprocate the significant 'moral' and military support that they had received from Tsar Nicholas I against the Hungarian Revolution in 1849 by siding with Russia against its British, French, Turkish and Piedmontese foes in the Black Sea region. On the contrary, in June 1854 an ungrateful Austria sent Russia an ultimatum demanding the withdrawal of its occupying forces from Moldavia and Wallachia (nascent Romania). Russia's armies were withdrawn and Austrian troops took their place, leaving Austria as the dominant power in the region and in control of almost the entire length of the Danube. However, this was a pyrrhic victory, for these moves left Austria without major allies. Russia attributed its own defeat to Austrian perfidy, while Britain and France concluded that the bloody and costly Crimean War could have been avoided altogether if Austria had actively supported them at the outset (instead of professing neutrality). In 1856 Austria was forced to withdraw its troops from Moldavia and Wallachia, which went on to become the virtually independent state of Romania under French patronage between 1859 and 1866 – temporarily negating the growth of Austrian influence in the Balkans.

These ill-judged and undignified Austrian manoeuvres during the Crimean War marked the end of nearly a century of fruitful co-operation between the Tsarist and Habsburg empires over the Balkans, Poland and Hungary, and the beginning of the mutual hostility and open rivalry in the Balkans which culminated in the First World War and the final disintegration of these imperial rivals. More immediately, however, by entering the Crimean War on the Anglo-French side, Piedmont obtained a promise of future French military assistance against Austria in northern Italy. This led to Franco-Piedmontese military victories over Austria in 1859, the Habsburgs' permanent loss of Lombardy and the formation of an anti-Austrian 'united' Italian state in 1860, and the Habsburgs' loss of Venetia in 1866.

The defeats of 1859 and the ever-growing unpopularity of bureaucratic centralism forced Bach to resign in July 1859. To bolster his own weakened position and authority, Franz Josef initially fell back upon a socially and politically conservative and quasi-federalist partnership between the crown and the loyalist aristocracies of the Habsburg Empire. The Polish aristocrat (and former viceroy of Galicia) Count Agenor Goluchowski became the new 'minister of state'. In 1860 considerable powers were devolved to landlord-dominated provincial diets, which were reconstituted for the purpose. The overwhelmingly conservative and ultra-loyal Galician Polish aristocracy gained substantial provincial autonomy for the first time, while Croatia, Transylvania, Bohemia and Moravia benefited to varying but more limited extents. In Hungary proper the aristocratic pre-1848 constitution of the Diet and the county system of local self-administration were restored, curtailing Austrian 'direct rule'. In October 1860 the so-called 'October Diploma' announced that most imperial legislation (excluding all military and foreign policy matters) would henceforth be submitted for inspection by the provincial diets and an augmented imperial Reichsrat, whose additional members were selected by Emperor Franz Josef from members of the provincial diets.

These changes did not satisfy the Magyar nobility. Magyar nationalism had been roused to fever pitch by the excitement of Italian unification and the cult around the Italian nationalist 'freedom fighter' Garibaldi, whose army of 'red shirts' had been joined by some Magyar veterans of 1848–9. Kossuth courted Emperor Napoleon III and concluded a pact with Cavour, the Piedmontese prime minister and 'midwife' of Italian unification. Magyar public opinion was also galvanized by the violent death of a young Magyar demonstrator in Budapest and the suicide of Count Istvan Szechenyi in March and April 1860, respectively. The Magyar leaders were not seeking a restoration of the limited, decentralized, aristocratic autonomy of the Metternich era, nor did they want to be represented in an imperial parliament (not even in a real one). They boycotted the augmented imperial Reichsrat and demanded the restoration of their modern 'liberal' constitution of April 1848, including a fully fledged Hungarian government and parliament at Budapest. On the other hand, Austrian German bureaucrats, the Viennese 'liberal' press and parts of the Austrian German bourgeoisie were up in arms against the October Diploma because it threatened to undo the 'unifying' centralizing achievements of the 1850s and jeopardize Austrian German dominance of the conduct of imperial affairs.

Faced with uncompromising Magyar nationalism and the realization that aristocratic federalism was a recipe for political paralysis which would weaken the Monarchy and alienate the Austrian German imperial bureaucrats and bourgeoisie without in any way placating the Magyars, Emperor Franz Josef back-tracked. In December 1860 the conservative Polish aristocrat Goluchowski was dismissed. He was replaced by an Austrian German 'liberal', Anton von Schmerling, whose chief task was to reaffirm 'centralism' and win back the wavering Austrian German 'liberals', bureaucrats and bourgeoisie. Through the so-called February Patent of February 1861 the Reichsrat was upgraded to the status of a bicameral imperial quasi-parliament, with an upper house nominated by Franz Josef and a 343-member lower house of representatives elected by the provincial diets. The diets (even the Hungarian one) were implicitly downgraded to the status of electoral colleges and organs of local government. Moreover, through so-called 'electoral geometry' (gerrymandering) as well as restrictive property qualifications and division of the electorate into separate curia, representation in the provincial diets and (more tellingly) in the Reichsrat was weighted strongly in favour of Germans.

These new arrangements were no more acceptable to the Habsburgs' non-German subjects than the October Diploma had been. The Magyar Diet decided to behave like a real Hungarian parliament, to persevere with the Magyar boycott of the imperial Reichsrat and to approve an Address to the Crown drafted by the 'liberal' landowner and lawyer Ferenc Deak, affirming the legality of the Hungarian constitutional laws passed in the spring of 1848. Continuing Magyar defiance led to the suspension of the Hungarian Diet and *comitat* system and to the return of the 'Bach hussars' and Austrian direct rule in Hungary from 1862 to 1865. Meanwhile, the Croatian Diet had resolved to boycott the Reichsrat and was suspended. The Czechs followed suit from 1863 onwards and the Galician Poles did so from 1864.

This added up to a de facto return to absolutism, which was barely mitigated by the existence of a very unrepresentative and widely boycotted Reichsrat. Even the privileged and over-represented Austrian and Bohemian Germans felt dissatisfied, partly because the February Patent of 1861 contained none of the provisions essential to a constitutional system. It made no provision for freedom of the press, for immunity from arbitrary arrest (even for members of the Reichsrat), for an independent judiciary or for the accountability of ministers to the Reichsrat. Tax levels, military matters and foreign policy remained outside the control of the Reichsrat. The imperial government could even govern and issue regulations on the emperor's authority when the Reichsrat was not in session (Taylor 1976: 107). What is more, the February Patent had been granted by the emperor's grace and could be revoked at will. 'The Reichsrat had not attained its position by struggle; therefore, despite its parliamentary appearance, it was a body without power.' The fact that the Germans owed their majority in the Reichsrat to a restricted franchise and 'electoral geometry' made them dependent on government support, rather than the government dependent on their support (p. 114). Moreover, by noisily applauding the government's intransigence towards the Magyar Diet in August 1861, the Reichsrat Germans betrayed their former 'liberal' principles and became subservient allies of the Habsburgs (p. 112). They decided that this was the way to safeguard the vaunted imperial customs union, economic liberalization and Germanic hegemony, against the importunate demands and aspirations of more 'reactionary' and/or overtly nationalistic Magyar, Polish, Czech and Croat notables. In Taylor's judgement, 'the decision taken in 1861 was the doom of stability and peace in central Europe . . . The Germans received an artificial majority in a sham parliament; in return they abandoned their liberal principles . . . and committed themselves to support the dynasty whatever its policy' (p. 114).

Few believed that this virtual restoration of Habsburg absolutism would last long, resting as it did on a narrow base of Austrian and Bohemian German support and the occasional show of force. Indeed, the ordinance restoring Austrian direct rule in Hungary in the autumn of 1861 was officially known as the *provisorium* (provisional regulation). The non-German subjects of the Habsburgs decided to sit it out.

In the autumn of 1864 the Reichsrat Germans finally baulked at the imperial government's intransigence and opted for an accommodation with the Magyars. As in 1848, Magyar domination of Hungary was a price that Austrian and Bohemian German 'liberals' and nationalists were willing to pay (at least temporarily) while they reinforced their own domination of the rest of the Monarchy. In late 1864 even Emperor Franz Josef started putting out feelers to Ferenc Deak, who had emerged as the de facto Magyar leader in succession to Kossuth and Szechenyi.

By 1862 exiled Kossuth had finally lost faith in either revolutionary war or Franco-Italian military intervention as the way to regain Magyar independence. In a complete volte-face, he now urged his Magyar compatriots to repair their relations with the Croats, the Serbs and the Romanians and, instead of scorning or oppressing them, promote an anti-Habsburg Danubian Confederation in which the Magyars could participate as partners-cum-leaders. He argued that the Magyars had to place themselves at the head of a multinational anti-Habsburg (and implicitly anti-Ottoman) Danubian liberation movement, if they were not to end up 'either in German bondage or torn asunder by the assaults of the awakening nationalities' (Jaszi 1929: 313).

Significantly, Kossuth's noble vision and change of heart terminated his practical political influence among the Magyars, although he remained a revered 'national hero' on account of his paramount role in 1848–49. 'Kossuth's prophetic warnings and his plan for confederation were rejected by the leading sections of the nobility, not because of their utopian nature, but because of their conciliatoriness, which came near to renouncing Hungarian supremacy and the territorial integrity of the country' (Hanak 1975c: 313). Any suggestion that the proud Magyar 'master race' should ally itself or associate on an equal footing with the 'backward' Slavic and Romanian 'peasant peoples' was anathema to the haughty Magyar nobility and strident Magyar nationalists. The latter groups preferred to strike a deal with the Austrian Germans, whom they regarded as 'true equals' and 'natural partners', despite the carnage and repression inflicted upon them by the Austrian Germans in the wake of the 1848 Revolutions, rather than to allow themselves to become associated with 'inferior' Balkan peoples (Taylor 1976: 122). Such attitudes erected enduring obstacles to almost all attempts to resolve the problems of Magyar minorities in (and relations with) Romania, Serbia, Croatia and Slovakia.

In 1863 and 1864 the Schmerling government faced mounting discontent, even within its 'natural' Austrian German constituency. The disaffection was exacerbated by the fiscal and monetary 'squeeze' which followed the war of 1859. In early 1865 Schmerling finally felt obliged to reconvene the temporarily suspended Magyar and Croatian diets. In an article published on 16 April 1865 Ferenc Deak disavowed any intention of weakening the essential foundations and integrity of the Habsburg Empire, within whose framework 'the basic laws of the Hungarian constitution should be given adequate scope'. In May he went on to acknowledge the existence of important matters of common concern to both Austria and Hungary. These reassurances cleared the way for the dismissal of Schmerling and his 'centralist' allies in July 1865 and the commencement of lengthy negotiations. These culminated in the May 1867 *Ausgleich* ('compromise') between the Magyars and their monarch, who came to Budapest in person to announce his intention of satisfying the *loyal* and *legitimate* aspirations of his Hungarian subjects (Hanak 1975c: 315; Taylor 1976: 122).

While internal considerations and dynamics were paramount, the rapprochement between the Magyars and their monarch was also facilitated by the external humiliations inflicted upon the Habsburg Empire by Bismarck's Prussia between 1863 and 1866. The August 1863 meeting of the still Habsburg-dominated German Confederation was boycotted by the King of Prussia, without whom the other German rulers would transact no business. That autumn Prussia also slammed the door on Austrian membership of the thriving Prussian-dominated German Zollverein (customs union), thereby marginalizing Austria in German economic affairs. In 1864 a joint Prussian and Austrian invasion of the Duchies of Schleswig and Holstein deprived Denmark of one-third of its territory, but it also showed many German princelings that they had a new Prussian 'boss' and began the forceful unification of most of Germany under the Prussian crown (completed by the Franco-Prussian War of 1870–1).

In early 1866 the Habsburgs prepared for an impending 'showdown' with Bismarck's Prussia. They appeared to have enlisted the support of most of the Catholic and some of the Lutheran German states against Prussian expansionism/'imperialism'. The Austrian foreign minister also made a secret agreement with Napoleon III that, in the event of the anticipated Habsburg victory over Prussia, Austria would cede Venetia to France (which would in turn reap the honour and rewards of ceding it to Italy) and obtain territorial compensation in Silesia and the Rhineland at Prussia's expense, in consultation with France. However, Bismarck outmanoeuvred the Habsburgs. In April 1866 he appealed to and allied himself with German 'liberalism' and nationalism in Prussia and elsewhere by proposing that the Diet of the German Confederation should henceforth be elected by adult male suffrage (like the Prussian parliament). Then in June 1866, having bought Italy's support by promising it Venetia, Prussia very rapidly invaded Hanover (a British appendage), Saxony, Kurhesse and Bohemia and, on 3–4 July 1866, decisively defeated the main Habsburg forces at Sadowa (Königsgrätz). Bismarck's quick-fire 'knockout blows' successfully averted a protracted and mutually destructive Austro-Prussian war and avoided any potentially costly French, British or Russian mediation between the two sides. Europe's other Powers, along with Austria, simply accepted Bismarck's fait accompli. The Treaty of Prague (23 August 1866) brought to an end centuries of Habsburg power and influence in Germany and Italy and eventually encouraged the Habsburgs to seek territorial compensation in the Balkans (with ultimately catastrophic consequences). It also imposed a small but humiliating indemnity on Austria and it sanctioned both the formation of a Prussian-dominated North German Confederation and Prussia's annexation of Hanover, Schleswig, Holstein, Nassau, Frankfurt and Kurhesse.

These peace terms were, nevertheless, nowhere near as harsh as they could have been. Bismarck stoutly resisted the King of Prussia's demands for extensive annexations of Habsburg territory (Kann 1974: 276). He also strove to preserve the Habsburg Empire as a defeated junior partner among the German states, not to destroy it. The continued existence of the Habsburg Empire was a bulwark against the creation of a Greater Germany, which would have been more than Bismarck and the Prussian Junker class could have hoped to control for long, and which might well have provoked the formation of anti-German coalitions in Europe. Educated Magyars, Czechs, Slovaks, Slovenes, Poles, Romanians, Russia, France, Italy and Britain appear to have greatly preferred the prolonged existence of the Habsburg Empire to the creation of a Greater Germany which would have dominated and destabilized Europe. Excluded from both Italy and Germany, the Austro-Hungarian Empire (as it became in 1867) still served as a useful barrier to either German or (alternatively) Russian hegemony over East Central Europe and the Balkans. Its prolonged existence conveniently put off having to address big questions which the European Powers preferred not to have to answer (that is, what to put in its place, or the questions which have plagued East Central Europe and the northern Balkans since 1918). To his great credit as a European statesman, Bismarck recognized the need to 'preserve Austria as she was in 1866', although this strongly contributed to a degree of 'suspended animation' in many areas of Austrian imperial politics from 1867 to 1918 (Taylor 1976: 127–9). In 1866, as in 1815, 'Austria was preserved to suit the convenience of others, not by her own strength' (p. 37). This signalled the beginning of the end of the Habsburg Empire as a military Power, although it continued to develop economically and culturally right up to the First World War.

THE AUSTRO-HUNGARIAN *AUSGLEICH* ('COMPROMISE') OF 1867

The defeats and humiliations of 1859–66 finally induced Emperor Franz Josef to seek far-reaching accommodations with the Austrian German 'liberals' as well as with the Magyar nobility, who had displayed exemplary loyalty and restraint during the crisis of 1866, in marked contrast to those of 1848 and even 1859. Franz Josef now needed their *active* support not only to ensure that he and the House of Habsburg survived the humiliating débâcles of 1859 and 1866, to which his extensive personal involvement in foreign and military affairs had very conspicuously contributed, but also to try to recoup some of the Habsburgs' losses. In October 1866 he entrusted Habsburg foreign policy to the former prime minister of Saxony, Baron (later Count) Ferdinand Beust, who was (mistakenly) considered to be more of a match for Bismarck. His primary political task was to try to construct a new anti-Prussian coalition, internally as well as externally, to try to turn the clock back to its position in 1863, if not earlier still. To stand even the slightest chance of success, this 'revanchist' strategy would require a comprehensive internal reorganization of the Habsburg Empire, including a complete reconciliation and a power-sharing partnership with the Magyar nobility and the Austrian German 'liberals' (Kann 1974: 276–7). The major flaw in all this was that these were the two groups who were least likely to welcome and enthusiastically support another war against Prussia. For, because they thought that they owed their big gains in 1867 to the defeat of Austria by Prussia in 1866, they similarly feared that these gains could be reversed after any future Austro-Hungarian victory over Prussia. Furthermore, Austrian Germans would have been most reluctant to go to war against a unified German national state, even one dominated by the widely detested Prussians, yet the terms of the 1867 *Ausgleich* made it almost impossible to seek (let alone attain) an all-round resolution of the Monarchy's ultimately fatal 'nationality problems' and thus made it harder rather than easier for Austria to 'get even with' Prussia.

In effect the Austro-Hungarian 'compromise' of 1867 instituted a union of two equal semi-sovereign states: Austria and Hungary. They would share the same monarch, a customs union, a single currency, common finances, common foreign and defence policies, unified diplomatic representation, joint armed forces and an integrated military command structure centred on Vienna. German would remain the language of military command and the lingua franca of the empire, while the Emperor of Austria/King of Hungary would retain sole jurisdiction over foreign and military affairs. Hungary would only be allowed to establish token armed forces of its own and would have little say in imperial military affairs. 'The Hungarian parliament's authority in military matters was limited to fixing the number of recruits, to voting on the completion of the ranks, and to deciding where the troops were to be stationed. The dynasty had absolute control over all other military concerns . . . The army acted as an independent power, often behaved in a provocatively anti-Hungarian manner and deliberately insulted national feelings' (Hanak 1975b: 119). This was to become the major bone of contention between the Magyars and the Austrian imperial authorities, culminating in a very tense 'standoff' in 1903–6 (which led to a brief suspension of the Hungarian parliament and constitution by the Austrian emperor and armed forces in early 1906).

Ministers continued to be appointed by and responsible to the Habsburg emperor/king rather than the Austrian and Hungarian parliaments. The few ministers-in-common were to be responsible to the emperor/king and to a committee comprising equal numbers of delegates from the two respective parliaments. They alone could deliberate and advise the emperor/king on matters of common policy, thereby removing many aspects of high policy from effective parliamentary scrutiny and control. The so-called 'common finances' were those sustaining the common policies and institutions of the empire, notably defence and foreign policy. These joint expenses were to be apportioned between Austria and Hungary in accordance with a ratio to be agreed between the respective parliaments once every ten years, as part of a so-called 'economic compromise' (which also covered such matters as external tariffs and trade, monetary affairs, railway routes and the decennial renewal of the customs union). It was initially decided to divide the empire's 'common expenses' 70:30, imposing a heavier fiscal burden on Austria than on Hungary, but in 1907 the ratio was altered to a more equitable 63.6:36.4. The negotiations and posturing which accompanied the decennial renewal of the 'economic compromise' were sometimes very fraught.

It was significant that the 1867 'compromise' was not concluded multilaterally, between the assorted representative bodies and peoples of Austria and Hungary. It was agreed bilaterally, between Emperor Franz Josef and self-appointed Magyar negotiators, over the heads of the various nationalities and their (indirectly) elected representatives. Even the Austrian Reichsrat, which had hitherto been intended to develop into a body representing the Habsburg Empire as a whole, was presented with an immutable *fait accompli*, as was the Hungarian Diet. This merely emphasized that neither body was a fully fledged parliament and that neither could exercise any positive control over the affairs of the empire as a whole, as distinct from those of its two increasingly separate 'halves'. Instead, the 'compromise' became something of a 'blocker's charter'. It allowed each side a veto on any fundamental alteration in the constitutional arrangements of the other and in the relationship between the two, thus obstructing any attempt to reach a more comprehensive settlement or accommodation with the non-German and non-Magyar subjects of the Habsburg emperor.

The *Ausgleich* helped to preserve the dominance of the two imperial 'master races': the Austro-Germans and the Magyars. Yet the fears and insecurity of the Magyars (concerning the fragility of their dominance and their incomplete autonomy within the Kingdom of Hungary) meant that they were never willing to take the risk of granting equal rights and status to the other nationalities within 'their half' of the empire. They also viewed with apprehension the persistent pressure for greater ethnic equality and popular participation in quasi-parliamentary institutions in the 'Austrian half' of the empire. The nub of the problem, in the eyes of the imperial authorities as well as the Magyar leadership, was 'how to cut the Habsburg Monarchy in two while leaving it in one piece' (Sked 1989: 194). The essence of the solution was encapsulated in the (perhaps apocryphal) words of the main Magyar negotiator, Count Gyula Andrassy, to an Austro-German colleague: 'You look after your Slavs and we'll look after ours' (p. 190). 'Andrassy desired an Austria centralized, liberal and German, just as Hungary would be centralized, liberal and Magyar . . . The Germans and the Magyars were to be the "Peoples of state"; as for the others, Andrassy said, the Slavs are not fit to govern, they must be ruled' (Taylor 1976: 130).

Nevertheless, the Austro-Hungarian 'compromise' satisfied no one. 'The Germans of the Monarchy came to detest it and many Hungarians also wanted to alter it. The other races of the Monarchy – quite properly – felt cheated by it . . . The "compromise" of 1867 had surrendered them to the master races' (Sked 1989: 188–9). In 1895 the leader of Austria's right-wing Christian Social Party, Karl Lueger, told the Reichsrat that he considered the Dual Monarchy to be 'the greatest misfortune which my fatherland has ever had to suffer' (p. 189). The Austrian public came to resent the seemingly 'sinister and predominant role of Hungary within the Monarchy', because the Magyars regularly vetoed any change in the status quo, while 'Hungarian public opinion still considered Hungary to be oppressed', because autonomous Hungary was still not allowed to assert its full sovereignty, independence and freedom of manoeuvre (pp. 190–4).

It is also illuminating to view the 1867 'compromise' through a Marxist prism, as the 'closing act in the period of bourgeois revolutions'. Following the failure of the 'liberal' and nationalist Revolutions of 1848–9 and of the neo-absolutist regime of 1849–66, the 'compromise' provided for 'an anti-democratic solution to the question of bourgeois transformation' and the development of capitalism. 'The Emperor, in order to save his Empire, gave his consent to moderate constitutional limitations on his unlimited power . . . The new system did not alter, indeed reinforced, national oppression . . . The system of big estates was not weakened but consolidated.' In this way the 'remnants of feudalism were preserved within the framework of capitalism', while the survivals of absolutism were 'wrapped in the forms of constitutionalism'. Thus the *Ausgleich* 'merely closed an era' without either accomplishing 'the bourgeois revolution' or solving its 'basic problems' (Hanak 1975c: 318–19). The ensuing incompleteness of this transformation was to be a major factor behind the mounting tensions and ambiguities of the so-called 'Dual Monarchy'.

THE 'AUSTRIAN HALF' OF THE MONARCHY AFTER THE *AUSGLEICH*, 1867–1918

Between 1867 and 1893 the 'Austrian half' of the Monarchy enjoyed two long spans of stable constitutional government. The first was under the Austrian German 'liberals' headed by Prince Karl von Auersperg (1867–8) and his brother Prince Adolf von Auersperg (1871–9), interspersed by six short-lived conservative chief ministers (1868–71). The second was under Count Eduard Taafe's so-called 'Iron Ring' of German, Polish and Czech conservatives, Catholics and landowners, from 1879 to 1893. From 1893 to 1914, however, the always fragile stability and composure of the Austrian polity was undermined by growing inter-ethnic tensions and rivalries, primarily between

Austrian and Bohemian ethnic Germans, on the one side, and Czechs, Slovenes, Croats, Hungarians (Magyars) and Jews, on the other. These tensions and rivalries ultimately rendered the Austrian half of the Monarchy ungovernable by parliamentary means and strongly contributed to the suspension of parliament (the Austrian Reichsrat) from March 1914 (four months *before* the start of the First World War) to May 1917. In the final analysis, the Monarchy was held together only by an iron frame of bureaucracy, a residual loyalty to the emperor, and the largely 'loyalist' armed forces.

The initial ascendancy of the Austrian German 'liberals', 1867–79, and the 'high tide' of liberal reform

Within the Austrian half of the Monarchy ethnic Germans constituted only one-third of the population, but they contributed two-thirds of all direct taxes. The Austrian German 'liberals' denied that they were merely a new elite which had hijacked the Austrian state for its own nefarious purposes. Like 'liberals' elsewhere in Europe and in the Americas during the nineteenth century, they maintained that wealth was the chief qualification for political responsibility and that 'the prizes in the economic struggle went to those that "earned" them . . . They were not democrats', but neither were they fanatical conservatives, reactionaries and/or nationalists (Whiteside 1967: 178–9, 184). The ascendancy of the ethnic German 'liberals' in Austria from 1867 to 1879 was substantially reinforced by a system of political representation which privileged property owners and tax payers (in common with 'liberal' parliamentary systems elsewhere in nineteenth-century Europe). On average a German paid twice as much tax as a Czech or an Italian, four and a half times as much as a Pole, and seven times as much as a South Slav (Jaszi 1929: 278–9). Nevertheless, the dominant position of ethnic Germans in the 'Austrian half' of the Monarchy 'rested less on inordinate parliamentary strength than on an economically privileged status anchored in various educational and social advantages' (Kann 1974: 426). As late as 1914, 80 per cent of the officials in fourteen central ministries (including the three 'joint' ministries), more than half of the students in higher education and of the higher clergy, and 78 per cent of the commissioned officers in the imperial armed forces were ethnic Germans (Whiteside 1967: 164–6; Zollner 1967: 222). Germans continued to dominate the economic, cultural and intellectual life of the Austrian half of the Monarchy, in spite of the impressive economic and cultural attainments of the nineteenth-century Czech renaissance (Jaszi 1929: 279–80). According to Whiteside, the 'open character of the German community' made it easy for other nationals to assimilate into it. 'Intelligent, ambitious people were attracted to it.' Consequently, 'German culture penetrated and influenced most of the Empire's peoples.' Capitalism reinforced the pre-eminence and integrative effect of Austrian German culture. 'It is doubtful whether any other ethnic-cultural group in the region could have performed the political, economic and cultural task of building and holding together the Empire . . . At any rate it was the Germans who had the human and material resources to fill the political and economic vacuum in Eastern Europe' (Whiteside 1967: 168–9). However, Whiteside somewhat overstates his case. These factors facilitated rather than justified Austrian hegemony.

To smooth the passage of the 1867 'compromise' through the Reichsrat, Emperor Franz Josef accepted an impressive array of 'liberal' legislation and an enhancement of German 'liberal' hegemony in Austria. In the Austrian *Reichsrat* which convened in May 1867, German 'liberals' had a two-thirds majority (Kann 1974: 338), even though ethnic Germans made up only one-third of the population. Five 'constitutional laws' passed in December 1867 strengthened individual liberties and the prerogatives of parliament (p. 339). Laws passed in May 1868 and May 1869 established secular civil marriage, secular compulsory state education (restricting the role of the clergy to religious instruction) and the legal equality of all denominations. Inter-denominational marriage was made easier, while in August 1870 the 1855 Concordat with the Vatican was repudiated, along with the 1870 papal encyclical proclaiming papal 'infallibility'. State supervision of church finances and administration was introduced in 1874.

The 1867–73 boom and the 1873 crash (*Krach*)

Between 1867 and 1873 the dominant position of the Austrian German 'liberals' was further reinforced by an unprecedented economic boom, known to historians as the *Gründerzeit*. Fuelled by the additional paper money issued to finance the wars of 1864 and 1866 and by net inflows of foreign capital (mainly from France and Belgium), there were speculative booms in banking, real estate and construction and the rail network more than doubled, with the result that by 1873 all the major towns and cities of German Austria, Bohemia and Hungary were linked to each other and to the outside world by rail. The railway mania in turn stimulated the growth of mining, metallurgy, engineering and grain production, while get-rich-quick company promoters launched numerous joint stock companies (including five joint stock banks). The heady *nouveau riche* atmosphere in Vienna at that time was perfectly caught (slightly after the event) by Johann Strauss jnr's 'fizzing' operetta *Die Fledermaus* (1874), a heady ode to champagne.

However, the great stock market 'crash' (*Krach*) of May 1873 in Germanic Central Europe (and hence much of East Central Europe as well) brought the *Gründerzeit* to an abrupt end, less than a month after the triumphal opening of a large World Exhibition in Vienna. The confidence of (and in) Austrian German 'liberalism' was severely shaken by the *Krach* and the ensuing six-year economic depression, which was accompanied by high interest rates, widespread bankruptcies, falling international grain prices and growing demands for social and commercial protectionism and increased state intervention in economic affairs. The *Krach* brought out into the open numerous corrupt or illicit or unsound financial dealings which had been rife during the *Gründerzeit*, some of them involving prominent 'liberal' politicians and tycoons. It also precipitated a major surge of popular (anti-capitalist) anti-Semitism (which persisted until the Second World War), as well as a retreat from 'liberalism'. The *Krach* and the subsequent scandals focused the minds of millions on the evils and hypocrisy of a 'liberal' regime which, 'while theorizing about liberty and equality, challenged their very existence'. They responded to the denunciations uttered by 'nationalist democrats, social-minded Catholics and even feudal aristocrats'. By the end of the decade many were ready to support 'political movements that wanted to replace the existing liberal system with some kind of social community organized around nationality, religion, class or occupational estate' (Whiteside 1967: 180). Thus began the retreat from 'liberalism' into various forms of corporatism, several of which bore terrible fruit during the first half of the twentieth century.

The fateful consequences of the Habsburg occupation of Bosnia-Herzegovina, 1878–1918

Emperor Franz Josef, who had never much liked the Austrian German 'liberals', finally dismissed them from office in 1879, after they had failed to applaud the Austrian military occupation of Bosnia-Herzegovina the previous year (sanctioned by the European Great Powers at the Berlin Congress of 1878). Franz Josef remained particularly 'sensitive' (that is, insensitive) over this issue because the occupation and later (1908) annexation of Bosnia-Herzegovina represented the only territorial gain during a reign overshadowed by humiliating military defeats and territorial losses. In due course, however, this acquisition dangerously magnified and inflamed 'the South Slav problem' within the Habsburg Empire and also introduced a new source of friction into relations between the Viennese imperial 'establishment' and the Magyar political elite. Many Magyars feared that any direct incorporation of additional South Slav territories and populations either into Austria or into the Monarchy as a whole would strengthen Slav demands for the conversion of the

Dual Monarchy into a Triple Monarchy, thus giving the Slavs formal parity with the Magyars and jeopardizing the fragile equilibrium and exclusive bilateral basis of the 1867 'compromise'. For these reasons Magyar political leaders (not unlike the Austrian German 'liberals') were very wary of Habsburg territorial ambitions in the Balkans and refused to permit Bosnia-Herzegovina to be fully incorporated either into Austria or even into the Monarchy as a whole. Any move of this sort would also have incensed many Russians and Serbs, as did the unilateral annexation of Bosnia-Herzegovina by the Monarchy in 1908. Since the Viennese imperial 'establishment' was equally loath to allow them to be incorporated into Hungary (as some Magyar 'hawks' would have wished), Bosnia-Herzegovina was confined to a quasi-colonial status *outside* the formal framework of the Monarchy, ostensibly under the 'protection' of the Habsburg armed forces and officials from the joint Austro-Hungarian Ministry of Finance. This regime resulted in mounting impoverishment, festering social problems, heavy-handed repression and provocatively high-profile support for the small Catholic (Croat) minority and the Catholic Church, in an 'unholy alliance' with the reactionary and oppressive Muslim landlord class and the conservative Muslim clergy, mainly to the detriment of the Orthodox Serb majority. Right up to the end of Austrian rule, more than 80 per cent of the population of Bosnia-Herzegovina remained illiterate. The most visible 'constructive' impact of Austrian rule was the building of grandiose Roman Catholic churches and cathedrals and showy 'imperial baroque' public buildings, especially in the capital Sarajevo. However, instead of blending with the beautiful vernacular architecture, they stuck out like sore thumbs, becoming the hated symbols of an overbearing, intrusive and alien regime. These divisive policies stoked up inter-communal tensions and grievances for the future.

In the Monarchy's defence, it has been claimed that the new overlords were 'extremely energetic in their efforts to develop the Bosnian economy'. By 1907 they had constructed 1,022 km of railway, more than 1,000 km of highway, bridges (121 of them), chemical plants, iron and steel works, cigarette and carpet factories, model farms, a model vineyard, a shariat school to train judges for the Muslim law courts, nearly 200 elementary schools, three high schools, a technical school, a teacher training college and an agricultural college, while also developing iron, copper and chrome mines as well as forestry (Malcolm 1994: 141–4). Free elementary education in state schools, in which members of each denomination were to receive separate religious instruction from their own clergy, was made compulsory in 1909 (pp. 143–4). By 1913 Bosnia's industrial workforce exceeded 65,000 persons (p. 141) and 41,500 serfs had been able to buy their freedom since 1879, although this still left more than 93,000 families in bondage (pp. 140–1).

Nevertheless, these vaunted achievements did more to confirm than to refute the essentially alien, incursive, disruptive and colonial character of Habsburg rule in Bosnia and Herzegovina. Many other colonial regimes were boasting similar 'achievements' at that time. Whatever the material benefits, the fact remained that the delicate, centuries-old co-existence and equilibrium between Bosnia's Muslims, Orthodox Christians and Catholics was fatefully disturbed by the sudden influx of large numbers of Catholic officials, colonists, soldiers and clergy. This was reinforced by Catholic pressures on non-Catholics to convert to Catholicism when marrying a Catholic and to raise the offspring of such marriages as Catholics. The number of (predominantly Catholic) Austro-Hungarian immigrants resident in Bosnia rose from 16,500 in 1880 to 108,000 in 1910 (Malcolm 1994: 143). While the Ottomans had latterly employed only 120 officials to rule Bosnia-Herzegovina, by 1910 the Habsburgs were employing 9,533 to do so (p. 138).

From 1882 to 1903 Benjamin Kallay, a former Magyar diplomat and future author of a respected history of the Serbs, ran the civil administration of Bosnia-Herzegovina while also serving as the joint finance minister of Austria-Hungary. Kallay boldly endeavoured to foster a distinctive Bosnian national identity that would both unite the area's Muslim, Orthodox Christian and Catholic inhabitants and keep them separate from their Serbian and Croatian neighbours (Malcolm 1994: 147–8). The pre-national or proto-national Orthodox, Catholic and Muslim religious affiliations and/or identities prevailing in Bosnia-Herzegovina at that time had not yet crystallized into Serb, Croat and Bosniak (Bosnian Muslim) ethnic identities. Had it been possible to keep Bosnia-Herzegovina completely sealed off from the outside world, Malcolm contends, Kallay's policy might have succeeded. However, it failed to elicit positive responses from the tolerant, cosmopolitan, civic-minded Muslims of Sarajevo, who had long maintained moderately civil relations with their Orthodox Christian, Catholic and Jewish neighbours, and Serbian and Croatian nationalist ideas did spread to the Orthodox and Catholic populations of Bosnia and Herzegovina 'through the very networks of priests, schoolteachers and educated newspaper readers which Austro-Hungarian policy had helped to bring into being' (pp. 148–9). Furthermore, government co-operation with the Muslim leadership in Sarajevo not only antagonized the more uncompromising Muslim leaders in Travnik and Mostar (who adopted intransigent positions 'in order to discredit their Sarajevan rivals'), but also aroused suspicion and resentment among those Catholic and Orthodox Christians who thought they should now enjoy a monopoly of official favour (pp. 145–7). At the same time, the Monarchy's increasingly aggressive, divisive and ham-fisted treatment of neighbouring Serbia and Croatia was fanning the flames of Serbian and Croatian nationalism and Yugoslavism. Thus the Monarchy's policy towards Bosnia-Herzegovina was doomed to failure by the inherent contradictions within its policies towards the South Slavs in general (p. 150). In this respect as in so many others, the Habsburgs unwittingly sowed and watered some of the seeds of later tragedies in the South Slav lands. It is therefore not altogether surprising that the shots which triggered the First World War were fired in Bosnia in June 1914.

The ascendancy of the conservative 'Iron Ring' in the 'Austrian half' of the Monarchy, 1879–93

After their ejection from office the Austrian German 'liberals' lost the elections of summer 1879 and were replaced by a conservative coalition of German, Polish and Czech Catholics and landowners cobbled together by Count Eduard Taafe. He persuaded the 'Old Czech' leaders to abandon their boycott of the Reichsrat by promising them increased provincial autonomy and linguistic/cultural equality with the Germans within Bohemia. Similar blandishments were offered to the conservative Catholic and landowning leaderships of Galicia and Slovenia. (Indeed, the Polish aristocracy had already been brought 'on side' by the granting of extensive administrative, educational and cultural autonomy to Galicia in 1868 and the creation of a Ministry for Galician Affairs in 1871.) As a result, Austria's non-German majority stopped trying to disrupt the new constitutional system, and instead competed for government favours and for jobs in the fast-expanding imperial and provincial bureaucracies. The governing coalition was held together by the premier's promises of a new road or railway line here and a new school or university there. The leaders of the rival national parties, bargaining with the prime minister and bustling self-importantly along the corridors of the huge Reichsrat building, 'ceased to press for any fundamental change of system'. Thus Taafe's political juggling act brought Austria a period of political stability, economic recovery and administrative devolution.

The hazardous long-term implications of the 1879 'Dual Alliance' between Austria-Hungary and Germany

The new conservative trend was consolidated by the (initially secret) 'Dual Alliance' of October 1879, which locked the Habsburg and Hohenzollern empires together in mutual embrace. As early as 1870 George Stratimirovich (a Serb member of the Hungarian parliament) had warned that, if it were to come about, 'this Austrian-Prussian alliance will certainly not secure the peace of Europe. On the contrary, the alliance of the Russian and French states which will become necessary [in response] is going to sow the seeds of a new world war and thus it is going to threaten our very existence' (quoted in Barany 1967: 249). While the astute Count Otto von Bismarck was in charge of German foreign policy, he averted such a potentially disastrous division of Continental Europe into two mutually hostile power blocs by keeping Germany on good terms with Russia (as a sort of 'fail-safe mechanism'). Bismarck engineered a precautionary three-year alliance of the Russian, Austrian and German emperors in 1881 and its renewal for another three years in 1884. In a change of tack in 1887 Bismarck then negotiated a secret Reinsurance Treaty with Russia, pledging that Russia and Germany would remain benevolently neutral towards one another if either were attacked by a third power. Thus, in spite of the (essentially defensive) 'Dual Alliance', Germany would not be obliged to support a Habsburg attack on Russia. Conversely, Russia would not be obliged to support France in a vengeful war against Germany. Furthermore, Bismarck repeatedly refused to give *carte blanche* support to the Habsburgs' expansionist ambitions in the Balkans. In 1876, indeed, Bismarck had told the German Reichstag that the Balkans were not worth the sacrifice of the limbs of a single Prussian soldier. After Bismarck's fall from grace in 1890, however, the inexperienced and inept Kaiser Wilhelm II threw Bismarckian caution to the wind and allowed the Reinsurance Treaty with Russia to lapse. The almost immediate consequence was the conclusion of a Franco-Russian alliance (1894) and the perilous division of Continental Europe into two mutually suspicious armed camps, palpably increasing the likelihood of conflict between them.

The 'Dual Alliance' of 1879 represented much more than a strategic or diplomatic move, even if its full significance was not apparent to the principal actors at the time. It was part of a more fundamental realignment within the Germanic world. In Germany in 1878 Chancellor Bismarck had ditched the predominantly Protestant north German National Liberals (the erstwhile champions of a Listian 'liberal' free-trading and laissez-faire Germany), in favour of a new alliance with the staunchly Catholic, protectionist, south German and pro-Austrian Centre Party. This realignment involved a decisive reorientation from political, social and economic liberalism to corporatism, protectionism and conservative étatism and the emergence of the so-called Central Powers as a cohesive conservative military, political and economic power bloc. The secret 'Dual Alliance' of 1879 was soon followed by a secret treaty under which the feckless Obrenovic dynasty transformed Serbia into a de facto Habsburg protectorate in 1881. In 1882, moreover, the 'Dual Alliance' was expanded into a secret 'Triple Alliance' with Italy, while Romania entered secret defence pacts with both Austria-Hungary and Germany in 1883. These secret treaties facilitated closer economic ties, driven by a steady growth of German investment, banking, industrial subsidiaries and trade in Austria-Hungary, Italy, Serbia and Romania, and by growing exports of Romanian grain, timber and oil to Austria-Hungary, Germany and Italy.

The damaging consequences of the growth of German 'ethnic' nationalism and pan-Germanism, 1879–1914

Count Taafe's 'Iron Ring' was finally shattered on the rocks of resurgent inter-ethnic conflict during the early 1890s. This problem had its roots in smouldering Austrian and Bohemian German resentment of the abrupt termination of their former exclusive political supremacy in Austria in 1879. They tended to blame the decline of German predominance on the alleged treachery and timidity of their political 'masters', including the dynasty. In the seminal Linz Programme of 1882, a number of disaffected pan-German 'liberals' boldly called for the metamorphosis of Austria (including Bohemia-Moravia, but shorn of Galicia and Dalmatia) into an integral German state enveloped in an economic union and military alliance with the German Empire and preserving only a dynastic tie ('personal union') with an otherwise independent Kingdom of Hungary. The principal authors of this 'liberal' pan-German manifesto were the militant pan-German Georg von Schönerer, the lawyer Robert Pattai, the writer Engelbert Penerstorfer, the Austrian Jewish physician (and future leader of the Austrian Social Democrats) Viktor Adler and the eminent Austrian Jewish historian Heinrich Friedjung. Like the pan-German 'liberals' of 1848, they looked to the wider 'German nation' to transform Austria into a unitary German state. In the final analysis true pan-Germans would have preferred an *Anschluss* (union) of Austria with Germany to the preservation of Austria-Hungary and, in this perspective, the Linz Programme can be seen as a 'liberal' trail-blazer for the Austrian Social Democratic and pan-German demands for *Anschluss* with Germany which were blocked by France in 1918–20 and 1929–31 (only to be accomplished by Hitler in 1938). Within two years, however, Schönerer finally broke with the 'liberals' and launched an overtly racist, anti-Semitic and anti-Catholic pan-German movement, the German National Association. While this failed to attract a mass following, it did achieve a sinister behind-the-scenes influence in organizations such as the Deutscher Schulverein (German Schools Association) and the Turnvereine (athletic clubs) patronized by Austrian German officials and pan-German intellectuals. It also served as an incubator of proto-Nazi ideology.

Austrian and Bohemian Germans saw themselves as increasingly beleaguered groups fighting a losing battle to hold back 'the barbarians' and preserve their own exclusive control of all the best schools, universities, museums, galleries and theatres, as well as the provincial diets and countless 'rotten boroughs'. Many 'disgusted' Austrian and Bohemian Germans did not know 'what the world was coming to' as their most hallowed institutions and preserves were gate-crashed, polluted and desecrated by 'inferior' non-German 'upstarts', especially Slavs and Jews. They therefore engaged in very tenacious rearguard actions against what they perceived to be insidious, subversive and quite outrageous Slav encroachments on their exclusive privileged positions and glorious ('sacred') heritage as 'the people of the state', while also becoming increasingly anti-Semitic.

The fall of Count Taafe's 'Iron Ring', 1893

In 1890 Germanic outrage bordered on apoplexy when a committee of moderate and conciliatory Czechs and Germans under Count Taafe's chairmanship decided to redivide ethnically mixed provinces along ethnic lines in an attempt to defuse inter-ethnic tensions. This decision provoked precisely the opposite of what was intended, namely an explosion of German and Czech indignation and decisive defeats for Taafe's moderate Czech and Bohemian German supporters in the 1890 elections in Bohemia, depriving the premier of much-needed parliamentary support. The premier then back-tracked in an attempt to placate the irate Bohemian Germans and win crucial parliamentary support from moderate Austrian Germans. However, this ungainly manoeuvre further antagonized the Czechs, who had hitherto been Count Taafe's most reliable supporters.

In desperation Count Taafe proposed to appeal over the heads of the 'bourgeois' nationalist and pan-German 'liberals' to the more conservative, deferential, loyalist and less nationalistic masses, by dramatically extending the franchise and the parliamentary representation of the lower classes. Such a stratagem might have worked in 1893. Active support for the querulous nationalist and 'liberal' movements still seemed to be largely confined to the professional and propertied classes, while divisive national and class consciousness still appeared to be relatively inchoate among the lower classes, especially non-Germans. Moreover, universal adult male suffrage had demonstrably served the counter-revolution well in France and Germany, just as Proudhon had predicted it would. In Austria, if Count Taafe had been allowed to introduce a wider franchise and greater parliamentary representation of the underprivileged classes in 1893, the 'bourgeois' nationalists and 'liberals' could well have lost out to the nascent 'mass party' of the right, the Catholic, 'loyalist' and anti-Semitic Christian Socials. Launched in 1887 by an erstwhile 'liberal' turned demagogue and anti-Semite, Karl Lueger, the Christian Social Party rapidly won mass support among conservative, Catholic, loyalist and mainly Austrian German traders, shopkeepers, small farmers and minor officials who envied, resented and felt threatened, slighted or cheated by 'big business', Jewish middlemen, the partly Jewish haute bourgeoisie, the substantially Jewish-owned 'liberal' press and the partly Jewish 'liberal' contingent in the Reichsrat. By rapidly winning over most of the potential lower middle-class, German-speaking voters in both urban and rural Austria, the Christian Socials fatally fractured the Austrian bourgeoisie and robbed both Austrian 'liberalism' and pan-Germanism of their potential mass support and political clout. Indeed, by 1895 Lueger was outpolling the hitherto dominant 'liberals' in Vienna's mayoral elections, although Emperor Franz Josef refused to allow such a disreputable demagogue to assume the mayoral office until after his fourth successive electoral triumph. That was in 1897, whereupon Lueger remained Mayor of Vienna until 1910.

However, the prospect of admitting the rude plebeian hordes into parliamentary politics alarmed not only Count Taafe's 'bourgeois' nationalist and 'liberal' opponents, but also his own conservative allies in the Reichsrat and in government. After all, electoral reform could have opened the doors not only to the far from 'respectable' Christian Socials, but also to the Marxist (and even more 'alarming') Austrian Social Democratic Party, launched in 1889 by the former 'liberal' Viktor Adler on an anti-capitalist, anti-militarist, anti-monarchist and anti-clerical platform. Faced with united 'liberal', conservative and pan-German opposition to the prime minister's proposed electoral stratagem, Franz Josef decided to dismiss Count Taafe from the premiership, although the emperor himself was to resort to a similar stratagem in 1907.

The gradual breakdown of constitutional government in the 'Austrian half' of the Monarchy, 1893–1914

From 1893 to 1895 the 'Austrian half' of the Monarchy was governed by a 'grand coalition' under Prince Alfred Windisgrätz, but it too foundered on the rocks of inter-ethnic conflict, this time between Germans and Slovenes in Styria. The polity was evidently becoming ungovernable by parliamentary means. The growing breakdown of a political system which had survived in either 'liberal' or conservative variants from 1867 to 1895 induced Franz Josef to put his faith in a high-minded non-partisan 'strongman'. He hoped that such a person would endeavour to cut Austria's 'Gordian knots' and overcome its creeping political paralysis by imposing bold but judicious 'solutions' on Austria's most divisive, destabilizing and seemingly insoluble problems. For this Herculean role the emperor shrewdly chose neither a German nor a Magyar, but Count Kasimir Badeni, the 'loyalist' but reputably 'liberal' Polish governor of Galicia.

Badeni got off to a flying start in 1896 by introducing a system of graduated personal income tax and a widely applauded electoral compromise. This involved the addition of a fifth electoral *curia* which would elect 72 Reichsrat deputies (out of a new total of 425) on the basis of adult male suffrage, thereby introducing a modicum of working-class representation for the first time. Badeni's boldest 'coup' occurred in relation to Bohemia. In 1879, as part of the political 'deal' concluded between Count Taafe and the Czech leadership, bilingualism had been imposed on Bohemia's officials of the 'outer service', that is, those dealing directly with members of the public. However, Bohemia's officials of the so-called 'inner service' (those dealing with other officials and with Vienna) had remained exclusively German speaking. In April 1897, however, Badeni decreed that even officials of the 'inner service' in Bohemia had to be fluent in both Czech and German. Although seemingly even-handed, such a change would have given the Czechs a near-monopoly of official posts in Bohemia, because as a matter of course most Czechs learned German as well as their 'mother tongue', whereas very few Bohemian Germans had learned Czech (nor were they willing to do so!). Badeni's language decree detonated an explosion of Germanic fury, whipped up still further by Schönerer's German National Association. There were mass demonstrations and riots all over Austria, backed up by angry meetings in many parts of Germany.

This backlash of 'Teutonic fury', which forced Badeni out of office in November 1897, was merely the culmination of the mounting inter-ethnic protests and violence which had scarred public life in Bohemia since the early 1880s (Bradley 1971: 135–8); and the underlying Germanic intransigence 'did more than anything else to destroy the Habsburg Empire' (Taylor 1976: 183). The Germans were not powerful enough to transform the 'Austrian half' of the Monarchy into a German national state, yet neither were they strong enough to thwart any other 'solution' to its inter-ethnic conflicts. This fostered an ever-deepening state of deadlock – and governmental gridlock – in the polity.

After the failure of Badeni, Franz Josef and his ministers virtually gave up the quest for definitive solutions to the so-called 'nationality problems' of the 'Austrian half' of the Monarchy. This rein-forced the emperor's innate pessimism, fatalism and sense of impending doom. As early as 1866 he had written to his mother: 'One just has to resist as long as possible, to do one's duty to the last and finally perish with honour' (quoted in Sked 1989: 229). This became a leitmotif of his long reign. It was as if he expected his house and his empire to go down in flames, sooner or later; he was await-ing a *Götterdämmerung*. Austrian politics was to become merely a holding operation, intermittently marred by violent outbursts of defensive aggression. There was a terrifying sense of drift, of living on borrowed time and of Austria's rulers merely reacting defensively to uncontrollable malign forces and events in wholly unchartered waters.

For their part, the Reichsrat party leaders were increasingly incapable of forming (let alone main-taining) a constitutional government. They preferred to jostle for positions and favours and to leave the responsibility for governing Austria to others. Hence the growing 'irresponsibility' of the Reichs-rat party leaders 'encouraged, even compelled, the Emperor to keep the real authority in his own hands', although that both further encouraged and enabled the parliamentary party leaders to con-tinue to evade their constitutional responsibilities (Taylor 1976: 170–2). It was a vicious circle. The actual business of government increasingly fell into the hands of 'faceless' state functionaries, selected by Franz Josef from the higher ranks of the imperial bureaucracy. Meanwhile the Reichsrat lost almost all influence on policy matters and became little more than a forum in which the prime minister (now merely the top state functionary) could from time to time meet with the parliamentary party leaders to hear grievances, strike bargains and grant favours (a new school here, a new road or railway route there), in order to keep them 'sweet' (pp. 198–9).

Ernst von Körber, who served as prime minister from 1900 to 1904, made further abortive attempts to settle the 'language question' in Bohemia and to 'buy off' Czech and Slovene national-ist discontent through programmes of public works and railway construction (known as 'politischer Kuhhandel', 'political cow-trading', the Austrian equivalent of American 'pork barrel' politics). However, even he had to govern largely by emergency regulations and imperial decrees.

The economy boomed during the premiership of Paul von Gautsch (1904–6), but there was a major crisis in relations between Austria and Hungary. This challenged the whole basis of the 1867 *Ausgleich* ('compromise') and the Dual Monarchy. From 1903 to 1906 the Magyars refused to supply their quota of soldiers for service in the Austro-Hungarian army unless Magyar was made the official 'language of command' of the Magyar contingents. This would in effect have created a separate Magyar army under Magyar officers, as very few non-Magyar soldiers could speak or write the very different Hungarian language. Magyar unity on the issue did not seriously crack until Emperor Franz Josef and the Habsburg authorities, having suspended Hungary's parliament and imposed military rule, threatened to introduce adult male suffrage for the election of a new parlia-ment. If enacted, this would have caused the Magyars to forfeit their 'in-built' parliamentary major-ity and political dominance within the Kingdom of Hungary.

During the premiership of Max von Beck (1906–8), Austrian–Hungarian relations were 'normal-ized' by the capitulation of most of the Magyar magnates and nobility and a peaceful revision and renewal of the pivotal 'compromise' (including the so-called 'economic compromise') in 1907. However, following the success of the 'sobering' threat to impose adult male suffrage on Hungary in 1906, Emperor Franz Josef sought to 'escape from the nationalist conflicts of middle-class politicians' by actually imposing direct adult male suffrage on a reluctant and rather apprehensive Austrian Reichsrat in 1907. The manoeuvre worked remarkably well. The 1907 Reichsrat elections, held under the new adult male franchise, returned the Christian Socials and the (still Marxist) Social Democrats as the two largest parties. Paradoxically, this represented 'a triumph for the imperial idea', in that both of these parties wished to preserve the territorial integrity of the Habsburg Empire (albeit in a federalized form in the case of the Social Democrats) and Franz Josef 'recovered greater freedom of action than he ever enjoyed since 1867' (Taylor 1976: 212). A budget was approved without recourse to emergency regulations and, most unusually, Beck even included some Reichs-rat members in his government. However, the 'honeymoon' was short lived. By 1911 even the Social Democrats had begun to split along ethnic lines, while the demagogic and anti-Semitic Christian Social Party soon dropped any pretence of high-minded Roman Catholic universalism and brazenly championed Austrian German supremacism and sectional interests.

Under Count Karl Stürgkh (1911–16), Austria's last long-serving premier, the Bohemian consti-tution was suspended (in 1913) amid resurgent inter-ethnic conflict in the Czech Lands, while the increasingly deadlocked and marginalized Austrian Reichsrat was itself prorogued from March 1914 (that is, four months *before* the outbreak of the First World War) until after the assassination of Count Stürgkh by the socialist Friedrich Adler (son of Victor Adler) in October 1916 and the death of Franz Jozef in November 1916.

The gradual breakdown of constitutional government in Austria was a seemingly unstoppable, albeit erratic, process. The multinational dynastic polity proved increasingly incapable of generat-ing and sustaining the minimum degrees of consensus and common allegiance necessary to bind it together and to make stable parliamentary government possible, despite the fact that this was a period of impressive economic advance and dazzling cultural and intellectual creativity. The illus-trious figures living and working in the Austrian half of the Monarchy at that time included Freud, Kafka, the poets Hoffmannstal and Rilke, composers such as Mahler, Schönberg, Berg, Dvorak, Janacek and Suk, artists such as Klimt and Kokoschka, the philosopher Mach, economists such as Menger, von Mises, Hayek and Schumpeter, and the Marxist theoreticians Hilferding and Bauer. Ironically, this intellectual brilliance and cultural ferment probably did more to destabilize than to stabilize the position of the monarchy, the Church, the bureaucracy and the armed forces, all of which found themselves increasingly under intellectual assault.

THE KINGDOM OF HUNGARY FROM THE 1867 AUSGLEICH ('COMPROMISE') TO 1917

In 1867, in the wake of the Austro-Hungarian 'compromise', the Magyar-dominated Transylvanian Diet was easily persuaded to vote itself out of existence and to allow Transylvania (whose inhabit-ants were 54 per cent Romanian and only 29 per cent Magyar) to be fully incorporated into a unitary Kingdom of Hungary, along with the largely South Slav Military Frontier regions (in what is now Croatia). However, under an agreement concluded between the Habsburg authorities and Croatian leaders in 1868, Croatia was allowed to retain its own Diet and official language, 45 per cent of its tax revenues and a measure of autonomy in purely internal, religious, educational and judicial affairs, although its governor/viceroy (*ban*) was to be appointed by (and answerable to) the Hungar-ian government in Budapest rather than to the Croatian Diet in Zagreb/Agram.

Between 1867 and 1871 the newly enhanced Kingdom of Hungary was governed by a coalition of moderate pragmatic 'liberals' and paternalistic (whiggish) aristocrats, headed by Count Gyula Andrassy and sustained in office by the parliamentary 'party' of Ferenc Deak. The founding statutes of the nascent Hungarian state, particularly the 1868 Nationality Act and the 1868 Education Act, made a very promising start down the road towards a unitary but relatively liberal polity based upon a broad and inclusive 'civic' conception of the emergent Hungarian nation-state (rather than a narrow, hard-edged and intolerant 'ethnic' or 'integral' conception of the ascendant Magyar nation dominating and aggressively 'Magyarizing' the numerous non-Magyars who had lived and worked for centuries on Hungarian soil).

The 1868 'Nationality Act', drafted by the progressive writer and minister of religion and education Baron Jozsef Eötvös (aided by Ferenc Deak), declared that 'all citizens of Hungary form, politically, one nation, the indivisible unitary Hungarian nation (*nemzet*), of which every citizen of the country, whatever his personal nationality (*nemzetiseg*), is a member equal in rights' (quoted by Sked 1989: 208). Eötvös clearly regarded the Magyars as just one *nemzetiseg* (nationality) among several within the historic political *nemzet* (nation) of Hungary (p. 209). In this usage, *nemzetiseg* was an *ethnic* label, whereas *nemzet* (nation) referred to a broader historic *territorial unit* and/or '*political nation*' which could accommodate several distinct nationalities and linguistic communities on a formally equal footing. The Magyar community, as the largest and strongest community within the 'historic' territories of the Kingdom of Hungary, would ostensibly be merely *primus inter pares*. This National- ity Act and the 1868 Education Act, which called for compulsory elementary schooling for all six- to twelve year-olds, did indeed respect the diversity of peoples and cultures within the Kingdom of Hungary (Jaszi 1929: 314–15). Ethnic minorities were formally permitted to conduct local govern- ment in their own language, and ethnic groups living together in considerable numbers were supposed to receive state education in their own language. Each nationality was to be free to develop its own national church or churches, while Hungary's Jewish minority was almost completely 'emanicipated' – granted most of the civil liberties and rights endowed on non-Jews.

If the Magyar ruling classes had remained true to the letter and spirit of this first flush of political and cultural liberalism, this semi-autonomous Kingdom of Hungary could conceivably have evolved into a polity akin to the United Kingdom (a 'union state') or even the Swiss Federation. However, in 1871 Eötvös died, while a disillusioned Deak withdrew from active politics (he died in 1876) and Andrassy was 'kicked upstairs' to the position of imperial foreign minister. Andrassy's successor as prime minister of Hungary, the former finance minister Menyhert Lonyay, lacked the political finesse and stature needed to hold the broad coalition together and to fend off vociferous demands from rowdy and nationalistic elements within the Magyar 'gentry', intelligentsia and nascent bourgeoisie for more aggressive 'Magyarization' of the state, public employment and the public education system. Furthermore, the 1873 'crash' and the subsequent slide in international grain prices, brought about by rapidly increasing American, Russian and Romanian grain exports, inflicted additional economic and social strains on a still relatively poor, polarized multi-ethnic and largely agrarian population. The 'ruined' Magyar landed gentry raised the loudest political clamour, although they were by no means the worst-afflicted victims. They increasingly demanded a monop- oly of state and professional employment for the sons of the Magyar nobility (quite literally 'jobs for the boys'), as 'compensation' for their (often exaggerated) reductions in seigneurial status and incomes. There was also significant peasant and proletarian unrest during the 1870s, but this was swiftly and firmly suppressed. Magyar governments would not tolerate the growth of either peasant or workers' movements until well into the twentieth century. Indeed, the 'ideology of [Hungarian] independence became – more or less consciously – a kind of *Verdrängungsideologie* (an ideology of repression) against all efforts which endangered the interests of the ruling classes' (Jaszi 1929: 359). The General Workers' Association, founded in 1868, was banned in 1872 (when its leaders were tried for 'treason') and was subjected to regular official harassment thereafter. Much the same fate befell the socialist Non-Voters' Party (the only name the authorities would allow it to use when it was established in 1878), the General Workers' Party of Hungary (formed by a fusion of the two embryonic socialist parties in 1880) and the (Marxist) Social Democratic Party of Hungary, estab- lished in 1890. Indeed, any political or social movement which challenged the hegemonic position of the Magyar ruling classes was liable to be repressed or charged with 'treason' (including 'subver- sion'), 'libel' or 'incitement of national hatred'. This was to be the fate of various Slovak, South

Slav, Romanian and Ruthene cultural societies and nationalist parties from 1876 onwards, as Magyar 'supremacism' intensified.

Forced 'Magyarization' and the repressive authoritarian rule of the so-called 'Liberal Party', 1875–1905

In 1875 the Magyar gentry malcontents fused with the depleted remnants of the ruling coalition to form the so-called Liberal Party. This amalgam soon became known as 'the government party', because it contrived to remain continuously in power for the next thirty years (until 1905) and because it comprised leading elements in the state bureaucracy as well as parliamentarians. From 1875 to 1890 the Liberal Party was dominated by Kalman Tisza, a prominent Calvinist landowner and a veteran of the Magyar nationalist revolution of 1848. A master of parliamentary and electoral manipulation and malpractice, Tisza ran a harsh Magyar landlords' police state behind a showy parliamentary and constitutional facade. Magyar 'liberalism', such as it was, soon 'betrayed the democratic ideas which represented the real value of 1848. Blind nationalism alone survived, narrow, stupid and corrupt' (D. Sinor, quoted by Barany 1967: 251).

The Kalman Tisza regime stepped up the creation of public service jobs for the crisis-stricken Magyar 'gentry', whose difficulties since the dissolution of serfdom were now being exacerbated by sagging international grain prices and the challenge of adapting to capitalism. Hungary's civil service had doubled from a mere 16,000 officials in 1867 to 32,000 in 1875. It was to double again by 1890 and yet again by 1914, when the total number of public employees (including the municipalities and state enterprises) reached 388,000 or 3.5 per cent of the working population (Janos 1982: 94). *The Magyar gentry, who had been staunch opponents of political centralization before 1867, became its most aggressive agents after 1867.*

This expanding army of state officials exercised inordinate central control over parliamentary elections and local government. They misused their powers of taxation, regulation, conscription and arrest to influence or intimidate voters, to forge ballot papers, to 'stuff' ballot boxes, to vet electoral registers and generally to perpetuate the Liberal Party in office. Moreover, some of the principal malefactors were allowed to stand for election in the 160 'rotten boroughs', which were safely 'in the government's pocket'. Such placemen came to constitute up to one-third of 'the government party' in the lower house of parliament, forming the nucleus of an almost unassailable parliamentary majority (Janos 1982: 95–7). Electoral manipulation and corruption were facilitated by Hungary's reliance on so-called 'open' rather than secret ballots in rural areas (enabling the local potentates to *see* that voters did as they were told), by restricting the franchise to less than 7 per cent of the adult population, and by blatant gerrymandering. Ironically, most of the 'rotten boroughs' were in areas where the Magyars were small, privileged and vulnerable minorities (dependent on government protection and favour) and the non-Magyar majorities were largely disenfranchised. These areas, whose Magyar populations represented only a small fraction of the total Magyar population in Hungary, returned a relatively high proportion of the Magyar members of parliament. These were the MPs who were most in league with the government. Thus Magyars representing somewhat less than half the total population of Hungary consistently 'won' more than 94 per cent of the seats in the lower house of parliament, gained more than 90 per cent of all official positions and held almost all the (hereditary) seats in the upper house of parliament. But this should not be allowed to overshadow or obscure the fact that not only the non-Magyar majority, but also the major concentrations of Magyars (including most of the poorer ones) were grossly under-represented in this supposedly 'representative' system of government. Conversely, through a combination of gerrymandering, vote rigging, intimidation and a restrictive franchise, the Magyar upper classes (especially those resident in largely non-Magyar areas) were grossly over-represented. Arguably, however, 'the new "constitutionalism" which the Compromise created . . . was only workable on the basis of a very restricted electoral law which was combined . . . in Hungary with administrative corruption and use of armed force' (Jaszi 1929: 349). Indeed, Hungarian 'parliamentarianism' was reduced to a mere charade under a regime which disenfranchised most of the adult population and 'terrorized the minority possessing the suffrage by the system of open ballot, corruption and mobilization of the army' (p. 363).

The Kalman Tisza regime also initiated much more aggressive 'Magyarization' policies in education, public administration, the legal system, the press, parliamentary representation and the promotion of cultural amenities, state enterprises (including railways) and agricultural colonization (Jaszi 1929: 318–36). These policies were to persist unremittingly until 1918 and went far beyond the haphazard 'Magyarization' stratagems of the 1840s. The Magyar ruling classes now dropped all pretence of respect for the diversity of peoples and cultures in Hungary. Since the Magyar ruling classes had been denied a fully independent Hungarian state, they were all the more determined to achieve complete hegemony and to 'lord it' over a fully 'Magyarized' Hungary. Denied 'their own' independent armed forces, they could (by way of compensation) enlist the help of Austrian bayonets to impose 'Magyarization' all the more ferociously, partly to vent their spleen on their perceived 'inferiors'.

Furthermore, the rapid growth of a Magyar state bureaucracy, the concurrent booms in Hungarian industry and infrastructure and the resultant influx of rustic Magyars into the main towns from the 1870s to the 1900s gave rise to a largely 'natural' and spontaneous 'Magyarization' of Hungary's hitherto predominantly German and Jewish urban populations. The population of Budapest rocketed from 202,000 in 1870 to 880,000 in 1910. It was in this period that the German and Jewish townspeople began to assimilate in earnest with the ascendant Magyars (from whom they had formerly remained quite separate) and to manifest the usual excessive zeal of 'new converts' (Jaszi 1929: 321, 324–5), while the Slovaks, South Slavs, Romanians and Ruthenes who were employed as cheap labour in urban industrial and construction work rapidly merged with their Magyar counterparts. The top-heavy concentration of 'modern' economic activity, political power, public employment and cultural amenities and patronage in booming Budapest exerted a powerful 'magnetic pull' on talent from the provinces, including the relatively few 'college-educated' Slovaks, South Slavs, Romanians and Ruthenes, and fostered a precocious yet remarkable flowering of 'modernist' cultural and scientific creativity. 'The intellectual splendour of the metropolitan city attracted into its sphere of influence all those elements of the country which were eager to embrace Western culture' (p. 325). Thus the meteoric rise of Budapest imparted a major additional impetus to cultural assimilation. To stand any chance of success in Budapest, aspiring musicians, writers, academics, artists, scientists, lawyers and churchmen usually had to be or 'become' Magyars, even if that involved changing their names, beliefs and identities. Magyarized Jews played prominent roles in the rise of Budapest and the spectacular scientific and cultural renaissance which it spearheaded – so much so that Karl Lueger, the anti-Semitic leader of Austria's Christian Social Party, habitually referred to Budapest and 'Judapest'.

Aggressive and repressive 'Magyarization', the forceful maintenance of Magyar supremacy and all the attendant social and political evils were, in the final analysis, bulwarks for the maintenance of feudal privilege in the face of festering ethnic and class antagonisms. The Magyar ruling classes found it expedient to play up and play upon Magyar phobias, especially vis-à-vis the 'inferior' nationalities. 'This fear complex . . . systematically developed by press and school and by parliamentarian and social oratory paralyzed all the efforts of three generations and made any serious social and economic reform impossible' (Jaszi 1929: 326).

It became axiomatic that either the ascendant Magyars would assimilate the non-Magyars or the latter would destroy the Hungarian state; that those who refused to learn the (difficult) Magyar language were traitors engaged in conspiracies to subvert the Hungarian state; and that there existed 'only one possible culture in the country, the Magyar culture' (Jaszi 1929: 320). The few non-Magyars elected to the Hungarian parliament were regularly shouted down or denounced as 'traitors' if they tried to speak out against forced 'Magyarization', while writers who dared to criticize forced 'Magyarization' in print were liable to be imprisoned either on charges of 'treason' or for 'incitement of national hatred' (pp. 327–8, 334–5, 338). Nevertheless, whether out of sheer ignorance or self-delusion, 'the majority of those who applied this system and the [Magyar] bourgeois and intellectual circles were deeply convinced that in Hungary there was no nationality persecution' and that the Magyars had conferred 'unparalleled . . . liberties and privileges' on the other ('inferior') nationalities. Consequently, 'it was regarded as unheard of ingratitude that these second-rank peoples rewarded this generosity by accusations and calumnies inciting foreign public opinion against the Magyar nation' (p. 337). Anyone who dared to criticize Hungarian conditions and practices had to be in the service of international conspiracies to subvert the Hungarian state and was immediately placed under 'suspicion of high treason'. 'Magyar domination was a command of destiny. Only a traitor could protest against it' (p. 338). Robert Seton-Watson, the eminent British specialist on the Balkans and East Central Europe who drew international attention to the seamy Magyar methods of national oppression and electoral chicanery before the First World War, was duly denounced by the Magyar press (p. 328).

The state employed various methods of forcible 'Magyarization'. As early as 1875–6 it suppressed several Slovak secondary schools. Then, starting with the 1879 (Primary) Education Act and the 1883 (Secondary) Education Act, it made more systematic efforts to 'Magyarize' the teaching profession, to extend compulsory instruction in and to curtail the use of non-Magyar languages, in flagrant violation of the 1868 Nationality Law. By 1900 more than four-fifths of all primary schools, five-sixths of all primary school teachers, 80 per cent of all secondary school pupils and 90 per cent of all students in higher education were formally Magyar-speaking (Jaszi 1929: 328–30). Magyar was made compulsory in all schools in 1883, while the 1907 Education Act not only imposed a special 'oath of loyalty' on all teachers, but also 'made them liable to dismissal if their pupils did not know Magyar' (Taylor 1976: 186).

More than 90 per cent of official posts were reserved for Magyars (Taylor 1976: 186), while 'all the cultural institutions of the country became instruments of Magyar national assimilation' (Jaszi 1929: 319). Many so-called Magyar Cultural Associations were established not so much 'for the cultural elevation of the Magyar masses' as for the harassment and intimidation of non-Magyar nationalists and cultural associations and the provision of 'sinecures for members of the privileged classes'. Other measures included the 'Magyarization' of place names (even in areas with few Magyar inhabitants) and 'Magyar agricultural colonization' (p. 336). In 1887 Lajos Mocsary, a prominent but increasingly isolated Magyar critic of aggressive 'Magyarization' policies, observed that 'the government does not regard as its proper task the checking of chauvinism in its wrong and aimless rampages but fosters it . . . This attitude gives rise to the surmise that all is allowed for the propagation of Magyarization, that the end sanctifies the means, that one can acquire by such deeds immortal merits' (quoted by Jaszi 1929: 339). 'Magyarization' engendered a cult of gratuitous violence against non-Magyars, perpetuated by upper- as well as middle- and lower-class thugs.

Jaszi foresaw that this whole programme was profoundly divisive and counter-productive, stirring up ill will and inter-ethnic conflict and using up scarce resources which could have been put to much more fruitful uses. For non-Magyars 'the Magyarizing drill of the elementary schools was good only for learning patriotic verses and songs by rote', with the result that 'they did not learn adequately either their mother-tongue or Magyar', while the time wasted on learning Magyar 'without obtaining the desired end' reduced the time available for all subjects (Jaszi 1929: 330). Yet the Magyar lower classes also lost out, because the state did not have sufficient resources to meet their basic educational and cultural needs and at the same time bestow/inflict Magyar education and culture upon the slightly larger non-Magyar population (pp. 328–9). Ironically, even among those non-Magyars who successfully progressed to a Magyar secondary or higher education, quite a few subsequently became ardent supporters of their own peoples' national claims (p. 330). Furthermore, 'forceful assimilation demoralized the ruling nation', engendering a kind of 'moral brutalization' of the perpetrators, whereas 'it elevates both intellectually and morally the better elements of the oppressed nationalities' (p. 340). Policies of forcible assimilation lowered the 'general standard of culture' by turning schools into 'a kind of chauvinistic nursery', thereby retarding the intellectual development of their pupils. Indeed, 'real assimilation' was rendered impossible: 'All real assimilation in modern times can be based only on the spontaneous exchange of spiritual and economic values.' The possibility of such an exchange (based on the 'spontaneous' processes of urbanization, economic development and 'natural' assimilation in post-1867 Hungary) was fatally impaired 'by the policy of forcible assimilation' (pp. 340–1, 325, 321). Responsibility for these deeply degrading, corrosive and counter-productive 'Magyarization' policies rested mainly on the blinkered Magyar upper classes (Jaszi 1929: 326, 336–7), who thus contributed strongly to the incipient disintegration of the Dual Monarchy.

During the early 1880s there was also a surge of virulent anti-Semitism in Hungary, fuelled by the continuing inflows of Jews from Poland and Russia and by their growing prominence in trade, finance, small-scale money-lending, industry, the professions and Hungary's cultural life. Magyar anti-Semitism culminated in the so-called Tiszaeszlar affair. In 1882, following the disappearance of a young girl from the village of Tiszaeszlar, the local Jews were accused of killing her for the purpose of ritual blood sacrifice. Their formal acquittal in 1883 unleashed a spate of anti-Jewish outrages in several counties. A new anti-Semitic party took off in the 1884 elections. However, many members of the Magyar 'establishment' realized that they needed the assistance of Jewish capital and commercial/financial expertise for their own solvency and that of the state, with the result that the 'party of government' soon decided to crack down on open expressions of anti-Semitism. Nevertheless, anti-Semitism simmered below the surface, especially among the lesser nobility, minor officials and sections of the peasantry and the petite bourgeoisie. It would resurface again from 1919 to 1922 and from 1931 to 1956, when various social groups found it expedient to blame their own and their country's woes on the Jews. Indeed, after the secession of Slovakia, Croatia and Transylvania in 1918, Jews replaced the Slovaks, South Slavs and Romanians as the favourite ethnic scapegoats of Hungary's 'declining classes'.

On the economic front the Kalman Tisza regime was under increasing pressure to respond to the deepening 'agrarian crisis' and, in particular, to come to the assistance of the Magyar nobility. In addition to providing more 'jobs for the boys' in the state bureaucracy, the increasingly interventionist Liberal Party inaugurated active programmes of industrial and infrastructural development, while at the same time enacting regressive and repressive rural labour legislation that was designed to assist landowners to weaken the position of rural labour, reduce rural wages, suppress agrarian unrest and impose a form of neo-serfdom.

Much has been made of the methods of state sponsorship of industrial and infrastructural development in Hungary from the 1880s to 1914. Since Hungary was prohibited from erecting tariffs against industrial imports from German Austria and the Czech Lands by the terms of the 1867 'compromise' and, what is more, it could not have afforded to run the risk of provoking retaliatory Austrian tariffs against Hungarian agricultural exports, the Magyar government devised more roundabout means of protection and promotion of Hungarian industry. In 1881 the first of several Industry Acts offered all new factories established in Hungary tax breaks and reimbursement of customs duties paid on equipment imported from outside the empire. Additional tax exemptions for new factories were introduced in 1884, while in 1890 economic stimulation was expanded in scope to include cash grants and credits to particular industries, manipulation of railway freight rates so as to favour Hungarian enterprises, and discrimination in favour of Hungarian companies in public procurement and in the allocation of state contracts. These policies culminated in the 1907 Industry Act, which distributed much larger subsidies on the basis of systematic studies of industrial bottlenecks and potential and more clearly formulated industrial priorities, concentrating 57 per cent of the projected subsidies on the textile industry (which offered the greatest scope for growth and import substitution right up to the 1930s).

After 1880 the state also became the driving force behind infrastructural development. By 1914 Hungary had 3,500 km of waterways navigable by steam vessels, while the Hungarian State Railways diversified into water transport in the 1880s, contributing to the growth of a Hungarian fleet of 338 steam vessels and 1,500 barges by 1914. More importantly, Hungary's railway network expanded from 7,200 km in 1880 to 22,200 km in 1913, largely as a result of state enterprise. By 1900 the density of railway lines per inhabitant and per square kilometre in Hungary had virtually caught up with that of Austria, was not far behind western Europe and far exceeded that of the Balkans, Poland and European Russia. The railways and railway construction boosted economic development in general, integrating product markets, increasing labour mobility, stimulating the land and capital markets, facilitating exports and imports, and providing the largest single market for Hungarian industrial products (Berend and Ranki 1974b: 37–9).

Yet, no matter how innovative or pioneering these policies were in the qualitative sense, quantitative research by Magyar economic historians has tended to downplay their relative importance in practice. They have calculated that, even at their peak, direct state subsidies to private industrial firms amounted to only 2 per cent of their total investment. 'Much more important was the fact that the state purchased 13 per cent of industrial production – indeed, in . . . machine-building it bought almost one-third of output' (Berend and Ranki 1974b: 55). By itself, however, state intervention could not wholly compensate for the weaknesses springing from low levels of economic development and capital accumulation. In itself it could only mobilize the modest resources at Hungary's disposal. 'By and large, state activity was effective only to the degree that it created attractive conditions for foreign capital, in particular by making investments secure and profitable. Thus the unique factor in the capitalist transformation was not so much direct state intervention as the influx and collaboration of foreign capital' (pp. 69–70). By 1913 36 per cent of Hungarian industry was foreign owned (p. 109). These are important qualifications to the influential theses put forward by Gerschenkron (1962, 1968), which have ascribed the crucial propulsive role in the economic development of Europe's so-called 'backward economies' from the 1880s to 1914 to direct state activity and intervention in the economy.

The Hungarian strategy for attracting foreign capital involved the maintenance of political stability, 'law and order', relatively low wages, the provision of tax incentives, the repression of strikes and organized labour, and official tolerance of foreign workers, foreign personnel and a broad range of religious denominations. In practice, the thirty-year tenure of the corrupt and repressive Liberal Party probably did more to attract than to repel foreign investors and entrepreneurs, who were not too concerned with democratic niceties. Indeed, the one area in which the regime was genuinely liberal was in matters of religion. Against fierce Habsburg, aristocratic and Roman Catholic opposition (especially in the upper house of parliament), the Liberal Party fought a long and eventually successful campaign to reduce the excessive power and influence of the Roman Catholic Church in education, marriage and family affairs and to establish freedom of religion and the equal status of various faiths and denominations (including Judaism). Between 1892 and 1894 Liberals, Calvinists, Lutherans, Jews, secularists and the anti-clerical left united to defeat the Roman Catholic right (just as they did a century later, in the June 1994 general election). Moreover, Protestant and Jewish entrepreneurs and immigrants, including numerous engineers, managers, technicians, doctors and lawyers, were attracted by the increasing secularism, doctrinal pluralism and religious tolerance of Hungarian society (a kind a revival of or return to pre-Habsburg traditions). Thus as early as 1875 'foreigners' made up 25 per cent of the working population of Budapest (Berend and Ranki 1974b: 79).

On the agrarian front the decisive interventions of the Magyar state were intended to strengthen the economic, social and political position of the Magyar landed elite vis-à-vis Magyar and especially non-Magyar farm servants and labourers. The Agricultural Labour Act of 1876 curtailed the personal liberties and equality before the law of farm labour, declared the hired labourer or farm servant to be 'under his master's authority', and gave landowners licence to humiliate or inflict corporal punishment upon their menials without fear of any legal 'comeback' from the victims. It also stipulated that farm servants or labourers who attempted to quit or change their jobs without their employer's consent were to be returned to their 'master' by the police or gendarmerie. The Penal Code of 1878 outlawed not only 'violent argument' and 'interference with the work of others' but any 'gatherings' in pursuit of higher wages. The Farm Servants Act of 1898 (popularly known as 'the slave law') went still further, forcing farm servants and labourers to enter into legally enforceable contracts with their employers, forbidding them either to leave their estates or to receive 'strangers' into their homes, and prescribing sixty-day prison terms for incitement to strike. Finally, the 1907 Farm Servants Act banned some remnants of 'feudal' labour services and corporal punishment of adults, but retained corporal punishment for teenagers, promised landowners military assistance 'on demand' against 'disobedient' employees and prescribed severe penalties for strikers.

These were in large part economic measures, intended to strengthen agricultural employers against their employees in order to reduce the estates' wage and other production costs and thereby protect investments and grain exports, while also cushioning landowners against the effects of the late nineteenth-century fall in grain prices and the difficult transition to a wage-labour economy. The Magyar ruling classes reached a consensus 'on the need to protect the profit margin of large agricultural production units in order to maintain the country's grain exports and the accumulation of domestic capital' (Janos 1982: 131). Yet these were also socio-political measures, designed to reintroduce elements of serfdom in a more modern capitalist 'police state' guise and thereby buttress the political monopoly and rural 'social control' exercised by the Magyar landed nobility, in the face of the mounting challenges posed by the birth of socialist movements and ideas, by organized labour and, among the non-Magyars who provided growing proportions of the estate owners' workforce as more and more Magyars migrated to the towns in search of higher wages, by the growth of nationalist movements and consciousness. In the final analysis the regime still regarded the Magyar landed estates as its main instruments of social and political control over Hungary's downtrodden but increasingly restive rural population.

In spite of all its repressive and regressive legislation, Hungary made striking economic and social progress from 1867 to 1914. Between these two dates the population of Budapest rose from 200,000 to 900,000, the railway network expanded from 2,200 km to 22,200 km, the growth of industrial output averaged 5 per cent per annum, agricultural output grew on average by 2 per cent per annum and the growth of national income averaged 3.2 per cent a year (Berend and Ranki 1974b: 73–4). The share of the workforce dependent on agriculture fell from 80 per cent in 1870 to 64.5 per cent in 1910, whereas the proportion engaged in industry, trade and transport rose from 11.5 per cent to 23.6 per cent over the same period (p. 74). Gross agricultural production more than doubled between 1867–70 and 1911–13 (p. 48). The late nineteenth-century fall in international grain prices both stimulated and was more than compensated by technical and structural changes. Over the period 1873–1913 there was a 70 per cent increase in grain yields per hectare, a 30 per cent expansion of the total cultivated area, a considerable diversification from grain crops into more intensive and remunerative livestock rearing and cultivation of potatoes, sugar-beet and other root crops, and a 60 per cent reduction in the proportion of arable land left fallow. In addition, there were major improvements in traditional farm implements. But these were later to be overshadowed by more spectacular advances in the use of both horse-drawn and steam-powered machinery on the larger estates. The number of steam threshers rose from 2,500 in 1871 to 30,000 by 1914, while the use of horse-drawn seed drills increased sevenfold between 1871 and 1895. Grain output nearly trebled between 1864–6 and 1911–13, but potato output increased sevenfold and the output of both sugar-beet and turnips increased more than twentyfold over the same period, while by 1900 more than 40 per cent of farm incomes came from livestock rearing (pp. 44–7). All in all, this amounted to a minor 'agricultural revolution', comparable to that which occurred in late Tsarist Russia (see Bideleux 1987: 11–18; 1990).

Not surprisingly, given this rich and diversifying agricultural resource base, food-processing continued to dominate Hungarian industrial development and, as early as 1884, Manfred Weiss opened Hungary's first food-canning plant ('the shape of things to come'). More remarkably, Hungary also emerged as a significant producer (and even exporter) of railway locomotives and rolling stock, flour-milling equipment, agricultural machinery and steam turbines for electricity generation (the Ganz Works and Mavag). It became a European pioneer in the manufacture of electric light bulbs (of which it remains a major producer and exporter today), electric transformers, watt-meters and electric locomotives. By 1914 Hungary was also a significant producer of chemicals (fertilizer and explosives), munitions and steel and it even produced its first tractors, lorries, cars and aircraft. This technological precociousness was partly the work of enterprising foreigners such as Abraham Ganz (of Swiss origin), but it must also be accredited to the promotion of scientific and technological higher education by an unusually 'developmental' Magyar state. Some of the 'leading names' (Kando, Blathy, Dery, Hevesy and Szilard) were clearly Magyars, precursors of such household names as Biro and Rubic.

It may appear even more paradoxical that the repressive (and in many ways regressive) Magyar state also presided over an 'educational revolution'. Attendance at elementary schools rose from 1.1 million in 1869 to 2.7 million in 1910 (or from 48 per cent to 89 per cent of the relevant six to twelve age group), although attendance at secondary schools only increased from 4 per cent to 5 per cent of the secondary age group. Adult literacy increased from 34 per cent in 1870 to 69 per cent in 1910 (nearly 80 per cent for males over the age of seven and 88 per cent for industrial employees). By 1914 Hungary also had 14,000 university students (Berend and Ranki 1974b: 26–8; Janos 1982: 156). The key to the apparent paradox was the fervent Magyar nationalist desire to make Hungary both 'great' and thoroughly Magyar. This involved the promotion of education as an instrument of Magyarization. Indeed, the share of the population recorded as 'Magyar' had risen from 37 per cent in 1837 to 48 per cent in 1910 in the kingdom as a whole and from 44 per cent to 52 per cent in 'Hungary proper' (that is, excluding Croatia-Slavonia).

However, this 'educational revolution' also broadened social and political horizons, raised expectations and increased Magyar and non-Magyar discontent with the outmoded political monopoly maintained by the Magyar ruling classes. This fuelled an intensification of social and political tensions in Hungary during the 1890s and 1900s, beginning with the fall of Kalman Tisza in 1890. During 1889–90 Tisza was obliged to 'steamroll' extremely unpopular 'Germanizing' reforms of the Habsburg armed forces through the Magyar-dominated Hungarian parliament, as part of a drive to modernize and expand the empire's defences. In doing so, however, he used up all his political credit with his nationalistic Magyar 'gentry' supporters and in 1890 he felt obliged to resign. Tisza's successors, the more 'liberal' Gyula Szapary and Sandor Wekerle governments (1890–2 and 1892–5 respectively), exhausted themselves in an ultimately successful campaign for anti-clerical 'secularizing' reforms. They were followed by the utterly intolerant, chauvinistic and repressive Banffy government (1895–9). This was eventually toppled by the incipient crisis in Austrian–Hungarian relations, precipitated by the provision for decennial renewal and revision of the precise terms of the 1867 'compromise'. Banffy's Liberal successors, the more emollient Kalman Szell (1899–1903) and the hardline 'strongmen' Count Karoly Khuen-Hedervary (1903) and Count Istvan Tisza (the son of Kalman Tisza, 1903–5), fell for similar reasons.

Hungary on the brink of revolution, 1905

In January 1905, amid increasing repression of mounting peasant, proletarian and ethnic unrest, the Liberal Party finally lost power in relatively 'free' and fiercely contested elections, which were called in an unsuccessful attempt to resolve the deepening deadlock in Austrian–Hungarian relations. The tyrannical Istvan Tisza was defeated by an unholy 'Coalition' of even more extreme Magyar nationalists, reform-minded 'liberals' and democrats, and disaffected conservatives, Catholics and aristocrats, who were united only by their opposition to Tisza's compliant behaviour towards Austria and Emperor Franz Josef. However, the emperor refused to allow the defiant 'Coalition' to form a government on its own terms (namely, radical revision of the terms of the 1867 'compromise'), while the 'Coalition' was not yet ready to form a government on Franz Josef's terms (acceptance of the status quo). During this standoff and the ensuing power vacuum, peasant and proletarian unrest escalated still further, spurred on by news of the unfolding 1905 Revolution in Russia. In June 1905, finally, Franz Josef prevailed upon the 'loyalist' general and former defence minister Geza Fejevary to form a government. However, the Fejevary government was voted down by the 'Coalition' majority in parliament, which then called for Magyar 'national resistance' in the time-honoured fashion: non-collection of taxes and non-delivery of army recruits.

Workers' protests climaxed on 'Red Friday' (15 September 1905), when a hundred thousand demonstrators encircled the parliament building in Budapest. But they shrank back from real revolution (entailing a transfer of political power to the streets and barricades) and eventually dispersed peacefully. Perhaps a revolutionary opportunity was missed, but it seems very unlikely that the left could have triumphed against the still well-organized and disciplined forces of 'reaction'. After this hollow and inconsequential show of strength, workers' unrest rapidly lost its sense of purpose and momentum.

On 3 October 1905, in Fiume, Croat and Serb leaders issued a 'resolution' declaring their readiness to support Magyar nationalist defiance of the Habsburgs in return for Magyar recognition of the 'national rights' of Croatia and Dalmatia, including a union of these two largely Croat-inhabited provinces which had long been divided between Hungary and Austria. But this pointed show of solidarity aroused more fear than hope in the hearts of Magyar nationalists, most of whom blithely assumed that it was their manifest destiny to dominate their 'inferior' neighbours.

Attempts to restore the status quo ante, 1906–10

In early 1906, when the imperial authorities and the Fejevary government stopped paying the salaries of Magyar officials, suspended the defiant parliament, imposed military rule and threatened to introduce universal suffrage (which could have deprived the Magyar parties of their parliamentary majority), the Magyar nationalist 'Coalition' rapidly caved in. Leading members of the 'Coalition' (including Ferenc Kossuth, son of Lajos Kossuth) joined a government headed by the former Liberal premier Sandor Wekerle (1906–10), which secretly agreed to renew the 1867 'compromise' virtually unchanged and defend the status quo in Hungary. The 'Coalition' ministers soon reneged on the positions they had taken when in opposition, thereby alienating their more radical supporters and exposing the unbridgeable divisions within their own ranks. However, by passing new Farm Servants and Industrial Acts and repressing peasant, proletarian and non-Magyar nationalist unrest, they contributed to a revival of business confidence and a fresh economic boom, which helped to buoy up the government and defuse economic discontents. Moreover, taking a leaf out of Bismarck's book, they expanded and centralized a nascent system of health insurance and established a system of compulsory accident insurance for industrial workers. This laid the foundations of a new conservative corporatism designed to defuse class antagonism and curb the popular appeal of the left.

Nevertheless, the urban working class, the peasantry and the intelligentsia had 'grown' considerably in education, consciousness, confidence and strength. During 1905 they had gained a small taste of power and a brief glimpse of freedom. It was now almost impossible to put the genie back into the bottle. The Social Democratic Party, the urban workers' movement and the Independent

Socialist Peasant Party of Hungary (established in 1906) gained steadily in membership, sophistication and organizational strength, at least until the fresh waves of repression unleashed by Istvan Tisza between 1913 and 1917. The radical and liberal sections of the intelligentsia found more effective and articulate expression in the journal *Huszadik Szazad* (*Twentieth Century*), under the intellectual leadership of Oscar (Oszkar) Jaszi and his Citizens' Radical Party (established in 1910), and in the radicalized Independence Party, headed by Mihaly Karolyi from 1913 onward. All these movements were working out potential alternatives to conservatism, oligarchy, Magyar supremacism and repression, the key characteristics of the existing state. Although their development was to be rudely interrupted by the Istvan Tisza regime of 1913–17 and the outbreak of the First World War, these movements would resurface with greatly enhanced strength, acuity and popular support in 1918.

The authoritarian ascendancy of Istvan Tisza, 1910–17

At the parliamentary and governmental levels, however, power slipped back into the hands of the former Liberal Party old guard, led by Istvan Tisza and reorganized in 1910 as the Party of National Work. It backed the government of Count Karoly Khuen-Hedervary, who returned to the premiership during 1910–11. He was toppled by united left-wing and Magyar nationalist opposition to an Army Bill in 1911. In May 1912 real power passed to Istvan Tisza who, as speaker of the lower house, steamrolled the troublesome bill through parliament (even evicting some opposition MPs) and faced down the mass protests and demonstrations organized by the workers' movement and the radical intelligentsia. In 1913 Tisza became prime minister and ruled Hungary with a rod of iron until he was forced to resign by the new, more liberal Emperor Karl in May 1917.

18 Capitalism and nationalism: the seeds of social revolution and imperial disintegration in Austria-Hungary, 1867 to 1918

THE ECONOMIC RESURGENCE OF AUSTRIA-HUNGARY, 1867–1914

The economic resurgence of the 'Austrian half' of the Habsburg Empire (which we shall sometimes refer to as 'Austria' for short) from the late 1860s to 1914 was stimulated and assisted by a number of factors: increased state expenditure on physical infrastructure (especially railways) and on armaments; growing industrial protectionism and cartelization; the creation of 'captive' export markets in Hungary and the Balkans; and strengthening economic ties with Germany, from which Austria's increasingly educated engineers, managers and workforce readily assimilated the latest technologies, business methods and banking practices.

Reflecting an earlier (much more negative) view of nineteenth-century Austria's economic performance, N. Gross (1973: 229) once wrote that 'the long-run decline of Habsburg from the status of a first rank power must have hampered economic growth at least because of the persistent costly efforts to halt or at least disguise the process'. However, it is now widely accepted that between 1880 and 1913 Austria's industrial output grew by about 3.6 per cent per annum on average, that is at approximately the same rate as that of Germany between 1870 and 1913 (Rudolph 1976: 235). Austria's industrial output roughly doubled between 1880 and 1895 and roughly trebled between 1880 and 1913 (Good 1984: 258–9). Furthermore, Austria's real per capita GNP grew at an average annual rate of 1.32 per cent between 1870 and 1913, roughly on a par with Switzerland (1.32 per cent) and Norway (1.35 per cent) and well ahead of Spain (0.25 per cent), Italy (0.81 per cent), Holland (0.93 per cent), Britain (1.0 per cent), Belgium (1.05 per cent) and France (1.06 per cent) during the same period. Only a few European countries did significantly better: Germany (1.51 per cent), Hungary (1.7 per cent), Denmark (2.19 per cent) and Sweden (2.39 per cent) (pp. 239–40). By 1913 the per capita GNP of the Germanic areas of Austria had drawn level with that of France and was only 10 per cent below that of Germany, while the per capita GNP of the 'Austrian half' of the Habsburg Empire was 38 per cent below that of France, 43 per cent below that of Germany, roughly on a par with Italy and about 44 per cent above that of Hungary (Good 1984: 219–20, 241–2).

Between 1880 and 1913 the average annual growth rate of Austria's former 'leading sectors' (food-processing and textiles) eased off to 2.7 per cent and 3.1 per cent respectively (Rudolph 1976: 13). This was partly because the rates of growth of demand for their products were tailing off slightly as particular markets approached saturation point and partly because the initially explosive growth potential of the technological advances which had revolutionized these industries was nearing exhaustion. Nevertheless, the Czech Lands and the Germanic areas of Austria were emerging as European technological leaders in several light industries, including sugar refining, brewing (Pilsener lager) and glass making. The new 'leading sectors' were engineering and metallurgy, which grew on average by 9.5 per cent and 7 per cent per annum respectively (p. 13). These industries directly benefited from the high levels of state expenditure on railway construction, the pan-European arms race, the relatively rapid development of engineering and metallurgical technologies, and the increasing industrial concentration, protectionism and cartelization in the decades leading up to the First World War. Protectionism, the arms race and high infrastructural expenditure particularly promoted the heavy industries which were emerging in Styria and (above all) the Czech Lands. By 1910, with just 36 per cent of the population of the Austrian half of the Empire, the Czech Lands were producing 58 per cent of its pig iron, more than 80 per cent of its cast iron, 86 per cent of its anthracite (hard coal), 84 per cent of its lignite (brown coal), 75 per cent of its chemicals, 94 per cent of its refined sugar, 59 per cent of its beer and more than 75 per cent of its textiles. In 1902 the Czech Lands provided in excess of 56 per cent of the industrial workforce and 68 per cent of Austria's mechanical horsepower (Rudolph 1976: 41). The introduction of the Gilchrist–Thomas process (1879) revolutionized the use of low-grade, highly phosphoric Bohemian and Moravian iron ores for steel making. The Skoda works (directed by Emil and Karl Skoda) had become the Monarchy's major producer of machinery and armaments by the 1900s.

Richard Rudolph has argued that the 'impressive growth' and industrial attainments of German Austria and the Czech Lands prior to the First World War were partly obscured or concealed by the presence of populous underdeveloped regions within the Austro-Hungarian Empire and customs union, and that it was as misleading to concentrate on per capita figures for the Habsburg Monarchy as a whole as it would be to do so 'for the British Empire as a whole' (pp. 9–10). Instead, he argued, areas such as Hungary or Galicia should be viewed as 'enclave economies' and 'the development of the Austro-Hungarian Monarchy may be seen as that of an industrializing region, the Austrian–Czech Land complex, which by its political power, in collaboration with the landed interests of its economic hinterland, and by means of its economic power, its role as a financial centre and its cartels, was able to develop itself at the expense of the enclave areas' (p. 10).

The main problem with this interpretation is that several distinguished Hungarian economic historians (including Ivan Berend, Gyorgy Ranki, Lajos Katus and Peter Hanak, who under Communist rule were obliged to work within officially mandated Marxist paradigms) have cogently demonstrated that the supposedly deprived and exploited economy of the 'Hungarian half' of the Habsburg Empire, which we shall refer to as 'Hungary' or the 'Kingdom of Hungary' for short, actually grew *even faster* than its Austrian counterpart between 1870 and 1913 and that it gained much more than it lost through its so-called 'dependence' on Austria. In particular, it gained in terms of political and economic stability and coherence, attraction of foreign (especially Austrian) finance and entrepreneurship, and preferential access to a secure market for its primary exports. This was not a zero-sum game: Austria's gain was not necessarily Hungary's loss. There were often reciprocal gains for both Austria and Hungary. Indeed, between 1867 and 1914 investment from outside Hungary (mainly from Austria) made up around 40 per cent of total investment in Hungary and something approaching 80 per cent of Austrian 'foreign' investment was destined for Hungary (Good 1984: 108). From the mid-1860s onwards, nevertheless, periods of faster growth in Hungary tended to coincide with periods of slower growth in Austria and vice versa (Komlos 1981: 10–11). Average annual rates of economic growth in Austria and Hungary were as shown in Table 18.1.

Table 18.1 Average annual rates of economic growth in Austria and Hungary (%)

	1867–71	1871–84	1884–98	1898–1907	1907–13
Austria	3.9	2.4	2.8	3.8	1.6
Hungary	1.4	5.1	3.3	2.4	5.3

'The mechanism for this pattern is to be sought in the flow of capital between Austria and Hungary' (Komlos 1981: 12). In particular, the 1873 crash encouraged a migration of capital from Austria, where speculators had over-invested during the 1867–73 *Gründerzeit*, to Hungary, which now seemed a safer bet. Conversely, as Austrian industrialization gradually regained momentum during the 1880s and 1890s, capital began to flow back to Austria and the Hungarian industrial boom of 1874–83 began to slow down. Finally, the industrial slow-down in Austria after 1907 was associated with a renewed outflow of capital from Austria into Hungary, where it financed another Hungarian industrial boom before the brief Austrian industrial revival of 1911–13 (reflecting sharply increased state spending on infrastructure and armaments, in apparent preparation for war).

The existence of various natural and man-made complementarities rendered the Austro-Hungarian economic relationship more mutually advantageous (symbiotic) than 'predatory' or 'exploitative'. By 1901 Hungary absorbed 35 per cent of Austria's exports and supplied 38 per cent of its imports, but Austria absorbed 72 per cent of Hungary's exports and supplied 79 per cent of its imports. In 1913 Hungary still accounted for 37 per cent of Austria's exports and 32 per cent of its imports, while Austria took 75 per cent of Hungary's exports and provided 72 per cent of its imports (Jenks 1967: 36). In 1913 Austria and Hungary exported only about 7 per cent of their combined GNP to markets outside the Monarchy. (Germany, by comparison, exported 14.6 per cent of its GNP, while the corresponding figure for France was 15.3 per cent.) In 1910, furthermore, Austria-Hungary accounted for only 5.6 per cent of European exports, compared with 20.4 per cent for Germany, 13.4 per cent for France, 23.7 per cent for Britain and 8.9 per cent for Russia (Good 1984: 109). The relative smallness of Austria-Hungary's export sector and the relatively high level of imperial autarky both reflected and reinforced the strong dependence on internal interregional trade, especially (but not exclusively) between Austria and Hungary. This adds weight to the observation that 'while nationalistic passions ran high . . . few men went so far as to advocate the atomization of the Empire. Such restraint may have been motivated in part by a fear of Austria-Hungary's powerful neighbours to the north and east, who were known for their ruthless treatment of minorities; and it may have been caused, perhaps to an even greater extent, by a widely shared realization that the customs union, for all its defects and imperfections, was an alternative preferable to the Balkanization of Central Europe' (März 1953: 135).

'FINANCE CAPITALISM', 'MONOPOLY CAPITALISM', RUDOLPH HILFERDING AND THE MARXIST-LENINIST ROUTE TO 'SOCIALISM'

Together with Germany and Switzerland, Austria was in the forefront of the development of European 'finance capitalism' and 'monopoly capitalism'. It was no accident that the first major treatise on cartels was written by the Austrian, Friedrich Kleinwächter (1883) or that entrepreneurial bankers and the creation of bank credit were to be so central to Joseph Schumpeter's influential theory of capitalist economic development. Moreover, the seminal Marxist analysis of the transformation of competitive and pluralistic 'liberal capitalism' into monopolistic 'finance capital' was written by another Austrian, Rudolph Hilferding (1910), who was later to serve as a socialist finance minister in Germany in 1923 and in 1928–9. Lenin's more famous analysis of 'monopoly capitalism' in 1917–18 added remarkably little to Hilferding's seminal insights.

In Austria, as in Germany, the growth of protectionism and of state and bank involvement in railway construction, arms production and the development of the affiliated heavy industries created an environment conducive to industrial concentration, cartelization and collusive/monopolistic practices. In north-western Europe and the USA, law courts and legislatures have generally regarded cartels and monopolistic arrangements in the private sector as illegal 'conspiracies in restraint of trade', detrimental to the 'public interest' and to the long-term health and vigour of a market economy. The Germanic world, by contrast, adopted much more permissive or even positively pro-cartel and pro-monopoly attitudes. The 'liberal' interlude in the German-speaking states during the 1850s and 1860s was only a temporary aberration on their part reflecting the short-lived ideological ascendancy and example of a 'liberal' Britain which was then at the peak of its power, success and influence. Austria, like Germany and Switzerland, never wholly 'kicked the habit' of forming collusive industrial and trade associations. Hence seventy-four voluntary associations of manufacturers were established in Austria between 1839 and 1892, mainly to lobby for protective tariffs (Good 1984: 218).

The connections and mutual support between these associations facilitated collusion, amalgamations and the subsequent growth of price-fixing and market-sharing agreements, particularly in those industries which were gradually insulated against potentially disruptive foreign competition by the raising of protective tariffs (Gross 1973: 258–9). Austria's first cartel agreement was established by rail producers in 1878, in the wake of the post-1873 depression. By 1890 there were eighteen such agreements, more than half of them in the mining and metallurgical sectors. Austria had 57 cartel agreements by 1900, 120 by 1909 (including 19 in mining and metallurgy, 12 in chemicals, 27 in textiles, 10 in glass making and 9 in food-processing) and 200 in 1912, by which time cartels had become the norm rather than the exception in Austrian industry (Good 1984: 219). 'As in Germany, the Austrian courts tended to view cartel arrangements as legally binding contracts', rather than as illegal conspiracies in restraint of competition (pp. 235–6). In Austria cartels were extolled as the way to avoid the 'anarchy' of competition, protect the small producer and safeguard industrial profit margins, firms, investments and jobs, thereby encouraging and facilitating investment in new technologies, scientific industries, rationalization and large industrial complexes and making the workforce less likely to fear and oppose change (p. 235).

Cartelization in turn paved the way for multiple or interlocking directorships, for the representation of bankers on boards of directors in industry and for increased intermarriage of industrial and banking families. Moreover, during the great 'crash' of 1873, the banks which survived had to foreclose on their 'overextended' industrial clients and thus acquired significant industrial assets. However, the 1873 'crash' also discouraged bankers from investing heavily in industry again until 1895, when Austria's banks began to promote a second *Gründerzeit* (Good 1984: 209; Rudolph 1976: 102–3). By 1914 the major Austrian banks had 'firmly embedded themselves in a number of major industrial firms' and banks held about 73 per cent of the share capital of joint stock mining and milling companies, about 80 per cent of that of the joint stock sugar companies and almost 100 per cent of that of the joint stock metal-working, machine-building and armaments companies (Rudolph 1976: 118–20). Similarly, by 1913 the five largest Budapest banks accounted for 57 per cent of all Hungarian bank credit, held 47 per cent of the capital of Hungary's industrial firms and controlled 225 of Hungary's 250 largest companies (Good 1984: 108; Janos 1982: 151). The bank of the Austrian Rothschilds, the famous Creditanstalt, eventually controlled nearly one-third of Austria's industrial assets, which was the main reason why its collapse in 1931 had such devastating economic repercussions.

Hilferding's *Das Finanzkapital* (1910) portrayed the bankers of the new era of 'finance capitalism' as essentially *parasitic* upon industry and agriculture and as products (even archetypes) of the putative 'advanced senility' of capitalism, in contrast to the more dynamic, heroic, competitive, innovative, buccaneering capitalism of the 'liberal era' and earlier. For Hilferding, the significance of the transformation of Austria's former 'liberal' capitalism into illiberal cartelized and monopolistic 'finance capitalism' was as much political as economic. 'Finance capitalism, in its maturity, is the highest stage of concentration of economic and political power in the hands of the capitalist oligarchy' (Hilferding 1981: 370). 'Finance capitalism' had ended the former separation of industrial, mercantile and banking capital, bringing them together 'under the common direction of high finance, in which the masters of industry and of the banks are united in a close personal association' (p. 301). This had fundamentally changed the relationship between the capitalist classes and the state. While capitalism was still an emergent and divided force, the bourgeoisie had struggled against mercantilism, against the privileges and monopolies of large trading and colonial companies and of the closed craft guilds, and against 'the centralized and privilege-dispensing state'. This became a battle for economic freedom, which in turn developed into 'a broader struggle for individual liberty against the tutelege of the state' (p. 301). Until the 1860s, therefore, the issues that agitated the bourgeoisie were 'essentially constitutional', that is, issues that 'affected all citizens alike, uniting them in a common struggle against reaction and the vestiges of feudal and absolutist-bureaucratic rule' (p. 337). However, the development of cartels and 'finance capitalism' had fundamentally altered political alignments and the balance of forces. 'Cartelization . . . co-ordinates the political interests of capital and enables the whole weight of economic power to be exerted directly on the state' (p. 338). Listian demands for *temporary* and *selective* protection of 'infant industries' gave way to organized lobbying for *permanent* protection of *established* industries, monopolies and cartels in order to help to make inflated profits on the home market, partly to subsidize exports and partly to finance higher investment (pp. 304–10.) 'Cartelization also strengthens the employers' position on the labour market and weakens that of trade unions' (p. 365), thereby inaugurating 'the ultimate phase of the class struggle between the bourgeoisie and the proletariat' (p. 367).

In Hilferding's view, the extraordinary centralization of economic control over private enterprises and production achieved by industrial concentration, cartelization, the intermarriage of banks and industry and the other contrivances of monopolistic 'finance capitalism' could also greatly facilitate the task of 'overcoming' capitalism (Hilferding 1981: 367–8). 'Once finance capital has brought the most important branches of production under its control, it is enough for society, through its conscious executive organ – the state conquered by the working class – to seize financial capital in order to gain immediate control of these branches of production' (p. 367). To establish socialism in societies in the grip of monopolistic 'finance capitalism', it would therefore be sufficient for the socialists to capture control of the biggest banks, because these already controlled the lion's share of large-scale industry, which in turn dominated most small producers. 'There is no need to extend the process of expropriation to the great bulk of peasant farms and small businesses because, as a result of the seizure of large-scale industry, upon which they have long been dependent, they would be indirectly socialized' (p. 368). This would allow expropriation to proceed gradually, 'precisely in those spheres of decentralized production where it would be a . . . politically dangerous process' (p. 368).

Hitherto, most Marxists had assumed that it would be necessary to wait patiently for many decades to allow capitalism to complete its 'historic' task of making the economy, society and the working class fully 'ripe' for socialism, that is, sufficiently productive, educated, politically conscious, class conscious and organized to be able to dispense with capitalism and capitalists. However, Hilferding's 'discovery' of the new possibilities opened up by an increasingly cartelized and monopolistic 'finance capitalism' offered to telescope the whole process into a much shorter time-span. It seemingly offered a short cut and a much quicker and easier transition to 'socialism'. Furthermore, Marxist socialism would no longer have to frighten and alienate the numerous small proprietors and small producers (the 'petite bourgeoisie') with threats of immediate post-revolutionary expropriation. Instead, 'since finance capital has already achieved expropriation to the extent required by socialism, it is possible to dispense with a sudden act of expropriation by the state and to substitute a gradual process of socialization through the economic benefits which ["socialist"] society will confer. While thus creating the final organizational prerequisites for socialism, finance capital also makes the transition easier in the political sense' (p. 368). At the same time 'the blatant seizure of the state by the capitalist class' in the era of monopolistic 'finance capitalism', together with the more naked use of 'the state apparatus' to serve capitalist interests, 'compels every proletarian to strive for the conquest of political power as the only means of putting an end to his own exploitation' (p. 368).

In addition, Hilferding maintained that the growth of industrial concentration, cartelization, monopoly and protectionism was intensifying the quest for captive markets, capital exports, imperialism and international tensions and conflicts. 'The old Free Traders believed in free trade not only as the best economic policy, but as the beginning of an era of peace. Finance capital abandoned this belief long ago . . . The ideal is now to secure for one's own nation the domination of the world' (p. 335). Eventually, 'as the expansion of the world market slows down, the conflicts between capitalist nations over their share in it will become more acute . . . The danger of war increases armaments and the tax burden' (p. 369). In the end, 'the policy of finance capital is bound to lead towards war, and hence to the unleashing of revolutionary storms' (p. 366).

Reinforced by the largely derivative theoretical writings of Lenin and Bukharin on 'finance capitalism', 'monopoly capitalism' and '(capitalist) imperialism' between 1915 and 1917, *Hilferding's novel ideas furnished the new theoretical and programmatic basis on which Marxist-Leninist Communist parties subsequently proposed to seize political power, capture control of the 'commanding heights' of the economy, and impose 'socialism' 'from above' on countries which were in the grip of the increasingly centralized economic systems created by cartelized and monopolistic 'finance capitalism'.* This was how Marxist-Leninist parties in Russia and subsequently in East Central Europe and the Balkans argued that *Communist seizures of power and Communist-led transitions to 'socialism' could (and indeed did) take place in the 'less developed' capitalist states of East Central Europe, the Balkans and Russia, rather than in the more liberal, prosperous and in these respects 'more developed' capitalist states of north-western Europe and North America.* The Habsburg Empire, Germany, Romania and Tsarist Russia were quite clearly in the grip of highly centralized, cartelized, protectionist and monopolistic forms of 'finance capitalism' by the early twentieth century (probably more so than Britain, France and the Low Countries). It was in this (limited) sense that they could be claimed to have become 'ripe' for (rather crudely conceived and implemented) 'transitions' to (even cruder) forms of 'socialism'. Increasingly centralized industrial, financial and infrastructural systems were indeed emerging in the central and easterly regions of Europe, under the aegis of monopolistic 'finance capital' promoted and buttressed by state tutelage. It was also the case that these emerging economic and state systems could be (and in most cases were) captured by sufficiently ruthless, opportunistic and determined Marxist-Leninist parties, which could then use their control of the 'commanding heights' of these highly centralized and concentrated economic systems to impose 'from above' their crude, doctrinaire, regimented and rather Spartan visions of 'socialism', even though (i) relatively few of the inhabitants of these countries manifested much desire to have these coarse, doctrinaire and coercive Marxist-Leninist visions of 'socialism' foisted upon them, and (ii) they were insufficiently educated and productive to attain anything remotely approaching economic 'abundance'. Consequently, all that could be achieved were mean, regimented, coercive, economically and culturally impoverished *parodies or travesties of 'socialism'*, which bore various uncomfortable resemblances to Europe's more short-lived fascist regimes.

Both non-Marxist and 'orthodox' Marxist critics of Europe's Communist regimes have argued that, even if crude and coercive parodies of 'socialism' could indeed be inflicted on largely unsuspecting, hostile or reluctant populations of Russia, East Central Europe and the Balkans, utilizing the centralized economic systems and the potentially coercive concentrations of power and control created by monopolistic 'finance capital' (alias 'monopoly capitalism'), most of these countries were nevertheless far from 'ripe' for less regimented, less Spartan and more widely acceptable versions of Marxist 'socialism'. Furthermore, nowhere in these regions has there even been strong evidence of majority support for Marxist movements, other than in Czechoslovakia, Yugoslavia, Albania and Greece in the exceptional circumstances of 1944–6. Only in one of these countries – Czechoslovakia – was there a sufficiently educated, class-conscious and productive popular base on which to attempt to build *a bona fide socialist system by consent rather than by coercion*. Indeed, if it had been allowed to do so, it is conceivable that Czechoslovakia could have pursued a 'democratic road to socialism' and 'socialism with a human face' in the late 1940s and subsequently. Moreover, despite the growing dependence of small producers and proprietors upon both bank credit and larger firms, and the unhealthy degrees of concentration of economic and political power and control in the hands of illiberal and undemocratic propertied oligarchies during the final decades of the Habsburg, German and Tsarist empires, Hilferding and the chief theoreticians of Marxism-Leninism undoubtedly overestimated the extent to which it would be viable for Marxist socialists to utilize the 'commanding heights' of these countries' economies to exercise effective centralized control over their large multitudes of small producers. The loose-reined financial and commercial control wielded by banks and large firms over dependent clients and small producers under (pre-electronic) monopolistic 'finance capitalism' was of a much lower order than the strict 'chains of command' and more comprehensive day-to-day control 'from above' which would have been nec-essary for the efficient functioning of a command economy. Even though the degrees of central control exerted by Europe's Communist regimes and central planning systems were among their most oppressive and unacceptable features, in practice they still fell far short of the 'total' control needed to achieve their largely inappropriate, premature and over-ambitious goals. Systems of central planning and control were ostensibly established, but the 'plans' were honoured more in the breach than in the observance, while the supposedly 'centrally planned' economies only functioned by tolerating a great deal of semi-legal or downright illegal economic activity which was not envis-aged in the 'plans'. When the high levels of oppression, hierarchy, piecework, and coercion and exploitation of workforces under Europe's former Communist regimes are also acknowledged, it becomes clear that these regimes never even came close to establishing authentic forms of social-ism of any kind, and that at best they established exceptionally crude and coercive forms of state capitalism which had more in common with fascism than with socialism. These are the main reasons why this book refrains from referring to Europe's former Communist regimes and the economic systems which they established as 'socialism'. In truth, far from having 'failed' or 'collapsed', no authentic forms of 'socialism' have ever been established and tested in practice anywhere.

NATIONALISM AND IMPERIAL DISINTEGRATION

The role of nationalism in the dissolution of the Habsburg Monarchy has continued to be the subject of vigorous historiographical debate. Some analysts have regarded the rise of nationalism as the chief cause of the empire's disintegration, but others have argued against the notion that it was the root cause, while some have even denied that nationalism constituted a serious threat to the empire's survival.

Oscar Jaszi's analytical framework: 'centripetal' and 'centrifugal' forces

In his seminal study of the opposing social forces involved in *The Dissolution of the Habsburg Monarchy* (1929), the eminent Magyar social scientist Oscar Jaszi identified eight supranational 'centripetal forces' which had held the empire together for centuries: 'The dynasty, the army, the aristocracy, the Roman Catholic Church, the bureaucracy, capitalism (represented in its majority by Jews), the free-trade unity and (however strange it may appear) socialism' (Jaszi 1929: 134).

The Austrian Habsburgs saw themselves as the divinely ordained, absolutist defenders of the easternmost bulwark of Roman Catholic Christendom against heretical religious reform move-ments (notably Hussitism, Lutheranism and Calvinism), against the 'infidel threat' of the Ottoman Turks (who laid siege to Vienna in 1529 and 1683) and, from 1815 to 1918, against revolution (whether it be republican, nationalist, socialist or atheist). They upheld a supranational purely dynastic conception of the state. 'The whole Empire was simply regarded as the extension of the *Hausmacht*, the patrimonial possessions of the dynasty' (p. 137). The 'most powerful pillar' of the

Habsburg Empire was its unified, German-speaking supranational army, created by and solely responsible to the monarch (p. 141). As late as 1910 'at least 85 per cent of its officers were Germans' (p. 279). The roles of the dynasty and its army were reinforced by those of the aristocracy and the Roman Catholic higher clergy as 'the chief maintaining elements of the absolutist power' (p. 220). In 1910 the Roman Catholic Church claimed the allegiance of 91 per cent of the population in Austria and of 60 per cent of the population in Hungary proper, partly by lumping in Uniates (Catholics of the Orthodox rite) with Roman Catholics (Jaszi 1929: 160).

The centralizing German-speaking imperial bureaucracy, deeply devoted to duty, uniformity and regulation, did its best to extirpate all forms of particularism and to perpetuate Metternich's *Polizeistaat*. Nevertheless, 'it represented a very honourable degree of order, accuracy, honesty and humanitarianism . . . and it could seldom be accused of brutality toward the poor and the oppressed' (Jaszi 1929: 166). In the end it even acquiesced in the growth of separate Magyar, Polish, Czech and South Slav bureaucracies (p. 167).

From 1850 to 1914 the diverse peoples of the Habsburg Empire supposedly enjoyed the benefits of free trade behind a common external tariff. This trade policy was intended to promote both imperial *autarkie* (self-sufficiency) and complementary specialization or interdependence between the diverse peoples and territories. 'There can be no doubt that, if all the possibilities of the free-trade policy had been utilized in the right way, the centrifugal and particularist tendencies could have been checked by the growing economic solidarity of the various nations' (Jaszi 1929: 185). Jaszi surmised that, if the various constituent territories of the empire had fully participated in sufficient levels of economic development, prosperity, mutual trade, division of labour and growing together, then their greatly enhanced interdependence might have overridden or outweighed the separatist 'centrifugal' forces, filling 'with a real content the economic framework created by the will of the Emperor' (p. 189).

Finally, the (Marxist) Austrian Social Democratic Party established in 1889 was a major supranational cohesive force in as much as it sought to transcend 'bourgeois' national rivalries and unite workers and labourers of all nationalities in the 'common struggle' for social justice. Its leading Marxist theoreticians, Karl Renner and Otto Bauer, denounced 'bourgeois' separatist aspirations and campaigned for cultural and educational autonomy and equality for the Monarchy's constituent ethnic groups within the framework of a supranational confederation or *Staatenstaat*, which could eventually serve as the model or embryo for a future European socialist polity transcending national differences and conflicts (Jaszi 1929: 178). In the end, paradoxically, the 'chief defenders' of imperial economic unity were *not* its rich beneficiaries, 'the German high bourgeoisie and the Magyar landed interests, but the leading theoreticians of socialism' (p. 181).

Jaszi argued that the 'centripetal forces' were ultimately incapable of holding the empire together, partly because 'these forces did not constitute a united front'. Only the dynasty, the army, the aristocracy and the Church were (albeit incompletely) 'united in a real political architectural scheme. The other four [centripetal forces] were conflicting with the first four and even with each other on important points' (Jaszi 1929: 134). Furthermore, some of the (erstwhile) forces of integration and cohesion became sources of imperial disintegration and dissention during the twilight years of the Habsburg Monarchy (p. 133). For example, the increasingly strident Magyar opposition to the maintenance of German as the sole language of command in the imperial army became a major rallying point for demands for 'total Hungarian independence' (p. 143), while the Hungarian bureaucracy 'developed into one of the chief separatist and centrifugal forces' (p. 169). Similarly, aristocratic power and property eventually became more of a liability than a source of cohesion and strength. By impeding agrarian change 'the landed oligarchy weakened the centripetal forces of the monarchy and at the same time increased the dissolving tendencies' (Jaszi 1929: 201). The Austrian Social Democratic Party also proved incapable of holding the ring. It was unable to unite the various national sections of the working class into a single, supranational party. Workers and socialists of the underprivileged non-metropolitan nations began to form their own *separate* socialist and trade union movements and organizations between 1907 and 1910, in time to compete (successfully) with the Austrian Social Democratic Party in the 1911 Reichsrat elections (Jaszi 1929: 184). Indeed, the empire's 'real problem' was not how to achieve 'the annihilation of all historical individualities . . . in the unity of a nationless superstate (as the Socialists . . . imagined), but to give fair opportunity to the nations to build up their own states . . . and to combine them as equal members of a confederation' (p. 246).

Likewise, capitalism and internal free trade failed to realize their full potential as 'the most decisive and efficient' centripetal forces (Jaszi 1929: 171). In both halves of Austria-Hungary, liberalism 'exhausted itself' in rarified constitutional and anti-clerical contests. It parroted the rhetoric of West European liberalism, 'but it was never in real contact with the popular forces of society', for whose interests and problems it displayed little sympathy or understanding (p. 171). Furthermore, as capitalism and the bourgeoisie increasingly fractured and developed along ethnic lines, liberalism was eclipsed by nationalism and anti-Semitism (p. 172). In the end 'Austrian capitalism developed serious centrifugal tendencies by fomenting racial and national struggles' (p. 173) and 'capitalism led inevitably toward the strengthening of national feeling and consciousness' (p. 176).

In the final analysis, the Habsburg Empire foundered on its inability to solve the national problem. 'All the centrifugal forces were national' or at least assumed nationalistic forms, whether as the 'particularism' of regional landlord interests, as the struggles of rising national bourgeoisies for occupational advancement (especially into administrative positions) or as the land hunger and demands for radical land redistribution emanating from the emergent peasant nations (Jaszi 1929: 215). From 1848 to 1918, after 'the hydra-heads of feudal particularism were already cut down', democratic nationalism was the major 'new force' which attacked the cohesion and integrity of the Habsburg Empire. Whereas the dynasty had defeated 'with comparative ease' the feudal particularism based on oppressive and outmoded seigneurial prerogatives, the new 'democratic nationalism', which sought to reconstruct the Habsburg domains on the basis of 'popular' (alias national) sovereignty, represented 'a higher principle of political organization which the dynasty could not conquer' (Jaszi 1929: 246–7). The Habsburg Empire was torn apart by a combination of 'the blind resistance of the privileged nations against the new forces and the exaggerated claims of the formerly oppressed when they became sufficiently powerful to reverse the situation' and turn the tables on their former masters (p. 267). For the most part the ruling groups were 'incapable of a sympathetic understanding with the national aspirations of the oppressed peoples'. The ruling groups 'did not try to solve the problem but rather to maintain their national privileges' (p. 216).

Jaszi concluded that there were five 'outstanding groups of causes which undermined the cohesion of the old patrimonial state': (i) the growing national consciousness of the various nations 'could not find a place for a true consolidation and adequate self-expression in the rigidity of the absolutist structure'; (ii) the 'economic and social pressure of the feudal class rule, allied with a usurious kind of capitalism', prevented the productive potential of each of the empire's constituent nations and territories from developing to the full; (iii) the growing indignation and mounting exasperation of the 'weaker nations' were intensified 'by the feeling of being a kind of colony for German capitalism' as well as for 'big Viennese finance'; (iv) insufficient 'civic education' meant that the constituent nations 'lived as . . . strangers to one another'; and (v) both 'the dynastic epic in Austria and the feudal [one] in Hungary were incapable of creating a sufficiently strong and cohesive state idea' (Jaszi 1929: 453).

In Jaszi's view, the 'growing dissolution and final collapse of the Habsburg Empire' had three main causes: (i) 'The continuous growth of the various nations', whose leaders increasingly realized that their hopes of a comprehensive federalization of the empire were 'fallacious', encouraging them to turn their thoughts to 'separation or secession'; (ii) the irredentism of adjacent states which aspired to liberate their compatriots living under Habsburg 'oppression'; and (iii) 'The disintegrating influence of the World War, which made the latent hatred between nations burst into flame', thereby allowing 'dissatisfied intelligentsias' to step up their struggles against the empire, while internal conflict and dissension 'gradually paralyzed the moral and economic forces of the monarchy' (Jaszi 1929: 454). Nevertheless, he insisted that 'the World War was not the *cause*, but only the final liquidation of the deep inner crisis of the monarchy' (p. 23).

More recent perspectives on the contributions of nationalism and capitalism to the dissolution of the Habsburg Empire

Some of Jaszi's claims and hypotheses have been challenged or even refuted. The nature and impact of nationalism in East Central Europe and the Balkans and the relationship between the rise of nationalism and imperial disintegration have remained subjects of intense debate. However, it is testimony to the ingenuity and erudition of Jaszi's theses and his analytical framework that they still provide the explicit or implicit point of departure and the conceptual underpinnings of most systematic analyses of the dissolution of the Habsburg Empire, at least among Anglophone historians. More recent research offered different answers, but it has remained heavily indebted to Jaszi for setting the agenda and for framing the key questions with such brilliance, insight and flair.

Jaszi, along with many other analysts, greatly underestimated the economic vigour of the Habsburg Empire during the nineteenth and early twentieth century and the resultant economic benefits to most of its constituent peoples and territories. The quantitative historical data assembled by Rudolph (1975, 1976, 1983), Katus (1970), Huertas (1977), Good (1979, 1980, 1984), Eddie (1985) and Komlos (1983a, 1983b), among others, have demonstrated beyond reasonable doubt that the rates of economic development achieved in both Austria and Hungary from the 1830s to 1913 compared quite favourably with those of most other parts of Europe and that interregional economic integration and convergence proceeded apace, despite (or perhaps even because of) the emergence of monopolistic finance capitalism and the exploitation of the imperial 'peripheries' by the metropolitan 'core'. Whatever its political, social and military failings, the traditional picture of the nineteenth-century Habsburg Empire as a severe economic 'laggard' or 'failure' is ill founded and misleading. Admittedly, 3.5 million people 'voted with their feet' by emigrating from Austria-Hungary between 1876 and 1914. However, this was not so very different from the concurrent mass emigration from Scandinavia, Germany, Italy, Greece, Spain and the United Kingdom. Mass emigration was more of a social safety-valve and a positive response to expanding global integration and opportunities than clear-cut evidence of relative economic failure.

Stephen Fischer-Galati has argued that the aspirations and demands of the leaders of autonomist and separatist movements 'carried little weight', because the central authorities believed that 'they were not representative of the wishes of the population' and that 'as long as Vienna was able to satisfy the socio-economic demands of the aristocracy and middle classes and hold out the prospect of improvement of the lot of the peasantry, all under the umbrella of *Kaisertreue*, the Empire was secure ... These considerations emphasize the politically innocuous nature of nationalism and nationalistic manifestation as such in the Habsburg state system' (Fischer-Galati 1963: 32–3). The integrity of the Habsburg Empire *did* come under serious threat in the South Slav lands and in Transylvania following the emergence of the independent states of Serbia and Romania in 1877–8. Nevertheless, 'the activities of Southern Slav and Romanian politicians as such did not alarm Vienna. Rather, the Monarchy's apprehension stemmed from the possibility of international, primarily Russian, support of ... nationalistic manifestations inside and outside the Empire', that is, the 'internationalization' of the empire's internal 'nationality problems' and the extension to Austria-Hungary of stratagems which had contributed to the gradual dismemberment of the Ottoman Empire (pp. 33–5). He concluded that 'only two phenomena' could have mortally threatened the Habsburg Empire: not nationalism as such, but either 'social revolution' or 'intervention by outside powers acting primarily as supporters of the nationalistic, unionistic aspirations of Romanian and Southern Slav politicians outside and inside the Empire' (p. 35).

The central defects of analyses of this kind concern the implicit underestimation of the independent mobilizing power of most modern nationalist movements, which develop a life of their own that can lead in directions which are unwelcome to their supposed 'sponsors' and 'manipulators'; and, conversely, to an overestimation of the extent to which such movements can be 'bought off'. Thus Magyar nationalism was by no means assuaged or satisfied by the special privileged status granted to the Kingdom of Hungary from 1867 to 1918. On the contrary, this privileged status encouraged Magyar nationalists to demand still greater independence for Hungary. Furthermore, Europe has been littered with examples of nationalist movements which have thrived on their nations' economic strengths and successes (most recently Flemish, Catalan, Basque, Scottish, Croat and Slovene nationalism), as well as ones which have expressed feelings of economic frustration and relative deprivation (for example Slovak, Kosovar, and nineteenth-century Irish nationalism). Secessionism is fuelled just as readily by economic success as by economic failure and/or deprivation.

Peter Sugar has argued that the examples of Switzerland and Great Britain demonstrate that the mere existence of several distinct nationalities within a single state was 'not enough to doom the Habsburg state' (Sugar 1963: 43) and that 'once the Slav revival passed its early cultural-linguistic stage . . . the idea of Slav unity was never a serious force in the Monarchy or a serious threat to Vienna' (p. 10). Likewise, Hugh Seton-Watson claimed that among Western Slavs 'the only common culture was Catholicism. That there was ever a specifically "Slav" culture common to Poles, Czechs and Croats is a myth' (Seton-Watson 1977: 118). Even a *united* Slav challenge need not have threatened imperial unity. So-called 'Austro-Slavism' could have provided a broader basis and mandate for imperial cohesion. The real threats to imperial unity came not from dreams of Austro-Slav unity, but from the emergence of numerous *separate* Slav national identities and loyalties, which gradually eroded or curtailed Czech, Slovak, Polish, Slovene and Croatian allegiance to the emperor and the empire.

The rise of nationalism was certainly a double-edged sword. In one sense it posed a serious threat to imperial cohesion and unity by creating new non-imperial foci of identity and allegiance. On the other hand, by further fragmenting the imperial polity and by pitting the various nationalities against one another, it made it easier for the Habsburgs to pursue a 'divide-and-rule' strategy against their increasingly restive subjects. Katherine Verdery has emphasized that the Habsburgs 'consciously played off each ethnic minority against another' and that Metternich himself declared that 'if the Hungarian revolts . . . we should immediately set the Bohemian against him, for they hate each other; and after him the Pole, or the German or the Italian' (Verdery 1979: 393–4).

It has been argued that 'there were no dominant nationalities in the Austro-Hungarian Monarchy. There were only dominant classes.' Thus the so-called 'nationality conflict' in Hungary was in reality a class conflict 'between the mainly Magyar upper class and both the Magyar and the non-Magyar lower classes', while the 'nationality conflict' in the Austrian half of the empire 'consisted primarily of clashes within the multinational propertied or educated class' (Deak 1967: 303). For many 'downtrodden' and 'exploited' workers, peasants, servants and labourers, it probably made little difference whether their 'oppressors' and 'exploiters' were 'aliens' or their own 'compatriots'. Some of the harshest and most blatant oppression and 'exploitation' took place within (rather than between) ethnic groups.

Nevertheless, particularly in the Austro-Hungarian Empire, class conflict frequently wore a national mask, and class hatreds were often further envenomed and inflamed by ethnic antagonism towards 'alien' landlords, traders, money-lenders, store-keepers and other (often Jewish) 'middlemen' or intermediaries, who increasingly came to be seen as agents and henchmen of malign political and economic systems and/or as obstacles to the fulfilment of both class and national aspirations. 'National' struggles often subsume or amalgamate with socio-economic economic 'class' struggles.

That is partly what gives them such explosive power. Most analyses of the Monarchy's 'nationality problems' have tended to focus upon the struggles and grievances of the subordinate 'underdog' nations against their 'overlords' and 'masters'. However, the defence of political, economic and educational dominance and privilege aroused almost as much heated debate and passion among the privileged nationalities (Austrian Germans, Magyars and to some extent Galician Poles) as did the struggles for greater equality and autonomy on the part of the underprivileged nationalities (Czechs, Slovaks, Ruthenes, South Slavs and Romanians).

In implicit criticism of Jaszi, Hans Kohn has claimed that 'it is a mistake to stress the unsolved nationality problems of the Monarchy as the fundamental causes of its fall. The integrating or disintegrating forces were not of decisive importance for the survival of the Monarchy' (Kohn 1967: 256). In Kohn's opinion it was the empire's foreign policy blunders, especially in the 1860s, the 1870s and the 1900s, 'and not the conflict of nationalities, which brought about the collapse of the Monarchy' (p. 259). In this respect, paradoxically, 'the dominant nationalities . . . contributed more to the disintegration of the Monarchy than did the Slavic or Romanian peoples . . . not so much by their resistance to timely domestic reforms as by their nefarious influence on foreign policy' (p. 256). The increasingly vulnerable Habsburg Empire should have espoused 'neutrality' and the territorial status quo, avoiding risky foreign policy adventures and estrangements. 'The alliance with the Prussian-German Empire, promoted by the Germans and Magyars in the Monarchy, and the occupation of Bosnia-Herzegovina were the most fundamental mistakes which carried within themselves the seeds of a coming catastrophe' (pp. 262–3).

However, it is unsound to assume that, just because the Habsburg Empire 'failed' to survive the First World War, it must already have been in terminal or progressive decline *before* that war. Alan Sked has argued that 'practically no one wanted to see the Monarchy break up . . . It was only defeat in war, therefore, which was to precipitate collapse; and that defeat was not certain until the early summer of 1918' (Sked 1989: 187). Thus the Habsburg Monarchy did not founder on its inability to contain or resolve its nationality problem; rather, 'it fell because it lost a major war'. Most of its subjects dutifully supported the Monarchy's war effort 'right up until the end. Before 1914, if anything, the nationality problem seemed to be abating. Its real weaknesses in 1914 were military and financial' (p. 264). 'At no point between 1867 and 1914 did the Monarchy even vaguely face the sort of challenge to its existence that it faced in 1848–49. The truth is that there was no internal pressure between 1867 and 1914 for the breakup of the Monarchy; no repudiation of the dynasty; while in some areas problems were actually being solved or compromises reached. At the same time, economic growth was continuing and the Monarchy was becoming more and more integrated in terms of living standards, infrastructure and finance' (p. 231). Thus, while commercial, industrial and agricultural integration proceeded apace (pp. 199–202), there emerged a mutually acceptable economic 'compromise' between Austria and Hungary in 1907 (pp. 232–3); and mutually acceptable linguistic and electoral accommodations were also reached in Moravia in 1905 and in Bukovina in 1910 (pp. 222, 225). Moreover, Romania (as an ally of Germany and Austria-Hungary) was unwilling to foment separatist tendencies in Transylvania (p. 212), while the main political forces in Croatia, Bohemia and Austrian Poland (Galicia) were still concentrating on making gains *within* rather than outside the imperial framework (pp. 217, 223–4). 'No major leader or party called for the destruction of the Monarchy' (Jelavich 1983b: 231).

The eminent Austrian Marxist Otto Bauer, who (like Jaszi) both analysed and participated in the dissolution of the Habsburg Empire, emphasized the close connections between the rise of nationalism, the First World War and the dissolution of the Habsburg Monarchy:

The accentuation of national antagonisms during the years preceding the War shook the Empire to its foundations. The Monarchy attempted to overcome its permanent crisis at home through war abroad. Consequently it plunged into the war, but this act made its existence dependent upon the outcome of the war. The terrible sacrifices of blood and treasure which the war exacted hit the Slav peoples doubly hard: they seemed to them to be sacrifices for an alien state and for a hostile cause. The longer the war lasted, the more the national revolutionary movement against Austria gathered strength ... Austria-Hungary was waging war not only against external enemies, but also against two-thirds of its own citizens ... and could only force its peoples to fight the external foe by using the coercive agencies of war-time Absolutism. (Bauer 1925: 14, 24, 27, 71–2)

Jiri Koralka has offered a subtle, perspicacious and undoctrinaire Marxist explanation of the relationship between the rise of nationalism and the disintegration of the Habsburg Empire. It avoided crude economic determinism, while emphasizing broad societal changes such as the rise of capitalism, the erosion of privilege and the political mobilization of the masses. In his view the fundamental challenge confronting the states of East Central Europe and the Balkans since the eighteenth century has been to embrace 'the great process of *social* change from the old, privileged, feudal society to a modern industrial society based upon the active participation of all inhabitants in social and political life' (Koralka 1967: 147). Therefore, 'the main reason for the disintegration of the Habsburg Empire was not nationalism as such, but the failure of the monarchy to create a national concept of its own which would be in harmony with the dynamic growth of modern capitalistic society' (p. 149). 'In Western Europe very heterogeneous ethnic groups and political territories were often united by dynasties into nation-states.' However, the Habsburgs scarcely even attempted to unify their heterogeneous domains into 'a West European-style nation-state', because they were 'overburdened for too long ... with the heritage of universalism of the Holy Roman Empire' (p. 148). They were repeatedly distracted by their dynastic ambitions in Italy, in the Netherlands, in Spain and, most fatefully, in Germany. The overstretched empire ultimately fell back upon a policy of trying 'to live with all the problems without ever really attempting to solve them' (p. 149). In the end the collapse of the empire was 'a logical consequence of the inability of the monarchy to create its own concept of a modern society. Wherever a *number* of modern national societies rather than a *single* modern society have evolved within an empire, it has been impossible to halt this development at the ethnic-cultural stage and prevent the formulation of political nation-state programmes' (p. 150).

The first duty of every Habsburg emperor was to defend the Habsburg patrimony, comprising a great diversity of territories and peoples, none of which held a position of absolute predominance. Thus, even though the majority of imperial officers and officials were German speaking (and German remained the lingua franca of administration, commerce and military command), the last four emperors could not afford to adopt German nationalism as a state ideology or to become exclusively identified with the interests and aspirations of their German-speaking subjects. With considerable justification, Emperor Franz Josef (1848–1916) viewed anti-clerical Austrian-German liberalism, nationalist pan-Germanism, the *Los von Rom* ('Break with Rome') movement and Karl Lueger's anti-Semitic Christian Social Party with deep suspicion and mistrust, as implicit challenges or threats to his power, authority and position as the ruler and 'spiritual custodian' of a Roman Catholic multinational empire. Indeed, he repeatedly annulled the election of the demagogue Karl Lueger as Mayor of Vienna. In an endeavour to retain at least the passive allegiance of his non-German subjects, especially the propertied classes among them, Franz Josef had to make a show of standing above narrow 'national' and 'sectional' interests; and, for much of his seemingly interminable reign, he ruled with the support of a predominantly Slavic, Catholic, conservative coalition (1879–93), *against* the faintly liberal, anti-clerical and pan-German leanings of the Austrian-German 'chattering classes' of that time. 'National consolidation' under the aegis of monarchical absolutism was a viable political strategy for the Hohenzollerns in Germany and, to a much smaller degree, for the Romanovs in Russia, but it was out of the question for the Habsburgs in Austria-Hungary.

Robert Kann has argued that 'the decline of the constitutional power of the monarch was even more a disintegrating force in the Habsburg Empire than nationalism. The common allegiance of the peoples under Habsburg rule was a very powerful centripetal factor in the eighteenth century. This feeling of common loyalty to the crown rapidly declined during . . . the next century, precisely when [it] was more necessary than ever to offset the increasing strength of centrifugal forces' (Kann 1967: 25, 29). Likewise, A.J.P. Taylor contended that 'the Habsburg monarchy was not a multinational empire; it was a supranational empire. Nations can perhaps co-operate if they have a common loyalty to bind them together . . . The Habsburgs had once provided the common loyalty; in the nineteenth century they failed to do so any longer, and it was this Habsburg failure, not the rise of the nationalities, which doomed their Empire' (Taylor 1967: 130–1).

These are important considerations, but in these instances Taylor and Kann underplayed the crucial impact of the rise of nationalism and specifically *national* allegiances in diminishing and eventually replacing or superseding popular (and especially middle-class) allegiance to the supranational Habsburg Monarchy. However, Kann did concede that 'nationalism was a much greater debilitating force in Austria-Hungary than anywhere else in Europe' (Kann 1967: 25), while in a different work Taylor conceded that during the nineteenth century the various nations of the Habsburg Empire 'began to have their own wishes and ambitions, and these proved in the end incompatible with each other and with the survival of the dynasty' (Taylor 1976: 21). These national movements were in large measure locked in a zero-sum game: the aspirations of each could only be met at the others' expense; and any attempt to meet their demands also weakened the Monarchy as a whole. Thus 'the Habsburg Monarchy and nationalism were incompatible; no peace was possible between them' (p. 40).

Nationalism not only asserted the interests and aspirations of the constituent peoples and territories of the empire at the expense of the centre. It also posited a different basis for relations between the constituent peoples and territories; a different political configuration ('nation-states', whether confederated or fully independent, in place of empire); and a different principle and source of authority and legitimacy (the nation/people and national/popular sovereignty, in place of the dynasty/monarchy). Furthermore, the scope for resentments, rivalry and conflict between the constituent 'nationalities' of the Habsburg Empire was made all the greater by the pervasiveness of Habsburg 'paternalism' and by the virtual absence of private (and hence independent) schools, universities, hospitals and railways, which by 1890 were nearly all state owned. In such a situation, 'the appointment of every school teacher, of every railway porter, of every hospital doctor, of every tax collector, was a signal for national struggle' (Taylor 1976: 173). Indeed, the underdevelopment of independent private activity helped to 'politicize' such appointments.

The major challenge to the survival of the Habsburg Empire came not from its less developed 'peripheries', but from the highly developed Czech Lands. The Monarchy could have survived the 'amputation' of territories mainly inhabited by Serbs, Romanians, Poles, Ruthenes and Italians, but an independent Bohemia was bound to kill it (Taylor 1976: 238–9). During the nineteenth century the Czechs were no longer oppressed and downtrodden *as a nation*, even if (or indeed because) more and more Czechs were oppressed and 'exploited' *as workers*, when Bohemia became the industrial heartland of the Habsburg Monarchy. The Czechs developed their own university and cultural life and major roles in the administration of Bohemia. They produced a capitalist class which very successfully oppressed and 'exploited' fellow Czechs. Nevertheless, the salient struggle in Bohemia was not the class struggle, but rather the struggle between Czechs and Germans. 'The Czechs could not be satisfied with the use of their language . . . They claimed, and had to claim, possession of their national home' (p. 204). However, because that would 'dethrone' the hitherto dominant Bohemian German propertied classes, the latter resisted tooth and nail. This bitter conflict had fateful consequences. To an even greater extent than Vienna, Bohemia became the crucible of the Germanic 'National Socialism' which later was exported to Weimar Germany during the 1920s. Furthermore, the self-pitying plight of the three million Bohemian Germans in interwar Czechoslovakia provided the pretexts for Hitler's two-stage incorporation of Bohemia into an expanded Nazi Germany in September 1938 and March 1939, which heralded the Second World War.

SCHEMES FOR THE 'FEDERALIZATION' OF THE HABSBURG EMPIRE

The twilight years of the Habsburg Empire witnessed a proliferation of liberal, Austro-Slav and Austro-Marxist schemes to reconstitute the imperial polity on new, democratic, multinational 'federal' foundations. Their exponents recognized 'the feebleness, the dead weight of bureaucracy, the conflict of national claims; yet all looked forward to a "solution". This solution, universally expected, was Federalism, the attractive name for diverse schemes' (Taylor 1976: 224). Because everyone recoiled in alarm at the prospect of the endemic conflict and economic collapse which could follow in the wake of imperial disintegration, there was a great thirst for 'solutions' and a great willingness to believe in them. 'Solutions' were all too easy to devise on paper. The problem was how to get one generally accepted (p. 225).

Austro-Slavs, Austrian Marxists and Austrian Liberals looked to Vienna and the Habsburgs for federal 'solutions' to the empire's 'nationality problems'. Yet to do so was 'to fail to understand the nature of the Monarchy' (Taylor 1976: 226). The Habsburgs generally 'strove to keep their dominions apart, not to bring them together'; they were afraid to unite them 'even in subjection' (pp. 12–13). With the possible exception of Josef II (1780–90), the Habsburg emperors saw their subjects as the servants of the dynasty rather than the other way around. Furthermore, according to Justus Freimund's treatise on *Österreichs Zukunft* (1867), 'Federalism is incompatible with the concept of a powerful monarchy. Federalism is possible only in a republic like Switzerland.' Austria could not tolerate freedom, as 'a free Austria is only a bridge to complete disintegration'. Yet, since the march of history was towards greater freedom, 'world history has passed judgement upon Austria and condemned her to fall' (quoted by Kann 1950b: 140). Kann challenges Freimund's dogmatic assertion that federalism is incompatible with monarchy. Nevertheless, he concludes that 'if the union of eastern central European peoples on a federal democratic basis should ever be achieved, it would have little in common with the setup in the Habsburg Empire' (p. 290).

All the 'eleventh-hour' schemes for a federalized multinational empire presupposed that Vienna and/or the Habsburgs would continue to provide overall co-ordination of central government, especially economic policy, foreign policy and military affairs. However, any thoroughgoing democratic federalization of the empire, granting genuine autonomy to all its ethnic and/or territorial subdivisions, was indeed incompatible with (or, at any rate, unacceptable to) this particular monarchy. '*Kaisertreue* precluded democratic reform and the reorganization of the Empire on the basis of ethnic or individual sovereignty' (Fischer-Galati 1963: 32). 'The Habsburgs . . . followed a purely dynastic policy of protecting their *Hausmacht* (patrimonial rights), emphasizing *Kaisertreue* (loyalty to the emperor and his family) and promoting a sort of dynastic patriotism. *Kaisertreue* held the Empire together until the end of World War I and made most national groups seek, almost to the last . . . a solution for their grievances within the state rather than in secession. This indicates not so much the success of the ruling family's policy as the inability of its subjects to find another principle on which even a substantial part of them could agree' (Sugar 1963: 2–4). Furthermore, the Habsburgs and the vast majority of Austrian Germans appeared to prefer an ever-closer partnership with the burgeoning German Empire to any form of power sharing with their Slav subjects, towards whom they displayed either patronizing condescension or haughty contempt.

In any case, it is doubtful whether any far-reaching federal reorganization of the Habsburg Empire could have resolved or defused its 'nationalities problem' for long, even if it had been possible to implement (or impose) such a 'solution'. The granting of substantial autonomy to the major subordinate ethnic groups and/or territorial subdivisions would probably have whetted their appetites for full independence, while reducing the capacity of the central authorities to hold the ring. No matter how much the imperial territory were to have been subdivided, some subdivisions would still have contained insecure, vulnerable and/or discontented ethnic minorities, some of whom might have sought 'union' with (or the 'protection' of) their co-nationals in neighbouring states and regions. Moreover, the constituent nationalities and territories of the Habsburg Empire remained extremely disparate in terms of levels of economic development, class configurations, educational attainments, geopolitical orientations and levels of national consciousness. To regard them as mutually compatible components of a viable, harmonious federation or confederation required wishful thinking of the first order; but optimism and blind faith are not sufficient bases on which to build viable state structures (Sugar 1967: 119). 'Men thought to alter the European position of the Habsburg Monarchy by changing its internal structure; in reality a change in its internal structure could only come about after a change, or rather a catastrophe, in its European position' (Taylor 1976: 225).

It is conceivable that any kind of East Central European federal or confederal union would have been riven by precisely the same inter-ethnic frictions, jealousies, rivalries and cultural fault-lines that had helped to destroy the Habsburg Empire in 1918. Indeed, it is arguable that the supranational Habsburg *Hausmacht* and *Kaisertreue* were *more* capable of holding the ring and papering over the cracks than any East Central European federation or confederation would have been, precisely because the dynasty constituted a strong *supranational* arbiter and focus of allegiance, standing above and policing inter-ethnic squabbles. The very existence of a large supranational empire limited the enormous scope for violent conflict (either within an ethnically structured multinational federation or between ethnically based states) in East Central Europe. As A.J.P. Taylor aptly put it, 'The Monarchy had not been a "solution"; it had rested on scepticism of the possibility of a "solution" and had therefore sought to conserve, though without faith, institutions which had long lost moral sanction' (Taylor 1976: 252). With regard to *motivations*, it may well be true that 'the Habsburg Monarchy was not a device for enabling a number of nationalities to live together' (p. 132). Nevertheless, objectively speaking, that was one of the vital functions it performed. In that sense the dissolution of the Monarchy in 1918 was a historic 'mistake', even if it appeared inevitable.

Against such a view, Adam Zamoyski has argued that 'most of the problems of Central Europe were created by Habsburg rule, whose vicious logic required that all subject peoples should be required to hate each other' (writing in *The Times*, 30 November 1995, p. 38). However, while the divide-and-rule tactics of the Habsburg Empire undoubtedly sowed the seeds of many subsequent conflicts in the so-called 'successor states', it would be churlish to deny that (for its own 'reasons of state') it kept such conflicts within certain bounds so long as the Habsburgs remained in control.

By 1918 all the major nationalities within the Habsburg Empire had their own written languages, literary traditions, historians, schools and nascent or fully fledged intelligentsias, who sought preferred placements in the emergent 'national' bureaucracies, schools, universities, legal professions and newspapers. Nevertheless, in the final analysis, the nationality problem was not merely a matter of schooling and public positions. These were merely the *hors d'oeuvres*. Sooner or later the emergent nations would seek or demand the power to determine their own destinies. In the final analysis 'most national groups in the Habsburg Empire, just like any others who were or felt oppressed, wanted statehood and not just national equality' (Kann 1974: 442). As a result of the defeat and disintegration of the Tsarist, Habsburg and Ottoman empires during the closing stages of the First World War, the national power seekers of the emerging East Central European nations attained 'national independence' rather sooner than they had anticipated. However, the experiences of the 1930s and early 1940s were soon to bring home to them the powerlessness of small and vulnerable nations situated in the 'marchlands' between Germany and Russia.

19   Life after death: partitioned Poland, 1795–1914

Following the third Partition of Poland-Lithuania in 1795 and the suppression of the last vestiges of the 1794 Kosciuszko rising, the prevailing moods in the Partitioned Commonwealth were ones of shock, apathy and fatalism, 'causing a temporary collapse of further political initiatives' (Skowronek 1982: 263). A supplementary Partition Treaty signed by Russia, Prussia and Austria in January 1797 secretly and chillingly declared that 'In view of the necessity to abolish everything which could revive the memory of the existence of the Kingdom of Poland . . . the high contracting parties are agreed and undertake never to include in their titles the name or designation of the Kingdom of Poland, which shall remain suppressed as from the present and forever' (quoted by Davies 1981a: 542). Significantly, as co-author of all the Partitions, the Tsarist regime claimed that it was merely recovering territories that had once been part of its ancient patrimony. In 1793 Empress Catherine the Great had even ordered the striking of a medal bearing the inscription: 'I have recovered what was torn away.' Nevertheless, this perception of her conduct was 'not shared by most of her contemporaries', while her immediate successors considered that the Partitions had been criminal acts (Wandycz 1974: 17). Nevertheless, Prussia similarly claimed that it had merely repossessed the lost patrimony of its Teutonic ancestors (Davies 1981a: 81), while in 1772 Austria decided to call its share of the first Partition 'the Kingdom of Galicia and Lodomeria'. These names were Latinized versions of Halicz and Vladimir, two medieval dukedoms to which the Habsburgs had unearthed long defunct Hungarian dynastic claims. However, Halicz 'formed only a small part of the acquisition', while 'Vladimir lay outside the region', and neither was ever restored to the Kingdom of Hungary (Wandycz 1974: 11). The additional territory which the Habsburgs annexed to Austria (not Hungary) in 1795 was christened New Galicia, cunningly exploiting their earlier sleight of hand to effect another. Yet the trick worked, for to this day historians generally refer to the areas annexed by Austria in 1772, 1795, 1815 and 1846 by the spurious name of Galicia.

These ruses and specious 'justifications' were meant to emphasize the apparent finality of the Partitions. The protestations of the Partitioning Powers that their claims to their new territories went far beyond mere 'rights of conquest' help to explain the policies they pursued and the tenacity of their conduct. Moreover, the Partitioning Powers appeared to be indissolubly bound together by their partnership in crime against the erstwhile Polish-Lithuanian Commonwealth. There was a fourth Partition of Poland in 1814–15, following the defeat of Napoleon and the Grand Duchy of Warsaw which he had sponsored from late 1807 to early 1813. Nevertheless, this was by no means the end of the road for Polish and Lithuanian political, economic and cultural life. Refusing to die, the disembodied Commonwealth lived on in the consciousness of the political classes until August 1939, when the Nazi–Soviet Pact (in effect the fifth Partition of Poland-Lithuania) finished the job which Friedrich the Great and Catherine the Great had begun. After that, although both Poland and Lithuania were subsequently 'reborn' more than once, the ideals of the Commonwealth were lost for ever.

FALSE DAWNS, 1797–1814

The solidarity of the Partitioning Powers was much weaker than has been commonly assumed. Sooner or later each of these Powers proved willing to use or to propitiate the Poles in attempts to steal a march on the other two. The three Partitioning Powers 'intrigued against one another' repeatedly, so it seems safe to conclude that the secret provision in the January 1797 Partition Treaty forswearing any future use of the word 'Poland' was 'directed against plans any of the three courts might have for reviving Poland, as much as it was against the Poles' (Wandycz 1974: 25). Yet the 'mad' Tsar Paul (1796–1801) soon freed Russia's most prominent Polish prisoners (including Kosciuszko, who returned to the United States), in return for promises never to take up arms against Russia again. He did so in celebration of the death of his mother, Catherine the Great, whom he hated. He also spent long hours with the dethroned Stanislaw Augustus discussing a plan to resurrect the former Polish Commonwealth and, when the former Polish king died in 1798, 'Paul gave him a state funeral and personally led the mourning' (Zamoyski 1987: 257). Tsar Paul's dedication to undoing his mother's 'achievements' contributed greatly to his own assassination by Russian nobles in 1801.

As early as October 1796, Napoleon Bonaparte's Polish aide-de-camp Jozef Sulkowski hinted that, if he triumphed in Italy, his master might be willing to lead French forces against Russia 'to force her to grant independence to Poland' (Wandycz 1974: 28). In December 1796, furthermore, Polish émigrés succeeded in persuading the somewhat nervous French Directory (government) to allow General Henryk Dabrowski, who had distinguished himself in the Kosciuszko rising, to form an ancillary 'Polish Legion' to fight under Napoleon against the Austrians in Italy, using émigré Polish officers like himself and Polish prisoners-of-war captured from the Austrian army (which had been recruiting heavily in Galicia). The small and undisciplined group of Polish émigrés who invaded Galicia from Ottoman-controlled Bukovina in July 1797 proved to be easy prey for the Austrians. Nevertheless, two additional 'Polish Legions' were successfully formed to fight alongside the French under General Jozef Zajacek in Italy in 1798 and under General Karol Kniaziewicz on the Rhine in 1800. Polish hopes and morale were further raised by Kosciuszko's arrival in Paris from the USA in 1800 (Wandycz 1974: 26–30). The rousing marching song of these 'Polish Legions' later became the Polish national anthem.

Between 1797 and 1801, 25,000–30,000 men served in the 'Polish Legions', which fought valiantly and with heavy losses in the battles of Trebia (1799), Marengo (1800) and Hohenlinden (1800). However, France managed to keep out of the wars with Austria and Prussia from 1801 to 1805, with the result that the 'Polish Legions' were relegated to policing duties in Italy, instead of fighting in the long-awaited campaign to liberate Poland-Lithuania. In 1802–3, against their wishes, they were sent to suppress a slave rebellion in the French colony of San Domingo (Haiti), where many of them died of swamp fever in a fight not *for* but *against* freedom (Davies 1981b: 296).

In 1800 there appeared an anonymous pamphlet entitled *Can the Poles Strike Out to Independence?* It was co-authored by Kosciuszko and his secretary Jozef Pawlikowski. They argued that the Poles could not count on the support of France or any other Power and must therefore mobilize their own social and military resources (including the peasantry) for a demotic 'war of independence' under a charismatic commander with dictatorial powers, on the pattern of the 1794 Kosciuszko rising (Wandycz 1974: 32). This became the founding statement of the Polish insurrectionary tradition. Kosciuszko warned his compatriots: 'Do not think that Bonaparte will restore Poland. He thinks only of himself . . . He is a tyrant whose only aim is to satisfy his own ambitions. I am sure that he will create nothing durable' (quoted by Davies 1981b: 295). Nevertheless, the 'Polish Legions' had given Napoleon a significant demonstration of Polish military valour and potential, while the survivors constituted a valuable cadre of officers and men trained in Napoleonic methods of warfare. They 'proved indispensable for the organization of the army of the future Duchy of

Warsaw', which put Poland back on the map (Wandycz 1974: 32). Furthermore, Polish contact with Napoleonic France helped to transform Polish nationalism into an ideology with an enlarged programmatic content, including an expanded conception of the political nation and of popular ('national') rights and obligations.

During the respite from war between 1801 and 1805, the Polish political torch passed from the émigrés in western Europe to a prominent Polish aristocrat in Russia. Sent to St Petersburg by the Czartoryski family as a virtual hostage and as a 'guarantee of good conduct' in 1795 (when he was twenty-five years old), Prince Adam Czartoryski charmed his way into the future Tsar Alexander's inner circle of reformist and liberal-minded friends and advisers. Czartoryski also engaged the sympathy of Russia's heir apparent for the Polish cause, even before the assassination of Tsar Paul catapulted Alexander and his close advisers into power in 1801. Czartoryski became Russia's foreign minister, a senator, a member of Alexander's council on education (charged with the expansion and modernization of education in Russia), and 'curator' of education within the former Grand Duchy of Lithuania, which Russia had acquired via the Partitions. Czartoryski seemingly 'succeeded in reconciling in his own mind the greatness of Russia with the eventual rebirth of Poland'. He evidently hoped that the emergence of a modernized and liberalized Russia would eventually oblige the other Partitioning Powers to give up their respective sectors of Poland, and that a 'reconstituted Polish state in close alliance with Russia, possibly ruled by a Romanov, could satisfy both Polish and Russian interests' (Wandycz 1974: 34). At the height of Czartoryski's influence in Russian affairs, the universities of Vilnius (Wilno) and Tartu (Dorpat) were relaunched. Under Czartoryski's curatorship (1803–23) the University of Vilnius 'flourished as the premier centre of Polish literature and learning' (Davies 1981b: 313) and was undergirded by a network of 430 feeder schools (Wandycz 1974: 95). However, Czartoryski also proposed that, in order to outbid the destructive and destabilizing influence of the French Revolution and Bonapartism, Russia (in partnership with Britain) should strive to initiate a reconstruction of Europe into Christian confederations, including two broad Slavic unions in the East. This would allow every nation rights of self-expression and liberty within a framework conducive to peace, harmony and the containment of aggressive instincts and aspirations (Kukiel 1955: 30–6, 156–7).

However, Napoleon was attacked in 1805 by Austria and Russia, whose combined forces were thoroughly beaten at Austerlitz in December. In 1806 the creation of a French-dominated Confederation of the Rhine precipitated a Franco-Prussian war which resulted in Napoleon's lightning victories at Jena and Auerstadt and his occupation of Berlin in October. This opened the way for Polish uprisings and a revived 'Polish Legion' to participate in the 'liberation' of Prussian Poland. After entering Berlin, Napoleon summoned General Dabrowski and Jozef Wybicki (an influential émigré) and urged them to seek Kosciuszko's support for a Polish uprising in Prussian Poland, taunting them that it was now up to the Poles to demonstrate whether they were really worthy to become a nation once more.

In the event, few Poles were in any hurry to re-establish a Polish state under French patronage. Polish radicals and émigrés with French republican connections and/or unhappy memories of the earlier 'Polish Legions' had every reason to mistrust Napoleon, who had avoided giving firm undertakings, while major Polish landowners were initially fearful of openly siding with Napoleonic France. Kosciuszko announced that he would co-operate with Napoleon only if three conditions could be met: an emancipation of the peasantry; the re-establishment of a Polish state extending from Gdansk to Riga, Odessa and the Carpathians; and the adoption of a political system modelled on that of Napoleon's arch-enemy Great Britain! Consequently, there were no Polish uprisings in support of the French 'liberation' of Poznan and Warsaw in November and December 1806 (Wandycz 1974: 36–8).

Once French control of both Warsaw and Poznan was a *fait accompli*, however, large numbers of Polish supporters quickly set aside their former mistrust of Napoleon and his regime and 'radical groups in Poland declared in favour of co-operation with France. Napoleon's victories over the Partitioning Powers appealed to the popular imagination and surrounded him with a halo of heroism' (Wandycz 1974: 39). For their part, conservative Polish landowners soon saw that their fears of French and/or Napoleonic 'radicalism' had been largely misplaced. Even before becoming a monarch, Napoleon had reined in revolutionary radicalism, nor did he wish to frighten the propertied classes of Poland-Lithuania and the Partitioning Powers by inciting social revolution. 'The last thing that Napoleon wanted to do was to unite all three Partitioning Powers against France' (p. 37), nor did he want to 'base his Polish policy on the support of the masses' (p. 39). On the contrary, like most upstarts, opportunists and dictators, he was eager to strike deals with the powers-that-be, if only they would accept him. He looked to Polish nobles and magnates for leadership and support. He gave the main portfolios in Warsaw's new Governing Commission to aristocrats. Prince Jozef Poniatowski (nephew of the last Polish king) was given command of the new Polish army, which by 1807 had nearly 40,000 men under arms. 'The left had no representatives in the governmental structure' (p. 40). Kosciuszko's reluctance to return to Poland at this critical juncture deprived the 'progressives' of a charismatic and universally respected leader. It is not known whether he was motivated primarily by his antipathy towards Napoleon, by his promises to the late Tsar Paul, by failing health (he died in 1817), or by a combination of all three!

The completion of Napoleon's conquest of Prussia (with Polish assistance) in June 1807 necessitated an 'answer' to the reopened Polish 'question'. Czartoryski strongly urged Tsar Alexander I (reg. 1801–25) to resurrect a Polish realm under Russian patronage in order to forestall the emergence of yet another Bonapartist puppet state. At their famous meeting at Tilsit aboard a raft on the River Niemen, Napoleon and Alexander offered each other the Polish crown, but at a price which neither would-be beneficiary was prepared to pay! In the end Gdansk was turned into a nominally independent 'free city' under French 'protection' and Russia took Bialystock, while the 2.6 million inhabitants of Wielkopolska and Mazovia were reconstituted as the Duchy of Warsaw. This was given the *Code Napoleón* and a French constitution which formally abolished serfdom, proclaimed the equality of all citizens before the law, recognized Roman Catholicism as the predominant religion, and guaranteed freedom of worship. Nevertheless, the plight of many peasants actually deteriorated, while in 1808 the political rights of Jews were suspended for ten years on the specious grounds that they were 'as yet unassimilated' (Wandycz 1974: 46–7). The Polish-speaking King of Saxony (an ally of Napoleon) formally became the Duchy's hereditary monarch, although he visited it just four times! Legislative power was vested jointly in the monarch (or his nominees) and in a bicameral Sejm, comprising a nominated Senate and an elective Chamber of Deputies. Yet the Duchy's official language was Polish and, in the eyes of many Poles, Poland was rising to fight another day. From 1808 onwards Polish men aged between twenty and twenty-eight became liable for up to six years' military service, mainly to fight in Napoleon's campaigns elsewhere in Europe. The army, which expanded from 30,000 men in 1808–9 to 100,000 in 1812, became a huge drain on the Duchy's human and fiscal resources.

In 1809 the Duchy was invaded by Austria, which was again at war with Napoleon. Having held the Austrians to a draw, the Duchy's military strategists (including Dabrowski and Poniatowski) shrewdly surrendered Warsaw to the Habsburgs but then proceeded to liberate Galicia. After the decisive defeat of Austria by Napoleon at Wagram in July 1809, the Duchy was allowed to annexe so-called New Galicia (including Krakow), which expanded the Duchy's territory to 155,430 square kilometres and its population to 4.3 million inhabitants (Wandycz 1974: 43, 53). In 1810, worn down by his divided loyalties to Poland and Russia, Czartoryski finally requested an indefinite 'leave of absence' from Tsar Alexander, who then assured him of his intention to restore a large Polish kingdom under Russian sponsorship. Word of this got back to an infuriated Napoleon, who accused Alexander of aggressive designs and duplicity. It was partly to forestall the Tsar's schemes (and perhaps to force him back into the French alliance system) that Napoleon assembled a *grande*

armeé of 600,000 men in the impoverished Duchy of Warsaw during the spring of 1812 in preparation for his invasion of Russia in June. Nearly 100,000 Polish soldiers took part in this campaign,
which aspired to 'liberate' large areas of Belarussia, Lithuania and Ukraine from Russian rule.
However, Napoleon failed to capitalize fully on the nationalism of the Polish and Lithuanian nobilities by allowing them to form explicitly 'national' regiments, other than the 35,000 Poles under
Poniatowski. Adding insult to injury, Napoleon entrusted Lithuania, Grodno and Minsk to a heavy-
handed Dutch military governor with no knowledge of the local conditions and languages. There
was no general mobilization of the Lithuanian nobility until December 1812 (Wandycz 1974: 59).
By then Napoleon was scuttling back towards Paris, passing through Warsaw without even a visit
to his longstanding Polish mistress Maria Walewska, 'who was left to pursue him to Paris, and
eventually to Elba' (Davies 1981b: 304). After fighting the Russian army at Borodino in September
1812 and witnessing the burning of Moscow the following month, barely 20,000 Polish soldiers
made it back to Poland. Warsaw fell to the Russians in February 1813, whereupon the Duchy
passed under de facto Russian military rule for two years, while awaiting decisions on its long-term
future at the Congress of Vienna in 1814–15.

All in all, the Napoleonic Wars had cruelly raised and dashed the hopes of the Polish and Lithuanian propertied classes. (The lower classes were still more acted upon than acting in their own
right.) Kosciuszko's instinctive distrust of Napoleon had largely been vindicated. Napoleon had
ruthlessly exploited the Polish 'patriots' for his own self-serving ends. Nevertheless, Napoleon had
helped to put Poland 'back on the map' in ways that would not have occurred without him. To that
extent Kosciuszko made a costly error of judgement. The Poles could conceivably have made larger
and more enduring gains if he had swallowed his misgivings and headed the renascent Polish state
and the Polish forces which participated in Napoleon's campaigns, even if he was too unwell to
play a more active role. All the same, however, the victorious Partitioning Powers made no renewed
attempt permanently to eradicate the name of Poland from European history at the glittering Congress of Vienna. Most of the erstwhile Duchy of Warsaw was incorporated into a reconstituted
Kingdom of Poland in 1815, albeit under Tsar Alexander's sceptre. The Napoleonic Wars and the
Duchy of Warsaw also bequeathed hopes and models of courage, devotion, action and statehood
which repeatedly inspired successive generations of Poles (and, to a lesser degree, Lithuanians)
right down to the Revolutions of 1989.

However, one must be aware of the many romanticized and nationalistic accounts of the outlook
and conduct of the Polish-Lithuanian nobility during the aftermath of the Partitions. Only a minority of the former *szlachta* managed to retain noble rank under their new imperial overlords. Countless thousands were downgraded to the status of commoners. The nobility as a whole lost most of
its former political prerogatives, sinecures and representative institutions, much of its previous
wealth and influence, and virtually all of its hitherto customary management and/or exploitation of
crown and ecclesiastical properties, even though its seigneurial privileges remained largely intact.
On discovering that they were now among the most 'superfluous people' in Europe, many demoralized and/or downgraded Polish-Lithuanian nobles threw themselves into a feckless and dissolute
existence in 'downsized' Warsaw or Krakow, in various provincial backwaters, or in foreign resorts,
spas, capitals and casinos, where some of them squandered or gambled away their remaining wealth.
Some dispossessed, déclassé or impoverished Polish nobles were susceptible to the appeal of French
revolutionary ideas and/or Bonapartism. However, this also intensified the alarm and anxiety felt by
those who had somehow managed to hang on to at least part of their former exalted status and
wealth, and rendered them all the more willing to collaborate and/or ingratiate themselves with the
Partitioning Powers. This makes it rather less surprising that the (mainly Polish or Polonized)
Lithuanian nobility presented an address to Catherine the Great in 1795 thanking her for taking over
their country, while the city of Warsaw issued a declaration acclaiming Russia's Field Marshal
Suvorov as a 'liberator' (Wandycz 1974: 21). Unfortunately, once Polish-Lithuanian nobles and

magnates were no longer even formally responsible for the well-being, security and good governance of the Commonwealth, this encouraged some of them to behave even more irresponsibly than before, while others recoiled in horror at the attitudes and conduct of their peers. This sorry predicament left Polish-Lithuanian nobles and magnates as deeply divided as ever.

After 1795 Poles and Lithuanians gradually had to come to terms with the deficiencies of the defunct Commonwealth and to nurture a new conception of the nation, one embracing not just the nobility but the whole population. They had to learn ways of challenging and dispensing with the outmoded privileges and leadership roles of the seigneurial classes and how to induct other social groups into the struggle to regain national independence (Fedorowicz 1982: 260).

THE DE FACTO FOURTH PARTITION OF POLAND-LITHUANIA, 1814–15

At the Congress of Vienna in 1814, Tsar Alexander I held out for the creation of an ethnically Polish kingdom, with himself as its hereditary constitutional monarch. However, because the predominantly Lithuanian, Belarussian and Ukrainian territories which Russia had acquired during the 1772, 1793 and 1795 Partitions were already being treated as integral parts of the Russian Empire (as Russia's 'western provinces'), the victorious Tsar expected the renascent Kingdom of Poland to be carved out of the former Prussian and Austrian shares of the Partitioned Commonwealth, in effect substituting Tsarist for Napoleonic patronage of the erstwhile Duchy of Warsaw. The Prussians would have been prepared to go along with this if they could have been generously compensated with even more valuable territorial gains in Germany (Saxony as well as the Rhineland). However, Austria, Great Britain and France mistrusted Alexander and were determined to minimize the westward expansion of Russia into Poland and of Prussia into Germany, partly for fear of upsetting the new balance of power in Europe. For his part, Alexander was offended by his partners' reluctance to entrust almost the whole of Poland to his tender loving care. Ironically, this induced him to treat his new Polish subjects with uncharacteristic leniency and liberality, despite their active complicity in Napoleon's fateful invasion of Russia in 1812. 'Although bitter towards the Poles . . . the Tsar did not seek revenge', and he was 'genuinely interested in the liberal experiment' in his Polish kingdom, which he 'visited almost annually and wanted to use . . . as an element to transform his empire' (Wandycz 1974: 61, 77). 'Alexander was neither vengeful nor blind to the opportunities of the Polish question' (Zamoyski 1987: 265). This most complex of Russian monarchs was underrated at the time and has remained so.

In the end, the Congress agreed to transform the core areas of the Duchy of Warsaw into a Kingdom of Poland, of which the Tsar would be king. However, Gdansk and most of Wielkopolska (renamed Posen or Poznania) were returned to Prussian rule, while Austria regained most of 'New Galicia' – minus Krakow, which became a nominally independent city-state. In Polish eyes the deal struck in Vienna 'amounted to a fourth Partition' (Halecki 1957: 9). However, as a result of the continuing diplomatic offensive and activity of Czartoryski, the Tsar's (probably genuine) desire to atone for the Partitions, and the patent inability of the other Partitioning Powers completely to 'stamp out' the indomitably Polish nation, the Vienna 'Final Act' contained a pledge that Poles would receive national representations and institutions 'in so far as compatible with the interests of the Partitioning Powers' (Article 1). It also called for 'the maintenance of free navigation, circulation of agrarian and industrial products and free transit' within and between the territories of the former Commonwealth (Article 14). For several decades after 1815, indeed, Poles continued to travel and communicate quite freely between the different parts of the former Commonwealth. 'Polish culture and learning continued to transcend political borders. None of the Partitioning Powers could conduct its Polish policy in isolation, and developments in one area, especially the Kingdom, affected the Polish situation everywhere' (Wandycz 1974: 62, 67). Therefore, when reading separate accounts of the different segments, one should keep in mind their perpetual interaction. Nineteenth-century Poles dismissively referred to the new frontier lines as 'the Prussian cordon' or 'the Austrian cordon', but in spirit the Commonwealth 'continued to exist in defiance of boundaries' (Zamoyski 1987: 267).

THE RUSSIAN-CONTROLLED 'CONGRESS KINGDOM' OF POLAND

With a territory of 127,000 square kilometres, the new Kingdom of Poland recognized by the Congress of Vienna in 1815 was somewhat smaller than its French-sponsored predecessor, the Duchy of Warsaw, but its population soared from 3.3 million in 1815 to more than 13 million by 1913 (Davies 1981b: 307). According to the 1897 census, 31.5 per cent of the population lived in towns and 72 per cent of the population was Polish (Wandycz 1974 206; Leslie 1980: 40).

Tsar Alexander allowed Polish aristocrats who had fought against him (but who were now at his mercy) to retain their landed estates and, where applicable, military positions. He also allowed the so-called Congress Kingdom to keep its own Sejm, government, laws, courts, armed forces, national guard, education system and official language. There were no vindictive 'purges' comparable to those initiated by subsequent Russian rulers. Warsaw was even allowed to open its first university in 1816, and by 1821 the kingdom had more than a thousand primary schools, continuing the educational reforms initiated during the 1770s and 1780s. Nevertheless, Russian rulers 'often refused to recognize the noble status of the poorest, peasant-like *szlachta*'. Large numbers of the latter were resettled on the Black Sea steppes, which Russia was busily colonizing (Wandycz 1974: 18). By 1864, as the joint result of these rustications, successive economic crises and the punishments meted out to noble participants in the uprisings of 1830–1 and 1863–4, more than half of the erstwhile *szlachta* had lost its former noble rank within the Congress Kingdom (Davies 1981b: 82).

The Constitutional Charter of November 1815, which was one of the most liberal-sounding constitutions of its time and which successive Tsar-Kings were sworn to uphold, promised personal and religious freedom (including freedom from arbitrary arrest and punishment), proclaimed the inviolability of private property, recognized Roman Catholicism as the majority religion and provided for a bicameral Sejm comprising a nominated upper house (Senate) and an elected lower house, albeit one whose members had to be landowners (Wandycz 1974: 74–5). At the opening of the 1818 session of the Sejm, however, the Tsar threw down the following (somewhat patronizing) challenge: 'The results of your labours will show me whether I shall be able to abide by my intention of expanding the concessions I have already made to you' (quoted by Zamoyski 1987: 266). As King of Poland, moreover, Alexander retained the power to appoint and dismiss ministers and officials, to convoke or amend its legislation, to conduct foreign policy, to control the police, to bypass the Sejm on budgetary matters and to act as ultimate arbiter.

The Congress Kingdom's standing army of 30,000 men, which was 'capable of rapid expansion in wartime', used Polish as the sole language of command, wore Polish colours and uniforms and absorbed 40 per cent of public expenditure (Davies 1981b: 311). 'Excellently trained and well administered, it was the pride of all Poles' (thus prefiguring the post-1918 and post-1945 Polish armies!). However, it was placed under the command of Alexander's brother, Grand Duke Konstantin, who was a typically Tsarist martinet and 'paradomaniac', even though his morganatic marriage to a Pole precluded any possibility of his acceding to the Russian throne and helped him to become genuinely enamoured of and protective towards his adopted country. In order to engender military dependence upon Russia, the Congress Kingdom was not allowed to establish armaments factories (Wandycz 1974: 77–8).

In the aftermath of the Napoleonic Wars numerous Polish landed estates throughout the former Commonwealth were very adversely affected by a slump in international grain prices, increased protection of some major western European markets against 'cheap' foreign grain (notably through the British Corn Laws passed in 1816), the loss of unimpeded access to Gdansk (Danzig) and other

Baltic ports, and Prussian state support for the Junker landowning nobility. These circumstances contributed to the financial ruin of many marginal or heavily mortgaged Polish landowners, some of whom had to sell or surrender their landholdings to creditors, bankers, burghers or non-Poles (including Prussian Junkers in Poznania, Masuria and Pomerania).

This agrarian crisis, following hard on the heels of the deeply unsettling effects of the French Revolution and Bonapartist reformism and opportunism, again forced questions of agrarian reform into the forefront of public attention and debate. This even resulted in the initiation of a Prussian-style 'landless emancipation' of the serfs in nearby Estland in 1816, in Kurland in 1817, in Livonia in 1819 and in Prussian-ruled Poznania in 1823. These reforms helped to transform landed estates into large-scale capitalist enterprises employing landless or almost landless wage labourers. Such hard-nosed solutions were rejected as being too risky and/or inhumane in the Congress Kingdom, in Russia's 'western provinces', in Russia proper and in the Habsburg Empire (including Galicia) at that time. Nevertheless, the agrarian question 'demanded a solution on economic, social and humanitarian grounds, and it was pregnant with political meaning. Depending on the kind of solution adopted, the peasant could become either a loyal subject of the Partitioning Powers or a politically conscious member of the Polish nation' (Wandycz 1974: 67). The Tsarist regime proved willing to go much further than the rulers of Prussian Poland and Galicia in its endeavours to use agrarian reform as a means of winning over or at least 'neutralizing' the peasantry and thus depriving the rebellious Polish-Lithuanian nobility of potential peasant support for secessionist and autonomist movements.

From the 1820s onwards, however, much the most effective alleviations of the agricultural crisis in the territories of the former Polish-Lithuanian Commonwealth stemmed from greatly expanded cultivation of potatoes, flax and sugar-beet, increased and improved crop rotation and sheep breeding, intensive rearing of pigs on potatoes and surplus grain, greatly increased production of vodka (from potatoes and surplus grain), sausage, beer, sugar, linen and woollen textiles, and greatly reduced reliance on grain as the staple subsistence and cash crop. This led to a corresponding diminished reliance on serf labour to cultivate grain, which in turn made it easier to contemplate and accommodate a more widespread abolition of serfdom. Broadly, the areas which abandoned serfdom first also pioneered the development of new cropping patterns, distilling, brewing and food-processing.

Within the Congress Kingdom, to a far greater extent than in either Prussian or Austrian Poland, the post-1814 agricultural crisis was also alleviated by the beginnings of more broadly based industrialization. From 1816 onwards the government and some forward-looking magnates of the Congress Kingdom successfully promoted coal, zinc and copper mining, zinc, copper and iron smelting, steel making and, less directly, distilling, brewing and the kingdom's mushrooming woollen and cotton textile industries. The latter were greatly assisted by the inclusion of the Congress Kingdom within the Russian imperial customs union. Direct access to the vast Russian market (from which Prussian, Austrian and Western competitors were increasingly excluded) not only gave the Congress Kingdom's native entrepreneurs a preferential position. It also encouraged Germanic and western European entrepreneurs, engineers and manufacturers of textiles and textile machinery to set up (or ally themselves with) firms in Congress Poland, both as part of a modern 'tariff-hopping' strategy and in order to take advantage of the ample availability of very cheap serf and ex-serf labour, which was largely surplus to local agricultural requirements. Moreover, some of the entrepreneurs, engineers and artisans involved in the hitherto burgeoning Poznanian textile industry, which now found itself severely squeezed by the more favoured and/or advanced textile producers of central and western Germany as a result of the Partitions, 'relocated' to the Congress Kingdom. Generally speaking, other than in distilling, brewing and food-processing, the industrialists or would-be industrialists of Poznania and Pomerania found it increasingly difficult to compete with the much stronger industries of Saxony, Silesia, Berlin and western Germany, while those of

Austrian Poland were even less able to compete with the burgeoning industries of Bohemia and German Austria. The Congress Kingdom, by contrast, succeeded in becoming the most highly industrialized territory of the far less industrialized Russian Empire. It was able to meet many of the industrial requirements of St Petersburg, Moscow and the Tsarist state, including a supply of military uniforms for the Russian armies that held it in subjugation! The Congress Kingdom's preferential economic position was placed in jeopardy by the liberalization of the Russian Empire's foreign trade during the 1850s and 1860s, which increasingly exposed the kingdom to industrial competition from the west, but this threat receded again when the Russian Empire's import tariffs were greatly increased during the 1880s and 1890s. The number of industrial workers in the Congress Kingdom rose to 75,000 in 1858, 150,000 in 1885 (when Poznania had only 28,000 and Galicia a mere 25,000) and 317,000 in 1913 (Wandycz 1974: 158, 202, 280).

Nevertheless, the narrowly economic advantages which the Congress Kingdom derived from being within the tariff walls of the Russian Empire were neither enough in themselves nor perceived with sufficient clarity (at least until the publication of Rosa Luxemburg's celebrated doctoral thesis on *Die Industrielle Entwicklung Polens* in 1898) to persuade Polish patriots to give up the struggle against irksome and increasingly repressive Russian tutelage. Moreover, although Tsar Alexander I was in principle prepared to grant the Poles of the Congress Kingdom a degree of autonomy and some constitutional civil rights, even this least illiberal of Russian Tsars bristled when Poles had the 'effrontery' to insist on exercising their vaunted 'rights' at all assertively. The long honeymoon between Alexander I and his new Polish subjects ended in 1820, when a couple of liberal opposition deputies 'sought to expose the arbitrariness of the government and its attempts to muzzle the Sejm'. The shocked Tsar interpreted such criticism as 'an attack on the monarchy', deprived the critics of their seats in the Sejm, dismissed the kingdom's liberal commissioner for education and religion, enhanced the extra-constitutional powers of Grand Duke Konstantin and refrained from convoking another Sejm until 1825 (Wandycz 1974: 84). In 1823, in Russia's 'western provinces', there were several dismissals, arrests and deportations of free-thinking Poles at the University of Wilno (Vilnius).

Russo-Polish relations rapidly deteriorated under Tsar Nicholas I (1825–55), who was deeply shaken at the very start of his reign by an abortive *coup d'état* by members of Russia's elite Guards Regiments in St Petersburg on 14 December 1825. These so-called Decembrists had links with secret opposition groups in Warsaw, whose 'ringleaders' were (on the Tsar's instructions) brought to trial before a Senate tribunal in 1828. However, the Tsar and Grand Duke Konstantin accepted neither the Senators' ruling that 'membership of an unapproved society did not in itself constitute a treasonable act', nor the lenient sentences imposed. The Senators' proceedings were annulled and the accused were subsequently 'transported in chains to Siberia' (Davies 1981b: 314). A classic pattern was emerging: 'having imposed a government and a Constitution on a satellite Poland, Russia could not countenance its legal functioning' (Zamoyski 1987: 269). In 1828, moreover, the Tsar initiated a vicious campaign of persecution and suppression against the Uniate Church in Russia's 'western provinces'. This culminated in the 'return' of the Uniate hierarchy to the Eastern Orthodox 'fold' in 1839, amid continuing popular resistance.

Polish anger at these flagrant violations of the Tsar's earlier manifesto promising to abide by the constitution and continue the policies of Alexander I contributed to the outbreak of a chaotic cadet-officers' uprising in Warsaw on 29 November 1830. This so-called 'November rising' began amid a serious economic crisis and an alarming cholera epidemic, a few months after the final overthrow of France's Bourbon regime and the attainment of Belgian independence from the Netherlands. However, the ineptitude of the mutinous cadets (who accidentally killed some of their own people) enabled conservative members of the kingdom's government to regain the political initiative. Out of a desire to avoid unnecessary bloodshed and burning of bridges, they allowed Grand Duke Konstantin safely to withdraw his Russian troops and officials from the Congress Kingdom to Russia (instead of holding them hostage) and tried to use the state of insurgency merely as a lever with which to extract constitutional guarantees and concessions from the Tsar. Unfortunately, Nicholas demanded unconditional capitulation and refused to negotiate, informing Grand Duke Konstantin that either Russia or Poland 'must now perish' (Davies 1981b: 320). On 25 January 1831, while a Russian invasion force assembled around Bialystok, the Sejm rashly voted to dethrone the Romanovs in the Congress Kingdom (emulating the recent Belgian dethronement of the House of Orange), thereby matching the Tsar's intransigence and transforming a hitherto restrained 'war of nerves' into a 'life-or-death' struggle for national independence. This also alienated the other Partitioning Powers, who had been enjoying Russia's discomfiture. In February Prince Adam Czartoryski emerged as president of a Polish National Government, which vainly scoured Europe for a new king while mobilizing more than 57,000 Polish servicemen, who initially inflicted heavy defeats and casualties on much larger and more heavily armed but cholera-stricken Russian forces. However, the kingdom's military actions were poorly synchronized with those of more than 20,000 Polish and Lithuanian rebels in Lithuania, Belarussia and Ukraine (Wandycz 1974: 112–15). More-over, the Polish leaders' reluctance to make a clean break with serfdom (for fear of alienating the mainstays of their own support, financial backing and officer class) inhibited them from fully mobi-lizing the peasantry, who could have turned their weapons against their 'masters'. By September 1831, therefore, the Congress Kingdom could no longer hold off the sheer weight of the Russian steamroller and Warsaw capitulated, while the Polish armies melted away and the political leaders fled abroad. For many Poles the cruellest cut came in 1832 when the Pope condemned the 'Novem-ber rising' and lauded the Tsar for suppressing it.

This time Tsarist retribution was merciless. Nicholas I lacked the magnanimity of Alexander I. About 360 people were sentenced to death (though most of these had already escaped abroad), several thousand landed estates were confiscated, half the Catholic convents and monasteries were closed, and more than 50,000 Polish and Lithuanian nobles and officers were banished to the back of beyond (Siberia, the Caucasus, beyond the Volga), some as convicts, others as low-ranking sol-diers. The kingdom's constitution, Sejm, army and institutions of higher learning were abolished, as was the University of Wilno, while Russian replaced Polish as the official language in Russia's so-called 'western provinces' (even in schools). The kingdom was in effect under Russian-administered martial law and its education system went to rack and ruin. By the late nineteenth century its adult literacy rates were even lower than those of Russia.

Nearly 8,000 educated Poles became political émigrés after 1831, 'and for the next fifteen years the centre of Polish intellectual life and political activities shifted abroad, mainly to France' (Namier 1946: 43–4). Those who remained in their old homelands found outlets and/or solace in practical ('organic') work, which did at least yield significant economic dividends. The newfound apoliti-cism of the Polish and Lithuanian propertied classes was reinforced by a ferocious peasant revolt in Galicia in 1846, which resulted in the deaths of some two thousand Polish landowners and encour-aged the Tsarist regime to register and regulate peasant rights and obligations in the 'western prov-inces' as a means of currying favour with the serfs at their masters' expense (see pp. 289, 295–6).

Industry and trade resumed their earlier rapid expansion following the elimination of the temporary tariff barriers established between Russia and the Congress Kingdom from 1832 to 1851 and were further stimulated by the Crimean War (1853–6). However, the political 'freeze' did not end until the death of Nicholas I in 1855. Polish attempts to use the Crimean War to reopen 'the Polish question' by military and diplomatic means came to naught. Nevertheless, Russia's humiliating defeats at British and French hands in Crimea did contribute to a thaw by igniting popular unrest in many parts of the empire, by sapping Nicholas I's will to live, and by helping to convince Tsar Alexander II (1855–81) that the emancipation of the serfs in both Russia and the Congress Kingdom could not be postponed any longer – he would have to grasp the nettle. This firm conviction prompted Alexander II to invite the kingdom's newly established Agricultural Society to formulate far-reaching proposals for peasant emancipation and agrarian reform in 1858. Formed ostensibly to promote 'improving landlordism', the 4,000 members and seventy-seven district branches of the Agricultural Society actually functioned as a surrogate Sejm for the Polish landed nobility. Its president, Count Adam Zamoyski, became the unofficial 'spokesman of the Poles in the Kingdom' (Wandycz 1974: 156). By February 1861 large crowds were cheering the arrival of delegates at its meetings!

Well before this, however, Russia's Crimean defeats and the death of Nicholas I had already aroused hopes, spirits and expectations, to which the new Tsar virtually had to respond. However, it proved difficult either to dampen or to satisfy these expectations of change. There is also much to be said for the Marxist view that the development of 'productive forces' in Russia and Poland had reached a point where it was both inhibited by and increasingly at odds with the prevailing 'social relations of production', and therefore had to change (see Bideleux 1994: 16–19).

In 1856 Alexander II announced his intention to initiate reforms in partnership with the propertied classes. He also appointed a (by Russian standards) liberal viceroy to the Congress Kingdom, amnestied the Poles who had been languishing in banishment since 1831, restored freedom of assembly and allowed the long-vacant Archbishopric of Warsaw to be filled, but also warned his Polish subjects not to indulge in impractical daydreams: 'Pas de rêveries, messieurs!' Long forbidden subjects were freshly debated as hundreds of new societies blossomed. There were calls for Jewish emancipation and assimilation; and the finest Russians (led by Alexander Herzen) promoted Russo-Polish reconciliation and co-operation in the interests of fraternal friendship, freedom and reform. Indeed, throughout the nineteenth century there were deep friendships and alliances as well as awful antagonisms between Russians and Poles (Zamoyski 1987: 308).

By 1861, however, the 'thaw' and rekindled Polish nationalism were spawning demands and expectations which the Tsarist regime was unwilling (and probably unable) to assuage, and mass demonstrations to which the authorities unfortunately over-reacted, causing unnecessary fatalities and even the suppression of the Agricultural Society. The initial terms on which serfs were gradually to be emancipated (from 1861 onwards) fell far short of public expectations and became a bone of bitter contention. During 1861 and 1862 the singing of patriotic hymns at huge Catholic masses in the Congress Kingdom and in Russia's 'western provinces' gave expression to rising nationalist fervour, foreshadowing the 'singing revolutions' of the Polish and other Baltic peoples during the late Tsarist and late Soviet periods. The imposition of martial law in the 'western provinces' and the Congress Kingdom in October 1861 did not dampen opposition, but simply drove it underground. During 1862 and 1863, indeed, Polish 'patriots' developed an elaborate underground state with its own administration, secret army, diplomatic representation and intelligence network, in preparation for a concerted armed insurrection. What the Poles lacked in regular military forces, compared with 1830–1, they now made up in superior morale, discipline and organization (prefiguring 1942–4). Sensing that something was afoot yet unable to track it down, the Russian authorities and their Polish collaborators (led by the conservative reformer Count Alexander Wielopolski) cunningly announced their intention to draft 30,000 young Polish males into military service on 14 January 1863. However, this ruse was forestalled by hastily bringing forward the start of the planned insurrection, which caught the authorities completely off guard.

The insurgents of the 'January rising' had to avoid direct engagements with the 45,000 Russian troops stationed in the kingdom. Yet they managed to keep up hit-and-run attacks on Russian garrisons, encampments and officialdom from January 1863 to May 1864 (and even longer in some areas) and forced the Russians temporarily to evacuate three-quarters of the localities they had occupied (Wandycz 1974: 172–7). The rising spread deep into Lithuania, Belarussia and Ukraine. It involved hundreds of Russian, Italian, German, French, British and Irish volunteers. While at any one time there were never more than 20,000–30,000 'insurgents in the field', approximately 200,000 people took part (p. 179). Remarkably, the actual identities of all but a few remained undetected and most of the 200,000 rebels 'simply melted away' at the end (Davies 1981b: 363). However, as in

1831, while several European Powers relished Russia's discomfiture, neither Prussia nor Austria could afford to have the rising succeed, and neither France nor Great Britain wanted to risk any military intervention on the insurgents' behalf.

To a far greater extent than Nicholas I, moreover, Alexander II was prepared to propitiate the peasantry by granting them additional land at their former masters' expense. However much the insurgents promised to accede to peasant aspirations or to prevent landowners from continuing to exact seigneurial dues from their former serfs, Alexander was willing to outbid them. Canny peasants probably twigged that, instead of putting their lives at risk by backing the insurgents' increasingly radical agrarian programme, they only needed to wait patiently to receive much the same agrarian gains (without risk!) from the Tsar. Indeed, the final terms on which the former serfs in Russia's 'western provinces' and the Congress Kingdom were emanicipated in 1864 were among the most favourable in East Central Europe and the Russian Empire.

In the aftermath of the 1863 rising more than 3,000 Polish and Lithuanian landed estates were confiscated (many were given to Tsarist officers or officials). Approximately 400 people were executed after due legal process (the number summarily shot or hanged is harder to establish), while tens of thousands were deported to Siberia and other similarly salubrious abodes. Warsaw became the capital of 'the Vistula Region' or 'the ten provinces', although the Congress Kingdom of Poland was not formally abolished until 1874. This territory was 'administered by Russians with Russian as the official language' (Wandycz 1974: 196) and in 1885 Russian also became the only language permitted in schools (Zamoyski 1987: 315). Neither 'the Vistula Region' nor 'the western provinces' was allowed the system of elected *zemstva* (provincial councils) established in Russia proper in 1864 or the elected municipal *dumi* (councils) introduced in the latter in 1870. Since they were also neither inclined nor encouraged to engage in Tsarist state service, the Tsar's Polish subjects again largely retreated from public political activity into 'organic work': the quiet construction of an economically and culturally renewed and strengthened Poland, an expanded industrial sector and a modernized infrastructure. In the longer term, however, this inevitably brought new players on to the political stage: an increasingly assertive bourgeoisie and 'bourgeois' political parties; several somewhat unassertive peasant parties; and politically awakened, partly Jewish and increasingly assertive industrial workers, trade unions and socialist parties. All of these would eventually challenge the former political ascendancy of the magnates, the nobility and the émigré intelligentsia during the 1890s and the 1900s.

The assassination of Alexander II in 1881 and the accession of Alexander III (reg. 1881–94) changed the political climate very much for the worse. In the first place these events precipitated a wave of officially condoned pogroms against Jews in Ukraine, Lithuania and, to a lesser degree, the former Congress Kingdom. These pogroms were both symptomatic of and conducive to a significant 'hardening' of official and even popular attitudes towards certain religious and ethnic groups (including Poles, Catholics and Armenians as well as Jews) and a deterioration of inter-ethnic and inter-denominational relations in general. Polish, Lithuanian, Ukrainian and Belarussian national movements, which had been parting company since the 1863–4 uprising and the subsequent repression and mutual recriminations, also became increasingly anti-Semitic, partly because the development of capitalism seemed to be expanding the roles of 'exploitative' Jewish middlemen and partly because growing urbanization was bringing ethnic Poles, Lithuanians, Ukrainians and Belarussians increasingly into competition with Jewish townspeople. The recurrent pogroms, which tended to be most violent in Ukraine, Belarussia and Lithuania, also provoked an unsettling influx of Jewish refugees (so-called 'Litvaks') into the *relative* safety and civility of the former Congress Kingdom, where Jews already made up more than 10 per cent of the population by 1881 (as was also the case in the 'western provinces'). Under Alexander III and Nicholas II (reg. 1894–1917), moreover, the Tsarist regime reverted to the repressive bigotry of Nicholas I, but applied it with the technology and ferocity of a more modern police state. For some people at least life in the western borderlands of the Russian Empire was becoming even nastier and more brutish than before, and this increasingly intemperate 'dog-eat-dog' climate was in no way alleviated by the rise of movements preaching class hatred! The growth of virulent nationalism was more often reinforced than dissipated or defused by the intensification of class antagonisms. When combined, they produced particularly poisonous and explosive cocktails.

Modern Polish, Jewish and (later) Lithuanian nationalist movements orientated towards the emerging entrepreneurial and professional classes developed rapidly during the 1880s and 1890s and began to establish cross-border ties between different parts of the former Commonwealth. Similarly, in areas primarily inhabited by Poles, Jews and Lithuanians, small socialist groups orientated towards the wage-earning working class (as distinct from the peasantry) sprang up during the 1880s. After a major workers' strike in Lodz in 1892 they coalesced into larger movements and parties in 1893–6, well before their Russian and Ukrainian counterparts. However, these socialists eventually forged ties with sister movements in Russia, Germany and Austria as well as between the various components of the former Commonwealth. Yet, while some people interpreted these links as manifestations of a reassuring growth of 'proletarian internationalism', others saw them as an additional cause for alarm. When it came to the crucial test, moreover, these vaunted 'bonds' did not prevent (and barely withstood) the outbreak of war in 1914.

In the former Congress Kingdom and in Russia's 'western provinces', even more than in Russia proper, the Russo-Japanese War of 1904–5 exacerbated already serious economic and social crises. These exploded into major anti-war and anti-Tsarist demonstrations, political as well as economic strikes and bloody clashes between workers and the Tsarist security forces (who were sometimes supported by the Polish propertied classes) from the autumn of 1904 to the summer of 1907, after which the fever temporarily subsided as the authorities resorted to increasingly draconian repression and divide-and-rule tactics. However, workers' unrest revived between 1912 and August 1914, whereupon the start of the First World War gave Tsarism a brief respite by allowing it to rally its Russian, Polish, Ukrainian, Jewish, Belarussian and Lithuanian subjects behind the war effort and to place would-be 'troublemakers' under military discipline.

THE 'PRUSSIAN ZONES' OF POLAND

The principal territories gained by the Hohenzollerns from the Polish-Lithuanian Commonwealth were West Prussia (1772–1807, 1815–1918), Mazovia and Bialystock (1795–1807), and, most importantly, Gdansk, Torun (Thorn) and Wielkopolska (1793–1807, 1815–1918). Prussian legal codes, administrative practices and personnel were introduced into these areas from 1795 onwards and elected provincial *sejmiki* were abolished, along with urban autonomy (Wandycz 1974: 14–15). The former crown estates and those belonging to insurrectionary nobles were first confiscated by the Prussian state and then sold to Germans (especially Junkers and bankers), ostensibly to raise revenue, but perhaps also to Germanize these newly annexed territories. There were also substantial Polish populations in Prussian Pomerania, Masuria (in East Prussia) and Silesia, and in 1800 Poles comprised more than 40 per cent of the population of the Kingdom of Prussia. From 1807 to 1815, however, Prussia lost most of its Polish territory to the Duchy of Warsaw, while at the Congress of Vienna in 1814–15 the Hohenzollerns also yielded Mazovia (including Warsaw) and Bialystock to victorious Russia, although they received rich compensation elsewhere (the Rhineland and part of Saxony). During the late 1790s the Hohenzollern-ruled areas of Poland experienced a grain boom which mainly benefited the bigger landowners, but this boom collapsed during the 1800s, under the combined impact of British blockades and Napoleon's Continental System. As a result, much of the Polish *szlachta* had to sell off land to wealthier Germans.

In 1815 Wielkopolska was reconstituted as the semi-autonomous Grand Duchy of Posen, alias Poznania. Its area was just 29,000 square kilometres and its population (80 per cent of which was

Polish speaking) was only 850,000 in 1815, rising to 2.15 million by 1911 (Davies 1981b: 120; Leslie 1971: 21). It had its own Landrat (Diet), elected by the nobility, and Polish was the official language in education, administration and the courts. By contrast, Pomerania, Upper Silesia and East and West Prussia were governed and educated in German, as integral components of the Kingdom of Prussia, with just a few concessions to the inchoate 'national' sensibilities of those inhabitants who spoke dialects of Polish as their mother tongues. However, many of the latter had an even weaker sense of 'Polishness' than did the mainly German-speaking inhabitants of Gdansk (Davies 1981b: 112) and the Prussian monarchy was able to promote the concept of 'the loyal Polish-speaking Prussian' with some success so long as (i) the Prussian state remained more monarchical than (German) 'national' and (ii) the Polish speakers of Pomerania, Masuria and Prussian Silesia retained essentially local identities and a stronger allegiance to the king than to the Polish 'nation'. By contrast the population of Poznania was classified as being 60 per cent Polish, 34 per cent German and 6 per cent Jewish during the 1840s (Wandycz 1974: 139). By 1911, as a result of significant population shifts, the Jewish share had fallen to 1.2 per cent (p. 286) and that of the Germans to 30 per cent, while the Polish share had risen to 68 per cent (Leslie 1971: 21).

The subjugation of Prussia's Polish subjects was aided by the circumstance that the exceptionally assiduous, efficient and law-governed Prussian civil service and armed forces were dominated by relatively educated and dutiful Protestant landowners (Junkers) whose power base lay mainly in areas with substantial Polish populations. It was doubly difficult for the relatively uneducated Poles to hold their own against a ruling class which presided over one of Europe's most developed education systems. This, besides producing such luminaries as Kant, Hegel, Fichte, Humboldt, Bunsen, Kleist and Lessing, acted as a cultural magnet and transformed Berlin and Königsberg into intellectual centres of the first order. 'Notwithstanding the authoritarian state, all political changes in Prussia were subjected to searching debate . . . In the absence of any comparable intellectual development in the Polish lands, many Poles were inevitably drawn into the world of German culture . . . Quite apart from official policy, therefore, many Poles in Prussia accepted that modernization went hand-in-hand with Germanization' (Davies 1981b: 118–19). 'By 1848, 82 per cent of children were attending schools' (p. 123). Many influential Poznanian Poles concluded that their only course was to try to become even more efficient, orderly, educated and industrious than their Prussian Protestant overlords, in order to beat the blighters at their own game! As one of them wrote in 1872, 'Learning, work, order and thrift, these are our new weapons . . . In this way you will save both yourself and Poland' (quoted in Wandycz 1974: 229).

There was a gradual dissolution of serfdom in most parts of Prussia between 1811 and 1853, although in Poznania the process was not initiated until 1823. But in Prussia, unlike the Congress Kingdom, Austria-Hungary and Russia, most of the former serfs were converted into landless agricultural labourers rather than independent peasant smallholders, while Junker dominance of the local law courts kept most of the agrarian population under landlord jurisdiction even after the dissolution of serfdom. For Prussia's Polish subjects the positive effects of formal personal emancipation were also offset by greatly increased burdens of taxation and compulsory military service (far in excess of anything imposed by the former Polish-Lithuanian Commonwealth).

After the abortive risings of 1830–1 in the Congress Kingdom, the Poznanian Landrat ceased to be convoked and some Poznanian Poles who had given succour to Polish insurgents had their property confiscated, while more than 250 Poznanian Poles were arrested during the Galician crisis of 1846. However, the latter group were set free following the outbreak of revolutionary unrest in Berlin on 20 March 1848 (Davies 1981b: 12). Many of the German liberals, radicals and nationalists of 1848 were anti-Russian. Some considered that 'one of the first acts of a newly united Germany should be to make war upon Russia' and that 'Poland should be erected into an independent state to act as a buffer between Germany and Russia' (Leslie 1971: 19). In the *Neue Rheinische Zeitung* on 19 August 1848, Marx and Engels declared that 'The establishment of a democratic Poland is a primary condition for the establishment of a democratic Germany . . . She must receive at least the frontiers of 1772 and . . . a considerable stretch of coast' (quoted by Namier 1946: 51).

However, in a debate in the German National Assembly in July 1848 on the future of Poznania, a German from East Prussia helped to sway German liberal-nationalist opinion away from its former sympathy for the Polish cause. 'Are half a million Germans . . . to be relegated to the position of nationalized foreigners subject to another nation of lesser cultural content than themselves?' he asked. 'Our right is the right of the stronger, the right of conquest . . . Mere existence does not entitle a people to political independence, only the force to assert itself as a state' (quoted by Namier 1946: 88). This naked appeal to *force majeure* was to set the tone for German–Polish relations thereafter. By the end of April 1848, moreover, the Prussian army had already suppressed the Poznanian Polish militias and National Committee which had emerged in March. After 1848 Poznania lost the last vestiges of its formal autonomy and was downgraded to a mere *Provinz* of the Prussian kingdom, as Germans veered from sympathy to hostility towards the Polish cause. This hardening of German attitudes seems even to have affected Engels, who wrote (to Marx) on 23 May 1851: 'The more I think about this business, the clearer it is to me that the Poles are *une nation foutue*, a serviceable instrument only until Russia herself is swept into the agrarian revolution. From that moment Poland loses all *raison d'être*. The Poles have never done anything in history except engage in brave, blatant foolery'! (quoted by Namier 1946: 52). Unlike Engels, however, Marx maintained his support for the Polish cause.

The position of Prussia's Polish provinces was radically transformed by the creation of Bismarck's German Empire in 1871. From having been one of several provinces of the Hohenzollern kingdom, Poznania now became a virtual colony of the German state. 'The imperial union of the German lands established Germanity as the touchstone of respectability, in a way that never pertained before' (Davies 1981b: 131). In 1872 German became the official language of instruction in all elementary schools (even in Poznania, where only religious education continued to be provided partly in Polish). In 1874 there was a ban on the use of Polish textbooks. In 1887 even the teaching of Polish as a 'foreign language' was discontinued in favour of English! Furthermore, teachers in state schools were no longer permitted to belong either to Polish or to Catholic organizations, while in 1876 German was made the exclusive language of administration, even in post offices, railway ticket offices and courts of law (Wandycz 1974: 235).

These measures coincided with Bismarck's infamous *Kulturkampf*, an attack on the alleged centrifugal and particularist tendencies of German as well as Polish Catholicism. The newly established German national state was determined to assert its temporal jurisdiction over the local branches of the Catholic Church, at a time when Pope Pius IX was challenging the authority and legitimacy of the new state by denouncing nationalism and encouraging ultramontanism. A series of German laws passed between 1872 and 1876 led to the expulsion of the Jesuits, the sequestration of Catholic Church properties, the severance of relations with the papacy and mass dismissals of Polish Catholic priests from teaching posts (mostly to be replaced by German Protestants). The conservative Polish Archbishop of Gniezno and Catholic Primate of Prussian Poland had initially been very willing to collaborate with the Prussian authorities against Polish nationalism, democracy and secular radicalism, supposedly to keep the universalist Catholic Church 'above' or 'out of' temporal politics (although it was nothing of the sort!). But in 1874 he was arrested and imprisoned (for two years) for refusing to acquiesce in the subordination of the Catholic Church to the state. This former 'collaborator' suddenly became a 'national hero'. The German Archbishop of Cologne, two Polish bishops, most Polish deacons and more than a hundred Polish parish priests were also imprisoned, while many more were harassed or dismissed from their positions. These anti-Catholic campaigns were targeted at German as well as Polish clergy, but they bit deeper and lasted longer in Germany's Polish provinces, where they were inseparable from equally acrimonious linguistic and educational issues (Wandycz 1974: 228–34).

During the 1880s, moreover, German publicists, academics and politicians started drawing attention to the substantial exodus of Germans from the Polish provinces to the more industrialized, urbanized and prosperous parts of the German Empire. This flight from the east (known as the *Ostflucht*) aroused German fears that, in spite of the state-sponsored Germanization programme, 'Germandom' (*Deutschtum*) was losing ground to 'Slavdom' and that Germany's grip on these provinces was therefore becoming less secure. The German backlash began in 1885–6 with the controversial expulsion of approximately 26,000 Poles and Polish Jews who held Russian or Austrian rather than German citizenship, even though some of these families had lived in Prussia for several generations (Leslie 1980: 32). In 1886, sensing that his own political position was becoming less secure, Bismarck also played up and pandered to German xenophobia by calling for the creation of a commission to buy up Polish-owned land in the east and colonize it with German peasants (Wandycz 1974: 236). The resultant Colonization Commission, endowed with a hundred million marks, was backed not just by German imperialists, but by National Liberals who saw peasant colonists as a useful counterweight to the excessive power of the Junkers in the 'eastern provinces' and also by Junkers who saw such colonists as a potential pool of cheap and/or dependent labour.

However, the main overall effect of the *Kulturkampf*, the Germanization programme and the Colonization Commission was to arouse, mobilize and even unite the Poles of Poznania, Pomerania, Masuria and Silesia in support of Polish nationalism, Catholicism and cultural resistance. The Poles were goaded into strikingly successful political, economic, educational and cultural counter-offensives, which actually *reversed* Germanization on the ground, despite further escalations of Germany's 'eastern' imperialism and colonialism.

Following the establishment of the pan-German Union in 1891, an association for the promotion of German interests in the 'eastern provinces' was launched in 1894. It was popularly known as the Hakata (after the initials of its founders, Hansemann, Kennemann and Tiedemann), before formally becoming the Deutscher Ostmarkverein in 1899. It enjoyed strong private, official and academic support and propagated a proto-Nazi *Lebensraum* programme and ideology. It systematically Germanized 'eastern' place names and public signs, fostered German cultural imperialism, and provided financial and other inducements for German farmers, officials, clergy and teachers to settle and work in the east. After Bismarck's fall in 1890, Kaiser Wilhelm II actively encouraged all this.

In response, the Polish and/or Catholic credit associations, agricultural co-operatives, mutual aid societies and land banks which had been launched in Prussia's 'eastern provinces' during the 1860s and 1870s were spurred to ever higher levels of activity. Polish farmers' *rolniki* ('circles'), whose membership rose tenfold between 1873 and 1914 (Wandycz 1974: 286), helped their members to undertake bulk purchases of seed, fertilizers, equipment and fuel, to secure more favourable terms for their produce, to buy additional land and to improve agricultural techniques and education (Davies 1981b: 192). In Poznania, Pomerania and Upper Silesia the Union of Credit Associations expanded its membership from 26,533 in 1890 to 146,312 in 1913, while its deposits rose more than twentyfold. (The resultant 'squeezing out' of middlemen contributed to the large-scale Jewish emigration.) Moreover, the Land Purchase Bank which the Poles established in 1897 was soon able to offer higher dividends and easier credit terms than were its German rivals, thanks to its efficient and close-knit network of operations; and between 1896 and 1904 there was a net 50,000 hectare increase in Polish landownership (Wandycz 1974: 286).

Many thousands of German peasants were settled in Prussia's 'eastern provinces' by the Colonization Commission, but fewer than half of these were inward migrants from other parts of Germany, and they proved all too willing subsequently to resell the land they had acquired (often to Poles!) in order to cash in on rising land prices (Leslie 1980: 35). Moreover, much of the money mobilized for the 'colonization' and Germanization of these 'eastern provinces' was diverted into the pockets of the Junkers, 'who made their patriotism a highly lucrative business' (Wandycz 1974: 237, 285–6).

Indeed, it is unclear to what extent the latter was the programme's true purpose, with nationalist colonial rhetoric serving mainly as a smokescreen with which to deceive the German public (which was not so eager to subsidize profiteers and Junkers). Whatever the case, the programme failed to halt (let alone reverse) the long-term decline of Poznania's German population, which fell from 666,083 in 1861 to 637,000 in 1911, while its Polish population rose from 801,372 to 1,463,000 over the same period (Leslie 1971: 21).

In addition, Poles began to take full advantage of the ubiquitous schools, literacy, public libraries, reading rooms and museums provided by the German state, while increasingly reserving their own educational and cultural expenditures for extensive private tuition in Polish language, literature, history and Catholicism (Wandycz 1974: 232, 235, 283, 285). This started a tradition which helped to maintain Polish culture and morale during the periods of Nazi and Communist rule. During the 1900s, moreover, Poles began to buy locally produced manufactures in preference to those from elsewhere, while the number of industrial workers in Poznania rose from 30,000 in 1875 to 162,000 in 1907 (p. 281). These trends led the German Ludwig Bernhard to conclude in 1910 that Prussia's Poles could be held up as a 'model of how a national minority can keep its independent existence and even strengthen it against a far stronger state authority'. Nevertheless, there was concern as to whether the Poles could have sustained this in the longer run, especially if the German state were to switch to 'a policy of unlimited oppression' (pp. 286–7). But we shall never know the answer to this question, because defeat in the First World War brought German hegemony to an abrupt end for most of the Prussian Poles.

GALICIA: HABSBURG POLAND

In 1822 Galicia had a territory of 77,300 square kilometres and a population of 4.8 million, which was approximately equal to the combined populations of Poznania and the Congress Kingdom (Davies 1981b: 143, 120, 307). Indeed, its population density in 1822 (sixty-two people per square kilometre) was roughly *double* that of either Poznania (twenty-nine per square kilometre in 1815) or the Congress Kingdom (twenty-six per square kilometre in 1815), by our calculations. By 1910, however, Galicia's population of 7.3 million had been far surpassed by that of the Congress Kingdom (nearly 13 million), which by then had a population density exceeding that of either Galicia or Poznania. (The figures were approximately 101, 94 and 74 people per square kilometre, respectively, by our calculations.) Between 1870 and 1914 approximately 1.1 million people emigrated from Galicia and roughly 1.2 million departed from Prussian Poland, while 1.3 million left the Congress Kingdom (Wandycz 1974: 276). Relative to population, the rate of emigration was higher from Galicia than from the former Congress Kingdom, but that of Prussian Poland was the highest. The most important reasons for Galicia's comparatively slow population growth were its extreme poverty, the relative lack of opportunity and its high morbidity rates, all of which were reflected in comparatively high adult and infant mortality rates. It was a landlocked and relatively stagnant economic backwater. According to Wandycz (1974: 330), Galicia's per capita income in 1913 was only $38, as against $63 for the relatively industrialized Congress Kingdom and $113 for a still relatively agrarian Prussian Poland. In a book published in Lwow in 1887, entitled *Galician Misery in Figures*, Stanislaw Szczepanowski provided the following evidence: that Galicia's per capita agricultural production was two-thirds that of the Congress Kingdom and Hungary and less than half that of France; that its *per capita* food consumption was less than half that of France and Great Britain and two-thirds that of Hungary; that the mortality rate was even higher in Galicia than in either Prussian Poland or the Congress Kingdom; that some 50,000 people were dying each year from malnutrition; and that conditions were worse than they had been in Ireland before the 1840s famine (Davies 1981b: 145–6). A major cause of these problems was lack of education: 77 per cent of the population above school age were illiterate in 1880 (Leslie 1980: 15).

On the other hand, Austria was the only one of the three Partitioning Powers that was Roman Catholic (and therefore respected Polish Catholicism) and which, as a ramshackle multinational conglomeration, made a point of preserving the cultural and ethnic diversity of its subjects (partly in order to divide and rule) instead of trying to homogenize them. Galicia was also relatively unscathed by fighting since it had not been involved in either the 1793 Partition or the 1794 uprising, and it had witnessed only light skirmishing in 1809 and 1813 (during the Napoleonic Wars). Northern Galicia was part of the Duchy of Warsaw from 1809 to 1814, yet Galicia never became a major battleground. After 1782, moreover, its peasants gained increased formal freedom to marry, change occupation and leave the land. Habsburg rule also introduced legal restrictions on the acquisition of peasant land by non-peasants and on the labour dues which could be demanded by landlords. On the downside, taxation and military service obligations greatly increased, labour obligations persisted until the 1850s (albeit on a reduced scale) and, in this landlocked, undiversified and uncommercialized economy, peasants remained rather dependent on landlords and vulnerable to seigneurial pressure (Wandycz 1974: 13).

The main perceived drawbacks of Austrian rule in Galicia during the period from 1815 to 1861 were its absolutism and its neglect of the interests of this poor, remote and strategically unimportant province. 'Galicia was for Austria a province beyond the Carpathians, the loss of which could never have threatened the Empire with disruption' (Leslie 1980: 26). As in Prussian Poland, the Congress Kingdom and Russia's 'western provinces', however, the lesser nobility rather lost out under Austrian rule. As Galicia's legal codes, administration and political institutions were 'Austrianized' from 1786 onwards, political *sejmiki* were replaced by a purely advisory Assembly of Estates dominated by magnates and the Catholic Church (Wandycz 1974: 12). By 1848 there were fewer than two thousand registered (noble) landowning families in Galicia, and three hundred of these were foreign (Davies 1981b: 143). Moreover, by making the landlord class responsible for collecting taxes, administering the law and furnishing recruits for the Habsburg armed forces, Austrian rule exacerbated the peasant–landlord tensions which erupted into widespread violence in 1846 (Wandycz 1974: 13).

In February 1846 an unsuccessful revolt by the Polish nationalist nobility in semi-autonomous Krakow sparked off a major rebellion of the exceptionally impoverished and downtrodden serfs of western and central Galicia against their Polish 'masters'. More than two thousand lives were lost on both sides. It has been hotly debated whether this serf rebellion was deviously incited by the Austrian authorities. Pyotr Wandycz has claimed that the Polish nationalist insurgents were 'massacred by peasant bands which had been mobilized and paid by the Austrian commander . . . The Galician administration, which had taken no preventive measures against the approaching revolution, fostered the peasants' antagonism toward the revolutionary nobles and connived at or in some cases engineered the peasant outbreaks' (Wandycz 1974: 134–5). However, Alan Sked has contended that 'the Habsburg authorities – despite later charges of connivance – knew nothing about what was going on and were appalled at the results of the blood-lust' (Sked 1989: 63). Either way, the conflicting accounts agree that thousands of Polish landlords and estate managers were killed by their cruelly oppressed serfs before the jacquerie was brutally suppressed by Austrian troops. The lesson was not lost on the Partitioning Powers, who thereby discovered the 'Achilles heel' of the Polish nationalist nobility. Metternich wrote to Field Marshal Radetzky: 'An extraordinary event has just taken place . . . The attempt by the Polish Emigration to start another revolution in the former Polish territories has been . . . smashed by the Polish peasantry . . . A new era, therefore, has dawned' (p. 64). The landlord class in Galicia was mainly Polish (or sometimes German), whereas the peasants were mainly Ruthenian (Ukrainian), especially in eastern Galicia. According to the 1822 census, 47.5 per cent of Galicia's population was Polish, 45.5 per cent was Ruthenian, 6 per cent was Jewish and 1 per cent was German (Wandycz 1974: 71). As a result of German and especially Jewish immigration, moreover, the ethnic composition became 45 per cent Polish, 41 per cent

Ruthene, 11 per cent Jewish and 3 per cent German by 1880 (Davies 1981b: 144). This was a potentially explosive mix. Indeed, the bloody peasant revolt of 1846 left Galicia's propertied classes deeply fearful of 'the masses', radicalism and anything that could reignite peasant hatred of the rich and powerful. After 1846, therefore, the Habsburgs could count on the calculated 'loyalism' of the shocked and chastened Galician nobility.

This helps to explain why there was so little social or educational change and reform, and no Galician revolution in 1848. Polish 'National Committees' were formed in Lwow (Galicia's capital) and in semi-autonomous Krakow in March 1848, and these petitioned the Habsburgs for Galician autonomy and emancipation of the serfs, but Krakow was subdued by Habsburg forces and bombardment in April 1848 (and forfeited its residual autonomy), while Lwow met a similar fate in November 1848.

In February 1861, in the wake of the humiliating eviction of the Habsburgs from Lombardy, Galicia was granted separate legal and administrative institutions, stopping short of autonomy. In December 1867, after even more humiliating Habsburg defeats in Germany and Venetia, Galicia was also granted an elective legislature (*sejm krajowy*) and a viceregal executive based in both Lwow and Krakow. At first less than 10 per cent of the population were enfranchised and the system of electoral *curia* (colleges) was weighted heavily in favour of Galicia's predominantly Polish landlords. However, there were mass demonstrations in Lwow in 1868 demanding further concessions. In response, the Polish language was given equal status with German in schools and law courts in 1868, in administration in 1869 and in the Jagiellonian University (in Krakow) in 1870. Galicia also gained an Academy of Sciences in 1872 and an Education Board to establish a comprehensive system of elementary schooling in 1873 (Davies 1981b: 150–1). After 1867 Galicia's Catholic Poles were in effect admitted into the exalted ranks of the 'master races' of the Habsburg Empire, alongside the Austrian Germans and the Magyars, although this also added fuel to the rising flames of resentment among the empire's underprivileged peoples.

Between the 1870s and the First World War, while Prussian Poland was being subjected to aggressive Germanization and Russia's 'western provinces' and the former Congress Kingdom were incurring equally aggressive Russification policies, Krakow and Lwow emerged as the cultural and intellectual capitals of Poland. They produced books, journals, newspapers, plays and *belles lettres* which transcended the Partition and spiritually reunified the Poles (Davies 1981b: 155), while the University of Lwow (established in 1817) and the Jagiellonian University gained strong international reputations in medicine, physics and history. Galician Poles were even permitted to celebrate the tercentenary of the Union of Lublin (1569), to erect a statue to their 'national bard' Adam Mickiewicz in Krakow in 1898, and to build a monument commemorating the five-hundredth anniversary of the Battle of Grunwald (1410). Galician Poles even rose to the ranks of Austrian prime minister (Kazimiercz Badeni), Austrian finance minister (Juljan Dunajewski) and Habsburg foreign minister (Count Agenor Goluchowski). Galicia's peasants, on the other hand, remained among the poorest and most downtrodden in Europe.

In Galicia (as elsewhere) the 1900s witnessed mounting peasant and proletarian unrest. In eastern Galicia this was reinforced by inter-ethnic tensions between the predominantly Polish (and Catholic) propertied classes and the mainly Ruthene (and Orthodox or Uniate) lower classes. Major peasant strikes in eastern Galicia in 1902–3 resulted in the appointment of a conciliatory and reform-minded viceroy, Count Andrzej Potocki, who put forward agrarian concessions designed to divide the malcontents by propitiating the more prosperous peasant proprietors. Nevertheless, the savage Tsarist repression of workers' demonstrations in Warsaw and St Petersburg in late 1904 and early 1905 encouraged workers in Lwow and Krakow to stage mass demonstrations in solidarity with their Polish and Russian 'comrades'.

The continued growth of trade unions, the strike movement and both socialist and nationalist unrest during 1905 encouraged radicals to demand, and the Austrian government to consider granting, universal direct suffrage. In October 1905, however, the representatives of Galicia's frightened propertied classes helped to vote down proposals for electoral reform in the Austrian Reichsrat (parliament), whereupon the increasingly polarized towns of Galicia, German Austria and Bohemia were convulsed by even greater political unrest and confrontations. On 28 November 1905 the Austrian government decided to meet halfway the seemingly revolutionary demands for universal direct suffrage, but was consequently voted out of office by representatives of the recalcitrant Austrian German and Galician propertied classes three months later. In the end, however, the Austrian Emperor Franz Josef resolved the crisis by intervening in favour of adult male suffrage. Fresh elections to the Austrian Reichsrat were held on that basis in 1907, with the result that Galicia's (Ruthene as well as Polish) nationalist, peasantist, Christian Democrat and socialist parties gained greatly increased political representation at the expense of the aristocratic ruling classes.

Much the same pattern was repeated in (unreformed) elections to the Galician Diet in February 1908, except that several Polish parties entered an electoral pact and trounced their Ruthene rivals. The latter felt aggrieved at this and, when a student belonging to the Ukrainian Social Democratic Party took it upon himself to assassinate Viceroy Potocki in April 1908, the Ruthene press and party leaders refused to condemn the murder, whereupon the more rabid Polish nationalists called for draconian reprisals against the Ruthene community. In fact, Potocki had been trying to broker a power-sharing deal between Galicia's Polish and Ruthene politicians, partly in a bona fide attempt to defuse conflict and avert further bloodshed, but also in order to play off one group against the other and thus retain power and institutions in the hands of the conservative aristocracy.

The new viceroy, the loyalist historian and educationalist Michal Bobrzynski, was prepared to grant the Ruthenes greater educational and cultural autonomy (including a university of their own in Lwow) in return for their acceptance of a 'junior partner' role in an autonomous and unitary Galicia governed by Polish aristocrats. The conservative 'rainbow coalition' which he assembled gained sweeping electoral endorsement in 1911. But in 1913 his compromise electoral reform deal, which would have fobbed off the Ruthenes with a mere 27 per cent of the seats in the Diet, was anathematized by Galicia's reactionary Catholic bishops and intransigent Polish nationalists. These denounced Bobrzynski as a 'traitor' and successfully bayed for his resignation. Faced with the threat of a concerted Ruthene campaign of non-co-operation and obstruction, however, the new viceroy secured the Diet's approval for a somewhat 'watered down' version of Bobrzynski's political deal and successfully held fresh elections on that basis. Nevertheless, the stage had now been set for a further 'war of attrition' between Ruthenes and Poles which a resurrected Poland would win by *force majeure* during the interwar period, only to have the tables turned against it by the clumsy might of the Soviet Union in September 1939.

SPIRITUAL SUSTENANCE: THE AMBIGUOUS POSITION OF THE CATHOLIC CHURCH

The Polish Catholic Church is generally regarded as a stalwart custodian and symbol of Polish national identity. During the Partition period, however, the role of the Church was ambiguous. It often provided spiritual strength and solace, and many of its clergy were active politically and educationally. Nevertheless, the dominant inclination of the church hierarchy was to 'render unto Caesar that which is Caesar's'. It accorded a much higher priority to the preservation of the Church as a supranational Catholic institution and ministry than to the preservation of the Polish national culture and identity. Indeed, Catholic bishops and the Pope not infrequently sided with the state authorities *against* Polish nationalists, even in Prussian Poland and in the Congress Kingdom.

During the seemingly interminable Partition period, the Polish sense of national identity and community was sustained, expanded and 'democratized' primarily by the vigorous development of Poland's language, literature and music. Poles were fortunate that, in contrast to modern Czech,

Slovak, Ukrainian, Lithuanian, Latvian, Finnish, Estonian, Hungarian, Romanian and Serbo-Croat, whose vocabulary, grammar and syntax were not fully fashioned and standardized until the middle or late nineteenth century, Polish was already 'a fully competent all-purpose instrument long before the Partitions' (Davies 1981b: 227).

The major figures in the development of Polish literature (and hence language) during the Partition period included Adam Mickiewicz (1798–1855), Juliusz Slowacki (1809–49), Zygmunt Krasinski (1812–59) and Henryk Sienkiewicz (1846–1916). However, Poland's most famous writer, Josef Korzienowski (1857–1924), 'defected' to the English language and adopted the name Joseph Conrad. The principal torch-bearers of Polish music, besides Frederyk Chopin (1810–49), were Stanislaw Moniuszko (1819–72), Henryk Wieniawski (1835–80), Ignacy Paderewski (1860–1941) and Karol Szymanowski (1882–1937).

Among these literary and musical figures, Adam Mickiewicz occupied a special position. Poles looked to him as a 'spiritual leader', verging on 'oracular high-priest' (Zamoyski 1987: 295). In his *Books of the Polish Nation and of the Polish Pilgrims* (1832) Mickiewicz popularized the idea that Poland was 'the Christ among nations'. Poland had been crucified in the cause of righteousness, but its crucifixion would expiate the sins of the world. That, in turn, would hasten its own resurrection. 'Poland will re-arise and free all the nations of Europe from bondage,' he declared (quoted by Namier 1946: 48). The political and spiritual significance of Polish national literature is further borne out by Russian estimates that by 1901 one-third of the population of the Congress Kingdom was involved in various forms of clandestine ('underground') education, based upon such writings (Davies 1981b: 235).

THE ROAD TO RESURRECTION

After 1815 some Polish patriots came to the conclusion that they could not depend on (or even hope for) active support from their foreign sympathizers, and that they would therefore have to rely on their own efforts (whether through national insurrection or collaboration with one or more of the Partitioning Powers). Others came to believe that efforts to resurrect or liberate Poland *without* external support would be futile and therefore settled for 'organic work' and/or collaboration until such time as more propitious external circumstances might emerge. Nevertheless, it took many Poles a long time to learn the bitter lesson that, however much their nation might be 'reborn' spiritually, culturally or materially, they could neither liberate themselves nor be liberated by sympathetic foreign Powers so long as the three 'Partitioning Powers' did not fall out among themselves. It was not until Germany and Austria decided to go to war against Russia in the summer of 1914 that the political resurrection of Poland became a serious possibility. Indeed, other than in the context of a general European war, active intervention in support of the Polish cause was deemed contrary to the interests of the western European Powers, both because it could have upset the European balance of power and because what they fundamentally desired was European peace, if only for commercial reasons, whereas (as in 1939) taking up the Polish cause had to involve war.

During the Partition era, the various Polish landed elites managed to maintain their own ascendancy and that of the 'Partitioning Powers' through varying degrees of collaboration with their foreign overlords and by co-opting (and even intermarrying with) segments of the rising Polish and Jewish bourgeoisies. Nevertheless, this fragile ascendancy was increasingly under challenge from emergent mass movements (whether nationalist, socialist or peasantist). There were serious possibilities of conflict between Austria and Russia, not only during the Crimean War of 1853–6, but also in the wake of the Russo-Turkish War of 1877–8 and during the Balkan crisis of 1908. In each of these instances, however, potential warfare between the 'Partitioning Powers' was successfully averted. A major risk of war between Austria and Prussia emerged during the Revolutions of 1848–9, as part of their continuing competition for supremacy in the Germanic world, and they actually came to blows over the same issue in 1866. In the event, however, war was avoided in 1848 and was kept within strict temporal and geographical limits in 1866, with the result that the stability of the Partitions was not threatened. Furthermore, Austria and Prussia acted with restraint during the risings which occurred in the Congress Kingdom and Russia's 'western provinces' in 1830–1 and 1863–4, just as Russia refrained from attempting to profit from the Galician revolt of 1846. In each of these cases the other Partitioning Powers were content to gloat from the sidelines while providing very limited co-operation in tracking down 'suspects'.

20   The Austro-Hungarian road to war, 1908–14

At the heart of the causes of the First World War lay Austria-Hungary's attempt to 'solve the South Slav problem' by subjugating Serbia without fully annexing it, in much the same way that it had taken control of Bosnia-Herzegovina in 1878 without fully absorbing it into the empire. The Habsburg Monarchy hoped thereby to recompense itself for its earlier losses in Italy and Germany and to prove that it was still a Great Power, even though this ran the risk of war with Russia – Serbia's main patron and protector. Germany, by contrast, had little interest in or motivation for the subjugation of Serbia. Between 1906 and 1908, Germany even helped Serbia to break free from Austria-Hungary's economic stranglehold by providing an alternative market for Serbia's vital exports of pigmeat. In the end, however, Europe was to pay a colossal price for Austria-Hungary's inability to restore its prestige, prove its virility and 'solve the South Slav problem' by more peaceful means.

During the 1880s and 1890s Serbia had become in effect a political and economic 'dependency' or 'client' of the Habsburg Empire, following the discomfiture of Russia by Europe's other Great Powers in 1878–81. In 1882 Austria-Hungary had signed a relatively liberal commercial treaty with Serbia. By 1903 60 per cent of the grain and 95 per cent of the livestock imported into the Habsburg Empire came from Serbia, which in turn obtained 87 per cent of its imports from Austria-Hungary (Jaszi 1929: 417). In 1903, however, Serbia's supine and pro-Austrian Obrenovic dynasty had been overthrown and replaced by the more assertive, pan-Slavic and pro-Russian Karadgeorgevic dynasty. Moreover, when the Austro-Hungarian *Ausgleich* (compromise) was renewed in 1906–7, the Magyar landed classes secured the erection of protective tariffs against Serbia's staple exports of agricultural products (especially pork) to the Monarchy. This trade war, commonly known as 'the pig war', obliged Serbia to gain greater economic independence by exporting its agricultural produce across Greek and Ottoman territory to new markets in western Europe and Germany and to obtain loans and armaments from France in place of Austria. Nettled by the Serbs' successes in these endeavours, the Habsburg Empire responded by formally annexing Bosnia-Herzegovina in October 1908, to the great fury of Serbian nationalists – not only those within Serbia itself, but also the many Serb nationalists living in Bosnia and Croatia. So long as Bosnia-Herzegovina had remained under supposedly 'temporary' military occupation by Austria-Hungary, Serb nationalists could still entertain serious hopes that the further disintegration of the Ottoman Empire would lead to a 'Greater Serbia' encompassing Bosnia-Herzegovina as well as Macedonia, Kosova and possibly Dalmatia, conferring the long-sought prize of unimpeded access to the sea. Formal Habsburg annexation of Bosnia-Herzegovina was intended to extinguish these aspirations to a 'Greater Serbia' and to force Serbia to accept a permanently landlocked and semi-dependent status (at that time Montenegro did not yet have a coastline to share with its Serbian 'cousins').

Serbian nationalists reacted to the Austro-Hungarian annexation of Bosnia-Herzegovina by staging angry mass meetings and by forming 'underground' nationalist associations committed to achieving 'Greater Serbia' by means of armed struggle – Narodna Odbrana (National Defence), Ujedjenje ili Smrt (Unification or Death; alias Crna Ruka, the Black Hand) and, within Bosnia, Mlada Bosna (Young Bosnia). However, the Russian foreign minister Izvolsky counselled the irate Serbian government to exercise restraint and 'do nothing which could provoke Austria and provide an opportunity for annihilating Serbia' (Malcolm 1994: 151).

In 1908, in an endeavour to provide a plausible pretext for declaring war on Serbia and for putting fifty-three Serb and Croat leaders in Croatia on trial for 'treason', the Austrian imperial authorities produced forged evidence of a Serb–Croat conspiracy against the Habsburg Empire. In March 1909 the Serbian government was given an ultimatum: either it must recognize and accept the Monarchy's annexation of Bosnia-Herzegovina, or the Habsburg Monarchy would declare war on Serbia. At the same time Germany told Russia that it must either give up its support for Serbia or face the risk of war with the Central Powers (Kann 1974: 414). Russia gave way, as it was still recovering from the Russo-Japanese War of 1904–5 (in which Russia had been defeated on both land and sea by the Japanese in the Far East) and the subsequent Revolution of 1905, and Serbia was obliged to follow suit.

Thereupon the Monarchy's plans for a war against Serbia were shelved, as the makers of Austro-Hungarian foreign policy belatedly woke up to the fact that *even a victorious war against Serbia would solve nothing*. Annexation of Serbia could only burden the Monarchy with even more embittered South Slavs, whereas, if it were not annexed, it would truly become the seething hotbed of frustrated pan-Serb ambition and South Slav discontent which Habsburg propaganda pictured it to be (Taylor 1976: 217). Serbia could not have been incorporated into the Habsburg Empire without further inflaming the already tense relations between the German Austrians and Magyar nationalists. Hungary's parliament might well have vetoed any move to bring Serbia into an expanded 'Dual Monarchy' – let alone the creation of a 'Triple Monarchy' granting equal status to Slavs and Magyars. Thus the Habsburg Monarchy could no more afford to acquire than to lose territory in the Balkans. Major territorial gains could have had much the same disintegrating effect as a serious defeat (Kann 1950b: 288). The best interests of the Habsburg Empire therefore lay in *preserving the territorial status quo*. Such a conclusion was reinforced by sober recognition of the latent weaknesses of the superficially imposing Habsburg armies. Emperor Franz Josef and Crown Prince Franz Ferdinand realized that these armies had become more effective against *internal* than external foes and that there was a real possibility that the Serbian 'David' might inflict humiliating defeats on an invading Habsburg 'Goliath' (as indeed it did in 1914, twice, before Germany came to the Monarchy's rescue).

However, while the Habsburgs pulled back from military action against Serbia in 1909, the damage had already been done. The Serbs were convinced that Austrian aggression had merely been postponed and 'therefore began an anti-Austrian policy in earnest' (Taylor 1976: 218). Furthermore, the falsely accused Serb and Croat leaders in Croatia engaged the eminent Czech professor Tomas Masaryk to bring a libel suit against the imperial authorities in Vienna. Between them, the so-called 'Zagreb treason trial' of 1909 and Masaryk's subsequent exposure of the Monarchy's official forgeries brought the Monarchy into damaging international disrepute by stripping away its veneer of respectability (pp. 219–20).

Since any immediate hope of 'liberating' Bosnia-Herzegovina from non-Slav rule had been temporarily doused by Austria-Hungary's formal annexation of these provinces in October 1908, Serbia and Montenegro turned their attention southwards, setting their sights on Macedonia, Albania and Kosova. Between October 1912 and May 1913, taking advantage of a major crisis within the Ottoman Empire (and with the Habsburg Empire helplessly looking on), Serbia, Montenegro, Greece and Bulgaria drove the remaining Ottoman forces out of Kosova, Macedonia, northern Albania and the Sandzak of Novi Pazar. This Balkan War, which almost doubled the territories of Serbia, Montenegro and Greece and raised South Slav nationalism to a triumphalist fever pitch, posed a major challenge to Austria-Hungary. 'The national principle had triumphed . . . The Balkans had been Austria-Hungary's "sphere of influence"; yet . . . her influence achieved nothing – even Albania was saved [from being carved up by the Balkan victors] only with Italian assistance' (Taylor 1976: 229). Indeed, with the almost complete expulsion of the Ottoman Empire from Europe, Austria-Hungary became the new 'sick man of Europe', although it was granted a brief respite by the fact that the Balkan victors fell out among themselves in the much briefer Balkan War of June and July 1913. During these Balkan Wars, significantly, Germany urged caution and self-restraint upon Austria-Hungary (p. 230).

The best-known catalyst of the outbreak of the First World War (and hence of the eventual dissolution of the Habsburg Empire) was the assassination of the Habsburg Archduke and Crown Prince Franz Ferdinand and his wife during their provocatively timed state visit to Sarajevo on 28 June 1914, the anniversary of the Battle of Kosova (the most important date in the Serbian nationalist calendar). Their assassin, the Bosnian Serb nationalist Gavrilo Princip, had been a student in Belgrade and had received some arms and assistance from an agent of the Serbian nationalist organization Narodna Odbrana (National Defence), who was also working for the head of Serbian military intelligence, Colonel Apis.

Taking advantage of an international wave of revulsion against this act of Serbian nationalist terrorism (even in Sarajevo, where the assassination of the Archduke and his wife was followed by anti-Serb demonstrations and attacks on Serbian shops and homes), on 23 July 1914 Austria-Hungary gave Serbia an ultimatum comprising ten demands for various measures to suppress Serbian nationalist activities inside and outside Serbia, nine of which were in fact accepted by the Serbian government. The ultimatum did not hold Serbia *directly* responsible for the Sarajevo assassination, but it justifiably complained that Serbia 'had tolerated the machinations of various societies and associations directed against the Monarchy, unrestrained language on the part of the press, glorification of the perpetrators of outrages and participation of officers and officials in subversive agitation' (Malcolm 1994: 156). Serbia's refusal to accept all ten of Austria's demands provided the pretext for Austria-Hungary to declare war against Serbia, which in turn precipitated a Russian military mobilization in support of Serbia. This then prompted Germany to declare war on Russia and its French ally, whereupon Britain was (ostensibly) drawn into the conflict by its treaty obligations as a guarantor of Belgian independence and neutrality, since German military strategy was premised upon an early knock-out blow against France via Belgium. However, as emphasized by the Bosnian Serb historian Vladimir Dedijer,

> To describe the Sarajevo assassination as either an underlying or an immediate cause of the 1914–18 war is to commit an enormity. It was an incident which under more normal international circumstances could not have provoked such momentous consequences . . . It was a truly unexpected gift . . . to the Viennese war party, which had sought, ever since the annexation crisis of 1908–9, a pretext for attacking Serbia, pacifying the South Slavs and extending Habsburg power to the very gates of Salonika. (Dedijer 1967: 445)

The outbreak of the First World War was *partly* a consequence of the deepening division of Europe into *mutually antagonistic power blocs*. This inflamed international tensions, made both 'national' and international politics more intemperate and violent, accelerated the European arms race and appeared to set the Germanic and the Orthodox Slavic worlds on a collision course.

Oscar Jaszi claimed that 'a mass-psychological situation' was emerging both within the Monarchy and on its borders which was pushing the whole system 'step by step toward explosion, making the struggle between Habsburg imperialism and Russian pan-Slavism more imminent from year to year' (Jaszi 1929: 420–1). Germany's Kaiser Wilhelm II referred to the approaching war as 'the last great battle between Teutons and Slavs'. However, Jaszi was also at pains to point out that the attribution of 'war guilt', in the sense of seeking out 'individual responsibilities', could be misleading or inappropriate because 'No diplomatic finesses, no . . . treaties of amity, could have avoided this explosion whose real roots were in the social, economic and national structure both of Russia and of the Dual Monarchy . . . One should not forget that the natural reactionary alliance . . . among the German, the Austrian and the Russian autocrats was not dissolved by their personal rivalry but under the pressure of a widely spread national public opinion' (pp. 422–3).

The existing European order was being simultaneously challenged and destabilized by significant spatial variations in the pace and pattern of industrial development and by the consequent shifts in the distribution of power and wealth within and between states. This made Europe's rulers very nervous and 'jumpy', increasing their readiness to resort to 'pre-emptive' wars, regardless of whether these were perceived as defensive or aggressive in nature. The growth of protectionism, cartels and monopolistic 'finance capital' had intensified the European scramble for 'captive markets' within Europe and for colonies and 'spheres of influence' outside Europe, even though Europe's major powers had already shown themselves capable of reaching agreement on the demarcation of their respective colonies and 'spheres of influence' in Africa and Asia. 'Conscious forces did not push the world to war in 1914. Most historians would now agree that the cause was a combination of an incapacity to work a complex system without a recognized arbiter and of the growth of anarchic forms of behaviour left unchecked until they became uncheckable. In fact, there was an inherent accelerator built into the system of aggressive competition for power and prestige' (Duchêne 1965: 231).

It was indeed becoming increasingly difficult for that states system to accommodate or cope with the severe challenges posed by the growth of nationalist movements and ideologies. In western Europe, for the most part, states had been able to harness nationalism to 'unify', strengthen and consolidate already existing or inchoate polities and allegiances. German and Italian 'national unification' harboured major destructive and disruptive potential, but this had been skilfully kept under control by the conservative legitimist statesmen – primarily Bismarck and Cavour. In the eastern half of Europe, however, nationalism and national unification were largely at odds with the existing (mainly supranational and imperial) state structures and boundaries. Above all, the Austro-Hungarian Empire was incompatible with the emerging conception of a new European order based upon sovereign national states.

However, while it is true that important elements in the European states system (along with the nationalist challenge to it) were powerfully conducive to war, it need not follow that all the states within that system were *equally culpable* or that no one state or group of states was particularly to 'blame' for the outbreak and rapid escalation of warfare in 1914.

Since the publication of Fritz Fischer's *Griff nach Weltmacht* (1963), it has been fashionable primarily to 'blame' Germany for 'causing' the First World War and therefore to make lenient judgements concerning Austro-Hungarian 'war guilt'. In line with Fischer's highly plausible reasoning, Noel Malcolm has maintained that 'Germany was pushing hard for a war, in order to put some decisive check on the growing power of Russia. The Austro-Hungarians were more hesitant, fearing Russia's involvement (as the protector of Serbia) as much as the Germans hoped for it' (Malcolm 1994: 157).

Nevertheless, we uphold the (unfashionable) contrary view that *Austria-Hungary was chiefly responsible for dragging Europe into the First World War,* mainly in foolhardy defence of its overweening sense of imperial honour and prestige, but also in reckless pursuit of imperial territorial self-aggrandizement in the Balkans in competition with Russia. We strongly reject the frequent portrayal of Austria-Hungary as a stabilizing factor in European diplomacy. It is clear to us that its rulers repeatedly considered themselves justified in rejecting peaceful diplomatic solutions to the Monarchy's problems. Austro-Hungarian rather than German ambitions, insecurities and sensitivities were the major destabilizing factors in European diplomacy between 1859 and 1914, both because 'imperial honour demanded that no territory be surrendered without a fight' and because, having lost its leading positions in Germany and Italy, the Monarchy was determined to recoup its losses by gaining 'a predominant position in the Balkans' (Sked 1989: 181–2).

Nevertheless, *war against Serbia – whether actively expansionist or merely as a pre-emptive strike – could have been averted.* The threat posed to Austria-Hungary by Serbian and South Slav nationalism was and has continued to be greatly exaggerated. *Serbia posed neither a direct nor an insurmountable threat to the Habsburg Empire.* Serbia had 'little interest' in acquiring Habsburg lands. 'The Serbs aspired to liberate their brothers still under Turkish rule and to recover all the territory once historically Serb; this ambition extended to Bosnia and Herzegovina, not beyond' (Taylor 1976: 228). Eastern Orthodox Serbia primarily aspired to create a Greater Serbia by expanding *southwards* (to liberate/unite with its South Slav co-religionists in Macedonia, Kosova and Bosnia) and *towards the sea*, and it was almost as hostile as the Habsburgs to the creation of a true South Slav state (pp. 190, 237). Even though a broad South Slav state was wished upon the Serbs in 1918 and again in 1945, few Serbs were really interested in anything more than a 'Greater Serbia'.

Only the vain Habsburg desire to avoid any further loss of imperial honour and prestige made war seem the only way out of the Austro-Serb confrontation. The negative repercussions of Austro-Hungarian acquiescence in a process of South Slav unification need not have been any greater than the consequences of Austria-Hungary's grudging and belated acceptance of the processes of Italian and German unification in the 1860s. Tragically, the Monarchy deliberately risked a world war 'rather than compromise internally or externally on the South Slav question' (Sked 1989: 255–7, 269).

There were some wise heads (for example, Serbia's former premier Vladan Georgievic) who attempted to pull both sides back from the brink, and as late as 1912 the Serb premier Nikola Pasic asked Tomas Masaryk to present far-reaching proposals for an economic union between Serbia and the Habsburg Monarchy (Jaszi 1929: 406–7). However, such overtures were contemptuously rebuffed by Austria-Hungary. As Count Polzer-Holditz, *chef de cabinet* to Emperor Karl (reg. 1916–18), recalled in 1928:

> Nobody thought of revising our Balkan policy, for this would have involved a complete change in our internal policy. The understanding that the hatred of Serbia . . . was caused by our customs policy, that the Southern Slavs did not want anything else than to unite themselves and to get an outlet to the sea, that by our Albanian policy we closed the last valve and therefore an explosion became inevitable; this understanding was never attained by the ruling elements. (quoted in Jaszi 1929: 420)

Thus there can be little doubt that 'responsibility for the war falls, in the first place, upon the Dual Monarchy' (Jaszi 1929: 423). Starting in the 1890s, there was a growing conviction in official and educated circles that the Germanic and Slavic worlds were locked on to a collision course (p. 420). The tragic stupidity was that 'nothing serious was undertaken for the solution of a vital problem, the colossal gravity of which was keenly felt by all intelligent observers . . . as the immediate cause of the approaching catastrophe' (p. 421). The 'defensively aggressive' Habsburg Empire embroiled Germany in foreign policy gambles and provocations in which Germany had little or no direct stake and over which it had even less control. 'Germany stood perfectly isolated in Europe, bound to Austria for life and death . . . Germany was compelled to follow its fatal ally into its leap to death' (Jaszi 1929: 426). 'Austria fixed the date of the conflict and Germany did not stop her ally. Here lies the primordial responsibility of Austria, motivated not by personal crimes of her statesmen, but by the social and national sins of the whole system'; by contrast, Germany's sin was one of 'omission' rather than 'commission' (p. 428). Furthermore, 'leading Viennese circles . . . precipitated the war because . . . the position of Austria would have become more untenable from year to year'. They feared that 'with the completion of those military reforms which were going on in Russia and France, and with the growth of anti-Austrian irredentistic propaganda, the odds for Austria would have become practically null' (p. 428). The war party in Vienna was eager for action. Germany's grave error, following the shock of the Sarajevo assassination, was in giving Austria-Hungary *carte blanche* to respond as it wished, instead of trying to restrain its aggrieved ally. Germany's rulers mistakenly assumed that Austria-Hungary would act responsibly. Count Czernin, one of the last Habsburg foreign ministers, later provided a virtual admission of Austro-Hungarian 'war guilt':

> It is, of course, impossible to say in what manner the fall of the Monarchy would have occurred had the war been averted. Certainly in a less terrible fashion than was the case through the war. Probably much more slowly, and doubtless without dragging the whole world into the whirl-pool. We were bound to die. We were at liberty to choose the manner of our death, and we chose the most terrible. (Czernin 1920: 38)

21   The impact of the First World War on East Central Europe

The intensification of inter-ethnic and class antagonisms in the decades preceding the First World War had shaken the Habsburg Empire to its very foundations. By 1914 it was clear that many prominent figures in the Monarchy hoped to override the permanent crisis at home through the successful prosecution of a war abroad. This well-known ploy, which had been used many times before, was expected to unite everyone in support of the throne and the war effort, to divert attention from internal discontents to external objectives, to make any manifestation of social or political dissent a treasonable offence and, if successful, to restore the Monarchy's former military élan, self-confidence, prestige and *esprit de corps*. It was, nevertheless, a high-risk stratagem, a desperate 'last throw', for it made the continued existence of the Monarchy dependent upon the outcome of the war (Bauer 1925: 71).

The Monarchy's declaration of war against Serbia on 28 July 1914 triggered off an international chain reaction which quickly escalated beyond the Habsburgs' control. The Habsburgs went to war in order to defend their battered imperial honour, pride and territorial integrity against the partly real, partly imagined, South Slav 'threat' and in an endeavour to prove that their empire was still a Great Power. These factors severely limited their strategic flexibility and freedom of manoeuvre during the war. The German government would have liked the Habsburgs to have ceded Trentino and parts of Dalmatia and Albania to Italy and at least part of Transylvania to Romania in order to induce the Italians and Romanians (who had been formally allied to Germany and Austria-Hungary since 1882–3) to enter the war on the side of the Central Powers against the Entente (Britain, France and Russia). However, the Habsburgs, the Austrian Germans and the Magyars were loath to accept any such deal. They had not gone to war against Serbia and its Russian protectors only to cede territory to Italy and Romania. Territorial gains in the South Slav lands would have provided meagre compensation for the loss of either Trentino or Transylvania. In any case the Magyar prime minister, Count Istvan Tisza, had accepted the Monarchy's declaration of war on Serbia in 1914 only on the (secret) condition that an Austro-Hungarian victory over Serbia must not result in the incorporation of additional Slavic inhabitants and territory into the Habsburg Empire, as this could only strengthen demands for a (federal) Triple Monarchy and thus destabilize the 1867 'compromise'. Indeed, since almost any territory that the Monarchy could realistically hope to gain by conquest would have been Slav-inhabited and therefore unacceptable to the Magyar leadership, Austria-Hungary in effect started the war only in order to bolster up its flagging morale, honour and prestige through a show of strength and virility! There was thus no real possibility of major territorial gains, even if the war had ended in an Austro-Hungarian victory.

By the time that a severely weakened Habsburg Monarchy finally gave in to German pressure to offer territorial blandishments to Italy in the spring of 1915, the Italian state had already decided that it could more reliably fulfil its expansionist ambitions by entering the war on the side of the Entente, which it did in May 1915. Romania followed suit in August 1916. It proved all too easy for

Britain, France and Russia to promise Italy, Romania and Serbia tasty morsels of Habsburg territory if they fought on the side of the Entente. These moves heavily counter-balanced Bulgaria's decision to enter the war on the side of the Central Powers in September 1915, although the detriment was partly mitigated by their rapid conquest of Romania between September and December 1916.

The precariousness of the 1867 'compromise' in effect permitted the Magyars to veto any Austrian or Habsburg attempt to mobilize more widespread and enthusiastic support for the war effort by offering to federalize and democratize the empire in a manner acceptable to the Austro-Marxists and/or the Austro-Slavs. Indeed, the Dual Monarchy system and the consequent failure to develop a highly centralized political and administrative structure (such as existed in the Russian Empire) made it harder to achieve an effective mobilization and concentration of forces and resources around the war effort.

Once the war had started, however, the goal of surviving and winning the war became an overriding end in itself. Within the Habsburg Monarchy there was at first surprisingly little overt opposition to the war. Many Austrian and Bohemian Germans hoped that the war would revive their waning dominance of the 'Austrian half' of the empire. Magyar nationalists relished the prospect of a latter-day German-backed 'anti-Slavic crusade', while millions of Polish Catholics welcomed a war against Orthodox Russia. Large numbers of Catholic Croats were only too eager to fight their Orthodox Serbian cousins. 'Only the Czechs were sullenly acquiescent' (Taylor 1976: 232). Indeed, after forty-eight years of relative peace (1866–1914), most of the Monarchy's inhabitants had little idea of what all-out war would involve, and those opposed to it were treated as 'traitors' (Kann 1974: 421). Furthermore, few people had foreseen the full impact of recent technological changes on the nature of warfare, which brought about death and destruction on an unimaginable scale.

THE COURSE AND CONDUCT OF THE WAR

From the outset, the First World War went disastrously wrong for the Habsburg Monarchy. The Austro-Hungarian forces unleashed against Serbia and Montenegro were soon driven back, enabling the Serbs to invade southern Hungary. Only after Bulgaria had actively sided with the Monarchy and Germany in September 1915 was it possible to reinvade Serbia and Montenegro, both of which were conquered by the Central Powers in December 1915. The Austro-Hungarian forces launched against Russia also suffered serious defeats, with the result that the Russians were able to invade most of Galicia (Austrian Poland) in late 1914 and early 1915. The Habsburg Empire was only spared further humiliations and loss of territory thanks to Germany's stunning victories over Russia (particularly at Tannenberg in August 1914 and at Gorlice in May 1915), which obliged Russia to deploy against Germany forces which would otherwise have been used for a full-scale invasion of Hungary as well as Austria.

The fact that Russia suffered some devastating and demoralizing defeats at the hands of a much more industrialized and well-equipped German Empire, culminating in the collapse of Tsarism and of the Russian war effort in 1917, should not be allowed to obscure the fact that *militarily Austria-Hungary proved to be no match for Russia – or even for Serbia*. Russia had been vigorously developing its heavy industries and reequipping and reorganizing its armed forces since 1908, in the wake of its humiliating defeats in the Russo-Japanese War of 1904–5. The military planners and strategists of the Central Powers had therefore been in favour of waging war on Russia sooner rather than later, as Russia's military strength was growing appreciably with every year that passed and the Russian economy had been expanding rapidly from 1908 to 1914. By 1914, in fact, Austria-Hungary's military expenditure was only about a quarter that of either Russia or Germany, about a third that of either Britain or France, and even below that of Italy (widely regarded as the 'least of the Great Powers'). Between 1878 and 1914, German armaments expenditure had quintupled, that of Russia, Britain and France had trebled, but that of Austria-Hungary had not even doubled (Taylor 1976: 229).

In 1913 Austria-Hungary had spent more than three times as much on beer, wine and tobacco as it did on its armed forces (Sked 1989: 262). Furthermore, the wartime strength of the Habsburg armed forces was 2.3 million men in 1914, compared with 5.3 million for Russia and 3.8 million each for Germany and France. Decades of Austro-Hungarian wrangling over military structures and budgets had taken their toll. The Habsburgs, the Austrian Reichsrat and the Magyars had regularly failed to agree on the form that any military reorganization or increase in military expenditure might take, who should control it and how it should be financed. Any attempt to reorganize or expand the Austro-Hungarian armed forces had engendered acrimony. Only the partial reassertion of Habsburg absolutism had averted complete deadlock on military matters during the 1890s and 1900s. For all these reasons, the still splendidly uniformed Austro-Hungarian armies were woefully underfunded and ill equipped for war, with the result that 'almost half of the regular army was killed in the campaigns of 1914' (Sked 1989: 258).

Consequently, during the First World War Austria-Hungary became increasingly dependent upon and subordinate to Germany, without which the Austro-Hungarian war effort would have ignominiously collapsed early in the war. In the words of Count Czernin: 'Without knowing it, we lost our independence at the outbreak of the war. We were transformed from a subject into an object' (Czernin 1920: 38). Indeed, it is often claimed that after 1915 the Austro-Hungarian Empire remained in existence only by courtesy of Germany and, in particular, Kaiser Wilhelm II's sentimental attachment to the Habsburg dynasty. 'Austria-Hungary was "saved" by Germany; this "saving" marked the real end of the Habsburgs. They had offered a tolerable alternative to German rule [in East Central Europe]; the alternative ceased to exist when the Germans took over the military and political direction of Austria-Hungary . . . Germany was now committed to a bid for the mastery of Europe; and the Habsburgs were no more than German auxiliaries' (Taylor 1976: 233–4).

During the winter of 1914–15 Professor Tomas Masaryk, the foremost Czech leader and the chief architect of the future Czechoslovak state, recognized that the hitherto sovereign Habsburg Empire had in effect been superseded by a German-controlled *Mitteleuropa* and that this threatened to obliterate permanently the limited autonomy and cultural freedoms which the Czechs, the Galician Poles and other subject peoples had acquired during the last decades of Habsburg rule – and which alone had made Habsburg dominion tolerable. The growth of Czech passive resistance to the war and the large-scale desertion of Czech soldiers (especially prisoners of war) to the side of the Entente demonstrated that sizeable sections of the Czech population were drawing similar conclusions. The incipient spiritual defection of the Czechs, formerly the most ardent Austro-Slavs, posed the most serious internal challenge to the continued existence of the Habsburg Empire. However, 'Masaryk did not "destroy" the Habsburg Monarchy; this was done by the Germans and the Magyars. What Masaryk did was to create an alternative' (Taylor 1976: 238–9). Even so, not until September 1918 was the Czechoslovak National Committee (led by Masaryk and Edvard Benes) recognized by the Western Powers as the 'government-in-exile' of a Czechoslovak state that did not yet exist (Sked 1989: 260). This decision, taken at a very late stage in the war, was nevertheless crucial because it was in effect incompatible with the preservation of Austria-Hungary (unlike the creation of a Polish or a Yugoslav state). The creation of a Czechoslovak state was bound to rip the heart out of the Habsburg Empire.

CRISES, MALNUTRITION AND INFLATION ON THE 'HOME FRONT'

During the First World War the ever-present tensions between the Austrian Germans and the Magyars, the two 'master races' of the Austro-Hungarian Empire, escalated into 'a real frenzy' (Jaszi 1929: 365). One of the underlying reasons for this was that in the course of the war, both in Austria and in Hungary, agricultural output shrank to roughly half the pre-war level, mainly because about half the male agricultural workforce and many (perhaps most) of the available horses had been dragooned into the armed forces, leaving behind insufficient manpower and draught animals to work the land as per normal (Berend and Ranki 1974a: 174–5; 1974b: 92).

In response to this agricultural crisis and to Magyar allegations that the predominantly Austrian German military leadership was wantonly using Magyar conscripts as 'cannon-fodder', the Hungarian government imposed stringent restrictions on deliveries of grain from Hungary to the 'Austrian half' of the Monarchy, which suffered growing food shortages and some malnutrition as a consequence.

The imperial authorities in Vienna in turn 'accused Hungary of promoting famine in the Monarchy by its selfish policy' (Jaszi 1929: 365). However, Hungarian economic historians have contended that 'Hungary was unable to send supplies, since she could not even take care of her own needs' (Berend and Ranki 1974a: 174). The bitterness and venom of the mutual recriminations also reflected the fact that, at bottom, the Austro-Hungarian 'compromise' of 1867 was 'born out of' mutual mistrust (Jaszi 1929: 350). Consequently, any massive crisis was almost certain to strain it to breaking-point. Indeed, Jaszi claimed that the antagonism between the two hegemonic nations, the Austrian Germans and the Magyars, was 'even greater than the conflict between the hegemonic nations and the second rank nations' (p. 365).

The Magyar decision to impose severe restrictions on Hungary's agricultural deliveries to Austria, along with first Russian and then German military devastation of grain-growing Galicia and the increasingly effective Anglo-French naval blockade against the Central Powers, meant that Austria suffered far greater wartime privations than did either Germany or the Western belligerents (Bauer 1925: 28). By 1918 the non-agricultural daily per capita consumption of flour had declined from a pre-war average of 380 grammes to 165 grammes for Austria and 220 grammes for Hungary, while daily per capita meat consumption fell from a pre-war average of 82 grammes to 17 grammes in Austria and 34 grammes in Hungary. 'The rural population suffered from brutal requisitioning' and, taking 1914 as 100, by June 1918 the cost of living index had risen to 1,082 for the population as a whole and 1,560 for urban workers (Sked 1989: 263). Industrial production, which held up remarkably well at first, eventually declined to about half the pre-war level in both Austria (including the Czech Lands) and Hungary as a result of increasingly acute fuel, raw material and manpower shortages and transport bottlenecks during 1917 and 1918 (Berend and Ranki 1974a: 174–5, 177).

Powerful inflationary pressures were at work both on the supply side (cost push) and on the demand side (demand pull) during the war. Despite wartime rationing and wage and price controls, money wages rose about fivefold in the course of the war. However, the inflationary pressures exploded with increased force when the war and wartime controls came to an end. The war efforts of the Central Powers were to a large extent financed by printing ever more banknotes, as was the post-war reconstruction. Consequently, the volume of Austrian crowns in circulation rose from about 3 billion in 1913 to 42.6 billion in 1918 and nearly 200 billion by 1921. In addition, there was a widespread loss of confidence in the currencies of the defeated and dismembered Powers at the end of the war. This, even more than the war-induced shortages and wartime wage rises, was what stoked up the hyperinflation that occurred throughout most of Germanic Central Europe as well as East Central Europe during the immediate aftermath of the First World War, wiping out much of the private savings of the region's middle- and upper-class inhabitants. Among the successor states of the Austro-Hungarian Empire, only Czechoslovakia 'contrived to avoid the harmful consequences of grave and prolonged inflation' (Berend and Ranki 1974a: 180–1). Furthermore, again with the sole exception of Czechoslovakia, all the so-called 'successor states' succumbed to authoritarian rule by the mid-1930s. It is commonly accepted that the widespread political alienation and disenchantment resulting from the destruction of most private savings by hyperinflation after the First World War played a significant part in that process (as it did in Germany as well).

COUNTING THE COSTS

The stresses and strains of sustaining a very overstretched Austro-Hungarian war machine took a heavy toll. In the course of the First World War 1.2 million Habsburg subjects were killed, 3.5 million were wounded and 2.2 million became prisoners of war, although many of the latter subsequently defected to the other side (Kann 1974: 483). As reported by Otto Bauer, a leading light in the Austrian Marxist opposition: 'The fearful losses of the army in the first months of the war necessitated a continuous calling up of new classes; militarism fetched children off the school benches, and old men marched with their sons. By brute force it was sought to drive the hungry workers into the war industries to work; the factories were militarized; workers were court-martialled; and military managers commanded the factories. The constitution was suspended, parliament closed, the press muzzled and the civil population made amenable to the summary justice of military courts' (Bauer 1925: 28). During the war the subject peoples of the Habsburg Empire increasingly pinned their hopes on an Entente victory. 'Austria-Hungary was waging war not only against external enemies, but also against two-thirds of its own citizens' (Bauer 1925: 24). 'The Habsburg Monarchy had to contend with the hostility of the Slav peoples', whom it could force to fight the external foe only 'by employing the coercive agencies of wartime absolutism' (p. 27). From the Slav standpoint, the Habsburg war effort was exacting 'terrible . . . sacrifices for an alien state and a hostile cause. The longer the war lasted, the more the national revolutionary movement against Austria gathered strength in the Slav lands' (p. 72).

THE DEATH THROES OF THE HABSBURG EMPIRE

The final breakdown of the Habsburg Monarchy began in the autumn of 1916. In September, amid deepening supply problems, receding hopes of an early end to the war, the evident collapse of any real danger of a Russian invasion of Austria-Hungary and mounting expectations that the USA would enter the war on the side of the Entente, serious labour unrest broke out in the war industries. Thereupon, aristocratic members of Austria's upper house requested the reinstatement of the Reichsrat. Premier Karl Stürgkh not only rejected this request, but instigated a harsh new crackdown on all opposition, sedition and dissent. This intransigence prompted the anti-war socialist Friedrich Adler (son of Viktor Adler, the founder of the Austrian Social Democratic Party) to break the political deadlock by assassinating the prime minister on 24 October 1916. Emperor Franz Josef, whose staid but august personage and sixty-eight-year devotion to duty had come to symbolize all that remained of the Habsburgs' battered authority, dignity and mystique, died not long afterwards – on 21 November 1916. His death seemed to mark the end of a hallowed institution, the loss of a safe anchor, the passing of an era and the loss of the main focus of loyalty to the empire.

The subsequent political 'show trial' of Friedrich Adler (18–19 May 1917) backfired on the Habsburg regime, because it gave him the perfect pulpit from which to present a detailed and heartfelt indictment of the regime and its conduct of the war. The trial helped to reignite the flame of the Socialist International and turned Friedrich Adler into an Austrian and international cause célèbre.

Emperor Karl (reg. November 1916 to October 1918), the great-nephew of Franz Josef, had not been 'raised in the tradition of Austria as the presiding power in the German Confederation and of the Habsburgs as Holy Roman Emperors . . . The aim of achieving peace . . . dominated his thinking' (Kann 1974: 474). Alarmed by the Russian Revolution and the fall of Tsarism in March 1917, the young Emperor Karl and Count Stürgkh's immediate successors (Ernst Körber, Heinrich Clam-Martinic and Ernst von Seidler) relaxed labour regulations in the war industries (18 May 1917), reconvened the Austrian Reichsrat (30 May 1917), obtained the resignation of the reactionary and repressive Istvan Tisza government in Hungary (5 June 1917), put out peace-feelers to the Western Powers (March–May 1917), restored constitutional government in Austria, amnestied Austria's political prisoners (July 1917) and rescinded the death sentences on Friedrich Adler and the Czech nationalist leader Dr Karel Kramar (July 1917).

The political relaxation in Austria and (to a lesser degree) Hungary during 1917 permitted a revival of party politics, trade unionism and the left. In January and February 1918, major strikes in key industries in Vienna and Budapest were followed by mutinies at Judenberg, Funfkirchen, Rumberg, Budapest and Cattaro (Kotor). The left drew inspiration from the boldness, anti-war stance and (apparent) initial successes of Russia's Bolshevik Revolution of October 1917 (November 1917, according to the Western calendar). Bolshevik influence on Austro-Hungarian workers, soldiers, sailors and intellectuals increased when, following the cessation of the war with Russia in December 1917 and the conclusion of a peace treaty between Russia and the Central Powers in March 1918, 'ten thousand prisoners-of-war who had witnessed the revolution in Russia returned home' (Bauer 1925: 38). Still, the mutineers who hoisted red flags in early 1918 also demanded peace on the basis of President Woodrow Wilson's famous Fourteen Points, announced in January 1918 (p. 37). This attested to the spread of American as well as Bolshevik influence. However, the left was unable to consummate its growing power and influence in Austria-Hungary at that time. The strikes and mutinies in January and February 1918 were easily suppressed by 'reliable' Habsburg forces:

> Even if Austrian militarism had no longer had at its command sufficient force to repel a revolutionary insurrection . . . an Austrian revolution could have had no other result than an invasion of Austria by the German armies . . . German imperialism was at the zenith of its power. The Russian army had melted away since the October Revolution. The gigantic armies of the German Eastern Front had become available . . . German armies would have occupied Austria in the same way as they shortly afterwards occupied an incomparably larger territory in Russia and the Ukraine . . . We realized how serious was the danger . . . We were aware that even the Czech revolutionaries feared a German invasion . . . for their tactics during the whole war were determined by the conviction that, so long as German imperialism remained undefeated, a Czech revolution could only lead to the occupation of Bohemia and Moravia by troops of the German Empire. (Bauer 1925: 34–7).

CONSEQUENCES OF THE MILITARY COLLAPSE OF THE CENTRAL POWERS

Eric Hobsbawm has argued that 'in deciding to suppress revolutionary agitation and continue a lost war, the authorities of the Habsburg Monarchy made sure that there would be a Wilsonian rather than a Soviet Europe' (Hobsbawm 1992: 129). Perhaps more by accident than by design, the Habsburg imperial authorities ensured that national/ethnic aspirations and mobilization would prevail over class/socialist aspirations in East Central Europe in 1918–19. Even so, in the eyes of many workers and peasants in this region at that time, the two would have appeared to go hand-in-hand or to be two sides of the same coin. In the end the former subject peoples of the Habsburg Empire and Tsarist Russia, who had hitherto aspired to a combination of social and national liberation, settled for national independence without very radical social change, under the protective umbrella of the victorious Western Powers (or so they thought). For defeated Germany, Austria, Hungary and Bulgaria, however, collapse led (at least temporarily) to punitive peace treaties and social revolution, with the result that nationalism here emerged 'not only as a milder substitute for social revolution', but also as the political mobilization of frustrated and deeply discontented ex-officers, officials and middle-class civilians towards counter-revolution and fascism (p. 130).

Nevertheless, it needs to be emphasized that the First World War had been neither initiated nor fought in order to create a new European order based upon the concepts of national self-determination and the nation-state. These were among the consequences, not the causes, of the war. Until as late as June 1918 the Western Powers had been anxious to preserve the Austro-Hungarian Empire as a counter-weight to Germany and Russia and thereby to avoid the creation of a power vacuum in East Central Europe which would probably be filled in due course either by a resurgent Germany or by Russia. Prior to June 1918 the dismemberment of the Habsburg Monarchy had never been on the agenda of the Western Powers. They had been willing to 'amputate' some of the Monarchy's territories, but such amputations would have been more of a recognition than a denial of the Monarchy's right to exist.

The entry of the USA into the war in April 1917 brought in its train the (seemingly) more high-minded and idealistic foreign policy and war aims of President Woodrow Wilson. He would attempt to bring peace to the world with his Fourteen Points, much as Moses had already tried and failed to do with his Ten Commandments. American entry into the war, combined with the collapse of the Russian Tsarist regime in February (March) 1917, replaced the old-fashioned brawl between the imperialistic Anglo-French–Russian Entente and the Central Powers with a more overtly ideological contest between the Western 'Allies' or 'Democracies', on the one side, and Absolutism, on the other.

Nevertheless, even the Fourteen Points (proclaimed in January 1918) envisaged only the *restructuring or federalization* of the Austro-Hungarian Empire, *not its complete dissolution or dismemberment* into a constellation of independent 'national' states. Point Ten merely stated that 'The peoples of Austria-Hungary, whose place among the nations we wish to see safeguarded and assured, should be accorded the freest opportunity for autonomous development.' In addition, Point Thirteen stated that 'An independent Polish State should be erected which should include the territories inhabited by indisputably Polish populations, which should be assured a free and secure access to the sea and whose political and economic independence and territorial integrity should be guaranteed by international covenant.' This clearly implied that the future Polish state should be co-terminous with the Polish nation and that Germany, Russia and Austria-Hungary would therefore have to cede territory to this resurrected state. But the Fourteen Points did not propose the creation of any other 'national' successor states apart from Poland. There was no mention of a Czech or a Slovak state. Indeed, some historians, economists, politicians and publicists continued to argue that it was either inappropriate or imprudent or even impossible to construct nation-states in East Central Europe and the Balkans. To do so would be politically and economically hazardous, and could pose a perpetual threat to European peace, prosperity and security (see, for example, Cole 1941). In some respects, such misgivings turned out to have been well founded.

By the autumn of 1918, however, three factors had finally persuaded the Western Allies that it was both necessary and safe to call into existence new 'national' states in Central and Eastern Europe: firstly, the continuing disintegration of Russia; secondly, the fatal Austro-Hungarian decision to stake everything on anticipated German victories on the Western Front in the spring and summer of 1918, following the imposition of a draconian peace treaty on Soviet Russia in March 1918 and the attendant German occupation of all Poland and most of Belarus, Lithuania and Ukraine; and, thirdly, the subsequent German military débâcle, caused mainly by German territorial over extension in the East as well as the long-delayed arrival of massive, well-equipped and well-fed American forces in Western Europe. It became temptingly easy to pull apart and paralyse the Habsburg Empire simply by granting official recognition to putative, self-appointed Polish, Czechoslovak and Yugoslav governments-in-exile. Moreover, the concurrent military foundering of Germany and the deepening disintegration of Russia seemed to render it safe (indeed imperative) to make 'national self-determination' the basis of a new states system in Central and Eastern Europe (if only to ward off the real or imaginary 'threats' of Bolshevism and 'red revolution'). In a single stroke, it seemed, the Western Powers curtailed the war, hit upon a simple 'magic formula' for a supposedly just and democratic new political order, and slew the Bolshevik beast. Western leaders with a penchant for panaceas were not fully aware that, while appearing to 'put to rest' the most pressing problems, they were sowing the seeds of even bigger ones.

On 4 September 1918, in an attempt to halt the carnage, Austria-Hungary called upon all belligerents to start peace negotiations immediately. However, the Western Allies rejected this appeal because they were now seeking surrender rather than negotiation. On 4 October 1918, following the capitulation of Bulgaria on 29 September, the Central Powers proclaimed their death-bed conversion to Wilson's Fourteen Points as the basis for a non-punitive peace. A Habsburg imperial manifesto promulgated on 16 October 1918 interpreted this as meaning local national autonomy for the subject peoples within a federal Austrian Monarchy, while Hungary was to remain unchanged. However, it was too late for this. Most Czechs, Poles and South Slavs would now be satisfied with nothing less than full national independence. On 18 October 1918, moreover, President Wilson publicly endorsed their demands.

On 27 October 1918 the last Habsburg imperial cabinet, headed by premier Heinrich Lammasch and foreign minister Julius Andrassy, accepted the secession of the Czechs, the Poles and the South Slavs. It also sought a separate peace and armistice from the Western Allies, in a belated endeavour to detach the Monarchy from Germany's fate and to salvage as much as possible of Austrian and Hungarian power and territory. When Austria-Hungary formally surrendered on 2 November 1918, Germany's High Command ordered a German invasion of Austria, but for some reason the order was not carried out (at least, not until 12 March 1938 . . .). Meanwhile, the predominantly ethnic German areas of Austria had established a socialist-led provisional government and adopted a republican constitution on 30 October 1918. However, Emperor Karl and his imperial cabinet did not abandon the pretence of a Habsburg Empire until 11 November. In the end Karl did not formally abdicate, but merely relinquished his powers and duties to the nascent German-Austrian Republic. This republic sought to accomplish a union (*Anschluss*) with Germany, but the Western Allies did not allow it to do so.

Hungary assumed de facto independence on 17 October 1918 and became a republic on 16 November 1918. Croatia and Slovakia seceded from Hungary on 29 and 30 October 1918, respectively. However, all these moves merely performed the last rites on an empire which had in reality died some months earlier. Indeed, much of its sovereignty had in effect been ceded to Germany by late 1914, while the true Habsburg spirit of tenacity and mediocrity had died with Franz Josef in November 1916. In that sense the First World War merely drove the final nails into the imperial coffin.

THE IMPACT OF THE FIRST WORLD WAR ON PARTITIONED POLAND: THE LONG-AWAITED OPPORTUNITY FOR POLAND'S RESURRECTION

The inability and/or unwillingness of the Partitioning Powers to pull back from the brink of war in July and August 1914 finally presented many Poles with the long-awaited opportunity to reassert Polish independence and sovereign statehood. Yet, paradoxically, most Poles probably did not fully appreciate this until the closing stages of the First World War. Most of the Poles elected to the parliaments of the Partitioning Powers dutifully voted for war credits and continued to support the respective 'war efforts'. By 1916 the armies of the 'Partitioning Powers' contained 2 million Poles, including 4 per cent of the population of the Congress Kingdom, 15 per cent of the Prussian Poles and 16 per cent of the Galician Poles. Between 1914 and 1918 about 450,000 Poles perished and nearly 1 million were wounded while fighting for the Partitioning Powers (Davies 1981b: 382). As part of their 'scorched earth' tactics, moreover, the retreating Tsarist forces forcibly evacuated about 800,000 people from the Congress Kingdom deep into Russia (Leslie 1980: 115), where ethnic Poles were on the whole abysmally treated.

The person who most vigorously exploited the opportunities opened up by the outbreak of the First World War was Josef Pilsudski (1867–1935), the future *generalissimo* and self-appointed custodian of Polish independence. This Polonized and impoverished Lithuanian noble, who had been banished to Siberia from 1887 to 1892, regarded Tsarist Russia (rather than Germany) as the major threat to the survival of the Polish nation. He dreamed of resurrecting a tolerant multinational commonwealth of Poles, Lithuanians, Jews, Baltic Germans, Ukrainians and Belarussians which would be large enough and strong enough to hold off Russia's 'Asiatic despotism' and 'barbarism'. Those who shared Pilsudski's anti-Russian orientation also feared that, in the words of a Polish proverb, 'while to the Germans we stand to lose our bodies, to the Russians we stand to lose our souls'. However, when Pilsudski resumed his budding political career in 1892, it was as a leading figure in the Polish Socialist Party (the PPS), which was founded near Wilno in 1893. He served as the editor of its main journal, *Robotnik* (*The Worker*), from 1894 to 1900, and he gave the PPS a strong nationalist orientation, albeit without rejecting its socialism and internationalism. He had concluded that, because the propertied classes of the former Commonwealth were for the most part collaborating with the Partitioning Powers, any hope of resurrecting it would primarily depend on the combined struggles of the multi-cultural proletariat, peasantry and intelligentsia for social justice. The PPS sought national equality and brotherhood for Poles, Lithuanians, Jews, Germans, Ukrainians and Belarussians, in opposition to Tsarist oppression, discrimination and despotism. Although Pilsudski was arrested by the Tsarist police in 1900, he soon escaped and continued his machinations against Tsarism from abroad. He even went to Japan to investigate the potential for joint operations against Tsarism during the Russo-Japanese War of 1904–5. His mind was evidently turning to military means of attaining his goal.

After the defeat of the 1905 Revolution in Russian and Congress Poland, Pilsudski moved to Galicia. Here he established a semi-clandestine military force (known as the Union of Active Struggle) in response to what he correctly saw as the growing prospect for military conflict between the Partitioning Powers in the wake of the Austrian annexation of Bosnia-Herzegovina in 1908, which set Austria and Russia on a collision course in the Balkans. Pilsudski initially envisaged that, in the event of war between the Partitioning Powers, his paramilitary units would move into Congress Poland and (in co-operation with the Austrian military but under his own command) foment a new Polish rising against Tsarism. This in turn would pave the way for the resurrection of a Polish-Lithuanian state. However, he changed tack when he realized the extent to which his chief political rivals, the National Democrats (NDs) led by Roman Dmowski (1864–1939), were prepared to collaborate with Tsarist Russia against Germany and Austria. Dmowski regarded German rather than Russian imperialism as the major threat to the survival of the Polish nation. Furthermore, because he valued ethnic homogeneity above the multi-ethnicity of the former Polish-Lithuanian Commonwealth, he was not anxious to 'recover' Lithuania, Belarussia and western Ukraine, or to include their inhabitants (especially Jews) in a reconstituted Polish state. He was therefore willing to collaborate with Russia against Germany and Austria, and he appeared to accept that the barbarities which Tsarism perpetrated against its non-Russian subjects were not very different from those that he as the champion of an 'ethnically pure' Poland would have liked to perpetrate against Poland's 'alien' minorities (especially the Jews), given the chance. He was a cold and calculating 'scientific' exponent of ethnic 'purification'. For all his faults, Pilsudski's growing vanity, militarism and megalomania were considerably less dangerous than Dmowski's surgical mentality.

Amid the military alerts and preparations precipitated by the Balkan Wars of 1912–13, Pilsudski decided that the role of his 7,000 *Strzelcy* (Riflemen) would be to 'agitate by means of war' and to show his compatriots that they could achieve success through their own military prowess in the service of one or more of the warring parties (Wandycz 1974: 327–8), as Polish soldiers had done during the Napoleonic Wars. Pilsudski's forces recruited 'leaders with pretensions to military ability', including Wladyslaw Sikorski, Edward Smigly-Ryd and Marian Kukiel. This bequeathed to post-1918 Poland 'an officer corps of dubious quality, but with a keen sense of its own importance in the body politic' (Leslie 1980: 109).

On 6 August 1914, five days after Germany declared war on Russia, Pilsudski led his new 'Polish Legions' into the former Congress Kingdom. He put out a proclamation from a (fictitious) Polish

National Government in Warsaw which had supposedly called upon Poles to rise up and allegedly appointed him as the supreme commander (donning the mantle of Kosciuszko). However, these operations met with a cool reception from Poles who feared being tainted by association with the rebels, or who had turned their backs on the discredited insurrectionary tradition, and by property owners who regarded Pilsudski either as an agent of the Central Powers (who had already razed the town of Kalisz) or as a dangerous socialist, revolutionary and dreamer (Wandycz 1974: 331–2). Nevertheless, the fact that Pilsudski had assembled Polish military forces which acquitted themselves reasonably well in combat and managed to maintain a semi-autonomous existence placed him in pole position for the power struggle in Poland at the end of the First World War. The defeated German military and political establishment chose to hand over the large areas which they still controlled to their erstwhile collaborator Pilsudski rather than to the Bolsheviks or to those Poles (including Dmowski) who had collaborated with the Entente. Sadly, the independence to which so many Poles had aspired for so long would prove 'something of a disappointment' (Zamoyski 1987: 340), not only because they could no longer conveniently blame every problem and defect on the Partitioning Powers, but also because their long-suppressed ambitions and grievances now exploded and collided with one another.

THE LONGER-TERM SOCIAL IMPACT OF THE WAR

The First World War precipitated major changes in the consciousness, attitudes and position of the peasantry, particularly in the eastern half of Europe. Millions of soldiers marched through or were billeted in villages, putting an end to centuries of rural isolation from events in the wider world. The war hastened the advent of rural trucking and bus services, which reached many of the villages not yet served by railways. During the Great War, moreover, millions of peasant conscripts were mobilized into national and imperial armies. They participated in bloody, momentous conflicts and upheavals and, having seen how other classes and nations lived and died, they frequently decided not to return to the limited horizons of humdrum village life after the war was over. Those who did return (if only to participate in post-war land redistributions) frequently remained unsettled and/or exercised unsettling influence on fellow villagers.

War-induced shortages of labour, horses, capital and fuel, rising land values, increased land taxes, rationalization of estates, and fear or anticipation of imminent peasant revolts caused widespread land transfers – initially, through the selling, mortgaging and/or leasing of land by big landowners, but later through land reforms and/or spontaneous land seizures as well. In Czechoslovakia and the Baltic States, but not yet in Poland or Hungary, this resulted in the final abolition or abdication of seigneurial control of the countryside. This profoundly challenged the structures of authority and of social deference to so-called 'superiors', who were widely regarded as having been responsible for the often callously cruel waste of millions of lives during the war. Only in reactionary Hungary and Poland did landlordism survive largely intact. Up to 1918, in a sense the Habsburg domains remained 'a collection of entailed estates, not a state; and the Habsburgs were landlords, not rulers . . . They could compound with anything, except with the demand to be free of landlords; this demand was their ruin' (Taylor 1976: 10). In this perspective, the widespread revolts and mutinies of peasants and predominantly peasant soldiers during the First World War also delivered the *coup de grâce* to Habsburg and Tsarist rule in East Central Europe.

EPILOGUE: THE HABSBURG IMPACT AND LEGACY IN EAST CENTRAL EUROPE AND THE NORTHERN BALKANS

No other European dynastic polity survived as long as that of the Austrian Habsburgs (1273–1918) or left so deep an imprint on European history. In most states governments and dynasties have come and gone, but territories have remained much the same, at least in the short term. In the case of the Habsburg Monarchy, by contrast, territories came and went, but the dynasty endured until 1918. To a far greater degree than most people realize, much of what has happened in East Central Europe since 1918 (and even since 1989) has implicitly been a consequence of the disappearance of the Habsburg Empire. Imperial political and economic union, security and order gave way to political and economic fragmentation, insecurity, disorder, instability, irredentism, revanchism, beggar-my-neighbour protectionism and international discord. During the late 1930s and early 1940s, the power vacuum left by the demise of the Habsburg Empire was filled by Nazi Germany. In one sense, the rise of Hitler and the catastrophic use which he made of German's enormous technological, economic and military power were 'Austria's revenge' for the long succession of military and diplomatic humiliations inflicted upon the Austro-Germans between 1859 and 1918. 'Hitler had learnt everything he knew in Austria – his nationalism from Schönerer, his anti-Semitism and appeal to the "little man" from Lueger. He brought into German politics a demagogy peculiarly Viennese' (Taylor 1976: 258). Hitler's peculiar hatred of Jews, Gypsies, Czechs and South Slavs (Yugoslavs), which was in large part responsible for the decisions and drive to implement the Holocaust against the Jews, the mass liquidation of the Gypsies and the dismemberment of Czechoslovakia in 1938–9 and of Yugoslavia in 1941, was much more Austro-German than north German in inspiration. This is not to deny that the German Empire under Kaiser Wilhelm II (reg. 1890–1918) and Weimar Germany (1918–33) manifested widespread anti-Semitism, some anti-Gypsy sentiments, some resentment of the perceived plight of Bohemian Germans within the Czech Lands, and some negative stereotyping or prejudices against Slavs (albeit without particularly singling out Yugoslavs or Serbs). However, we doubt whether these sentiments *on their own* were sufficiently strong and/or widespread among north Germans to have actually resulted in genocide against the Jews and the Gypsies and dismemberment of Czechoslovakia and Yugoslavia. Hitler's accession to power in 1933, the resultant annexations of Austria and the so-called Sudetenland in 1938, and the increased power and prominence which this gave to south Germans (mostly from Austria, Bohemia and Bavaria), all imported particularly virulent Austrian German, Bohemian German and Bavarian resentments, anxieties, phobias and hatreds into a German polity which had hitherto been dominated by north Germans, especially Protestant Prussians. These additional factors help to explain both why and even how the Third Reich – a considerably expanded Germany – went to the extremes of actually carrying through mass genocide and the dismemberment of Czechoslovakia and Yugoslavia.

During the Cold War era a chorus of American and émigré scholars lamented the disintegration of the Austro-Hungarian Empire at the end of the First World War and the loss of the opportunity to transform it into a federalized, multinational buffer state separating Germany and Russia. In the judgement of George Kennan (1979: 423), a prominent American diplomat, adviser and specialist on Russian and East Central European affairs during the Cold War, 'The Austro-Hungarian Empire still looks better as a solution to the tangled problems of that part of the world than anything that has succeeded it'. Its demise engendered a motley assortment of small, vulnerable and far from homogeneous nation-states and a power vacuum which was most likely to be filled by Germany and/or Russia. In the event the void was filled first by Nazi Germany (thereby engulfing Europe in the Second World War and the Holocaust) and then, from 1945 to 1989, by the westward extension of Soviet power into the Balkans and East Central Europe.

Part III

From national self-determination to fascism and the Holocaust: the Balkans and East Central Europe, 1918–45

22 The post-1918 political order in the Balkans and East Central Europe

The question of why democracy generally 'failed' in the Balkans and East Central Europe between the two World Wars is one of the most crucial issues in the history of the twentieth century. This failure effectively undermined the 1919–20 peace settlements, facilitated the expansion of Nazi Germany and Fascist Italy, and thereby engulfed Europe in another World War, which in turn paved the way for a huge territorial extension of Communist power in Europe and Asia between 1945 and 1949, a major escalation of the 'Cold War', and a forty-year east–west partition of Europe.

Part III is in large measure an extended answer to this pivotal question of why democracy 'failed' in East Central Europe and the Balkans between the two World Wars. Some writers have argued that the entire project of basing a new political order on the concepts of national self-determination and 'national' states with borders corresponding to 'ethnic divisions' was doomed to failure from the start. They have maintained that this project was inherently flawed and/or that, amid the complex ethnic mosaics of East Central Europe and the Balkans, it was simply not realizable – or even that it was a recipe for disaster. In the English-language literature, two of the most trenchant exponents of this position were the eminent British socialist G.D.H. Cole (Cole 1941) and the development economist Doreen Warriner (1950). Others have argued that the project was in the main a sound one, but that it was compromised by wartime promises, Great Power ambitions, fear of Bolshevism and economic and strategic considerations, and was therefore not applied in a sufficiently just, consistent and resolute manner. Hugh Seton-Watson wrote a seminal English-language formulation of this line of argument (Seton-Watson 1945). However, a third school of thought has argued that the project was basically sound, that it was implemented as justly, consistently and resolutely as was possible in the circumstances, and that, given two or three decades of European peace and prosperity, the new order would gradually have gained deeper and healthier roots and wider acceptance, while many of the disputes and bones of contention would eventually have been resolved either by compromise or by plebiscite or, in the last resort, by *force majeure*. In this perspective, what ultimately scuppered the project was the largely exogenous 1930s Depression and the (not unrelated) spread of fascism. In the English-language literature, this stance has been expounded most cogently by Joseph Rothschild (1974).

In practice there is much to be said in favour of each of these three perspectives and lines of argument. The new political order was indeed seriously flawed, perhaps even fatally so. Nevertheless, it could have produced much healthier or more positive results than it did if it had not been compromised by the wartime promises, selfish geopolitical ambitions and highly partisan conduct of the victorious Western Powers, who dispensed 'victors' justice' (favouring their friends and allies), instead of trying to implement their high-flown declared principles (especially national self-determination) as consistently and equitably as was possible in the circumstances. Yet the post-1918 settlement and the new political order were later further undermined by the rise of fascism (starting already in the 1920s) and by the hugely debilitating impact of the 1930s global Depression.

Map 5 The Balkans and East Central Europe, *c.*1930

HOW THE FALLACIOUS AND DESTABILIZING DOCTRINE OF NATIONAL SELF-DETERMINATION COMPOUNDED THE CURSE OF 'ETHNIC COLLECTIVISM'

Prior to 1918, East Central Europe and most of the Balkans had been ruled for centuries by supranational empires. The peace settlements of 1919–20 marked the first ever attempt to reconstruct East Central Europe on the basis of 'national' states and national self-determination, while taking further the pre-1914 moves in this direction in the Balkans. The Treaty of Versailles, which was signed by defeated Germany on 28 June 1919, settled the western frontiers of Poland and Czechoslovakia, but large German minorities who would have preferred to be 'united' with Germany were left under Polish and Czech rule. The Treaty of St Germain, which was signed by dismembered Austria on 10 September 1919, determined German Austria's new borders with Poland, Italy, Czechoslovakia and Yugoslavia (officially the Kingdom of Serbs, Croats and Slovenes) and prevented the fulfilment of the desire on both right and left for political and economic union (*Anschluss*) with Weimar Germany. The Treaty of Neuilly, which was signed by defeated Bulgaria on 27 November 1919, fixed the new frontiers between Romania, Yugoslavia, Greece and Bulgaria, in denial of Bulgarian territorial claims to Macedonia, western Thrace and southern Dobrudja. The Treaty of Trianon, which was signed by a truncated Hungary on 4 June 1920, settled the hotly disputed frontiers of Czechoslovakia, Romania and Yugoslavia with the humbled Magyar state, yet the deeply resented loss of Slovakia, Transylvania, Banat, Vojvodina and Croatia-Slavonia left nearly 3 million Magyars outside the diminutive new Hungary, which also felt severed from the bulk of its 'natural' economic hinterland. Lastly, on 10 August 1920, the government of the dismembered Ottoman Empire signed the Treaty of Sèvres, which awarded Greece eastern Thrace, several Aegean islands and (in effect) parts of western Anatolia, including the major port of Smyrna/Izmir. However, this treaty was never ratified by the Turks, while the Greek state soon overreached itself. In 1921–2 a successful Turkish nationalist counter-offensive re-established full Turkish possession of western Anatolia and some of the Aegean islands. This was confirmed by the Treaty of Lausanne (signed on 24 July 1923), which also ratified Europe's only large-scale post-1918 'population exchange', whereby about 1.1 million Greek refugees (mostly from Smyrna/Izmir) were resettled in Greece and about 380,000 Muslims were expelled from Greece to Turkey (Clogg 1992: 101). Otherwise, with this one major exception, the architects of post-1918 Balkans and East Central Europe mainly endeavoured to draw the new state boundaries to fit the existing (ethnic) distribution of populations, rather than to 'adjust' or relocate populations to fit the existing or pre-determined state boundaries (as occurred on a massive scale, involving the relocation of about 20 million people, at the end of the Second World War).

When President Woodrow Wilson enunciated his Fourteen Points to the US Congress on 8 January 1918, he loftily proclaimed that 'justice' should be done by 'all peoples and nationalities' and that political boundaries should be drawn in accordance with 'historically established lines of allegiance and nationality'. This probably sounded very fine, straightforward and reasonable to an American audience. However, perhaps because he was American rather than European, Wilson was seemingly unaware that 'historically established lines of allegiance and nationality' simply did not exist in Europe (nor did they exist in Africa or Asia, for that matter!). Nations and nationalities were relatively recent mental constructs, which were not even based on uniformly applicable criteria. They had been variously defined in terms of 'national' language or 'national' religion or common territory or shared history or dynastic allegiance. Therefore, far from being objectively identifiable, the extent of 'national' territories and the 'correct' positioning of national boundaries on a relatively densely populated landmass were often bound to be fiercely disputed matters, and this was bound to be the case in the domains of the disintegrating multinational empires of East Central Europe and the Balkans. One nation's 'justice' was often another nation's 'injustice'. However, President Wilson knew that the instincts of the US Congress were essentially isolationist and that it would be almost impossible to persuade most Americans to accept a more interventionist US role in Europe unless this was conceived in terms of a moral and ideological 'mission' to settle Europe's quarrels once and for all, by imposing a more just, principled and uniform 'new order' on that troubled (sub)continent. He felt the need to appeal to the moral crusading instincts of American 'liberals' and evangelical Christians. Like the Truman Doctrine of 1947, the principle of national self-determination and the Fourteen Points were designed largely for American domestic consumption. With his pious, priggish and puritanical upbringing and cast of mind, Wilson preached his doctrines with great steadfastness and certainty and a quasi-religious fervour, even though they proved 'difficult to apply in any extensive or binding way' to the complex political realities of post-1917 Europe (Schulz 1972: 24–5, 85). Wilson assumed that the whole world was steadily evolving towards 'liberal' democratic nation-states and laissez-faire market economies. This so-called 'Wilsonian heresy' derived from nineteenth-century Positivist and 'evolutionist' assumptions concerning the supposed inevitability of 'Progress', capitalism, industrialization and the ascendancy of the bourgeoisie. These reinforced Wilson's belief that the system of sovereign 'national' states which was seen as having triumphed and prospered in most of nineteenth-century *western* Europe would be equally appropriate and would produce similar results in the post-1917 Balkans and East Central Europe.

The peace treaties of 1919–20 did indeed establish state boundaries which 'approximated more closely to ethnical divisions than any previous system in the history of Eastern Europe' (Seton-Watson 1945: 269). However, Wilson's high-flown principles could never have been fully realized in practice. They had already been compromised by the extravagant promises which Britain and France had made during the war, often in the form of binding treaty obligations and formal declarations, in order to persuade countries such as Italy, Greece and Romania to fight against (rather than for) the Central Powers. Likewise, as a result of wartime undertakings given to the Serbian government-in-exile and to Czech émigrés (particularly Masaryk and Benes), the Allies refused to allow Croat, Slovene or Slovak delegations to receive a hearing at the Paris Peace Conference in 1919. In addition, the victorious Western Powers were understandably concerned to ensure economic viability, easily defendable frontiers and the largest possible territories for the new or expanded pro-Western states (Poland, Czechoslovakia, Romania and Yugoslavia), in the hope that this would transform them into stronger and more dependable 'bulwarks' not only against future 'revanchism' within or by Europe's defeated states (Germany, Austria, Hungary and Bulgaria), but also against Soviet Communism. Largely as a consequence of this, they received much more generous allocations of territory and economic resources than a stricter application of national self-determination would have permitted, while other would-be 'nations' such as Ukraine, Belarussia, Slovakia, Croatia, Slovenia and Macedonia were completely denied either national autonomy or independent statehood (although the Austrian Germans had this thrust upon them against their wishes!). Political, military and economic expediency frequently won out against Wilson's proclaimed principles, to his considerable chagrin. Indeed, particularly for Britain, France and their European allies, 'The fundamental purpose of the 1919 Peace Settlement in Eastern Europe was to create a *cordon sanitaire* of new states between the two dangerous Great Powers, Germany and Russia' (Seton-Watson 1945: 362).

For various reasons, therefore, the much-vaunted principle of national self-determination was not applied as consistently as it might have been. The victorious Western Powers actively favoured those nations which had sided with them during the war, to the detriment of the defeated enemy nations and a 'defeatist' Soviet Russia, which had concluded a 'separate peace' with Germany and its allies at Brest-Litovsk on 3 March 1918. They most strongly favoured the new states which partly owed their existence to Western sponsorship and were therefore expected to remain staunchly pro-Western and actively opposed to the 'Soviet threat' and the 'revanchism' of the former enemy nations.

However, it soon became apparent to many that the victorious Western Powers had seriously miscalculated. Instead of serving as a high moral principle that would make no distinction between victors and vanquished and would therefore be acceptable to both, the manifest inequities and inconsistencies in the application of the principle of national self-determination meant that it came to be seen as a symbol of Western perfidy, hypocrisy and duplicity. This was the dominant perception not only in the former 'enemy nations', but also in Italy, Greece and other countries which felt cheated or 'let down' by the terms of the peace settlement. This in turn intensified their angry hostility to that settlement and contributed to the rise of fascism in the Balkans, East Central Europe and Germanic Central Europe, as well as in Italy. Thus, even those nations which had been treated most favourably by the Western Powers did not always remain staunchly pro-Western, anti-Soviet and hostile to the former Central Powers. Italy, which had sided with the Western Powers less out of any sense of obligation to do so than because of expectations (indeed promises) of major territorial gains at the end of the war, felt 'cheated' by the subsequent thwarting of its imperialistic ambitions in the Balkans and in the Aegean. In practice, the Peace Conference mainly awarded Italy territories to which the state could stake a plausible claim in terms of national self-determination, namely Trentino and Istria, and denied it most of the territorial gains which it claimed (and Britain and France had promised) in the Balkans. During the 1920s and 1930s, therefore, Italy sided with the 'revisionist' nations, which were demanding revisions of the peace settlement in their own favour. This contributed strongly to the emergence of the Rome–Berlin Axis in 1936. Moreover, most of the 'successor states' in the Balkans and East Central Europe sought 'accommodation' with the Axis Powers and loosened their links with the Western Powers, although this was mainly attributable to the failure of the West to offer the 'successor states' adequate material, moral and military support in the face of the 1930s Depression and the rise of both Fascist Italy and Nazi Germany. In the end, as the balance of power shifted in the Axis Powers' favour, it even became possible for Hitler to turn the tables on the Western Powers by invoking the principle of national self-determination for the Germans of Austria, Bohemia and the Baltic region, as a means of overturning the peace settlement and 'destroying its keystone, Czechoslovakia', in 1938–9 (Warriner 1950: 64). Indeed, a liberal German assessment of the peace treaties concludes that 'the "system of Versailles" failed not because the treaties were worthless, not because mistakes were made, but primarily because there was no timely or far-sighted attempt to revise these treaties and to continue the necessarily unfinished work of the Paris Peace Conference' (Schulz 1972: 236). This particular failure can be attributed not only to lapses and lack of imagination on the part of Britain and France, but also to the great misfortune that the 'moral author' of the peace settlement, who bore the chief responsibility for ensuring that it 'worked' and that it received adequate material, moral and military support, failed to get it ratified by the US Congress. America's refusal even to join the League of Nations, which was Wilson's brainchild, deprived that body of much needed power, resources and authority. The USA reverted to its former 'isolationism' in 1920 and Wilson died soon afterwards, a broken and disillusioned man.

Nevertheless, the problems which arose from inequities and inconsistencies in the way that the principle of national self-determination was applied were not the most fundamental ones. Overall, the number of people 'liberated from alien rule' by the restructuring of the Balkans and East Central Europe was about three times greater than the number of people newly subjected to 'alien' rule (Rothschild 1974: 4). For the most part, moreover, the various anomalies and departures from a strict application of the principle of national self-determination in 1918–20 were not purely arbitrary or gratuitously offensive. They were in fact intended to accommodate legitimate and often well-founded economic and security concerns and to contain potential aggressors (especially Hungary, Germany and Soviet Russia), even though they were sometimes inconsistent with the proclaimed principle of national self-determination and were thus ultimately conducive to the very dangers that they were intended to limit or forestall. Unfortunately, various vital economic and security considerations could not be reconciled with the principle of national self-determination, which was therefore often overridden in such contexts. The anger and/or frustration of nations which felt unjustly treated was partly offset by the long-delayed satisfaction of the nationalist aspirations of the Poles, the Czechs, the Romanians and the Serbs, and the important roles this played in preserving them from the violent political and social upheavals that convulsed Russia and (to much lesser degrees) Hungary, Austria, Bulgaria and Germany in the wake of their defeats and territorial losses (Rothschild 1974: 13). While it is normal to focus on the anger and discontent aroused by the peace treaties, it should be emphasized that Germany (the most voluble complainant) was by no means the most harshly treated. Indeed, compared with the territorial losses and economic hardships inflicted on Russia, Hungary, Austria and Bulgaria, those inflicted on Germany were very slight (see pp. 330–2). Conversely, some other nations felt an initial glow of satisfaction which helped to carry them through their post-First World War hardships.

By the 1940s it was widely believed that the principle of national self-determination was 'simply not workable'. Most of the difficulties derived from the same root cause: the attempt to impose a system of 'tidy national states on to an untidy patchwork of nationalities'. This was bound to give rise to intractable and disruptive problems, because it was impossible either to draw boundaries that would create homogeneous national states or to incorporate everybody into the state 'to which by nationality they belonged' (Warriner 1950: 64; cf. Cole 1941: 63–8, 93–105).

However, the so-called 'nationality problems' of the interwar Balkans and East Central Europe were made even more insoluble by the implicit assumptions that a 'nation-state' ought ideally to be 'ethnically homogeneous' and that people who were not members of the majority ethnic group *ipso facto* did not strictly 'belong' to or in that state, even though their forebears might have lived and worked there for centuries. This spurious and pernicious conception of 'ethnic homogeneity' as the ideal basis for 'national statehood' was espoused by the Western statesmen gathered at the Paris Peace Conference and accepted by the governments of most of the 'successor states', in the mistaken belief that they were thereby transposing the western European system of 'nation-states' on to the Balkans and East Central Europe. In reality they were doing nothing of the sort, since such 'ethnic homogeneity' has never existed in western Europe (any more than it has done in the Balkans and East Central Europe) and it had rarely been regarded as either a basis or a prerequisite for 'national statehood' in western Europe. *All European peoples are mongrels and every western European state is a mélange*, the product of many centuries of migration, 'folk wandering', acculturation and intermarriage. In western Europe states have often defined 'nations', but 'nations' have rarely defined states. In western Europe, so-called 'nationality' has normally been conferred by established citizenship of a particular state, rather than by innate 'ethnic' attributes. Therefore the endeavour after the First World War to construct 'national' states in the Balkans and East Central Europe on the basis of a pernicious ideal of 'ethnic homogeneity', which racists rapidly translated into concepts of (and demands for) ethnic or racial 'purity', was based on a grotesque misreading of western European history and too much reading of dangerous German 'idealist' and/or and romantic nationalist ideologues.

This tragic error contributed greatly to the disruptive and potentially explosive 'ethnic minority' problems which bedevilled the Balkan and East Central European 'successor states'. That is to say, if genuinely western European conceptions of the nation, nationality and the 'nation-state' had been transposed to the new or reconstituted states of East Central Europe and the Balkans, all the people whose families had been living and working there for centuries would have been defined and treated as full citizens and 'nationals' of those states, irrespective of their ethnic affiliations.

What actually happened was that *the largest 'ethnic group' in each state constituted itself as 'the titular nation' and sole proprietor of the state*, while all other 'ethnic groups' were classified as (implicitly 'alien' and barely tolerated) 'ethnic minorities', even though these minorities had often contributed greatly to the culture and economic development of those societies for hundreds of years past. Thus the narrow and exclusive manner in which Balkan and East Central European nations were conceived and defined further reinforced the already strong institutionalization of patterns of ethnic collectivism, political and social exclusion, and antagonistic or adversarial relationships between the ethnic majorities and minorities. This frequently prevented the latter from playing the fullest possible roles in the further development of the 'successor states' in which they resided, and it often called their loyalty to them into question.

It is not inconceivable that the often narrow, exclusive and illiberal 'ethnic nationalisms' and 'ethnic collectivism' which had flourished among the Germanic people(s), in East Central Europe and in the Balkans since the later nineteenth century pre-determined these unhealthy and potentially dangerous outcomes. Nevertheless, *the principle of national self-determination placed a huge additional premium on 'ethnic homogeneity'* because, in its absence, national self-determination would be either unworkable or a recipe for inter-ethnic conflict. Indeed, national self-determination is an extreme form of the 'winner takes all' syndrome, for whoever has a majority at the outset is likely to hold on to it indefinitely, while the ethnic minorities almost invariably become permanent political underdogs or at best second- or third-class citizens. Also, because the nature and 'ownership' of the state were in effect determined by actual or implicit plebiscites (that is, by the perceived relative sizes of self-defined ethnic groups on the ground), the high-sounding principle of national self-determination created pernicious new incentives for 'ethnic purification' or 'ethnic cleansing' of the new or expanded state, in order to secure and/or strengthen the 'ownership claims' of the 'titular' ethnic group in each state. In effect, President Woodrow Wilson's eloquent enunciation of the principle of national self-determination inadvertently gave the green light to vicious ethnic chauvinism and ethnic collectivism by suggesting that, if a particular ethnic group was in the majority within a specified area, then that gave it *a moral right* to impose its culture and identity on everyone living within that territory.

These considerations lend weight to the warning by the eminent American legal theorist Ronald Dworkin that 'self-determination is the most potent – and the most dangerous – political ideal of our time' (Dworkin 1996: 21–2). Even though colossal harm has been inflicted by more overtly totalitarian ideologies such as Communism and Italian Fascism, their impact pales by comparison with those resulting from literal or fundamentalist interpretations of the seductively high-sounding but dangerous and fallacious principle of national self-determination, which was but taken to its logical conclusion in the Holocaust and other programmes of ethnic 'purification' or 'cleansing' and genocide.

Significantly, the Western sponsors of the new political order in the Balkans and East Central Europe saw only too clearly that the results of their handiwork would still leave significant vulnerable and insecure 'perpetual national minorities' within most of the 'successor states' and that this could pose major problems for a long time ahead. Above all, in spite of the proclamation of national self-determination as the founding principle of the new order, it would remain inherently impossible for every 'nation' to have a state of 'its own', nor would it be possible for every person to reside in his or her own 'national state'. However, *instead of going back to the drawing board to reconsider the inherently flawed basis of the new order, they decided to treat the symptoms rather than the root causes of the minority problems.* Under pressure from the American Jewish lobby and American 'experts', the Western Powers forced each of the new or enlarged 'successor states' reluctantly to sign 'minority protection treaties' which supposedly obliged them to uphold certain basic laws, respect the fundamental rights of ethnic and religious minorities, and grant aggrieved minorities a right of appeal to the newly established League of Nations, whose approval would 'in principle' have to be sought for any change in the laws governing fundamental human rights. However, only the relatively liberal rulers of Czechoslovakia accepted such conditions willingly, 'and even they failed to observe their undertakings. The Ruthenes . . . were never to obtain their own Diet any more than the Slovaks were to have their own assembly or law courts.' In practice, education, law and administration in Czechoslovakia remained overwhelmingly in Czech hands, 'although the Ruthenes did secure most of the available jobs as roadmenders' (Longworth 1994: 68–9).

The resultant treaty provisions conflicted with widespread fear, mistrust or resentment of ethnic minorities and invited accusations of hypocrisy and double standards, since similar arrangements would never have been accepted by France for Algeria or by the United Kingdom for Northern Ireland, for example. They also virtually invited Italy's Fascists and other ultra-nationalists to take up the cause of the Italian minorities in Yugoslavia and Albania, Germany's Nazis and other ultra-nationalists to champion the 'rights' of the German (*Volksdeutsche*) minorities in Poland and Czechoslovakia, the Horthy regime and other Magyar ultra-nationalists to fan the grievances of the Magyar minorities in Romania, Yugoslavia and Czechoslovakia, and the International Macedonian Revolutionary Organisation (IMRO) and other Macedonian Slav ultra-nationalists to incite violence and carry out assassinations on behalf of the Macedonian Slav community in Yugoslavia, as preludes to fascist military incursions into the host countries. 'Minority protection' proved to be a very double-edged sword.

The first of these 'minority protection treaties' was signed by Poland on the same day as the signing of the Versailles Treaty (28 June 1919), as a heavy hint that Poland's vital territorial gains from defeated Germany were directly linked to future Polish observance of the rights of the large German, Jewish, Ukrainian, Belarussian and Lithuanian minorities. Similar treaties were signed by Czechoslovakia, Greece, Yugoslavia and Romania in the autumn of 1919 and the summer of 1920, immediately after the treaties of St Germain, Neuilly and Trianon, dropping analogous hints (Schulz 1972: 200). Occasional appeals were made to the League of Nations under the terms of these treaties, 'but the grievances were not removed and no means was found . . . of enforcing the . . . obligations assumed. The Treaties were resented by the Successor States as limitations of their sovereignty, while the minorities complained that they were quite ineffectual as guarantees of their rights' (Seton-Watson 1945: 269).

Nevertheless, during the 1920s and 1930s the Balkan and East Central European states were able to ignore and violate the rights of minorities with almost complete impunity. During the 1930s quite ferocious Polish oppression of Ukrainians, Belarussians and Jews, along with Romanian persecution of Magyars and Jews and persistent Czech and Serbian refusal to grant federal autonomy to their major 'national minorities', drew barely a protest from the Western liberal democracies, other than from the American Jewish lobby and some Ukrainian, Belarussian, Slovak and Croatian émigrés operating as private citizens. The Western Powers were mildly interested in these states as potential 'bulwarks' against German revanchism, Italian Fascism and Soviet Communism, but barely at all in their internal policies and politics or the actual treatment of their inhabitants by the 'powers that be' (the dominant ethnic groups, churches and public institutions). There were no major attempts to make financial or other assistance available to these states conditional upon their respect for and protection of minority rights or fundamental human rights. Nor was there any attempt to apply League of Nations sanctions to 'successor states' which ignored or violated such rights. This naturally encouraged the aggrieved German, Magyar, Italian, Greek and Macedonian minorities in the interwar East Central European and Balkan states to seek 'protection' or 'assistance' from their ethnic and cultural 'mother countries' (Germany, Hungary, Italy, Greece and Bulgaria, respectively), 'against the pressures of the "host" state' (Rothschild 1974: 12). However, even this option was unavailable to 'stateless nations' such as the Jews and Gypsies and, in effect, to Slovaks, Croats, Slovenes, Ukrainians and Belarussians.

Basing her work on an analysis of the 'national' population censuses of 1930–1, Warriner (1950: 68) estimated that the national minorities of the Balkan and East Central European successor states 'numbered in all some 25 million (including 3.6 million Jews) out of a total population of some 90 million'. Besides the Jews, the major 'ethnic' components were 6 million Germans (3.2 million in

Czechoslovakia, 1 million in Poland, 0.8 million in Romania, 0.5 million in Hungary and 0.5 million in Yugoslavia), 5.4 million Ukrainians and Belarussians (4.3 million in Poland, 0.6 million in Romania and 0.5 million in Czechoslovakia) and 2.7 million Magyars (1.5 million in Romania, 0.7 million in Czechoslovakia and 0.5 million in Yugoslavia). It should be emphasized, however, that the censuses from which Warriner obtained her data were 'national' censuses in more senses than one. The 'national' census authorities massaged the census returns and angled the questionnaires in order to understate the size of the ethnic minorities and to overstate the size of the dominant or titular 'nations'. Thus the census-takers in Czechoslovakia did not distinguish between Czechs and Slovaks, while those of Yugoslavia lumped together Serbs, Croats, Montenegrins, Bosnian Muslims, Macedonians and Bulgarians (Polonsky 1975: 157, 160, 162). The number of Jews was understated everywhere, not least because many Jews were in large measure assimilated, often declaring the language of their 'host country' to be their first language or 'mother tongue'. In reality, therefore, 'national minorities' probably numbered at least 30 million people or about one-third of the total population of the Balkans and East Central Europe. Even in defeated Bulgaria and Hungary, which the peace treaties had reduced to their 'ethnic core territories', national minorities made up 10 per cent of the population, while in other more populous states the proportion was more than 30 per cent (Polonsky 1975: 20).

With good reason, most ethnic minorities perceived their plight to be much worse in the new or expanded 'national states' of East Central Europe and the Balkans than it had ever been in the former Habsburg and Ottoman empires, which were more multinational and cosmopolitan than overtly 'national' in nature and had for the most part allowed their diverse 'nationalities' to enjoy considerable degrees of cultural-cum-religious autonomy. The attainment of full 'national' independence and statehood, whether in 1878 (for most Balkan states) or in 1918 (for East Central Europe), gave the 'titular nation' (dominant ethnic group) of each of the so-called 'successor states' a sometimes 'long-awaited' opportunity to claim sole and often fiercely exclusive possession of the state apparatus and all state-funded institutions. Each 'titular nation' promoted its own language and culture as the 'official' language and culture of the state, while doing as little as possible (or worse) for the languages and cultures of the ethnic minorities. Indeed, the desire to 'nationalize' the language and culture of the state was a major driving force behind the rapid expansion of state universities and compulsory state schooling during the interwar years. For the nationalistic members of the dominant 'titular nations', this was the moment of triumph. They rejoiced in their new-found 'national freedom', even when it increasingly took the form of political dictatorship! For ethnic minorities, however, it raised the prospect of a permanently underprivileged status and eventual cultural 'extinction'. However, few people foresaw that, for some ethnic minorities, this process would eventually culminate not only in loss of citizenship, but even in mass expulsions ('ethnic cleansing') or mass extermination ('ethnic purification' or genocide) during the 1940s. While most western European nationalisms were rooted in relatively liberal and inclusive 'civic' conceptions of the nation and citizenship which were encased and encoded in the constraining framework of constitutionally limited government and the rule of law, East Central European and Balkan nationalisms were not constrained to anything like the same degree and were predominantly based upon innately illiberal and exclusive Germanic 'ethnic' conceptions of the *Volk*, kinship, descent or, in Ignatiev's apt phrase, 'blood and belonging' (Ignatiev 1993).

The Wilsonian 'new order' in East Central Europe and the Balkans was also criticized from many other angles. For example, G.D.H. Cole, an eminent British socialist, argued that 'the idea of nationality as a basis for independent statehood is obsolete . . . The independence of small states, and indeed of all states save the largest and richest in developed resources, is impractical now . . . The utmost "independence" that any small state can hope for in the future is a false independence, behind which lies the reality of complete domination by a greater neighbour' (Cole 1941: 13).

Cole's strictures may not have been applicable to every small state. Sweden and Switzerland, for example, were not noted for subservience to powerful neighbours and retained considerable freedom of manoeuvre. However, there is widespread agreement that the formally 'independent' successor states were in fact economically, psychologically and strategically 'dependent' on the Western Powers during the 1920s and the early 1930s. Thus their formal independence was largely an illusion and, once the initial 'national euphoria' had died down, not a very comforting one. Cole also expatiated on the damaging economic consequences of the Wilsonian 'new order' in the Balkans and East Central Europe: 'It would be possible to enlarge at almost any length on the absurdities of the European frontiers of 1939 from the standpoint of economic convenience and well-being . . . It is often suggested that these absurdities were caused by the folly of the statesmen of 1919. But in truth the cause of the trouble goes much deeper. It was utterly beyond the bounds of possibility so to draw the frontiers of Europe that each "nation" should constitute a separate state and at the same time preserve the essential units of economic co-operation. No doubt this would not have mattered if the nation-states had been prepared to treat their independence as purely "political", and to refrain from putting up any barriers in the way of the free intercourse . . . But, though it was in practice impossible for the small states to be economically independent of the great, this limitation on their powers made them only the more determined to practise economic independence at one another's expense' (Cole 1941: 103–4).

Despite the fact that prudent economic considerations resulted in some significant deviations from a strict application of the principle of national self-determination, many borders were nevertheless 'drawn so as to cut right across the natural units of production and exchange' (Cole 1941: 104). Many towns and ports were detached from their former economic hinterlands, while many villages were deprived of access to their traditional grazing lands. The new frontiers frequently ruptured existing rail and trade networks, while lumping together railway systems which were previously almost unconnected (e.g. those of Slovakia and the Czech Lands, those of the disparate parts of Romania and those of the South Slav territories) or even based on different railway gauges and incompatible rolling stock (the different parts of Poland). Moreover, traffic on the Danube slumped as a result of the 'Balkanization' of the Danube basin and the river never recovered its pre-1918 role as the main economic artery of the Balkans and East Central Europe. Its importance vanished along with that of the Habsburgs and the unified Danubian culture and cuisine which they had helped to foster. It was the end of an economic, cultural and culinary era, but one which might fruitfully be revived in the twenty-first century, as eastward enlargement of the European Union revives Danubian integration. Two eminent Hungarian Marxists lamented that 'The creation of independent states in the place of great empires, the dissolution of large territorial and economic units, the contraction of some countries to a third of their former size and the expansion of others to twice or even three times their former extent in land and population, the economic condition of countries pieced together out of territories at different stages of economic development and taken from different states – all these circumstances created a radically new situation. Even in normal conditions, a considerable period of time, in fact an entire historical era, would have been required to complete the adjustment to new conditions, the integration into a unified economic whole, the opening up of new development possibilities and the attainment of a steady and sustained rate of economic growth. But history did not allow the problem to be presented in this fashion. The needs of the new order became apparent at a moment when the problems of the transition from a war to a peace economy were being added to the already difficult problems faced by an economy crippled by war, and all clamouring for immediate solution. The simultaneous appearance on the scene of all these problems brought about complete economic chaos' (Berend and Ranki 1969: 170).

Against this pessimistic view, the revisionist Czech economic historian Vaclav Prucha argued that 'despite the postwar feelings of hopelessness, even the greatly reduced territories of Austria and Hungary proved viable. For the neighbours of these two countries the breakdown of the clumsy and conservative system of a multinational monarchy which involved pumping funds to Vienna and

Budapest and which was linked with the privileges of the Austro-German and Hungarian landed gentry . . . and the Catholic Church, dynamized the efforts of politicians and the population to prove their capability of building up and managing the new states' (Prucha 1995: 40–1). However, without wishing to deny that the establishment of independent nation-states did have liberating and energizing effects in the aftermath of the First World War, we are even more struck by the magnitude of the problems which soon weighed them down. Not only did the new states have to deal with problems of reconstruction, 'but they literally had to create new administrations and national economies out of the motley collection of territories which they had inherited. Even worse, they were left to accomplish these tasks with little help from the West, apart from the short-lived American relief aid. Consequently, salvation was sought in restrictive trade policies, currency depreciation and inflation in a effort to achieve self-sufficiency and to promote structural change . . . Though there was an initial boost to activity and exports, once inflation got out of control it probably did more harm than good' (Aldcroft and Morewood 1993: 33).

'WINNERS' AND 'LOSERS': THE PEACE SETTLEMENTS OF 1919–20

The chief gainer from the 1919–20 peace settlements was Romania which, through its acquisition of Bessarabia from Russia, southern Dobrudja from Bulgaria, and Transylvania, Bukovina and the Banat from Austria-Hungary, more than doubled its territory. These gains were all the more remarkable since Romania had signed a separate peace with the Central Powers in December 1917 and only re-entered the war on the Allied side on 10 November 1918, one day before the armistice! They were mainly attributable to the Allies' obsessive fear of 'Bolshevism' and their consequent willingness to maximize the size and strength of four states (Poland, Czechoslovakia, Yugoslavia and Romania) which were intended not only to guard the Balkans and East Central Europe against any potential revival of the Central Powers, but (more immediately) to constitute a *cordon sanitaire* against 'the Bolshevik plague'. (The original *cordon sanitaire* was a line of quarantine posts along Europe's borders with the Ottoman Empire, intended to reduce the risk of bubonic plague spreading into Europe from the more disease-prone Ottoman domains.)

The Poles also did extremely well out of the 1919–20 peace settlements. Having co-operated with and fought on both sides during the First World War, they were nevertheless treated as 'victorious Allies' at the end of it, while still keeping the gains Pilsudski had made by working with the Central Powers against Tsarist Russia. Moreover, following the Polish victory in the Russo-Polish War of 1920, the Western Powers allowed the Poles to hang on to large swathes of predominantly Ukrainian and Belarussian territory (amounting to half the land area of interwar Poland), in clear breach of the principle of national self-determination.

The new order in East Central Europe and the Balkans was, in Otto Bauer's Austrian Marxist perspective, the combined result of 'the bourgeois national revolution of the Slav nations and the victory of Entente imperialism'. The national revolution freed the Czechs, South Slavs and Poles from alien rule and it initiated a period of democracy (albeit a short one in the cases of Poland and Yugoslavia). At the same time, however, 'the victory of Entente imperialism . . . falsified and distorted all the results of the national revolution' (Bauer 1925: 125). The victorious West 'has so drawn the frontiers of the new states that the national problems which disrupted the Habsburg Monarchy have again arisen in the new states'. In the case of Czechoslovakia, the Czechs 'can only rule by force the Germans, Slovaks, Magyars and Ruthenes who are included in her territory', while from the outset Yugoslavia was riven by 'the resistance of Croats and Slovenes to Great Serbian centralization' (p. 277). In Bauer's view, 'Any accentuation of the internal difficulties of the Czech and South Slav states can only favour the counter-revolutionary forces which have seized power in Italy and Hungary. Every collision between Serbia and Croatia will offer the Italian Fascisti an opportunity to realize their plans of domination over the Adriatic. The Magyar officer caste hope for much from the Magyar *irredenta* in Slovakia and Transylvania.' Thus fear of Italian imperialism and Magyar revenge 'keeps the whole area of the former Danube Monarchy in a state of latent war-like tension' (pp. 277–8). Bauer's fears were well founded, although he failed to foresee the even greater threat that would eventually be posed by a resurgent Germany. This underestimation of the potential threat from Germany was characteristic of the 1920s (other than in France), and was not just a typically Austrian or Marxist oversight.

Bauer believed that 'the fear of the Entente bourgeoisie at the spread of the social revolution . . . was responsible for the Czech state overflowing the boundaries of the Czech people' and that the same consideration 'also applies to Poland, which sprawls far beyond the national frontiers of the Polish people. Aggrandized at the expense of Russia and Germany, thereby incurring the enmity of both . . . Poland is forced to become a tool of French imperialism against the German Republic and the Russian Revolution' (Bauer 1925: 126). Indeed, Bauer suggested that the crucial roles of the Western Allies in defeating the Central Powers and in calling into existence the new Slav states would render the latter unduly dependent upon and 'subservient to the bourgeoisie of Western Europe' (pp. 76, 79, 126). This unhealthy psychological dependence and subservience heightened the panic and sense of betrayal when the West proved unwilling or unable to provide effective assistance to its Slav protégés during the 1930s.

In a similar vein, Oscar Jaszi warned that none of the nations nurtured within the womb of the Habsburg Empire had produced a truly self-conscious and self-confident bourgeoisie, 'capable, as in the great Western states, of directing the evolution of the state'. In this sense, the 'successor states' remained politically stunted, like many post-colonial states elsewhere in the world (Jaszi 1929: 171).

THE LATENT TRIUMPH OF GERMANY

One of the major (and often overlooked) consequences of the 1919–20 peace settlement was that, by dividing the former Habsburg territories between no fewer than seven small and medium-sized countries, it further enhanced the relative strength of Germany vis-à-vis central and the eastern half of Europe. The trenchant verdict of Jacques Bainville (a French nationalist) was that 'Germany was preserved but Europe was broken up' (Schulz 1972: 224). This kind of judgement tends to arouse consternation and moral indignation among those who have been unduly influenced by a powerfully persuasive book by John Maynard Keynes, entitled *The Economic Consequences of the Peace* (published in 1919), which forcefully argued that Germany was too harshly treated by the victors at Versailles. Germany was certainly disarmed, excessively burdened with 'reparations' and 'war guilt', and compelled grudgingly to relinquish Alsace-Lorraine, parts of Upper Silesia, Prussian Poland, parts of Schleswig-Holstein, its colonies and, temporarily, the Saar coal basin. Keynes also correctly argued that, in view of the sheer magnitude and centrality of its economy, economic recovery in Germany was essential to the economic recovery of Europe. Furthermore, if humiliation and economic collapse were to drive the Germans to embrace Bolshevism, this great concentration of people in the centre of the Continent could pull the rest of Europe towards a similar fate. There was indeed a case for reducing the astronomical 'reparations' demands, which hung like a Sword of Damocles over German economic recovery, and for a fairer apportionment of 'war guilt'. However, in his understandable desire to make his case as strongly as possible, Keynes misled many of his readers into thinking that, as a result of the way it had been treated by the victors, Germany was now 'down and out' and no longer in a position to threaten or dominate its neighbours. He also gave powerful ammunition to the 'revisionist' cause, which was soon to include the Nazis. Many of his readers were inclined to underestimate Germany's latent or residual strengths and the degree to which it had actually been *strengthened* vis-à-vis its eastern and south-eastern neighbours by the peace settlement taken as a whole. This was one of the reasons why so many people were to be surprised by the apparent suddenness and speed of the revival of Germany's strength and of its capacity to dominate East Central Europe and the Balkans after 1933.

In reality the resurgence of Germany's strength was not surprising at all. It was implicitly there all along, merely awaiting a Siegfried to 'kiss' new life into the sleeping Brünnhilde. The Versailles Treaty had left Germany's major strengths (its 'high technology' and the industrial and education systems which produced it) *largely intact*, not least because there had been no fighting on German soil between 1914 and 1918, while the war effort had broadly *accelerated* the development of Germany's relatively advanced technologies and production systems. During the 1920s, despite widespread unemployment, Germany was still Europe's technological leader in the electrical, metallurgical, engineering, machine tools, chemicals, petrochemicals and synthetic products industries – the industries of the future and the ones which the Nazis deployed to such devastating effect after 1933. The territories that Germany lost in 1918–19 were (in the main) relatively poor and depressed agricultural and mining areas, to most of which Germany had little or no legitimate claim in terms of the doctrine of national self-determination (which Germany professed to accept and uphold), and they were mostly inhabited by non-Germans. Moreover, Germany's colonies had been acquired very late in the day, after all the richest pickings had been seized by Britain and France, and were probably more of a liability than an asset. Their loss left Germany free from vainglorious extra-European 'imperial burdens' and distractions (unlike Britain and France) and allowed it to concentrate minds and resources on the further development of the advanced industries and technologies which could conquer Europe both economically and (under Hitler) by other means. The 'reparations' demanded under the Versailles Treaty were indeed astronomical and based on an unduly one-sided attribution of 'war guilt'. Yet during the 1920s the sums actually paid were quite modest (relative to the size and underlying strength of the German economy) and were largely offset by substantial capital inflows from the USA. During the 1930s Germany soon stopped paying 'reparations', initially because President Hoover of the USA pronounced a 'moratorium' and from 1933 onwards because the Nazis repudiated the whole shenanigan. The true significance of the 'reparations problem' was almost entirely political and psychological rather than economic. Indeed, in an otherwise mischievous book, A.J.P. Taylor trenchantly argued that the victorious Western Powers had two options in 1919. Either they could treat Germany leniently and magnanimously, clear it of 'war guilt' and rehabilitate it fully into the new community of nations, in order to promote full reconciliation and 'best behaviour' all round. Or, if they were bent upon holding Germany solely responsible for the war, imposing a punitive territorial settlement and 'making Germany pay', the victorious Western Powers should have occupied and partitioned Germany (as they did in 1945), in order to be in a position to uphold the punitive settlement and enforce 'reparations'. In the event, the victors fell between two stools. They inflicted territorial losses, 'war guilt' and 'reparations' and prohibited any 'union' with German Austria and the German-inhabited parts of Bohemia, but they stopped short of partition and occupation of Germany. Thus they renounced the surest means of enforcement, while simultaneously antagonizing much (perhaps most) of the German 'nation'. First East Central Europe and later the whole of Europe were to pay the price of the Western Powers' inconsistency (Taylor 1964: 41–88).

The dangers implicit in this basic mistake, however, were compounded by the strengthening of interwar Germany vis-à-vis its eastern and south-eastern neighbours. A peace settlement based on the principle of national self-determination necessarily left Germany as Europe's largest country in terms of population, if one discounts truncated and devastated Soviet Russia. Indeed, 'Germany had gained through the replacement of the Habsburg Empire as a neighbour, which for all its debilities had still been a major power, by a large number of frail and mutually hostile successor states in the Danubian area . . . and through the substitution of Poland and the Baltic states in lieu of Russia as her immediate eastern neighbours' (Rothschild 1974: 5). Germany would soon find itself able to threaten and dominate an increasingly disunited Balkans and East Central Europe far more effectively than it could have done before the First World War. By 1939 'Germany's economic hegemony over East-Central Europe was more categorical than it could have been in 1913, demonstrating that the political advantages that accrued to her from the replacement of the Habsburg Empire by several smaller states were paralleled by economic opportunities' (p. 24). Similarly, an Austrian historian has argued that 'despite all the burdens imposed on Germany by the peace treaties, the power potential of the German Empire in 1919 remained unimpaired'. Its territorial losses were 'insignificant compared with the losses inflicted on Russia'. Germany was fortunate that 'no plans were ever made by the Allied Powers to partition the German Empire, even though the dismemberment of the *Reich* into the sovereign states in existence before 1870 . . . would have been in no way contrary to the course of modern Germany before the Franco-Prussian War' (Fellner 1968: 24–5). Indeed, it was by means of military intimidation and conquest that Bismarck had dragooned the many particularist German kingdoms and principalities into a 'unified' German Empire, which in 1918 was still of relatively recent origin. The Western Powers should perhaps have restored the independence of Bavaria, Saxony and Hanover in 1918–19, in order to match the more spontaneous disintegration of the Habsburg Empire and to have made Europe – and the World – a safer place.

23 From revolution and counter-revolution to fragile stabilization and recovery, 1918–29

The First World War precipitated the dissolution of three supranational empires: the Habsburg Monarchy, Tsarist Russia and the Ottoman Empire. A new political order in the Balkans and East Central Europe was ushered in, based on the concepts of national self-determination and sovereign 'national' states. In reality, however, the so-called successor states were far from being homogeneous 'nation-states'. To be sure, powerful forces of imperial disintegration had already been at work both in East Central Europe and in the Balkans before 1914. The Austro-Hungarian Empire had suffered damaging defeats and loss of prestige in 1809, 1859 and 1866, while the Ottoman Empire had been forced to retreat gradually from the Balkans between 1687 and 1912. Independent Balkan 'national' states and an autonomous Hungary had emerged in the course of the nineteenth century. Nevertheless the process of imperial disintegration was greatly accelerated by the First World War, which Lenin saw as 'a tremendous historical crisis, the beginning of a new epoch. Like any crisis, the war has aggravated deep-seated antagonisms and brought them to the surface, tearing asunder all veils of hypocrisy, agitating all conventions and deflating all the corrupt or rotten authorities' (Lenin 1964: 98). Without the stresses and strains and crippling defeats engendered by the First World War, the Habsburg, Tsarist and Hohenzollern empires might well have survived for several more decades, either by making timely concessions to disaffected social and ethnic groups or, conversely, by intensifying the repression of such groups.

Like the other major wars in twentieth-century Europe, the First World War originated and had its major effects in eastern, not western, Europe. The powerful poems and images inspired by the often senseless and horrific carnage in the relatively static trench warfare on the Western Front have helped to distract attention from the even greater carnage and destruction inflicted by the much more mobile warfare on the Eastern Fronts. There were several theatres of war in East Central Europe and the Balkans. Poland was the major battleground between Germany and Russia and between Austria-Hungary and Russia. It was also the scene of further fighting between Soviet Russia and the resurrected Polish state in 1919 and, more seriously, in 1920. The battle lines shuttled back and forth across a prostrate Poland, causing widespread devastation and loss of life, while the Russian and Germanic protagonists escaped relatively unscathed in comparison. The Eastern Fronts did not get bogged down in mud, in contrast to the low-lying and easily flooded fields of Flanders. In the Balkans there were concurrent conflicts between Serbia and Austria-Hungary, between Romania and Austria-Hungary, between Bulgaria and her Balkan neighbours, and between Christians and Turks. For this segment of Europe the First World War was in a sense 'the Third Balkan War', a direct sequel to the Balkan Wars of 1912 and 1913. In all, there were six years of almost continuous conflict, both in Poland (1914–20) and in the Balkans (1912–18). The severity of the human and socio-economic costs has been outlined in chapters 9 and 21.

THE REVOLUTIONS OF 1918–19

It has been argued that the dissolution of the Habsburg Empire in October 1918 was 'not a revolution but only a national and constitutional upheaval', since 'the existing social and economic order was preserved in the former provinces of the Habsburg Monarchy . . . and the administrative apparatus remained intact', albeit under 'national' rather than supranational political masters. Indeed, the dissolution of the Habsburg Empire was accomplished 'not along the lines of Communist or even socialist ideology', nor 'in fulfilment of the pan-Slav ideology which was regarded as the real danger for the multinational empire before 1914, but almost entirely in a legal manner' (Fellner 1968: 19, 23). What occurred was 'only a change of guard'. Beneath the 'superficial political changes, the social structure continued untouched; the economic system was shaken by crises but remained intact in its structure; the moral, political and practical value systems were preserved' (pp. 97–8). In Fellner's view, the 'steps taken by the Social Democratic leaders to prevent a revolution' offer an explanation as to 'why only a political reorganization and not a social upheaval took place in 1918' and, furthermore, 'why the republicanizing of the Central European states was not followed by the democratizing of the social order' (p. 20).

This provocative line of argument provides a salutary antidote to the temptation to exaggerate the scale and violence of the restructuring of East Central European society in the wake of the imperial disintegration that occurred in 1917–18. All the same, Fellner has overstated his case. Admittedly, the 'international proletarian revolution' prophesied by many Russian and East Central European Marxists (and much feared by Europe's propertied classes) failed to materialize outside Russia (from October/November 1917 onward) and the short-lived Hungarian Soviet Republic under Bela Kun (from March to July 1919). The only other radical regime in the Balkans and East Central Europe after the First World War was the 'peasantist dictatorship' established by Aleksandur Stamboliski in Bulgaria from 1919 to 1923. Both Stamboliski and Bela Kun were soon overthrown by very bloody counter-revolutions. Yet this does not mean that the Balkans and East Central Europe circumvented social revolution in the wake of the First World War. Rather it serves to emphasize that the social revolutions unleashed in the post-1917 Balkans and East Central Europe were more akin to the French Revolutions of 1789 and 1848 than to the Bolshevik Revolution which began in Russia in October/November 1917. The political ideas that prevailed in the Balkans and East Central Europe in 1918 were those of the French Revolution (Seton-Watson 1945: 154). With the partial exceptions of Poland and Hungary, the post-1917 social revolutions in the Balkans and East Central Europe involved significant redistributions of land from the old (often 'alien') estate-owners to the peasantry, major extensions of political participation and voting rights (usually to all adult males) and the establishment of comprehensive 'national' (often fiercely nationalistic) systems of free, compulsory and (to varying degrees) secular state education. They also transferred power from the old supranational imperial aristocracies, armies and bureaucracies to the emerging peasant and bourgeois 'national' states, in which the old landed, military and bureaucratic elites certainly retained disproportionate influence and wealth but no longer monopolized political power and office. Power passed to rising 'national bourgeoisies' (the professions, the intelligentsias, managers, capitalists and non-noble officers and officials), as career structures were opened up to 'talent' and all of the monied and educated classes. The old elites were rarely dispossessed, but they survived only as components of the expanding propertied and professional ruling classes.

'War is sometimes a kind of revolution.' The First World War destroyed several petrified political structures. 'In consequence, a great number of state embryos . . . grew into an independent life and for many millions of people the road was opened to national and social emancipation.' At the same time, however, 'war is a very crude and poor substitute for reason and morality. Like revolution, it can solve problems only in an incomplete and summary way, arousing new difficulties and injustices' (Jaszi 1929: 454–5).

According to Otto Bauer, the leading light of Austrian Marxism at that time, the final dissolution of the Habsburg Empire in October 1918 'was a national and democratic revolution' in which various national governments comprising 'the leaders of the parties of the bourgeoisie, the peasantry and the workers supplanted the dynasty, its supranational bureaucracy, its generals and its diplomats'. However, these same events, while marking the completion of various national struggles for independent statehood, also 'awakened the Social Revolution' and let loose 'the class struggle' within each of the newly independent nations (Bauer 1925: 53). 'The Social Revolution which arose out of the war proceeded from the barracks rather than the factories . . . The four years' suppression of the dignity of the soldiers now revenged itself in a wild outburst of hatred for the officer' (p. 56). However, 'revolution in the barracks immediately provoked a revolution in the factories'. During the war industrial workers had been placed under military discipline and control, but now 'the whole authority of private enterprise and its organs crumbled with the collapse of military power', while the 'self-consciousness and the self-reliance of the workers were powerfully reinforced' (p. 60). Thus the East Central European revolutions of 1918 'inflicted a severe blow upon the capitalist mode of production'. Industry had been harnessed to the war effort. But, with the end of the fighting, 'the machines suddenly came to a stop' (p. 130). Almost immediately a whole new literature on the socialization of production appeared. 'The faith of capitalist society in itself was undermined' (p. 131), as 'shattered industry could not absorb the masses of workers returning from the Front or thrown on the streets by the idle war industries' (p. 132). The restoration of labour discipline was delayed by the workers' state of exhaustion at the end of the war, by the 'passionate excitement into which they were plunged by the revolution' and by the irregularity of fuel and raw material supplies, which rendered regular uninterrupted work impossible (p. 140). 'Many employers, discouraged by the collapse . . . made no effort to adapt their undertakings to peacetime production . . . They preferred to withdraw their capital . . . and turn it into foreign securities' (p. 133).

Like all revolutions, Bauer maintained, this one was achieved by the use of force. But the force that made the revolution possible had been expended, not in the city streets and barricades, but on the First World War battlefields on which the 'obsolete' imperial polities and armies had been 'smashed' (Bauer 1925: 65). The war, which began as 'a struggle of powerful imperialistic groups', became in the end 'a struggle between two political systems' (p. 70). 'The victory of the Western Powers over the Central Powers was the victory of bourgeois democracy over the oligarchical, military monarchies. It was the greatest and bloodiest revolution in the history of the world' (p. 71). Indeed, more than 8 million people had perished in the course of the conflict, not counting the additional 8 million who perished in the ensuing Russian civil war (1918–21) and Russo-Polish War (1920). Moreover, the success of the Czechs, the Poles and the South Slavs in attaining independent statehood constituted 'a bourgeois revolution' in the sense that 'it broke the power of the Habsburgs, the German-Austrian bureaucracy and the Magyar gentry', replacing it with 'the rule of the Czech, the Polish and the Jugo Slav bourgeoisies, organized in the new national states' (p. 76).

In view of the longstanding debate on the extent to which the French Revolution can properly be described as a 'bourgeois revolution', it should be emphasized that labelling a revolution 'bourgeois' does not necessarily imply (let alone require) that it was actively brokered and led by the industrial, commercial and financial bourgeoisie, or even that the revolution was perceived by them to be directly in their own interests. Traders, bankers and industrialists are not often noted for political courage or daring. They have tended to fear revolution and to support the status quo, because violent and/or cataclysmic political and social upheavals can (at least in the short term) damage property, business confidence and existing commercial networks, especially those that depend on state contracts and patronage. In the case of the Austro-Hungarian Empire, the traders, bankers and industrialists were for the most part 'risk-averse' socially and politically conservative Germans and Jews, rather than political leaders of the secessionist 'nations'. In Marxist terms, nevertheless, the revolution of 1918–19 (like that of 1789) helped to weaken and 'disarm' the old ruling class and the former social hierarchy. It cleared the decks for more 'unfettered' development of capitalism and the transfer of power to the ascendant 'national' bourgeoisies of the nascent national states of East Central Europe. As in France in 1789, the principal leaders and brokers of the revolution were not businessmen but members of the professional wing of the bourgeoisie (lawyers, teachers and journalists). Their 'historic role' was to enact a 'bourgeois democratic revolution' which would promote and consolidate the inchoate political and social ascendancy of the capitalist classes, even if at the time few of them were wholly conscious of the full significance and long-term consequences of their actions. The contours of the emerging political landscape were the outcome of a kaleidoscope of conflicting interests which, as remarked by Longworth (1994: 65), 'are difficult enough to comprehend in retrospect and were certainly not fully understood by the main protagonists'.

Indeed, any attempt to explain the revolution in terms of the pursuit of material self-interest is complicated by the fact that, between 1918 and 1923, large sections of the long-established bourgeoisie were impoverished by the unexpected severity of the economic collapse and the subsequent hyperinflation. 'Thousands who had been rich before the war could only prolong their existences by selling old furniture and jewellery and letting rooms to strangers' (Bauer 1925: 198). The real gainers were spivs, speculators and profiteers, who amassed new fortunes during the war and the subsequent hyperinflation and reconversion to a peacetime economy, while the bourgeoisies that emerged triumphant in the 1920s were by no means synonymous with the old imperial bourgeoisies. It is perhaps hardly surprising that so many downgraded and resentful Austrian and Bohemian Germans subsequently became attracted to Nazism.

REGIME CONSOLIDATION DURING THE 1920S

For the Balkans and East Central Europe after the First World War, the most immediate internal political problem bequeathed by the dissolution of Europe's 'eastern empires' was how to establish a new basis for authority, loyalty and obedience. This need was to a large extent met by 'ethnic' nationalism. The authority and legitimacy of the new states and regimes was essentially 'national'. The main motivations for loyalty and obedience among the new 'peoples of the state', that is the new dominant ethnic groups, were generated by 'ethnic' nationalism. As noted by Rothschild (1974: 4), however, the interwar Balkans and East Central Europe provide the classic illustrations of the limitations and drawbacks as well as the strengths and advantages of nationalism as a legitimizing ideology. It may have engendered majority attachment, obedience and loyalty to each of the new states, even in the particularly difficult cases of Yugoslavia and Czechoslovakia, but it did so at the price of permanently and damagingly alienating substantial minorities. Indeed, if nationalism had been capable of contributing significantly to the dissolution of great empires, then it was certainly capable of setting in motion forces which could lead to the disintegration of Czechoslovakia and Yugoslavia (as was seen between 1938 and 1941 and yet again in the early 1990s), interwar Poland (viz. September 1939) and perhaps, at some future date, Russia, Ukraine, Macedonia, Moldova, Estonia or Latvia. Indeed, if one accepted the premises of nationalism and took them to their logical conclusion, the unravelling process seemed 'natural and legitimate and no end could be set to it' (Carr 1945: 24). Many people must by now have asked: 'Where will it all end?' In western Europe national unification and integration essentially promoted the consolidation of large numbers of small political entities into a lesser number of larger 'national' states, whereas in the Balkans and East Central Europe nationalism and the creation of 'national' states had the very opposite effect (Rothschild 1974: 1). Between the wars, on balance, nationalism proved to be the major 'curse' of the Balkans and East Central Europe. National grievances, whether they were real or imaginary, justified or unjustified, provided pretexts for dictatorial and oppressive rule and leverage points for Nazi and fascist influence, interference, encroachment and (eventually) domination. In the meantime, economic nationalism and 'national' tariff walls restricted regional economic integration, gains from trade and specialization and, in the long run, the whole scope for economic development (Warriner 1950: 64). Thus economic development was ultimately 'boxed in' by economic nationalism, while political nationalism rendered the region increasingly vulnerable to external interference and domination – the very opposite of what nationalism was supposed to do, in the eyes of its proponents.

During the interwar years almost every state in the Balkans and East Central Europe was governed by a rapidly expanding 'national bourgeoisie' which took over the state apparatus, gradually displaced some 'non-national' elements from the professions, commerce and finance, hijacked most of the political parties (including the peasant and social democratic parties) and drew in new recruits via the greatly expanded 'national' education systems (Seton-Watson 1945: 123–6). 'The task of the ruling classes of the Eastern European countries after 1918 was to attract to themselves new elements, in order to strengthen themselves against possible revolutionary forces. They needed greatly to increase the number of people interested in the preservation of the existing regimes, but had to guard against being swamped by new recruits' (p. 125). In Poland and Hungary 'national bourgeoisies' governed in partnership with the old 'national' aristocracies, which held on to power thanks to the exceptional strength of their nationalist credentials as well as their continuing control of the countryside and large parts of the professions (and, in Hungary and parts of Poland, official posts). On the economic front the Polish and Magyar aristocracies were 'placated' by the protection and subsidies accorded to the agricultural products of the big landed estates, but in most respects the policies pursued were those favoured by the 'national bourgeoisies' (p. 127).

According to Rothschild, however, the 'ruling class' in the Balkans and East Central Europe in the interwar period 'was not, contrary to conventional assumptions, the bourgeoisie, which was quite weak and either dependent on state subsidies or else ethnically "alien" and hence vulnerable. Rather it was the bureaucracy, which was allied with and recruited from the intelligentsia' (Rothschild 1974: 17). 'Both its civilian and military components were recruited from the so-called intelligentsia, which, in turn, was simply identified by its possession of academic diplomas.' This educated class was mainly recruited from the gentry, the middle class and the peasantry. 'It might rule in association with the landed and entrepreneurial class, but it was never a mere tool of the aristocracy or the bourgeoisie' (p. 19).

In point of fact, these differing conceptions of the ruling class in the interwar Balkans and East Central Europe ('the bourgeoisie' versus 'the bureaucracy') are not as far apart as they appear to be. The dispute is partly a matter of semantics. In its original pre-Marxist usage, which is the one employed by Seton-Watson, the term 'bourgeoisie' was not limited to the capitalist or entrepreneurial classes. The 'bourgeoisie' also comprised middle-ranking officers and officials and the liberal professions. In the agrarian or semi-agrarian states of the interwar Balkans and East Central Europe, as in late eighteenth-century France, the typical 'bourgeois' was not a capitalist entrepreneur but an office-holder, a lawyer or a doctor. Thus Rothschild's strictures mainly apply to the narrower Marxist usage of the term 'bourgeoisie' to refer to the capitalist/entrepreneurial propertied classes rather than to Seton-Watson's broader use of the term. Indeed, Rothschild's claim that the ruling 'bureaucracy' was recruited from 'the intelligentsia' is even more problematic, given the mainly radical or oppositional overtones of the word 'intelligentsia' before and during the interwar period.

The 'neo-mercantilist' industrialization programmes launched by the Balkan and East Central European states during the 1920s were motivated by economic nationalism. The new regimes perceived that industrial nations were stronger than agrarian ones. Therefore, in a Europe of nation-states, each of the successor states was determined to build up industries of its own. 'A new industrial system would give the state a greater degree of international prestige, security and independence. It would offer the ruling class a means of enriching itself. It would provide employment for a considerable number of young men of the ruling class . . . Lastly, it would give employment to part of the labour overflow from the countryside' (Seton-Watson 1945: 126–7). Aside from land reform and the expansion of education and non-agricultural employment opportunities, however, the needs of the peasants were largely neglected by Balkan and East Central European governments, which mainly 'devoted themselves to such economic activity as directly benefited the ruling class' (p. 128). Moreover, through their heavy reliance on high import duties, the profits on state monopolies of items such as salt, matches and tobacco and indirect taxes on articles of popular consumption, the taxation systems were 'calculated to make the poorer classes pay for the economic programme of the ruling class' (p. 131).

During the 1920s, with the significant exception of Czechoslovakia, the Balkan and East Central European states were also very dependent on inflows of foreign capital (mainly from western Europe) to finance their sometimes ambitious infrastructural and industrialization programmes. Indeed, by 1929 foreign ownership of industrial share capital stood at about 48 per cent in Bulgaria, 44 per cent in Yugoslavia, 40 per cent in Poland and 28 per cent in Hungary (Berend and Ranki 1974a: 236–7; 1974b: 109). Only the fiercely nationalistic Bratianu 'Liberals', who dominated Romanian politics from 1922 to 1928 under the slogan 'Prin noi insine' ('By ourselves alone'), erected serious obstacles to foreign investment. This was partly the result of the Bratianu brothers' unsuccessful attempt to bring about private 'national' control of Romania's largely foreign owned oil industry, which was by 1927 the sixth largest in the world and the largest in Europe (excluding the USSR). But even Romanian industry remained to a large extent foreign owned. Moreover, the Romanian National Peasant Party, which won a landslide victory in the 1928 elections, launched a (short-lived) 'open door' policy, in reaction to the corrupt and regressive economic nationalism of the Bratianu clientele ('capitalism in one family').

Nationalists did have substantial grounds for concern and resentment over the magnitude of Balkan and East Central European dependence on foreign capital and the resulting 'political inter-ference' by foreign creditors, although some of the grievances would not cut much ice in 'liberal' and socialist circles either then or now. Heavy dependence on foreign capital was seen as a partial negation of 'national' independence and of the nationalist goal of 'national' self-reliance. It increased Western leverage and influence on the Balkan and East Central European states. Some foreign investors even criticized the nationalistic economic and cultural policies and the increas-ingly xenophobic and anti-Semitic attitudes and behaviour of the Polish, Hungarian and Romanian 'national bourgeoisies'. Many nationalists feared that Western investment might reinforce Western cultural influence and spread 'liberal' and secular Western values, although they actually had little to fear on that account! More seriously the (mainly extractive) industries in which Western inves-tors were willing to invest most heavily were not the ones which Balkan and East Central European governments and nationalists would have favoured. Above all, partly as a result of the political instability of the region and fears that the new 'national' frontiers could eventually be challenged by Germany, Hungary, Bulgaria or the USSR (threatening the region's peace and economic stabil-ity), the Balkan and East Central European states were able to borrow only at relatively high rates of interest and their economies became burdened by very onerous debt-service obligations. This was naturally seen as impairing the capacity of Balkan and East Central European states to under-take much-needed economic and social programmes on the domestic front (Seton-Watson 1945: 130). Nevertheless, whatever its drawbacks, foreign capital helped to restore and even increase Balkan and East Central European industrial production. By 1929, relative to 1913, real industrial output had increased by about 12 per cent in Hungary, 18 per cent in Austria, 37 per cent in Romania, 40 per cent in Bulgaria and Yugoslavia, and a remarkable 72 per cent in Czechoslovakia. (The figure for Europe as a whole was 27 per cent.) Only war-battered Poland had failed to regain its 1913 level of industrial production by 1929 (Berend and Ranki 1974a: 240).

It has been argued that a prerequisite for 'regime consolidation' in an emergent parliamentary democracy is the successful integration of a plurality of competing groups and interests with the state, which develops as a set of 'rules and structures relating to, and the personnel of a central authority exercising sovereign powers over, a defined territorial unit' (Arter 1993: 31). In the would-be parliamentary democracies of the post-1918 Balkans and East Central Europe, the nascent political parties and party systems were cast in crucial roles 'as agencies of national integration', responsible for 'mobilizing, socializing and organizing mass electorates, recruiting a new class of political leaders and building a pro-system consensus'. On the other hand, less auspiciously, 'parties could serve as channels for the articulation of dissenting, anti-systemic sentiment', expressing ideological and/or territorial opposition to and challenging the legitimacy of the new states (p. 32). The newly established Communist parties, the uncompromisingly separatist or autonomist ethnic minority parties, some of the peasant parties and most of the neo-fascist movements and parties of the successor states fell into the latter role, contributing to the premature death of genuine parliamentary democracy (if it was not 'still-born') in Hungary, Bulgaria, Poland, Yugoslavia and Albania during the 1920s, as well as in Austria, Romania and finally Czechoslovakia during the 1930s.

The party systems of most of the successor states were from the outset plagued by excessive fragmentation. Thus in Poland nearly a hundred political parties, including five different peasant parties, participated in elections during the first half of the 1920s and more than thirty gained representation in parliament. The Czechoslovak parliament had seventeen political parties by 1920 (none with more than a quarter of the seats) and much the same was true of Yugoslavia (Longworth 1994: 72–3). Parliaments were so fractionalized and fractious that it was often difficult to assemble and hold together stable governing coalitions capable of taking tough decisions, decisive action and the long view. Short-term considerations were almost always uppermost. Only in Austria was there a well-defined two-party cleavage offering voters a clear choice between the sharply contrasting political, social and economic programmes of the left and right, but the republic was riven by the violent mutual hatred between the Marxist socialism of 'Red Vienna' and the reactionary and equally doctrinaire Catholicism of the Alpine provinces. In several of the successor states most political parties were 'personal coteries united by loyalty to an individual rather than a political programme or ideology'. Political support was usually maintained 'by a system of rewards and sanctions within the elite and from the elite downwards' (Schöpflin 1993: 21). For the most part voters were looking for charismatic 'saviours' with panaceas, rather than disciplined parties offering coherent programmes. Moreover, the successor states mostly comprised territories which had previously been divided between very different states and these frequently had widely differing legal and administrative traditions, ethnic compositions, political orientations and levels of development, along with little or no experience of inter-party negotiation, compromise and parliamentary rule.

None of the states of the Balkans and East Central Europe between the two World Wars (not even Czechoslovakia) was able to integrate its ethnically and regionally diverse inhabitants into a unified all-embracing class structure and 'civil society', to make a single whole. Both the will and the means were lacking. This in turn strongly contributed to their failure to develop unified bodies of public opinion which could exercise effective control over the political sphere (Schöpflin 1993: 19). It also exacerbated the failure to promote responsible and accountable government, other than in Czechoslovakia. The various social and ethnic groups may have been 'cohesive within themselves . . . but they lacked any . . . sense of participating in the same political venture' (p. 24). Thus the state was more dominant (and autonomous actors were fewer and weaker) in the interwar Balkans and East Central Europe than in Western countries. The power of the state was occasionally challenged, but these challenges were usually emasculated or suppressed, with the result that the autonomy of social classes and other groups failed to grow. What is more, the sense of reciprocal obligation between social and ethnic groups and between rulers and ruled, while not entirely non-existent, was 'weak', as was the autonomous rule of law (p. 11). 'The state exercised a paramountcy over society that the latter could do little to modify' (p. 13), partly because Balkan and

East Central European cities lacked the high degree of civic pride and autonomy enjoyed by most Western cities (p. 17).

Under the quasi-parliamentary regimes of the early interwar years heads of government were usually chosen from and by the political elite. The government then 'elected' a parliament to serve it. Thus governments normally determined the timing and outcome of elections, instead of elections determining who was to be in government. Rarely did an incumbent government lose an election. Elections were usually just charades that sometimes had to be gone through in order to confirm new governments in office or to renew the existing government's 'mandate', while 'deselecting' some potentially troublesome parliamentary opponents. However, a government did not need to control the whole of the electorate, but only a proportion that would give it de facto control of public affairs and policy-making. Governments mainly relied upon bribery, patronage, gerrymandering, electoral fraud, restriction of the franchise and (in the last resort) violence and intimidation to maintain themselves in office (Seton-Watson 1945: 155; Arter 1993: 45; Schöpflin 1993: 21; Longworth 1994: 73–4). Even Hungary achieved a stable quasi-parliamentary regime after 1921, but only by intimidating, disenfranchising or 'buying off' the most discontented sections of the population and restoring the use of 'open' (rather than secret) ballots in rural areas, thereby placing rural voters at the mercy of the great landowners, rural officials and the police. Only 27 per cent of the population was permitted to vote after the disenfranchising of all men under the age of twenty-four, women under the age of thirty (unless they had three children or a 'high school' education) and anyone with fewer than six years' schooling.

The political and economic rhetoric of the post-1918 Balkans and East Central Europe often sounded quite radical, whether it was nationalist, peasantist, socialist, Communist, étatist, fascist or neo-liberal. However, the principal propagators of this rhetoric were 'the educated and semi-educated class . . . whose material interests were opposed . . . to those of the peasants and workers, whom they kept in place by police terror and mulcted by taxation' (Seton-Watson 1945: 154). There were many parallels with the outcome and social/ideological contradictions of the French Revolution. Indeed, most of the political struggles in the interwar Balkans and East Central Europe took place 'between different small groups within narrow ruling classes, over the heads of the peoples'. To most of the office-holders and power-brokers 'the masses' were little more than 'electoral currency, the passive objects of their policy' (p. 256).

In a vignette that could be applied with equal justice to the Communist period, Seton-Watson lamented that 'the Balkan official does not like to work. He considers himself so fine a fellow that the state and the public should be proud to support him for life, and should not ask him to make efforts that will tax either his intellect or his character.' Balkan officials would happily chat over cups of Turkish coffee for hours while peasants queued, patiently awaiting various permits and receipts. After all they had already been waiting for justice for centuries, so a few more hours would not make much difference. Indeed, Balkan bureaucracy involved 'obscure and complicated formalities and documents, the result of an accumulation of laws and taxes superimposed since the beginning of time', yielding constant sources of 'revenue to the bureaucrat and annoyance to the citizen'. Corruption was endemic. Most officials were so poorly paid that they could not support their families without taking bribes and, since the laws were 'often cumbrous, stupid, inefficient and oppressive', there was no shortage of bribe payers. Frequently, however, official decisions were referred to a higher level and, after further days or weeks of delay, the citizen could be 'summoned to the capital, at his own expense in time and money, to settle some trifling formality' (Seton-Watson 1945: p. 147).

Much more insidious, however, was the corruption of the upper echelons. 'In Eastern Europe the greatest fortunes are made not in industry or banking but in politics' (Seton-Watson 1945: 148). Petty corruption could have been cured by increasing official salaries, but it was far harder to find a cure for upper-class corruption. Government ministries in most of the successor states 'possessed large "discretionary funds", of which the ministers often embezzled part or all. Ministers of finance enriched themselves by selling protective tariffs to industrialists', and senior factory inspectors from ministries of labour also found industrialists most appreciative of the omission of any mention of certain 'minor irregularities and deficiencies' in their routine inspection reports (p. 148). In inter-war Poland, Hungary and the Balkans, moreover, taxes were often 'collected with the utmost bru-tality', particularly from the peasantry (p. 148). There was not infrequent use of physical violence and confiscation of vital assets for non-payment of taxes and 'there was no redress against adminis-trative abuses'. Of course there were legal rights and courts of appeal, but 'all this remained on paper'. Peasants who complained of abuses were often denounced as 'Communists', beaten, hauled before military tribunals and 'sentenced either to prison or to forced labour'. Indeed, 'ruthlessness and brutality were widespread all over Eastern Europe except Czechoslovakia and even there they were not unknown' (pp. 148–9). The worst abuses occurred in recently annexed 'backward' frontier areas with mixed populations, such as Bessarabia, Bukovina, Macedonia and, in Poland, the prov-inces of Polesia and Volhynia, whose inhabitants 'lacked the political and cultural standards of the advanced regions and had neither material nor moral weapons with which to defend themselves'. In such areas, 'officials could beat, rob and rape as they pleased'. They branded anyone who resisted or protested a 'Bolshevik' or an 'enemy of the state', and often eventually turned 'even the poten-tially loyal part of the population into real Communists and separatists' (pp. 153–4).

With the exception of Czechoslovakia the successor states lived in constant fear of 'Bolshevism', which was one of the main motivations for their hastily conceived land reforms, largely cosmetic welfare provisions and rather more impressive educational achievements. With some justification the new regimes 'prided themselves particularly on the progress made in education'. Numerous schools were built in regions where they had previously been lacking. Systems of compulsory and universal elementary schooling were established in each state. A few regions continued to suffer illiteracy rates in excess of 80 per cent throughout the interwar period (for example, parts of Bosnia and Bessarabia and much of Albania). However, Seton-Watson contended that this could not be blamed entirely on governments. 'Often children needed at home for work in the fields were not allowed by their parents to go to school' (p. 139). (A similar problem re-emerged in Albania during the early 1990s.) Moreover, even where great progress was made in educating the rising genera-tions, there remained widespread illiteracy among older people, except in the highly educated Czech Lands. Nevertheless, during the interwar years illiteracy rates in the Balkans and East Central Europe were greatly reduced and genuine attempts were made 'to enable poor children of talent to obtain a higher education', albeit more so in Czechoslovakia, Bulgaria, Yugoslavia and Romania than in the more 'feudal' states (p. 139).

The more rapid expansion of education awoke an impressive 'appetite for knowledge', while the intellectual perhaps attained 'greater prestige in Eastern Europe than anywhere else in the world' (p. 140). This was to be of crucial importance in the subsequent political history of the Balkans and East Central Europe (right down to the fall of the Communist regimes and the transition to democ-racy and market economies after 1989). During the interwar years Balkan and especially East Central European universities produced many distinguished intellectuals, writers and scientists and considerable sums were spent on the provision of scientific and medical facilities, particularly in Czechoslovakia and at the universities of Krakow, Budapest and Warsaw (p. 140). However, the immediate results were not always positive ones. Most students were of relatively humble origin and needed some financial assistance from the state to enable them to continue their studies. For such persons access to university education was seen as the gateway to individual social advance-ment. 'It was assumed that every student who passed his examinations had a right to a job in the state apparatus. The job might be of little importance, but it conferred great prestige on the son of a peasant or village priest . . . A university diploma was considered a claim on the state for the rest of one's life' (Seton-Watson 145: 126, 142). (This was a foretaste of the so-called 'diploma disease' which has also afflicted many developing countries in other parts of the world.) The investments made by Balkan and East Central European states in higher education became 'disproportionately large' vis-à-vis their investments in primary education and 'the absorptive capacities of their still basically agrarian economies' (except in the case of the industrialized and more comprehensively educated Czech Lands). Soon more graduates were being churned out than could find gainful employment. Consequently, the 'land hunger' of the peasantry was mirrored by the 'office hunger' of the intelligentsia. This strongly contributed to the 'proliferation of political parties more concerned with patronage than with policy' (that is, 'jobs for the boys') and to the growth of swollen, nepotistic bureaucracies whose 'tenacious but essentially stagnant power' stultified the political development of the successor states (Rothschild 1974: 20). The notable exception was again the industrialized and well-educated Czech Lands, which were more capable of absorbing the Czech intelligentsia into gainful employment. But, contrary to claims that 'social mobility was low to very low' in the interwar Balkans and East Central Europe (Schöpflin 1993: 24), it is clear that the growth of bloated state bureaucracies and 'bourgeois' ruling classes involved considerable upward mobility, as emphasized by Seton-Watson (1945: 123–6).

The most persistent and widespread educational problems in the interwar Balkans and East Central Europe concerned the chronic shortages of properly qualified teaching staff, rampant nepotism in educational appointments and 'grave deficiencies in the content and quality of the education provided' (Seton-Watson 1945: 140). For example, the teaching of history was often little more than crude indoctrination in narrow-minded xenophobic nationalism, with exaggerated emphasis on medieval heroics. 'The youth of each nation was taught to regard its neighbours as inferior' (p. 141). In higher education the much-needed medical, agricultural and engineering sciences remained underdeveloped. This was 'the more striking in view of the overcrowding of Law Faculties, whose students in many cases received no more than a training in chauvinism as a preparation for a bureaucratic post'. Moreover, the over-production of law graduates was 'largely responsible' for the mounting problems of graduate unemployment, which provided 'a generous supply of "Führers" for the various fascist movements of Eastern Europe' (pp. 144–5). Especially in Poland and Romania, the universities became veritable hotbeds of fascism and anti-Semitism during the 1920s and 1930s, and the 'impatient and discontented idealism' of the intelligentsia was 'exploited by governments and politicians for the basest purposes' (pp. 142–3). The shock-troops of the Romanian, Polish and Hungarian fascist movements were recruited from such a background, initially into the employ of corrupt governments, political parties and the police ('as toughs, agents provocateurs, strike-breakers or Jew-baiters') before graduating to careers of more blatant political criminality (pp. 143, 206–7; Longworth 1994: 84–6; Crampton 1994: 160–7).

More insidiously the arrogant, dishonest, xenophobic nationalism nurtured by most of the Balkan and East Central European education systems 'at best encouraged chauvinism and at worst helped to destroy all conceptions of morality'. Indeed, it was 'not confined to the schools and universities, but extended to the press, publications of all sorts, the theatre, official propaganda'. Not surprisingly the ruling classes formed in such an environment 'had no sense of responsibility towards other classes, no understanding of the principle of individual liberty' (Seton-Watson 1945: 143). At the same time the 'young generation was brought up to hate and despise other nations . . . and to see in any proposal for collaboration with other states a poisonous intrigue of Reds, Jews and Freemasons', making them 'easy prey' to anti-Semitic, anti-democratic and fascist demagogues and agitators. Moreover, little was done to promote the study of the languages, cultures, societies and histories of neighbouring peoples. The consequent 'lack of cultural relations between the Eastern European states was one of the fundamental reasons for their failure to collaborate against common external enemies' (p. 145). This problem has persisted into the 1990s. In contrast to the major efforts to promote mutual knowledge, understanding and reconciliation between the peoples of France, Germany, Italy, the Low Countries and Scandinavia after the Second World War, the peoples of the eastern half of Europe still know relatively little about one another. Indeed, under the so-called 'national Communism' of the 1970s and 1980s they were mainly 'force fed' fiercely nationalistic accounts of their own histories and negative stereotypes of their neighbours. Throughout the Communist era it was made very difficult for inhabitants of the Balkans either to visit one another's countries or to learn each other's languages, even if they wanted to do so. (There was rather more cultural contact between the peoples of East Central Europe.) Significantly, most of the non-Romanian Balkan participants in an academic conference on the Balkan states held in Bucharest on 29–30 August 1994 informed us that they had never set foot in Romania before and that lack of mutual knowledge and understanding was still a major impediment to Balkan political co-operation and economic integration. Even at the time of writing (2006), it remained relatively difficult and expensive for the inhabitants of the Balkan states to visit one another, and they still knew relatively little about each other, although entry into the EU improved this situation considerably for the East Central European and Baltic States in 2004 and was set to do so for Romania and Bulgaria as well in 2007.

For all their faults the quasi-parliamentary regimes in the Balkans and East Central Europe in the 1920s still allowed some political and cultural pluralism, some diversity (if not always 'freedom') of expression and some (albeit limited) political and legal means of redressing certain types of individual and collective grievance. These regimes were in no sense 'totalitarian'. As emphasized by Seton-Watson (1945: 156), 'It would be a mistake to pretend that there was no difference between pseudo-parliamentarianism and open dictatorship. Under the former there were at least a few safety valves.' Gradually, however, the many failings of the pseudo-parliamentary regimes and the corrupt self-serving political parties brought so-called 'democracy' into disrepute. 'Disillusioned by the old parties, the people looked for new men', men who claimed to be able to cleanse society of corruption, chicanery, incompetence and 'cleptocracy'. 'Extremist movements of Left and Right gained ground', promising charismatic leadership, vision, reform, moral regeneration and a new sense of common purpose, with action instead of words and strong government in place of talking shops, trickery and drift. The onset of the 1930s Depression accelerated the growth of domestic and international tensions, popular disenchantment with 'democracy' and the groundswells of support for authoritarian panaceas, fascism and Communism, but the rot had set in much earlier. In important respects the new order erected in the aftermath of the First World War was inherently flawed and sooner or later most of the successor states proved incapable of meeting the political and economic challenges posed by the twentieth century. Confronted by their own incompetence and the rising tides of popular disillusionment, deprivation and discontent, 'the ruling classes became more and more frightened'. They increasingly resorted to repression (except in relatively resilient and liberal Czechoslovakia) and, recognizing that they were no longer able to sustain pseudo-democratic facades, they allowed the last trappings of 'democracy' to be chipped away bit by bit (or even did the job themselves). Thus, except in Czechoslovakia, quasi-parliamentary rule gradually gave way to royal, nationalist, military or fascist dictatorship. If the tumultuous events of 1918–19 amounted to a real (albeit limited and flawed) 'revolution', those of the 1920s and 1930s were a creeping 'counter-revolution', accelerated by the rise of fascism and the onset of the 1930s Depression,

24 The 1930s economic Depression and its consequences

A major cause of the economic crises which convulsed interwar Europe was the fact that European capitalism had exhausted the dynamic technological and growth potential of the products and processes which it had developed and exploited with such spectacular success during the eighteenth and nineteenth centuries. To a considerable degree, Europe fell victim to its own past achievements. European markets for cotton, woollen and linen textiles, processed foods and drinks, footwear, steel, coal, ships, railway construction and railway equipment were approaching saturation point, and the ageing textile, coal, steel, shipbuilding and railway industries were facing problems of overcapacity which could only be temporarily assuaged by the exceptional demands generated by the two World Wars. In principle, there was still considerable scope for the further development of industries such as these in the Balkans and East Central Europe, except in the already industrialized regions of the Czech Lands. In practice, however, financial difficulties and constraints, the growth of Western protectionism and the relatively small size and low purchasing power of the Balkan and East Central European 'national' markets limited their potential. Certainly it was impossible to replicate the easy profits and the largely unimpeded export-led expansion experienced by several of the Western industrial pioneers during their heyday. The once lucrative non-European markets for Europe's 'traditional' industrial products were under threat from the gathering pace of industrialization and rising levels of protectionism in Asia, Latin America and Australasia.

Many Marxists mistook the mounting crisis for the long-heralded terminal crisis of capitalism. In reality, however, a new generation of 'high-technology' capitalist products and processes was already germinating in the West, particularly in the USA and Germany. However, their long-term significance and dynamic potential were obscured and prevented from being fully realized (in both senses of the word), first by the severity of the 1930s Depression and later by the temporary revival of older industries under the impact of rearmament and the outbreak of the Second World War. It was not until the 1940s in the USA and the 1950s in Western Europe that the new 'high-tech' industries (mainly consumer durables) became sufficiently massive to 'take up the slack' by absorbing the resources discarded or left unemployed by the older 'declining' industries. However, the latter were to be given a further lease of life by 'étatist' (state-sponsored) development of import-substituting metallurgical, engineering, shipbuilding, coal and textile industries in the Balkans and East Central Europe and parts of the 'developing world' from the late 1930s onward, while the West was gradually making the transition to 'high-technology' capitalism.

The 1930s Depression probably hit the Balkans and East Central Europe harder (proportionately) than almost any other region in the world. It is commonly portrayed as an externally induced affliction, the consequence of the interplay of momentous economic forces in the dominant Western economies (primarily the USA, Britain, Germany and France), over which the puny Balkan and East Central European states could exercise little or no influence, let alone control: their inhabitants were alleged to be hapless passive victims. Balkan and East Central European governments have thus been largely absolved of any 'blame' or responsibility for the ensuing catastrophes. Different policies and/or politicians, it is commonly assumed, could only have slightly curtailed the devastating impact of the Depression on the Balkans and East Central Europe. There was indeed very little room for manoeuvre, very little that could have been done, given the weakness, fragility and highly exposed position of the Balkan and East Central European states in the face of much larger world market forces and the magnitude of the waves that pounded these small vessels. Nevertheless, the Balkans and East Central Europe were significantly involved in the causes as well as the consequences of the 1930s Depression. It was not merely passive and acted upon; it also acted.

The First World War and its immediate aftermath caused widespread disruption and some devastation of primary commodity production in both western and (especially) eastern Europe, mainly as a result of the massive mobilization of manpower, horses and transport for the war effort. This, combined with high wartime prices and inflated demand for certain categories of raw materials and fuels, stimulated large increases in agricultural and mineral production in the Americas, Africa, Asia and Australasia. Yet during the mid-1920s, particularly in the central and eastern parts of the Continent, European farmers and mining companies started borrowing heavily in an all-too-successful endeavour to regain their pre-war levels of production. However, partly as a result of the massive 'population deficit' and reductions in purchasing power brought about by the war and its aftermath, Europe's effective demand for primary products either did not revive with comparable alacrity or could not become large enough to absorb both the restored European output and the increased non-European output. Therefore the markets for primary products remained relatively weak, even when European industry surpassed pre-war levels of output.

In the Balkans and East Central Europe, as elsewhere in the world, over-production and cut-throat competition forced farmers and mineral producers to accept lower prices in vain attempts to increase their shares of the market. Hence, during the years immediately preceding the Wall Street Crash of October 1929, primary commodity prices weakened. Except for highly developed Czechoslovakia, the Balkans and East Central Europe were most adversely affected by the sagging international prices of grain and timber (Romania, Hungary and Poland), coal (Poland and Romania), non-ferrous metals (Yugoslavia and Hungary), tobacco (Bulgaria) and even oil (Romania) during the latter half of the 1920s, as was also the case for the Soviet Union and the Baltic States. Only industrialized Czechoslovakia was not adversely affected by the weakness of demand for and the prices of primary commodities, which helps to explain the buoyancy of the Czechoslovak economy at that time. Indeed, Czechoslovak farmers were given adequate tariff protection against cheap imports.

The USA, as the world's largest producer and exporter of mineral and agricultural products, was also affected by the weakening of commodity prices and the consequent negative effects on land values. This was an important factor in the onset of the Depression there. Moreover, the falling real incomes and purchasing power of farmers and mineral producers, especially in the Balkans and East Central Europe and the Americas, reduced their capacity to purchase west European and local manufactured goods. The Wall Street Crash sent primary commodity and real estate prices tumbling even faster, further reducing the real incomes of primary commodity producers and their effective demand for industrial products. The consequences were magnified even more by the abrupt cessation of lending to primary commodity producers, who had for a short time borrowed money in an attempt to sustain their mid-1920s expenditure levels despite the weakening of commodity prices. In the Balkans and East Central Europe, not only did new domestic lending cease, but so did capital inflows from the West. Thus, as in the USA (powerfully portrayed by John Steinbeck's *The Grapes of Wrath*), many Balkan and East Central European banks were forced to start calling in existing loans from heavily mortgaged farmers and mineral producers. (In contrast to the USA, however, Balkan and East Central European farmers were rarely forced off their land.) This inevitably exposed the extent to which their clients were unable to pay interest on (let alone repay the principal of) their loans, which had been secured on properties whose value was now plummeting. That in turn undermined public confidence in a number of Central European banks, culminating in the collapse of Austria's illustrious Creditanstalt and various other central and eastern European finance houses during 1931. Like the *Krach* (crash) of 1873, the cataclysmic banking crisis of 1931 further undermined investors' confidence and business confidence and liquidity in Germanic Central Europe and hence neighbouring East Central Europe and the Balkans as well, greatly deepening and prolonging the 1930s Depression in this part of the world (including, by now, Czechoslovakia, which could not isolate itself from the crises in neighbouring states).

This was by no means the end of Balkan and East Central European woes. In the West most industrialists were able to respond to declining products prices and demand by 'moth-balling' or cutting back capacity, freezing or even reducing nominal wages and laying off workers, in order to cut costs and stave off bankruptcy. Moreover, many were able to come together in quite strong and stable national and international cartels to curb competitive price cutting and to restrict their members' output in a co-ordinated fashion, often with government backing (even in the supposedly 'liberal' USA and UK). Increased tariffs and import controls were also quite effective in protecting western European farmers, manufacturers and mineral producers (especially coal mining) against cheap imports and alleged 'dumping'. Indeed, this potent protectionism was crucial to the strength and stability of western European cartels and state farm support schemes, which might otherwise have been undercut and undermined by low-priced imports. For various reasons, however, the agricultural and mineral export economies in the Balkans and East Central Europe and elsewhere were not able to defend themselves so effectively. This was partly attributable to the structural rigidities in their economies and societies, which prevented them from adjusting as quickly and flexibly as some Western economies did (e.g. Sweden and the UK). With the exception of the industrialized Czech Lands (whose recovery from the 1930s Depression was severely impeded by a menacing stand-off between the Czechs and the increasingly pro-Nazi Bohemian Germans after 1933), the countries of the Balkans and East Central Europe were capable of producing only a limited range of products. This was not for want of trying. Despite the great hardships, privations and budgetary constraints, there was considerable state (and some private) investment in further education and training and in the creation of new industries (even if these were often military rather than civilian in orientation). The peoples of the Balkans and East Central Europe were not deficient in would-be entrepreneurs and 'enterpreneurial spirit'. The influential claims to the contrary, especially by Gerschenkron (1962), have simply overlooked the great groundswell of private enterprise in the eastern half of Europe from the late nineteenth century until either the start of Soviet collectivization in 1928–9 or the tidal wave of bankruptcies and bank collapses in Central, East Central and Balkan Europe in 1930 and 1931 – not to mention the strong revival of private enterprise in most parts of East Central Europe and the Balkans since 1989, which Gerschenkron did not live to see. Even the millions of so-called 'kulaks' in the Balkans and East Central Europe were essentially entrepreneurs, as were the reviled Russian middlemen and 'rich peasants' from whom they acquired their deeply derogatory name (by a Leninist legerdemain). The peoples of the Balkans and East Central Europe made valiant efforts to overcome economic adversity during the 1930s, as did many other Depression-stricken societies. The real problem was that their low levels of economic development, the continued predominance of low-technology agriculture, the shortage of industrial and technical skills, and the (resulting) limited versatility and purchasing power of the bulk of the population made it doubly difficult to adjust to economic shocks and setbacks by rapidly diverting financial resources and manpower into new lines of economic activity in order to change the product mix and reap higher economic returns on the investments and (often heroic) efforts that were made. Moreover, in so far as most Balkan and East Central European farmers necessarily relied on unpaid or low-paid family labour, it was impossible for them to reduce their costs significantly by reducing wages and/or by laying off workers (in the manner of Western industrialists). Their costs were relatively fixed in the sense that they could not be reduced much further. There was no 'fat' to be trimmed. Conversely, most of the extractive industries were relatively capital intensive and most of their capital had already been (literally) 'sunk' in mine-shafts and oil wells. So they too were unable to cut their costs substantially by reducing wages and/or laying off workers, since wages were already a small part of their overall production costs. Either way, as primary commodity prices fell, primary producers desperately tried to compensate by increasing their production volumes. However, while this seemed to be a rational response for each individual farmer and mine-owner to make, it actually worked to their collective disadvantage. The primary commodity producers of the Balkans and East Central Europe were to remain locked into a vicious downward spiral of commodity prices until the rise of Nazi Germany, public works programmes, rearmament and a UK housing boom revived some of the western European economies in the late 1930s.

Thus the crucial behavioural difference was that, when faced with falls in the prices of their respective products, manufacturers tended to reduce their output levels and industrial prices were soon stabilized at new (albeit lower) levels, whereas farmers and mine-owners tended to increase their output volumes and this pushed the prices of their products down still further.

Furthermore, since average primary commodity prices more than halved between 1929 and 1933 (while average industrial prices fell by much less), industrialists and industrial workers reaped the benefits of a significant improvement in the terms of trade of industrial versus primary commodities. By the same token the highly industrialized West gained at the expense of primary producers everywhere. Thus a given volume of industrial products could now be exchanged for an increased volume of primary products. This, in combination with the abrupt cessation of capital inflows, greatly magnified the depression in the primary export economies (including most of the Balkan and East Central European countries). The latter were further disadvantaged by the fact that most primary commodity cartels and government-backed commodity price stabilization schemes were both intrinsically difficult to sustain and not very successful. This was mainly the result of the very large numbers of separate and widely dispersed producers involved in producing and exporting most of the principal primary commodities. The chance of producers breaking ranks rises in proportion to the number of cartel members. Products such as oil, gold, diamonds and platinum (produced by a relatively small number of companies and countries) were more amenable to cartelization, but unfortunately the Balkans and East Central Europe were generally not well endowed with these.

Between 1929 and 1933, mainly as a result of the slump in primary commodity prices, the nominal value of export earnings fell by about 66 per cent for Poland, 62 per cent for Hungary, 58 per cent for Romania and Yugoslavia, and 56 per cent for Bulgaria (Berend and Ranki 1974a: 248). Over the same period, for similar reasons, nominal agricultural incomes fell by about 59 per cent in Poland, 58 per cent in Romania, 52 per cent in Bulgaria and 36 per cent in Hungary (p. 245). Among the occupational groups hardest hit by the Depression were cattle exporters. Between 1929 and 1933 the nominal value of cattle exports fell by 89 per cent for Poland, 86 per cent for Bulgaria, 73 per cent for Romania and 59 per cent for Yugoslavia, as most Western and Central European states severely restricted or even prohibited cattle imports altogether in order to protect their own farmers (p. 247).

The decline in the nominal value of industrial output between 1929 and 1932 amounted to about 11 per cent in Romania, approximately 17 per cent in Yugoslavia and Bulgaria, 24 per cent in Hungary, 37 per cent in Poland and 40 per cent in Czechoslovakia (Berend and Ranki 1974a: 250–4). The fall in industrial output was less marked in the Balkans than in more industrialized countries. The simple reason for this was that initial Balkan industrial output was so small that the contraction in domestic demand for industrial products there was easily offset by restricting industrial imports into the region (p. 249), while there were few industrial exports from the Balkans either before or after 1929.

There has been much less Western awareness of the impact of the 1930s Depression on the largely agrarian countries of the Balkans and East Central Europe than of its impact on the industrial countries of western and Germanic Central Europe. The main reason for this, apart from the 'closeness to home' factor, was that in the industrial countries the burden of adjustment to the Depression fell heavily on wage and employment levels, causing very visible and readily quantifiable increases in poverty and dole queues. Furthermore, these adverse effects could be quite readily alleviated through public works programmes, welfare benefits and lower interest rates on loans. The effects of the Depression on the more exposed, vulnerable and impoverished agricultural and mineral-export economies of the Balkans and East Central Europe were more severe, but less conspicuous, less easily quantifiable, more 'internalized' and not so readily susceptible to effective alleviation. Balkan and East Central European countries really did have little option but to slash imports and public expenditure by imposing draconian import restrictions, foreign exchange controls and deflationary austerity programmes. The types of policies that alleviated the Depression in industrialized Germany, Britain and Sweden would not have achieved similarly positive results in the more rigid and constrained primary export economies. They were less able to undertake or finance anti-cyclical programmes and were more dependent on a revival of exports, even though most of them did take some significant steps down the path of 'import-substituting industrialization'. Indeed, the curtailment and increased real cost of industrial imports and the sharply contracting real returns on and scope for 'traditional' primary exports gave local entrepreneurs major new incentives to invest in increased 'national' production of manufactured goods, irrespective of the explicit economic decisions made by the governments of agricultural and mineral-exporting countries and the serious structural impediments to any major economic reorientation.

Fundamentally, especially if they were also small countries without any major industries and large urban markets of their own, the predominantly agrarian and mineral-exporting countries of the Balkans and East Central Europe were asymmetrically dependent on unimpeded access to the markets, finance, services and 'know-how' of the major industrial countries. When this access was curtailed during the 1920s and (to a much greater degree) the 1930s, the functioning of most Balkan and East Central European economies was seriously impaired, but there was little they could do about it. Their own protectionism (which was inspired and guided more by strident and simplistic economic nationalism than by judicious 'selective retaliation') could secure their meagre 'national' markets, but it could not secure vital export markets. Indeed, the world-wide movement towards ever-increasing levels of protectionism placed the relatively poor, weak, small and trade-dependent states of the Balkans and East Central Europe at a steadily increasing disadvantage vis-à-vis industrial countries with large internal markets (the USA and Germany) and those with 'captive' imperial markets (Britain and France). However, since most of the Balkan and East Central European states were themselves built upon the pernicious doctrines of political and economic nationalism, which increasingly repressive and authoritarian rulers embraced as the whole basis of their legitimacy and of their own (often very limited) thinking, they were in no position to object in principle to the growing and extremely damaging political and economic nationalism of the USA and of Europe's major industrial powers.

In international economic relations, power and control lay overwhelmingly in the hands of the 'core' industrial countries (the USA, Germany, Britain and France) rather than the agrarian and mineral-exporting 'peripheries' of the capitalist system. International trade was largely conducted on terms that better suited the former, while the latter were obliged to accommodate themselves to this uncomfortable reality as best they could. Thus the interwar years provided the clearest possible demonstration that small 'nations' can afford to be fiercely 'nationalistic' only so long as the bigger and stronger 'nations' do not follow suit. Otherwise the small 'nations' will find themselves squeezed out of the major 'national' markets and, in any ensuing battle of the titans, the small 'nations' are bound to be the main losers. Small countries, especially if they are essentially exporters of primary commodities, usually benefit from and often depend upon an open, liberal, non-nationalistic political, economic and international order, even if nationalists are sometimes too blinkered to see that. In a Europe built on concepts of political and economic nationalism (a Europe of zealously 'national' states), all lose out from the ensuing 'Balkanization' of the Continent, but the smaller, weaker and most trade-dependent countries referred to here stand to lose the most. For them nationalism can be a recipe for de facto subordination and relative stagnation rather than 'liberation'.

Balkan and East Central European governments met in Warsaw in August 1930 in the vague hope of agreeing on a co-ordinated response to the onset of the Depression. But they were unable to agree on any framework of regional co-operation or 'collective economic security', since they were at the same time bitterly competing to sell similar products in much the same export markets and were vying for 'national' advantage, one against another. Amid a climate of intense economic and political nationalism, all proposals for regional co-operation and integration fell on deaf ears. These states were therefore doomed to embrace nationalistic 'beggar-my-neighbour' and *sauve qui peut* responses to the Depression, including increased tariffs, import licensing, exchange controls, closed bilateral trading arrangements, competitive devaluations, debt moratoria, remission of internal debts, repudiation of external debts and the establishment of official 'national' crop procurement and marketing agencies (or 'boards'). Above all, in the wake of a persistent depression and the concurrent cessation of almost all Western investment in the Balkans and East Central Europe (partly causing and partly caused by the discontinuation of their debt-service payments from 1931 onwards), the rulers of Poland, Hungary and the Balkan states embarked on étatist programmes of import-substituting industrialization (comparable to those initiated by many Latin American states in the same period). These were largely motivated by economic nationalism and a growing desire to bring many hitherto independent economic activities under increasingly extensive state control, by a xenophobic and/or anti-Semitic desire to eliminate 'aliens', middlemen, 'speculators', rentiers and potential 'fifth columnists' from the industrial, commercial and financial sectors, by the pressure to provide 'jobs for the boys' (especially the sons of the 'national bourgeoisies' and the ruling oligarchies) and by 'strategic' concern to foster armaments production and potential war industries in order to enhance their illusory 'national' security. 'Governments increased their control over cartels and took over a number of industries, particularly those connected with war production' (Seton-Watson 1945: 130).

The most ambitious state-directed industrial projects were Hungary's 'Billion Pëngo Plan' (1938–40) and Poland's 'Central Industrial Region' (1936–9), both designed to build up war industries in and around their capital cities, well away from their more vulnerable frontier regions. In Czechoslovakia from 1936 to 1938, during the premiership of the Slovak Milan Hodza, there was a major programme to promote industrial development in Slovakia, partly in endeavours to alleviate poverty and lack of industrial employment there and thus to assuage the socio-economic discontent which was feeding the growth of Slovak nationalism, but also partly because Slovakia was perceived to be less vulnerable to annexation by Nazi Germany. In Yugoslavia, likewise, the Stojadinovic government (1935–9) fostered state-funded chemical and metallurgical enterprises. In Romania King Carol II (1930–40) and his court camarilla, who personally acquired large chunks of the armaments, textile and sugar industries, played similar roles, while lining their own pockets (Seton-Watson 1945: 131, 210). Yet in the short term (and in most cases even in the longer run) this kind of import-substituting industrialization mainly substituted inferior and costlier home-produced manufactures for cheaper and superior quality imported ones. High tariffs, import restrictions and foreign exchange controls protected 'articles whose price was 50 to 300 per cent above that formerly paid for importing them from Western Europe. Many such "artificial" industries could not be defended on grounds of strategic necessity. They benefited the small number of persons directly interested in them and their cost was borne by the poorer section of the town population and, to a lesser degree, by the peasantry' (p. 131). In effect, increased protectionism and exchange controls encouraged 'rent-seeking' behaviour and allowed local industrial monopolists to make inflated profits by shielding them from foreign competition, to the great detriment of most local users of their products (including other industries which were more dependent on locally manufactured inputs). We see no valid objection to 'natural' or spontaneous import-substituting industrialization based on products in which the countries under consideration had actual or potential comparative cost advantages, on rational responses to shifting terms of trade and on continued exposure to the disciplines provided by foreign competition and the world market. Much could have been achieved in this direction in the 1930s Balkans and East Central Europe. However, excessive, indiscriminate and permanent protectionism, 'jobs for the boys' and very corrupt allocation of state contracts and subsidies encouraged 'rent seeking', racketeering, inefficiency, waste, fraud, misallocation or mis-appropriation of resources and damaging distortions of the market system in general. Furthermore, the sort of import-substituting policies adopted in the 1930s, rooted as they were in economic nationalism, eventually curtailed or negated their own effectiveness by emphasizing the pursuit of autarky (self-sufficiency) and thus forgoing many potential gains from greater international trade, specialization and investment. Ironically, not until the 1950s did import-substituting industrialization attain a sufficiently large scale to transform fundamentally the income, employment and productive potential of the mainly primary export economies of the Balkans, East Central Europe and Latin America, but by then the circumstances which had originally 'justified' the over-zealous pursuit of import-substituting industrialization had long ceased to exist and were but a distant memory!

25 The plight of the peasantry: towards a re-evaluation of peasant poverty and aspirations

THE AWAKENING OF 'PEASANT EUROPE'

From the 1860s to 1929, from Ireland to the Urals, peasants were 'on the move' and 'on the make'. As late as 1929, peasants still comprised around half the inhabitants of Europe as a whole and almost three-quarters of the population of the eastern half of Europe. Peasants were emerging as a conscious class with specific social, economic and political interests and aspirations, although at first these were often articulated on their behalf by bourgeois politicians and the intelligentsia, who sometimes used peasants for their own ends. The protracted dissolution of serfdom in East Central Europe and parts of the Balkans between the 1840s and the 1880s, the slowly increasing availability of rural schooling, the growing contact with the slowly expanding ranks of the rural intelligentsia (including village teachers, doctors and local government personnel) and the rural industrial proletariat (including railwaymen and miners), the eye-opening experiences provided by more universal military service and occasional employment in the towns, the widening of peasant horizons by national market integration and railway networks, and growing peasant awareness (as well as resentment) of their remaining disadvantages, all awakened peasants to the growing need to defend their interests and organize themselves politically and economically. By 1905–7 there were major peasant-based mass movements in Ireland, France, Scandinavia, Latvia, Estonia, Lithuania, Poland, Ukraine, Russia and Romania. (The great Romanian peasant revolt of 1907 was partly inspired by the peasant revolts in the Russian Empire in 1905–6.) Moreover, during 1906–14 there was a spectacular growth of peasant co-operatives in some countries, consciously modelled on the trail-blazing Danish co-operatives of the 1880s and 1890s. Thus by 1914 most Danish, Swedish, Finnish and Romanian and more than one in three Russian and Irish peasant households belonged to marketing and/or credit co-operatives.

Peasantist movements were also reaping the harvest of the momentous nineteenth-century romantic, folkloristic, ethnographic, philological, 'völkisch' and Slavophil 'rediscoveries' or 're-inventions' of vernacular peasant cultures. These began to bridge the chasm which had separated elite culture from popular culture since the Enlightenment. This went hand in hand with the emergence of the vernacular languages and newly created literatures of long-submerged peasant nations and proto-nations (Latvian, Estonian, Lithuanian, Finnish, Ukrainian, Czech, Slovak, Croat, Serb, Bulgarian, Greek, Romanian, Albanian, Slovene, Macedonian and Irish). These linguistic-literary 'revivals' may often have been instigated initially by outsiders (for example, Germans, Swedes and Catholic clergy), but their consequences went far beyond the original intentions, sometimes dramatically shifting the rural balance of power in favour of hitherto downtrodden peasantries and throwing alien landed elites on to the defensive, notably in Latvia, Estonia, Finland, Ukraine, the Czech Lands, Croatia, Bulgaria and Ireland. The great groundswells of peasant radicalism and hitherto submerged peasant-national cultures in late nineteenth- and early twentieth-century Europe coincided with a growth in the relative economic strength of peasant smallholders in the course of national-revolutionary struggles to establish independent, predominantly peasant nation-states and to dispossess alien landed nobilities.

The gradual enfranchisement of peasants, the growth of peasant co-operatives, the steady extension of education and cheap transport, the rise of agricultural protectionism and even the 'progress' of industrialization, far from 'de-peasantizing' the countryside (as predicted by classical Marxism), were expanding the potential for intensive small-scale livestock-rearing, dairying, horticulture, viticulture and arboriculture, and granting a new lease of life to an increasingly commercialized peasant smallholder agriculture, while increasingly denying large-scale agriculture the captive pool of docile cheap labour on which its profitability had depended. The slump in international grain prices from 1874 to 1896 had hit hardest precisely those farms which employed wage labour to produce grain on a large scale for international markets, and benefited those smallholders who were net purchasers of grain. The self-employed, self-exploiting family labour of the peasant farm was also much more motivated and responsive to changing conditions than the underpaid wage labourer who only did what he was told (and no more) and who had good reason to slack when no one was watching. Agriculture based on hired hands incurred all sorts of supervision and managerial costs which simply did not arise among the more flexible and self-reliant smallholders, who could reap more fully the fruits of their own labour. This contributed to the famed 'tenacity' of peasant farmers during periods of severe economic depression, such as the early 1930s. Periods of increased hardship did not automatically result in a major exodus from the land. The growing economic strength of peasant agriculture was reflected in generally rising levels of peasant consumption. Peasant diets became more varied (including more meat, vegetables, white bread, fruit, coffee, tea, sugar and beer) and some even took up smoking. They bought increasing quantities of footwear, cheap washable clothing, matches, kerosene and kerosene lamps. Even where such goods were heavily taxed, peasant consumption of them continued to rise inexorably. Hence Europe's expanding light industries were able to count on this expanding peasant market for their goods.

Many peasants and, more particularly, agricultural labourers largely or completely missed out on these rising rural consumption standards. The impoverished peasantry of Austrian Poland (Galicia) suffered acute Malthusian population pressures on their meagre landholdings and the Romanian peasantry were grievously exploited under the rapacious 'arenda' system. Many remote mountainous regions experienced damaging overgrazing by sheep and goats, deforestation, soil erosion and rural depopulation, especially in the Balkans. These factors swelled the massive European emigration to the New World, although areas such as these remained the exception rather than the rule. For most of the lower-lying regions of the Balkans and East Central Europe this was a period of agricultural intensification and rising per capita crop production (Bideleux 1987: 13, 23, 250; 1990).

Thus the proletariat was not the only class 'on the move' in post-1917 Europe. There was also a groundswell of peasant-based movements right across Europe, from Ireland and Scandinavia through Germany to the Slav world. This so-called 'Green Rising' was accelerated by the emergence of self-consciously peasant nation-states in Ireland, the Baltic region, East Central Europe, the Balkans and Ukraine, by the central role of the peasantry in the Russian Revolutions of 1917, by the subsequent radical land reforms in the Balkans, Soviet Russia and the Baltic States, by the growing politicization of peasantries during and after the Great War, by electoral competition between rival political parties and by the international ideological appeal of 'blood and soil' nationalism, Gandhian ideas and Russian agrarian socialism (the latter mainly among Slavs and Romanians). Moreover, the widespread adoption of universal suffrage and compulsory elementary schooling in post-1917 Europe benefited the peasantry more than any other class, as did the continuing spread of co-operative networks. 'And what has happened in Europe since the War has been a vast victory for the peasants, and therefore a vast defeat for the Communists and the capitalists,' wrote G.K. Chesterton in 1923. 'In a sort of awful silence the peasantries have fought one vast and voiceless pitched battle with Bolshevism and its twin brother, which is Big Business, and the peasantries have won' (Chesterton 1923: 8).

THE LAND REFORMS OF THE 1920S

In 1918 the economies of the Balkans and East Central Europe were mainly agricultural, with peasants and farm labourers constituting around 80 per cent of the population in Bulgaria, 78 per cent in Romania, 75 per cent in Yugoslavia, 63 per cent in Poland, 55 per cent in Hungary and 34 per cent in Czechoslovakia (Seton-Watson 1945: 75). Large landed estates dominated the agriculture of the former Austro-Hungarian Empire, Poland and Romania, while peasant smallholdings predominanted in Yugoslavia and Bulgaria. After the land reforms of the 1920s. however, peasant smallholdings became dominant everywhere except Poland and Hungary.

The 1920s land reforms were not conceived as economic measures and they should not be judged as such (Seton-Watson 1945: 80). 'It should be clearly understood that the motives of the reforms were political, social and nationalist, not economic' (p. 79). They were hastily concocted preemptive measures, designed to defuse peasant 'land hunger' and social unrest in the wake of the First World War and to deflect the potential political 'fall out' from the Russian Revolutions of 1917. There was also a widespread feeling among the educated classes that 'as the peasantry had borne the brunt of the war, and had proved itself in the greatest crisis yet known in human history to be in fact the backbone of the nation, it deserved to be given its share of the wealth of the nation. This thought was to override all other arguments' (pp. 79–80).

The land redistributions that were carried out (as distinct from the more radical ones that had been promised) involved the dispossession of thousands of 'alien' landlords. However, so long as the latter received nominal payments of compensation (in ritual obeisance to the sanctity of private property), this was seen as a price well worth paying for the sake of greater political stability and social peace. Moreover, the triumphant nationalists welcomed such expropriations as a form of so-called 'nostrification' of their nation's productive resources. Thus the redistribution of land hitherto owned by German landlords in the Czech Lands and western Poland, by Magyar landlords in Transylvania, Slovakia and the Vojvodina, and by formerly pro-Ottoman Muslim landowners in Bosnia-Herzegovina, encountered little resistance, since the interests of these dispossessed 'alien' landlords were not represented in the new or expanded 'national' states (Seton-Watson 1945: 77–8). Large landed estates remained dominant only in Poland and Hungary, whose native nobilities had played leading roles in public life and in the national movement before the First World War. They therefore managed to hang on to their great economic power and possessions after the attainment of national independence (p. 78).

Precisely because the land reforms had not been conceived as economic measures, they were widely judged to have suffered from numerous inadequacies which condemned them to economic failure. Thus, according to Seton-Watson (1945: 80–1), the owners of the new or expanded holdings lacked the requisite technical knowledge and equipment to make an economic success of them, and 'the new governments paid little attention to the improvement of agriculture or the assistance of peasant owners until the World Depression forced these tasks upon them'. Furthermore, even before the onset of the 1929–33 Depression, Balkan and East Central European agriculture faced severe competition from grain-producing areas outside Europe. 'It was cheaper to transport grain raised on the highly capitalized farms of America by sea from New York or Buenos Aires to Hamburg than to bring the products of the less capitalized estates of Hungary (not to mention the uneconomic holdings of the Balkans) a few hundred miles. American competition more than balanced the . . . disappearance of Russian wheat from the world market.' This increased competition was felt 'more by the big and medium proprietors than by the smallholders, but it influenced directly or indirectly the whole agricultural population of Eastern Europe' (pp. 81–2). During the 'comparative prosperity' of the mid-1920s, however, 'the wealthier peasants had borrowed money . . . in order . . . to improve their lands. The poorer peasants also borrowed money in order to buy food in the critical period . . . before the harvest, when their supplies from the previous harvest had run out . . . Loans were made at a high rate of interest, particularly those made by money-lenders . . . The fall of agricultural prices enormously increased the burden of these debts, since the peasant now received half as much for his products as earlier, while . . . his debt remained the same' (p. 83). At the same time the fragmentation of landholdings was proceeding apace, because in most parts of the Balkans and East Central Europe inherited land was by custom divided equally between the surviving sons. 'If the holding consisted of land of different qualities, devoted to different kinds of production, then each son must have a piece of each type . . . A holding of a few acres may consist of as many as forty small strips, separated from each other by several miles. Large acres of culti-vated land are wasted in the form of paths enabling owners to walk from one strip to another. The strips are incapable of efficient production' (p. 81). Between the two World Wars, according to Warriner (1950: 143), 'The average East European farm produced about one-third as much as a peasant farm in Western Europe, yet each acre had to feed and employ twice as many people.' (By Western Europe, it appears she meant Britain, France, Germany, the Low Countries and Denmark.)

Seton-Watson was, nevertheless, somewhat overstating his case. There were indeed serious defi-ciencies in Balkan and East Central European agriculture and agrarian arrangements between the wars, but these problems need to be kept in proportion. Per capita grain and potato output in the Balkans and East Central Europe remained nearly double that of southern Europe, about 25 per cent above that of France, about 5 per cent above that of Germany and only 3 per cent below that of Denmark, while average annual grain yields per hectare remained about 17 per cent above those of southern Europe and only 22 per cent below those of north-western and Germanic Central Europe (Bideleux 1987: 250–1, tables 11 and 12). Furthermore, per capita holdings of livestock in the Balkans and East Central Europe remained about the same as those of Europe as a whole (excluding the Soviet Union) and considerably above those of southern Europe (p. 254). In addition, Seton-Watson himself has pointed out that on balance crop yields and rural living standards were no higher in Hungary, which had a predominance of large landed estates, than in either Bulgaria or Yugoslavia, where there was a preponderance of peasant smallholdings (Seton-Watson 1945: 102). From 1934 to 1938 the average annual grain yield was 1.5 tonnes per hectare in Hungary and 1.1 tonnes per hectare in Poland (with a similar predominance of large landed estates), as against 1.7 tonnes per hectare in Czechoslovakia, 1.4 in the case of Yugoslavia, 1.2 in Bulgaria and 0.9 in Romania (Bideleux 1987: 251, Table 12). The interwar years also witnessed considerable diversifi-cation away from allegedly 'monocultural' grain production into more lucrative and labour-inten-sive crops and livestock products which were better suited to small-scale peasant agriculture, as noted by Rothschild (1974: 353) and Berend and Ranki (1974a: 296).

In 1934, interestingly, Henry Tiltman reported that among Bulgarians 'the word has gone forth that there is money in strawberries, peas and wine, whereas the world has too much wheat . . . In the task of transforming the country from a farm into a garden the peasants are assisted at every turn by a government awake to the vital issues at stake. Since her old markets have disappeared, Bulgaria must win new markets for her new crops. Therefore every precaution is being taken to ensure that each chicken, egg, crate of fruit and bottle of wine exported will be of a quality calculated to assist and not retard the progress of the country. To this end, a system of inspection based on the Danish model has been instituted and strict methods of grading adopted' (Tiltman 1934: 68).

On the whole, Balkan and East Central European agricultural productivity and rural living stand-ards were evidently much more affected by environmental factors (terrain and climatic conditions) and by levels of urbanization and industrialization, than by whether the agricultural sector was dominated by peasant smallholdings or large landed estates. Yet Seton-Watson's somewhat gloomy and exaggerated views on the allegedly negative 'parcellizing' effects of the 1920s land reforms and of peasant farming nevertheless were and continue to be widely shared, for example, by W. Moore (1945: 26–35, 87–94), Political and Economic Planning (PEP 1945: 26–33), Warriner (1950: xii–xiii, 142–4), Berend and Ranki (1974a: 288–95), Cochrane (1993: 851) and Crampton (1994: 35). Thus, according to Thompson (1993: 844), 'Land reform in Eastern Europe during the interwar period did not bring prosperity to the peasantry . . . Man–land ratios in Eastern Europe changed little or [even] fell slightly by 1930 because agrarian reform did not relieve rural overpopulation . . . The major effect of the interwar agrarian reforms was to hasten slightly the structural transformation of agriculture in Eastern Europe.' On the other hand, Cochrane (1993: 851) contends that the 1920s land reforms 'failed on the whole to alter significantly the structure of agriculture'. She rightly emphasizes the importance (then as now) of promoting appropriate infrastructural support for agriculture through the development of 'co-operatives, credit institutions, new marketing structures and extension services' (p. 855), but she quite misleadingly claims that 'most . . . governments failed to follow up the land reforms with the instutitions or infrastructure needed to support the new farmers . . . Extension services throughout the region were virtually unheard of' (p. 853). 'To the extent that the reforms of the 1920s failed to improve conditions for the rural population, it was because this necessary support was lacking' (p. 855). We shall shortly provide more evidence to the contrary. Rural infrastructure developed considerably and there were important agricultural changes.

In our view, the problems of rural poverty in the interwar Balkans and East Central Europe did not hinge upon land tenure arrangements. To think that they did is to bark up the wrong tree. One can no more blame the serious and widespread poverty simply on the legacies of the former predominance of the large landed estate than on its opposite, the effects of the 1920s land reforms and the growing preponderance of peasant smallholdings (however much either explanation might fit with one's political and economic prejudices!). Nor can one simply attribute the problems to the effects of rural population growth. By this period the density of agricultural population per hectare of arable land was indeed considerably higher in the Balkans and East Central Europe than in France, Germany or the United Kingdom (Moore 1945: 197–204). However, there was serious and widespread rural poverty in the Balkans and East Central Europe long before the emergence of problems of rural 'overpopulation'. Conversely, with higher levels of education and agricultural technology, Balkan and East Central European landed estates and peasant agriculture would easily have been capable of sustaining such high rural population densities (comparable to those in countries as diverse as the Netherlands, Belgium, Norway and Finland). Fundamentally, rural poverty in the interwar Balkans and East Central Europe mainly resulted from (and took the form of) long-standing social and cultural deprivation and neglect. Most of the peasants and agricultural labourers in these regions still suffered from inadequate education, a deficiency of public health and sanitation provisions, a lack of clean tap water and a prevalence of unhygienic housing and life-styles. As observed by Seton-Watson (1945: 95), lack of education had made it difficult for peasants 'to understand the importance of hygiene or to make the best even of the scanty resources of food that are at their disposal'. Moreover, 'The majority of smallholders live in such wretched hovels that even the best hygiene experts would have difficulty in making much of them. One bed will hold six or seven persons, including children. In parts of Bosnia and other poor regions the cow or the pig sleeps in the same room as the family' (p. 92). 'The living conditions of the Hungarian rural proletariat are similar to those of the smallholder class of neighbouring countries. Families are packed into small, unhygienic rooms. Some have their own tiny houses, others are crowded together in barracks provided by the estate' (p. 102). In Bucharest there is an outstanding museum of traditional peasant dwellings gathered from various parts of Romania. They look very spruce and picturesque in their museum park setting, but many of them are amazingly small, dark, cramped, fire-prone and poorly insulated, while others clearly used to be little more than crudely covered 'holes in the ground'. Interwar East Central Europe and especially the Balkans had some of Europe's lowest literacy rates (Bideleux 1987: 227, table 3), the highest rates of infant mortality (p. 225, table 2) and the highest incidence of diseases such as tuberculosis, typhoid, scarlet fever, smallpox, diphtheria, whooping cough and cholera outside the Soviet Union.

If this was the essence of rural poverty in the interwar Balkans and East Central Europe, land reform per se could not substantially eliminate it, just as the land tenure arrangements (old and new) were not its main direct cause. Even where landed estates were expropriated and redistributed among the peasantry, most peasant smallholdings were only augmented by between 10 per cent and 35 per cent, and the short-term benefits were soon cancelled out by surging rural population growth. Thus land reforms could offer only temporary palliation of peasant 'land hunger'.

The principal consequences of the land reforms were (like the dominant motives) more political and social than economic. Indeed, by breaking (or at least diminishing) the power of the old landlord class, they did help to reduce some longstanding impediments to effective peasant organization, co-operation and self-help. All but the most enlightened landlords and rural officials had tended to oppose anything that might tip the rural balance of power in favour of the peasantry. More lasting solutions to rural poverty were primarily to be found in the significant expansion of rural education, agronomic assistance and other measures designed to enhance the capacity of the peasants to help themselves. For, other than in the Czech Lands, Balkan and East Central European industrial sectors were not yet big enough to be capable of absorbing large rural labour surpluses (even if these industries had developed much more rapidly than they did), while the scope for rural emigration from the Balkans and East Central Europe to North America was being severely curtailed by the introduction of ever tighter (North) American immigration quotas. As reported by Henry Tiltman (1934: 72), Bulgarians (among others) had 'discovered the vital truth that the key to the future prosperity of agrarian nations is to be found in education and then more education'.

Rather more was achieved on this front than writers such as Seton-Watson (1945), Berend and Ranki (1974a), Thompson (1993) and Cochrane (1993) have realized or cared to admit, although many of the measures adopted necessarily took time fully to bear fruit. Centuries of social and cultural deprivation could not be rectified overnight. The most important reforms lay in the establishment of free, compulsory and universal schooling in rural areas, a process which began well before the First World War. By the 1930s school enrolments as a percentage of the total population were (other than in Albania) mostly on a par with western Europe (Bideleux 1987: 22, table 3).

Of course it was still widely believed that peasants did not need much education on the grounds that the alleged simplicity of peasant agriculture put a low premium on formal knowledge and training. Moreover, many landowners, officials and townspeople did not want the peasants to gain knowledge and skills that would help them to organize, to lobby for legislation and resources and to think for themselves. Even Mitrany was ambivalent. On the one hand, he regarded 'improved education' (together with improved transport and administration) as one of the three crucial prerequisites 'if the standard of rural life is to be raised'. On the other hand, he claimed that 'hitherto such education as has been provided has on the whole rather weakened the village. It has done little to adapt the peasants to life and farming in scattered rural communities, and it has tempted the abler of the young villagers away to the towns and to the professions. This has had the additional result that most of the countries of the region were burdened with a restless intellectual proletariat' (PEP 1945: 14–15).

Nevertheless, it is an incontrovertible fact that Europe's most educated peasantries were also its most healthy, dynamic and prosperous ones (mainly to be found in Denmark, Sweden, Finland, Switzerland, the Netherlands and, more recently, in Austria and the Czech Lands). Educated peasants were increasingly receptive to new implements, technologies, cropping practices, seed varieties, building and fencing materials and ideas about sanitation and human and animal hygiene. They were also more responsive to peasant parties, agricultural co-operation and new forms of finance, marketing, food-processing and political lobbying, bringing increased access to rural services and agronomic assistance, and bypassing or squeezing out the most ruthless and manipulative middlemen. By 1937 the number (and membership) of agricultural credit co-operatives was 6,080 (1,440,784) in Czechoslovakia, 3,736 (816,007) in Poland, 1,008 (421,507) in Hungary, 4,638 (905,420) in Romania, 4,283 (414,645) in Yugoslavia and 1,899 (216,538) in Bulgaria, while the number (and membership) of dairying and other agricultural marketing/processing co-operatives was 2,579 (486,385) in Czechoslovakia, 5,176 (1,082,551) in Poland, 22,435 (746,462) in Hungary, 1,906 (219,207) in Romania, 3,204 (233,939) in Yugoslavia and 1,640 (202,256) in Bulgaria (PEP 1945: 154). In addition, the (largely rural) membership of consumer co-operatives was 805,544 in Czechoslovakia, 373,516 in Poland, 127,428 in Hungary, 29,063 in Romania, 86,983 in Yugoslavia and 84,449 in Bulgaria (p. 155).

It needs to be emphasized that, until well after the second World War, the major advances in European peasant farming were *rarely* based on large-scale agricultural mechanization and heavy use of chemical fertilizers. The large-scale machinery pioneered on large American and British farms during the nineteenth century was usually too expensive and in any case unsuitable for use on Europe's peasant smallholdings. The expensive chemical fertilizers pioneered in Prussia were also used much more sparingly by peasant farmers, mainly in kitchen gardens rather than for staple grain crops. Peasants usually felt that the per hectare returns on grain cultivation were too low to justify a heavy use of mineral fertilizers, and they were probably correct. Instead, the major advances in European peasant agriculture up to the Second World War were mainly based on changes in cropping patterns, including the introduction of new crops (such as root crops and legumes) and new higher-yielding seed varieties, and improvements in farm tools and other small-scale equipment. Receptivity to these forms of agricultural innovation was partly a function of farm size and wealth, but was mainly a function of level of the farmer's capacity to reason and to find out about newly available seed varieties, crops, tools and small-scale equipment, by reading seed and equipment catalogues, newspaper advertisements and farmers' magazines. We therefore reject Warriner's view that 'what prevented the peasant from improving their methods was not ignorance' (Warriner 1950: 144). Overcoming ignorance, in our view, was the key to overcoming poverty and 'backwardness'. The expanding peasant membership of agricultural credit and marketing co-operatives (itself closely correlated with rising levels of peasant education and consciousness) also helped to increase awareness of the new farm tools, seed varieties, crops and agricultural techniques. Just as significantly, perhaps, rising levels of education led to increased awareness of the importance of personal hygiene and of the need regularly to change and wash clothes, to boil drinking water, to clean up water supplies, to drain unsavoury, disease-ridden bogs and ditches, to develop safe ways of using or disposing of 'night soil', and to house livestock separately from humans.

Significantly, Tiltman (1934: 70–1) reported that the knowledge and skills needed to carry out the above-mentioned transformation of Bulgaria 'from a predominantly corn-growing nation to a variety of . . . more lucrative forms of cultivation have been supplied by an agricultural education system which is equal to that existing in any other European country. This system has at its apex the Faculty of Agriculture . . . of the University of Sofia and includes four agricultural high schools, fifteen practical agricultural schools (seven or eight of which are reserved for women), thirty winter schools for adult peasants and a network of agricultural continuation schools, of which in June 1933 110 had already been opened out of 800 projected. These continuation schools will, when completed, cover every large village and town throughout the country. Every child who has completed . . . primary school is obliged to attend an agricultural continuation school for two terms of four months each. During these terms, held in winter months, boys are given instruction in modern methods of farming with special reference to the type of cultivation predominating in the region where the school is situated, while girls are taught home-making, cooking, sewing, care of children and the rudiments of hygiene.'

Leaving aside the 'sexism' of these role divisions (which was nonetheless fully consonant with social expectations at that time), interwar Bulgaria was laying the foundations of its subsequent agricultural prowess (1950s to 1970s). Bulgarian achievements in this regard also warn us to beware the temptation to paint too bleak a picture of the interwar Balkans and East Central Europe. There were some patches of light to relieve the gloom. Indeed, the life-style of the Bulgarian peasantry was undergoing a vital transformation. 'The Bulgarian people have been "lifted off the floor" . . . The poorest Bulgarian peasant today generally has his land, his house, some pieces of furniture and his self-respect . . . And with this psychological transformation the health of the people has improved. The death rate, though still high, is falling . . . The peasantry live in modern two-roomed dwellings, often built of designs supplied by the state, and their animals are housed separately. The earth floors have been replaced by brick and wood. There are windows that open . . . Many . . . now sleep on beds and eat sitting at tables. Separate plates for each person have replaced the old communal bowl. Electric light, even, has come to some of the villages' (Tiltman 1934: 83).

In short, Bulgaria's peasants were belatedly entering the twentieth century. However, it has been forcefully argued that even the most marked intensification of agriculture would have only 'half' relieved the agrarian problems of the interwar Balkans and East Central Europe. The other 'half' of the solution (accepting that large-scale emigration had ceased to be feasible) could have come only from faster industrialization. This was the way to increase aggregate demand for higher value farm products, supply increased inputs of fertilizer and farm equipment and remove so-called 'surplus' population from the land (Warriner 1950: xii–xiii, 144; Seton-Watson 1945: 115–17). 'By the nineteen-thirties a large proportion of the peasant population was "surplus" – in the sense that it could have left the land without reducing agricultural production. The size of this surplus population cannot . . . be exactly estimated, since it took the form of half-employment for most of the farm population. But the various estimates that have been made agree that it was large, amounting to between one-quarter and one-third of the total population on the land . . . The pressure of population on the land meant that small farms were divided into ever smaller units. Methods of farming remained primitive, because the peasants were too poor to invest in machinery and livestock, and of necessity kept most of their land under grain . . . For this widespread poverty the only remedy would have been industrialization. But to this the obstacles were shortage of capital and the lack of an internal market due to the poverty of the peasants . . . Peasant poverty therefore created a vicious circle' (Warriner 1950: xii).

Instead of totally rejecting such arguments (which mistakenly equate agricultural advance with mechanization and increased use of chemicals supplied by industry), we would strongly emphasize the other side of the equation. Other than in already highly industrialized Czechoslovakia, rapid town-centred large-scale industrialization *on its own* could have relieved only one half of the agrarian problems of the interwar Balkans and East Central Europe. The other 'half' of the solution needed to come from the intensification of agriculture and from dispersed, small-scale, labour-intensive, rural industrialization: firstly, because capital and industrial skills and 'know-how' were indeed in short supply; and secondly, because it was bound to take two or three decades for Balkan and East Central European industrial sectors and urban infrastructures to become large enough to become capable of fully absorbing the rural 'population surplus' (especially as most industries are intrinsically more capital- and skill-intensive than agriculture). In the meantime, as argued by Balkan and East Central European peasantist parties, it would have been easier, safer and more cost effective to have emphasized the development of peasant agriculture and rural industries *in situ*, rather than to transplant millions of peasants to overcrowded and undercapitalized urban-industrial sectors. Indeed, a great deal hinged upon the forms of industrialization and the types of industry that were to be promoted. The peasantist parties cogently argued that, in peasant societies, industrial priorities and the pattern of industrialization pursued ought primarily to have been geared to meeting the 'basic needs' of the peasantry. This was desirable not only because the latter constituted the vast majority of the population, but also because this would have fostered a harmonious and symbiotic relationship between industrial and agricultural development. Agricultural sectors would have provided markets and raw materials for Balkan and East Central European industries, which in turn would have provided markets and industrial inputs for agriculture, while minimizing infrastructural costs and social upheaval. Indeed, there was 'no need for industrialization in Eastern Europe to lead to the vast unhealthy urban agglomerations that exist in the West' (Seton-Watson 1945: 118). The lopsided emphasis on large-scale, capital-intensive, town-centred heavy industries and mining, favoured by Balkan and East Central European dictators, economic nationalists, Communist parties, military interests and some influential Western development economists (including Doreen Warriner, Maurice Dobb and Alexander Gerschenkron) has proved to be a very dirty and costly mistake, for which the Balkans and East Central Europe are still paying a high social, economic and environmental price.

THE PEASANTIST MOVEMENTS IN THE BALKANS AND EAST CENTRAL EUROPE

Major peasant movements emerged in almost every country in the interwar Balkans and East Central Europe, engaged in a common quest to end 'feudal' landlordism and build in its place a democratic society based on peasant proprietors united in co-operative movements. The natural constituency for peasantism was still considerably larger than that for Marxian socialism, fascism or liberalism. Only in Slovakia, Slovenia, Hungary and Poland did agrarian parties remain strongly under (Catholic) ecclesiastical influence. Only under the reactionary Sanacja regime in Poland (1926–39), under the counter-revolutionary Horthy regime in Hungary (1920–44) and under the repressive Zog regime in Albania (1924–39) did landed oligarchies survive almost intact. But even in Poland and Hungary peasant parties eventually united (in 1931 and 1939 respectively) in support of radical programmes, laying the foundations for their sweeping electoral victories in 1945.

In Czechoslovakia, however, the Agrarians were consistently the largest party in every parliament and in every government from April 1920 to September 1938. This was an impressive achievement. The Agrarian Party became 'so strongly organized, so deeply entrenched in the provincial and local government apparatus, so thoroughly involved in the co-operative and banking systems' that it became the quintessential party of government, 'indispensable to any and every cabinet coalition', without selling out its predominantly peasant clientele (Rothschild 1974: 97). In Romania Iuliu Manin's National Peasant Party (formed by merger in 1926) won a landslide victory in the genuinely free elections of December 1928 (pp. 299–301). Its election platform promised to clean up Romania's corrupt system of government, to dismantle the protectionism that had enriched a few industrialists at the expense of consumers (mainly peasants) and to foster further expansion of rural education, health care, extension services and peasant co-operatives. Last but not least, interwar Croatia was consistently dominated by the Croatian Peasant Party (established in 1904), first under Stjepan and Ante Radic and subsequently under Dr Vladko Macek, while Slovenia was dominated by the Catholic, peasantist and very educative Slovene People's Party and its affiliated credit and marketing co-operatives.

The major exception to the democratic and non-violent precepts and orientation of most of the peasant movements in the interwar Balkans and East Central Europe was Aleksandur Stamboliski's Peasant Union (formerly Agrarian Union, established in 1901), which ruled Bulgaria from October 1919 to June 1923. 'Regarding "the city" and its inhabitants as sinful and parasitical . . . Stamboliski's actions often degenerated into a brutal . . . externalization of hitherto frustrated peasant resentments.' His fascistic paramilitary Orange Guard became the scourge of the 'parasitic' bourgeoisie and of political opponents and rivals, and 'he almost appeared to be less interested in benefiting the peasants than in harassing the other classes' (Rothschild 1974: 338).

Stamboliski and many of his active supporters were wiped out in June 1923 in a very bloody military coup which was actively supported by a vengeful urban bourgeoisie and by nationalist extremists, while the Communists and Social Democrats gloated on the sidelines, relishing the nemesis of their major rival. Stamboliski's only lasting achievements were a very egalitarian land reform (partly reversed by his successors in 1924); a more enduring expansion of rural education, co-operatives and credit facilities; a durable system of compulsory national labour service (in place of military service); and the displacement of private grain merchants by a state grain corporation, although this proved to be a very mixed blessing.

Stamboliski had perpetrated his excesses in the name of the peasantry, comprising about 80 per cent of the population. However, his Peasant Union had obtained only 32 per cent, 38 per cent and 53 per cent of the votes in the 1919, 1920 and 1923 elections, respectively, despite Orange Guard harassment and intimidation of rival parties in 1920 and 1923. Much of the peasantry evidently did not support him, although for a time his excesses brought the peasantry as a whole into disrepute. The whole tragedy was an object lesson in the dangers of basing a movement on violent class hatred and megalomania, rather than a reflection on peasants as such.

In Europe since the late nineteenth century large-scale industrialization and the spread of Marxian socialism had increasingly distanced urban-industrial workers' movements from peasantist movements and fostered often bitter ideological divisions between them. Marxist orthodoxy was too abstract, academic and doctrinaire to elicit much support from independent peasant farmers. It failed to recognize that in countries where peasants still constituted the bulk of the population, economic 'progress' or 'development' would be somewhat meaningless or even fraudulent if peasants did not benefit. However strongly the Marxist parties attacked and criticized specific abuses and disadvantages which weighed heavily on the peasantry, such parties could not lastingly or legitimately win the hearts and minds of a class that they had written off as being hopelessly and necessarily 'doomed' to gradual extinction by large-scale capitalist or socialist industrialization, or of a class which for Marxists epitomized reactionary petit bourgeois attachment to private property and petty capitalism. Marxism and peasantism were worlds apart. Marxists, like capitalists, asked how the land could be made to yield a maximum return with a minimum of labour and sought to maximize economies of scale. Peasants asked how the land could be made to support the maximum number of autonomous peasant and rural industrial households organized in villages and rural co-operatives in order to preserve peasant communities, values, rituals and ways of life. Marxist orthodoxy was coldly economistic, whereas peasantism addressed wider human values and concerns (Mitrany 1951: 50, 126–7).

However much Marxist parties attacked the exploitation, abuses and alienation inherent in capitalist industrialization, they fully intended to move or 'progress' in the same direction as capitalist industrializers, only their industrial society would be under the control of socialists or Communists. It would be capitalist industrialization without the capitalists. The Marxist parties only supported the radical land reforms as temporary political expedients which, by terminating the power of the oppressive and parasitic landlord class, would 'neutralize' the peasantry and clear away potential impediments to rapid large-scale industrialization (and, implicitly, the proletarianization of the peasantry). They rarely showed any interest in radical agrarian reform as a means of giving a new lease of life to peasant agriculture, as they feared that this could only retard the processes of large-scale industrialization and proletarianization upon which orthodox Marxism based its vision of the future. While piously disavowing any intention of ever forcibly dispossessing the peasantry of their vital smallholdings, the Marxist parties remained wedded to the supposedly 'inevitable' and 'progressive' conversion of peasants into proletarians – that is, to a form of 'voluntary euthanasia' for the peasantry as a class!

In contrast, the peasantist movements aspired to move in an altogether different direction, inspired by a different vision of society. They envisaged a 'co-operative society', distinct from both capitalism and Marxist industrial collectivism. In their view full democracy could only be achieved if peasants were to break the political monopoly of the urban and rentier classes, so that society could be governed 'from below' and not 'from above'. Peasants would have to liberate and assert themselves as a class just as other classes were doing or had done.

Representatives of peasant movements in Poland, Yugoslavia, Czechoslovakia, Hungary, Bulgaria, Romania and Greece met in London in July 1942 to produce a joint statement of policies and objectives. It began thus: 'Believing, in the words of the bible, that we are all members of one body, we maintain that the raising of the peasant's standard of life is the necessary precondition for the progress of the whole nation ... The main basis on which a sound and progressive agricultural community can be built up is that of individual peasant-owned farms. We do not, however, believe that the peasant can live in isolation, and we recognize the desirability of voluntary co-operation in land cultivation.' They called for measures to curb land speculation and the mortgaging and distraint of farmland, in order to 'safeguard the peasant against dispossession or alienation of his land'. To overcome fragmentation, 'the holdings of each peasant must be consolidated ... either by voluntary co-operation ... or by machinery set up by the law'. In the peasantist view, 'The strength of the peasantry depends on the strength of their common institutions as much as on their ownership of the land ... The peasants themselves should control marketing, credit and the supply of agricultural equipment by their own institutions, democratically organized.' Co-operative organization 'should be extended to factories for processing agricultural produce, to the markets of the products thus made, to village communities engaged in special types of production and to the promotion of agricultural education'. In areas of rural overpopulation, 'Industries, so far as possible on a co-operative basis, are required to provide the necessary employment. They should be mainly devoted to the processing of local agricultural or forest products. We are convinced that, by these measures, we can raise the standard of living of peasants and avoid excessive concentration of production in large towns.' The statement also envisaged national and international regulation of agricultural procurement prices and the development of comprehensive health care, sanitation, housing, rural banking and insurance, rural electrification, irrigation, drainage, water conservation, hydro-electric power, fertilizer and equipment supply, and seed and livestock improvement schemes. All would combine state support with local and co-operative control and initiatives by the peasants themselves. (The full text of this important document is translated in F. Gross 1945: 113–17.)

Voluntary, democratic intra-village co-operation was expected to address every need of village life, but collective agriculture on the Soviet model was rejected because of its regimentation, its subordination of peasants to the Communist Party, the state and central planning, and its suppression of peasant autonomy, freedom, initiative, rituals and values. Vladko Macek, leader of the Croatian Peasant Party during the 1930s and 1940s, declared that peasants would not happily accept forms of rural collectivism which would 'turn the peasant into a serf of the state', especially where they had only recently freed themselves from 'feudal serfdom'. In his view 'it is possible to turn the village into an economic unit. Every peasant holding produces partly for the needs of the peasant family and partly for the market.' The former 'should remain the business of the peasant family' but the latter was evolving 'towards co-operative production as a common concern of the village as a whole. Where there is a lack of land, new possibilities of earning a livelihood must be created within the village, ranging from home industries to village factories. But the peasant's connection with the land must not be severed, he must not be driven from the soil' (quoted in Mitrany 1951: 116–17, 143).

The very survival of peasant movements and democracy were closely intertwined in the Balkans and East Central Europe. Both were under recurrent threat from the fascist and/or royalist authoritarian right and from the Marxist left, but the peasantist movements remained the highest and most authentic expression of popular and intelligentsia aspirations. The absence of large urban proletariats and Marxist parties, other than in industrialized Czechoslovakia, left the peasantist movements as the major vehicles for political mobilization and radical reform. They attracted the support of much of the radical-democratic intelligentsia, who in turn provided articulate leadership and reinforced their radical-democratic orientation. Balkan and East Central European intellectuals from peasant families increasingly studied, romanticized, took pride in and wrote about their humble rustic origins, which 'formerly they had tried to leave behind them' (Mitrany 1951: 131–3, 141). During the interwar period the Balkans and East Central Europe experienced a Russian-style 'movement to the people' (almost a pilgrimage) by so-called village-explorers, ethnographers, agronomists, folklorists and composers (most famously Bartok, Kodaly and Enescu). There was also a corresponding change in peasant attitudes to rural clergy, village schoolteachers and intellectuals. 'The village now wanted service, not direction, and priests and teachers could retain their influence only in so far as they helped their villagers to work out their problems in their own way' (p. 133).

Unfortunately, except in liberal Czechoslovakia, the peasantist movements did not manage to retain and expand their footholds in government. Poland's two main peasant parties played prominent roles in government between 1920 and 1926. Thus Wincenty Witos, leader of the larger party and an influential political broker, even became prime minister in 1920, in 1923 and again on 10 May 1926. After Marshal Pilsudski's coup on 12 May 1926, however, political power was monopolized by the authoritarian Sanacja (Regeneration) regime until 1939, when Poland was once more 'partitioned' between Germany and Russia. The peasantist parties of Hungary and Bulgaria took years to recover from the 'white terror' that followed the overthrow of Bela Kun's Bolshevik regime in August 1919 and from the bloodbath that accompanied the overthrow of Aleksandur Stamboliski's peasantist regime in June 1923. In Yugoslavia the strength of the peasantist movements remained heavily concentrated in areas inhabited by Croats and Slovenes, thus making few inroads into Serb dominance of central government. In practice their major function was to give the Croatian and Slovene peasantries significant degrees of de facto local autonomy in the face of obdurate Serbian dominance of the Yugoslav state.

The peasant parties undeniably suffered from certain innate handicaps. Most peasants were still poor, uneducated, diffident and difficult to organize. Able young peasants were precisely those most likely to migrate to the towns or to the Americas, although levels of education and consciousness were rapidly rising and the rate of rural exodus was in fact decelerating. But the peasantist movements also fell victim to the singularly vicious conjuncture of world depression, fascism and neo-mercantilism ('beggar-my-neighbour' trading policies). In Romania, for example, the National Peasant Party government was soon riven by dissension over how to cope with the sudden collapse of export and tax revenues and with the deliberately divisive tactics of a king bent on becoming a royal fascist dictator. In the Balkans and East Central Europe, as elsewhere, the Depression and the accompanying decline in tax and export revenues scuppered schemes of democratic social reconstruction by causing public expenditure cuts, widespread financial defaults, increased ethnic tension and irredentism. This provided a fertile breeding ground for both urban and rural fascism. Furthermore, the continuing popularity of the peasantist movements and their proven ability to make effective use of the democratic rights written into most of the Balkan and East Central European constitutions 'frightened the ruling groups as the socialist movement never had done' (Mitrany 1951: 121). It made them prime targets of the political malpractice and persecution perpetrated by monarchs, dictators, fascists and corrupt urban 'machine politicians'. Prominent peasantist politicians such as Stjepan Radic and the former Romanian finance minister Virgil Madgearu (1928–31) were murdered. Others, such as Wincenty Witos and the former Romanian prime minister Iuliu Maniu were imprisoned. Nevertheless, most of the Balkan and East Central European peasantist parties endeavoured to uphold the democratic principles enshrined in their official statutes and programmes. But 'this steadfastness in conduct, this unwillingness to sully their democratic principles, also meant that the peasant parties were unable to check the spreading Reaction while reactionary forces everywhere never hesitated to wreck them by corruption or violence' (Mitrany 1951: 122,

129). Furthermore, although 'no other party or movement could by offering a basis for democratic progress provide a check alike both to fascism and Bolshevism', Western governments made little attempt to bolster the interwoven fortunes of the peasant parties and democracy in the interwar Balkans and East Central Europe (p. 129). The West failed to foresee the terrible price that Europe would pay for these 'sins of omission'. (Such shortsightedness is not entirely a thing of the past.) The Second World War was primarily unleashed by the unchecked advances of fascism in the Balkans and East Central Europe, which led in turn to the post-war Soviet domination of these regions and a new East–West division of Europe.

These political and economic setbacks forced the peasantist movements into a period of intense self-examination and self-renewal from which they were to emerge strengthened in 1945, but not before they had undergone the ordeal of fascist domination, during which millions of peasants demonstrated extraordinary capacities for active and passive resistance. Historically, peasants have been the great passive resisters. During the Second World War, however, peasants also became mainstays of the major Balkan and East Central European resistance movements.

26   The failure of democracy

Looking back over interwar Europe as a whole, one can see that popular expectations had been greatly raised by the consequences of the First World War, the peace settlements, the principle of national self-determination, the proclamation of democracy, the rise of mass movements and the promises of social reform. Unfortunately, these heightened expectations were fulfilled only to very limited degrees during the 1920s, before the battered hopes were finally dashed to pieces by the onset of the 1930s Depression. On a more positive note, most states did enact significant land reforms, broaden the franchise and expand educational opportunities. However, these constructive projects further raised expectations and, overall, the 1920s did not – and indeed could not – live up to the high hopes held out in 1918–19. There were too many conflicting or mutually exclusive desires. Some of the dreams were impossible to fulfil. Moreover, other than in Czechoslovakia, many reforms were bedevilled by corruption, incompetence and economic adversity, while the new regimes and political parties increasingly lost touch with their popular constituencies and succumbed to authoritarian, charismatic or personalistic forms of leadership. Many of the things that were done (or not done) in the name of 'democracy' merely served to bring democratic ideals into disrepute. Many people, not all of whom had innately fascist or Communist leanings, became disillusioned or impatient with the Balkan and East Central European travesties of 'democracy' and yearned for 'strong government', sometimes in order to defend the status quo against perceived threats from 'profiteers', 'speculators', 'aliens', Jews, Bolsheviks or 'anarchists', but in other cases to bring about 'moral' and/or 'national' regeneration and major social, political or economic changes. There were disturbing parallels in Europe's post-Communist states during the 1990s.

Other things being equal, the economic vicissitudes and the changes in popular mood and attitude might have been expected to result in the mushrooming of support for the Communist parties. These very plausibly portrayed the rampant corruption, unrelieved economic hardships, deficiencies of the agrarian reforms, naked oppression of workers, peasants and ethnic minorities, and the growing concentration and abuse of wealth and power as the inevitable consequences of the deepening 'crisis of capitalism', the allegedly fraudulent nature of 'bourgeois democracy' and the growing recourse of capitalism to fascist or quasi-fascist methods of containing the crisis and the attendant intensification of class struggle and inter-ethnic conflict.

In the long run, ironically, nothing did more to enhance the moral and political standing of the (mostly outlawed) Communist parties than the way in which conservative and authoritarian politicians, publicists and ecclesiastics habitually denounced as 'Communist' anyone who campaigned for social justice or who criticized official corruption, speculation, chauvinism, oppression or the abuse and excessive concentration of power and wealth. The constant barrage of anti-Communist invective (emanating from groups that were so blatantly corrupt, chauvinistic, exploitative and oppressive) encouraged many non-Communists to take the Communists more seriously and to accord them increased respect, if only in recognition of their apparent political courage and integrity.

Balkan and East Central European rulers thus unwittingly conferred on the Communist parties a status and mystique out of all proportion to their actual strength and deeds and contributed to the Communists' accession to power after the Second World War.

In the short term, however, the officially orchestrated fear of 'Bolshevism' (encouraged by France and Britain as much as by Nazi Germany and Fascist Italy) meant that the chief beneficiaries of the popular disenchantment with 'bourgeois democracy' and laissez-faire capitalism were the various ultra-nationalist and quasi-fascist movements that emerged in the interwar Balkans and East Central Europe and those rulers in these regions who tried to emulate Fascist and Nazi methods of popular 'mobilization' and government. However, the increasingly fascist or quasi-fascist movements and regimes of the later 1930s and the early 1940s were to prove no more capable of fulfilling popular expectations than supposedly 'democratic' parties and governments had been during the 1920s. By 1942 those Balkan and East Central European states that had been allowed to survive had become mere pawns in the Nazi and fascist plans for Axis domination of Europe. In practice these authoritarian states, which were supposed to be the apotheosis of the 'national' principle, forfeited without a fight all but the outward trappings of national sovereignty. However, while it is all too easy to condemn the puny Balkan and East Central European regimes for accommodating themselves to the hegemonic ambitions of Nazi Germany and Fascist Italy, it should be remembered that the leading 'appeasers' were the governments of Britain and France. Arguably, only these two states were in a position really to stand up to Mussolini and Hitler and to give a lead to others to do likewise. If strong and democratic Britain and France felt unable to face down Hitler and Mussolini before 1939, what chance or reasonable expectation was there that the smaller and more vulnerable authoritarian nationalistic states of the Balkans and East Central Europe should do so?

It can be argued that, having 'called into existence' the new or expanded nation-states of the interwar Balkans and East Central Europe and having determined that the new political order should be based upon the principle of national self-determination, the victorious Western Allies were under some obligation to assist these fledgling states to attain political stability and economic prosperity. Moreover, having rolled back Russia, it was clearly in the interests of the Western democracies to develop the Balkan and East Central European states and economies as counter-weights to Italy and a temporarily emasculated Germany. Otherwise the latter would eventually fill the resultant vacuum in the heart of Europe and again pose a potential threat to the West. Yet during the 1920s Western stabilization loans and private investment went mainly to Germany and Austria rather than to the Balkans and East Central Europe. The stabilization and economic revival of Germany was, admittedly, crucial to the peace and prosperity of Europe as a whole, as John Maynard Keynes had forcefully argued in 1919. But the Western democracies made a fatal error in leaving the Balkan and East Central European states largely to fend for themselves, aside from some small loans and modest Western investment in extractive and processing industries in the region. Indeed, it has been argued that the principal weaknesses of the post-1918 peace settlements resulted not so much from intrinsic defects as from 'the failure of the Allied Powers to make the necessary effort and sacrifices' to uphold and enforce them. These failings were compounded by the additional international tensions and antagonisms generated by the classification of the newly established Poland, Czechoslovakia and Yugoslavia and expanded Romania as victorious Allied states, while Austria, Hungary, Bulgaria and Germany were treated as 'enemy states' and saddled with 'war guilt' and reparations (Mamatey 1967: 234–6).

The Balkan and East Central European states would have been more able to withstand the 1930s Depression and Italian and German blandishments, threats and encroachments if they had been able to attain some semblance of regional solidarity, economic integration and collective security. But this was precluded by 'the multiple divisions and rivalries that were born of competing territorial claims, ethnic-minority tensions, socioeconomic poverty, mutually irritating psychologies and sheer political myopia' (Rothschild 1974: 8). In effect, a strong defensive union of Balkan and/or

East Central European states was rendered impossible by the same factor that had helped to tear asunder the Habsburg Monarchy: 'the conflict between master and subject nations' (Taylor 1976: 257).

The Little Entente established by Czechoslovakia, Yugoslavia and Romania in 1920–1 was primarily directed against Hungarian revanchism, while the Balkan Entente established by Greece, Turkey, Romania and Yugoslavia in 1934 was essentially directed against anticipated Bulgarian revanchism. But there was no provision for joint resistance to potential German, Italian or Soviet aggression. Thus the defensive regional alliances were largely directed against states that were too small on their own to pose much of a threat, rather than against the major potential external threats to Balkan and/or East Central European security. Moreover, the non-participation of Poland, which misguidedly put its faith in its bilateral links with France and non-aggression pacts with the Soviet Union (1932) and Nazi Germany (1934) and rather looked down its nose at the smaller and less 'aristocratic' Balkan and East Central European states, combined with the ostracizing of Hungary and Bulgaria, further reduced the efficacy of these Ententes as possible means of promoting regional unity and co-operation and protecting the Balkans and East Central Europe against German, Italian or Soviet interference and aggression.

In 1936–7 the Czechoslovak premier Milan Hodza actively canvassed the creation of an economic bloc comprising the Little Entente plus Poland, Austria, Hungary and Bulgaria, both to promote closer intra-regional ties and to counter growing German economic hegemony. But Poland, Yugoslavia, Romania and Hungary were afraid of offending Nazi Germany. Moreover, Romania and Yugoslavia were not yet ready for full reconciliation and equal partnership with Hungary and Bulgaria. Yet Hungary expected concessions and improved treatment of the substantial minorities in Czechoslovakia, Romania and Yugoslavia, as preconditions for any Magyar participation in the proposed economic union, which was also viewed 'with misgivings' by Italy and Germany. Only the Austrian government, which was trying desperately to fend off Nazi pressure, welcomed the Czechoslovak initiatives. (Hodza's overtures and negotiations are described in Hodza 1942: 125–39.)

Rejoicing in their recently acquired national independence, the fledgling states of the Balkans and East Central Europe were also extremely reluctant to accept any limitations or reductions of their sovereignty in order to secure greater regional harmony, stability, peace and prosperity. The First World War had ended in acceptance of the principles of untrammelled national sovereignty and self-determination, not supranational confederation, as the foundations on which the new political order in the Balkans and East Central Europe should be built. In the economic sphere, similarly: 'The first efforts of the new states were directed towards making a clean break with their old economic ties and towards attaining as far as possible, complete economic independence. They regarded it as their main task to eliminate . . . the division of labour prevailing in the former empire[s] and to make themselves independent of even those regions which had up till then been their natural market for some goods and their main source of supply for others. The newly independent states quickly walled themselves in with import prohibitions and high protective tariffs . . . Thus the barriers which had been erected to promote self-sufficiency . . . divided the Central and East European states more deeply from each other than from those of western Europe' (Berend and Ranki 1969: 176–7). Trade between the Balkan and East Central European states shrank to 10–15 per cent of their total foreign trade. Conversely, 75–80 per cent of their exports went to western Europe, which in return supplied 70–80 per cent of their imports (p. 178).

Furthermore, extreme political and economic nationalism in many ways impeded the resolution of Balkan and East Central European economic problems, both by diverting precious resources into the creation of tin-pot military-industrial complexes and by further fragmenting ('Balkanizing') the states in these regions into 'national' economic units that were too small to provide adequate markets for state-sponsored import-substituting industrialization. Autarkic economic development was difficult to attain in countries as large and as diversely endowed as the Soviet Union and Nazi Germany, but it proved even more difficult, costly and inappropriate in countries as small as Hungary and Bulgaria.

Nevertheless, despite all the debilitating intra-regional problems and conflicts confronting the interwar Balkan and East Central European states, it can plausibly be argued that 'the fundamental cause of the collapse lies not in the faults of these states, but in the policy of the Great Powers of the West' (Seton-Watson 1945: 412). Rothschild agrees that 'one must assign greater responsibility for the catastrophe of 1939–41 to the malevolence, indifference or incompetence of the Great Powers than to the admittedly costly mistakes of these states' (Rothschild 1974: 25). Moreover, in the opinion of A.J.P. Taylor (1976: 259), the Western Powers 'had nothing to offer eastern Europe except protests; quite apart from military aid, they were not even prepared to assist the shifting of industrial power to Eastern Europe, which is the only solution to "the German question"'.

The US retreat into isolationalism and protectionism during the 1920s and 1930s was mirrored by British and French preoccupation with empire and, in trade policy, the development of 'imperial preference' and protectionism. These inward-looking and defensive outlooks also engendered a 'bunker mentality' in the military sphere, epitomized by excessive French reliance on the notorious Maginot line. It would therefore only be a matter of time before first Fascist Italy and later Nazi Germany advanced into the resultant economic and military vacuums on the Continent, virtually unopposed as Russia had been temporarily sidelined.

Initially the new rulers of the Balkans and East Central Europe thought that they had at last miraculously escaped Germanic hegemony without falling under Russian domination. 'The basis of this miracle was alliance with France.' However, this proved to be one of the great delusions of the interwar system and contributed to the latter's undoing, for it encouraged the new or expanded victor states to rely on the apparent strength of post-1918 France, whereas the French state was in fact looking to its new Balkan and East Central European allies (Poland and the Little Entente) to compensate for its own lack of strength (Taylor 1976: 259). France's Maginot mentality, combined with British and French reluctance to 'guarantee' the new international borders established in the Balkans and East Central Europe between 1918 and 1921 (in contrast to their willingness to extend such guarantees to West European borders in 1925), rapidly reduced the credibility of France's alliance commitments in the East. 'That credibility was finally flushed away by her passive acceptance of Hitler's remilitarization of the Rhineland' on 7 March 1936, after which Hitler could pick off his Balkan and East Central victims one at a time, without fear of French retaliation on his western flank (Rothschild 1974: 8). This also nurtured a belief that he could attain most of his expansionist ambitions without prematurely plunging Germany into all-out war.

Furthermore, instead of reinforcing its military alliances by promoting strong commercial ties, France traded very little with its Balkan and East Central European allies, heavily protected its own agriculture against their staple agricultural exports and obstructed some of their attempts to develop the refining or processing of their own mineral resources, many of which were owned and/or exploited by French companies. Nor did France actively encourage closer commercial ties (let alone economic co-operation and integration) between its Balkan and East Central European allies. The members of the Little Entente maintained closer commercial ties with their 'revanchist' enemy Hungary than they did with each other, while Czechoslovakia and Yugoslavia traded more with Germany and Italy respectively than they did with their Little Entente partners.

Nazi Germany easily established its hegemony over the Balkan and Hungarian economies during the later 1930s by offering them assured markets and seemingly favourable terms for their staple agricultural and mineral exports, in return for payment in non-convertible German marks which could only be held in 'blocked' accounts in the Reichsbank and used only to purchase German products. Indeed, a leading British socialist even ventured to suggest that: 'The peasants of those countries of Southern and Eastern Europe which were most subject to German economic penetration

. . . were perhaps better off with Germany as a market for their produce, even on highly disadvantageous terms, than with no market at all . . . This, as well as the fear among the upper classes in these peasant states of revolutionary uprisings grounded in hunger and despair, explains the ease with which Nazism was able to penetrate their countries both economically and with its political ideas . . . The Germans were in a position to offer a market; and that, on almost any terms of exchange, was better than nothing' (Cole 1941: 73–4).

However, Hungary and the Balkan states (other than Italian-dominated Albania and British-dominated Greece) acceded to Germany's bilateral trading arrangements not just because these were the only economic lifelines that were thrown to them, but also because they fell into the then common error of underestimating the economic and military capabilities and expansionist ambitions of Nazi Germany, while overestimating those of Fascist Italy and the Soviet Union. In practice, despite persistent Soviet hostility towards the 1919–20 peace settlements and the ensuing nationalist and anti-Communist regimes, there was little evidence of serious Soviet territorial ambitions in the interwar Balkans and East Central Europe, other than in response to the German threat from 1939 onward. Hungary and the Balkan states soon became 'utterly dependent on continuing German purchases, supplies, spare parts and infrastructure' (Rothschild 1974: 24). When the world economy and commodity prices recovered somewhat in the late 1930s, under the stimulus of international rearmament, these countries found it much harder to disentangle themselves from Germany's clutches than it had been to enter them. Moreover, they almost certainly failed to recognize the full magnitude of the threat posed by Nazism until it was too late to escape from its suffocating embrace, and even then it took time to appreciate the enormity of the consequences. Only Poland and Czechoslovakia, with their problematic German minorities, proximity to Germany, living memories of German domination and exports that competed with (rather than complemented) those of Germany, felt directly threatened by a resurgent Germany and resisted its economic charms.

All the while British, French and American introversion and their inertia in regard to the Balkans and East Central Europe encouraged *sauve qui peut* attitudes and a fateful belief that the Western Powers increasingly saw the renewed German ascendancy over the region as something natural, positive and inevitable. This in turn induced most of the Balkan and East Central European states to adapt themselves to the new facts of life as best they could. Thus the relative ease with which Nazi Germany established its dominion over these states arose partly from the ideological, economic, ethnic and sectarian fissures and weaknesses of the region, but also from the passivity of the other Powers. These ripening apples essentially fell into Hitler's lap while the Western Powers stood to one side, even if they did not completely avert their gaze. As argued by Warriner (1950: xiv), 'Western Europe so far as it was interested in eastern Europe at all, was interested in keeping it backward, as a source of cheap food and cheap labour.' If the Western Powers had been able to have their way in the Balkans and East Central Europe in 1945–7, 'they would have put back into power the same kind of government which [had] existed before, and whose failure led to Fascism'. During the Second World War they elaborated 'no new policy' for the Balkans and East Central Europe: they supported the émigré governments in London, 'at best, liberal politicians of the old style, at worst, near-Fascists'. It therefore fell to the Communists to break the deeply flawed moulds of the successor states. Indeed, while the Western Powers had learnt little from the failure of the 1919–20 peace settlements in the Balkans and East Central Europe, the Soviet Union and the Communist parties of these regions had learned a great deal: 'Their conception of the future was clear, and so also was their grasp of the strategy of gaining power' (p. xiv).

Warriner astutely observed that the real significance of the Balkan and East Central European revolutions of 1945–50 lay not only in the political transformation, including 'the destruction of the old ruling groups', but also in 'the economic dynamic' that accompanied it. 'What eastern Europe primarily needed was the industrial revolution and, without the shift in the European balance of power resulting from Soviet victory, it would never have come' (Warriner 1950: xiii). There is also much to be said for her view that: 'Democracy needs a middle class to make it work, and in eastern Europe as a whole there was no strong middle class, because there had never been an industrial revolution. The "bourgeois revolution" of 1919 was abortive because there was no wind to fill the sails of the new liberal constitutions. It was only in Czechoslovakia that the new pattern did work, because the country was already highly industrialized and had a strong middle class' (pp. x–xi).

Democracy rests not only on formal rules, safeguards and procedures, but also upon the existence of a multiplicity of independent social groups that are willing and able to defend and uphold civil rights and work against excessive concentration of power and authority in too few hands, while at the same time supporting and accepting the need for viable executive, legislative and judicial institutions and the rule of law. Autonomous social groups can both curb and yet sustain authority by sharing it, that is, acting as intermediaries who constrain one another and the state and yet help to order particular spheres of economic, social and political life. Such roles are by no means confined to the middle classes. Autonomous trade unions and peasant associations are also vital to the maintenance of democratic liberties and dispersed authority. Thus the weakness of most of the trade unions and peasant associations, as well as of the middle classes, strongly contributed to the early demise of democracy in the interwar Balkans and East Central Europe (other than in Czechoslovakia).

Nevertheless, democracy also failed to take root in the interwar Balkan and East Central European states because 'the Western Powers themselves did not support it . . . In reality, Britain and France were concerned with the small nations only as a *cordon sanitaire* against Russia: so long as the dictatorships were anti-Soviet it did not matter if they were also anti-democratic' (Warriner 1950: ix–x). The West hardly protested against the suppression of democracy and the violation of minority rights in Hungary and Bulgaria during the 1920s, and in Poland, Yugoslavia and Romania during the 1930s. To paraphrase Neville Chamberlain's words on his return from Munich in September 1938, these were 'faraway countries' about which Westerners knew little and cared even less. Western governments, newspapers and public opinion have only ever become concerned with the dangers to 'democracy' in the Balkans and East Central Europe when the threats have come from the left rather than from the right, and there have been major prices to pay for the West's persistent double standards.

By late 1939 German economic dominance over the Balkans and East Central Europe was even more complete than it had been on the eve of the First World War, indicating that the geopolitical advantages which accrued to Germany as a result of the replacement of the Habsburg Empire by a collection of much smaller states were matched in the economic sphere (Rothschild 1974: 24). Nevertheless, even though the Hungarian, Bulgarian, Yugoslav and Romanian economies were tightly bound to the German economy by late 1939, their ruling elites initially played 'hard to get' when Hitler endeavoured to translate economic ties into concrete military commitments to the Rome–Berlin Axis between 1938 and 1941. Economic dependence did not automatically engender unflinching military and political subservience (Crampton 1994: 37).

Paradoxically, the fate of East Central Europe and the Balkans was sealed, not by the manifest weaknesses of Poland, Hungary and the Balkan states, but by the demise of the seemingly strong Czechoslovak Republic. Hitler shrewdly singled out Czechoslovakia (rather than Poland) as the weakest link in the encircling chain of potentially hostile states allied to France. On account of its major industrial resources and strategic location, the artificial creation of Czechoslovakia (underwritten by France and Britain) was the keystone of Balkan and East Central European security and the 1919–20 peace settlements. However, Hungary, Poland and Nazi Germany harboured implicit or explicit designs on Czechoslovak territory and, once begun, the dismemberment of Czechoslovakia would destabilize the entire region by fully exposing the fickleness of the French, British, Balkan and East Central European ruling elites and the fragility of Europe's post-1918 frontiers, alliances and balance of power. Moreover, the extremely multinational composition of the

Czechoslovak state was fundamentally at odds with the implicitly 'ethnic' principle of national self-determination around which the 1919–20 peace settlements were formally framed and legitimized. Nearly a quarter of Czechoslovakia's population was German and the eastern half of the country contained large and somewhat disaffected Slovak, Ruthene and Magyar minorities. The ascendant Czechs constituted little more than one-third of the total population, yet they tended to call the shots, dominate public employment and cultural provisions, and resist even the most moderate demands for a federal state. They did so partly out of fear that any substantial concession of federal autonomy to the main ethnic groups or regions would fan rather than douse the flames of ethnic separation, thus jeopardizing the security and cohesion of the state. President Tomas Masaryk (1918–35) and his 'anointed' successor Edvard Benes (1935–8) did their best to promote the ideal of a tolerant multi-cultural state, but they did not succeed in fostering a 'civic' Czechoslovak nation commanding the allegiance and affections of the vast majority of its putative members. Therefore, even though foreign minister Benes issued a diplomatic note on 20 May 1919 claiming that his government's goal was 'to make the Czecho-Slovak Republic a sort of Switzerland' (Wiskemann 1938: 92), he never believed in this sufficiently to commit either himself or his cabinet colleagues to a Swiss-style federation. However, while the Czechs were confronted with an acute political dilemma, many Slovaks felt cheated by the persistent non-fulfilment of their demands for federal autonomy. Since Slovakia was severely lacking in higher education, large towns and modern industries, and had been under Magyar rule even longer than Wales has been part of the United Kingdom, most Slovaks felt little cultural or economic solidarity with the Czechs and primarily aspired to some sort of autonomy within a federalized state. Taken in isolation, Slovak autonomy could conceivably have done more to strengthen than to weaken the cohesion of the Czechoslovak state. The dilemma for the Czechs was that they could hardly concede federal autonomy to the Slovaks without offering the same to the larger, richer and more educated German minority, yet such a concession would have made it easier for a resurgent Germany to prise apart the constituent elements of this multinational state. It is significant that the Slovaks and the Ruthenes won their long-sought autonomy only when the Czechoslovak state was coerced into surrendering its predominantly German-inhabited territories (the so-called Sudetenland) to Germany at Munich in September 1938 and that this was but the prelude to the complete disintegration of interwar Czechoslovakia. The security and cohesion of Czechoslovakia were indeed indivisible.

In the opinion of Milan Hodza, premier of Czechoslovakia from 1935 to 1938, the new order established in the Balkans and East Central Europe in 1918–19 was not a complete failure. In his view, the region had to 'share all the pains of a new Europe which could not succeed in being created in a pacific way by diplomatic channels and which had to emerge out of blood and toil and suffering, like all great achievements and political settlements' (Hodza 1942: 5–6). During the interwar period, Hodza contended, it was 'the noble task of many of the Slav intellectual leaders to open the windows of their peoples' cultural homes to let in the fresh air of Western civilization. The twenty years of political independence meant also cultural self-determination.' This allowed the formerly downtrodden and/or subjugated peoples of the Balkans and East Central Europe to 'quench their burning spiritual thirst' and strike a new balance between 'German and all-European cultural influences' (p. 171). Nevertheless, the problems besetting the new order in the interwar Balkans and East Central Europe were so severe and so numerous that the surprise is not that most of the so-called 'successor states' soon degenerated into authoritarian nationalist, royalist or military dictatorships, but that they nevertheless managed to maintain their sovereignty and territorial integrity for some twenty years before succumbing to Hitler's New Order. Indeed, the most enduring achievement of the successor states was that 'they legitimized their sovereign existence' in the eyes of the world, so much so that neither Hitler nor Stalin succeeded in permanently wiping them off the political map of Europe (Rothschild 1974: 24). During and after the Second World War the international community took it for granted that these states should be re-established as fully sovereign entities at the earliest opportunity, just as it had taken for granted the existence (and the right to exist) of the Habsburg and Ottoman empires in much the same region not long before. The Great Powers have great powers of collective amnesia.

27   The lure of fascism: towards a reinterpretation

During the 1930s almost all the ruling oligarchies in the Balkans and East Central Europe sought authoritarian nationalist and quasi-fascist means of resolving or containing the acute tensions, political pressures and military challenges engendered by the 1930s Depression and the growing power and territorial/hegemonic ambitions of Fascist Italy and (after 1933) Nazi Germany. The growth of protectionism, exchange controls, import and export licensing arrangements, étatist import-substituting industrialization, debt remission and agricultural price support schemes greatly increased state control over the Balkan and East Central European economies. As if introverted and illiberal political and economic nationalism were not enough, most of these states sought additional ideological and geopolitical support and justification for these policies by developing closer economic and political relations with Italy and (from as early as 1932 onwards) Germany. They also began to emulate some of the trappings, style, rhetoric, institutions, cultural policies, political violence, intimidation and 'mass mobilization' techniques of first the Fascist and later the Nazi regimes. Indeed, these were often at least in part defensive tactics or a type of insurance policy, adopted in the (vain) hope of fending off potential external political interference, military threats and/or territorial encroachments by submitting to the economic wishes and political tutelage of the emerging fascist Powers.

Nowadays, for obvious reasons, Mussolini's ambitions in this region are less well known and are usually taken less seriously than those of Adolf Hitler. At least until the mid-1930s and possibly until 1940 or 1941, however, Mussolini's much-trumpeted military 'might' was widely overestimated and Fascist Italy was (with some justification) perceived to be posing the major immediate threat to the Balkan states, along with the rather exaggerated 'Soviet threat'. Fascist Italy harboured imperial designs upon Albania, Dalmatia and large swathes of Slovenia, Croatia, Bosnia, Macedonia and Greece, hoping to replicate the Roman dominance and 'civilization' of the Balkans in ancient times and to turn the Adriatic and the Aegean seas into 'Italian lakes' once more. Mussolini also aspired to a domineering and protective patron–client relationship with the rulers of Austria, Hungary, Romania and Bulgaria. Fascist Italy aimed to fill the power vacuum in the Balkans, south-central Europe and the eastern Mediterranean created by the demise of the Austro-Hungarian and Ottoman empires. To this end it aided and abetted Hungarian, Austrian and Bulgarian 'revisionism' and authoritarian-corporatist tendencies, as well as Macedonian nationalist and Croatian fascist terrorism.

The ruling oligarchies also often resorted to the creation of fascist or quasi-fascist states in the hope of heading off, undercutting or politically 'neutralizing' potential threats and challenges from the more wayward, anarchic and violent fascist and quasi-fascist movements which were emerging in most of the Balkan and East Central European states, most notably Corneliu Zelea Codreanu's violent and unruly 'Iron Guard' in Romania (see pp. 387–8, 395–6) and Ferenc Szalasi's 'Arrow Cross' in Hungary (see pp. 388, 439–42). Concurrently, Roman Dmowski's National Democrats (who constituted Poland's main opposition party) were becoming increasingly fascist in their ideology, rhetoric, leadership cult, authoritarianism, anti-Semitism and use of paramilitary affiliates, youth movements and other 'mass mobilization' techniques, posing an analogous challenge to the increasingly fascist 'colonels' regime' (1935–9). Alignment with Fascist Italy also gave the small but very violent Croatian Catholic-fascist *Ustasa* movement (founded by Ante Pavelic in 1929) some hope of eventually taking Yugoslavia apart and creating an 'independent' fascist state of Croatia strong enough to incorporate large chunks of Bosnia, Herzegovina, Serbia and Montenegro. Moreover, for gym teacher Konrad Henlein's neo-Nazi *Sudetendeutsche Partei* (which suddenly mushroomed into the major political party of Bohemia's self-styled 'Sudeten Germans' in the mid-1930s) and for the Catholic-nationalist and increasingly fascist Slovak People's Party (which became Slovakia's major political party during the interwar years), the birth of Nazi Germany translated into a practical possibility the dream of dismembering Czechoslovakia. Likewise, for the 'revisionist' states of the Balkans and East Central Europe (Hungary, Austria and Bulgaria), political and economic alignment with the emerging fascist Powers transformed the prospects for wholesale 'revision' of the hated 1919–20 peace settlements from hopelessly unrealistic pipe-dreams into imminent practical possibilities and held out the promise of a total subversion of the victors' 'new order'.

The awesome power, dynamism, ruthlessness and successes of Italian Fascism and German National Socialism clearly encouraged the increasingly authoritarian nationalist, royalist and military regimes that were emerging in the Balkans, East Central Europe, the Baltic States, the Iberian Peninsula and Latin America to foster fascist or quasi-fascist movements, institutions and one-party systems, both in order to capitalize on fascism's apparent capacity to inspire, unite, reinvigorate and mobilize 'the nation' (alias 'the people') and in the hope of eliminating or neutralizing more violent, radical and subversive challenges 'from below'. 'States of lesser power, especially new or restored states, generally take as their model the political institutions and values of the seemingly strongest and most successful Great Power of the day' (Rothschild 1974: 21). After 1933 Western parliamentary democracy seemed increasingly effete, ineffectual and adrift, in contrast to the apparent strength, dynamism and sense of purpose of the fascist states. To the admirers of Mussolini and Hitler fascism became the *Zeitgeist*, the Spirit of the Age, the wave of the future.

However, it is often argued that the fascist or quasi-fascist parties, institutions and organizations created 'from above' by more traditional authoritarian rulers (often co-opting state officials, army officers and leaders and personnel of established and 'respectable' political parties) were fundamentally different from the more autonomous, active, radical, 'mobilizatory' fascist movements and parties that 'conquered power' for their leaders and active supporters. 'All imitations of fascism and its style could not hide the essentially different spirit' (J. Linz 1979: 21). The most widely favoured explanation for this alleged fundamental difference is the contention that, although a number of Balkan, East Central European and Baltic states seemed to offer 'fertile ground' for fascism, they had not yet attained either the 'minimum degree of political freedom' or the requisite 'level of economic, social, cultural and political development' that would have allowed fascism to develop into an organized, disciplined 'mass movement'. Moreover, 'the urban classes that could have provided the ideological leadership of fascist-type movements were, as state bourgeoisies, too closely tied to the bureaucratic, military, professional and commercial establishment' (p. 49).

In a similar vein, Hugh Seton-Watson (1945: 257) contended that the dictatorships which emerged in the interwar Balkans and East Central Europe were 'not Fascist regimes in the proper sense of the word'. From 1938 to 1940 King Carol II of Romania 'tried to ape Fascism' through his (single-party) Front of National Rebirth, but it 'never succeeded in raising the minimum of popular enthusiasm necessary for Fascism'. At the same time: 'Specifically Fascist movements, such as the Polish National Radicals, the Hungarian Arrow Cross Party and the Romanian Iron Guard, failed in their purposes. The Eastern European Dictatorships relied not even on artificially stimulated popular enthusiasm, but on police pressure . . . These regimes had no such basis of support as those of Hitler or Mussolini. They were able to survive because they had a firm grip on the bureaucratic and military machines, because the peoples were backward and apathetic, and because the bourgeoisie would always support them in case of need. Certainly a part of the bourgeois and intellectual classes suffered from these regimes . . . But if ever the regime were radically threatened from below, the great majority of bourgeois and intellectuals would rally round it' (p. 257).

These authoritarian regimes may have proclaimed national unity, moral regeneration, non-party objectivity and strong government, but in Seton-Watson's view they were 'no more than greedy, corrupt and brutal class regimes'. Their leaders were 'stupid, timorous, dishonest and pettily cunning men' who, when faced with major internal and international problems, 'could only hesitate, temporise and take the line of least resistance' (Seton-Watson 1945: 156). According to Joseph Rothschild, the Balkan and East Central European dictatorships 'would not or could not emulate the totalitarian dynamism of Hitler . . . Their commitments were essentially bureaucratic and conservative, at most technocratic and oligarchical. Projecting no mass ideology, they either failed or refused to elicit mass support. Despite their sonorous rhetoric . . . they proved petty, brittle, often irresolute' (Rothschild 1974: 21).

Thus we seem to have come to a fork in the road. Either we can adhere to a narrow, uniform, 'purist' conception of fascism, which would carry the very misleading implication that fascism as such was a relatively marginal, extraneous, peripheral phenomenon in the interwar Balkans and East Central Europe. Or we can uphold a broader, more variegated conception of fascism, which would allow us to include the seemingly (and often self-avowedly) fascist movements, organizations and regimes in these regions among the diverse 'national' varieties of fascism that emerged in Europe between the wars. This would make possible a greater appreciation of the multifaceted nature of European fascism, as well as the pervasive impact and significance of fascism in the interwar Balkans and East Central Europe. Both approaches raise conceptual difficulties. But it will be argued that, on balance, the second approach has decisive advantages.

THE LIMITATIONS OF THE 'PURIST' APPROACH

The 'purist' approach starts from the premise that 'true' unadulterated Fascism (with a capital 'F') was a uniquely Italian phenomenon which could not be replicated outside Italy, just as 'pure' undiluted National Socialism was a uniquely Germanic response to peculiarly German and Austrian problems, preoccupations and ideological currents. This conveniently allows the 'purists' to discount or play down the significance of the increasingly fascist pretensions and proclivities of the dictatorships, political parties, movements and organizations in the Balkans and East Central Europe which openly proclaimed their adherence and political indebtedness to fascism, on the (questionable) grounds that these were not 'the real McCoy'. The 'purist' approach thus makes it much easier to maintain the (not always innocent) impression that fascism was essentially an extraneous, skin-deep phenomenon in the Balkans and East Central Europe and to contend that it was in essence a peculiarly Italian and Germanic malady which was 'imported' into or even 'imposed' as a result of increasing Italian and German domination of these regions. Thus one of the standard texts on fascism maintains that 'the right-wing dictatorships of interwar Europe lacked many of the essential ingredients of fascist regimes. Poland, Romania, Greece and Yugoslavia were ruled by varying forms of military dictatorships of a conservative type which, although they suppressed the left, never went as far as the totalitarian dictatorships of the fascist type.' The fascist movements of the Balkans and East Central Europe 'remained on the fringe of the radical right until, in some cases such as Hungary, Croatia and Slovakia, they gained power thanks to German armies of occupation. They were thus imported regimes which did not reflect the social structure and political dynamics of the countries which they dominated' (Kitchen 1976: 88).

Such wholesale discounting of the self-avowedly fascist movements and regimes which emerged in the Balkans and East Central Europe during the late 1930s and early 1940s is misleading and unsound. Rather, the methods, institutions and illiberal nationalist ethos of government throughout the interwar Balkans and East Central Europe were steadily degenerating into distinctive 'eastern' forms of fascism, with the partial exception of Czechoslovakia (this was only a partial exception, because Slovakia and the so-called Sudetenland had spawned movements which helped to usher in fascist regimes in 1938–9). This process of degeneration was driven not only by circumstantial factors, such as the 1930s Depression, widespread economic misery and the rise of Fascist Italy and Nazi Germany, but also by the inherent flaws in the new order erected in the Balkans and East Central Europe after the First World War. Avowedly fascist movements and individuals were infiltrating and/or influencing the entire machinery and ethos of most of the Balkan, Baltic and East Central European states, which in turn increasingly sponsored and/or adopted such movements in order to bolster their legitimacy and authority and to mobilize more active and widespread support. Thus fascism, far from being an alien, marginal or 'imported' phenomenon, was becoming an increasingly pervasive, hegemonic ideology and *Weltanschauung* in this part of the world. The notion that the fascist regimes which emerged with German support in Hungary, Croatia and Slovakia were merely 'imported regimes which did not reflect the social structure and political dynamics of the countries which they dominated' is actually quite preposterous. However, it perfectly illustrates the contortions and distortions into which 'purists' are forced by their vain attempts to uphold narrow and restrictive conceptions of fascism and to 'explain away' other avowedly or seemingly fascist phenomena that fall outside their rigid definitions. It is necessary to reject 'the familiar procedure of first arbitrarily elevating either the Italian or the German experience of fascism to paradigmatic stature and then focusing a quest for the "essence of fascism" upon whichever movement is felt to embody this essence most completely. A method of this kind inevitably ends with results which are as arbitrary as the point from which it began' (O'Sullivan 1983: 40–1).

To be fair, Kitchen added that, although Nazi Germany and Fascist Italy furnished 'the best examples of fascism in action', it would nevertheless be 'a serious mistake to limit a definition of fascism to these two forms', for that 'would make it impossible to analyse fascist dangers in the present day' (Kitchen 1976: 88). Yet this did not prevent him from discounting the authenticity of the fascist features of *most* of the regimes established in the Balkans, East Central Europe and Austria during the late 1930s and early 1940s, on the spurious grounds that some (but by no means all) of these regimes emerged as a result of the presence and support of German military forces. In the few cases where the latter really did play crucial roles, one can point to a very pertinent and instructive parallel: no one even dreams of arguing that the Balkan and East Central European regimes which emerged partly or even mainly as a result of the presence and support of Soviet military forces in the region after the Second World War were *ipso facto* not genuinely Stalinist. Moreover, even if they were in large measure alien or 'imported' regimes, there is no denying that they soon succeeded in harnessing and mobilizing considerable indigenous 'activism' and support, as also occurred under some partly 'imported' fascist regimes, such as the Tiso regime in Slovakia (late 1938 to early 1945) and the fascist *Ustasa* regime in Croatia (1941 to early 1945). In common with many 'purists', Kitchen also expressly denied the fascist credentials of Salazar's avowedly corporative *Estado Novo* in Portugal, Franco's dictatorship in Spain, the Metaxas regime in Greece, the Peronist regime in Argentina and 'the dictatorships of the underdeveloped world' (pp. 88, 91). However, while it is always correct to question whether this or that regime really was fascist, it is difficult to see what other fascist regimes he has in mind, when he has discounted all the prime candidates! Indeed, even more than Linz, Kitchen insisted that 'Fascism is a phenomenon of developed industrial states. If capitalism has not reached a certain level of development, the particular relationships between classes which are characteristic of fascist movements are not possible. Only in advanced capitalism can there be a powerful capitalist class, a large and organized working class with a potentially revolutionary ideology which calls for a radical restructuring of society, and a large petite bourgeoisie which is caught in the contradictions between capital and labour and is unable to find any way out of its social, economic and political dilemmas' (p. 83).

If these widely accepted stipulations are correct, then 'genuine' fascism was largely impossible in the interwar Balkans and East Central Europe – other than in the highly industrialized Czech Lands, which did indeed produce one of the most popular and impassioned fascist movements, in the form of Konrad Henlein's Sudetendeutsche Partei. However, Kitchen's rather rigid quasi-Marxist insistence on a particular 'threshold' level of capitalist development as a precondition for real fascism runs up against a number of fundamental objections. Most absurdly, it would appear to preclude the possibility of genuine fascism in the actual birthplace of fascism! Italy, the 'mother country' of fascism, was not much more industrialized, educated or capitalist than East Central Europe (and less so than either the Czech Lands or German Austria). Indeed, large-scale industrialization only got under way in Italy in the mid-nineteenth century and accelerated in the 1880s and 1890s, more or less concurrently with East Central Europe and only two to three decades ahead of the Balkan states (excluding Albania). Not until the 1930s did industry's share of Italian national income overtake that of agriculture (partly because agricultural prices fell more than industrial prices) and it was not until the 1950s that industry's share of the Italian workforce surpassed that of farming. Within Italy, moreover, the main strongholds of Fascism were not in the relatively industrialized, educated, class-conscious and capitalist north. There the relatively large and strong working class strove to remain loyal to the beleaguered left-wing parties and trade unions in the early 1920s, while big business and the bourgeoisie were strongly orientated towards Giovanni Giolitti's Liberal Party. Only the big northern landowners actively courted the Fascists, by employing them as bailiffs and bully-boys to beat up 'Bolshy' tenants, share-croppers and farm workers. The political bastions of Fascism were in Emilia, Tuscany and central Italy, areas with a preponderance of small-scale artisanal and market towns. Here droves of young 'action hungry' ex-servicemen, unemployed persons, students, lapsed or disillusioned socialists, malcontents, blacklegs and plain thugs joined the seemingly radical and dynamic Fascist *squadri* (squads) and, with money, vehicles and weapons supplied by reactionary and apprehensive property-owners and state officials, set about crushing the 'Red Peril' in the early 1920s by breaking boycotts and strikes, attacking socialist and trade union offices, print-shops and meetings, or hunting down and beating the life out of socialist workers and radicalized share-croppers. In one sense, Fascism was an enormous Mafia-style protection racket which (almost inevitably) got out of control and not only terrorized its intended victims, but soon started blackmailing and intimidating its well-to-do sponsors and taking over the state. Ironically, the Fascists found it hardest to penetrate southern Italy, as this was already 'sewn up' by longstanding local patronage, intimidation and protection racketeering networks (including, of course, the Sicilian Mafia). By their very nature, however, these patrons and protection racketeers were ready to co-operate with and 'deliver' support to whoever controlled the central government in Rome, in return for certain 'favours' and a free hand in local affairs (at least until they were 'bought off' by US money in 1942–3, to facilitate the Allied landings and advances in southern Italy).

One can in fact stand Kitchen's thesis on its head. As emphasized by William Kornhauser (1960: 197–8), 'the most highly developed capitalist societies have experienced the smallest fascist movements and the strongest commitments to democratic values on the part of the business community, and . . . it has been in the less industrial countries (e.g. Italy) and in countries in which the state assumed a major responsibility for industrial development (e.g. Germany) that fascist movements have been strong and have commanded at least some business support'. Moreover, the burgeoning of extremist mass movements (whether of the right or the left) has mainly occurred during the early stages of large-scale urbanization and industrialization (particularly if these began as eruptive rather than gradual processes), before the towns, factories and labour movements increased their capacity to absorb numerous new entrants into the urban population, workforce and organizations capable of effectively defending their new class interests. These early phases of urbanization and industrialization were the ones in which the greatest social deprivation and disruption, discontinuity of community and family life, and disorientation of helpless individuals were most likely to occur (pp. 125, 145, 150–8).

Furthermore, although Kitchen's views are often couched in a pseudo-Marxist language, 'true' Marxists would be the first to insist that degrees of 'ripeness' for fascism should be judged on an international rather than a narrowly national basis, that is by assessing the economic, social and political conditions, trends and balance of forces in the whole or large parts of Europe rather than in each individual country separately considered.

In the final analysis the 'purist' approach is not very useful. It essentially ducks the difficult questions posed by the existence of more widespread and clearly recognizable 'fascist' or 'quasi-fascist' phenomena. Arguably it is an intellectual cop-out. For, even if it were to be generally accepted that the term 'fascism' ought only to be applied to the Italian Fascist movement and regime and possibly to the German Nazi movement and regime, it would then become much harder to come up with satisfactory labels and explanations for the 'quasi-fascist' or 'para-fascist' phenomena which are often (in a broader sense) characterized as 'fascist'. As argued in one of the most influential books on fascism: 'There is evidently an imperative need for a term for those political systems (and their corresponding strivings) which differ as much from the democratic-parliamentary type as from the Communist, yet which are not merely military dictatorships or conservative regimes' (Nolte 1969: 569).

This statement is particularly pertinent to the Balkan and East Central European dictatorships of the later 1930s and early 1940s, most of which developed into much more ferocious, far-reaching, militant, 'mobilizatory', activist, anti-Semitic and therefore 'fascistic' polities than the relatively complacent, corrupt and self-serving conservative-authoritarian military, monarchical or nationalist regimes from which they had emerged, like monstrous insects out of hairy chrysalides. Kitchen conceded that after the First World War 'there were movements in almost all European states which showed distinct fascist tendencies. They rejected the idea of parliamentary democracy. They opposed the organized working class . . . they were violently nationalistic. They subscribed to a vague anti-capitalism. They preached submission to authority, discipline and an irrational sense of community' (Kitchen 1976: ix).

Labels such as 'quasi-fascism', 'para-fascism', '*ersatz* fascism' or 'pseudo-fascism' are cumbersome and unduly dismissive, often failing to do justice to either the dangers or the importance of the phenomena so described. Furthermore, narrowly restricting the use of the term 'fascism' to Italy and possibly Germany does not make the more widespread cognate phenomena 'go away'. They still have to be explained. In varying degrees, moreover, they shared or participated in the broader European trends towards increasingly illiberal and belligerent nationalism, xenophobia, anti-Communism, étatism, autarky, corporativism, authoritarianism, the cult of the 'infallible' and charismatic plebeian leader, the glorification of war and conquest, the promotion of martial values, the routine use of electoral and governmental violence against actual or potential opponents and rivals (including initial coalition partners and dissident elements within fascist movements and regimes) and an 'activist' and 'mobilizatory' style of politics, which were also the principal hallmarks of 'fascism'. Hence one might as well call them 'fascist'. Accordingly, our preferred approach is to recognize not only the pertinent 'local' differences between Italy, Germany, East Central Europe, the Balkans, the Baltic States and the Iberian Peninsula, but also the existence of a widespread twentieth-century phenomenon to which the term 'fascism' has been aptly and fruitfully applied (initially by the Marxists who were its first targets, victims and consistent ideological opponents). This broad-brush approach usefully allows us to treat the avowedly fascist parties, movements and regimes that were emerging in the interwar Balkans and East Central Europe as *sui generis* national or regional variants of fascism, 'creatively' adapted to local conditions.

FASCISM VERSUS GERMANIC NATIONAL SOCIALISM

In important respects Italian Fascism had more in common with kindred movements and regimes in the Balkan and Iberian peninsulas and East Central Europe than it did with Germanic National Socialism. As remarked by one of the most influential writers on fascism and so-called 'totalitarianism': 'After the First World War, a deeply anti-democratic . . . wave of semi-totalitarian and totalitarian movements swept Europe; Fascist movements spread from Italy to nearly all Central and Eastern European countries . . . yet even Mussolini, who was so fond of the term "totalitarian state", did not attempt to establish a full-fledged totalitarian regime and contented himself with dictatorship and one-party rule. Similar non-totalitarian dictatorships sprang up in prewar Romania, Poland, the Baltic States, Hungary, Portugal and Franco Spain' (Arendt 1966: 308–9).

Some of the dictators (including Mussolini) would certainly have liked to have established 'totalitarian' regimes and even boasted that they were in the business of doing so. In truth, however, these countries were not sufficiently strong or populous to enable their rulers to engage in 'total domination': 'Without much scope for the conquest of more heavily populated territories, the tyrants in these countries were forced into a certain old-fashioned moderation lest they lose whatever people they had to rule' (Arendt 1966: 310). These 'tinpot' dictators had to husband their meagre resources and simply could not afford to take either such extreme measures or such enormous gambles as the much more powerful and ruthless Nazi regime did. The dictatorships of the smaller and less powerful states had to be more cautious, circumspect and ready to compromise, in order to preserve their more limited power. The Nazi propaganda minister Joseph Goebbels noted in his diary in 1942 that Fascism was 'nothing like National Socialism. While the latter goes deep down to the roots, Fascism is only a superficial thing.' Similarly in 1943 a speech by the Nazi SS leader Heinrich Himmler declared that 'there is absolutely no comparison between Fascism and National Socialism as spiritual, ideological movements . . . Fascism and National Socialism are two fundamentally different things' (both quoted in Arendt 1966: 309). While Mussolini's Fascist movement was content to seize power and establish the Fascist 'elite' as the uncontested rulers of Italy, the more fanatical, formidable, 'totalitarian' Nazi movement was never content to rule by external means alone. The Nazis devised and discovered coercive, ideological and judicial techniques of 'dominating and terrorizing human beings from within', as did the Stalinist regime in Soviet Russia (pp. 323–5). This gave them much more 'total' or pervasive political, economic, social and cultural control.

The more typical goal of most fascist movements and regimes, including Mussolini's Fascists and the kindred movements and regimes which emerged in the Balkans and East Central Europe during the 1930s and early 1940s, was merely to gain control of government and fill all major and minor public offices with party members, in order 'to achieve a complete amalgamation of state and party'; hence the supposedly 'ruling' party became merely 'a kind of propaganda organization for the government. The system is "total" only in a negative sense, namely in that the ruling party will tolerate no other parties, no opposition and no freedom of public opinion' (Arendt 1966: 419). This type of one-party dictatorship normally 'leaves the original power relationship between state and party intact; the government and the army exercise the same power as before, and the "revolution" consists only in the fact that all government positions are now occupied by party members' (p. 419). Thus the ruling party's power only comprises its monopoly or near-monopoly of public office, rather than any absolute supremacy of the party over the state. By contrast, the more radical and 'totalitarian' Nazis, like their Communist cousins, consciously strove 'to maintain the essential differences between state and movement and to prevent the "revolutionary" institutions of the movement from being absorbed by the government' and thereby becoming politically emasculated (p. 419). For Arendt, one of the distinguishing features of the more 'totalitarian' regimes is that 'all real power' and decision-making is concentrated in the higher echelons of the ruling party rather than in 'the state and military apparatuses', which become increasingly pliable instruments in the hands of the party leadership (p. 420). Therefore the frequent observation that fascist or neo-fascist parties never achieved absolute supremacy over state and military institutions in the increasingly authoritarian nationalist regimes in the Balkans and East Central Europe during the late 1930s and early 1940s does not in itself constitute evidence that these regimes had not become fascist. It merely reinforces the view that they were in important respects closer to the original Italian Fascist model than was Hitler's much more 'totalitarian' Nazi regime.

Italian Fascism was spawned by a semi-agrarian, semi-industrial, semi-educated and strongly clientelistic society with an unchallenged monarchy, a commanding and relatively autonomous Catholic Church, powerful and aggressive propertied classes, and an overweening and corrupt state bureaucracy. In southern Italy the poorest and least educated sections of Italian society continued to be dominated by big landowners and/or mafias (by origin, protection racketeers) and remained relatively inaccessible or unresponsive to Fascism. In order to win and retain power Mussolini had to adjust to these constraining 'facts of life', which to the end remained strong enough to prevent the Fascists from attaining a 'total' ascendancy over Italian society. The Fascists were therefore never able to achieve a 'total mobilization' of Italian society and resources, to Mussolini's occasional chagrin, and the human resources at his disposal always left much to be desired. This was to be the crucial 'Achilles heel' of Mussolini's regime, especially during the Second World War.

This was much more like the situation in the increasingly authoritarian and fascist states of the Balkans and East Central Europe than the one in Nazi Germany. Like his Balkan and East Central European counterparts, Mussolini found it necessary and/or expedient to seek accommodations with the 'powers that be', namely the established Church, the monarchy, the military establishment and the propertied classes. More out of weakness than any innate preference for 'moderation', Mussolini had been forced into formal recognition of their continuing spheres of autonomy and their paramount influence over important aspects or sectors of national life. For example, the Catholic Church continued to enjoy ecclesiastical autonomy and exercised increased control over educational and family matters after the Lateran Treaties of 1929. Indeed, Italian Fascism always had to contend with the rival authority, influence and legitimacy of the Roman Catholic Church, which (however much it consorted with the Fascist regime or professed to be 'above politics') continued to preach its own distinctive doctrines, values and codes of conduct. These were fundamentally at variance with those of Fascism. In Fascist Italy, as in several Balkan and East Central European states (but unlike Nazi Germany), the fascist movement and the *Führerprinzip* even had to co-exist or 'co-habit' with a monarchy whose legitimacy pre-dated and thus owed nothing to that of fascism. Constitutionally the King of Italy still out-ranked Il Duce and, in the last resort, Vittorio Emanuele III could dismiss the Fascist leader from prime ministerial office (as he eventually did, with the formal approval of the Fascist Grand Council, in July 1943).

The crucial result of all this was that in Fascist Italy, as in the increasingly authoritarian and fascist states of the Balkans and East Central Europe, there remained significant elements of pluralism and spheres of relative autonomy which the fascists never managed to suppress completely. This in turn allowed the continued expression of dissent within and between the various segments of the political, military, bureaucratic, ecclesiastical and social 'establishment', as well as the emergence of a substantial wartime opposition and resistance movement which drew significant support from dissident members of the 'establishment' and the propertied classes. Indeed, fascism was accepted with less conviction, with less fanaticism, or in a more conditional, calculated and opportunistic manner in Italy than in Germany. The same can be said of the Balkans and East Central Europe. Thus in 1943, when the Axis Powers began to suffer major military reverses, key sections of the population began to turn against fascism in Italy, as in the Balkans and East Central Europe and unlike Nazi Germany. The less extreme (that is, less 'totalitarian') nature of Italian and Balkan and East Central European fascism was what made possible the eventual emergence of widespread, open, internal opposition to fascism there (Kolinsky 1974: 59–60).

German National Socialism, by contrast, was a product of one of Europe's most advanced and highly educated industrial societies, with neither a monarchy nor a preponderant 'national' church (the Germans being divided between Roman Catholicism and several Protestant churches). Germany also had a somewhat discredited landed nobility, military hierarchy and state bureaucracy and a severely curtailed and restricted military establishment, as a result of its defeat in 1918 and the punitive Versailles Treaty of 1919. It was therefore relatively easy for the Nazis to 'reach' and penetrate all sectors of German society and to establish Nazi hegemony over the state apparatus and large sections of the propertied classes, the churches and the armed forces during the 1930s. The fact that most Germans were much more educated than most of the inhabitants of Italy, East Central Europe and the Balkan and Iberian peninsulas seems to have made them more (not less) susceptible to fascism. Indeed, about one-third of the (half million) officials and leaders of the Nazi Party in 1935 were teachers by profession. Support for National Socialism, extreme nationalism and pan-Germanism was particularly marked among university students and professors (Kolinsky 1974: 87–8). One-quarter of the future SS elite had doctorates, while in the elections to student councils in German universities during the academic year 1930–1 Nazi candidates received 40 per cent or more of the votes cast in fourteen of the eighteen universities for which such data survive, and 50 per cent or more of the votes in nine of them (Kornhauser 1960: 188). It does not necessarily follow that all highly educated people were inherently susceptible to fascism, but students and university professors were very strikingly over-represented within most of the major fascist movements, including those of the interwar Balkans and East Central Europe (Seton-Watson 1945: 142–5, 195, 206–7; Carsten 1967: 183; Weber 1964: 90–1, 97; Linz 1979: 26, 53). Intelligentsias had long been purveyors of extreme forms of cultural and ethnic nationalism in Germany, Austria, the Baltic States, and the Balkans and East Central Europe. These 'national intelligentsias', which had discovered or invented 'the nation' and propagated national myths, were the groups most likely to get excited or up-in-arms over nationalist issues. The less educated classes tended to be preoccupied by more mundane bread-and-butter problems, aspirations and discontents. Thus large doses of education were not in themselves likely to encourage rejection of fascism. On the contrary, the almost uniformly high standards of education and the consequent cultural unity and technological prowess of the German people helped the Nazis to achieve a more 'total' control and mobilization of German society and resources than was possible in either Italy or the Balkans and East Central Europe at that time. Thus, although about 150,000 Germans died as a result of their opposition to Nazism, German resistance remained 'fragmented, individualized; it never attained the public force of an open resistance movement' (Kolinsky 1974: 59).

There were also significant doctrinal differences between Fascism and National Socialism which emphasized or reinforced the closer affinities between the Italian and Balkan and East Central European varieties of fascism. Mussolini repeatedly put forward the goal of a 'corporative' society, conceived in ways that drew upon (but also perverted) anarcho-syndicalist as well as Catholic social doctrines. On his own admission, 'in the great river of Fascism are to be found the streams which had their source in Sorel, Péguy, in the Lagardelle of the *Mouvement Socialiste* and the Italian syndicalists who between 1904 and 1914 brought a note of novelty into Italian socialism' (Mussolini 1932: 168–9). Mussolini's 'corporative' doctrine did not aspire to abolish or transcend social classes. Instead, it purported to defuse class conflicts by enmeshing the entire working population in a sector-by-sector network of 'syndicates' or 'corporations' (representing employers, employees, the self-employed, the major professions and the state), within which terms and conditions of work were to be negotiated and conflicts resolved by a combination of conciliation and arbitration. 'Fascism recognizes the real exigencies for which the socialist and syndicalist movement arose, but, while recognizing them, wishes to bring them under the control of the state and give them a purpose within the corporative system of interests reconciled within the unity of the state. Individuals form classes according to the similarity of their interests; they form syndicates according to differentiated economic activities within these interests' (pp. 166–7). Moreover, according to the Charter of Labour promulgated by the Fascist Grand Council in April 1927, 'only the juridically recognized syndicate which submits to the control of the state has the right to represent the entire category of employers or workers for which it is constituted, in safeguarding its interests vis-à-vis the state and other occupational associations, in making collective contracts of work binding on all the members of that category, in levying contributions and exercising over its members functions delegated to it in the public interest . . . The Labour Court is the organ by which the state intervenes in the settlement of labour disputes . . . after the corporative organ has first made an attempt at conciliation' (pp. 184–5).

Mussolini also eulogized the Italian 'nation' and 'race' and Italy's age-old contributions to European civilization, but he nearly always did so in cultural, historical, non-biological terms. More tellingly, he presented the Italian 'nation' and 'race' as a creature and servant of the state, rather than vice versa: 'Against individualism, the Fascist conception is for the state . . . Fascism reaffirms the state as the true reality of the individual . . . For the Fascist, therefore, everything is in the state and nothing human or spiritual exists, much less has value, outside the state. In this sense Fascism is totalitarian . . . It is not the nation that generates the state . . . Rather the nation is created by the state, which gives the people . . . a will and therefore an effective existence . . . The keystone of Fascist doctrine is the conception of the state . . . For Fascism the state is an absolute before which individuals and groups are relative . . . It is the state alone that grows in size and power. It is the state alone that can solve the dramatic contradictions of capitalism' (Mussolini 1932: 166–7, 175–7).

Thus, far from seeing the Fascist 'corporative' project as being uniquely applicable to Italy or as something only realizable by a 'master race' with markedly superior 'racial characteristics', Mussolini proudly proclaimed it to be 'exportable' and applicable to other countries, especially those with strong 'corporative' or syndicalist traditions of their own. Otherwise it would have been hard to sustain Mussolini's characteristically extravagant claim that 'the Corporative System is destined to become the civilization of the twentieth century'. For many the appeal of the 'corporative' model was very seductive. It purported to offer a constructive 'third way' between Communism and laissez-faire capitalism. It conjured up visions of social unity and harmony in place of class division and strife. It facilitated and reinforced industrial and agricultural collusion, cartelization, monopolistic practices and protectionism. It seemed to offer greater long-term job security for those in work. It made it easier for fascists, nationalists, syndicalists, social Catholics, social monarchists and technocrats to work together, under the illusion that they were all united in a common cause. Some of its proponents even claimed that the 'corporative' system was a form of 'functional' or 'producers' democracy', purportedly superior to corrupt, phoney and divisive parliamentary democracy. Lastly its seemingly universalist, collaborationist, consensual rhetoric appeared to convert the naked coercive power of fascist regimes into legitimate authority, thereby conferring an aura of legitimacy and respectability on regimes which in reality rested on regimentation, repression and intimidation (O'Sullivan 1983: 132–7; Kolinsky 1974: 56–8; Kitchen 1976: 50–5). Significantly, Mussolini's 'corporative' rhetoric did indeed evoke positive responses and some emulation in the Balkans, East Central Europe, Austria, Portugal, Spain, Belgium and France (especially under Marshal Pétain's Vichy regime).

Mussolini's 'corporative' project is often glibly dismissed as 'little more than an elaborate ideological facade' (Kolinsky 1974: 56, 117) or 'merely a further enhancement of Mussolini's dictatorship' or 'only a technique for extending state control over society' or 'nothing more than the most ordinary protectionism' (O'Sullivan 1983: 136). According to Kitchen (1976: 51–2), 'The "corporative state" never existed in fact, for there was no new economic policy, no fundamental change in the structure of the economy . . . and no real authority to the *Consiglio delle Corporazioni* or to the minister of corporations . . . They remained subordinate to the traditional bureaucracy.' In Kitchen's view, Fascist 'corporativism' was merely a means of controlling labour, while granting private monopolies and cartels a free hand to control prices and restrict competition to their own advantage (pp. 52–5). If that were the case this would explain *part*, but not all of the considerable appeal of the Fascist 'corporative' project outside Italy.

It is significant that Palmiro Togliatti, the long-serving leader of the Italian Communist Party and one of the more discerning 'fighters' against Fascism, took the Fascist 'corporative' project rather more seriously. In a series of lectures delivered in Moscow in 1935 he warned fellow Communists that 'corporativism is not only a propaganda tool, a demagogic slogan fascism uses for the masses, but is also a reality: corporativism is the organizational form fascism has given and is endeavouring to give to Italian society and especially to certain aspects of the activity of the state' (Togliatti 1976: 87). 'It is no accident that the Catholic Church and the Vatican substantially accept Italian corporativism and that in Austria, where fascism is bound more closely to the Catholic Church than in Italy, fascism has immediately set about rebuilding the state apparatus on a corporative basis' (p. 91). In Togliatti's view, 'fascist corporativism' was a conservative, capitalist attempt to develop a conservative, capitalist means of 'overcoming' the interwar 'crisis of capitalism' (p. 93). Viewed from another angle, and recalling 'the creation of the committees for industrial mobilization that organized the economy for war' during the First World War, 'the corporative structure is the groundwork for an organization of production keyed to war' (pp. 102–3). At the same time 'the corporations are an instrument for the ideological propaganda of class collaboration', for 'the destruction of every democratic liberty' and 'for suppressing any attempt by the working masses to liberate themselves' (p. 103).

The Nazis, by contrast, propounded and implemented more extreme 'totalitarian' concepts of the 'organic' state, the *Führersprinzip* and *Gleichschaltung*, that is total subordination of the entire institutional complex of society to a single focus of power and authority (Kolinsky 1974: 91). Instead of belonging to various sectoral 'syndicates' or 'corporations', each of which would preserve the particularism of individual trades and professions (in the manner of medieval guilds), the entire workforce was to belong to a single German Labour Front with 25 million members, controlled by a single overarching bureaucracy (pp. 92–3). As emphasized by Werner Sombart in his book on *German Socialism* (1934), the Nazi goal was 'a total ordering of the German *Volk*' which would be 'uniform, born of a single spirit and extended from a single central point systematically over the entire social life' (quoted by O'Sullivan 1983: 132). In the Third Reich membership of separate social classes was (eventually) supposed to be superseded by total immersion in and subordination to an 'organic', racially 'purified' nation conceived as a single organism and *Volksgemeinschaft*. The Nazis upheld an essentially racial (*völkisch*) conception of an economy and society in which only the 'Aryan' Nordic/German 'master race' would be fully eligible to participate and 'realize itself'. For Mussolini the state was paramount and nations, social groups and individuals could only have the meaning, value and existence with which the state endowed them. For Hitler, however, 'the state is only a vessel and the race is what it contains. The vessel can have meaning only if it preserves and safeguards the contents. Otherwise it is worthless' (quoted by O'Sullivan 1983: 173). Thus Hitler's racial ('biological') conception of society was the very opposite of Mussolini's essentially non-racial, socio-economic, statist and almost universalist 'corporative' project.

In the Fascist conception of the state and society there were autonomous or semi-autonomous state and 'corporative' institutions which stood between the Leader and his people, mediating and implicitly constraining his purportedly absolute power and authority. By contrast, Nazi ideology posited a wholly direct unchecked, unmediated relationship between the Führer and his nation. In more traditional dictatorships the dictator makes no claim to be the 'tribune' or representative of the people over whom he rules. However, in Nazi ideology the Führer was not merely the sole representative and 'tribune' of the people, but also the direct embodiment of the nation and the national 'will'. This, rather than any state office or title he might hold or the process by which he rose to pre-eminence, was the source of his legitimacy and absolute authority. State institutions derived authority and legitimacy from the Führer, rather than vice versa (O'Sullivan 1983: 156–8). However, the Führer 'depends just as much on the "will" of the masses he embodies as the masses depend on him. Without him they would lack external representation and remain an amorphous horde; without the masses the leader is a nonentity.' Hitler trenchantly expressed this relationship between the Führer and the nation in his speech in Berlin on 30 January 1936: 'All that you are, you are through me; all that I am, I am through you alone' (Arendt 1966: 325).

In Italy, as in the Balkans and East Central Europe, fascism was also a response to the political fragmentation and weakness of the bourgeoisie. This was cogently explained by Palmiro Togliatti in an article published in *L'Internationale Communiste* on 5 October 1934: 'The Italian bourgeoisie did not possess a strong political organization before the advent of fascism.' There was a multiplicity of political parties, 'but they mainly had an electoral and local character, without well-defined programmes, and from the standpoint of political organization and cadres they were insubstantial'. During the late nineteenth and early twentieth century Italy's leading 'bourgeois' politicians, especially Giovanni Giolitti, had been 'anxious not to create strong bourgeois parties equipped with a well-defined programme and solidly organized, but on the contrary to impede the formation of such parties. Their art of government consisted, rather, in breaking up the existing parties and forming a parliamentary majority through compromises, corruption, manoeuvres etc.' However, when this mode of bourgeois hegemony and government was challenged by the emergence of more solid, disciplined, programmatic mass parties (such as the Socialist Party and the Catholic Partito Popolare), the 'bourgeoisie's whole system of government was thrown out of kilter'. In the ensuing crisis, 'Fascism . . . set itself the task of creating a solid, united political organization of the bourgeoisie . . . Fascism has given the Italian bourgeoisie what it had always lacked, namely a strong, centralized, disciplined, *single* party equipped with its own armed force' (Togliatti 1976: 137–8). There was a gap to be filled and the Fascists set out to fill it. This almost exactly mirrored the political situation in the fledgling states of the Balkans and East Central Europe, where the political parties of the bourgeoisie were even more fragmented, unstable, corrupt, manipulable and weak, and was quite unlike the political situation in Weimar Germany which had several strong and well-organized programmatic political parties representing the bourgeoisie. In this respect, therefore, the rise of Fascism in Italy was more closely paralleled in the Balkans and East Central Europe than in Germany. Such a contention does not rest on the banal thesis that fascism was simply created by the bourgeoisie in an endeavour to override a serious crisis in its rule and/or the capitalist system. Rather it suggests that, among other things and with varying degrees of success, Italian and Balkan and East Central European fascists saw (and sometimes seized) some golden opportunities to make themselves *the* party of the 'national' bourgeoisie, by thrusting themselves into the political limelight, by mobilizing new political constituencies and by viciously attacking Marxist labour movements (and/or vulnerable ethnic minorities), thereby seizing the political initiative, 'calling the shots' and violently upstaging or usurping the customary 'prerogatives' of the older 'bourgeois' parties.

Fascist ideologists and the first Italian writers and foreign commentators on the emergence of Italian Fascism initially presented it as a uniquely Italian response to peculiarly Italian problems, preoccupations and ideological currents and as a consummation of Italy's belated and incomplete national unification, industrialization and debut as a European Power. Very soon, however, Italian writers, foreign observers and the Fascists themselves noticed the emergence of similar movements and manifestations in other parts of Europe and commented on their affinities with Italian Fascism (Linz 1979: 19). While claiming to have developed a uniquely Italian synthesis of Catholic, corporative, syndicalist and nationalist traditions, the Fascists were at the same time only too pleased to be seen as the pioneers and pace-makers of a major new trend in European politics. This boosted their self-importance and vanity. Thus in 1932 Mussolini boasted that, just as 'the nineteenth century has been the century of Socialism, Liberalism and Democracy', so 'this century may be that of authority, a century of the "Right", a Fascist century' (Mussolini 1932: 175). 'If every age has its own doctrine, it is apparent from a thousand signs that the doctrine of the present age is Fascism' (p. 178). 'Fascism . . . has . . . the universality of all those doctrines which, by fulfilling themselves, have significance in the history of the human spirit' (p. 179). This was indeed the form in which fascism permeated the 1930s Balkans and East Central Europe. Thus the frequent denials that the purportedly fascist movements and regimes that emerged in the Balkans and East Central Europe during the 1930s and early 1940s were genuinely fascist rest not only on an unwarranted 'purism' concerning the nature of fascism, but also on exaggerations of the *affinities* between Italian and German forms of fascism as well as the *differences* between the Italian, Balkan and East Central European varieties of fascism. In many ways, therefore, the relationship of German National Socialism to Italian Fascism was one not so much of kinship as of rival poles of attraction; and identifying the important differences between Fascism and National Socialism helps to highlight the greater similarities between Italian Fascism and the 'lesser fascisms' that emerged in Austria, the Balkans, East Central Europe and the Iberian Peninsula, without which there would not be much point in employing the word 'fascism' as a generic term.

Indeed, despite the racial overtones of Balkan and East Central European 'integral'/'ethnic' nationalism, xenophobia, anti-Semitism and 'ethnic purification' programmes, it seems that Mussolini's non-racial statism, activism, voluntarism and corporativism had more of an appeal among Balkan and East Central European fascists and authoritarian rulers than did Hitler's much more dangerous racial doctrines, with their insistence on the primacy of (spurious) 'racial' characteristics and considerations, on the attainment of (bogus) 'racial purity' and 'racial hygiene', on the mass extermination of Jews, Gypsies and other alleged 'vermin' and 'degenerates', and on the Germans as the supposedly Aryan 'master race'. The incumbent authoritarian nationalist rulers in the Balkans and East Central Europe clearly had more to gain from Mussolini's étatism, activism, voluntarism and corporativism, which could buttress their power and authority and mobilize the population 'from above' in support of state-sponsored projects and objectives, than they did from Hitler's potentially much more wayward, subversive and destructive racial doctrines, 'racial determinism' and 'eugenics'. Moreover, the easiest and most promising way for fascists to achieve 'hegemony' over Balkan and East Central European states and societies was by 'infiltrating' and slowly taking over the existing ('ready made') authoritarian nationalist regimes from within, gradually making them their own and further intensifying their increasingly fascist features and spirit: a 'top-down' strategy, leading to a form of 'fascism from above' rather than 'fascism from below'. Fascists did not need to overthrow democracy in the Balkans and East Central Europe, as it was already being curtailed for them by frightened monarchs and military rulers. Czechoslovakia, the major exception, was surrendered to the Axis Powers by the frightened British and French governments in September 1939.

Among the Balkan and East Central European countries, only the Croatian fascist *Ustasa,* the Romanian Iron Guard and General Ion Antonescu's National Legionary State enthusiastically emulated Hitler's mass extermination policies. However, *Ustasa* genocide was directed not so much against Jews and Gypsies as against Orthodox Serbs, in operations intended to achieve the 'ethnic cleansing' (using a modern term) of a Greater Croatia. The motivation derived more from vicious and fanatical 'integral' or 'ethnic' nationalism than from real racialism. Indeed, the *Ustasa* found it impossible to identify consistent 'racial' or 'biological' differences between Croats and Serbs, who had been formed from much the same Balkan 'melting pot' and even used the same spoken language (Serbo-Croat). Therefore they were often able to distinguish Serbs (and Bosnians and Jews) from Croats only on the basis of religious rather than 'ethnic' affiliation or spurious 'racial characteristics'.

The pervasive stench of virulent religious, economic, political and sometimes racial anti-Semitism was the only major respect in which Balkan and East Central European fascism can be said to have resembled Hitler's National Socialism more than Mussolini's Fascism. Unlike the contrived and half-hearted anti-Semitism adopted by Italian Fascism after 1938 (from fear of being upstaged by the Nazis), Balkan and East Central European anti-Semitism was 'home spun', not an 'alien' importation. Polish, Romanian, Hungarian, Slovak, Croat and Ruthene 'integral nationalism' had become rabidly anti-Semitic by the mid-1930s, well before these countries fell under German domination. Polish, Romanian and Hungarian Jews were subjected to official restrictions and occasional pogroms and their positions became increasingly vulnerable and insecure. By the time of the German invasion of Poland in September 1939, one in three Polish Jews had been beggared by punitive taxation and a government-backed boycott of all Jewish economic establishments (see Crampton 1994: 174–6 and Heller 1977, although these claims are disputed by Davies 1981b: 240–6 and Marcus 1983). Ironically, if Nazi Germany and the Soviet Union had not invaded Poland in September 1939, it is quite conceivable that 1930s and early 1940s Poland would now be remembered primarily for its own severe maltreatment of the Jews, rather than for the heroism, courage and tenacity of the Polish resistance to the German occupation and the terrible sufferings which most Poles were forced to endure. Nazi Germany and the Soviet Union inadvertently saved Poland's reputation. The premiership of the virulently anti-Semitic Hungarian national socialist Gyula Gömbös from 1932 to 1936 was mercifully cut short by his premature death in 1936, but Hungary's Jews were subjected to even more dangerous and life-threatening anti-Semitic measures from 1938 onward – and only partly under pressure from Nazi Germany.

Balkan and East Central European anti-Semitism was nasty and bestial, but it was also calculating and opportunistic. It was inspired mainly by envy, xenophobia, blinkered anti-capitalism and anti-Communism and muddle-headed Christian vindictiveness, rather than by pseudo-scientific racial doctrines, but among some Croatians and Romanians it attained levels of ferocity and fanaticism comparable to Hitler's lethal, pseudo-biological, racialist fanaticism.

RIVAL CONCEPTIONS OF FASCISM: METHODS, IDEOLOGY AND 'STYLE'

There is remarkably little agreement as to which political parties, movements and regimes deserve to be labelled 'fascist', just as there has been no agreed definition of fascism and no consensus on its 'natural constituency', what it stood for or where it was located in the left–right spectrum. It cannot simply be bracketed with conservative nationalist parties and regimes committed to a stout defence of the status quo, as fascism was often quite radical and vociferously opposed to the established political, social and international order. Many of its most active adherents were attracted to it as a purportedly radical (or even revolutionary) movement or regime which would establish a 'new order' substantially different from the status quo. Yet there is no generally accepted threshold beyond which authoritarian nationalist movements or regimes can clearly be said to have become fascist. The former 'shade off' into the latter.

The form, orientation and content of fascist parties, movements and regimes were not 'predetermined' by the existence of a 'revered' common body of scriptures and doctrines, a standard constitutional template and rule book, and an overarching international organization and 'papal' authority, in the way that their Communist counterparts were. Unlike Stalinism, fascism was not a monolithic phenomenon. In one sense, of course, every manifestation of fascism was of necessity unique, reflecting the particular conjuncture of forces and events in each country and in the Continent as a whole at the time of its emergence and of its subsequent struggle for political power and popular support. Each exploited and drew upon its own specific national roots, traditions, preoccupations, ideologies and political, social, cultural and economic context. Fascism was, to a large extent, nationalism taken to extremes. In this respect, however, the seminal Italian and German variants were *no more* unique than any other form and they differed from one another just as fundamentally as they did from the other varieties. The tendency for analysts of fascism to make this self-evident and inevitable national uniqueness of the various forms of fascism a pretext for 'purism' is not only a cop-out. It is also an implicit admission that these analysts are unable to distinguish between the general and the particular and to recognize that each unique national manifestation of fascism was just one of many possible variants or expressions of a more general and deep-seated twentieth-century phenomenon, brought about by a distinctive new stage in the development of European capitalism (according to most Marxist analyses of fascism) and/or by the rise of increasingly illiberal and extreme forms of nationalism, racism, political 'activism' and 'mass' politics, tending towards (but rarely achieving) more 'totalitarian' forms of governance and 'mass mobilization' (according to many liberal analyses of fascism).

Consequently, any manageable and readily comprehensible conception or definition of something as diverse and multifaceted as fascism is inevitably partial. But this need not be an unmitigated disadvantage. One of the main functions of any coherent and illuminating definition is to 'edit' complex and variegated phenomena so as to make them more manageable and intelligible to the human brain. By considering and making use of various different definitions of fascism it is possible to draw out or focus attention on various important aspects or dimensions of the phenomenon. But it is unlikely that any single definition can ever encompass every major facet and manifestation of fascism. Indeed, attempts to construct all-inclusive composite definitions of fascism tend to become either too bland (by focusing on the lowest common denominators) or too complicated and unwieldy. Either way the results tend not to be very enlightening. Linz (1979: 25) unwittingly illustrates the contortions and difficulties involved in any serious attempt to construct a comprehensive, composite definition of fascism: 'We define fascism as a hypernationalist, often pan-nationalist, anti-parliamentary, anti-liberal, anti-Communist, populist and therefore anti-proletarian, partly anti-capitalist and anti-bourgeois, anti-clerical or at least non-clerical movement, with the aim of national social integration through a single party and corporative representation not always equally emphasized; with a distinctive style and rhetoric, it always relied on activist cadres ready for violent action combined with electoral participation to gain power with totalitarian goals by a combination of legal and violent tactics. The ideology and above all the rhetoric appeals for the incorporation of a national cultural tradition selectively in the new synthesis . . . with new organizational conceptions of mobilization and participation.'

This is not only unwieldy, but also misleading, as not all these specific ingredients were present in every plausible example of a fascist movement and/or regime, while the important socio-economic aspects of fascism are not even mentioned. One can learn more about fascism by considering the implications of several more partial conceptions or definitions, taking only one or a few strands at a time, than by reaching out for more comprehensive or all-inclusive definitions of fascism. Our preferred procedure will not yield a consistent and coherent overall picture of fascism, but this faithfully reflects the fact that fascism really was a very eclectic, incoherent and contradictory phenomenon. Indeed, it is often described as a rag-bag or mish-mash of half-baked phobias, precepts and crude ideas. That is why no one is in a position to lay down the law on what did or did not constitute 'true' fascism. It is nonsensical to try to be 'purist' about something so eclectic and incoherent. It is more fruitful to consider its appalling diversity and many-sidedness.

Significantly, one of the crucial tasks of any effective fascist leader was to hold the disparate elements together by creating and sustaining the illusion that the 'ideas' he put forward and the movement he led were coherent. He mainly did so by embodying or drawing together all the potentially conflicting strands in his own person and by concentrating fascist phobias and hatreds on a single 'arch-enemy' (usually the Communist, the Jew or the Communist-Jew). In *Mein Kampf* (1925) Hitler shrewdly observed that the 'art of leadership . . . consists in consolidating the attention of people against a single adversary and taking care that nothing will divide that attention . . . The leader of genius must have the ability to make different opponents appear as if they belong to one category.' Otherwise, if 'the vacillating masses find themselves facing an opposition that is made up of different groups of enemies, their sense of objectivity will be aroused and they will ask how it is that all the others can be in the wrong and they themselves, and their movement, alone in the right' (quoted in O'Sullivan 1983: 125).

It is often emphasized that most fascist movements, including Mussolini's Fascists and Hitlers's Nazis as well as those in eastern and south-western Europe, were ready 'to enter into coalitions' and 'make compromises with the Establishment, to gain access to power' (Linz 1979: 27). This was by no means peculiar to the Balkans and East Central Europe. 'In both Italy and Germany the old political leaders thought that they could bend the Fascist movement to their purposes' (Kolinsky 1974: 119). This would usually prove to be an awful delusion, but by the time they realized their mistake it was often impossible to turn the clock back.

During their ascent to power, fascists often found themselves allied with illiberal conservatives in defending and celebrating the virtues of the nation, the family, hierarchy, order, discipline and patriotism 'against common enemies perceived as undermining these institutions and values', even though fascism was nevertheless 'bent on revolutionizing their content in ways which would eventually transform, marginalize or sweep away conservative elites' (Griffin 1993: x). Fascist leaders, including Mussolini and Hitler, received crucial help from members of the ruling elites and from high-ranking army officers. 'Without this, there would have been . . . no Mussolini government. Without the support rendered by the Bavarian government and army, the National Socialists would not have become a mass party . . . in the early 1920s. Later, the ambiguous role of the *Reichswehr* leaders and their deep contempt of the [Weimar] Republic proved of inestimable value to Hitler, as did the financial contributions which he received from certain industrialists' (Carsten 1967: 234).

The scenario was broadly similar in the Balkans and East Central Europe. Thus the Romanian Garda de Fier (Iron Guard) 'would not have become a mass movement if it had not been supported for a time by King Carol and industrialist circles', while 'in Hungary the army provided invaluable help for the Fascists' (Carsten 1967: 234–5). However, Carsten also emphasizes that 'the Fascist movements did aim at a fundamental change of the political structure . . . and replacement of the [old] ruling groups by a new elite', even though they continued to make extensive use of 'the old experts, civil servants and generals' once in power. Nevertheless, the balance of power increasingly shifted from the old elite to 'new leaders who often came from entirely different social groups, far below the level of the old ruling classes. The Fascist "revolution" was not fought out in the streets and on the barricades, but in the ministries and government buildings' (p. 236).

In these *crucial* respects, the differences between the increasingly fascist regimes of the Balkans and East Central Europe and those of Italy and Germany were merely ones of speed and degree. The former got off to a slower and more hesitant start and some of the Balkan and East Central European fascist movements may have had less public support, resulting in a slower and more tentative displacement of power from the old elites to the fascists. Nevertheless, the basic direction and dynamics were fairly similar.

THE GROWING BASES OF SUPPORT FOR FASCISM IN THE BALKANS AND EAST CENTRAL EUROPE DURING THE LATE 1930S

In December 1937, in the last 'free' Romanian general election of the interwar period, Corneliu Zelea Codreanu's Iron Guard officially gained 15.6 per cent of the vote, while Alexandru Cuza's anti-Semitic and ultra-nationalist League of National Christian Defence obtained a further 9.2 per cent, taking the combined fascist and quasi-fascist vote to nearly 25 per cent of the total, on a 66 per cent turn-out (Rothschild 1974: 310). However, 'the actual fascist vote was well above that percentage. In fact, the King's decision . . . to hand over the government to the right-wing coalition of Octavian Goga and A.C. Cuza was a clear reflection of his realization that the country was leaning toward the extreme right' (Fischer-Galati 1971: 117).

In May 1939, in the first Hungarian election held under secret ballot, the votes obtained by the various 'fascist and national socialist parties' added up to about 37 per cent of the total (Barany 1971: 77). Indeed, the 250,000-member Arrow Cross (the largest of these parties) on its own gained 25 per cent of the vote and the outbreak of the Second World War strengthened 'hopes for a total fascist transformation coming from above, from the government' (Ranki 1971: 71).

In the Czechoslovak parliamentary election of May 1935, 62 per cent of the so-called 'Sudeten German' vote went to the neo-Nazi Sudetendeutsche Heimatfront, which had been established in 1934 by an insanely ambitious gymnastics instructor called Konrad Henlein. In the summer 1938 municipal elections, after Hitler had annexed Austria and begun to stake claims to the so-called 'Sudetenland', Henlein's party won an extraordinary 91 per cent of the German vote (a very rare attainment in freely contested elections).

These voting statistics considerably understate the true magnitude of the base of public support for fascism in the interwar Balkans and East Central Europe. Overt electoral support was really just the tip of a very dangerous iceberg, because Balkan and East Central European 'integral nationalism' and modes of government were also becoming increasingly fascist during the mid- to late 1930s. This was most strongly the case in Hungry, Romania, Poland, Bulgaria and Greece, as in nearby Austria and the Baltic States. Only the Czechs (and to lesser degrees) the Albanians and Serbs clearly resisted the lure of fascism.

Even where fascist movements did win public office, the apparent inability of the liberal parliamentary democracies to deal effectively with the daunting structural economic, social, political and ethnic problems of the interwar period left openings for fascists to set the agenda and call the shots. To many people it appeared that 'the Devil had all the best tunes'. The fascist parties and regimes appeared to be the ones which could get things done and put the unemployed back to work (or at least get them off the streets, whether into barracks or jails or back to the land). The fascist 'ethos of power' seemed to signify a capacity for regeneration.

RIDING THE TIGER: THE CASE OF ROMANIA, 1938–41

In the last resort, just as Mussolini and Hitler crushed the socially radical wings of their own movements once they had gained state power, so some Balkan and East Central European rulers were prepared to crush the anarchic and potentially subversive autonomous fascist movements if this seemed necessary for the preservation of 'order'. For example, when faced with the growing strength of Corneliu Zelea Codreanu's wayward Iron Guard (see pp. 387, 395–6), Romania's King Carol inaugurated a one-party 'corporative' state headed by himself. This was modelled on Antonio Salazar's Christian authoritarian coporativist *Estado Novo* in Portugal, rather than on Hitler's Germany or Mussolini's Italy, and was regarded as far too conservative by the radical and wayward Iron Guard (Ioanid 2000: 43). Carol appointed the 'hypernationalist' Orthodox Patriarch Miron Cristea to the office of prime minister, while independent political parties and movements were banned and gradually suppressed. In the ensuing crackdown, hundreds of Guardists were imprisoned and/or murdered. Codreanu himself was imprisoned in April 1938 and then garrotted (along with thirteen fellow Guardist prisoners) the following November, supposedly 'while trying to escape'. However, many of the Guardists who survived this repression became hell-bent on avenging the deaths of these 'martyrs' by murdering their opponents and rivals as well as Jews.

In September 1939, emboldened by Hitler's lightning conquest of Poland, a group of Guardists assassinated King Carol's principal 'strongman' Armand Calinescu, who as interior minister had spearheaded the crackdown on Guardists in 1938 and had succeeded the deceased Patriarch Cristea as premier in March 1939. Calinescu's death was followed by further repression of the Iron Guard, with many more dead Guardists becoming revered 'martyrs' and 'saints' laid up in various Orthodox churches (Carsten 1967: 189). In early 1940, however, under mounting pressure from the Axis states (whose ranks he had refrained from formally joining), King Carol allowed thousands of Guardists to be released from prison or to return from exile and to join his one-party regime, whereupon they began to avenge the deaths of the Guardist 'martyrs' by murdering sundry royalists, Communists and Jews.

The uneasy alliance between Carol and the Iron Guard soon unravelled, partly because the Soviet Union occupied and annexed Bessarabia (present-day Moldova) and northern Bukovina on 28–30 June 1940. The USSR had reserved the 'option' to do this in secret clauses attached to the notorious Nazi–Soviet Pact of August 1939, even though northern Bukovina had never before been part of a Russian state or empire, Bessarabia had been Russian-controlled only from 1812 to 1918, and the inhabitants of both regions were largely ethnic Romanians. The hasty forced withdrawal of Romanian security forces from Bessarabia and northern Bukovina 'was a heavy blow to Romanian prestige and triggered severe reactions', including numerous killings of Romanian Jews – mainly by angry and/or disgruntled Romanian soldiers, 'but sometimes by Romanian or Ukrainian mobs' (Ioanid 2000: 38–40). Even though hardly any Romanian Jews belonged to the tiny and unpopular Communist Party of Romania (which then had fewer than a thousand members) and most Romanian Jews were deeply fearful of the implications of these Soviet annexations and what they might portend for the future, Romanians increasingly associated Jews with Communism and blamed them for Soviet misdeeds (p. 39). At least 450 Romanian Jews were killed in Galati and Dorohoi in late June and early July 1940, and Romanian anti-Semites started expelling Jews from Moldavia's rural areas during July and August 1940 (Ioanid 2000: 41–3, 61).

Even worse followed. Hitler forced King Carol to cede northern Transylvania to Hungary on 30 August 1940 and South Dobrudja to Bulgaria on 7 September 1940. Romania had now been deprived of one-third of its previous population and territory. These losses completely discredited King Carol in the eyes of his subjects – left, right and centre. Fearing for his life, he either decided to go into exile or was forced to do so by the head of the armed forces, General Ion Antonescu, and by the Iron Guard. Carol abdicated his throne to his nineteen–year-old son Mihai (Michael), who thereupon appointed General Ion Antonescu as premier, with full powers to govern as he saw fit, and the Iron Guard leader Horia Sima as deputy premier. (Hitchins 1994: 445–55, 476; Ioanid 2000: 43). However, although Antonescu managed to preserve what was left of the Romanian state, he did so at the price of *completely subordinating* it to the needs and ambitions of the Third Reich – not only as its principal supplier of crucial petroleum, but also as an important provider of imported food and raw materials for the German war effort and as the 'southern anchor of the German eastern front' (Hitchins 1994: 456–8).

On 14 September 1940 General Antonescu and the Iron Guard proclaimed a 'National Legionary State', in which Antonescu adopted the title of *Conducator* (Leader) and the Iron Guard was to be the only legal party. At first the elated Iron Guard appeared to have the upper hand over the dejected military, who had been humiliated and demoralized by the unchallenged dismemberment of Greater Romania (Rothschild 1974: 315). From 24 September 1940 to 24 January 1941, however, the Iron Guard sporadically ran amok. It almost indiscriminately incarcerated and/or beat up thousands of Jews, seized large amounts of Jewish property, and killed about 136 Jews as well as at least 64 non-Jewish liberals, royalists, prominent peasantists (including Virgil Madgearu) and even the august Romanian ultra-nationalist historian Nicolae Iorga (Ioanid 2000: 44–60).

The Iron Guard received messages of support and congratulation from leading members of Germany's Nazi Party and the SS, including Heinrich Himmler (Ioanid 2000: 46–7, 52). However, the escalating violence, especially the wave of sixty-four assassinations and five attempted assassinations of prominent non-Jewish Romanians on 26 and 27 November 1940, 'sent shock waves through the Romanian political class: no one was safe, anyone could be arbitrarily executed' (p. 46). In addition, Antonescu and Germany's military leaders, the Foreign Office and Economics Ministry became increasingly alarmed by the very damaging impact of the Iron Guard's mayhem, confiscations and bloodletting on the Romanian economy, which (as already mentioned) was the key supplier of petroleum and a major provider of food and raw materials to the Third Reich (p. 52). Therefore, when Antonescu visited Hitler on 14 January 1941 for crisis talks, the Führer urged him to 'get rid of . . . fanatical militants who think that, by destroying everything, they are doing their duty' (p. 53). After his return to Romania, Antonescu prepared for a crackdown on militant Guard-ists by dismissing the 'Romanianization commissar' on 18 January and the interior minister and the police chief on 20 January, but this prompted the Iron Guard to rise up against him from 20 to 24 January 1941, demanding his resignation and the establishment of a 'pure' Legionary State under Horia Sima (p. 54). However, Hitler greatly preferred the efficient, disciplined and dependable Romanian military-fascists led by Antonescu to the more fanatical, wayward and disruptive fascist Iron Guard, which was more of a liability than an asset to the German war effort. Hitler therefore personally ordered German troops to be made available to assist Antonescu's brutal suppression of the Iron Guard in late January, during which 374 people (including more Jews as well as soldiers and Guardists) were reportedly killed and another 380 were wounded (p. 54). Antonescu then for-mally dissolved the National Legionary State and purged the Iron Guard of its 'hooligan' elements. More than nine thousand 'Legionaires' were arrested, several leading members of the Iron Guard (including Horia Sima) were sentenced to hard labour for life (although all but one escaped abroad, mostly with German help), and those declared guilty of the murder of sixty-four prominent Roma-nians on 26–7 November 1940 were sentenced to death (p. 55). Nevertheless, Antonescu retained some of the less wayward ex-Guardists as functionaries in his military-fascist dictatorship, which had a more pragmatic, disciplinarian, corporative, technocratic orientation than a 'pure' Iron Guard regime would have had.

From June 1941 to August 1944, Antonescu committed twenty-seven Romanian army divisions to the German-led invasion of the Soviet Union, in which about 300,000 Romanians perished and about 200,000 were wounded (Rothschild 1974: 318). Many of the surviving Legionaries and Iron Guardists found solace and/or met 'martyrs' deaths' in this war, which was undertaken partly as a quasi-religious crusade against 'Judaeo-Communism' and 'the new Antichrist', but also as a way of retrieving northern Bukovina and Bessarabia from Soviet control. Romanians also hoped to regain northern Transylvania from Hungary. However, because Hungary was allied to Nazi Germany, this was only achieved after Antonescu was overthrown in August 1944 and Romania re-entered the war on the side of the Soviet Union against Nazi Germany and Hungary, at the cost of another 111,000 Romanian lives and 59,000 wounded (Rothschild 1974: 318).

'GARRISON STATES'

Like Admiral Horthy's Hungary and Admiral Tojo's Japan, General Antonescu's Romania increas-ingly conformed to Harold Lasswell's concept of 'the garrison state'. In 1941 Lasswell speculated that 'the trend of our time is away from the dominance of the specialist on bargaining . . . and toward the supremacy of the specialist on violence, the soldier . . . In the garrison state all organized social activity will be governmentalized; hence the role of independent associations will disappear . . . Not only will the administrative structure be centralized, but at every level it will tend to inte-grate authority in a few hands' (Lasswell 1941: 455, 462–3). In such a state 'at least in its introduc-tory phases, problems of morale are destined to weigh heavily . . . It is easy to throw sand in the gears of the modern assembly line; hence there must be a deep and general sense of participation in the total enterprise of the state if collective effort is to be sustained' (p. 458). The changing nature of modern warfare (or the emergence of what came to be known as 'total war') was tending 'to abolish the distinction between civilian and military functions'. For a variety of reasons, therefore, in 'the garrison state there must be work – and the duty to work – for all. Since all work becomes public work, all who do not accept employment flout military discipline. For those who do not fit within the structure of the state there is but one alternative – to obey or die' (p. 459). Moreover, the 'rulers of the garrison state will be able to regularize the rate of production, since they will be free from many of the conventions that have stood in the way of adopting measures suitable to this purpose'. However, 'they will most assuredly prevent full utilization of modern productive capacity for non-military consumption purposes', for they will retain 'a professional interest in multiplying gadgets specialized to acts of violence' (pp. 464–5). Garrison states would have to try to perpetuate siege mentalities 'as a means of maintaining popular willingness to forego immediate consumption' and also 'in order to preserve those virtues of sturdy acquiescence in the regime which they so much admire and from which they so greatly benefit'. However, they would also tend to employ 'militaristic ritual and ceremony' as surrogates for (hazardous) real wars. 'The tendency to ceremonialize rather than to fight will be particularly prominent among the most influential elements in a garrison state' (pp. 465–6).

There were unmistakeable trends towards this type of state in post-Depression Europe, Asia and Latin America. Lasswell also alluded to the need to distinguish 'the garrison state' from 'the party propaganda state, where the dominant figure is the propagandist, and the party bureaucratic state, in which the organization men of the party make the vital decisions' (p. 455). In keeping with this distinction, we differentiate the fascist 'garrison state' from the fascist 'party state'. Antonescu's Romania and, to a lesser degree, Horthy's Hungary can be categorized as fascist 'garrison states', since the military leadership managed to retain the upper hand over civilian and paramilitary fascists, who nevertheless played important mobilizing and legitimizing roles and turned these states into more than mere military dictatorships. Conversely, Mussolini's Italy and Hitler's Germany were fascist 'party states', in the sense that their fascist leaders managed to remain somewhat more important than the military hierarchy, the state bureaucracy, old ruling classes and, in Italy's case, the Catholic Church and the monarchy.

However, these distinctions were not absolute, but mainly differences of emphasis. The active co-operation of most of the state bureaucracy, the military hierarchy, the old ruling classes and (in Italy) the Church and the monarchy was essential to the survival and to the implementation of the projects and policies of Hitler and Mussolini, just as the different arms of the political Establishment needed each other's active support for the implementation of major projects and for the retention of political power in increasingly fascist Hungary and Romania (and, in different ways, in clerico-fascist Slovakia and monarcho-fascist Bulgaria). Military and paramilitary fascists could not have ruled unaided in Hungary or Romania any more than the mainly civilian fascist parties could have ruled solely by their own efforts in Italy or Germany. Extensive interpenetration and co-operation between the fascists and other elements in the political 'Establishment' was essential. Conversely, open conflict between military and paramilitary civilian fascists (of the sort that broke out in Romania in 1940–1) was potentially fatal to the survival of fascist regimes if it was not quickly brought under control.

Hitler evidently preferred to have Romania controlled by a 'reliable' military *Conducator* (Leader) who could be trusted to keep order, toe the line, enthusiastically contribute to the Axis invasion of the Soviet Union and deliver the vital Romanian oil, grain and raw materials needed by the German war machine as it prepared for the ultimate military challenge, rather than to have Romania terrorized by 'unreliable' and disruptive hooligans (Carsten 1967: 192). Antonescu subsequently became one of Hitler's most valued, decorated and respected foreign allies. He was even allowed to disagree with the Führer occasionally. Nevertheless, Hitler still took Horia Sima and other leading Guardists into asylum in Germany, in case they should be needed at a later stage. Indeed, when King Mihai and some prominent anti-fascists toppled Antonescu and sided with the Allies against Hitler in August 1944, the Nazis made unsuccessful last-ditch moves to establish Horia Sima as the leader of a Romanian fascist government-in-exile (Rothschild 1974: 317).

FASCIST MOVEMENTS AS POLITICAL 'LATECOMERS'

The fascist movements were relative 'latecomers' on the party political scene, in the sense that they arose considerably later than liberal, conservative, socialist, Christian, republican, agrarian and 'traditional' nationalist parties and after the 'crystallization' of party systems and allegiances (Linz 1979: 13–14). Fascist movements were therefore often unable to gain the support of the social groups at whom they initially targeted their appeals and frequently found themselves obliged to champion the interests of miscellaneous social groups who were (or felt themselves to be) politically and socially neglected because they were not specifically targeted or served by the older and more established political parties. Thus in many countries the fascists remained 'minority movements with little or no electoral appeal', and only the will to power of their core activists and the methods to which they were prepared to resort turned them into serious 'contenders for power' (p. 15). Even in Italy fascism did not gain prominence primarily through its electoral appeal (the Italian Fascists remained very much a minority party on the eve of their 'seizure' of power), but rather through its lethal combination of violence, intimidation and terror with electoral participation (p. 25). Fascist parties and movements did not experience steady and continuous growth, but aimed at the acquisition of power by less orthodox means. They did not aspire to become just one party among many, each representing particular sections of the electorate, but *the* party of the whole nation (p. 14). Fascist movements tended to set themselves the 'goal of representing the whole national community, integrating all classes, overcoming class conflict and appealing to former supporters of old parties on account of common national interests in conflict with . . . groups defined as alien' (p. 19). Indeed, they did not enduringly capture distinctive class bases of support comparable to those of the socialist, Communist, peasantist, liberal and conservative parties. In their doctrinal and programmatic eclecticism and their willingness to pick up potential support from almost any quarter, they were more like the 'catch-all' parties of today, with a heavy dependence on support from volatile, 'foot-loose' floating voters (pp. 13, 16, 20). Indeed, European fascism was to a considerable extent 'a conjunctural phenomenon', the product of the unique circumstances of the post-First World War crises and the 1930s Depression, 'attracting supporters from a heterogeneous social base largely on the basis of generational cleavages rather than class characteristics and allegiances' (p. 14).

This recognition that fascism was a relative latecomer on the party political scene also helps to explain why fascism was to such a large extent defined by the things it opposed: Communism; the rhetoric of class struggle; materialism; (independent) organized labour; parliamentary democracy; political and economic liberalism; individualism; pacifism; cosmopolitanism; internationalism; international 'finance capital' and Jewry; 'Anglo-Saxon' imperialism; the 1919–20 peace settlements; rentiers, capitalist 'speculation' and 'unearned' income; and feminism, homosexuality and miscegenation (to name only the fascists' favourite bugbears!). On their own, however, these 'anti' positions were not enough, for they could alienate even more potential adherents than they attracted (Linz 1979: 29–30, 38).

SURROGATES FOR ACTIVISM AND RADICALISM

Especially for veterans of the First World War and for males who entered adulthood during the turbulent 1920s, fascist movements also had a positive appeal based on their paramilitary organizations, strong-arm tactics, violent nationalist rhetoric, the promise of a 'comradely' and egalitarian yet disciplined and hierarchical 'new order', and their distinctive new styles, symbols, salutes, songs, chants, ceremonies, marches, mass rallies and eye-catching shirts. Thus the particular appeal of fascist movements to the ex-servicemen, students and young men who formed the initial nucleus of most fascist movements and the hard core of founder members who were most likely to rise to the top 'cannot be understood simply in terms of their ideology or their programmatic positions' (Linz 1979: 54). For ex-servicemen who experienced acute difficulties in readjusting to civilian employment, society and attitudes after the First World War, fascist militias offered a continuation of wartime heroics, camaraderie, military values and the idealization of war and men of violence. In contrast to the more gradual and orderly demobilization of European armies after the Second World War, the demobilizations of 1918–19 were over-hasty and chaotic, contributing to the emergence of high unemployment, vigilantism, hooliganism and unruly paramilitary violence among ex-servicemen. Significantly, the attractions of fascist or proto-fascist militias were far greater for ex-servicemen than for serving military personnel, who normally preferred to advance their military careers through exaggerated displays of strictly 'professional' and 'apolitical' loyalty to the 'powers that be' (pp. 56–61). For students and young men, on the other hand, fascism seemed to satisfy a desire for romantic gestures, heroic deeds, action rather than words, to be somebody, and involvement in daring collective exploits on behalf of 'the nation'. Fascist militias, paramilitary organizations and ceremonials substituted obedience and readiness to fight for reason and debate, and offered opportunities for pseudo-military violence, excitement and camaraderie, to males who had been influenced or even inspired by romanticized stories of the First World War but were too young to have served in it. For these deluded 'greenhorns', the fascists' bold coloured shirts expressed a modernist rejection of convention, individualism and humdrum, grey-suited, 'bourgeois conformity' (pp. 53–60). In view of the particular appeal of fascism to young adult and adolescent males, it is significant that more than half the population of the Balkans and East Central Europe was under the age of thirty during the interwar period and that in the countries with high birth rates, such as Poland and the Balkan states, this proportion was even higher (Longworth 1994: 78). In this respect the 'natural constituency' for fascism was larger in the Balkans and East Central Europe than in north-western Europe and Germanic Central Europe.

The hierarchy proposed by fascism aimed to transcend class division and class conflict, to dissociate social status from accidents of birth and social opportunity, to instil harmony and 'national' consensus, and slowly to redefine high social status on the basis of service to (and position in) the fascist movement. Although fascist movements invariably *failed* to carry out their promised social 'revolutions' against big landed property, big business and 'parasitic finance capitalism', active involvement in the fascist movements and in their affiliated mass organizations provided *surrogate forms of social advancement* for many thousands of plebeian fascist officials. Most fascist movements did indeed recruit and create elites which were not limited to people of high educational, class or occupational status, but were 'open to all, irrespective of social origin, willing to devote their energies to the movement' (Linz 1979: 37).

NATIONALISM, REGENERATION AND REBIRTH

It is sometimes argued that fascism was above all a form of nationalism. For example, Linz (1979: 28) states that 'Nationalism was the central appeal of fascism movements' (p. 47). Thus it can be difficult to decide whether particular movements were 'fascist' or merely 'extreme nationalist' and in some instances, such as the Slovak People's Party, 'a movement that is not originally fascist becomes increasingly fascist' (p. 28). Our interpretation of Balkan and East Central European nationalism fully concurs with his contention that 'in Eastern Europe integral nationalism would often be fascist or quasi-fascist' (p. 18). The basic reason for this was that nearly one-third of the inhabitants of the Balkan and East Central European 'successor states' were members of so-called 'national minorities', not merely because the population was more 'mixed' than in other parts of Europe, but more fundamentally because 'nations' had been defined in narrow, exclusive, 'ethnic' terms. This way of defining 'nations' fuelled nationalist demands for ethnic 'purification' or 'cleansing' in order to rid 'national' territories and populations of supposedly 'alien' elements who had often been peacefully and productively living in their midst for many generations. However, we should also keep in mind the latent fascist potential within most forms of nationalism. 'Obviously, if the nation was the highest good, if it was the worldly incarnation of the divine spirit at work in history, if it was an absolute necessity for the well-being and the self-fulfilment of its citizens, then its interest must be supreme; no petty rights like property and individual liberty could be set up against it, because property, individual liberty and cultural self-expression existed only in and through the nation. The part . . . might quite properly be subordinated and sacrificed to the interests of the whole' (Weber 1964: 21). As the Jacobin leader St Just observed at the height of the French Revolution, 'There is something terrible in the sacred love of the fatherland; it is so exclusive as to sacrifice everything to the public interest, without pity, without fear, without respect for humanity' (quoted by Kedourie 1993: 18).

According to Roger Griffin, 'fascism is best defined as a revolutionary form of nationalism, one which sets out to be a political, social and ethical revolution, welding the "people" into a dynamic national community under new elites infused with heroic values' (Griffin 1993: xi). In his view, the distinctiveness of fascist ideology primarily lies in 'its core *myth* of national rebirth' (p. xii), and it is 'the vision of a revolutionary new order which supplies the affective power of an ideology' (p. 35). In the case of fascism, the 'mobilizing vision is that of a national community rising phoenix-like after a period of encroaching decadence which all but destroyed it' (p. 38). Under certain conditions 'the fascist vision of a vigorous new nation growing out of the destruction of the old system can exert on receptive minds the almost alchemical power to transmute black despair into manic optimism'. This helps to explain the rapidity with which a fascist movement could transform the mood of a country and 'win a substantial mass following', by promising 'to substitute . . . 'youth, heroism and national greatness' for 'gerontocracy, mediocrity and national weakness' and to usher in 'an exciting new world in place of the senescent, played out one'. The critical factor was whether the fascists struck the right note and said what people wanted to hear at the time, not the feasibility or human implications of the fascists' declared goals (p. 39).

Fascism reflected deep anxieties concerning 'the modern age', in particular 'fears that the nation or civilization as a whole was being undermined by the forces of decadence' (Griffin 1993: viii). That was why it promised to 'renovate', 'rejuvenate', 'remould', 'restore' or 'resurrect' the nation and to create a 'new man', a revolution of 'Youth' and a new and more fulfilling type of state and society; and it saw war as 'an intrinsically regenerating force in the life of the nation' (p. 74). Partly for such reasons, the rulers of Hungary and Romania did not need much persuading to participate in the Axis invasion of the Soviet Union, launched in June 1941.

It is striking that fascism developed mainly in 'nations' which had attained 'national' unity and statehood relatively recently (to say 'late' is to imply the existence of a specious divinely ordained or natural 'timetable' against which the timing can be judged) and thus had not yet established such stable and securely anchored 'national' identities and political systems as the longer established 'nation-states'. In 1932 Mussolini himself declared: 'Fascism is the doctrine most fitted to represent the aims, the states of mind, of a people, like the Italian people, rising again after many centuries of abandonment or slavery to foreigners' (Mussolini 1932: 178). This promise of a consummation of recently attained 'national' independence, statehood and unity was one of the fundamental features which Italian Fascism had in common with fascist and other extreme nationalist movements and regimes in the Balkans, East Central Europe, the Baltic States, Finland, Greece and Germany and, in varying degrees, extreme nationalist movements and regimes in newly independent states outside Europe. However, it was not a universal characteristic of fascist or quasi-fascist regimes, if Salazar's Portugal, Peronist Argentina or 1940s Spain are considered to be fascist or at least quasi-fascist. Moreover, it should be stressed that the 'decadence' against which German National Socialism and writers such as Moeller van den Bruck and Ernst Jünger were reacting in Weimar Germany was a much blacker, more profound and more desperate spiritual, philosophical and cultural crisis than the relatively superficial political and economic corruption, enervation, sterility and wheeler-dealing in relation to which fascism was partly a reaction and partly a consequence in Italy, the Balkans, East Central Europe, the Baltic States and the Iberian Peninsula. This is one reason why the National Socialist reaction (including the notorious book burning and purges of 'cosmopolitan', materialist and 'degenerate' writers, artists, musicians and intellectuals) was so much more extreme or 'totalitarian'. The German national and racial rejuvenation and rebirth promised by the Nazis was supposed to be attained through racial and cultural 'purification' and a rediscovery of the 'folk community' and institutions 'which peculiarly German conditions had forged' (Weber 1964: 81).

EUROPEAN CHRISTIANITY AND FASCISM

Almost all forms of fascism relied heavily on concepts of 'rebirth', 'revival' and 'resurrection', but in the Balkans and East Central Europe such concepts still had strongly *religious* as well as secular nationalist overtones. The major Romanian, Croatian, Slovak, Polish and Hungarian manifestations of fascism and anti-Semitism had distinctly religious complexions, drew moral, personal, institutional and practical support from substantial sections of the clergy of the respective 'national churches', and relied heavily on religious imagery, concepts and rituals.

Michael Mann has tried to draw a clear distinction between the supposedly religious sources and motivations of pre-modern xenophobia and purgative 'cleansing' and the supposedly modern and secular sources and motivations of the even more murderous twentieth-century manifestations of xenophobia and purgative 'cleansing' (Mann 2005: 34–69). However, this religious–secular distinction is actually quite difficult to maintain in practice. Extreme nationalism, fascism, the Holocaust against the Jews, the atrocities of the Croatian fascist *Ustasa* against Serbs and Montenegrins during the 1940s and various other manifestations of religious, racial and ethnic 'cleansing' and xenophobia in the Balkans and East Central Europe during the nineteenth and twentieth centuries continued to be pervaded by Christian ideas, language, imagery and (presumably) motives, and were often aided and abetted by Christian churches. The very notions of 'cleansing' or 'purification' and the associated notions of 'renewal' and 'rebirth' originated in certain forms of religious fervour, fanaticism and millenarianism and seem never to have shaken off their originally religious or eschatological characteristics, even if the modern decline of religion has resulted in substantial 'secularization' of 'cleansing' and 'purificatory' mindsets. Secular modern racism and anti-Semitism have *supplemented* rather than *supplanted* older religious and millenarian demonologies, xenophobias and drives to exorcize perceived inner demons or repel external threats.

For example, the 'spiritual core' of the Romanian Iron Guard was the so-called Legion of the Archangel Michael, founded by Corneliu Zelea Codreanu in 1927 (Heinen 2006). Its origins can be traced back to an Association of Christian Students (which Codreanu and his cronies had established at the University of Iasi in 1922) and to Codreanu's alleged 'visions' of the Archangel Michael while he was serving a prison sentence in 1923–4. The Legion was essentially a violently nationalistic and anti-Semitic 'Christian Brotherhood', dedicated to an ultra-nationalist form of religious revivalism. It thus despatched so-called 'Brotherhoods of the Cross' to propagate its gospel in Romanian villages, schools and universities. The Legionary elite was to be 'forged' and 'purified' through fire and struggle. Legionaries were to eschew all excess, luxury and sexual immorality, in order to lead relatively ascetic lives of practical service to others and thus win 'converts' by example. Rule Number 3 in the Legionaries' *Manual* (written by Codreanu) was the 'Rule of Silence: speak little. Say what has to be said. Speak when you need. Your oratory is the oratory of the deed. You act; let others talk' (quoted in Weber 1964: 100). However, this life of asceticism and service to others was also intended to expiate sin, for Legionaries were even exhorted to kill. In the words of their *Manual*, 'When I have to choose between the death of my country and that of a thug, I prefer the thug to die; and I am a better Christian if I do not let him hurt my country and lead it to perdition' (Weber 1964: 103). Moreover, every Legionary had to swear 'to work for the ever deeper popular penetration of the new spirit of Work, Honesty, Sacrifice and Justice' and 'believe in a new Romania which we shall conquer through Jesus Christ and through integral nationalism, acting through the country's Legions' (Weber 1964: 100). Codreanu also explained that Romania was 'dying for the lack of *men*, not for lack of programmes . . . It follows that the Legion of the Archangel Michael shall be more a school and an army than a political party . . . The finest souls that our minds can conceive, the proudest, tallest, straightest, strongest, cleverest, cleanest, bravest and most hardworking that our race can produce, this is what the Legionary schools must give us!' (pp. 167–8).

The Legion of the Archangel Michael has therefore been described tentatively as 'a religiously founded movement or a rebirth or a reawakening of the Orthodox Church' (Turczynski 1971: 111) and as 'a "born again" Christian Orthodox movement' within which Codreanu's role was to be 'the earthly representative of the Archangel Michael' (Fischer-Galati 1984: 28). Legionary meetings were often accompanied by hymns, prayers or religious services and sometimes led to torch-lit processions and 'Calvary crusades' through villages. Legionary 'martyrs' were often venerated in the manner of Christian 'saints'. The Legion used the language of medieval religious chiliasm. According to Codreanu, 'The ultimate goal is not life. It is *resurrection*. The resurrection of nations in the name of Jesus Christ the Saviour . . . A time will come when all the world's nations will arise from the dead, with all their dead . . . That *final* moment, "resurrection from the dead", is the highest and most sublime goal for which a nation can strive' (quoted in Fischer-Galati 1970: 330). This is utter drivel, but it was apparently delivered and received with religious conviction and po-faced solemnity.

Members of the Croatian fascist *Ustasa* were similarly conceived to be participants in a form of militant, violent, crusading, Catholic order, a latter-day version of the Order of Teutonic Knights. Indeed, at least one organization affiliated to the *Ustasa* was called the Crusaders (*Krizari*) (Djordjevic 1971: 132). Moreover, many Croatian Catholic priests in Italy (including the Vatican) as well as in Croatia itself worked for the *Ustasa* in the belief that, if they did not do so, the Balkans would eventually fall under the thrall of atheist Communism. Their ruthlessness reflected a belief that they were engaged in a fight to the death against the Devil's agents, including Orthodox (that is, pro-Russian) Serbs as well as overt Communists and Jews.

Nationalist and anti-Communist Catholic clergy also played high-profile roles in Slovak fascism and anti-Semitism, although this particular brand of anti-Semitism had the slight saving grace of being largely religious rather than racial (and genocidal), as was also the case in Hungary. This did not save the majority of Slovak and Hungarian Jews from the Nazi death camps. However, unlike their German counterparts, most Slovak and Hungarian fascists did not want the Jews to be exterminated, but 'merely' to be expelled to countries willing to receive them after the end of the Second World War – or sooner, if it could be arranged.

The religious fervour of Balkan and East Central European fascism is partly to be explained by the fact that, for the most part, these were still mostly agrarian, provincial, church-dominated societies with limited mental horizons. With the exception of the Czech Lands, where fascism was largely confined to the Bohemian Germans (alias 'Sudeten Germans'), these societies were much less urban, less anonymous, less sophisticated and less secular than either Germany or north-western Europe. In as much as Balkan and East Central European fascists sought to tailor their language and their message to the audiences they addressed, they may have calculated that religious concepts and imagery would be most readily understood and absorbed by peasants, worker-peasants, rural labourers and first-generation industrial workers. What is more, Balkan and East Central European fascists could easily exploit and draw upon living traditions of religious anti-Semitism – mainly Roman Catholic ones, but Eastern Orthodox ones in Romania.

The religious tone and the 'religious infrastructure' of the fascist movements of the Balkans and East Central Europe must also be attributed to the fact that in these areas nationalism was already saturated with religious imagery, fervour, concepts, language and goals and was often strongly supported by 'national' churches and nationalist clergy. West European nationalism is often described as a kind of secular religion, but most Balkan and East Central European nationalisms were not yet secularized in the 1930s. As in Northern Ireland, it was partly religion that gave Balkan and East Central European nationalisms their particularly sharp, bigoted, fervent, intolerant and doctrinaire edge. Orthodoxy was central to Romanian, Serb, Montenegrin, Macedonian-Slav, Greek and Bulgarian nationalism and national identity, just as Roman Catholicism was central to Polish, Croatian, Slovene, Austrian and Slovak national identity, although it was less so for the more secular and multi-denominational Czechs and Hungarians. Moreover, Eastern Orthodox Christianity encouraged submergence of the individual into the collective or corporate body of the faithful, while Roman Catholicism not only emphasized obedience to authority and the state but also promoted 'corporative' or 'corporatist' social doctrines and partnerships which heavily overlapped with those promoted by the Austrian, Polish, Slovak, Slovene and Croatian fascist movements (as well as by the Fascists in Italy, the Falangists in Spain and the Salazarist *Estado Novo* in Portugal).

Peter Sugar has stressed that dominant national religions and the accommodating and sometimes supportive attitudes of dominant national churches, together with the open or tacit support given by schools, universities, state bureaucracies and the military, gave Balkan and East Central European fascist movements and doctrines *major footholds* within the main power structures in these regions. This helps to explain why these fascist movements, unlike those in western Europe, 'could operate within the existing system and could wait for their moment' (Sugar 1971b: 153). Sugar concludes that these footholds and the 'native' or home-spun content of Balkan and East Central European fascism were strong enough to have produced something which, 'without Mussolini's choice of label for his party, we would possibly not have called fascist, but which, in their essence and numerous manifestations, would have amounted to nearly the same thing', even if Fascist Italy and Nazi Germany had never existed (p. 156).

However, precisely because of the close connections between Balkan and East Central European fascisms and nationalisms, fascist movements never flourished among the Czechs or the Serbs during the interwar period. There were small Czech and Serb fascist movements (Sugar 1971b: 49–51, 61–2, 129–31, 136–8), but most 'nationally minded' Czechs and Serbs had enough sense to see that fascism and their big fascist neighbours posed the greatest dangers to their 'national' survival. Thus for them fascism was simply a threat, not a salvation. Unfortunately, most of the Balkan and East Central European fascist movements either failed to recognize or were undeterred by the fact that, by promoting fascism and collaboration with Nazi Germany and/or Fascist Italy, they were diminishing rather than strengthening their 'national' sovereignty, security and chances of survival.

FASCISM AS A NEW STYLE OF POLITICS

One of the most useful and illuminating characterizations of fascism has been provided by Noel O'Sullivan (1983). He presents fascism not as an aberration, but as the most extreme manifestation of one of the main currents in modern European civilization (pp. 63–4, 80). He defines fascism as 'an activist style of politics' which conceived 'the highest good for man' to be 'a life of endless self-sacrifice spent in total and highly militant devotion to the nation-state' and 'unconditional allegiance to a fascist "leader" whose arbitrary personal decree is the sole final determinant of right and wrong'. In practice this amounted to a demand for absolute obedience to the 'leader', regardless of how he had acquired or exercised his power and a total absence of formal constitutional restraints (p. 33). This involved a wholesale rejection of the 'traditional limited style of politics' and of a political order based upon states, within which political communities are governed and held together by common bodies of law and clear distinctions between the public and private domains, with strong constitutional restraints on the acquisition and use of power within specific historically determined territories and jurisdictions. An 'activist style of politics' substitutes an ideology and a sense of 'mission' (or 'shared purpose') as the basis of the new political community. It establishes an all-embracing and all-intrusive political order (abolishing the distinction between public and private domains). It dispenses with formal constitutional restraints on the acquisition and use of power. It refuses to regard existing frontiers and jurisdictions as inviolable and it endeavours to redefine frontiers in accordance with its own militant ideological mission and precepts (pp. 34–7). Fascism was 'the most extreme, ruthless and comprehensive expression of this new style of politics' (p. 41). It was revolutionary in the sense that it consciously 'set out to destroy the state concept upon which . . . limited politics had been based for the previous five centuries' and replaced it with 'a style of politics in which there was no intrinsic regard for legality; in which state and society were to be submerged into one all-pervasive movement; in which all constitutional constraints upon power were excluded, in principle at least; and in which the nation . . . was an essentially fluid entity whose territorial limits were to be determined solely by the ideological fanaticism of the fascist leaders' (p. 39). It glorified war, perpetual 'struggle', strength, youth, vigour, the heroic spirit and martial values (pp. 44, 70–4).

Fascism thus transformed politics into a millenarian crusade to build a new social and political order purged of all evil, corruption, decadence and alien elements. In the new order there were to be no laws, rules or morals other than those ordained by the leader, while 'freedom' was redefined as unconditional self-sacrifice, devotion and obedience to the 'leader', who alone embodied and expressed the 'will' of the nation (O'Sullivan 1983: 58–63). Fascism also involved the transformation of politics into spectacular public ceremonies, rituals, games, marches and singing festivals, orchestrated by the fascist regime, in order to engender more 'total' and 'active' identification with the national political community, a more complete sense of 'organic' political and social unity, and more 'total' and 'active' devotion and obedience to the fascist movement and regime (pp. 94–9).

O'Sullivan singles out five core ideas in the fascist *Weltanschauung*: (i) 'corporatism', in the sense of an 'all-embracing vision of an organic, spiritually unified and morally regenerated society' within which the divisions and conflicts will be defused and/or transcended in order to release citizens from petty, everyday, 'egotistical concerns' and facilitate more total devotion and service to the nation and its leaders (pp. 132–4); (ii) the need for unrelenting, perpetual 'struggle' (pp. 138–9); (iii) the 'leadership principle' (*Führerprinzip*), establishing the fascist 'Leader' as the sole, infallible embodiment and expression of the nation's destiny and will, the focus of all loyalty, self-sacrifice and solidarity, and the source of all law and authority (pp. 149–53); (iv) a 'messianic mission' of conquest and domination (pp. 161, 166–7); and (v) the pursuit of autarky, neo-mercantilism and étatism (pp. 170–1).

O'Sullivan concludes that 'the intellectual appeal of fascism derived principally from the skill with which it exploited the oldest and most potent of human dreams, the dream that is of creating spiritual unity and purity within societies whose institutions had come to appear divisive and corrupt' (p. 181). His stimulating essay sheds light not only on the fascist movements and regimes in Italy and Germany, but also on those that emerged in the Balkans and East Central Europe. It is hard to accept his assertion that the latter were 'either copies of the two main ones or else stooge regimes created by them' (p. 34), since every fascist movement and regime had its own national roots and distinctive features in addition to the common characteristics. Nevertheless, the main thrusts of his thesis are well born out by Mussolini's pronouncements on Fascism in 1932:

> Fascism desires an active man, one engaged in activity with all his energies . . . It conceives of life as a struggle . . . Life, therefore, as conceived by the Fascist, is serious, austere . . . Fascism

disdains the 'comfortable' life . . . Fascism is a religious conception in which man is seen in immanent relationship with a superior law and an objective will that transcends the particular individual and raises him to conscious membership of a spiritual society . . . Above all, Fascism believes neither in the possibility nor in the utility of perpetual peace . . . War alone brings to their highest tension all human energies and puts the stamp of nobility on the peoples who have the courage to meet it . . . Thus the Fascist . . . looks upon life as duty, ascent, conquest. (Mussolini 1932: 165, 170–1).

The Fascist *Statuto* of December 1929 similarly emphasized the militant, crusading, ultra-nationalist, 'activist' character of Fascism:

The National Fascist Party is a civil militia for all the service of the nation. Its objective: to realize the greatness of the Italian people. From its beginnings . . . the party has always thought of itself as in a state of war, at first in order to combat those who were stifling the will of the nation . . . and from henceforth to defend and increase the power of the Italian people. Fascism . . . is above all a faith . . . under the impulse of which the new Italians work as soldiers, pledged to achieve victory in the struggle between the nation and its enemies. (reprinted in Oakeshott 1940: 179).

The principal limitation of O'Sullivan's incisive characterization of fascism, as with many others which focus primarily on the distinctive methods, ideology and 'style' of fascist movements and regimes, is the relative neglect and near-dismissal of the much debated economic and class basis, dimensions and context of fascism. These other aspects are, by contrast, central to most Marxist and sociological conceptions of fascism. It is to these that we now turn our attention. We shall give special consideration to the official Communist interpretations and explanations of fascism, particularly those published by the Communist International (Comintern). These not only shed important light on the pivotal relationship, competition and 'struggle' between Communism and fascism in interwar Europe, but also elucidate the basis on which Europe's Communist parties – especially those of the Balkans and East Central Europe – aspired to win power by 'leading the fight against fascism'.

28   The Comintern 'theory of fascism' and its long-neglected role in rationalizing the Communist seizures of power in 1945–8

Most of the well-known Marxist luminaries in interwar Europe initially saw fascism as the 'death rattle' of senescent capitalism, as a 'pre-emptive strike' against the Marxist left and the proletariat, or as a drastic last-ditch response to the long-awaited (and supposedly 'terminal') crisis of 'decaying' or 'moribund' monopolistic 'finance capitalism'. This momentous crisis had begun with the First World War and its tempestuous aftermath, lifted slightly during the mid-1920s economic recovery and deepened dramatically with the onset of the 1930s Depression. The First World War had substantially expanded the size, reduced the deference and obedience, and raised the political and class consciousness of Europe's industrial proletariat, as the war industries drew in millions of new (usually unskilled) recruits. Millions of former soldiers and munitions workers became unemployed in 1919–20. However, in the turbulent wake of the First World War Europe's toiling masses were less docile and less tractable than they had been in the late nineteenth century (although the contrast with the very unsettled years between 1900 and 1914 was less marked). There was very widespread unrest in Europe's countryside as well as in urban areas, but it was more tightly orchestrated in the towns. In both town and country, nonetheless, there were frequent strikes, boycotts and 'sit-ins', and employers experienced great difficulty in restoring labour discipline, the profitability of their enterprises and 'management's right to manage' (that is, high-handed autocratic styles of management, giving no 'say' to hired workers). Therefore employers widely resorted to lock-outs, harassment and aggressive strong-arm tactics against organized labour, often with the full backing of European governments, which since the 1890s had become increasingly vigorous and heavy-handed in the 'labour taming' methods they employed, even in the 'liberal' democracies.

On the political front, old-fashioned governments and 'liberal' politicians had been accustomed to the very limited popular participation in political life before the 1914–18 war, even in the parliamentary states. They found it exceedingly difficult to cope with the recently enfranchised, increasingly educated, more and more unionized and politically 'mobilized' working-class and peasant voters. Popular discontents and increasingly insistent demands accelerated the rise of the new mass parties of both the left and the illiberal nationalist right, which in turn 'gate-crashed' many formerly sedate and patrician political institutions. Europe's 'oiks' and 'riff-raff' gained access to its gentlemen's clubs. In the face of this social upheaval, European governments all too readily resorted to repression, police harassment and other forms of aggressive suppression or dispersal of general strikes, 'sit-ins', marches and mass protests, whether in Britain, France, Sweden, Germany, Italy, Spain, Portugal, Austria or the Balkans and East Central Europe. Acute labour unrest and the repressive responses it evoked from governments, industrialists and landowners were part of a Europe-wide confrontation between 'property' and 'labour', between the 'haves' and the 'have-nots'. (By the early 1920s even the Bolshevik Revolution had begun to 'devour its own children', as Lenin's regime resorted to repression of strikes and labour unrest and to 'Taylorism', involving piece rates and time and motion studies.)

Despite heated and often acrimonious arguments over minor differences of interpretation, most Marxists were broadly in agreement that the frightened and crisis-stricken propertied classes were flailing out at the revolutionary left with the mad fury of a mortally wounded monster. Thus Italian Fascism was seen as merely the local Italian variant of European capitalism's desperate last counter-revolutionary offensive against organized labour and the Marxist left. Fascism was seen as a kind of protection racket in which fascist thugs interposed themselves between the propertied classes and the toiling classes and offered the former 'protection' against the latter. At first industrialists, land-owners, state officials and traditional political bosses called the shots and the fascist thugs were the underlings, but the latter gradually gained the upper hand over their easily intimidated paymasters during the offensive against their proletarian and/or Marxist prey. In the words of an early *Resolution on Fascism* passed by the Executive Committee of the Communist International (ECCI) on 23 June 1923:

> Fascism is a characteristic phenomenon of decay, a reflection of the progressive dissolution of capitalist economy . . . Its strongest root is the fact that the imperialist war and the disruption of the capitalist economy which the war intensified and accelerated meant for broad strata of the petty and middle bourgeoisie, small peasants and the 'intelligentsia', instead of the hopes they cherished, the destruction of their former condition of life and especially their former security. The vague expectations which many in these social strata had of a radical social improvement, have also been disappointed. (reprinted in Degras 1960: 41)

This same Comintern Resolution on Fascism explicitly stated that such feelings of insecurity, dis-appointment, disillusionment and frustration, which often propelled disaffected and alienated indi-viduals towards fascism, were by no means confined to the petty and middle bourgeoisie: 'They have been joined by many proletarian elements who, looking for and demanding action, feel dissat-isfied with the behaviour of all political parties. Fascism also attracts the disappointed and declassed, the rootless in every social stratum, particularly ex-officers who have lost their occupation since the end of the war' (Degras 1960: 41). The *Resolution on Fascism* passed by the Fifth Congress of the Comintern in July 1924 similarly affirmed that fascism 'has its roots in the middle class doomed to decay as a result of the capitalist crisis, and in the elements (such as ex-officers) declassed as a result of the war, and partly also in the embittered proletarian elements whose revolutionary hopes were disappointed' (Degras 1960: 139).

THE 'MASS SOCIETY' INTERPRETATIONS OF FASCISM, WHICH WERE ANTICIPATED BY THE COMINTERN

These Comintern *Resolutions* strikingly foreshadowed the view, normally attributed to 'mass society' theorists such as Hannah Arendt (1966: 305–39) and William Kornhauser (1960: 14–15, 179–82ff.), that social support for fascism came not only from one class, but from disappointed, disillusioned, discontented or marginalized members of various social classes and from *déracinés*, *déclassés* or disorientated individuals who had been cut adrift from their class moorings and were thus quite likely to be seeking new affective attachments (or a new 'sense of belonging') of the sort that fascism could offer. Since this is one of the most central and contentious themes in the whole literature on fascism, it calls for further elucidation.

The central thesis of 'mass society' theorists is that modern 'totalitarian movements', that is, movements which aspire to create 'totalitarian' regimes, 'are fundamentally mass movements rather than class movements'. That is to say, 'although fascism tends to recruit a disproportionate number of its adherents from the middle class and Communism attracts more of its adherents from the working class, these movements cannot be understood merely as political expressions of the middle class and the working class respectively. For in both cases a large proportion of the movement is composed of people who possess the weakest rather than the strongest class ties. Furthermore, both movements tend to draw many adherents from all major social classes' (Kornhauser 1960: 14–15). This is partly a simple question of political arithmetic. 'Any political enterprise which aspires to power on the basis of popular support will have to command the allegiance of sizeable numbers of people from both the middle and working classes, because the size of these classes makes it a necessity. This is true even when a political group depends for primary support on only one class' (p. 194). But that is not all. The nub of the 'mass society' theory is 'the hypothesis that all social classes contributed to the social base of totalitarian movements, and that in particular it is the socially uprooted and unattached members of all classes who support these movements first and in the greatest numbers. This implies that unattached intellectuals, marginal members of the middle class, isolated industrial and farm workers have been among the major social types in totalitarian movements' (p. 182). Substitute the word 'fascist' for the word 'totalitarian' and this formulation could have been taken as one of the seminal Comintern pronouncements on fascism!

These pronouncements clearly and unambiguously anticipate Kornhauser's contentions that 'fascist movements . . . are not adequately conceived as middle class phenomena' and that 'fascist movements rely on working class support for a significant portion of their following' (p. 196). Thus in 1933 42 per cent of Nazi party members were 'manual and service workers', not far below their 52 per cent share of the workforce, while in 1922 43.5 per cent of Italian Fascist party members were workers (p. 219). In Hungary in 1940 workers similarly constituted 41 per cent of the membership of Ferenc Szalasi's fascist party, which by then had more than 100,000 members (Barany 1971: 77).

In the Balkans and East Central Europe the middle classes were far too small to constitute a mass base for fascism in the way that they did (along with many workers and peasants) in Germany, for example. Furthermore, most of the East Central European and (to lesser degrees) Balkan middle classes were to considerable degrees composed of Jews and other vulnerable ethnic minorities who were usually more alarmed than attracted by the rise of violent, ultra-nationalist, xenophobic, anti-Semitic and increasingly fascist movements and regimes (especially in Hungary, Romania and Poland). In the Czech Lands, the Czech 'national bourgeoisie' was similarly terrified and/or repulsed by the rise of fascism, which threatened both the existence and the cherished ideals of the multi-ethnic Czechoslovak state.

Therefore, even if many writers have managed to get away with very misleading claims that fascism was a narrowly or specifically middle-class, 'bourgeois' phenomenon in Germany or France or Italy, such arguments are complete non-starters in the Balkan and East Central European context, where the mass base for fascism had to come from other social classes besides the relatively small and/or predominantly anti-fascist bourgeoisies.

The 'mass society' social perspective on fascism is frequently counterposed to that of 'most' Marxists, in the mistaken belief that the latter saw fascism as simply a (middle-) class phenomenon (see, for example, Kornhauser 1960: 198–207; Kolinsky 1974: 74–93, 116–20; Cohan 1975: 146–72). However, it is (and was) perfectly possible to see fascism as being primarily a response to (and consequence of) a profound 'crisis of capitalism', without also seeing it as a narrowly or exclusively middle class or 'bourgeois' phenomenon. After all, the interwar 'crisis of capitalism' threatened the security and livelihoods of workers and peasants as well as the middle-classes. People of all classes lost out or felt extremely worried and insecure as a result of that crisis. Thus it is not surprising that the Comintern identified the social basis and support for fascism in much the same way as the 'mass society' theorists did. The Communist leaders had their intellectual limitations, but they were not stupid and quite a few were astute social observers and intellectuals. In this respect at least, the alleged crudity or rigidity lies less in the official Comintern view of the social basis of fascism than in the eyes of critics who either have not read and thought about the Comintern pronouncements with sufficient care or prefer to caricature the Comintern stance because it was in some other respects deeply objectionable and dangerous.

The June 1923 Comintern *Resolution on Fascism* also implicitly acknowledged the dangerous and disturbing political ambiguities which made fascism a direct rival as well as an opponent of Communism. Communism and fascism were the two main competing forms of radical activism, purportedly dedicated to the total economic, social, political and spiritual reconstruction and cleansing (that is, 'purging') of society in the twentieth century. Fascism was in a sense Communism's alter ego: 'In the period of revolutionary ferment and proletarian risings, fascism to some extent flirted with proletarian revolutionary demands. The masses which followed fascism vacillated between the two camps . . . But with the consolidation of capitalist rule and the general bourgeois offensive they threw themselves definitely on to the side of the bourgeoisie . . . The bourgeoisie immediately took fascism into paid service in their fight to defeat and enslave the proletariat . . . Although fascism by its origin and its exponents also includes revolutionary tendencies, which might turn against capitalism and its state, it is nevertheless becoming a dangerous counter-revolutionary force . . . The triumph of fascism in Italy spurs the bourgeoisie of other countries to take the same course in defeating the proletariat . . . It is the task of the conscious revolutionary vanguard of the working class to take up the struggle against victorious fascism . . . The fascist forces are being organized on an international scale, and it is consequently necessary to organize the workers' struggle against fascism internationally' (reprinted in Degras 1960: 41–2).

THE HAZARDS OF INDISCRIMINATE LABELLING

The 1923 and 1924 Comintern *Resolutions on Fascism* saw the fascists as 'shock troops' who were not themselves exclusively bourgeois, but who were placing themselves at the service of the frightened, anti-Communist bourgeoisies, even though this involved the betrayal or compromising of the more radical revolutionary elements in the fascist programme and camp following. Indeed, that was the easiest way for the fascists to win state power and gain the upper hand over their 'bourgeois' paymasters. Genuine Western liberals viewed the rise of Fascism with varying degrees of horror and patrician distaste, seeing it as a negation of Western liberal norms of governance and law-abiding conduct, as indeed it was. As Mussolini himself proclaimed in 1932, 'In the face of Liberal doctrines, Fascism takes up an attitude of absolute opposition both in the field of politics and in that of economics' (Mussolini 1932: 173). Seen from a Communist standpoint, however, the Fascist offensive against the Marxist parties and labour movements in 1920s Italy did not at first seem so very different from the counter-revolutionary offensive unleashed by 'capital' against 'labour' in the 'liberal' parliamentary democracies at about the same time. According to the *Resolution on Fascism* passed by the Fifth Congress of the Comintern in July 1924: 'Fascism is one of the classic forms of counter-revolution in the epoch when capitalist society is decaying, the epoch of proletarian revolution . . . Fascism is the bourgeoisie's instrument for fighting the proletariat, for whose defeat the legal means at the disposal of the state no longer suffice . . . As bourgeois society continues to decay, all bourgeois parties, particularly social democracy, take on a more or less fascist character . . . Fascism and social democracy are two sides of the same instrument of capitalist dictatorship. In the fight against fascism, therefore, social democracy can never be a reliable ally of the fighting proletariat' (reprinted in Degras 1960: 138–9).

It should be remembered that to the predominantly Communist targets of Europe's counter-revolutionary offensives it did not initially seem to make a huge difference whether these assaults were the work of fascists, conservatives, nationalists, 'liberals', socialists or social democrats. Indeed, Europe's Communist parties condemned as 'social fascists' the German, Polish and other social democratic parties that initiated or acquiesced in offensives against labour militancy and the far left in the hope of promoting the stabilization and recovery of capitalism and 'bourgeois' parliamentary rule in Western and East Central Europe. They denounced these so-called 'social fascists' as 'traitors' to the class they claimed to represent and as de facto allies of the overt fascists who were blatantly out to annihilate the revolutionary left and all radical proletarian and peasant movements. However, this was a fatal misrepresentation and misunderstanding of the position of social democracy vis-à-vis fascism, as the Comintern and its affiliated Communist parties implicitly recognized in 1935, by performing a volte-face and belatedly urging co-operation with social democrats in the creation of broad 'popular fronts' against fascism.

Admittedly, Europe's socialist and social democratic parties were in full retreat from Marxism and openly proclaimed that a strong recovery of Europe's market economies and parliamentary democracies was in the best interests of their still predominantly working-class constituencies. This meant having to come to terms with the necessity and virtues of the capitalist system, which in turn involved a sometimes painful acceptance of the need for relatively strict fiscal, monetary and labour discipline and for curbing the disruptive and often violent or intimidating activities of the revolutionary and anti-democratic left, to allow both capitalism and democracy to function. Thus there were genuine disagreements and partings of minds between Europe's increasingly 'gradualist' or 'reformist' social democratic and socialist parties, on the one hand, and the revolutionary, anti-capitalist and anti-democratic left, especially the Communist parties, on the other. The socialists and social democrats were inherently more committed to the defence of democracy than were the Communists, who merely wanted to take advantage of democratic liberties in order to expand their own anti-democratic movements and activities in preparation for the projected establishment of Communist 'dictatorships of the proletariat'.

The Programme of the Communist International (1928), which was binding on all the affiliated Communist parties in Eastern and Western Europe, reaffirmed the 'historic mission of achieving the dictatorship of the proletariat' (Comintern 1929: 58) through 'a combination of strikes and armed demonstrations and, finally, the general strike against the state power of the bourgeoisie' (p. 61). It openly and unashamedly advocated violence and rejected peaceful constitutional methods: 'The conquest of power by the proletariat does not mean peacefully "capturing" the ready-made bourgeois state machinery by means of a parliamentary majority . . . The conquest of power by the proletariat is the violent overthrow of bourgeois power, the destruction of the capitalist state apparatus (bourgeois armies, police, bureaucratic hierarchy, the judiciary, parliaments etc.) and the substitution in its place of new organs of proletarian power, to serve primarily as instruments for the suppression of the exploiters' (p. 23).

Europe's increasingly 'Bolshevized' Communist parties began to apply the label 'fascist' to virtually all the repressive, authoritarian, anti-Marxist governments and movements that willingly promoted or participated in the propertied classes' offensives against militant labour and the revolutionary left. Not only Mussolini's avowedly Fascist regime, but also the authoritarian regimes established in Hungary in 1920, in Bulgaria and Spain in 1923, in Albania in 1925, in Poland and Lithuania in 1926, in Yugoslavia in 1929, in Portugal, Austria and Germany in 1933, in Latvia and Estonia in 1934, in Romania in 1938 and in Spain (for a second time) and Slovakia in 1939, came to be described as 'fascist' in Marxist literature. In the late 1930s, indeed, 'leading Hungarian politicians frequently boasted that Hungary was the first country in Europe to introduce fascism, and they even insisted that Horthy's "white terror" and the subsequent system manifested the features of the ideology and practical system that conquered Germany and Italy' (Ranki 1971: 65). While conceding that the word 'fascism' was 'not part of the vocabulary of the Hungarian counter-revolutionaries', Ranki nevertheless affirmed that the 'white terror' of 1919–20 (and the regime it established) comprised 'several features that were also characteristic of the rising fascism in Germany and Italy', including 'a political system that mercilessly persecuted both the labour movement and, in general, democratic ideas and their proponents' while stressing 'the importance of the Hungarian "race" and the idea of a strong national state. It became the first official ideology of this sort in Europe' (p. 65).

However, Ranki also recognized that Hungary's international isolation and 'total economic bankruptcy' in the early 1920s and the consequent need for Western recognition and economic assistance obliged Horthy and his new premier, Count Bethlen, to muzzle the more wayward fascist elements headed by Gyula Gömbös and to promote a more liberal facade for the time being (p. 68), just as Mussolini did during his first two years in power.

STALIN ON THE DEEPENING 'CRISIS OF CAPITALISM' IN THE EARLY 1930S

The awesome deepening of the 'crisis of capitalism' after 1929 seemed to account for the further proliferation and hardening of fascist regimes during the 1930s. The official Soviet view was presented by Stalin in his 'political report' to the June 1930 Congress of the Communist Party of the Soviet Union (CPSU). He began by emphasizing the universality of the crisis. 'The illusions about the omnipotence of capitalism are collapsing.' This crisis was 'not a mere recurrence' of previous capitalist crises. This one had 'most severely affected the principal country of capitalism, its citadel, the United States'. In addition, the 'industrial crisis in the chief capitalist countries' had become 'interwoven with the agricultural crisis in the agrarian countries', the one exacerbating and prolonging the other. Moreover, the monopolistic structure of twentieth-century capitalism encouraged 'the capitalist combines' to endeavour to maintain the 'high monopolistic prices' of their products 'in spite of over-production'. This rendered the crisis 'particularly painful and ruinous for the masses . . . who constitute the main consumers' and could only impede its resolution. 'The present crisis is developing on the basis of the *general crisis* of capitalism, which came into being already in the period of the imperialist war, and is sapping the foundations of capitalism.' The crisis 'is laying bare and intensifying the contradictions between the major imperialist countries . . . between the victor countries and the vanquished . . . between the imperialist states and the colonial and dependent countries'. Hence 'the bourgeoisie will seek a way out of the situation through further fascistization in the sphere of domestic policy', while 'in the sphere of foreign policy the bourgeoisie will seek a way out through a new imperialist war' (Stalin 1955a: 243–61).

At the January 1934 Congress of the CPSU, Stalin gloated that the 'continuing crisis of capitalism' was 'now in its fifth year, devastating the economy of the capitalist countries year after year and draining it of the fat accumulated in previous years'. He attributed the unprecedented duration and magnitude of the crisis to the following factors. Firstly, 'the industrial crisis has affected every capitalist country without exception, which has made it difficult for some countries to manoeuvre at the expense of others'. Secondly, 'the industrial crisis has become interwoven with the agrarian crisis which has affected all the agrarian and semi-agrarian countries'. Thirdly, 'the agrarian crisis has grown more acute' causing a technical 'retrogression of agriculture'. Fourthly, 'the monopolist cartels which dominate industry strive to maintain high commodity prices, a circumstance which . . . hinders the absorption of commodity stocks'. Fifthly and most importantly, 'the industrial crisis broke out in the conditions of the *general* crisis of capitalism, when capitalism no longer has . . . the strength and stability it had before the war and . . . when industry has acquired, as a heritage from the war, chronic under-capacity operation of plants and . . . millions of unemployed'. Moreover, despite the resistance of 'the monopolist cartels', most commodity prices nevertheless fell, further undermining the position of debtors and 'unorganized' commodity producers ('peasants, artisans and small capitalists') vis-à-vis creditors and 'capitalists united in cartels'. Thus capitalism had 'succeeded in somewhat alleviating the position of industry', but mainly 'at the expense of farmers . . . and at the expense of peasants in the colonies and economically weaker countries, by further forcing down prices for the products of their labour'. In addition, the 'intensified struggle' for markets had given rise to increased dumping, protectionism and 'extreme *nationalism* in economic policy', straining international relations and sowing the seeds of 'military conflicts' conducive to 'a new redivision of the world . . . in favour of the stronger states'. That was why the ruling classes of the capitalist countries were 'so zealously destroying . . . the last vestiges of parliamentarianism' and 'fascism has now become . . . fashionable . . . among war-mongering bourgeois politicians'. Hence the triumph of fascism in Germany in 1933 was to be seen 'not only as a symptom of the weakness of the working class and a result of the betrayals of the working class by Social Democracy', but also as further evidence that the bourgeoisie was 'no longer able to rule by the old methods of parliamentarianism and bourgeois democracy' and could 'no longer . . . find a way out of the present situation on the basis of a peaceful foreign policy'. It was 'compelled . . . to resort to terrorist methods of rule . . . and . . . a policy of war' (Stalin 1955b: 288–92, 297–300).

Few liberals, let alone Marxists, foresaw that within two decades capitalism and 'bourgeois democracy' would be enjoying a new lease of life in an era of unprecedented economic buoyancy, technological dynamism, welfare provision and popular participation in pluralistic parliamentary regimes. The belief that capitalism was in 'terminal' crisis was by no means confined to the Marxist left. There were deep-seated fears for the future even among 'liberal' economists. The so-called 'under-consumptionist' school (which provided many of the theoretical underpinnings, personnel and policy prescriptions of the American 'New Deal' in the mid-1930s) feared that the increasingly monopolistic structure of American and European industry and finance was causing profits and the growth of investment and productive capacity to outstrip the growth of wages, purchasing power and hence consumption, leading to chronic problems of over-capacity or 'under-consumption'. Moreover, the so-called 'stagnationist' school headed by Alvin Hansen (and strongly influencing John Maynard Keynes) argued that European and American capitalism had lost forever the vigour, dynamism, trade expansion, mass migration, high profits, buoyant demand and seemingly limitless opportunities generated by the European population explosion, the Industrial Revolution and the colonizing 'expansion of Europe' into the New World between the late eighteenth and the early twentieth century. This was now perceived as an unrepeatable 'one-off' experience. Moreover, with the exhaustion of fortuitous external stimuli, the secular decline in European birth rates, the cessation of mass migration, the increasing closure of markets and the apparent saturation of demand, there seemed to be no guarantee that the American and European economies would ever again expand fast enough either to generate full employment or to avert a disastrous decline in rates of profit, with the result that investment would eventually dry up and laissez-faire capitalism and the profit motive would cease to be viable (let alone dynamic). Consequently, many European and American economists, politicians and intellectuals were slowly coming to the conclusion that laissez-faire capitalism was not only incapable of providing full employment (with all the social and political dangers that this would involve), but was literally 'running out of steam' and might even be 'doomed'. For many the only means of escape seemed to lie in some form of socialism or étatism or fascism.

COMINTERN'S RESPONSE TO THE RISE OF NAZI GERMANY

In December 1933, in response to Hitler's rapid and brutal consolidation of Nazi rule and his government's swift moves to reactivate the mighty German economy and rearm the German Reich, the Comintern Executive Committee promulgated new *Theses on Fascism, the War Danger and the Tasks of Communist Parties*: 'The fascist government of Germany, which is the chief instigator of war in Europe, is provoking trouble in Danzig, in Austria, in the Saar, in the Baltic countries and in Scandinavia and, on the pretext of fighting against Versailles, is trying to form a bloc for the purpose of bringing about a new bloody carving up of Europe for the benefit of German imperialism . . . Europe has become a powder-magazine which may explode at any moment' (reprinted in Degras 1965: 300).

These same Comintern pronouncements anticipated that the coming conflict would culminate in an assault on the USSR. 'The bourgeoisie want to postpone the doom of capitalism by a criminal imperialist war and a counter-revolutionary campaign against the land of victorious socialism' (p. 301). The deepening world crisis and the approaching war(s) were seen as posing mortal threats to the very survival of the Soviet Union and of Europe's Communist parties, while also strengthening their chances of finally overthrowing European capitalism. Matters would soon be forced to a head. Intensified fascist repression of revolutionary forces 'cannot, in conditions when capitalism is shaken, for long frighten the advanced strata of the toilers'. Indeed, 'the indignation which this terror has aroused even among the majority of workers who followed the social democrats makes them more susceptible to Communist agitation and propaganda' (p. 299). The economic crisis had sharpened all the contradictions of capitalism: 'The great task of the international proletariat is to turn this crisis of the capitalist world into the victory of the proletarian revolution . . . The great historical task of international Communism is to mobilize the broad masses against war even before war has begun, and thereby hasten the doom of capitalism . . . In fighting against war, the Communists must prepare even now for the transformation of the imperialist war into civil war' (reprinted in Degras 1965: 299–303).

THE PRIMACY OF THE CONTEST BETWEEN COMMUNISM AND FASCISM

The Communists' contempt for liberalism and social democracy sprang partly from a belief that the only two forces which really counted in interwar Europe were Communism and fascism, which were now pitted against one another in readiness for the final showdown. There was an implicit mutual respect and understanding between Communists and fascists which was largely absent from their attitudes to other political movements and ideologies. Like the fascists, most Communists then believed that the liberal democracies were a spent force and that twentieth-century European liberalism and social democracy were mere masks for the monopolistic and imperialistic 'finance capital' which had superseded nineteenth-century liberal capitalism. Thus interwar Europe's liberals and social democrats were inherently 'soft' on fascism, which they would rather 'appease' than resist. This view was greatly reinforced when the prime ministers of Britain and France, Chamberlain and Daladier, virtually handed Czechoslovakia to Hitler on a plate in September 1938. In his report to the March 1939 Congress Stalin wryly remarked that 'one might think that the districts of Czechoslovakia were yielded to Germany as the price of an undertaking to launch a war on the Soviet Union' (Stalin 1955c: 368).

Both Hitler and the Communists believed that in the approaching 'battle of the Titans' (Greater Germany and its minions versus the Soviet Union), the defeated side would probably lose everything. The stakes could not have been higher. A fascist victory would lead to the extinction of Communism (not to mention European humanist civilization). Conversely, a Communist victory would hasten the downfall of European capitalism and permit a massive extension of Communist rule into Central, Eastern and perhaps even Western Europe, in a different version of 'the end of history'. Therefore, whatever the costs, it came to be seen as the sacred duty of all Communists to do whatever was necessary to ensure the survival of 'the socialist fatherland', without which all would be lost.

Thus the Nazi–Soviet Pact of August 1939, under which Nazi Germany would invade the western half of Poland while the Soviet Union invaded the eastern half, was partly 'justified' in Communist eyes as buying time for the further industrialization, rearmament and military reorganization of the Soviet Union, while keeping its powder dry for the eventual showdown with the Axis Powers. In the words of a distinguished Soviet military historian and biographer of Stalin, the Nazi–Soviet Pact of August 1939 'appears extremely tarnished, and morally an alliance with the Western democracies would have been immeasurably preferable. But neither Britain nor France was ready for such an alliance. From the point of view of state interest the Soviet Union had no other acceptable choice. A refusal to take any step would hardly have stopped Germany . . . In any case, Britain and

France had both signed similar pacts with Germany in 1938 and were conducting secret talks with Hitler in the summer of 1939 with the aim of creating an anti-Soviet bloc' (Volkogonov 1991: 356–7).

The December 1933 Comintern *Theses* also promulgated an influential but much criticized Communist definition of fascism:

> Fascism is the open, terrorist dictatorship of the most reactionary, most chauvinist and most imperialist elements of finance capital. Fascism tries to secure a mass basis for monopolist capital among the petty bourgeoisie, appealing to the peasantry, artisans, office employees and civil servants who have been thrown out of their normal course of life, and particularly to the declassed elements in the big cities, also trying to penetrate into the working class . . . Having come to power, fascism pushes aside, splits and disintegrates the other bourgeois parties (for instance Poland) or dissolves them (Germany and Italy). This striving of fascism for political monopoly intensifies the discord and conflicts in the ranks of the ruling class which follow from the internal contradictions in the position of the bourgeoisie who are becoming fascistized. (reprinted in Degras 1965: 296–7)

BEWARE OF CARICATURES OF THE COMINTERN *THESES* ON FASCISM

It needs to be emphasized that these Comintern *Theses* embody a broad and far from monolithic conception of fascism (hence the references to the 'internal contradictions' of fascism, to the conflicts within the capitalist ruling classes and to Pilsudski's Poland as a form of fascist state). Moreover, these same *Theses* insisted that 'fascist dictatorship is not an inevitable stage of the dictatorship of the bourgeoisie in all countries' (p. 297) and that 'the Communist parties must first of all brush aside the fatalistic, defeatist line of the inevitability of a fascist dictatorship' (p. 302). Hostile caricatures of the official Communist view of fascism often overlook or wilfully ignore these important points. The Communist parties did *not* see fascism as a new 'highest stage of capitalism', towards which all 'advanced' capitalist states must inevitably evolve. Rather, they saw it as the most extreme ('most reactionary' and 'most chauvinistic') form of capitalist regime, examples of which were also (not surprisingly) to be found among the fiercely nationalistic and less developed capitalist states of Eastern, Central and Southern Europe, but *not in north-western Europe* (at least not before the German occupations of the Low Countries, France, Denmark and Norway in 1940). This was most clearly spelled out in a set of lectures given in Moscow in 1935 by the Italian Communist leader Palmiro Togliatti. He insisted that 'transition from bourgeois democracy to fascism' was not 'inevitable', since 'imperialism' (alias monopoly capitalism or finance capitalism) 'does not necessarily give birth to the fascist dictatorship . . . England, for example, is a great imperialist state in which there is a democratic parliamentary regime . . . Take France, the United States, etc. In these countries you will find tendencies toward the fascist form of society, but the parliamentary forms still exist' (Togliatti 1976: 4–5). The December 1933 Comintern *Theses* similarly insisted that 'fascist dictatorship is not an inevitable stage of the dictatorship of the bourgeoisie in all countries' (Degras 1965: 297).

This somewhat belies Kitchen's claims that the 1930s Comintern view was that fascism was 'a strikingly crude example of vulgar-Marxist determinist economism', that is, economic determinism (Kitchen 1976: 10, 29, 47, 65, 81). Criticisms of this sort fail to understand that the Communist parties were founded (even premised) upon a Leninist *rejection* of strict economic determinism in favour of an almost reckless/adventurist voluntarism. The Comintern and its affiliated Communist parties very plausibly contended that the turn to fascism was a widespread 'bourgeois' response to the profound 'crisis of capitalism' in interwar Europe. However, they did not claim that there was anything automatic, inevitable or rigidly economically determined about the passage from 'bourgeois parliamentarianism' to fascism, even though there obviously were strong economic and political forces pushing states in that direction.

TOWARDS A 'POPULAR FRONT' AGAINST FASCISM, 1935–9

The Comintern saw increased support for Communism as the *natural* popular reaction to the proliferation and 'hardening' of fascist regimes amid the profound (possibly terminal) 'crisis of capitalism' during the 1930s. If the Communist parties played their cards right, it was believed, they could turn the situation to their own advantage. But the Communist leaders did not expect Europe simply to fall into their laps. They expected to have to fight for it. As Stalin lucidly explained in an interview with H.G. Wells in July 1934: 'Capitalism is decaying, but it must not be compared with a tree which has decayed to such an extent that it must fall to the ground of its own accord. No, revolution, the substitution of one social system by another, has always been a struggle, a painful and cruel struggle, a life and death struggle. And every time the people of the new world came into power they had to defend themselves against the attempts of the old world to restore the old power by force' (Stalin 1955c: 35).

Accordingly, resolutions passed by the August 1935 Comintern Congress warned 'against dangerous illusions about an automatic collapse of the fascist dictatorship', emphasized that 'only the united revolutionary struggle of the working class at the head of all toilers will bring about the overthrow of the fascist dictatorship', and reaffirmed that the transformation of the deepening crisis of capitalism into a 'victorious proletarian revolution' depended 'solely on the strength and influence of the Communist parties among the broad masses of the proletariat, on the energy and self-sacrificing devotion of the Communists' (reprinted in Degras 1965: 360, 355). This was *extreme voluntarism*, the very *opposite* of the economic determinism of which the Communist parties have frequently been accused.

The August 1935 Comintern Congress also approved a significant change of attitude towards Europe's social democratic parties, which even the March 1934 *Theses* of Comintern's Agitprop Department had blamed for the latest triumphs of fascism: 'In the conditions when the last and "decisive battle" is approaching, a cleavage in the working class is the main source of its weakness . . . This cleavage is the result of the treachery of social democracy, a result of its policy of saving bourgeois rule from the proletarian revolution' (Degras 1965: 324).

In reality the Communists' refusal to co-operate with so-called 'social fascists' had fatally divided the German left, scuppering all attempts to reconstruct moderate centre-left alternatives to the ultra-nationalist right, reinforcing 'bourgeois' and 'petty bourgeois' fear of 'the Communist threat' and helping the Nazis to gain power in January 1933, despite having won just 33 per cent of the vote (less than the 37 per cent combined share of the Communists and the socialists) in the November 1932 Reichstag elections (Kolinsky 1974: 77–8). Belatedly learning from their momentous mistake, the Communist parties decided to foster and support broader anti-fascist coalitions known as 'Popular Fronts', although by then the Nazis were firmly entrenched in power and the German left had been crushed. Now social democrats were no longer to be denounced as 'social fascists' and cold-shouldered, but to be treated as comrades-in-arms in the struggle against fascism. However, it should be stressed that the adoption of the 'Popular Front' policy did not involve any fundamental change in the official Communist conception of fascism. Georgi Dimitrov, the Bulgarian Communist president of the Comintern (and future dictator of Bulgaria) simply reaffirmed the December 1933 Comintern definition of fascism (Degras 1965: 359). What is more, only the Communist parties' tactics began to change, not their goals. The 1935 Comintern Congress offered 'unity' between Communist and social democratic parties, but only on condition that 'the necessity of the revolutionary overthrow of the bourgeoisie and the establishment of the dictatorship of the proletariat in the form of Soviets be recognized' (pp. 368–9).

The August 1935 Comintern Congress passed a *Resolution on the Danger of a New World War*, warning that the 'frantic arming of fascist Germany' had given rise to 'a new intensified race for armaments throughout the capitalist world . . . The countries which have gone farthest in preparing for war (Germany, Japan, Italy, Poland) have already placed their national economy on a war footing'. The fear was expressed that these war-mongering 'fascist governments' would endeavour to reconcile their rivalries 'at the expense of the Soviet Union. The danger of the outbreak of a new imperialist war daily threatens humanity' (reprinted in Degras 1965: 373–4). The same *Resolution* affirmed that, if such a war were to start, 'the Communists will strive to lead the opponents of war . . . to struggle for the transformation of the imperialist war into a civil war against the fascist instigators of war . . . for the overthrow of capitalism' (pp. 377–8). This partly contradicts claims that, as a result of the Popular Front policy, the Comintern (and the USSR) renounced its former goal of fomenting international revolution. The disavowals of revolution would no longer hold if the Popular Fronts failed to hold fascism in check. Indeed, the Communist parties' undying commitment to the overthrow of capitalism was reaffirmed in an article by Georgi Dimitrov (as leader of the Comintern) in November 1939, after the outbreak of war in Europe: 'As the war goes on, the indignation of the masses will grow and the anti-war movement will become more extensive. The most furious persecution by the bourgeoisie will not hold up and stifle the struggle of the working people against the imperialist war. The historic role of the Communist vanguard of the working class is at the present moment to organize and take the lead of this struggle . . . The working class is called upon to put an end to the war after its own fashion, in its own interests, in the interest of the whole of labouring mankind and thereby to destroy once and for all the fundamental causes giving rise to imperialist wars' (reprinted in Degras 1965: 458–9).

This prognosis proved to be wildly over-optimistic, from a Communist standpoint. As in the First World War, most of Europe's workers loyally supported the war efforts of the states they lived in. Only the substantial Communist-led wartime resistance movements that developed in the Balkans and East Asia directly led to the establishment of some new Communist regimes. However, the May Day Manifesto issued by the Comintern Executive on 30 April 1938 demonstrated a clearer grasp of the threats hanging over both eastern and western Europe. Already German fascism, having swallowed Austria, was 'preparing an attack on Czechoslovakia. Together with Polish fascism, it strives for the occupation and partition of Lithuania.' Germany was 'crouching for a spring upon the Balkans . . . It threatens Belgium, Holland, Switzerland, and the Scandinavian countries. It surrounds France with a fascist ring and reckons to take it unawares with a sudden blow. Like a beast of prey, it scours far and wide to procure raw materials . . . and human reserves for a large-scale war against the land of socialism' (reprinted in Degras 1965: 420). This was a reasonably accurate prediction except that, instead of acting in concert with 'Polish fascism' (as suggested by the German-Polish Pact of 1934), German fascism decided to devour Poland as well.

MUNICH AND THE ORIGINS OF 'NATIONAL COMMUNISM'

The Anglo-French 'betrayal' of Czechoslovakia to the 'fascist camp' in September 1938 marked a major turning-point in the history of Communism. Indeed, it precipitated a fundamental repositioning of the Comintern and European and Asian Communist parties vis-à-vis nationalism. There had already been some 'softening' of Communist attitudes towards nationalism since 1935, under the impetus of the Popular Front policy approved in that year (and a desire to win over 'centrist' parties and opinion to more resolute resistance of the fascist Powers). Until September 1938, however, Communist parties continued to be seen as inherently 'internationalist' and 'anti-national'. After all, Communist doctrine had repeatedly disavowed nationalism and patriotism in favour of 'proletarian internationalism', proclaiming the 'solidarity' of working peoples of all nations against 'bourgeois nationalist' trickery, duplicity and oppression of working people. Moreover, it was widely known that the world's Communist parties took their 'orders' from the Comintern headquarters in Moscow. Hence there was widespread nationalist and public suspicion of Communists, who were routinely regarded as 'traitors' who would readily 'betray' their countries. 'Being a Communist implied being an agent of a foreign power, which to most people seemed abhorrent.' Indeed, 'the greatest deterrent to people becoming Communists' was 'the feeling that Communism implied disloyalty to one's country' (Hammond 1958: 282). This, along with their 'godlessness' or atheism, was certainly the Communist parties' biggest electoral liability and a favourite taunt by their rivals. Public hostility to Communist parties was particularly strong in countries such as Poland and Romania, which not only nursed longstanding grievances against Russia but also felt that their 'territorial integrity' and 'national' security were threatened by the Soviet Union's apparent designs on their eastern marchlands and by Polish and Romanian Communist parties which (in the name of 'proletarian internationalism') really were prepared to countenance (and even participate in) the imminent dismemberment of Poland and Romania by the Soviet Union. In actual fact the eastern half of Poland was mainly inhabited by Ukrainians, Belarussians and Lithuanians. Thus, by the principle of national self-determination, they did not properly 'belong' to Poland. But this highly inconvenient fact did not cut much ice with Polish nationalists, most of whom were grimly determined to hang on to the Ukrainian, Belarussian and Lithuanian territories and populations that they had conquered in 1919–20. They deeply resented all Soviet and Communist intimations of the need to 'liberate' these territories from (genuine) Polish 'oppression' and implicitly to 'reunite' them with their co-nationals in the Ukrainian and Belarussian Soviet Republics and in Lithuania. Soviet designs on Bukovina and Bessarabia (now Moldova) were not similarly underpinned by Wilsonian 'ethnic' justifications, however, since 'ethnic' Romanians were clearly in the majority and the Slavs formed small minorities. Soviet 'claims' to their territories were purely 'historical' in the case of Bessarabia (which had been annexed to the Russian Empire from 1812 to 1918) and 'strategic' in the case of northern Bukovina, which had never previously tasted the blessings of Russian rule before it was annexed by the Soviet Union in June 1940. In making these annexations, Stalin was to act more as a 'big power' imperialist than as a revolutionary Marxist championing world revolution.

However, the September 1938 Munich agreement between Chamberlain, Daladier, Hitler and Mussolini (to dismember Czechoslovakia) handed Europe's Communist parties the golden opportunity to put themselves forward as the only 'reliable' champions of 'collective security' and as the 'true defenders' of European nations against the fascist menace and 'bourgeois liberal' trickery. After Munich, indeed, the Czechoslovak centrist parties which had misguidedly put so much faith in the Western Powers suffered severe crises of confidence and loss of support, whereas the Czechoslovak Communist Party experienced such a strong upsurge of popularity that it took its members quite a while to get used to it! (But this was the fundamental reason why the Communist Party became Czechoslovakia's most popular party during the 1940s, winning 38 per cent of the vote in the 1946 elections.)

The Comintern was quick to capitalize on this unexpected 'gift horse' and turn of events. In a 'Manifesto' issued in November 1938 it claimed that, by reaffirming its readiness to defend Czechoslovakia against Germany (if France would do likewise), 'the Soviet government, during the Czechoslovak crisis, showed how agreements should be kept and collective security defended . . . The Munich agreement was not only a blow at Czechoslovakia. It is a conspiracy against the small nations which Britain and France are betraying to the fascist plunderers.' It was asserted that Czechoslovakia could have been saved, as Germany was not yet fully prepared for war: 'Ranged against Germany were forces on whose side was the overwhelming preponderance. Czechoslovakia possessed an excellent army and was protected by a first class system of fortresses. The British and French fleets were in a position to blockade Germany. Action by the Soviet Union would have given rise to a powerful wave of the anti-fascist movement in defence of the just cause of the peoples. Faced by such forces, German fascism would have had no alternative but to retreat. But the British bourgeoisie who dragged France in the wake of their policy did not want to permit this political defeat of the fascist gendarme of Europe. Britain and France did everything possible to compel Czechoslovakia to capitulate' (reprinted in Degras 1965: 430).

COMINTERN'S ESPOUSAL OF 'PROLETARIAN PATRIOTISM'

The Comintern decided to cast the Communist parties and the working classes in the roles of true patriots and bona fide custodians of national liberty and independence in the struggle against Europe's fascists and 'false' patriots. 'The condition for a successful struggle to strengthen the cause of peace is to replace the governments of national treachery and shame in the countries menaced by fascist blows . . . A government of real national salvation cannot pursue the ruinous path of capitulation. It will conduct a ruthless struggle against capitulators and agents of foreign fascism . . . It will disarm the fascist leagues and make the working class organizations the mainstay of the country's defence. It will conduct a consistent policy of collective security and will not shrink from employing sanctions against the aggressor' (p. 432). Most tellingly of all, it declared that 'the task of the working class now is to head the liberation struggle of the enslaved nations and the defence of the peoples threatened by foreign domination. The nation is not the gang of fascists, reactionary financiers and industrial magnates who rob and betray the people. The nation is the many millions of workers, peasants and working people generally – the people that is devoted to its country, cherishes its liberty, and defends its independence . . . The working class is the backbone of the nation, the bulwark of its liberty, dignity and independence' (p. 432).

In performing this volte-face and embracing the nationalist and patriotic sentiments which they had eschewed for so long, the Communist parties imparted a whole new significance to the Popular Front policy which they had launched in 1935. Identification with 'the people' suddenly translated into neo-populist and/or nationalist identification with the *narod*, the nation, *la patrie*, the fatherland, paving the way for the anti-fascist centre-left Patriotic or Fatherland Fronts which became the Trojan horses through which Balkan and East Central European Communist parties went on to establish so-called 'People's Democracies' in the aftermath of the Second World War. 'The Workers', whom Communists had hitherto held up as the historic bearers of 'proletarian internationalism' *in opposition* to reactionary 'bourgeois nationalism', were suddenly hailed as the supreme and unsullied embodiments of 'the nation' and national virtue, using much the same kind of language as fascist and extreme nationalist propagandists. With brazen inconsistency, however, Communist parties continued to use the language and imagery of 'proletarian internationalism' whenever it suited them, *alongside* that of the new 'patriotic' working class. Europe's more principled (internationalist) Marxists were disgusted by this unprincipled ideological 'sell-out', pandering to primitive national and patriotic pride and prejudice. Nevertheless, shedding the stigmas of 'treason' and 'disloyalty' opened the way for a number of Communist parties to win unprecedented 'national' followings in 1940s Czechoslovakia, Yugoslavia, Albania, Greece, Italy, France, China and Vietnam. Communists were able to turn the tables on the right by stealing their thunder (that is, by appropriating the emotive language and imagery of patriotism for their own use) and many new or young voters unsuspectingly 'fell' for this Communist stratagem. Moreover, in the course of their often bitter and heroic struggles against European and East Asian fascism and/or imperialism during the 1940s, the Yugoslav, Albanian, Italian, Chinese and Vietnamese Communist parties were successfully metamorphosed into patriotic 'freedom fighters' and 'national liberation movements', vindicating and validating their new patriotic credentials by the extraordinary courage, tenacity, endurance and ferocity of their fighting.

Chalmers Johnson has argued that the major Communist successes in the Balkans and East Asia during the 1940s would not have occurred if the parties in question had not abandoned their former anti-national positions and rhetoric and transformed themselves into anti-fascist and anti-imperialist 'national liberation movements', whose rapidly growing popular support and political appeal owed more to patriotism than to Communism. In his view, the scale, scope and savagery of the Axis occupation of Yugoslavia and the Japanese invasion of China left the inhabitants 'little or no room for accommodation to the new order' (Johnson 1962: 157–8, 164). The persistent brutality of the subsequent 'mopping up', counter-insurgency and 'bandit extermination' operations and the reprisals against villages and towns that tried to resist raised the levels of popular political and national consciousness 'in countries . . . where previous "national movements" had appealed only to educated elites' (pp. 23, 30, 172–4). The invaders unwittingly curtailed the former 'parochialism and political indifference among the peasants' and, 'mobilized by an unavoidable military challenge' yet 'bereft of their traditional foci of loyalty, the peasantry stood ready to resist the invaders but lacked effective leadership. The Communist party filled the need. Possessing a valuable cadre of battle-tested and militarily competent veterans, as well as a commitment to war as a mode of social change the Communist party was not only willing but eager to lead' (pp. 156–8, 166). In the case of Yugoslavia, membership of the outlawed Communist Party had dwindled from 80,000 in 1920 to just 3,000 in 1929 and 1939 (p. 165). But about 1,200 Yugoslav Communists gained combat training and experience in 'the fight against fascism' during the Spanish Civil War (1936–9) and contributed a nucleus of military commanders to the Yugoslav Partisan forces, who numbered some 800,000 members by 1945 (pp. 166, 173). Johnson concluded that 'the demands of national crisis rather than the logic of Communism brought the Chinese and Yugoslav Communist Parties to power' (p. 180) and that 'popular Communism without a basis of nationalism does not exist' (p. 179).

Johnson's thesis is very persuasive, but he was mistaken in treating 'national Communism' as something that was peculiar to Yugoslavia and China during the 1940s (p. 7). By the late 1930s the Comintern was eagerly extolling patriotism (as distinct from more predatory forms of nationalism), not least because Stalin had decided to rehabilitate and make use of Great Russia nationalism within the Soviet Union in anticipation of the long-awaited fascist invasion of his own domains. The new 'patriotic appeal' of Communism was also exploited to considerable effect in 1940s Czechoslovakia, Albania, Greece, Vietnam, Bulgaria, France and Italy (despite the temporary embarrassments and confusion caused by the Nazi–Soviet Pact from August 1939 to June 1941). Moreover, Johnson's insistence that the successes of the Yugoslav Communist Party during the 1940s were based on an identification with nationalism (pp. 175, 178, 184) is misleading and problematic, as in Yugoslavia nationalism chiefly took the form of crude, fratricidal, almost racist, Croat and Serb 'ethnic' nationalism. The Partisans and the Yugoslav Communist Party did sometimes exploit or pander to these crude forms of nationalism at the local/tactical level. But the Communists triumphed partly because they were the only major political force in Yugoslavia that managed (for the most part) to rise above 'ethnic' nationalism by credibly championing a supranational Yugoslavism. This was 'nationalist' only in the laudable sense of trying to persuade the various Yugoslav ethnic groups or 'nations' to stop killing each other and to unite against the external predators who had ravaged and dismembered their country. Likewise, the Czechoslovak Communist Party mainly upheld the civic Czechoslovak ideals of Masaryk and Benes, rather than the more self-centred, tetchy and introverted Czech and Slovak 'ethnic' nationalisms.

WHY THE OFFICIAL COMMUNIST *THESES ON FASCISM* MERIT SERIOUS CONSIDERATION

Some of the mainstream Western literature on fascism seems to discount the official Communist interpretations of this 'excrescence' of European civilization simply on the basis that Communist pronouncements represent the official 'party line' and must therefore be crude, simplistic, reductionist or suspect, almost by definition (see, for example, O'Sullivan 1983: 17–19 and Griffin 1993: 3–4). However, while we deplore the hideous excesses perpetrated by most Communist parties and regimes, we do not believe that the official Communist interpretations of fascism can or should be lightly dismissed. They are no more suspect, deficient or partisan than some of the other partial or one-sided conceptions or interpretations which have strongly illuminated particular facets of fascism without offering a comprehensive or rounded explanation, especially those that analyse or conceptualize fascism virtually in the abstract or with insufficient regard for its specific social and economic context and sources of social and political support, for example Nolte (1969) and O'Sullivan (1983).

On the contrary, just as Nolte and O'Sullivan furnish valuable fresh insights into the ideology, discourse, style and antecedents of fascism, so the official Communist interpretations shed important and interesting light on the socio-economic dimensions of fascism, which many other approaches have tended to neglect or deliberately ignore. The Communist interpretations also usefully emphasize the centrality of the titanic struggles between fascism and Communism (in contrast to the weak-kneed 'appeasement' of fascism by the Western democracies) and the critical roles that these played in the subsequent expansion of Communist power in the Balkans and East Central Europe and the widespread popular support which it enjoyed for a time in Italy and France.

Furthermore, until the commencement of the Nazi-sponsored genocide of the Jews in the late 1930s, the first and foremost target of fascist thuggery and persecution was the so-called 'Bolshevik menace'. Many of Europe's leading Communist analysts of fascism felt or witnessed these fascist verbal and physical assaults at first hand and as part of a more widespread offensive by Europe's increasingly crisis-stricken, frightened and aggressive propertied classes against the Marxist left, independently organized labour and a putative 'Soviet threat' in the wake of the Bolshevik Revolution and the massive economic disruption and social unrest bequeathed by the First World War. If only for these reasons, the Communist interpretations of fascism merit serious consideration, just as one cannot and should not lightly dismiss Jewish accounts of the subsequent Holocaust. From our standpoint, the chief virtues of the official Communist interpretations of fascism are that they aptly portray it as: (i) a widespread, multifaceted phenomenon which was inextricably linked to the general interwar 'crisis of capitalism' and of 'liberal'/'bourgeois' parliamentary democracy; (ii) a phenomenon which developed not only in the mind and in the realms of ideology, but also in specific social and economic contexts and with specific sources of social and political support; (iii) part of a wider drift towards economic nationalism, étatism and authoritarianism; and (iv) part of a 'crusade' against 'Bolshevism' and independently organized labour in most of the capitalist world, including the increasingly repressive, anti-Bolshevik, ultra-nationalist regimes of East Central Europe and the Balkans.

At least in their initial stages, fascist movements usually managed to combine two potentially contradictory thrusts or manifestations of class antagonism: a 'prole-bashing' hostility to militant labour and the Marxist left; and seemingly radical hostility to 'finance capitalism', rentiers, 'parasites' and economic intermediaries ('middlemen'). Marxists are often criticized for emphasizing the role of the former to the relative neglect of the latter. 'By assuming fascism to be an essentially anti-proletarian force, they play down its antagonism to the ethos of laissez-faire economics, consumerist materialism and the bourgeoisie, and are unable to take seriously its claim to be the negation of nineteenth-century liberalism rather than its perpetuation in a different guise,' according to Griffin (1993: 4). However, these criticisms are misplaced and/or misinformed. Marxists, including the Comintern and most Communist party leaders, were among the first to recognize the important roles played by the anti-capitalist rhetoric in mobilizing mass support for fascist movements, as noted above. Furthermore, Marxism not only recognized the huge significance of the metamorphosis of nineteenth-century 'liberal capitalism' into twentieth-century 'monopoly capitalism', but also produced some of the most perceptive and influential analysts of that transformation (including

Hilferding, Bukharin, Lenin, Bauer, Gramsci, Togliatti and Vargas). Most Marxists directly related the emergence and historic significance of fascism to the replacement of liberal capitalism by monopolistic 'finance capitalism'. Griffin's accusation that Marxists were 'unable to take seriously' fascism's claim that it was 'the negation of nineteenth-century liberalism rather than its perpetuation in a different guise' is therefore preposterous. Nevertheless, Marxists were quite correct to emphasize that 'prole-bashing' anti-Bolshevism was a much more pronounced, pervasive and persistent feature of fascist ideology than its superficial and ephemeral anti-capitalism. Indeed, all successful fascist leaders (including Mussolini and Hitler) sought accommodations with the 'powers that be' and the propertied classes in the course of their ascents to power and depended on the active co-operation of the military, the state bureaucracy and the propertied classes once they were installed in office, even if this involved the betrayal and frequent suppression of the radical anti-capitalist elements in their own movements. 'Fascism was not the creation of capitalism since the sources of support for the former were quite varied', yet fascism could not have operated 'against the fundamental interests of big business if it wanted to achieve its aim of military conquest' (Kolinsky 1974: 84). Moreover, most industrialists in Europe's later industrializing countries not only accepted fascist economic nationalism and étatism, but were 'accustomed to regarding state activity as an essential framework for economic development' (p. 85). In a well-received speech to the *Industrie-Klub* in Dusseldorf in January 1932, Hitler declared: 'In my view it is to put the cart before the horse when today people believe that by business methods they can . . . recover Germany's power position, instead of realizing that the power position is also the condition for the improvement of the economic situation . . . There can be no flourishing economic life which has not before it and behind it the flourishing powerful state as its protection . . . There can be no economic life unless behind this . . . there stands the determined political will of the nation absolutely ready to strike – and to strike hard' (quoted by Kolinsky 1974: 84). Fascism was neither the creature nor the servant of big business, but in order to enhance its military potential it needed to protect industrial interests. It also 'deepened the interpenetration of organized business and the state' by bringing big business 'into a more bureaucratized relationship with the state' (p. 121). Fascism attracted the propertied classes into a Faustian pact with the Devil by offering 'a spectacular solution to the problem of stability' (p. 119) as well as an expeditious resolution of the crisis of capitalism (p. 83).

RIVAL SOCIO-ECONOMIC INTERPRETATIONS OF FASCISM

Socio-economic explanations of fascism are by no means restricted to Marxists. For example, James Barrington Moore Jnr postulated the existence of 'three main historical routes from the preindustrial to the modern world', via bourgeois-democratic revolution, Communist revolution and fascism (Moore Jnr 1969: xii). He saw the fascist route as a limited 'revolution from above', occurring in industrializing societies in which the old landed ruling classes managed to avoid either losing power to or being overthrown by the bourgeoisie and/or the lower classes. In such societies the 'bourgeois impulse' was much weaker than in those that experienced bourgeois-democratic revolutions. 'If it took a revolutionary form at all, the revolution was defeated. Afterwards sections of a relatively weak commercial and industrial class relied on dissident elements in the older and still dominant ruling classes, mainly recruited from the land, to put through the political and economic changes required for a modern industrial society . . . Industrial development may proceed rapidly under such auspices. But the outcome . . . has been fascism' (pp. xii–xiii).

This interpretation implicitly depends upon an exceptionally broad conception of fascism. But, whatever one's reservations about that aspect of his thesis, Barrington Moore is surely correct in his assumption that the old landed ruling classes tried to use fascism for their own purposes (pp. 450–1), not only in Italy, Germany, Japan and the Iberian Peninsula, but also in parts of the Balkans and

East Central Europe (especially Hungary and Poland). Nevertheless, fascism was not created by the scions of the old landed ruling classes. They merely sought to manipulate and hide behind their ple-beian fascist politicians, towards whom they maintained a considerable aristocratic *hauteur*. Indeed, it was mostly the landed lesser nobility (rather than the magnates) who became actively involved in fascist or quasi-fascist organizations and activities and tried to infiltrate and gradually take over the conservative authoritarian nationalist regimes that ruled these countries. Moreover, defence of the power and privileges of the old ruling class was not integral to fascist programmes and ideologies. The frequent collaboration between fascist dictatorships and the old landed classes was 'a contin-gent historic circumstance rather than an essential feature of the regime' (Gregor 1979: 312). Indeed, fascist regimes often found themselves irksomely constrained or even impaired by their dependence upon the collaboration of the old ruling classes, who for their part later made some attempts to throw off or escape from the fascist embrace. In any case, the collaboration of the old ruling classes was just one of several important strands in fascism. Therefore, while Barrington Moore has thrown some new light on this, he has provided a rather incomplete and one-dimensional explanation of fascism as a phenomenon.

A.J. Gregor has more provocatively portrayed Mussolini's Fascist dictatorship as a prototype of the 'mobilizing, developmental regimes that have become so prominent in the twentieth century', especially in countries experiencing 'delayed industrialization' (Gregor 1979: ix, xii, 171, 327). In contrast to the many writers who have maintained that Mussolini and his Fascist movement never developed a substantial and definitive political and economic philosophy and programme, Gregor is second to none in arguing that 'Fascism, prior to its advent to power, advertised a specific pro-gramme addressed to immediate problems that afflicted the national economy' (p. 127). 'Long before Fascism became a successful mass-mobilizing movement, it entertained ideological, doctri-nal and programmatic commitments which it acted out once in power.' These were the work of 'the most aggressive and youthful revolutionary syndicalists', including Angelo Olivetti, Sergio Panun-zio, Roberto Michels, Edmondo Rossoni and Massimo Rocca (p. 117). 'Fascism was the direct and documented heir of revolutionary syndicalism' (p. 97). Even though their programme was not implemented in earnest until the 1930s, 'Fascists early anticipated a corporative and revolutionary state that would displace the ineffectual parliamentary regime. That new state would undertake extensive intervention in labour relations; it would institute tariff protection (and, by implication, subventions) for selected industries . . . Fascists expected that their strong state would provide the impetus for the expansion and modernization of the entire economic infrastructure of the nation' (p. 131). Thus the Fascists fashioned 'an ideology of rapid modernization and industrialization', fos-tered an ethos of work, sacrifice and 'class-collaboration', and promoted 'the expansion of a dynamic, interventionist and hegemonic state' under 'a charismatic and heroic leader who would incarnate the process' (p. 314). According to Gregor, 'what is essential for all mass-mobilizing, developmental regimes is not their respective class bases, but their developmental programme . . . These regimes must domesticate labour to an economy of high productivity but minimal consump-tion. To that end, they will try to orchestrate consensus . . . through the invocation of national myths and appeals to the providential leader' (pp. 312–13).

Gregor's critics have argued that he has underplayed the specificity and exaggerated the coher-ence and consistency of the Fascist ideology and economic programme. Indeed, the 'modernizing' and 'developmental' tendencies and accomplishments of the Fascist regime were not as strong as he suggests, and most authoritarian nationalist regimes have neither had such a strongly developed party base nor rested upon such charismatic leadership as that developed by Mussolini (O'Sullivan 1983: 22–3, 187–9). However, while accepting that the differences can be as important as the simi-larities, it seems to us that Gregor has highlighted a significant facet of the fascist and quasi-fascist regimes. Indeed, his approach yields useful insights that are even more readily transferable to the fascist and quasi-fascist regimes of the interwar Balkans and East Central Europe than they are to

Nazi Germany. But these by no means exhaust the socio-economic roles and significance of such regimes. Each approach and interpretation offers only an incomplete and partial explanation of fascism. This is as true of the 'mass society' interpretations of fascism (e.g. Kornhauser 1960; Arendt 1966) as it is of the Communist ones.

THE SUPERIORITY OF CIRCUMSPECT AND MULTIFACETED INTERPRETATIONS OF FASCISM

In his 1935 lectures on fascism Togliatti prudently warned that 'fascism must not be viewed as something which is definitively characterized; that it must be seen in its development, never as something set, never as a scheme or a model, but as the consequence of a series of real economic and political relations resulting from real factors – from the economic situation, from the struggle of the masses' (Togliatti 1976: 26). He also emphasized that fascism 'is an eclectic ideology ... Fascist ideology contains a series of heterogeneous ingredients ... It serves to solder together various factions in the struggle for dictatorship over the working masses and to create a vast movement for this scope. Fascist ideology is an instrument created to bind these elements together' (p. 9). Fascist rule had become increasingly 'totalitarian' in the course of vain attempts to cope with the heterogeneity and the inherent instability and 'contradictions' of its social support (pp. 22–3, 25–6). 'Fascism was not born totalitarian; it became so' (p. 24). However, as he pointed out in an article published in 1934, it would be a 'grave theoretical and political error to think that the setting up of the fascist dictatorship suppresses the contradictions among the various groups of the bourgeoisie' and an even graver mistake to imagine that 'by creating a fascist organization that embraces the majority of the population and all the forms of its life, fascism can ultimately suppress the fundamental antagonism that exists between the class content of the fascist dictatorship and the interests and aspirations of the working classes'. Quite the reverse: 'sheltered by this would-be "totalitarianism" and monolithic system, capitalist exploitation is increasing considerably, creating the objective conditions for an extreme sharpening of the class struggle that can be contained only for a certain period of time, exploding in the end with all the more force and impetus' (p. 140), as indeed it did in Italy, France, East Central Europe and the Balkans in 1945–6. In conjunction with the (not unrelated) expansion of Soviet power, this 'action recoil' played a crucial role in the Communist seizures of power in the Balkans and East Central Europe at that time.

29   The impact of the Second World War and mass genocide, 1939–45

THE PIVOTAL 'WAR OF ANNIHILATION' IN THE EASTERN HALF OF EUROPE

The titanic struggle for control of the eastern half of Europe, between the Axis Powers, on the one side, and the Soviet Union and its Communist supporters in parts of the Balkans and East Central Europe, on the other, was the pivotal contest of the Second World War. Relative to the 'wars of annihilation' and 'fights to the death' unleashed by the German invasions of western Poland in September 1939 and eastern Poland in June 1941 and the German-led Axis invasions of Yugoslavia in April 1941 and the USSR in June 1941, the battles fought in western Europe and north Africa during the Second World War were mere sideshows with limited objectives and much lower death tolls. The warfare in the eastern half of Europe had a savage no-holds-barred bestiality which by comparison made the conduct of the Axis forces in western Europe seem relatively tame and rule-governed. Furthermore, by 1943 or 1944 the Jews, the Roma (Gypsies) and most of the Slavs in the eastern half of Europe were grimly aware that victory for the Third Reich over the Soviet armed forces could mean total annihilation for millions of their kinsfolk and the reduction of the vast majority of the survivors to subhuman conditions of servitude to the alleged 'master race', and that the fate of the whole of the eastern half of Europe therefore depended on whether the seemingly primitive, barbaric and technologically puny Soviet Union could somehow – and against all the odds – manage to defeat the Third Reich. Tragically, 'the tide of war turned too late' to save most of Europe's Jews, the vast majority of whom lived in the eastern half of Europe, even though the Soviet Union ultimately emerged victorious (C. Browning 2005: 427).

Unlike the vast majority of wars (including those which Germany has fought against western European states), the German invasion of Poland and the Axis invasions of Albania, Greece, Yugoslavia and the Soviet Union were not limited wars aimed merely at inflicting somewhat humiliating military defeats on these countries, making modest territorial acquisitions at their expense, and establishing superiority and/or overlordship over them, whilst leaving their societies, economies and territories still largely intact. Fascist Italy aimed at the total subjugation and absorption of Albania, Greece and western Yugoslavia; Nazi Germany aimed at the total dismemberment and pulverization of Poland and Yugoslavia; and Nazi Germany's political and military leaders characterized their war against the Soviet Union as a 'war of destruction', aiming at the total annihilation of the so-called 'Judaeo-Communists' and the economy and society of Soviet Russia (Hilberg 1985: 100; C. Browning 2005: 213–14). In addition to regarding Jews, Gypsies and 'Judaeo-Communists' as 'vermin' to be exterminated, the Nazis also regarded Russians, Poles and most Yugoslavs as inferior species, fit only to be 'hewers of wood and drawers of water'; and the Polish intelligentsia was 'marked for extermination, no matter what it did' (J.T. Gross 1979: 47, 74–5, 92, 233; 2006: 5; C. Browning 2005: 71). Hitler's propaganda minister Joseph Goebbels noted in his diary on 10

October 1941: 'The Führer's verdict on the Poles is devastating. More like animals than human beings, totally stupid and amorphous' (quoted in C. Browning 2005: 46).

Consequently, the inhabitants of East Central Europe, the Balkans and the Soviet Union suffered vastly more than the Western states during the Second World War. Nazi Germany and its Austrian, *Volksdeutsche*, Italian, Magyar, Slovak, Romanian, Croatian, Bulgarian, Bosniak, Kosovar, Ukrainian, Belarussian, Lithuanian and Latvian collaborators not only killed around three-quarters of the 5 million Jewish inhabitants of East Central Europe and the Balkans, but also caused the deaths of around 20 million (mainly Russian) Soviet citizens, nearly 2 million ethnic Poles, tens of thousands of Roma (Gypsies), and hundreds of thousands of Yugoslavs, Greeks and Albanians, among others.

From late June 1941 to May 1945 the Soviet Union bore the main burden of the land war against Nazi Germany. From June 1941 to June 1944, Hitler deployed '80 or 90 per cent of his land forces against Russia . . . According to German military sources, Hitler guarded the Atlantic coast with 59 second rate divisions, while 260 of his divisions, including the best, fought on the Russian front' (Deutscher 1966: 485–6.) Between 75 and 80 per cent of German losses of 'men and materiel were incurred on the Eastern Front' (Davies 2006: 244). From mid-1941 to mid-1944 'the Soviet Union never fought less than 90 per cent of the German army, and even after the Normandy landings the western Allies fought only about a third of the Wehrmacht. The British and Americans were content with a situation in which the very high casualties that would be necessary to defeat the Germans would be borne by the Soviets . . . At no time were the British and the Americans prepared to adapt their own strategy to meet Soviet requirements', nor did they create a second front in Europe to reduce the burden on the Soviet Union in 1942, and the Mediterranean strategy which they adopted in 1943 did not significantly relieve the military pressure on the Soviet Union (Ponting 1995: 96–7). Although the Western Allies delivered vital supplies of aircraft, tanks, lorries and jeeps from 1941 to 1944, Western deliveries of tanks and aircraft never exceeded 10 per cent of Soviet output and 'dropped to 3 per cent after late 1942' (p. 128). This is sometimes portrayed as magnanimous Western aid to the USSR in its fight against Nazi Germany, but it was really very meagre assistance given in the hope that the USSR would defeat Germany in modes of warfare which only a regime like Stalin's could have sustained for any length of time. Indeed, Stalin had already sacrificed millions of Soviet lives during the 1930s, although precisely how many millions has remained hotly disputed. The Western liberal democracies simply did not have the stomach to bear casualties on the scale entailed by land war against the main German armed forces at the peak of their strength in 1941–3, nor the large casualties involved in the capture of major German-held cities during 1944–5. Of about 20 million *combat* deaths during the Second World War, fewer than 600,000 were incurred by the UK and the USA combined and 2.3 million were incurred by Germany, whereas roughly 13 million were incurred by the Soviet Union (Ponting 1995: 203). Thus Nazi Germany was primarily defeated by the Soviet Union, especially by its ethnic Russian citizens.

Norman Davies has recently attempted to play down the paramount role of the Russians in defeating Nazi Germany, by pointing out that 'Russians formed only 55–60 per cent of the population' of the Soviet Union and that 'by far the heaviest civilian casualties of the war were incurred in the western, non-Russian borders of the USSR: among Balts, Byelorussians, Jews, Poles and Ukrainians' (Davies 2006: 241–2). However, his argument is very misleading. Although the western borderlands of the Soviet Union almost certainly did account for a high proportion of the 20–27 million Soviet lives alleged to have been lost during the Second World War, these areas fell under German control very quickly during the Axis invasion of the Soviet Union and were therefore unable to play major roles in defeating Nazi Germany. On the contrary, it is widely acknowledged that many Ukrainians, Belarussians and Balts initially welcomed the German forces as liberators and that many members of these same ethnic groups went on to 'collaborate' with the occupation forces and even participate in the Nazi-orchestrated mass extermination of Jews and of many

Russians taken as forced labourers or prisoners of war, or work as brutal guards in Nazi forced labour, POW and concentration camps (Gross 1979: 190–5; Beevor 2004: 113; Polonsky and Michlik 2004: 26, 438; Hilberg 1985: 139). Well over a million largely non-Russian Soviet citizens worked or fought for Nazi Germany against the Soviet Union (Beevor 2004: 113). Therefore the ethnic Russian population of the Soviet Union bore the brunt of the fighting against Nazi Germany and, as Davies himself admits, incurred most of the 13 million Soviet combat deaths (Davies 2006: 245). On the eve of the Second World War most European countries were ruled by authoritarian nationalist or fascist regimes and, as Mark Mazower has cogently argued, the dominant trends in Europe were leading away from liberalism and democracy towards various forms of authoritarian nationalism, fascism and beggar-my-neighbour protectionism (Mazower 1998: 2–3, 20–7). Paradoxically, it was the defeat of Nazi Germany by the Soviet Union which reversed these trends and thereby launched western Europe on a new course towards liberal/social democracy, welfare states and economic integration after 1945, even though this was not at all what Stalin and his Soviet regime had intended at the time. Although they mostly prefer to forget this, western Europeans are heavily indebted to the Russians for the freedom, prosperity and economic integration which they have enjoyed and largely taken for granted since the 1950s – and which has been extended to East Central Europe and (in smaller measure) the Balkans since 1989.

The especially massive scale of the depredations, deportations and loss of life in Poland, Yugoslavia, Greece and Albania, which (relative to their respective population sizes) far exceeded anything experienced in the West and was comparable only to what the Soviet Union suffered, helps to explain why these four countries produced Europe's largest resistance movements: in Yugoslavia there were the Communist-led Partisans, with nearly a million adherents by early 1945, as well as Colonel Draza Mihajlovic's smaller Serbian nationalist Cetnik forces; in Poland the pro-Western Armia Krajowa (Home Army) had an estimated 350,000 members in 1943 (Gross 1979: 281) and more than 300,000 'sworn-in members' at its peak (J.T. Gross 2006: 5), but there were also some other smaller forces, including a Communist-led Armia Ludowa (People's Army); in Greece the Communist-led National People's Liberation Army (ELAS), which comprised around 60,000 active combatants by October 1944 (Clogg 1992: 128), tied down 200,000–300,000 occupation troops and successfully disrupted Axis supply lines, and there was also a (Venizelist) right-wing National Republican Greek League (EDES) led by a shady, ambitious and macho Colonel Napoleon Zervas; and in Albania there was a Communist-led National Liberation Front (LNC), launched in September 1942, as well as a smaller republican-nationalist *Balli Kombetar* (BK, National Front) guerilla movement launched in October 1942. These movements fought tenaciously not only against fascism, but for the future control of their respective countries by creating so-called 'facts on the ground' (de facto control of territory).

By the end of the Second World War, several million Slavs, Jews, Greeks and Albanians had joined anti-fascist resistance movements. For many the main motives may have been to save their skins or to avoid seizure for forced labour. Their active resistance to the Axis Powers and their collaborators evoked barbaric Germanic and (to much lesser degrees) Italian reprisals. The Axis Powers took especially ferocious and systematic reprisals against attacks by resistance movements in Yugoslavia, Greece, Albania and Poland. In Yugoslavia in September 1941, for example, German military commanders issued orders that a hundred local people (especially Jews) were to be killed for every German killed by the local resistance movements, while fifty locals were to be killed for every German wounded (C. Browning 2005: 338–9). Whatever their motives, these resistance movements also made heroic contributions to the defeat of Nazi Germany by the Soviet Union and to the restoration of the possibility of freedom, democracy and prosperity in western Europe.

The emergence of a Czech resistance movement, which began in October 1939 and culminated in the assassination of the infamous 'Protector' and SS leader Reinhard Heydrich in May 1942, also led to savage German reprisals, including wholesale executions, deportations to concentration camps, martial law and mass extermination of Jews and Gypsies. Most notoriously, all the adult males in the village of Lidice were massacred in retaliation for Heydrich's death, and the entire village was razed to the ground. However, reprisals of this sort were almost commonplace in Yugoslavia, Greece and Albania.

Romania and Hungary also incurred large death tolls and heavy war damage despite the absence of large-scale anti-fascist resistance. This resulted from their participation in Nazi Germany's invasion of the Soviet Union in 1941–3 and in the Nazi-led Holocaust; the impact of the Soviet invasion of their respective territories; and their subsequent participation in the Soviet-led war against Nazi Germany in late 1944 and early 1945.

THE DEATH TOLLS IN EAST CENTRAL EUROPE AND THE BALKANS

During the Second World War, roughly the following numbers of people perished:

- 4.5–5 million Polish citizens, including 2.9–3 million Polish Jews (Polonsky and Michlik 2004: 7; Gross 2006: 4)
- 947,000–1 million Yugoslav citizens, including *c*.60,000 Yugoslav Jews (Covic 1991: 35; Lampe 1996: 380);
- 840,000–950,000 Romanian citizens, including 420,000–520,000 Romanian Jews (Wiesel *et al.* 2005: 388, on the death toll for Jews; and Rothschild 1974: 318 and Romania 1974: 9 for non-Jews);
- 900,000–1,050,000 inhabitants of 'greater Hungary', including 500,000–550,000 Jews (Braham 2001 and Kontler 2002: 387 for Jews; and Kontler 2002: 387 and Hoensch 1994: 163 for non-Jews);
- *c*.708,000 Greeks, including 60,000 Greek Jews, 1941–9 (Koliopulos and Veremis 2002: 258, 295);
- 125,000–135,000 Czechs, including 70,000–80,000 Czech Jews (Sayer 1998: 14 and Wandycz 2001: 232);
- 57,000–67,000 Slovak Jews (Toma and Kovak 2001: 130–2, and Liptak 2000: 264);
- 35,000–45,000 people in Bulgarian-controlled territories, including *c*.11,000 Macedonian and Greek Jews (interpolated from McIntyre 1988: 88 and Todorov 2001: 11, 23);
- more than 28,000 inhabitants of Albania (Marmullaku 1975: 59).

In the cases of Yugoslavia, Albania and possibly Greece, the casualties probably resulted less from conflict with the Italian and German occupation forces than from the economic collapses, malnutrition, disease and internal conflicts (civil wars within the overarching European war) which these military occupations precipitated.

The above totals are by no means definitive. In recent years, estimates of the numbers of people who perished during the Second World War in East Central Europe and the Balkans have been repeatedly revised *downwards* by sober and reputable demographers and social and economic historians who have been carefully reconsidering the evidence and some of the biases and assumptions underlying the calculations on which earlier 'guesstimates' ultimately rested. Immediately after the Second World War, there was a natural, spontaneous and all-too-human tendency to exaggerate the undeniably enormous scale of the casualties and suffering experienced by almost all of the former belligerents. In addition, the scale of these casualties was often deliberately inflated by post-war regimes, whether democratic or authoritarian, and by their academic and propagandistic champions in often highly competitive attempts to enlist domestic and foreign sympathy and/or enhance the legitimacy of those regimes, which invariably sought to present themselves as the promoters of peace in these war-torn lands.

Another conscious or unconscious factor which appears to have contributed to the inflation of estimates of the numbers of wartime deaths was widespread resentment of the post-1960s surge in international (and especially Western) attention to the utterly horrific fates suffered by Europe's Jews, especially East Central European and Balkan Jews, which had the largely unintended effect of diverting international attention from the proportionately much smaller but nevertheless heavy casualties and privations of non-Jews during the war years.

However, perhaps the largest upward bias in the earlier calculations of the numbers of deaths which occurred during the Second World War resulted from the fact that, as a result of the outbreak of war in Europe in 1939 and the political, social and economic upheavals during the immediate post-war years, no careful and thorough population censuses were held between 1930 or 1931 and 1950 or 1951. It was therefore all too easy to assume that the large population 'shortfalls' or 'deficits' which were laid bare by the censuses held in 1950 or 1951 (calculated by contrasting the new census results with the population totals which would have been reached if the population growth rates established between the 1920/1 and 1930/1 censuses had continued unabated) were largely attributable to the greatly increased mortality resulting from the war itself, the widespread increases in the incidence of malnutrition, disease and starvation, and (above all) the atrocities and genocide committed against Jews and (to lesser degrees) Roma (Gypsies), ethnic Serbs, ethnic Montenegrins, ethnic Greeks and ethnic Albanians. In particular, during the 1950s the Communist regimes and their official demographers and historians failed to make adequate allowance for the major reductions in birth rates which occurred not only during the early to mid-1940s but also during the 1930s – under the impact of the global economic Depression, growing recourse to contraception and eugenics, the rise of fascism and fascist xenophobic attitudes, and other sources of popular anxiety about the future. As in the Soviet Union during the 1930s (Bideleux 1987: 122–3), the major shares of the demographic 'shortfalls' or 'deficits' which emerged in East Central Europe and in the eastern Balkans between 1930/1 and 1950/1 were attributable to reduced birth rates rather than to increased death rates. In effect, most of the 'missing people' had never been born.

Nevertheless, while downward revisions have repeatedly been made to official and academic estimates of how many people died in East Central Europe and the Balkans during the Second World War, especially in the case of Yugoslavia (where the total has been reduced from the official Communist regime claim of 1.7 million to just under 1 million), *the revised death tolls are still enormous and utterly dwarf those experienced by belligerent and/or occupied countries in the western half of Europe.* Consequently, while the overall population *rose* by roughly 7.2 per cent between 1940 and 1950 in western Europe (here defined as the UK, Ireland, France, the Low Countries, the Federal Republic of Germany, Austria, Switzerland, Scandinavia, Spain, Portugal and Italy), over the same period the overall population remained roughly unchanged in the western and southern Balkans (Yugoslavia, Albania and Greece) and *fell* by roughly 6.8 per cent in East Central Europe and the eastern Balkans (Romania and Bulgaria) and by roughly 7.7 per cent in the Soviet Union (calculated from Macura 1976: 22, who cites UN sources).

RESPONSES TO DIFFERING PATTERNS OF MILITARY AND ECONOMIC SUBORDINATION

According to a major comparative study of the ways in which European countries responded to military and economic subordination to the Axis Powers and/or the Soviet Union between 1938 and 1945 (Deak *et al.* 2000), the prime determinant was how the overlords behaved:

Everywhere, the comportment of the occupied population was 'occupier-driven', to use a term aptly coined by Jan Gross. This means that generally the population . . . reacted to the behaviour of the German, Soviet, and other occupying powers. Where the Germans behaved correctly, as was the case, at least initially, in Western Europe, the populace also tended to behave correctly towards the Germans, irrespective of the presence or absence of any racial affinity with the Germans. In occupied Denmark the German army felt so confident of popular and official compliance that within a few weeks of the country's invasion in April 1940, it reduced the . . . occupation forces to . . . less than ten thousand men. This was far less than the total number of Danish army and armed police forces in the country, both of which the German occupiers . . . allowed to continue to function. Similarly, in France, certainly not a fellow 'Nordic country', German . . . forces in mid-1942 consisted only of three battalions, some 2,500 or 3,000 men, far too few to be able to maintain order or carry out the deportation of the Jews. These functions were performed by the French police on behalf of the Germans. On the other hand, in Yugoslavia, where the Germans' Croatian fascist Ustasha allies unleashed a reign of utter terror, there was almost immediate massive armed resistance. (Deak 2000: 6–7)

The wartime experiences of the subordinated and/or occupied countries varied greatly (Gross 2000: 17–19). Under the stimulus of artificially high wartime levels of aggregate demand, countries such as Hungary, Slovakia, Austria and even the Nazi-controlled Czech Lands initially experienced large increases in industrial output and employment between 1939 and 1942, while Romanian and Bulgarian industries expanded more modestly (Gross 2000: 17–19; Berend and Ranki 1974a: 320–3, 328–33). In these countries, ironically, it was the hugely increased demand and public spending generated by the Second World War which finally succeeded in overcoming the mass unemployment and the attendant impoverishment and economic misery of the 1930s Depression, whereas most of the peacetime civilian remedies tried out in the 1930s had conspicuously failed. During the 1930s, most European governments had remained too hidebound by neo-classical fiscal and monetary 'orthodoxies' to reflate their economies sufficiently to attain major reductions in mass unemployment. This was even true of Mussolini's Italy and most other authoritarian nationalist and fascist states. The major exception was Nazi Germany, where the bold deficit spending policies of Dr Schacht restored full employment by 1936, while the subsequent major rearmament programme actually created mounting labour shortages, supply bottlenecks and inflationary pressures in 1938–40. Remarkably, even in the so-called Warthegau area, located between the rivers Vistula and Oder in German-occupied Poland, industrial employment trebled between 1940 and 1943 (Gross 2000: 17).

The initial wartime booms and the return to full or near-full employment in 1940–2 were major reasons why so many people in so many countries did not oppose the outbreak of war and in some cases actively welcomed it. In most of the countries which Hitler occupied and/or subordinated, there was initially much wider acceptance of and 'collaboration' with the Nazis than active resistance, while several western European states which were 'defeated and occupied by the German army early in the war later became virtual allies' (Deak 2000: 8–9). Furthermore, in the western borderlands of Ukraine and Belarus, the eastern half of Poland, the Baltic States and Bessarabia (now Moldova), each of which experienced annexation and very brutal treatment by the Soviet Union from either September 1939 or May–June 1940 to June 1941, the German invaders and their Hungarian and Romanian allies were initially welcomed widely as 'liberators' in June–July 1941 (Stola 2004: 399), as had also been the case in Austria in March 1938. Nevertheless, because Nazi policies made heavy demands even on allies and would-be supporters, sooner or later 'all of Germany's allies eventually turned against Germany' (Deak 2000: 9).

At the other extreme, most of occupied Poland experienced terrible economic privations and devastation from late 1939 onward, as did Axis-occupied Greece, Yugoslavia, Albania and the western regions of the Soviet Union from 1941 onward. It was therefore scarcely surprising that these areas put up the fiercest resistance to their foreign occupiers. Indeed, 'Poland was the only place in Hitler's Europe where the defending army never surrendered to the invader, and where the resistance movement began to organize without waiting for a provocation' (Deak 2000: 7). Nevertheless, even in Poland there were German estimates in 1943 that they could count on 850,000 to a million native 'collaborators' (Gross 1979: 166).

In the end, material losses attributable to the impact of the Second World War were equivalent to about 30 per cent of national assets or three to four years' output in Poland and Yugoslavia, about two years' output in the case of Hungary, about one year's output in Czechoslovakia, and about four months' output in the cases of Bulgaria and Romania (Berend and Ranki 1974a: 340–1).

The industrial, agricultural and mineral resources of the Balkan and East Central European states were systematically plundered and/or harnessed to the Axis war machine, with no coherent long-term plans to enhance the development of the occupied countries. In the case of Poland, for example, 'The original intention of the German occupiers was to set up a social system geared entirely to the possibility of unlimited exploitation of the subjugated populace', and 'the purpose of German occupation policies was to exploit Polish society to the point of literally destroying it' (Gross 1979: xii, 297). By 1943 more than 80 per cent of the Polish population's needs were (barely) being met through the black market (p. 109). To smaller degrees, this was also the fate of the other 'eastern' countries occupied by and/or allied to Nazi Germany: 'the main value of the occupied territories to Germany was as an area for exploitation, in the least sophisticated sense' (Milward 1965: 31). The distinction between 'eastern' countries allied to Germany and those occupied by it became increasingly blurred.

By November 1943, moreover, voluntary migrant workers from East Central Europe and to lesser degrees the Balkans made up more than 11 per cent of the Third Reich's population (Gross 1979: 81). In addition, Nazi Germany used several million forced labourers (virtual slaves), the vast majority of whom either had been taken from the Slav countries it had occupied or were Slav prisoners of war. All told, Germany's 7.5 million foreign workers 'constituted over a fifth of its civilian workforce' by the end of the war (Maddison 1976: 468–9). Between 1.3 and 1.5 million of the 15 million inhabitants of the so-called 'General Gouvernement' in Poland were sent to work in Germany, in addition to the 400,000–480,000 Polish prisoners of war released for labour and the Poles sent to concentration camps there (Gross 1979: 78).

By 1943 or at the latest by 1944, the effects of the Nazis' ruthless and relentless determination to suck in or appropriate whatever resources they could from their allies and from the countries they occupied had begun seriously to undermine their economies, societies and regimes and the functioning of the so-called 'New Order'. In this sense, the Nazi 'New Order' was self-undermining: the occupied and/or subordinated countries simply 'seized up' and became increasingly incapable of functioning effectively as satellites of the Third Reich and/or Fascist Italy. There were four main reasons for this: they were being bled dry by Axis demands; their collaborationist and/or military occupation regimes lacked legitimacy; these conditions increasingly generated active and passive resistance movements of various sorts and magnitudes; and many of these countries also suffered the effects of British naval blockade and/or increasingly heavy Allied bombardment.

THE AXIS 'NEW ORDER' IN GREECE

The dynamics outlined above are especially well brought out in Mark Mazower's trenchant analysis of the ultimately self-undermining effects of the Axis New Order in Greece (Mazower 1993):

> Reflecting Hitler's own tendency to view the subjects of his European New Order as sources of raw materials, food and labour rather than as potential political associates, Berlin and Rome sought to govern Greece through the existing political machinery headed by a designedly weak political leadership. But the Greek state bureaucracy, never impressive for its efficiency, seized up in the face of exorbitant Axis demands, and was pushed towards an acute fiscal and monetary

crisis within a few months. Inflation, black-marketeering, food shortages and eventually famine itself marked the collapse of the national economy. Athens could no longer feed itself, still less rule the country. For ordinary Greeks, worried by the prospect of hunger and economic break-down, it became vital to band together. When the state lost its authority, alternative social group-ings emerged. (Mazower 1993: xviii)

In the eyes of Adolf Hitler, the Wehrmacht (the German army), the Reich foreign ministry and the Italian Fascist regime, the 'sole function' of the new puppet regime in Greece was 'to keep the administration of the country going in accordance with Axis wishes. Events soon demonstrated, however, that the government's very weakness would prevent it from carrying out that task' (Mazower 1993: 20). The Reich and especially Italy demanded and levied 'exorbitant occupation costs', and these became the biggest bone of contention between the military occupation forces and the Greek civil administration: 'In practice, no rigid [clear] distinction between the civil and mili-tary spheres of administration was really possible' and 'not even the military spoke with one voice', since the German and Italian occupation forces had conflicting interests and priorities. This set the stage 'for bureaucratic infighting of Byzantine complexity' (p. 22).

Hitler insisted that the expression 'occupation costs' was a misnomer, because the German occu-pation forces were 'in fact *rebuilding* roads, bridges and rail-links which would serve the Greeks as well as the Axis' and (in his view) 'the Greeks had not contributed enough to this effort'; he there-fore responded by refusing to reduce his demands and instead proposed that the expression *Bezat-zungskosten* (occupation costs) be replaced by the more positive expression *Aufbaukosten* (construction costs) (Mazower 1993: 67). However, the economic disruption resulting from war and occupation and the collapse of Greece's long-established reliance on trade with Britain and France, combined with large-scale military requisitioning to feed German and Italian occupation forces and rumours of worse to come, caused Athens to endure 'the worst scenes of starvation seen in occupied Europe outside the concentration camps' during the winter of 1941–2, while the puppet regime headed by Georgios Tsolakoglu was 'torn apart by the economic crisis' (pp. 22, 67).

Following Nazi Germany's loss of its footholds in North Africa in late 1942, Greece's role changed from that of 'forward supply base to a likely centre of operations in its own right'. Antici-pating an Allied invasion somewhere in the Aegean in 1943, the Wehrmacht began a massive mili-tary build-up in Greece during that year. As a result, 'Further increases in the *Besatzungskosten* were demanded' (Mazower 1993: 71), resulting in the printing of vast sums of paper money in des-perate attempts to meet German demands in 1943–4. This led to hyperinflation which in turn caused a 'proletarianization' of the population. 'The Greeks were now reported to be "95 per cent" hostile to the Axis. Yet the Wehrmacht still refused to scale down its demands' (p. 71). Hyperinflation led to a collapse in the value of money and in the functioning of a market economy, a reversion to barter in place of a cash economy and (by 1944) the almost complete paralysis of the economy and the machinery of state, with the result that the Wehrmacht's demands could no longer be met and its functioning was jeopardized (p. 72).

Greek resistance movements grew rapidly from 1942 to 1945, headed by the Communist-led EAM/ELAS. 'In the mountains of "Free Greece" a surrogate state emerged to challenge the falter-ing legitimacy of the Athens government' (Mazower 1993: xviii). Although EAM/ELAS sought to dominate the resistance and 'terrorized its opponents', it was also 'unquestionably popular . . . War kept many guerrillas too concerned about their day-to-day existence to think very long about what would happen after Liberation' (p. xix).

The Wehrmacht responded with a series of anti-guerrilla operations, based on reprisal killings and the arrest of civilian hostages. Violence . . . became the chief way of reasserting German control over the countryside. Terror became the basis for rule in urban areas . . . But these policies proved incapable by themselves of wiping out the resistance and may have even been counterproductive. By 1944, EAM/ELAS was claiming that its support extended to more than one million members. (Mazower 1993: xviii–xix)

However, the resultant political polarization caused the middle ground of Greek politics to disappear by late 1944: 'two armed camps faced one another, most dramatically in Athens. There lay the origins of the bitter feuding and street battles which led after Liberation to outright civil war' (Mazower 1993: xix). In Greece, Anglo-American intervention and Soviet non-interference ensured the eventual victory of monarchist forces over the more popular Communist-led anti-fascist resistance movement in 1948–9. By contrast, geopolitical factors and Soviet military might ultimately tipped the military and political outcomes of the Second World War in favour of Communist-led forces in Poland, Hungary, Romania and Bulgaria, while in Yugoslavia, Albania and Czechoslovakia the Communists movements triumphed mainly through their own efforts and their capacity to transcend internal ethnic divisions and rivalries.

THE IMPACT OF RELIGIOUS, RACIAL AND ETHNIC ATROCITIES AND SYSTEMATIC MASS GENOCIDE

In the Balkans and East Central Europe during the Second World War, even more people perished as a result of religious, racial and ethnic atrocities and systematic mass genocide than as a result of the more direct impact of the war itself. However, it is somewhat arbitrary to try to distinguish between the direct impact of the Second World War and the other atrocities, including systematic mass genocide, which took place under the cover or even partly as a result of this war.

The Axis invasions of Austria, the Czech Lands and (above all) Poland, Greece, Yugoslavia and the Soviet Union were the main causes of the huge scale of the Nazi-led Holocaust against Europe's Jews and the smaller-scale genocide against Gypsies and various Slavic peoples (primarily Poles, Serbs and Russians). Despite the virulence of Nazi anti-Semitism, relatively few Jews lived in Germany proper (515,000 in 1933, falling to 350,000 in 1938, according to Hilberg 1985: 158). More than 80 per cent of Europe's Jews lived in the eastern half of Europe, primarily in Poland (numbering 3.1 million by religious affiliation, or 9.8 per cent of the population, in 1931), Czechoslovakia (numbering 357,000 by religion, or 2.4 per cent of the population, in 1930), Hungary (724,000 by religion, or 4.9 per cent of the population, in 1941), Romania (757,000 by religion, or 4.2 per cent of the population, in 1930), Austria (190,000 in 1938), Greece (80,000 in 1938) and the Soviet Union (about 2.2 million in the western borderlands of the Soviet Union in 1939) (Rothschild 1974: 36, 90, 196, 284; Mazower 1993: 256; Hilberg 1985: 107, 158).

The issues raised by these enormous crimes against humanity have remained the biggest and most contentious issues in modern Balkan and East Central European history, and they therefore require at least as much attention as the war within which they occurred. However, there is an increasingly vast and complex literature on the religious, racial and ethnic atrocities and programmes of genocide carried out in East Central Europe and the Balkans during the late 1930s and the 1940s. Therefore, we cannot pretend even to begin to do justice to these matters in the space available to us. Nevertheless, we shall attempt to convey the broad orders of magnitude and the main contours of the crimes committed, the principal issues raised by them, and the main ways in which they have been perceived and/or treated.

During the Second World War between 5.1 and 5.8 million European Jews, including at least 4.3 million in East Central Europe and the Balkans and 0.7 million in the Soviet Union, 'perished at the hands of the Nazis and their, mostly East European, helpers' (Deak 2000: 5; Hilberg 1985: 338–9; Engel 1999; Stola 2004: 386). Concurrently, tens of thousands of Roma (Gypsies) and hundreds of thousands of South Slavs (mostly Serbs and Montenegrins) perished at the hands of Croatian and

Bosniak fascists, Catholic and Muslim bigots and their collaborators, while tens of thousands of Muslim ethnic Albanians and Bosniaks perished at the hands of Bulgarian, Macedonian Slav, Serbian and Montenegrin ultra-nationalist fanatics and Orthodox Christian bigots. In addition, especially in the wake of the Soviet occupation of the eastern half of Poland in September 1939, the Soviet annexations of Bessarabia (Moldova), northern Bukovina and the Baltic States in June–July 1940 and the Soviet re-annexations of all the areas in 1945, hundreds of thousands of Poles, Ukrainians, Belarussians and Balts and not a few Jews were killed, deported to labour camps or otherwise persecuted by the Soviet regime, although the precise numbers of Soviet victims remain the furthest from being ascertained.

Until late 1939 it had seemed just about feasible for the Nazis to attain their so-called 'solution to the Jewish question' in Germany by means of induced emigration and piecemeal expulsion of German Jews. Emigration, depressed birth rates and (not yet enormous) sporadic killings of Jews had already reduced Germany's Jewish population from roughly 515,000 in 1933 to around 331,000 in May 1939 (Hilberg 1985: 41, 158). The annexation of Austria in March 1938 placed Austria's 190,000 Jews under Nazi control (p. 158), while the occupation of the Czech Lands in March 1939 brought another 357,000 Jews (by religion) under Nazi control (Rothschild 1974: 90). Nevertheless, the Nazi leaders were still thinking primarily in terms of forced emigration and expulsion of Jews, rather than genocide (C. Browning 2005: 25, 81–3, 89).

The German conquest of the western half of Poland in September 1939 placed about 1.7 or 1.8 million Polish Jews under Nazi control, while 'the outbreak of war now threatened to constrict even further the already fast diminishing avenues of emigration . . . Thus the conquest of Poland inevitably set in motion a search for a new kind of solution to the Nazis' Jewish problem' (Browning 2005: 12). In the eyes of many Germans, 'Easy victory over Poland seemed to confirm the Germans as a *Herrenvolk* or "master race" deserving and destined to rule over inferior Slavs'; and this 'reignited' the radical racist 'eliminationist' elements within Nazism, while the state of war released the Nazi regime from previous 'restraints and inhibitions' by making harsh measures against 'the enemy' and 'potential enemies' appear 'justified by national interest' (pp. 12–13). 'Poland was thus destined to become a "laboratory" for Nazi experiments in racial imperialism, an area where they tried to turn into reality ideological slogans such as *Lebensraum* (living space), *Volkstumskampf* (ethnic or racial struggle) . . . and *Endlösung der Judenfrage* (Final Solution to the Jewish Question)', although this did initially entail 'much trial and error' (p. 14).

At least since the late nineteenth-century German assaults against Catholic Poles (the so-called *Kulturkampf* – see pp. 292–3, above), and even more strongly since Germany's humiliating defeat in the First World War, many members of Germany's military and other elites had come to regard Poles and 'eastern Jews' (*Ostjuden*) as 'primitive and inferior, fit only for colonial rule by a German master race' and 'as inherently treacherous and anti-German and hence threats to security' (Browning 2005: 16). However, Poland's non-aggression treaty with Germany in 1934, along with its participation in the dismemberment of Czechoslovakia in the autumn of 1938, had encouraged Hitler to assume that Poland would be willing to cede some of its partly German-inhabited territories in return for German help in making much larger compensating territorial gains at Soviet expense in Ukraine and Belarus. It was only *after* Poland refused to continue to play along with Hitler's stratagems in early 1939, and instead obtained a British 'guarantee' of military support against Germany in March 1939, that Hitler became deeply enraged against it and ordered the German military in April 1939 to start preparing to invade Poland no later than September 1939 (p. 13). Hitler was henceforth intent on ferociously punishing Poland for having crossed him.

Nevertheless, 'Nazi plans for racial policy and Lebensraum in Poland took shape only during September [1939], not before' (Browning 2005: 25). By late September 1939 the Nazis had formulated 'a grandiose plan of demographic engineering based on racial principles' which would involve brutally relocating 'hundreds of thousands, indeed ultimately millions' of Jews and non-Jewish

Poles eastwards in order to free up *Lebensraum* for millions of German colonists in the territories which Germany was occupying (p. 27). 'The broad support for German racial imperialism in the east was one foundation upon which the future consensus for the mass murder of the Jews would be built' (p. 28). Indeed, the creation of *Lebensraum* for millions of Germans in Poland 'could not . . . be accomplished without a solution to the Jewish question as well' (p. 26), because Poland was home to more than 3 million people of the Jewish faith (Rothschild 1974: 36).

However, at this stage Germany's military leaders were still trying not to get the Wehrmacht directly involved in the dirty work of pulverizing and forcibly relocating Jewish and/or Polish populations. Instead, this task was entrusted primarily to the so-called Einsatzgruppen (special task forces) of Himmler's Schutzstaffel (SS, Nazi security guards). These 'mobile killing units', which later orchestrated and carried out mass shootings of Soviet Jews and so-called 'Judaeo-Communists' in the German-occupied western borderlands of the Soviet Union from late June 1941 to 1943, first cut their teeth in Poland from October 1939 onward. By the end of 1940 the Germans had already executed 50,000 mainly civilian Poles, whether non-Jews or Jews (Browning 2005: 35). This prepared the ground for the mass murder of civilians in former Soviet territories, which in turn served as the prelude to the more scientific and industrialized mass extermination of West European, East Central European, Central European, Baltic and Balkan Jews in gas chambers from early 1942 to November 1944.

During 1940, however, it was still officially envisaged that occupied Europe's 'Jewish problem' would be 'solved' primarily by forced emigration and expulsion. After the fall of France in May 1940, many Nazis were proposing that most of Europe's Jews would be deported to the island of Madagascar, rather than exterminated (Browning 2005: 81–3, 89). However, this ceased to appear feasible after Nazi Germany's failure to defeat Britain in the 'Battle of Britain' in late 1940 – not least because, without first neutralizing Britain and obtaining the use of its navy, it would be difficult to transport more than 2 million European Jews to Madagascar.

Nazi Germany's invasion of the Soviet Union in late June 1941 'raised the stakes' much higher. This 'murderous war of destruction' paved the way for 'the systematic mass murder of first Soviet and then European Jewry' (Browning 2005: 214). This war drew not only hundreds of thousands of Germans, but also hundreds of thousands of Hungarians, Romanians, Slovaks, Croats, Bosniaks, Balts, Ukrainians and Belarussians, into an all-out 'crusade' against Jews and Soviet 'Judaeo-Communism'. Millions of Ukrainians and Belarussians who had experienced Soviet forced collectivization of agriculture and the mass deportations and privations which had accompanied this during the 1930s, as well as millions of the predominantly Ukrainian, Belarussian, Polish, Baltic and Romanian inhabitants of the territories annexed by the Soviet Union either in September 1939 or in June–July 1940 (under the terms of the August 1939 Nazi–Soviet Pact), sought vengeance against the allegedly 'Jewish' Communists whom they held responsible for their own recent tribulations. There were undoubtedly Jewish officials in the Communist Party of the Soviet Union (CPSU) and in the Soviet security forces who had played prominent roles in Soviet forced collectivization, deportations and purges during the 1930s and in the Soviet annexation of (and subsequent atrocities and brutalities in) the eastern half of Poland (western Ukraine and western Belarus) in September 1939 and in Bessarabia (Moldova), north Bukovina and the Baltic States in June–July 1940. Anti-Semites seized on this to escalate greatly their Christian and/or racist propaganda against Jews and 'Judaeo-Communism' from late June 1941 onward. Nevertheless, it needs to be stressed that Jews were only small minorities within the CPSU and in the Soviet security services. The vast majority of the 'Communist' thugs responsible for atrocities and brutalities were non-Jewish. Moreover, there were strong anti-Semitic undercurrents within the CPSU, especially from the late 1930s to the 1970s, and from October 1939 to June 1941 (as in 1945–53 and 1966–78) Jews were among the chief *victims* of the persecution, repression, purges, deportations and associated atrocities carried out by the Soviet security services, the CPSU and affiliated Communist parties (see

Gross 2000: 92–113; 2006, *passim*). Nevertheless, the anti-Semitic 'crusade' against 'Judaeo-Communism' during the early 1940s was as lethal as it was doltish. Between June and December 1941, in eastern Poland, Bessarabia and Bukovina as well as in the longstanding western border-lands of the Soviet Union, between 500,000 and 800,000 Jews were killed (2,700 to 4,200 per day on average), and by the end of that year large areas were reported to be 'free of Jews' (*Judenrein*). Simultaneously, Soviet prisoners of war (mainly Russians) were dying in German POW camps 'at a rate of 6,000 per day', resulting in a total of more than 2 million deaths by spring 1942 (Matthäus 2005: 244).

Christopher Browning has cogently argued that the systematic killing of Jews and Russians on this horrific scale on the eastern war front, combined with the intoxicating initial speed of the Axis penetration of Soviet territory from June to September 1941, was decisive in focusing Nazi minds from September or October 1941 onwards on 'a new conception of how the Final Solution might be implemented – through massive deportation [of Jews] to factories of death equipped with facili-ties to kill on an assembly-line basis through poison gas' (C. Browning 2005: 316–18, 321–9).

Quite independently, yet far from accidentally, another branch of the German military also launched systematic mass shootings of 'Judaeo-Communists', Serbs and Gypsies (Roma) in Serbia during September and October 1941, even *before* the launching of 'industrialized' genocide (pp. 336–45). Indeed,

the massacres in Serbia in the fall of 1941 were an anticipation of the Final Solution, for ulti-mately all [Serbian] Jews were killed because they were Jews . . . Once partisan resistance drove the Germans to impose upon themselves the obligation to fulfill the maximum reprisal quota, all Serbs were at risk, but male Jews were doomed . . . Even if local in its origins, this systematic mass murder of Jews outside Soviet territory had wider implications concerning German prepar-edness for the Final Solution. Not only on the eastern front but also elsewhere in Europe, the German military viewed the Jews as part of the wider 'enemy' against whom 'ruthless' meas-ures were justified. The German Foreign Office . . . proved itself equally accommodating to mass murder . . . Undersecretary [Martin] Luther moved on his own initiative to reach an agree-ment with Heydrich on a 'local solution' to the troublesome Jewish problem in Serbia. Such ini-tiative from below obviated the necessity for orders from above . . . Thus a commonalty of interests had emerged between the Wehrmacht, SS and Foreign Office to kill the male Jews of Serbia even before the Final Solution to murder all the Jews of Europe was in operation. It is no wonder that, when instituted, the European-wide murder program would meet no meaningful resistance from any organized segment of German society. (Browning 2005: 346)

Independently of what was occurring on the eastern front and in Serbia, local dynamics combined with wider strategic considerations similarly propelled the German military towards systematic mass shooting of Jews in eastern Galicia (in southern Poland) during the autumn of 1941, after Germany acquired this territory and its 500,000 Jews (10 per cent of the population) in June–July 1941. However, there was a major difference between the situation here and the one in Serbia. As in other parts of eastern Poland seized from the Soviet Union at that time, 'the native population – predominantly Ukrainian – unleashed pogroms against the Jewish communities in Lwow, Tarnopol and elsewhere', with the acquiescence and even encouragement of the German occupiers, but without waiting for their direct involvement (Browning 2005: 347).

The implementation of the Holocaust was widely facilitated by the widespread presence of sub-stantial German minorities in East Central Europe and the Balkans. During the 1930s there were about 740,000 Germans in Poland, about 3.2 million in Czechoslovakia, 478,000 in Hungary, 500,000 in Yugoslavia and 745,000 in Romania, although there were only about 4,000 Germans in Bulgaria (Rothschild 1974: 36, 89, 192, 203, 284, 328) and even smaller numbers in Greece and

Albania. These communities constituted major potential German 'fifth columns' within the allied and/or occupied countries, and in many (though not all) cases these Germans proved grievously susceptible to the temptations and opportunities created by Nazism. Regardless of whether they were actively sympathetic to the Nazis, these so-called *Volksdeutsche* found themselves 'suddenly thrust into the position of masters' and many became 'intoxicated by the opportunity to brutalize, plunder, drive off or murder their Polish and Jewish neighbours with impunity' (Browning 2005: 13–14), while simultaneously serving as agents of German policy and domination.

However, because Browning is pre-eminently a specialist on Germany's pivotal role in the Holocaust, his analyses of the concatenation of major causes and catalysts of the Holocaust have mainly focused on the role of Germans. His relatively brief treatment of the parts played by Balts, Ukrainians, Belarussians and Romanians is excessively German-centred, mainly because he largely relied on accounts provided by German participants and observers (Browning 2005: 268–77). He explains that 'As most of the available contemporary documentation originated from the Einsatzgruppen [mobile killing squads orchestrated by the German SS], it is not surprising that other agencies – German as well as non-German – appear less important' (p. 272). However, this statement is somewhat misleading, in that ever-increasing quantities of non-German documentation of the important roles played by non-Germans in the Holocaust and other acts of genocide are becoming available. It is more the case that, as a specialist on the Nazi regime, he has paid much less attention to the roles played by non-Germans in the Holocaust and has therefore tended to make much less use of non-German sources. Nevertheless, he is on stronger ground in claiming that 'Whatever crimes non-Germans committed, it was the Germans who, by establishing a pattern of systematic persecution, posed a much deadlier threat to Jewish existence' (p. 277). However, this underplays the *concurrent and closely related yet semi-independent dynamics* which unleashed mass killings of Jews by Hungarians, Romanians and Croats between 1940 and 1944, some of which pre-dated the full subordination of these countries to Nazi Germany (summarized on pp. 439–46, below). Likewise, it is becoming increasingly implausible to attribute the significant participation of Balts, Ukrainians and Belarussians in the Holocaust and the much smaller-scale acts of genocide committed by Poles wholly to the opportunities, incentives and other dynamics initiated by German occupation of their respective countries (on Poland, see pp.434–8, below).

While Axis and Soviet invasions and/or alliances provided *the main contexts and frameworks* within which the atrocities and systematic genocide took place, they were by no means the whole explanation. The Polish state had *already* begun to commit atrocities against Ukrainians in 1930, and Poles had already embarked on systematic mistreatment of their Jewish 'neighbours' and compatriots from 1935 to 1939. This was *before* the Nazi–Soviet invasion of Poland in September 1939 and even longer before the Nazi invasion of eastern Poland and the Soviet Union in June–July 1941 (see Rothschild 1974: 64, Crampton 1994: 174–6, and Heller 1977, although the perspectives they offer have been disputed by Davies 1981b: 240–66 and Marcus 1983, among others). Similarly, Hungarian anti-Semites crossed the Czechoslovak border and started murdering Jews in parts of Czechoslovakia even *before* Hungary started formally annexing those areas on 10 November 1938, in the wake of the notorious September 1938 'Munich agreement' to dismember Czechoslovakia (Gryn 2001: 74–5). Likewise, Romanian fascists began to murder substantial numbers of Jews during the late 1930s, *before* the country became formally allied to the Axis Powers and *before* the partial dismemberment of Romania during 1940 (Wiesel et al. 2005: 390). Thus, while the military occupation of some countries by Nazi Germany and the growing subordination of other fascist states to Nazi Germany's power and influence undoubtedly hastened the Holocaust and promoted 'exterminationist' currents within the wider traditions of European/Christian anti-Semitism, there is considerable evidence that parts of East Central Europe and the Balkans were already moving towards *smaller-scale extermination of Jews* before these regions fell more directly under German influence and/or control. It is thus unsound to see and portray the anti-Semitic atrocities and systematic genocide committed in East Central Europe and the Balkans simply as responses to the growing power influence of Nazi Germany, hugely important though that was.

It is also important not to overlook the mass killings of Poles, Romanians, Magyars, Balts and (very significantly) Jews which officials, security services and 'Communist' supporters of the Soviet regime carried out in 1939–41 in the Polish, Baltic and Romanian territories which the USSR occupied and annexed either in September 1939 or in May–June 1940 under the terms of the August 1939 Nazi–Soviet Pact and which it brutally repossessed in late 1944 and early 1945. However, these killings appear to have been somewhat smaller in scale and have certainly been less well documented and quantified than the genocide carried out by fascist, nationalist and Christian anti-Semites and xenophobes during the 1940s. There are hugely conflicting claims concerning the scale of the killings, deportations and deaths in captivity of the diverse ethnic and religious groups who inhabited eastern Poland, Bessarabia, northern Bukovina, the Baltic States, Ukraine and Belarussia. The attribution of responsibility for these deaths is also hotly contested. Sober and balanced explanations, characterizations and assessments of the terrible occurrences in these areas between 1905 and 1956 will become possible only after a great deal more research has been completed on these much less exhaustively investigated mass killings, which (at least within the territories concerned) have long been widely regarded as having been genocidal in nature and intent. For example, Jan Gross has claimed that Ukrainian nationalists, many of whom collaborated with the Nazis from late June 1941 to late 1944, 'murdered sixty to eighty thousand Poles in eastern Poland between 1941 and 1944' (J.T. Gross 1979: 192–3). In his view, 'Old scores were being settled . . . and a policy of fait accompli was being pursued. It was argued that in the event the Germans were defeated and the weakened Russians pushed back east, the Western Allies could not refuse Ukrainian claims to statehood in territories that by that time would be virtually *Polenrein* [free of Poles] . . . With silent German blessing, Ukrainians were pushing out or openly exterminating the Poles living in the Western Ukraine (not to mention the Jews . . .) . . . Ukrainians were setting the stage for their ultimate takeover [of these areas] in the aftermath of the war' (pp. 194–5). In retaliation Polish partisans, mainly members of the Polish nationalist Home Guard, 'killed entire populations of isolated Ukrainian hamlets' (p. 194). The figures given in claims of this sort need to be treated with great caution, as they usually include a great deal of tendentious guesswork about matters on which there is very little reliable and uncontested information.

The killing of European Jews did not come to a halt with the capitulation of Germany in May 1945. This provides further evidence that Germans were by no means the only murderous anti-Semites in Europe during the 1930s and 1940s. It appears that between 500 and 1,500 Jews were killed by anti-Jewish violence in Soviet-'liberated' Poland in 1945–6, most notoriously in the August 1945 pogrom in Krakow and in the July 1946 pogrom in Kielce (Gross 2006: 35). In addition, the 'purges' carried out both within and by Europe's Communist regimes during the late 1940s and the early 1950s had strong anti-Semitic undercurrents and especially targeted Jews for imprisonment, execution and deportation to labour camps.

Reassignments of territory from one state to another in 1938–40 and again in 1945 also resulted in the perpetration of numerous atrocities, some of which involved heavy loss of life. For example, Jan Gross has endorsed the view (widespread among Germans) that the expulsion of millions of Germans by Poles during the Soviet-sponsored transfer of Pomerania, East and West Prussia and much of Silesia from Germany to Poland in 1945 was 'exceedingly brutal and resulted in the death of many thousands' of Germans (Gross 2006: 35). More than 500,000 Germans allegedly perished between December 1944 and January 1945, while trying to escape from East Prussia after it had been cut off from the Reich by Soviet armed forces (Woods 1972: 68). However, during 2006 President Lech Kaczinski and the Polish government headed by his twin brother Jaroslaw Kaczinski repeatedly protested against the holding of an exhibition in Germany commemorating the casualties and sufferings of the millions of Germans who had to flee from what became known as Poland's 'western territories'. There was also considerable Czech violence against Germans during the expulsion of more than 3 million Bohemian Germans from the Czech Lands in 1945–6, although this resulted in much less loss of life than the concurrent expulsion of millions of Germans by Poles (Sayer 1998: 242–3). In addition, hundreds and possibly thousands of ethnic Romanians were robbed, raped or killed by both regular and irregular ethnic Hungarian forces engaged in 'score set-tling' during and after the transfer of northern Transylvania from Romania to Hungary following the so-called 'Second Vienna Arbitration' (by Nazi Germany and Fascist Italy) on 30 August 1940. Conversely, hundreds and possibly thousands of ethnic Hungarians were robbed, raped or killed by both regular and irregular ethnic Romanian forces engaged in 'score settling' during and after the Soviet-backed Romanian repossession of northern Transylvania in the autumn of 1944. Until 1949 there were also small and isolated pockets of armed resistance to the forcible (re)incorporation of the Baltic States and (formerly Romanian) Banat into the Soviet Union in 1945 (Milin 2000).

Very few of the ethnic and religious groups in East Central Europe and the Balkans came out of the Second World War with their reputations unsullied by varying degrees of complicity in atroci-ties of one kind or another. Contrary to the thesis advanced by Daniel Goldhagen (1996), so-called 'eliminationist' anti-Semitism and analogous expulsive or genocidal tendencies were by no means peculiar to the Germans, even though the exceptional size and power of the Third Reich helped to make Germans by far the biggest perpetrators of such crimes. Nevertheless, even a polity as large and powerful as Nazi Germany was able to implement the Holocaust only with the willing help of hundreds of thousands – possibly millions – of non-German Europeans. Administratively and logis-tically, the Holocaust was an immensely complex operation which diverted huge human resources from the Axis war effort and, with bitter irony, became a costly burden which contributed signifi-cantly to the eventual defeat of the Axis states (Hilberg 1985: 270–4). Therefore, as Christopher Browning has pointed out in relation to the countries which experienced German occupation, 'Without the active support of mayors, city councils, housing offices, and a plethora of local admin-istrators, the identification, expropriation, and ghettoization of the Jewish population, especially in rural areas, would have exceeded the limited logistic capacities of German occupation agencies' (Browning 2005: 275). Much the same holds for countries 'allied' to Germany, especially Hungary, Romania, Croatia, Slovakia, Fascist Italy, the Low Countries and Vichy France. Germans were by no means the only 'willing executioners' of Jews. The scale of non-German complicity and active participation in the 'final solution of the Jewish question' and in smaller and less systematic atroci-ties and programmes of genocide against other ethno-cultural groups has remained relatively under-investigated. However, these dimensions have gained increasing attention in the wake of the fall of Europe's Communist regimes, the subsequent opening up of East Central European, Balkan and former Soviet archives relating to the treatment of minority groups during the 1930s and 1940s, and the growth of investigative journalism, independent media and the internet (see Polonsky and Michlik 2004: 26–9; Braham 1997; 2004; Ioanid 2000; Wiesel *et al.* 2005; and Browning 2005; besides the studies of western European complicity cited on p. 449).

CHRISTIANS, CHURCHES AND THE HOLOCAUST

Many parts of a still predominantly church-going Christian Europe evinced sympathy or even active support for fascist movements. This seems to have derived partly from the fact that most of Europe's fascist movements included the establishment of 'corporative-Christian' states among their declared central objectives, and partly from the fact many (perhaps most) European Christians were at that time still mildly or in some cases virulently anti-Semitic and regarded the fascist move-ments as providential instruments and allies in the paramount struggle against the 'real scourge' or 'real enemy' of European Christendom: Marxist-Leninist Communism, alias 'Judaeo-Communism' or 'Judaeo-Bolshevism', which many Christians regarded as a 'Jewish conspiracy' to subvert

European Christian values and civilization. During the late 1930s and early 1940s, this seems to have been the stance or the order of priorities of many (perhaps most) European Christian clergy, including Popes Pius XI and Pius XII, Cardinal August Hlond (the then head of the Polish Catholic Church) and Cardinal Aloys Stepinac (the then head of the Croatian Catholic Church) (Cornwell 2000; Goldhagen 2002: 39–49, 81, 104–5, 141). Christian clergy were much more conspicuous and prominent *in support* of anti-Semitic Slovak, Croatian, Romanian, Polish, Austrian, French and Hungarian fascist and/or ultra-nationalist movements than they were in the same countries' *anti-fascist* movements or in publicly *condemning* fascism and anti-Semitism. Similarly, both then and subsequently, the popes and cardinals of the Roman Catholic Church were far more forthright in their condemnations of the evils of Communism than they were in their relatively rare and muted criticisms of genocidal fascist regimes (often mere chidings and private rebukes). Whether they meant to or not, they certainly managed to convey strong impressions that, even though the Roman Catholic Church did not actively and publicly instigate or approve of genocide, it nevertheless regarded it as a 'lesser evil' than so-called 'Judaeo-Communism'. Considering the millions of Europeans (including a great many European Jews) who perished in Communist purges, prisons and concentration camps, possibly on a scale which ultimately exceeded the total number of deaths attributable to fascist movements and regimes, many people seem to have taken the view that Roman Catholic Church leaders were not necessarily mistaken in regarding fascism and genocide as 'lesser evils' than Communism. Indeed, Norman Davies has recently reiterated longstanding East Central European (especially Polish) complaints that the West has been much more concerned with the crimes committed by *fascist* regimes than with those committed by the Soviet Union and its *Communist* allies, because (i) the West was much more directly affected by the crimes which the fascist regimes committed and the war which they fought than they were by the crimes committed by the Soviet Union and other Communist regimes, and (ii) the UK and the USA quickly realized that the Soviet Union was crucial to the defeat of Nazi Germany and its Balkan and East Central European allies between 1941 and 1945 and therefore felt obliged to ignore or at least play down many of the crimes committed by the Soviet regime and its accomplices (Davies 2006: 243–8). By contrast, most of the Christian clergy in the Balkans and East Central Europe appear to have been primarily concerned with the safety of their respective churches and co-religionists (often including Jewish converts to Christianity), and were therefore much more inclined to denounce Communism than fascism, racism and anti-Semitism. This weighing of evils does help to *explain*, albeit without *exculpating*, the relative silence or acquiescence of the Roman Catholic Church vis-à-vis the Holocaust.

In most of the European states allied to and/or occupied by the Axis Powers, especially France, the Low Countries and Austria as well as East Central Europe and the Balkans, the most typical Christian reactions to the terrible plight of the Jews seem to have been ones of sullen indifference or cold contempt rather than compassion, with numerous outbreaks of anti-Semitic violence (Szarota 2000). In the words of Ian Kershaw, 'the road to Auschwitz was built by hatred, but paved with indifference' (Kershaw 1983: 277). Among church-going Christians, there seems to have been a widespread perception or belief that Jews were getting their 'just deserts', whether for being 'Christ-killers', atheistic 'Judaeo-Communists', 'Bolshevik scum', 'filthy capitalists', or parasitic 'leeches' ('blood-suckers') extorting excessive rates of interest (usury) from hapless Christian peasantries. Such attitudes came as a traumatic and devastating shock to the Jewish communities which had contributed so much to the economic and cultural development of East Central European and the Balkans over so many centuries and which, despite widespread Christian anti-Semitism, had long regarded these areas as 'home' and the Christian inhabitants as their 'neighbours' and 'compatriots'.

During the summer of 2006 there was an illuminating exhibition in Bratislava Castle entitled 'The Way of the Cross', dealing with the prominent role of the cult of the crucifixion of Christ in the Roman Catholic Counter-Reformation in southern Germany, Austria and East Central Europe and in the subsequent development of Roman Catholicism in East Central Europe. The exhibition helped to persuade Robert Bideleux that this cult must have strengthened Roman Catholic perceptions, images and consciousness of the Jews as 'Christ-killers'. The particular virulence of Catholic anti-Semitism in East Central Europe may have been yet another dimension of the 'collateral damage' inflicted by the Catholic Counter-Reformation in these regions. The long-held Christian perception of the Jews as 'Christ-killers', much less evident today but still widespread during the 1930s and 1940s, was inextricably bound up with the cult of the crucifixion of Christ. This was by no means peculiar to the Roman Catholic Church – it was also manifest in the Eastern Orthodox Christian imagery and language of many Romanian anti-Semites, especially Corneliu Zelea Codreanu's Legion of the Archangel Michael (Heinen 2006; Weber 1964: 100–3, 168) and Alexandru Cuza's National Christian Party. However, it does appear to have been especially prevalent within East Central European Catholicism, at least until the 1940s. This helps to explain the main way in which East Central European anti-Semitism differed from German – especially Nazi – anti-Semitism, which by the 1930s had become much more secular, racial, pseudo-scientific and biological.

POLISH ANTI-SEMITISM AND COMPLICITY IN THE HOLOCAUST

The historian Jan Gross has powerfully publicized the scale and intensity of anti-Semitic attitudes and conduct in Poland during the 1940s (Gross 2000: 81–117; 2001; 2003; 2006). His book *Sasiedzi* (2000), which was first published in English in 2001 as *Neighbours: The Destruction of the Jewish Community in Jedwabne, Poland*, became an international best-seller, and unleashed a major national and international debate on the degrees of Polish complicity in the Holocaust. The issues raised by Polish attitudes and behaviour towards Jews during and immediately after the Second World War, which Gross succeeded in transforming into the most controversial issue in Poland's recent history, have aroused far stronger reactions in Poland than the issues of responsibility for the crimes committed by Communists and their 'fellow travellers' during the four decades of Communist rule in Poland (Jedlicki 2004: 237). In large part, this is because the issues raised, along with the attitudes and atrocities which Gross has publicized, have so strongly challenged the widely preferred self-image of the Poles as heroes, victims and martyrs who stoically suffered and courageously fought against both Nazi German and Soviet Communist occupation and oppression (Gross 2003: 173–4). Some major contributions to this debate are available in English (see Brand 2001 and Polonsky and Michlik 2004).

While most modern histories of Poland have sought to promote the romantic self-image of Poles as victims, heroes and martyrs valiantly struggling against both German and Soviet military occupation and subsequent Communist rule, a much smaller but increasingly influential body of work on Polish attitudes and conduct towards Jews from the 1930s to the 1960s has presented many Poles in a much more negative light – in particular, as indifferent or contemptuous 'bystanders' or as active supporters of, or accomplices in, the enormous crimes against humanity carried out against Jews on Polish territory during the 1940s (see Polonsky and Michlik 2004: 1–43). However, many Polish nationalists, along with some Western admirers of the indomitable courage and desire to be free which millions of Poles undeniably displayed between 1939 and 1989, have claimed that Poland's national pride, honour and integrity have been besmirched by those who have been determined to investigate fully and publicize the more disreputable values, attitudes and conduct which were also sadly manifested by many Polish patriots during that same half-century. Thus a battle has been raging between those who promote somewhat edited, sanitized and whitewashed accounts of twentieth-century Poland, and those wish to present the whole truth. Members of the latter group and members of their families have been subjected to considerable vilification, hate mail and harassment by Polish nationalists (see Gross 2003: 175–6, 178, 256–7). Prior to the publication of *Neighbours*, Polish claims that the Holocaust enacted during the German occupation of Poland was almost entirely the work of the German occupying forces and a small number of non-German 'collaborators' were widely accepted at face value. Although it had been challenged in various ways many times before, this comfortable myth was finally exploded by the publication of *Neighbours*.

THE JEDWABNE MASSACRE, 10 JULY 1941

The small eastern Polish town of Jedwabne, which had a population of around 2,500 people in 1939, experienced twenty months of Soviet military occupation and oppression from September 1939 to June 1941. Soon after the start of the German invasion of the Soviet Union on 22 June 1941, however, the Soviet administration, the Soviet occupying forces and their local collaborators were driven out of the eastern half of Poland, while the newly arriving German occupation forces were widely welcomed as 'liberators' – other than by the Jewish inhabitants of eastern Poland, who justifiably feared Nazi rule even more than Soviet rule (Gross 2003: 55). Gross forcefully argued that on 10 July 1941 the ethnically Polish inhabitants of Jedwabne brutally, callously and opportunistically murdered all of the town's 1,600 or so Jewish inhabitants and subsequently appropriated Jewish property for their own use; and that at least 92 of the roughly 225 adult and ethnically Polish male residents of this town (that is, getting on for half of its adult male population) participated in these atrocities (Gross 2003: 87–8). Gross also claimed that only a few German soldiers and Gestapo personnel were present in Jedwabne at the time, because the German army was preoccupied by its ongoing invasion of the Soviet Union (pp. 64–5); that this massacre was co-ordinated by Jedwabne's mayor Marian Karolak (p. 73); and that after the war several ethnically Polish witnesses testified in court that the Jedwabne massacre had been carried out only by Poles and that German participation was limited to taking photographs of these Polish crimes against humanity (pp. 79–80). Gross intimated that eastern Poland had had a long history of anti-Semitic violence, including pogroms and other 'beatings of local Jews' – especially at Christian festival times such as Easter, when Catholic priests 'evoked in their sermons an image of Jews as God-killers' – and that the Jewish communities there had become accustomed to providing gifts and paying protection money to the secular as well as religious authorities, in attempts to mitigate such violence (pp. 38–9). He advised his readers:

> We must remember that in the background of anti-Jewish violence there always lurked a suspicion of ritual murder, a conviction that Jews use for the preparation of Passover matzoh the fresh blood of innocent Christian children. It was a deeply ingrained belief among many Polish Catholics . . . After all, rumours that Jews were engaging in these practices drew incensed crowds into the streets of Polish *cities* at a moment's notice even after the Second World War. This was the mechanism that triggered the most infamous postwar pogroms, at Cracow in 1945 and in Kielce in 1946. (Gross 2003: 123–4)

Gross quoted at length the handwritten testimony of Menachem Finkelsztajn, a Jew from the village of Radzilow in Grajewo, who claimed that 800 Jews had been killed by their ethnically Polish neighbours in his native village on 7 July 1941; that 1,200 Jews had similarly been killed by their ethnically Polish neighbours in the nearby village of Wasosz on 5 July 1941; that, amid the temporary power vacuum left by the Soviet forced retreat from eastern Poland, Poles had 'immediately cozied up to the Germans'; that there 'were no German authorities, as the army moved on and did not leave power to anyone'; and that 'propaganda started coming out from the upper echelons of Polish society which influenced the mob, stating that it was time to settle scores with those who had crucified Jesus Christ, with those who take Christian blood for matzoh and are a source of all evil in the world' (Gross 2003: 57–65). Gross also stated that 'there is no reason to single out Jedwabne as a place where relationships between Jews and the rest of the population during those twenty months of Soviet occupation were more antagonistic than anywhere else' (p. 43). He quoted Dr Zygmunt Klukowski, the director of a country hospital near Zamosc in Poland, who wrote despairingly in his diary on 26 November 1942:

> Peasants afraid of reprisals catch Jews in hamlets and bring them to town or sometimes kill them on the spot. In general some terrible demoralization has taken hold of people with respect to the Jews. A psychosis took hold of them and they emulate the Germans in that they don't see a human being in Jews, only some pernicious animal, which has to be destroyed by all means, like dogs sick with rabies, or rats. (Gross 2003: 161–2)

Gross was implying that what took place in Jedwabne was not a freakish aberration, but part of a more widespread phenomenon. However, his claims have evoked various objections.

The Polish historian Bogdan Musial has accused Gross of 'neglect of the historical context', 'cavalier treatment of sources', reliance on a 'scant selection' of unreliable sources, and 'numerous contradictions, erroneous interpretations, unhistorical speculations, and false statements' (Musial 2004: 305, 313, 340). Furthermore, Musial claimed that there was 'sufficient evidence in the sources used by Gross to indicate that the murder of 10 July 1941 was planned, organized, and conducted by the Germans with some Polish participation . . . The Jedwabne massacre took place two weeks after the entry of the Germans [into the region], making it difficult to speak of a sudden, autonomous explosion of anti-Jewish violence there' (p. 336). Dariusz Stola, a Polish specialist on Polish–Jewish relations whom Gross has quoted approvingly (Gross 2006: 260), has similarly questioned whether the massacre of Jedwabne's Jews on 10 July 1941 'can be construed as an unintended effect of an unorganized, largely chaotic social process . . . It seems more than sheer coincidence that concurrently with the crime in Jedwabne, German authorities conducted or staged genocidal killings of Jews in many other localities, which followed specific orders of German leaders to "intensify . . . efforts at self-cleansing by anticommunist and anti-Jewish activists" and make it appear . . . spontaneous' (Stola 2004: 387). Stola also found it 'hard to believe that Karolak, the German-appointed mayor of Jedwabne, invented the idea of killing all Jews in town and then requested that the German authorities agree to the murder and send for this occasion a special group of [German] officers with photographic equipment' (p. 390).

David Engel has emphasized that 'the present state of historical research does not allow for an unambiguous determination of the extent to which the events in Jedwabne were typical or extraordinary. Gross has uncovered traces of similar occurrences in two nearby towns, Radzilow and Wasosz, and there is evidence of murderous violence against Jews by aroused Polish mobs in other localities around Lomza, such as Stawiski and Szczuczn. However, such behaviour does not appear to have been a general phenomenon, even in the specific region under discussion . . . For this reason there are at present no scholarly grounds for viewing the Jedwabne incident as indicative of a general pattern' (Engel 2004: 412).

Some Polish historians have also claimed that, because Gross was a sociologist by training, he had 'never learned the historian's craft: the search for and evaluation of sources' (Polonsky and Michilik 2004: 380). However, this is *ad personam* criticism and a *non sequitur*: most of Gross's published output has consisted of widely respected works of history, as Szarota has implicitly acknowledged elsewhere (p. 416).

On 9 July 2002 a twenty-month investigation by Poland's official Institute of National Remembrance (IPN), which began its work in September 2000, concluded that at least forty Poles (rather than German occupation forces) had carried out the massacre of Jews in Jedwabne on 10 July 1941. Twelve people had been convicted by a Communist court in 1949 for allegedly assisting Germans to carry out the massacre, and the lawyers in charge of the new investigation stated there was no new evidence on which to base new charges against the perpetrators of the massacre (*IHT*, 10 July 2002, p. 5). Radoslaw Ignatiew, the special prosecutor who headed the enquiry, described Jan Gross's estimate of the number of victims (1,600) as 'improbably high'. He warned that further investigation was needed before a final estimate of the number of victims could be reached. Exhumations had found the remains of between forty and fifty victims in one mass grave, while the number of bodies in a second mass grave could not be verified. The enquiry concluded that German forces had been present during the massacre and had inspired the killings, but it had uncovered no incontrovertible evidence of an active German role. 'We have to conclude that the role of the local population was decisive in the perpetration of this criminal act' (The *Guardian*, 10 July 2002, p. 13).

THE WIDER CONTEXT

In October 2002 the IPN published a book entitled *Wokol Jewabnego (Around Jedwabne)*, which concluded that Poles had indeed been responsible for massacring more than a thousand Jews in Second World War pogroms which had previously been blamed on the German occupation forces. IPN files indicated that, after the Second World War, more than a hundred Poles were charged with having participated in massacres of Jews, twenty-seven had been found guilty, four death sentences had been handed out, and one had been enforced. The authors had investigated thirty pogroms which took place in north-east Poland in 1941. Krzysztof Persak, one of the authors of the book, stated that 'The most important discovery made during our work was that the Jedwabne massacre was not an isolated incident but part of a wider phenomenon . . . At this stage of investigation, we can certainly say that the number of Jewish victims exceeded a thousand or even two thousand' (*The Independent*, 4 November 2002, p. 9). An earlier study by Jan Gross had already intimated that there had been significant Polish involvement in 'bloody pogroms' against Jews in June–July 1941 in Bolechow, Boryslaw, Borczow, Brzezany, Buczacz, Czortkow, Drohobycz, Dubna, Grodek Jagiellonski, Jawarow, Kolomyja, Korycin, Krzemieniec, Lwow, Razilow, Sambor, Sasow, Schonica, Sokal, Stryj, Szumsk, Tarnopol, Tluste, Trembowla, Tuczyn, Wizna, Woronow, Zaborow and Zloczow during the German invasion of the eastern half of Poland and the western regions of the USSR (Gross 2000: 105, 125). Nevertheless, Jan Gross has conceded that, while the atrocities committed by ethnic Poles against Polish Jews during the Second World War 'were opportunistic, Poles did not seek the opportunity to commit them. Those crimes would not have taken place but for the circumstances created under Nazi occupation. Poles did not want the Nazis to occupy their country, and they did everything possible, with commendable bravery, to stave them off' (Gross 2006: 249–50).

The claims made by Jan Gross and his supporters are broadly consistent with the breadth of Christian anti-Semitism in interwar Poland, which 'was unquestionably one of the countries most affected by this obsession. Its ideological leaders never stopped developing ideas for depriving millions of Polish citizens of their rights and property and banishing them from the country. The only groups to actively oppose such ideas were the Socialists and the Communists and the liberal faction of the intelligentsia' (Jedlicki 2004: 241). The boycotts and punitive levels of taxation against Jewish shops and businesses orchestrated by Poland's Sanacja regime and by the Polish nationalist (and increasingly fascist) National Democratic Party in 1936–9 are alleged to have reduced one-third of Polish Jews to penury by August 1939 (Crampton 1994: 174–76; Heller 1977). However, as already mentioned, these claims have been disputed by Norman Davies (1981b: 240–66) and Joseph Marcus (1983), among others. Dariusz Stola has also claimed that interwar Polish anti-Semites stopped short of advocating extermination of Jews: 'As far as I know, such an idea had not appeared in the prewar anti-Semitic writings in Poland. Although the rhetoric of Polish anti-Semites was often eliminatory in nature, they saw emigration of a considerable proportion of Polish Jews as their solution to the Jewish question' (Stola 2004: 389).

In late 1940 Jan Karski reported to the Polish government-in-exile in London that 'understanding' of the plight of Polish Jews was 'lacking among the broader masses of the Polish society. Their attitude towards the Jews is ruthless, often without pity' (Gross 2000: 82). This view is corroborated by much of the evidence which Gross has assembled. However, some of his own documentation qualifies this view slightly. For example, a report sent to the Polish government-in-exile in London in autumn 1941 claimed that 'The inhuman terror to which the Jews are subjected is universally condemned and evokes a lot of pity', although the same report added that 'the social and particularly the economic isolation' to which the Jews were also being subjected was 'generally approved' by the Polish population (p. 83).

ANTI-SEMITISM AND VIOLENCE AGAINST JEWS ELSEWHERE

Even though Polish anti-Semitism and violence against Jews has latterly attracted a great deal of international publicity and attention, the scale of Polish complicity in the Holocaust was actually much smaller than that of countries such as Austria, Hungary, Romania, Lithuania, Latvia, Slovakia and France. 'In all of the countries conquered by the Soviets after 1939, there were horrible acts of terror against Jews in the summer and autumn of 1941. They died at the hands of their Lithuanian, Latvian, Estonian, Ukrainian, Russian and Belarussian neighbours' (Michnik 2004: 438). General Walter Stalecker reported at the time that 'Lithuanians had killed as many as 1,500 Jews in one night in Kaunas at the end of June 1941. Other sources estimate that in the Kaunas massacre as many as 10,000 Jews were murdered, and that pogroms broke out in at least forty Lithuanian towns. A recent study of western Ukraine . . . has described how pogroms erupted in as many as thirty-five places after the Nazi invasion of the Soviet Union and resulted in the deaths of between 28,000 and 35,000 victims . . . Within the ethnically Polish area, there were fewer such incidents' (Polonsky and Michilik 2004: 26).

The media publicity generated by the Jedwabne controversy has fostered a highly misleading impression that Poles were exceptionally anti-Semitic and unusually willing to participate in the Holocaust. However, as Jan Gross has acknowledged,

> Opportunistic complicity with anti-Jewish Nazi policies was a universal phenomenon in occupied Europe – as much an experience of Jews and their neighbours in Paris, Amsterdam, Vienna and Salonika as it was in Warsaw, Wilno, Riga, Minsk, Tarnopil, and Lwow. . . Poland's anti-Semitism was the standard brand, widespread in the countries of Christian Europe and the United States at the time. The only difference was that three and a half million Jews lived in Poland on the eve of the war (far more than in any other country occupied by the Germans) and the Nazis proceeded to murder them right there. In the process, 'bystanders' were incrementally drawn into complicity . . . Deep religiosity compelled individual Catholics to shelter and help human beings facing mortal peril and save many a Jewish life. But rescuers represented a small minority, ostracized in their own milieus. (Gross 2006: 249)

The magnitude of the debate aroused by the publication of *Neighbours* is testimony to the willingness of courageous and articulate elements within the Polish intelligentsia, media, academia and political establishment to confront and debate their country's past openly, critically and honestly, in contrast to the long-persistent propensities towards Holocaust-denial in several other countries which have much more to be ashamed of in this regard. Several other East Central European, Baltic and Balkan peoples, along with France and the Low Countries participated in genocide on much greater scales than did the Poles, whose anti-Semitic record was by no means the worst. The scale and intensity of the debate reinforces a recurring theme of this book: that the most burning issues in East Central European and Balkan history and politics antedate the Communist era.

Hungarian complicity in the Holocaust, 1939–45

Hungary's ruling aristocratic oligarchy, headed by the 'Regent' Admiral Miklos Horthy, looked on with mounting apprehension in 1938–9, as Austria, the Czech Lands and the western half of Poland were overrun by Germany. Nevertheless, Hungary's rulers sought to exploit this fraught situation in order to make long-sought territorial gains at the expense of Czechoslovakia, Romania and Yugoslavia. They did so by supporting the Axis Powers *politically*, while trying not to get drawn into a formal state of war with anybody. Hungary thereby managed to regain possession of southern Slovakia and part of Ruthenia (Sub-Carpathian Ukraine) in November 1938; the rest of Ruthenia in March 1939; the northern half of Transylvania in November 1940; and the Vojvodina region in northern Yugoslavia in April 1941. In all, in the space of thirty months, the Horthy regime regained about 80,000 square kilometres, or almost half the territory Hungary had lost in 1918–19. While about half of the 5 million additional inhabitants thus acquired by Hungary were ethnic Magyars, the other half were non-Magyars, including 'over a million Romanians, 700,000 Germans and half a million Ruthenians, besides Slovaks, Serbs and Croats', yet few Magyars questioned the 'rightfulness' of these changes (Kontler 2002: 377).

At least until late 1942 (and economically until late 1943), these stratagems brought substantial rewards and only minor losses or costs, and each new success made Hungary's rulers increasingly confident that they could escape or at least postpone the eventual 'come-uppance' for their 'ill-gotten gains'. However, this Faustian pact with the Axis 'Devil' was from the outset a very high-risk strategy. Since 1936 successive prime ministers had started out with moderate programmes, but had 'ended up by being more radical and more pro-German than Horthy would have liked them to be. The main reason for this was that these politicians were invested with an impossible task: to fight Bolshevism in every one of its manifestations; to rely on Germany for political, military and economic help; and to reduce the Jewish presence in the economy and society, yet also to keep the domestic fascists at bay and [simultaneously] preserve Hungarian independence vis-à-vis Nazi Germany' (Deak 2000: 51).

Active complicity in and acceptance of major territorial gains which were only made possible by Nazi Germany's military might and favour inescapably resulted in Hungary becoming ever more deeply beholden to its Nazi 'godfathers'. From 1942 to 1945 terrible prices were paid for this. Hungary's rulers appear to have had strong, persistent and well-founded forebodings that this would be the case yet sadly they proved unable or too morally weak either to pull back from this course or to forgo the major territorial and population gains which it provided. A large part of the explanation for this was that not only Hungarian nationalists but also many otherwise 'progressive' and liberal-minded Hungarians had remained deeply convinced that Hungary had morally just 'God-given' and 'historic' claims to the territories which it had lost in 1918–19 and which they now sought to repossess, even though they also seem to have known deep down that regaining them as gifts from Nazi Germany was playing with a fire that would ultimately burn their own house down. They also persuaded themselves and much of the Magyar population that the Axis Powers would win the war and that fascism was 'the new wave of the future'. By hitching their fortunes to the Axis Powers, many Magyars evidently thought that they were plugging into and harnessing the fascistic *Zeitgeist* or spirit of the age. Significantly, the 250,000-member Hungarian fascist ('Hungarist') Arrow Cross and its allies obtained about 750,000 votes (37.5 percent of the 2 million votes cast) in the relatively free (secret ballot) parliamentary elections which were held on 28–30 May 1939 (Barany 1971: 77). However, their chickens came home to roost all too quickly. While striving to preserve as much Hungarian autonomy as possible up to the German military occupation of Hungary in March 1944,

Hungary's rulers nevertheless found that their country was increasingly trapped in Nazi Germany's steadily tightening economic and geopolitical 'noose'. It found itself increasingly dependent on Nazi Germany for export markets, technology transfers and other vital imports, as well as increasingly surrounded by states allied to Nazi Germany, greatly reducing its room for manoeuvre. One consequence of having accepted Nazi favours was that Hungary's aristocratic oligarchy, which had on the whole been relatively tolerant and welcoming towards Jewish capitalists and towards Hungary's increasingly educated and professionally qualified Jewish population since the early nineteenth century, suddenly felt obliged to enact increasingly drastic anti-Semitic laws in 1938, 1939, 1940 and 1941, albeit simultaneously insisting to Nazi leaders that the Jews were vital to Hungary's economic dynamism and well-being. In addition, Hungary's rulers felt obliged to sign the Anti-Comintern Pact in 1940, to participate actively in the German war against the Soviet Union from June 1941 to late 1944, and to start expelling Hungarian Jews to the Nazi concentration camps during 1941.

Randolph Braham, widely regarded as the leading authority on the Holocaust in Hungary, has estimated that Hungary's anti-Jewish measures had already 'claimed approximately 64,000 Jewish lives by early 1944. Approximately 40,000 to 50,000 of these were labor servicemen; 17,000 to 18,000 so-called "alien" Jews who were deported in the summer of 1941 and murdered near Kamenets-Podolsk; and the remainder the victims of massacres in and around Ujvidek early in 1942. Nevertheless, the bulk of Hungarian Jewry survived the first 4 ½ years of the war thanks to the physical protection of the conservative-aristocratic government' (Braham 2001).

In mid-March 1944, however, Horthy belatedly attempted to switch sides in the war, whilst striving to hang on to the territorial gains which Hungary had made courtesy of Nazi Germany. His fickleness precipitated a full-scale German military occupation of Hungary on 19 March 1944. At this critical stage in the war with the USSR, however, the Nazis calculated that they still needed to keep Horthy at least nominally in power in order to minimize disruption to their own military and economic war effort, rather than risk replacing him with the fanatical Hungarian fascist Arrow Cross movement led by Ferenc Szalasi.

On 19 March 1944, about 825,000 people who were regarded as Jews by race and/or religion (including thousands of Jewish refugees from Poland, Slovakia, Austria, Croatia and Romania) were still alive on Hungarian-controlled territory, which included northern Transylvania, southern Slovakia, Carpathian Ruthenia and Vojvodina (Deak 2000: 65). Between May and July 1944, however, about 430,000 of these people (more than half the total) were deported to the Nazi death camps (p. 64). 'With only a minimum of German assistance, the Hungarian authorities collected nearly half a million Jews from the countryside and sent [about 430,000 of] them to Auschwitz. The brutality of this procedure defies imagination', and it was carried out 'before the eyes of an indifferent public' (pp. 53, 59, 64). 'Approximately 132,000 Jews were deported to Auschwitz during May and June 1944 from Hungarian-ruled northern Transylvania' (Wiesel *et al.* 2005: 388), which was probably the worst affected part of 'Greater Hungary'. According to Randolph Braham, 'in no other country was the Final Solution programme – the establishment of the central and local Jewish Councils, the isolation, expropriation, ghettoization, concentration, entrainment and deportation of the Jews – carried out with as much barbarity and speed as in Hungary' (Braham 1997: 39–40). In response to American, British and papal protests and warnings against these deportations in June 1944, the Western Allied landings in Normandy and Soviet military advances into Romania, Horthy 'finally emerged from seclusion and reasserted his authority in July, forbidding any further deportations' (Deak 2000: 64). He dismissed Laszlo Endre and Laszlo Baky, the chief Hungarian organizers of the deportations, which officially ceased on 6 July 1944. By then, however, it was too late to save the 430,000 Jews who had already been deported (p. 64).

Hungarian conduct during these deportations was, at best, very mixed. While some non-Jewish Hungarians tried to help Jews or to resist and/or protest against the Holocaust in Hungary, at considerable risk to themselves and their families, it appears that the vast majority stood by and that a substantial minority were complicit in the round-ups, killings and deportations of Jews. Although the notorious Adolf Eichmann came to Hungary in March 1944, he brought a team of fewer than two hundred Nazi SS personnel. The deportation of about 430,000 Jews to Nazi death camps was therefore

> chiefly the work of the new Hungarian government under General Dome Sztojay as well as of the provincial and municipal authorities, the cruel and greedy gendarmes and, to a certain extent, the Jewish Councils. This means that thousands of Hungarians played an active role in the deportations; conversely, there is no evidence of anyone forcibly resisting the deportations. Some county prefects and mayors resigned . . . others were dismissed, but all were easily replaced, usually by their deputies. Most Catholic bishops and other church leaders protested in letters to the government, but only one or two went so far as to criticize openly a regime whose vast majority consisted of professing Christians. A few bishops took the risk of protesting to the Gestapo or of intervening for individuals, but only one or two tried to enter the ghetto in order to bring solace even to the 'Christian Jews' there. Nor . . . did the [Hungarian underground] resistance movement undertake any action [to help Jews]. On the other hand, many convents, monasteries, Catholic social organizations, individual priests, and thousands of civilians offered shelter to Jews who had not been deported, especially toward the end, when the Russians were near and public opinion had begun to turn against the Arrow Cross. (Deak 2000: 64)

Although some of Horthy's critics have intimated that he could and should have resigned or threatened to resign at some point between March and July 1944 in order 'to show his opposition to such horrors', it has nevertheless been pointed out that, 'if he had done so, even the Budapest Jews and the many thousands of Jewish men who had been drafted into the Hungarian army as forced labourers would also have been deported to Auschwitz. Further, power would have fallen into the lap of the Arrow Cross'; nevertheless, 'Horthy really cared little for others beyond those whom he considered "good" Jews, the decorated war veterans and the capitalists, some of whom came close to being his personal friends' (Deak 2000: 54).

Horthy took Hungarians by surprise on 15 October 1944 by authorizing a radio broadcast announcing that he had 'informed a representative of the German Reich that we were about to conclude an armistice with our former enemies and to cease all hostilities against them' (Horthy 2000: 321). Few Hungarians were then aware of the secret armistice negotiations which had been going on between certain members of the Horthy regime and the Soviet authorities, but Germany's fairly competent and very extensive intelligence networks informed the Nazi leadership, the German military leadership and the Arrow Cross leaders that negotiations of some sort were taking place. Furthermore, it had become obvious that Horthy was deeply uneasy about his own position, the adverse course the war was taking, and the mounting human, military and economic costs that Hungary was incurring, and that Horthy and his closest confidants felt increasingly tempted to 'cut and run' if an opportunity to do so arose. After all, King Vittorio Emanuele III and General Badoglio had already succeeded in extricating Italy from its alliance with Germany in July 1943; King Mihai and his closest confidants had done the same for Romania on 23 August 1944; and during September and October 1944 parts of Slovakia were in full-scale revolt against the country's pro-Nazi Catholic-fascist regime and continued participation in Germany's war effort. It was only to be expected that Horthy and parts of the Hungarian population would try to follow suit. Germany's rulers had therefore made contingency preparations to replace Horthy and his more moderate associates with more fanatically fascist and anti-Semitic personnel, if and when the need arose.

Following the 'defeatist' radio broadcast on 15 October 1944, Horthy's palace in Budapest was swiftly surrounded by German forces. Further radio broadcasts explained that Horthy's announcement had been 'misunderstood' and that Hungary would continue to fight at Germany's side. The next day Horthy was forced to give up his own position as regent of Hungary and to appoint the Arrow Cross leader Ferenc Szalasi in place of General Geza Lokatos as prime minister. Szalasi adopted the title 'Nation Leader', in emulation of Hitler's position as Führer of the Third Reich. The Arrow Cross and its pro-Nazi collaborators in Hungary's state bureaucracy, gendarmerie and armed forces, who had already insinuated themselves into key positions in Hungary between 19 March and 15 October 1944, were finally installed fully in power by Nazi Germany at this time in a last-ditch attempt to ensure that Hungary would fight to the finish alongside the Third Reich and comply in full with Hitler's 'final solution of the Jewish question'. These groups immediately unleashed a ferocious reign of terror, attempted to make all of Hungary's remaining economic resources more completely available to Germany, and sought (largely unsuccessfully) to mobilize 1.5 million able-bodied Magyars aged between twelve and seventy for military and/or labour service, in a desperate but obviously futile endeavour to repel the incipient Soviet invasion of Hungary and help store up the failing German war effort. Although Ferenc Szalasi was a rabid Christian anti-Semite on traditional Christian/religious grounds, there were indications that he personally did not support the extermination of the Jews and instead preferred the option of using Hungary's Jews as forced labourers on public works projects until they could emigrate and/or be forcibly relocated to countries willing to accept them once the war was over (Carsten 1967: 180; Weber 1964: 90, 95). Nevertheless, he had been placed in power to do Hitler's bidding. He proved incapable of halting the round-up of Jews in rural Hungary, which the Arrow Cross movement and parts of the Hungarian bureaucracy and gendarmerie reactivated (following its suspension by Horthy in July), in preparation for further deportations of Jews to the Nazi extermination camps. Many more Hungarian Jews were killed or died during these 'round-ups', while in captivity, or while trying to escape.

However, partly because the Nazis began to close down their extermination camps in late 1944 in attempts to hide the horrific scale of their crimes against the Jews, most of the still surviving (mainly urban) Hungarian Jews were concentrated in the hastily established and increasingly overcrowded, under-provisioned and under-heated Budapest ghetto, where many of them died of malnutrition, cold, gunshots or beatings. Although the Arrow Cross and the Hungarian gendarmerie incurred condemnation for this (both at the time and subsequently), in practice 'confining the Jews to a ghetto instead of deporting them actually contributed greatly to the survival of about 150,000 in Budapest' (Karsai 2000: 244).

Nevertheless, between 1941 and 1945 (inclusive), about 550,000 Hungarian Jews perished, mainly as a result of the executions, beatings, round-ups and deportations of Jews carried out between March 1944 and February 1945 (Braham 2001). Over the same period, around 500,000 non-Jewish Hungarians perished, mainly while fighting alongside German and Romanian forces in the Soviet Union in 1942–3 or while fighting to either defend or liberate their country and/or defeat Nazi Germany in late 1944 and early 1945 (Kontler 2002: 387). In addition, in 1944–5 somewhere between 250,000 (Hoensch 1994: 163) and 600,000 (Kontler 2002: 287) mainly (but not entirely) non-Jewish Hungarians were deported to Soviet prisons and labour camps, from which a significant proportion never returned to Hungary (and were mostly presumed to have died in Soviet captivity).

The Hungarian historian Laszlo Kontler contends that Horthy's failure to pull Hungary out of the war before it was occupied by the Germans in March 1944 'immensely increased' the subsequent 'reconstruction tasks' and robbed Hungary of any residual standing and respect which it might otherwise have gained in the eyes of the Allies (Kontler 2002: 388), but this argument is not fully convincing. Romania, which successfully extricated itself from the war against the Allies through a change of regime on 23 August 1944, then found itself obliged to fight alongside the Allies against Germany and by doing so incurred even heavier casualties (including the loss of more than 300,000 lives) and extensive economic damage. Yet in some ways it was still treated quite harshly (punitively) as a former 'enemy state' after the war ended. Through their *folies de grandeur* and their rash and intrinsically evil Faustian pacts with Nazi Germany, both Hungary and Romania managed to get themselves into 'no win' situations during the Second World War, and in the end both countries paid dearly for this. 'Ironically, it appears in retrospect that had Hungary continued to remain [*sic*] a militarily passive but politically vocal ally of the Third Reich instead of provocatively engaging in essentially fruitless . . . diplomatic maneuvers, the Jews of Hungary might possibly have survived the war relatively unscathed' (Braham 1994a: 233–4), like the Jews of Bulgaria.

After the war, Admiral Horthy enjoyed a comfortable and peaceful exile in the coastal resort of Estoril (near Lisbon) until his death in 1957, under the protection of the Portuguese dictator Antonio Salazar and with financial support from some wealthy Hungarian Jews who felt gratitude for Horthy's sporadic and half-hearted attempts to limit the impact of the Holocaust in Hungary. However, the official reburial of Horthy in Hungary during the autumn of 1993, which was orchestrated by Hungary's first post-Communist government, contributed to the defeat of that government in the Hungarian elections of 1994 (Deak 2000: 40).

THE GENOCIDE PERPETRATED UNDER GENERAL ION ANTONESCU 1940–3

From September 1940 to October 1943 the Romanian military-fascist regime headed by General Ion Antonescu actively participated in Hitler's 'final solution of the Jewish question'. Although there were probably about 800,000 Jews living in Romania in early 1940, only about 315,000 Jews remained under Romanian rule after it lost one-third of its territory and population to the USSR, Hungary and Bulgaria between June and September 1940 (Hitchins 1994: 483).

Jews made up about 7 per cent of the total population (and 27 per cent of the urban population) of Bessarabia and about 11 per cent of the total population (and 30 per cent of the total population) of Bukovina in 1930 (Ioanid 2000: 14; Rothschild 1974: 289), and about 330,000 Jews were still living in Bessarabia and northern Bukovina when these territories were annexed by the USSR in late June 1940 (Mann 2005: 305). Some of these Jews subsequently 'collaborated' with or even became members of the Soviet regime, the Red Army or the Communist Party of the Soviet Union (CPSU). As Jews, they understandably felt somewhat safer from total annihilation under brutal Soviet rule than they did under genocidal Romanian and/or German rule. This resulted in the participation of *some* Jews in atrocities committed by the Soviet military and civil authorities in Bessarabia and northern Bukovina, especially against known or suspected Romanian, Hungarian and German nationalists, anti-Semites and fascists. This in turn helped the Antonescu regime to portray the Jews 'as the most important internal enemy, as agents of London or Moscow, and as the principal cause of Romania's economic difficulties'; indeed, 'acceptance of these lies outweighed fear' as an explanation for the almost complete absence of Romanian protests against the regime's horrific treatment of Romanian and Ukrainian Jews (Wiesel *et al.* 2005: 390).

However, although anti-Semitic Romanian nationalists and fascists regularly ranted against 'Judaeo-Communism', they greatly exaggerated both the proportion of Jews who became Communists and the proportion of Romania's Communists who were Jews (about 10 per cent at that time), in much the same way that Polish nationalists greatly exaggerated the numbers of Jews who participated in Soviet atrocities against Poles in eastern Poland between September 1939 and June 1941 and subsequently used this as a bogus pretext for anti-Semites to take savage reprisals against Jews. They also ignored or overlooked the fact that, as many Jews had anticipated and feared, Jews were among the chief targets and victims of the Stalinist Soviet regime in Soviet-occupied eastern Poland from autumn 1939 to June 1941 (Gross 2000: 92–115) and in Soviet-occupied Bessarabia and northern Bukovina from late June 1940 to June 1941 (Ioanid 2000: 39). Anti-Semitic equation of Jews with Communism was not merely unfounded, but a bitterly ironic travesty of the facts.

From late June 1941 to August 1944 Romania fought alongside Nazi Germany against the Soviet Union. This enabled Romania temporarily to regain possession of Bessarabia and northern Bukovina until early 1944. In addition, Nazi Germany entrusted the Romanian military with the administration of south-western Ukraine (including Odessa) from late 1941 to early 1944. Although the Antonescu regime's anti-Jewish policies 'drew strength from the long history of anti-Semitism within Romania's political and intellectual elites' (Wiesel *et al.* 2005: 390), participation in the Second World War as an ally of Nazi Germany against the Soviet Union 'transformed what might otherwise have remained a period of severe anti-Semitic outbreaks into a true Romanian Holocaust' (Ioanid 2000: 108).

When the USSR lost Bessarabia and northern Bukovina to the German–Romanian–Hungarian invasion launched in June 1941, up to 130,000 Jews (between one-third and two-thirds of the Jewish inhabitants of these territories) prudently fled eastwards with the retreating Red Army and the CPSU (Hitchins 1994: 485). Most of these survived the war – the main exceptions being those who subsequently perished either fighting for the Soviet Union, or in Soviet captivity, or as prisoners captured by the Axis forces. By contrast, most of the Jews who remained in Bessarabia and northern Bukovina were either killed by the mainly Romanian occupation forces between June and September 1941 or deported to camps in Romanian-administered 'Transnistria', where they were joined by up to 100,000 Jews deported from Moldavia, Wallachia and southern Transylvania. In Transnistria up to 200,000 Jews 'suffered waves of killings, deliberate starvation and cruel treatment . . . Only 50,000 Jews survived to the end of 1943' (Hitchins 1994: 485; Mann 2005: 305). Radu Ioanid estimated that, between them, the Antonescu regime, Romania's security forces and the Iron Guard were responsible for the deaths of at least 250,000 Jews (Ioanid 2000: 289). Raul Hilberg put the figure at 270,000 (1985: 339), which Ioanid deemed reasonable (Ioanid 2000: xxi).

An International Commission for the Study of the Holocaust in Romania was established by President Ion Iliescu in the summer of 2003 in an attempt to resolve once and for all the various claims and counter-claims concerning the intensity of anti-Semitism and the scale of genocide in Romania during the Second World War. According to this Commission's Final Report, 'in the territories under Romanian control, between 280,000 and 320,000 Romanian and Ukrainian Jews were murdered or perished during the Holocaust. In addition, approximately 135,000 Romanian Jews living under Hungarian rule in northern Transylvania also perished' (although the latter deaths cannot be blamed on Romanians), as did about 5,000 Romanian Jews who had been deported or forced to emigrate by the Romanian authorities to other Axis states (Wiesel *et al.* 2005: 387–8).

More specifically, this Commission concluded that between 45,000 and 60,000 Romanian and Ukrainian Jews were killed in Romanian-controlled Bessarabia and Bukovina between June and December 1941 – mainly by Romanians, but also by German troops stationed there. Between 105,000 and 120,000 of the Romanian Jews who were deported by the Romanian authorities to Romanian-administered Transnistria in 1941–3 perished as a consequence. In addition, between 115,000 and 180,000 of the native Jewish inhabitants of Transnistria were liquidated, especially in Odessa and in the districts of Golta and Berezovka. Furthermore, at least 15,000 Jews were killed by Romanians alone in Romania's old core regions (the Regat), especially in the pogrom of late June and early July 1941 in Iasi (Moldavia's capital city, in which Jews had made up half the population in 1930) and in rural Moldavia. However, far fewer were killed in Wallachia, where Jews had made up only about 5 per cent of the population. The Romanian authorities had also deported about 25,000 Gypsies (Roma) to Transnistria, where about 11,000 of these perished (all from Wiesel *et al.* 2005: 388). Consequently,

Of all Nazi Germany's allies, Romania bears responsibility for the greatest contribution to the extermination of Jews, apart from Germany itself. The massacres committed in Iasi, Odessa, Bogdanovca, Dumanovca and Peciora, for example, were among the most hideous crimes committed against Jews during the Holocaust. Romania committed a genocide against the Jews, and the survival of Jews in some regions does not change this reality. (Wiesel *et al.* 2005: 392).

When it saw which way the wind was blowing, the Antonescu regime began to pull back from its genocidal policies in October 1942, thus starting even before the Axis defeat at Stalingrad. Antonescu staunchly resisted German demands for the deportation of Romanian Jews to the Nazi death camps. Because of the crucial importance of Romanian oil, food and raw materials to the Axis war effort and his well-attested respect for and trust in Antonescu, Hitler accepted this (as he also did in the Bulgarian case), and he refrained from instigating a German invasion of Romania to enforce full compliance with the Final Solution. Instead, from December 1942 onwards, Antonescu began to seek ways to dispatch Romania's surviving Jews to Palestine, using them as bargaining chips in his clumsy and ultimately unsuccessful pursuit of a 'separate peace' with the Allies (Mann 2005: 306; Hitchins 1994: 486). Deportations of Romanian Jews to Transnistria definitively halted in March–April 1943. 'This change of policy resulted in the survival of at least 292,000 Romanian Jews' (Hitchins 1994: 391). This is consistent with claims that by the 1950s around 300,000 Romanian Jews were living in Israel, while 23,000 remained in Romania (Ross 1992). The survival rate for Jews was thus higher in Romanian-controlled territory than in most of the other countries allied to and/or occupied by Nazi Germany (Mann 2005: 303), even though Romania had the third or fourth highest level of complicity in the Holocaust – exceeded only by Germany, Austria and possibly Hungary.

It is nonetheless disturbing that many Romanians have continued to revere Antonescu as a saviour-figure and as a national hero in whom they can take pride. During the 1990s many streets were named after him, public statues were erected to him and nostalgic films were made about him. Romania was the only country in post-Nazi Europe to have accorded such respect to a genocidal dictator – albeit ostensibly for his role in 'liberating' Bessarabia and northern Bukovina from Soviet control in 1941 (Ioanid 2000: viii–ix, xxiii–xxiv). Many Romanians have continued to deny that many of their forebears were willing accomplices in the Holocaust, preferring to uphold the convenient fiction that it was nearly all the work of the Germans (*IHT*, 2 August 2002, p. 3). To some degree, these attitudes were reflections of the extent to which the Communist regime and the first Iliescu regime (1990–6) had helped to suppress evidence that hundreds of thousands of Romanian and Ukrainian Jews had perished at the hands of the Antonescu regime and/or the Iron Guard.

GENOCIDE IN THE 'INDEPENDENT STATE OF CROATIA' (NDH)

Although Jews were by far the main victims of calculated programmes of genocide during the Second World War, they were by no means the only ones. Croatian Catholic fascists and ultranationalists killed more than 300,000 Serbs and Montenegrins on the territory of the 'Independent State of Croatia' (NDH). This regime was established in April 1941 by Ante Pavelic and his fascist *Ustasa*, with the active support of many Catholics, Bosniaks (Bosnian Muslims) and the Axis Powers. The NDH comprised not only 'Croatia proper', but also much of Slovenia, Slavonia, Bosnia and Herzegovina, within which the *Ustasa* and its Catholic collaborators forced many Orthodox Christian Serbs and Montenegrins to embrace Catholicism (on pain of death) and carried out widespread 'ethnic cleansing'. The *Ustasa* had a relatively free rein, partly because Croatia was incapable of contributing much to the wider Axis war effort and partly because it had never had a large Jewish population. Nevertheless, the savagery with which it carried out 'genocide' against the Serbs shocked the local Italian and German occupation forces.

In the late 1940s the Yugoslav Communist regime informed the UN that the number of war deaths in Yugoslavia had been 1.7 million, including about 600,000 Serbs, Montenegrins and Jews who had allegedly perished at the *Ustasa* concentration camp at Jasenovac. This greatly inflated estimate of the death toll was uncritically accepted in most foreign writing on Yugoslavia (including our own). This helped to reinforce claims that the Communist-ruled Yugoslav federal system was the most efficacious 'cure' for Serb supremacism and for the genocidal Croatian and Bosniak backlash which had occurred between 1941 and 1945.

More recently, however, estimates of the numbers of Yugoslavs killed by fellow Yugoslavs during the 1940s have been revised downwards, not only by Croatian ultra-nationalists eager to play down the scale of Croatian crimes against humanity, but also by Serbian and Croatian historians and demographers who appear to be primarily interested in veracity. On the basis of census data from before and after the Second World War, the Serbian émigré academic Bogoljub Kocevic estimated that the number of Yugoslav deaths attributable to the *Ustasa* regime and the Second World War was around 1 million. Implicitly, the rest of the 'demographic deficit' for that period reflected the wartime reduction in birth rates rather than increased mortality (Lampe 1996: 380). This was broadly supported by subsequent calculations (by Vladimir Zerjavic and other Croatian academics, but based on work by Serb as well as Croat historians) that about 947,000 Yugoslavs perished between 1941 and 1945, including about 487,000 Serbs, 50,000 Montenegrins, 207,000 Croats, 86,000 Muslims (Bosniaks), 60,000 Jews and 30,000 Slovenes. On these estimates, 78 per cent of Yugoslavia's Jews, 8.1 per cent of its Muslims (Bosniaks), 7.3 per cent of its Serbs and 5.0 per cent of its Croats perished (Covic 1991: 35). These figures are compatible with the just claims that Jews, Serbs and Montenegrins were by far the most numerous victims in 1940s Yugoslavia, even though many Croats and Bosniaks appear to have perished either while perpetrating genocide or as a result of acts of resistance and/or retaliation against genocidal attrocities.

SLOVAK COMPLICITY IN GENOCIDE UNDER THE TISO REGIME, 1942–4

During the interwar period Slovak nationalists had nursed considerable resentments against Czech dominance of Czechoslovakia and Czech refusal to countenance the conversion of this unitary state into a federation conferring extensive autonomy on its principal ethnic groups. While Czechoslovakia was being dismembered in October–November 1938 (under the terms of the infamous September 1938 'Munich agreement' between Britain, France, Germany and Italy), the Hlinka Slovak People's Party (HSLS) seized the opportunity to proclaim Slovak autonomy on 6 October 1938 and form a Slovak government headed by the HSLS leader Dr Jozef Tiso (himself a Catholic priest). During November 1938 the nationalistic, strongly Roman Catholic and increasingly anti-Semitic and 'clerico-fascist' HSLS consolidated an autonomous authoritarian regime in Slovakia by outlawing the Communist Party (which went underground), by prohibiting the functioning of the Social Democratic Party and Jewish parties, and by absorbing most of the other Slovak parties, although it did not dare to interfere with the 60,000–member German Party (the Deutsche Partei, DP) and the Hungarian Party, which represented many of the 60,000 Magyars still left in Slovakia. The HSLS also expanded its name to the Hlinka Slovak People's Party: Party of Slovak National Unity (HSLS-SSNJ), and on 18 December 1938 this presented a single list of candidates in plebiscitary elections to a new Slovak parliament in which representatives of the old HSLS obtained fifty-four of the seventy seats (Toma and Kovac 2001: 115). The dismemberment of Czechoslovakia was completed on 14 March 1939, when Nazi Germany invaded the rest of Bohemia-Moravia while Hungary invaded and annexed Ruthenia and a slice of Slovakia containing about 40,000 inhabitants (pp. 121–2).

A somewhat truncated Slovakia became a formally independent Slovak State, with an area of 38,004 square kilometres and a population of about 2,655,000 (whereas in 1920 Slovakia had been allowed an area of 49,006 square kilometres and a population of about 2,998,000) (Liptak 2000: 244, 259). Fiercely nationalistic, anti-Communist and frequently anti-Semitic Catholic clergy played leading roles in this new polity. However, Slovak anti-Semitism was largely *religious rather than racial* and was *not (or not yet) exterminationist*. Almost all of Slovakia's anti-Semites (including Dr Tiso) advocated assisted relocation and/or forced deportation of Slovakia's citizens of Jewish faith (not 'race') to any state(s) willing to receive them, rather than the extermination of the Jews. After Slovakia adopted a republican constitution in July 1939, the Slovak parliament elected Dr

Tiso to the new post of President of the Republic, enabling the more racist and exterminationist anti-Semite Dr Vojtech Tuka to take over the vacated premiership.

During 1939 and 1940 Jews were still able to emigrate from Slovakia. Starting in September 1940, however, the Slovak parliament empowered the government to exclude Jews (expressly defined by *religion*, not 'race') from many public institutions and occupations, to 'Aryanize' and/or confiscate their businesses and property, to freeze their bank accounts, and to restrict their dress and rights of movement (Spiesz *et al.* 2006: 216). In September 1941 the neo-Nazi prime minister, Vojtech Tuka, pushed through a whole raft of much more explicitly racist laws known as the 'Jewish Code', modelled on Nazi Germany's racially anti-Semitic Nuremburg laws, although President Tiso 'granted numerous exemptions' (Toma and Kovac 2001: 130–1; Spiesz *et al.* 2006: 216–17).

In January 1942, finding itself 'unable to deliver a negotiated quota of 20,000 Slovak migrant workers to Germany', the Tiso regime 'offered to supplement them with Jewish workers' (Spiesz *et al.* 2006: 220). In response, 'German officials informed the Slovak government that Hitler had decided to create a special state for Jews on occupied Polish territory . . . Jews were supposedly to manage it themselves and perform agricultural, trade and other physical work there' (p. 216). As a result, between 25 March and 20 October 1942 the Slovak Republic deported between 57,000 and 60,000 Slovak Jews, between 45,000 and 57,000 of whom perished in or on their way to the Nazi extermination camps in German-occupied Poland (Liptak 2000: 264; Toma and Kovac 2001: 130–2). However, whether in response to repeated Vatican protests against Slovakia's anti-Semitic laws and the deportation of around two-thirds of Slovakia's Jews, or because President Tiso and some of his ministers belatedly became aware that these Jews were being starved, cruelly and degradingly treated, and exterminated, the deportation of Slovak Jews was halted from October 1942 to August 1944 (Toma and Kovac 2001: 130–2). Slovakia then appeared for a time to become a relative 'safe haven' for Jews, and Jewish organizations started urging Polish and Hungarian Jews who could do so to take refuge there.

However, the major anti-German and anti-fascist uprising in central Slovakia from early August to late October 1944 precipitated a large influx of German armed forces, including the SS. These forces not only crushed the Slovak uprising but also instigated further round-ups of Slovak Jews. Between 13,000 and 13,500 of them were deported to the Nazi death camps between September 1944 and March 1945 – 10,000 to 12,000 of these perished (Liptak 2000: 264; Toma and Kovac 2001: 130–2). The residue survived mainly as a result of the liberation of the death camps by the Red Army in April 1945 (Spiesz *et al.* 2006: 231). Overall, however, between 57,000 and 67,000 of 85,000–90,000 Slovak Jews (between two-thirds and three-quarters of the total) perished (Liptak 2000: 264; Toma and Kovac 2001: 130–2; Wandycz 2001: 232), including a majority of those who fell under Hungarian rule from 1938 or 1939 to 1945. Although Slovak apologists try to defend Dr Tiso and his regime mainly on the basis of claims that he and his predominantly Christian support-ers allegedly went to great lengths and took considerable risks to try to save as many Slovak Jews as possible from extermination, it is very significant that the proportion of Slovak Jews extermi-nated was either as high or almost as high as that for Czech Jews (three-quarters, according to Wandycz 2001: 232), even though Bohemia and Moravia were directly occupied by Nazi Germany and directly exposed to the SS from March 1939 to early 1945. The efforts of Dr Tiso and his Slovak Christian supporters to 'save' as many Slovak Jews as possible were therefore either greatly exaggerated or largely ineffectual.

BULGARIA AND GREECE DURING THE HOLOCAUST

Even in those countries where the dominant churches did not publicly support fascist movements and/or anti-Semitism, only rarely did the churches take prominent roles in actively opposing and condemning these evils. However, the courageous and high-profile roles of the leaders and clergy of the national (autocephalos) Orthodox Churches in Bulgaria and Greece in denouncing and actively resisting anti-Semitism and genocide and in completely thwarting the planned mass deportation of Bulgaria's Jewish citizens to the Nazi death camps constituted exceptional stands against anti-Semitism by European Christians (Chary 1972; Todorov 2001; Mazower 1993: 256–561). Other than in Thessaloniki, there was more *philo-Semitism* than anti-Semitism among Greeks: 'Overall, Greeks showed a remarkable generosity of spirit towards the Jews' (Mazower 1993: 257–61). Nevertheless, the vicious policies of the Axis Powers ensured that, of the 70,000–80,000 Jews in Greece in 1940, fewer than 10,000 survived (Mazower 1993: 256).

Admittedly, Tsar Boris III, his prime minister Bogdan Filov and the Bulgarian state apparatus and armed forces actively participated in the Holocaust in March 1943 by forcibly rounding up and deporting to the Nazi death camps the 11,355 Jewish inhabitants of the Bulgarian-occupied parts of Macedonia and Thrace, only twelve of whom survived the war (Todorov 2001: 8–9). Subsequently, however, Bulgarian clergy, parliamentarians, academics, writers and journalists mounted a successful campaign to persuade the Tsar and his prime minister skilfully and doggedly to resist German pressure for mass deportation of the Jewish inhabitants of Bulgaria proper (48,400 people or 0.8 per cent of the population, according to the 1934 census, quoted by Todorov 2001: 4). We have discussed this campaign and the somewhat paradoxical reasons for its success more fully elsewhere (Bideleux and Jeffries 2007: 80–3).

The only comparable stands taken by church leaders and Christian clergy elsewhere in Europe were those taken by the leaders and clergy of the Danish and Norwegian Lutheran churches – with remarkable success in the Danish case (fewer than two hundred Danish Jews perished), but with tragically little success in the Norwegian case. However, the successful Danish stance did not call for anywhere near as much moral courage as the tragically unsuccessful stand taken by the Greek Orthodox clergy and church leaders. Because Nazi Germany treated Nordic Denmark with much respect and leniency and maintained only half an infantry division (fewer than 10,000 men) in Denmark (Deak 2000: 6), Danish Christians managed to smuggle all but 481 of the 7,500 Jews in Denmark at that time to safety in Sweden during October 1943. Even when the Germans realized what had happened, they treated the Danes very gently, in sharp contrast to the ferocity of the reprisals which the German occupation forces in Greece meted out against thousands of courageous Greeks.

Bulgaria became the only Axis-aligned European state in which more Jews were alive at the end of the war than at its start (Chary 1972: xiii), and it also succeeded in keeping out of the German-led war against the Soviet Union. As a result, it incurred relatively low casualties and war damage and was even allowed to make a net territorial gain (Dobrudja) at the end of the war.

HAZARDS OF STEREOTYPING AND CRUDE APPORTIONMENT OF 'BLAME'

The foregoing accounts are not intended to establish an invidious and ultimately specious 'hierarchy of blame', but rather to emphasize that almost none of the ethnic groups discussed has had a record to be proud of and that it is dangerous as well as unjust to suppose that particular ethnic groups can be cast exclusively in the roles of villains or monsters. Life is rarely that simple. In Hobbesian environments characterized by the warfare of 'all against all', the continual struggle simply to survive tends to involve almost everyone in varying degrees of complicity in misdeeds of varying degrees of ghastliness. Those of us who have had the great luck never to have found ourselves in such positions are poorly placed (let alone equipped) to pass judgement on the actions of those who have had the misfortune to find themselves trapped in such predicaments.

In highlighting the unusual degrees of Romanian, Hungarian, Slovak and Croatian complicity in genocide during the Second World War, we have no wish to caricature these nations as having stronger innate propensities towards crimes against humanity and genocide than others. On the contrary, we believe that crimes against humanity and genocide have mainly resulted from circumstantial rather than innate factors, and we share Istvan Deak's belief that 'every ethnic group harbours its share of potential murderers who can be readily mobilized to commit violence' (Deak 2001: 56). As a rule, no one ethnic group is innately worse than another, and today's villains have often been yesterday's victims (and vice versa). The chief culprits are not so much *particular* ethnic groups as the mindsets of devotion and subservience to *ethnic and/or religious collectivism*, the pursuit of intrinsically dangerous concepts of ethnic, racial or religious 'purity' and 'purification' (alias 'cleansing'), and the defence of bogus ethnic claims and aspirations, wherever and in whatever form they manifest themselves.

Nor do we wish to suggest that there were greater innate propensities to commit atrocities and other violent crimes against Jews in East Central Europe and/or the Balkans than in western and Germanic Central Europe. After all, there was also large-scale Austrian and French participation and considerable Dutch, Norwegian and Italian complicity in and profiteering from deportations of Jews to Nazi death camps and other violence against Jews (Fraenkel 1967; Marrus and Paxton 1981; Presser 1969; Petrow 1974; Michaelis 1978). In the countries occupied by Nazi Germany, several million people – or between 2 and 3 per cent of the population – were subsequently accused of having collaborated with the Nazis (Deak 2000: 4).

Admittedly, the assaults on Jews by East Central European, Balkan, Baltic, Ukrainian and Belarussian peoples were on the whole much more spontaneous, chaotic and disorganized than the increasingly systematic, scientific and industrialized liquidation of the Jews in death camps orchestrated by the Nazi regime (although the initial huge mass killings carried out by German and Austrian SS Eisatzgruppen in Poland in 1939–41 and on Soviet territory in 1941–4 were second to none in their primitive barbarity). This contrast reflects the fact that Germany was a highly educated, scientific and industrialized country with highly professionalized and relatively efficient and disciplined security forces and bureaucracies, whereas most of the Balkan and East Central European states were still predominantly agrarian, church-dominated, semi-educated, and relatively inefficient, undisciplined and corrupt – much more like Fascist Italy than Nazi Germany. The anti-Semitism which pervaded these regions was still predominantly Christian rather than secular and racial, and perhaps as a consequence it was less scientific, totalistic and unremittingly exterminationist than was Nazi anti-Semitism. These differences were what ultimately made Nazi anti-Semitism so much *more* (rather than less) lethal, appalling and barbaric than its allegedly 'less civilized' or 'more primitive' East Central European, Balkan, Baltic, Ukrainian and Belarussian counterparts.

The contributors to *The Politics of Retribution in Europe: World War II and its Aftermath* have cogently argued that it is extremely difficult to maintain clear and defensible distinctions between 'resistance' and 'collaboration', or between 'resisters' and 'collaborators' (Deak *et al.* 2000). Istvan Deak has emphasized that 'the extent of the material and human losses suffered by European states, and their postwar treatment, depended on luck, geography and great power politics. At no time was their postwar fate a function of wartime merits and demerits; witness the relative luck of National Socialist Austria, collaborationist France, and fascist Slovakia, but also the catastrophic experiences of anti-Nazi Poland' (Deak 2000: 55).

The paramount needs of societies which have been afflicted by seriously debilitating internal divisions and conflicts over the past century are to defuse the root causes of those internal divisions and conflicts, to dwell on the future rather than the past, to heal old wounds, to put old grievances to rest, and to knit back together again. The politics of retribution and revenge, focused upon the vilification, rooting out, prosecution and punishment of the 'guilty parties', may not be the most effective way of meeting these paramount needs. There are few positive gains to be made from continually reopening old wounds and grievances. It has often been virtually impossible to establish clearly and precisely where ultimate responsibility for crimes and evils lay, with the result that it is all too easy to vilify and punish the wrong people or to apportion blame too indiscriminately. This engenders new injustices, wounds and grievances. There is a great deal more work to be done on establishing the extent of the crimes committed during the 1930s and 1940s, the scale of political, police, military and popular complicity in those crimes, and how and why they came about. This is necessary in order to overcome the widespread tendencies towards selective amnesia and denial, to help many countries to face up to and come to terms with what happened on their territories during those decades, and to gain fuller understanding and recognition of the traumas and sufferings of the victims and those connected to them.

Simplistic 'black-and-white' moral judgements and the crude apportioning of blame, exemplified by Daniel J. Goldhagen (1996; 2002), are best avoided. It is more important to try to understand and explain more fully the very difficult pressures and predicaments which turned large numbers of seemingly 'ordinary' people into conscious or unconscious, willing or unwilling, and major or minor accomplices of some horribly unsavoury movements, tendencies and regimes. As Vaclav Havel repeatedly emphasized in relation to life under Europe's Communist regimes, for most people minor acts of complicity were part of daily life and of their struggles to do the best they could for themselves and/or their families. Even the most unlikely regimes (such as those of Admiral Horthy in Hungary, Dr Tiso in Slovakia and Tsar Boris III in Bulgaria) intermittently held out against the enormous pressures exerted on them to engage in wholesale ethnic and/or racial 'purification' or 'cleansing' of their own countries, albeit with very mixed results in terms of helping to save many people from extermination during the Second World War. Two or three Balkan and East Central European regimes that were tied or 'allied' to Nazi Germany may on balance have done more to frustrate than to facilitate Hitler's 'Final Solution'. Sixty years on, there is still much that is being debated and revised, and much that remains unresolved. If this is true of the late 1930s and early 1940s, it is equally true of the enormous political crimes committed under Communist rule (especially during the late 1940s and the 1950s) and during the Yugoslav 'wars of dissolution' in the 1990s. It is therefore also crucial to beware of rushing into over-hasty and simplistic moral judgements and apportionment of blame and retribution with regard to those more recent crimes, which also require thorough and circumspect investigation and debate in pursuit of truth, reconciliation and societal healing, rather than the perpetration of new injustices and the creation of new climates of uncertainty, insecurity and fear on the basis of premature and/or superficial ('black and white') judgements and conclusions (see pp. 22).

THE LONGER-TERM IMPACT OF THE SECOND WORLD WAR AND MASS GENOCIDE ON BALKAN AND EAST CENTRAL EUROPEAN SOCIETIES

The Second World War polarized political and social attitudes across much of Europe. This in turn caused a 'polarisation of politics' and persuaded millions of people to join resistance 'cells' (Mazower 1993: xvi). The prominence of Communists in several resistance movements, above all those of Greece, Yugoslavia and Albania, led many people to see them no longer as 'anti-national' subversives, but rather as stalwart patriots largely untainted by collaboration with fascism. The (actually quite limited) collaboration of Communist parties with Nazi Germany and its allies following the August 1939 Nazi–Soviet Pact seems to have been widely forgiven and perhaps even partly forgotten, because of the central roles, great courage and extraordinary tenacity of large numbers of Communists in the anti-fascist resistance movements from late June 1941 onward. Simultaneously, with the partial exception of the Czech Lands, the old (interwar) ruling establishments and right-wing nationalist movements were in large measure discredited and deprived of their previous 'patriotic credentials' by the high degrees to which their members succumbed to and/ or 'collaborated' with fascism and demonstrated their unwillingness and/or inability to uphold and safeguard their countries' independence and sovereignty during the war.

Like a tidal wave, occupation swept away old structures, and changed the entire landscape. It forced upon Europe a regime whose brutality it [Europe] had inflicted on other continents, but had not expected to suffer at home. The shock caused established systems of thought and rule to disintegrate. In this way, Nazi rule acted as a catalyst for a series of unpredictable political and social reactions'. (Mazower 1993: xiv)

The crucial roles played by the Soviet Union in the defeat of the Third Reich, Hungary, Romania and Bulgaria and in the subsequent 'liberation' of East Central Europe and the eastern Balkans from fascist rule also promoted widespread respect bordering on admiration for Europe's Communist parties, even though this was mitigated somewhat by the equally widespread fear of potential Soviet domination and by the often atrocious conduct of the Soviet armed forces, whose soldiers raped more than two milllion German and Polish females (often repeatedly and in gang rapes) and systematically plundered German towns and villages (Beevor 2004: 25, 28–37, 46, 65–7, 106–8, 117–23,188, 326–7, 406–15; Beevor and Vinogradova 2006: 320, 326–7 337; Naimark 1995, chapter 2). Many members of the Balkan and East Central European intelligentsias who had been embittered by fascist persecution and/or disillusioned by the failure of the interwar regimes to solve their countries' social and economic maladies were widely drawn to Marxism as an ideology which claimed (and for a time appeared) to eschew nationalist and religious bigotry and to supply the keys to understanding the recent course and future direction of history. Communism promised to build a better world and, albeit at awesome social cost, it appeared to have demonstrated its strength and viability in Stalin's Soviet Union.

In the wake of the fearful and painful political and economic debacles brought about by the defeat of fascism, many millions of unemployed or insecure workers and intelligentsia gravitated towards Communist movements which seemed capable of delivering huge expansions of industrial employment and massive upward social mobility on the Soviet model. For similar reasons, the still numerically preponderant peasantries of East Central Europe and the Balkans mainly looked to resurgent peasantist parties to enact radical land redistributions and build up voluntary rural co-operative networks responsive to peasant needs and aspirations (Mitrany 1951). Within the anti-fascist Popular Front coalitions of Communists, socialists, peasantists, liberals and Christian democrats which emerged in East Central Europe and the Balkans during and immediately after the Second World War, there was a broad consensus on the urgent need for radical land reform, the expropriation of German and Italian property, the expulsion of Hitler's German collaborators, planned economic reconstruction, comprehensive welfare systems, and public ownership of banks, large-scale industries and public utilities.

The upshot was that many (perhaps most) people in the Balkans and East Central Europe became psychologically prepared for a very thoroughgoing post-war reconstruction in which radical proletarian and peasantist movements had seemingly won some sort of moral right to determine the agenda and 'call the shots'. From 1944 onwards, nearly all the 'anti-fascist' parties in these regions stoutly resisted the perceived 'half-measures' and 'sell-outs' which had so fatally compromised and disarmed the ineffectual governments and large parts of the equally ineffectual liberal, democratic and radical opposition forces during the interwar years. Not just among Communists, but also among peasantists, socialists, social democrats, liberals and Christian democrats, there was a very widespread determination *not* to repeat the mistakes of the interwar years, *not* to settle for half-measures and *not* to allow the wily old oligarchies to retrieve their former positions. Consequently, even in the relatively free elections held in Czechoslovakia in May 1946, the Communist Party emerged as by far the largest political party, with a 38 per cent of the vote. The Communist alliance with the still semi-Marxist Social Democratic Party obtained more than half the votes cast. However, while these elections are commonly described as 'free', it needs to be pointed out that the Communists' electoral success was greatly facilitated by the fact that the Agrarian Party, the most popular political party in interwar Czechoslovakia and the natural rallying-point for democratic opposition to the Communists, had been banned (along with the quasi-fascist Slovak People's Party) because a few Agrarians had allowed themselves to be used by Nazi Germany after 1938.

The experiences of the Second World War also played crucial roles in providing legitimacy for the post-war regimes. 'War is a myth-creating experience in the life of every society. But in Eastern, Central and Southern Europe it is continuously a source of vivid, only too often lethal, legitimization narratives' and in Poland (as elsewhere) the 'memory, indeed symbolism, of collective national martyrology during the Second World War is paramount for the self-understanding of Polish society in the twentieth century. Every town has its sacred sites commemorating victims' (Gross 2003: 143).

The Second World War also fostered stronger social bases and popular demands for democracy. In the case of Poland, for example, 'The most sweeping result of the occupation was the democratization of Polish society: differences of class, status and power among Poles disappeared under the weight of German terror. This period also saw the mobilization of large masses of people into politics' (Gross 1979: 291). Polish public opinion became increasingly hostile to the old elites: '"The masters", "the educated", "the well brought up", "the leaders" . . . all were under attack. There was a widespread feeling across the whole political spectrum that Poland after the war should be a country of "the people", of "the masses"' (Gross 1979: 172–3).

Whether under enemy occupation or under regimes whose legitimacy was eroded by their servility towards the Third Reich and Fascist Italy, societies were thrown back on their own resources and were thereby obliged to become more self-reliant. The traditional 'verticality' of power relations and power structures temporarily gave way to the 'horizontal' ties and relations pertaining to and promoted by autonomous social, familial and communal institutions and solidarity – namely, to organic versions of civil society. For example, the German and Soviet occupations of Poland destroyed the Polish state, but 'the outlawed political, professional and voluntary associations' remained in existence and continued to function' and 'the infrastructure of the society, although somewhat depleted, was still standing' (Gross 1979: 264). Consequently, the 'underground' Polish resistance movement was not only 'an anti-German conspiracy' but also an 'underground state', with a rudimentary 'apparatus of administration, for education, for welfare, and for cultural activity' (p. 283), helping 'to work against social atomization' (p. 287).

Thus there were some new foundations and 'moral resources' on which to base radical reconstruction and swift recuperation, but there were also new fears, grievances, enmities, injustices and desires for revenge or retribution, many of which were cynically manipulated and exploited by nascent Communist regimes for their own often pernicious purposes.

THE ECONOMIC LEGACIES OF THE SECOND WORLD WAR

Most of the major banks, large-scale industries and public utilities in East Central Europe and the Balkans were taken into state ownership by fascist, military occupation or collaborationist regimes during the 1930s and early 1940s, chiefly through the confiscation of Jewish properties, German-imposed mergers between local and German firms, and very unequal production and delivery contracts and licensing agreements imposed by the Third Reich on every one of the East Central European and Balkan countries – almost regardless of whether they were formally 'allies' or occupied countries. This in turn left Nazi Germany in de facto control of most of the major banks, public utilities and large-scale industries in both regions (Berend and Ranki 1974a: 320–5, 328–38; Gross 1979: 96).

Consequently, the centre-left Popular Front coalitions which took power in East Central Europe and most of the Balkans during the immediate aftermath of the Second World War simply inherited banks, industries and public utilities which had already been 'nationalized' during the war by the fascist, military occupation or collaborationist regimes. These assets were generally retained in the hands of the new post-war regimes to use as they saw fit, instead of being restored to their pre-war owners, many of whom had either perished (especially if they were Jewish) or emigrated or were about to be incarcerated, killed or driven to emigrate. In these ways, the Communist parties in both regions propagated the thesis that fascism and the Second World War had jointly created the financial, institutional and public ownership infrastructures and the degrees of concentration of production and ownership needed for the rapid conversion of these economies into centrally planned 'socialist' economies, in much the same ways that Lenin argued that the artificially accelerated development of increasingly concentrated and centralized 'finance capitalism' or 'monopoly capitalism' had done in Russia between the 1890s and 1917 – especially during the First World War (Lenin 1948: 32, 108; 1969: 41, 46, 87, 89; 1972: 9–12). In each case, it was argued, the Communist parties and their socialist 'allies' and 'fellow travellers' were able simply to take over the already highly concentrated and centralized economic and institutional infrastructures and rapidly adapt them to their own purposes. Thus in-built trends towards concentration, centralization, étatism and mass-production technologies within 'monopoly capitalism' and 'finance capitalism', reinforced by two World Wars which were themselves claimed to have to have resulted from the logic and dynamics of capitalism, had created and bequeathed almost 'ready-made' the economic, institutional, technological, social and political prerequisites for Soviet-style 'socialism'. It was simply up to the industrial proletariats, acting through their so-called 'vanguard' Communist parties, to seize control of the newish 'commanding heights' of these countries and economies and use them to carry out 'socialist' programmes of egalitarian state-directed economic, institutional and educational development and usher in Marxist-Leninist 'brave new worlds'.

THE DISPLACEMENT OF HOPES AND DREAMS FROM FASCIST AND NATIONALIST DYSTOPIAS TO SOCIALIST ONES

These circumstances, together with widespread perceptions that the interwar experiments with democracy had generally 'failed' and that the region's fascist and quisling regimes had led ultimately to defeat, disgrace and collapse, had effectively prepared the ground for the establishment of Communist-led regimes and centrally directed economies, even though it was not yet a foregone conclusion that these would take the form of Stalinist dictatorships in all cases. In the words of the Nobel prize-winning Polish writer Czeslaw Milosz,

> To understand the course of events in Eastern and Central Europe during the first postwar years, it must be realized that the prewar social conditions called for extensive reforms. It must further be understood that Nazi rule had occasioned a profound disintegration of the existing order of things. In these circumstances, the only hope was to set up a social order which would be new . . . So what was planned in Moscow as a stage on the road to servitude was willingly accepted in the countries concerned as though it were true progress. (Milosz 1953: x)

Milosz went on to explain why he and so many other writers and intellectuals had felt that it was futile and counter-productive to resist the expansion of Communist power in their part of the world:

> given the postwar circumstances, the Party was the only power that could guarantee peace, reconstruct the country, enable the people to earn their daily bread, and start schools and universities, ships and railroads functioning. One did not have to be a Communist to reach this conclusion. It was obvious to everyone. To kill Party workers, to sabotage trains carrying food, to attack labourers who were trying to build factories was to prolong the period of chaos. Only madmen could commit such fruitless and illogical acts. (Milosz 1953: 103)

The post-war socio-economic transformations of East Central Europe and the Balkans after the Second World War were further expedited by the greatly increased ethnic homogeneity of these regions. This resulted primarily from the extermination of more than 4 million East Central European and Balkan Jews and the flight or expulsion of between 13 and 15 million *Volksdeutsche* from the eastern half of Europe to a truncated and partitioned Germany in 1945–7 (Deak 2000: 4), but also from the major post-war territorial changes: the westward displacement of Poland; the restoration of northern Transylvania to Romania and of South Dobrudja to Bulgaria; and the incorporation of almost all of the predominantly Ukrainian- or Belarussian-inhabited territories which had formerly belonged to interwar Poland, Czechoslovakia, Hungary or Romania into an expanded Soviet Union. This drastic surgery reduced potential obstacles to change and may also have made these already brutalized, numbed and shell-shocked societies even more ready to accept – or less able and willing to resist – further social engineering and surgery, albeit this time carried out under brutal Communist-cum-Soviet auspices.

Another crucial dimension of the impact of the Second World War and foreign military occupation, whether German, Italian, Hungarian, Romanian, Bulgarian or (in 1939–41 and again at the end of the war) Soviet, was the colossal moral damage and disintegration inflicted on whole societies. In his relatively idealized and optimistic 1970s analysis of the impact of the German and Soviet occupations of Poland during the Second World War, Jan Gross mainly emphasized the effects which tended to reinforce social solidarity, egalitarian sentiment and the 'democratic revolution' (Gross 1979: 172–3, 305). However, his more recent and much more jaundiced and critical analyses of Polish responses to the German and Soviet occupations have emphasized the pervasive 'moral disintegration . . . the breakdown of cultural taboos that prohibit the murder of innocent human beings' (Gross 2003: 158). 'People subject to Stalin's or Hitler's rule were repeatedly set against each other and encouraged to act on the basest instincts . . . Every conceivable cleavage in society was eventually exploited, every antagonism exacerbated . . . Secret police encouraged, and thrived on, denunciations: *divide et impera* writ large. In addition . . . people became, to varying degrees, complicitous in their own subjugation' (Gross 2003: 4). In addition to recruiting people fired by idealistic commitment to social change and to serving 'the people' and 'the cause' (however misguided), the nascent Communist regimes (like their fascist precursors) thrived on recruiting ruthless opportunists and careerists, 'people devoid of all principles' (Gross 2003: 165). Contrary to the stereotypical popular anti-Semitic perceptions of the emerging Communist regimes as products of 'Judaeo-Communism', these regimes may actually have recruited more anti-Semites than Jews (p. 167).

The themes of Gross's earlier and more recent important work on Poland during the Second World War are complementary rather than contradictory. The focus of his earlier work was on how Polish society managed to continue to function and cohere under German and Soviet occupation, despite the complete destruction of the official Polish state, and on the qualities of courage, self-sacrifice and solidarity which helped Poles to rise to the challenges and survive. The focus of his more recent work has been on how that same society was simultaneously brutalized and detached from its moral constraints and moorings, to the point where some Poles were prepared to murder and/or rob their Jewish neighbours in cold blood, and very few were prepared to take the huge risks (not just to themselves but to their families) involved in any attempt to give Jews help and/or protection.

In conclusion, while acknowledging the degrees to which the Second World War evoked much courage and stoicism and inspired noble aspirations and strong demands for long-overdue social changes, it is even more important to recognize the sheer brutalization and demoralization of peoples by the bestial 'war of destruction' which engulfed the eastern half of Europe. Noble courage and brutal depravity emerged side by side and out of much the same conditions. 'This was a war that no one had quite survived' (Kovaly 1997: 45). There were no real winners: to varying degrees, even if they survived the Second World War (and well over 30 million did not), most of the inhabitants of the eastern half of Europe came out of the war degraded, bereaved and profoundly damaged, brutalized and desensitized to suffering. This provided a large part of the explanation, albeit not an exculpation, of the base and brutal conduct of many people (especially police and other officials and their Soviet overlords) under the Stalinist regimes which emerged in the Balkans and East Central Europe during the aftermath of the Second World War.

Part IV

In the shadow of Yalta: the Communist-dominated Balkans and East Central Europe 1945–89

30   The East–West partition of Europe, 1945–89

The victories of the Soviet Union and certain Communist-led resistance movements over 'fascism' towards the end of the Second World War reduced the isolationism implicit in Soviet 'socialism in one country' by extending Soviet tutelage and Communist ascendancy into East Central Europe and the Balkans. By early 1945 these regions had been recognized by both Britain and the United States to be legitimate Soviet 'spheres of influence', in return for implicit Soviet acquiescence in the maintenance and/or establishment of a preponderance of British and/or American influence in areas such as Greece, Japan, Latin America and the oil-rich Middle East. In his war memoirs Winston Churchill described how he had scribbled the following percentages on a sheet of paper, during bilateral discussions between himself and Stalin in Moscow on 9 October 1944:

Romania	Russia 90 per cent
	The others 10 per cent
Greece	Great Britain 90 per cent (in accord with the USA)
	Russia 10 per cent
Yugoslavia	50–50
Hungary	50–50
Bulgaria	Russia 75 per cent
	The others 25 per cent

Churchill pushed the paper over to Stalin, who after only a slight pause 'took his blue pencil and made a large tick upon it, and passed it back to us. It was all settled.' After a long silence, Churchill asked: 'Might it not be thought rather cynical if it seemed we had disposed of these issues, so fateful to millions of people, in such an offhand manner? Let us burn the paper.' 'No, you keep it,' Stalin replied (Churchill 1989: 852–3). Perhaps in an attempt to allay his own sense of unease, Churchill tried to justify this extraordinary deal in a letter circulated to his 'colleagues at home'. He explained that these percentages were 'not intended to prescribe the numbers sitting on commissions for the different Balkan countries, but rather to express the interest and sentiment with which the British and Soviet governments approach the problems of these countries'. He even added that they could 'in no way' tie the hands of the USA, which had not been a party to the deal (although it seems not to have occurred to him that *other European* governments might be entitled to a say in the matter). Nevertheless, he acknowledged that 'Soviet Russia has vital interests in the countries bordering the Black Sea, by one of whom, Romania, she has been most wantonly attacked . . . and with the other of whom, Bulgaria, she has ancient ties.' In the case of Yugoslavia, 'the numerical symbol 50–50 is intended to be the foundation of joint action . . . to favour the creation of a united Yugoslavia . . . and also to produce a joint and friendly policy towards Marshal Tito'. In the case of Hungary: 'As it is the Soviet armies which are obtaining control . . . it would be natural that a major share of influence should rest with them' (pp. 855–6). Hungary and most of the Balkans were thus consigned to the Communist 'sphere of influence' in late 1944. Moreover, Stalin even refrained from assisting the Greek Communists in the subsequent Greek Civil War and in return he expected Britain to keep its side of the bargain, by allowing Tito a free hand in Yugoslavia and leaving the Russians a free hand in Bulgaria, Romania and Hungary.

Churchill later claimed that the 'informal and temporary arrangement which I had made with Stalin during my October visit to Moscow could not, and so far as I was concerned was never intended to, govern or affect the future of these wide regions once Germany was defeated' (p. 876). Nevertheless, the 'percentages agreement' proved remarkably durable, reflecting as it did the real distribution of power and influence in the region. However, there is no denying that the deal was possible partly because Churchill and Stalin had similarly imperialist mindsets. Moreover, at the Yalta meeting between Churchill, Stalin and Roosevelt in February 1945, it was agreed that 'Russia should advance her western frontier line into Poland as far as the Curzon Line' and that, by way of compensation, Poland 'should receive substantial accessions of German territory' (p. 943). This would leave Poland dependent on future Soviet support against potential German revanchism and thus very effectively caught in the Soviet net. As president of a country that still thought of itself as a former colony and as an anti-imperialist power (despite its own imperialism in Latin America and the Philippines and its commanding 'hegemonic' position in the Western world), Roosevelt may have found the old-fashioned European imperialism of his British and Soviet counterparts some-what distasteful, but he was prepared to play along with it in order to bring the wars against Germany and Japan to speedier conclusions. The price for this would be paid by the inhabitants of East Central Europe and most of the Balkans, who were to be left to the tender mercies of a triumphal but battle-scarred, impoverished and punitive Soviet Union. In 1988 the Hungarian philosopher Mihaly Vajda voiced a widespread fear that 'Western Europe is convinced that the main condition of its freedoms is the subjection of East Central Europe. After all, if the status quo worked out at the end of the Second World War was once upset, anything might happen'(Vajda 1988: 336). That was one reason why the European Community/Union was in no hurry during the 1990s to agree on a firm timetable for the admission of any of Europe's post-Communist states to full membership. Communist rule had collapsed and the Cold War had ended, but during the 1990s the institutional-ized east–west partition of Europe remained largely intact. During that decade the Balkan and East Central European post-Communist states continued to live in the shadow of Yalta, and many of their inhabitants believed that the old 'political Yalta' had merely given way to a more enduring 'economic Yalta'. It was not until the early 2000s that this situation really began to change – mainly for East Central Europe and the Baltic States, but also in more limited ways for the post-Communist Balkan states.

For millions of Soviet citizens who did not give a damn about Communism as such, control of East Central Europe and much of the Balkans had been perceived as a *reward* for a momentous and hard-won Soviet victory over 'fascism' at the end of the Second World War. Grimly, there were also many who saw it as an opportunity for vengeful rape and pillage. Thousands of East Central European women were sexually assaulted by their Red Army 'liberators', whose conduct mimicked the bestiality of the defeated Axis Powers. For several years Hungary, Romania, Bulgaria, Austria and Germany had been in Soviet eyes 'fascist' enemy states. Hundreds of thousands of inhabitants of East Central Europe, the Balkans and the Baltic States had indeed fought alongside or collabo-rated with Nazi Germany against the Soviet Union during the Second World War, and many had done so quite willingly or even enthusiastically. Thus the political and economic arrangements imposed on the Balkans and especially East Central Europe after the war were in some respects quite blatantly and unashamedly vengeful and punitive, as was the Soviet suppression of the Hun-garian Revolution of October 1956. Balkan and East Central European states were required to provide some of the coal, oil, industrial equipment, technology, rolling-stock and other resources used in the reconstruction of the Soviet Union, which as a result of the Second World War had suf-fered terrible privations, devastation and the loss of 20–27 million lives (estimates vary). However, the Soviet Union levied economic 'tribute' not only from the defeated former 'Axis states', but also from its supposed wartime 'allies', the Poles and the Czechs. It has been claimed that, between 1945 and Stalin's death in 1953, the Soviet Union received a net transfer of resources from East Central Europe and the Balkans on a scale roughly comparable to the net transfer of resources from the United States to Western Europe under the Marshall Plan (Marrese 1986: 293). Former Axis states were in effect forced to pay substantial reparations to the Soviet Union, while others were forced to pay a similarly heavy price for their so-called 'liberation' from fascist rule by the Red Army. Such payments were perhaps not wholly unwarranted, in view of the enormous sacrifices and suffering which most of the Soviet population had been forced to endure in order to free itself and thereby Europe from Nazism. However, they fell exceedingly hard on the Poles, who had suf-fered even more than the Eastern Slavs (Russians, Belarussians and Ukrainians) during the war, not least through the cruel defeat of the Warsaw Uprising of August–September 1944, in which around 200,000 Poles perished (Crampton 1994: 199). This levying of economic 'tribute' was rapidly cur-tailed following the widespread social and political unrest which erupted in parts of East Central Europe (and in much lesser degrees the Balkans) from 1953 to 1956, while from the 1960s to the 1980s the Soviet Union became a large-scale net supplier of heavily subsidized energy and raw materials to East Central Europe and some of the Balkan Communist states. Thus the net transfer of resources was by no means as unidirectional as has often been claimed by East Central Europeans in particular.

Not surprisingly, the West heard a great deal more about Russian/Soviet misdeeds in and levying of 'tribute' from the East Central European and Balkan Communist states than about the mineral resources and technologies which the latter later received from the Soviet Union, often on very favourable terms. However, when these states 'slipped the leash' in 1989, many Russians who had endured or fought in the Great Patriotic War against fascism understandably felt that their country had been unjustly deprived of legitimate and hard-won fruits of victory. Later still, after Soviet forces were withdrawn with moderately good grace from Germany and East Central Europe, there was further Russian resentment that there had been almost no reciprocal concessions to or gains for Russia. To many Russian 'patriots', it appeared that the former fascist states had finally emerged as 'the real victors' after all. This was a major reason why some Russian ultra-nationalists and embit-tered 'old stagers' continued to dream of an eventual reimposition of Russian control over parts of East Central Europe and the Baltic States. Further resentments were aroused by what for many was the 'humiliating' break-up of the Soviet Union and termination of Russia's erstwhile 'superpower' status in 1991. Thus the rantings and ravings of the Russian ultra-nationalist politician Vladimir Zhirinovsky and his ilk played upon Russian feelings and beliefs that went beyond the 'loss of empire' syndrome. In narrowly economic terms, post-1945 Soviet hegemony over East Central Europe and parts of the Balkans may ultimately have been more of a liability than an asset. Never-theless, it may have satisfied atavistic desires for power, control and revenge; and, in geopolitical and military terms, it had helped to turn the Soviet Union into a 'superpower'. Conversely, the 'Revolutions of 1989' brought all of this to an end.

The precise consequences of the recognition of a post-war Soviet 'sphere of influence' in East Central Europe and much of the Balkans had not been immediately obvious or clear cut in 1945, however. At that time British and American strategists mainly understood 'spheres of influence' to mean informal hegemony, in the manner of British and US capitalist imperialism in Latin America, the Arab world and Greece, whereas Stalin undoubtedly envisaged more far-reaching forms of dominance over East Central Europe, the Baltic States and most of the Balkans. It was relatively easy and straightforward for powerful capitalist states to achieve economic dominance over their 'dependencies' by indirect ('informal') means, which conveniently avoided most of the potential

risks and drawbacks of more direct political forms of control. By contrast, both the innate characteristics and the war-ravaged condition of the Soviet economy after the Second World War rendered it virtually impossible for the Soviet Union to dominate its newly gained 'sphere of influence'
primarily by 'informal' economic means. In order to establish such dominance, which was semi-
legitimated even in official British and American perceptions by the Soviet Union's paramount
roles in defeating the Third Reich, Hungary, Romania and Bulgaria and in 'liberating' East Central
Europe and the eastern Balkans from fascist rule, the Soviet Union had to rely primarily on more
direct political and latent military forms of control. This was further reinforced by the very nature
of the Soviet 'command economy', in that the overwhelming preponderance of state ownership and
central planning in the Soviet Union was bound to politicize its relations with its new 'allies' and
'dependencies'. Soviet domination was probably incapable of operating in any other way.

Since the 1930s, moreover, Stalin had been grooming various (often little known) Communist
activists to take power in sundry European states in the wake of the eventual overthrow of fascism.
In Soviet eyes the liberal capitalist states of the West were inherently 'soft' on fascism, which they
had often 'appeased' and always regarded as a potential ally or weapon in the 'containment' of
Communism. Therefore, notwithstanding the various temporary 'tactical' deals which he struck
with European fascist states during the 1930s, Stalin saw the Second World War as essentially a
struggle between Communism and fascism – and not between fascism and the supposedly effete
Western democracies. Consequently, the comprehensive defeat of European fascism in 1944–5,
mainly at the hands of the Soviet Union and the Communist-led resistance movements in Yugoslavia, Albania, Greece and parts of Italy and France, was expected *ipso facto* to 'deliver' most of
Europe to the victorious forces of Communism. In the apt words of the Nobel prize-winning Polish
writer Czeslaw Milosz, 'The philosophy of History emanating from Moscow is not just an abstract
theory. It is a material force that uses guns, tanks, planes and all the machines of war and oppression. All the crushing might of an armed state is thrown against any man who refuses to accept the
new Faith' (Milosz 1953: 221).

Nevertheless, it remained possible for such an extension of Communist power and Soviet 'influence' to take several different forms: (i) direct incorporation of additional 'nations' into an expanded
USSR as new or expanded Soviet republics – the fate which befell the Baltic States, Bessarabia
(Moldova), western Ukraine and western Belarussia; (ii) the establishment of Communist-controlled Popular Front coalition governments in formally independent People's Democracies, constitutionally responsible for managing their own economic, social and political affairs in 'indissoluble
alliance' with the Soviet Union, as occurred in East Central Europe and much of the Balkans; (iii)
Soviet acceptance of genuinely independent Communist-ruled states, as eventually transpired in
relation to the Yugoslav Federation and Albania; (iv) Soviet tolerance and recognition of 'friendly'
neutral states which were not permitted to join any actually or potentially anti-Soviet Western
organizations but were otherwise free to determine their own destinies, as was to be the fate of post-
1955 Austria and Finland.

The fourth variant proved to be the least problematic in the long run. Indeed, Finland eventually
even profited from its 'special relationship' with the Soviet Union, as did Austria from its 'special
relations' with East Central Europe and northern Yugoslavia. However, hopes that so-called 'Finlandization' might also become the norm for the East Central European 'People's Democracies'
were to be thwarted by the persistence of the Cold War and by the simple calculation that, the larger
the number of 'Finlandized' states, the greater the probability that they would eventually escape
from the Soviet 'sphere of influence' as they gradually became richer, stronger and more
Westernized.

The third variant (autonomous revolution) was only feasible in those countries where the Communist Party could win and retain power without direct Soviet intervention and support – namely,
in Yugoslavia, Albania and Czechoslovakia. This could also have been the outcome in Greece, but

for heavy British and American intervention on the side of Greek monarchist forces against the Communists during the Greek Civil War of 1946–9. The fact that the Soviet Union exerted strong pressure on the Czechoslovak Communist Party to act in accordance with Soviet wishes should not obscure the fact that, if Stalin had been willing to leave well alone there, the large, popular and widely respected Czechoslovak Communist Party might have been able to lead Czechoslovakia down a 'democratic road to socialism' during the late 1940s and early 1950s. Indeed, until the Communists subverted Czechoslovak democracy in 1947–8, Czechoslovakia offered the best prospects in Europe for an authentic 'democratic socialism'. To the great misfortune of most Czechs and Slovaks and the socialist cause, however, 'democratic socialism' proved to be as unacceptable to Moscow in 1948 as it would be during the 'Prague Spring' of 1968.

The first variant (direct incorporation into the Soviet Union) was the tidiest. It was also the one most in keeping with Marxist-Leninist and Luxemburgist precepts concerning the need to transcend the outmoded 'bourgeois' nation-state by 'uniting' all workers (irrespective of creed, nationality or race) into a single supranational 'workers' state' in the interests of 'proletarian solidarity' against counter-revolutionaries and capitalist imperialism. However, this variant also burdened an impoverished and war-ravaged USSR with full economic and political responsibility for the peoples and territories absorbed thereby, and it was therefore the most costly option. Furthermore, if Stalin had tried to apply it to post-war Poland and/or to other East Central European States, he could conceivably have precipitated a Third World War – this time between the West and the Soviet Union.

The second variant (the establishment of formally independent 'People's Democracies') prevailed partly as a result of the challenges and constraints imposed by the Cold War and the US-sponsored European Recovery Programme (ERP), commonly known as the Marshall Plan. However, it soon displayed all the drawbacks consequent upon the indirect imposition of largely inappropriate and increasingly unpopular political and economic models and precepts by means of inherently unstable quisling regimes, against which some of the inhabitants of East Central Europe, Romania and Bulgaria were likely to rebel at every opportunity – as indeed they did in 1953, 1956, 1968, 1970, 1976, 1980 and 1989. The foundation and subsequent development of the Council of Mutual Economic Assistance (CMEA), commonly known to the West as 'Comecon', can partly be seen as an ultimately self-defeating endeavour by the Soviet Union to counter these challenges and problems in its own 'backyard' by curtailing the East Central European and Balkan Communist states' links with their former markets and suppliers of machinery, equipment, capital and technology in the West and by fostering mechanisms for closer co-ordination, synchronization and bonding of their economic plans with those of the USSR. By helping to entrench and perpetuate authoritarian and over-centralized political and economic models and by 'locking' the relatively capital-deficient and mineral-deficient East Central European and Balkan Communist states into lopsided and overly capital- and mineral-intensive patterns of economic development which were incapable of becoming self-supporting or self-reliant, the Comecon experiment simply magnified and exacerbated the problems it was supposed to overcome or alleviate. Adding insult to injury, Comecon restricted the Balkan and East Central European states' access to the Western products, technologies and markets which really were capable of alleviating their problems, while making them increasingly dependent on subsidized Soviet energy supplies to support the inefficient and environmentally devastating patterns of industrial development foisted upon them by the Soviet Union and its client regimes. This contributed to the growth of East Central European and Balkan resentment of Soviet tutelage, especially when these so-called 'satellite states' were also expected to show 'gratitude' for Soviet munificence despite never having freely chosen the patterns of economic development which increasingly necessitated the large and heavily subsidized Soviet inputs into their increasingly dysfunctional economic systems.

31   The emergence of Communist regimes in the Balkans and East Central Europe, 1945–60

It is often assumed that the revolutionary changes which occurred in the Balkans and East Central Europe in the aftermath of the Second World War simply resulted from the presence of powerful Soviet forces in these regions. Stalin probably *did* regard East Central Europe and much of the Balkans as a protective cordon or buffer zone between the Soviet Union and an increasingly hostile West. He may even consciously have held these regions *hostage* against the implicit danger that a 'gung ho' USA might be tempted to drop atomic bombs on Moscow, as it already had done on Hiroshima and Nagasaki. Nevertheless, the realities were a great deal more complex than such perspectives would suggest. The Communist regimes were not established merely 'at the point of the bayonet', although Soviet military might did play a major part. There was also widespread local support for radical social and economic change, if not always for Communist parties as such. More generally, widespread perceptions and even admiration of the Soviet Union as the principal 'liberating power' in East Central Europe and in the eastern Balkans, as the chief victor over European fascism, and as the architect and builder of a 'brave new world', undoubtedly played important roles in the expansion of Communist power and Soviet influence in post-war East Central Europe and the Balkans – regions in which both democracy (of sorts) and fascism had been tried and found wanting during the 1920s and 1930s. It should also be emphasized that Soviet armed forces were not present when Communist parties seized and consolidated power in Czechoslovakia and in Albania (both of which felt that they had been somewhat 'betrayed' by the Western powers in 1938 and 1939, respectively) and that they provided only minor and very belated assistance to Tito's Partisans in Yugoslavia. Moreover, there would probably have been an autonomous Communist revolution in Greece (as well as in Yugoslavia, Albania and Czechoslovakia) if Britain and the USA had not intervened militarily on the side of the not very popular Greek monarchists against the seemingly popular and successful Greek Communist movement. A more accurate summary would be that the social upheavals and the emergence of Communist-led regimes in East Central Europe and the Balkans during the second half of the 1940s and the widespread (but far from ubiquitous) presence of the Red Army were mutually reinforcing joint consequences of the Second World War.

THE 'COLD WAR' CONTEXT: REVISIONIST PERSPECTIVES

The extension of Communist power and Soviet 'influence' in the Balkans and East Central Europe between 1945 and 1950 has usually been analysed in the context of an east–west 'Cold War' which supposedly erupted at that time. Contrary to the conventional wisdom, the ideological 'Cold War' between Marxist-Leninist Communism, on the one side, and Western liberal democracy and capitalism, on the other, did not begin between 1945 and 1950. It had really begun in 1918, with the consolidation of the Bolshevik regime in Russia and the commencement of Western political and military interventions against the Bolsheviks. Overt or latent ideological and economic competition between Communism and Western liberal democracy and capitalism continued throughout the interwar period and even during the Second World War, even though it was overshadowed by other issues and conflicts for much of that time. The notion of the Cold War as something that began in the late 1940s may have appealed to the new generations who were clawing their way up the Soviet hierarchy, but for seasoned 'Old Bolsheviks' it was merely a media catchphrase for something that had been going on since 1918. 'Molotov, just like Stalin, never recognized the Cold War as a new stage in international relations', and their thinking remained tied to Leninist postulates, classic 'balance of power' and 'territorial security' concepts, and the demarcation of 'spheres of influence' (Zubok and Pleshakov 1996: 37, 73, 89). After the defeat of Germany and Japan in 1945, admittedly, the Cold War did occupy centre-stage to a greater extent than before. Seen through Soviet eyes, however, the post-1945 period *did not* represent a major departure from patterns established during the interwar period, but was merely a resumption of the ideological antagonism between 'the two camps' which had *started in 1918* and had only *temporarily* abated during the Grand Alliance against the Axis Powers (1941–5). The dropping of American atomic bombs on Hiroshima and Nagasaki in August 1945, combined with the realization that the Americans were in a position to do the same to Moscow and Leningrad, did help to reignite Soviet insecurity and paranoia (Zubok and Pleshakov 1996: 7, 27–34, 40–3), but it changed the nature of the Cold War considerably less than might have been expected. Contrary to some simplistic Western allegations that the Soviet Union was implacably 'daggers drawn' towards the capitalist world from beginning to end, it can be argued that Soviet conceptualizations of the relationship between the USSR and the capitalist 'camp' were always *deeply ambivalent*, even under Stalin. Strident Soviet insistence on the 'impossibility' of a durable stabilization of, and peaceful co-existence with, capitalism continually alternated with a more sober and pragmatic recognition of the 'necessity' of peaceful co-existence with a capitalist world system which seemed set to survive for the foreseeable future. Successive shifts in Soviet thinking on these matters were determined as much by changing economic and geopolitical considerations and contexts as by changing ideological imperatives. Just as Tsarist Russia had vacillated between periods of accommodation and periods of confrontation with other parts of Europe, and between periods of outward-looking Westernism and periods of introverted Slavophilism and 'Eurasianism', so did the Soviet Union.

THE EVOLUTION OF SOVIET RELATIONS WITH THE WEST, 1918–47

In order to comprehend official Soviet thinking on East–West relations between 1945 and 1950 and avoid jumping to simplistic or misleading conclusions on these matters, it is necessary to provide a brief analysis of the manner in which the Soviet Union and its relations with the West had developed thus far.

Judged by classical Marxist criteria, the Bolshevik seizure of power in an economically and socially 'backward' and agrarian Russia in October 1917 had been 'premature', but Lenin had succeeded in persuading his Bolshevik colleagues to launch the Bolshevik Revolution in Russia on the basis of several very rash assumptions: (i) that their own *coup d'état* would almost immediately act as a catalyst for Marxist socialist revolutions in Germany, France and Poland; (ii) that new Marxist socialist regimes in Europe's more industrialized countries would soon be willing and able generously and obligingly to provide much of the finance, machinery and technology needed for 'the construction of socialism' in underdeveloped Russia, along the lines suggested by Friedrich Engels in his famous 1875 article on 'Social Relations in Russia' and his Preface to the 1882 Russian edition of *The Communist Manifesto*; and (iii) that the increasing global ascendancy of monopoly capitalism and finance capitalism had created radically new international conditions and a new transnational economic infrastructure which made it economically as well as politically feasible and vitally necessary to launch Marxist socialist revolutions and proceed forthwith to the overthrow of capitalism and the 'construction of socialism' in Russia, without first having to wait for countries such as Russia to become highly industrialized and proletarianized before embarking on such a course (Bideleux 1987: 11, 23–7, 104–5). Bolshevik revolutionary strategy-cum-foreign policy was therefore initially subordinated to the goal of fomenting revolution elsewhere in Europe – especially in the highly industrialized Germanic 'motherland' of Marxism.

By the early 1920s, however, it was already becoming crystal clear to the Bolshevik leadership that Europe's 'revolutionary wave' was subsiding, that Russia's beleaguered and fledgling Soviet regime would therefore have to depend largely on its own efforts and resources, and that the Soviet government would therefore have to work out some sort of *modus vivendi* with the other major European states as well as with Soviet Russia's socially preponderant peasantry and small private entrepreneurs. This shedding of naive illusions opened the way for a much more circumspect and conciliatory 'New Economic Policy' (1921–7), the 'fence-mending' Treaty of Rapallo with Germany (1922), the subsequent 'normalization' of Soviet economic and diplomatic relations with most Western countries, and substantial inflows of Western capital, technology, engineers and managerial personnel into Soviet Russia from 1924 to 1930.

Trotsky warned the 1922 Congress of the Communist International (Comintern) that 'we shall have to engage in large-scale transitional operations through the market over many years' and that 'market relations have a logic of their own, whatever goals we may have in restoring them', but he also emphasized that this would help to ensure that 'available resources are directed where they are most needed – into branches producing goods for personal or productive consumption by workers and peasants . . . Only after gaining success in agriculture and light industry can real impetus be given to engineering, metallurgy, coal, oil' (Bideleux 1987: 105–6).

In 1926 Trotsky presented the classic arguments in favour of 'peaceful co-existence' between the Soviet Union and the West. He pointed out that, since the factory industries of pre-revolutionary Russia had found it necessary to import almost two-thirds of their plant and equipment, 'it will hardly be economically advantageous for us to produce more than two-fifths or at most one-half of our own machinery'. Any headstrong attempt to adjust 'in one leap to the production of new machinery' would cause potentially devastating economic distortions and disequilibria. There were ways in which such constraints could be minimized: 'Every foreign product that can fill a gap in our economic system – raw material, intermediate goods and consumer goods – can under certain conditions accelerate our reconstruction.' Furthermore, 'the dialectics of history involve capitalism assuming temporarily the role of creditor to socialism . . . Our present order rests not only on the struggle of socialism against capitalism, but also, within limits, on co-operation between socialism and capitalism.' Of course, 'loans, concessions and greater dependence on exports and imports involve dangers'. However, 'there is a greater, opposite danger. It consists of delaying our economic progress.' Besides, 'the more diverse our international economic relations, the harder it will be for our enemies to disrupt them' (Trotsky 1926: chapters 8–12).

Trotsky was in these respects a thoroughgoing *internationalist* and thus a true Marxist, in contrast to Stalin's advocacy of introverted economic nationalism and protectionism masquerading as socialism. In 1928 Trotsky again emphasized that 'By introducing the New Economic Policy . . . we created a certain place for capitalist relations in our country, and for a prolonged period ahead we must recognize them as inevitable' (Trotsky 1928: 31). Even though he continued to give political encouragement to revolutionary socialist movements, from 1922 onwards Trotsky consistently advocated *economic moderation and peaceful co-operation with the capitalist states* during the 'construction of socialism' in Soviet Russia. This was also broadly the position taken by the chief economist of the so-called Left Opposition, Evgeny Preobrazhensky, as well as such well-known Bolshevik moderates as the finance minister Grigori Sokolnikov, the central banker Lev Shanin, the planner Vladimir Bazarov and the trade minister Leonid Krasin during the mid-1920s (Bideleux 1987: 83–114).

In its initial formulations, even Stalin's keynote doctrine of 'socialism in one country' was essentially a *holding operation* rather than a harbinger of autarky, xenophobia and domestic coercion. In his *Foundations of Leninism* (1924), Stalin maintained that for the Soviet regime 'the whole point is to retain power, consolidate it, make it invincible', until such time as the 'proletarian revolution' is victorious in other countries. In December 1925 Stalin assured the Fourteenth Congress of the Communist Party of the Soviet Union (CPSU) that 'a certain temporary equilibrium of forces has been established between our country . . . and the countries of the capitalist world, an equilibrium which has determined the present period of "peaceful co-existence" . . . What we at one time regarded as a brief respite after the war has become a whole period of respite' (Stalin 1954: 267–8). Later in the same report Stalin contended that, as a result of the Bolshevik Revolution, 'The world split into two camps: the camp of imperialism and the camp of anti-imperialism' (p. 288). Stalin's 'two camps' doctrine thus originated in 1925, rather than in 1947 (as is often misleadingly suggested). This doctrine did not imply that the Soviet Union would be perpetually at war with a stable and monolithic capitalist bloc united against it. On the contrary, Stalin emphasized from the outset that 'there is no unity of interests and no solidarity' in the capitalist camp and that 'what reigns there is a conflict of interests, disintegration, a struggle between victors and vanquished, a struggle among the victors themselves, a struggle among all the imperialist countries for colonies, for profits', as a result of which 'stabilization in that camp cannot be lasting' (pp. 288–9). However, while Trotsky and other leading figures were arguing that Soviet Russia needed greater access to Western products, capital, technology, managerial expertise and markets, Stalin emphasized the extent to which the ailing economies of capitalist Europe needed to regain access to the Soviet Union's natural resources and large market (pp. 294–6). Furthermore, while Trotsky, Preobrazhensky, Shanin, Sokolnikov, Bazarov and Krasin rejected economic nationalism in favour of full exploitation of the potential gains from *foreign* trade, investment, loans, technology and managerial expertise, Stalin declared that 'we must exert all efforts to make our country an economically self-reliant, independent country based on the home market; a country that will serve as a centre of attraction for all the other countries that little by little drop out of capitalism and enter the channel of socialist economy. That line demands the utmost expansion of our industry' (Stalin 1955a: 306). Stalin's immediate, overriding priorities were to develop large-scale heavy industries, especially fuels and metallurgy (pp. 323–4). From 1926 onward, as he consolidated his power, Soviet industrial investment went mainly into heavy industry. The resultant disproportions, strains and shortages propelled the USSR down a path of lopsided and coercive industrialization, although the horrific human and economic implications of this economic strategy did not become fully apparent until the 1930s (Bideleux 1987: 100, 118, 124–7). Nevertheless, the successive published 'variants' of the First Five-Year Plan (1928–32) actually envisaged that the USSR would remain a market economy with a preponderance of smallholder agriculture. All this was premised upon a continuance of high levels of East–West trade and substantial American, German and British involvement in the modernization and expansion of important branches of the economy, including the oil, chemical, engineering, mining and timber industries. Despite the war scare of 1927 and the show trial of a group of foreign engineers on charges of being 'saboteurs' and 'spies' in 1928, the Soviet Union could not afford major confrontations with the principal capitalist states at that critical juncture. In 1935, moreover, the Soviet foreign minister Maxim Litvinov emerged as a leading proponent of 'collective security', and the Soviet Union signed treaties of mutual assistance with France and Czechoslovakia. Hitler's remilitarization of the Rhineland in March 1936 and the Nazi annexation of Austria in March 1938 prompted Litvinov to step up Soviet offers of participation in collective security arrangements to 'contain' Nazi expansionism.

During the 1920s and 1930s the USSR was also eager to establish closer relations with the USA. In Bolshevik eyes, the USA was a 'new' society (like the USSR), in contrast to decadent western and central Europe, and the First Five-Year Plan relied in large measure on importing and copying

American technology to modernize the oil industry, mining, metallurgy and transport (as documented in Sutton 1968–72). Many Bolsheviks, from Lenin downwards, were mesmerized by American technology, industrial organization and 'scientific management' (Taylorism, time and motion studies, ergonomics), and they especially sought US business partners, methods and machinery. On 6 December 1921 the Soviet state newspaper *Izvestiya* declared that 'the US is the principal force in the world . . . all possible means will have to be employed somehow or other to come to an understanding with the US' (quoted in Kennedy-Pipe 1995: 23). Soviet courtship of the USA intensified in the wake of Japan's occupation of Manchuria in 1931, and the establishment of diplomatic relations between the USA and the USSR in November 1933 was directed against Japanese as well as Nazi expansionism. In 1938 Litvinov sought a formal military pact with the USA, but he was rebuffed by the Americans (Kennedy-Pipe 1995: 24–6).

The 1930s Depression and its political repercussions profoundly affected the course of the internal development of the Soviet Union and Soviet perceptions of the capitalist world. The collapse in the world market prices of the Soviet Union's staple exports of oil, grain, timber and minerals, along with the widespread adoption of protectionism and 'anti-dumping' measures in Europe, America and Asia, obliged the USSR to become more 'closed' and autarkic, even though this substantially raised the costs of Soviet industrialization and agricultural mechanization programmes (Dohan 1976). Nevertheless, since self-reliance was also one of Stalin's most frequently stated goals from 1925 onward, this movement towards autarky cannot solely be blamed on adverse world market conditions.

We have already emphasized that the Soviet/Comintern pronouncements on fascism during the 1930s furnished a new Marxist rationalization of the eventual Communist take-overs in East Central Europe and the Balkans during the late 1940s (see chapter 28), in much the same way that Lenin's *Imperialism: The Highest Stage of Capitalism* and associated writings provided a new rationale for the Bolshevik seizure of power in Russia in 1917. It has also passed largely unnoticed that these pronouncements paved the way for the altered Soviet conception of the 'imperialist camp' which was reasserted during the high point of the Cold War during the late 1940s (see pp. 471).

Victory over Germany gave the Soviet regime a new lease of life, a broader base of popular support, new cadres and a fresh crop of heroes and heroines. Between 1941 and 1945 the CPSU recruited 8.4 million new members, 80 per cent of whom were from the armed forces. Thus two-thirds of the post-1945 CPSU had joined during the Great Patriotic War, which played much the same legitimizing and 'charismatizing' role for post-war Soviet leaders as participation in the Russian Revolutions and the Civil War of 1918–21 had done for their predecessors (S. Linz 1985). For forty-five years, thousands of books, war memorials and military bookshops sustained strong public awareness of the stupendous Soviet war effort. Nevertheless, the Soviet triumphalism of Stalin's final years can easily obscure the fact that, unlike the USA, the war-ravaged USSR became a 'superpower' largely by default: Germany had been occupied by the Allies and dismembered, France took nearly fifteen years to recover from the humiliating defeats of 1940 and those in Indo-China and Algeria after the war, Japan was occupied by the United States, and Britain's contributions to victory had sapped its economic and military strength. The 'superpower' role was a far greater strain on the USSR than on the USA. The US economy had grown by about 50 per cent during the war, whereas Soviet national income was about 20 per cent smaller in 1945 than in 1940. In 1950 Soviet national income and industrial output were merely 31 per cent and less than 30 per cent, respectively, of those of the USA, even on official Soviet calculations (USSR 1977: 95). Therefore, in its struggle for military parity with the USA, the USSR had to devote a vastly greater proportion of its much lower per capita output to military purposes. The physically and emotionally drained Soviet peoples were in no mood to take on this labour of Sisyphus, which the Soviet regime inflicted upon them willy-nilly. At the start of the Second World War, moreover, Stalin had been quite out of his depth, which compounded the strain. 'He came to strategic wisdom only through blood-spattered trial and error' (Volkogonov 1991: 452). By 1945 the sixty-five-year-old leader was exhausted (p. 497). He was physically 'at the point of collapse . . . A statesman in his condition generally either retires or delegates responsibility for world affairs to trusted subordinates', yet 'Stalin did neither' (Zubok and Pleshakov 1996: 26).

In such a context, the presumption of many Western Cold Warriors that a victorious USSR was now bent on world domination by escalating the Cold War and displacing the USA from Europe appears highly implausible. Indeed, three decades of hostile capitalist encirclement had induced a defensive 'bunker' mentality. 'There is little evidence that before the Marshall Plan Stalin had any master plan for immediate expansion. He had to digest what he had already gained during the war' (Zubok and Pleshakov 1996: 130). Significantly, the Red Army was reduced from 11.3 million men in May 1945 to 2.9 million in 1948 (Kennedy-Pipe 1995: 85). Moreover, with France temporarily out of action and Britain at breaking point, both Stalin and Molotov looked to the USA for indispensable assistance in keeping the Germanic peoples prostrate and divided. Stalin 'wanted a US presence in Europe, but at the same time he wanted to deny it influence in what he considered to be his part of Europe' (p. 67). 'Every Soviet proposal for post-war Europe, and specifically the plans for Germany and Austria, envisaged a US or British military presence' (p. 44). Stalin even 'tried to persuade his Western Allies to arrive in Austria at the same time as the Red Army' (p. 50), in order to establish tripartite rather than solely Soviet control (p. 56). Having suffered so much in the titanic struggle against Greater Germany (including Austria), the foremost Soviet fear was that Germanic power might revive as speedily as it did after the First World War. At Tehran in 1943 Stalin asserted that German hegemonism would rear its ugly head again within twenty years unless the Germanic peoples were dealt with very harshly, because he did not believe that the Germans could change their 'national character', and as a result he 'foresaw the German question as requiring long-term political and military cooperation between East and West' (p. 42). At a meeting with Yugoslav leaders in Moscow in April 1945, Stalin reaffirmed his belief that German power 'will recover, and very quickly. It is a highly developed country with an extremely skilled and numerous working class and technical intelligentsia. Give them twelve to fifteen years and they'll be on their feet again' (M. Djilas 1963: 90–1).

Stalin's immediate aim was therefore not world domination, let alone world revolution, but the much more limited one of creating a protective glacis of buffer states bound to the Soviet Union by treaties and ties of military, economic and ideological dependence. He regarded the territories 'liberated' by the Red Army as rightly belonging to a new Soviet 'sphere of influence', just as he recognized countries occupied by the Western Allies as belonging to *their* 'spheres of influence'. If the United States and Britain expected a free hand to foster pro-Western regimes in Italy, Japan, Greece, Libya, Egypt, Iraq, Iran, the Philippines and Japan, without direct Soviet 'intrusion' into *their* spheres, why did they presume to dictate the terms on which East Central European and Balkan states were to be governed once they had been 'liberated' by the Red Army and/or Communist-led resistance movements? Stalin informed the Yugoslav leadership in April 1945: 'whoever occupies a territory also imposes on it his own social system. Everyone imposes his own system as far as his army has the power to do so. It cannot be otherwise' (Djilas 1963: 90). Similarly, he told a Yugoslav delegation which visited Moscow early in 1948: 'The West will make Western Germany their own, and we shall turn Eastern Germany into our own state' (p. 119). The Soviet occupation forces 'Bolshevized' eastern Germany, 'not because there was a plan to do so, but because that was the only way they knew how to organize society' (Naimark 1995: 467).

Literature drawing on hitherto unpublished memoirs and documents dealing with the 1940s and early 1950s has tended to confirm that the Soviet leadership truly believed that the co-operation with the Western powers which had begun during the Second World War was set to continue for several years after the war (Zubok and Pleshakov 1996: 27–34). In view of the enormous loss of life, physical devastation and sheer exhaustion incurred by the Soviet Union and the immense debt of gratitude that the West owed to the Soviet peoples for their paramount role in defeating Hitler, it was widely believed that the West would help to rebuild the USSR's shattered economy and society and that it had incurred a huge moral obligation to do so. This made the dropping of American atomic bombs on Hiroshima and Nagasaki in August 1945 all the more shocking in Soviet eyes. These awesome acts, undertaken without prior consultation with America's Soviet ally, were seen as being directed as much against the USSR as against Japan, and as a demonstration of the fate that would befall the Soviet Union if it tried to reap the spoils of its hard-won victory over Germany – thereby enabling the West to renege on its moral debts to the 'heroic Soviet peoples' and on the 'spheres of influence' agreed at Yalta (Zubok and Pleshakov: 41). According to Yuli Khariton, one of the 'fathers' of the first Soviet atomic bomb, 'The Soviet government interpreted Hiroshima as atomic blackmail against the USSR' (p. 42). Some Western academics have concurred that those bombs were indeed dropped more in order to intimidate the Soviet Union than to shorten the war and save lives (Alperovitz 1995).

Nevertheless, the initial Soviet preparations for post-war reconstruction continued to be premised on the previously anticipated provision of Western (especially American) assistance at least for a few years after the end of the war, and for a time Stalin continued to negotiate with Western governments and restrain Communist revolutionary movements outside the Soviet 'spheres of influence' explicitly recognized by his erstwhile Western allies in Moscow, Yalta and Potsdam in 1944–5. The death of Roosevelt in April 1945, Churchill's loss of office in July 1945 and the use of atomic bombs against Hiroshima and Nagasaki in August 1945 *severely strained but did not break* the relationship between Stalin and his Western allies. Stalin and Molotov still sought large-scale Western assistance for Soviet reconstruction and expected the West to respect the Soviet Union's freely acknowledged 'legitimate interests' in East Central Europe and the Balkans. Conversely, they accepted that Britain and the United States were similarly entitled to do as they saw fit in their own 'spheres of influence', even if this involved some unwelcome 'dollar diplomacy' in Europe (Zubok and Pleshakov 1996: 105). They also initially welcomed the Marshall Plan (which took them by surprise) as a return to some sort of 'Lend–Lease aid' or as 'no-strings-attached assistance to the anti-Nazi allies' (including the Poles and the Czechs), with the result that Molotov participated in the preliminary discussions in Paris in June 1947 (p. 104). Molotov still accepted that the USA had useful roles to play in Germany in particular and in Europe more generally (p. 101). Indeed, Soviet fear of any potential revival of Germanic might was so strong, and Soviet perceptions of the diminution in British and French power were so acute, that Soviet political and military leaders still looked to the USA to assist in the continued subjugation and containment of German power into the indefinite future. This also explains why Stalin eventually consented to 'French help in maintaining an effective stranglehold on Germany', having previously opposed French involvement on the grounds that France had discredited itself militarily, economically and politically (Kennedy-Pipe 1995: 53–5).

Therefore, the *decisive factor* in swinging the Soviet leaders against the Marshall Plan in July 1947 was not the implicit extension of US economic influence in Europe, nor even the invidious strings attached to receipt of Marshall Aid, but *the American determination to include Germany (along with other former 'enemy states') in the European Recovery Programme*. Influenced by the famous tract by J.M. Keynes on *The Economic Consequences of the Peace* in 1919, many British and American economists, politicians and publicists had come to consider the economic recovery of Germany to be essential to the economic recovery of Europe, and in their view it was absolutely vital to secure full German participation in the Marshall Plan. In Soviet eyes, however, this was a treacherous Western bid to restore Germany's economic and hence military power, and thereby to turn the tables on the USSR and renege on their moral obligations and commitments to it. The Marshall Plan came to be seen as 'a large-scale attempt by the United States to gain lasting and preeminent influence in Europe' and as 'a far-reaching design to revive German military-industrial potential and to direct it, as in the 1930s, against the Soviet Union' (Zubok and Pleshakov 1996: 50).

These perceptions help to make proper sense of the infamous speech on the 'two camps' delivered by Andrei Zhdanov at the founding meeting of the new Communist Information Bureau (alias Cominform) in September 1947. This tirade against Western perfidy not only marked a *return* to the 'two camps' rhetoric developed by Stalin during the interwar years, but expressed a quite plausible suspicion that Western capitalist 'imperialists' were again prepared to harness German might to another right-wing crusade to roll back Soviet influence in post-war Europe, just as they had hoped that the Munich agreement of September 1938 would have deflected Nazi expansionism eastwards against the USSR in 1939:

> The reactionary imperialist elements all over the world, notably in Britain, America and France, had reposed great hopes in Germany and Japan and chiefly in Hitler's Germany: firstly as in a force most capable of inflicting a blow on the Soviet Union . . . secondly, as in a force capable of smashing the revolutionary labour and democratic movement in Germany herself and in all countries singled out for Nazi aggression and thereby strengthening capitalism generally. This was the chief reason for the prewar policy of 'appeasement' and encouragement of fascist aggression, the so-called Munich policy . . .
>
> Of all the capitalist powers, only one – the United States – emerged from the war not only unweakened but even considerably stronger economically and militarily . . . But America's aspirations to world supremacy encounter an obstacle in the USSR, the stronghold of anti-imperialist and antifascist policy . . . Accordingly, the new expansionist and reactionary policy of the United States envisages a struggle against the USSR . . . and against the emancipationist, anti-imperialist forces in all countries . . . The vague and deliberately guarded formulations of the 'Marshall Plan' amount in essence to a scheme to create a bloc of states bound by obligations to the United States . . . Moreover, the cornerstone of the 'Marshall Plan' is the restoration of the industrial areas of Western Germany . . . It is the design of the 'Marshall Plan' . . . to render aid in the first place, not to the impoverished victor countries, America's allies in the fight against Germany, but to the German capitalists, with the idea of bringing under American sway the major sources of coal and iron needed by Europe . . . and of making the countries which are in need of coal and iron dependent on the restored economic might of Germany. (Zhdanov 1947: 38–41)

This speech conveyed the real sense of betrayal felt by the Soviet leadership and a deep resentment of the central role accorded to western Germany in the Marshall Plan, as well as the often neglected elements of continuity with the 1930s Comintern *Theses* on fascism and the Western policy of 'appeasement'. The Soviet Union was thus induced to adopt increasingly antagonistic postures towards the West. Some revisionist writings have suggested that in such circumstances even a moderately nationalistic Russian regime would not have reacted very differently, so profound was the sense of shock and betrayal. In response to the Western decisions to offer Marshall Aid to Germany in 1947 and to launch a separate west German currency in 1948, Stalin mounted a blockade of West Berlin in 1948–9. This was intended to challenge, *not* the US presence in Germany per se, but Western claims to West Berlin and to Western pre-eminence in Germany, defeat of which had after all been achieved largely by the USSR (Kennedy-Pipe 1995: 6). However, this Soviet reaction merely reinforced US influence and leadership in the West. 'Stalin's actions in 1947–1948 were based upon the correct assumption that he was not risking war with the West. But he had miscalculated the effect of his preventive moves' (Zubok and Pleshakov 1996: 49–52).

Renewed Soviet insistence on the 'impossibility' of peaceful co-existence between the Soviet bloc and the capitalist states climaxed in the paranoia of Stalin's final years. At the same time, however, the establishment of Communist China and the breaking of the Western monopoly on atomic weapons in 1949 appears to have persuaded Stalin that the Eurasian balance of power had shifted in the Communist camp's favour and that it was now safe to risk a Communist invasion of South Korea. The USA, having lost its Kuomintang ally, seemed to be making preparations to retreat from mainland Asia. Stalin realized that the Communist offensive in Korea would violate the existing delimitations of 'spheres of influence' and that *in extremis* this could precipitate a Third World War. However, he thought that it was safer to run such risks in 1950, while Germany and Japan were still subjugated by foreign occupation forces, than to wait until such time as the West would be strengthened by a Western-sponsored revival of the former Axis Powers. Apropos East Asia, Stalin stated: 'If war is inevitable, let it happen now, and not in a few years, when Japanese militarism will be restored as a US ally, and when the United States and Japan will have a beach-head on the [Asian] continent . . . in the form of Syngman Rhee's Korea' (Zubok and Pleshakov 1996: 62–3, 66–7). However, the scale of the American counter-offensive in Korea took Stalin by surprise; and it not only resulted in an unwanted escalation of the Korean War and the East–West arms race but also hastened the fulfilment of one of Stalin's worst nightmares, 'the rearmament of West Germany, with the help of some of Hitler's former generals' (pp. 64–5, 69–70).

Stalin's extension and strengthening of Communist control over East Central Europe and most of the Balkans in 1945–50 can therefore be characterized most accurately as *defensive aggression* and as an expansion of the essentially autarkic '*bunker mentality*' of his doctrine of 'socialism in one country', rather than either as part of a premeditated plan to ditch his wartime alliance with the main Western Powers or as the first steps in a bid to bring Europe as a whole and/or the world under Communist control. This did not make Communist rule and/or Soviet domination any more comfortable for the inhabitants of the new 'People's Democracies' or Communist states established in East Central Europe and the Balkans. On the contrary, it resulted in their being much more roughly treated than they probably would have been if Stalin had really been bent on fomenting a Europe-wide Communist revolution, using the new Communist states in East Central Europe and the Balkans as show-cases for the blessings of Communist rule.

THE KEY CHALLENGE FOR THE COMMUNIST PARTIES: THE EMASCULATION OF EAST CENTRAL EUROPEAN AND BALKAN PEASANTRIES, 1945–7

The peasantries confronted the increasingly Communist-dominated governments of post-war East Central Europe and the Balkans with their biggest initial challenge, not least because peasants were still in a majority everywhere (except for relatively industrialized Czechoslovakia and East Germany, where they respectively made up only 36 per cent and 26 per cent of the population by 1950). The discredited former rulers were summarily exiled, imprisoned or executed for their mis-deeds. In view of their shared Marxist heritage and working-class following, the socialist parties often felt obliged to play along with Communist Party policies, salami tactics (picking off opponents slice by slice), rent-a-mob demonstrations and the intimidation or liquidation of opponents, until their active or passive complicity in Communist crimes or foul play made it very difficult for them to resist being incorporated into forcibly merged Communist-led parties and regimes in 1947–8. The middle classes, deprived of property and economic opportunities, were 'rapidly reduced to poverty and impotence', but the peasants 'could neither be crushed like the middle class nor cowed and absorbed like the socialists' (Mitrany 1951: 171). The Communists therefore initially concili-ated the peasant parties and 'neutralized' the peasantry by backing and helping to implement radical peasantist land reforms, while surreptitiously strengthening their grip on key state institutions (especially the state security apparatus) behind the scenes.

The land reforms of 1945–7 in effect completed those of 1918–23. However, they not only redistributed many of the still surviving landed estates of Hungary, Poland and eastern Germany (the rest being turned into state farms), but also took land from many medium-sized farms (without compensation in Romania, Yugoslavia and Albania) and discriminated in favour of the poorer peasants and landless labourers. In addition, although the redistributed land was received as inheritable personal property, it could not be sold or let or mortgaged without official permission. The transitory, tactical nature of these agrarian reforms was indicated by the speed with which they were implemented (less than a month in the cases of Hungary and Romania!) and the consequent lack of preparation, including the frequent absence of proper registers and surveys of the land in question. Nevertheless, by discriminating in favour of poor peasants and landless labourers at the expense of so-called 'rich peasants' and by striving to affiliate poor peasants and radical peasantist groups to the proletarian parties, the Communists succeeded in fomenting some dissension and conflict within the peasantry and within the peasantist movements, thereby facilitating the pursuit of 'divide and rule' tactics towards both. Communist politicians were also frequently photographed (for the media) handing out title deeds to the new landholders, in order to win political credit and gratitude in the eyes of the peasantry.

RURAL COLLECTIVIZATION, 1948–64

In contrast to the more firmly entrenched Stalinist regime in the Soviet Union, however, the relatively precarious and fragile Communist regimes established in East Central Europe and the Balkans between 1945 and 1948 simply could not afford to 'liquidate' millions of so-called 'kulaks' ('rich peasants' and village traders and money-lenders). Nor could they risk mass starvation and agricultural sabotage in the interests of rapidly achieving rural collectivization, involving the establishment of large-scale state farms and agricultural producers' co-operatives (APCs) in place of independent peasant smallholder agriculture. Nor indeed was there any need for them to do so, although this begs the question of whether collectivization had really been 'necessary' in the Soviet Union. (The arguments are critically assessed in Bideleux 1987: 11, 36–7, 54–6, 62–9,77–9, 110–13, 118–23, 194–220.) Wholesale rural collectivization was accomplished in stages and without widespread violence or destruction in Bulgaria, Romania, Hungary, Czechoslovakia and East Germany between 1948 and 1960 and in Albania between 1955 and 1964. Although it did involve officially acknowledged 'excesses', 'errors', 'distortions' and 'violations of the principle of voluntariness' in parts of Czechoslovakia, East Germany, Bulgaria and Hungary, such occurrences appear to have been more the exception than the rule (Bideleux 1987: 200). Indeed, while rural collectivization was being carried out in each of these states, there were actually slight increases in overall livestock numbers (with the exception of horses, which were being rapidly replaced by tractors all over Europe at that time). This contrasted sharply with the massive destruction of livestock that had accompanied forced rural collectivization in many parts of the Soviet Union during the 1930s and again in 1945–9 (Bideleux 1987: 122, 201, 205–8). This in turn refuted simplistic claims and assumptions that rural collectivization is necessarily violent and destructive – it could be, but it did not have to be so.

Several factors made the costs of rural collectivization in East Central Europe and the Balkans much lower than they had been in the USSR under Stalin. There was broader and more careful preparatory discussion and briefing on the precise forms and functions to be assumed by collectivized agriculture in each area. There was much more widespread use of transitional forms and differential compensation payments, in recognition of the fact that some peasant households were contributing much more land, capital or livestock to the new APCs than others. Peasants were often encouraged to join APCs by the offer of favours and privileges. Former landless labourers who had acquired land during the 1945–7 land reforms but lacked the means to farm it properly proved especially susceptible to official blandishments. Moreover, both Czechoslovakia and the German Democratic

Republic (GDR) were much more highly industrialized than the Soviet Union and were in a position to furnish most of the equipment and fertilizer inputs needed to make collectivized agriculture
tolerably productive in these two countries and, to some extent, in the neighbouring Communist
states as well. In addition, the already 'tractorized' Soviet Union exported more than 100,000 tractors to East Central Europe and the Balkans between 1946 and 1962. Above all, whereas Stalin's
regime had automatically branded all successful farmers as 'kulaks' and 'class enemies' who were
to be 'liquidated' and debarred from joining APCs, the East Central European and Balkan Communist regimes made greater efforts to utilize such farmers in the formation of successful farming co-
operatives, sometimes even making them farm chairmen or managers, secure in the knowledge that
they would be surrounded and closely watched by their poorer brethren (Bideleux 1987: 201–2).
Thus collectivized agriculture was considerably better placed to realize at least some of its potential
economic, social and technical advantages in much of East Central Europe and the Balkans during
the 1950s than it had been in the Soviet Union during the 1930s. For once, *some* lessons had been
learned from earlier mistakes.

   In Poland and Yugoslavia, on the other hand, fierce resistance from peasants, many of whom had
actively participated in the armed wartime resistance against the Axis Powers, led to the early abandonment of wholesale rural collectivization in these two countries during the early 1950s (Bideleux
1987: 61–3). The fact that Poland nevertheless managed to carry out large-scale centrally planned
industrialization with no more difficulty or lack of success than some of its collectivized East
Central European neighbours further calls into question the economic, social and political 'necessity' and desirability of rural collectivization, even from an 'orthodox' Communist standpoint.
Only Poland's so-called 'western territories' (the areas appropriated from Germany in 1945) were
to be substantially collectivized, and here the creation of APCs was mainly a means of rapidly set-
tling large numbers of Poles on good farmland which German farmers had been forced to quit and
thereby giving greater permanence to these territorial acquisitions (not unlike the use of kibbutzim
to colonize Israel's 'occupied territories'). In the final analysis, the Polish and Yugoslav Communist regimes were not quite as obdurate, inhuman and unyielding as Stalin's had been. They knew
when and how to pull back from potential human and economic disasters, instead of blundering and
bludgeoning onward heedless of the human and economic costs.

FORCED INDUSTRIALIZATION, FROM 1948 TO THE 1960s

From the late 1940s to the early 1960s the East Central European and Balkan Communist states
mobilized rapidly growing inputs of labour, capital, energy and raw materials in order to achieve
rapid industrialization and impresssive rates of growth. However, this was based not so much on
increased productivity or the more efficient use of resources (so-called 'intensive' growth) as on the
massive mobilization of ever-increasing but inefficiently used capital, labour, energy and raw material inputs (so-called 'extensive' growth). Since this involved the prodigal exploitation of natural
resources, this has also been described as a kind of 'slash and burn' economy. Furthermore, in sharp
contrast to Western capitalist patterns of industrialization, priority was given to heavy rather than
light industries and to the growth of 'forced savings' and investment rather than personal consumption. Thus the economic development of the East Central European and Balkan Communist states
was propelled, not by the mass production and consumption of *consumer goods* (as in every instance
of Western industrialization), but by the mass production of *producer goods* such as steel, machinery, chemicals, coal and oil, which were *mostly consumed by industry itself rather than by final
consumers*, and as a result there were few positive effects on popular living standards (these Communist industrialization strategies are critically assessed in Bideleux 1987: 144–60.) Moreover,
overall control was exercised by means of highly centralized, mandatory and supposedly comprehensive planning and resource allocation, rather than by market forces and financial discipline,

although the so-called centrally planned economies were never as centrally and comprehensively controlled in practice as they appeared to be in principle, because genuinely comprehensive central planning was actually unattainable (pp. 141–3).

Industrialization is rarely (if ever) a painless or costless process, but the social, political and economic costs of these very lopsided, 'extensive' and crudely regimented and coercive Communist development strategies were inordinately high. They involved the relative neglect of consumer needs and the service sector (with the partial exceptions of education and health care), unprecedentedly rapid urbanization, acute urban overcrowding, chronic shortages, massive recruitment of women into mostly menial and/or low-paid occupations, widespread use of coercion, repression, 'show trials', purges and intimidation, and major errors and waste in the over-centralized resource allocation and distribution systems. Much of what was produced never reached its intended users, while many perishable products became unfit for consumption before reaching their intended consumers. Despite (and often because of) the suffocating and terrifying control of society by a monolithic state and an all-pervasive party and official ideology, these systems provided no effective mechanisms or incentives to control costs, profligacy, inefficiency and waste, no effective means of ensuring that what was produced was what users wanted, and very little public accountability for what was done (or left undone).

Post-war reconstruction and Stalinist industrialization rapidly changed the nature of the Balkan and East Central European Communist states. In 1945 most of their inhabitants had still lived in agrarian settings, most towns had still served as provincial market-places for the surrounding rural areas, and policy debate was still centred on agrarian reform and peasant aspirations. By 1960, however, agriculture and peasants had been eclipsed by industry and workers, and non-agricultural households constituted the following proportions of the population: 83 per cent in the GDR, 74 per cent in Czechoslovakia, 61 per cent in Hungary, 56 per cent in Poland, 46 per cent in Bulgaria and 34 per cent in Romania. Millions of young adult peasants had moved from the countryside to the towns, although many non-agricultural households continued to reside in rural areas. Thus Poland's urban population soared from 7.5 million in 1945 to 14.4 million in 1960 (rising from 32 per cent of the total population to 48 per cent), while Bulgaria's rose from 26 per cent of the total population in 1948 to 38 per cent in 1960. Between 1950 and 1960 the population of Belgrade grew from 368,000 to 585,000, that of Bucharest from 886,000 to 1,226,000, Budapest from 1,571,000 to 1,805,000, Gdansk from 170,000 to 286,000, Sofia from 435,00 to 687,000, Warsaw from 601,000 to 1,136,000, Wroclaw from 279,000 to 429,000 and Zagreb from 280,000 to 431,000 (Mitchell 1978: 12–14). In Poland urban blue-collar employment increased by 10 per cent per annum from 1947 to 1958, while new recruits from the peasantry were able to find jobs without having either to complete their schooling or improve their skills and qualifications, with the result that by 1958 42 per cent of urban workers had 'incomplete elementary education bordering on illiteracy' (Kolankiewicz and Lewis 1988: 41). Similar situations pertained in Bulgaria, Romania and Yugoslavia, but conditions were much worse in Albania.

Many towns became giant building sites. In both Poland and Yugoslavia more than one-third of the pre-war housing stock and nearly half the factories had been destroyed during the Second World War, while serious urban devastation had also occurred in Hungary and eastern Germany during the closing stages of the war. Some cities were lovingly and sensitively restored to their former beauty, but more often than not economic austerity and the sheer magnitude of the housing and reconstruction problems resulted in a prevalence of cheap, drab, quickly dilapidated, system-built blocks of flats. (However, given the scale of the problems, this might have been the outcome whatever the regime.) Urban living standards plummeted, because too many resources were tied up in huge projects of long gestation, while headlong industrialization forced millions of former peasants to live in hut camps or in grim apartment blocks close to gigantic and grossly polluting industrial complexes, either in the middle of nowhere or on the outskirts of soulless new industrial towns with few amenities and even less character. Post-war food shortages also persisted as peasants reacted negatively to rural collectivization, the vilification of kulaks and the imposition of often unremunerative compulsory delivery quotas, while the low priority accorded to agricultural investment and the mass exodus of young men from the villages further depressed agricultural productivity. The suppression of 'free'(independent) trade unions and the explosive growth of the urban working classes, largely through the arrival of millions of 'new recruits' from the countryside, also resulted in widespread social fragmentation, disorientation, 'deracination' and 'atomization', further reducing their ability to resist economic oppression and exploitation in all its forms. The vulnerability of the working classes was reinforced by the fact that the potential leaders of working-class protest were frequently promoted to junior and sometimes senior managerial positions, further dissipating any residual 'proletarian solidarity'. War-weary, battered and demoralized populations fell victim to predatory authoritarian regimes as easily as they had done during the interwar years.

FROM INITIAL ENTHUSIASM TO EMBITTERED DISILLUSIONMENT, 1950–6

Not surprisingly, the initial left-wing and working-class enthusiasm for the Stalinist development strategy soon wore off and eventually turned to bitter disillusionment. The ambivalent feelings aroused by the initial phase of Communist rule were aptly described by Czeslaw Milosz: 'After the experiences of the War, none of us, not even nationalists, doubted the necessity of the reforms that were being instituted. Our nation was going to be transformed into a nation of workers and peasants and that was right. Yet the peasant was not content, even though he was given land; he was afraid. The worker had not the slightest feeling that the factories belong to him, even though he worked to mobilize them with much self-denial and even though the propaganda assured them that they were his . . . This was, indeed, a peculiar Revolution . . . it was carried out entirely by official decree' (Milosz 1953: 166–7).

Sociological studies of the workers' protests which occurred in the GDR, Hungary and Czechoslovakia during the summer of 1953 and in Poland and Hungary during the summer and autumn of 1956 have emphasized that the strongest protests came precisely from those elements that had originally provided the Communist regimes with their most enthusiastic support. Foremost among these were young workers, socialist intellectuals (many of whom ended up being imprisoned in 1949–53), radical journalists, peasants who had 'risen' into the industrial proletariat, and young men who had volunteered to 'induct' the peasantry into the supposed benefits of Stalinist socialism and collectivized agriculture. Those who had denounced the Stalinist economic strategy from the outset could take a few crumbs of satisfaction from seeing their dire predictions fulfilled, whereas those who had been indifferent or apathetic at the start often remained so. However, those who had fervently believed that Stalinist industrialization and collectivization were the fast roads to the 'promised land' of socialism generally felt the most disillusioned and betrayed by the mostly dismal results of Communist rule. Their naive fervour, idealism and courage frequently led them to open criticism and complaint, usually followed by punitive demotion to inferior jobs and housing or, in the more serious cases, to arrest, imprisonment or even execution. This trajectory was powerfully portrayed in Andrzej Wajda's brilliant film, *Man of Marble* (1977).

The number of Communist Party members 'purged' between 1948 and 1953 was about 90,000 in Bulgaria, 200,000 in Romania, 200,000 in Hungary (which had only about a third as many inhabitants as Romania), 300,000 in East Germany, 370,000 in Poland and a colossal 550,000 in Czechoslovakia, according to Brzezinski (1967: 97). In the case of Hungary, according to other estimates, around 150,000 Communists were imprisoned, 2,000 were summarily executed and 350,000 were expelled from the ruling party over the same period (Rothschild 1989: 137). In the case of Czechoslovakia about 130,000 people (more than 1 per cent of the population) were sent to prisons, labour camps and mines (Sword 1991: 60). It is broadly agreed that Poland, which had already suffered terrible 'purges' and blood-letting during the Second World War, was the East Central European country least afflicted by post-war 'purges'. Conversely, Bulgaria, Czechoslovakia and Hungary, which had emerged from the war relatively unscathed, were much more affected by post-war 'purges'. The Communist-led 'Fatherland Front' government in Bulgaria was very quick to establish punitive 'People's Courts' in autumn 1944–5 and these reportedly tried and either imprisoned or executed a higher proportion of its population as 'fascists', 'war criminals' and 'collaborators' than any other country in Europe (Oren 1973: 88). The post-war purges in Czechoslovakia and Hungary got off to a slower start than those in Bulgaria, but ultimately claimed even more victims.

THE HUNGARIAN REVOLUTION OF OCTOBER-NOVEMBER 1956

The upheaval in Hungary in the autumn of 1956 was not simply an attempted 'counter-revolution' instigated by Catholic, peasant and 'bourgeois nationalist' opponents of Communist rule, as Soviet interventionist propaganda maintained and many Western observers and commentators were equally keen to believe. It also involved a campaign for 'real socialism', a radical attempt by embittered and disillusioned workers and intelligentsia to bring about *a more authentic socialist revolution* with more far-reaching gains for the working class and the peasantry. A network of workers' councils emerged in Hungarian factories and working-class suburbs in late October and November 1956. According to Bill Lomax, the struggles of Hungarian workers and workers' councils were mainly directed against the monolithic control exercised by the ruling party bureaucracy over the workforce and the means of production through party-appointed managerial and trade union personnel and through shop-floor party cells and informers. In November 1956, 'Party-appointed managers were given the boot by the workers, Party organizers were driven out of the factories, and so were those union officials who had never given a damn for the workers' interests. The workers' councils were then set up as organizations through which the workers themselves could control their factories' (Lomax 1976: 201–3). On 27 November the Central Workers' Council of Greater Budapest issued a protest against official proposals to confine workers' councils to purely economic functions and a proclamation that 'the real interests of the working class in Hungary are represented by the workers' councils' (p. 201). Indeed, the workers' councils 'did not set themselves up as a new privileged elite or a new bureaucratic caste . . . On the contrary, even the executive members of the Central Workers' Council spent the full working day on the factory floor.' Its members were expected to report back regularly to the workers and were subject to recall and replacement (p. 202). Thus the Hungarian working class 'both smashed the former state power ruled over by the Communist Party and reopened the road to that society which had been the original aim of Marxism and socialism – in which hierarchy would give way to equality, in which political institutions would be replaced by popular organs' (p. 203).

THE AFTERMATH OF THE HUNGARIAN REVOLUTION OF NOVEMBER–DECEMBER 1956

The conflicting objectives and ideologies of the rival left-wing and right-wing participants in the abortive Hungarian Revolution of 1956 facilitated its bloody suppression by the Soviet armed forces and their Hungarian collaborators headed by Janos Kadar, who served as leader of the ruling party from October 1956 to May 1988. The casualties included more than 2,000 Hungarians executed and 2,000 others killed, and around 13,000 wounded, while over 15,000 Hungarians were imprisoned and more than 200,000 took refuge in the West (Molnar 1971: 240, 249). The almost complete disintegration of the ruling party, many former members of which openly sided with the Revolution and/or handed in or destroyed in their party membership cards, both forced and allowed

Kadar to rebuild his party almost from scratch after 1956. However, in order to crush the Hungarian Revolution, 'every independent organization of the working class had to be smashed' (Lomax 1976: 194–5). Indeed, the working class bore the brunt of the repression, partly because the 'greatest armed resistance to the Soviet forces occurred in the large iron and steel centres of Dunapentele, Ozd and Miscolc, and in the mining regions of Borsod, Dorog, Tatabanya and Pecs. In Budapest itself the Soviet military authorities had to concentrate their heaviest armoured units on the workers' suburbs, where the workers had occupied their factories and continued to defend them for several days against the Soviet tanks', whereas 'the fashionable middle-class districts ... were hardly touched' (p. 149).

THE POLISH UPHEAVALS OF 1956–7

A network of workers' councils similar to that in Hungary also arose in Poland in the wake of the suppression of workers' protests in Poznan in June 1956 (in which 113 people were killed by the Polish army and security police) and the campaign to restore the 'national Communist' Wladislaw Gomulka to the ruling party's leadership. An official decree legalized the mushrooming workers' councils in November 1956, but confined them to dealing with a narrow range of economic and social matters at the local level. It prohibited attempts to organize a nationwide federation of workers' councils capable of bringing concerted political pressure to bear on the regime or of playing an effective role in policy-making at the national level (Brzezinski 1967: 350). By September 1957 three-quarters of the 1,936 eligible industrial enterprises had established workers' councils, but in April 1958 these were further emasculated by being subordinated to a so-called Workers' Self-Government Conference in which elected representatives of workers' councils were outnumbered by official party and trade union appointees and the proceedings were chaired by the party secretary (p. 356). Polish workers' councils thus became mere 'grievance boards', serving as barometers and safety valves rather than as harbingers of authentic industrial democracy or 'workers' control'. Working-class discontent was more muzzled than assuaged, but this did not provide a durable resolution of the recurrent conflict between the ruling party and the workers in whose name it ruled, as Gomulka and his successors were to discover to their cost during the Polish crises of 1970, 1976, 1980–2 and 1988–9.

THE LEGACIES OF THE HUNGARIAN AND POLISH UPHEAVALS

The East Central European and Balkan Communist regimes were much more profoundly challenged by workers' grievances than by counter-revolutionary 'bourgeois', nationalist and religious discontents. The latter undoubtedly existed, but the combined effects of fascism, the Second World War and Stalinism had ensured that bourgeois nationalists and liberals and the Christian churches lacked a strongly organized class base and that the Communist regimes could glibly dismiss them as 'enemies of the people' and/or as epigones of the former 'exploiting classes'. Their howls of pain and protest could be treated both as confirmation that the Communist regimes were successfully achieving their objectives and as a pretext for the repression of 'counter-revolutionary elements' bent on overthrowing Communist rule. Mass unrest among workers and the socialist intelligentsia, supposedly the twin pillars of Communist rule, was much more threatening and embarrassing. It was nipped in the bud in 1953–8 by repression sugared with concessions to the incipient consumerism of both wage and salary earners and to widespread desires for social and economic security, stability and upward mobility. However, the price paid was *the death of revolutionary élan and socialist idealism*, which were superseded by cynical 'deals' and compromises and by pragmatic appeals to grasping and acquisitive self-interest. Buying off wage and salary earners' discontent in this way involved the Communist regimes in far-reaching 'sell-outs', drawing most sections of society into implicit and deeply corrupting 'social contracts' with their Communist rulers. These took a heavy toll on economic and administrative efficiency. The success of such political strata-gems would largely depend upon how successfully (or otherwise) the Communist regimes could maintain high rates of economic growth and rising consumption levels, which alone could enable them to deliver on their side of the implicit social contracts.

However, these were objectives which none of the Balkan and East Central European Commu-nist regimes could attain on their own. Consequently, they would ultimately depend on how suc-cessfully they could escape or surmount the constraints and austerities of 'boxed in' national self-reliance by promoting transnational and/or supranational economic co-operation, division of labour and integration within Comecon, which could also offer increased access to the large markets and even larger mineral resources of the Soviet Union. It is therefore important to consider the achievements and the inherent shortcomings of Comecon, even though Western analysts have com-monly regarded it as a sham and as a bureaucratic irrelevance. The long-term survival of Commu-nist rule in East Central Europe and the Balkans ultimately depended in large measure on how well (or otherwise) Comecon could perform.

THE RISE OF COMECON, 1949–60: THE MAIN MECHANISM FOR INSTITUTIONALIZING THE SOVIET BLOC

Comecon, the official name of which was the Council of Mutual Economic Assistance (CMEA), was founded in 1949, at the height of the East–West division and Cold War confrontation in Europe. In parallel with the inter-party Communist Information Bureau (Cominform, founded in 1947) on the ideological front and the inter-governmental Warsaw Pact (established in 1955) on the military/political front, Comecon was intended to enhance the solidity and cohesion of the Soviet bloc. It was as much a by-product of the Second World War and the ensuing East–West division of Europe as were the nascent supranational and inter-governmental institutions of Western Europe.

The establishment of Comecon was in part a consequence of Stalin's decision to veto the desired participation of the Balkan and East Central European Communist states in the European Recovery Programme, which had been announced by American secretary of state George Marshall in June 1947, although the precise nature and importance of the causal connections are still under debate. The USA seemingly offered so-called Marshall Aid to all the European states that were struggling to recover from the Second World War, including the Soviet Union and the emerging 'People's Democracies' in East Central Europe and the Balkans. Soviet representatives participated in some of the preliminary discussions, but their sudden withdrawal from the July 1947 Paris conference on the European Recovery Programme contributed to 'the division of Europe into two parts' (Brabant 1989: 9). In those East Central European and Balkan states that were not yet fully under Communist control at that time, namely Czechoslovakia, Hungary and Poland, the Communist parties were still formally espousing moderation, gradualism and a 'middle way' between Soviet 'socialism' and Western capitalism (for fear of frightening the numerous peasant and 'petit bourgeois' voters), and their increasingly Communist-dominated coalition governments initially signalled their interest in receiving Marshall Aid. They did so in spite of the fact that the 'strings' attached to Marshall Aid pledged the recipients to restore market economies with convertible currencies and to promote multilateral integration of their economies with those of the members of the Organization of Euro-pean Economic Co-operation (OEEC). The OEEC was to be responsible for allocating Marshall Aid and for upholding the liberal integrationist economic conditions on which it was to be granted. The recipients were thus bound to be drawn into the economic orbit of the richer Western capitalist economies. Presumably in order to prevent this happening in East Central Europe and most of the Balkans, which were still supposed to be in the Soviet 'sphere of influence', in July 1947 Stalin ordered the Czechoslovak and Polish governments to reverse their earlier decisions to accept

Marshall Aid. The Communist and socialist ministers in these governments meekly complied, thereby precipitating serious crises in their relations with the so-called 'bourgeois' ministers in the ruling 'Popular Front' coalitions. Many socialist politicians submitted to Communist pressure partly out of a (misguided!) commitment to left-wing and working-class 'solidarity', but also from fear of losing working-class and trade union support to the Communists and because of actual and potential reprisals from the increasingly Communist-controlled security forces.

This was a moment of truth, the signal for the Communist parties rapidly to establish more complete control of the so-called 'People's Democracies' during late 1947 and early 1948. The forced rejection of Marshall Aid not only foreclosed opportunities for gradual reconstruction by market methods, utilizing Western economic and technological assistance and mutual gains from liberalized multilateral trade, but also heralded their incipient subjection to more blatant forms of Soviet control. If Poland and Czechoslovakia had been allowed to accept Marshall Aid, other People's Democracies would almost certainly have followed suit and much of East Central Europe and the Balkans could have slipped out of Soviet and/or Communist control (which was still far from secure). Significantly, the strong revival of Czechoslovak foreign trade in 1946 had been almost entirely with its traditional Western trading partners rather than with its new Soviet 'ally' (Rothschild 1989: 93). However, once the hitherto semi-autonomous Polish and Czechoslovak governments had bowed to Stalin's will, none of the others dared to step out of line, apart from the exceptionally battle-hardened and self-reliant Communist rulers of Yugoslavia. The Yugoslav Communist regime had not yet embraced the more liberal course for which it later became famous. The source of its rift with the Soviet Union in 1948 was not doctrinal heterodoxy, nor a desire to seek an accommodation with the West, but rather its headstrong refusal to submit to Soviet dictates. This fell foul of Stalin's innate mistrust of Communists who gave him anything less than blind and unquestioning obedience.

Thrown back on their own meagre resources, the East Central European and Balkan Communist-led regimes found themselves obliged to retreat into much more autarkic and coercive methods of resource allocation and mobilization modelled on those employed in Stalin's Soviet Union (and not so very different from those used by the Nazis during the Second World War).

On 25 January 1949 most Communist newspapers and news agencies published a short communiqué announcing that an economic conference representing the Soviet Union, Czechoslovakia, Poland, Hungary, Romania and Bulgaria had met in Moscow on 5–8 January and, 'in order to establish still broader economic co-operation among the countries of People's Democracy and the USSR', had instituted a Council for Mutual Economic Assistance 'on the basis of equal representation, and having as its tasks the exchange of experience in the economic field, the rendering of technical assistance to one another and the rendering of mutual assistance in regard to raw materials, foodstuffs, machinery, equipment etc.' (reprinted in Vaughan 1976: 132–3). Albania joined Comecon the following month, while a newly established and Communist-controlled 'German Democratic Republic' (GDR) followed suit in 1950.

The precise motives and objectives of this unheralded announcement have long been matters of speculation and debate, as we still have no windows into Stalin's inscrutable mind. At the time it was widely believed that the creation of Comecon was part of a slowly unfolding plan for Soviet domination of post-fascist Europe. However, Western 'revisionist' historians of the Cold War have long maintained that such a plan never existed, and we share the view that Stalin was mainly reacting defensively to unforeseen Western challenges and provocations, improvising as he went along (see pp. 468–70). The Soviet leadership correctly perceived that Marshall Aid was (among other things) an indirect attempt to subvert or renege upon the apportionment of Soviet and Western 'spheres of influence' agreed in Moscow, Yalta and Potsdam in 1944–5, since the strings attached to it were bound to enmesh the recipients firmly in the Western economic sphere. Indeed, President Truman needed to persuade Congress that the Marshall Plan was an anti-Communist programme, the economic counterpart to the so-called 'Truman doctrine' on the 'containment' of Communism. (They were, in Truman's apt phrase, 'two halves of the same walnut'.) Had he not made this move, the instinctively isolationist and parsimonious US legislature might well have refused to approve the requisite financial appropriations. Significantly, the above-mentioned communiqué announcing the formation of Comecon stated that the Soviet Union and the People's Democracies 'did not consider it possible to submit to the Marshall Plan dictate', because it supposedly violated their 'sovereignty' and 'the interests of their national economies'. However, having prohibited the People's Democracies from participating in the US-sponsored European Recovery Programme and the OEEC, the Soviet leadership may have felt obliged to offer them some sort of substitute, both by way of compensation for the opportunities forgone and as a means of propping up their ailing economies, which had been severely damaged by the subsequent collapse of their trade with the West. Indeed, the same communiqué noted that 'the Governments of the United States of America, Britain, and of certain other countries of Western Europe, had been, as a matter of fact, boycotting trade relations with the countries of People's Democracy and the USSR'.

Stalin's motives for allowing the establishment of Comecon are sometimes seen as 'more negative than positive'. Thus he was more 'anxious to keep other powers out of neighbouring buffer states . . . than to integrate them', and he 'envisaged Comecon as the economic counterpart of the Cominform, which he had instituted in 1947' (Wallace and Clarke 1986: 1). Indeed, Comecon was often dismissed in the West as little more than a figleaf with which to cover the nakedness of Soviet domination of East Central Europe and the Balkans, as an artificial contrivance designed to confer a semblance of solidity and of economic and institutional legitimacy on the emerging Soviet bloc, and as a way to discourage East Central European and Balkan economic links with the West and to redirect the foreign trade of the new People's Democracies towards the Soviet Union. Nevertheless, Schiavone contends that the motives for the creation of Comecon were 'not reducible to the Soviet desire to oppose to the OEEC an East European organization. The establishment of the OEEC certainly served as an incentive, but it seems to have provided no more than an occasional prompting for the establishment of a multilateral co-operation body, the need for which was already felt' (Schiavone 1981: 16). Since 1848, indeed, there had been dozens of projects and schemes for customs unions and political federations or confederations in East Central Europe and the Balkans, although some of these had been expressly directed against the Russian and/or Communist 'menace'.

In any case, the emergence of Communist regimes and so-called centrally planned economies in East Central Europe and the Balkans obliged these states to place their economic and political relations with each other and the Soviet Union on a new and more coherent footing, partly because Western economic sanctions were rapidly cutting them off from their traditional export markets and from many former Western suppliers. The new regimes were to be drawn together by common political systems and precepts, similar development strategies, geographical proximity and security considerations. They were also driven into each others' arms by the new international trade and payments systems that were emerging in the capitalist West. 'GATT's insistence on nondiscriminatory treatment of trade partners was at odds with the notion of socialist integration and solidarity and in any case was not observed by the industrialized West in its trade policies vis-à-vis planned economies' (Brada 1988: 654). The Western emphasis on currency convertibility was inconsistent with the conception of central planning prevalent among CMEA members. Moreover, the centrally planned economies required an international regime to mediate trade among them even more than did market economies. 'Among the latter, trade takes place between private agents at market-determined prices. States need to interact with each other only to set the rules for such transactions, to enforce contracts, and to promote the functioning of markets. Among planned economies international trade is a state monopoly. Therefore markets cannot function, since each transaction confronts a monopolist with a monopsonist. As a result . . . there is less information, transactions are much costlier to negotiate, and states must interact with each other directly as parties to each transaction rather than merely as creators and guarantors of the rules of the game' (p. 655).

The pricing formulae employed by Comecon fixed intra-CMEA prices for several years at a time. Moreover, the absence of meaningful exchange rates and of domestic prices that reflected relative costs and scarcities obliged the Comecon states to take (lagged) world market prices as a reference point. (Hence the old dictum that Comecon could never have taken over the whole world, because then it would no longer have known what prices to charge.) Brada argued that this pricing system was particularly advantageous to centrally planned economies. Firstly, the maintenance of stable prices reduced 'transaction costs'. In the absence of these stable pricing formulae, the centrally planned economies would have had to undertake more frequent trade negotiations 'with no starting point for the prices at which trade would take place' and no certainty that 'prices obtained in negotiations with one country would resemble those achieved with other countries', thus making trade negotiations exceedingly costly and time consuming. Secondly, the use of stable pricing formulae in international transactions helped to maintain stable contexts for central planning. Thirdly, the systematic over-pricing of manufactured goods relative to fuels and raw materials offered the East Central European and Balkan members of Comecon artificially high returns on their production of manufactures that were often 'not up to world standards'. This gave them considerable protection against risk and competition as well as compensation for 'the high investment costs of modernizing and developing industries to serve the Soviet market', while providing the Soviet Union with substantially larger supplies of manufactured goods from East Central Europe and the Balkans than would otherwise have been the case, at overall costs that were lower than those of producing these manufactures itself (Brada 1988: 656–7). Such arrangements also economized on the Comecon members' scarce earnings of hard currency, much as the OEEC and the associated European Payments Union did within post-war Western Europe.

Some members were bound to derive larger benefits from the intensification of intra-CMEA relations and cohesion than others, just as some would incur larger costs than the rest. The main tangible and measurable costs of the collective benefits that Comecon could confer on its participants would be borne by those members who could either have sold their major exports more dearly, or have purchased their import requirements more cheaply, in non-CMEA markets. Nevertheless, even if the individual balance-sheets of costs and benefits varied considerably between members and over time, there was a basic presumption that all members would reap some net benefits from Comecon membership. These benefits were not just economic, but also came in the form of the increased internal and external legitimacy, security, stability and room for manoeuvre procured for Balkan and East Central European Communist regimes, since increases in the economic strength, political stability and international stature of the Soviet Union could also enhance the standing of its client states. Members would benefit from increases in the economic strength, political stability and international standing of Comecon as a whole.

However, Vladimir Sobell has argued that the supposed benefits of Comecon membership should really be regarded as partial mitigation or compensation for some of the inherent drawbacks of the whole economic system. Indeed, co-operation and specialization within Comecon could be seen as ways of alleviating 'the disadvantages associated with participation in the grouping' or as damage-limiting responses to 'the fundamental political error' of instituting this type of economic system in the first place. Likewise, the fact that the energy-importing members of Comecon participated in investment in energy projects on Soviet territory was not a 'sign of efficient integration', but rather 'an expression of a fundamental disorder' in the socialist system: the importing countries were 'unable to offer the USSR goods and services of sufficient "hardness" to motivate it to invest in additional energy infrastructure'. Indeed, experts and officials from these states testified that joint investment was 'not only an inefficient strategy' but also a 'considerable strain on their economies' (Sobell 1984: 248–9).

Sobell also pointed out that the criteria by which Comecon integration was evaluated in the West were somewhat inappropriate. The CMEA was never intended to maximize integration through trade, but rather to provide a protected environment within which to maximize the power, stability and economic growth of the 'socialist' states. Comecon should be assessed primarily by the extent to which it satisfied these criteria, rather than by its failure to maximize classical gains from trade: 'When judged by the criteria operating in a market environment Comecon integration appears as a passive and wasteful process: participation in the grouping leads to losses due to undertrading with non-members which are only partially made good by intra-group trade (leaving aside the losses from sub-optimal specialization on account of the lack of a rational intra-CMEA price system). On the other hand when judged by the criteria dominating the study of economics in most of Eastern Europe the verdict would be radically different. Undertrading would be regarded as a positive measure ensuring that domestic production planning is isolated from the disruptive effects of the capitalist markets; the disproportionate trade with member countries would be seen as a sign of active integration designed to reap natural advantages stemming from countries having the same socio-political systems' (Sobell 1984: 3).

East Central European and Balkan Communist backing for Soviet denunciations of Marshall Aid from July 1947 onward and for the 1948–9 Soviet blockade of West Berlin (following the unilateral introduction of the Deutschmark in the Western zones of occupation in June 1948) led to an escalation of Western economic sanctions against the nascent Soviet bloc (Brabant 1989: 41). From March 1948 onwards all American exports to Communist-controlled states were subject to government licensing. 'The scope of the boycott was extended on 3 April 1948 by the statutes of the Marshall Plan.' Participants in the European Recovery Programme (ERP) were debarred from trading in eastern European goods subject to US controls. This policy was formalized by the establishment of the Co-ordinating Committee for Multilateral Trade Controls (COCOM) in 1950 (p. 17). Thus, even though the original US motivations were at least partly philanthropic, the ERP really did become an economic weapon in the incipient Cold War. This most adversely affected those East Central European states which were still heavily dependent on trade with the West. Western economic sanctions drove these states deeper into the economic and political embrace of the Soviet Union. The creation of Comecon accordingly reflected a need to enhance and to demonstrate Soviet bloc 'solidarity' in the face of Western economic sanctions and provocations, which in turn 'reinforced the economic arguments for the gradual elaboration of a common regional economic policy for Eastern Europe, including the USSR' (p. 18).

It has also been argued that Nikolai Voznesensky, who served as the influential chairman of the Soviet State Planning Commission from 1937 to 1949, was keen to place Soviet economic relations with the East Central European and Balkan Communist states on a more regular and law-governed footing. This would have removed them from the jurisdiction and interference of capricious Communist politicians, while also enhancing the role of more 'rational' and predictable economic mechanisms and of technocrats like himself (Kaser 1967: 21–6, 32–5). However, the dismissal and arrest of Voznesensky in March 1949, not long after the death of his Leningrad 'patron' Andrei Zhdanov in August 1948, eliminated the pivotal Soviet proponent of a more 'rational' economistic conception of Comecon and facilitated its subsequent emasculation by Stalin. The continuing absence of criteria whereby economic goals, performance, output, inputs, costs and demand could be adequately measured, compared, evaluated and aggregated was to become the rock on which Comecon integration would eventually founder (pp. 26, 32–8). 'The implications for Comecon of the Voznesensky approach were . . . trade arrangements based on the analysis of comparative costs and permitting the evaluation of multilateral exchanges . . . A "law of value" operating between Comecon members would have furnished criteria for . . . rational specializations undertaken in the context of co-ordinated long-term planning' (p. 35).

Voznesensky's precise role and position in the seminal preliminary debates on the appropriate structure, powers, functioning and economic basis of Comecon will remain a matter of conjecture until the relevant records have been investigated more fully. Nevertheless, Voznesensky 'stood for a rational economy – it is unclear whether centralized or decentralized – that made sensible use of prices'. By contrast, Stalin and Voznesensky's successors on the economic front rejected 'the use of the price mechanism, both nationally and internationally, in favour of continued physical planning'. Stalin thus 'found himself saddled with an organ he had indeed allowed to be born, but could not personally work with' (Wiles 1968: 313).

If the ideas, policies, procedures and supranational institutions and mechanisms discussed by Comecon officials, economists and technocrats in 1949–50 had actually been implemented at that time, when the new centrally planned economies were still inchoate and malleable, it is conceivable that Comecon could have developed much more advantageously and that East Central European and Balkan industrialization and inter-state specialization could have proceeded in a less arbitrary, less autarkic and more 'rational' fashion. This would certainly have avoided a great deal of wasteful duplication and would have been far more efficacious than the belated attempts to pull these processes back on to more efficient and 'rational' paths during the 1960s and 1970s, by which time the autarkic and dysfunctional features of the East Central European and Balkan centrally planned economies were much more deeply entrenched and difficult to correct (Ausch 1972: 44; Brabant 1989: 26, 40–1). According to Sandor Ausch, Hungary's representative at Comecon headquarters in Moscow in 1949 and from 1962 to 1964, 'the concrete form of our production relations (the system of direct plan instruction) is hindering to an ever-increasing extent the unfolding of a more efficient intra-regional co-operation'(Ausch 1972: 226). Indeed, each member of Comecon continued to strive for a high level of industrial and agricultural self-reliance, because each mistrusted the ability and willingness of the other members to deliver what they were supposed to deliver under the terms of Comecon's later 'specialization agreements'.

More far-reaching integration of the East Central European and Balkan economies could have been achieved either through the adoption of market principles (that is, enterprise autonomy, prices broadly reflecting relative costs and scarcities, convertible currencies and multilateral trading) or by erecting supranational Comecon agencies with the power to plan production, control trade, direct investment and assign specializations for the Soviet bloc as a whole, from Berlin to Vladivostok. The first option, which was increasingly canvassed by liberal economic reformers, never became politically feasible, because its inherent logic pointed to the eventual abandonment of central planning and Communist Party control of (and interference in) the economy. Such a scenario was as unwelcome to most Communist apparatchiki, who stood to lose power, status and control, as it was attractive to most reformers. It would have relieved the Communist parties of economic responsibilities which they were ill fitted to discharge, but it would also have removed the central *raison d'être* of Communist rule. The second option was taken rather more seriously. It appears that on 18 January 1949 the six founder members of CMEA signed (but never ratified) a 'protocol' on the establishment of a 'common economic organization' and a supranational economic institution which would 'formulate a common economic plan for the harmonious development of the entire region, including the USSR'. It would have been granted 'plenipotentiary economic powers' to 'dovetail the member economies', ensure 'supplies of essential inputs for the region's industrialization' and promote 'regional complementarities', specialization, standardization, transnational investment, co-ordination of national economic plans and exchange of scientific and technical information (Brabant 1989: 20). According to Milan Cizkovsky (writing in 1970), 'the prerequisites for organizing supranational unified planning were intentionally created with the decision to co-ordinate the plans, the main goal being the gradual planned elimination of all attributes of the national economies as autonomous economic units. Therefore, a supranational system should have resulted and, in consequence, the absoluteness of state sovereignty would be negated' (quoted by Brabant 1989: 34).

In April and August 1949, the first and second Council Sessions of Comecon apparently discussed 'the co-ordination of national economic plans to foster production specialization and co-operation', the close meshing of trade plans for key commodities, the introduction of multilateral clearing and realistic exchange rates, the elaboration of 'a common economic plan for the harmonious development of the entire region', mutual aid to counteract the effects of Western economic sanctions against CMEA members, the enforcement of Comecon's analogous economic boycott of independent-minded Yugoslavia, and comprehensive scientific and technical co-operation, which would result in the sharing of know-how and the standardization of weights, measures, industrial standards and product specifications to Soviet norms (Brabant 1989: 31–6). However, while this more centralized and proactive second option seems superficially compatible with the retention of centrally planned economies and the 'guiding roles' of the Communist parties, in practice it would have transferred ultimate control of economic processes from *national* economic planners and industrial ministries to *supranational* planners and Comecon industrial directorates and, even more radically, from Communist politicians and apparatchiki to economic planners and technocrats. Although the precise reasons for the early rejection of this second option have not yet been fully documented, it is clear that its long-term implications would have been as unwelcome to *national* economic planners and industrial ministries as they were to *national* Communist Party bosses and their henchmen, all of whom would have suffered large losses of power, function and status. They decided to safeguard their highly prized powers and perquisites by defending the principle of national economic sovereignty. This was the formal pretext for the recurrent rejection of supranational institutions, agencies, projects and powers within Comecon. Indeed, as early as 26 January 1949, the two main Polish newspapers, *Trybuna Ludu* and *Zycie Warzawy*, proclaimed that the form assumed by the new CMEA 'would strengthen sovereignty', while the Romanian *Universul* saw it as 'protecting the rights and sovereignty of members'(quoted in Kaser 1967: 15). Moreover, it seems likely that Stalin vetoed the entire project for a thoroughgoing supranational integration of the Comecon countries (along with the more 'rational' and technocratic system of central planning that such a project would have required) not merely out of uncharacteristic regard for the interests and sensibilities of his Communist acolytes in the Balkans and East Central Europe, but also because it could have acquired a momentum, logic and power base of its own, outside Soviet control. Stalin evidently preferred more informal and direct methods of intervention in the affairs of the East Central European and Balkan states through the Soviet embassies and the legions of Soviet agents attached to them. By 1950 the Soviet Union was directly supervising the policies of these states and 'substantial components of national economic planning were entrusted to Soviet advisers and technicians, primarily through the so-called Soviet embassy system' (Brabant 1989: 22).

Stalin's sudden emasculation of Comecon in the summer of 1950 seems to have taken its personnel by surprise. As testified by Milan Cizkovsky, 'it was certainly not known . . . that the activity of the CMEA would come to a complete standstill for the next three years' (quoted by Brabant 1989: 38). Partly as a result of the outbreak of the Korean War on 25 June 1950 and the enhanced priority for autarkic Stalinist methods of resource mobilization and industrialization, the Soviet Union 'abruptly ceased active participation in the CMEA's Bureau' and instead relied on its 'embassy system of meddling in other countries' affairs directly'. Comecon's third Council Session was therefore delayed until November 1950 and, to the Bureau's surprise, it decided to confine Comecon to 'practical questions of facilitating mutual trade' for the time being (p. 39). Nevertheless, partly as a result of the severity of Western economic sanctions, by 1953 intra-CMEA trade accounted for nearly 80 per cent of the foreign trade of the Member States, which had conducted less than 13 per cent of their trade with one another in 1938 and would transact only 54 per cent of their foreign trade with one another by 1983, following the revival of East–West trade (Robson 1987: 225–6).

If Stalin had allowed Comecon to develop in the manner envisaged by its April and August 1949 Council Sessions, it could have become an institutional 'buffer' mediating the East Central European and Balkan members' relations with each other and, more importantly, with the Soviet Union. For the People's Democracies, this would have been safer, more politically correct and less unequal than direct bilateral relations with an 'overbearing' USSR. However, Stalin was unwilling to countenance the emergence of any regional organization that would make it easier for them to keep the Soviet 'bear' at bay or to 'gang up' to impose a majority policy on the Soviet Union. It is conceivable that Stalin deliberately stymied Comecon in order to keep the East Central European and Balkan Communist states divided and powerless against him. 'The central body, the Council Session, had to reach unanimous agreement in order to respect the sovereign rights of its Member States. It could not make decisions, only recommendations. These had to be ratified subsequently by all governments and, even if so ratified, still had to be translated into policy by all governments acting separately' (Wallace and Clarke 1986: 4).

Thus the Soviet Union initially limited (rather than encouraged) multilateral exchange and co-operation between the East Central European and Balkan members of Comecon. It negotiated bilateral treaties with each of them, fostered direct Soviet supervision and 'guidance' of their economic development (in flagrant violation of the vaunted sovereignty which had been the pretext for prohibiting multilateral integration on a more equal footing), and forced them all to pursue relatively uniform 'closed in' patterns of development which maximized economic duplication and costly import-substitution and minimized the scope for fruitful resource-saving complementarities, integration and specialization. They all tended to develop similar strengths and weaknesses, while the development of command economies concentrated economic influence and decision-making in the hands of central economic ministries and planning bureaucracies which naturally became increasingly reluctant to cede powers and functions to any supranational body. Ironically, routine Soviet violations of their political sovereignty made them cling all the more tenaciously to their formal economic sovereignty, which was their main area of limited autonomy (Brabant 1989: 4). During the early 1950s, however, 'Comecon was a sham. Stalin ruled Eastern Europe, as he ruled the Soviet Union, by other than constitutional means' (Wallace and Clarke 1986: 3–4). Precisely because Comecon was an organization formally based on the professed sovereignty and equal status of its members, Stalin did not have much use for it (Wiles 1968: 314). From the outset Stalin viewed his new East Central European and Balkan 'allies' with considerable suspicion, as they were too Westernized, untested and unstable for his liking. He therefore endeavoured to restrict their contacts not only with the West, but also with each other and with the USSR. He did not trust them enough to allow Comecon to realize more than a fraction of its true potential, and it would remain permanently scarred by this early experience.

Some important initial steps were nonetheless taken at this time. In particular, the Council Session of Comecon hosted by Bulgaria in August 1949 passed a seminal resolution on the pooling or sharing of technology among its Member States, which came to be known as 'the Sofia principle'. Instead of setting up an elaborate patents system and scientific protectionism to safeguard the advantages of technological leaders, as has been standard Western practice, they agreed to make their technologies available to one another for a nominal charge (mainly to cover the costs of providing technical documentation). This system was much disliked by the more industrialized members of Comecon (Czechoslovakia and the GDR). The latter stood to gain very little in return for the technologies they passed on to their less developed partners (especially the Soviet Union, Bulgaria, Romania and, somewhat later, Cuba, Mongolia and Vietnam). Anthony Sutton has documented (albeit with some exaggeration) the considerable extent to which Soviet economic development was based upon the systematic transference, adaptation and copying of foreign technologies, blueprints, products and processes. The seminal infusions of Western technology into the Soviet economy occurred during the later 1920s and early 1930s, when many Western firms entered various types of management or service contract within the Soviet Union and resourceful Soviet engineers and scientists systematically copied Western prototypes, ingeniously adapting them to

Soviet needs and production possibilities. The first two Five-Year Plans, including the huge new fleets of trucks, tractors and locomotives, were in large measure based on 'pirated' Western technology. But by the mid-1940s, in spite of deriving some benefits from American wartime assistance, the increasingly isolated Soviet economy had largely exhausted the potential of its now obsolescent 1920s and 1930s technologies. It stood in desperate need of large new transfusions of foreign technology in order to ward off technological stagnation. These were obtained partly through the heavy-handed removal of plant, equipment, products, prototypes, blueprints and even scientific personnel from Soviet-occupied East Germany (on a scale that gave a whole new meaning to the concept of 'technology transfer'). In addition, Czechoslovakia, Hungary and Poland were obliged to 'share' their technological know-how with the USSR and (to a lesser extent) Bulgaria and Romania under the Sofia principle (Sutton 1968–72). Similarly, some of the Western technologies acquired or 'imported' by individual East Central European and Balkan Communist states and enterprises during the 1960s and 1970s were passed on to their partners under Comecon's 'scientific and technical co-operation' arrangements. Arguably, this was the substantive meaning of the 'mutual economic assistance' in Comecon's official title. However, the Sofia principle was downplayed after 1968, in recognition of its implicit discouragement of original and/or expensive technological research and development (and Czech and East German grievances on this score). Moreover, as the Soviet Union itself developed more expensive and/or sophisticated military, metallurgical, aircraft and energy technologies, it became less willing to give these away to its Comecon partners largely free of charge.

The revamping of Comecon in the wake of Stalin's death in March 1953 and the Hungarian Revolution of October–November 1956

Following Stalin's death in March 1953, there were various attempts to 'relaunch' Comecon as a new and more equitable economic partnership and to use it as a substitute for more invidious forms of Soviet hegemony over East Central European and Balkan Communist states. The Council Sessions of March and June 1954 established a permanent Comecon secretariat and a standing conference of representatives of member countries. They also initiated a series of 'specialization agreements' designed to curb costly industrial duplication and import-substitution, especially in those states that lacked the appropriate resource base to sustain autarkic neo-Stalinist patterns of industrialization. In 1956 ten permanent standing commissions were established to promote specialization and co-operation in particular sectors (Brabant 1989: 46–7, 52–4). Comecon was revitalized, and its scope extended, partly in response to an extension of the range of tasks and challenges confronting the Soviet Union under its frenetic new party leader, Nikita Khrushchev (1953–64). The Soviet Union increasingly relied on the Balkans and especially East Central Europe to provide the types of machinery, equipment, manufactured consumer goods and foodstuffs that were in short supply domestically and to provide 'captive' markets for Soviet-produced plant, machinery, armaments and oil (Mellor 1971: 14). (The Soviet Union initially faced difficulties in breaking into international oil markets controlled by Western multinational oil companies.) The December 1955 and May 1956 Council Sessions of Comecon called for the co-ordination and synchronization of national Five-Year Plans. In practice, however, most of the attempts at plan co-ordination at this time were limited to bilateral *ex post* harmonization of the trade implications of national economic plans and failed to achieve *ex ante* harmonization of either trade intentions or planned production (Brabant 1989: 51). In any case, the 'specialization agreements' of 1954–6 were largely nullified by the social and political upheavals of 1956 (which precipitated many hasty revisions of trade and production priorities in the hope of defusing discontent), while plan synchronization and co-ordination was derailed in 1957 by the sudden abandonment of the 1956–60 Soviet Five-Year Plan (Brabant 1989: 47; Mellor 1971: 15).

Comecon was 'relaunched' yet again in the wake of the November 1956 invasion of Hungary. The Member States hoped that, by fostering higher living standards, less costly patterns of economic growth and stronger economic bonds within Comecon, they would be spared a repetition of anything so drastic as a full-scale military invasion of one of their own 'allies', since the 1956 invasion had starkly confirmed the lack of legitimacy and popular support of the East Central European and Balkan Communist regimes and had severely dented their confidence and international standing. The 1957 Moscow Declaration ostensibly relaunched relations between the Comecon states on a new basis of mutual respect, non-interference and equality. The June 1957 and June 1958 Council Sessions of Comecon initiated preparations for the introduction of multilateral clearing (including the use of the 'transferable ruble' as a unit of account in intra-CMEA clearing) and for the establishment of a CMEA clearing bank. In May 1958 a special Comecon 'economic summit' launched preparations for more far-reaching specialization of production, to be achieved by multilateral, supranational *ex ante* co-ordination of plans under the aegis of fifteen sectoral and two functional Standing Commissions. The June 1958 Council Session approved new rules on the pricing of goods traded within Comecon, in an attempt to promote more equitable and multilateral trading and to shield intra-CMEA trade from the vagaries of the world market, while that of December 1959 belatedly adopted a Comecon Charter, partly inspired by the 1957 Treaties of Rome (Brabant 1989: 54–60). The Charter defined the status and functions of the Council Session ('the highest organ'), the executive committee ('the principal executive organ'), the standing commissions and the secretariat. While it proclaimed 'the sovereign equality of all member countries', it also committed them to 'the consistent implementation of the international socialist division of labour'. (The complete text is translated in Vaughan 1976: 138–44.) The supranational 'integrationist' implications of this particular formulation may not have been immediately apparent to all the signatories of the Charter, but they opened a more substantive chapter in Comecon's development, while also sowing the seeds of future dissension.

32 'National Communism'

The 1960s began as a period of rising expectations and relative optimism in East Central Europe and the Balkans. At the start of the decade the ruling parties and many of their political opponents seemed to share a belief that it would be possible to work towards a mutually acceptable *modus vivendi*. This was reinforced by optimistic assumptions that (other than in recession-stricken Czechoslovakia) rapid economic development would allow the East Central European and Balkan economies simply to grow their way out of political, social and economic difficulties. It appeared that the harsh austerities, privations, terror and coercion of the 1940s and 1950s had gone for good, allowing the inhabitants of these states to reap the fruits of an expanded infrastructural and industrial base, albeit one that had been constructed at exorbitant social and economic cost. It was now hoped that, with appropriate streamlining or reform, the centrally planned economies could be made more efficient and responsive. At the same time the rapidly increasing Soviet output of oil, coal, natural gas, iron ore and electric power enabled the Soviet Union to satisfy a growing proportion of the rapidly expanding energy and raw material requirements of the increasingly mineral-intensive East Central European and Balkan industries. In effect, the Soviet Union became willing to underwrite and prop up the expansion of these relatively fragile, mineral-deficient and internationally uncompetitive economies (and thus bind them more closely to itself) by forgoing payment in hard currency for its 'hard' commodity exports and by providing markets for East Central European and Balkan manufactured exports, many of which were of poor quality and/or design and could not easily have been sold elsewhere. In addition, in an endeavour to make the new economic systems less rigid and more palatable, the Soviet regime also allowed the East Central European and Balkan states greater leeway to chart their own courses towards 'socialism' and to humour and conciliate their citizens, although Moscow still laid down the overall political and economic parameters and insisted upon unswerving adherence to the Warsaw Pact and the so-called 'leading role' of the Communist parties. Officially, 'national roads to socialism' were deemed necessary and permissible, but Western-style political pluralism was not. On the whole, however, the increased room for manoeuvre granted to the East Central European and Balkan Communist regimes enhanced public confidence in their capacity to deliver advances in social and economic welfare. So-called 'national Communism' was also an attempt to cultivate specifically 'national' support and allegiances in order to remedy the general lack of legitimacy of several (some would say all) of the Communist regimes, especially those that owed their existence mainly to Soviet political or military interventions and hegemony in East Central Europe and the eastern Balkans.

By its very nature, 'national Communism' developed or found expression in very diverse 'national' forms. Therefore, the most appropriate way to convey what it meant is to provide brief vignettes of the forms it took in each of the East Central European and Balkan Communist states.

'NATIONAL COMMUNISM' IN POLAND UNDER WLADISLAW GOMULKA, 1956 TO 1970

By the early 1960s the Gomulka regime had become the epitome of 'national Communism'. Since 1956 the ruling party had forsworn forced collectivization of agriculture, relaxed travel and publishing restrictions, conciliated Poland's overwhelmingly Catholic workers, peasants and intellectuals, and forged a mutually advantageous *modus vivendi* with the still powerful Roman Catholic Church, whose Polish primate Cardinal Wyszynski had been released from prison (like Gomulka himself) in 1956. Since then, the state had relaxed its control of ecclesiastical appointments, religious instruction in the Catholic faith had been restored in the schools, Catholic lay organizations had been licensed to publish their own newspapers and Catholic chaplains had been appointed to state hospitals and prisons. In return, the Church implicitly undertook not to rock the boat politically and to be a force for political and social restraint and moderation. Poland's Roman Catholicism was allowed to flourish, not just as the principal focus and ingredient of national identity, but as the major legally permitted alternative set of beliefs and values which could compete with official Marxism-Leninism and atheism.

At the same time, Gomulka's grandiose industrial projects (including the development of giant steelworks, shipyards and coal mines) enhanced Poland's international standing and national self-esteem. By the mid-1960s, however, he was succumbing to delusions of Polish grandeur and to old-fashioned neo-Stalinist authoritarianism. He became increasingly out of touch with the problems and hardships experienced by ordinary citizens in an over-centralized, lopsided and severely strained economy. In the end the heavy-handed suppression of student unrest in the spring and summer of 1968 and of workers' strikes and mass protests in Poland's Baltic ports and shipyards two years later precipitated Gomulka's removal from office in December 1970.

'NATIONAL COMMUNISM' IN THE GERMAN DEMOCRATIC REPUBLIC (GDR) UNDER WALTER ULBRICHT (1953–71) AND ERICH HONECKER (1971–89)

The most paradoxical manifestations of 'national Communism' occurred in the German Democratic Republic, the European state that was most conspicuously lacking in either national or international legitimacy and support. It was an entirely artificial creation, arising out of the defeat and subsequent partition of the Third Reich at the hands of the victorious Allied Powers. It was sometimes portrayed as a new incarnation of the erstwhile Kingdoms of Prussia and Saxony. In reality, however, large swathes of the former Prussian and Saxon 'homelands' had been permanently lost to Poland, Czechoslovakia and the Soviet Union. Furthermore, the East German Communist regime initially dissociated itself from the rather murky and disreputable Prussian past, preferring instead to present itself as the 'new broom' that would rid or 'cleanse' the 'eastern zone' of Germany of that severely tainted legacy, whereas the (West) German Federal Republic was allegedly controlled by the self-same capitalist 'monopolies' and 'cartels' that had repeatedly endeavoured to gain control of Europe, with such catastrophic results.

The infamous Berlin Wall was erected in 1961 in order to increase the GDR's seclusion from the outside world and to staunch an economically debilitating haemorrhage of (mainly young) professional and skilled East Germans to the West. The Wall was more than a monument to the deficiencies of the GDR. It also signalled the determination of the East German regime to win at least a semblance of legitimacy, popular support and public acceptance, by making a serious attempt to catch up with and surpass West Germany both economically and in terms of its social, cultural and sporting provisions and achievements, by emphasizing the German provenance of Marxism, and by presenting the GDR as the most 'advanced' Marxist-Leninist state and as a custodian of Marxist 'orthodoxy'. The bid to win popularity and legitimacy by matching and overtaking West German living standards was doomed from the start, especially as large numbers of East Germans were able to make direct comparisons by watching the increasingly glamorous and glamorized images of the West projected by West German television. With more justification, however, the GDR claimed to have the most educated, competent, orderly and scientific civil bureaucracy, economic planners and industrial planners in the Soviet bloc. In a belated endeavour to enhance its prestige and authority, it emphasized a conception of Marxism as 'the science of society' and of the Marxist regime as a sort of scientocracy, engaged in the 'scientific' organization and planning of the economy and society by natural and social scientists recruited on the strength of their scientific merit and credentials. This intensified the regime's efforts to draw the country's leading managers, technocrats and natural and social scientists into the ruling elite. As under the Nazi regime, the process was facilitated by the growing awareness among ambitious managers, technocrats and other professional personnel that 'loyal service' to the ruling party could bring meteoric advancement and other rewards, at the expense of those who refused to succumb to such blandishments. At least in the short term, these orientations may have enhanced the status and performance of East German industry, economic planning, science, technology, technical education, health care, sport and classical music-making, without entailing any politically risky decentralization of decision-making or relaxation of the regime's control of the economy and society. Nevertheless, the hard line and essentially cautious leadership of the GDR inadvertently offended the equally conservative Soviet leadership in 1969–71, in the wake of the August 1968 invasion of Czechoslovakia. The Brezhnev regime took exception to the increasingly headmasterly and presumptuous sermonizing and pontification of the East German party leader, Walter Ulbricht, the (heretical) reductionism of the GDR's 'scientocratic' conceptions of Marxism and of the Marxist regime, the implicit downgrading of the importance of the working class (and of non-scientific or non-technocratic party stalwarts recruited from the working class), and the corresponding dilution of orthodox Marxist-Leninist doctrine on the class basis of society and on class struggle as the prime mover of social change. According to the West German statesman Willy Brandt, 'Ulbricht rated as a persistent bore . . . German pedantry (Eastern version) reigned supreme. It can truly be said that the German bent for thoroughness received a special imprint in the GDR' (Brandt 1978: 184). In 1971 Ulbricht was replaced by a more faceless and deferential party leader, the 'master wall-builder' Erich Honecker (who remained in power until November 1989). He subsequently attempted to cultivate a more conventional form of 'national Communism' by posing as a custodian of the previously reviled heritage of Friedrich the Great's Prussia and Lutheranism. Martin Luther and Richard Wagner were promoted alongside Marx as 'national' heroes, although perhaps the only traits that all three had in common were their Germanness and their anti-Semitism (even though Marx was a Jew and Wagner feared he might be one!).

THE CZECHOSLOVAK REFORM MOVEMENT (1963–8) AND THE 'PRAGUE SPRING' OF 1968

The most widely applauded and appealing attempt to map out a distinctive 'national road to socialism' emerged during the so-called Prague Spring. The Czechoslovak reform movement of 1963–8 did not try to jettison either 'socialism' or the hegemonic 'leading role' of the Communist party, but instead sought to establish 'socialism with a human face'. The need for reform was widely accepted (not least among senior members of the Communist Party) as an antidote to the economic and political stagnation to which Czechoslovakia had succumbed by the early 1960s (in this respect, the Prague Spring was a precursor of Gorbachev's *perestroika* in the Soviet Union). The Czechoslovak economy had boomed during the 1950s, when it had successfully exported large quantities of engineering and metallurgical products to its rapidly industrializing Comecon partners, as well as to China, North Korea, India and Egypt. During the early 1960s, however, as the industrializing

Communist states became less dependent on Czechoslovak producer goods exports, Czechoslovakia's rapidly obsolescing heavy industries went into decline. At the same time, internal economic rigidities and inappropriate neo-Stalinist methods and priorities impeded attempts to develop high-technology industries and to revive and modernize the country's once renowned light industries, which had been damaged both by the expulsion of 3 million 'Sudeten' Germans from Czechoslovakia in 1945–8 and by the state's neglect of investment in light industry during the 1950s. To technocratic reformist demands for economic liberalization, led by the Communist economist Professor Ota Sik, were added intelligentsia demands for political and cultural liberalization, Slovak autonomy, complete rehabilitation of victims of the 1948–52 purges, and the restoration of the German-speaking Czech-Jewish writer Franz Kafka (1883–1924) to a place of honour in the pantheon of great Czechoslovak writers. The Czechoslovak reform movement culminated in the installation of the benign and liberal-minded Slovak Communist Alexander Dubcek as leader of the Czechoslovak Communist Party in January 1968, the liberal-minded 'war hero' General Ludvik Svoboda as president of Czechoslovakia in March 1968, and the liberal-minded 'reform Communist' Josef Smrkovsky as speaker of the revitalized Czechoslovak parliament in April 1968. In an attempt to prevent Czechoslovakia from being invaded by Warsaw Pact forces in the way that Hungary had been in 1956, these new Czechoslovak leaders bent over backwards not to alienate the Soviet leadership. They studiously avoided any commitments to terminate the political monopoly of the Communist Party, to withdraw Czechoslovakia from the Warsaw Pact, to de-collectivize agriculture or to restore 'capitalism' in Czechoslovakia. Nevertheless, the liberal Action Programme of April 1968, the abolition of censorship, the infectious exuberance of the 'liberated' Czech and Slovak populations, and even the very existence of the liberal-minded Dubcek regime uncomfortably exposed the hypocrisy, falsehoods and coercion on which Europe's other Communist regimes still rested.

During the night of 20–21 August 1968, following a protracted war of nerves, Czechoslovakia was invaded by a million Warsaw Pact troops. The next day Soviet officials abducted Alexander Dubcek, Josef Smrkovsky, the prime minister Oldrich Cernik and the Popular Front chairman Frantisek Kriegel to Moscow. The Warsaw Pact invasion of Czechoslovakia was launched in the name of 'proletarian internationalism'. On 25 September 1968 *Pravda* published the so-called 'Brezhnev doctrine', proclaiming that the decisions of the peoples and the Communist parties of the so-called 'socialist countries' should 'damage neither socialism in their own country nor the fundamental interests of other socialist countries', and that the suppression of 'counter-revolution' was the joint responsibility and duty of all 'socialist countries'.

As a result of intercession by President Svoboda, widespread Czechoslovak refusal to co-operate with the invaders, and Moscow's initial inability to find a hard-line collaborator capable of controlling the situation, the abducted Czechoslovak leaders were released, reinstated and given a chance to prove through initially successful appeals for restraint that they (alone) could control Czechoslovakia at that time. However, Dubcek and his colleagues were unable to prevent major public demonstrations against the Warsaw Pact occupation forces: firstly in late October 1968; again in early November 1968; then in sympathy for the self-immolation of young Jan Palach in Wenceslas Square in January 1969; and yet again in March 1969, after Czechoslovakia beat the Soviet Union in an internationally televised ice-hockey match. This last event unleashed such an uncontrollable outpouring of popular jubilation on the streets of Prague that the following month Dubcek was obliged to relinquish the Communist Party leadership to Dr Gustav Husak, a hard-line Slovak Communist and quisling. The Husak regime subsequently sacked, demoted or imprisoned several hundred thousand supporters of the Prague Spring and put Czechoslovak society into a kind of 'deep freeze', from which it did not thaw until the momentous autumn of 1989. In the meantime, most of the population withdrew into extreme privacy ('internal emigration'), consumerism, careerism, cynicism or corruption.

The Czechoslovak reform movement had been dominated by the country's relatively large and well-educated intelligentsia. This was to be a source of both strength and weakness. Its leaders were articulate and commanded great moral and intellectual respect. They displayed an unusual breadth of interests and concerns. In contrast to the Hungarian Revolution of October–November 1956, however, the Prague Spring failed to evoke large-scale peasant and working-class participation, and the Warsaw Pact invasion of Czechoslovakia in August 1968 did not meet with widespread and tenacious armed resistance from these quarters. The Prague Spring was to some extent another Revolution of the Intellectuals (like that of 1848) and that contributed to its failure. The prominent roles played by dissident intelligentsia in the Czechoslovak reform movement also made it relatively easy for Moscow to denounce it as a 'counter-revolution' directed against the interests of the working class and 'the workers' state', while the conspicuous roles played by a few Czech-Jewish intellectuals prompted slanderous Soviet allegations that the movement was part of an international Zionist conspiracy to subvert the Soviet bloc.

ENVER HOXHA'S ALBANIA: THE HERMIT STATE

One of the most extreme versions of 'national Communism' emerged in Albania. Albania is surrounded by Serbian, Montenegrin, Greek and Italian neighbours who have not only harboured 'historic' or 'strategic' claims on Albanian-inhabited territory, but have repeatedly attempted to carve up the country between them. It is therefore not surprising that Albania's local potentates have tended to look to Great Power 'patrons' and 'protectors' (the Ottoman Turks, Italy, the Soviet Union and China), before subsequently discovering or deciding that each of these putative 'protectors' was really just another would-be overlord and predator. Albania attained a precarious national independence during the interwar years, only to find itself annexed by Fascist Italy (its erstwhile 'patron') in 1939. During the early 1940s there arose rival Albanian nationalist, royalist and Communist resistance movements, which fought each other as well as the Italian occupation forces. Following the collapse of Fascist Italy in 1943, the country was invaded by the Nazis in order to prevent it from falling into Allied hands. Before long, the Allies switched their support from the ambivalent royalist and republican nationalist resistance movements to the more consistently effective and anti-fascist Communist forces led by Enver Hoxha. The latter gradually gained the upper hand and, having captured Tirana from the retreating Germans in November 1944, proceeded to establish a hard-line Communist regime. Repeated Anglo-American attempts to overthrow the Hoxha regime in 1947, 1949, 1950 and 1952 were foiled with the help of the infamous British double agent Kim Philby. He not only played a pivotal role in the organization of these Albanian adventures but also disclosed the relevant details to the Soviet security services, which in turn tipped off Hoxha, with the result that hundreds of British- and American-backed insurgents were killed or captured by the Albanian authorities virtually on arrival (Jelavich 1983b: 378–9). These operations, combined with a deepening resentment against pervasive Yugoslav Communist tutelage and interference in Albania's internal affairs, caused a rapid deterioration in Hoxha's relations with his former British, American and Yugoslav wartime allies. This helped to transform this relatively Westernized, cosmopolitan and middle-class Marxist intellectual, who had been a student in France and Belgium during the 1930s, into Europe's most paranoid and xenophobic Communist dictator. During the late 1940s and early 1950s he turned to and increasingly modelled himself upon Stalin. His severance of all links with Yugoslavia in 1948 resulted in increased Albanian dependence on Soviet economic and technical assistance during the 1950s. However, Khrushchev's famous 'secret speech' denouncing Stalin in March 1956, the Soviet invasion of Hungary in November 1956, Khrushchev's acceptance of the need for 'peaceful co-existence with the West' and the concurrent rapprochement between the Soviet Union and Yugoslavia, all contributed to Hoxha's decision to side with Mao's China against the Soviet Union during the 1960s Sino-Soviet schism. Henceforth, Hoxha denounced the Soviet Union as a 'revisionist' and 'social imperialist' power. In his memoirs, Hoxha described Stalin as having been 'kindly and considerate', whereas he portrayed Khrushchev as a 'blackmailer' who wanted to turn Albania into a 'fruit-growing colony'. Soviet tutelage and assistance gave way to reliance on Chinese economic aid and technicians during the 1960s. All the while Albania continued to develop a modern education system, agriculture (including irrigation), hydro-electric power and some large-scale centrally planned extractive and processing industries, but not much else. Under Hoxha, Albania avoided the so-called 'capitalist scourges' of unemployment, inflation, income tax, private cars, pop music, blue jeans, short skirts, pornography, foreign investment, foreign credits and external debt. Adult illiteracy rates were reduced from about 85 per cent (in 1938) to less than 10 per cent within the space of just two generations, while average life expectancy rose from thirty-eight (in 1938) to seventy-one (in 1985). However, under Hoxha Albanian society became highly regimented and living standards remained very low. Taking his cue from Mao's China, Hoxha inaugurated an egalitarian 'proletarian cultural revolution' and radical programmes of 'workers' control' in 1966. In 1967 he proceeded to ban foreign travel, Western influences and all religious institutions and practices, while proclaiming Albania to be the world's first 'atheist state'. More than two thousand churches and mosques were either pulled down or turned into warehouses, clinics, classrooms or so-called 'state museums of atheism and religion', while the former clergy were either 're-educated' in prison and labour camps or forced to retire. Apart from simple emulation of the egalitarian, 'proletarian', xenophobic and anti-religious features of Mao's Proletarian Cultural Revolution (1966–9), these policies seem to have been intended to curb any potential threats to national unity and state security and to insulate Albanians from foreign or transnational ideologies and cultural influences. During the 1960s and 1970s the Albanian economy, education system and health services continued to develop, but Hoxha's autarkic, xenophobic, isolationist policies and excessive regulation and regimentation of society eventually engendered severe forms of economic, social and political stagnation and corruption, especially after he severed relations with China in 1978, having accused the new post-Maoist leadership of succumbing to capitalism and 'social revisionism'.

'NATIONAL COMMUNISM' IN ROMANIA UNDER GHEORGHE GHEORGHIU-DEJ (1952–65) AND NICOLAE CEAUSESCU (1965–89)

In Romania 'national Communism' manifested itself partly as a reassertion of interwar traditions of economic nationalism, encapsulated in the Bratianu Liberals' slogan *Prin noi insine* ('By ourselves alone'), and partly in reaction to the overbearing conduct of the Soviet regime and its Romanian 'sepoys' towards Romania from 1944 to 1952, during the ascendancy of Petru Groza and a coterie of so-called 'Moscow Communists' (Ana Pauker, Emil Bodnaras, Vasile Luca and Teohary Georgescu). These 'Moscow Communists' were former Romanian exiles who had spent the early 1940s in Moscow, where they had been groomed by the Soviet regime as the future rulers of a Soviet 'client state'. In 1952, however, the so-called 'Moscow Communists' were ousted by resentful and hitherto subordinate 'home Communists', headed by the Communist Party leader Gheorghe Gheorghiu-Dej and some of his wartime associates (Chivu Stoica, Ion Gheorghe Maurer and the then almost unknown Nicolae Ceausescu). They had spent much of the Second World War together in various Romanian prisons, where they had forged close personal ties. Aside from purging the widely reviled 'Moscow Communists', their decisive first step was to dissolve the unpopular joint Soviet–Romanian companies ('Sovroms') which had been established in order to exploit Romania's natural wealth with the 'assistance' of Soviet capital, technology and technical personnel – and, in large measure, for Soviet benefit. In addition, partly as a reward for 'loyal' (perhaps even enthusiastic) Romanian participation in the armed suppression of the Hungarian Revolution of October–November 1956, the ascendant 'native Communists' secured the full withdrawal of the Soviet military forces which had been stationed in Romania since late 1944. Having thus been freed from the permanent presence of Soviet 'occupation forces' (with 1962 being the last year in which Warsaw Pact military exercises were held on Romanian territory), during the early 1960s Romania's new 'home Communist' rulers angrily rejected Comecon proposals that their relatively underdeveloped country should specialize in the production and exportation of primary products and import more sophisticated manufactures from its more industrialized Comecon partners instead of attempting to develop a high-tech industrial base of its own.

There was continued emphasis on autarkic ('self-reliant') development of heavy industries such as steel, oil and chemicals under Nicolae Ceausescu, who smoothly succeeded Gheorghiu-Dej as Communist Party leader in 1965. In contrast to other European members of Comecon, Ceausescu refused to break off relations either with China (during the 1960s Sino-Soviet schism) or with Israel (over the Arab–Israeli War of 1967). Furthermore, in a speech to 100,000 people assembled in the Piata Republicii on 21 August 1968, Ceausescu condemned the Warsaw Pact invasion of Czechoslovakia, in which his regime refused to participate (Catchlove 1972: 108–9). This courageous stance initially exacerbated fears that independent-minded and militarily vulnerable Romania could be invaded even more easily than either Czechoslovakia or Hungary, but it considerably enhanced Ceausescu's domestic and international reputation. There was also a temporary relaxation of the censorship of books, films and plays, an upsurge in the screening of Western films and a more enduring rehabilitation of non-Communist literary classics. Consequently, Ceausescu was courted not merely by China and Israel, but also by the West, which for a time mistook his nationalism for liberalism and regarded him as a useful thorn in the Soviet Union's side. Nevertheless, Ceausescu's Romania remained a hard-line Stalinist regime in terms of its domestic policies and priorities, and it degenerated into a particularly venal, inbred, incompetent and paranoid 'socialism in one family', as Ceausescu's extended family gradually monopolized the perquisites of office and cracked down on anyone who dared to criticize them for doing so. By the 1970s Ceausescu was beginning to exhibit symptoms of 'obsessive compulsive despotic disorder'.

'NATIONAL COMMUNISM' IN BULGARIA UNDER TODOR ZHIVKOV (1956 89)

Like Romania, Communist Bulgaria was initially ruled by so-called 'Moscow Communists', who had taken refuge in Moscow during the Second World War. In this case they were headed by some quite high-ranking figures in the international Communist movement, most notably Georgi Dimitrov, who had won international fame as an outspoken defendant in Hitler's Reichstag fire show trial in 1934 and as president of the Communist International (Comintern) from 1935 to 1943, before serving as prime minister of Bulgaria from 1947 until his (natural) death in 1949. He was succeeded as prime minister by his brother-in-law, Vulko Chervenkov (1949–56). Nevertheless, as in Romania, during the 1950s the 'Moscow Communists' were gradually ousted by so-called 'home Communists' led by Todor Zhivkov, who had spent the war years in Bulgaria and served as leader of the Bulgarian Communist Party from 1954 to 1989. However, in spite of his assiduous promotion of 'native Communists' and certain Bulgarian writers and musicians, his partial adoption of nationalist political and historical rhetoric, and his subsequent harassment of ethnic minorities such as Pomaks (Islamicized Slavs), the Roma (Gypsies) and Turks, in his external relations Zhivkov did not emulate the more overtly nationalistic posturing of Romania's 'home Communists'. As a largely Slavic and Eastern Orthodox state with a national language very close to Russian, Bulgaria had long regarded Russia as a patron and protector. When Comecon began to promote increased economic specialization among its member states in 1962, Bulgaria readily accepted its *assigned role* as a major supplier of fresh and processed Mediterranean agricultural and horticultural products to the Soviet Union and East Central Europe. (The foundations for successful production and exportation of relatively lucrative and intensive agricultural and horticultural products had already been laid during the 1930s – see pp. 357–7). In return for this and for Zhivkov's unwavering slavish 'loyalty' to the Soviet Union on international and doctrinal matters, such as the invasion of Czechoslovakia and the severance of relations with China and Israel, Bulgaria received steadily increasing deliveries of subsidized Soviet fuels and raw materials, industrial equipment, nuclear power plants and technological assistance, much of which facilitated Bulgarian industrialization.

'REFRIGERATOR COMMUNISM' IN HUNGARY UNDER JANOS KADAR, 1961–88

'National Communism' developed most successfully in Hungary under Janos Kadar, the Communist Party leader who had participated in the Soviet invasion of his own country in November 1956 and remained in power until May 1988. From late 1961 onward, after political repression and the re-collectivization of Hungarian agriculture had brutally but effectively reimposed party control and persuaded the Soviet regime that its new Hungarian 'collaborators' had put their political house in order, Kadar offered an olive branch to the Hungarian intelligentsia, working class, peasantry and even Catholics by promulgating the slogan 'those who are not against us are with us'. To this end, political censorship and travel restrictions were progressively relaxed, the political police were reined in, there was increased observance of due legal process and the rule of law, the state negotiated a concordat with the Roman Catholic Church (in 1964) and most of Hungary's political prisoners were gradually amnestied, released and rehabilitated. In effect, Kadar offered Hungarians increased economic and cultural freeedom as a substitute for more radical changes in the country's political system. This 'pact with the Devil' particularly appealed to those who were weary of revolutionary upheaval, repression, privation and anxiety about the future. In addition, non-party luminaries were increasingly encouraged to play prominent roles in intellectual and cultural life, in public administration and in programmes of economic reform. In their eagerness to expand and to take full advantage of the new freedoms, Hungarian writers, film-makers and musicians did much to repair and restore their country's international standing. Ironically, the unsavoury origins of the Kadar regime also gave it a latent advantage. More than 85 per cent of the 800,000 people who were members of the ruling party in the autumn of 1956 had left it by 1958 (Molnar 1971: 251). Thus the need and the opportunity to rebuild the ruling party in his own image helped Kadar to retain full control of the pace, direction and extent of his liberalization and reform programmes. This enabled him largely to avoid (or at least contain within safe limits) potentially hazardous infighting between hard-line 'dogmatists' and reforming 'revisionists' within the governing elite. (Nevertheless, conflicts of this sort did contribute to a temporary setback in the reform process during the 1970s and to the regime's final downfall in 1988–9.) Furthermore, the fact that Kadar was so clearly the master of his own house made him invaluable, perhaps even indispensable, to the Soviet leadership, which therefore gave him a relatively free hand to pursue liberalization and reform in accordance with his own judgement of what was politically acceptable and sustainable.

In the rural sector, which still accounted for about half of Hungary's population in the 1960s, the new collective farms were granted unprecedented commercial and managerial autonomy in recognition of their (hitherto ignored) formal legal status as autonomous self-managed agricultural producers' co-operatives. Peasant hostility to collectivization, evinced by a mass exodus from collective farms in 1956, was also mollified by official encouragement of private side-lines or by-employments within the re-collectivized sector, by the resultant proliferation of rural industrial co-operatives and by a rapid expansion of rural services and amenities. The collective farmers responded by vigorously expanding Hungary's agricultural production and exports, especially food and wine exports to Western markets, thus reinforcing the revival in Hungary's international visibility and standing. During the 1960s food and drinks production provided one-third of Hungarian employment and gross material product and nearly half of the country's hard currency earnings (Bideleux 1987: 188). Agriculture was in fact the seedbed of Hungary's so-called 'market socialism', as the new commercial and managerial freedoms which produced such successful results in this sector were gradually extended to the food-processing, catering, retailing, personal services and handicrafts sectors. Then in January 1968, while Soviet and Western attention was nervously fixed upon the more dramatic political and economic changes that were being introduced in neighbouring Czecho-slovakia, the Kadar regime quietly inaugurated a comprehensive and carefully prepared New Economic Mechanism in Hungary. Henceforth, industrial productivity growth, innovation and responsiveness were to be promoted by encouraging industrial enterprises to establish direct con-tractual relations with one another and with their final customers at home and abroad, to become self-financing, and to use repayble interest-bearing credits in place of outright grants from the state budget. State subsidies were sharply reduced and mandatory central directives and centralized allo-cation of supplies were largely superseded by indirect economic regulators, such as fiscal and mon-etary instruments, credit policy, wage and price controls, foreign trade licences and multiple exchange rates. Consequently, by 1971 manufacturing enterprises were funding two-thirds of their fixed investment, mandatory output targets had been largely abandoned, only 3 to 4 per cent of the 'intermediate' (producer) goods used by industry were centrally allocated and Hungary had ceased to be a command economy, even though large-scale state industry remained state owned (Granick 1975: 242–82). As a counter-weight to the increased commercial and financial autonomy and powers of enterprise managers, the still party-controlled trade unions were exhorted to become more active in defending and representing workers' interests. Indeed, the 1967 labour code gave them a regularly used right to veto some management decisions and unions retained major roles in national policy-making, in the maintenance of labour discipline and in the administration of holi-days, sick leave and social welfare benefits. Enterprise managers were neither empowered nor per-mitted to dismiss workers at will, and industrial over-manning and inefficiency were supposed to be reduced mainly through mergers and redeployment rather than through socially disruptive and politically hazardous plant closures and dismissals. Nevertheless, in spite of fears that the new system would be plagued by labour immobility, labour turnover averaged 32–36 per cent per annum from 1968 to 1971 (pp 245–7). Moreover, the worker's lot was far from being a bed of roses. The sheer size of Hungarian industrial enterprises was more conducive to hierarchy, inequality and workers' alienation than to the growth of workers' participation, control and contentment, as emphasized by Miklos Haraszti in his famous report on the soulless work regime at the Red Star tractor factory (Haraszti 1977). By 1973 Hungary had, on average, 1,070 employees per industrial enterprise, which was more than ten times the average for many Western states (Bideleux 1987: 147).

All the same, many Hungarians prospered under Kadar's reforming rule. For some people, Kadarism signified a purely materialistic 'refrigerator Communism': better food, consumer dura-bles, fashion goods, weekend cottages in the countryside and foreign travel. Yet for others it also held out the promise of a spiritual release from the grim repressiveness and restrictions of Stalinism and the initial post-1956 regime. Within the limits dictated by prudence and by memories of 1956, it allowed the natural energy, ebullience and creativity of the Hungarian people to effervesce into economic and cultural achievement. However, the Kadarist social contract was very vulnerable, and it is perhaps remarkable that it survived for so long. There was an ever-present danger that the economic and cultural fermentation which it both required and evoked could bubble out of control, outgrowing the political limits set by Kadar and by Hungary's Soviet overlords. Most Hungarians realized that their country was constantly 'on probation', at least during the 1960s and 1970s, and this was a source of deep-seated resentments which eventually burst out into the open in the late 1980s. Furthermore, in owing its origin to a Soviet military intervention, and in being unable to admit the truth about the course of events from October 1956 up to the execution of Imre Nagy on 16 June 1959, the Kadar regime always lacked political legitimacy. Its survival therefore depended upon a qualified and pragmatic popular acceptance of its promise of limited and conditional liberalization and sustained increases in economic prosperity. This made the regime and its small, mineral-deficient economy exceptionally vulnerable to external factors which were beyond Kadar's control, especially to international economic fluctuations.

YUGOSLAVIA UNDER 'WORKERS SELF-MANAGEMENT' AND 'MARKET SOCIALISM', 1950s–1980s

The circumstances of its birth gave Marshal Tito's Yugoslav Communist regime the freedom and authority to define its own distinctive 'Yugoslav road to socialism'. Yugoslavia had been liberated from fascism by the often heroic resistance of a million Communist-led Partisans, with meagre assistance from the West, the Soviet Union and the Serbian nationalist Cetniks. The Communists created the one Yugoslav movement that succeeded in transcending the country's perilous religious and ethnic divisions and drawing substantial support from each of its constituent ethnic groups. At first, however, their hard-won 'liberation' of Yugoslavia transformed the leading Yugoslav Communists into headstrong, unremitting ultra-Stalinists. Against Stalin's wishes, they actively supported the Communist side in the Greek Civil War (1945–9), lorded it over Hoxha's Albania and talked of creating a Communist-ruled Balkan Federation strong enough to stand up to Soviet hegemonism. In 1947, contrary to Soviet advice, the Yugoslav leadership launched the premature and over-ambitious Five-Year Plan for rapid state-directed development of heavy industries and mechanized large-scale collective agriculture, for which they expected the Soviet Union to provide a large part of the requisite resources (especially fuels, equipment, capital and technical assistance). This Stalinist development strategy was singularly inappropriate for Yugoslavia, which lacked an appropriate human and natural resource base. The mainly mountainous terrain did not readily lend itself to large-scale mechanized cultivation, the requisite economic and political centralization could only revive interwar resentments of Serbian domination, and it was highly unlikely that peasants who had successfully resisted fascism would now meekly submit to forced collectivization. When Tito's regime refused to come to heel, Yugoslavia was 'excommunicated' from the Soviet bloc in 1948 – not as the result of any developmental or ideological heterodoxy, but for getting 'too big for its boots' and trying to be even more Stalinist than Stalin. Deprived of crucial imports and technical assistance from the Soviet Union and Czechoslovakia, the Yugoslav economy was plunged into crisis. Initial headstrong attempts to persevere with ultra-Stalinism unaided from 1948 to 1950 actually deepened the crisis still further, and Tito's regime probably survived only because it was unexpectedly bailed out by massive Western aid (amounting to more than US$2 billion at 1950s prices) during the 1950s. (By way of comparison, American Marshall Aid to the whole of Western Europe came to US$13 billion at early 1950s prices.)

The quest for a distinctively Yugoslav road to socialism began after the ignominious collapse of Tito's initial over-ambitious ultra-Stalinism in 1950. Henceforth, to have any real chance of success, the Communist regime would have to build on its vaunted capacity to transcend Yugoslavia's religious and ethnic divisions. Since no ethnic group constituted an absolute majority of the population, a Soviet-style federation dominated by the largest ethnic group would have been neither acceptable nor workable in a country which had been riven by inter-ethnic and inter-denominational strife as recently as the Second World War. That made it all the more vital to move towards a system that could devolve decision-making to local or regional institutions, in the hope that this would assist and encourage the diverse nations living within the Yugoslav Federation to live and work together peacefully and constructively. However, since mere regional devolution could just as easily have reinforced the strong centrifugal tendencies in Yugoslav society, there was an even stronger case for devolving power to the lowest possible levels, that is to individual enterprises and local communes. This came to be seen as the framework most capable of peaceably holding Yugoslavia together.

An embryonic system of 'workers self-management' emerged in 1950, when elected workers councils with key roles in enterprise management were established in almost all industrial enterprises employing more than thirty workers each. By 1952 there were workers councils in 8,800 industrial enterprises, including 4,187 enterprises with fewer than thirty workers apiece. Between them these employed more than a million workers. According to the June 1950 Basic Law on workers councils, 'state economic enterprises, as the property of the people, shall be managed by working collectives on behalf of the social community, within the framework of the state economic plan . . . Working collectives will exercise this right of management through the workers councils' (quoted in Singleton 1976: 126).

The development of Western and Algerian ideas on workers' participation and industrial democracy and Tito's central role in the launching of the non-aligned movement in 1955 provided additional motives for distancing his own Communist regime doctrinally from those of the Soviet bloc. The 1958 Programme of the League of Communists of Yugoslavia (as the party was renamed in 1953) warned that managing the economy and society 'exclusively through the state apparatus inevitably leads to greater centralization of power' and thence to 'bureaucratic-étatist deformities' and the betrayal of socialism. The preferred 'way out' of the cul-de-sac of state socialism was to instigate forms of direct participatory democracy and direct producers' control of the means of production. Thus the state was expected gradually to 'wither away' as socialist consciousness and new autonomous forms of collectivism developed. The state was intended to become 'less an instrument of coercion and more and more an instrument of social self-government, based on the consciousness of the common material interests of working people and on the concrete needs of their producing organizations'. The League of Communists of Yugoslavia (the SKJ) was still expected 'to give ideological guidance in the process of socialist development . . . But this does not confer any special prerogatives or privileges on members of the League' (quoted in Singleton 1976: 135–6). To these ends, compulsory deliveries of farm produce to the state were discontinued in 1950, enterprise managers ceased to be central government appointees after 1951, rural collectivization and command planning were finally abandoned in 1952, and public administration was largely devolved to local communes and the constituent republics of the Yugoslav Federation in 1953, leaving only five ministries (employing less than 4 per cent of public officials) in the hands of central government. The 1963 Constitution extended the principle of 'self-management' to education, health and social administration, introduced 'rotation' of all elective offices (other than Tito's 'presidency for life') and prohibited individuals from simultaneously holding office in the state apparatus and in the SKJ or in both federal and republican bodies. Yet until 1965, for the most part, Yugoslavia continued to be managed from the centre and in accordance with political rather than economic criteria, while in practice decentralization was mainly to republics and local communes rather than to enterprises. Most prices were still regulated by central or republican authorities and banks, credit, foreign trade and most investment remained centrally controlled. Most enterprise directors continued to be political appointees, chosen through elaborate systems of patronage and clientelism, rather than freely elected representatives of the workforce. Indeed, so long as enterprises had little political or commercial autonomy, there was not much scope for genuine workers' self-management.

During 1965 and 1966, however, the champions of full decentralization and enterprise autonomy decisively outmanoeuvred and defeated the centralizers (who were headed by the Serb security chief Alexander Rankovic) and breathed new life into the hitherto cosmetic or even moribund system of self-management. During the 1960s and 1970s Tito's increasingly decentralized and confederal Yugoslavia managed to achieve very rapid economic growth, which was buoyed up by booming tourism earnings and large remittances from emigrants to Western Europe (mainly from so-called *Gastarbeiter* working in Germany, Austria and Switzerland).

Table 32.1   Official figures for the average annual rate of growth of Gross Social Product in Yugoslavia, 1952–80

Years	Growth (%)
1952–62	8.3
1961–5	6.8
1966–70	5.7
1971–5	5.9
1976–80	5.2

Source: Jeffries (1993: 319).

The impressive expansion of the Yugoslav economy during the 1960s aroused widespread international interest in its systems and doctrines of 'self-management' and 'market socialism', even among non-Marxists. Yugoslavia was widely acclaimed as having hit upon a viable 'third way' between Communism and capitalism, and many Western as well as Communist bloc and Third World economists elaborated increasingly sophisticated theories of so-called 'Illyrian models' of 'market socialism' and 'workers' self-management' and theoretical models of the behaviour of 'self-managed' enterprises.

The Tito regime also managed to contain the demands for even greater autonomy which erupted in (largely Albanian) Kosova in 1968 (and again in 1981) and in Croatia from 1970 to 1972. At least until Tito's death in 1980, it seemed that rampant consumerism, judicious federalism and the Marshal's firm hand and 'divide and rule' tactics were keeping the upper hand over potentially fractious and fratricidal sectarianism and 'ethnic' nationalism. There was widespread peaceful co-existence, inter-marriage and mutual reconciliation between diverse ethnic and religious communities, most notably in Bosnia-Herzegovina, and there were some genuine grounds for hope that inter-ethnic hatreds were being assuaged by constructive achievement and that secularization was at last taking the sting out of age-old religious tensions.

Nevertheless, critics claimed that full-blown self-management (lasting from 1965 to 1974) gave insufficiently accountable and often monopolistic enterprises undue licence to do as they pleased, with highly inflationary, inegalitarian and anti-social consequences, even when enterprise directors took decisions in collusion with their workers. Moreover, officially registered unemployment rose from an average of 7 per cent of the workforce in the 1960s to an average of 10 per cent in the 1970s and 13 per cent in the 1980s. Therefore, from 1974 onwards, enterprises were to varying degrees circumscribed by various investment and price controls, planning agreements, 'social compacts' and macro-economic stabilization programmes, in (ultimately unsuccessful) endeavours to limit the resultant over-investment, wage inflation, excess demand, overexpansion of money supply, trade deficits and mounting foreign indebtedness. The years from 1974 to 1982 are known as the 'social planning period', because the 'social compacts' and 'self-management agreements' of those years represented compromises between centralization and decentralization. 'Social compacts' were not legally binding. They mainly covered broad policy objectives, such as prices and pay at the republican and inter-republican level, and were concluded between territorial authorities, 'economic chambers', trade unions and the Communist Party. 'Self-management agreements' were legally binding contracts dealing with investment and the delivery of goods and so on, concluded between enterprises and so-called Basic Organizations of Associated Labour. So-called 'contractual planning', which acted in conjunction with (rather than in place of) the market, involved information exchange and agreements between government authorities, trade unions and 'economic chambers' (bodies representing enterprises). After 1983 there was increased reliance on market forces and financial disciplinary measures, since 'social planning' suffered from serious problems such as collusion (in place of competition) and the difficulty of actually enforcing contracts (Ben-Ner and Neuberger 1990: 786–7).

Meanwhile, beneath a seemingly calm political exterior, local Communist potentates were cultivating and consolidating increasingly 'national' clienteles and fiefdoms within the constituent republics of the Yugoslav Federation and within Serbia's autonomous regions of Kosova and Vojvodina, which attained virtual republican status during the 1970s. These developments fuelled the centrifugal forces and aspirations which were eventually to tear Yugoslavia apart during the early 1990s (almost as brutally as they had done during the early 1940s). The violent disintegration of the SFRY in 1990–2 might conceivably have been avoided if its Communist rulers (particularly at the republican level) had not mobilized, manipulated and exploited 'ethnic' nationalism for their own purposes, especially in order to cling to power by fomenting 'states of emergency' which served to prolong their authoritarian rule (see pp. 519–25). The gradual metamorphosis of Yugoslavia's republic-level Communist politicians into authoritarian nationalist rulers was accomplished with consummate Machiavellian skill, but at a terrible human and economic cost. The noxious legacies could take decades to overcome.

THE DARK SIDE OF 'NATIONAL COMMUNISM'

Thus the evolution of the East Central European and Balkan Communist regimes towards 'national Communism' was, in varying degrees, a retrograde rather than a progressive trend. It was naively welcomed by many myopic Western commentators as a retreat from the rigours of Communist internationalism and as an attempt to gain greater political legitimacy by pandering to deep-rooted (and mostly brutish) nationalist traditions and aspirations. However, it also paved the way for increased discrimination and fulmination against ethnic and religious minorities, be they Jews, Gypsies, Turks, Magyars, Albanians or whatever, and it made the eventual transitions to 'post-Communism' much nastier and more fraught with dangers of intolerance, authoritarianism, demagogy and inter-communal violence. As Godfrey Hodgson remarked in 1991, 'Everywhere reconstruction is hindered by the revival of nationalism; not only the jealousies of nation states, but the ancient aspirations and resentments of the buried nations and provinces that were treated as so many estates to be exploited by the Russian, German, Austro-Hungarian, Turkish, Nazi and Stalinist empires' (writing in *The Independent on Sunday*, 13 October 1991). The greatest bounties that Communism could have offered this region were rooted in its formal 'internationalist' commitment to the goal of transcending inter-ethnic and inter-denominational jealousies and conflicts, which were the bane of Eastern Central Europe and the Balkans during the twentieth century. Communist rule did initially suppress, contain or restrain the destructive nationalist and religious aspirations of the interwar period and the early 1940s. Even before the gradual abandonment of 'internationalism' in favour of 'national Communism', however, the Stalinist purges of 1948–52 were strongly influenced by crude 'ethnic' stereotyping, hatreds and vendettas. In succumbing to nationalist demagogy and mindsets, the Communist regimes muffed their main chance to do something creditable in this fatally riven region.

THE INTERNATIONAL SOCIALIST DIVISION OF LABOUR, 1960–8

During the 1960s East Central European economists and reformers increasingly looked to the development of foreign trade and other external economic relations as important ways of increasing economic specialization, economies of scale, factor productivity and the returns on investment. This was seen as a basis for more 'intensive' patterns of economic growth, making more productive use of more slowly growing resource inputs, now that the previous potential and scope for 'extensive'economic growth had been largely exhausted. They were also prodded in this direction by the example of Western Europe (which was achieving impressive increases in output and factor productivity partly on the basis of increased economic integration) as well as by fears that East Central European access to West European markets might in time be curtailed by the 'group preferences' of the European Community (Brabant 1989: 65).

Mainly for these reasons, the December 1961 Council Session of Comecon approved the Basic Principles of the International Socialist Division of Labour. These proclaimed that each socialist country would draw up its own economic development plan on the basis of 'the concrete conditions in the given country, the political and economic goals set out by the Communist and Workers Parties, and the needs and potentialities of all the socialist countries', thus combining 'the development of each national economy with the development and consolidation of the world economic system of socialism as a whole'. The explicit objectives of this International Socialist Division of Labour were 'more efficient social production, a higher rate of economic growth, higher living standards. . . industrialization and gradual removal of historical differences in economic development levels of the socialist countries, and the creation of a material basis for their more-or-less simultaneous transition to Communism'. (Most of the text is reproduced in Kaser 1967: 249–54.) The planned International Socialist Division of Labour would contribute to 'the maximum utilization of the advantages of the socialist world system . . . the determination of correct proportions in the national economy of each country . . . the rational location of production . . . the effective utilization of labour and material resources, and . . . the strengthening of the defensive power of the socialist camp'(quoted in Brabant 1989: 67). While the 'principal means' of realizing these objectives would continue to be the 'coordination of economic plans', this would have to be 'strong and stable' since 'any deviation, even by a single country, would inevitably lead to disturbances in the economic cycle in the other socialist countries' (Kaser 1967: 251). More controversially, the Basic Principles talked of 'concentrating production of similar products in one or several socialist countries', exploring 'the possibilities for further specialization in agricultural production' and 'resultant recommendations for specialization and cooperation' (pp. 252–4). This appeared to imply that some states could be asked to concentrate on agriculture while others would specialize in industry. In November 1962, moreover, Khrushchev proclaimed the need for 'a common single planning organ . . . composed of representatives of all countries coming to CMEA' (quoted in Smith 1983: 183).

In practice, however, the Comecon states did little to implement the Basic Principles, whose implicit supranationalism was resisted by Czechoslovakia, Hungary, Poland and, most volubly, Romania (Brabant 1989: 69–70). They generated more vituperation than integration. Romania's increasingly nationalistic Communist elite was committed to autarkic forced industrialization and indignantly denied that Comecon had any right to 'recommend' a self-respecting sovereign state to specialize in agriculture. In April 1964 the Central Committee of the Romanian Communist Party issued a public declaration that industry, not agriculture, held the key to the 'harmonious, balanced and ever-ascending . . . growth of the whole national economy' and that the proposed transfer of some economic responsibilities 'from the competence of the respective state' to supranational bodies was unacceptable for two main reasons: (i) 'The planned management of the national economy is one of the fundamental, essential, inalienable attributes of the sovereignty of the socialist state' and the chief means by which it 'achieves its political and socio-economic objectives'; and (ii) 'The state plan is one and indivisible', since centrally planned 'management of the national economy as a whole is not possible if the questions of managing some branches or enterprises are . . . transferred to extra-state bodies'. (The full text is reproduced in Vaughan 1976: 148–50.) In a sense, this was a new unilateral declaration of Romanian independence.

Beyond the nationalist claptrap there lurked serious operational considerations. Comprehensive *national* economic planning really did depend upon untrammelled *national* economic sovereignty. It was becoming increasingly clear to East Central European and Balkan economists that the proposed surrender of various planning and co-ordinating functions to Comecon agencies would not only further impair national economic planning, but also reproduce at the supranational level (and in greatly magnified forms) most of the rigidities, diseconomies, disincentives and malfunctions that already bedevilled central planning at the national level (Brabant 1989: 70). Politically, it would have increased the preponderance of Soviet predilections over those of its much smaller Balkan and East Central European 'vassals'.

Ironically, the Soviet Union had declined to impose supranational planning and a thoroughgoing international socialist division of labour in the early 1950s, when it still had the power to do just that, whereas by the early 1960s the Soviet leadership had acquired the will but forfeited the power to do so (Wiles 1968: 311). Furthermore, the emergence of major East Central European reform movements between 1961 and 1968, along with the more enduring expansion of East–West trade and 'co-operation', somewhat reduced the pressure to develop intra-CMEA 'co-operation' and integration, which could indeed have restricted East Central European and Balkan room for manoeuvre (both in the pursuit of domestic economic restructuring and in the cultivation of West European economic partners). Conversely, the significant 1960s expansion of East–West economic relations (including subcontracting and the importation of 'turnkey' installations) seemed to reduce 'the need to adapt the CMEA economic structures to the fundamental requirements of more ambitious economic reforms' (Brabant 1989: 77). It was in many ways easier and more immediately rewarding for the centrally planned economies to expand their links with the West than with each other. This was not merely the line of least resistance, but also the avenue of maximum advantage, as East–West trade offered increased access to much-needed Western products, equipment, technology, finance, design and more modern production, management and marketing systems.

Intra-CMEA co-operation, specialization and integration did nonetheless make some headway during the 1960s, mainly by side-stepping the resistance of 'national' vested interests. There were expanded roles for Comecon's sectoral and functional standing commissions, mirroring sectoral and 'neo-functionalist' approaches to West European integration. Six new standing commissions were established, including ones to deal with standardization, scientific and technical co-operation, statistics, and currency and finance. This was supplemented by increased reliance on bilateral and trilateral joint ventures and the exchange of East Central European and Balkan manufactures, equipment and foodstuffs for Soviet oil, gas, coal, metal ores and nuclear technology. Comecon's physical cohesion was considerably enhanced by the construction of the Druzhba (Friendship) oil pipeline, in order to increase East Central European and Balkan reliance on imported Soviet oil (and on re-exports of refined oil products to earn precious hard currency), and the Mir (Peace) electricity grid, in order to 'even out' power supplies. An International Bank for Economic Co-operation was founded in 1963, in an unsuccessful attempt to facilitate multilateral intra-CMEA 'clearing' via the new 'transferable ruble'. In 1967, moreover, Comecon adopted the so-called 'interested party principle'. This allowed individual member states simply to opt out of any Comecon project they did not like, permitting the rest to go ahead unencumbered by awkward or reluctant participants. In the last resort, a member state could veto a Comecon project or policy which was deemed to threaten its vital national interests, since Comecon's joint decision-making still rested ultimately on unanimity or consensus among 'equal' and 'sovereign' member states.

As mentioned before, the tenacious predominance of bilateralism over multilateralism could only have been overcome either by supranational central planning of Comecon as a single economy or by the adoption of market mechanisms (including convertible currencies and realistic pricing). However, the first option would have increased Soviet dominance and was therefore resisted by both the more market-orientated and the more nationalistic member states, while the second option would have allowed the more commercially minded members (Hungary, Czechoslovakia and Poland) to draw away from Comecon towards the West and was therefore unacceptable to the USSR and its 'hard-line' allies. In the long run, therefore, Comecon was destined to fall between two stools.

33 From the crisis of 1968 to the 'Revolutions of 1989'

REPRESSION, ANTI-ZIONISM AND EAST–WEST DÉTENTE

The optimism of the 1960s was seriously deflated by a crackdown on mounting student unrest and on the radical-liberal intelligentsia in Poland in March 1968 and by the Warsaw Pact invasion of Czechoslovakia in August 1968. These acts of repression were accompanied by a barrage of virulent 'anti-Zionist' propaganda orchestrated by the Soviet Union. In the wake of the defeat of the Soviet Union's Arab allies during the six day Arab–Israeli War of June 1967, it was alleged that 'Zionist' Jews in Israel, the United States and the Soviet bloc were acting as agents of American imperialism in a three-pronged international conspiracy to subvert Communist rule in the eastern half of Europe, to deny the Palestinians an independent homeland and to provide pretexts for the US presence and US interventions in the Middle East. Accordingly the Soviet media and other 'anti-Zionist' publications highlighted and wilfully exaggerated the important (but far from hegemonic) role played by a few Jewish intellectuals, dissidents and 'refuseniks' (Jews who had been refused permission to emigrate) in the eastern European dissident and reform movements. There was a very thin line separating Soviet 'anti-Zionism' from more traditional forms of anti-Semitism and anti-intellectualism. Official 'anti-Zionism' stirred the embers of a residual popular anti-Semitism and anti-intellectualism within the Soviet bloc (especially in Poland), thereby helping to alienate the radical-liberal intelligentsia from potential proletarian and peasant support. Indeed, 'anti-Zionism' was not just a diversionary tactic that damagingly isolated and vilified Jews, but also a means of isolating and discrediting the radical-liberal intelligentsia and dissidents in general, although Jews obviously bore the brunt of this latterday 'counter-reformation'. This inevitably fuelled Jewish fears and anxieties, with the result that many Jews who had hitherto been 'loyal' Soviet or East Central European citizens (often as doctors, scientists, lawyers, academics and journalists) or even members of the ruling Communist parties were harassed, blocked in their careers, demoralized, disillusioned and driven to seek permission to emigrate either to the West or to Israel.

Despite the widespread climate of repression, 'anti-Zionism', anti-intellectualism and demoralization in East Central Europe at the end of the 1960s, a more subdued and pragmatic optimism was rekindled in the early 1970s by the continuing reforms in Kadar's Hungary, by the intial two or three year 'honeymoon' period of political relaxation and social reconciliation which followed the accession of Edward Gierek in Poland in December 1970 and Erich Honecker in the GDR in May 1971 and, above all, by the process of East–West détente initiated by Willy Brandt's *Ostpolitik* in 1969 (reinforced by President Nixon's path-breaking visit to Moscow in 1972). West Germany's non-aggression treaties with the Soviet Union and Poland in 1970 and its state treaty with the GDR in 1972 paved the way for greatly increased East–West commerce, contacts, credit and technology transfers, as the West gradually followed Willy Brandt's lead.

As early as 1968 the West German foreign minister Willy Brandt declared his 'clear conviction that reconciliation of Poles and Germans will someday have the same historical importance as the friendship between Germany and France' (Brandt 1968: 272), although he had already formed this view long before that (Brandt 1978: 183). He also seized the opportunity presented by the Prague Spring to normalize West German relations with Czechoslovakia in 1968. But the principal thrust of his *Ostpolitik* was towards German–Polish reconciliation. On 7 December 1970, the day that he signed the treaty normalizing relations between the Federal Republic and Poland and ratifying the Oder–Neisse frontier between the two states, Brandt went down on his knees in front of the memorial to those who had died in the Warsaw Ghetto. 'This gesture, which attracted worldwide attention, was not "planned", though I had certainly debated earlier that morning how best to convey the special nature of this act of remembrance at the Ghetto monument . . . Oppressed by memories of Germany's recent history, I simply did what people do when words fail them . . . My gesture was intelligible to those willing to understand it' (p. 399). As one unnamed reporter wrote afterwards: 'Then he knelt, he who has no need to, on behalf of all those who ought to kneel but don't' (p. 399). This visit opened the way to a similar thaw in West German relations with other East Central European states, including the GDR. Another (unanticipated) effect was to deprive the Polish Communist regime and its Soviet overlord of the claim that they were defending Poland's post-1945 frontier against pent-up German revanchism.

The high-point of East–West détente was the 1975 Helsinki Final Act, which established the Conference on European Security and Co-operation (CSCE). At the time this was condemned by many Western conservatives and Cold Warriors as an abject act of 'appeasement' towards the Communist regimes of the Soviet bloc (or as another Yalta), because it ostensibly involved a general acceptance of the territorial status quo in Europe. Certainly, the Soviet Union had long advocated the holding of a major international conference to bestow international recognition on the GDR and on the post-1945 borders of Poland, and this was what it obtained at Helsinki in 1975. However, the so-called third 'basket' of the Helsinki Accords also committed all signatories to respect 'civil, economic, social, cultural and other rights and freedoms, all of which derive from the inherent dignity of the human person' (Stokes 1993: 24). They spelled out these rights and freedoms in great detail, giving East Central European, Soviet and (to lesser degrees) Balkan dissidents a legal basis on which they could challenge their governments through Helsinki Watch Committees established to monitor observance of the provisions of the Final Act. This threw Europe's Communist regimes on to the defensive. Instead of endorsing the status quo, the Final Act was 'a charter for change. Instead of legitimizing the Soviet sphere of influence, it legitimized Western intrusion into it . . . Instead of confining itself to interstate relations, it reinforced the principle that peace depends also on how states treat their people' (Davy 1992: 19).

At the time, Governor Ronald Reagan appealed to all Americans to oppose the Helsinki Final Act. Another prominent right-wing Republican Cold Warrior, Professor Richard Pipes, claimed that Helsinki 'legitimized Russia's conquests' in the Balkans and especially East Central Europe (Davy 1992: 249), as did British right-wingers such as Margaret Thatcher. Pipes even claimed that 'weariness and disillusionment with war and politics and, second, the pursuit of material wealth as a by-product of the social revolution have, between them, sapped the political will of [Western] Europe' to resist Soviet hegemonism, while Leo Labedz warned that the 'pseudo-detente which led up to Helsinki will eventually lead to the Finlandization of Western Europe as surely as Yalta resulted in the satellitization of Eastern Europe' (p. 265). The opponents of détente were regarded as 'hawks', while its defenders were labelled 'doves'. However, these labels were utterly misleading, in that 'détente was in many ways more threatening to Soviet interests than the confrontational policies advocated by the hawks' (p. 237). Ironically, the 'hawks' greatly underestimated the strength of the West, which they mistakenly saw as engaging in a process of 'moral disarmament', whereas the exact opposite was the case (p. 257). Indeed, 'without the Final Act and the Western interest it aroused, opposition in Eastern Europe would have been weaker, less coherent, easier to suppress' (p. 251).

In the longer term, by supporting the re-emergence of autonomous civil and political associations and activities and increased concern for the rule of law, Helsinki 'paved the way for a *smoother* transition to democracy when the [Communist] regimes crumbled because it had fostered alternative structures and authorities to take their place' (Davy 1992: 263). Conversely, any return to East–West confrontation (as advocated by the 'hawks') would have provided pretexts for increased repression, a siege mentality, seclusion, austerity and a renewed domestic 'freeze' within the Soviet bloc.

Why did the Soviet leadership sign a treaty which was so profoundly against its real interests? Part of the explanation was that Brezhnev, having invested so much in the Helsinki initiative, had a large personal stake in securing an agreement and Western recognition of Europe's existing frontiers, while 'the nature of the Soviet system' made it difficult for anyone to tell him that he had blundered! Brezhnev also mistakenly believed that he could simply implement the bits he liked and 'bury the rest under a mound of verbiage' (Davy 1992: 19). In addition, 'Soviet officials had also acquired a very personal stake in the Helsinki process because it enhanced their own positions and gave them the opportunity of trips to the West', while 'East European regimes had developed a strong interest in the economic and political benefits of détente' (p. 21). Furthermore, for all his failings, Brezhnev did see the dangers posed to all Europeans, East and West, by the unbridled escalation of the Cold War arms race. It was Leonid Brezhnev, *not* Mikhail Gorbachev, who first proclaimed that 'whatever may divide us, Europe is our common home. Common fate has linked us through centuries, it links us today too.' These pregnant words were uttered by Brezhnev in Berlin in November 1981, in opposition to NATO deployment of cruise missiles in Western Europe and the attendant escalation of the arms race in Europe (Stokes 1993: 74). However, it was Gorbachev who had the courage to take the Helsinki process to its logical conclusion. In 1987 he declared that 'Security can no longer be assured by military means', for 'the arms race is lowering the level of security, impairing it' (Gorbachev 1988: 141). The advent of nuclear weapons had made security indivisible. 'It is either equal security for all or none at all. Universal security in our time rests on the recognition of the right of every nation to choose its own path of social development, on the renunciation of interference in the domestic affairs of other states, on respect for others in combination with an objective self-critical view of one's own society. A nation may choose either capitalism or socialism. This is its sovereign right. Nations cannot and should not pattern their life either after the United States or the Soviet Union' (pp. 142–3). These were the additional implications that Gorbachev discerned and acted upon in the Helsinki process and in the concept of 'the common European home'. In these respects he towered above his Soviet predecessors and President Reagan, both morally and intellectually. In 1987 Gorbachev warned that the USA was seeking 'to bleed the Soviet Union white economically, to prevent us from carrying out our plans of construction by dragging us ever deeper into the quagmire of the arms race' (p. 219). The reckless expansion of nuclear arsenals 'is not our choice. It has been imposed upon us', because 'the United States is not ready to part with its hope of winning nuclear superiority' (pp. 218, 239). Gorbachev believed that, like nuclear war, the nuclear arms race was 'unwinnable' (p. 138). At the Reykjavik summit in October 1986, he warned President Reagan that 'our meeting could not produce one winner: we would both either win or lose' (p. 240). On this point, however, Gorbachev was mistaken. In the course of the 1980s, the Soviet system was forced to its knees, thereby scuppering *perestroika* and confounding Khrushchev's early 1960s boast that 'We will bury you'.

SOCIALIST ECONOMIC INTEGRATION DURING THE 1970S AND 1980s

Until the late 1960s the term 'integration' was a taboo word in Communist circles. It carried connotations of 'monopoly capitalist' collusion against workers and consumers (in the hope of postponing the elusive but long-predicted 'terminal crisis of capitalism'). Consequently, the intra-regional projects and policies of the European members of Comecon were largely confined to 'fraternal' inter-party and inter-governmental co-operation, modest 'mutual economic asssistance' and minimal *ex post facto* harmonization of national economic plans (Brabant 1989: xxi). Economic integration became Comecon's formal goal only after the 'special' Council Session of April 1969, at which Communist leaders discussed ways and means of keeping member states 'in line' and 'on side' in the aftermath of the August 1968 Warsaw Pact invasion of Czechoslovakia. Subsequent progress towards greater integration between the European members of Comecon from 1969 to 1989 was limited, not by a lack of official blueprints and declarations, but by the existence of very deep-seated barriers or impediments to integration between sovereign centrally planned economies. It was possible to attain 'hyper-integration' between Soviet republics, as these were components of a single supranational state, tightly controlled by a single centre of power. By the same token, however, inter-state integration was virtually a contradiction in terms for the centrally planned economies. Their development strategies were neither conceived nor implemented with wide-ranging economic co-operation as a central or paramount concern. Nor was Comecon ever endowed 'with the power to promote desirable or expedient dependences among its members' (Brabant 1980: 9–10). Integration within Comecon was also hindered by the extremely disparate nature of its membership, exacerbated by the admission of underdeveloped and non-European Mongolia in 1962, Cuba in 1972 and Vietnam in 1978 (as a matter of political expediency), and by the overwhelming asymmetry between the Soviet Union (a real 'superstate') and the motley assortment of small and medium-sized members. Some of these became in a sense merely extra-territorial 'appendages'or 'extensions' of the Soviet Union. Indeed, Bulgaria was sometimes described as the sixteenth Soviet republic, and there was a well-known ditty: 'Kuritsa ne ptitsa, Bolgaria ne za granitsa' (A hen is not a bird, Bulgaria is not abroad). Indeed, for many purposes, it was more meaningful to think of Comecon as an imposed monolith and (from 1955 onwards) as the economic arm of the Warsaw Pact (the only 'defensive alliance' that repeatedly invaded its own member states!), rather than as the vehicle for voluntary co-operation, mutual assistance and (belatedly) integration between 'equal' and 'sovereign' member states that it always professed to be. In 1983 the Soviet Union accounted for 88 per cent of Comecon's territory and 60 per cent of its population (Comecon 1984: 7). Soviet priorities and preferences naturally predominated and the vast disparities between the Soviet Union and the other member states inevitably fostered more suspicion and animosity than mutual trust. Intra-CMEA co-operation and integration inevitably became 'a contest in which each participant endeavoured to extract the maximum advantage at the minimum price' (Brabant 1980: 3). Hence the Soviet bloc was never quite as monolithic as its leaders (as well as many Western commentators) would have liked us to believe. Indeed, Comecon's persistent emphasis on inter-state 'co-operation' and 'mutual assistance' and on the co-ordination of national economic plans did more to *reinforce* than to reduce the primacy of individual Member States over the collectivity, while post-Stalinist 'national assertion' placed additional obstacles in the path of any far-reaching integration within Comecon. To a far greater degree than the European Community, Comecon was a *Europe des patries* or, better still (in the words that de Gaulle actually used), a *Europe des états*.

In 1989 the Balkan and East Central European members of Comecon accounted for no more than 4 per cent of world trade. These states and their enterprises endeavoured to minimize their dependence on potentially unreliable external suppliers. Comprehensive, mandatory economic planning was found to be less difficult in relatively self-sufficient and secluded economies than in ones heavily dependent on foreign trade, the volume and composition of which lay largely outside the control of national economic planners. Indeed, 'planners do not see foreign trade as a desirable pursuit in its own right but merely as an additional source of supplies, the volume and composition of which is contingent on the requirements of the production plan' (Sobell 1984: 4). In most centrally planned economies, foreign trade was legally a state monopoly, in order to safeguard state control of the economy and of the terms and extent of any foreign involvement, and it had to be channelled through cumbersome and often corrupt state agencies and foreign trade corporations. Thus it was limited to what these were willing and able to handle. This extreme institutional separation of domestic producers from foreign customers also increased the unresponsiveness of the former to the needs and desires of the latter. In addition, the use of arbitrary, over-valued multiple exchange rates typically resulted in formal accounting 'losses' on exports and profits on imports. This effectively ruled out any meaningful calculation of relative costs, economic returns and gains from trade. Endemic shortages of 'hard' currency, the inability of most state enterprises to penetrate and hold their own in internationally competitive markets, and the failure to develop convertible currencies and rational price mechanisms that could have facilitated multilateral trading brought about a predominance of bilateral trading. The volume of trade was limited to the quantities and types of products that the weaker partner could manage to export. Each partner was discouraged from running a trade surplus and this acted as a further disincentive to increase exports. Indeed, most of the better products were reserved for particular domestic projects, since producers and planners were essentially judged and rewarded in accordance with the domestic performance of high priority or high profile industries and projects, especially those of strategic importance. Consequently, with exceptions such as Soviet oil and gas, the products available for export were to a large extent unwanted 'left-overs'. The centrally planned economies thus found it difficult to trade with one another. Economic integration became even harder to achieve as the centrally planned economies became more highly industrialized and produced a wider range of products. That was a principal reason why dependence on intra-CMEA trade peaked in the early 1950s and then slowly declined until Comecon's collapse in the early 1990s.

The scope for intra-CMEA trade and integration could have been increased by stronger moves towards market mechanisms, multilateralism and currency convertibility, which would have increased the latitude for autonomous integrative forces. However, such moves were strongly resisted by most of the Communist Party and central planning hierarchies, not least because they would have downgraded the overriding priority given to defence and heavy industry (the military-industrial complex), thereby increasing the consumer orientation of these economies and allowing the more successful and market-orientated members of Comecon to reduce their economic dependence on the Soviet Union. There would also have been a loss of 'captive' markets and suppliers, while the increased exposure to international competition and market forces would have threatened the solvency and survival of many obsolete, inefficient or feather-bedded industries and enterprises, as indeed came to pass after 1989. Yet, while it was obvious to all that the so-called 'full market solution' to Comecon integration would depend on currency convertibility, multilateralism and prices reflecting relative costs, returns and scarcities, it was insufficiently appreciated that supranational central planning, specialization and division of labour within Comecon as a whole had remarkably similar prerequisites. For, in the absence of convertible currencies, multilateral payments systems and realistic prices and exchange rates, supranational central planners would not have been able to make rational decisions, calculations or comparisons.

However, except in the cases of Yugoslavia and Hungary, Balkan and East Central European moves towards 'market socialism' were unceremoniously halted by the August 1968 Warsaw Pact invasion of Czechoslovakia and the subsequent suppression and/or emasculation of the 'reform' movements. For a time even the Hungarians had to tread carefully: they talked merely of a New Economic Mechanism (inaugurated in January 1968), rather than of 'reform' or 'market socialism' as such. However, even if the reform movements were emasculated politically, the Communist regimes still had to try to surmount the tightening resource constraints and the deteriorating economic performance which had contributed to the emergence of reform movements in the first place. Therefore, despite (or even because of) the resultant setbacks to fundamental systemic change and East–West trade, it seemed all the more necessary to foster increased trade, assistance, co-operation and cohesion between members of Comecon, in the hope of enhancing economic performance, 'buying off' economic and social discontents, and reducing the likelihood of another blatant and traumatic Warsaw Pact invasion of a 'fraternal' state in the near future. The 1968 invasion has even been described as 'a watershed in CMEA relations' (Brabant 1989: 78). It was certainly the major impetus behind the convocation of a 'special' Council Session of Comecon in April 1969, ostensibly to celebrate the organization's twentieth anniversary, and the proclamation of a new panacea: Socialist Economic Integration (SEI). However, it was one thing to proclaim this and another to agree on what it meant and how to achieve it. During the later 1950s and the early 1960s it had been agreed that each Communist regime would have to chart its own 'national road to socialism', although the Soviet regime arrogantly reserved the right to prescribe the destination (and, if necessary, change the driver!). By 1969, however, the various economic systems and policy preferences of the Communist regimes had become too diverse, entrenched and mutually incompatible to lend themselves to a common conception and mode of integration. The Complex Programme for the Further Extension and Improvement of Co-operation and the Development of Economic Integration by the CMEA Countries, published by Comecon in 1971, was therefore an incoherent hotchpotch of disparate ingredients cooked up by seventeen different committees. 'No attempt was ever made to weave these propositions into anything remotely resembling a coherent, let alone comprehensive, concept of SEI and how it should or could be fostered'(Brabant 1989: 86). However, there was a more positive interpretation: 'the document is significant in that it imbued the organization with an unprecedented spirit of pragmatism: the fundamental issues were left unresolved but co-operation schemes went ahead regardless; Romanian opposition was bypassed by *de facto* abandonment of the single-member veto in favour of the "interested party" principle' (Sobell 1984: 16). In effect, Comecon fell back on rather British methods of 'muddling through'.

It may be objected that the European Community never had a coherent, clear-cut, comprehensive and generally accepted concept of integration either, and yet Western Europe has made significant progress towards 'ever closer union' since the 1950s. The crucial difference is that, once 'national' barriers to the free movement of goods, capital, labour and services have been largely eliminated and a permissive framework of institutions and ground rules has been established, integration between market economies will normally proceed automatically, even while the politicians and bureaucrats are asleep. To set in motion the economic integration of the six founder members of the European Economic Community, all that was really required was a limited 'compact of abstention': an agreement to remove all restrictions on trade between the Six and subsequently to refrain from impeding cross-border flows of goods, capital and labour within the resultant 'common market'; indeed, 'agreeing on a number of specific things that governments will not do is much easier than arriving at a positive agreement on a line of action to be taken in common' (Shonfield 1973: 14). Integration within Comecon, by contrast, was much more dependent on continuous active intervention by economic planners and politicians and a consensus on what they were trying to achieve, if they were not to cancel each other out by pulling in different directions. In practice, it was limited to what could be agreed in advance between mutually mistrustful Communist states and incorporated into their current and prospective five-year plans. Unless they ceased to be centrally planned economies, they could not easily generate or accommodate spontaneous, decentralized, cross-border or transnational trade, investment, migration or joint ventures.

Integration between the Comecon states was also restricted by their historic rivalries, frictions and animosities and by the additional tensions and mutual suspicion and mistrust generated by the very unequal, oppressive, hegemonic and intrusive relationship between the Soviet Union and its

Balkan and East Central European 'allies'. Indeed, whereas 'capitalist' integration helped Western Europe to side-step and surmount the bitter legacies of its recent past, East Central Europe and the Balkans had the opposite experience. These regions came out of the Second World War at least as disunited, aggrieved, suspicious and resentful as they went into it. The Soviet Union was able to muzzle or suppress many of the mutual enmities and suspicions between its East Central European and Balkan 'vassals', but it did little to dissipate or defuse the underlying sentiments. There was no comprehensive post-war settlement and reconciliation between former belligerents in East Central Europe and the Balkans, comparable to that achieved by the Marshall Plan, the OEEC and the European Coal and Steel Community in Western Europe. Nor did East Central Europe and the Balkans ever achieve the levels of prosperity and hedonistic consumerism and oblivion that helped to soothe, dissipate and divert attention from inherited enmities and resentments in post-1940s Western Europe.

In view of all these impediments, 'Socialist Economic Integration' had to assume roundabout and limited forms, rather than 'head on' and comprehensive ones. Since it was impossible to agree on common approaches to pricing, economic reform, multilateralism, currency convertibility and intra-CMEA capital and labour mobility, Comecon had to settle for suboptimal or second-best solutions. It had to limit itself to whichever half-measures and sector-specific programmes its disparate membership would accept and in which not everyone would have to participate. This was consistent with the 1967 'interested party' principle, which appears to have been reaffirmed as part of the price paid by the Soviet Union for East Central European and Balkan 'fraternal assistance' in the invasion of Czechoslovakia. Thus in 1971 an International Investment Bank was established to finance and facilitate intra-CMEA co-operation on transnational investment projects, especially in energy production, power-grids, pipelines, mining, transportation, chemicals, metallurgy and machine-building. In 1975, 1980 and 1985, moreover, the Comecon states cobbled together a series of five-year 'concerted plans for multilateral integration measures', which were intended to synchronize with their national five-year plans and to resource and co-ordinate transnational projects in key sectors such as the energy and extractive industries. These projects were pushed by the Soviet Union as a way of getting its Balkan and East Central European 'partners' to shoulder part of the increasing investment and production costs of the fuels and other minerals which they consistently imported from the Soviet Union at considerably less than world market prices (and sometimes re-exported to the West to make a nice hard-currency profit) in return for supplies of 'soft' East Central European and Balkan manufactured goods. However, from their own very different standpoint, most East Central Europeans resented having to defray some of the costs of developing the economy of their hated overlord and oppressor. It is possible to see both points of view. In 1975 it was also proposed that Comecon members should adopt a cluster of binding, collective 'target programmes' to relieve bottlenecks in the production and transportation of energy, raw materials, foodstuffs, industrial consumer goods and transportation and to increase inter-state specialization in the various branches of engineering. However, these did not become operational until the 1980s, when the trade flows covered by these 'specialization agreements' do not seem to have exceeded 25 per cent of all intra-CMEA trade in engineering products or 10 per cent of total intra-CMEA trade (Robson 1987: 225; Brabant 1989: 91–3).

From the early 1970s onward, the Soviet Union and most of the other European members of Comecon began to devolve some of their economic planning, allocation and decision-making tasks to giant industrial combines and/or 'industrial associations'. This was done partly with the aim of reducing the so-called 'operational and informational overload' on central planners in increasingly complex and industrialized centrally planned economies by establishing intermediate tiers of economic decision-making, and partly in the hope of replicating the dynamic roles of huge, highly integrated and increasingly science-based industrial combines and conglomerates in the Western and East Asian capitalist economies. The new industrial associations and combines were expected to develop strong research, development, design and supply capabilities, to reap increased economies of scale and to 'internalize' the more detailed planning and allocation functions, by transforming these into managerial tasks performable within giant enterprises or groups of enterprises. In theory, this would free up the overloaded central economic organs to concentrate on their overarching macro-economic roles. It was also hoped that these industrial associations and/or combines would foster decentralized 'horizontal' contractual links with one another to supplement (and partly supplant) the 'vertical' chains of command extending from the central planning and supply agencies and industrial ministries to the myriad industrial enterprises. All this was expected to have a major impact on intra-CMEA integration, by facilitating the autonomous development of direct transnational links, investment, joint ventures and scientific and technical co-operation between industrial associations and/or combines in different Comecon economies.

In practice, however, the new conglomerations or groupings of enterprises were often unwieldy, conservative, risk averse and bureaucratic. They tended to reproduce most of the deficiencies, errors and rigidities of the central planning and supply organs and industrial ministries, which they were supposed to ameliorate. They were often little more than additional intermediate links in essentially unchanged 'vertical' chains of command. Indeed, it was never clearly explained how the 'horizontal' links which the industrial associations and combines were supposed to foster would intermesh with the 'vertical' chains of command radiating from the central planning and supply organs and economic ministries. It can be argued that, in order to have any chance of functioning in accordance with some idealized (or nightmarish) cybernetic vision, a command economy needs to have clearly defined and free-standing chains of command. Any cross-currents are more likely to generate disorganization and chaos than increased efficiency and productivity. In any case, the 'really existing' centrally planned economies lacked most of the financial, commercial, legal and distributive infrastructure that sustains or facilitates autonomous 'horizontal' links between industrial enterprises in developed market economies. Industrial associations and combines were therefore unable to foster many direct 'horizontal' links within (let alone between) the centrally planned economies. In the absence of market economies there was nothing to propel companies inside Comecon into co-operating across national borders, as in the West. Prices did not reflect real costs, while artificial exchange rates between Comecon currencies and the absence of a convertible currency meant that it was virtually impossible to determine whether direct ties were profitable (Leslie Collit, *FT*, 22 July 1987, p. 2).

THE ROAD TO 1989

From 1973 to 1978, while the Western world went into economic recession in the wake of the quadrupling of OPEC oil prices in 1973–4, the economies of the East Central European and eastern Balkan Communist states continued to grow, in some cases even faster than they had done during the 1960s. This superficially impressive feat was made possible by several special factors. These economies became increasingly dependent on the Soviet market and on imports of under-priced Soviet oil and gas, which were largely to be paid for by stepping up exports of agricultural and (mostly 'soft') manufactured products to the Soviet Union. In addition, the Soviet Union provided its European 'satellite' states with considerable amounts of power-generating equipment and technology (including nuclear power plants) on concessionary terms. These forms of Soviet 'assistance' helped not only to cushion most of these economies against adverse trends in their terms of trade and in their access to Western markets, but also to continue to grow (albeit at diminishing rates) through most of the 1970s. However, while increased dependence upon the Soviet Union helped to shield these economies from the potentially damaging effects of recession and higher oil prices in the capitalist world, in the longer term it further impaired their capacity to export successfully to the West.

At the same time, the increasingly nationalistic and independent-minded Romanian and Albanian Communist regimes were increasingly denied such Soviet 'assistance'. However, they had significant, albeit rapidly diminishing, mineral resources of their own. Albania, which had ceased to be an active member of Comecon since 1960, also received considerable Chinese economic assistance in return for supporting China in the Sino-Soviet disputes of the 1960s and the early 1970s.

There was a major Western debate about the scale, direction and significance of the (implicit) transnational subsidies resulting from the trade patterns that developed within Comecon. The debate raised complex and emotive issues to which we cannot fully do justice here, but we shall highlight the main issues. Notwithstanding the substantial economic and technical assistance rendered to Cuba, Vietnam and Mongolia between 1960 and 1990, Comecon never undertook any large-scale fiscal transfers between its European Member States, analogous to those engendered by the Common Agricultural Policy and the so-called 'structural' and 'cohesion' funds within the European Community. Debate mainly centred on the implicit transfers (so-called 'trade subsidies') generated by the systematic deviations of intra-CMEA prices from world market prices, especially the fact that from 1973 to 1990 large quantities of Soviet oil and natural gas were supplied to East Central European and Balkan Communist states at prices that were substantially below those paid in the capitalist world. The most influential Western view was that this implicit Soviet subsidization of these states represented a politically motivated endeavour to 'underwrite' the further development of these rather shaky centrally planned economies, to defuse economic discontents, to encourage and reward compliance with Soviet wishes and security arrangements, to give preferential treatment to the states that most loyally toed the line, and to maintain (or even enhance) the cohesion of the Soviet bloc without periodic recourse to military invasions (Marrese and Vanous 1983; Marrese 1986; Reisinger 1992). However, some analysts, particularly Holzman (1986a, 1986b), Desai (1986) and Brada (1985, 1988), favoured more narrowly economic explanations of the implicit subsidies. They argued that within any trade bloc in which internal prices systematically deviate from those on the world market, some members will benefit and others will lose out; and that, in the case of Comecon, this was not necessarily the result of concerted Soviet attempts to reward loyalists and penalize recalcitrants. Thus the vagaries of the Common Agricultural Policy have similarly given rise to gainers (most notably the Netherlands, Ireland and Denmark) and losers (especially Britain) within Western Europe. Brada argued that 'such subsidies are far from unique and arise whenever a number of countries engage in preferential trade among themselves'. Indeed, the magnitude of the Soviet subsidies to its CMEA partners was 'not at all unusual' and their existence depended 'neither on the planned nature of these economies nor on Soviet hegemony over Eastern Europe'. Instead, they arose because intra-CMEA trade, like intra-EC trade, was 'not carried out at world market prices' (Brada 1988: 641–3). Moreover, the growth of implicit Soviet subsidies to East Central European and Balkan states after 1973 was a largely fortuitous consequence of factors beyond Soviet control, primarily the large rises in world oil prices in 1973–4 and in 1979–80 (pp. 646, 657). 'Soviet subsidies to Eastern Europe were basically related to a slow adjustment of CMEA oil and gas prices to the two "energy shocks" of the 1970s' (Poznanski 1993: 923). Instead of exaggerating the role of political considerations (in the manner of Marresse and Vanous), the distribution of implicit gains and losses among Comecon members could be just as plausibly explained by the fact that, within Comecon as a whole, mineral resources were relatively abundant, whereas capital was perennially scarce. Consequently, viewed purely in terms of relative factor endowments, the more capital-rich member states (the GDR, Czechoslovakia and, to a lesser extent, Hungary) were most likely to benefit at the expense of the relatively mineral-rich ones (the Soviet Union and, to a lesser extent, Romania) (Brada 1988: 652–3). Nevertheless, many East Central Europeans and Bulgarians have indignantly dismissed any suggestion that they were therefore being subsidized by the Soviet Union or that they were in some way benefiting from Soviet largesse. They have retained a strong belief that they were underpaid for their own exports to the Soviet Union. In their eyes the magnitude of the implicit 'subsidies' has been greatly exaggerated (as a result of excessive attention to the easily quantifiable trade in oil and gas, to the relative neglect of the less easily evaluated trade in manufactures). If they existed at all, such subsidies were meagre compensation for the coercive imposition of economic systems and development strategies that were utterly inappropriate to the particular economic needs and factor endowments of East Central Europe and Bulgaria, keeping them much poorer than they would have been if they had been allowed to adopt economic systems and strategies of their own choosing (Koves 1983; Poznanski 1993).

There was broader agreement that, at least in the short term, the 1970s East–West détente facilitated increased inflows of Western capital and technology into the still expanding East Central European and Balkan economies. There was an uncontrolled proliferation of East–West joint ventures, production licensing agreements and imported 'turnkey' installations, many of which were financed by recycled 'petrodollars', as Western banks often incautiously re-lent to Eastern Central European and Balkan Communist regimes some of the oil 'windfalls' deposited in them by the newly rich oil states. These regimes eagerly accepted Western loans, investments, joint ventures, industrial installations and 'technology transfers' as substitutes for more fundamental reforms in their socio-economic systems. Admittedly, in the absence of far-reaching systemic reforms to increase their economic efficiency, they were unable to reap in full the potential benefits or 'payoff' that could have been obtained from such transfers. Nevertheless, in the wake of the ill-fated Prague Spring, most of Europe's Communist regimes perceived radical reforms to be socially and politically dangerous. (The exceptions were Kadar's Hungary and Tito's Yugoslavia.) 'Technology transfer' and import-led growth, largely financed by foreign loans, seemed to offer politically safer means of modernizing the East Central European and Balkan economies, both by raising productivity and by expanding the range of products and equipment available.

All the same, increased reliance on Western capital, technology and firms had unanticipated political and social repercussions. Increased contact with Western visitors (both tourists and businesspeople), together with the proliferation of amenities catering to their needs, helped to diffuse Western values, consumerism and pop culture, especially among the young. The resultant Westernization of East Central European, Yugoslav, Bulgarian and Romanian attitudes, values, dress and leisure activities was, in the end, just as corrosive of Communist influence on the minds of the young as any radical systemic reform. Moreover, through their clumsy attempts to curb the growing influence of rock concerts, Western pop music, blue jeans and consumerism, the ageing dictators made themselves seem increasingly old fashioned, puritanical, out of touch and ridiculous, especially in the eyes of the young.

Excessive reliance upon Western capital and technology transfers posed equally serious economic hazards. Production licensing agreements, such as that between the Polish Ursus tractor plant and Massey-Ferguson-Perkins, often incurred great expense for relatively little benefit (Stokes 1993: 19). Debt-service payments became very burdensome, absorbing resources which could have been spent on much-needed infrastructure or imports, and by the late 1970s they had begun to exceed any fresh inflows of Western capital. The latter quickly dried up as East Central European and Balkan credit ratings fell. Some of these states even had difficulty in completing existing projects involving Western capital or equipment and in obtaining Western spare parts. This further impaired their capacity to increase exports on the scale anticipated or required. Indeed, these states found themselves under increasing pressure to expand their exports to the West to service their uncomfortably large hard-currency debts at the very moment when the further doubling of OPEC oil prices in 1979 plunged the West into another economic recession, which in turn further depressed Western demand for (and raised trade barriers against) imports from them. This time, moreover, the Soviet Union was less able to come to the rescue. The 1979–82 world recession coincided with the nadir of the Brezhnev 'years of stagnation', during which Soviet economic growth sharply decelerated and crucial sectors such as oil, coal, iron and steel stopped growing altogether. The Soviet Union's inability to continue supplying ever-increasing quantities of fuel and raw materials on preferential terms also reduced its willingness and capacity to absorb (in return) ever-increasing quantities of obsolete and/or poor quality industrial products, some of which must have contributed to the deterioration in Soviet economic performance. The East Central European and Balkan Communist states were therefore caught in a 'two-way squeeze' between a stagnating Soviet economy and a recession-stricken West. The crisis was compounded by the simultaneous termination of East–West détente and the start of the 'new Cold War', precipitated by a dramatic escalation of the nuclear arms race (1978–84), the Soviet invasion of Afghanistan (December 1979), the accession of Ronald Reagan to the US presidency (1980–8) and the imposition of martial law in Poland (December 1981).

From 1979 to 1983 the economies of the Balkan and East Central European Communist states were plunged into acute economic recessions from which they still had not fully recovered in 1989, when the 'iron curtain' finally lifted. Between 1979 and 1989, these economies hardly grew at all in real per capita terms and, in the extreme cases of Romania and Poland, experienced severe economic contractions and drastic reductions in living standards. Moreover, it was later revealed that the relative success of the GDR and Bulgaria during the 1980s was more apparent than real and that the full magnitude of their economic crises, infrastructural decay and mounting external indebtedness had been obscured by the selective suppression and falsification of economic and social statistics, and partial concealment of the sheer scale of the costly environmental damage incurred through the reckless development of their chemical, metallurgical, lignite and power-generating industries (social, economic and environmental costs that would continue for many years to come). In the early 1990s it became clear just how much of the Western capital and equipment imported during the 1970s had been wasted on 'white elephants' or diverted into luxurious accommodation and social amenities for the political, managerial and military elites (the 'edifice complex'), instead of being used for the originally intended modernization of industry and physical infrastructure. The worst affected countries were Poland and Romania.

LURCHING FROM CRISIS TO CRISIS IN POLAND, 1976–89

In Poland the resultant shortages, hardships, sporadic repression of student and labour unrest, and official attempts to conceal the full dimensions of the mismanagement of the economy, the misappropriation of funds and the ensuing economic and social crisis aroused more open and politically active opposition to the Gierek regime. A belated attempt to restore market equilibrium in Poland in 1976 by decreeing large rises in retail food prices sparked off widespread and sometimes violently suppressed strikes and protests, forced Gierek to rescind the decreed price increases and precipitated the formation of a prominent Committee for Workers' Defence (KOR) in 1976, partly in order to promote increased solidarity between intelligentsia and working-class opponents of the regime. Led by Adam Michnik, Jacek Kuron, Jan Lipski and Edward Lipinski, KOR began to circulate an illegal fortnightly news-sheet called *Robotnik* (*The Worker*), which publicized oppression and abuses and provided guidance to workers' protests from 1977 to 1980. The movement also had the tacit support of the Catholic Church. KOR was not suppressed by Edward Gierek, perhaps because he had lived in the West and was anxious to safeguard his international reputation as the builder of a new Poland. He seemed to accept that it was more prudent to allow intellectuals to criticize and let off steam than to try to repress them (Stokes 1993: 28–9).

Out of the blue, the election of Cardinal Karol Wojtyla to the papacy in 1978 and his fully televised triumphal return to Poland as Pope John Paul II in 1979 gave an enormous uplift to Polish Catholic nationalism and national self-confidence at a critical juncture in the country's history. In the words of an outstanding Western commentator on Polish affairs, this was an awakening: 'The Pope did nothing so crude as to attack the regime openly or urge the people to rise. Instead, he spoke straight past the government to the real feelings, the real memories of the Poles', and he 'evoked an ancient Christian nation, as if Communist rule was a transient phenomenon of little importance'. The upshot was that 'Poles felt a surge of returning confidence. Given freedom, the people could organize Polish life for itself, true to its own sense of what was just and appropriate.' The visit was both a catharsis and an exorcism. In public attitudes towards the ruling Communists, hatred gave way to 'something even more ominous: a contemptuous indifference'. It also became increasingly apparent that 'the Polish nation was mature and strong enough to make its own choices', without the irksome tutelage of either the party or the state (Ascherson 1988: 192).

In this highly charged situation, the new prime minister, Edward Babiuch, made another abortive attempt to raise retail food prices and introduce measures to boost exports of foods that were in short supply in Polish shops in June 1980. These ill-judged actions triggered a growing wave of peaceful strikes and sit-ins in the big Baltic shipyards and in the vast Silesian steelworks and coal mines during July and August 1980. To everyone's surprise, the Polish authorities allowed KOR to act as an 'information exchange' and pass reports on the strikes and sit-ins to foreign news agencies and radio stations, which in turn broadcast much of this information back to Poland. A major strike and sit-in at the Lenin shipyard in Gdansk brought to prominence a (hitherto little known) dissident marine electrician, Lech Walesa, who began to negotiate with government representatives on behalf of his fellow workers, closely advised by Jacek Kuron, Adam Michnik and Catholic Church leaders. The negotiations were soon being televised to the outside world, making it virtually impossible for the government to extricate itself from this clever political trap without losing face. Walesa's team negotiated the following far-reaching concessions, which were embodied in the so-called Gdansk Agreement of 31 August 1980: the right to strike and to form independent trade unions; increased wages; public broadcasts of Sunday mass; a relaxation of censorship; reform of welfare provisions; selection of enterprise managers on the basis of ability rather than party affiliation; and a commitment to a thorough overhaul of the entire economic system in consultation with the new independent trade unions. 'Not since the revolutions of the nineteenth century had a European people forced such a treaty on its own rulers. In a Communist system . . . the agreements were almost unimaginable. They were possible only because in Poland . . . the party's "leading role" had become an official sham. The reality was a sort of crude pluralism' (Ascherson 1988: 198). Thus KOR was even permitted to play a crucial role in brokering the agreement, partly because its most prominent intellectuals and the government negotiators, divided though they were politically, 'sprang from the same Warsaw milieu and spoke the same language' (p. 196). Much the same was true of the metropolitan intelligentsias and bureaucrats of Prague, Budapest, Belgrade and even Sofia, Tirana and Bucharest.

These mass protests and the Gdansk Agreement soon resulted in the rapid emergence of Solidarnosc (Solidarity), an independent trade union claiming 10 million members (in a country with 35 million inhabitants). Indeed, 'as one strike committee after another all over Poland adopted the outline of the Gdansk Agreement, adding local points of their own, Solidarity swelled into a nationwide organization'(Ascherson 1988: 198).

Gierek was obliged to resign in September 1980. His successor, the rather colourless Communist apparatchik Stanislaw Kania, soon proved incapable of dealing with the deepening crisis. The situation was not helped by the way in which Solidarity encouraged its members to believe that they could enjoy the potential benefits of political and economic liberalization without forgoing job security, over-manning and fixed prices, and to refuse to recognize any link between remuneration and productivity. At grass roots level, Solidarity also encouraged strikes, wage demands and a ban on weekend work for miners, thereby exacerbating shortages and inflation and further depressing production, real incomes and exports. National income contracted by about a quarter between 1980 and 1982, while the annual inflation rate jumped to 18 per cent in 1981 and 109 per cent in 1982. During 1981 Solidarity wielded power without responsibility. It did not make a bid for formal governmental responsibility, partly because it still saw itself as 'only a trade union' and partly because it feared that any such move might precipitate a Warsaw Pact intervention in Poland. Nevertheless, many people on both sides came to believe that, if the Communist authorities did not destroy Solidarity, then Solidarity would finish off the party. At heart, the fiercely Catholic members of Solidarity detested materialist and atheist Communism. Conversely, with the notable exceptions of those who 'defected' to Solidarity (as a more authentically working-class organization than the Polish United Workers Party!), many Communists saw Solidarity as a reactionary and national-chauvinist 'God squad', bent on suppressing Marxist-Leninist materialism and atheism. Such attitudes militated against any durable truce, accommodation or *modus vivendi* between the two sides. Yet neither side was really capable of completely vanquishing the other. They were condemned to a protracted and mutually debilitating political stalemate and war of attrition.

General Wojciech Jaruzelski, who had been Poland's defence minister since 1968, became prime minister in February 1981 and leader of the ruling party in October 1981, in bids to restore 'discipline', halt the downward spiral of production and consumption and avert potential Soviet military intervention. At first it was widely hoped that the army would act as a 'non-political patriotic force', placing the national interest above divisive ideology, and that Jaruzelski would emerge as a patriotic authoritarian nationalist ruler in the Pilsudski mould. Yet, even after Jaruzelski's declaration of martial law in December 1981, the military found it exceedingly difficult to arrest the economy's downward slide (Ascherson 1988: 211–13). Under the martial law regime (December 1981 to July 1983), key industries were placed under military discipline and thousands of Solidarity and KOR activists were interned or beaten up or killed (mainly by the hated ZOMO security police). Solidarity was outlawed in 1982, driving it underground. Industrial production nevertheless continued to contract in 1982 and it remained below the (already falling) 1979 level throughout the 1980s. Moreover, despite the lack of fresh infusions of Western capital during the 1980s, the continually accumulating arrears on debt-service payments increased Poland's hard-currency debt to the West from $25 billion in 1981 to $43 billion in 1989, while its average annual inflation rate merely fell to about 15 per cent in the mid-1980s before climbing back up to 60 per cent in 1988 and 244 per cent in 1989. Military rule, Communism's last recourse, was deemed a failure, even if it had pre-empted a potential Warsaw Pact invasion of Poland in 1981–2. The military regime missed its chance to carry out a radical reform of the economy in 1982–3, while its opponents were in disarray and in retreat. Poland was locked on to a treadmill from which it would have been very hard to escape without a fundamental regime change.

Their painful experiences since the late eighteenth century had taught the Poles that they could hasten their own destruction as a nation if they were to resort to unchecked conflict among themselves. This hard lesson made the nation and its leaders reluctant to push any confrontation to its logical extreme. This had helped to restrain Poland's first Communist leaders from indulging in full-blown Stalinist purges and show trials in the late 1940s and early 1950s. It had also contributed to the avoidance of a bloody outcome to the Polish crisis of 1956 (in contrast to the Hungarian Revolution of 1956 and the resultant Soviet invasion of Hungary in November of that year). 'This inner tolerance, which has made Poland such a mature society in comparison to Germany or Russia, had led to a history of half-measures, of belligerent words and symbols accompanied by only hesitant deeds. The nation had suffered for this, but because of this it had also survived' (Ascherson 1988: 207). The martial law regime was indeed a characteristically Polish half-measure, carried out with a brutality that 'appalled and alienated the nation', yet 'not brutal enough to terrorize the Poles into passivity' (p. 215). Most of the regime's opponents concluded that 'the price of all-out resistance was too high', while the regime concluded that 'the price of reducing Poland to conformity and obedience was also too high' (p. 218). Thus Jaruzelski was unable to achieve his main political aim of a 'national reconciliation' that marginalized Solidarity. Nor was he able to broaden his power base. His Patriotic Front of National Rebirth (PRON), established in 1982, 'never acquired a convincing life of its own'. After July 1983, when the army formally returned to barracks, 'his only tool of government was the state, which often meant the security police'. Furthermore, his regime was neither able nor willing to destroy the distinctive pluralism of Polish society. Even though the press was strictly censored, Poles continued to speak out and, with Solidarity driven underground, 'the influence of the Catholic Church increased enormously' (pp. 216–17).

Church mediation and Jaruzelski's evident desire to propitiate Poland's Western creditors by introducing a small dose of much-needed economic liberalization and by refraining from an unrestrained reign of terror also helped Solidarity to survive. Indeed, Solidarity continued to pose an ever-present threat to Communist rule because it had successfully exposed the lack of legitimacy and 'proletarian' credentials of the ruling party, with the result that from 1980 onwards Europe's Communist regimes were increasingly on the defensive. Whether they resorted to repression or concession, they could not credibly claim to be the true representatives and custodians of the working class. Thus the emergence of Solidarity in 1980 had marked the beginning of the end of Communist rule in Europe, even though Poland and (less overtly) Romania and Albania constituted the only cases in which the main challenges to Communist rule came overwhelmingly 'from below', from the working class.

During 1983, in a vain endeavour to win international respectability and 'national reconciliation', Pope John Paul II was again allowed to visit Poland, martial law was formally rescinded (in return for the lifting of US trade sanctions), censorship was relaxed, most political detainees were released and a programme of economic reform was announced (although it did not go very far in practice). But in 1984 overt opposition to the regime was reignited by the shockingly brutal murder of the popular priest Jerzy Popieluszko by members of the security police. This barbaric act helped to derail Jaruzelski's 'controlled liberalization' strategy, as its perpetrators presumably intended. Consequently, the political and economic stalemate and war of attrition continued until August 1988, when the hated interior minister, General Czeslaw Kiszczak, broke the deadlock by proposing 'round table talks' between the principal elements in Polish society, including the Catholic Church and Solidarity. In addition the hitherto passive lower house of parliament (the Sejm) unprecedentedly voted down the government in September 1988, clearing the way for the formation of a new administration headed by the 'reform Communist' Mieczyslaw Rakowski, in consultation with church leaders. The remarkably open and constructive 'round table talks' of February and March 1989 resulted in a formal agreement on extensive political and economic reforms (including the re-legalization of Solidarity) on 5 April 1989.

This paved the way for the holding of contested multi-party elections to the Sejm and a new upper house (the Senate) in June 1989, although sixty-five of the hundred seats in the Sejm were reserved for the Communists and their allies. Solidarity candidates duly won ninety-nine of the hundred Senate seats and all thirty-five of the freely contested seats in the Sejm. Meeting in joint session, the two houses narrowly elected General Jaruzelski president of the republic, but the Communists were largely deserted by their hitherto passive coalition partners and were thus thwarted in their attempts to form a government under General Kiszczak. In August 1989, finally, a Solidarity-dominated government was formed under Tadeuz Mazowiecki, a widely respected Catholic intellectual who was at that time close to Lech Walesa. In Poland the Communist abdication of power was mercifully non-violent and in that respect the Polish Communists did perform a valuable last service to their country. Yet Communist rule had ended in total failure, amid an incipient economic and social collapse and runaway inflation.

OBSESSIVE-COMPULSIVE DESPOTIC DISORDER IN ROMANIA, 1977–89

In Romania, not altogether dissimilarly, the economic miscalculations of the 1970s (such as the overexpansion of oil-refining and the petrochemical industry, when Romania's proven oil reserves were being rapidly depleted), the mounting shortages, the large-scale corruption and misappropriation of funds by the Ceausescu kleptocracy, the bloodily suppressed Jiu valley coal miners' strike in July 1977 and the spectre of Solidarnosc all induced the Communist regime to tighten its grip. The Western capital borrowed during the 1970s had helped to expand the country's inefficient and capital-intensive heavy industries far beyond Romania's capacity either to meet their voracious energy requirements or to feed its fast-growing non-agricultural population. Western capital and technology transfers had served as substitutes rather than as catalysts for the radical reforms needed to make Romania's economy more efficient. By 1977 this longstanding net exporter of oil and foodstuffs had become a net importer of such products. As a result, without in any way curbing the excesses of the extended ruling family, from late 1981 to late 1989 Ceausescu put Romanians through the most draconian austerity programme of any state in the Soviet bloc. It even included power cuts and the rationing of food and petrol. In 1987 a state of emergency was declared in the energy sector, which was gradually subjected to military discipline and control from 1985 onwards. The various economic reforms announced by the Ceausescu regime were largely cosmetic exercises. Moreover, as a result of the austerity drive, the country's $10 billion foreign debt (which had to be rescheduled in 1981) was almost entirely repaid by 1989, so as to deny Romania's increasingly critical Western creditors any handle on the Romanian state. But the human and economic costs of these policies were enormous. They included the widespread neglect and rapid decay of Romania's social infrastructure (hospitals, schools, housing, services) and severe strains on the social fabric, as was to be revealed to the world by lurid photographs of the shocking conditions in Romanian orphanages and homes for the mentally retarded after the fall of Ceausescu at the end of 1989. Despite sporadic social unrest among peasants, workers (notably in the city of Brasov in November 1987) and the large Magyar minority in Transylvania, there was no let up, only brutal repression. The more he sullied his international reputation, the greater was Ceausescu's determination to repay the foreign debt and root out potential 'subversion' (the hated state security police, the Securitate, allegedly recruited one in five adult males), and the more he played up crude 'ethnic' nationalism, xenophobia and persecution of the country's sizeable Gypsy and Hungarian minorities. In 1988 he started to implement his infamous 'systematization' programme. This aimed to erase more than 7,000 villages (those with fewer than 3,000 inhabitants) and to resettle their former inhabitants in 550 'agro-industrial centres' by the year 2000, ostensibly in order to increase the cultivable area, modernize rural infrastructure and reduce the differences between town and country. Viewed from another angle, however, millions of Romanian, Hungarian and Romany villagers were to be bulldozed out of the relatively safe havens provided by their traditional close-knit small communities and herded into soulless 'bugged' apartment blocks, within which their opinions and activities could be more easily monitored by networks of police 'spies' and 'informers'. This particularly aroused fears among Romania's increasingly victimized ethnic minorities. Fortunately, owing to lack of time and money, the programme had not progressed very far before Ceausescu was overthrown. But it contributed significantly to the growth of inter-ethnic tensions in Transylvania, where the concurrent official persecution of the Hungarian Lutheran pastor Laszlo Tokes in the relatively liberal university city of Timisoara evoked mass protests from Romanians as well as Hungarians and became the catalyst of the widespread confrontations between the Securitate, ordinary citizens (especially students) and the mainly conscript army, which precipitated the violent overthrow of the Ceausescu cabal in December 1989. It is not yet clear just how 'spontaneous' the Romanian Revolution of 1989 really was. There were numerous indications that some of Ceausescu's former henchmen had a hand in his overthrow and execution and that they were all too ready to step into the dead man's shoes. The indecent haste with which Ceausescu and his wife were put to death (without due process of law) on Christmas Day 1989 may well have been intended (in some quarters at least) to stop the dictator making any damaging revelations concerning the new regime's senior personnel, many of whom had been Ceausescu's cronies at one time or another. Nevertheless, there is little doubt that the acute social and economic crises and inter-ethnic tensions of the 1980s created the flammable materials which the leaders of the new National Salvation Front were able to exploit for their own ends.

ALBANIA'S ECONOMIC COLLAPSE, LATE 1980s

The even more severe social and economic crisis that developed in Albania during the late 1980s was primarily a result of the country's growing international isolation rather than the problems afflicting the Comecon states. Following the death of Mao Zedong in 1976 and the subsequent retreat from Maoism in China, Hoxha soon fell out with China's new leaders, whom he denounced as 'revisionists'. After Hoxha's death in 1985 power passed to Ramiz Alia, whose daughter was married to Hoxha's son. But Hoxha's widow Nexhmije continued to wield considerable (hard-line) backdoor influence in an endeavour to keep power 'within the family', and President Alia initially ruled out any attempt at an Albanian *perestroika*. This left Albania completely bereft of friends and benefactors, with the result that its hitherto dynamic economy stagnated during the 1980s (although its population was growing by more than 2 per cent per annum, the fastest rate of population growth in Europe). According to the *Statistical Yearbooks* published by the Communist regime, Albania's officially recorded Gross National Income increased only 1.5 per cent per annum from 1980 to 1985 and contracted by 1.1 per cent per annum from 1985 to 1990, after growing by 4.6 per cent per annum during the 1970s, 7.4 per cent per annum during the 1960s and 9.1 per cent per annum during the 1950s (Pashko 1996: 65). By 1989, 9 per cent of the workforce was unemployed (p. 5) and nearly 40 per cent of Albanian children were suffering from malnutrition (according to World Health Organization data, cited in the *FT*, 14 December 1991, p. xx). The economy of Communist-ruled Albania finally collapsed between 1990 and 1992, when (according to early estimates) net agricultural output more than halved, industrial output fell to about one-quarter of its 1989 level and GDP fell by more than one-third. Officially recorded unemployment peaked at 39 per cent of the workforce in 1992, while the average annual rate of inflation rocketed to 36 per cent in 1991 and 226 per cent in 1992. Food rationing had to be introduced in 1991 and there was also a mass exodus from the countryside (where the collective farm system was rapidly crumbling), in addition to the much-publicized emigration of thousands Albanian 'boat people', desperate to escape from the collapsing urban sector and a restrictive and politically bankrupt Communist regime. By 1992 Albanians were heavily dependent on emergency aid from the West (including food aid) for their survival.

THE CRISES AND FINAL DISINTEGRATION OF THE YUGOSLAV FEDERATION (SFRY), 1987–92

Yugoslavia's economic growth rates began to tail off in the late 1970s and fell disastrously during the 1980s. By 1990 the earlier international interest in and enthusiasm for Yugoslav 'market socialism' and 'self-management' had died almost as completely and suddenly as international interest in the utterly discredited models of the 'command economy' and 'state socialism' (in reality, 'state capitalism') which had developed in other Communist states.

Table 33.1   Official figures for the average annual rate of growth of Gross Social Product in Yugoslavia, 1981–91 (per cent)

Years	Growth (%)
1981–5	1.1
1986	3.5
1987	−1.1
1988	−2.0
1989	0.8
1990	−7.5
1991	−15.0

Source: Jeffries (1993: 319, 472).

In addition, the already alarmingly large economic disparities between the more developed and the less developed republics and autonomous regions had continued to widen. In 1952 average income per head in Slovenia was about four times that of Kosova, but by 1989 this disparity had doubled to eight to one. Furthermore, while Slovenia's unemployment rate in 1989 was a mere 2.7 per cent (Steinherr and Ottolenghi 1993: 230), Kosova's rose from 18.6 per cent in 1971 to 27.5 per cent in 1981 and 57 per cent in 1989 (Vickers 1998: 189, 223). Yugoslavia had also become heavily indebted as a result of massive borrowing from abroad during the 1970s. By 1979 the hard-currency debts of European Communist states to Western countries had risen to the levels shown in Table 33.2.

Table 33.2   Hard-currency debts of European Communist states, 1979 (US $)

	Total (US $ billion)	**US $ per inhabitant**
Yugoslavia	17	780
Hungary	7.5	700
Poland	19.5	557
Romania	7	320
Bulgaria	4	455
Czechoslovakia	3.5	233
USSR	10.2	39

Source: (Bideleux 1987: 270):

In this respect, Yugoslavia (along with Hungary) found itself in by far the worst plight of any of the European Communist states, in large part because of its relatively easy access to Western credit. As the most 'Westernized' Communist state, it had in effect succumbed most fully to the fateful temptations of 'credit card spending', while the application of compound interest caused such debts to spiral exponentially.

Yugoslavia also became acutely inflation prone. The annual inflation rate averaged 33.3 per cent during 1974–9 and 48.7 per cent during 1980–5, before soaring to 89.8 per cent in 1986, 120.8 per cent in 1987, 194.1 per cent in 1988 and 1,256 per cent per annum in 1989 (Jeffries 1993: 319). It was widely concluded that the 'self-management' system had ceased to be viable, that it encouraged the payment of wages at the expense of ploughed-back profits, that borrowed funds were inefficiently used because interest rates were kept artificially low and enterprise closure was effectively ruled out, and that 'self-managed' enterprises exercised undue influence over the banks (which they had in many cases established in the first place).

The federal government headed by Ante Markovic, January 1989 to December 1991

Ante Markovic, who served as prime minister of the Yugoslav Federation from January 1989 to 20 December 1991, made a valiant last-ditch attempt to 'save' the Yugoslav economic system and the SFRY from complete collapse. The so-called Markovic programme comprised two distinct phases The first phase, initiated in December 1989, involved an IMF-inspired macro-economic stabilization and austerity programme, combined with micro-economic liberalization measures. In effect, this offered a combination of macro-economic 'shock therapy' and, at the micro-economic level, 'big bang' institutional reform. During 1990 hyperinflation was 'tamed' to a remarkable degree and with great speed by restrictive fiscal and monetary policies, a six-month pay freeze and the simultaneous introduction of a new currency on 1 January 1990, the 'new dinar', the international exchange rate of which was pegged to the value of the Deutschmark (as were wages and salaries). This fixed exchanged rate was intended to hold until 30 June, but in the event it was maintained until 1 January 1991. At the same time, both retail and producer prices and foreign trade were extensively liberalized, while the main banks were transformed into either private or limited liability joint stock companies, partly in an attempt to subject the banks themselves and the enterprises which borrowed from them to more stringent financial discipline. By early 1990 only 20 per cent of retail prices and 24 per cent of industrial producer goods prices remained subject to controls, and by the year's end all indirect price controls had been abolished. Nevertheless, the annual inflation rate plummeted from 1,252 per cent in 1989 to 121 per cent in 1990 (Jeffries 1993: 471–73). By May 1990 the inflows of foreign exchange were exceeding the outflows (a good indicator of reviving domestic and international confidence), and summer 1990 witnessed booming levels of foreign tourist arrivals in Yugoslavia (Lampe 1996: 348). Although the January–June 1990 pay freeze was painful, it had dramatic results and there was palpable relief and gratitude that wages and salaries were once again worth something, as one of the authors witnessed at first hand during August 1990. The public mood seemed to be broadly optimistic (even in Bosnia) and, despite international concern and some evidence of nagging unease about the growing assertiveness of Serbian and Croatian nationalists (especially Milosevic, Tudjman and the leaders of the Croatian Serb and Bosnian Serb communities), few people seemed to have any inkling that inter-ethnic conflicts of terrible proportions were shortly to engulf Yugoslavia. The atmosphere was very much one of 'business as usual', especially in the tourist areas, although many people may well have been 'putting on a brave face' in an endeavour to 'will away' the gathering storm clouds, while others probably preferred not even to think about what might be about to happen.

Buoyed up by the initial successes of the first phase of the Markovic reform programme, there was a considerable revival of Yugoslav economic confidence, confidence in the federal political system and hope for the future during 1990. As a result, at least until mid-1990 the most popular politician in Yugoslavia as a whole and even in Serbia itself was the liberal and reform-minded Croatian technocrat Ante Markovic – not Slobodan Milosevic (Lampe 1996: 349; Miller 1997: 158). On the strength of his initial successes and popularity, and in a bold endeavour to 'relaunch' the SFRY on a new liberal-cosmopolitan and non-Communist footing, on 29 July 1990 Markovic launched an Alliance of Reform Forces of Yugoslavia (ARFY, Savez reformskih snaga Jugoslavije) as a new political party whose *raison d'être* was to mobilize and unite large sections of the intelligentsia, professional people, managers, entrepreneurs and well-educated liberal-minded young people in support of the reform programme and to 'fight back' against the pernicious champions of intolerant and vindictive ethnic collectivism. Unfortunately, in the multi-party elections held in each of the Yugoslav republics in the course of 1990, most Yugoslavs voted for nationalist parties preaching ethnic collectivism, rather than for the ARFY and similarly liberal-minded parties. In most cases, the ARFY obtained only 5 per cent of the votes cast, although in Bosnia-Herzegovina (the republic with the most to lose from the impending descent into 'ethnarchy') the ARFY obtained

14 per cent of the vote (Lampe 1996: 349). The second phase of the Markovic reform programme was launched on 29 June 1990, the main emphasis being on the transition to a more Western-style market economy. The August 1990 Law on Social Capital initiated the transformation of 'self-managed' and 'socially owned' enterprises into joint stock share-holding companies. The situation was not completely clear, but the Markovic government seemed particularly keen on worker share ownership playing an important role. Tragically, no agreement or consensus was reached on the way forward, either within the federal government or among the various constituent republics, with the result that the stabilization and reform programmes promoted by Markovic at the federal level ultimately fell victim to the renewed political disintegration of the SFRY.

If there ever was any real chance of the Markovic programme succeeding, Slobodan Milosevic effectively killed it off in December 1990 by carrying out a colossal financial coup-cum-theft which left a gaping hole in the federal budget, thereby undermining any hope of maintaining the monetary discipline needed to bring the still-powerful inflationary pressures under control. In December 1990, without either prior consultation with other governments or authorization from the National Bank of Yugoslavia, and at a time when Markovic was limiting federal expenditure and was urging (and depending on) the governments of the individual Yugoslav republics to do likewise, the Serbian government led by Milosevic's Socialist Party of Serbia (SPS) secretly usurped more than half of the total Yugoslav public borrowing rights for 1990 to pay off huge arrears of public wages, salaries and pensions and boost public spending in Serbia. This was done partly in order to enhance Milosevic and the SPS's chances of winning the first multi-party elections in Serbia in December 1990 (by effectively bribing Serb voters to vote for them), and partly to blast a huge hole in Markovic's anti-inflation programme – thereby killing two birds with one stone. As a consequence, during 1991 and 1992 inflation escalated out of control again, and the new dinar was devalued with ever-increasing frequency as the economic situation rapidly deteriorated again.

During 1990–2, confronted by resurgent inter-ethnic conflict, seemingly uncontrollable inflationary pressures and incipient economic collapse, most Yugoslavs – who had initially shown great faith in and support for Markovic – finally lost confidence in the capacity of the Markovic government and the Communist regime to deal with the multiple crises which were engulfing the SFRY. In the course of 1990 quite freely contested multi-party elections were held in each of the Yugoslav republics (even Serbia). As a result, non-Communist governments were elected during 1990 in Croatia, Slovenia, Macedonia and Bosnia-Herzegovina, whose respective parliaments passed declarations of independence in June 1991 (Croatia and Slovenia) and February 1992 (Macedonia and Bosnia-Herzegovina), which also received strong support in popular referenda. The SKJ had disintegrated in early 1990 (paradoxically, it was the first Yugoslav-wide institution to do so). However, most of the separate Leagues of Communists in most of the Yugoslav republics successfully 'changed horses' and reinvented themselves either as liberal, governmentally experienced and reform-minded social democratic parties (in Slovenia and Macedonia) or as pragmatic and governmentally experienced nationalist parties (in Serbia and Montenegro) and performed well in multi-party elections. Either way, the result was a comprehensive abandonment of Communist precepts and doctrine and a general retreat from Yugoslavism and federalism, although the 'successor' parties in Slovenia, Macedonia and Bosnia-Herzegovina and Markovic's liberal-cosmopolitan ARFY did make energetic (albeit ultimately unsuccessful) attempts to hold together a much looser form of Yugoslav confederation.

The bloody disintegration of the SFRY, 1990–5

Armed clashes between Croats and autonomist or secessionist members of the Serb minority in Croatia first began during the spring and summer of 1990 and became more serious from March 1991 onwards. In the wake of the declarations of independence by Croatia and Slovenia on 25 June

1991, the federal Yugoslav People's Army (JNA) made a ham-fisted attempt to hold the Yugoslav Federation together by force by intervening militarily in Slovenia between 25 June and 18 July 1991. However, through lack of 'intelligence' (in both senses of the word!) the JNA had failed to anticipate that the Slovenes would put up effective armed resistance and that the West would condemn rather than support its heavy-handed operations. The JNA was quickly thrown into disarray and humiliated in a series of brief clashes with the well-prepared 'special forces' (essentially paramilitary police units) of the Slovene Ministry of the Interior and with Slovenia's Territorial Defence Force. On 18 July 1991 the shame-faced JNA announced that it was beginning a permanent face-saving withdrawal of all its forces from Slovenia. It then turned its attention to an attempt to prevent the secession of Croatia or, failing that, to assist the secession of the Serb-inhabited areas from a seceding Croatia and their inclusion in a Serb-dominated 'rump Yugoslavia'.

The JNA, having freed itself from any residual political control by the increasingly defunct Yugoslav Federation, backed the secessionism of the substantial Serb minorities living in Croatia. Warren Zimmerman, the last US ambassador to Yugoslavia, recalled that 'The fighting in Croatia began with the illusion of evenhandedness. The JNA would step in to separate the Serbian and Croatian combatants. During the summer of 1991, however, it soon became apparent that the JNA, while claiming neutrality, was in fact turning territory over to Serbs' (Zimmerman 1995: 13). There was particularly ferocious fighting between Serb and Croatian forces from July to December 1991, during which time the JNA seized control of about one-third of Croatia's territory. The town of Vukovar first came under JNA shelling in August 1991, while in October 1991 the Yugoslav army also started shelling the very vulnerably located city of Dubrovnik. Zimmerman subsequently commented that a humanitarian military intervention by NATO to halt this fighting 'was simply too big a step to consider in late 1991. I did not recommend it myself – a major mistake. The JNA's artillery on the hills surrounding Dubrovnik and its small craft on the water would have been easy targets. Not only would damage to the city have been averted, but the Serbs would have been taught a lesson about Western resolve that might have deterred at least some of the aggression against Bosnia. As it was, the Serbs learned another lesson – that there was no Western resolve, and that they could push about as far as their power could take them' (p. 14).

By early 1992 there was a stalemate between the two sides, partly because both Milosevic and Croatia's President Franjo Tudjman were turning their attention to plans to partition most of Bosnia-Herzegovina between Serbia and Croatia. This respite allowed UN peacekeeping forces to patrol some of the predominantly Serb-inhabited areas of Croatia from early 1992 onward. However, intermittent skirmishing between the two sides continued until the summer of 1995, when two lightning counter-offensives by Croatia's revamped and rearmed forces succeeded in recovering almost all the territory that Croatia had lost and driving out most of its Serb inhabitants. By then the Serb–Croat war had claimed more than 20,000 lives.

During 1991–2 federal authority rapidly collapsed. On 12 March 1991 the federal collective presidency declared itself 'paralysed'. Serbia at first refused to allow the Croat Stipe Mesic to take up the rotating post of federal Yugoslav president when it was his turn to do so on 15 May 1991. The EU imposed an arms embargo on the whole of the former Yugoslavia in July 1991 and the UN Security Council followed suit on 25 September 1991. Serbia, in league with Montenegro, assumed control of the federal presidency and government on 3 October 1991. Stipe Mesic formally resigned from the federal presidency on 5 December 1991, declaring that 'Yugoslavia no longer exists'. The resignation of the federal prime minister, Ante Markovic, on 20 December 1991 placed the final nail in the coffin of the SFRY.

Starting in March–April 1992, the JNA gave increasingly overt support to the Serb communities in Bosnia-Herzegovina against the Muslim Bosniaks and the Bosnian Croats, precipitating even greater carnage. On 27 April 1992 Serbia and Montenegro declared a new Federal Republic of Yugoslavia (FRY). This new 'rump Yugoslavia' became an international pariah until it was partially 'brought in from the cold' by Milosevic's imposition of an embargo on the Bosnian Serbs in August 1994. On 30 May 1992 the UN Security Council imposed a trade embargo on the new FRY. The embargo excluded foodstuffs and medicines, but it included oil products and cigarettes, which therefore provided easy profits for sanctions-busting smugglers and hugely enriched the various emerging mafias. The most notorious of these mafia networks were those controlled by the Bosnian Serb warlords-turned-gangsters Radovan Karadzic, Ratko Mladic and Arkan, but they had powerful counterparts in Albania, Bulgaria, Macedonia and Romania, where they also contributed to the extensive gangsterization (criminalization) of economic activity.

Other sanctions against the FRY included the cutting of international air links, the freezing of its public and private assets held abroad, reductions in the size of diplomatic missions to Belgrade, and a ban on cultural, scientific and sporting contacts with Serbia and Montenegro. On 10 July 1992 NATO and the Western European Union (WEA) invoked powers to stop and search Adriatic shipping, especially if its cargoes were thought to be bound for Serbia via Montenegro. On 22 September 1992 the UN General Assembly refused to recognize the FRY as the legal successor to the old Yugoslavia, and on 16 June 1993 it was expelled from the UN seat formerly held by the former SFRY. On 16 November 1992 the UN Security Council voted for even tougher sanctions against the FRY, with the use of force authorized. Stop and search powers were initiated along the Danube and in the Adriatic, while third-country transit traffic passing through Serbia or Montenegro henceforth needed permission from the UN sanctions committee. Also on 16 November 1992 NATO and the WEU agreed to a full naval blockade of the Adriatic.

The disintegration of the SFRY had been both bloody and complex. The collapse of Europe's Communist regimes eliminated the last vestiges of any external threats to the Yugoslav lands and peoples. This reduced the previously perceived need to maintain a cohesive SFRY and unleashed a bestial struggle for territory between the Yugoslav successor states. Nationalism was shrewdly exploited by ex-Communists such as Slobodan Milosevic and Franjo Tudjman for their own ends. The American columnist William Pfaff commented that there was 'a common but irresponsible and unhistorical inclination to treat violence as somehow endemic to the Balkans and therefore insoluble, a matter of "ancestral hatreds" or "the clash of civilizations". This simply is not true . . . The war in Yugoslavia was not some spontaneous upheaval of peoples. It was launched with deliberation and calculation by certain political figures from the old Communist Yugoslavia – Slobodan Milosevic and Franjo Tudjman chief among them – who believed that they could expand their power after Tito's death by awakening and exploiting the nationalism of Serbs, Croats, Slovenes and Muslims, while attacking the principle of the multinational federal state' (*IHT*, 8 October 1996, p. 8). Likewise, his fellow columnist Anthony Lewis contended that 'the savagery was not caused by "ancient hatreds", that chestnut produced by Western leaders as an excuse for inaction. It resulted from "the conscious actions of nationalist leaders"' (*IHT*, 17 September 1996, p. 8). Warren Zimmerman argued that 'The break-up of Yugoslavia is a classic example of nationalism from the top down – a manipulated nationalism in a region where peace has historically prevailed more than war and in which a quarter of the population were in mixed marriages. The manipulators condoned and even provoked local ethnic violence in order to engender animosities that could then be magnified by the press, leading to further violence . . . Milosevic's Serbia was at the heart of the complex of issues that destroyed Yugoslavia . . . In the Balkans, intellectuals tend to be standard bearers of nationalism; in Serbia this is carried to fetishistic lengths. A lugubrious, paranoid and Serbo-centric view of the past enables the Serbs to blame everyone but themselves for whatever goes wrong' (Zimmerman 1995: 2–3).

Milosevic himself played the pivotal role in the disintegration of Yugoslavia by thwarting all attempts to salvage it in the form of a looser confederation. He strove to carve out a 'Greater Serbia' by backing (Eastern Orthodox) ethnic Serbs in the other republics. He only began to distance himself from the belligerent Bosnian and Croatian Serb paramilitary forces and gangster networks when their activities finally began to threaten his own hold on power in Serbia in 1993–5. In parallel,

Croatia's President Franjo Tudjman also tried to carve out a 'Greater Croatia' by backing secessionist Bosnian Croat (Catholic) paramilitary forces and gangster networks in Bosnia and Herzegovina. As early as 25 March 1991 Tudjman and Milosevic held a meeting at which they agreed to partition Bosnia-Herzegovina between a Greater Serbia and a Greater Croatia, leaving only a small residue of its territory in the hands of the (Muslim) Bosniaks.

The Western Powers and Russia (which traditionally supported the Serbs) managed to avoid being drawn onto opposite sides in the Yugoslav conflicts, which was clearly a positive factor. However, the attempts of these powers to bring peace to the region were ineffectual until October 1995. By then, after more than 120,000 deaths and the displacement of more than 2 million people from their homes, the conflicts had started to burn themselves out anyway, so the USA cannot take a great deal of credit for the peace accords which it finally brokered at Dayton, Ohio in November 1995.

THE DEATH THROES OF THE COMMUNIST REGIMES IN EUROPE

Conditions may have been less grim in other parts of the eastern half of Europe. Nevertheless, there was a widespread revulsion against the pervasive corruption, kleptocracy, police brutality, surveillance, irksome restrictions, baronial power and perversion or concealment of truth that characterized Europe's Communist regimes. Citizens increasingly resented the perennial shortages and the time spent queuing or fruitlessly searching for goods in short or highly erratic supply. Even in relatively well-stocked East Germany, Czechoslovakia and Hungary, the spread of Western comparators (aided by growing access to Western visitors, cultural goods and radio and television broadcasts) produced a threatening escalation of expectations and discontent. It became natural for eastern Europeans to compare their own plight with the situation of their relatively prosperous Western neighbours, rather than with other even worse-off eastern Europeans.

At the same time, various ecological and peace movements and some of the Protestant churches intensified public environmental concerns during the 1980s, as increasing numbers of Soviet nuclear power plants and/or nuclear weapons were installed in the Balkans and East Central Europe. The nuclear disaster at Chernobyl (in Ukraine) in April 1986 was especially important. The environmental damage caused by neo-Stalinist economic development, with its heavy reliance and emphasis on old-fashioned ('smoke-stack') metallurgical, power-generating and chemical industries which were poisoning and acidifying the air and water supplies, was also a source of mounting concern. Thus Ecoglasnost, an environmental group demanding greater openness and veracity about the environmental costs of neo-Stalinist patterns of industrialization, was to play a prominent role in the toppling of the Zhivkov regime in Bulgaria in November 1989. By then, however, the economic and social programmes of Europe's Communist regimes had lost all credibility and, after a decade of stagnation and retrogression, even the ruling parties were losing faith in their capacity to lead their countries out of the deepening economic and social impasse in which they found themselves. This loss of faith, capacity and credibility seems rather more calamitous than the often alleged 'loss of legitimacy', given that most of these regimes had never had much legitimacy in the first place! Loss of legitimacy was mainly a problem for the Albanian and Yugoslav Communist regimes, which had always been heavily dependent upon autonomous internal support

THE DEMISE OF THE SOVIET BLOC

There were some last-ditch attempts to breathe new life into Comecon during the 1980s, in a vain attempt to revitalize the increasingly moribund centrally planned economies. A major Comecon 'economic summit' held in Moscow in June 1984 called for an accelerated transition to 'intensive growth', through a more 'rational' use of Comecon's resources, closer co-ordination of national economic plans, a strengthening of bilateral ties between Comecon states and an 'active utilization of commodity–money relations', in addition to co-operation and plan co-ordination. Moreover, the Soviet leaders served notice that low-priced deliveries of fuel and raw materials to Balkan and East Central European states would be increased (to make good unilateral reductions imposed on them in 1982) only in so far as they upgraded their shoddy exports to the Soviet Union (Brabant 1989: 114–16). However, instead of having the intended effect, this further encouraged Balkan and East Central European Communist states to expand their economic relations with the West, the more so since the Soviet Union was doing the same.

Much was expected of Mikhail Gorbachev when he became Soviet leader in March 1985 and caught the world's attention with his programmes of *perestroika* (restructuring), *uskorenie* (acceleration), *demokratizatsiya* (democratization) and *glasnost* (openness). The December 1985 Council Session of Comecon approved a Comprehensive Programme to Promote Scientific and Technological Progress of the Member Countries of the CMEA up to the Year 2000, calling for increased scientific and technical co-operation in the fields of electronics, information technology, automation, robotics, nuclear energy, new materials and biotechnology, with the declared aim of doubling output per worker by 2000. As a substitute for more fundamental systemic change, which could have aroused formidable opposition from powerful vested interests, Gorbachev and his chief economic mentor, Abel Aganbegyan, basically gambled on finding a quick technological fix for the problems of the Soviet economy and Comecon: 'Especially important is the preferential development of external economic ties within the framework of the CMEA . . . Of key significance here is the implementation of programmes of scientific technological progress with these countries . . . Since we must overcome the current trends and achieve a qualitative breakthrough in the development of the forces of production, we can no longer rely on the evolutionary form of scientific and technological progress. It cannot guarantee radical increases in economic efficiency. Such radical increase can only be assured by *revolutionary changes* in scientific and technological progress, with the transition from the old generation of technology to fundamentally new technological systems . . . Science will increasingly become a "direct productive force", as Marx foresaw, and a fundamental integration of science with production will take place as large scientific and production associations will become the bases of scientific and technological progress . . . By the year 2000 . . . the renewal of plant and machinery . . . will be running at 6 per cent or more per year. Virtually no machinery that is now in use will then remain . . . This is to be assured by trebling machine-building output over the fifteen years' (Aganbegyan 1988: 38, 84, 220).

Comecon's new scientific and technical co-operation programme reflected Gorbachev's essentially voluntarist and directive approach to the acceleration of economic growth, involving the imposition of new priorities and technologies 'from above' on a largely unchanged economic system. The programme failed, however, because it grossly underestimated both the extent and the negative consequences of the institutional isolation of the centrally planned economies (and their scientific communities) from each other and from the outside world, and the (not unrelated) inability of centrally planned economies to match the continuous and all-pervasive pressures on capitalist economies to innovate in order to survive in increasingly competitive environments (Bideleux 1987: 151–5). The Gorbachev regime made too many commitments on too many fronts, thereby overstretching and overheating the Soviet economy. Bottlenecks and shortages were not relieved but exacerbated, while the other European members of Comecon resented being asked to contribute scarce capital to projects that were chiefly of interest to the Soviet Union and were always placed under the overall direction of Soviet scientific institutions. In any case, the hastily cobbled together scientific and technical co-operation programme emerged slightly too late to be incorporated into the new 1986–90 five-year plans (Brabant 1989: 117–21).

In 1985 the Soviet regime also launched an initiative which unwittingly hastened Comecon's demise. If the likely consequences had been fully understood, it would surely have acted differently. In June of that year the secretary general of Comecon, Vyacheslav Sychov, sent a letter and a draft joint declaration to the new president of the EC Commission, Jacques Delors, proposing reciprocal diplomatic recognition and relations between the European Community and Comecon, within the parameters of 'their respective competences' (Pinder 1991: 24). This signalled a tacit acceptance that the European Community could directly negotiate trade agreements with individual Comecon members. Unlike the European Community, Comecon had never been recognized as a legal person and its members had never empowered it to negotiate trade treaties on their behalf. In October 1985 the EC commissioner for external relations, Willy De Clercq, informed the European Parliament that the draft joint declaration could be accepted in principle, provided that mutual recognition and relations were accompanied by a normalization of bilateral relations between the European Community and Comecon's individual member states, which would then accredit diplomatic representatives to the EC, negotiate trade agreements with it and cease to oppose European Community representation on other international bodies. De Clercq sent Comecon and each of its members a letter to this effect in February 1986. By May all had formally accepted this twin-track approach to 'normal relations' between the two groups and their individual Member States, paving the way for formal negotiations between Comecon and the European Community to commence in September 1986 (p. 25). The negotiations were prolonged by a dispute over the status of West Berlin, but the much-needed joint declaration of mutual recognition, reciprocal relations and co-operation on matters of joint interest was finally signed on 25 June 1988. This enabled the European Community to conclude trade and co-operation agreements with each of the European members of Comecon, starting with Hungary in December 1988, Poland in December 1989 and the Soviet Union, Czecho-Slovakia (as it briefly became known), Romania and Bulgaria in 1990. These were soon superseded by so-called 'Europe Agreements' (beefed-up Treaties of Association), which were concluded with Poland, Hungary and Czecho-Slovakia in December 1991 and with Romania and Bulgaria in late 1992.

Gorbachev's 'Sinatra doctrine'

In July 1989, moreover, on the eve of the revolutions that ended Communist rule, Mikhail Gorbachev made a major declaration at the Council of Europe: 'The political order of one country or another changed in the past and may change in the future. This change is the exclusive affair and choice of that country. Any interference in domestic affairs and any attempt to restrict the sovereignty of states, both friends and allies or any others, is inadmissible' (quoted in Arter 1993: 237). The so-called 'Sinatra doctrine' (that they could 'do it their way') reversed the previous 'Brezhnev doctrine' concerning the alleged 'limited sovereignty' of the 'fraternal' states (by which Brezhnev had tried to justify the Warsaw Pact invasion of Czechoslovakia in 1968) and gave the green light to sweeping reforms in the Balkans and especially East Central Europe. These states were being allowed to go their own ways. By the same token, however, this was seen as absolving the Soviet Union of any further obligations towards them. Henceforth they would have to 'stand on their own feet', unconstrained but also unsupported by the Soviet Union. Given that the economic systems and industrial structures inherited from the Communist regimes generated comparatively high inputs of energy per unit of output (GDP), the economic cost (energy bills) of cutting their umbilical cords to the former Soviet Union has remained high, even as long afterwards as 2006.

In January 1990 Czecho-Slovakia threatened to secede from Comecon if the other members did not agree to put it into liquidation. In the event a commission was established to assess the options and a Comecon meeting held in Prague in March 1990 proposed a rapid switch from multilateral to bilateral co-operation and plan co-ordination. In reality, however, there were no longer any plans to co-ordinate, since the new five-year plans for 1991–5 never even got off the drawing-boards.

Unfortunately, the trials and tribulations of the reassertion of untrammelled national sovereignty

by the Balkan and East Central European post-Communist states and the marketization, liberalization and privatization of their economies were seriously exacerbated by this hasty abandonment of
the economic interdependencies that had been so laboriously nurtured during Comecon's forty-one-
year life-span. From 1 January 1991, as proposed by the Soviet Union in 1989, all intra-CMEA
trade was officially to be conducted in hard currencies and at world market prices, although this
switch was already well under way in 1990. This signalled the end of Soviet willingness (and even
ability) to meet the ever-increasing energy needs of the Balkan and East Central European states on
concessionary terms.The cost of the implicit shifts in the terms of trade was, as a percentage of
GNP, about 4 per cent for Bulgaria, 2 per cent each for Hungary and Czechoslovakia, 1.5 per cent
for Romania and slightly below 1 per cent for Poland (*FT*, 21 December 1990, p. 6). The volume of
intra-CMEA trade fell by about 15 per cent in 1990 and more than halved in 1991. The OECD estimated that this, combined with the costs of the switch to trading in hard currencies and at current
world prices, accounted for as much as two-thirds of that year's 10–15 per cent decline in Balkan
and East Central European output (*Economic Outlook*, June 1992, p. 43).

Partly as a result of the collapse of intra-CMEA trade in 1990–1, trade with the European
Community rose to about 50 per cent of the foreign trade of the Balkan and East Central European
states by 1992, from a mere 25 per cent in 1989. Nevertheless, trade with these states still accounted
for only 1.7 per cent of the European Community's foreign trade in that year, that is, less than the
value of EC trade with countries such as Austria or Sweden at that time (*FT*, 7 June 1993, p. 13).
Conversely, the share of other former members of Comecon in the foreign trade of the Balkan and
East Central European states had fallen to less than 25 per cent by 1993, from an average of just
over 50 per cent in 1988. Thus the post-Communist states in East Central Europe and the Balkans
exchanged asymmetrical trade dependence on the Soviet Union for an equally asymmetrical
commercial dependence on the European Community. The final Council Session of Comecon was
held in Budapest on 28 June 1991. The organization was to be disbanded within ninety days (that
is, by 28 September 1991). It is an exaggeration to claim, as Jonathan Eyal did, that Comecon
amounted to 'little more than a medieval bazaar in which second-rate economies transacted barter
deals and cheated each other' (*The Independent*, 22 February 1995, p. 15), but few mourned its
demise. It may have been beyond redemption, but the manner of its passing would have inflicted
less pain and fewer costs if it had been more dignified and gradual. The export niches which the
Balkan and East Central European Communist states had carved for themselves as suppliers of
highly specific products to the former Soviet republics were somewhat incautiously thrown to the
wind.

Unfortunately, the somewhat unhappy experience of externally imposed 'mutual economic
assistance' and co-operation within Comecon had not helped to prepare either the peoples or the
rulers of the East Central European and Balkan post-Communist states to work closely together in
pursuit of further integration with the European Union and for the construction of interim arrangements to promote the requisite economic integration within these regions, both in order to salvage
some of the fruitful interdependences that emerged in the Communist era and to overcome Western
doubts as to whether the post-Communist states were really capable of sinking their differences and
becoming worthy partners in a wider Europe. Writing on the eve of the Revolutions of 1989, the
Czechoslovak dissident Miroslav Kusy remarked that 'economic integration within the Soviet bloc
has essentially taken place at such exalted levels that it does not affect daily life in the countries
involved in such a way as to make all inhabitants directly aware of it . . . and generate in them a
feeling of belonging to the bloc, a shared sense of East Europeanness' (Kusy 1989: 95).

THE 'REVOLUTIONS OF 1989'

The collapse of the Communist regimes in East Central Europe, Bulgaria and Romania during 1989 and in Yugoslavia and Albania during 1990–1, should not be attributed simply to the severity of the economic, social and environmental crises over which they presided during the 1980s. Measured in terms of telephones, televisions, washing machines, refrigerators, teachers, doctors, nurses, hospital beds or housing space per thousand inhabitants, living standards in these countries had been considerably lower during the 1950s and 1960s than they were in the late 1980s. The major difference was that the Communist parties could still put forward plausible 'socialist' solutions to the problems of the 1950s and 1960s and hold out credible 'socialist' visions and hopes for the future, whereas they could neither offer nor even see any credible 'socialist' way out of the economic, social and environmental crises of the 1980s, which were in that sense 'terminal'. By the late 1980s even 'market socialism' had fallen into disrepute, partly because the experiments in economic liberalization and decentralization in Hungary and Yugoslavia had run into the sand – into seemingly insoluble difficulties. In addition, partly as a result of the neo-liberal counter-revolution in Western economic governance during the late 1970s and 1980s, market socialism and other so-called 'middle ways' between full-blown socialism and capitalism had ceased to be intellectually fashionable, in sharp contrast to the 1950s and 1960s. Few people, in either East or West, believed in them any longer. Reformist half-measures were ceasing to be acceptable. There now seemed to be a straight choice between various viable forms of capitalism and various 'failed' and utterly discredited forms of so-called 'socialism'.

There was growing cynicism, a crisis of belief and a loss of vision at all levels. Even though the Communist regimes managed to conceal the full magnitude of the 1980s crises from the public and even from Western specialists on the eastern half of Europe, key personnel within those regimes sensed that the game was up and completely gave up the search for 'socialist' solutions to the profound systemic crises afflicting Europe's Communist states. Indeed, Poznanski, Kolakowski and others have gone so far as to argue that the growing alienation of the masses was not in itself sufficient to cause and/or explain the demise of Communist rule in Europe. The Communist parties themselves were, paradoxically, 'an equal or more essential force in the collapse'; and 'this self-destruction was in response not so much to the frustrated masses' as to the Communists' own appreciation of 'the grim future that lay ahead'. Party leaders 'stopped believing', while the party faithful 'lost faith in what used to be perceived as the historic mission of the apparatus' (Poznanski 1992: 204). The floundering ruling strata were at a complete loss as to what to do. In 1989 they lost control of a situation in which they had never expected to find themselves. This was a major reason why (other than in Romania) the demise of Communist rule in Europe evoked so little violent resistance from Communist 'diehards' and 'barons', who found themselves incapable of offering any viable 'socialist' solutions. The only obvious way out of the general crisis of Marxist-Leninist regimes was 'to relax the political structures and change property rights so that strong social groups interested in economizing on resources were reintroduced' (p. 93).

Significantly, Marxists have long argued that revolutions usually occur (i) when there is a fatal split within a ruling class which has lost faith in its own capacity to govern and to resolve crises, (ii) when the prevailing mode of production and social relations of production have reached the limits of their productive potential and have become a brake on any further development of society's productive forces, (iii) when a large section of the educated classes no longer supports the status quo and (iv) when there is growing demoralization and discontent among the toiling classes. All these insights were clearly applicable to Europe's Communist states during the 1980s. The ruling parties were manifestly losing faith in their own doctrines and competence to govern, there were paralysing splits between hard-line 'dogmatists' and more liberal 'reformers', the economies of Europe's Communist states were visibly stagnating or contracting, there was a widespread 'defection' of the intelligentsia, and most workers felt badly let down or even betrayed by these self-proclaimed 'workers' states'. There was also a widespread moral revulsion of the ruled against the mendacity, mediocrity, sleaze and corruption of the Communist rulers, who had long ceased to command any respect. Their continuing claims to a monopoly of truth, wisdom and virtue became all the more derisory or repugnant. As argued by Ernest Gellner, 'the sleazy but . . . relatively mild squalor of the Brezhnev years proved far more corrosive for the image of the faith than the total, pervasive, random and massively destructive terror of Stalinism. That terror could at least be seen as the fearful but appropriately dramatic heralding of a totally new social order, the coming of a new man . . . The squalor, on the other hand, heralded nothing at all except, perhaps, more squalor' (Gellner 1996: 3). 'When the *nomenklatura* killed each other and accompanied the murderous rampage with blatantly mendacious political theatre, belief survived; but when the *nomenklatura* switched from shooting each other to bribing each other, faith evaporated' (p. 41). Consequently, the Communist regimes even proved incapable of achieving re-legitimation or self-renewal through competitive, pluralistic elections, as Gorbachev's limited Soviet experiments in *demokratizatsiya* soon demonstrated.

Not surprisingly, therefore, 'revisionist' and reform-minded Marxists played seminal roles in the gradual breakdown of Communist rule and in the struggles for freedom in the eastern half of Europe, especially in Poland, Hungary, Czechoslovakia and Yugoslavia (Michnik 1985: 135–48). In the words of Adam Michnik, the doyen of Polish dissent (and like Leszek Kolakowski and Jacek Kuron, himself a lapsed Marxist), new forms of 'critical Marxism' left official Communism 'with its teeth kicked in'. Critical Marxists pioneered the re-creation of an 'independent space' for philosophical discourse and the revival of political engagement and activism in place of apathetic acceptance of the apparent unassailability of the Communist regimes (Taras *et al.* 1992: 3–12). By producing profoundly damaging (neo-)Marxist critiques of 'actually existing socialism', by having the courage and the capacity to challenge it on its own terms and from within, and by exposing intrinsic failings which tended to get overlooked by liberal and right-wing critics attuned to very different agendas and discourses, dissident Marxism hit the Communist regimes where it hurt most. It was second to none in undermining Marxism as an official ideology and reducing it to a hollow shell.

The social and political upheavals of 1989–91, which ended Communist rule in the eastern half of Europe, were in large measure 'revolutions from above' stage-managed by white-collar intelligentsias, reform Communists and 'closet reformers' within the Soviet security police (KGB). Even the apparently spontaneous demonstrations of popular hostility to the dying Communist dictatorships were to considerable extents prepared and informed by 'passive revolutions' (in the Gramscian sense), that is, by significant shifts in the balance of power, values, aspirations and ideas, which in turn established the cultural and political leadership and hegemony of the white-collar intelligentsia in eastern European societies. Through their growing dominance of the media and information services, white-collar intelligentsias and reform Communists committed to political and economic liberalization were able to manipulate the symbols and ideology of the incipient revolutions and indicate to the population at large what was taking place, how and when popular pressure ('people power') could most effectively be applied, and where mass demonstrations should assemble or converge.

The Communist dictatorships had sown the seeds of their own destruction. The future ruling class was being nurtured, as always, within the womb of the old system. The centrally directed industrialization, mass education and 'scientific-technological revolution' promoted by Communist regimes had elevated both the so-called 'creative intelligentsia' and the white-collar professional, managerial and technical intelligentsia to 'leading' (guiding) roles in eastern European societies. By the 1980s such groups constituted 20–30 per cent of the workforce, according to official classifications and calculations. Since the 1960s, conversely, the old 'blue-collar' working class had steadily shrunk as a proportion of the workforce and had become increasingly differentiated, heterogeneous and, in its upper echelons, 'embourgeoised'. As in the West and in the Soviet Union, increased mechanization, complex control systems and the 'scientific-technological revolution' had progressively reduced the importance of manual labour while enhancing that of technical, professional and managerial skills, expertise and training. Moreover, the ruling parties and so-called 'techno-bureaucratic personnel' were increasingly recruited from the ranks of the intelligentsia rather than the shrinking 'blue-collar' working class. Indeed, while it remained fashionable to dwell on antagonisms between the intelligentsia at large and the narrower party-state bureaucracy, in reality the intelligentsia was not sharply separated from but increasingly overlapped with the party-state bureaucracy. As the Hungarian sociologist Ivan Szelenyi pointed out in 1979, the borderline between the intelligentsia and the party-state bureaucracy was 'a very shaky one in terms of personal career patterns. Many university graduates with high academic ambitions enter the party bureaucracy' and, 'from the point of view of material privilege, it is practically impossible to distinguish between the techno-bureaucracy and the intelligentsia. Their living standard is practically identical' (Szelenyi 1979: 59). He also argued that the all-pervasive roles of central planning under the highly 'teleological' (goal-orientated) and 'redistributive' Communist regimes had enhanced the ideological and managerial roles and social status of the intelligentsia far above that attained under capitalism, placing the intelligentsia rather than capitalists in the driving seat and transforming the intelligentsia into a type of secular priesthood that not only managed social resources but also arrogated exclusive rights to prescribe society's goals and values. This virtually 'integrates the whole intelligentsia into a dominating class' (pp. 65–6). Furthermore, by the mid-1950s in Poland and Hungary, by the 1960s in Czechoslovakia, Yugoslavia and the GDR and by the 1980s in the rest of eastern Europe, the growing 'creative' and 'technical' intelligentsias fostered by Europe's Communist regimes were chaffing against the crudities, the narrow-mindedness, the excesses and the irksome tutelage of one-party rule. However, in contrast to the archetypal nineteenth-century radical/oppositional intelligentsias (who characteristically led precarious existences on the margins of society and of the economy and were essentially independent of the state), the new intelligentsias fostered by the Communist regimes mainly consisted of state employees whose power, aspirations, special status, privileges and sense of importance and vocation were largely determined by their positions and roles as servants and functionaries of hegemonic state institutions, even after the collapse of Communist rule. They remained very dependent on somewhat humbled and impoverished but still dominant states to protect and provide for them and to give them a continuing status and sense of importance in the new post-Communist societies, despite (or even because of) the fact that many of their former functions had become redundant or superfluous as a result of the dismantling of command economies and Communist regimes. Many found themselves in extremely vulnerable, impoverished and wholly unenviable positions. Not surprisingly, therefore, their enthusiasm for political and economic liberalism was tempered by an acute awareness of their continuing dependence on the state and by a prudent reluctance to bite the hand that had not only nurtured and fed them but had also given them their sense of usefulness and public worth. The initial predominance of the intelligentsia was reinforced by the fact that an entrepreneurial business class was only just beginning to emerge and was not yet politically effective at the time of the Revolutions of 1989–91. This and the continuing preponderance of the state sector, which could not be privatized overnight, left the 'hegemonic' leading roles of the intelligentsia and state functionaries almost unchallenged for the time being.

Poland and, to much lesser degrees, Romania and (in 1991) Albania provided the only clear-cut examples of worker-led rejections of Communist rule. Nevertheless, even the Solidarity-led government formed in June 1989 was completely dominated by the liberal-minded intelligentsia, to the disgust of many of Solidarity's 'blue-collar' grass-roots supporters, thousands of whom were soon to be made redundant or dismissed from their jobs by agents and official receivers appointed by the Solidarity-led government as a result of the economic 'shock therapy' which it administered in

1990–1. The major problem for most of eastern Europe's 'blue-collar' workers was that, except in Poland (where Solidarity was indeed in a position to provide genuinely independent grass-roots union representation and defence of the interests of workers, but was placed in an invidious position when Solidarity intellectuals took up the principal reins of government), the capacity of workers to represent and defend their interests during the demise of Communist rule and the 'command economies' was limited by the fact that the existing official trade unions were greatly weakened and discredited by their close links with and subservience to the now defunct Communist parties and regimes. Moreover, the fact that many of eastern Europe's heavy industries were grossly overmanned, inefficient, struggling to survive and, in effect, surplus to requirements (especially after the Communist regimes collapsed and the Cold War ended) placed most of the region's 'blue-collar' workers in extremely weak bargaining positions.

THE CONSPICUOUS PASSIVITY OF THE PEASANTRY

Peasants played strikingly passive roles in the Revolutions of 1989 to 1991. Although most peasants had received raw deals during the 1950s, their plight had on the whole improved substantially during the 1960s and 1970s. The basic reason for this reversal of fortunes was, paradoxically, that agriculture had come to be seen as a problem sector. During the Stalinist era, when eastern Europe's still mainly agricultural economies were able to maintain a basic self-sufficiency in agricultural products despite the rapid growth of urban-industrial sectors, the remuneration and resource requirements of eastern European agriculture had been assigned relatively low priorities. By the 1960s and 1970s, however, as the growth of urban-industrial sectors, incomes and effective demand for agricultural products began to outstrip the growth of domestic agricultural output, agricultural remuneration, resource requirements and state subsidies were gradually accorded a higher priority, in an endeavour to minimize urban food shortages, workers' discontent and the expenditure of scarce foreign exchange on imports of agricultural products. Nevertheless, the Communist regimes' persistent reluctance to raise official retail food prices (partly for fear of provoking urban unrest), combined with an accelerating growth of disposable money incomes in the towns, meant that aggregate demand for agricultural products continued to outstrip the more moderate growth of farm output. Indeed, it was in the interest of the farm population to make only modest increases in agricultural deliveries to the state distribution networks. For, so long as agriculture remained a 'problem' in the eyes of the state, farmers could expect to receive increased farm subsidies, remuneration and investment from the state and to be allowed increasingly to engage in lucrative sidelines, private enterprise and petty pilfering, to which farm officials increasingly turned a blind eye because they were either in on the game or fearful of alienating a still somewhat resentful peasant population. Conversely, if farmers had delivered enough agricultural produce to satisfy rapidly growing demand, agriculture would have ceased to be seen as such a serious problem and the state would have treated them less generously, while farm officials could have become stricter. It therefore paid the farm populations to provide only the most perfunctory fulfilment of their obligations to the state and to the collective farms, and increasingly to concentrate on their private 'home improvements' and increased private production of not only food but clothing, footwear, jewellery and drinks for their own consumption and for the relatively high-priced 'free' and 'black' markets. These private activities increasingly diverted resources from the collective and state farms, both legally and illicitly, but that was the state's problem – not the peasantry's. Even during the relative stagnation of the 1980s, the real incomes and assets of the farm populations continued to increase as states desperately pumped in more and more resources in vain endeavours to reinvigorate collective and/or state farm systems, while persistent urban food shortages perpetuated the opportunities for private profiteering and blackmarketeering. In effect, farmers got their own back for the hardships and privations to which they had been subjected during the 1940s and 1950s. In the process, however, they became less interested in radical change. Like their West European counterparts, eastern European farmers had much to fear from the freer trade, price reforms, withdrawal of subsidies, runaway inflation and loss of captive markets that could result from a change of political and economic regime.

THE CATALYTIC ROLES OF 'REFORM COMMUNISTS'

During 1990 it gradually came to light that 'closet reformers' in the Soviet KGB (state security police) had also played significant roles in the subversion of the hard-line Communist regimes in East Germany, Czechoslovakia and Bulgaria in November 1989 and in Romania the following month. Their aim was not to end but to prolong Communist rule, by replacing embarrassingly hard-line rulers with more palatable and pragmatic 'reform Communists' in the Gorbachev mould. It was envisaged that these reform Communists would initiate managed transitions to more market-oriented and pluralistic but still Communist-led regimes, more in keeping with the liberal image projected by Soviet *perestroika* and *glasnost* and the 'reform Communism' pioneered in Hungary. These manoeuvres misfired, however. They triggered changes which rapidly went far beyond what 'reform Communists' and the KGB had intended. The KGB-backed 'reform Communists' lost out because of a complete loss of faith in and rejection of the ruling Communist parties, other than in their new 'socialist', National Salvation Front and Serbian nationalist incarnations in Bulgaria, Romania and Serbia, respectively. In most cases, moreover, 'reform Communists' still had the cautious mindsets of enlightened and paternalistic planners, aiming at limited reforms 'from above' rather than more radical initiatives 'from below'. They were afraid of the working classes and of any real spontaneity and, as soon as large numbers of eastern Europeans displayed a will to move beyond the limited agenda of 'reform Communism' in late 1989, the 'reform Communists' lost their political power base almost overnight. They suddenly became 'yesterday's men', as they were quickly overtaken by events.

The Revolutions of 1989 (to 1991) took Western specialists on the eastern half of Europe (among others) by surprise because their underlying assumptions about Communist regimes overestimated their resilience and staying power and underestimated the extent to which civil society in the region was able to foster alternative political cultures which could erode the increasingly threadbare political legitimacy of Communist rule. These revolutions were the result of a prolonged systemic crisis, allied to the unwillingness of the Soviet leader Mikhail Gorbachev to emulate his predecessors by employing force to keep Communists in power.

Furthermore, command economies could function only so long as commands were generally obeyed. As the ruling elites became increasingly divided as to how to react to the systemic crisis, civil society lost some of its former fear of the seemingly formidable apparatus of repression, while the diminution of fear decreased the disposition to obey. Nevertheless, the Revolutions of 1989 might not have succeeded if Gorbachev had not unilaterally renounced old habits of Soviet military-political intervention in East Central European politics. The emergence of the Gorbachev regime was probably a necessary (though not a sufficient) precondition for the democratization of Europe's hitherto Communist states.

Gorbachev's team may have decided as early as the autumn of 1986 to renounce the use of force in the Balkan and East Central European states and had an ideal opportunity to inform their Communist Party leaders of this at the CMEA summit held in Moscow on 10–11 November 1986. 'Gorbachev realized that the Europeanization of the Soviet Union could not proceed without the de-Sovietization of Eastern Europe' (Dawisha 1990: 198). Conversely, Gorbachev's concept of a 'common European home' dovetailed with the East Central European intelligentsias' strong belief in the oneness of Europe and it reinforced their efforts to deepen or renew their emotional and cultural ties with the West, implicitly turning away from Russia. At the same time, paradoxically, Gorbachev's programme of *perestroika* profoundly influenced East Central Europe and the Balkans by providing a potent model and symbol of reform from above and liberalization, by licensing or even igniting a ferment of ideas, debate and demands for reform in other Communist states, and by encouraging some prominent East Central European and Balkan Communists to try to ape Gorbachev (pp. 208–10). Thus the imperatives of Soviet *perestroika* destabilized East Central Europe and parts of the Balkans during the late 1980s, in much the same way that Khrushchev's 'de-Stalinization' programme had done in 1956. Furthermore, by abandoning the hitherto customary requirement of Soviet approval of successors to East Central European and Bulgarian Communist Party leaders after 1985, Gorbachev ended a direct channel of Soviet supervision of its East Central European 'allies' and Bulgaria (Light 1994: 154–5), although the KGB continued to operate behind the scenes from Soviet embassies in these countries at least until the end of 1989.

Gorbachev's announcement in 1988 that Soviet troops would be withdrawn from Afghanistan was widely seen not just as a blow to the aura of Soviet invincibility and to Soviet military morale, but also as tangible confirmation of his renunciation of Soviet military interference in the affairs of 'fraternal socialist states'. This also helped to lift the veil of fear which had hitherto kept mounting hostility to or alienation from Communist regimes in check.

Gorbachev's marked reluctance to express approval of the Berlin Wall, let alone the Soviet invasions of Hungary in 1956 and Czechoslovakia in 1968, reduced the security and legitimacy of the Honecker, Kadar and Husak regimes, because Honecker had risen to power as the man who oversaw the building of the Berlin Wall in 1961 and the GDR's role in the 1968 invasion of Czechoslovakia, while both Kadar and Husak headed quisling regimes initiated by Soviet invasions. Without his having to issue explicit disavowals or condemnations, the distaste with which Gorbachev regarded the unsavoury hard-line rulers of the GDR, Czechoslovakia, Bulgaria and Romania became plainly visible to millions of television viewers who watched the official television coverage of his public meetings with and visits to East Central European and some Balkan Communist leaders. It was also difficult to disguise the pointed contrast between the spontaneous enthusiasm of the crowds that greeted Gorbachev during his visits to East Central Europe and their sullen indifference to their own rulers. Europe's hard-line Communist regimes were further undermined when there was no public Soviet protest either against the opening of Hungary's border with Austria in May 1989 or against Hungary's decision officially to allow East German 'holiday-makers' to escape through that bolt-hole to the West on 10 September 1989. This and Gorbachev's refusal to sanction a military crackdown on mounting East German popular demands for freedom in October 1989 increased the pressure on the regime to allow East Germans freely to cross the Berlin Wall on 9 November 1989, thereby imparting an unstoppable momentum to German unification and to further popular challenges to brittle Communist authority in other East Central European and Balkan states. As Vaclav Havel remarked on 9 April 1990, 'We all know how much harder our road to freedom would have been if the great work of renewal in our society had not been linked with the name of President Gorbachev' (Havel 1994b: 63).

Nevertheless, Gorbachev was mainly 'reacting to events rather than initiating them'(Light 1994: 154). There is no suggestion that he was acting out a master plan for the dismantling of Communist rule in the eastern half of Europe. Rather, he hoped to ensure its survival by encouraging the deposition of hard-liners in favour of reformers in his own image. However, the undermining of hard-liners unleashed forces which also dethroned the reform Communists.

In the final analysis, Gorbachev precipitated the democratization of Europe's Communist states not so much by what he consciously *did* as by what he *was*, namely a tonic, a beacon of hope, a humane voice of reason and an opponent of falsehood, intimidation, sleaze and hypocrisy. In some ways he was quite out of tune with the darker forces that were unleashed by the democratization of Europe's Communist states and the long retreat from Communist 'proletarian internationalism'. For example, when he visited the victims of the devastating earthquake which struck Armenia in 1988, he was understandably shocked and angered to discover that some Armenians were much more interested in the line he would take in Armenia's territorial dispute with the neighbouring Soviet Republic of Azerbaijan than in what was to be done to assist the earthquake victims lying on the ground all around them (Roxburgh 1991: 122–3). Gorbachev avoided military invasions and crackdowns, other than in Georgia and the Baltic Soviet republics where Soviet forces may conceivably have defied his wishes, although the evidence is ambiguous. (Most Georgians and nationalists of the Baltic States seemed convinced of Gorbachev's complicity, but we were not.) Gorbachev thus contributed to the remarkably low levels of violence employed by either side (other than in Romania and Yugoslavia) during the demise of Communist rule in Europe. By adopting a new foreign policy and persevering with it even after it was visibly contributing to the Soviet Union's loss of its major external 'sphere of influence', Gorbachev 'created the conditions in which democratic forces within Eastern Europe could come to the fore, and Western democratic and market forces could penetrate the region', even though 'only the East Europeans themselves were in a position to ensure that the outcome was democracy' (Light 1994: 163–4).

Part V

Post-Communist transformations

34 Post-Communist political transformations: debunking 'democratic transition' and 'democratic consolidation'

In 1989 East Central Europe and most of the Balkans embarked on an arduous 'triple transformation': from Communist dictatorship to pluralistic democracy; from centrally administered to market economies; and from Soviet imperial hegemony to fully independent nation-statehood. This was the third time that these regions had embarked on such far-reaching transformations during the twentieth century. East Central Europe and much of the Balkans underwent a comparable 'triple transformation' after the First World War: from semi-absolutist monarchies to ostensibly democratic regimes; from a supranational imperial order to an order based on fully independent nation-states; and from a social order dominated by imperial bureaucracies and armies and large landed estates to societies with a preponderance of peasant farmers, dominated by national bureaucracies, national armies and ascendant national bourgeoisies. East Central Europe and most of the Balkans embarked on yet another 'triple transformation' in 1945–6: from fascist imperial domination to independent national statehood; from fascist dictatorship to pluralistic democracy; and from fascist (autarkic) administered economies to more open, semi-planned market economies.

The post-1918 transformations came to grief on the rocks of illiberal 'ethnic' or 'integral' nationalism, irredentism, revanchism, beggar-my-neighbour protectionism and increasing 'asymmetrical' commercial dependence on a resurgent German Reich and, to a lesser extent, Fascist Italy. The post-1945 transformations were stymied by an extension of Soviet imperial hegemony over East Central Europe and most of the Balkan states and by the imposition of neo-Stalinist regimes and programmes of coercive, centrally planned industrialization and rural collectivization, the (initial) positive appeal of which rested in part on their presumed capacity to transcend the ethnic, irredentist and economic problems which had plagued these regions from 1918 to 1947. Regrettably, 'ethnocracy' and 'ethnic collectivism' were still very much alive in the Balkans and East Central Europe during the 1990s and early 2000s. This was more obviously the case in the Balkans than it was in East Central Europe, mainly because Hitler, Stalin and their allies had 'surgically homogenized' the populations of East Central Europe during the 1940s and 1950s, whereas Balkan populations had remained much more heterogeneous.

The previous attempts to build a 'new order' in East Central Europe and the Balkans on the basis of fully independent nation-states had coincided with crises arising from the concurrent social and economic transformations and the attendant disruption of natural or long-established trade patterns. These crises had fostered extreme nationalism and social unrest, had reduced popular support for liberal democracy and 'free market' economics, and had precipitated external intervention in Balkan and East Central European affairs. Unfortunately, the post-1989 transformations re-created similar conditions and opportunities in former Yugoslavia during the first half of the 1990s and came close to doing so in some other localities. Although the Communist regimes had been officially atheist and internationalist and had frequently persecuted clergy, active 'believers' and outspoken independent-minded nationalists, they had nevertheless fostered various forms of 'official nationalism' and (except in Albania) had in large measure tolerated the dominant 'national' religions, in vain and ultimately self-undermining attempts to compensate for perceived deficiencies in their own political legitimacy and popular support from the 1960s to the 1980s. This left nationalism and 'national' religions as the only available value- and belief-systems that were immediately capable of filling the spiritual and ideological vacuums opened up by the decline and eventual fall of the moribund Communist dictatorships. Furthermore, the initial 'national euphoria' unleashed by the collapse of Communist rule both enhanced the influence of exclusive and potentially intolerant 'ethnic nationalism' and national religions, and aroused expectations which could not rapidly be fulfilled, and the initial hopes of imminent prosperity soon dissolved into grim realization that the market too could be a tyrannical and unforgiving master.

The situation was exacerbated by the fact that there had never been much of a politically and economically independent middle-class constituency for either political or economic liberalism in the eastern half of Europe. It rapidly proved to be almost as difficult to create flourishing liberal democracy and dynamic liberal capitalism with insufficient capital and without highly developed bourgeoisies, as it had previously been to create genuinely 'proletarian' dictatorships and well-functioning centrally planned economies with insufficient capital and without highly developed industrial proletariats. The independent entrepreneurial and professional middle classes of East Central Europe and the Balkans, which were still comparatively small after the First World War, had been further reduced in size by the mass extermination of most East Central European and Balkan Jews during the Second World War, the subsequent emigration of most of the few surviving Jews, and the hasty departure or expulsion of more than 10 million Germans from East Central Europe and (in smaller measure) from the Balkans in 1945–7. Besides horrific suffering and loss of human life, these man-made catastrophes also inflicted enormous economic and political costs, since Jews and Germans had (between them) made up at least half of the Balkan and East Central European independent urban professional and entrepreneurial middle classes prior to the Second World War. The Stalinist regimes established in the Balkans and East Central Europe during the later 1940s swiftly completed the work begun by illiberal and xenophobic nationalists and fascists, by bringing all public institutions and activities under Communist control and thereby destroying the last vestiges both of 'civil society' and of the legal, administrative, educational and cultural impartiality of the state. Indeed, Balkan and East Central European politics remained very violent during the late 1940s and early 1950s, because the post-war anti-fascist 'Popular Front' coalitions sought 'retribution' against many thousands of known or suspected fascists and their wartime 'collaborators', even before the ascendant Communist parties instituted large-scale 'purges' against tens of thousands of actual or potential opponents (see Deak *et al.* 2000: Parts I and III). The surviving members of the decimated interwar intelligentsias and the professional and entrepreneurial middle classes were either 'liquidated' by these purges and the attendant suppression of almost all independent activity, or else 'swamped' by the large, malleable and subservient 'technical' and 'creative' intelligentsias fostered by the Stalinist regimes. Significantly, these new intelligentsias were in large measure recruited from the educated upper layers of the working class and the peasantry, thereby 'buying off' and/or 'creaming off' the potential spokesmen or ringleaders of proletarian and peasant opposition and discontent, while simultaneously creating a new 'privileged class' which consciously owed its positions and perquisites to Communist favour and patronage.

As a consequence, one of the major actual or potential initial impediments to the maturation of liberal forms of democracy in East Central Europe and the Balkans during the early 1990s was the fact that (other than in the Czech Lands) independent and impartial political and civil institutions had barely existed hitherto. Even those that did emerge had been largely destroyed by the combined effects of intolerant 'ethnic' nationalism and authoritarianism, the 1930s Depression, fascism, the Second World War, the Holocaust and neo-Stalinist dictatorship, all of which had helped to decimate, emasculate or drive abroad the ethnic and social groups that were most capable of producing or recreating autonomous, pluralistic and liberal-minded 'civil societies'.

James Barrington Moore Jnr greatly oversimplified matters when he famously coined the phrase 'No bourgeoisie, no democracy' (Moore 1969: 418). In much of Western Europe the establishment and/or maintenance of liberal democracy and fundamental civil rights owed a great deal to the struggles and contributions of the burgeoning industrial working classes and their trade unions (see Therborn 1978; Reuschemeyer *et al.* 1992), while in the Balkans and East Central Europe similar roles were played by the peasant(ist) parties and movements (see Mitrany 1951: 124–9). Nevertheless, the destruction and emasculation of independent intermediary classes has usually made it *more difficult* to establish and/or sustain liberal democracy. Successful establishment of *liberal democracy* (as distinct from the various forms of *illiberal democracy* which now abound) has therefore tended to depend on the *prior or concurrent emergence* of *liberal practices and customs and a robustly liberal legal/institutional infrastructure* (Parekh 1992), as well as 'a plurality of independent groups jealously guarding their autonomy'; and both sets of prerequisites need to be strong enough to be capable of obliging the 'pre-existing ruling groups progressively to share their power and privileges with wider and wider sections of society' (Kornhauser 1960: 135, 141).

Similarly, the long-term survival of liberal democracy has usually depended upon the maintenance and/or emergence of the rule of law, limited government, extensive civil rights and liberties, and a rich diversity of responsible and autonomous social groups. It requires 'limitations on the use of power by majorities as well as minorities', involving not only 'constitutional checks and balances (e.g., separation of powers), but also a system of social checks and balances', typically in the form of a multiplicity of autonomous competing 'interest groups' (Kornhauser 1960: 130). In the absence of 'constitutional rule, backed by a system of social checks and balances', there are insufficient safeguards against the potential 'tyranny of the majority' and/or an overweening state (p. 131). In the absence of autonomous, articulate and effectively organized pressure 'from below', it is all too easy for ruling elites to abuse and augment their powers and privileges, to stonewall, and (sometimes literally) to get away with murder, while policies are also less likely to be thrashed out and debated as much as they need to be. Conversely, a plurality of independent social groups not only works *against excessive concentration(s)* of power and authority in too few hands, but also *supports and sustains authority by sharing it.* Autonomous social groups act as 'intermediate authorities capable of ordering limited spheres of social life', while simultaneously supporting and enlarging 'the sphere of liberty' by constraining each other and by inducing the state to seek mutual accommodation within a framework of rights of free association, freedom of expression, the rule of law, and limited government (p. 136).

The strength and vigour of liberal democracies and liberal market economies depend as much on the size, health and vitality of these intermediate layers, networks and associations, which stand and mediate between the state and individual citizens, as they do on having formal legal and institutional infrastructures capable of sustaining limited government, the rule of law and strongly 'horizontal' power relations, power structures and 'level playing fields' (Putnam 1993, 2000, 2002; Pharr and Putnam 2000; Fukuyama 1995). In this respect, economics and politics have tended to go hand in hand. In recent decades the world's most dynamic economies have tended to be those with the most vigorous intermediate associations and networks, most notably the East Asian 'tiger' economies and post-Maoist China, rather than the more liberal but less vigorously 'associational' and 'networked' Western democracies (Ian Davidson, *FT*, 1 February 1995, p. 14; and, more generally, Fukuyama 1995). Crudely neo-liberal free-marketeers in the Thatcherite and/or Reaganite moulds have mistakenly equated civil society with the market and individuals, overlooking the degrees to which both democracy and market systems rest on the autonomous intermediate institutions, associations, ties and networks and standards of probity which neo-liberal policies have done so much to weaken, emasculate, undermine or erode, especially in the USA, the UK and Latin America since the 1980s 'neo-liberal counter-revolution' in economic governance. In the absence of sufficiently strong social supports, the state is left standing omnipotent over an atomized mass of increasingly isolated and defenceless individuals, which is probably quite the opposite of what any sincere and well-meaning neo-liberals intended.

CONCEPTUAL CRITICISMS OF THE 'DEMOCRATIC TRANSITION' AND 'DEMOCRATIC CONSOLIDATION' LITERATURE OF THE 1980s AND 1990s

The huge literature on so-called 'democratic transition' and 'democratic consolidation' written by political scientists during the 1980s and 1990s generated (along with a great deal of turgid new jargon!) some moderately useful conceptual distinctions and taxonomies which helped to generate more variegated and nuanced conceptualizations of processes of democratization. So-called 'democratic transition' widely came to be seen as 'a process of regime change commencing at the point when the previous authoritarian regime begins to be dismantled, abruptly or gradually'. During this phase 'democratic rules of procedure have to be negotiated and accepted; institutions have to be restructured; and political competition has to be channelled along democratic lines'. So-called 'democratic consolidation', by contrast, widely came to be seen as a lengthier process involving 'the removal of the uncertainties that invariably surround transition and the full institutionalization of the new system, the internalization of its rules and procedures and the dissemination of democratic values' (Pridham *et al.* 1994: 2), to the point where democracy becomes 'the only game in town' (Linz and Stepan 1996: 5).

In addition to contingent economic and social circumstances, various studies of 'democratic consolidation' in southern Europe and Latin America sought to emphasize the crucial importance of so-called 'elite settlements' and 'elite convergence', that is, processes which encouraged elites to engage in 'politics as bargaining' rather than 'politics as war'. These 'elite settlements' were seen as involving formal pacts: 'previously disunified and warring elites suddenly and deliberately reorganize their relations by negotiating compromises on their most basic disagreements, thereby achieving consensual unity and laying the basis for a stable democratic regime'. By contrast, 'elite convergence' was seen as involving 'a series of deliberate, tactical decisions by rival elites that have the cumulative effect . . . of creating elite consensual unity', perhaps over the space of a generation. It has been argued that elite convergence often occurs in two stages. During the first stage, 'some of the warring factions in a disunified national elite enter into sustained, peaceful collaboration in order to mobilize a reliable electoral majority, win elections repeatedly, and thereby dominate government'. During the second stage, 'the major elite factions opposing this coalition tire of continuous government by their ideological and programmatic opponents', but, instead of resorting to violent conflict, 'they conclude that there is no way to challenge their rivals' hegemonic position except . . . by forming an electoral coalition . . . to compete according to the regime's rules, implicitly or explicitly acknowledging the legitimacy of its institutions'. In the main, 'this is accompanied by a reduction of ideological and programmatic polarization in the party system' (Higley and Gunther 1992: xi–xii).

In certain respects, the 'democratic transition' and 'democratic consolidation' literature made considerable advances on the previously influential 'modernization theories', which over-optimistically perceived or treated democratization as an inevitable concomitant of economic, educational and technological development. Modernization theories have implicitly or explicitly presupposed fairly high degrees of economic and technological determinism. They have also rested on an underlying assumption that the West has been acting as a 'role model' and/or 'vision of the future' for other parts of the world and that, as the latter become more economically developed, urbanized and educated, they will increasingly resemble the West. Much the same was true of North–South and East–West 'convergence theories', which were in effect variants or extensions of modernization theory.

The principal virtues of the new 'transitologists' and 'consolidologists' have been that they have tended to take major account of the roles of circumstantial factors and human volition in democratization. They have emphasized that democratization has *not* been the almost *automatic* concomitant of economic, technological and educational advance (as many 'modernization theorists' assumed) and that it could suffer *impediments or even reverses as well as advances*, even in quite well-educated and economically developed societies. The most extreme example of such a reverse was of course Weimar Germany, which, despite being one of the most economically, educationally and technologically advanced countries in interwar Europe, both engendered and quite rapidly succumbed to the Nazi movement. Moreover, the Nazis gained especially strong followings among German university graduates, professors and schoolteachers, some of the most educated segments of German society (Kolinsky 1974: 87–8; Kornhauser 1960: 188).

Nevertheless, despite the usefulness of some of its terminology and insights, some of the most central implicit or explicit assumptions underlying the 'democratic transition' and 'democratic consolidation' literature have been seriously misleading or even fundamentally flawed. Much of this literature has relied on relatively shallow, mechanistic, teleological conceptions or understandings of democracy, democratization and political change. Its conceptual language and formulations misleadingly imply or presuppose that 'democratic transitions' and 'democratic consolidations' are finite and for the most part unilinear processes, involving movement from broadly comparable and clearly identifiable starting points towards broadly comparable and clearly identifiable final destinations; that democratization passes through fairly regular and predictable intermediate stages; that elites are more or less free to choose 'off the shelf' or out of a democratic 'toolkit' whatever political arrangements they fancy; and that political and economic elites are usually capable of establishing and 'consolidating' democracy from the top downwards, with quite minimal input from the rest of society. The literature is implicitly or explicitly elitist, in as much as it has assumed that political and economic elites have been the key players and that they are broadly capable of (pre)determining political outcomes, as matters of human volition. At the same time, the literature has also been strongly mechanistic, in that it has assumed that pulling particular 'levers' in particular directions at key moments will produce broadly predictable outcomes.

In practice, however, processes of democratization have varied enormously. They have proceeded from very diverse points of departure and have arrived at widely varying institutional embodiments or outcomes, even among the countries which are routinely lumped together as 'the West' and/or as 'liberal democracies'. Yet, even in the West, *no one knows the final destinations towards which democracy and processes of democratization are moving*. The main reasons for this are that the advent of large-scale transnational capitalism, globalization, growing concentration of corporate power, rapidly developing information technologies, newly emerging modes and networks of communication, and ever-widening international (and possibly domestic) disparities of income, wealth, education and power, are *continually changing the nature and context* of the never-ending quest for the maximum (albeit often limited and/or illusory) scope for democratic control, accountability, scrutiny and debate. Furthermore, the enormous and still growing power of the global forces and networks of global capitalism and information technology and the (possibly resurgent) power of organized religion mean that, even (or perhaps especially) in the West, *liberal democracy is by no means 'the only game in town'*. In the various concurrent 'games', moreover, *the goalposts are continually being moved, the characteristics of the players and the playing field are continually being metamorphosed and reconceptualized, and the nature of the games themselves are also repeatedly being reconceptualized*. It is therefore highly debatable how much democratic scrutiny, debate, control, accountability and legitimacy there really is – even, or perhaps especially, in the increasingly transnational and globalized power relations and power structures which dominate the so-called 'Western liberal democracies'. In addition, as a result of the mounting threats to basic civil liberties posed by the growing obsession of increasingly Islamophobic and xenophobic Western states and media with terrorism and the ever-increasing police powers of detention, surveillance and monitoring authorized by anti-terrorist legislation and made possible by technological advance, the dominant trajectory of 'Western liberal democracies' could just as easily be towards Orwellian dystopias as towards further deepening or strengthening of 'liberal democracy'. If this is the case, the terminology of 'democratic consolidation' will become increasingly meaningless. Anyone who imagines that 'democracy' is something that can be 'consolidated' once and for all, anywhere, is living in a world of self-delusion and make-believe.

In any case, the word 'democracy' is an umbrella term covering many different forms of democratic polity and governance. It is routinely used fairly indiscriminately to refer not only to a wide range of 'really existing' systems of government, but also to an abstract ideal and yardstick against which the much murkier 'really existing' and allegedly 'democratic' political systems can be measured, judged and (in most cases) found wanting. Many Western 'transitologists' and 'consolidologists' have complacently tended to assume that Western liberal democracy is 'the norm' towards which most or even all processes of democratization are ultimately converging. Others have glibly presumed that the new political systems emerging from the so-called 'Third Wave of Democratization' can be acknowledged as being *genuinely democratic* only in so far as they conform to Western conceptions of liberal democracy. Either way, they have unwarrantedly made the West the implicit or explicit ultimate arbiter of what does or does not constitute 'democracy'.

Nevertheless, many (perhaps most) of the new political regimes which emerged from the late twentieth-century 'wave' or 'waves' of democratization have at best produced various kinds of democratic 'facade', behind which highly monopolistic or oligopolistic finance capitalism operates according to its own rules, dynamics and power structures. In most cases, this has given rise to varying degrees and forms of 'illiberal democracy', which have been subjected to illuminating critical analyses by Guillermo O'Donnell (1993, 1996, 1998), Fareed Zakaria (1998, 2003) and the late Claude Aké (1995). O'Donnell has argued that the most important factor in determining whether or not democracy develops in deep, predictable and law-abiding liberal forms is the strength or weakness of what he calls (mutual, legal) 'horizontal accountability' between public institutions and associations, in addition to the establishment of the (electoral) 'vertical accountability' of public office-holders to their electorates. In the absence of strong 'horizontal accountability', only very weak and shallow forms of democracy will be attainable and sustainable in practice. Nevertheless, as O'Donnell (1996) has emphasized, 'these forms have usually been more *long-lasting* than *transitory*; and it is therefore misleading to label them as "transitional".'

This makes it all the more prudent to consider whether we are witnessing 'the universalization of democracy or its final demise?' Having posed this crucial question, Claude Aké boldly replied that even Western political systems have come

> under unrelenting . . . pressure to reconstruct the meaning and practice of democracy in consonance with . . . an increasingly trivial notion of popular participation. The apparent universalization of democracy is the consummation of this process. Democracy has been trivialized to the point where it is no longer threatening to power elites. Elites are delighted to proclaim their democratic commitment, knowing that it demands very little of them. Democracy has been universalized in a highly devalued form . . . The end result is not really democracy. Democracy has been displaced by something else which has assumed its name while largely dispensing with its content. Liberal democracy has atrophied in a long process of devaluation and political reaction in which it has lost redeeming democratic elements. (Aké 1995: 79)

As a result there has emerged 'a trivialized version of liberal democracy in which democracy is merely the institutionalization of multiparty elections which are only significant as allocations of power rather than [as] an exercise of the popular will' (p. 84). Aké discussed this paradoxical 'democratization of disempowerment' primarily as a phenomenon afflicting developing countries dominated by the IMF, the World Bank and other manifestly undemocratic power holders. However, it is significant that European *demoi* are also finding it increasingly difficult to maintain any far-reaching control, debate and scrutiny in relation to the locus and exercise of power and the content and framing of legislation and policy – hence the often abysmal voter turn-outs in European elections and the constant complaints about 'democratic deficits', which are only partly attributable to the effects of European integration (see Bideleux 2001a: 229–30). Very pertinently, a collaborative study of *The Breakdown of Democratic Regimes* (directed by the most eminent 'transitologists' Juan Linz and Alfred Stepan) found that during the interwar era democratic regimes were not so much overthrown by anti-democrats as gradually atrophied, corrupted and dismantled from within, often by politicians and officials who claimed or even believed that they were engaged in struggles to 'save democracy' either from external threats or from itself – from its own lapses, deficiencies and excesses (Linz and Stepan 1978).

For these and other reasons, it is by no means certain that Western forms of 'liberal democracy' have become or will ever become 'the norm' for the world as a whole, or that they will remain so in the West, even though 'democracy' in various guises has become the standard appellation of the new political systems which have replaced or superseded various overt forms of one-party and/or military dictatorship in much of Europe, Latin America and Asia and in some parts of Africa since 1974.

Another fundamental problem underlying the approaches adopted by 'democratic transition' and 'democratic consolidation' theorists is that political systems are never simply the fruits of the wishes of their participants. They are in large measure societally constrained, and sometimes even societally determined. To a great extent, Western political science has tended to attribute the illiberal conditions in which most of humanity lives to the alleged prevalence of illiberal attitudes, values, belief-systems and 'political cultures' in those 'other' societies. The influential polymath Ernest Gellner forcefully argued that 'Men are born into and live within the institutions and culture of their society, which they often take for granted . . . A culture is a system of prejudgement. Social institutions and cultures are seldom chosen: they are our fate, not our choice . . . But, generally speaking, the democratic model ignores the fact that institutions and cultures *precede* decisions rather than *follow* them' (Gellner 1996: 185). Explanations of this sort often appear to rest upon lazy, condescending, complacent or even racist Western cultural stereotypes and caricatures of non-Western peoples, religions, 'mentalities' and cultures. Nevertheless, whatever the *explanation*, there is widespread agreement that much (probably most) of humanity has long been ensnared by illiberal systems which are deeply entrenched, tenacious and persistent, and are far from being products of conscious societal choice. This is implicit in the above-mentioned analyses by O'Donnell, Zakaria and Aké.

Our 'take' on these matters is that most of humanity has lived for millennia under profoundly tenacious and deeply entrenched vertically structured power relations and power structures which have repeatedly reasserted themselves whenever they have been challenged from 'below', 'above' or 'outside'; that *this* is the normal condition of humanity (if there is such a thing!); and that only in (largely fortuitous) exceptional circumstances have a few very fortunate parts of the globe succeeded for a time in replacing the usual 'verticality of power' with the more horizontally structured and law-governed civil societies, civil economies and 'level playing fields' which are the indispensable preconditions for the very *possibility* of liberal democracy and liberal capitalism (Bideleux 2001a, 2005a; 2007; Bideleux and Jeffries 2007: xi–xiii, 1, 5–16, 72, 122–3, 141–3, 180–2, 200, 230–1, 323–8, 361, 400, 504–6, 587).

By contrast, much of the strongly elitist 'democratic transition' literature has misleadingly abstracted the analysis of political systems and institutions from their social and cultural contexts and has thereby underplayed the degrees to which they are structurally, socio-economically and/or culturally conditioned and constrained. In practice, political institutions – like attitudes and 'mentalities' – are *dependent* rather than *independent* (determining) variables. Democracy can only become firmly established if and when it is strongly undergirded by the often unplanned or fortuitous prior existence and/or rapid emergence of more horizontally structured civil societies and civil economies based upon the rule of law, limited government and relatively autonomous or free-standing social networks and groupings which are willing to champion and abide by relatively impartial civil codes of law and conduct. A liberal-democratic constitutional regime becomes (moderately) secure only when 'its ways have become engrained in the habits and instinctive reactions – *dans les moeurs* – of the political nation: it safeguards civilized life, but it presupposes agreement and stability as much as it secures them' (Namier 1946: 31), but it is therefore never fully secure – let alone 'consolidated'.

The official publications of Europe's former Communist regimes routinely propagated a crude Marxist economic determinism which insisted that the socio-economic 'base' determined the nature of a society's political and ideological 'superstructure', even though the actual development of the Communist states was an extreme demonstration of the opposite (from Lenin to Gorbachev, Europe's Marxist-Leninist parties and regimes were doggedly voluntarist, and the voluntarism of these parties and regimes quite blatantly determined the very lopsided and increasingly dysfunctional character of their economic systems!). In turning against the crude economic determinism pedalled by the erstwhile Communist regimes, the inhabitants of East Central Europe, the Baltic States and the Balkans had to beware of falling into the opposite error of assuming that the superstructure could operate autonomously, largely unaffected by the nature of the 'underlying' socio-economic system and context. Unfortunately, the 'democratic transition' and 'democratic consolidation' literature fostered new forms of voluntarism. These encouraged widespread expectations and beliefs that (liberal) democracy and highly marketized economic systems could swiftly be implanted and consolidated 'from above' (that is, by the new and/or metamorphosed ruling elites), even though the inhabitants of these countries had not been actively prepared for and habituated to such systems, and even though they had not inherited ready-made infrastructures and practices of liberal institutions, rule of law and 'horizontal' as well as 'vertical' accountability, on to which liberal democracy could easily be grafted – as had been the case in much of western Europe when universal suffrage was established after the First World War.

As a consequence of all these factors, the recurrent struggles from the 1950s to the 1990s to establish stronger and more firmly rooted political and judicial accountability, political and economic 'level playing fields' and the rule of law in East Central Europe and the Baltic States took much longer than had been widely anticipated to curb the deeply entrenched 'verticality' of the power relations and power structures and the endemic political clientelism and corruption inherited from the past.

Since the early 1990s (most recently in 2004–6, reflected in very low voter turn-outs), there has repeatedly been widespread popular disenchantment with the new governing elites and varying degrees of popular disillusionment with the inability of either democratization or marketization to produce 'instant' socio-economic benefits and/or 'quick fixes' for the malfunctions of the polities and economies inherited from the former Communist regimes, as well as varying degrees of popular nostalgia for the (perceived) greater socio-economic security, equality of opportunity and upward mobility which many people think they had under the former Communist regimes. Western perceptions of East Central European and Baltic disillusionment and 'reform fatigue' almost certainly contributed to the long delays before the East Central European and Baltic States were finally given the 'green light' in December 2002 to enter the European Union in May 2004.

In the post-Communist Balkan states, the unrealistic expectations raised by unduly voluntaristic and mechanistic conceptions of democratization and marketization were even more quickly and cruelly dashed. It is taking them even longer than it has taken the East Central European and Baltic States to curb pervasive and deeply entrenched 'verticality' of power relations and power structures, including 'ethnocracy', 'ethnic collectivism', political clientelism, deep-seated corruption and the power of organized criminal networks, as preconditions for the establishment of effective political and judicial accountability, political and economic 'level playing fields', limited government, the rule of law, and autonomous and vigorous civil societies and civil economies.

While most accounts of modern Balkan political and economic change have favoured cultural explanations of this 'Balkan predicament', attributing it primarily to illiberal cultures, belief-systems, value-systems, attitudes, mentalities or mindsets which are often deemed to be innate characteristics of the inhabitants of the Balkan Peninsula, our companion volume on the post-Communist Balkan states has argued that such explanations are at least partly based on Western cultural stereotyping and caricatures of the unfortunate inhabitants of those states and that political cultures, mentalities, belief-systems, value-systems and mindsets are mainly *dependent* rather than *independent* variables (determining factors). Instead, we have come to regard widely tenacious 'ethnocracy', 'ethnic collectivism', clannish clientelism, corruption and the scale and power of organized crime mainly as products and expressions of strongly entrenched power relations and power structures, rather than as products and expressions of particular mentalities, political cultures or mindsets (see Bideleux and Jeffries 2007: 5–16, 180–2, 323–8, 587). If they are well founded, a major implication of our preferred perspectives on Balkan polities and societies is that the prevailing forms of polity and society are far from having been products of unfettered choice, least of all for the politically marginalized majority of the population, and that it therefore makes little sense to hold the population at large responsible for the predicaments in which they find themselves (see pp. 27–37, 58, 87–90, 96, 98–109, 121–2 and Bideleux 2005 and 2007).

EMPIRICAL OBJECTIONS TO SOME INFLUENTIAL THESES PROPAGATED IN THE 'DEMOCRATIC TRANSITION' LITERATURE OF THE 1980s AND 1990s

Aside from raising fundamental *conceptual* objections to the often simplistically mechanistic and teleological assumptions which underlie many of the most influential conceptualizations of the challenges and requirements of post-Communist democratization (and marketization, for that matter), it is also necessary to raise *empirical objections* to some of the themes which were put about by the 'democratic transitions' literature of the 1980s and 1990s.

It has sometimes been claimed that the range and magnitude of the problems and challenges faced and posed by democratic transitions and consolidation were far greater in Europe's post-Communist states than they had been in Greece, Portugal, Spain and most parts of Latin America during the 1970s and 1980s (see, for example, Higley and Gunther 1992: 344–7 ff.; and Pridham *et al.* 1994: 7–9, 52–3, 168–71). The numerous newly democratized states of southern Europe and Latin America already had longstanding market economies (even though many of them contained many very poor people), whereas Europe's post-Communist states needed to change their economic systems at the same time as they metamorphosed from one-party dictatorship towards liberal democracy. In Europe's post-Communist states, it has often been argued, democratization was accompanied by greatly increased economic and social disruption, insecurity and hardship. Secondly, it has usually been claimed that, with the possible exception of Castro's Cuba, the authoritarian regimes of twentieth-century southern Europe and Latin America had never suppressed the plurality and autonomy of social and economic groups to anything like the degrees that Europe's Communist regimes had done. Most of Europe's post-Communist states had to (re-)create (or at least permit) a greatly increased plurality of autonomous social and economic groups, whereas it has been widely assumed that the new democratic regimes of Latin America and southern Europe were able to take for granted the prior existence of such groups and that this facilitated economic change and responsiveness as well as democratization. Thirdly, it has been widely assumed that democratic transitions and consolidation in southern Europe and Latin America were not faced with and obliged to contend with problems of irredentism and/or inter-ethnic antagonism on anything like the scale that many states in the eastern half of Europe have been, not only in recent years but also in earlier decades of the twentieth century. This was not said in order to deny that most southern European and Latin American states contain some unreconciled ethnic or racial minorities, but simply to suggest that minority problems were generally smaller and less of a threat to the territorial integrity of existing states than had been the case in much of the Balkans and East Central Europe. Only Poland, Hungary, Slovenia and, since 1993, the Czech Republic were relatively free of major 'minority' problems, but even they were not entirely free of such difficulties. Many Czechs have displayed open hostility towards their Gypsy minority since the early 1990s, and many Poles have continued to harbour resentments against Poland's small German minority and/or the almost non-existent Jewish minority (see Gross 2006), while some Hungarians have continued to nurture irredentist resentments towards Romania (with regard to Transylvania), Serbia (with regard to Vojvodina) and Slovakia (with regard to certain Magyar-inhabited areas in southern Slovakia) and/or against Hungary's Gypsy minority and/or the largely non-existent Jewish minority. Many Slovenes, for their part, have increasingly displayed open hostility towards the growing Slav and Albanian Muslim minorities who moved to Slovenia after the break-up of the SFRY.

However, while they were not wholly without substance, such contrasts were somewhat glib or overstated. Thus, while democratization clearly took place in even less favourable circumstances and to the accompaniment of even more painful and fundamental changes of economic system in Europe's post-Communist states than was the case in countries such as 'post-authoritarian' Italy, Spain, Portugal, Greece, Chile, Uruguay, Argentina and Venezuela, it was by no means clear that democratization in the eastern half of Europe took place in conditions that were markedly more difficult to those prevalent in other Latin American states which have been to varying degrees afflicted by endemic criminal, social and political violence, grinding poverty, widespread drugs-related problems, very low standards of education, extensive slums and shanty towns, minimal health and social welfare provisions, chronic mass unemployment, exceptionally unequal distributions of income, wealth and power, and enduring legacies of racial oppression and slavery. In spite of all their problems, Europe's post-Communist states have inherited relatively well-educated and largely urban populations with considerable occupational skills, experience and social support structures, as well as largely industrialized economies with substantial (albeit somewhat run-down) physical and social infrastructures. Indeed, while the states of southern Europe and Latin America have never experienced forms of authoritarian rule that were as all-pervasively doctrinaire, systematic, party-based and 'totalitarian' as those created by Europe's Stalinist regimes, *the Communist regimes attached much greater importance to education, skills, social protection, full employment, social awareness, social solidarity and (at least in their official propaganda) the work ethic*. These were very important compensating advantages. Furthermore, after the worst excesses of Stalinism abated (following Stalin's death in 1953), a limited plurality of autonomous social groups *did* (re-) emerge in most of Europe's Communist-ruled states – especially in Yugoslavia, Poland and Hungary, but also to lesser degrees in Czechoslovakia, the Baltic States and East Germany. These countervailing advantages need to be offset against the ways in which the democratization of Europe's post-Communist states is perceived to have been beset by difficulties which did not loom as large in other regions which underwent democratization during the later twentieth century.

Influential contributors to the comparative 'democratic transitions' literature have also maintained that, while democratization (allegedly) took place within largely autonomous states in southern Europe and Latin America, most of the formerly Communist-ruled states in Eastern Europe lived under Soviet domination and therefore had to regain their full sovereignty before they could consummate their transitions to democracy. One book claimed that 'in no case is the impact of foreign powers on political developments as great as in Eastern Europe. Indeed, before the Soviet proclamation of the "Sinatra Doctrine" . . . the wave of democratization that swept across Eastern

Europe in 1989 was virtually unimaginable' (Higley and Gunther 1992: 347). In Latin America and southern Europe, according to Laurence Whitehead (1986: 5), 'Local political forces operated with an untypically high degree of autonomy. The international setting . . . seldom intruded too conspic-uously on an essentially domestic drama.' In East Central Europe, by contrast, 'the Communist parties . . . were turned into accomplices of foreign imposition, and of the suppression of popular rights and aspirations. This is the fundamental reason why all later attempts to stabilize Communist rule through liberalizing it were doomed to failure' (Whitehead 1994: 55). 'By 1989 "democracy" in East Central Europe was universally equated with the dismantling of an externally imposed system of Communist rule' (p. 34).

Thus, nowhere else were the *international dimensions* of regime change as important as they were in the democratization of the Balkans and East Central Europe, according to Geoffrey Pridham (Pridham *et al.* 1994: 7–8). Judy Batt, a leading British specialist on the East Central European states, argued that these states were 'characterized by a uniquely *low* degree of autonomy. The "penetratedness" of East European politics was of a qualitatively different order than that identified by scholars pursuing the theme of "linkage" of domestic and international politics elsewhere.' The Kadar and Husak regimes were even installed by 'Soviet military intervention, replacing reformist regimes which had overstepped the limits set by Moscow. These limits were subsequently codified in the so-called "Brezhnev Doctrine" which attempted to define a set of ideological principles to be observed by all Communist regimes.' Furthermore, Soviet dominance was 'institutionalized in "the leading role of the Communist party", whose leaders were appointed by Moscow and subject to close supervision. A back-up chain of control was also maintained through the security forces, which were run directly by the Soviet KGB and which, in times of crisis, clearly . . . were answera-ble primarily to Moscow.' Indeed, 'the military structures were fused in the Warsaw Treaty Organi-zation, and were unable to operate independently'. What is more, 'the East European economies . . . were tied into the Soviet-dominated trading bloc . . . which greatly limited room for manoeuvre in economic policy . . . The transition to democracy was only possible once the entire international structure of the Soviet system collapsed' (Batt 1994a: 168–9).

The drawing of such contrasts was not wholly unwarranted, but the differences were considera-bly overstated. Major Western Powers had long been prepared to accept (and sometimes to assist) authoritarian regimes in southern Europe and Latin America. During the Cold War, right-wing dic-tatorships which opposed actual or imagined 'Communist threats' tended to be applauded by the United States as 'defenders of freedom' and were sometimes amply rewarded for doing so. More-over, while it is clear that there was considerable formal and informal Soviet penetration of most of the Communist-ruled states in East Central Europe and much of the Balkans (the main exceptions being post-1950s Albania and Yugoslavia), we should not overlook the extent and significance of informal American penetration of many of the states in southern Europe and especially Latin America during the Cold War era, not least through the activities and (often undue and sometimes illicit) influence of American multinational companies, but also those of the CIA and other federal agencies. American attitudes often had a major bearing on whether Latin American and southern European states were ruled by dictators or democrats (even if the difference sometimes appeared to be merely cosmetic). In East Central Europe, the Baltic States and the Balkans, the advent of the Gorbachev regime in Soviet Union in 1985 did help to make possible conditions in which demo-cratic forces could become more assertive and influential. However, this was not so very different from the ways in which the policies (and even the mere existence) of the then European Community helped to create conditions in which democratic forces could prevail in Spain, Portugal and Greece (Bideleux 1996, 1999, 2003). Nor was it totally unlike the ways in which the USA under President Jimmy Carter pressed for greater democracy and observance of human rights in Latin America and parts of Asia during the late 1970s. Therefore, while there is no denying the importance of external influences and constraints on the democratization of the Balkans and East Central Europe, we should beware of the temptation to exaggerate the extent to which these regions differed in this respect from southern Europe, Latin America or even, for that matter, countries such as South Africa, Taiwan, South Korea and the Philippines.

'Democratic transition' analysts ('transitologists') were on much firmer ground when they emphasized the peculiarly large international *significance and consequences* of the East Central European and Balkan 'Revolutions of 1989'. The so-called 'democratic transitions' in Latin America, southern Europe, the Philippines, South Korea and Taiwan caused only a few small ripples in the international states system. By contrast, the democratization of the post-Communist East Central European, Baltic and Balkan states abruptly ended the bipolar East–West division of the world into mutually antagonistic power blocs which had prevailed from 1945 to 1989, thereby contributing to a transformation in international power structures and power relations. The 'Revolutions of 1989' were in that sense events of global and epochal significance, like the French Revolution of 1789 (which changed the face of Europe and Latin America), the Russian Revolutions of 1917 (which went on to divide the world into two ideologically opposed armed camps), and even the convulsions in East Central European and the Balkans in 1918 (which ushered in the era of national self-determination, not just locally but ultimately on a world scale). As a consequence of the anti-Communist Revolutions of 1989–91, the division of Europe into three rival regional groupings (the EC, EFTA and Comecon) came to an end and hopes of constructing a 'united Europe' were rekindled. In some quarters the Revolutions of 1989 were even hailed as harbingers of 'the end of history', as the final triumph of Western liberal democracy and liberal capitalism over all rival ideologies and economic systems, although the sometimes tortuous trajectories of democratization and liberalization in the eastern half of Europe (and elsewhere!) since 1989 have amply demonstrated that the jubilation was premature. Outcomes often take unforeseen turns, especially when the battle lines are radically redrawn.

THE REORIENTATION OF THE BALKANS AND EAST CENTRAL EUROPE SINCE 1989

The first priority of the post-Communist states in the Balkans and East Central Europe was quite rightly to create or restore formal democratic institutions, rights and procedures. However, the formal provisions to this effect only became secure in so far as they were accompanied and/or followed by a vigorous development of civil societies with liberal and multi-cultural 'civic' conceptions of the nation-state. By definition, however, 'civil societies' could not simply be created or re-created 'from above'. Creatures of the state tend to remain dependent upon and subservient to the state. However, the penury, retrenchment and atrophy of the post-Communist states obliged them to vacate many 'social spaces' which had to be filled or taken over by autonomous civil associations and individuals, if they were not to remain under the control of the former Communist *nomenklatura* and/or criminal elements. Going beyond any private motives and ambitions which they cherished, Balkan and East Central European professionals, legitimate entrepreneurs, writers, journalists, broadcasters, trade unions and farmers' organizations found themselves confronted with a historic opportunity and responsibility to maximize their autonomy and self-reliance and to minimize their dependence on the state, in order to secure the conditions in which the moves to pluralist liberal democracy and market economies could be consummated. Their degrees of success in this regard proved to be even more important in determining their countries' fortunes than either the crumbs of assistance received from the West or the more technical tasks of managing the liberalization, marketization and privatization of their economies. If they had flunked or passed up this historic opportunity and responsibility, they would have been among the first to suffer and they would have had no one else to blame, for the creation or re-creation of vibrant, autonomous and pluralistic 'civil societies' was not something that could be done for them by the state or politicians or foreign assistance. Indeed, the post-Communist states lacked the capacity and/or wherewithal to direct a vast panoply of social and economic activities, and any lingering insistence that they should attempt to do so in an endeavour to provide universal economic and social security could only have led back to forms of authoritarian paternalism and corporatism which had already been tried and found wanting. This did not mean that they had to embrace a minimalist role for the state, but rather that they had to beware of the dangers posed by expecting too much of the state, especially in circumstances where so much of the existing state apparatus and personnel had been inherited from a rather murky past and the rule of law was not deeply and securely entrenched. State tutelage could only be as effective as the quality and resources of the state apparatuses which were available to exercise it.

Unfortunately, the high hopes aroused in late 1989 and early 1990 were soon dashed by the grim realities of falling output, soaring inflation, mounting unemployment, fiscal retrenchment, continuing infrastructural decay, an intractable environmental crisis and simmering inter-ethnic tensions (particularly in the Balkans and Slovakia). The generous and optimistic sentiments which were widely expressed during the initial 'national' jubilation were bound to evaporate when varying degrees of political and economic 'liberalization' not only failed to deliver the anticipated rapid improvements in living standards, but also plunged most people into extremes of economic and social hardship for which they were largely unprepared and for which there were inadequate 'social safety nets'. Indeed, a major report released by UNICEF in early 1994 claimed that the collapse of Europe's command economies and Communist regimes had precipitated a slump in birth rates and major increases in poverty, death rates, morbidity rates, malnutrition, truancy, family breakdowns and violent crime, with the result that by 1993 conditions in the eastern half of Europe were even worse than those in Latin America during the so-called 'lost decade' of the 1980s or in western Europe during the 1930s Depression (*The Independent*, 28 January 1994, p. 10).

This did not surprise many Western specialists on the eastern half of Europe, but it did wrong-foot those exultant Western politicians and pundits who had subscribed to the naive belief that the ending of Communist rule would automatically usher in secure democracy, vigorous market economies, vibrant civil societies and a new era of sweetness and harmony. Most Western specialists on the former Soviet bloc took the gloomier view that the 'natural' reaction or backlash against more than forty years of Communist rule was more likely to assume the form of resurgent 'ethnic' nationalism and illiberal religious revivalism than of profound and enduring support for and commitment to political and economic liberalism.

Incompletely reconstructed ex-Communists continued to run Romania until 1996, Slovakia and Bulgaria until 1998, Croatia until 1999 and Serbia until 2000. Such problems were not entirely absent from Poland or Hungary either, while large sectors of the economies of Serbia, Montenegro, Bulgaria, Macedonia, Bosnia and Albania fell under the control of organized criminal networks, blackmarketeers, armed thugs, and traffickers in fuel, drugs, arms, cigarettes and prostitutes. These elements were much boosted and enriched by the uneven, leaky and highly dysfunctional UN sanctions applied by the West to the Yugoslav successor states from 1992 to 1995 (see Bideleux and Jeffries 2007: pp. 14, 65–72, 102–6, 121–3, 177–9, 218, 246, 277, 288, 300–4, 308, 313, 325, 358, 361, 365, 382, 400, 402, 467–8, 479, 493, 501, 504, 506, 533, 561, 571, 579, 591–2).

Any circumspect and liberal-minded observer was bound to harbour doubts about the durability of political and economic liberalism in conditions of severe economic contraction, retrenchment, high inflation, acute social hardship, environmental crisis and widespread dilapidation and infrastructural decay, which were the immediate legacies of Communist rule. There had been a restoration of free elections, to be sure, but secure democracy involved much more than the holding of free elections, just as the restoration of market economies entailed far more than the mere 'freeing' of prices. The new political systems were 'still in their early infancy', politicians and parties were unsure of their roles, politics centred on 'personalities rather than programmes or parties', and the 'accumulated experience of the West' proved hard to apply or to relate to the conditions in which these countries found themselves (Patricia Clough, *The Independent*, 24 April 1992, p. 19). Free elections and price liberalization unleashed irrational and unruly forces which, paradoxically, made it all the more difficult to consummate the perilous 'transitions' to pluralistic parliamentary democracy and thriving private-enterprise economies. The problems were compounded by the continuing prevalence of 'ethnic' nationalism and religious dogmatism, and the related failure of liberal values, concepts of limited government and the rule of law to put down deep roots in Balkan and (to a lesser degree) East Central European societies and cultures.

Unfortunately, the intelligentsia-turned-politicians who spearheaded the overthrow of Communist rule were not necessarily the most suitable persons to provide leadership and direction during the consolidation of democracy and market economies. Indeed, by early 1995 politicians and parties with roots in the former Communist regimes were back in power in most of the Balkan and East Central European states. The major exception was the Czech Republic, where both President Vaclav Havel and Premier Vaclav Klaus managed to ride out the popular hardships, disillusionments and resentments which had by then toppled most of the leaders of the 'Revolutions of 1989'.

Fortunately, many of the 'new look' or 'reconstructed' ex-Communist politicians were, for the most part, almost as strongly committed to liberal democracy and market systems as the anti-Communists, intellectuals and former dissidents whom they had unseated. In the minds of many voters, perhaps, the 'reconstructed' ex-Communists held out the prospect of a more modest pace of change and the provision of stronger social safety nets for the victims of macro-economic stabilization and micro-economic restructuring, but they also promised to bring greater experience of governing and of 'getting things done'. To varying degrees, many ex-Communists embraced or resuscitated long dormant social democratic traditions which were more in tune with the economic and social philosophies which prevailed in the European Union than were those of their more clerical, sectarian and nationalistic rivals, many of whom were more uncompromising, intemperate, xenophobic, anti-Western or étatist than the more hard-headed, circumspect and pragmatic ex-Communists.

The qualities and outlooks that had brought many former dissidents national and international acclaim and respect as dogged and unyielding opponents of the Communist regimes were not necessarily the ones needed in government, not least because the major issues and choices confronting governments and parliaments were no longer as black-and-white as they had previously been. During periods of very difficult and often painful adjustment, there is a high premium on conciliation, the healing of old wounds, clarity of vision, political acumen and sound judgement, and ex-Communist politicians often turned out to have these qualities in greater abundance than their more 'heroic' former opponents. For example, an editorial in the *Financial Times* passed the following judgement on the presidency of Lech Walesa, who had risen to prominence as the doughty leader and talisman of Poland's strongly Catholic anti-Communist Solidarity movement: 'His undoubted qualities of courage and cunning and his intuitive understanding of ordinary peoples' desires and fears made him an effective saboteur of Communist rule . . . With all his accumulated prestige, Mr Walesa could have been a great president, taking the lead in strengthening the institutional base to underpin post-Communist rule. Instead he has shown himself incapable of understanding that democracy is based on the rule of law and respect for democratic institutions. His declared role model is Marshal Pilsudski, the interwar military dictator; his political style, ironically, is that of the all-powerful Communist party first secretary, hectoring and intriguing behind the scenes' (*FT*, 7 February 1995, p. 19).

THIRD TIME LUCKY?

In October 1993 Hungary's then foreign minister, Geza Jeszenszky, wrote: 'Three times in recent history Western powers have promised liberation to the peoples of Eastern Europe, but the East

European nations finally won freedom for themselves. Today, however, a crisis of confidence is emerging on both sides: the West is questioning Eastern Europe's ability to make good use of freedom, while East Europeans are voicing doubts about the seriousness of Western helpfulness. In my region people feel disoriented and increasingly unhappy. They find themselves in a polluted environment wasted away by redundant industries. The attractions of consumer society beckon but prove unobtainable, except to the old political bosses, who profit in commercial business. The spirit of compassion and tolerance was not cultivated under Communism. This social environment creates space for the demagoguery of onetime Communists now donning national colours, as well as for the resurgence of extremist (neo-Stalinist and/or neo-Nazi) tendencies.' In Jeszenszky's view, East Central European and Balkan democrats were determined to persevere with political reform and economic transformation and to overcome extremism, but they needed 'stronger and better-directed support from the developed democracies. Carrot and stick policies do not seem to work in Eastern Europe . . . We in Eastern Europe are not asking for miracles. However, as new members of the community of democratic nations, we believe that we are within our rights when asking for strong leadership, clearly articulated priorities and decisive action by those with the resources and the moral responsibility to prevent the backsliding of Eastern Europe' (Geza Jeszenszky, writing in *IHT*, 22 October 1993, p. 8). In October 1993 the Czech dissident playwright-turned-president Vaclav Havel similarly warned that 'Twice in this century Europe has paid a terrible price for the narrow-mindedness and lack of vision of its democracies . . . Democratic Europe cannot afford a third failure' (Havel 1994b: 242–3).

In some ways the post-1989 democratic transformations were even more fraught with difficulties than the post-1918 and post-1945 attempts had been. Much of the industrial capacity inherited from the Communist regimes was either technologically obsolete or environmentally hazardous or produced goods for which there was no longer a market. If stringent commercial and health and safety criteria had been ruthlessly applied, large parts of the hard-won East Central European and Balkan industrial capacity (including most of its power stations) would have had to be closed down, with massive loss of employment. This was most strongly borne out by the slump in total output and employment which took place during the early 1990s in East Germany, the most industrialized of the former command economies. Between 1989 and 1993, the total number of jobs in East Germany shrank from 9.3 million to 6.2 million, manufacturing employment fell from 3.2 million to 1.3 million (that is, by 60 per cent) and the number of people working on the land dropped from more than 920,000 to 210,000 (that is, by 70 per cent), while the size of the population available for work declined from 10.8 million to 8.2 million, mainly as a result of emigration to the West. By March 1994, 1.3 million people (16.8 per cent of the workforce) were registered as unemployed, but in reality 37 per cent of the diminished workforce were without employment in March 1994 and, if the absolute size of the available workforce had not shrunk by 2.6 million, this percentage would have been even higher (*FT*, Survey, 4 May 1994, pp. ii, iv). Moreover, between 1989 and 1991 East German GDP fell by 45 per cent, while the total number of hours worked plummeted from 8.9 billion to 4.0 billion (*FT*, 17 July 1992, p. 16, and 13 September 1991, p. 17). This devastating contraction occurred because, in addition to the loss or collapse of hitherto captive Comecon markets which had previously absorbed more than 65 per cent of East German exports, the somewhat precipitate incorporation of East Germany into the German Federal Republic (and hence into the West European economy) in 1990 had prematurely exposed it to the full blast of market forces and competition from much more advanced Western products and producers.

Admittedly, East Germany gained much-publicized advantages from massive eastward fiscal transfers within reunified Germany, which provided various forms of 'life support' for redundant East Germans and helped to conceal the true magnitude of the job losses. In 1993, for example, financial transfers from western to eastern Germany amounted to DM 170 billion ($100 billion) or 5 per cent of West Germany's GDP, with the result that total East German expenditure that year was almost twice the value of its output (*FT*, 14 October 1993, p. 15). However, these advantages were offset by the immediate loss of the political and economic autonomy, leverage, insulation and self-defence mechanisms which would have been furnished by the retention of a separate East German state, currency and trading system with the power to preserve some of the more positive social, scientific and cultural features of the former East German regime and to set its own tariffs, excise duties, import quotas and exchange rates at levels that would have allowed most enterprises to survive in the face of fierce Western competition, as was the case in post-Communist Poland, Hungary and the Czech Republic. Instead, the exchange rate at which East German marks (and hence prices and production costs) were converted into Deutschmarks at the time of the German economic and monetary union in mid-1990 was set too high to allow much of East German industry to have any real chance of holding its own against Western products.

In 1918 and 1945, by contrast, the Balkan and East Central European economies were suffering from severe human losses, war damage and dislocation, but they were much less industrialized (than in 1989) and they did not have to contend with such extensive closures of industrial capacity. Even if they were still subject to wartime controls, they were already market economies. Therefore, they did not need to undergo a profound change of economic system at the same time as they embarked on economic reconstruction and stabilization programmes.

When the Balkan and East Central European states embarked on the post-1989 transformations, most of them were burdened by large foreign debts (see table 33.1 on p. 520, above) and heavy debt-service payments, inherited from the foregoing Communist regimes. In 1918 and in 1945, by contrast, the newly independent states started with relatively clean slates, although they incurred considerable foreign debts during the 1920s.

In other ways, however, the post-1989 metamorphoses to pluralistic liberal democracy and independent national market economies initially appeared much easier and more hopeful than the post-1918 and post-1945 attempts. This time around the Balkans and East Central Europe were not having to recover from the devastating effects of total war. Furthermore, it was widely assumed that, because of the redrawing of state boundaries and the elimination of most of the former Jewish and German communities of the Balkans and East Central Europe and many of their Gypsies during the 1940s, the scope for renewed inter-ethnic conflict had been greatly reduced. In addition, the Balkans and East Central Europe no longer appeared to be menaced by dangerous or potentially dangerous neighbours, while the West appeared to be much more willing and able to assist the economic recovery and reconstruction of the Balkans and East Central Europe in the early 1990s than it had been after 1918 or after 1945. Finally, relative to 1918 and 1945, the existence of a peaceful, prosperous and highly integrated European Community appeared to hold out the prospect of much more propitious political and economic frameworks and mechanisms through which the Balkans and East Central Europe could gradually be (re)integrated into the mainstream of European development.

Unfortunately, some of the supposed advantages of the post-1989 transformations proved to be much *weaker* than they had appeared at first glance. Although this time the Balkans and East Central Europe were not recovering from a World War, they were struggling to recover from a state of economic collapse, high levels of inflation, severe infrastructural neglect and decay, acute social strains, the draining effects of the Cold War, the lopsided economic priorities of Communist rule, and life-threatening environmental crises, while in Yugoslavia inter-ethnic tensions boiled over into catastrophic fratricidal conflicts. On the economic front, the tasks which the Balkans and East Central Europe confronted turned out not to be so very different from those involved in the reconversion of a ravaged and run-down war economy to civilian production. Furthermore, even though the ethnic map of the Balkans and East Central Europe had been subjected to drastic surgery since 1918, a considerable potential for violent inter-ethnic conflict had nevertheless survived, sadly vindicating the view that no (acceptable) amount of resettlement and/or redrawing of Balkan and East

Central European state boundaries could either satisfy all conflicting territorial claims or allow all peoples to occupy discrete territories (or even cantons, in cases such as Bosnia-Herzegovina and Macedonia), because many peoples and territories remained inextricably intermingled. Indeed, the territorial expedients and stratagems which Marshal Tito had adopted in his attempts to 'cut Serbia down to size' and thereby allay non-Serb fears of potential Serbian dominance of Yugoslavia back-fired disastrously during the early 1990s, when the Serbs brutally reversed some of the territorial losses inflicted on them by the Yugoslav Constitutions of 1946 and 1974. In the mid-1990s, more-over, there were still sizeable aggrieved and vulnerable ethnic minorities in Serbia, Croatia, Macedonia, Bulgaria, Romania, Albania, Greece, Slovakia and the shattered remains of Bosnia-Herzegovina. Poland had dormant territorial disputes with Lithuania and the Czech Republic, as did Italy with Slovenia and Germany with Poland. In addition, Greece temporarily revived old territo-rial disputes with Albania and the Macedonian Slavs, while Hungary had anxieties concerning the plight of the 3 million Hungarians living in neighbouring Romania, Slovakia and Serbia.

35 Post-Communist economic transformations: from dirigiste capitalism to more liberal forms of market capitalism

One of the great dangers confronting Europe's post-Communist states was that the traumas of socio-economic transformation and painful disappointment at the parsimony, protectionism and pusillanimity of the West could foster rapid disillusionment with democracy and the market system. Except in those states which had already established semi-marketized economies while the Communists were still in power (Yugoslavia and Hungary), there was bound to be a very difficult interval between the abandonment of centrally administered economic systems and the emergence of fully functioning market economies. The guarantees, subsidies and certainties of the former centrally administered economies were forfeited a considerable time before new marketized systems could get up and running. During that painful interval, most people suffered from greatly increased hardships, loss of job security, considerable reductions in state provision of free education and health care and low-cost public housing, and unaccustomed levels of inflation. Economic transformation was made even harder by the rapid collapse of the patterns of trade and specialization established within Comecon and by the fact that the eastern half of Europe had to a large extent 'missed the boat' in the information technology, electronics and biotechnology revolutions. It was not just lagging far behind Japan and the West. It was also far behind many of the 'new industrial countries'. To the end, Europe's Communist regimes had remained wedded to old-fashioned 'smoke-stack' industries which only had limited export and growth potential. The replacement of these ossified, moribund industries with more viable new industries, service activities and 'knowledge economies' and 'information/network societies' was bound to be a painful and protracted process.

THESE TRANSFORMATIONS WERE NOT FROM 'SOCIALISM' TO CAPITALISM'

It needs to be emphasized from the start that it is highly misleading to regard the post-Communist economic transformations as having been from various forms of 'socialism' to 'capitalism'. Admittedly, the economic systems established by the former Communist regimes did replace heavy reliance on market mechanisms and relatively unfettered market forces to allocate resources and to motivate managers and employees with varying forms and degrees of economic planning and either state or social ownership of the main means of production. Nevertheless, they continued to employ *wage labour* to generate and appropriate '*surplus value*', albeit mainly in the hands of state and/or party bureaucracies rather than private capitalists, and they did so primarily in order to produce commodities *for sale* on state-regulated markets. These economic systems were just as hierarchical and exploitative as the wide range of Western economic systems which go under the name of 'capitalism' or 'the market economy', and they treated 'their own' workers and peasants far more brutally and oppressively than did Western market economies (see Bideleux 1987: 81, 115–27, 133–4, 144–63, 205–11). The exploitative, hierarchical, corrupt and self-serving nature of Europe's

Communist states and regimes was powerfully portrayed by the prominent Yugoslav Communist-turned-dissident Milovan Djilas in his famous Marxist critique of the *The New Class* (Djilas 1957) and by Miklos Haraszti in his famous Marxist account of the plight of *A Worker in a Worker's State* (1977), both of which followed in the distinguished footsteps of Leon Trotsky's devastating Marxist critique of Stalin's Soviet Union (Trotsky 1937). The economic systems which most Western writers on the former Communist regimes have chosen to call 'socialism', for reasons which range from conceptual woolliness to cynical attempts to discredit socialism (which has really never yet been put to the test anywhere), were hugely oppressive and inefficient bureaucratic travesties of 'socialism': fiercely exploitative, extremely hierarchical and (especially during the Stalinist era) based on piecerates. Far from being 'socialist', these economic systems were for the most part extreme forms of (étatist) 'state capitalism', which bore more resemblances to fascist economic systems and capitalist war economies than to any bona fide forms of 'socialism'. From 1968 onward Hungary experimented with so-called 'market socialism', which was a semi-marketized form of 'state capitalism', and from the 1960s onward the Yugoslav Communist regime experimented with ostensibly 'self-managed' enterprises which were formally owned by and responsible to their employees. However, not even these experiments were in any meaningful sense 'socialist' – they remained just as hierarchical, exploitative and corrupt as the more centralized 'command economies' (see Bideleux 1987: 126–7, 147, 161, 178–93; Haraszti 1977; Lydall 1989; and Estrin 1983, 1991).

The so-called 'centrally planned economy' remained an *aspiration*, instead of becoming a reality, because so-called 'central planners' lacked the supernatural powers of clairvoyance which alone could have made it possible for them to draw up internally consistent and operationally viable plans for whole economies for even one year ahead (let alone for five years ahead!). Furthermore, like Nazi Germany and Fascist Italy, the Communist states were riddled with bureaucratic infighting, clientelism, corruption, networking and blackmarketeering. This made the term 'centrally planned economy' as much of a misnomer as the term 'socialism'.

Consequently, the economic metamorphoses which took place at the end of Communist rule were not from 'socialism' (or even 'centrally planned economies') to 'capitalism'. Instead, they need to be understood as transformations from various forms of 'state capitalism' to more liberalized and marketized forms of capitalism. The changes primarily involved major shifts from highly 'vertical' economic power relations and power structures to more 'horizontal' ones, that is, to systems in which enterprises interacted more with one another than with state bureaucracies. To accomplish this, it was necessary to introduce the rule of law, more stringent financial discipline (so-called 'hard budget constraints'), the institutional infrastructure of market systems (so-called 'market institutions'), effective competition and more 'level playing fields', as well as openly to promote private enterprise, private ownership and self-help, while lifting the 'veil of fear' on which the former 'command economies' had depended to make central 'commands' effective.

Therefore, before market systems could even begin to work effectively in the Balkans and East Central Europe and start to help these regions hold their own with the much more technologically advanced and vigorously competitive Western and East Asian economies, it was necessary to establish the requisite legal, financial and telecommunications infrastructure and to bring about extensive industrial de-concentration (in order to foster economic pluralism and inter-enterprise competition) as well as effective regulation of monopolies (to curb abuse of monopolistic powers). There is really no such thing as a free market. In order to work effectively, markets need to be governed by rules, institutions and laws. In a nutshell, the changeover from centrally planned command economies to more decentralized, market-orientated economic systems which could enhance lower-level accountability and decision-making required not only 'proper macro-economic policies and institutions but also well-defined behavioural rules for integrating the decisions of decentralized agents . . . Perhaps of utmost importance is rule certainty for all economic agents' (Brabant 1989: 404–5).

Samuel Brittan, one of the leading lights of the monetarist and neo-liberal counter-revolution in Western economic orthodoxy, commented that 'Only a fool would have expected a successful capitalism to emerge from the ashes in a couple of years. The fact that a carefully nurtured system of law, legislation, customs and habits and – of course infrastructure – is required should surprise no-one except a few equilibrium economists' (writing in *FT*, 9 November 1992, p. 10).

Furthermore, the effective functioning of market economies also depends on the existence of an 'enterprise culture' which extends far beyond the 'hucksterism' of blackmarketeers, brokers, speculators and gangsters. As argued by Robert Heilbroner, 'hucksterism does not develop the attitudes of innovation and management that modern corporate life requires, much less the skills of accountancy or finance' (writing in *IHT*, 17 September 1991, p. 8). The so-called 'hucksters' who were often quoted as evidence of the existence of 'enterprise cultures' in Europe's post-Communist states mainly knew about so-called 'dealing' and corruption, how to buy and sell in captive or monopolistic 'sellers' markets', how to corner scarce supplies, how to misappropriate public property and funds, and how to obtain 'favours' and 'protection' from corrupt government agencies and officials, often in league with so-called 'mafias' or networks of gangsters. Unfortunately, they actually had very little knowledge or experience of large-scale corporate manufacturing and provision of services in sophisticated and fiercely competitive product markets, as the economies in which they operated had long been highly monopolistic and sealed off from the outside world.

Another major problem was that the implementation of radical marketizing reforms and 'structural adjustment', including the promotion of small businesses and the restructuring of state enterprises to make them fit for privatization, was bound to require considerable initial inputs of capital. Initially, substantial amounts of capital could only come *either* from the West *or* from native black marketeers, embezzlers and other criminal elements, as these were the only major possessors of liquid capital.

It was very much in the West's interests for much of the 'pump-priming' or 'seed' capital to come from the West, in order to help develop the Balkans and East Central Europe into successful low-cost, export-orientated production bases which would greatly help Europe (as a whole) to meet the formidable competition and other challenges posed by the meteoric rise of the dynamic industrial export economies of East Asia. The East Central European states are indeed becoming Europe's 'tiger economies', and several of the post-Communist Balkan states are poised to follow suit (see the economic growth rates in Tables 35.1 and 35.2). Most of Europe's post-Communist states possess substantial reserves of relatively cheap, underemployed, skilled and educated labour with a strong drive to prosper – or to try (at least) to escape from dull, grey and monotonous poverty.

Conversely, wherever (or in so far as) the West failed to come forward with sufficient short-term assistance, know-how and long-term venture capital to help kick-start Balkan and East Central European economic recoveries, it found itself having to 'do business' with lack-lustre states and economies run by seasoned gangsters or criminal elements and/or often seedy former members of the Communist-era *nomenklatura*, who came to be known as '*nomenklatura* capitalists'. Unfortunately, Western parsimony, meanness and lack of vision and imagination helped the latter outcome to prevail during the 1990s and early 2000s in the Balkans, as was also the case in most of the former Soviet republics.

Partly for these reasons, we were among the early advocates of mobilizing Western aid to the economies of East Central Europe and the Balkans on a Marshall Plan scale, rejecting the counter-arguments that they were incapable of absorbing and making effective use of aid on that scale and that aid would act as a deterrent to the taking of painful measures (thereby allegedly transforming them into permanent 'basket cases'). Large-scale aid granted on appropriate conditions could have helped to cushion responsible but 'fragile' governments and societies during the inevitably very painful early stages of economic transformation. Indeed, as in the case of the Marshall Plan, large-scale technical aid could have helped to increase the absorptive capacity of these economies by helping them to create the institutions of a market system. It would have been prudent as well as benign to have given these countries a great deal more help in setting up the political institutions of liberal democracy, in order to help keep them freer from the rampant corruption and organized crime which became rife in much of the Balkans, the former Soviet republics and some parts of East Central Europe.

Professor Jeffrey Sachs, the Harvard economist who served as an economic adviser to Poland from 1989 to 1991 and subsequently in Russia, forcefully argued that Western aid could 'help sustain political support for the reforms long enough for them to take hold. The Marshall Plan did not provide Europe with the funds for economic recovery. It provided governments with enough financial backing to achieve economic and political stability, give hope to the population and thus make economic recovery possible' (writing in *IHT*, 16 May 1991, p. 6). Sachs warned that 'In the absence of a generous and visionary approach by the West . . . it will prove impossible to achieve success in the reforms – no matter how resolute Eastern Europe is with its actions' (Sachs 1994: 6). Schemes such as the widely praised PHARE programme and the UK 'Know-How Fund' were useful as far as they went, but they were peanuts by comparison with the actual financing needs of most of Europe's post-Communist states (see pp. 589–90, below). Sachs also railed against some of the advice offered and some of the conditions laid down for aid by the IMF: 'Rather than concentrating nearly all its efforts on budget-cutting, as it does now, the IMF should aim to combine fiscal restraint with ample foreign loans, exchange rate stabilization, increasing central bank independence and debt relief, all designed to restore confidence in the currency and in the government's ability to honour its (restructured) debts.' In his view, Western aid packages should have been large enough to help mobilize sufficient support to enable the early post-Communist governments to continue providing essential services. The IMF should have done much more to help governments to mobilize international financing of budget deficits during the acutely painful early stages of the reform process, thereby reducing the risks that 'fragile' governments might be brought down by hostile reaction to heavy spending cuts and tax increases (Jeffrey Sachs, writing in *The Economist*, 1 October 1994, p. 28).

We concurred wholeheartedly with Sachs's advocacy of generous Western aid to Europe's post-Communist states. Unfortunately, the West appears largely to have taken for granted the very things which these countries most lacked, including the rule of law, a modern commercial banking system, ethnically impartial states, efficient tax-collection systems, and effective bankruptcy and redundancy laws. For lack of more generous, enlightened and easily affordable Western financial assistance, recovery from the early 1990s economic collapse and the establishment of the rule of law have both been much slower and less complete than they need have been.

THE CASE FOR 'BIG BANG'/'SHOCK THERAPY' STRATEGIES (AS AGAINST 'GRADUALISM')

This is not the place to try to unravel all the twists and turns of a debate in which there was considerable disagreement on terminology as well as on more substantive issues. Our own view is that the virulence of the debate often hid substantial areas of agreement. We have examined the vicissitudes and complexities of marketization, liberalization and privatization in more detail in individual Balkan states elsewhere (Bideleux and Jeffries 2007), and we are currently engaged in doing the same for individual East Central European states, but it seems appropriate to offer an overview of the main challenges and pitfalls here. Part of the problem has been the propensity of economic theorists to try to impose neat cut-and-dried categories on a messy world. The term 'shock therapy' has often been used virtually interchangeably to refer to both (i) severe austerity measures (alias 'macro-economic stabilization'), and (ii) rapid and comprehensive change in the economic system (alias 'micro-economic restructuring'). At other times, however, the term 'shock therapy' has been used in a narrower sense, referring only to (i). Public understanding of the issues and choices involved would have been increased if 'shock therapy' had been used exclusively to refer to (i) and if the term 'big bang' had been used exclusively to refer to (ii), as these are two very different (albeit usually complementary) policies or phenomena. However, the inconsistencies of current usage have obliged us to use the composite term 'big bang'/'shock therapy'.

Two of the leading proponents of 'big bang'/'shock therapy' have been Leszek Balcerowicz, who served as Poland's finance minister from 1989 to 1992 and has been the governor of Poland's central bank more recently, and Harvard's Professor Jeffrey Sachs, who served as economic adviser to Balcerowicz from 1989 to 1991. Balcerowicz argued that it was a fallacy to believe, when dealing with hyperinflation, that a gradualist approach would be milder in its social consequences. 'What is crucial in such circumstances is to change the basic monetary conditions and to eliminate or at least reduce inflationary expectations. In such a situation a consistent and credible radical stabilization is much more likely to succeed and could be far less costly than a gradualist approach', because 'tough stabilization and comprehensive liberalization seem to be the necessary conditions for any meaningful structural change'. Such an environment 'encourages many state enterprises to restructure, transferring their resources to the private sector, and/or to change their sphere of operations' (Balcerowicz 1994: 38–40).

Balcerowicz put forward a number of arguments in favour of comprehensive liberalization of most prices: (i) it was necessary to make maximum use of the initial political 'honeymoon period' to push through as many of the painful-but-necessary reforms as possible; (ii) it was a necessary (and largely sufficient) means of removing widespread shortages quickly, which was in turn necessary for consumers' well-being and for the more efficient operation of enterprises; and (iii) slow price liberalization would have prolonged the existence of highly distorted pricing structures, with the result that the performance of enterprises could not have been judged reliably and the so-called 'soft budget constraint' would have persisted longer if loss-makers had been able to deflect the blame for their poor economic performance on to distorted prices (Balcerowicz 1994: 42). Balcerowicz argued that the actual choice in Europe's post-Communist states was between either 'maintaining widespread price controls with the corresponding shortages and distortions, or liberalizing prices within initially very imperfect market structures'. To be effective, in his view, comprehensive price liberalization had to be complemented by comprehensive liberalization of foreign trade (p. 28), which in turn was needed to provide the competition which was lacking in economies dominated by state monopolies.

In a similar vein, Sachs emphasized the need to take full advantage of the 'unique opportunity to make an economic breakthrough to the market and a political breakthrough to democracy', the necessity to compensate for the 'lack of experienced personnel in the ministries' through maximum reliance on market forces, and the belief that merely 'tinkering with the old system would produce no results' (Sachs 1994: 43). 'The key idea was to break decisively with the Communist system, to end halfway reform ... Balcerowicz understood extremely well from the experience of Latin America that to break the back of a hyperinflation, half measures cannot work. The stabilization measures must be extraordinarily tough' (p. 45).

The five main prongs of the Sachs–Balcerowicz strategy were: (i) draconian macro-economic stabilization; (ii) rapid micro-economic liberalization; (iii) privatization (controls on the private sector could be removed very quickly, but the privatization of large enterprises inevitably took much longer than the privatization of small ones); (iv) the establishment of a 'social security net' (especially an unemployment compensation scheme); and (v) the mobilization of international financial assistance (Sachs 1994: 45–7). In the Polish case, 'First, to eliminate shortages and to allow markets to function, virtually all prices were decontrolled ... Second, to cut the budget deficit and eliminate hyperinflationary pressures, most subsidies to households ... and industry were slashed or eliminated ... Overall budget spending was restrained, through sharp cuts in public

Table 35.1 Selected economic indicators for East Central European and Baltic states, 1990–2006

(a) Rates of growth of GDP (percentage change in real terms)

	1990	1991	1992	1993	1994	1995	1996	1997	1998	1999	2000	2001	2002	2003	2004	2005	2006	1999–2006
Poland	-11.6	-7.0	2.6	3.8	5.2	7.0	6.0	6.8	4.8	4.1	4.2	1.1	1.4	3.8	5.3	3.4	5.0	3.5
Hungary	-3.5	-11.9	-3.1	-0.6	2.9	1.5	1.3	4.6	4.9	4.2	5.2	4.3	3.8	3.4	4.6	4.1	3.5	4.1
Czech Republic	-1.2	-11.5	-3.3	0.6	2.2	5.9	4.3	-0.8	-1.0	1.2	3.9	2.6	1.5	3.2	4.7	6.1	6.2	3.7
Slovakia	-2.5	-14.6	-6.5	-3.7	4.9	6.7	6.2	6.2	4.1	1.5	2.0	3.8	4.6	4.5	5.5	6.1	6.4	4.3
Slovenia	-4.7	-8.9	-5.5	2.8	5.3	4.1	3.5	4.6	3.8	5.6	4.1	2.7	3.5	2.7	4.2	4.0	4.5	3.9
Lithuania	–	-6.2	-4.3	-16.0	-9.8	3.3	4.7	7.3	5.1	-1.7	4.7	6.4	6.8	10.5	7.0	7.5	7.0	6.0
Latvia	–	-10.4	-34.9	-14.9	2.2	-0.9	3.7	8.4	4.8	3.3	6.9	8.0	6.4	7.2	8.3	10.2	9.0	7.4
Estonia	–	-13.6	-14.2	-9.0	-2.0	4.3	3.9	9.8	4.6	0.3	7.9	6.5	7.2	6.7	7.8	10.5	8.9	7.0
Average	–	–	–	–	3.9	5.5	4.8	5.0	3.8	3.5	4.3	2.5	2.4	4.0	5.2	4.7	5.3	4.0

(b) Rates of inflation (annual average, per cent)

	1990	1991	1992	1993	1994	1995	1996	1997	1998	1999	2000	2001	2002	2003	2004	2005	2006
Poland	586.0	70.0	43.0	35.0	32.0	28.0	20.0	15.0	12.0	7.3	10.1	5.5	1.9	0.8	3.5	2.1	1.6
Hungary	29.0	35.0	23.0	23.0	19.0	28.0	24.0	18.0	14.0	10.0	9.8	9.2	5.3	4.7	6.8	3.6	4.0
Czech Republic	9.7	57.0	11.1	21.0	9.9	9.1	8.3	8.5	10.7	2.1	4.0	4.7	1.8	0.2	2.8	1.9	2.9
Slovakia	10.8	61.0	10.1	23.0	13.0	9.9	5.3	6.1	6.7	10.6	12.0	7.3	3.0	8.5	7.5	2.7	4.5
Slovenia	555.0	118.0	207.0	33.0	21.0	14.0	9.9	8.4	7.9	6.1	8.9	8.4	7.5	5.6	3.6	2.5	2.5
Lithuania	–	225.0	1021.0	410.0	72.0	40.0	25.0	8.9	5.1	0.8	1.0	1.5	0.3	-1.2	1.2	2.7	3.1
Latvia	–	172.0	951.0	108.0	36.0	25.0	18.0	8.4	4.7	2.4	2.6	2.5	1.9	2.9	6.2	6.7	6.2
Estonia	–	211.0	1076.0	90.0	48.0	29.0	23.0	11.0	8.1	3.3	4.0	5.8	3.6	1.3	3.0	4.1	3.6
Average	–	–	–	–	–	–	–	–	–	5.3	6.6	5.6	3.2	2.9	4.3	3.3	3.6

(c) Rates of unemployment (end of year, per cent of labour force) (mid-year for Slovenia, annual average for Estonia)

	1990	1991	1992	1993	1994	1995	1996	1997	1998	1999	2000	2001	2002	2003	2004	2005
Poland	6.1	11.8	13.6	16.4	16.0	14.9	13.2	8.6	10.4	13.4	15.1	17.5	20.0	20.0	19.0	17.6
Hungary	1.7	7.4	12.3	12.1	12.4	12.1	11.8	11.6	10.1	7.0	6.4	5.7	5.8	5.9	6.3	7.3
Czech Republic	0.7	4.1	2.6	3.5	3.2	2.9	3.5	5.2	7.5	8.7	8.8	8.1	7.3	7.8	8.2	7.9
Slovakia	1.6	–	–	12.2	14.6	13.1	12.8	12.5	15.6	19.2	18.0	18.7	17.9	17.4	17.1	15.3
Slovenia	–	7.3	8.3	9.1	9.1	7.4	7.3	7.1	7.6	7.4	6.6	7.0	6.5	6.7	6.5	7.2
Lithuania	–	0.3	1.3	4.4	3.8	17.5	16.4	14.1	13.3	14.6	16.4	17.4	13.8	12.4	11.4	8.3
Latvia	–	0.6	3.9	8.7	16.7	18.1	19.4	14.8	14.0	14.3	14.4	13.1	12.4	10.6	10.4	8.7
Estonia	–	–	–	6.5	7.6	9.7	10.0	9.6	9.8	12.2	13.6	12.6	10.3	10.0	9.6	7.9

Sources: Various issues of the annual EBRD *Transition Report*, supplemented by UN Economic Commission for Europe; UN, *World Economic and Social Survey*; and IMF, *World Economic Outlook*.

Table 35.2   Selected economic indicators for the post-Communist Balkan states, 1990–2006

(a) Rates of growth of GDP (percentage change in real terms)

	1990	1991	1992	1993	1994	1995	1996	1997	1998	1999	2000	2001	2002	2003	2004	2005	2006	1999–2006
Albania	–10.0	–27.7	–7.2	9.6	8.3	13.3	9.1	–10.9	8.6	13.2	6.5	7.1	4.3	5.7	6.7	5.5	5.0	6.8
Bulgaria	–9.1	–11.7	–7.3	–1.5	1.8	2.9	–9.4	–5.6	4.0	2.3	5.4	4.1	4.9	4.5	5.7	5.5	6.0	4.8
Romania	–5.6	–12.9	–8.8	1.5	3.9	7.1	3.9	–6.1	–4.8	–1.1	2.1	5.7	5.1	5.2	8.4	4.1	6.5	4.5
Croatia	–7.1	–21.1	–11.7	–8.0	5.9	6.8	5.9	6.8	2.5	–0.9	2.9	4.4	5.6	5.3	3.8	4.3	4.6	3.8
Serbia and Montenegro	–7.9	–11.6	–27.9	–30.8	2.5	6.1	7.8	10.1	1.9	–	–	–	–	–	–	–	–	–
Serbia	–	–	–	–	–	–	–	–	–	–18.0	5.2	5.1	4.5	2.4	9.3	6.3	6.5	2.7
Montenegro	–	–	–	–	–	–	–	–	–	–6.7	3.1	–0.2	1.7	1.5	3.7	4.1	5.5	1.6
Bosnia and Herzegovina	–	–	–40.0	0.00	20.8	86.0	37.0	15.6	9.6	5.5	4.3	5.3	3.0	6.0	5.8	5.0	5.6	
Republic of Macedonia	–9.9	–7.0	–8.0	–9.1	–1.8	–1.1	1.2	1.4	3.4	4.3	4.5	–4.5	0.9	2.8	4.1	4.0	4.0	2.5
Average	–	–	–	–	3.9	6.0	2.2	1.1	0.6	–2.2	3.7	4.7	4.9	4.6	6.9	4.7	5.9	4.2

(b) Rates of inflation (annual average, per cent)

	1990	1991	1992	1993	1994	1995	1996	1997	1998	1999	2000	2001	2002	2003	2004	2005	2006
Albania	0.0	35.5	226.0	85.0	22.6	7.8	12.7	33.2	20.6	0.4	0.1	3.1	5.2	2.4	2.9	2.3	2.3
Bulgaria	26.3	333.5	82.0	73.0	96.3	62.0	123.0	1082.0	22.2	0.7	9.9	7.4	5.9	2.3	6.1	5.0	3.0
Romania	5.1	170.2	210.4	256.1	136.7	32.3	38.8	154.8	59.1	45.8	45.7	34.5	22.5	15.3	11.9	9.5	6.5
Croatia	611.0	123.0	666.0	1518.0	98.0	2.0	3.5	3.6	5.7	4.2	6.2	4.9	2.2	1.8	2.1	3.3	3.5
Serbia and Montenegro	593.0	121.0	9,237.0	*	3.3	78.6	94.3	21.3	29.5	–	–	–	–	–	–	–	–
Serbia	–	–	–	–	–	–	–	–	–	37.1	60.4	91.1	21.2	11.3	9.5	17.2	13.0
Montenegro	–	–	–	–	–	–	–	–	–	67.6	97.1	22.6	18.2	6.7	2.2	2.6	3.5
FBiH	–	–	–	–	780	–4.4	–24.5	14.0	5.1	–0.9	1.9	1.9	–0.2	0.2	–0.3	2.1	8.5
Republika Srpska	–	–	–	–	1,061.0	12.9	16.9	–7.3	2.0	14.1	14.0	7.0	1.7	1.8	2.2	2.7	7.0
Republic of Macedonia	608.0	115.0	1,664.0	338.0	126.0	16.0	2.3	2.6	–0.1	–0.7	5.8	5.3	2.4	1.1	–0.3	0.1	2.0
Average	–	–	–	454.0	81.0	42.0	52.0	189.0	24.0	22.1	31.9	24.0	11.0	5.8	4.9	5.7	5.0

* 116.5 to the power of 10 x 12 (hyperinflation)!

(c) Rates of unemployment (end of year, per cent of labour force)

	1990	1991	1992	1993	1994	1995	1996	1997	1998	1999	2000	2001	2002	2003	2004	2005
Albania	9.5	9.2	27.9	28.9	19.6	16.9	12.4	14.9	17.8	18.4	16.8	14.5	15.8	15.0	14.5	14.7
Bulgaria	1.8	10.5	15.3	16.4	12.8	11.1	12.5	13.7	12.2	17.0	16.4	19.5	16.8	13.7	12.0	10.1
Romania	0.0	3.1	8.2	10.4	10.1	8.2	6.6	8.9	10.3	6.8	7.1	6.6	8.4	7.0	6.3	5.9
Croatia	–	14.1	17.8	16.6	17.3	17.6	15.9	17.6	18.6	13.6	16.1	15.8	14.8	14.3	13.8	12.3
Serbia and Montenegro	–	21.0	24.6	23.1	23.1	24.6	25.8	25.8	25.1	–	–	–	–	–	–	–
Serbia	–	–	–	–	–	–	–	–	–	25.5	24.4	25.5	27.6	30.3	31.7	–
Montenegro	–	–	–	–	–	–	–	–	–	–	37.3	36.5	36.7	33.5	31.3	27.3
Bosnia & Herzegovina	–	–	–	–	–	–	–	37.0	38.0	39.3	39.6	40.3	40.9	42.0	43.0	44.5
Republic of Macedonia	23.0	25.0	26.0	28.0	30.0	36.0	39.0	42.0	41.0	32.4	32.1	30.5	31.9	36.7	37.2	36.5

Sources: Various issues of the (annual EBRD) *Transition Report*, supplemented by UN Economic Commission for Europe, *Economic Survey of Europe*; UN, *World Economic and Social Survey*; and IMF, *World Economic Outlook*.

investment and subsidies. Monetary policy was also tightened substantially. Cheap credits to industry were discontinued, and the central bank rediscount rate . . . was raised sharply, even brutally . . . To establish a free-trade regime, the currency was sharply devalued and made convertible from the start . . . Existing restrictions on international trade were almost entirely lifted . . . and tariffs were kept low' (pp. 48–9). Indeed, the highly monopolistic or oligopolistic structure and behaviour of the existing industrial structure prompted maximum reliance on international competition to discourage giant enterprises from responding to reduced state subsidies simply by raising prices (pp. 49–50). These measures inflicted great hardship on Poland's blue- and white-collar workers and in so doing tore apart the Solidarity movement and contributed strongly to the subsequent electoral defeat of the Solidarity-led government in which Balcerowicz served as finance minister, but they also swiftly halted Poland's (socially as well as well as economically) debilitating hyperinflation and turned it into the first post-Communist state to achieve sustained economic recovery. Indeed, thanks to this massive 'kick-start', Poland has remained the post-Communist state with the largest percentage increase in GDP since 1989 (see Tables 35.1 and 35.3).

Table 35.3 Selected comparative economic indicators for post-Communist East Central European, Baltic and Balkan States

	GDP per capita in 2005 ($)	Real GDP in 2005 (% of 1989 level)	Private sector share of GDP, 2005 (%)	External debt (% of GDP, 2005)	Remittances as% of GDP, 2004
Poland	7,809	148	75	52.3	1.7
Hungary	10,911	123	80	70.1	0.5
Czech Republic	12,231	121	80	42.1	0.4
Slovakia	8,632	128	80	57.7	1.5
Slovenia	17,337	131	65	64.0	1.0
Lithuania	7,568	98	75	46.6	1.7
Latvia	6,618	99	70	93.5	2.0
Estonia	9,688	123	80	89.1	1.8
Average	–	133	–	–	1.8
Albania	2,730	138	75	22.0	13.5
Bulgaria	3,381	94	75	69.3	0.3
Romania	4,295	104	70	36.2	0.1
Croatia	7,721	98	60	88.1	3.5
Serbia and Montenegro	3,117	58	55	62.4	17.3
Bosnia and Herzegovina	2,353	60 (2004)	55	31.1	22.1
Macedonia	2,839	88	65	44.8	4.2
Average	–	97	–	–	–
Russia	4,874	88	65	25.7	0.3
Ukraine	1,671	59	65	29.6	0.6

Note: The figures for 2005 are EBRD provisional estimates, those for 2006 are EBRD projections, and the remittance figures for 2004 are estimates.

Sources: Various issues of the annual EBRD *Transition Report*, supplemented by UN Economic Commission for Europe, *Economic Survey of Europe*; UN, *World Economic and Social Survey*; and IMF, *World Economic Outlook*.

THE CASE FOR GRADUALISM

Josef Van Brabant argued that outside advisers had 'obfuscated the tasks of the transformation by focusing too much on pitting the potential virtues of shock therapy [in the broad inclusive sense of the term] against the potential drawbacks of gradualism. All too often many of the participants in these debates have ignored that any substantial transformation programme must embody elements of both. Not only that, these elements can only be tailored relative to the specific conditions of time and place . . . rather than in terms of a preset technocratic blueprint' (Brabant 1993: 94–5). Advocacy of a 'big bang' approach was open to accusation of ducking out of the need to decide on the most appropriate sequencing of reforms in each particular case. It had long been recognized that restructuring and privatization of large-scale enterprises would inevitably take a considerable time to be implemented and to start producing the desired effects. The proponents of 'big bang'/'shock therapy' appeared to have underestimated the time needed to accomplish the transformation of the economic system (for example, the time needed for behaviour patterns, attitudes and institutions to change) and the capacity of new and inexperienced governments to change everything at once. This was likely to give rise to costly mistakes. Except perhaps in the case of post-Communist Hungary, which already had major cadres of officials, politicians and entrepreneurs familiar with the requirements of marketization, the almost ubiquitous lack of personnel qualified to deal with the changed political, administrative and economic conditions was also bound to slow the pace of reform and restructuring.

Some economists argued that it was very hazardous to liberalize prices in a 'big bang' fashion when the authorities did not possess effective instruments of monetary control and that 'the big bang argument for total price decontrol is flawed if the important actors bidding for scarce resources have soft budget constraints'; indeed, 'until budget constraints are hardened, uncontrolled bidding by state enterprises will cause the producer price level to increase indefinitely' (McKinnon 1994: 462).

Other critics of the 'big bang'/'shock therapy' approach argued that its proponents neglected to examine existing institutional structures and how to change them in order to reach the goal of creating a Western-style market economy, and instead focused on ways, means and strategies 'to replace these structures entirely. There is complete disdain for all that exists' (Murrell 1993: 113). Murrell argued that a more sophisticated understanding of the sources of capitalist success would require a focus on mechanisms capable of generating growth and change, rather than on equilibrium models. In Schumpeterian fashion, he emphasized the dynamic roles played by innovation, rather than static allocative efficiency. His evolutionary approach stressed 'the existence of rigidities in organizational behaviour and the importance of entry and exit processes to the dynamism of capitalism' (Murrell 1992a: 52). During the transformation period, he argued, privatization of existing publicly owned enterprises should have been given a lower priority than policies to promote the growth of new private firms (pp. 36, 46). He advocated fuller and more effective use of existing structures. Thus 'during the transition there might be a case for direct controls on state enterprises to promote macro-economic stability, rather than relying upon solely market-based measures' (p. 47).

Neuber criticized the 'big bang' approach on the grounds that 'Although the creation of market-enhancing institutions figures in the transition blueprints, their lagged creation is not seen as an indispensable condition for the initial stages. Underlying that faithful leap into a market setting characterized by a hybrid institutional environment is the neoclassical assumption that markets operate in a frictionless world, the institutions of which do not play any instrumental role' (Neuber 1993: 514). 'The erroneous belief in the automaticity of market-based incentives and signals, especially when coupled with the advocacy of wholesale import of institutions that neglects the existence of surviving institutions, however much disliked, has led to a vast underestimation of the difficulties and subtleties involved' (p. 527).

The late Alec Nove strongly advocated state-directed investment programmes designed to counteract the severe contractions of investment and output which universally accompanied the end of Communist rule and the initial moves from dirigiste to more market-orientated and privatized economies. During this critical phase, 'The danger is not of "creative destruction" as envisaged by Schumpeter, but just of destruction, de-industrialization, with nothing creative taking its place. Here, in my view is *the* Achilles heel of the transition models. The necessary adjustments on the supply side . . . require investment' (Nove 1994: 865). The chances of success would be higher if 'the government, instead of giving sole emphasis to macro-economic stabilization, launched and publicized a recovery programme, and mobilized opinion and private (and foreign) capital to that end' (p. 869).

Europe's post-Communist governments tended to subsidize most of their existing publicly owned enterprises, even in Poland, the Czech Republic and Hungary. Bankruptcies and closures were rare, and implicit and explicit subsidies continued. Even so, unemployment rose alarmingly, placing heavy burdens on state budgets. 'In these circumstances, arguments for a "gradualist" approach, not to the restructuring programme as a whole but to the rate of run-down of production and employment in state firms, are gaining ground. It will often be less costly in both social and fiscal terms to maintain employment than [to] close down an enterprise, and there is no reason to think the growth of new private firms will be impeded as a result' (Jackman 1994: 344). Expanding private firms were recruiting their employees primarily from those still employed in the state sector rather than from the growing pools of unemployed people (p. 334.)

Was it feasible for Europe's post-Communist states successfully to emulate China's post-Maoist 'gradualism'?

China since 1978 has been by far the most successful example of a clearly *gradualist* approach to economic restructuring and reform. Its rapidly growing economy cannot help but impress, and its huge successes have presented advocates of 'big bang'/'shock therapy' with quite a challenge. Woo tried to argue that 'gradual reform . . . was not the optimal reform for China' (Woo 1994: 306), but China's remarkably long-sustained high rates of economic growth have somewhat negated his argument! The more usual response by champions of the 'big bang'/'shock therapy' approach has been to argue that the economic circumstances in China have been very unusual and that this has rendered the post-Maoist model of economic gradualism not readily transferable to the very different Balkan and East Central European contexts. In 1978 China did not face severe inflationary pressures, its foreign debt was low, and it still had a largely agrarian economy. Abundant, cheap labour was readily available to supply the fast-growing non-state sector of the economy, and China was thus able to postpone potentially destabilizing fundamental restructuring and reform of its still relatively modest-sized state-run industrial sector. Conversely, the much more highly industrialized countries of the Balkans and especially East Central Europe were much less able to delay the restructuring and privatization of their large and generally inefficient state-run industrial sectors, notwithstanding the great socio-economic hardships and risks of political instability which this would necessarily entail. It was also argued that China's highly successful township-village enterprises, which managed to perform well even in the absence of conventional property rights, could only flourish in a Confucian culture (Sachs and Woo 1994; Layard 1993; Weitzman 1993; Weitzman and Xu 1994.) However, we fundamentally mistrust 'culturalist' claims of this sort, because they come uncomfortably close to cultural stereotyping of whole peoples, which in turn is not far removed from racial stereotyping. Furthermore, prior to the 1970s the 'Confucian cultures' of several major East Asian peoples were habitually being caricatured as major *cultural impediments* to capitalism, private enterprise, 'modernization' and socio-economic advancement. We are more persuaded by arguments that China's *political and socio-economic circumstances* since the late

1970s have been much more favourable to gradualism than was the case in the Balkans and East Central Europe. China's Communist Party has remained very firmly in control, not least because the Tiananmen Square massacre of summer 1989 served notice that it would ruthlessly suppress any direct challenge to its power and authority. This in turn has made it much more feasible for post-Maoist China to pursue a very controlled and carefully co-ordinated process of gradual marketization and privatization, while postponing potentially destabilizing political restructuring and liberalization into the distant future. These options were simply not available to Europe's post-Communist states, whose economies were much more industrialized and were in most cases in the grip of deep and multifaceted crises which urgently required drastic and very painful surgery. Just as importantly, their populations comprised large, well-educated and politically conscious intelligentsias and industrial working classes, who by 1988–9 were strongly rebelling against continued tutelage by Communist regimes, most of which were by then disintegrating. China's methods and accomplishments since 1978 have therefore been neither politically nor economically feasible in Europe's post-Communist states, whatever the attractions of the post-Maoist Chinese model of gradualism. Moreover, while China's gradualism might superficially appear more attractive because of its undeniable economic achievements, it does not begin to match the greatly increased political and cultural freedoms that have been won by the East Central European, Baltic and Balkan peoples, even if 'the jury is still out' with regard to the extent and durability of the freedoms won by the inhabitants of most of the post-Soviet successor states .

THE CASE FOR CIRCUMSPECTION AND PRAGMATISM

We find ourselves broadly in agreement with a major report published by the World Bank in 1996, which concluded that 'Differences between countries are very important, both in setting the feasible range of policy choice and in determining the response to reforms. Which works best, rapid or gradual reform? This question has no single or simple answer. Nevertheless, for the bulk of these economies the answer is now clear: fast and more consistent reform is better' (World Bank 1996: 143). 'A country's starting circumstances, both economic and political, greatly affect the range of reform policies and outcomes open to it. Within this range, however, the clear lesson of the past few years' reforms is that, regardless of the starting point, decisive and consistent reform pays off' (p. 9). 'In every case what matters is the breadth of the policy reforms attempted and the consistency with which they are maintained' (p. 21). 'Consistent policies, combining liberalization of markets, trade and new business entry with reasonable price stability, can achieve a great deal – even in countries lacking clear property rights and strong market institutions' (p. 142).

In practice, it is impossible to change 'everything at once'. Therefore, the real questions revolve around *how much* can or should be attempted all at the same time, as well as the optimal *sequencing* of reforms. During the early and mid-1990s we were sceptical about the wisdom and the feasibility of 'big bang' solutions, but we were equally aware that simply changing the economy as little and as slowly as possible would be a recipe for economic catastrophe. Indeed, the vaunted 'gradualism' of President Kravchuk's regime in Ukraine during the early 1990s led to the worst of all worlds: simultaneous hyperinflation and economic collapse, giving rise to the pejorative term 'Ukrainianization'.

We therefore see merit in the idea of (i) a 'critical mass' of co-ordinated measures on a sufficient scale to provide an irreversible and ongoing momentum to the reform process; and (ii) a credible programme for which a democratically elected government must seek and maintain popular approval (as stressed by the UN Economic Commission for Europe 1993: 9). Choosing the appropriate mix and scale of measures best suited to particular countries remains a political art rather than an economic 'science'. The initial circumstances vary between countries, such as the size of the private sector, the extent of previous reforms, the burden of foreign debt and the availability of aid.

Clearly, chronic inflation had to be tackled as a matter of dire urgency. Nevertheless, any adverse effects on output and employment needed to be taken into account, and care had to be taken to ensure that the magnitude of the stabilization measures was proportionate to the scale of the inflationary problem.

The debate really came down to what was politically and economically feasible. The Swedish economist Anders Åslund, a prominent advocate of 'big bang'/'shock therapy', contended that 'the interesting limitation is what is practically and politically possible, and nothing else' (Åslund 1994: 37). It also had to be borne in mind that in reality 'the range of sensible strategies is limited and there may be little margin for choice' (Portes 1994: 1180). Most of the alleged protagonists in the debate could probably agree that as much as possible should be done as quickly as possible, but the snag is that this begs all sorts of crucial questions, because deciding how much is possible (and how quickly) remains essentially a matter of intuition and judgement rather an exact science. There was and is little room for arrogance or dogmatism in such momentous matters, affecting the well-being of many millions of people. Pragmatism and acute circumspection are the prime requirements.

In 1994 the UN Economic Commission for Europe emphasized that many of the achievements of the years 1990–4 were 'more likely to impress professional economists and international officials than the long suffering electorates of the countries concerned'. Indeed, 'with the possible exception of the Czech Republic', there was 'widespread disillusionment with the transition process and dissatisfaction with the fall in living standards: the essentially political task of organizing and maintaining popular support for the ultimate objectives of market-based economies and democratic institutions remains as urgent as ever' (UN Economic Commission for Europe 1994: 1). It conceded that the official published economic statistics probably overstated the depth of the initial falls in output in Europe's post-Communist states. Nevertheless, 'Even though the overall reliability and accuracy of macro-economic statistics may legitimately be questioned because of difficulties connected with measuring changes in real output and demand levels under conditions of high inflation and rapidly growing unregistered private sector activities, it is very unlikely that even more elaborate and accurate estimates would yield a fundamentally different picture of the macro-economic performance of transition countries' (p. 58).

By the mid-1990s there was growing recognition that the process of marketization was too important simply to be entrusted to a free-for-all 'dash for the market', and that the economic transformation needed to be orchestrated and regulated by the state in an endeavour to protect the most vulnerable sections of society and ensure that the privatization process was not abused by 'management buyouts' and members of the former Communist *nomenklatura* through 'insider privatization', and/or by mafia-style networks of criminals, blackmarketeers and traffickers, who were the only major holders of liquid capital.

We accept that severe inflationary pressure had to be combated because, if this malady was not quickly brought under control, it was capable of causing hyperinflation, loss of confidence in the currency, a flight from production (into hoarding and speculation), and total economic collapse. In such cases, shock therapy was imperative, delay was dangerous, and no 'softer options' were either available or effective. Poland's first Solidarity government grasped this particular nettle in 1990 and, after experiencing a large contraction in recorded output between 1989 and 1991, Poland became the first post-Communist state to achieve positive growth (in 1992), thanks to the rapid growth of exports and the private sector. However, internal dissension over the enormous pain and hardships inflicted on its mainly blue- and white-collar supporters helped to tear the Solidarity movement apart and to return Poland's ex-Communists to power at the head of a 'new look' coalition of socialist and peasant parties in 1993. In the case of the increasingly centrifugal Socialist Federal Republic of Yugoslavia (SFRY), the power, authority and collective decision-making of the federal government had become so weakened that it was unable to persevere with remedial measures of sufficient strength and duration to bring the inflationary pressures under control, despite premier Markovic's brave attempt to do so in 1990. The subsequent descent into hyperinflation contributed to the accelerating disintegration of both the economy and the SFRY in 1991.

However, other less dire situations allowed considerably greater room for manoeuvre. The former Communist states with still viable economies were able to embark on more gradual and cautious transitions to the market. Nevertheless, the zealots of 'big bang'/'shock therapy' have argued that their approach is always necessary in order to get the pain over with as quickly as possible, instead of prolonging the agony. In the first place, as soon as reformers started dismantling the old system, its malfunctions increased exponentially – with very negative effects on output, employment, prices, distribution and living standards. It was therefore vital to get the new system up and running as rapidly as possible, in order to arrest the contraction and initiate new growth at the earliest opportunity. Secondly, as a result of the complementarity and interdependence between macro-economic stabilization, structural (or systemic) change and the various components of a market system (all of which would need to be put in place simultaneously in order to attain optimal results), a gradual or piecemeal transition would most probably yield damagingly 'suboptimal' economic results and would therefore risk alienating parliamentary and popular support for the government of the day and for the transition to the market. Thirdly, the more any government prolonged the agony of transformation by proceeding cautiously and gradually, the greater would be the risks of a neo-Communist, neo-fascist or ultra-nationalist backlash against the entire reform programme, including liberal democracy and free market economics. Both politically and economically, *there was often a unique 'window of opportunity' for wholesale systemic change which had to be seized and used to the full*. If that opportunity was missed, or if the change was implemented too cautiously and gradually, the entire momentum of reform could be lost or, worse still, the systemic malfunctions and loss of output and employment resulting from an incomplete or piecemeal introduction of the various components of the new system could throw the whole trajectory of reform into reverse, as it did at times in Serbia under Slobodan Milosevic during the 1990s and in Slovakia under Vladimir Meciar during the mid-1990s. Simply put, the 'big bang'/'shock therapy' approach to systemic change meant striking while the iron was still hot, and promoting restructuring and liberalizing reforms simultaneously across the board.

Looked at purely in the abstract, as the most direct means of getting from A to B, the economic and political arguments for 'big bang'/'shock therapy' appear very plausible. However, too much 'shock' can be counter-productive and lead to a backlash against the market reform process, particularly as the 'pain' is largely here and now, while many of the benefits take time to appear and are dependent on the success of the reforms. Yet 'big bang'/'shock therapists' reply that, if one proceeds more cautiously, the pain will still be immediate, but the benefits will take even longer to materialize and there will still be the increased risk of a backlash, and that it is therefore it is safer and more advantageous to proceed as fast as possible. Nevertheless, *what is 'possible' is more a matter of politics than economics*. In the words of Marshall Goldman, 'As economists we can draw up any reform plan that we want; but in a democracy . . . the leaders can only push so far' (*IHT*, 23 February 1995).

In several post-Communist states that had embarked on programmes of macro-economic stabilization, enterprise managers (among others) soon decided that they could not (or would not) tolerate any further financial stringency and started creating their own forms of credit by ceasing to pay their bills and taxes or delaying payment long enough for galloping inflation drastically to reduce the amounts they would have to pay (in real terms). However, this mushrooming growth of inter-enterprise credit (or debts) and corporate tax arrears merely added fuel to the fires of inflation by undermining monetary policy. That made it still more advantageous to defer payments. This is a phenomenon long familiar in Latin America. Once it takes hold of a country, it makes any kind of macro-economic stabilization exceedingly difficult to achieve, especially when the authority and credibility of the government are weak (and any 'non-payment' crisis does much to reduce these still further).

In the less liberal post-Communist states, the most likely danger was that democratization and marketization would 'get stuck half-way'. In other words, these states would have many of the outward trappings but little of the substance or, worse still, most of the pain with few of the benefits. It would be very easy for them to become caught in the so-called 'transition trap' or even to succumb to a 'creeping' counter-revolution. The initial window of opportunity for a clean break with the past was, for a variety of reasons, evidently missed in countries such as Serbia, Croatia, Albania, Romania and Bulgaria. Their long-suffering citizens subsequently had to settle for the long haul. However, it became much more difficult to push forward programmes of political and economic reform and fundamental structural change in countries that were already mired in mounting unemployment, inflation, poverty, crime, gangsterism, apathy and cynicism, and after the former Communist *nomenklatura* had had time to regroup, change their outward appearance and capture (or acquire) large chunks of the new semi-marketized and quasi-democratic systems. All of Europe's post-Communist states embarked on marketization, but some wavered between different types of market economy – primarily between those that were relatively open, law-governed and free from excessive state interference and those that were closed, corrupt and 'dominated by insiders fighting for government-allocated privileges' (Chrystia Freeland, *FT*, 3 September 1995, p. 16).

Creating capitalism amid a shortage of legitimate capitalists and capital proved at least as difficult as consolidating democracy without sizeable middle classes. On the political front, ruling elites could foster makeshift substitutes for 'the missing bourgeoisie'. On the economic front, however, finding effective substitutes for the missing capitalists and capital which do not lead back to étatism and excessive concentration of power in the hands of easily corrupted state functionaries was rather more difficult. The challenges posed by privatization were much greater in post-Communist states than in the West. In the West, 'privatization' has merely involved relatively modest transfers of assets from the state into private hands within already well-established market economies with highly developed capital market institutions. In the post-Communist East, by contrast, it entailed wholesale transformation of the nature of the economic system and the creation of the institutions of a liberal market economy virtually from scratch (Clague and Rausser 1992: 18).

RECENT ECONOMIC ACHIEVEMENTS AND PROBLEMS

Thumbnail assessments of the economic performance and problems of individual East Central European and Balkan countries are deferred until the next chapter, because they are invariably intertwined with evaluations of the significance and impact of EU membership (see pp. 607–14). We have provided more detailed analyses and assessments of economic policies and economic change in individual Balkan post-Communist states in Bideleux and Jeffries (2007), and a companion volume providing similar country-by-country evaluations of East Central Europe's post-Communist states is not far from completion. Here we limit ourselves to a few broad-brush indications of the overall economic record.

By 1994, with the notable exceptions of Bosnia and Macedonia, the East Central European and Balkan post-Communist states were achieving significant economic growth. By 1994, again with the exception of Bosnia, they were also making substantial headway towards the establishment of viable independent market economies. Radically shock-therapied, liberalized and privatized Poland consistently led the way during the 1990s. It was followed initially by Albania, Slovenia and the Czech Republic, and was later joined by the Baltic States, Hungary and Slovakia. However, it is difficult to discern a consistent overall correlation between economic radicalism and performance. Radically reformed Poland experienced rapid and strong economic recovery from 1992 onward, but so did cautious and gradualist Slovenia (from 1993 onward) and more mildly Romania (1993–5 only) and the Czech Republic (1993–6 only), while radically liberalized and privatized Macedonia has trailed among the laggards (see Tables 35.1, 35.2 and 35.3).

Remarkably, the very high levels of inflation which almost invariably accompanied the collapse of the Communist-era economic systems and the liberalization of prices had been largely brought under control through stringent monetarist policies by 1993 in East Central Europe, by 1994 in Latvia and Albania, by 1995 in Estonia, Romania, Croatia, Bosnia and Macedonia, by 1996 in Lithuania, by 1997 in Serbia-Montenegro, and by 1998 in Bulgaria (Tables 35.1 and 35.2).

Table 35.4 Percentage of workforce employed in knowledge-intensive services and medium-/high-tech manufacturing, 2002

	Knowledge-intensive services	Medium- high-tech manufacturing
Sweden	47.0	7.3
Denmark	44.0	6.3
UK	40.8	6.7
France	35.5	6.8
Germany	31.8	11.4
Italy	27.5	7.4
EU-15 average	33.3	7.4
Estonia	30.9	3.4
Hungary	26.4	8.5
Lithuania	24.7	2.6
Latvia	24.7	1.9
Slovakia	24.0	8.2
Czech Republic	23.9	8.9
Slovenia	22.8	9.2
Bulgaria	22.2	5.3
Romania	12.8	5.5

Source: European Commission, Press Release, Stat/03/127, 7 November 2003, pp. 1–2 (Data not provided for Poland and Malta).

Table 35.5 Cars, personal computers and computers linked to the internet per 100 inhabitants, 1999/2000

	Cars	PCs	PCs linked to Internet
EU-15 av'ge	46.1	24.8	2.3
Slovenia	42.6	25.3	1.2
Estonia	33.9	13.5	2.1
Czech Republic	36.2	10.7	1.2
Latvia	23.5	8.2	0.8
Hungary	23.5	7.4	1.2
Slovakia	23.6	7.4	0.5
Poland	25.9	6.2	0.4
Lithuania	31.7	5.9	0.4
Bulgaria	24.4	2.7	0.2
Romania	13.9	2.7	0.2
(Turkey)	(6.8)	(3.2)	(0.1)

Source: European Commission, Press Release, Stat/01/129, 13 December 2003, p. 4.

Table 35.6   Hourly labour costs in industry and services (in euros), 2000

EU-15 average*	22.70	Accession states' average	4.21
Sweden	28.56	Cyprus	10.74
Denmark	27.10	Slovenia	8.98
Germany	26.54	Poland	4.48
France	24.39	Czech Republic	3.90
UK	23.85	Hungary	3.83
Austria	23.60	Slovakia	3.06
Netherlands	22.99	Estonia	3.03
Ireland	17.34	Lithuania	2.71
Spain	14.22	Latvia	2.42
Greece	10.40	Romania	1.51
Portugal	8.13	Bulgaria	1.35

*Excluding Italy and Belgium, for which data were unavailable.

Notes: Average hourly labour costs are total annual labour costs divided by the total number of hours worked during the year.

Source: EU Press Release STAT/03/23, 3 March 2003, p. 2

The figures presented in Tables 35.4 and 35.5 on the proportions of the workforce employed in 'knowledge-intensive services' and (to lesser degrees) in 'medium- and high-technology manufacturing' in 2002 (Table 35.4) and on the numbers of cars, personal computers and computers connected to the internet per 100 inhabitants in 1999 (Table 35.5) help to make concrete the magnitude of the technical/economic chasm still to be bridged between the EU-15, on the one hand, and East Central Europe, the Baltic States, and Bulgaria and Romania, on the other.

It will take several decades to overcome these enormous East–West economic and technological disparities, even if the economic booms taking place in most of the East Central European, Baltic and Balkan post-Communist states during the early and mid-2000s were to continue unabated. However, it is unlikely that such booms can be sustained for very long. Some of the booming economies in these regions have begun to experience labour and skills shortages (notably the Baltic States and to lesser degrees Poland and the Czech Republic), others have run up colossal budget and external trade deficits relative to GDP (especially Hungary), and most have been artificially boosted by highly problematic, distorting and fragile real estate-cum-property-development booms which further exacerbate already widening internal inequalities and could easily crash. In the western Balkans, moreover, high levels of unemployment and poverty and still unresolved territorial status problems could easily reignite violent conflicts and jeopardize the region's still very fragile political stability. It would be prudent to try to forestall the crises that could result from over-heating economies and bursting property and stock market bubbles by reining in the booms, settling for less strenuous and more sustainable rates of economic growth, and preparing the inhabitants of these regions for a long haul. The figures in Table 35.6 suggest that comparisons of per capita GDP understate the magnitude of Europe's east–west (and also north–south) disparities in hourly labour costs.

THE 'NEW WESTERN DOMINATION' OF THE EAST CENTRAL EUROPEAN, BALTIC AND BALKAN STATES

There are potential benefits to be gained by host countries in attracting direct foreign investment and wider benefits to be gained by Europe as a whole in terms of capital flows helping to unite Europe. However, there have also been dangers that the post-Communist East Central European, Baltic and Balkan states could become 'informal colonies' and/or 'captive' markets of the major

Western European economic powers and providers of very cheap labour to subsidiaries and subcontractors of Western multinationals. Adam Burgess, in his *Divided Europe: The New Domination of the East* (1997), was one of the first to argue that this was what was happening, although his warnings were perhaps premature, in as much as the privatization of the region's major industries and service providers was not completed until the late 1990s or early 2000s in most cases.

Such a pattern of development would help the EU economies to withstand growing competition from outside Europe. West European investors could be primarily interested in 'cherry-picking' the strongest or most promising East Central European, Baltic and Balkan enterprises, while leaving the rest to founder, pocketing any available subsidies or investment grants, spiriting away key personnel and their technological know-how, or simply making 'a quick killing', before turning their attention elsewhere. West European entrepreneurs may be less interested in sustainable long-term development for the benefit of Balkan and East Central Europeans than in 'rent seeking', monopolistically capturing new markets, and subjugating the Balkan and East Central European economies to West European industrial and finance capitalism. They are primarily there to make money. For example, there have been widespread criticisms and complaints that Western companies have been buying up and monopolizing banks, gas distribution, telecommunications services and the generation of electricity in the Balkan and East Central European post-Communist states, without reducing charges and/or raising standards of provision very greatly. This may be too cynical a picture, but it is a necessary antidote to any idea that capitalist Western Europe and the EU are engaged in a great philanthropic venture. Nevertheless, it is worth recalling Joan Robinson's legendary remark that if there is anything worse than being exploited by foreign capital, it is *not* being exploited by foreign capital.

36 The 'return to Europe': the gradual integration of East Central European and Balkan post-Communist states into the EU and NATO

This chapter outlines and analyses the so-called 'return to Europe' – the gradual integration of the East Central European and Balkan post-Communist states into the European Union since the mid-1990s – as well as the ways in which this process has interacted with the political and economic transformations which have been taking place in these regions. Admittedly, the expression 'return to Europe' is somewhat misleading, in as much as the East Central European and Balkan states never really 'left' Europe, and their 'European credentials' are second to none. Nevertheless, no other expression adequately captures the widespread feeling and/or perception that these countries are being reconnected and reintegrated into the 'mainstream' of European affairs, from which they were temporarily side-lined not only by the now defunct Communist regimes but also by their authoritarian nationalist predecessors. This chapter also provides a short outline and assessment of Western assistance to Europe's post-Communist states during the 1990s and a brief résumé of their ongoing integration into NATO.

THE FUNDAMENTAL TRANSFORMATION: FROM 'VERTICALLY STRUCTURED' TO 'HORIZONTALLY STRUCTURED' POLITIES, ECONOMIES AND SOCIETIES

In March 2004, on the eve of the accession of the five East Central European and three Baltic states to the European Union, the EU Commission claimed with considerable justification that 'For the acceding countries, the accession process has served as a catalyst for change, accelerating the implementation of complex and difficult political, institutional and economic reforms. The conclusion of the process is a significant achievement that was based on sustained commitment over many years' (EU Commission 2004: 4). The protracted quest for membership of the EU has indeed been the major 'driver of change' in East Central Europe and the Baltic States, and it remains so in the post-Communist Balkan states. It has been the single most important factor driving the crucial overarching transformation from the previous prevalence of vertical power relations and vertical power structures towards polities, economies and societies based on the prevalence of horizontal power structures and power relations. This transformation is in essence what both defines and makes possible the rule of law, substantial equality before the law, limited government, liberal parliamentary/representative democracy, law-governed civil societies, 'level playing fields', and civil (rule-governed) market economies.

In the East Central European and Baltic states which joined the EU in May 2004, the struggles to fulfil the so-called 'Copenhagen Criteria' and 'Madrid Criteria' for EU membership helped to foster growing cross-party consensuses on macro-economic policies, privatization, restructuring of institutions and industries, judicial and legal reform, and the promotion and protection of human and minority rights. This in turn helped to promote the rule of law, equal citizenship (equal civil rights and equality before the law), political stability, 'level playing fields', and the development of more fully marketized and liberalized economies. The net effect was slowly to *restructure and/or reorientate* these countries away from the prevalence of 'vertical' power relations and power structures, from the primacy of 'primordial' ethno-cultural ties, and from clientelistic and 'ethnic collectivist' conceptions of the polity, by nurturing and strengthening horizontally structured impersonal ties and civil societies and civil economies based upon limited government and the rule of law. All this was inherently complex and far from easy to accomplish. Nevertheless, it has been accomplished to impressive degrees.

This transformation, which has both *driven* and been *driven by* the quest for EU membership, has made much greater headway in East Central Europe and the Baltic States than it has in the post-Communist Balkan states. This is the fundamental reason why the 'European Council' (meeting of EU heads of state and government) in Copenhagen in December 2002 decided to allow the five East Central European states (Poland, Hungary, the Czech Republic, Slovakia and Slovenia) and the three Baltic States (Lithuania, Latvia and Estonia) to enter the EU in May 2004, together with the considerably more prosperous Republic of Cyprus and Malta. By contrast, the post-Communist Balkan states' drive for EU membership has been seriously retarded by well-founded perceptions that *highly clientelistic, clannish, semi-criminalized vertical power relations and power structures* have been much more deeply and tenaciously entrenched in these states (as argued on pp. 610–13 and in Bideleux 2007: 119–20).

It is crucial to recognize the transformative roles of the EU itself, including the very fact of its existence and its availability as the basis of an emerging and commodious supranational legal order and civil association in Europe, as well as the strong (albeit fluctuating) drive of the governments and 'political classes' in these regions towards first attaining and then consummating EU membership. Nevertheless, for the sake of historical veracity, we must also lament the woeful degrees to which the EU initially dragged its feet (especially from 1990 to 1997), the quite breathtaking niggardliness of the economic and technical assistance offered by hugely affluent western European states to their vastly poorer 'eastern cousins' (Germany's comparatively open-handed generosity has been a partial exception to this generalization), the extraordinarily mean and harsh terms on which the East Central Europe and the Baltic States were allowed to enter the EU in May 2004, and the shameful degrees to which the EU and its western European members have engaged in invidiously intrusive, prescriptive, peremptory and patronizing tutelage over and 'micro-management' of the post-Communist East Central European, Baltic and (above all) Balkan states. This tutelage has sometimes assumed quasi-colonial proportions.

These criticisms are in no way intended to denigrate 'European ideals' and the European integration project. On the contrary, we are strongly committed to the goals of pan-European integration and convergence: a Europe united on the basis of a robust overarching legal and institutional order and framework which both fosters and makes possible the *peaceful and fruitful co-existence of a rich diversity* of European cultures and values (*rather than* foolish and dangerous dreams of a more *monolithic* European identity based upon imposed *homogeneity of culture and/or values*, which can only be a recipe for suffocation, stultification and strife). Nevertheless, we have been repeatedly struck by *how little* (rather than how much) the EU and the comparatively prosperous western European states have *actively* done to help finance and accelerate the transformation of Europe's far poorer post-Communist economies and societies and thereby promote 'real' (as distinct from merely formal) East–West convergence and integration within Europe. There is insufficient awareness in the West that the death throes and the aftermath of Communist rule in the eastern half of Europe during the 1980s and 1990s resulted in large *increases* (rather than reductions) in Europe's East–West economic disparities; and that, partly for this reason, but also as a consequence of greatly increased socio-economic inequality and the collapse of the 'social safety nets' hitherto provided by the former Communist regimes, life has in many ways become *much harder* (rather than easier) for most people in Europe's post-Communist states since the demise of the Communist regimes. The restructuring of polities, economies and societies required by democratization, marketization, liberalization and the quest for membership of the EU has been hugely painful for all but a few people 'on the make', no matter how necessary and desirable such restructuring might be in the longer term. Nevertheless, the West has done precious little either to alleviate the pain or to accelerate the recovery (see pp. 581–2, 585–95).

The scale of Western meanness and myopia needs to be kept in mind in order to begin to understand the depth of the *disillusionment, disenchantment and even bitterness* felt by many (perhaps most) inhabitants of Europe's post-Communist states towards the West and the EU, not only among unrepentant Communists and anti-Western nationalists, but also (or even especially) among people who are profoundly convinced of the necessity and long-term desirability of the massive and arduous transformations which these countries have been undergoing. The frequent description of their feelings as 'reform fatigue' is a *colossal understatement*. They are profoundly *weary* and often *resentful* of the long tunnels of hardship through which they have had almost to claw their way, largely unaided (but much preached at and berated!) by the West. The raw ambivalence of East Central European and Baltic sentiments towards western Europe and the EU were revealingly reflected in the distressingly low voter turn-outs for most of the referenda on entry into the EU which were held in the East Central European and Baltic States in 2003 and in the even lower voter turn-outs for their first elections to the European Parliament on 12 June 2004, just over a month after joining the EU (see Tables 36.2 and 36.5 on pp. 604 and 607).

The enormous asymmetries of power and wealth between western Europe, on the one side, and the post-Communist East Central European, Baltic and Balkan states, on the other, have meant that western Europe has persistently been able to get away with its niggardliness and its arrogant, patronizing, intrusive and irksome tutelage towards the new and prospective 'eastern' members of the EU. This has been reinforced by the hard-headed and pragmatic acceptance by the governments and the greater part of the 'political classes' of the post-Communist East Central European, Baltic and Balkan states that they really do have 'nowhere else to go'. Their only viable long-term option has been to join the EU, even though many feel that their treatment and the terms of entry imposed upon them by the EU-15 have been mean, harsh and humiliating. Indeed, the so-called 'negotiations' for EU membership were nothing of the sort, and the terms of entry were imposed on a 'take-it-or-leave-it' basis by western European states which knew only too well that they had the prospective 'eastern' members 'over a barrel'. In place of authentic two-way negotiation of the terms of entry, the candidates for EU membership had no choice but to transpose the entirety of the so-called *acquis communautaire* (more than 80,000 pages of existing EU rules, regulations and legislation) into their own 'domestic' or 'national' law as rapidly as feasible, with no leeway (other than over the length of any 'transitions' towards full compliance) and with the minimum of contestation or debate. They were also required to develop and to demonstrate the 'administrative and judicial capacity' to implement and enforce this *acquis communautaire*. The so-called 'negotiations' involved little more than regular unilateral and subjective assessments by the EU Commission of the degrees to which candidate states had adopted or complied with the *acquis* and had developed and demonstrated the 'administrative and judicial capacity' to implement and enforce it. There was negligible give-and-take over the pitifully small net financial transfers which these relatively poor states could expect to receive after accession. Quite literally, 'beggars' were not allowed to be 'choosers'.

WHY EU MEMBERSHIP IS NEVERTHELESS CRUCIAL FOR THE POST-COMMUNIST EAST CENTRAL EUROPEAN, BALTIC AND BALKAN STATES

In intensely practical and life-determining ways, it has never been so crucial as it is now to be considered 'European' and part of 'Europe'. Conceptions and meanings of Europe have become increasingly bound up with the ongoing 'construction of Europe', which is often portrayed as the natural culmination of 'the European idea' and of innumerable projects for its realization, harking back to medieval Christendom, the Renaissance and the Enlightenment. Since the demise of the former Soviet bloc (and with it the notion of a world divided into a Western capitalist 'First World', a Communist 'Second World' and a formerly colonial or quasi-colonial 'Third World'), membership of the European Union has become all the more important as a badge of acceptance, respectability and First World status. It has become quite literally the chief 'passport' to unrestricted access to European Union product, capital and labour markets, to major life-enhancing opportunities in schooling, higher education, business, mobility, networking and funding. To be able to claim to be 'European', and to be able to back up that claim with appropriate documentation, has become almost as important as it was to be able to say 'Civis Romanus sum' in Roman times. Perceived and documented possession or non-possession of a 'European' identity ('credentials') and citizenship of a state which is a member of the European Union increasingly determines who is allowed to live and work in the European Union – and who is not. This has become a major determinant of the life chances of tens of millions of people, as many citizens of Europe's post-Communist states, Turkey and the semi-'Europeanized' Maghreb states (Morocco, Algeria and Tunisia) have been learning to their cost.

The EU now provides an overarching political, economic and legal framework and 'order' for about two-thirds of all Europeans (the exact proportion depending, in large measure, on how 'Europeans' are defined and where Europe's outer perimeters are drawn). As in Western Europe, so in East Central Europe, in the Baltic States and even in the post-Communist Balkan states, the EU is increasingly the major arena within which the main rules, laws, institutional frameworks and policy frameworks which set the main parameters for the conduct of European political and economic activity are collectively and consensually negotiated, formulated, enforced and upheld. The European Union can be most accurately characterized as a post-democratic supranational 'liberal legal order' (in a Hayekian sense) or as a supranational 'civil association' (in an Oakeshottian sense), rather than as a democratic project or entity (for further elucidation, see Bideleux 2000, 2001a, 2001b; Hayek 1960, 1973; and Oakeshott 1962, 1975).

The European Union is not merely *based upon* the rule of law. In essence, *it is the rule of law*. The EU is both an expression of, and a major contributor to, the growth of what has come to be called 'regulatory governance' (Majone *et al.* 1996) and the so-called 'judicialization of governance' (Stone Sweet 2000). At the national as well as at the supranational level Western, East Central and Baltic Europeans are increasingly governed by unelected bodies and appointed (rather than elected) officials, acting in regulatory, judicial or quasi-judicial capacities.

In this context, the effects of EU membership on East Central Europe and the Baltic States can and should be regarded as *the consummation* of the new Members States' shift from the age-old primacy of vertical power relations and power structures (buttressed by various forms of ethnic and confessional collectivism, clientelism and mafia-style gangsterism) to *an emerging primacy of horizontally structured civil societies, economies and polities based primarily upon the rule of law, limited government and growing approximations to equality before the law* (equal rights and obligations of all citizens). Thus, even though EU membership has necessarily entailed difficult surrenders of *some* of the hard-won national sovereignty, autonomy and national-democratic control, scrutiny and accountability which the previously Soviet-dominated East Central European and Baltic states gained by breaking asunder the Soviet bloc (or which Slovenia gained by playing a leading role in breaking asunder the Socialist Federal Republic of Yugoslavia), the post-Communist states which entered the EU in May 2004 made enormously valuable compensating gains in doing so. By joining the EU, they locked themselves into a very robust supranational legal order and civil association which is greatly increasing the strength, pervasiveness and durability of limited government and the rule of law – the linchpins of liberty and of genuinely liberal forms of democracy and market economy.

Even though the EU is riddled with seemingly insurmountable 'democratic deficits' and (for this and other reasons) cannot and should not be regarded as a *democratic* project or polity, it can confer membership of an immensely valuable supranational legal order which deeply entrenches and greatly extends the remit of the rule of law, limited government and equality before the law on a supranational basis. This increasingly gives all its states and citizens equal rights and equal obligations by placing them under an overarching jurisdiction and a growing body of laws which are equally applicable to all.

These are profound long-term gains, vastly more valuable than the relatively trivial and ephemeral agricultural subsidies and 'structural funds' (transfer payments) on which most attention has mistakenly been focused. The benefits of EU membership ought not to be evaluated primarily in terms of a superficial, short-term and often fallacious *economic calculus*, as many politicians and academic and media analysts simple-mindedly assume, especially in the UK. Instead, the benefits should be evaluated in terms of the European Union's *enduringly transformative potential*: the ways in which it *cumulatively* changes national and transnational power relations, power structures, opportunity structures, incentive structures and (most valuably of all for individuals) mobility and life chances. Therein lies the true greatness of Jean Monnet's vision. As his former assistant (and best biographer) the late François Duchêne was fond of putting it, the internal and external relations of the EU and its Member States have in large measure been '*domesticated*' and embedded within a supranational civil (legal) framework (Duchêne 1994: 369, 404–6). In using the word 'domesticated', Duchêne meant mainly that a whole range of matters which had previously been dealt with by European ministries of foreign affairs, foreign trade and defence as part of *international relations* (relations between sovereign states) are now being dealt with in the largely civil and judicial ways that states deal with 'domestic' matters, within a single legal framework, as if they were living within a single polity. However, Duchêne was also simultaneously using the word 'domesticated' in the sense of 'tamed' and made 'civil' or 'civilian' (as distinct from 'brutish' and 'military'). Disputes between the countries which are now members of the EU used to be resolved by the *flexing of muscles*, by *force majeure*, and ultimately by *going to war*. Within the new EU framework and order, by contrast, they are resolved by transnational negotiation and mediation, by *negotiating* until solutions with which the parties concerned can live are reached, or, if that is not possible, by *going to court* – ultimately to the Court of Justice of the European Communities in Luxembourg or, on matters outside EU jurisdiction, to the European Court of Human Rights in The Hague. These frameworks have created an unprecedented new supranational civil legal order in Europe and an utterly new civil, juridical and 'domesticated' basis for politics, for relations between EU Member States, and for relations between these states and their citizens.

The countries in greatest need of being locked into the EU supranational civil legal order have been the East Central European, Baltic and Balkan post-Communist states. EU membership offers them and the rest of Europe the best hope (conceivably the only hope) of finally overcoming the tensions, grievances, disputes, minority problems, economic problems and geopolitical vulnerabilities which afflicted them more than any other part of Europe during the twentieth century – and which dragged them and many millions of other people into two World Wars. As argued more fully elsewhere (Bideleux 2001a, 2001c, 2002a, 2005a; Bideleux and Jeffries 2007: ch. 11), most of the territorial, size-related, minority-related and economic problems facing the post-Communist East Central European, Baltic and Balkan states can be *mitigated* or *alleviated* but cannot be fully overcome or resolved within the narrow and confining framework of the nation-state. In most cases, *the nation-state framework is part of the problem to be solved, rather than part of the solution*. For example, most of these states are too small and/or impoverished to offer viable self-sufficient markets and sources of key inputs for their industries, development of which is greatly constrained by being dominated by local monopolists and/or being 'boxed into' their limited national markets. Furthermore, no matter how much effort is made to protect and enhance the rights of ethnic minorities, such minorities are nevertheless bound to remain second- or even third-class citizens in states which have largely remained 'ethnocracies' – states which are quite tenaciously regarded as belonging exclusively to the dominant/titular ethnic group, to be used as the elected representatives of that group see fit.

By contrast, the EU supranational civil legal order and 'civil association' represents and has created a cosmopolitan legal framework which is increasingly placing states and peoples of widely differing size, wealth, strength, creeds and ethnicities on relatively equal legal footings with regard to the ever-widening range of matters that come under EU jurisdiction, such as rights of movement, consumer rights, environmental rights, gender equality and (above all) the Single Market, which is striving to establish a so-called 'level playing field'. The EU also makes it possible for elected and/ or appointed representatives of small states to participate on an increasingly equal footing with those from big states in transnational debates and deliberations on the policies and future development of the EU, to degrees that were quite impossible in the 'old Europe' of sovereign states in which the larger states imposed their own interests, agendas and wishes by *force majeure* and rode roughshod over those of small states. The Low Countries and later Ireland were the first to reap and appreciate such benefits in practice, but they also have particular significance for the new and prospective EU Member States, as most of these are small (the only exceptions being Poland, Romania and Turkey) and relatively poor (the exceptions being Cyprus, Malta and Slovenia).

It also needs to be stressed that the benefits of EU membership outlined above pertain to the EU *as it is has evolved in practice*, rather than to an abstract and unattainable vision of perfection. No useful purpose is served by pretending that the EU can be made much more democratic and egalitarian (or less technocratic and elitist) than it currently is. If the EU were to be made much more democratic in the majoritarian sense, enabling the elected representatives of (transitory) majorities to impose their wishes or aspirations on various out-voted minorities, this would allow the large member states to out-vote the smaller ones – and some of the above-mentioned benefits of EU membership for small states would largely be nullified. Nevertheless, the member states most tenaciously opposed to the creation of a 'federal Europe' (Britain, Denmark, Sweden, the Czech Republic and Poland) would strongly resist such an arrangement, because a democratized European Union could only be a federation of some sort. Conversely, if comprehensive safeguards for the interests, aspirations, cultures and identities of small states were to be built into some sort of EU-wide 'consociational democracy', in which major decision-making, policy-making and law-making would be based on negotiation and agreement between elected and/or appointed representatives of each of the constituent nations and ethnic groups, this could rapidly become even more elitist than the current arrangements, while severely circumscribing the operation of democratic procedures and most likely becoming a recipe for gridlock – or, at the very least, for even slower and more cumbersome decision-making and law-making than at present. Notwithstanding its blatant elitism and glaring 'democratic deficits', an EU run by unelected appointed officials who are only remotely and indirectly accountable to the EU 'citizenry' probably remains the only politically viable and operationally effective structure on which all Member States can agree, even if this does not correspond to anybody's ideal arrangement. Furthermore, making any vision of the EU fully operational necessarily entails the creation and acceptance of a technocracy to regulate and administer it. Hankering after an EU without a technocracy is mere wishful thinking.

Most of the heated debates about the EU's undeniable elitism and 'democratic deficits' lose sight of the fact that the EU's legitimation is not primarily democratic, but rather procedural (juridical) and functional (performative). The EU is required to conform to procedures which have been negotiated and agreed in advance by a mixture of elected and appointed representatives of the member states. Likewise EU accountability is largely procedural or juridical rather than radically democratic, and the EU is judged chiefly by the value and quality of the outcomes it achieves and/or the functions it performs. EU collective decisions are not made by majoritarian democratic procedures (a democratically elected majority imposing its wishes or aspirations on everyone else), nor even in most cases by so-called 'qualified majority voting' (assigning population-based weights to the representatives of each member states). Only a minority of EU decisions are put to a vote at all (Bomberg and Stubb 2003: 51–3). Instead, the EU operates and makes decisions primarily by highly consensual negotiations between a mixture of appointed and elected representatives of the member states, who generally continue to negotiate on any issues which any member states consider to be matters of 'vital national interest' until unanimous agreement is reached on frameworks, packages or compromises which the representatives of all the member states think they can live with and persuade their governments and parliaments to accept. This is accepted by the member states, partly because the European Union's main *raison d'être* is to reach agreement on common *procedures*, *institutions* and *policies*, on ways of doing things in step with one another, and on setting *mutually acceptable parameters*, chiefly in order to make it possible for these states to co-exist with the minimum of friction and mutual impairment, for their mutual benefit, security and prosperity. Contrary to the perceptions in some quarters, the Brussels bureaucracy very rarely *imposes* decisions, policies, regulations, directives or legislation on the Member States 'by diktat' or on its own initiative, partly because it has little power to do so. Most of the laws, rulings, regulations and directives emanating from the Commission itself merely fill the gaps and iron out defects or inconsistencies in the policies, decisions and legislation collectively and consensually negotiated and agreed between appointed and elected representatives of those same Member States. The Commission's powers and remit are largely confined to prompting and cajoling the Member States to implement and comply with such policies, decisions and laws.

Thus, even though only states which are perceived to be liberal democracies are permitted to join the EU, and even though the EU's supranational civil legal order or civil association provides a juridical and institutional superstructure which is strongly *supportive* of liberal democracy, liberal market economies, limited government, level playing fields and liberal civil societies at the national and sub-national levels, *the EU is not itself a democratic entity*. The EU's functions and characteristics have much more to do with the *rule of law* than with democracy as such. It is chiefly by strengthening the rule of law and making it more pervasive as the framework for all political and economic activity that EU membership has helped to consummate the post-1989 transformations of the East Central European, Baltic and (in due course) Balkan states.

Unfortunately, much of the burgeoning academic literature on 'eastward enlargement' of the EU and on the so-called 'Europeanization' of the East Central European, Baltic and Balkan states has done much more to obscure the saliency and centrality of the fundamental transformations which these states have undergone. Many of the analysts who have been publishing in the West on eastward enlargement of the EU and its relationship to the political, economic and social transformation(s) in Europe's post-Communist states have never been specialists on the history, politics and economic development of these states, to which they have only relatively recently begun to give attention – often in quite superficial ways. This has resulted in widespread reliance on employing and applying ready-made Western jargon, nostrums and conceptual toolkits (developed mainly in relation to quite different Western problems, trajectories and experiences) to conceptualize, analyse and explain the changes taking place in East Central Europe, the Baltic States and the Balkans and the nature of the challenges they face, instead of endeavouring primarily to understand, conceptualize and explain the integration of the East Central European, Baltic and Balkan regions into the European Union and the accompanying changes in governance on their own terms and in the light of their own rich histories and intellectual traditions. Western jargon and conceptualizations are poor substitutes for in-depth study of the countries under examination. The most insightful and illuminating analyses have been those produced by East Central European, Baltic and Balkan analysts who have witnessed and experienced these transformations and challenges at first hand and from the inside, and who have formulated their own 'home-grown' ways of understanding, conceptualizing and explaining them – for example, Agh (2003), Dimitrova (2004), and various contributors to Rupnik and Zielonka (2003), Pettai and Zielonka (2003), and Dobre and Coman (2005).

WESTERN EUROPE'S FALTERING FIRST STEPS TOWARDS INTEGRATING EAST CENTRAL EUROPE INTO THE EUROPEAN COMMUNITY, 1991–7

Jean Monnet and the 'founding fathers' of the European Communities never intended their brain-child to remain an exclusively Western European club. Admittedly, there is remarkably little documentary evidence to back up this claim. However, the late François Duchêne assured us both personally and in his publications that 'Monnet never thought of the Community as confined to the original Six'; indeed, on 28 March 1958 Monnet told the Economic Affairs Committee of the Council of Europe Assembly that 'Our Community is neither a little Europe nor a closed Community', and this stance was implicit in Monnet's treatment of European union 'as the only solution for German unity. This could hardly have taken place without changes affecting the whole of central Europe – which has proved to be the case' (Duchêne 1994: 379). In a speech delivered on 15 January 1959, however, the West German foreign minister, Heinrich von Brentano, explicitly stated that 'just as the European economic communities we have created are not intended to be restrictive, nor would a European political community be. It would be open to any European country prepared to accept the necessary political conditions in the interests of all' (Brentano 1964: 161).

On 9 December 1989, amid the great excitement and optimism generated by the Revolutions of that year in East Central Europe, a European Council meeting of EU heads of state and government affirmed that the European Community and its Member States were 'fully conscious of the common responsibility that devolves upon them in this decisive phase in the history of Europe'. The first post-Communist governments of East Central Europe, the Baltic States and the Balkans attached great importance to the so-called 'return to Europe', a slogan that embodied a whole web of aspirations: for fast-track entry into the European Union; for the rapid adoption of Western-style laws, institutions and market systems (which some people thought would soon result in Western-style living standards); for freer travel and migration; for major cultural, economic and geopolitical reorientations; and for international acceptance as 'normal' countries.

The 'Europe Agreements' of 1991–6

The first post-Communist governments initially entertained high hopes of a rapid 'return to Europe', starting with the conclusion of bilateral trade and co-operation agreements between the EC and several East Central European and Balkan states in 1988–90. These hopes were reinforced by the EC's conclusion of bilateral 'Europe Agreements' ('enhanced Treaties of Association') with Hungary, Poland and Czecho-Slovakia in December 1991 and with Romania and Bulgaria in late 1992. These treaties provided for a phased reciprocal reduction and removal of trade barriers over a ten-year period and held out the possibility (but as yet no firm promise) of accession to the European Union as Europe entered the new millennium. Following the 'velvet divorce' of the Czech Republic and Slovakia on 31 December, the EU signed replacement 'Europe Agreements' with these separated states in October 1993. Additional 'Europe Agreements' were signed with Lithuania, Latvia and Estonia in June 1995 and with Slovenia in June 1996. The 'Europe Agreements' with Poland and Hungary took effect in 1994; those with the Czech Republic, Slovakia, Bulgaria and Romania did so in 1995; those with the Baltic States came in force in 1998, and the one with Slovenia did so in 1999.

Contrary to initial Balkan, Baltic and especially East Central European expectations, however, *the European Community was very slow to start (re)integrating Europe's former Communist states into the mainstream of European development*. The 'Europe Agreements' signed in 1991–2 seemed, in the words of Jacques Attali (the founding president of the EBRD), to have been designed to 'restrict their access to key Western markets rather than to integrate them' (quoted in *FT*, 29 October 1992, p. 19). The agreements did so mainly by maintaining various 'safeguard' and 'anti-dumping' provisions (so-called 'contingent protection', which could and would be invoked against any 'disruptive' exports from Europe's former Communist states), as well as stringent EC restrictions on imports of agricultural products, processed foods, drinks, steel, chemicals, textiles, footwear, clothing and other so-called 'sensitive goods'. These happened to be the main existing and potential East Central European, Baltic and Balkan exports to the West. Such restrictions were to be maintained for at least ten years after the 'Europe Agreements' took effect. The European Community adopted this restrictive and defensive attitude in spite of the fact that such exports posed little threat to EC producers, since they amounted to less than 1 per cent of EC output (and less than 4 per cent of EC imports of each of the products in question) and were being more than offset by increased EC exports to East Central Europe, the Baltic States and the Balkans (*FT*, 19 October 1992, p. 6; 7 June 1993; 18 June 1993, p. 15).

The 'Copenhagen Criteria' of June 1993

The European Council hosted in Copenhagen in June 1993 belatedly spelled out more explicit conditions for admission: 'Membership requires that the candidate country has achieved stability of institutions guaranteeing democracy, the rule of law, human rights and respect for and protection of minorities, the existence of a functioning market economy as well as the capacity to cope with competitive pressures and market forces within the Union. Membership presupposes the candidate's ability to take on the obligations of membership, including adherence to the aim of political, economic and monetary union' (Baldwin 1994: 155). In addition to laying down conditions that candidate countries would have to be able to meet before being admitted to full membership of the European Union, the June 1993 European Council in Copenhagen stipulated that 'The Union's capacity to absorb new members, while maintaining the momentum of European integration, is also an important consideration in the general interest of both the Union and the candidate countries' (*Enlargement Newsletter*, 6 June 2006, p. 2).

Concerns relating to the EU's 'absorption capacity' have subsequently provided the most widely acceptable grounds for exercising prudent caution in the pursuit of further enlargement of the EU, as neither the existing nor prospective members of the EU have anything positive to gain from any form or scale of enlargement which could fatally impair the future viability of the EU. In our view, indeed, the only serious and acceptable objections to the eventual admission of the western Balkan states and Turkey into the EU are claims that the current structures and procedures of the EU could find it difficult to accommodate either a large number of additional members (up to ten more) or a state with a population as large as that of Turkey. These objections cannot be lightly dismissed, and they represent a position that can be upheld without necessarily subscribing to any negative judgements concerning the intrinsic merits and/or 'European credentials' of the western Balkan states and/or Turkey. Such considerations will weigh even more heavily when the EU is forced to consider (as it will be, sooner or later) the increasingly strong claims and aspirations of countries such as Ukraine, Moldova, Belarus, Georgia and Armenia to eventual membership of the EU, if only in order to avert or reverse the marginalization of these states from the main currents of European affairs and economic development. Perhaps for these reasons, in 2006 the EU Commission felt it necessary to provide a fuller formulation of the 'absorption capacity' criterion: 'The pace of enlargement must take into consideration the EU's absorption capacity. Enlargement is about sharing a project based on common principles, policies and institutions. The Union has to ensure that it can maintain its capacity to act and decide according to a fair balance within institutions; respect budgetary limits; and implement common policies that function well and achieve their objectives' (*Enlargement Newsletter*, 6 June 2006, p. 2).

The major transformations needed to meet the Copenhagen Criteria were bound to take time, however, as they involved fundamental changes in the structures of power and ownership, as well as in political and cultural values, attitudes, assumptions, mentalities, and the ways that East Central European and Balkan nations and states had been accustomed to seeing and defining themselves and each other. The creation or restoration of strong and healthy 'civil societies', which are necessary prerequisites for 'civil economies' as well as for secure parliamentary democracies, was bound to be equally difficult and protracted (Rose 1992: 13–26).

Early in their quest to become sufficiently democratic, law-governed and peaceful to be deemed eligible for membership of the European Union, the East Central European, Baltic and Balkan states were formally expected to subscribe and commit themselves to the EU's cosmopolitan ethos and rules. For example, all citizens of the EU, regardless of nationality, are formally granted equal rights under the (old) Article 7 of the Treaty of Rome. This was (in principle, at least) fundamentally at odds with the invidious ethnic exclusion and discrimination which pervaded much of the Balkans, Estonia, Latvia and parts of East Central Europe during the 1990s, and it still poses significant challenges and problems for them. However, in order to avoid accusations of double standards or hypocrisy, the EU-15 ought also to have been prepared to uphold and enforce the same rules more consistently among themselves.

THE 'FIRST WAVE' OF APPLICATIONS FOR EU MEMBERSHIP, MARCH 1994 – JANUARY 1996

Recognizing that the 'Europe Agreements' were in practice a device to delay (rather than expedite) the entry of post-Communist states into the EU, the East Central European, Baltic and eastern Balkan governments decided to take the bull by the horns and formally apply for full membership of the EU sooner rather than later. Hungary submitted its application in March 1994, Poland in April 1994, Slovakia and Romania in June 1995, Latvia in October 1995, Estonia in November 1995, Lithuania and Bulgaria in December 1995, the Czech Republic in January 1996, and Slovenia in June 1996. In almost all of these countries, there were very high levels of parliamentary and elite support for these applications, even though at the time there appeared to be little immediate prospect of the applications either being taken seriously by the EU or making much tangible difference to the pace and direction of the enlargement process.

However, according to Eurobarometer polls conducted between 1992 and 1996 (see Table 36.1), *popular* approval of the EU was much weaker, partly as a result of the great hardships which most

Table 36.1 Levels of positive public approval for the EU, 1992–6 (per cent)

	1992	1993	1994	1995	1996
Hungary	34	36	32	30	33
Poland	48	37	42	46	58
Czech Republic	45	37	34	36	33
Slovakia	35	44	37	31	34
Estonia	32	31	29	30	24
Latvia	40	40	35	35	26
Slovenia	45	30	37	35	35
Romania	55	45	51	50	65
Bulgaria	51	42	37	27	42

Source: Henderson (1999: 186).

people were suffering and perceptions that these were being exacerbated by the meanness and foot-dragging of western Europe and the EU. Except in Romania, the decisions to submit applications for EU membership were thus very much *an elite affair*, not unlike the original founding of the European Communities in western Europe during the 1950s.

Ever since the collapse of the Austro-Hungarian Empire in 1918, East Central Europe had been an economic and power vacuum waiting to be filled, usually by Germany and/or Russia: 'nature abhors a vacuum.' After 1989, this power vacuum could again have been filled by Germany, but to its credit the government led by Helmut Kohl strongly took the view that it would be both safer and more rewarding for all concerned if this time the vacuum were to be filled by the EU rather than by a reunified Germany acting on its own. This stance was clearly spelled out in a position paper on Europe written by senior members of Germany's ruling Christian Democratic Union, Karl Lamers and Wolfgang Schäuble (Kohl's then second-in-command and heir apparent):

> Now that the East–West conflict has come to an end, a stable order must be found for the eastern half of the continent . . . This is in the interests of Germany in particular since, owing to its position, it would suffer the effects of instability in the East more quickly and directly than others. The only solution which will prevent a return to the unstable prewar system, with Germany once again caught in the middle between East and West, is to integrate Germany's central and eastern European neighbours into the (west) European postwar system and to establish a wide-ranging partnership between this system and Russia. Never again must there be a destabilizing vacuum of power in Central Europe. If (west) European integration were not to progress, Germany might be called upon, or be tempted by its own security constraints, to try to effect the stabilization of Eastern Europe on its own and in the traditional way . . . Hence Germany has a fundamental interest both in widening the Union to the East and in strengthening it through further deepening. Indeed, deepening is a precondition for widening. Without such further internal strengthening, the Union would be unable to meet the enormous challenge of eastward expansion. (translated as 'Reflections on European policy', in *European Access*, October 1994, no. 5, pp. 11–12)

The Kohl government became the most important intra-EU advocate of eastward enlargement of the EU (Gower 1999: 8). Chancellor Kohl's determination to bring East Central Europe into the EU as soon as feasible was driven 'not by economics but politics, just as it was when he made his expensive dash for German unification. He no more wants Germany's eastern neighbours left languishing in a no man's land between Europe and Russia than he wants its eastern border exposed to instability' (*The Economist*, 15 July 1995, pp. 35–6).

The 'pre-accession strategies' of 1994–5 and the 1995 EU 'White Paper' on *Preparation of the Associated Countries of Central and Eastern Europe for Integration into the Internal Market of the Union*

The 'pre-accession strategies' championed by the powerful EU Commissioners Sir Leon Brittain, Hans van den Broek and Henning Christophersen in 1994–5 recognized the tactical advantages of producing a European Union White Paper setting out a list of concrete steps which the East Central European and Balkan states would be required to take or implement in order to make themselves 'eligible' for EU membership. This more positive, prescriptive approach, which sought to repeat the successful strategy behind the 1985 White Paper on the creation of a Single European Market, represented a major advance on the European Union's previous foot-dragging passivity towards East Central Europe and the Balkans. However, critics argued that this approach placed excessive emphasis on technocratic economic and commercial preparations for EU membership, to the relative neglect of the much more difficult and fundamental changes or reorientations which were required in the political and cultural spheres. Andrei Plesu, Romania's former foreign minister and the founder of the influential New Europe College in Bucharest, warned that 'an exclusive emphasis on legal and fiscal integration transforms Europe into a scheme, a strictly technical framework, a simple managerial recipe. "Europe" develops the regrettable appearance of a set of criteria that must be passed and loses the aura of an attractive model, a project that inspires emulation' (Plesu 1997: 53–6). President Vaclav Havel voiced similar views (Havel 1994b: 240–5, 291–302).

The Madrid European Council, December 1995, and continued EU foot-dragging

The European Council meeting of EU heads of state and government in Madrid in December 1995 asked the Commission to start preparing detailed reports on the scope, feasibility and implications of eastward enlargement of the EU, including the preparation of Opinions on each of the applicant states (formal recommendations on whether or not to recognize the applicants as official candidates and to open formal membership negotiations with them). The summit envisaged that the start of membership negotiations with eligible post-Communist candidates would coincide with the opening of negotiations with Cyprus and Malta. The meeting also approved the so-called 'Madrid Criteria', which emphasized that prospective member states must henceforth demonstrate that they possess the 'administrative and judicial capacity' to comply with, implement and enforce the EU *acquis communautaire*. This became a crucial supplement to the much more widely known Copenhagen Criteria of June 1993.

During most of the 1990s, however, the European Community/Union remained very reluctant to commit itself to a firm timetable for the first phase(s) of eastward enlargement, although it did make provision for regular 'structured dialogue' with the states concerned. Confronted by seemingly intractable wrangles and problems of their own, most of the existing EU states were in no hurry to admit new member states, even though the states with which the EU had signed Treaties of Association had been given to believe that they would become full members in due course. It should perhaps be recalled that it took six years to negotiate mutually acceptable terms of Spanish and Portuguese entry (even though the potential problems posed were much smaller), that Greece had to wait nearly twenty years for its Treaty of Association to 'ripen' into full membership of the EC, and that Turkey has been waiting since 1964 (although it did not formally apply for membership until 1987).

Western economic and technical assistance to Europe's post-Communist states was initially furnished within an essentially unaltered structure of East–West relations. There was little attempt to change or challenge long-established frameworks. Timorous Western governments were only too happy to abdicate responsibility to the EC Commission which, in the words of Heinz Kramer, 'resorted mainly to well-established means and procedures in EC foreign relations'. These had two main prongs: 'help for the promotion of self-help'; and 'integration by organized free trade' (Kramer 1993: 222). EC/EU aid and trade commitments to East Central Europe, the Baltic States and the Balkans were developed in ways that reinforced rather than recast the prevalent bilateralism and massive asymmetries of power. Increased aid and trade were simply to be 'added on' to existing structures, keeping the recipient countries in the position of economic dependents or supplicants at the gate. This was a bureaucratic strategy for preserving as much as possible of the status quo. The grafting of increased EC or EU aid to and trade with post-Communist states on to existing EC structures minimized disturbance to the current members, institutions and procedures, avoided any fundamental reconsideration of Europe's architecture, and dampened the quest for new structures more capable of bridging the East–West divide. Thus the more ambitious proposals for a (Pan-)European Confederation put forward by President Mitterrand in 1990 and by President Havel in 1991 were almost immediately kicked into touch. This was unfortunate because the launching of a (Pan-)European Confederation dealing primarily with matters of European security and high politics could have avoided some of the dilemmas which the EU and NATO later confronted over how to deal with Russia and Ukraine. Such a European Confederation could have provided viable security guarantees to East Central European and Balkan states and the smaller ex-Soviet republics within an overarching framework that need not have excluded or antagonized Russia. It could also have provided a more appropriate and effective forum for handling border disputes and threats to minority rights, of the sort that reignited long dormant inter-ethnic conflicts in the Caucasus region and former Yugoslavia, as well as inter-ethnic confrontations and/or tensions in Moldova, Transylvania, Slovakia, Ukraine, Latvia and Estonia.

The Stability Pact of March 1995

After the failure of Presidents Havel and Mitterrand to win support for a Pan-European Confederation in 1990–1, the French government headed by Edouard Balladur hosted a conference on stability in Europe in Paris on 26–27 May 1994, with the express purpose of promoting a so-called Stability Pact designed to constrain, forestall and defuse border and ethnic minority problems of the sort that had devastated much of the former Yugoslavia. An additional condition for entry into the EU and NATO was to be the signing of 'good neighbour' accords, with guarantees of borders and minority rights. Bilateral agreements were to be signed within one year. Together with existing friendship agreements, these were to form part of the Stability Pact. The countries taking part were Bulgaria, the Czech Republic, Hungary, Poland, Romania, Slovakia, Estonia, Latvia and Lithuania. Italy, which was demanding compensation for property allegedly seized by Yugoslavia after the Second World War, debarred Slovenia from participating as a full member. A non-binding set of principles to 'render irreversible the advance of democracy and institute durable good-neighbourliness in Europe' was agreed at a meeting held in Paris on 20–21 March 1995.

   Under this rubric, the prime ministers of Hungary and Romania signed a 'basic treaty' (of 'reconciliation and friendship') on 16 September 1996. The long-disputed borders between the two states were declared to be inviolable. Although ethnic Hungarians in Romania were granted human rights, the treaty did not recognize their 'collective rights' or grant them autonomy. Nevertheless, the treaty required both countries to protect the civil liberties and cultural identities of historic ethnic minority communities. Such communities were guaranteed the right to be educated in their mother tongues, and to use their mother tongues in administrative and judicial proceedings, wherever there were substantial concentrations of ethnic minority inhabitants. Analogous provisions were made with regard to road signs, print media, broadcasting and other aspects of the communal life of minorities. Each country committed itself in the treaty to support NATO and EU membership for the other (*IHT*, 19 September 1996, p. 8). It was hoped that this treaty, concluded and ratified in the face of virulent protests from intransigent nationalists on both sides, would become an exemplar, encouraging and facilitating the settlement of similar disputes elsewhere in the region.

THE MEAGRENESS OF WESTERN ASSISTANCE TO EUROPE'S POST-COMMUNIST STATES DURING THE 1990s

Western politicians, economists and political commentators said and wrote a great deal about the need for a new 'Marshall Plan' to assist the 'transitions' to the market and parliamentary democracy in East Central Europe and the Balkans and recognized that it was in the self-interest of the West (especially Western Europe) to provide such assistance. Thus Richard Gephardt, then majority leader in the US House of Representatives, wrote after the abortive coup by Soviet hardliners in August 1991: 'The United States and its allies cannot escape the consequences of economic and political collapse in the countries of the former Soviet bloc. Not only will Washington face the potential of new military threats if strife and turmoil intensify, but it will also miss the chance to create new jobs and investment in its own economy by taking advantage of expanding markets in the East. . . It is crucial to show the people who have fought for freedom that their courage will be rewarded' (writing in *IHT*, 1 September 1991, p. 6). On 27 December 1991 an editorial in *The Independent* gave expression to a similar belief in 'virtuous circles': 'There can hardly be a higher interest for the West than that democracy should take root in the former Soviet bloc. If it does so, Russia will cease to pose a military threat for the first time in centuries. With the Russian lands pacified, Central Europe, too, might no longer generate the tensions and rivalries that have dragged the Continent into so many wars . . . Then, as market economies spread eastward and new members are drawn into the European Community, an area of huge economic potential will emerge, spreading its benefits far beyond Europe.'

The PHARE Programme

On the joint initiative of Jacques Delors and US President George Bush, the lead role in mobilizing and co-ordinating Western assistance to Eastern Europe was entrusted to the EC Commission. As a French Catholic socialist with a trade union background and as president of the EC Commission (1985–95), Delors was seen as the ideal person to empathize and develop Western ties with the new Catholic/Solidarity government in Poland and the new Catholic/nationalist Democratic Forum government in Hungary. Moreover, the hard-pressed president of an 'imperialistically over-stretched' USA was only too eager to relinquish the main responsibility for mobilizing and co-ordinating Western efforts in the post-Communist East to the EC. This arrangement also seemed to accord with the professed Western preference for multilateral rather than bilateral relationships with Europe's post-Communist states, in order to ensure that both the burdens and the potential benefits would be distributed more equitably and in a manner that would encourage rather than discourage multilateral integration with and between the intended beneficiaries. The principal outcomes of the July 1989 G7 summit were: (i) the setting up of a 'Group of Twenty-Four' aid donors (the G24) comprising all the large and medium-sized Western states (including Japan); and (ii) an initial EC-sponsored programme of aid for Poland and Hungary, which was given the acronym PHARE (*Pologne, Hongrie: activité pour la restructuration économique*; the word *Phare* means 'lighthouse' or 'beacon of light' in French). This name became something of a misnomer, however, when PHARE was extended to include Czechoslovakia, Romania, Bulgaria and Yugoslavia in May 1990; Albania, Lithuania, Latvia and Estonia in December 1991 (when the shattered Yugoslav Federation was excluded from its remit); and Slovenia in 1992. The main emphases were on micro-economic and technical assistance for agriculture, food aid, the distribution and processing of food, restructuring of industrial enterprises and banking, urgent projects to raise energy efficiency and safety, retraining, the encouragement of (small-scale) private enterpise, the provision of rudimentary social 'safety-nets' and the promotion of democratic procedures, legal reform, minority rights and civil society' (PHARE 1994: 7). PHARE tried not to involve itself in programmes of macro-economic stabilization, which were seen as tasks for the IMF, nor in large-scale programmes of structural adjustment, which were to be left to the World Bank and the International Finance Corporation.

The Tempus Programme

In May 1990 the EC also launched the Trans-European Mobility Programme for University Studies (TEMPUS). This was designed to promote links, co-operation and student and staff exchanges between EC institutions of higher education and those in East Central Europe, the Baltic States and the Balkans and to help the latter to change the structure and content of their higher education and research and to upgrade their books and equipment.

The European Bank for Reconstruction and Development (EBRD)

Despite US misgivings, the European Community summit held in Strasbourg in December 1989 approved President Mitterrand's proposal for the establishment of a European Bank for Reconstruction and Development (EBRD). The EBRD was formally inaugurated on 15 April 1991. Headquartered in London, its twenty-three-member board of directors was headed by Jacques Attali. There were thirty-nine participating countries and two institutional shareholders. Shareholding was as follows: EC countries, the EC Commission and the European Investment Bank, 53.7 per cent; the seven (former) Warsaw Pact members plus Yugoslavia, 13.5 per cent (the Soviet Union had a 6 per cent shareholding, but its eligibility for loans was limited to the stipulated one-third paid-in capital for at least a three-year period); the USA, 10 per cent; Japan, 8.5 per cent; and the EFTA countries, 10.7 per cent. Other members included Malta, Cyprus, Mexico, Egypt, Morocco, Liechtenstein and Israel. The EBRD was capitalized at Ecu 10 billion, one-third of the capital being paid in and the remainder on call. The aim was 'to promote private and entrepreneurial initiative in the Central and Eastern European countries committed to and applying the principles of multi-party democracy, pluralism and market economics'. Funds could be used for loans at market rates of interest, investment in equity capital, joint ventures, underwriting guarantees and technical assistance grants. Sixty per cent of funding was to be devoted to the development of the private sector, although state enterprises in the process of being privatized were eligible (recipients in the private sector were to be commercially viable but unable to attract private capital). The remaining 40 per cent was to be used for infrastructure investments such as transport and communications. In February 1992 it was decided that 60 per cent of its funds were to be allocated to East Central Europe, the post-Communist Balkan states and the three Baltic republics, while the remaining 40 per cent were to go to eleven other former Soviet republics (the 'missing republic' was Georgia). The former Soviet Union's 6 per cent shareholding in the EBRD was then reallocated among the Soviet successor states.

Jacques Attali, the EBRD's first president, declared that 'The vision was and is to build the first pan-European institution, in order to make totally irreversible the end of the split of the European continent in two', and he expressed the hope that, in helping to transform the post-Communist states into democracies and market economies, the EBRD would metamorphose into a truly 'pan-European institution', much as the European Coal and Steel Community mutated into the Common Market (*FT* interview, 15 April 1991, p. 25). Unfortunately, the EBRD soon gained a reputation for lavishing more money on itself than on its intended clients, and Attali resigned in the summer of 1993 after a highly critical audit committee report. However, the EBRD's initial low disbursement rates were not entirely the fault of either Attali or the EBRD. Attali had attempted to secure a relaxation of the restrictions placed upon the EBRD. He had also suggested that a soft-loan facility be set up to help convert defence to civilian production and to restructure sectors such as nuclear power. The USA and in particular its treasury secretary Nicholas Brady, resisted such proposals, partly as the result of the well-known US aversion to public enterprise as well as its misgivings about setting up the EBRD in the first place. In some eyes, especially American ones, the EBRD involved an expensive and unnecessary 'European' duplication of functions that were already being performed to US satisfaction by institutions such as the World Bank. Attali's protest that 'The bank has more money than it has projects' had fallen on deaf ears (*FT*, 13 April 1992, p. 2). Richard Portes, an eminent Western specialist on Europe's east–west economic relations, strongly defended Attali 'because he brought excellent people to the bank and because he was an eloquent public voice for eastern Europe and the right western policies for dealing with the region . . . Those who saw no need for the bank ignored the historic importance of its mission and the unique profile of its activities' (letter to *FT*, 29 June 1993, p. 14). By the time of Attali's dismissal, ironically, the expansion of private enterprise in Eastern Europe was rapidly increasing the number of potential borrowers who fell within the EBRD's narrow remit, causing most of the problems that had bedevilled the Attali presidency to evaporate. Meanwhile, the EBRD had lost a leader with a large vision.

Jacques de Larosière, a former managing director of the IMF and governor of the Bank of France, was appointed as Attali's successor on 19 August 1993. On 8 November 1993 a radical reorganization of the EBRD was approved. Its division into a development banking department (responsible for infrastructure projects) and a merchant banking department (responsible for encouraging the private sector) was scrapped. There was to be greater concentration on expanding operations and locating personnel within the recipient countries.

The EBRD's record for net disbursements rose from Ecu 127 million in 1992, to Ecu 409 million in 1993, Ecu 591 million in 1994 and Ecu 988 million in 1995. On 15 April 1996 the EBRD gained unanimous approval from its sixty shareholders to double its capital base to Ecu 20 billion. By then there were fifty-eight member countries, Bosnia and Herzegovina having been admitted on 11 April 1996. The EBRD agreed that it should start preparing for an eventual 'gradation' away from the more advanced countries of East Central Europe towards the less developed countries of the Balkans and the former Soviet Union. In 2005 the EBRD formally announced that it now regarded the East Central European and the Baltic States as 'normal' economies capable of standing on their own feet, and that it would henceforth concentrate its assistance on the more 'needy' Balkan and post-Soviet states.

Crumbs from the rich West's tables

Programmes such as PHARE, TEMPUS, the European Training Foundation (ETF) and Technical Assistance to the CIS (TACIS) did assist the post-Communist transformations. By 1993 PHARE and TACIS, both managed by the EU, were channelling about 70 per cent of the West's technical aid to post-Communist states (*The Economist* 10 April 1993, p. 21). By the end of 1992 Ecu 2.3 billion ($2.6 billion) had been committed by PHARE, although only Ecu 888.8 million had actually been paid out (*BCE*, December 1993/January 1994, p. 18). By the end of 1994 Ecu 3.8 billion had been committed by PHARE and Ecu 1.7 billion by TACIS.

Nevertheless, the sum total of EU-co-ordinated Western assistance to East Central Europe, the Baltic States and the Balkans was tiny, not only in relation to the needs of the recipients and the magnitude of the stakes for Europe as a whole, but also in relation to the vast sums which the West continued to spend on defence despite the demise of the Soviet threat and the Warsaw Pact. From 1991 to 1993, total official Western aid disbursements to Europe's former Communist states amounted only to 2.7 per cent of the recipients' combined GDP (World Bank 1996: 138). Western annual aid commitments to the Balkans and East Central Europe amounted to only $20–25 billion in 1991 and 1992 (*FT*, 17 April 1991, p. 2). This was equivalent to less than 0.3 per cent of the EC's annual GDP. Compared with the external financing needs of the post-Communist Balkan states and East Central Europe, the $70–90 billion annual transfer payments from western to eastern Germany, and the $500 billion that the Group of Seven (G7) leading industrial economies spent on defence in 1990, these Western aid commitments were trifling amounts. William Pfaff remarked that 'more money is being paid annually to the West from the East in loan interest and loan repayments, than the East European countries have yet received from the West' (*IHT*, 14 September 1991, p. 6).

Perversely, the West proved itself willing to spend vastly more on winning the Cold War than on securing the subsequent peace. In 1995, despite the recession of the former Soviet threat, defence expenditure still stood at $263 billion in the USA, $56 billion in Japan, $37 billion in France and $34 billion in Britain (*FT*, 11 October 1995). Nor has Western defence spending fallen dramatically since 1990 or 1995. In 2005, the USA spent $472 billion on defence, while the rest of NATO spent $266 billion (*The Economist*, 25 November 2006, p. 23).

At 1.5 per cent of American GDP, the Marshall Plan had been much more generous relative to the main donor economy's income. Furthermore, while 80 per cent of Marshall Aid had been in the form of non-repayable grants, most of the Western 'aid' to East Central Europe and the Balkans during the early 1990s took the form either of loans, which would eventually increase the recipients' already massive indebtedness and heavy burdens of debt service, just when they were supposed fully to open up their economies to EU exports, or of trade credits and guarantees to Western firms in order to promote Western exports to the region.

During the mid-1990s the money allocated to East Central Europe, the Baltic States, Bulgaria and Romania under the PHARE programme averaged out at only 10 Ecu (roughly $10 or £6) per person per year for the recipient countries (Mayhew 1998: 17). This would have been just about enough to buy each of the inhabitants of the recipient countries one modest restaurant meal per annum! Furthermore, these programmes were criticized for possessing weak monitoring systems, duplicating the work of other organizations, and being over-centralized, unwieldy, and constrained by short-term budgets (*BCE*, April 1995, pp. 37, 44–8).

Why was so little concrete Western support forthcoming for the reconstruction and recovery of Europe's post-Communist states?

In the first place, there was no longer a fear of 'the Soviet threat'. This had undoubtedly been a major determinant in the scale of American Marshall Aid to western Europe in 1947–51. During the early 1990s, the West's new bogeys were predominantly Islamic, whether in the shape of Saddam Hussain, Iranian ayatollahs, Islamic fundamentalism in Algeria, Tunisia, Egypt and Turkey, or millions of North African, Kurdish and Turkish migrants fleeing civil strife, mass unemployment and actual or potential political and religious persecution. Far from encouraging Western generosity towards Europe's post-Communist states, these new bogeys prompted French and southern European calls for a major reallocation of European Union resources away from eastern Europe towards a strengthening of Europe's 'southern flank' through the 'Euro-Med Partnership' with North African and Levantine states launched in 1996. Beyond these xenophobic anxieties lay 'Latin' fears that, combined with the accession of Austria, Sweden and Finland to the European Union in January 1995, eastward enlargement of the EU would shift the European Union's centre of gravity towards a resurgent *Mitteleuropa*. Therefore, in November 1994 the French premier, Edouard Balladur, wrote: 'To avoid being . . . marginalized by the enlargement of the EU to the north and east, France must set itself several objectives: to deepen further the Franco-German relationship, to develop co-operation with the UK particularly in defence, and to tighten its links with Italy and Spain' (quoted in *FT*, 30 November 1994, p. 2).

Western European states were also preoccupied with their own internal problems during most of the 1990s, including the effects of prolonged economic recession, high unemployment and sometimes sizeable budget deficits. It was singularly unfortunate that the mammoth tasks of building liberal, pluralistic parliamentary democracies and market economies in the eastern half of Europe coincided with the onset of severe economic recession in the West and with politically problematic and divisive moves towards deeper integration within the EC, including the fraught negotiation, ratification and implementation of the increasingly unpopular Maastricht Treaty (1991–3).

Furthermore, the EC/EU was ill equipped to play the co-ordinating roles assigned to it (which may have been one reason why it was given these roles in the first place!). Composed of twelve (from 1995 fifteen) quarrelsome, cantankerous and mutually competitive nation-states, it was still a somewhat introverted organization, which during most of the 1980s and 1990s was intensely preoccupied with its own internal problems, disputes and objectives. With nominal control over a mere 1.2 per cent of the EC/EU's GDP, it possessed neither the wherewithal nor the political muscle and strength of resolve to mobilize sufficient resources and challenge existing power relations and power structures sufficiently to break the mould of the east–west division of Europe. It still lacked well-developed institutions, procedures and competences for dealing with external relations, as was demonstrated by its dismally ineffectual handling of the 1990/1 Gulf crisis and of the conflicts in former Yugoslavia between 1991 and 1995. Unfortunately, the development of common regional, social, industrial and agricultural policies and the veto powers of individual member states had left the EC/EU hostage to producer interests which were more effectively organized and better placed to apply pressure on national governments and EC institutions than were western European consumers, who would have been net beneficiaries of unrestricted access to products from Europe's former Communist states, and the governments of these states had even less influence on the EC. The EC/EU was also hostage to its principal paymasters. All these elements were well placed to block any radical overtures to Europe's post-Communist states, whether in terms of economic assistance, trade liberalization or fundamental changes in Europe's overall 'architecture'.

Western Europe's self-absorption, lack of vision, and 'sins of omission', 1990–7

By the mid-1990s, admittedly, even the most mean-spirited Western governments, parliaments, economists and political commentators were becoming increasingly aware of the scale of support required by East Central Europe and the Balkans, while the tragic armed conflicts in the Yugoslav lands were confronting Western governments with the high costs which Europe as a whole could incur if greatly increased Western support for 'Eastern' recovery and restructuring was not forthcoming. Nevertheless, with the notable partial exception of Germany, each western European state continued to hope that *other* Western states would dig deeper into their pockets to provide this much-needed assistance for 'Eastern' reconstruction and recovery, while still hoping to cash in on the new commercial opportunities thereby created by others. Furthermore, the existing members of the EU (including Germany) continued to expect most of the hardships, sacrifices and burdens of adjustment to be borne by 'easterners'. There was little willingness to face up to the reciprocal adjustments and sacrifices which needed to be made by and within the EU. As Jacques Attali stated in 1994: 'Western Europe has no global vision of a continental union. Everybody is fixated with their own national problems. We really need a new generation of visionary statesmen' (The *Guardian*, Supplement, 26 January 1994, p. 7).

West European governments and citizens alike were far more concerned to preserve and protect their relatively high levels of affluence, their relatively low levels of unemployment, their high welfare benefits, and their dominant positions in European and global affairs, than to share their wealth with the East Central European, Baltic and Balkan States and to incorporate these states into the EU. The East–West partition of Europe from 1945 to 1989 and the massive economic collapse which the vast majority of post-Communist states suffered during the early 1990s substantially increased east–west economic disparities to the great advantage of western Europeans, and most western Europeans have subsequently been exceedingly reluctant to share their advantages with relatively impoverished 'eastern cousins'. Up to 1997, EU policies towards the post-Communist East Central European, Baltic and Balkan states remained much more reactive than proactive and appeared to be designed to offer as little as possible, as late as possible, with the maximum scope for procrastination, delay and foot-dragging. Little was done to accelerate the integration of the applicants into the nascent Single European Market and into the policy deliberations of the EU.

At the same time, however, it needs to be acknowledged that the applicant states were seeking entry into a club with an already established rule book, rather than into a freely negotiated collective bargain (Preston 1997: 228), and that the European Community/Union's primary duties were to preserve its own political and institutional viability and to uphold and defend the cosmopolitan ideals of its founding fathers, because this club would otherwise have ceased to be worth joining. This genuinely and legitimately limited the extent to which the EC/EU could make substantive concessions in order to accommodate new members, although it was too often used as a cover or pretext for sheer meanness. Furthermore, it can also be conceded that premature admission of East Central European, Baltic and Balkan states to the EC/EU could have been as damaging as it was in the case of East Germany (via German reunification) in 1990.

The principal western European 'sins of omission' during the 1990s included the initial failures (i) to spell out the steps which Europe's post-Communist states would have to take in order to make themselves eligible for EC membership in due course, (ii) to provide generous economic and technological assistance for carrying out of the requisite changes, (iii) to give these states potent inducements to pursue an economic union of their own in the interim, and (iv) to provide a clear and generous timetable for the removal of EC barriers against their exports. More positive action programmes and stronger economic support and incentives were needed to encourage governments, parliaments and populations in East Central Europe, the Baltic States and the Balkans to 'stay the course' of extremely painful and politically costly economic liberalization, to persuade more Western firms to invest in these regions (secure in the knowledge that their products would soon be assured of unimpeded access to the EU market), and to help stimulate and sustain export-led economic recoveries in these regions. Export markets were crucially necessary because the markets within the post-Communist states were in most cases small and levels of domestic purchasing power were very low, as a result of the declines in their (already very meagre) real incomes during the late 1980s and early 1990s. For the most part, the socio-economic recovery of East Central Europe, the Baltic States and the Balkans could only occur to the degrees that these regions could earn sufficient hard currency to service their often extremely burdensome foreign debts and/or to pay for resurgent fuel requirements, most of which had to be imported. By retarding the growth of their exports to the vastly richer western European markets, EC/EU import restrictions not only held back the economic recovery and long-term economic growth of these regions, but also substantially delayed their potential eventual accession to the EU (on the grounds that their economies were still too weak to withstand EU membership!).

Not surprisingly, many inhabitants of the post-Communist East Central European, Baltic and Balkan states became increasingly disenchanted or even embittered by the sufferings and hardships induced by their rush to the market, by the delayed appearance of many compensating benefits (most of which are beyond the reach of the poorer sections of the population), and by the European Community's evident stand-offishness, delaying tactics and prevarication on anything relating to increased access to EC/EU markets and a timetable for the first wave(s) of eastward enlargement of the EC/EU. This contributed to a cooling of popular enthusiasm for the 'return to Europe'. In early 1994 a Eurobarometer poll found that positive evaluation of the EU had declined to 37 per cent in the four Visegrad states (Kolankiewicz 1994: 478).

The governments and 'educated classes' of East Central Europe and the Baltic and Balkan states also felt increasingly offended by the EC's defensive, niggardly and patronizing language and attitudes. In the words of the former Polish finance minister, Leszek Balcerowicz: 'Western governments do not seem to realize their own potential to damage or increase the chance for successful economic reform in the former socialist countries through actions that appear to be quite marginal to them ... What for Western countries is a marginal restriction of access to their markets may cause great harm to countries undergoing radical economic reform, reducing their chances of success' (cited in *IHT*, 7 December 1993, p. 9). In December 1994 the Czech President Vaclav Havel lamented that

> the birth of a new and genuinely stable European order is taking place more slowly and with greater difficulty and pain than most of us had expected five years ago. Many countries that shook off their totalitarian regimes still feel insufficiently anchored in the community of democratic states. They are often disappointed by the reluctance with which that community has opened its arms to them. The demons we thought had been driven for ever from the minds of

people and nations are dangerously rousing themselves again, and are surreptitiously but systematically undoing the principles upon which we began to build the peaceful future of Europe. (Vaclav Havel, *The New York Review of Books*, 2 March 1995, p. 43)

The preponderance of 'hub-and-spoke' relations between the EU and the candidate states, and the relative neglect of preparatory integration between candidate states

The European Union insisted on negotiating with the candidate states individually, rather than as a group. For their part, instead of co-ordinating their relations with the EU, each of the East Central European and Baltic states sought to steal a march on its neighbours. This, together with the abrupt disintegration of 'Czecho-Slovakia' during 1992, severely damaged the concept of 'Central Europe' as a distinct and cohesive region and the credibility of projects of East Central European integration, such as the Visegrad grouping launched in February 1991 and the Central European Free Trade Area (CEFTA) inaugurated in March 1993.

The major drawback of the so-called 'hub-and-spoke' relations between the EU and the candidate states was that such relationships did little to encourage multilateral trade, co-operation and integration between the candidate states, in addition to integration between them and the EU. The economist Richard Baldwin argued that bilateral 'hub-and-spoke' free trade agreements (FTAs) tended to 'marginalize the "spoke" economies, since factories in the "spokes" have artificially lower market access than factories in the hub. Consequently, hub-and-spoke FTAs render an artificial deterrent to investment in the outer economies.' This in turn made the 'outer' or 'spoke' economies 'even smaller than they need be', thereby reducing the profitability of EU firms seeking to do business in the spoke economies and reinforcing the tendency for firms to locate in the hub rather than in the spokes (Baldwin 1994: 133–4). Furthermore, once entrenched, it would be possible for the adverse effects of such a situation to persist long after its initial causes had ceased to apply, since 'five or ten years of hub-and-spoke bilateralism' would give production locations within the EU a head-start over those in the spoke economies, and even EU membership for the latter within ten years 'might not be enough to offset the initial head-start' gained by producers located within the 'hub' at the outset (p. 135).

In an attempt to overcome such disadvantages, the 'spoke' economies naturally endeavoured to attract foreign direct investment by offering foreign investors protection against imports from other 'spoke' economies. 'If this pandering-for-investment becomes quite common, the spoke economies may eventually become "Balkanized". That is, foreign multinationals may be enticed into locating inefficiently small production facilities in each spoke economy. Having done this, the multinationals . . . that have invested in inefficiently small facilities in several spoke economies may resist efforts to liberalize spoke–spoke trade' (Baldwin 1994: 138). Such patterns were emerging in the production of cars and televisions in East Central Europe during the 1990s. 'Hub-and-spoke' relations not only marginalized the 'outer' or 'spoke' economies but discouraged economic relations between them. This increased the need to map out 'a clearer path to accession that would multilateralize the Europe agreements so as to create a comprehensive free trade area, then deepen integration in an approach to something like the EU–EFTA "European Economic Area"' (Portes 1994: 1188–9).

The preponderance of 'hub-and-spoke' relations between the EU and the candidate states during the 1990s sharply contrasted with the much more far-sighted multilateralism of the architects of the Marshall Plan in 1947–8. The Marshall Plan had astutely made the receipt of Marshall Aid conditional upon the recipient states sinking their differences and coming together in an Organization of European Economic Co-operation (OEEC), which was tasked with working out a joint European Recovery Programme (ERP) designed to foster multilateral trade, co-operation, integration, mutual reconciliation and market integration between its members. According to George Kennan (who headed the US State Department's Policy Planning Staff at the inception of the Marshall Plan), if the Americans had not insisted on this, 'the United States would have been confronted with a whole series of competing national demands, all padded and exaggerated for competitive purposes, all reflecting attempts to resolve economic problems within national frameworks rather than on an all-European basis . . . By insisting on a joint approach, we hoped to force the Europeans to begin to think like Europeans, and not like nationalists, in their approach to the economic problems of the continent' (Kennan 1979: 337). Another major difference was that the countries which took part in the ERP and the OEEC had 'historically developed complementary trade patterns . . . Intra-regional trade amounted to 60–70 per cent of total trade.' In early 1990s East Central Europe, by contrast, intra-regional trade was 'a very modest fraction of total trade – less than 5 per cent for Hungary and Poland, and less than 10 per cent for the Czech Republic and Slovakia', while the longstanding jealousies, rivalries and mutual suspicions that had bedevilled relations between the states and nations of East Central Europe and the shared loathing of the phoney co-operation and mutual assistance imposed in the Communist era by Comecon had killed off any local enthusiasm for intra-regional co-operation and integration (Inotai 1994: 37–8). These were further reasons why *leadership for integration probably had to come at least partly from outside East Central Europe* if progress was to be made, even though the European Union was in no rush to provide such leadership. Furthermore, the East Central European governments dragged their feet with regard to intra-regional integration, not only because they found it very difficult to work together, but also because they feared that the EU might come to regard a successful Visegrad grouping or CEFTA as a *substitute* (rather than a preparation) for membership of an expanded EU.

At the very least, the European Community/Union owed it to East Central Europe to be more open and honest about what it considered to be possible or impossible within a given time frame, if only to concentrate minds on the construction of more substantial interim schemes of intra-regional integration and co-operation and to reduce the extent to which the preponderance of 'hub-and-spoke' relations between the EC/EU and the candidate countries marginalized them and discouraged economic relations among them. Unfortunately, the EC/EU did little to counteract the unhelpful effects that its own successes and powers of attraction were having on neighbouring countries and regions. 'The EC congratulates itself on its powers of integration internally and the "magnetic attraction" it exercises on those around it. What has not been sufficiently noted is that this powerful magnetic pull tends to provoke the disintegration of other federal or co-operative structures in the neighbourhood. The EC may preach local and regional co-operation, but the audience is not interested. What the audience sees is a rich and powerful club, membership of which eclipses the value of any local association. Every nation or potential nation . . . starts to think how it could get in and how, above all, it must not be held back by association with less wholesome or less fortunate neighbours' (Edward Mortimer, *FT*, 7 July 1993, p. 16). It was understandable that the EC/EU felt flattered by its own attractiveness, as demonstrated by the growing queue of prospective candidates for membership. Nevertheless, the EC/EU could have made more effort to limit the resultant disintegrative effects on neighbouring countries and regions by stipulating that they must pursue integration among themselves as a precondition for closer links with and assistance from the EC, instead of dealing with each of them separately on a divisive and hegemonic 'hub-and-spoke' basis.

The EC/EU, which was supposed to be promoting integration and 'European-mindedness', unfortunately did precisely the opposite in the East Central European, Baltic and Balkan regions during the 1990s and early 2000s. By mainly dealing with the candidate states bilaterally, it encouraged each of the East Central European, Baltic and Balkan governments to think only in terms of their own nation, national economy and national interests, rather than 'like Europeans'. This tendency was further exacerbated by EC/EU insistence on assessing and negotiating terms of entry with the current applicants individually, rather than as a group. This was divisive and encouraged the candidates to look upon each other as rivals rather than as partners. Furthermore, the fixation of the first post-Communist governments and parliaments of the East Central European and Baltic states on eventual accession to the EC/EU strongly discouraged vigorous development of appropriate precursors to EC/EU membership. This was unfortunate, as an interim scheme to foster political and economic integration and supranational institutions within East Central Europe, going far beyond the modest commitments to East Central European free trade and inter-governmental co-operation agreed at the Visegrad meeting in February 1991 and through CEFTA, could have helped to prepare the East Central European states for eventual membership of the EU by developing and demonstrating their capacities for constructive participation in joint institutions, for resolving bitter intra-regional disputes and for promoting 'national reconciliation' and closer relations between former foes. It could also have assisted the East Central European states to speak with one voice and to strengthen their very weak negotiating positions, both during the membership negotiations (1998–2002) and after their eventual entry into the EU in May 2004.

The drawbacks of 'hub-and-spoke' bilateralism strengthened the case for admitting all ten of the East Central European, Baltic and Balkan candidates for EU membership simultaneously, instead of divisively admitting some countries ahead of the others. This would also help to avoid the potential creation of damaging new political and economic barriers and divisions between East Central European and Baltic states admitted to the EU and those 'left outside', such as the introduction of stringent visa requirements for travel and restrictions on the importation of so-called 'sensitive goods' (foodstuffs, textiles, footwear, chemicals, steel) from the latter states to the former. This would have been particularly invidious in the case of Slovakia, if (as had seemed possible until 1999) it had found itself unable to join the European Union at the same time as the Czech Republic and Hungary, with which it had been united in a single state until 1992 and 1918 respectively, particularly as the Slovak minority in the Czech Republic would then be much better placed than the Czech and Hungarian minorities in Slovakia. For similar reasons, Hungary actively lobbied for early admission of Romania into the EU, in order to increase the likelihood that the large ethnic Hungarian minority in Transylvania would not be left stranded 'on the wrong side' of the increasingly heavily monitored and policed external frontier of an emerging 'fortress EU'. By the same token, the admission of East Central Europe and the Baltic States to the EU was bound to erect new barriers and divisions between them and their former Soviet bloc partners further to the east and south-east, unless trade and travel restrictions between the EU and the western Balkan and European CIS states were relaxed prior to the eastward enlargement of the EU. However, such a situation was probably unavoidable in the short term, given the manifest unreadiness of the western Balkan and CIS states for EU membership. In April 2001 it was announced that from June 2001 onward Russians, Ukrainians, Belarussians, Moldovans and Bosnians would require visas to enter Hungary, which became the first candidate country to adopt EU standards in this regard (*IHT*, 28 April 2001, p. 2). This set a precedent which the other candidate countries felt obliged to follow, out of fear of jeopardizing their EU membership negotiations.

THE EU COMMISSION'S *AGENDA 2000: FOR A STRONGER AND WIDER EUROPEAN UNION* (JULY 1997)

In its *Agenda 2000* reports, published in July 1997, the EU Commission laid down some very exacting 'preconditions' for the admission of East Central European, Baltic and Balkan states to full membership of the EU, premised upon an implicit expectation that the first wave of new accessions would commence in 2002 or 2003 (EU Commission 1997: 61–2, 73–4). It was by no means a foregone conclusion that these preconditions would be strictly upheld by the governments of the EU-15. Nevertheless, the enormity and complexity of the challenges of eastward enlargement of the EU made it likely that successive European Councils would adhere to most of the Commission's forcefully argued stipulations. This offered the EU and its existing member states pleanty of scope for procrastination – that is, for further delaying the entry of fomerly Communist-ruled states into the Union.

The Commission called upon the applicant states to reform their judiciaries and police forces, strengthen the rule of law, and take further steps to integrate ethnic and religious minorities into the body politic (pp. 40, 42). It deemed that only half the applicants could be regarded as 'functioning market economies' as of 1997, but that the other applicants 'should be able to meet this first economic criterion early in the next century'. In addition, new entrants would 'need to be able to produce products conforming to European [Union] technical requirements' (pp. 42–3), and would have to adopt and comply with the obligations of Stage 2 of the European Union's project of Economic and Monetary Union (the establishment of the euro as the European Union's supranational currency). This implies central bank independence, coordination of economic policies (national convergence programmes, multilateral surveillance, excessive deficit procedure, etc.), and adherence to the relevant provisions of the stability and growth pact. New Member States will forego any central bank financing of public sector deficits as well as privileged access of public authorities to financial institutions. They shall have completed the liberalization of capital movements. Also, they are expected to participate in an exchange rate mechanism and avoid excessive exchange rate changes . . . As in previous enlargements, the European Council has ruled out any idea of a partial adoption of the *acquis* . . . However, none of the applicants has yet been able to transpose a large proportion of Community laws in the single market into national legislation and a major effort is needed before accession' (pp. 44–5). 'The Union does not envisage any kind of second-class membership or opt-outs' (p. 51).

In addition, the applicants would be required to establish 'the structures needed to apply new regulations, for example environmental and technical inspections, banking supervision, public accounts and statistics', for which they could receive PHARE assistance. 'There are also widespread problems of corruption which are now being tackled by most governments' (p. 46). Before accession, applicants would have to have made 'every effort to resolve any outstanding border dispute' and any trade disputes with current members of the EU (p. 51), a stipulation which primarily affected Slovenia vis-à-vis Italy (as well as Turkey vis-à-vis Cyprus). Entrants would also have to raise their low standards of public health, unemployment relief, farming, and health and safety at work and to upgrade their food-processing plants, for which they would need transition periods and PHARE assistance (pp. 47–8). Likewise, they would have to undertake 'massive investments' in transport, environmental protection and nuclear safety, for which there would also have to be substantial transition periods and external assistance (pp. 49–50).

Collectively and even individually, these stipulations were bound to be extremely difficult to fulfil, unless the candidates were granted much greater financial assistance than had been contemplated hitherto. Either these preconditions would have to be relaxed considerably when it came to the crunch, or the EU's chief paymasters would have been pressed to fork out much more than they were willing to pay, or eastward enlargement would have to be delayed much longer than the report envisaged. The first option was the one implicitly adopted in practice. Rather than foot the bill for more assistance or further delay the entry of the East Central European and Baltic states, the Commission and the EU turned a blind eye to the fact that it remained unaffordable for the new members to comply in full with Western environmental, public service and health and safety standards.

With regard to the EU-15, the Commission insisted that the new EU currency (the euro) would have to be already 'in place' and that 'all the Union's policies must be developed and deepened in order to build a wider and stronger Europe'. In addition, it called for dates to be set for the re-weighting of votes in the Council of Ministers, a reduction in the number of Commissioners to one per member state, an Inter-govermental Conference to reform the EU's institutions and Treaty provisions, and 'the introduction of qualified majority voting across the board', prior to the first wave of eastward enlargement (p. 13). It also proposed acceptance of the phasing out of structural funding for regions and states where per capita GDP had risen above 75 per cent of the EU average, bearing in mind that successive eastward enlargements would significantly reduce that average (p. 63). It envisaged that 'the absorption of new members would have to be accommodated within a tight budgetary framework' (p. 11), that the Union would have to continue to operate within an 'own resources ceiling maintained at 1.27% of Union GDP' (p. 66), and that enlargement 'will inevitably provoke a deterioration in the budgetary positions of all the current Member States' (p. 68).

We do not criticize the stance adopted by the EU Commission in *Agenda 2000*. It had a moral and legal duty to point out all that would have been required to accomplish an eastward enlargement which complied fully with EU regulations and Treaty obligations and conformed to the standards attained in the much richer EU-15. There was a large dose of realism in its assessment of the actual financial parameters within which any eastward enlargement of the EU could be expected to take place. Given the inescapable meanness of the much richer EU-15, reflected in their collective unwillingness to foot the bills for assisting the new Member States to comply in full with EU regulations and Treaty obligations and to conform to the standards of the EU-15, the choice was between further delaying enlargement or turning a blind eye to a lowering of standards. The crucial importance of entry into the EU in consummating the transformations taking place in East Central Europe and the Baltic States meant that it was more important not to delay further the eastward enlargement of the EU than to insist on full conformity and compliance, even though this virtually predetermined that the May 2004 enlargement would take place on terms that were undeniably suboptimal and would need to be redressed in years to come – as and when additional budgetary resources became available through further growth of the EU budget and/or from the anticipated 'growth dividends' in the economies of the new Member States.

However, even the most modest proposals for institutional and procedural changes designed to maintain the EU's viability provoked resistance from vested interests with the power to veto any major departures from the status quo. This problem was compounded by the fact that most of the prospective entrants were small states, accession of which would further exacerbate the tensions between large and small states within the EU. The smaller members of the EU were loath to accept any reductions in their disproportionate influence and representation in EU institutions, policy-making and decision-making, while the larger member states were very reluctant to accept any further increases in the collective capacity of the small states (comprising a minority of the EU's population) to out-vote the larger states (containing the vast majority of EU citizens). In addition, prominent German, Austrian and later French, Dutch and Belgian politicians began to signal that they would only accept eastward enlargement of the European Union if it was linked to restrictions on freedom of movement of labour from the new Member States, whose average wage rates were only about 10–15 per cent of those obtainable in Austria, Germany, France, the Netherlands and Belgium. During the mid-1990s, moreover, Greece repeatedly threatened to veto eastward enlargement of the EU if this preceded the admission of Cyprus to the EU, while Turkey repeatedly threatened to veto eastward enlargement of NATO if there was no attempt to accommodate vital Turkish and Turkish Cypriot interests in these matters. However, the improvements in Greek–Turkish relations from 1999 onward considerably reduced the likelihood of difficulties from this particular quarter.

THE DIVISIVE 1997 DECISION TO PROCEED WITH A 'TWO-WAVE' EASTWARD ENLARGEMENT OF THE EU

On 16 July 1997 the EU Commission recommended that Poland, Hungary, the Czech Republic, Slovenia and Estonia should be invited to open membership negotiations with the EU in early 1998. These invitations were formally approved at a European Council meeting (of EU heads of state or government) in Luxembourg on 13 December 1997, where it was also decided that Romania, Bulgaria, Slovakia, Latvia and Lithuania should be given special EU aid to help them meet the conditions necessary for membership negotiations to begin. However, the divisive decision to open membership negotiations with only five of the ten formerly Communist-ruled candidate states caused great consternation and despondency in Romania, Bulgaria, Slovakia, Latvia and Lithuania, who thenceforth intensively lobbied the EU-15 to open up the membership negotiations to include all of the post-Communist candidate states.

THE EU'S 'CHANGE OF HEART', OCTOBER–DECEMBER 1999: THE DECISION TO BRING ALL THE POST-COMMUNIST CANDIDATE STATES INTO THE FOLD DURING THE 2000s

It did not take long for the EU Commission and the governments of the EU Member States to become aware of (i) the demoralizing negative impact of their 1997 decision not to open EU membership negotiations with Romania, Bulgaria, Slovakia, Latvia and Lithuania; (ii) the need to be seen to be taking much bolder and more decisive action to bring more of the former Communist states into the EU fold, in order to give the governing elites of the candidate countries stronger incentives to persevere with economically, socially and politically painful reforms and restructuring; and (iii) the fragility of Balkan stabilization efforts, together with the damaging effects of continuing Balkan instability on their own societies and economies. Britain and France (which were bearing the brunt of European military interventions in the Balkans), Italy (which had led the EU military intervention in Albania in 1997) and Germany (which had most to gain from increased stability in East Central Europe and the Balkans), each had strong motivations to bring about a fundamental change of tune. Romania had garnered considerable EU goodwill by assisting the Italian-led military intervention to subdue the major insurgency in Albania in 1997. Furthermore, during the March–June 1999 Kosova War, Romania and Bulgaria gave NATO much more wholehearted support and co-operation than did the three new NATO member states (the Czech Republic, Hungary and Poland), partly by allowing NATO forces to use Romanian and Bulgarian military facilities.

Above all, the EU Commission found itself becoming ever more deeply involved in increasingly intense and extensive deliberations, debates, investigations and monitoring in the candidate states. Partly as a consequence of this, on 13 October 1999 the Commission recommended that Romania, Bulgaria, Latvia, Lithuania, Slovakia and Malta should be allowed to begin membership negotiations in March 2000.

This recommendation was ratified by the European Council meeting in Helsinki on 10 December 1999. A fully flexible, multi-speed accession process was envisaged. Each candidate was to be permitted to proceed on merit, including the possibility for those countries which began membership negotiations in 2000 to catch up with the front-runners. It was announced that, by the end of 2002, the EU would in principle be ready to 'welcome' as new members any or all the twelve countries with which it had already opened or was about to open membership negotiations, provided they were deemed to have met in full the Copenhagen and Madrid Criteria. As a result of these decisions, the six 'front-runners' (Hungary, Poland, the Czech Republic, Slovenia, Estonia and Cyprus) implicitly lost the favoured positions they had previously enjoyed. They were henceforth to be treated and judged on exactly the same footing as the six additional candidates. To their credit, however, the perceived 'front-runners' accepted these changes in good spirit and did not sulk over the fact that their aspirations would no longer automatically take priority over those of their less 'EU-ready' neighbours.

At Helsinki on 11 December Turkey was also added to the list of official candidate countries, albeit with unusually strict stipulations concerning respect for human rights and normalization of relations with Greece and Cyprus. However, it was agreed that the formal decision on whether to start membership negotiations with Turkey would not be taken until the meeting of EU heads of government scheduled for December 2004.

However, despite the optimistic gloss put on the accession schedule in Helsinki, diplomats stipulated that it was likely to be 2004 at the earliest before any of the candidate countries could join the EU. Günther Verheugen, who had been serving as EU Commissioner for Enlargement since August 1999, announced that the existing Member States' ratification of new entrants would only begin after the existing members of the EU had agreed on and approved a further reform of the European Union's constituent treaties. It was decided to aim to complete the ratification of these reforms by the end of 2002 and the ratification of individual candidates' treaties of accession to the EU during 2003. Verheugen also insisted that the unanimous decision by the existing Member States to start talks in January or February 2000 with six additional candidate countries would not be allowed to slow down the existing negotiations with the first six (*FT*, 11 December 1999, p. 6; 13 December 1999, p. 10). In his own words: 'From now on negotiations will be carried out on a country-by-country basis, taking account of each country's state of preparations. Therefore negotiations will progress according to merit, and progress largely depends on the candidates' own efforts, which is why a target date for accession cannot be set yet. All we can do is name a target date for the EU to be ready to take the first accession decisions. This date will be 2002, as long as the EU carries out the institutional reforms necessary to ensure a proper functioning of a Union of twenty-seven or twenty-eight members – and providing that negotiations with candidate countries have reached a conclusion' (*BCE* December 1999: 17).

The November 2000 EU Commission reports on *Progress Towards Accession*

On 8 November 2000 the EU Commission published frank assessments of the candidate countries' *Progress Towards Accession*. It bluntly stated that 'corruption, fraud and economic crime' were 'widespread in most candidate countries', 'discrediting the reforms' and causing a 'lack of confidence' among citizens. Roma (Gypsies) faced 'widespread discrimination in social and economic life', and 'trafficking in women and children' was a growing problem in some of the candidate countries. The reports still did not specify a target entry date for the first wave of new members, but they stipulated that transitional measures and all outstanding issues would be addressed by the EU-15 with the most advanced candidates by June 2002 at the latest. Bulgaria and Romania were judged to be lagging far behind the East Central European candidate states (*FT*, 8 November 2000, p. 10; 9 November 2000, p. 22; *The Economist*, 12 November 2000, p. 73).

The European Council at Nice, 7–11 December 2000, and the Treaty of Nice

A fraught five-day European Council meeting of EU heads of state and government, hosted by President Jacques Chirac in Nice from 7 to 11 December 2000, managed to reach agreement on various reforms in the structures, operation and procedures of the EU, which were deemed essential to accommodate ten to fifteen additional Member States. New voting weights in the Council of Ministers were assigned to existing and prospective members and the range of areas subject to qualified majority voting was greatly expanded. The EU leaders also promised to speed up the entry of the former Soviet bloc counties into the EU and expressed the hope that the necessary internal reforms would be completed in time for the candidate countries which met its conditions to be able to take part in the European Parliament elections scheduled for June 2004.

The Treaty of Nice, and hence the eastward enlargement of the EU, was temporarily placed in jeopardy on 7 June 2001, when a referendum in Ireland rejected this Treaty (albeit with a low turnout). Many Irish feared that Ireland could be disadvantaged by the eastward enlargement of the EU, which the Treaty of Nice was intended to facilitate. The Treaty needed to be ratified by all fifteen of the existing EU members before it could take effect, but the Irish electorate was the only one in the EU to be given the opportunity to vote on it. Fortunately for the candidate countries, however, Ireland ratified the Nice Treaty in a fresh referendum held on 20 October 2002. This allowed the ratification of the Treaty to be completed and cleared the way for the East Central European and Baltic enlargement of the EU to go ahead without constitutional or legal impediment. The Treaty came into force on 1 February 2003.

The November 2001 Commission reports on *Progress Towards Accession*: acceptance of a 'big bang' enlargement of the EU

On 13 November 2001 the EU published another set of annual progress reports on the twelve applicants for EU membership with which negotiations were under way. The reports implied that the EU was heading for a 'big bang' enlargement, involving the accession of up to ten new members in 2004. It had hitherto been envisaged that a small advance guard would constitute the first wave of entrants, with others joining later in stages. Behind these carefully worded documents lay highly political calculations, in which the position of Poland was pivotal. Poland's progress had been overtaken by that of other candidate states, but Poland enjoyed the powerful support of Germany, which, for historical reasons, considered the projected 'eastward enlargement' of the EU to be politically impossible – indeed, almost pointless – without the Poles. However, if Poland were to be admitted, the Commission knew it would have great difficulty in turning away smaller candidate countries which were closer to meeting in full the Copenhagen and Madrid Criteria, including Slovenia, Slovakia, Latvia and Lithuania. There were also concerns over the potential for the erection of new barriers between neighbouring states by admitting the Czech Republic while excluding Slovakia, or by admitting Estonia while keeping out Latvia and Lithuania (*The Independent*, 14 November 2001, p. 20). Thus, even though the reports could not make overt political judgements, since the terms of reference confined the Commission to making technical assessments of each candidate's readiness for EU membership, the political logic pointed increasingly to a 'big bang' enlargement involving ten or more new members (*The Economist*, 17 November 2001, p. 41). The Commission also argued that, in the wake of the 11 September 2001 al-Qaeda attacks on the World Trade Center in New York, a strong and united Europe was all the more important 'to ensure peace, security, freedom and prosperity for all its citizens' (*FT*, 14 November 2001, p. 12).

In these reports, the Commission deemed that twelve candidate countries had met the Copenhagen political criteria (the exception was Turkey). It considered that the Copenhagen economic criteria, requiring new entrants to have functioning market economies capable of withstanding the competitive pressures and market forces within the EU, had been fully met only by Cyprus and Malta. However, the Czech Republic, Estonia, Hungary, Latvia, Lithuania, Poland, Slovakia and Slovenia were judged already to be functioning market economies, which were expected to become capable of coping with competitive pressures and market forces within the EU in the near future, provided they continued to follow EU policy prescriptions. In addition, Bulgaria was deemed close to being a functioning market economy and, with further hard-headed restructuring, it was expected to become capable of coping with competitive pressure in the medium term. However, Romania was considered to have met neither of the economic criteria. Its difficulties were deemed to be severe, although it was perceived to be making progress. The Commission reports also made it clear that Bulgaria and Romania were some way from meeting the so-called Madrid Criteria, relating to their administrative and judicial capacities (see pp. 585, 601, 610–11).

More specifically, Slovenia and Malta were praised for their economic and legislative progress; Poland was told to reform further its labour-intensive farm sector; Hungary, the Czech Republic, Latvia and Lithuania were told to crack down on corruption; the Czech Republic was called upon to halt the trafficking of women and children; Slovakia and Hungary were told to improve the treatment of their Roma populations; and Estonia was told that it must show greater respect for the rights of Russian speakers. Other outstanding problems included civil service and banking reform in the Czech Republic, Latvia's administrative capacity and practices, Lithuania's huge and unsafe Ignalina nuclear plant, the slowness of Slovenia's privatization programme, 'some non-transparent fiscal practices' and uncertainty over pension and health-care reform in Hungary, and the slowness and timidity of social security reform in the Czech Republic, Slovakia and Slovenia (*The Economist*, 17 November 2001, p. 41; *FT*, 14 November 2001, p. 12).

EU Commission recommendations, October 2002

In its report entitled *Towards the Enlarged Union*, published in October 2002, the EU Commission deemed that Poland, Hungary, the Czech Republic, Slovakia, Slovenia, Estonia, Latvia, Lithuania, Cyprus and Malta would be ready for EU membership from the beginning of 2004. It recommended that entry negotiations should be concluded by the end of 2002, with a view to signing their Treaties of Accession in April 2003. Its recommendations were based on rigorous and fairly objective assessments of the state of readiness of each candidate country. The report contended that Bulgaria and Romania would not be ready for membership until 2007, especially with regard to their administrative and judicial capabilities (the Madrid Criteria). However, in an endeavour to ensure that they really would be ready for EU membership by then, it recommended that there should be intensified monitoring and pressure on these two states to carry out further legal, judicial and administrative reforms. The report also recommended that the EU should enhance its support for Turkey's pre-accession preparations and provide additional resources for this purpose.

After enlargement, the Commission, as 'guardian of the Treaty', would remain responsible for ensuring proper implementation of EU law in the new Member States, employing the same methods and rigour as in existing Member States. The report recommended that, in relation to the first two years of membership, the Accession Treaties should include specific safeguard clauses concerning the internal market (including food safety) and the field of justice and home affairs, in order to allow the Commission to react more flexibly to potential problems during that initial period of membership. This would complement the Commission's usual instruments designed to ensure compliance with EU law.

The Commission's various findings, conclusions and recommendations were examined and largely accepted by a meeting of EU heads of state and government in Brussels on 24–25 October 2002. On 18 November 2002 the EU-15 foreign ministers tentatively agreed that the ten new Member States would be allowed to enter the EU on 1 May 2004, just in time to participate in the European Parliament elections scheduled for 12 June 2004 (*IHT*, 19 November 2002, p. 4). It was also decided that these so-called 'accession states' would be allowed to participate fully in the forthcoming Inter-Governmental Conference (IGC) on the Future of Europe, which was drawing up a proposed EU Constitution. This was intended to give them equal status with the EU-15 in these deliberations, including the implicit right to block any unacceptable changes to the existing EU Treaties (*FT*, 19 November 2002, p. 8).

THE COPENHAGEN EUROPEAN COUNCIL, 12–13 DECEMBER 2002: THE FINAL GO-AHEAD FOR EASTWARD ENLARGEMENT OF THE EU 'ON THE CHEAP'

This meeting of EU heads of state or government, chaired by Denmark's prime minister, Anders Fogh Rasmussen, concluded the fraught negotiations on the terms on which ten states would enter the EU in 2004. It was confirmed that the new members should be admitted on 1 May 2004.

Disputes over funding continued up to the last minute, with the Polish and Czech representatives in particular doing their utmost to secure less niggardly financial provisions for the new entrants. The Polish negotiating team had hoped to extract an additional €2 billion ($2.01 billion) from the fifteen existing EU members for the ten candidate states during 2004–6, on top of the €40.4 billion already proposed for that three-year period. In the end it was agreed that the EU would pay an extra €433 million to the ten new entrants, raising the gross cost of this 'eastward enlargement' to €40.8 billion for the years 2004–6. Poland, which comprised more than half the population of the ten new Member States, obtained the largest share of the increase, including €108 million for improved border controls and additional farm support. The Polish government was also allowed to gain early access to €1 billion of cash earmarked for future infrastructure projects, albeit taken out of its existing allocation of EU 'structural funds'. The other nine candidates were to receive an extra €300 million.

Last-minute negotiations by the Baltic States focused on Lithuania's Ignalina nuclear power plant and on levels of farm support. Lithuania agreed to close the Soviet-era plant in return for an extra €30 million over three years to ensure that it could be closed safely. Thus the EU, which had already spent hundreds of millions of euros on increasing the safety of Lithuania's Soviet-built Ignalina nuclear power plant, now agreed to spend a further €300 million by 2009 on closing it down – classic EU logic! In addition, Estonia cut a deal on EU farm support, designed to ensure that it did not begin its membership of the EU as a net contributor to the EU budget (*The Baltic Times*, 19–25 December 2002, p. 1).

This enlargement was projected to cost €40.8 billion *gross* during the years 2004–6 (*FT*, 14 December 2002, p. 6). However, according to documents released by the EU Commission on 16 December 2002, the *net cost* of this enlargement was projected to be €10.3 billion during the years 2004–6. This was mainly because, while receiving EU budgetary expenditures, the new Member States would simultaneously be required to pay €15 billion in contributions to the EU budget and because, in addition, large parts of the structural and agricultural funds to which the new members were in principle entitled were unlikely to be taken up in practice. Enlargement would therefore cost only about €9 per year per citizen of the EU-15. Two years previously, extrapolating from *Agenda 2000*, experts had been predicting that the cost would be about €30 per person. The EU Commission also estimated that EU infrastructural spending, farm support and other financial transfers would generate the following annual receipts per person in 2005 (the first full year of EU membership): about €67 for Poland; €49 for Hungary; €41 for Slovenia (the richest post-Communist state); and €29 for the Czech Republic. By way of comparison, some existing EU Member States would receive the following amounts per person: Greece €437; Portugal €211; Spain €126; and relatively rich Ireland €418 (*IHT*, 17 December 2002, p. 1).

This was very blatantly 'eastward enlargement on the cheap'. Some West European politicians even *boasted* of their 'success' in reducing the net cost of the East Central European and Baltic enlargement of the EU to just one-third of the amount envisaged in *Agenda 2000* by being even less generous to the new members than had been proposed in that already niggardly document. During the first years of East Central European and Baltic membership of the EU, the governments of the EU-15 were only prepared to allow the very much poorer new members to receive 25 to 30 per cent of the levels of per capita farm support and structural funding received by the much richer EU-15. It needs to be emphasized that even Portugal, Greece, southern Spain and southern Italy, the main net recipients of EU structural funds, were relatively rich by comparison with the new Member States. Ireland, Denmark and France, the biggest net per capita recipients of EU farm support, were extremely rich by comparison.

Thus, far from being one of Europe's 'finest hours' or a visionary demonstration of pan-European generosity, this momentous juncture in European history showed Western Europe at its most dismally selfish, myopic and mean-spirited. The East Central European and Baltic States were being given a few token crumbs from the tables of rich western Europe. The scale of West European meanness and myopia almost beggared belief. This was undoubtedly a major reason for the low voter turn-outs in most of the East Central European and Baltic referenda on joining the European Union during 2003, and for the even lower East Central European and Baltic voter turn-outs in the June 2004 European Parliament elections (see Tables 36.2 and 36.5 on pp. 604 and 607).

Nevertheless, with heavy hearts and considerable bitterness, most of the governments, parliaments and active voters of the East Central European and Baltic states accepted that there was no choice but to persevere with entry into the European Union, even though the EU-15 forced them to do so on utterly demeaning and humiliating terms. The new entrants really did have 'nowhere else to go'. As expressed in the apt title of a book written mainly by Balkan, Baltic and East Central Europeans, these countries felt 'driven to change' (Dimitrova 2004: 1). The process involved huge and very prolonged economic hardship, with a very dim light at the end of their very long tunnel, yet they felt that they had no option but to persevere. However, it is incumbent on all honest commentators and champions of European integration to record that the attendant hardships, sacrifices and 'adjustments' (a really atrocious euphemism!) were thrust almost entirely on to the relatively impoverished supplicants in the east, because rich Western Europe was too mean to make *any* significant financial sacrifices whatsoever for the sake of greater European unity, real convergence or even token recompense for the injustice of 'Yalta'.

Ratification of the East Central European and Baltic enlargement of the EU, 2003

The 'ratification year' got off to a depressing start. In January 2003 the US defence secretary Donald Rumsfeld denounced France and Germany for opposing the American drive for military action against Iraq. Rumsfeld described France and Germany as 'old Europe', out of step with the 'new Europe' made up of formerly Communist-ruled states (*IHT*, 19 February 2003, p. 1).

In a so-called 'Letter of Eight' signed in January 2003, Hungary, Poland, the Czech Republic, Spain, Italy, Portugal, Denmark and Britain openly supported the US-led occupation of Iraq. This move further exposed divisions within the EU over how to deal with Iraq and Saddam Hussein. In addition, ten post-Communist states belonging to the so-called 'Vilnius Group', namely Estonia, Latvia, Lithuania, Slovakia, Slovenia, Bulgaria, Romania, Croatia, Macedonia and Albania, signed a collective letter backing the US-led occupation.

On 17 February 2003 the French president Jacques Chirac crudely berated the East Central European, Baltic and Balkan candidates for EU membership for having openly sided with the USA, Britain, Italy and Spain over Iraq. 'They missed a good opportunity to keep quiet,' he declared. 'When you are in the family, after all, you have more rights than when you are asking to join and knocking on the door.' Chirac crudely threatened the ten countries scheduled to join the EU in 2004 that their pro-American leanings could be 'dangerous' for them, since their accession treaties had not yet been ratified. He reserved his most blatant threats for Bulgaria and Romania, two countries which had historic cultural links with France and whose cause French governments had championed, but which he claimed had done their best to 'reduce their chances of entering Europe' by openly supporting the USA (*FT*, 19 February 2003, p. 8).

Chirac's intemperate, condescending and ignoble outburst caused widespread offence in the East Central European, Baltic and Balkan states. They felt that they had been deliberately lectured, patronized, insulted by a very undistinguished west European politician who was trying to set himself up as their 'new headmaster', chastising them as if they were naughty school children. This probably contributed to the low turn-outs which characterized several of the East Central European referenda on EU membership during 2003 (Table 36.2). The accession treaties for the ten prospective new members were nevertheless duly signed in Athens on 16 April 2003.

Table 36.2   Results of East Central European and Baltic referenda on EU membership, 2003

Country	Date	% 'Yes'	% 'No'	Voter Turn out (%)
Slovenia	23 March	89.6	10.4	60.29
Hungary	12 April	83.8	16.2	45.62
Slovakia	16–17 May	92.5	6.2	52.15
Poland	7–8 June	77.5	22.5	58.85
Czech Republic	13–14 June	77.3	22.7	55.20
Lithuania	10–11 May	89.9	8.9	63.4
Estonia	14 September	66.8	33.1	64.0
Latvia	20 September	67.0	32.3	72.5

Source: Goetz (2005: 268) and *FT*, 22 September, p. 8

The European Council in Rome, 12–13 December 2003

At the European Council meeting of EU heads of state and government hosted by Italy on 12–13 December 2003, the leaders of the twenty-five existing and prospective members of the EU failed to reach agreement on the EU Constitution proposed by the IGC on the Future of Europe, chaired and drafted by the former French president Valery Giscard d'Estaing. The meeting stumbled on how to apportion power among large and small states. The main issue was a proposal to discard the voting system which the European Council at Nice had agreed in December 2000. This had given Spain and Poland, which each had less than half the population of Germany, almost as large a voting weight as Germany. Spain and Poland had been intent on keeping these voting weights, but they now found themselves relatively isolated, because the other EU states preferred to jettison the Nice system in favour of an arrangement known as the 'double majority', which stipulated that in order to become law EU legislation would in future have to gain the approval of at least half of the Member States representing at least 60 per cent of the total EU population.

Problems renewing a 'Partnership and Co-operation Agreement' with Russia, early 2004

The EU had signed a pact with Russia in December 1997, setting out the frameworks for Russia–EU political and trade relations for the next ten years. However, this accord now needed to be modified to take account of the EU's eastward enlargement. Moscow was eager to exact a price for its acquiescence in a geopolitical change which would further increase Russia's marginalization in European affairs and economic development. It sought visa-free access for Russian citizens to the new EU members, especially ethnic Russians who had been left stateless when the three Baltic States declared their independence in 1991. In addition, Russian officials claimed that the eastward enlargement of the EU could cost Russia's economy between $150 million and $300 million a year, mainly because of the extension of EU-wide quotas and tariffs to countries with which Russia had hitherto had preferential bilateral trade agreements. Russia sought compensation for the loss of its tariff privileges in the new EU states, but its case was weakened by calculations that, while the new Partnership and Co-operation Agreement would result in Russia facing new or increased import tariffs on *some* of its exports to its former 'satellites', the average level of import duties on Russian exports to those countries would fall (*FT*, 25 February 2004, p. 18).

The EU and Russia finally reached an agreement on 27 April 2004. This resolved most of Russia's concerns about the impact of the EU's enlargement on its own economy, especially on its trade with former Soviet bloc countries. German Gref, Russia's minister of trade and economic development, conceded that the net impact on Russian trade would be negligible. The two sides agreed to finesse some contentious issues in a separate non-binding statement. This affirmed a previous agreement to allow Russia free transit of goods to Kaliningrad and noted that, on average, tariffs on Russian imports would fall from 9 per cent to 4 per cent. However, the statement also made it clear that some important issues were left for negotiation, including tariffs on Russian agricultural products and the shipment of nuclear fuel to reactors in East Central Europe and the Baltic States. Another contentious issue involved the status of ethnic Russians in the newly expanded EU, mainly in Latvia and Estonia. Russia had been pressing the EU for a pledge to push the 'social integration' of such ethnic minorities in the new Members States, but Latvia and Estonia had resisted this. The statement simply reaffirmed the commitment of the two sides to protect human rights and persons belonging to minority groups (*IHT*, 28 April 2004, pp. 1, 6).

ENTRY OF EAST CENTRAL EUROPE AND THE BALTIC STATES INTO THE EU, 1 MAY 2004

This enlargement increased the EU's population by 20 per cent (from 375 million to 450 million) and its territory by 25 per cent, but its GDP by barely 5 per cent. The EU's combined GDP now exceeded that of the United States, but the USA (with a population of only 290 million) still had a higher per capita GDP. Most of the new Member States had relatively high proportions of their workforce employed in agriculture and their accession greatly increased the cultivated area of the EU (see Tables 36.3 and 36.4).

Table 36.3 Percentage shares of agriculture in total employment and in GDP, 2001

	In total employment	In GDP
Czech Republic	4.9	3.4
Estonia	7.1	4.7
Hungary	6.1	1.9
Latvia	15.1	4.0
Lithuania	16.5	6.9
Poland	19.2	2.9
Slovakia	6.3	4.1
Slovenia	9.9	2.9
EU-15	4.3	2.0

Source: Eurostat statistics, cited by Broussolle (2005: 946).

Table 36.4 The effects of successive EU enlargements on EU agricultural resources

	Increase in agricultural output (%)	Increase in agricultural population (%)	Increase in cultivated area (%)
The 1973 enlargement (from 6 to 9 members)	19	17	42
The 1981 and 1986 enlargements (from 9 to 12 members)	32	54	41
The 1995 enlargement (from 12 to 15 members)	3	5	7
The 2004 enlargement (from 12 to 25 members)	54	134	46

Source: Broussolle (2005: 946).

There has been much discussion of the effects that eastward enlargement of the European Union could have on the Common Agricultural Policy (CAP). Many agricultural economists claimed (or even hoped!) that the admission of countries such as Poland, Romania and Hungary would wreck the CAP (and the present structure of EU finances) by greatly increasing the cost of farm subsidies and the agricultural surpluses which the EU would have to absorb, dump or destroy. However, if such predictions had been correct, some of the current members of the EU would almost certainly have vetoed the eastward enlargement, rather than acquiesce in the destruction of the CAP. Those who hoped to use EU enlargement as a means of wrecking the CAP were thus barking up the wrong tree.

In any case, the supposed effects of the eastward enlargement on the CAP were greatly exaggerated, probably for political motives. The problems posed were more political than economic, they were not insurmountable, and they were likely to diminish quite rapidly. The entry of the Czech Republic, Slovenia and Slovakia posed no major challenges to the CAP, in view of their smallness and/or infertile terrain and, in the case of the Czech Republic and Slovenia, their relatively high levels of industrialization and urbanization. Like Portugal and Greece, these three countries were net importers of temperate farm products, thereby helping to relieve pressures on the CAP. The real problems concerned the admission of Poland and (in 2007) Romania, because their relatively unproductive farmers were so numerous, and of Hungary and (in 2007) Bulgaria, because their farms were relatively productive and export-orientated. However, if the 70 per cent reduction in East Germany's farm workforce between 1989 and 1993 is at all indicative, we can expect the East Central European agricultural population to slump as and when opportunities for leaving the land (including emigration) open up. This in turn should lead to some reductions in cultivated area, restraining potential increases in agricultural output. As in the West, not many young East Central Europeans want to remain on the land for ever more. Few can resist the lure of the cities, with their wider ranges of occupations and amenities. Thus the potential threat has been somewhat exaggerated by the alarmists, many of whom want either to scrap or to 'repatriate' EU farm support, which they regard as little more than a very costly and corrupt system of 'outdoor relief' for ne'er-do-well farmers. The more blinkered critics fail to grasp that the CAP was an essential component of the political contract that created the EEC and that the motives for its creation were not merely to placate rural political constituencies and anxious Frenchmen, but also to banish the *national* agricultural protectionism, which, if it were allowed to reappear in the form of repatriation of farm support, would soon prompt tit-for-tat *national* protectionism in other sectors and quickly unravel the invaluable achievements of the Common Market (not to mention its sequel, the Single European Market). Indeed, it needs to be more widely understood that the CAP is not merely a system of farm support, but also a system of food security and a small fee (or 'insurance premium') which Europeans pay to prevent a return to the national agricultural protectionism and beggar-my-neighbour trade wars which bedevilled interwar Europe. It costs less than 0.5 per cent of the European Union's GDP.

The elections to the European Parliament, 12 June 2004

Even though this was the first opportunity for East Central Europeans, Balts and Estonians to take part in EU elections, the levels of turn-out were even more dismal in the new members of the EU (27 per cent on average) than in the EU-15 (50 per cent on average) and in the EU as a whole (45.3 per cent on average) (see Table 36.5). 'Of the eight new central European members, only Lithuania had a turnout above the EU average, and then only because it held a presidential election at the same time. Slovakia, with a turnout of 16.7 per cent, set the record for abstention' (*The Economist*, 19 June 2004, p. 42).

Table 36.5   Voter turn-outs in the European Parliament elections, 12 June 2004 (per cent)

New members		Older members			
Poland	20.4	France	43.1	UK	38.9
Hungary	38.5	Germany	43.0	Greece	62.8
Czech Republic	27.9	Netherlands	39.1	Portugal	38.7
Slovakia	16.7	Belgium	90.8*	Spain	45.9
Lithuania	46.1	Italy	73.1	Austria	49.0
Latvia	41.2	Luxembourg	90.0*	Finland	41.1
Estonia	26.9	Ireland	61.0	Sweden	37.2
Slovenia	28.3	Denmark	47.9		
Cyprus	71.2				
Malta	82.4				

Note: * voting is mandatory

Source: FT (15 June 2004, p. 15).

Agreement on an EU Constitution, Brussels, 18 June 2004

On 26 March 2004, a meeting of the heads of state or government of the twenty-five existing and prospective EU states had agreed to conclude a final deal on the proposed EU Constitution no later than the European Council scheduled for 17 June 2004. The Polish government and the new Spanish government had indicated their readiness to compromise on this matter (*FT*, 27 March 2004, p. 7; *IHT*, 27 March 2004, p. 8).

Last-minute negotiations focused on the proposed new voting system within the EU Council of Ministers. Germany, France, the UK and Italy were very reluctant to accept any further increases in the collective capacity of the small states to out-vote the larger states, which contained the vast majority of EU citizens. The governments of Poland and Spain accepted a revised 'double majority' voting system. The original proposal had been that a law would pass if it had the support of at least half the twenty-five member states, representing 60 per cent of the EU population. The new deal raised the respective voting thresholds to 55 per cent of the member countries representing 65 per cent of the population, with the added provision that a blocking majority had to come from at least four countries. This made it easier for Poland and Spain to block laws they did not like, while preventing 'the big three' (France, Germany and the UK) from being able to do so on their own (*The Economist*, 26 June 2004, p. 41).

EAST CENTRAL EUROPE'S FIRST THREE YEARS IN THE EU, 2004-6

From 2004 to 2006, after entering the EU in May 2004, East Central Europe and the Baltic States experienced significant accelerations in economic growth and (in most cases) reductions in unemployment (see Table 35.1). These states also experienced property and stock-market booms, increased emigration (leading to increased remittances from emigrants), and buoyant inflows of foreign direct investment (FDI). Total inflows of FDI into East Central Europe were dwarfed by the massive inflows of FDI into East Asia. Nevertheless, East Central Europe was receiving rather more FDI than East Asia in per capita terms – and a great deal more in per capita terms than South Asia, Africa and Latin America (see UNCTAD 2004: 367–71; UNCTAD 2005: 303–7; and UNCTAD 2006: 299–302).

In a review of East Central Europe's first two years in the EU, delivered to the European Policy Centre in Brussels on 19 May 2006, the EU enlargement commissioner Olli Rehn justifiably declared that the process of integrating the East Central European states into the EU had been 'the main driving force' in the region's 'spectacular economic and democratic transformation' and that the 'Cassandras' had been 'proved wrong', in as much as none of the 'catastrophes' predicted by the critics of this enlargement had materialized. The European Union's institutions had not been paralysed, and its budget had not collapsed. Furthermore, the economies of the EU-15 had not been undermined by the low-waged newcomers, while the industrial and agricultural sectors of the new Member States had not collapsed under the blast of intensified competition. On the contrary, east-ward enlargement was having positive effects on the economies of both the old and the new member states (*Enlargement Newsletter*, 6 June 2006, p. 1).

For the EU economy as a whole, the new East Central European and Baltic member states repre-sented major assets, resources and opportunities, rather than burdens, problems or liabilities. With relatively low labour costs, low taxes, low unionization, low living costs, slightly antiquated and run-down but nevertheless serviceable physical and educational infrastructures, guaranteed access to the Single European Market, and workforces with relatively strong education, skills, flexibility, and motivation to work and prosper, these economies were well placed to become Europe's new 'tiger economies'. It was therefore economically rational for western European industrial firms to continue to relocate much of their manufacturing and assembly work in the new Member States and for western European trading firms to increase their reliance on East Central European and Baltic suppliers, in order to take advantage of their major potential as low-cost export-orientated manufac-turing bases capable of holding their own against low-cost competitors outside Europe. Conversely, it was economically rational for the more expensive but more highly trained workforces of western Europe to play to their comparative advantages by concentrating even further on the service indus-tries and knowledge-intensive activities which already accounted for more than 70 per cent of western Europe's GDP and offered the most favourable prospects for competing successfully in global markets.

Another consequence of EU membership was increased emigration from East Central Europe and the Baltic States. Between May 2004 and October 2006, Britain alone received roughly 511,000 migrant workers from these states, including 300,000 from Poland. However, most of these were only temporary migrants, and the majority returned to their countries of origin within a year. Large numbers of these migrants went to Ireland and Sweden as well, and each month Poland was losing the equivalent of a small town. During the summer of 2006 several other EU states, influenced by studies which concluded that the British and Irish economies had not suffered and almost certainly benefited from these labour inflows, decided to lift their previous restrictions on migrants from East Central Europe and the Baltic States. The host countries ought not to view these migrants as prob-lems. They are, for the most part, educated, skilled, motivated, flexible and adaptable workers, who alleviate skills and labour bottlenecks and make few demands on the welfare state, according to many British employers and the UK Home Office. A greater cause for concern was whether the East Central European and Baltic States could afford to lose so many skilled, educated and motivated young adults, even allowing for the value of their homeward remittances.

EAST CENTRAL EUROPE: ECONOMIC CHANGE AND INTEGRATION WITH THE EU

Poland, whose cataclysmic economic-cum-political crisis and runaway inflation during the late 1980s made brutal macro-economic 'shock therapy' and 'big bang' restructuring almost unavoida-ble during the early 1990s, was thereby virtually forced to become the pace-maker of East Central European economic liberalization, restructuring and privatization. This not only limited the scale of its economic contraction in 1990–1, but also enabled Poland to become the first European post-Communist state to achieve positive economic growth (in 1992) and the first to regain its 1989 level of GDP (in 1998). Nevertheless, Poland's unemployment rate has remained painfully high, fluctuating between 13 and 20 per cent of the workforce from 1995 to 2005 (see Table 35 (c), on p. 562) before at last dropping below 12 per cent in early 2007.

During the late 1990s and early 2000s, unfortunately, Poland lost much of its earlier reforming momentum and sense of direction. Persistently high unemployment, the other great hardships incurred during Poland's economic transformation, and popular perceptions that Poland had been forced to wait an unwarrantedly long time before being admitted to the EU in 2004 seriously eroded popular support for the strongly pro-EU socialist and liberal currents in Polish politics, as did the numerous corruption scandals in which they were implicated during the same period. All these factors contributed to the triumph of conservative, Europhobic, xenophobic and homophobic populist parties in the September 2005 parliamentary election, placing the earlier political and economic achievements of post-Communist Poland in serious jeopardy. During 2006, to the great chagrin of Polish liberals and socialists, the regime led by the identical twins Lech and Jaroslaw Kaczynski very divisively initiated a witch-hunt against former Communists and Communist-era informers employed in public service positions (including the education system). It simultaneously adopted increasingly hostile stances towards Germany and homosexuals, and somewhat tetchy and uncooperative ones towards the European Union. The Polish economy enjoyed a boom during the mid-2000s, reaping the long-awaited economic rewards of entry into the European Union. However, the Kaczynski brothers manifested no enthusiasm for preparing Poland to fulfil the clause in its EU accession treaty requiring it to adopt the euro and join the euro-zone.

Slovenia, which in the early 1990s was already the richest and most marketized of the post-Communist states, returned to modest but steady positive economic growth from 1993 onward, albeit with 7–9 per cent of the workforce unemployed. Buoyed up by tourism and by relatively high per capita inflows of foreign direct investment, the EU decided in 2006 to allow Slovenia to adopt the euro and enter the euro-zone in January 2007. Slovenia was the first post-Communist state to attain this honour. However, Lithuania only narrowly missed being allowed to do so at the same time (it was excluded on a mere technicality), and it was well placed to join the euro-zone in 2008.

The relatively highly educated and skilled workforce, healthy public finances, low internal and external debts, and low inflation rates which the Czech Republic inherited from the Czechoslovak Communist regime made it possible to carry out a gradualist and seemingly successful programme of economic liberalization, privatization and restructuring during the first half of the 1990s under the aegis of Vaclav Klaus. Klaus served as Czechoslovakia's finance minister from December 1989 to June 1992 and as Czech prime minister from June 1992 to November 1997. The country achieved positive economic growth with relatively low unemployment from 1993 to 1996. Thereafter, however, the gradualist reform programme fell into major disarray as a result of the half-heartedness of Klaus's approach to economic restructuring and reform, which contributed to the financial scandals and political crises of 1996–8. The Czech Republic resumed respectable rates of economic growth under the Social Democrats from 2000 to 2006, albeit with 8–9 per cent unemployment. During the 1993–6 and 2000–6 periods, Czech economic growth was bolstered by comparatively high per capita inflows of foreign direct investment (FDI), especially from multinational manufacturers attracted by the Czech Republic's educated, skilled and disciplined workforce and its well-developed infrastructure. The predominantly Eurosceptical Czech political establishment was in no hurry to fulfil the Czech Republic's EU accession treaty commitment to adopt the euro and join the euro-zone, even though its economy would soon be in a position to do so.

Hungary, which had already established a semi-marketized economy under its Communist regime from 1968 to 1989, confounded optimistic Western predictions by recording a very lacklustre economic performance during the mid-1990s (see Table 35.1). However, it achieved considerably faster economic growth (4.3 per cent per annum) with 6–7 per cent unemployment rates from

1997 to 2006. Like the Czech Republic, Hungary was buoyed up by comparatively high per capita inflows of foreign direct investment from multinational manufacturers, attracted by Hungary's relatively well-educated and skilled workforce and its nodal position in the wider European economy. However, Hungary's economic prospects were placed in jeopardy when successive governments, of all political stripes, ran up unsustainably high budget and trade deficits during the early and mid-2000s. The country was enveloped in political crisis after revelations in October 2006 that the socialist party had won the April 2006 parliamentary election by blatantly and persistently lying to the public about the magnitude of Hungary's deficits and the severity of the macro-economic measures needed to reduce them to manageable levels. Hungary's official target date for adoption of the euro and entry into the euro-zone had to be put back to 2011. However, in view of the magnitude of Hungary's largely self-inflicted crisis, many Western financial analysts regarded 2014 as more realistic target date.

Slovakia incurred growing Western opprobrium while it was governed by a series of populist, neo-Communist, ultra-nationalist, and increasingly corrupt and authoritarian coalition governments headed by Vladimir Meciar, from 1992 to 1995 and from 1995 to 1998. It was largely because of this that Slovakia was initially excluded from the intended 'first wave' of East Central European entrants into the European Union. However, the radical economic liberalization, privatization and tax-cutting programmes carried out by the neo-liberal governments headed by Mikulas Dzurinda from 1998 to 2006 helped Slovakia to emerge as a 'dark horse' economic success during the early 2000s, paving the way for its entry into the EU in May 2004, simultaneously with the other East Central European states. Under Dzurinda, Slovakia gained renown for low flat-rate taxation policies, which raised work and investment incentives and helped the economy to attract high inflows of FDI, most notably in car production. Bratislava, Slovakia's capital city and virtually an economic suburb of Vienna, became the major magnet for foreign direct investment and accounted for a quarter of Slovakia's GDP in 2005. Until mid-2006 Slovakia was considered fairly certain to join the euro-zone by 2009. However, the unexpected election of a centre-left populist-nationalist coalition government headed by Robert Fico in July 2006 raised widespread doubts as to whether this goal would remain attainable. Fico's critics regarded his fairly extravagantly 'populist' election pledges and his reliance on populist and nationalist coalition partners as scarcely compatible with the levels of 'fiscal prudence' deemed necessary to maintain the previous low inflation, low interest rates, low budget deficits and high inflows of FDI.

THE BALKANS: ECONOMIC CHANGE AND INTEGRATION WITH THE EU

Compared with East Central Europe, the economic picture for most of the post-Communist Balkan states has remained much grimmer. Bulgaria, Romania, Croatia, Serbia and Montenegro missed 'windows of opportunity' for radical economic liberalization and restructuring during the early 1990s, chiefly because their polities and societies were dominated by corrupt, clientelistic and deeply entrenched vertical power structures which strongly resisted radical change. Their initial moves towards liberal democracy and liberal market economies were half-hearted and more formal than substantial. Partly for these reasons, significant economic contractions occurred in Bulgaria in 1996–7, in Romania in 1997–9, in Serbia in 1999 and (more modestly) Croatia in 1999, flagging up their ongoing economic vulnerability. By contrast, Albania experienced a rapid and almost complete collapse of its previous economic system and power structures during the early 1990s, but what took their place proved to be very unstable and resulted in a 7 per cent contraction of GDP in 1997.

In 2005, official unemployment levels remained extremely high in Kosova (more than 50 per cent), Bosnia (around 40 per cent), Macedonia (usually in excess of 35 per cent) and Serbia (around 30 per cent); and they exceeded 19 per cent in Bulgaria as recently as 2001 and 18 per cent in

Albania as recently as 1998–9. Official unemployment levels in the Balkan post-Communist states would have been even higher but for the fact that high proportions of their populations had emigrated since the end of Communist rule. While 10–15 per cent of the population left Bulgaria and Romania during the 1990s, much higher proportions left Kosova, Bosnia, Serbia, Montenegro and Albania, with the result that their economies became heavily dependent on remittances from émigré workers (see Table 35.3). In 2004 remittances amounted to between three and four times the net inflows of foreign direct investment into Bosnia, Serbia and Albania, and to between 100 and 167 per cent of the value of their export earnings (EBRD 2006a: 4–5). In the short term, emigration and remittances helped to relieve pressures on these economies, but in the longer run emigration has deprived them of many of their ablest and/or most enterprising people. Remittances may have begun a downward trend in 2005, as longstanding emigrants began to put down roots in their (mainly EU) host countries and loosen their links with their countries of origin. Another major problem has been that high levels of organized crime, racketeering and corruption have taken heavy economic and social tolls on the inhabitants of Serbia, Kosova, Bulgaria, Macedonia, Croatia, Montenegro and (to a lesser degree) Romania, and are bound to continue to do so for many years to come. One only has to consider the example of Italy to realize how long it can take to extirpate deeply entrenched gangsterism.

There was great relief in Bulgaria and Romania in September 2006, when the EU decided to allow these two countries to enter the EU on schedule in January 2007, yet this was mixed with annoyance that they were to continue to be subjected to close monitoring by the EU Commission even after their entry into the EU. However, the annoyance was not altogether warranted, in as much as there was still much to be done in both countries to bring racketeering, high-level corruption and organized crime under control and to establish more fully the rule of law. Their admission to the EU was of crucial significance, because there would be much greater scope, support and incentives for overcoming their ongoing problems *within* the EU than *outside* it (Bideleux and Jeffries 2007: 121–4, 182, 586–7). Rising expectations that EU entry would indeed come about in January 2007 had already helped to accelerate economic growth and reduce unemployment in Bulgaria and Romania from 2001 onward (see Table 35.2), while also stimulating increased inflows of foreign direct investment and booms in property development. This in turn helped to reduce Bulgarian and Romanian emigration from the substantial levels of the 1990s and lent weight to official claims that entry into the EU would not precipitate a further huge exodus of Bulgarians and Romanians to other EU Member States. This, combined with official and business community perceptions that the British, Irish and Swedish economies had reaped considerable economic benefits from large inflows of cheap, skilled, flexible and highly motivated workers from the East Central European and Baltic states between May 2004 and October 2006, encouraged nearly half the EU-15 to decide to allow Bulgarians and Romanians to enjoy free movement from the moment they became EU members in 2007, instead of exercising their powers to restrict entry for the first seven years. However, mainly because Britain had received an influx of roughly 511,000 East Central Europeans and Balts between May 2004 and October 2006 (more than ten times the number predicted, precipitating xenophobic reactions from some UK politicians and the media), Tony Blair's UK government decided to restrict entry of Bulgarians and Romanians. The Irish government followed suit, pointing out that Ireland too had received several times as many East Central European and Baltic migrants as predicted. Viewed in purely economic terms, however, these restrictions were misguided because (as mentioned on p. 608) the 2004–6 wave of East Central European and Baltic migrants had made substantial net contributions to the British and Irish economies, helping to keep their economic growth rates significantly above the EU average without dramatically increasing unemployment (since they mainly relieved labour and skill shortages). These migrants had also made minimal claims on UK and Irish welfare provisions. However, as in other EU Member States in 2004, irrational xenophobia triumphed over economic rationality.

From 2000 to 2005, successive Croatian governments aspired to obtain their country's accession into the EU at the same time as Bulgaria and Romania. However, Croatia continued to pay heavy economic and political prices for having supported the authoritarian ultra-nationalist Tudjman regime through the 1990s and for its subsequent reluctance to arrest and hand over for trial the Croatians indicted by the ICTY (International Criminal Tribunal for former Yugoslavia) in The Hague for the war crimes and crimes against humanity which they allegedly committed during the 1991–5 war with the Serbs and in Bosnia. The resultant uncertainties caused economic growth and foreign direct investment in the country to be considerably lower than they would otherwise have been, while also delaying Croatia's headway towards EU membership. Croatia still had not fully regained its 1989 level of GDP in 2005 (Table 35.3), although it finally did so in 2006. Croatia has largely had itself to blame for the fact that it missed a brief 'window of opportunity' during 2004 and early 2005 to clinch a deal on EU entry in 2008 or 2009, hard on the heels of Bulgaria and Romania. Croatia's continued foot-dragging vis-à-vis the ICTY was chiefly responsible for this major setback. Furthermore, the strong growth of 'enlargement fatigue' in the EU during 2005 and 2006 made it increasingly unlikely that Croatia would be allowed to enter the EU before 2010 at the earliest. The resultant uncertainties concerning Croatia's future were likely to perpetuate its relatively modest economic growth and suboptimal inflows of foreign direct investment, despite the country's considerable tourism potential.

The Republic of Macedonia (ROM) stands next in line for EU membership, having signed a Stabilization and Association Agreement (SAA) with the EU in 2001 and having been granted official EU candidate status in 2005. However, the ROM's relatively lack-lustre economic growth and more than 35 per cent unemployment, combined with renewed attempts by the new Slav Macedonian nationalist government elected in June 2006 to marginalize the ROM's large ethnic Albanian minority (25 per cent of the population), contributed to the EU's reluctance during 2006 to set a target date for the start of formal membership negotiations. Like Croatia, the ROM missed golden opportunities to make greater headway towards EU membership during the window of opportunity which opened in 2004 and early 2005. Unfortunately, continued uncertainty over its future status vis-à-vis the EU was likely to preclude any dramatic amelioration in its very difficult economic situation.

Albania signed an SAA with the EU on 12 June 2006, after three long years of negotiation. However, continuing high levels of corruption, racketeering, organized crime and violence in Albania prevented rapid implementation of the SAA, and by early 2007 it seemed likely that the country might have to wait several years before gaining official candidacy for EU membership. Nevertheless, Albania's economy grew by roughly 6.8 per cent per annum from 1999 to 2006 (see Table 35.2), mainly as a result of its very low wages, its low initial economic base, high levels of remittances from the large Albanian diasporas in the EU and North America, and buoyant earnings from drug smuggling, arms dealing, money laundering and people trafficking (Pond 2006: 25).

Between 1992 and 1995, Bosnia and Herzegovina suffered the loss of around 100,000 lives, the expulsion of more than two million people from their homes, and massive military devastation of the economy. Recovery from those cataclysmic years has been painful and slow. Bosnia's rates of economic growth after 1995 look respectable on paper (Table 35.2), but its official unemployment rates have remained exceedingly high (more than 40 per cent of the workforce) and the state has remained vulnerably dependent on Western economic aid and local spending by the UN administration and peacekeeping forces. This, together with continuing tensions and mistrust between its three main communities, contributed to Bosnia's failure to bring its negotiations for an SAA with the EU to a successful conclusion during 2006. That in turn was likely adversely to affect Bosnia's prospects for self-sustaining economic development.

During the 1990s Serbia's economy was debilitated by the costs of warfare, UN trade and financial embargoes, massive emigration of (mostly well-educated) young adults to escape the draft, maintaining large security forces, and subsidizing the secessionism of Bosnian and Croatian Serbs. The economy was also systematically exploited for personal gain by President Slobodan Milosevic and his cronies. Considering the circumstances, Serbian economic activity recovered remarkably resiliently in 1995–7, after Serbia's belligerence towards Croatia and Bosnia, and again in 2000–6, after the Kosova conflict of 1998–9. However, Serbia has continued to incur heavy costs from organized crime, corruption, considerable political and economic isolation, and uncertainties over its future status vis-à-vis the EU. These factors have discouraged much-needed foreign direct investment. Although Serbia was belatedly allowed to start negotiating an SAA with the EU in October 2005, these negotiations were suspended in spring 2006 as a result of the Serbian establishment's persistent failure/reluctance to arrest and hand over for trial in The Hague Serbs indicted by the ICTY for war crimes and crimes against humanity, which they allegedly committed during the wars of 1991–5 and 1999. Nevertheless, in order to strengthen the position of Serbian liberals vis-à-vis the ultra-nationalist Serbian Radical Party (which topped the poll in the January 2007 elections), and in order to give Serbia increased incentives to comply with ICTY demands, the EU Member States announced in March 2007 that a compliant Serbia could attain official candidacy for EU membership as early as 2008.

From 1992 to 2000, as the junior partner in a Serb–Montenegrin binary state, Montenegro was caught in the backwash from Serbian nationalism, Serbia's wars with its neighbours and UN sanctions. This resulted in debilitating isolation of the Montenegrin economy, substantial parts of which fell under the control of racketeers who had been spawned and enriched by sanctions-busting operations. Even after the fall of President Milosevic in October 2000, Montenegro's room for manoeuvre remained severely limited by the terms of its union with Serbia. Even the looser State Union of 2003–6, brokered by Javier Solana and the EU, proved too restrictive. Thus, even though Montenegro was able to start negotiating an SAA with the EU in late 2005, it was not an independent state and its negotiations were repeatedly placed in jeopardy by the shenanigans of its domineering Serbian cousins within the State Union. The 616,000 inhabitants of Montenegro were only able to start taking proper care of their own interests by voting (by a 55.5 per cent majority) in May 2006 to become an independent state. This was consummated remarkably smoothly during the summer of 2006, and Montenegro was henceforth able to continue its negotiations with the EU unimpaired. These negotiations quickly bore fruit with the signing of a Stabilization and Association Agreement with the EU in March 2007, but subsequent negotiations for official candidate status and EU membership were likely to be very protracted, in view of the smallness and vulnerability of the Montenegrin state and economy, along with the saliency of corruption and racketeering (see Bideleux and Jeffries 2007: 504–11).

Kosova has been desperately in need of EU membership, if only to help relieve its massive unemployment rate (50–70 per cent of the workforce) by obtaining greater freedom of movement to EU states and by making itself more attractive to foreign businesses and investors. However, before taking even the first steps towards EU membership, Kosova (like Montenegro) has had to pursue recognition as an independent state, because in practice the EU deals directly only with independent states and only independent states can take on the obligations of EU membership. Although Kosova has remained on course to be granted some sort of conditional independence during 2007, this embryonic statelet was bound to remain anything but independent economically. Any formal independence was therefore likely to remain somewhat illusory. Since Kosova has also become deeply mired in corruption, racketeering, crime and violence, EU membership has remained a fairly remote prospect even though by early 2007 the EU commission was already encouraging Kosova's government to regard and pursue this as a viable medium-term goal.

During 2006 it became increasingly apparent that none of the ailing western Balkan economies were likely to obtain stimulus and/or relief in the form of EU membership any time soon. This made it all the more urgent for the EU to take effective steps to prevent these states from becoming increasingly marginalized, both economically and as a consequence of EU visa restrictions (see Bideleux and Jeffries 2007: 578–9, 593). One major way in which both the EU and its individual Member States could contribute to this would be by promoting the growth of European tourism and actively investing in tourist/transport infrastructure in the western Balkans, bearing in mind the roles which European tourism has played in developing Spain, Portugal, Greece, Cyprus and Malta and in integrating them into the wider European economy, community and culture.

THE GRADUAL ADMISSION OF EAST CENTRAL EUROPEAN, BALTIC AND BALKAN STATES TO *PARTNERSHIP FOR PEACE* AND SUBSEQUENTLY TO NATO

On 21 October 1993 NATO decided to adopt a US proposal that non-aligned and former Communist countries should be offered a Partnership for Peace rather than immediate membership. The idea was formally accepted at the NATO summit held in Brussels on 10–11 January 1994 as a way of reconciling conflicting pressures: (i) the eagerness of the East European and Baltic states in particular to join in order to benefit from NATO's security guarantees (especially after the December 1993 general election in Russia and the failure of the West to deal with the crisis in Bosnia); (ii) the desire to avoid a security vacuum in Eastern Europe; (iii) the danger of stirring nationalist passions in a Russia perceiving potential isolation (on 10 January 1994 Vladimir Zhirinovsky warned that the incorporation of Eastern Europe 'would mean NATO took the path of preparing for World War Three'); (iv) the fear of involving NATO in a still unstable region and drawing new lines of division in Europe; and (v) the fear of weakening NATO if countries not yet ready for membership were to be admitted. Russia joined the Partnership for Peace on 31 May 1995. By mid-1996 there were twenty-seven participants in the programme: Albania, Armenia, Austria, Azerbaijan, Belarus, Bulgaria, the Czech Republic, Estonia, Finland, Georgia, Hungary, Kazakhstan, Kyrgyzstan, Latvia, Lithuania, Macedonia, Malta, Moldova, Poland, Romania, Russia, Slovakia, Slovenia, Sweden, Turkmenistan, Ukraine and Uzbekistan (*The Economist*, 1 June 1996, p. 22).

The prelude to the first eastward enlargement of NATO

During the autumn of 1993, the Clinton administration decided to press for gradual eastward enlargement of NATO and 'a package of policy initiatives designed to reassert American international leadership and defy the critics who had been charging that Clinton was weak and vacillating in the foreign policy arena' (Smith 1999: 53). At a NATO summit in Brussels in January 1994, President Clinton 'pushed for a clear statement that NATO was open to expansion' (p. 54). A communiqué issued on 11 January 1994 stated: 'We expect and would welcome NATO expansion that would reach to democratic states to our east, as part of an evolutionary process, taking into account political and security developments in the whole of Europe.' No former Communist country and member of the North Atlantic Co-operation Council would be excluded from *consideration* as a future member, although at this stage there was no *guarantee* of membership, no timetable was laid out and no detailed and specific eligibility criteria were listed (as distinct from the general requirement that candidates for NATO membership had to be democracies which accepted existing national territorial boundaries and which ensured democratic/civilian control of the military). What was promised was closer co-operation with NATO on a bilateral, individually tailored basis, which might lead to membership in the fullness of time. The idea was to sign a standard framework; individual deals could be worked out in detail later. The forms of co-operation included: information exchange; transparency in defence planning and budgeting; joint planning, exercises and training (including preparation for peacekeeping duties); and consultation with any country that faced 'a direct threat to its territorial integrity, political independence or security'.

The Western European Union offered 'associate partner' status to Bulgaria, the Czech Republic, Hungary, Poland, Romania, Slovakia, Estonia, Latvia and Lithuania on 9 May 1994. In September 1995 NATO published *A Study on NATO Enlargement* which, like the 'Copenhagen Criteria' promulgated by the EU in 1993, for the first time spelled out conditions to be met by aspiring NATO members:

(i)   a functioning democratic political system and market economy;
(ii) treatment of minority populations in accordance with OSCE guidelines;
(iii) resolution of all outstanding disputes with neighbours and a commitment to the peaceful settlement of disputes generally;
(iv) [The ability and willingness to make] a military contribution to the alliance and achieve interoperability with other members' forces;
(v)   Democratic-style civil-military relations. (Greenwood 2005: 11)

In the same month a European Council meeting in Essen decided that negotiations for the accession of new EU members would not be initiated until after the completion of the 1996–7 Inter-Governmental Conference (IGC) on reform of the EU, whose conclusions were embodied in the 1997 Treaty of Amsterdam. Faced with the prospect that eastward enlargement of the EU would be put on ice for the time being, whereas the chances of admission to NATO seemed to be improving, some East Central European leaders played up the importance of joining NATO. For example, President Vaclav Havel stated: 'For reasons of security, being accepted into NATO is indeed even more urgent for us than being accepted into the European Union . . . Now the time is really ripe to seriously negotiate about our membership in NATO; it alone offers a security guarantee. Integration in the European Union remains a long-term process' (quoted by Morrison 1995: 80).

On 8 July 1997, NATO invited the Czech Republic, Hungary and Poland to begin accession talks. Romania and Slovenia were not invited to do so, even though a majority of European NATO members (led by France) had supported their admission. The US Clinton administration insisted that only three post-Communist states should be invited to join in the first instance. However, during a visit to Bucharest on 11 July 1997, President Clinton described Romania as one of the 'strongest candidates' for inclusion in the second wave of invitations.

The entry of Poland, Hungary and the Czech Republic into NATO, 12 March 1999

Poland, Hungary and the Czech Republic became members of NATO on 12 March 1999 at a signing ceremony held in the American town of Independence, Missouri, where NATO had been founded on 4 April 1949. This move increased NATO's membership from sixteen to nineteen states and played well with the public in the new Member States, which naturally interpreted it as a mark of strong Western approval for their headway in developing liberal parliamentary democracies and largely marketized economies.

However, the former president of the Soviet Union, Mikhail Gorbachev, declared that he felt 'betrayed' by this eastward enlargement of NATO and accused the West of humiliating Russia and taking advantage of its current weakness in a manner resembling the Allies' treatment of defeated Germany after the Second World War (*IHT*, 13 March 1999, p. 4). This 'eastward enlargement' of NATO did indeed breach the promise which the leaders of the Western democracies had given to Gorbachev in November 1990, when as Soviet president he had gracefully acceded to Western calls for the rapid reunification of Germany and the rapid and complete withdrawal of Soviet forces from Germany, in return for a solemn undertaking from the Western leaders that NATO would *not* be expanded eastwards. Nevertheless, the Yeltsin regime prudently decided to make the best of a bad job. It accepted that it was unable to prevent the eastward enlargement of NATO. It ended its boycott on contacts with NATO on 23 July 1999 by taking part in a NATO meeting in Brussels. When NATO secretary general George Robertson visited Russia on 16 February 2000, he and President Vladimir Putin issued a joint statement that 'the two sides aimed to intensify their contacts and become a cornerstone of European security' (*FT*, 17 February 2000, p. 12). There was growing recognition by the Russian establishment that Russia (like the West) had a direct interest in promoting security and stability in East Central Europe and that this could be achieved through NATO membership. In practice, even though elite opinion in Russia has (understandably) been more sensitive and prickly about eastward enlargement of NATO than about eastward enlargement of the EU, the latter has been more damaging than the former to Russia's long-term interests, because eastward enlargement of the EU is what really increases Russia's marginalization in European affairs, leaving it sidelined in an increasingly integrated Europe. However, prickliness and sensitivity over Russia's hugely diminished military and territorial standing seems to have blinded much of Russia's elite to the greater real threat to Russia's future standing posed by eastward enlargement of the EU.

Admittedly, Russia was unlikely to aspire to become a member of the EU in the foreseeable future. As a major Asian and Pacific power, Russia had other 'fish to fry'. Nevertheless, even if it is too large and problematic to be accommodated within the EU, the West would be unwise to try to freeze Russia (or Ukraine, for that matter) out of the 'common European home'. This would amount to a new Yalta. Moreover, there can be no lasting security for East Central Europe, the Baltic States or the Balkans so long as Russia remains a 'loose cannon'. If the main justification for binding Germany ever more closely into the EC and the EU has been that Europe cannot afford to have a German loose cannon rolling around on the European deck, this logic applies just as strongly to Russia. We should therefore be moving towards a barrier-free 'single European space', linking together several regional sub-groupings with varying commitments to varying forms of deeper integration. So long as Russia remains 'out in the cold', NATO can offer the states in Russia's 'front yard' only illusory forms of security.

In 1996 Jack Matlock Jnr, the last American ambassador to the Soviet Union (1987–91), warned that: 'Much of recent Russian recalcitrance can be traced to a feeling that their country is being left out of the European security club. As a loner, Russia will always be a problem. Washington must reassure Moscow that it places a high priority on creating a European security structure to which Russia is a party. Whether that is done through a treaty relationship between Russia and NATO, an augmentation of the authority of the Organization for Security and Co-operation in Europe, or some other mechanism is less important than the commitment to include Russia . . . provided Russia does not threaten other countries or violate its OSCE obligations' (Matlock 1996: 49). The emphasis should be on creating a pan-European security structure and a barrier-free 'single European space', in which all who are willing and able to abide by a set of common rules and norms should be allowed to participate on an equal basis.

The NATO summit in Prague, 21–22 November 2002

At the NATO summit held in Prague on 21–22 November 2002, the first such meeting ever to be hosted by a former Communist country, formal invitations were extended to Estonia, Latvia, Lithuania, Bulgaria, Romania, Slovakia and Slovenia to become full members of NATO in May 2004 (allowing time for the ratification process). The seven new NATO members agreed to adhere to prescriptive 'Membership Action Plans' (MAPs) for several more years (*IHT*, 22 November 2002, p. 8). Albania and Macedonia were deemed to be next in line for NATO membership. A communiqué issued by the NATO leaders stated: 'We encourage both countries to redouble their reform efforts.' An entrance ticket was also dangled before Croatia, but it was warned that full co-operation with the ICTY in The Hague was a prerequisite. NATO leaders even hinted that Serbia could join the alliance eventually, although it would first have to join NATO's Partnership for Peace (*The Guardian*, 22 November 2002, p. 16). Thenceforth, NATO stipulated that henceforth all aspirants to NATO membership would *first* have to serve an apprenticeship in Partnership for Peace, and would later have to participate in the formalized Membership Action Plan (MAP) process (Greenwood 2005: 7).

The NATO summit in Vilnius, 29 November 2006

Here NATO leaders gave Croatia, Macedonia and Albania strong signals that they would be admitted as full members of NATO in 2008. In addition, the NATO leaders decided formally to invite Bosnia-Herzegovina, Montenegro and even Serbia to join the Partnership for Peace (PfP) programme, despite the fact that Belgrade had not yet arrested and handed over Ratko Mladic and Radovan Karadzic for trial by the ICTY. This move involved the United States, the UK and the Netherlands performing a dramatic volte-face, since they had been repeatedly telling Serbia that it could not join PfP until it complied with the requirements of the ICTY. This long-overdue policy reversal was undertaken in a last-ditch attempt to undercut support for the ultra-nationalist Serbian Radical Party in advance of the parliamentary elections which took place in Serbia in January 2007 (*IHT*, 30 November 2006, p. 4; *FT*, 30 November 2006, p. 6).

Our companion volume on the post-Communist Balkans, published two weeks before this NATO summit, fiercely criticized the hitherto prevailent Western hard-line policy requiring total Serbian and Croatian compliance with ICTY demands. In our view, this policy had merely served to strengthen popular support for unrepentant ultra-nationalists and to tear apart and undermine the liberal coalitions that had managed to gain power in Serbia and Croatia after termination of the authoritarian nationalist regimes of Slobodan Milosevic and Franjo Tudjman, respectively (Bideleux and Jeffries 2007: 231–2, 324–8). The hard-line policy was utterly counter-productive, and the NATO volte-face fully vindicated our criticisms.

Serbia, Montenegro and Bosnia were formally admitted into the PfP programme on 14 December 2006. PfP, which had originally been conceived *as a substitute* for NATO membership, had by this time become the crucial first *step towards* eventual membership. The NATO Secretary General, Jaap de Hoop Scheffer, declared that Bosnia had 'finally moved from the Dayton era to the Brussels era'. It was simultaneously reaffirmed that Croatia, Macedonia and Albania were expected to join NATO in 2008 (*IHT*, 15 December 2006, p. 3).

CONCLUSION

In the East Central European, Baltic and Balkan post-Communist states, cross-party consensuses on macro-economic policies, privatization, restructuring of institutions and industries, and judicial and legal reform have been gradually built and strengthened in response to the June 1993 'Copenhagen Criteria', which laid down that full-blown liberal democracy and liberal capitalism combined with the rule of law and respect and protection for human and minority rights were the prime preconditions for EU membership. This in turn has further promoted limited government, equal civil rights, equality before the law, political stability, more 'level playing-fields', and more fully marketized and liberalized economies. The drive towards EU membership has helped to consummate *the restructuring and reorientation* of the candidate states away from the dominant 'vertical' power relations and power structures and clannishly clientelistic conceptions of the polity, towards more horizontally structured civil societies and civil economies based upon limited government, the rule of law, and more impersonal ties. These major changes and 'adjustments' were inherently complex, painful and difficult, but they have nevertheless been accomplished to remarkable degrees and with impressive alacrity. Many of the inhabitants of these countries felt that they had been 'driven to change' (Dimitrova 2004: 1–8). Yet it was on this basis that eight of these countries were allowed to enter the EU in May 2004 and two more – Romania and Bulgaria – were allowed to enter in January 2007.

Pursuit and attainment of EU and NATO membership has helped to defuse century-old ethnic and territorial tensions between and within some of the new Member States. This in turn has contributed to major force reductions, abolition of military service, much freer movement, and enhanced levels of transparency and confidence, with the result that armed conflict and military coups are now almost unthinkable in East Central Europe, the Baltic region and the eastern Balkans, thereby stabilizing and civilianizing these states and fostering a more liberal and democratic ambience (Epstein and Gheciu 2006: 322–3; Vachudova 2005: 7). Having constructed a remarkably stable and robust supranational legal order with strong commitments to promote and protect fundamental human and minority rights and freedoms and non-discrimination between citizens, the eastward enlargement of the EU is strengthening rights and freedoms, the rule of law, and physical and psychological certainty and security in its new Member States.

These major positive changes have helped to offset indications that rates of membership in voluntary associations, levels of employment in the 'formal civil society sector', and levels of interpersonal trust have remained considerably lower in the East Central European, Baltic and Balkan post-Communist states than in most Western states (Tarrow and Petrova 2007: 76; Howard 2003: 80; Badescu and Uslaner 2003: 71, 89, 198). It is also noteworthy that the widely acclaimed democratization and liberalization of post-Francoist Spain, post-Salazarist Portugal and post-Pinochet Chile were accompanied by *comparatively low levels of membership in voluntary associations* (McDonough *et al.* 1998; Howard 2003: 80) and *comparatively high levels of interpersonal mistrust* – in the Portuguese and Chilean cases, considerably higher than in East Central Europe or even Russia (Badescu and Uslaner 2003: 71-2). Seen in this light, post-Communist democratization in East Central Europe was probably no less secure than the justly celebrated Iberian democratizations.

Furthermore, EU membership has locked the new member states into an institutional system which requires the maintenance of liberal forms of capitalism, the rule of law and (at the national and sub-national levels) liberal democracy. This can mitigate the numerous media reports since mid-2006 of a serious 'crisis of democracy' in the East Central European states, as well as mounting Western fears that these states may have been allowed to enter the EU prematurely and that they could now be 'slipping back into their bad old ways', after having been allowed entry. In many ways, this widely perceived 'crisis of democracy' in East Central Europe merely indicates that these states are beginning to face much the *same kinds* of difficulties as older West European democracies do in sustaining *substantive* (as distinct from purely *formal*) liberal democratic governance under conditions of advanced capitalism and high levels of global and regional integration. The Czech Republic, for example, has latterly experienced voter alienation, political apathy, low election turnouts, low or falling membership in political parties, widespread perceptions of official corruption, and the trivialization of media content (Drucker and Druckerova 2006). Such problems are also to be found in various supposed heartlands of Western liberal democracy, including the UK and the USA. It therefore makes more sense to regard them as problems of democratic 'maturity' than as part of the 'growing pains' of so-called 'new democracies'.

37 Epilogue: some final reflections on the fate of modernist projects in East Central Europe and the Balkans

The prevailing approaches to democratization and marketization in Europe's post-Communist states have misleadingly assumed that these projects can and should be contained within the existing national states. In practice, however, these supposedly 'national' units and processes will have to be supplemented in various ways if they are to be capable of retaining the semblance of national autonomy on which they depend. Most of the purportedly 'national' states that have been established in Eastern Europe since the late nineteenth century have not been 'self-made' states on the British and French models, but have owed their legitimacy and existence to international recognition (primarily from the Western Powers, but also from Russia, Germany, Turkey and Italy). Therefore, they have always found it difficult to sustain the claims that states usually make to exclusive jurisdiction over what they consider to be 'their own internal affairs' and to fend off external scrutiny of (and often interference in) their conduct of those affairs. Furthermore, in an increasingly globalized, regionalized and interdependent world, the locus of policy-making and decision-making is gradually shifting back from nation-states to international regulatory institutions such as the World Trade Organization, the IMF, the World Bank and NATO, and to macro-regional regulatory confederations such as the EU. As yet, however, there is not a great deal of democratic accountability in the workings of such international and macro-regional organizations. They remain essentially 'cartels of governments', which side-step democratic processes and take decisions over the heads of elected parliaments. However, since their policy-making and decision-making roles largely deal with matters that transcend national boundaries, it would not be very helpful or constructive to bring them within the jurisdiction of national parliaments. That would just be a recipe for chronic international or inter-parliamentary bickering, deadlock and immobilism. Increased national assertion can at best achieve only an illusion of increased democratic control of supranational policies, processes and organizations Chasing such chimeras can only reinforce beliefs that 'democracy does not work' and reduce public support for the democratic institutions on which Europe's post-Communist states have initially pinned their hopes.

The putative supranational alternatives propagated under the rubric of 'cosmopolitan democracy' are largely exercises in self-delusion and wishful thinking. To apply the term 'democracy' to international institutions run by appointed (rather than elected) officials simply empties it of any substantial content and/or meaning. The most that can be viably and realistically constructed in order to provide some effective constraints and/or limits on power and authority at the supranational level is a binding supranational framework of rules and law – a supranational 'civil association' or legal order, of which the most fully fledged example is the European Union (Bideleux 2000, 2001a, 2001b).

During the twentieth century the collapse of multinational empires often resulted in the fragmentation of their former territories into a profusion of small successor states animated by an upsurge of liberated nationalism. This was certainly the outcome in the Balkans and East Central Europe after the collapse of the Ottoman, Habsburg and Tsarist empires, and more recently in the Commonwealth of Independent States since the collapse of the Soviet empire. The decisive challenge facing politicians in these regions has been to find ways of accommodating ethnic loyalties and nationalism consistent with raising incomes and maintaining peace and security. The post-Communist governments of East Central Europe and the Balkans have wished to side-step this challenge by gaining rapid accession to the EU and NATO, but this is not enough. They also 'need to construct voluntary supranational organizations of their own that are strong enough to referee quarrels, to keep borders open to trade and to protect the human rights of minorities. They need to build a moral equivalent of the old empires' (*IHT* editorial, 10 June 1992, p. 8). The basis of their polities needs to be moved away from the building of rather exclusive, intolerant and egotistic 'ethnic' nation-states towards the construction of more open, inclusive and tolerant societies embedded in supranational and loosely confederal 'civil associations', if these region are to escape endemic conflict, instability, national messianism and the attendant dangers of a resurgence of various forms of authoritarianism, Caesarism and religious or ethno-cultural collectivism. Far from suggesting that this will be quickly and/or easily realizable, we are merely suggesting that it offers the only hope.

With regard to the historical significance of the end of Communist rule in the eastern half of Europe, we do not consider that this in any sense marked 'the end of history' or the final irreversible triumph of liberal democracy. The 'demons' of nationalist and religious exclusiveness, intolerance and bigotry are still very much alive, and it may be premature to write the 'final obituaries' on Communism. After all, when Zhou Enlai was asked what was the significance of the French Revolution of 1789, he famously replied that it was still 'too early to say'. Instead, we share the view that the collapse of Communist rule in Europe marked the termination of one of the most extreme expressions of the various 'modernist projects' set in motion by the Renaissance and the Enlightenment. In the words of Vaclav Havel in February 1992, 'The modern era has been dominated by the belief, expressed in different forms, that the world – and Being as such – is a wholly knowable system governed by a finite number of universal Laws that man can group and rationally direct for his own benefit. This era, beginning in the Renaissance and developing from the Enlightenment to socialism, from positivism to scientism, from the Industrial Revolution to the information revolution, was characterized by rapid advances in rational, cognitive thinking. This, in turn, gave rise to the proud belief that Man, as the pinnacle of everything that exists, was capable of objectively describing, explaining and controlling everything that exists, and of possessing the one and only truth about the world. It was an era . . . of belief in automatic progress brokered by the scientific method. It was an era of systems . . . It was an era of ideologies, doctrines, interpretations of reality, an era when the goal was to find a universal theory of the world and thus a universal key to unlock its prosperity. Communism was the perverse extreme of this trend' (Havel 1994b: 177).

Marx and Engels fondly believed that 'the rational order dreamt of by the Enlightenment, based on consent and truth, not only *could* come about, but in the end inevitably *would* come about' (Gellner 1996: 35). The Communist parties and regimes saw themselves as the ultimate secular scientocracies of the new age, the culmination of the drive to place Man (ultimately, just one man – and never a woman!) in control of everything. The degeneration and collapse of Europe's Communist regimes dramatically exposed the hollowness, the fraudulence and the self-delusions behind such claims, and also delivered a powerful warning to those who would rush in to fill the Communists' vacated 'shoes' and podia. Nevertheless, it is still too soon to announce the death of the modernist project. Neo-liberal 'market fundamentalists' who dogmatically believe that secular laissez-faire capitalism (rather than Communism or fascism) holds the keys that will unlock the secrets of prosperity, peace and social as well as scientific and technological progress are still in its thrall. So are the latter-day champions of unilinear and/or 'top-down' modernization and democratization theories. It cannot be assumed that 'market fundamentalism' and laissez-faire capitalism or dogmatic doctrines and conceptions of democratization will always carry all before them or that they can furnish 'all the answers'. The moral is *caveat emptor*. Beware of doctrines claiming to have found the universal cognitive keys and panaceas. They are most likely to lead to tyranny and to endanger both humans and Nature.

BIBLIOGRAPHY

* Asterisks denote strongly recommended further reading, including those works which have deeply influenced Robert Bideleux, the main author of this book.

MAIN PERIODICALS, NEWSPAPERS AND REPORTS USED

Business Central Europe (BCE)
Transition Reports (EBRD)
The Economist
Eastern Europe Newsletter (EEN)
Financial Times (FT)
The Guardian
International Herald Tribune (IHT)

BOOKS AND JOURNAL ARTICLES

*Abou-El-Haj, R.A. (1991) *Formation of the Ottoman State*, Albany, N.Y.: SUNY Press.

Abramsky, C., Jachiczyk, M. and Polonsky, A. (eds) (1984) *The Jews in Poland*, Oxford: Blackwell.

Acton, J.E.E.D. (Lord Acton) (1956) *Essays on Freedom and Power*, London: Thames and Hudson.

Aganbegyan, A. (1988) *The Challenge: Economics of Perestroika*, London: Hutchinson.

Agh, A. (1998) *Processes of Democratization in the Central European and Balkan States*, Budapest: Hungarian Centre for Democracy Studies.

*—— (2003) *Anticipatory and Adaptive Europeanization in Hungary*, Budapest: Hungarian Centre for Democracy Studies.

*Aké, C. (1995) 'The democratisation of disempowerment in Africa', in J. Hippler (ed.), *The Democratisation of Disempowerment*, London: Pluto, pp. 70–89.

Aksakov, K. (1889) *Polnoye sobranie sochinenii*, vol. I, Moscow.

Aldcroft, D. and Morewood, S. (1993) 'Eastern Europe since Versailles', *Economic Review*, vol. 10, no. 3.

—— (1995) *Economic Change in Eastern Europe since 1918*, Cheltenham: Edward Elgar.

Ali, R. and Lifschultz, L. (1994) 'Why Bosnia?', *Third World Quarterly*, vol. 15, no. 3, pp. 367–401.

Ali, T. (ed.) (2000) *Masters of the Universe? NATO's Balkan Crusade*, London: Verso.

*Allcock, J. (2000) 'Constructing the Balkans', in J. Allcock and A. Young (eds), *Black Lambs and Grey Falcons*, Oxford: Berghahn, pp. 217–40.

Alperovitz, G. (1995) *The Decision to Use the Atomic Bomb*, London: Fontana.

*Anderson, P. (1979) *Lineages of the Absolute State*, London: Verso.

Andreades, A. (1948) 'The economic life of the Byzantine Empire', in Baynes and Moss (1948).

Andric, I. (1949) *The Bridge over the Drina*, London: George Allen and Unwin; originally published Belgrade: Prosveta, 1945.

Antohi, S. and Tismaneanu, V. (eds) (2000) *Between Past and Future: The Revolutions of 1989 and their Aftermath*, Budapest: Central European University Press.

Arendt, H. (1966) *The Origins of Totalitarianism*, 3rd edn, New York: Harcourt, Brace and World.

Arnakis, G. (1963) 'The role of religion in the development of Balkan nationalism', in Jelavich and Jelavich (1963).

Arter, D. (1993) *The Politics of European Integration in the Twentieth Century*, Aldershot: Dartmouth.

*Ascherson, N. (1988) *The Struggles for Poland*, London: Pan.

—— (1995) *Black Sea*, London: Jonathan Cape.

Ashdown, P. (2006) 'The way ahead for Europe and the western Balkans', lecture delivered by Lord Paddy Ashdown at the London School of Economics, 8 March 2006.

Åslund, A. (1994) 'Lessons of the first four years of systemic change in Eastern Europe', *Journal of Comparative Economics*, vol. 19, no. 1.

Aston, T. (ed.) (1965) *Crisis in Europe, 1560–1660*, London: Routledge and Kegan Paul.

Ausch, S. (1972) *Theory and Practice of CMEA Co-operation*, Budapest: Akademiai Kiado.

Avakumic, I. (1971) 'Yugoslavia's fascist movements', in Sugar (1971b).

Babeti, A. and Ungureanu, C. (eds) (1998) *Europa Centrala: Memorie, paradis, apocalipsa,* Bucharest: Polirom.

Babinger, F. (1978) *Mehmed the Conqueror and his Time*, Princeton: Princeton University Press.

Badescu, G. and Uslaner, E. (eds) (2003) *Social Capital and the Transition to Democracy*, London: Routledge.

*Bakic-Hayden, M. (1995) 'Nesting orientalisms: the case of former Yugoslavia', *Slavic Review*, vol. 54, no. 4, pp. 917–31.

*—— (2002) 'What's so Byzantine about the Balkans?', in Bjelic and Savic (2002) pp. 61–78.

*Bakic-Hayden, M. and Hayden, R.M. (1992) 'Orientalist variations on the theme "Balkans": symbolic geography in recent Yugoslav cultural politics,' *Slavic Review*, vol. 51, no. 1, pp. 1–15.

Balcerowicz, L. (1989) 'Polish economic reform, 1981–88: an overview', in Economic Commission for Europe (1989).

—— (1993) 'Transition to market economy: Central and East European countries in comparative perspective', *British Review of Economic Issues*, vol. 15, no. 37.

—— (1994) 'Common fallacies in the debate on the transition to a market economy', *Economic Policy*, vol. 9, no. 19 (supplement), pp. 16–50.

Baldwin, R. (1994) *Towards an Integrated Europe*, London: CEPR.

Barany, G. (1967) 'Hungary: the uncompromising compromise', *Austrian History Yearbook*, vol. 3, part 1, pp. 234–59.

—— (1971) 'The dragon's teeth: the roots of Hungarian fascism', in Sugar (1971b).

*Barford, P. (2001) *The Early Slavs: Culture and Society in Early Medieval Eastern Europe*, London: British Museum Press.

—— (2005) 'Silent centuries: the society and economy of the northwestern Slavs', in Curta (2005) pp. 60–102.

Bartha, I. (1975) 'The development of the bourgeois national reform movement' and 'Towards bourgeois transformation, revolution and war of independence, 1790–1849', in Pamlenyi (1975).

Basch, A. (1944) *The Danube Basin and the German Economic Sphere*, London: Kegan Paul.

Batt, J. (1988) *Economic Reform and Political Change in Eastern Europe: A Comparison of the Czechoslovak and Hungarian Experiences*, London: Macmillan.

—— (1991) *East Central Europe from Reform to Transformation*, London: Pinter (Chatham House Papers: Royal Institute of International Affairs).

—— (1994a) 'The international dimension of democratization in Czechoslovakia and Hungary', in Pridham *et al.* (1994).

—— (1994b) 'The political transformation of East Central Europe', in Miall (1994).

*Bauer, O. (1925) *The Austrian Revolution*, London: Leonard Parsons.

Baynes, N. and Moss, H. (eds) (1948) *Byzantium: An Introduction to East Roman Civilization*, Oxford: Clarendon Press.

Beardmore, W. trans. (1948) 'Manifesto of the first Slavonic Congress to the Nations of Europe', *Slavonic Review*, vol. 26, no. 67, pp. 303–13.

Beevor, A. (2002) *Berlin: The Downfall, 1945*, rev. edn, London: Penguin.

Beevor, A. and Vinogradova, L. (2006) *A Writer at War: Vassily Grossman with the Red Army, 1941–1945*, London: Pimlico Press.

Bell, J.D. (1977) *Peasants in Power: Alexander Stambolinski and the Bulgarian Agrarian National Union, 1899–1923*, Princeton: Princeton University Press.

Ben-Ner, A. and Neuberger, E. (1990) 'The feasibility of planned market systems: the Yugoslav visible hand and negotiated planning', *Journal of Comparative Economics*, vol. 14, no. 4.

*Berend, I. (1986) 'The historical evolution of Eastern Europe as a region', *International Organization*, vol. 40, no. 2, pp. 329–46.

Berend, I. and Ranki, G. (1969) 'Economic problems of the Danube region after the break-up of the Austro-Hungarian Monarchy', *Journal of Contemporary History*, vol. 4, no. 3, pp. 169–85.

*—— (1974a) *Economic Development in East-Central Europe in the Nineteenth and Twentieth Centuries*, New York: Columbia University Press.

—— (1974b) *Hungary: A Century of Economic Development*, Newton Abbot: David and Charles.

Berktay, H. and Faroqi, S. (eds) (1991) 'New approaches to state and peasant in Ottoman history', *Journal of Peasant Studies*, vol. 13, nos 3–4 (special issue), pp. 1–263.

Bernal, Martin (1987–91) *Black Athena: The Afro-Asian Roots of Classical Civilization, vols I–II*, London: Free Association Press.

Betts, R. (1931) 'The Regulae Veteris et Novi Testamenti of Matej z Janova', *Journal of Theological Studies*, vol. 32, no. 128, pp. 344–51.

*—— (1947) 'The place of the Czech Reformation in the history of Europe', *Slavonic and East European Review*, vol. 25, no. 65, pp. 372–90.

Bialostocki, J. (1985) 'Borrowing and originality in the East-Central European Renaissance', in Maczak *et al.* (eds) (1985).

Bideleux, R. (1987) *Communism and Development*, London: Methuen. [First published 1985.]

—— (1990) 'Agricultural advance under the Russian village commune system', in R. Bartlett (ed.), *Land Commune and Peasant Community in Russia*, London: Macmillan, pp. 196–218.

—— (1994) 'Alexander II and the emancipation of the serfs', in P. Catterall and R. Vine (eds), *Europe 1870–1914*, London: Heinemann, pp. 13–24.

—— (1996) 'The southern enlargement of the EC: Spain, Portugal and Greece', in Bideleux and Taylor (1996) pp. 127–53.

—— (1999) 'La Grèce: Ni intérêts nationaux, ni idéaux fédéralistes', in A. Landuyt (ed.), *Europe: Fédération ou nations*, Paris: SEDES, pp. 205–27.

—— (2000) 'Dopo la democrazia: l'Unione Europea come ordine giuridico liberale sovranazionale', in A. Landuyt (ed.), *L'Unione Europea tra rifflessione storica e prospettive politiche e sociali,* Siena: Protagon Editori, pp. 15–48.

—— (2001a) 'Civil association: the European Union as a supranational liberal legal order', in M. Evans (ed.), *The Edinburgh Companion to Contemporary Liberalism*, Edinburgh: Edinburgh University Press, pp. 225–40.

—— (2001b) 'Europeanization and the limits to democratization in East-Central Europe', in G. Pridham and A. Agh (eds), *Prospects for Democratic Consolidation in East-Central Europe*, Manchester: Manchester University Press, pp. 25–53.

—— (2001c) 'What does it mean to be European? The problems of constructing a pan-European identity', in G. Timmins and M. Smith (eds), *Uncertain Europe*, London: Routledge, pp. 20–40.

—— (2002a) 'Extending the European Union's cosmopolitan supranational legal order eastwards: the main significance of the forthcoming eastward enlargement of the European Union', in M. M. Tavares Ribeiro (ed.), *Identidade Europeia e Multiculturalismo*, Coimbra: Quarteto, pp. 129–64.

—— (2002b) 'The new politics of inclusion and exclusion: the limits and divisions of Europe', in A. Plesu and L. Boia (eds), *Nation and National Ideology: Past, Present and Prospects*, Bucharest: New Europe College, pp. 28–49.

—— (2003) 'Imigração, multiculturalismo e xenofobia na União Européia: Para um estado policial europeu?', in M.M. Tavares Ribeiro (ed.), *Europa em Mutação*, Coimbra: Quarteto, 2003, pp. 243–61.

—— (2004) 'Tra oriente e occidente: la Grecia e l'integrazione europea', in A. Landuyt (ed.), *Idee d'Europa e integrazione europea*, Bologna: Il Mulino, pp. 299–342.

—— (2005a) 'The Balkans and the European Union: a difficult road', in A. Landuyt and D. Pasquinucci (eds), *Gli allargamenti della CEE/UE, 1961–2004*, vol. I, Bologna: Il Mulino, pp. 659–83.

—— (2005b) 'Denmark's ambiguous roles in the eastward enlargement of the European Union: from Copenhagen to Copenhagen', in A. Landuyt and D. Pasquinucci (eds), *Gli allargamenti della CEE/UE, 1961–2004*, vol. I, Bologna: Il Mulino, pp. 263–87.

—— (2007) '"Making democracy work" in the eastern half of Europe: explaining and conceptualizing divergent trajectories of post-communist democratization', *Perspectives on European Politics and Societies*, summer 2007.

Bideleux, R. and Jeffries, I. (1996) 'Nationalism and the post-1989 transitions to democracy and market economies in the Balkans: a historical perspective', in Jeffries (ed.) (1996) pp. 173–92.

—— (1998) *A History of Eastern Europe: Crisis and Change*, 1st edn, Abingdon: Routledge.

—— (2007) *The Balkans: A Post-Communist History*, Abingdon: Routledge.

Bideleux, R. and Taylor, R. (eds) (1996) *European Integration and Disintegration: East and West*, London: Routledge.

Biermann, R. (1999) 'The Stability Pact for south eastern Europe: potential, problems and perspectives', Discussion Paper C56, Zentrum für Europäische Integrationsforschung, Rheinische Friedrich Wilhelms-Universität, Bonn.

Biraben, J.N. and Le Goff, J. (1975) 'The plague of the Early Middle Ages', in R. Forster and C. Ranum (eds), *Biology of Man in History*, Baltimore: Johns Hopkins University Press, pp. 48–80.

Birnbaum, H. (1993) 'On the ethnogenesis and protohome of the Slavs: the linguistic evidence', *Journal of Slavic Linguistics*, vol. 1, no. 2, pp. 352–74.

Bizzell, W. (1926) *The Green Rising*, New York: Macmillan.

*Bjelic, D. and Savic, O. (eds) (2002) *Balkan as a Metaphor: Between Globalization and Fragmentation*, Cambridge, Mass.: MIT Press.

Black, C. (1963) 'Russia and the modernization of the Balkans', in Jelavich and Jelavich (1963).

Blanchard, I. (1989) *Russia's Age of Silver: Precious Metal Production and Economic Growth in the Eighteenth Century*, London: Routledge.

Blum, J. (1957) 'The rise of serfdom in eastern Europe', *American Historical Review*, vol. 62, no. 4, pp. 807–36.

—— (1978) *The End of the Old Order in Rural Europe*, Princeton: Princeton University Press.

Bogucka, M. (1982) 'Polish towns between the sixteenth and eighteenth centuries', in Fedorowicz (1982).

Bomberg, E. and Stubb, A. (eds) (2003) *The European Union: How Does It Work?*, Oxford: Oxford University Press.

Booth, K. (ed.) (2001) *The Kosovo Tragedy: The Human Rights Dimension*, London: Frank Cass.

Bourne, K. (1970) *The Foreign Policy of Victorian England*, Oxford: Clarendon Press.

Brabant, J. van (1980) *Socialist Economic Integration*, Cambridge: Cambridge University Press.

—— (1989) *Economic Integration in Eastern Europe*, London: Harvester Wheatsheaf.

—— (1991) 'Renewal of co-operation and economic transition in Eastern Europe', *Studies in Comparative Communism*, vol. 24, no. 2.

—— (1993) 'Lessons from the wholesale transformations in the East', *Comparative Economic Studies*, vol. 35, no. 4.

—— (1994) 'Trade, integration and transformation in Eastern Europe', *Journal of International Affairs*, vol. 48, no. 1.

Brada, J. (1985) 'Soviet subsidization of Eastern Europe: the primacy of politics over economics', *Journal of Comparative Economics*, vol. 9, no. 1, pp. 80–92.

—— (1988) 'Interpreting Soviet subsidization of Eastern Europe', *International Organization*, vol. 42, no. 4, pp. 639–58.

Bradley, J. (1971) *Czechoslovakia: A Short History*, Edinburgh: Edinburgh University Press.

Braham, R. (1994a) *The Politics of Genocide: The Holocaust in Hungary*, 2nd edn, New York: Columbia University Press.

—— (1994b) *The Tragedy of Romanian Jewry*, New York: Columbia University Press.

—— (1997) 'The Holocaust in Hungary: a retrospective analysis', in Cesarani (1997) pp. 29–46.

—— (2001) 'Hungary and the Holocaust: the nationalist drive to whitewash the past' (Part 1) in *East European Perspectives*, Radio Free Europe/Radio Liberty Reports, vol. 3, no. 18, http://www.rferl.org/reports/eepreport/2001/10/18–171001.asp, accessed on 4 April 2006.

—— (ed.) (2004) *The Treatment of the Holocaust in Hungary and Romania during the Communist Era*, East European Monographs, New York: Columbia University Press.

Brand, W. (ed.) (2001) *Thou Shalt Not Kill: Poles on Jedwabne*, Warsaw: Towarzystwo 'Wiez'.

Brandt, W. (1968) 'A peace policy for Europe', in K. Harprecht (ed.), *Willy Brandt: Portrait and Self-Portrait*, London: Abelard-Schuman (1972).

—— (1978) *People and Politics: The Years 1960–1975*, London: Collins.

Braudel, F. (1975) *The Mediterranean and the Mediterranean World in the Age of Philip II*, 2 vols, London: Collins-Fontana.

*—— (1981, 1982, 1984) *Civilization and Capitalism, 15th–18th Century*, 3 vols, London: Collins.

*—— (1995) *A History of Civilizations*, Harmondsworth: Penguin.

Brenner, R. (1989) 'Economic backwardness in Eastern Europe in the light of developments in the West', in Chirot (1989).

Brentano, H. van (1964) *Germany and Europe*, London: André Deutsch.

Brittan, L. (1994) *Europe: The Europe We Need*, London: Hamish Hamilton.

Brock, P. (1957) *The Political and Social Doctrines of the Unity of Brethren*, Gravenhage: Mouton.

Brotton, J. (2002) *The Renaissance Bazaar*, Oxford: Oxford University Press.

Broussolle, D. (2005) 'L'Agriculture française a-t-elle des raisons de craindre l'élargissement et les réformes de la PAC?', in A. Landuyt and D. Pasquinucci (eds), *Gli allargamenti della CEE/UE, 1961–2004*, vol. II, Bologna: Il Mulino, pp. 943–66.

Brown, J. (1970) *Bulgaria under Communist Rule*, New York: Praeger.

—— (1991) *Surge to Freedom*, London: Adamantine Press.

Brown, L.C. (ed.) (1996) *Imperial Legacy: The Ottoman Impact on the Balkans and the Middle East*, New York: Columbia University Press.

*Brown, P. (1971) *The World of Late Antiquity*, London: Thames and Hudson.

*Browning, C. (2005) *The Origins of the Final Solution*, London: Arrow Books.

Browning, R. (1975) *Byzantium and Bulgaria*, London: Temple Smith.

Brubaker, R. (1992) *Citizenship and Nationhood in France and Germany*, Cambridge, Mass.: Harvard University Press, 1992.

—— (1996) *Nationalism Reframed*, Cambridge: Cambridge University Press.

Brucan, S. (2000) *Romania in deriva*, Bucharest: Editura Nemira.

Bryant, C. and Mokrzycki, E. (1994) *The New Great Transformation: Change and Continuity in East-Central Europe*, London: Routledge.

Brzezinski, Z. (1967) *The Soviet Bloc*, Cambridge, Mass.: Harvard University Press.

Bugajski, J. (1995) *Nations in Turmoil: Conflict and Co-operation in Eastern Europe*, Boulder, Col.: Westview Press.

Bulliet, R. (2004) *The Case for Islamo-Christian Civilization*, New York: Columbia University Press.

Bulmer, S. and Lequesne, C. (eds) (2005) *The Member States of the European Union*, Oxford: Oxford University Press.

Burgess, A. (1999) 'Critical reflections on the return of minority rights regulation to East/West affairs', in K. Cordell (ed.), *Ethnicity and Democratization in the New Europe*, London: Routledge.

Burke, U.P. (1985) 'Introduction: A Note on the Historiography of East Central Europe', in Maczak *et al.* (eds) (1985).

Burnheim, J. (1985) *Is Democracy Possible?*, Cambridge: Polity Press.

Callinicos, A. (1991) *The Revenge of History*, Cambridge: Polity Press.

Cameron, R. (1966) *Banking in the Early Stages of Industrialization*, Oxford: Oxford University Press.

Campbell, J. (1963) 'The Balkans: heritage and continuity', in Jelavich and Jelavich (eds) (1963).

Carabott, P. (ed.) (1995) *Greece and Europe in the Modern Period: Aspects of a Troubled Relationship*, London: Centre for Hellenic Studies, King's College.

Carr, E. (1945) *Nationalism and After*, London: Macmillan.

Carsten, F. (1967) *The Rise of Fascism*, London: Batsford.

Catchlove, D. (1972) *Romania's Ceausescu*, Tunbridge Wells: Abacus Press.

Cesarani, D. (ed.) (1994) *The Final Solution: Origins and Implementation*, London: Routledge.

—— (ed.) (1997) *Genocide and Rescue: The Holocaust in Hungary, 1944,* Oxford: Berg.

Chandler, D. (1999) *Bosnia: Faking Democracy after Dayton*, London: Pluto Press.

Chary, F.B. (1972) *The Bulgarian Jews and the Final Solution, 1940–44*, Pittsburgh, Pa.: University of Pittsburgh Press.

Chesterton, G.K. (1923) 'Introduction', in Irvine (1923).

Childs, D. (1988) *The GDR: Moscow's German Ally*, 2nd edn, London: Unwin Hyman.

Chirot, D. (ed.) (1989a) 'Causes and consequences of backwardness', in Chirot (1989b).

—— (1989b) *The Origins of Backwardness in Eastern Europe: Economics and Politics from the Middle Ages until the Early Twentieth Century*, Berkeley: University of California Press.

Churchill, W. (1989) *The Second World War*, Harmondsworth: Penguin.

Cipolla, C. (1970a) *The Economic Decline of Empires*, London: Methuen.

—— (1970b) *European Culture and Overseas Expansion*, Harmondsworth: Penguin.

—— (1976a) *Before the Industrial Revolution*, London: Methuen.

—— (ed.) (1976b) *The Fontana Economic History of Europe, vol. V: The Twentieth Century, Part One*, V Glasgow: Collins-Fontana.

—— (ed) (1976c) *The Fontana Economic History of Europe, vol. V: The Twentieth Century, Part Two*, V Glasgow: Collins-Fontana.

Clague, C. and Rausser, G. (eds) (1992) *The Emergence of Market Economies in Eastern Europe*, Oxford: Blackwell.

Clapham, J. and Power, E. (eds) (1942) *The Cambridge Economic History of Europe from the Decline of the Roman Empire*, Cambridge: Cambridge University Press.

Clissold, S. (ed.) (1968) *A Short History of Yugoslavia*, Cambridge: Cambridge University Press.

Clogg, R. (1992) *A Concise History of Modern Greece*, Cambridge: Cambridge University Press.

Cobban, A. (1969) *The Nation State and National Self-Determination*, Glasgow: Collins.

Cochrane, N. (1993) 'Central European agrarian reforms in a historical perspective', *American Journal of Agricultural Economics*, vol. 75, no. 3, pp. 851–6.

Cohan, A. (1975) *Theories of Revolution*, London: Nelson.

Cohen, L. (1993) *Broken Bonds: Yugoslavia's Disintegration and Balkan Politics in Transition*, Boulder, Colo.: Westview Press.

—— (2002) *Serpent in the Bosom: The Rise and Fall of Slobodan Milosevic*, Boulder, Colo.: Westview Press.

Cole, G.D.H. (1941) *Europe, Russia and the Future*, London: Gollancz.

Coles, P. (1968) *The Ottoman Impact on Europe*, London: Thames and Hudson.

Collingwood, R. (1946) *The Idea of History*, Oxford: Clarendon Press.

—— (1994) *The Idea of History*, rev. edn (with lectures, 1926–8) Oxford: Oxford University Press.

Comecon (1984) *Statisticheski ezhegodnik stran-chlenov Soveta ekonomicheskoi vzaimopomoshchi*, Moscow: Comecon Secretariat.

Comintern (1929) *The Programme of the Communist International, 1928*, London: Modern Books.

Connor, W. (1979) *Socialism, Politics and Equality: Hierarchy and Change in Eastern Europe and the USSR*, New York: Columbia University Press.

Contogeorgis, G. (2003) 'La Grèce moderne: un paradigme national issu du cosmosystème hellénique', *Pôle sud*, no. 18, pp. 113–30.

Cornwell, J. (2000) *Hitler's Pope: The Secret History of Pius XII*, Harmondsworth: Penguin, 2000.

Coudenhove-Kalergi, R. (1926) *Pan Europe*, New York: Knopf.

Covic, B. (ed.) (1991) *Croatia between War and Independence*, Zagreb: Skolska knjiga.

Crainic, N. (1938) 'Programmul statului etnocratic', in his *Ortodoxie si etnocratie*, Bucharest: Cugetarea, 1938; reissued 1997, Bucharest: Albatros.

*Crampton, R. (1994) *Eastern Europe in the Twentieth Century*, London: Routledge.

—— (1997) *A Concise History of Bulgaria*, Cambridge: Cambridge University Press.

*—— (2002) *The Balkans since the Second World War*, London: Longman.

Croan, M. (1989) 'Lands-in-between: the politics and cultural identity in contemporary Eastern Europe', *East European Politics and Societies*, vol. 3, no. 2, pp. 176–97.

*Curta, F. (2001) *The Making of the Slavs: History and Archeology of the Lower Danube Region*, Cambridge: Cambridge University Press.

*—— (ed.) (2005) *East Central and Eastern Europe in the Early Middle Ages*, Ann Arbor: University of Michigan Press.

—— (2006) *Southeastern Europe in the Middle Ages, 500–1250*, Cambridge: Cambridge University Press.

Czernin, O. (1920) *In the World War*, New York: Harper and Brothers.

Czobor-Lupp, M. and Lupp, J.S. (eds) (2002) *Moral, Legal and Political Values in Romanian Culture*, Romanian Philosophical Studies 4, Washington, D.C.: Council for Research in Values and Philosophy.

Dalrymple, W. (2005) 'Foreword', in MacLean (2005) pp. i–xxv.

Darby, H.C. (1976) 'Medieval and Turkish Greece', in Heurtley *et al.* (1967), pp. 35–51, 77–90.

—— (1968) chapters 1–8 of Clissold (1968), pp. 8–153.

*Davies, N. (1981a) *God's Playground: A History of Poland, vol. I: The Origins to 1795*, Oxford: Clarendon Press.

*—— (1981b) *God's Playground: A History of Poland, vol. II: 1795 to the Present*, Oxford: Clarendon Press.

—— (1986) *Heart of Europe: A Short History of Europe*, Oxford: Oxford University Press.

—— (2006) *Europe East and West*, Oxford: Oxford University Press.

Davy, R. (ed.) (1992) *European Détente: A Reappraisal*, London: Sage/RIIA.

Dawisha, K. (1990) *Eastern Europe, Gorbachev and Reform*, Cambridge: Cambridge University Press.

Dawisha, K. and Parrot, B. (eds) (1997a) *The Consolidation of Democracy in East-Central Europe*, Cambridge: Cambridge University Press.

*—— (eds) (1997b) *Politics, Power, and the Struggle for Democracy in South-East Europe*, Cambridge: Cambridge University Press.

Deak, I. (1967) 'Comment', *Austrian History Yearbook*, vol.3, part 1, pp. 303–8.

*—— (1979) *The Lawful Revolution: Lajos Kossuth and the Hungarians, 1848–49*, New York: Columbia University Press.

—— (2000) 'Introduction' and 'A Fatal Compromise? The Debate over Collaboration and Resistance in Hungary', in Deak *et al.* (2000), pp. 3–14, 39–73.

—— (2001) 'Heroes and Victims', *New York Review of Books*, vol. 48, no. 9, 31 May.

*Deak, I., Gross, J. and Judt, T. (eds) (2000) *The Politics of Retribution in Europe: World War II and its Aftermath*, Princeton: Princeton University Press.

Dedijer, V. (1967) *The Road to Sarajevo*, London: Macgibbon and Kee.

Degras, J. (ed.) (1956) *The Communist International, 1919–1943, vol. I: Documents, 1919–22*, London: Oxford University Press.

—— (ed.) (1960) *The Communist International, 1919–1943, vol. II: Documents, 1923–28*, London: Oxford University Press.

—— (ed.) (1965) *The Communist International, 1919–1943, vol. III: Documents, 1929–43*, London: Oxford University Press.

Delaisy, F. (1924) *Les Deux Europes*, Paris.

Desai, P. (1986) 'Is the Soviet Union subsidizing Eastern Europe?', *European Economic Review*, vol. 30, no. 1, pp. 107–16.

Deutsch, K. (1969) *Nationalism and its Alternatives*, New York: Knopf.

Deutscher, I. (1966) *Stalin: A Political Biography*, Harmondsworth: Penguin.

Diehl, C. (1948) 'From AD 1204 to AD 1453' in Baynes and Moss (1948) *Byzantium: An Introduction to East Roman Civilization*, Oxford: Clarendon Press.

Dimitrov, V., Goetz, K.H., Wollmann, H., Zubek, R. and Brusis, M. (2006) *Governing after Communism: Institutions and Policymaking*, Lanham, Md.: Rowman and Littlefield.

*Dimitrova, A. (ed.) (2004) *Driven to Change: The European Union's Enlargement Viewed from the East*, Manchester: Manchester University Press.

Djilas, A. (1991) *The Contested Country: Yugoslav Unity and Communist Revolution, 1919–1953*, Cambridge, Mass.: Harvard University Press.

Djilas, M. (1957) *The New Class*, London: Thames and Hudson.

—— (1963) *Conversations with Stalin*, Harmondsworth: Penguin.

Djordjevic, D. (1971) 'Fascism in Yugoslavia, 1918–1941', in Sugar (1971b).

Dobre, A.M. and Coman, R. (eds) (2005) *Romania si integrarea europeana*, Iasi: Institutul European.

Dohan, M.R. (1976) 'The Economic Origins of Soviet Autarky, 1927/28–1934', *Slavic Review*, vol. 35, no. 4, pp. 603–35.

Dolukhanov, P. (1996) *The Early Slavs*, Harlow: Longman.

*Donia, R. and Fine, J. (1994) *Bosnia and Hercegovina*, London: Hurst.

Dragovic-Soso, J. (2002) *Saviours of the Nation: Serbia's Intellectual Opposition and the Revival of Nationalism*, Ithaca: McGill–Queens University Press.

Drakulic, S. (1993) *The Balkan Express*, New York: Norton.

Drucker, J. and Druckerova, A. (2006) 'Country report: the Czech Republic', in Freedom House, *National in Transit (2006)*. Available at http://www.freedomhouse.org.

Duby, G. (1974) *The Early Growth of the European Economy*, Ithaca: Cornell University Press.

Duchêne, F. (1965) 'Britain in a harder world', *Journal of Common Market Studies*, vol. 3, no. 3, pp. 315–28.

—— (1994) *Jean Monnet*, New York: Norton.

Dunn, A.W. (1994) 'The transition from polis to kastron in the Balkans', *Byzantine and Modern Greek Studies*, vol. 18, pp. 60–80.

Duray, M. (1989) 'The European ideal: reality or wishful thinking in Eastern Europe', in Schöpflin and Wood (1989).

Dvornik, F. (1962) *The Slavs in European History and Civilization*, New Brunswick: Rutgers University Press.

Dworkin, R. (1996) *Freedom's Law*, Cambridge, Mass.: Harvard University Press.

Dyker, D. and Vejvoda, I. (eds) (1996) *Yugoslavia and After*, London: Longman.

EBRD (2005a) *Transition Report: Update* (April), London: European Bank for Reconstruction and Development.

—— (2005b) *Transition Report*, London: European Bank for Reconstruction and Development.

—— (2006a) *Transition Report: Update* (April), London: European Bank for Reconstruction and Development.

—— (2006b) *Transition Report*, London: European Bank for Reconstruction and Development.

Economic Commission for Europe (1989) *Economic Reform in the European Centrally Planned Economies*, Economic Studies 1, New York: UN.

Eddie, S. (1985) 'Economic policy and economic development in Austria–Hungary, 1867–1913', in H.J. Habakkuk and M. Postan (eds) *The Cambridge Economic History of Europe*, vol. VIII, Cambridge: Cambridge University Press.

Engel, D. (1999) *The Third Reich and the Jews*, Harlow: Longman.

—— (2004) 'Introduction to the Hebrew edition of *Neighbors*', in Polonsky and Michlik (2004) pp. 408–13.

Epstein, R. and Gheciu, A. (2006) 'European security after the Cold War', in P. Heywood *et al.*, *Development in European Politics*, Basingstoke: Palgrave, pp. 318–36.

Estrin, S. (1983) *Self-management: Economic Theory and Yugoslav Practice*, Cambridge: Cambridge University Press.

—— (1991) 'Yugoslavia: the case of self-managing market socialism', *Journal of Economic Perspectives*, vol. 5, no. 4.

EU Commission (1997) 'Agenda 2000: for a stronger and wider Union', *Bulletin of the European Union*, Supplement 5/97, May 1997.

—— (2003) 'Communication from the Commission to the Council and the European Parliament: Wider Europe – Neighbourhood: A New Framework for Relations with our Eastern and Southern Neighbours', Brussels: Commission of the European Union, COM (2003) 104 Final.

—— (2004) 'Report from the Commission: The Stabilization and Association Process for South East Europe, Third Annual Report', Brussels: Commission of the European Union, 30.3.2004, COM (2004) 202 Final.

Europa (1992) *Eastern Europe and the Commonwealth of Independent States 1992*, London: Europa Publications.

European Council (1997) *Presidency Conclusions: Luxembourg European Council*, Brussels: European Union.

Evans, R. (1973) *Rudolph II and his World*, Oxford: Oxford University Press.

—— (1979) *The Making of the Habsburg Monarchy*, Oxford: Oxford University Press.

Evans, S.G. (1960) *A Short History of Bulgaria*, London: Lawrence and Wishart.

Fallmerayer, J.P. (1830) *Geschichte der Halbinsel Morea während des Mittlelalters*, vol. I, Stuttgart.

*Faroqhi, S. (1997) 'Crisis and change, 1590–1699', in H. Inalcik and D. Quataert (eds), *An Economic and Social History of the Ottoman Empire, 1300–1914*, vol. II, Cambridge: Cambridge University Press, pp. 411–636.

*—— (2004) *The Ottoman Empire and the World Around It*, London: I.B. Tauris.

*—— (2005) *Subjects of the Sultan: Culture and Daily Life in the Ottoman Empire*, London: I.B. Tauris.

Fedorowicz, J. (ed.) (1982) *A Republic of Nobles: Studies in Polish History to 1864*, Cambridge: Cambridge University Press.

Feher, F. (1988) 'Eastern Europe's long revolution against Yalta', *Eastern European Politics and Societies*, vol. 2, no. 1, pp. 1–35.

—— (1989) 'On making Central Europe', *Eastern European Politics and Societies*, vol. 3, no. 3, pp. 412–47.

Fellner, F. (1967) 'Comment', *Austrian History Yearbook*, vol. 3, part 3, pp. 238–49.

—— (1968) 'The dissolution of the Habsburg Monarchy and its significanace for the new order in Central Europe: a reappraisal', *Austrian History Yearbook*, vol. 4.

*Findley, C.V. (2005) *The Turks in World History*, Oxford: Oxford University Press.

Fine, J., jnr (1976) *The Bosnian Church: A New Interpretation*, Boulder, Colo.: Westview Press.

*—— (1987) *The Late Medieval Balkans: A Critical Survey from the Late Twelfth Century to the Ottoman Conquest*, Ann Arbor: University of Michigan Press.

*—— (1991) *The Early Medieval Balkans: A Critical Survey from the Sixth to the Late Twelfth Century*, Ann Arbor: University of Michigan Press.

*Finkel, C. (2005a) *Osman's Dream: The History of the Ottoman Empire, 1300–1923*, New York: Basic Books.

—— (2005b), ' "The treacherous cleverness of hindsight": myths of Ottoman decay', in MacLean (2005) pp. 148–74.

Fischer, F. (1967) *Germany's Aims in the First World War*, London: Chatto and Windus.

Fischer-Galati, S. (1963) 'Nationalism and *Kaisertreue*', *Slavic Review*, vol. 22, no. 1.

—— (ed.) (1970) *Man, State and Society in East European History*, New York: Praeger.

—— (1971) 'Fascism in Romania', in Sugar (1971b).

—— (1984) 'Autocracy, orthodoxy and nationality in the twentieth century: the Romanian case', in *East European Quarterly*, vol. 18, no. 1, pp. 25–33.

Fraenkel, J. (ed.) (1967) *The Jews of Austria*, London: Valentine Mitchell.

Frank, A.G. (1998) *ReOrient*, Berkeley: University of California Press.

Fukuyama, F. (1995) *Trust*, New York: Free Press.

Gaddis, J.L. (1997) *We Now Know: Rethinking Cold War History*, Oxford: Clarendon Press.

*Gagnon, V. (2004) *The Myth of Ethnic War: Serbia and Croatia in the 1990s*, Ithaca: Cornell University Press.

Gallagher, T. (2001) *Outcast Europe: The Balkans, 1789–1989*, London: Routledge.

—— (2003) *The Balkans since the Cold War: From Tyranny to Tragedy*, London: Routledge.

*—— (2005) *Theft of a Nation: Romania since Communism*, London: Hurst.

Garton Ash, T. (1986) 'Does Central Europe exist?', in Schöpflin and Wood (1989).

Gati, C. (1990) *The Bloc that Failed*, Bloomington: Indiana University Press.

Gellner, E. (1996) *Conditions of Liberty: Civil Society and its Rivals*, Harmondsworth: Penguin.

Georgiev, V. (1966) 'The Genesis of the Balkan Peoples', *Slavonic Review*, vol. 44, no. 103, pp. 285–97.

Geremek, B. (1982) 'Poland and the cultural geography of medieval Europe', in Fedorowicz (1982).

Gerolymatos, A. (2004) *The Balkan Wars*, Staplehurst: Spellmount.

Gerschenkron, A. (1962) *Economic Backwardness in Historical Perspective*, Cambridge, Mass.: Harvard University Press.

—— (1968) *Continuity in History and Other Essays*, Cambridge, Mass.: Harvard Unversity Press.

Gierowski, J. (1982) 'The international position of Poland in the seventeenth and eighteenth centuries', in Fedorowicz (1982).

Gimbutas, M. (1971) *The Slavs*, London: Thames and Hudson.

Glenny, M. (1990) *The Rebirth of History: Eastern Europe in the Age of Democracy*, Harmondsworth: Penguin.

—— (1992) *The Fall of Yugoslavia*, Harmondsworth: Penguin.

—— (1999) *The Balkans 1804–1999*, London: Granta.

Goetz, K. (2005) 'The new member states and the EU: responding to Europe', in Bulmer and Lequesne (2005), pp. 254–80.

Goffman, D. (2002) *The Ottoman Empire and Early Modern Europe*, Cambridge: Cambridge University Press.

Gojda, M. (1991) *The Ancient Slavs: Settlement and Society*, Edinburgh: Edinburgh University Press.

Goldhagen, D.J. (1996) *Hitler's Willing Executioners: Ordinary Germans and the Holocaust*, New York: Alfred Knopf.

—— (2002) *A Moral Reckoning: The Role of the Catholic Church in the Holocaust and its Unfulfilled Duty of Repair*, London: Little, Brown.

Goldstein, I. (1999) *Croatia: A History*, London: Hurst.

—— (2002) 'Invention and in(ter)vention: the rhetoric of Balkanization', in Bjelic and Savic (2002).

Goldsworthy, V. (1998) *Inventing Ruritania*, New Haven: Yale University Press.

Good, D. (1979) 'Issues in the study of Habsburg economic development', *East Central Europe*, vol. 6, no. 1.

—— (1980) 'Modern economic growth in the Habsburg Monarchy', *East Central Europe*, vol. 7, no. 2.

—— (1984) *The Economic Rise of the Habsburg Empire, 1850–1914*, Berkeley: University of California Press.

—— (1994) *Economic Transformation in Central and Eastern Europe*, London: Routledge.

Goody, J. (1996) *The East in the West*, Cambridge: Cambridge University Press.

Gorbachev, M. (1988) *Perestroika: New Thinking for our Country and the World*, London: Collins.

Gordy, E. (1999) *The Culture of Power in Serbia*, University Park, Pa.: Pennsylvania State University Press.

Gow, J. (1997) *Triumph of Lack of Will: International Diplomacy and the Yugoslav War*, London: Hurst.

Gower, J. (1999) 'EU policy to Central and Eastern Europe', in Henderson (1999), pp. 3–19.

Gramsci, A. (1971) *Selections from the Prison Notebooks*, London: Lawrence and Wishart.

Granick, D. (1975) *Enterprise Guidance in Eastern Europe*, Princeton: Princeton University Press.

Grant, M. (1978) *A History of Rome*, London: Book Club Associates.

Gray, J. (2000) *The Two Faces of Liberalism*, Cambridge: Polity Press.

Greenwood, D. (ed.) (2005) *The Western Balkan Candidates for NATO Membership and Partnership*, Harmonie Paper 18, Groningen: Centre of European Security Studies.

Gregor, A. (1969) *The Ideology of Fascism*, London: Collier-Macmillan.

—— (1979) *Italian Fascism and Developmental Dictatorship*, Princeton: Princeton University Press.

Grekov, B.D. (1959) *Kiev Rus*, Moscow: Foreign Languages Publishing House.

Grell, O. (1994) 'Scandinavia', in Scribner *et al.* (1994).

Griffin, R. (1993) *The Nature of Fascism*, London: Routledge.

Grochulska, B. (1982) 'The place of the Enlightenment in Polish social history', in Fedorowicz (1982).

Gross, F. (1945) *Crossroads of Two Continents*, London: Oxford University Press.

*Gross, J.T. (1979) *Polish Society under German Occupation: The Generalgouvernement, 1939–1944*, Princeton: Princeton University Press.

—— (2000) 'Themes for a social history of war experience and collaboration' and 'A tangled web: confronting stereotypes concerning relations between Poles, Germans, Jews, and Communists', both in Deak *et al.* (2000), pp. 14–35, 74–129.

—— (2001) *Upiorna dekada trzy eseje o stereotypach na temat zydow, Polakow, Niemcow i komunistow 1939–1948*, Krakow: Universitas.

*—— (2003) *Neighbours: The Destruction of the Jewish Community in Jedwabne, Poland, 1941*, London: Random House (first published 2001).

—— (2006) *Fear: Anti-Semitism in Poland after Auschwitz*, Princeton: Princeton University Press.

Gross, N. (1973) 'The Habsburg Monarchy, 1750–1914', in C. Cipolla (ed.), *The Fontana Economic History of Europe,* vol. IV: *1750–1914*, part one, Glasgow: Collins-Fontana, pp. 228–78.

Gryn, H. (2001) *Chasing Shadows*, Harmondsworth: Penguin.

Gunst, P. (1989) 'Agrarian systems of Central and Eastern Europe', in Chirot (1989b).

Gyuzelev, V. (1981) 'Bulgaria: 1300 years', in G. Bokov (ed.), *Modern Bulgaria: History, Policy, Economy, Culture,* Sofia: Sofia Press, pp. 17–33.

Habermas, J. (1992) 'Citizenship and national identity: some reflections on the future of Europe', *Praxis International*, vol. 12, no. 1, pp. 1–19.

Haddock, B. and Caraiani, O. (1999) 'Nationalism and civil society in Romania', *Political Studies*, vol. 47, no. 2, pp. 272–94.

Halasz, Z. (ed.) (1960) *Hungary*, Budapest: Corvine.

Halecki, O. (1950) *The Limits and Divisions of European History*, New York: Columbia University Press.

—— (ed.) (1957) *Poland*, New York: Praeger.

Haldon, J. (1985) 'Some considerations on Byzantine society and economy in the seventh century', *Byzantinische Forschungen*, vol. 10, pp. 75–112.

—— (1993) *The State and the Tributary Mode of Production*, London: Verso.

—— (1995) *State, Army and Society in Byzantium*, Aldershot: Variorum.

*—— (1997) *Byzantium in the Seventh Century*, Cambridge: Cambridge University Press.

—— (2000) *Byzantium: A History*, Stroud: Tempus.

Hall, R. (2000) *The Balkan Wars, 1912–1913*, London: Routledge.

Hammond, T. (1958) 'Origins of national communism', *Virginia Quarterly Review*, vol. 34.

—— (ed.) (1975) *The Anatomy of Communist Takeovers*, New Haven: Yale University Press.

Hanak, P. (1975a) 'The Dual Monarchy, 1867–1914', in Pamlenyi (1975).

—— (1975b) 'Economics, society and sociopolitical thought in Hungary during the age of capitalism', *Austrian History Yearbook*, vol. II.

—— (1975c) 'The period of neo-absolutism, 1849–1867', in Pamlenyi (1975).

—— (1989) 'Central Europe: a historical region in modern times', in Schopflin and Wood (1989).

Haraszti, M. (1977) *A Worker in a Worker's State*, Harmondsworth: Penguin.

Hare, P., Radice, H. and Swain, N. (1981) *Hungary: A Decade of Reform*, London: Allen and Unwin.

Harvey, A. (1989) *Economic Expansion in the Byzantine Empire, 900–1200*, Cambridge: Cambridge University Press.

Haussig, H. (1971) *A History of Byzantine Civilization*, London: Thames and Hudson.

Havel, V. (1985) *The Power of the Powerless*, ed. J. Keane, New York: M.E. Sharpe.

—— (1991) *Open Letters: Selected Writings, 1965–1990*, New York: Alfred Knopf.

—— (1993) *Summer Meditations*, New York: Vintage.

—— (1994a) 'A call for sacrifice: the co-responsibility of the West', *Foreign Affairs*, vol. 73, no. 2.

*—— (1994b) *Towards a Civil Society: Selected Speeches and Writings, 1990–1994*, Prague: Lidove Noviny Publishing House.

—— (1996) 'The Hope for Europe', *New York Review of Books*, vol. 38 (20 June), pp. 38–41.

Hay, D. and Betts, R. (1970) *Europe in the Fourteenth and Fifteenth Centuries*, London: Longman.

Hayek, F. (1939) 'Economic conditions of inter-state federation', *New Commonwealth Quarterly*, vol. 5 (September), pp. 131–49.

*—— (1960) *The Constitution of Liberty*, London: Routledge and Kegan Paul.

—— (1973) *Law, Legislation and Liberty*, vol. I, London: Routledge and Keegan Paul.

Heinen, A. (2006) *Legiunea 'Arhanghelul Mihail'*, Bucharest: Humanitas.

Held, J. (ed.) (1992) *The Columbia History of Eastern Europe in the Twentieth Century*, New York: Columbia University Press.

Heller, C. (1977) *On the Edge of Destruction: Jews of Poland between the Two World Wars*, New York: Columbia University Press.

Henderson, K. (ed.) (1999) *Back to Europe: Central and Eastern Europe and the European Union*, London: UCL Press.

Herodotus (1996) *The Histories*, Harmondsworth: Penguin.

Heurtley, W.A., Darby, H.C., Crawley, C.W. and Woodhouse, C.M. (1967) *A Short History of Greece*, Cambridge: Cambridge University Press.

Higley, J. and Gunther, R. (1992) *Elites and Democratic Consolidation in Latin America and Southern Europe*, Cambridge: Cambridge University Press.

*Hilberg, R. (1985) *The Destruction of the European Jews*, abridged edn, New York: Holmes and Meier.

*Hilferding, R. (1981) *Finance Capital*, London: Routledge and Kegan Paul. [Originally published as *Das Finanzkapital*, Vienna, 1910.]

Hinsley, F. (1973) *Nationalism and the International System*, London: Hodder and Stoughton.

*Hitchins, K. (1994) *Rumania, 1866–1947*, Oxford: Clarendon Press.

Hobsbawm, E. (1965) 'The crisis of the seventeenth century', in Aston (1965), pp. 5–58.

—— (1992) *Nations and Nationalism since 1870*, Cambridge: Cambridge University Press.

Hodgson, M. (1993) *Rethinking World History: Essays on Europe, Islam and World History*, Cambridge: Cambridge University Press.

Hodza, M. (1942) *Federation in Central Europe: Reflections and Reminiscences*, London: Jarrolds.

Hoen, H. (ed.) (2001) *Good Governance in Central and Eastern Europe: The Puzzle of Capitalism by Design*, Cheltenham: Edward Elgar.

Hoensch, J. (1994) *A History of Modern Hungary, 1867–1994*, Harlow: Longman.

Hoffman, G. (1967) 'The political bases of the Austrian nationality problem', *Austrian History Yearbook*, vol. 3, part 1 pp. 121–46.

Holborn, H. (1967) 'The final disintegration of the Habsburg Monarchy', *Austrian History Yearbook*, vol. 3, part 3, pp. 189–205.

Holzman, F. (1976) *International Trade under Communism*, New York: Basic Books.

—— (1986a) 'Further thoughts on the significance of Soviet subsidies to Eastern Europe', *Comparative Economic Studies*, vol. 28, no. 3.

—— (1986b) 'The significance of Soviet subsidies to Eastern Europe', *Comparative Economic Studies*, vol. 28, no. 1.

Horthy, M. (2000) *Admiral Nicholas Horthy: Memoirs*, Safety Harbour, Fla.: Andrew Simon; originally published New York, 1957.

Howard, M.M. (2003) *The Weakness of Civil Society in Post-Communist Europe*, Cambridge: Cambridge University Press.

Hristov, H. (1985) *A History of Bulgaria*, Sofia: Sofia Press.

Huertas, T. (1977) *Economic Growth and Economic Policy in a Multinational Setting: The Habsburg Monarchy, 1841–1865*, New York: Arno Press.

Huntington, S. (1991) *The Third Wave: Democratization in the Late Twentieth Century*, Norman, Okla.: University of Oklahoma Press.

—— (1993) 'The clash of civilizations?', *Foreign Affairs*, vol. 72, no. 3, pp. 22–49.

—— (1998) *The Clash of Civilizations and the Remaking of World Order*, London: Touchstone.

Hupchick, D. (2002) *The Balkans*, New York: Palgrave Macmillan.

Hus, J. (1972) *The Letters of John Hus*, Manchester: Manchester University Press.

Ignatiev, M. (1993) *Blood and Belonging: Journeys into the New Nationalism*, London: Chatto and Windus.

Ignotus, P. (1972) *Hungary*, London: Benn.

Imber, C. (2002) *The Ottoman Empire, 1300–1650*, Basingstoke: Palgrave Macmillan.

Inalcik, H. (1969) *The Ottoman Empire: The Classical Age, 1300–1600*, London: Weidenfeld and Nicolson.

—— (1991) 'The emergence of big farms, *ciftliks*: state, landlords and tenants', in Keyder and Tabak (1991), pp. 17–34.

*—— (1997) 'The Ottoman state: economy and society, 1300–1600', in Inalcik and Quataert (1997) vol. I.

*Inalcik, H., and Quataert, D. (eds) (1997) *An Economic and Social History of the Ottoman Empire, 1300–1914*, 2 vols, Cambridge: Cambridge University Press.

Inotai, A. (1994) 'Transforming the East: Western illusions and strategies', *The Hungarian Quarterly*, vol. 35, no. 133.

International Commission on the Balkans (2005) *The Balkans in Europe's Future*, Sofia: Centre for Liberal Strategies, April.

Ioanid, R. (2000) *The Holocaust in Romania: The Destruction of the Jews and Gypsies under the Antonescu Regime, 1940–1944*, Chicago: Ivan Dee.

Irvine, H. (1923) *The Making of Rural Europe*, London: Allen and Unwin.

Islamoglu-Injan, H. (ed.) (1987) *The Ottoman Empire and the World Economy*, Cambridge: Cambridge University Press.

Issawi, C. (1989) 'The Middle East in the world context', in G. Sabagh (ed.), *The Modern Economic and Social History of the Middle East in its World Context*, Cambridge: Cambridge University Press.

Jackman, R. (1994) 'Economic policy and employment in the transition economies of Central and Eastern Europe: what have we learned?', *International Labour Review*, vol. 133, no. 3.

Jackson, G. (1966) *Comintern and Peasant in Eastern Europe, 1919–1930*, New York: Columbia University Press.

Janos, A. (1982) *The Politics of Backwardness in Hungary, 1825–1945*, Princeton: Princeton University Press.

Jardine, L. (1996) *Worldly Goods: A New History of the Renaissance*, Basingstoke: Macmillan.

Jardine, L. and Brotton, J. (2000) *Global Interests: Renaissance Art between East and West*, London: Reaktion Books.

*Jaszi, O. (1929) *The Dissolution of the Habsburg Monarchy*, Chicago: Chicago University Press.

Jedlicki, J. (2004) 'How to grapple with a perplexing legacy', in Polonsky and Michlik (2004), pp. 237–46.

Jeffries, I. (ed.) (1981) *The Industrial Enterprise in Eastern Europe*, New York: Praeger.

—— (1990) *A Guide to the Socialist Economies*, London: Routledge.

—— (1992a) 'The impact of reunification on the East German economy', in J. Osmond (ed.), *German Unification*, London: Longman.

—— (ed.) (1992b) *Industrial Reform in Socialist Countries: From Restructuring to Revolution*, Aldershot: Edward Elgar.

—— (1993) *Socialist Economies and the Transition to the Market: A Guide*, London: Routledge.

—— (1996a) *A Guide to the Economies in Transition*, London: Routledge.

—— (ed.) (1996b) *Problems of Economic and Political Transformation in the Balkans*, London: Pinter.

—— (2002a) *Eastern Europe at the Turn of the Twenty-First Century: A Guide to the Economies in Transition*, London: Routledge.

—— (2002b) *The Former Yugoslavia at the Turn of the Twenty-First Century: A Guide to the Economies in Transition*, London: Routledge.

Jeffries, I., Melzer, M. and Breuning, E. (eds) (1987) *The East German Economy*, London: Croom Helm.

Jelavich, B. (1983a) *A History of the Balkans, vol. I*, London: Cambridge University Press.

—— (1983b) *A History of the Balkans, vol. II*, London: Cambridge University Press.

Jelavich, C. and Jelavich, B. (eds) (1963) *The Balkans in Transition*, Berkeley: University of California Press.

—— (1977) *The Establishment of the Balkan National States, 1804–1920*, Seattle: University of Washington Press.

Jelavich, C. and Rath, R. (eds) (1967) in Rath, R.J. and Jenks, W.A. (1967), vol. 3, parts 1, 2 and 3, pp. 32–61.

Jenks, W.A. (1967) 'Economics, constitutionalism, administration and class structure in the monarchy', *Austrian History Yearbook*, vol. 3, part 1.

Jenkins, R.J.H. (1966) *Byzantium: The Imperial Centuries*, London: Weidenfeld and Nicolson.

Johnson, C. (1962) *Peasant Nationalism and Communist Power*, Stanford, Calif.: Stanford University Press.

Johnson, L. (2002) *Central Europe: Enemies, Neighbors, Friends*, 2nd edn, Oxford: Oxford University Press.

Jones, E. (1981) *The European Miracle*, Cambridge: Cambridge University Press.

Jones, E.L. (1988) *Growth Recurring: Economic Change in World History*, Oxford: Clarendon Press.

*Kafadar, C. (1995) *Between Two Worlds: The Construction of the Ottoman State*, Berkeley: University of California Press.

Kaminski, A. (1975) 'Neo-serfdom in Poland-Lithuania', *Slavic Review*, vol. 34, no. 2, pp. 253–68.

Kaminsky, H. (1967) *A History of the Hussite Revolution*, Berkeley: University of California Press.

Kann, R. (1950a) *The Multinational Empire*, vol. I, New York: Columbia University Press.

—— (1950b) *The Multinational Empire*, vol. II, New York: Columbia University Press.

—— (1967) 'The dynasty and imperial idea', *Austrian History Yearbook*, vol. 3, part 1, pp. 11–30.

—— (1974) *A History of the Habsburg Empire, 1526–1918*, Berkeley: University of California Press.

Kaplan, M. (1986) 'L'économie paysanne dans l'Empire byzatin du Vème au Xème siècle', *Klio*, vol. 68, pp. 198–232.

—— (1992) *Les hommes et la terre à Byzance du VIe au XIe siècle, Propriété et exploitation du sol*, Paris: Publications de la Sorbonne.

Kaplan, R. (1993) *Balkan Ghosts: A Journey through History*, New York: St Martin's Press.

Karpat, K. (1972) 'The transformation of the Ottoman state, 1789–1908', *International Journal of Middle East Studies*, vol. 3, no. 3, pp. 243–81.

—— (1984) *Ottoman Population, 1830–1914*, Madison: University of Wisconsin Press.

Karsai, L. (2000) 'The people's courts and revolutionary justice in Hungary, 1945–46', in Deak *et al.* (2000), pp. 233–51.

Kasaba, R. (1988) *The Ottoman Empire and the World Economy: The Nineteenth Century*, Albany: State University of New York Press.

Kaser, M. (1967) *Comecon: Integration Problems of Planned Economies*, Oxford: Oxford University Press.

—— (1981) 'The industrial enterprise in Bulgaria', in Jeffries (1981).

—— (1986) 'Albania under and after Enver Hoxha', US Congress, Joint Economic Committee, Washington, D.C.: Government Printing Office.

Kaser, M. and Radice, E. (eds) (1986) *The Economic History of Eastern Europe*, vols. I and II, Oxford: Oxford University Press.

Katus, L. (1970) 'Economic growth in Hungary during the age of dualism, 1867–1913', in E. Pamlenyi (ed.) *Socio-Economic Researches on the History of East-Central Europe*, Budapest: Akademiai Kiado.

Kaufmann, T. (1995) *Court, Cloister and City: The Art and Culture of Central Europe, 1450–1800*, London: Weidenfeld and Nicolson.

Kavka, F. (1960) *An Outline of Czechoslovak History*, Prague: Orbis.

—— (1994) 'Bohemia', in Scribner *et al.* (1994).

Kazhdan, Alexander (1993) 'State, feudal and private economy in Byzantium', *Dumbarton Oaks Papers*, no. 47, pp. 83–100.

Keane, J. (ed.) (1993) *Civil Society and the State: New European Perspectives*, London: Verso.

Kedourie, E. (1993) *Nationalism*, 4th edn, London: Hutchinson.

Kennan, G. (1979) *The Decline of Bismarck's European Order: Franco-Russian Relations, 1875–1890*, Princeton: Princeton University Press.

Kennedy, P. (1989) *The Rise and Fall of the Great Powers*, London: Harper-Collins Fontana.

Kennedy-Pipe, C. (1995) *Stalin's Cold War: Soviet Strategies in Europe, 1943–1956*, Manchester: Manchester University Press.

—— (1997) *Russia and the World since 1917*, London: Arnold.

Kenney, P. (1996) *Rebuilding Poland: Workers and Communists, 1945–50*, Ithaca: Cornell University Press.

Kershaw, I. (1983) *Popular Opinion and Political Dissent in the Third Reich*, Oxford: Oxford University Press.

Keyder, C. (1991) 'Introduction: large-scale commercial agriculture in the Ottoman Empire?', in Keyder and Tabak (1991) pp. 1–15.

*Keyder, C. and Tabak, F. (eds) (1991) *Landholding and Commercial Agriculture in the Middle East*, Albany: State University of New York Press.

Kidd, M., Malinovsky, W. and Wittlin, J. (eds) (1943) *For Your Freedom and Ours: Polish Progressive Spirit through the Centuries*, New York: Frederic Ungar.

Kiraly, B. (1975) 'Neo-serfdom in Hungary', *Slavic Review*, vol. 34, no. 2, pp. 269–78.

Kirschbaum, S. (1995) *A History of Slovakia*, New York: St Martin's Press.

Kiss, C. (1987) 'Central European writers about Central Europe', in Schöpflin and Wood (1989).

Kissinger, H. (1957) *A World Restored: Metternich, Castlereagh and the Problems of Peace, 1812–22*, London: Weidenfeld and Nicolson.

Kitchen, M. (1976) *Fascism*, London: Macmillan.

Kitromiledes, P. (1995) 'Europe and the dilemmas of modern Greek conscience', in Carabott (1995).

Klaniczay, T. (1992) 'Hungary', in Porter and Teich (1992).

Kleinwächter, F. (1883) *Die Kartelle: ein Beitrag zur Frage der Organisation der Volkswirtschaft*, Innsbruck.

Kochanowicz, J. (1989) 'The Polish economy and the evolution of democracy', in Chirot (1989b).

*Kohn, H. (1944) *The Idea of Nationalism*, New York: Macmillan (2nd edn 1961).

—— (1967) 'Was the collapse inevitable?', *Austrian History Yearbook*, vol. 3, part 3, pp. 250–66.

Kola, P. (2003) *The Search for Greater Albania*, London: Hurst.

Kolankiewicz, G. (1994) 'Consensus and competition in the eastern enlargement of the EU', *International Affairs*, vol. 70, no. 3, pp. 477–95.

Kolankiewicz, G. and Lewis, P.G. (1988) *Poland: Politics, Economics and Society*, London: Pinter.

Kolinsky, M. (1974) *Continuity and Change in European Society*, London: Croom Helm.

Koliopoulos, J. and Veremis, T. (2002) *Greece: The Modern Sequel*, London: Hurst.

Komlos, J. (1981) 'Economic growth and industrialization in Hungary, 1830–1913', *Journal of European Economic History*, vol. 10, no. 1, pp. 5–46.

*—— (ed.) (1983a) *Economic Development in the Habsburg Monarchy*, New York: Columbia University Press.

—— (1983b) *The Habsburg Monarchy as a Customs Union: Economic Development in Austria–Hungary in the Nineteenth Century*, Princeton: Princeton University Press.

Konrad, G. (1984) *Antipolitics: An Essay*, London: Harcourt, Brace and Jovanovich.

—— (1986) 'Is the dream of Central Europe still alive?', *Cross Currents: A Yearbook of Central Europe Culture*, vol. 5, pp. 109–21.

Konrad, G. and Szelenyi, I. (1979) *The Intellectuals on the Road to Class Power*, New York: Harcourt, Brace and Jovanovich.

Kontler, L. (2002) *A History of Hungary*, Basingstoke: Palgrave.

Koralka, J. (1967) 'Comment', *Austrian History Yearbook*, vol. 3, part 1, pp. 147–55.

Korbonski, A. (1990) 'CMEA, economic integration, and *perestroika*, 1949–89', *Studies in Comparative Communism*, vol. 33, no. 1.

Kornai, J. (1986) 'The Hungarian reform process: visions, hopes and reality', *Journal of Economic Literature*, vol. 29 (December).

—— (1990) *The Road to a Free Economy*, New York: W.W. Norton.

—— (1992) *The Socialist System*, Oxford: Oxford University Press.

Kornhauser, W. (1960) *The Politics of Totalitarianism*, 3rd edn, London: Routledge and Kegan Paul.

Kostanick, H. (1963) 'The geopolitics of the Balkans', in Jelavich and Jelavich (1963).

Kovaly, H.M. (1997) *Under a Cruel Star: Life in Prague, 1941–1968*, New York: Holmes and Meier.

Koves, A. (1983) 'Implicit subsidies and some issues of economic relations within Comecon', *Acta Oeconomica*, vol. 31, no. 1, pp. 125–36.

—— (1992) *Central and East European Economies in Transition: The International Dimension*, Boulder, Colo.: Westview Press.

Kozyrev, A. (1995) 'Partnership or cold peace?', *Foreign Policy*, no. 99, pp. 3–14.

Kramer, H. (1993) 'The European Community's response to the "new Eastern Europe"', *Journal of Common Market Studies*, vol. 31, no. 2.

Krastev, I. (2004) *Shifting Obsessions: Three Essays on the Politics of Anti-Corruption*, Budapest: Central European University Press.

Krekovic, E., Mannova, E. and Krekovicova, E. (2005) *Myty nase slovenske*, Bratislava: Academic Electronic Press.

Krofta, K. (1932) 'Bohemia in the fourteenth century', in J. Bury (ed.), *The Cambridge Medieval History*, vol. VII, Cambridge: Cambridge University Press.

—— (1936) 'Bohemia in the fifteenth century', in J. Bury (ed.), *The Cambridge Medieval History*, vol. VIII, Cambridge: Cambridge University Press.

Kukiel, M. (1955) *Czartoryski and European Unity*, Princeton: Princeton University Press.

Kumar, K. (1992) 'The 1989 revolutions and the idea of Europe', *Political Studies*, vol. 40, no. 3, pp. 439–61.

Kundera, M. (1984) 'The tragedy of Central Europe', *New York Review of Books*, vol. 31, no. 7 (26 April), pp. 33–8.

Kusy, M. (1989) 'We, Central European East Europeans', in Schöpflin and Wood (1989).

Kymlicka, W. (1995) *Multicultural Citizenship*, Oxford: Oxford University Press.

Kymlicka, W. and Opalski, M. (eds) (2001) *Can Liberal Pluralism be Exported? Western Political Theory and Ethnic Relations in Eastern Europe*, Oxford: Oxford University Press.

Lafore, L. (1971) *The Long Fuse*, Philadelphia: Lippincott.

Laiou, A. (1977) *Peasant Society in the Late Byzantine Empire*, Princeton: Princeton University Press.

—— (ed.) (2002) *The Economic History of Byzantium: From the Seventh through the Fifteenth Century*, Cambridge, Mass.: Dumbarton Oaks, Harvard University.

Lampe, J. (1975) 'Varieties of unsuccessful industrialization: the Balkan states before 1914', *Journal of Economic History*, vol. 35, no. 1, pp. 56–85.

—— (1989) 'Imperial borderlands or capitalist periphery? Redefining Balkan backwardness, 1520–1914', in Chirot (1989b).

*—— (1996) *Yugoslavia as History*, Cambridge: Cambridge University Press.

*—— (2006) *Balkans into Southeastern Europe*, New York: Palgrave Macmillan.

*Lampe, J. and Jackson, M. (1982) *Balkan Economic History 1550–1950*, Bloomington: Indiana University Press.

Lasswell, H. (1941) 'The garrison state', *American Journal of Sociology*, vol. 46, no. 4, pp. 455–68.

Layard, R. (1993) 'Comment', *Transition*, vol. 1, no. 3.

Lefort, J. (1993) 'Rural economy and social relations in the countryside', *Dumbarton Oaks Papers*, no. 47, pp. 101–13.

Lemerle, P. (1959) 'Recherches sur le regime agraire à Byzance: La terre militaire à l'époque des Comnènes', *Cahiers de civilisation médiévale*, vol. 2, no. 3, pp. 265–81.

*—— (1979) *The Agrarian History of Byzantium, from the Origins to the Twelfth Century*, Galway: Galway University Press.

Lenin, V.I. (1948) *Imperialism: The Highest Stage of Capitalism*, London: Lawrence and Wishart.

—— (1964) *Collected Works*, vol. XXI, Moscow: Progress Publishers.

—— (1969) *State and Revolution*, Moscow: Progress Publishers.

—— (1972) *On the Development of Heavy Industry and Electrification*, Moscow: Progress Publishers.

—— (1975) *Selected Works in Three Volumes*, Moscow: Progress Publishers.

Leslie, R. (1971) *The Polish Question*, London: Historical Association.

—— (1980) *The History of Poland since 1863*, Cambridge: Cambridge University Press.

Lewis, B. (1961) *The Emergence of Modern Turkey*, London: Oxford University Press.

—— (2002) *What Went Wrong? Western Impact and Middle Eastern Response*, London: Phoenix.

—— (2005) *From Babel to Dragomans: Interpreting the Middle East*, London: Phoenix.

Lewis, P. (2000) *Political Parties in Post-Communist Eastern Europe*, London: Routledge.

Lewis, P.G. (1994) *Central Europe since 1945*, Harlow: Longman.

Liashchenko, P. (1949) *History of the National Economy of Russia*, New York: Macmillan.

Light, M. (1994) 'The USSR/CIS and democratization in Eastern Europe', in Pridham *et al.* (1994).

Linz, J. (1979) 'Some notes toward a comparative study of fascism in sociological historical perspective,' in W. Laqueur (ed.), *Fascism: A Reader's Guide*, Harmondsworth: Penguin, pp. 13–78.

*Linz, J. and Stepan, A. (eds) (1978) *The Breakdown of Democratic Regimes*, 3 vols, Baltimore; Johns Hopkins University Press.

—— (1996) *Problems of Democratic Transition and Consolidation*, Baltimore: Johns Hopkins University Press.

Linz, S. (ed.) (1985) *The Impact of World War II on the Soviet Union*, Totowa, N.J.: Rowman and Littlefield.

Lipset, S.M. (1959) 'Some social requisites of democracy', *American Political Science Review*, vol. 53, no. 1, pp. 69–105.

—— (1960) *Political Man*, New York: Doubleday.

Lipshich, E.E. (1945) 'Vizantiiskoye krestianstvo I slavianskaya kolonizatsiia', *Vizantiiski sbornik*, (Moscow/Leningrad), pp. 96–143.

—— (1947) 'Slavanskaya obshchina I ee roli v formirovanii vizantskogo feodalizma', *Vizantiiskii vremennik*, vol. 26, pp. 144–63.

Liptak, L. (2000) 'Slovakia in the twentieth century', in Mannova (2000), pp. 241–305.

Lomax, B. (1976) *Hungary, 1956*, London: Allison and Busby.

Longworth, P. (1994) *The Making of Eastern Europe*, London: Macmillan.

Lydall, H. (1989) *Yugoslavia in Crisis*, Oxford: Clarendon Press.

McCarthy, J. (1995) *Death and Exile: The Ethnic Cleansing of Ottoman Muslims, 1821–1922*, Princeton: Darwin Press.

—— (1997) *The Ottoman Turks*, London: Longman.

—— (2001) *The Ottoman Peoples and the End of Empire*, London: Arnold.

Macartney, C. (1969) *The Habsburg Empire, 1790–1918*, London: Weidenfeld and Nicolson.

Macartney, C. and Palmer, A. (1962) *Independent Eastern Europe*, London: Macmillan.

McDonough, P. *et al.* (1998) *The Cultural Dynamics of Democratization in Spain*, Ithaca: Cornell University Press.

Macek, J. (1958) *The Hussite Movement in Bohemia*, Prague: Orbis.

—— (1992) 'Bohemia and Moravia', in Porter and Teich (1992).

McFarlane, B. (1988) *Yugoslavia: Politics, Economics and Society*, London: Pinter.

*McGowan, B. (1981) *Economic Life in Ottoman Europe: Taxation, Trade and the Struggle for Land, 1600–1800*, Cambridge: Cambridge University Press.

—— (1997) 'The age of the Ayans, 1699–1812', in Inalcik and Quataert (1997) vol. II, pp. 637–758.

McIntyre, R. (1988) *Bulgaria: Politics, Economics and Society*, London: Pinter.

McKinnon, R. (1994) 'Financial growth and macro-economic stability in China, 1978–92: implications for Russia and other transitional economies', *Journal of Comparative Economics*, vol. 18, no. 3.

MacLean, G. (ed.) (2005) *Reorienting the Renaissance*, Basingstoke: Macmillan.

McNeill, W.H. (1964) *Europe's Steppe Frontier*, Chicago: University of Chicago Press.

—— (1979) *Plagues and Peoples*, Harmondsworth: Penguin.

Macura, M. (1976) 'Population in Europe, 1920–1970', in Cipolla (1976a), pp. 1–87.

Macurek, J. (1948) 'The achievements of the Slavonic Congress', *Slavonic Review*, vol. 26, no. 67, pp. 329–40.

Maczak, A. (1982) 'The structure of power in the Commonwealth of the sixteenth and seventeenth centuries', in Fedorowicz (1982).

—— (1992) 'Poland', in Porter and Teich (1992).

Maczak, A., Samsonowicz, H. and Burke, U. (eds) (1985) *East-Central Europe in Transition: From the Fourteenth to the Seventeenth Centuries*, Cambridge: Cambridge University Press.

Maddison, A. (1976) 'Economic policy and performance in Europe', in Cipolla (1976b), pp. 403–40.

Magas, B. (1993) *The Destruction of Yugoslavia*, London: Verso.

*Magas, B. and Zanic, I. (eds) (2001) *The War in Croatia and Bosnia-Herzegovina 1991–1995*, London: Frank Cass.

Magris, C. (1989) *Danube*, London: Harvill Press.

Majewski, W. (1982) 'The Polish art of war in the sixteenth and seventeenth centuries', in Fedorowicz (1982).

Majone, G. (1992) 'Regulatory federalism in the European Community', *Government and Policy*, vol. 10, no. 3, pp. 299–316.

Majone, G., Baake, P., Baldwin, R., Cases, L., Demarigny, F., Everson, M., Laudate, L., Perschau, O. and Weale, A. (1996) *Regulating Europe*, London, Routledge.

Makkai, L. (1975a) 'From the Battle of Mohacs to 1711', in Pamlenyi (1975).

—— (1975b) 'The independent Hungarian feudal monarchy to the Battle of Mohacs (1000–1526)', in Pamlenyi (1975).

—— (1975c) 'Neo-serfdom: its origins and nature in East-Central Europe', *Slavic Review*, vol. 34, no. 2, pp. 225–38.

—— (1975d) 'The origins of the Hungarian people and state', in Pamlenyi (1975).

*Malcolm, N. (1994) *Bosnia: A Short History*, London: Macmillan.

—— (1998) *Kosovo: A Short History*, London: Macmillan.

Malowist, M. (1959) 'The economic and social development of the Baltic countries from the fifteenth to the seventeenth centuries', *Economic History Review*, vol. 12, no. 2, pp. 319–57.

—— (1974) 'Problems of the growth of the national economy of Central Eastern Europe in the late Middle Ages', *Journal of European Economic History*, vol. 3, no. 2, pp. 319–57.

Mametey, V. (1967) 'Legalizing the collapse of Austria-Hungary at the Paris Peace Conference', *Austrian History Yearbook*, vol. 3, part 3, pp. 206–37.

Mango, C. (1980) *Byzantium*, London: Weidenfeld and Nicolson.

*Mann, M. (1988) *States, War and Capitalism*, Oxford: Blackwell.

—— (1993) *The Sources of Social Power, vol. II: The Rise of Modern Nations and Classes, 1760–1914*, Cambridge: Cambridge University Press.

—— (2004) *Fascists*, Cambridge: Cambridge University Press.

—— (2005) *The Dark Side of Democracy: Explaining Ethnic Cleansing*, Cambridge: Cambridge University Press.

Mannova, E. (ed.) (2000) *A Concise History of Slovakia*, Bratislava: Historical Institute of the Slovak Academy of Sciences.

Mansfield, P. (1992) *A History of the Middle East*, Harmondsworth: Penguin.

Marcus, J. (1983) *Social and Political History of the Jews in Poland, 1919–39*, The Hague: Mouton.

Marer, P. (1974) 'Soviet economic policy in Eastern Europe' in US Congress Joint Economic Committee, *Reorientation and Commercial Relations of the Economies of Eastern Europe*, Washington D.C.: Government Printing Office.

Markova, Z. (1981) 'Bulgarian national revival', in G. Bokov (ed.), *Modern Bulgaria: History, Policy, Economy, Culture,* Sofia: Sofia Press, pp. 34–66.

Marmullaku, R. (1975) *Albania and the Albanians*, London: Hurst.

Marrese, M. (1986) 'CMEA: effective but cumbersome political economy', *International Organisation*, vol. 40, no. 2.

Marrese, M. and Vanous, J. (1983) *Soviet Subsidization of Trade with Eastern Europe*, Berkeley: Institute of International Studies.

Marrus, M. and Paxton, R. (1981) *Vichy France and the Jews*, New York: Basic Books.

Marton, S. (ed.) (2006) *Europe in its Making*, Iasi: Institutul European.

März, E. (1953) 'Some economic aspects of the nationality conflict in the Habsburg Empire', *Journal of Central European Affairs*, vol. 13, no. 2, pp. 123–35.

Matlock, J. (1996) 'Dealing with a Russia in turmoil', *Foreign Affairs*, vol. 75, no. 3.

Matvejevic, P. (1989) 'Central Europe seen from the east of Europe', in Schöpflin and Wood (1989).

Matthäus, J. (2005) 'Operation Barbarossa and the onset of the Holocaust, June–December 1941', in C. Browning (2005), pp. 244–308.

May, A. (1951) *The Hapsburg Monarchy, 1867–1914*, Cambridge, Mass.: Harvard University Press.

Mayhew, A. (1998) *Recreating Europe*, Cambridge: Cambridge University Press.

*Mazower, M. (1993) *Inside Hitler's Greece*, New Haven: Yale University Press.

*—— (1998) *Dark Continent: Europe's Twentieth Century*, Harmondsworth: Allen Lane/ Penguin.

—— (2001) *The Balkans*, London: Phoenix Press.

Meier, V. (1999) *Yugoslavia: A History of its Demise*, London: Routledge.

Mellor, R. (1971) *Comecon: Challenge to the West*, New York: Van Nostrand.

Miall, H. (ed.) (1994) *Redefining Europe*, London: Pinter.

Michaelis, M. (1978) *Mussolini and the Jews*, London: Oxford University Press.

Michnik, A. (1985) *Letters from Prison and Other Essays*, Berkeley: University of California Press.

—— (2004) 'Poles and the Jews: how deep the guilt?', in Polonsky and Michlik (2004), pp. 434–9.

Michta, A. (ed) (1999) *America's New Allies: Poland, Hungary and the Czech Republic*, Seattle: University of Washington Press.

Mikus, J. (1977) *Slovakia and the Slovaks*, Washington D.C.: Three Continents Press.

Milin, M. (2000) *Rezistenta anticomunista din munti Banatului*, Bucharest: Fundatia Academia Civica.

Miller, N. (1997) 'The Republic of Macedonia: finding its way', in Dawisha and Parrott (1997b), pp. 226–84.

Miller, W., White, S. and Heywood, P. (1998) *Values and Political Change in Postcommunist Europe*, Basingstoke: Macmillan.

Milosz, C. (1953) *The Captive Mind*, London: Secker and Warburg.

—— (1986) 'Central European attitudes', in Schöpflin and Wood (1989).

Milward, A. (1965) *The German Economy at War*, London: Athlone Press.

—— (1992) *The European Rescue of the Nation-State*, London: Routledge.

Mitchell, B. (1978) *European Historical Statistics, 1750–1970*, London: Macmillan.

Mitrany, D. (1930) *The Land and the Peasant in Romania*, London: Oxford University Press.

—— (1945) 'Introduction', in PEP (1945)

*—— (1951) *Marx against the Peasant*, Chapel Hill, N.C.: University of North Carolina Press.

Molnar, M. (1971) *Budapest 1956*, London: Allen and Unwin.

Monnet, J. (1976) *Mémoires*, Paris: Fayard.

Moore, J.B. jnr (1969) *Social Origins of Dictatorship and Democracy*, Harmondsworth: Penguin.

Moore, W. (1945) *Economic Demography of Southern and Eastern Europe*, Geneva: League of Nations.

Morrison, J. (1995) *NATO Expansion and Alternative Future Security Alignments*, Washington, D.C.: National Defense University Press.

Murrell, P. (1992a) 'Evolution in economics and in the economic reform of the centrally planned economies', in Clague and Rausser (1992).

—— (1992b) 'Evolutionary and radical approaches to economic reform', *Economics of Planning*, vol. 25, no. 1.

—— (1993) 'What is shock therapy? What did it do in Poland and Russia?', *Post-Soviet Affairs*, vol. 9, no. 2.

Musial, B. (2004) 'The pogrom in Jedwabne: critical remarks about Jan T. Gross's *Neighbours*', in Polonsky and Michlik (2004), pp. 304–43.

Mussolini, B. (1932) 'The doctrine of fascism', translated in Oakeshott (1940).

Naimark, N. (1995) *The Russians in Germany: A History of the Soviet Zone of Occupation, 1945–49*, Cambridge, Mass.: Harvard University Press.

Namier, L. (1946) *1848: The Revolution of the Intellectuals*, London: Geoffrey Cumberlege.

Nardin, T. (1983) *Law, Morality and the Relations of States*, Princeton: Princeton University Press.

Nelson, G. (1993) 'Agricultural policy reform in Eastern Europe', *American Journal of Agricultural Economics*, vol. 75, no. 3.

Neuber, A. (1993) 'Towards a political economy of transition in Eastern Europe', *Journal of International Development*, vol. 5, no. 5.

Nolte, E. (1969) *Three Faces of Fascism*, New York: Mentor.

Nove, A. (1994) 'A gap in transition models? A comment on Gomulka', *Europe-Asia Studies*, vol. 46, no. 5.

Nugent, N. (ed.) (2004) *European Union Enlargement*, Basingstoke: Palgrave Macmillan.

Oakeshott, M. (ed.) (1940) *The Social and Political Doctrines of Contemporary Europe*, London: Basic Books.

—— (1962) *Rationalism in Politics and Other Essays*, London: Methuen.

—— (1975) *On Human Conduct*, Oxford: Clarendon Press.

Obolensky, D. (1974) *The Byzantine Commonwealth*, London: Weidenfeld and Nicolson.

O'Donnell, G. (1993) 'On the state, democratization and some conceptual problems', *World Development*, vol. 21, no. 8, pp. 1355–69.

*—— (1996) 'Delegative democracy', in L. Diamond and M. Plattner (eds), *The Global Resurgence of Democracy*, 2nd edn, Baltimore: Johns Hopkins University Press.

*—— (1998) 'Horizontal accountability in new democracies', *Journal of Democracy*, vol. 9, no. 3.

Oisteanu, A. (2001) *Imaginea evreului in cultura Romana*, 2nd edn, Bucharest: Humanitas.

Okey, R. (1982) *Eastern Europe, 1740–1980*, London: Hutchinson.

—— (1992) 'Central Europe/Eastern Europe: behind the definitions', *Past and Present*, no. 137, pp. 102–33.

Oren, N. (1973) *Revolution Administered: Agrarianism and Communism in Bulgaria*, Baltimore: Johns Hopkins University Press.

Ostrogorsky, G. (1942) 'Agrarian conditions in the Byzantine Empire in the Middle Ages', in John Clapham and Eileen Power (eds), *The Cambridge Economic History of Europe from the Decline of the Roman Empire*, vol. I, Cambridge: Cambridge University Press, pp. 194–223.

*—— (1968) *History of the Byzantine State*, Oxford: Blackwell, 1968.

*O'Sullivan, N. (1983) *Fascism*, London: Dent.

—— (2004) *European Political Thought since 1945*, Basingstoke: Palgrave.

Owen, D. (1996) *Balkan Odyssey*, London: Indigo-Cassell.

Palacky, F. (1948) 'Letter sent by Frantisek Palacky to Frankfurt', *Slavonic Review*, vol. 26, no. 67, pp. 303–8.

Palairet, M. (1997) *The Balkan Economies c.1800–1914*, Cambridge: Cambridge University Press.

Palmer, A. (1970) *The Lands Between: A History of East Central Europe since the Congress of Vienna*, London: Weidenfeld and Nicolson.

Pamlenyi, E. (ed.) (1975) *A History of Hungary*, London: Collets.

Pamuk, S. (1987) *The Ottoman Empire and European Capitalism*, Cambridge: Cambridge University Press.

—— (2000) *A Monetary History of the Ottoman Empire*, Cambridge: Cambridge University Press.

Parekh, B. (1992) 'The cultural particularity of liberal democracy', *Political Studies*, vol. 40 (s. 1), pp. 160–75.

Pashko, G. (1991) 'The Albanian economy at the beginning of the 1990s', in Sjöberg and Wyzan (1991).

—— (1993) 'Obstacles to economic reform in Albania', *Europe-Asia Studies*, vol. 45, no. 5, pp. 907–21.

—— (1996) 'Problems of the transition in Albania, 1990–94', in Jeffries (1996b), pp. 63–82.

Pavlowitch, S. (1999) *A History of the Balkans, 1804–1945*, Harlow: Longman.

—— (2002) *Serbia: The History behind the Name*, London: Hurst.

Paxton, R. (2004) *The Anatomy of Fascism*, Harmondsworth: Penguin.

PEP (Political and Economic Planning) (1945) *Economic Development in South-East Europe*, London: Oxford University Press.

Peter, K. (1994) 'Hungary', in Scribner *et al.* (1994).

Petersen, R. (2002) *Understanding Ethnic Violence: Fear, Hatred and Resentment in Twentieth-Century Eastern Europe*, Cambridge: Cambridge University Press.

Petrow, R. (1974) *The Bitter Years: The Invasion and Occupation of Denmark and Norway, April 1940–May 1945*, New York: William Morrow.

Pettai, V. and Zielonka, J. (eds) (2003) *The Road to the European Union, vol. II: Estonia, Latvia and Lithuania*, Manchester: Manchester University Press.

PHARE (1994) *Operational Programmes 1994*, Update no. 4, Brussels: PHARE Information Office, European Commission.

Pharr, S. and Putnam, R.D. (eds) (2000) *Disaffected Democracies: What's Troubling the Trilateral Countries?*, Princeton: Princeton University Press.

Pinder, J. (1991) *The European Community and Eastern Europe*, London: Pinter.

Plesu, A. (1997) 'Towards a European patriotism: obstacles as seen from the East', *East European Constitutional Review*, Spring–Summer, pp. 53–6.

Polisensky, J. (1974) *The Thirty Years' War*, London: New English Library.

—— (1975) *The Little Dictators*, London: Routledge.

Polonsky, A. (ed) (1990) *My Brother's Keeper? Recent Polish Debates on the Holocaust*, London: Routledge.

Polonsky, A. and Michlik, J. (eds) (2004) *The Neighbours Respond: The Controversy over the Jedwabne Massacre in Poland*, Princeton: Princeton University Press.

Pomeranz, K. (2000) *The Great Divergence: China, Europe and the Making of the Modern World Economy*, Princeton: Princeton University Press.

Pond, E. (2006) *Endgame in the Balkans: Regime Change European Style*, Washington, D.C.: Brookings Institution Press.

Ponting, C. (1995) *Armageddon*, New York: Random House.

—— (2000) *A World History*, London: Chatto and Windus.

—— (2002) *Thirteen Days: The Road to the First World War*, London: Chatto and Windus.

Porter, R. and Teich, M. (eds) (1992) *The Renaissance in National Context*, Cambridge: Cambridge University Press.

Portes, R. (1994) 'Transformation traps', *Economic Journal*, vol. 104, no. 426.

Poznanski, K. (ed.) (1992) *Constructing Capitalism*, Boulder, Colo.: Westview Press.

—— (1993) 'Pricing practices in the CMEA trade regime: a reappraisal', *Europe-Asia Studies*, vol. 45, no. 5, pp. 923–30.

Presser, J. (1969) *The Destruction of the Dutch Jews*, New York: Dutton.

Preston, C. (1997) *Enlargement and Integration in the European Union*, London: Routledge.

Pridham, G. and Gallagher, T. (eds) (2000) *Experimenting with Democracy: Regime Change in the Balkans*, London: Routledge.

Pridham, G., Herring, E. and Sandford, G. (eds) (1994) *Building Democracy? The International Dimension of Democratization in Eastern Europe*, London: Leicester University Press.

Prodi, R. (2000) '2000–06: shaping the new Europe: presentation to the European Parliament', *Bulletin of the European Union*, Supplement 1/2000, pp. 5–13.

Prout, C. (1985) *Market Socialism in Yugoslavia*, London: Oxford University Press.

Prucha, V. (1995) 'Economic development and relations, 1918–89', in J. Musil (ed.), *The End of Czechoslovakia*, Budapest: Central European Press.

Pryor, F. (1963) *The Communist Foreign Trade System*, London: Allen and Unwin

*Putnam, R.D. (1993) *Making Democracy Work*, Princeton: Princeton University Press.

—— (2000) *Bowling Alone*, New York: Simon and Schuster.

—— (ed.) (2002) *Democracies in Flux*, Oxford: Oxford University Press.

Puto, A. (2006) 'Albania: one step closer', TOL, 15 June.

Quataert, D. (1993) *Ottoman Manufacturing in the Age of the Industrial Revolution*, Cambridge: Cambridge University Press.

*—— (1997) 'The age of reforms', in Inalcik and Quataert (1997) vol. II, pp. 759–943.

—— (2005) *The Ottoman Empire, 1700–1922*, Cambridge: Cambridge University Press.

Ramet, S. (1997) *Whose Democracy? Nationalism, Religion and the Doctrine of Collective Rights in Post-1989 Eastern Europe*, Lanham, Md.: Rowman and Littlefield.

—— (ed.) (1998) *Eastern Europe: Politics, Culture and Society since 1939*, Bloomington: Indiana University Press.

Ranki, G. (1971) 'The problem of fascism in Hungary', in Sugar (1971b).

Rath, J. (1957) *The Viennese Revolution of 1848*, Austin: University of Texas Press.

Rau, Z. (1991) *The Reemergence of Civil Society in Eastern Europe and the Soviet Union*, Boulder, Colo.: Westview Press.

Raupach, H. (1969) 'The impact of the Great Depression on Eastern Europe', *Journal of Contemporary History*, vol. 4, no. 4, pp. 75–86.

Reddaway, W. (ed.) (1941) *The Cambridge History of Poland, 1697–1935*, Cambridge: Cambridge University Press.

—— (1950) *The Cambridge History of Poland to 1696*, Cambridge: Cambridge University Press.

Reisinger, W. (1992) *Energy and the Soviet Bloc: Alliance Politics after Stalin*, Ithaca: Cornell University Press.

Reuschemeyer, D., Stephens, E. and Stephens, J. (1992) *Capitalist Development and Democracy*, Cambridge: Polity Press.

Robson, P. (1987) *The Economics of International Integration*, London: Unwin Hyman.

Romania (1974) *Romania*, Bucharest: Editura Eniclopedia Romana.

Rose, R. (1992) 'Toward a civil economy', *Journal of Democracy*, vol. 3, no. 2, pp. 13–26.

Ross, G. (1992) 'Survival in Romania', *New York Review of Books*, vol. 39, no. 10, 28 May.

*Rothschild, J. (1974) *East-Central Europe between the Two World Wars*, Seattle: University of Washington Press.

—— (1989) *Return to Diversity: A Political History of East-Central Europe since World War II*, London: Oxford University Press (2nd edn 1994).

Roxburgh, A. (1991) *The Second Russian Revolution*, London: BBC Books.

Rudolph, R. (1975) 'The pattern of Austrian industrial growth from the eighteenth to the early twentieth century', *Austrian History Yearbook*, vol. 11.

—— (1976) *Banking and Industrialization in Austria-Hungary, 1873–1914*, Cambridge: Cambridge University Press.

—— (1983) 'Economic revolution in Austria? The meaning of 1848 in Austrian economic history', in Komlos (1983a).

*Runciman, S. (1968) *The Great Church in Captivity: A Study of the Patriarchate of Constantinople from the Eve of the Turkish Conquest to the Greek War of Independence*, Cambridge: Cambridge University Press.

*—— (1969) *The Fall of Constantinople 1453*, Cambridge: Cambridge University Press.

—— (1970) *The Last Byzantine Renaissance*, Cambridge: Cambridge University Press.

Rupnik, J. (1990) 'Central Europe or Mitteleuropa?', *Daedalus*, vol. 119 (winter), pp. 249–78.

Rupnik, J. and Zielonka, J. (eds) (2003) *The Road to the European Union, vol. I: The Czech and Slovak Republics*, Manchester: Manchester University Press.

Rustow, D. (1970) 'Transitions to democracy: towards a dynamic model', *Comparative Politics*, vol. 22, no. 3, pp. 337–63.

Sachs, J. (1994) *Poland's Jump to the Market Economy*, Cambridge, Mass.: MIT Press.

Sachs, J. and Woo, W. (1994) 'Structural factors in the economic reforms of China, Eastern Europe and the former Soviet Union', *Economic Policy*, vol. 9, no. 18, pp. 101–45.

Sakwa, R. (2002) *Russian Politics and Society*, 3rd edn, London: Routledge.

Samsonowicz, H. (1982) 'Polish politics and society under the Jagiellon Monarchy', in Fedorowicz (1982).

Sayer, D. (1998) *The Coasts of Bohemia: A Czech History*, Princeton: Princeton University Press.

Schiavone, G. (1981) *The Institutions of Comecon*, London: Macmillan.

Schimmelfennig, F. and Sedelmeier, U. (eds) (2005) *The Europeanization of Central and Eastern Europe*, Ithaca: Cornell University Press.

Schmitt, B. (1958) *The Origins of the First World War*, London: Historical Association.

Schnytzer, A. (1982) *Stalinist Economic Strategy in Practice: The Case of Albania*, London: Oxford University Press.

—— (1992) 'Albania: the purge of Stalinist economic ideology', in Jeffries (1992b).

Schöpflin, G. (1993) *Politics in Eastern Europe*, Oxford: Blackwell.

—— (1994) 'The rise of anti-democratic movements in post-Communist societies', in Miall (1994).

*Schöpflin, G. and Wood, N. (eds) (1989) *In Search of Central Europe*, Totowa, N.J.: Barnes and Noble.

Schulz, G. (1972) *Revolutions and Peace Treaties 1917–1920*, London: Methuen.

Schwartz, E. (1989) 'Central Europe: what it is and what it is not', in Schöpflin and Wood (1989).

Scribner, R. (1994) 'A comparative overview', in Scribner *et al.* (1994).

Scribner, R., Porter, R. and Teich, M. (eds) (1994) *The Reformation in National Context*, Cambridge: Cambridge University Press.

*Seton-Watson, H. (1945) *Eastern Europe between the Wars*, Cambridge: Cambridge University Press.

—— (1977) *Nations and States*, London: Methuen.

—— (1985) 'What is Europe, where is Europe? From mystique to politique', *Encounter*, vol. 65, no. 2.

Shafir, M. (1985) *Romania: Politics, Economics and Society*, London: Pinter.

Shaw, S. (1962) 'The aims and achievements of Ottoman rule in the Balkans', *Slavic Review*, vol. 21, no. 4, pp. 617–22.

—— (1963) 'The Ottoman view of the Balkans', in Jelavich and Jelavich (1963).

Shaw, S. and Shaw, E. (1977) *A History of the Ottoman Empire and Modern Turkey*, 2 vols, Cambridge: Cambridge University Press.

Shevtsova, L. (2005) *Putin's Russia*, Washington: Carnegie Endowment.

Shonfield, A. (1973) *Europe: Journey to an Unknown Destination*, Harmondsworth: Penguin.

Simecka, M. (1985) 'Another civilization? An other civilization?', in Schöpflin and Wood (1989).

—— (1987) 'Which way back to Europe?', in Schöpflin and Wood (1989).

Singleton, F. (1976) *Twentieth Century Yugoslavia*, London: Macmillan.

Sirc, L. (1979) *The Yugoslav Economy under Self-management*, London: Macmillan.

Sjöberg, Ö. and Wyzan, M. (eds) (1991) *Economic Change in the Balkan States*, London: Pinter.

Sked, A. (1989) *The Decline and Fall of the Habsburg Empire, 1815–1918*, London: Longman.

Skowronek, J. (1982) 'The direction of political change in the era of national insurrection, 1795–1864', in Fedorowicz (1982).

Skwarczynski, P. (1956) 'The problem of feudalism in Poland up to the beginning of the sixteenth century', *Slavonic and East European Review*, vol. 34, pp. 292–310.

Smith, A.D. (1995) *Nations and Nationalism in a Global Era*, Cambridge: Blackwell.

Smith, A.H. (1983) *The Planned Economies of Eastern Europe*, London: Croom Helm.

Smith, M.A. (1999) 'The NATO factor', in Henderson (1999) pp. 53–67.

Sobell, V. (1984) *The Red Market*, Aldershot: Gower.

Soisson, P. (1977) *The World of Byzantium*, Geneva: Minerva.

Southern, R.W. (1959) *The Making of the Middle Ages*, London: Arrow Books.

Spiesz, A., Caplovic, D., Bolchazy, L., and Kopanic, M. (2006) *Slovak History*, Wauconda, Ill.: Bolchazy-Carducci.

Spinka, M. (1968) *John Hus: A Biography*, Princeton: Princeton University Press.

—— (1972) *The Letters of John Hus*, Manchester: Manchester University Press.

Spulber, N. (ed.) (1963) 'Changes in the economic structure of the Balkans, 1860–1960', in Jelavich and Jelavich (1963).

Stahl, Henri (1980) *Traditional Romanian Village Communities: The Transition from the Communal to the Capitalist Mode of Production in the Danube Region*, Cambridge: Cambridge University Press.

Stalin, J. (1954) *Works*, vol. VII, Moscow: Foreign Languages Publishing House.

—— (1955a) *Works*, vol. XII, Moscow: Foreign Languages Publishing House.

—— (1955b) *Works*, vol. XIII, Moscow: Foreign Languages Publishing House.

—— (1955c) *Works*, vol. XIV, Moscow: Foreign Languages Publishing House.

*Stavrianos, L. (1958) *The Balkans since 1453*, New York: Holt, Rinehart and Winston.

—— (1963) 'The influence of the West on the Balkans', in Jelavich and Jelavich (1963).

Steinherr, A. and Ottolenghi, D. (1993) 'Yugoslavia: was it a winner's curse?', *Economics of Transition*, vol. 1, no. 2.

Stoianovich, T. (1960) 'The conquering Balkan Orthodox merchant', *Journal of Economic History*, vol. 20, no. 2, pp. 234–313.

—— (1962) 'Factors in the decline of Ottoman society in the Balkans', *Slavic Review*, vol. 21, no. 4, pp. 623–32.

—— (1963) 'The social foundations of Balkan politics, 1750–1941', in Jelavich and Jelavich (1963).

—— (1967) *A History of Balkan Civilization*, New York: Knopf.

—— (1994) *Balkan Worlds*, Armonk, N.Y.: M.E. Sharpe.

Stokes, G. (ed.) (1991) *From Stalinism to Pluralism*, Oxford: Oxford University Press.

—— (ed.) (1993) *The Walls came Tumbling Down*, Oxford: Oxford University Press.

Stola, D. (2004) 'Jedwabne: how was it possible?', in Polonsky and Michlik (2004).

Stone Sweet, A. (2000) *Governing with Judges*, Oxford: Oxford University Press.

Struve, P. (1942) 'Medieval agrarian society in its prime: Russia', in Clapham and Power (1942).

Sugar, P. (1963) 'The nature of non-Germanic societies under Habsburg rule', *Slavic Review*, vol. 22, no. 1, pp. 1–30.

—— (1967) 'The rise of nationalism in the Habsburg Empire', *Austrian History Yearbook*, vol. 3, part 1 pp. 121–46.

—— (1971a) 'External and domestic roots of East European nationalism', in Sugar and Lederer (1971).

—— (ed.) (1971b) *Native Fascism in the Successor States, 1918–1945*, Santa Barbara, Calif.: ABC-Clio Press.

—— (1977) *Southeastern Europe under Ottoman Rule, 1354–1804*, Seattle: University of Washington Press.

—— (ed.) (1995) *Eastern European Nationalism in the Twentieth Century*, Washington, D.C.: American University Press.

Sugar, P. and Lederer, I. (eds) (1971) *Nationalism in Eastern Europe*, Seattle: University of Washington Press.

Sutton, A. (1968–72) *Western Technology and Soviet Economic Development*, 3 vols, Stanford: Stanford University Press.

Svoronos, N. (1973) *Etudes sur l'organisation intérieure, la société et l'économie de l'Empire Byzantin*, London: Variorum.

Sword, K. (ed.) (1991) *The Times Guide to Eastern Europe*, 2nd edn, London: Times Books.

Szarota, T. (2000) *U progu Zaglady: Zajscia antyzydowskie I pogromy w okupowanej Europie*, Warsaw: Wudawn.

Szelenyi, I. (1979) 'The position of the intelligentsia in the class structure of state socialist societies', *Critique*, nos 10–11, pp. 51–76.

Szucs, J. (1988) 'Three historical regions of Europe', in J. Keane (ed.), *Civil Society and the State*, London: Verso, pp. 291–333.

Tamas, G.M. (1996) 'Ethnarchy and anarchism', *Social Research*, vol. 63, no. 1.

Taras, R. (ed.) (1992) *The Road to Disillusion: From Critical Marxism to Postcommunism in Eastern Europe*, Armonk, N.Y.: M.E. Sharpe.

Tarrow, S. and Petrova, T. (2007) 'Transactional and participatory activism in the emerging European polity: the puzzle of East Central Europe', *Comparative Political Studies*, vol. 40, no. 1, pp. 74–94.

Taylor, A.J.P. (1940) *The Habsburg Monarchy*, vols I and II, London: Macmillan.

—— (1964) *The Origins of the Second World War*, Harmondsworth: Penguin.

—— (1967) *Europe: Grandeur and Decline*, Harmondsworth: Penguin.

—— (1976) *The Habsburg Monarchy, 1809–1918*, Chicago: University of Chicago Press.

Tazbir, J. (1982) 'The fate of Polish Protestantism in the seventeenth century', in Fedorowicz (ed.) (1982).

—— (1994) 'Poland', in Scribner *et al.* (1994).

Therborn, G. (1978) 'The rule of capital and rise of democracy', *New Left Review*, no. 103, pp. 3–41.

Thompson, S. (1993) 'Agrarian reform in Eastern Europe following World War I', *American Journal of Agricultural Economics*, vol. 75, no. 3.

Thompson, S.H. (1933) 'Pre-Hussite heresy in Bohemia', *English Historical Review*, vol. 48, no. 189, pp. 23–42.

Tiltman, H. (1934) *Peasant Europe*, London: Jarrolds.

Tismaneanu, V. (ed.) *The Revolutions of 1989*, London: Routledge,

Todorov, T. (2001) *The Fragility of Goodness*, London: Weidenfeld and Nicolson.

*Todorova, M. (1994) 'The Balkans: from discovery to invention', *Slavic Review*, vol. 53, no. 2, pp. 453–82.

*—— (1997) *Imagining the Balkans*, Oxford: Oxford University Press.

Togliatti, P. (1976) *Lectures on Fascism*, New York: International Publishers.

Toma, P. and Kovac, D. (2001) *Slovakia: From Samo to Dzurinda*, Washington, D.C.: Hoover Institution Press.

Topolski, J. (1981) 'Continuity and discontinuity in the development of the feudal system in Eastern Europe', *Journal of European Economic History*, vol. 10, no. 2, pp. 373–400.

—— (1982) 'Sixteenth century Poland and the turning point in European economic development', in Fedorowicz (1982).

Touraine, A. (1997) *What is Democracy?*, Boulder, Colo.: Westview Press.

Toynbee, A. (1954) *A Study of History*, vol. VIII, London: Oxford University Press.

Treadgold, W. (1997) *A History of the Byzantine State and Society*, Stanford: Stanford University Press.

Trotsky, L. (1926) *Toward Socialism or Capitalism?*, New York: International Publishers.

—— (1928) *The Real Situation in Russia*, New York: International Publishers.

—— (1937) *The Revolution Betrayed*, repr. New York: Pathfinder Press, 1972.

Turczynski, E. (1971) 'The background of Romanian fascism', in Sugar and Lederer (1971).

UNCTAD (2004) *World Investment Report, 2004*, Geneva: UN.

—— (2005) *World Investment Report, 2005*, Geneva: UN.

—— (2006) *World Investment Report, 2006*, Geneva: UN.

UN Economic Commission for Europe (1993) *Economics Survey of Europe in 1992–93*, New York: United Nations.

—— (1994) *Economic Survey of Europe in 1993–94*, New York: United Nations.

Urbanczyk, P. (2005) 'Early state formation in East Central Europe', in F. Curta (2005), pp. 139–51.

USSR (1977) *Narodnoye khoziaistvo CCCP za 60 let*, Moscow: Statistika.

Vachudova, M. (2005) *Europe Undivided*, Oxford: Oxford University Press.

Vajda, M. (1986) 'Who excluded Russia from Europe?', in Schöpflin and Wood (1989).

—— (1988) 'East Central European perspectives', in J. Keane (ed.), *Civil Society and the State*, London: Verso.

Vasiliev, A. (1952) *History of the Byzantine Empire*, Oxford: Blackwell.

Vaughan, R. (ed.) (1976) *Postwar Integration in Europe*, London: Edward Arnold.

Veiga, F. (2002) *La Trampa Balcánica*, Barcelona: Grijalbo Monadori.

Veinstein, G. (1991) 'On the *ciftlik* debate', in Keyder and Tabak (1991) pp. 35–55.

Verdery, K. (1979) 'Internal colonialism in Austria-Hungary', *Ethnic and Racial Studies*. vol. 2, no. 3, pp. 378–97.

Veremis, T. and Daianu, D. (eds) (2001) *Balkan Reconstruction*, London: Frank Cass.

Vickers, M. (1998) *Between Serb and Albanian: A History of Kosovo*, London: Hurst.

—— (1999) *The Albanians*, London: I.B. Tauris.

Vlasto, A. (1970) *The Entry of the Slavs into Christendom*, Cambridge: Cambridge University Press.

Volkogonov, D. (1991) *Stalin: Triumph and Tragedy*, London: Weidenfeld and Nicolson.

Vucinich, W. (1962) 'The nature of Balkan society under Ottoman rule', *Slavic Review*, vol. 21, no. 4, pp. 597–616.

—— (1963) 'Some aspects of the Ottoman legacy', in Jelavich and Jelavich (1963).

—— (1965) *The Ottoman Empire: Its Record and Legacy*, Princeton: Van Nostrand.

Wallace, W. and Clarke, R. (1986) *Comecon, Trade and the West*, London: Pinter.

Wallerstein, I. (1974a) *The Modern World System: Capitalist Agriculture and the Origins of the European World Economy*, New York: Academic Press.

—— (1974b) 'The rise and future demise of the world capitalist system', *Comparative Studies in Society and History*, vol. 16, no. 4, pp. 387–415.

Wandycz, P. (1974) *The Lands of Partitioned Poland, 1795–1918*, Seattle: University of Washington Press.

—— (1992) *The Price of Freedom: A History of East-Central Europe from the Middle Ages to the Present*, London: Routledge.

*—— (2001) *The Price of Freedom: A History of East-Central Europe from the Middle Ages to the Present*, 2nd edn, London: Routledge.

Warriner, D. (1950) *Revolution in Eastern Europe*, London: Turnstile Press.

Weber, E. (1964) *Varieties of Fascism*, New York: Van Nostrand.

Weiler, J. (1999) *The Constitution of Europe*, Cambridge: Cambridge University Press.

Weitzman, M. (1993) 'Economic transition: can theory help?', *European Economic Review*, vol. 37, nos 2/3.

Weitzman, M. and Xu, C. (1994) 'Chinese township–village enterprises as vaguely defined co-operatives', *Journal of Comparative Economics*, vol. 18, no. 2.

Whitehead, L. (1986) 'International aspects of democratization', in G. O'Donnell, P. Schmitter, and L. Whitehead, (eds) (1986) *Transitions from Authoritarian Rule*, vol. III, Baltimore: Johns Hopkins University Press.

—— (1994) 'East-Central Europe in comparative perspective', in Pridham *et al.* (1994).

Whiteside, A. (1967) 'The Germans as an integrating force in imperial Austria', *Austrian History Yearbook*, vol. 3, part 1 157–99.

Wiesel, E., Friling, T., Ioanid, R. and Ionescu, M. (eds) (2005) *Comisia Internationala pentru Studierea Holocaustului in Romania: Raport Final*, Bucharest: Editura POLIROM.

Wiles, P. (1968) *Communist International Economics*, Oxford; Blackwell.

Wilkes, J. (1992) *The Illyrians*, Oxford: Blackwell.

Wiskemann, E. (1938) *Czechs and Germans*, London: Oxford University Press.

Wolf, E.R. (1982) *Europe and the People without History*, Berkeley: Uniersity of California Press.

Wolff, L. (1994) *Inventing Eastern Europe*, Stanford: Stanford University Press.

Woo, W. (1994) 'The art of reforming centrally planned economies: comparing China, Poland and Russia', *Journal of Comparative Economics*, vol. 18, no. 3.

Woodhouse, C. (1977) *Modern Greece: A Short History*, London: Faber.

Woods, W. (1972) *Poland: Phoenix in the East*, Harmondsworth: Penguin.

Woodward, S. (1995) *Balkan Tragedy*, Washington, D.C.: Brookings Institution Press.

World Bank (1996) *World Development Report: From Plan to Market*, New York: Oxford University Press.

Wright, W. (1975) 'Neo-serfdom in Bohemia', *Slavic Review*, vol. 34, no. 2, pp. 239–52.

Wyczanski, A. (1982) 'The problem of authority in sixteenth-century Poland', in Fedorowicz (1982).

Wyrobisz, A. (1982) 'The arts and social prestige in Poland between the sixteenth and eighteenth centuries', in Fedorowicz (1982).

Zakaria, F. (1998) 'The rise of illiberal democracy', *Foreign Affairs,* vol. 76, no. 6, pp. 22–43.

—— (2003) *The Future of Freedom*, New York: Norton.

*Zamoyski, A. (1987) *The Polish Way: A One Thousand Year History of the Poles and their Culture*, London: Murray.

Zeman, J. (1977) *The Hussite Movement and the Reformation in Bohemia, Moravia and Slovakia, 1350–1650*, Ann Arbor: University of Michigan Press.

Zhdanov, A. (1947) 'The two camp policy', reprinted in Stokes (1991) pp. 38–42.

Zielonka, J. (ed.) (2001) *Democratic Consolidation in Eastern Europe, vol I: Institutional Engineering*, Oxford: Oxford University Press.

Zielonka, J., and Pravda, A. (2001) *Democratic Consolidation in Eastern Europe, vol II, International and Transnational Factors*, Oxford: Oxford University Press.

Zientara, B. (1982) 'Melioratio terrae: the thirteenth-century breakthrough in Polish history', in Fedorowicz (1982).

Zimmerman, W. (1995) 'The last ambassador: a memoir of the collapse of Yugoslavia', *Foreign Affairs*, vol. 74, no. 2.

Zollner, E. (1967) 'The Germans as a disintegrating force', Austrian History Yearbook, vol. 3, part 1 pp. 201–33.

*Zubok, V. and Pleshakov, C. (1996) *Inside the Kremlin's Cold War: From Stalin to Khrushchev*, Cambridge, Mass.: Harvard University Press.

Zürcher, E. (2001) *Turkey: A Modern History*, 3rd edn, London: I.B. Tauris.

*—— (2004) *Turkey: A Modern History*, 4th edn, London: I.B. Tauris.

Index

Routledge History

The Balkans
A Post-Communist History

Robert Bideleux and Ian Jeffries

An excellent companion volume to the successful *A History of Eastern Europe*, this is a country-by-country treatment of the contemporary history of each of the Balkan states: Albania, Bulgaria, Romania, Croatia, Serbia, Bosnia and Herzegovina, Macedonia, Montenegro and Kosova.

Focusing on political and economic continuities and changes since the 1980s, *The Balkans* includes brief overviews of the history of each state prior to the 1980s to provide the background to enable readers to make sense of the more recent developments.

With a distinctive conceptual framework for explaining divergent patterns of historical change, the book shifts the emphasis away from traditional cultural explanations and concentrates on the pervasive influence of strongly entrenched vertical power-structures and power-relations. An invaluable book for all students of Eastern European history.

ISBN10: 0-415-22962-6 (hbk)
ISBN10: 0-415-22963-4 (pbk)

ISBN13: 978-0-415-22962-3 (hbk)
ISBN13: 978-0-415-22963-0 (pbk)

For ordering and further information please visit:
www.routledge.com

Routledge History

Eastern Europe in the Twentieth Century – And After

2nd edition

R.J. Crampton

Covering all key Eastern European states and their history right up to the collapse of communism, this new edition of *Eastern Europe in the Twentieth Century – And After* is a comprehensive political history of Eastern Europe taking in the whole of the century and the geographical area.

Focusing on the attempt to create and maintain a functioning democracy, the new edition now:

- examines events in Bosnia and Hercegovina

- includes a new consideration of the evolution of the region since the revolutions of 1989–91

- surveys the development of a market economy

- analyzes the realignment of Eastern Europe towards the West

- details the emergence of organized crime

- discusses each state individually

- includes an up-to-date bibliography.

Eastern Europe in the Twentieth Century – And After provides an accessible introduction to this key area which is invaluable to students of modern and political history.

ISBN10: 0-415-16422-2 (hbk)
ISBN10: 0-415-16423-0 (pbk)

ISBN13: 978-0-415-16422-1 (hbk)
ISBN13: 978-0-415-16423-8 (pbk)

For ordering and further information please visit:
www.routledge.com

Routledge History

Atlas of Eastern Europe in the Twentieth Century

Richard and Ben Crampton

Marshalling 129 maps, numerous diagrams and incisive textual commentary, the *Atlas of Eastern Europe in the Twentieth Century* draws a definitive picture of the changing shape of Eastern and some of central Europe from the beginning of the twentieth century to the present, charting the emergence of a volatile world from the abrupt collapse of the communist system. An invaluable guide to a complex subject, this *Atlas*:

- gives a general introduction to the physical, ethnic and religious composition of the region

- includes summary maps of Eastern Europe in 1900, 1923, 1945 and 1994

- charts the ebb and flow of the first and second world wars in Eastern Europe

- presents detailed information relating to consituent territories, elections, economic developments, land holding patterns for key individual countries in the inter-war years

- provides crucial social and economic data, evidencing changes under communist domination

- gives maps of the new states of the post-communist years with details of elections and economic indicators for Albania, Belarus, Bosnia-Hercegovina, Croatia, The Czech Republic, Estonia, Latvia, Lithuania, Macedonia, Moldova, Slovakia, and others.

- contains an extensive glossary listing the major towns of the area under their linguistic variants.

ISBN10: 0-415-06689-1 (hbk)
ISBN10: 0-415-16461-3 (pbk)

ISBN13: 978-0-415-06689-1 (hbk)
ISBN13: 978-0-415-16461-0 (pbk)

For ordering and further information please visit:
www.routledge.com

Routledge History

The Economy of East Central Europe, 1815–1989

Stages of Transformation in a Peripheral Region

David Turnock

From a widely published expert in the field, this major survey reviews two centuries of modernization and examines the dramatic changes in the economies of Eastern Europe.

Uniquely taking the broader historical picture into account, David Turnock brings together the entire scope of the modernization process, from the first phase of modern national development in the Balkans and the impact of imperial systems on the area as a whole, to the feeling of 'unfinished business' at the end of the Second World War. He continues up to the present-day state of transition, evaluating the contrasts in the region between the northern and southern states, domestic division between dynamic and backward areas, and the increasing emphasis on the opening up of frontier regions.

Wide in scope and including detailed and informative chronologies, this book will prove an invaluable asset to students of European history and economics.

ISBN10: 0-415-18053-8 (hbk)
ISBN13: 978-0-415-18053-5 (hbk)

The East European Economy in Context: Communism and Transition

David Turnock

Since 1989, the former communist countries of Eastern Europe have witnessed a profound and dramatic upheaval. The economic coherence of this region, formerly maintained through the adoption of the Soviet system of government, has fractured. In this book, David Turnock examines the transition from Communist to free-market economies, both within and between the states of Eastern Europe. He offers a comprehensive discussion of the background to this change, as well as detailing the variations which have taken place in each country.

Beginning with a review of the historical background, Turnock considers Eastern Europe in relation to the imperial systems of the rest of Europe in the eighteenth and nineteenth centuries. He also examines the region in relation to the global perspectives of growth.

ISBN10: 0-415-08626-4 (hbk)
ISBN13: 978-0-415-08626-4 (hbk)

For ordering and further information please visit:
www.routledge.com